# Get started with your **Connected eBook**

Redeem your code below to access the **ebook** with search, highlighting, and note-taking capabilities; **case briefing** and **outlining** tools to support efficient learning; and more.

1. Go to www.casebookconnect.com
2. Enter your access code in the box and click **Register**
3. Follow the steps to complete your registration and verify your email address

## ACCESS CODE:
Scratch off with care.

If you have already registered at CasebookConnect.com, simply log into your account and redeem additional access codes from your Dashboard.

Is this a used book? Access code already redeemed? Purchase a digital version at **CasebookConnect.com/catalog**.

If you purchased a digital bundle with additional components, your additional access codes will appear below.

"I liked being able to search quickly while in class."

"Being able to highlight and easily create case briefs was a fantastic resource and time saver for me!"

"I loved it! I was able to study on the go and create a more effective outline."

9781543819809

# International Human Rights

ASPEN CASEBOOK SERIES

# INTERNATIONAL HUMAN RIGHTS

## PROBLEMS OF LAW, POLICY, AND PRACTICE

### SEVENTH EDITION

**HURST HANNUM**
PROFESSOR OF INTERNATIONAL LAW EMERITUS
THE FLETCHER SCHOOL OF LAW AND DIPLOMACY
TUFTS UNIVERSITY

**S. JAMES ANAYA**
UNIVERSITY DISTINGUISHED PROFESSOR AND
NICHOLAS DOMAN PROFESSOR OF INTERNATIONAL LAW
UNIVERSITY OF COLORADO LAW SCHOOL

**DINAH L. SHELTON**
MANATT/AHN PROFESSOR OF LAW EMERITUS
GEORGE WASHINGTON UNIVERSITY LAW SCHOOL

**ROSA CELORIO**
ASSOCIATE DEAN FOR INTERNATIONAL AND COMPARATIVE LEGAL STUDIES
AND BURNETT FAMILY DISTINGUISHED PROFESSORIAL LECTURER IN
INTERNATIONAL AND COMPARATIVE LAW AND POLICY
GEORGE WASHINGTON UNIVERSITY LAW SCHOOL

To contact Customer Service, e-mail customer.service@aspenpublishing.com, call 1-800-950-5259, or mail correspondence to:

Aspen Publishing
Attn: Order Department
PO Box 990
Frederick, MD 21705

Printed in the United States of America.

1 2 3 4 5 6 7 8 9 0

ISBN 978-1-5438-1980-9

**Library of Congress Cataloging-in-Publication Data application is in process.**

# About Aspen Publishing

Aspen Publishing is a leading provider of educational content and digital learning solutions to law schools in the U.S. and around the world. Aspen provides best-in-class solutions for legal education through authoritative textbooks, written by renowned authors, and breakthrough products such as Connected eBooks, Connected Quizzing, and PracticePerfect.

The Aspen Casebook Series (famously known among law faculty and students as the "red and black" casebooks) encompasses hundreds of highly regarded textbooks in more than eighty disciplines, from large enrollment courses, such as Torts and Contracts to emerging electives such as Sustainability and the Law of Policing. Study aids such as the *Examples & Explanations* and the *Emanuel Law Outlines* series, both highly popular collections, help law students master complex subject matter.

**Major products, programs, and initiatives include:**

- **Connected eBooks** are enhanced digital textbooks and study aids that come with a suite of online content and learning tools designed to maximize student success. Designed in collaboration with hundreds of faculty and students, the Connected eBook is a significant leap forward in the legal education learning tools available to students.

- **Connected Quizzing** is an easy-to-use formative assessment tool that tests law students' understanding and provides timely feedback to improve learning outcomes. Delivered through CasebookConnect.com, the learning platform already used by students to access their Aspen casebooks, Connected Quizzing is simple to implement and integrates seamlessly with law school course curricula.

- **PracticePerfect** is a visually engaging, interactive study aid to explain commonly encountered legal doctrines through easy-to-understand animated videos, illustrative examples, and numerous practice questions. Developed by a team of experts, PracticePerfect is the ideal study companion for today's law students.

- The **Aspen Learning Library** enables law schools to provide their students with access to the most popular study aids on the market across all of their courses. Available through an annual subscription, the online library consists of study aids in e-book, audio, and video formats with full text search, note-taking, and highlighting capabilities.

- Aspen's **Digital Bookshelf** is an institutional-level online education bookshelf, consolidating everything students and professors need to ensure success. This program ensures that every student has access to affordable course materials from day one.

- **Leading Edge** is a community centered on thinking differently about legal education and putting those thoughts into actionable strategies. At the core of the program is the Leading Edge Conference, an annual gathering of legal education thought leaders looking to pool ideas and identify promising directions of exploration.

# Summary of Contents

This casebook is intended to introduce students to the established and developing international law on human rights. There is now a substantial body of this law, which encompasses substantive norms; procedural rules; and national, regional, and global institutions, whose mandate it is to promote, monitor, and supervise international human rights. Human rights issues are a concern today of nearly every national government, whether a country's goal is to expand or to constrain their impact on state (and increasingly non-state) behavior. Human rights law has become an integral part of international law per se, and no one with pretensions of being an international lawyer can ignore its content entirely. Additionally, advocates for a range of causes can look to international human rights law as a valuable tool.

At the same time, international human rights law—as it is generally understood—does not encompass every social good or even every international norm whose purpose is to improve the human condition. Among the issues that are highly relevant to the lives of billions of people but that are not addressed in depth in this coursebook are theories of economic development, broad issues of social equality, refugees, and migration. Other important concerns that are addressed only in terms of their particular relationship to international human rights law are international criminal law, trade, business, protection of the environment, and climate change. And, of course, many moral, social, and philosophical issues appropriately lie beyond the reach of international law of any kind.

The materials in this book are generally organized around the foundational features and diverse components of the international human rights system. Distinct problems related to human rights are introduced to illustrate the real issues that face human rights lawyers and how those issues might be addressed through international (and domestic) processes involving internationally-recognized human rights norms. The book provides a survey of the sources and content of these norms and related policies, and of the institutions and procedures that exist to advance compliance with them. Whenever possible, the book makes use of primary sources, such as treaties, international and domestic jurisprudence, UN resolutions, and other documents emanating from various human rights bodies and procedures. Original explanatory text bridges these materials and provides context for them. Comments and questions are added to guide and provoke discussion of the materials.

The first five chapters consider broadly the substantive content of contemporary international human rights law. The first three chapters highlight contemporary human rights issues, including racial discrimination, and examine the historical development of human rights law through treaties, customary law, and so-called "soft law" instruments. Responses to concerns about the environment, indigenous peoples, minorities, and older persons are discussed to show the dynamic nature of international human rights law. Chapter 4 examines the scope of states' obligations under international human rights law, including with regard to private acts of violence against women and others. It also considers the obligations or responsibilities that might be assigned to other actors, including international organizations and business enterprises. Chapter 5 introduces the related norms of international humanitarian law (the laws of war) in the context of the Russian-Ukraine conflict and the "war on terror," focusing on the relationship between international human rights and humanitarian law. Chapter 5 also includes a brief introduction to international criminal law, a subject that is now offered in many law schools as a separate course.

Chapter 6 serves as an introduction to the discussion of international human rights norm implementation, focusing on the crucial element of domestic enforcement of human rights norms. International human rights law restricting use of the death penalty provides a backdrop for discussion of the capacity of United States courts to apply international human rights norms. Chapter 6 also provides a comparative perspective with materials on South African and other domestic systems.

The next three chapters deal with supervisory mechanisms created by the United Nations and regional human rights regimes. Chapter 7 discusses the expansive system of human rights mechanisms within the UN. Substantively, the Inter-American materials in Chapter 8 consider the regional responses to the phenomenon of enforced disappearance, suppression of expression and protest, challenges to democratic governance, and other issues. The materials on the European system in Chapter 9 highlight issues of cultural diversity and religion. Chapter 9 also considers newer human rights institutions in the Arab world and Asia.

This seventh edition of the book is substantially reduced in volume from prior editions, such that it is better designed for use in a one-semester, three-hour course or seminar at the law school or university level. With some omissions, the book also could be used in a shorter seminar, although balancing depth and breadth of coverage is always difficult. While a background in international law would certainly be helpful to both students and teachers, it is not required for an adequate understanding of most of the materials. Some of the particularly technical legal issues, such as domestic implementation, might be omitted if the book is used in a school or department of international relations, as opposed to a law school. Many of the materials focus on the United States by way of example, given the expectation that this book will mostly be used in US classrooms. Overall, however, the materials are relevant to the practice of international human rights globally.

This coursebook is designed to engage the student in thinking about concrete issues and the application of human rights law to the "real world." Philosophical issues are addressed at various points in the book, but our primary purpose is to explore the practice of human rights in depth. Many of the problems addressed lend themselves to student role-playing, and the materials present different perspectives and positions on many of the more hotly-contested issues in human rights. For all of its sophistication, human rights law—indeed, international law in general—is in constant movement, and many of the materials present the student with alternatives that are actively under discussion rather than offer the "correct" answer to every question. The materials do not attempt to provide a synopsis of human rights law for the casual reader; rather, they are intended to focus attention on the theoretical and legal underpinnings of the international human rights regime and on its practical implications for contemporary, cutting-edge issues.

Finally, this book strives to present a picture of international human rights law as it is and as it is in fact developing, not as we might wish it to be. Human rights advocates can justifiably claim a great deal of success since the adoption of the Universal Declaration of Human Rights in 1948, and the shield of sovereignty that protected states from external criticism over how they treated their own citizens is gone forever. At the same time, however, the mere adoption of new declarations or the issuance of progressive opinions by independent experts does not automatically create effective international law. International law is under increasing challenge today on a number of fronts, both within and beyond the United States, and human rights law is not immune to that challenge. "North-South" issues; the unilateral use of force by states; economic, political, and institutional instability; a near obsession with "terrorism" as well as nationalist movements pose challenges to the structure and normative foundation of international law itself. Only with a full understanding of the constraints within which international law operates can students (and activists) move forward in the most effective manner possible. There is no dichotomy between realism and idealism, because both are necessary; however, neither cynicism disguised as realpolitik nor willfully exaggerated claims for the power of law are useful, and we have tried to avoid them both.

The first edition of this book was published in 1979, when issues such as domestic enforcement of human rights norms, international criminal accountability, and the use of force against human rights violators were little more than theories. It is a tribute to the prescience of the authors of that first edition, Richard B. Lillich and Frank C. Newman, that many of the subjects addressed over 50 years later and the general approach of the book largely remain. Of course, those who have used previous editions will notice that substantial material in this edition is different from that in the sixth edition, as the 21st century continues to bring significant changes and challenges to the field of human rights.

This seventh edition of the book was compiled by S. James Anaya and Rosa Celorio. While Hurst Hannum and Dinah Shelton did not directly participate in the production of this 7th edition, their many contributions to prior editions remain reflected and incorporated into substantial parts of this edition. We are most grateful for those contributions and the foundations they provided for this edition.

S. James Anaya
*Boulder, Colorado*

Rosa Celorio
*Washington, D.C.*

October 2022

This edition of the coursebook was greatly facilitated by the support that S. James Anaya and Rosa Celorio received from their respective universities and from the many colleagues, friends, and loved ones. In particular, S. James Anaya is grateful to his wife, Jana Happel, for her loving support for this and other projects. Additionally, he thanks Alexandra Kinsella and Kelsea Suarez for assisting with research for several parts this book and for providing useful comments on drafts of parts of the text.

Rosa Celorio is grateful to Eric, Sebastian, and her family for all of their love and support with all of her projects and work. She also thanks her Research Assistant Sabrina Rodriguez and Traci Emerson Spackey, Foreign and International Law Librarian at GW Law School, for their support with research incorporated in different parts of this book. Lastly, she thanks James, Dinah, and Hurst for letting her share these pages with them, and for all of their mentoring throughout this process.

The editors also wish to express their appreciation to the following authors, periodicals, and publishers for their permission to reproduce materials from their publications.

"All of My Body Was Pain." Human Rights Watch (May 27, 2020). https://www.hrw .org/report/2017/11/16/all-my-body-was-pain/sexual-violence-against -rohingya-women-and-girls-burma#. Licensed under CC BY-NC-ND 3.0 US.

"Russia-Ukraine Conflict: From Making Molotov Cocktails to Taking up Arms, How Ukraine's Every Man is Standing Up to Russian Troops," Firstpost (February 28, 2022), https://www.firstpost.com/world/russia-ukraine-conflict-from-making -molotov-cocktails-to-taking-up-arms-how-ukraines-every-man-is-standing-up-to -russian-troops-10414511.html.

Al-Midani, Mohammed Amin. "Human Rights Bodies in the League of Arab States," Jinan Human Rights Journal, Vol. 3 (June 2012). Reprinted with permission from the author.

Alexander, Amanda. "A Short History of International Humanitarian Law," The European Journal of International Law, Vol. 26, No. 1 (2015). Oxford University Press. Copyright © 2015.

Alston, Philip. "Human Rights Responses to the Populist Challenge." Journal of Human Rights Practice, Vol. 9, Issue 1 (February 1, 2017). Oxford University Press. Copyright © 2017.

Alston, Philip. Report of the United Nations Special Rapporteur on Extreme Poverty and Human Rights on the Human Rights Policy of the World Bank. UN Doc. A/70/274 (2015). The United Nations.

Anaya, James. Report of the Special Rapporteur on the Rights of Indigenous Peoples – Extractive Industries and Indigenous Peoples. UN Doc. A/HR/C/ 21/47 (2012). The United Nations.

Anaya, James. Report of the Special Rapporteur on the rights of indigenous Peoples. U.N. Doc. A/HRC/24/41 (2013). The United Nations.

Anaya, James. Indigenous Peoples in International Law (2nd ed. 2004). Oxford University Press. Copyright © 2004.

Bachelet, Michelle. "Ukraine: High Commissioner cites 'new and dangerous' threats to human rights" (March 3, 2022), https://www.ohchr.org/en/statements/ 2022/03/ukraine-high-commissioner-cites-new-and-dangerous-threats-human -rights.

Bradley, Curtis A. "The Juvenile Death Penalty and International Law," Duke Law Journal, Vol. 52, No. 3 (December 2002). Duke University School of Law. Reprinted with permission from the author.

Buergenthal, Thomas. "The Evolving International Human Rights System," The American Journal of International Law, Vol. 100, No. 4 (October 2006). Reprinted with permission from the American Society of International Law.

Bush, George W. Address to a Joint Session of Congress and to the American People (Sept. 20, 2001), https://georgewbush-whitehouse.archives.gov/news/ releases/2001/09/20010920-8.html.

Celorio, Rosa. "Discrimination and the Regional Human Rights Protection Systems: The Enigma of Effectiveness," University of Pennsylvania Journal of International Law, Vol. 40, Issue 4 (2019). The University of Pennsylvania Carey Law School. Copyright © 2019.

Charlesworth, Hillary. Feminist Methods in International Law, American Journal of International Law, Vol. 93 (1999). Cambridge University Press. Copyright © 1999.

Committee on Economic, Social, and Cultural Rights, The Nature of States Parties Obligations (Art. 2, para. 1). General Comment No. 3, UN Doc. E/1991/23 (1990). The United Nations.

Committee on the Elimination of Discrimination against Women, Violence against Women. General Recommendation No. 19, UN Doc. A/47/38 (1992). The United Nations.

Committee on the Elimination of Racial Discrimination, Decision 1 (68) – United States of America, Early Warning and Urgent Action Procedure. U.N. Doc. CERD/C/USA/DEC/1 (2006). The United Nations.

Committee on the Elimination of Racial Discrimination, Right to Self-Determination, General Recommendation XXI, UN Doc. A/51/18 (1996). The United Nations.

Compilation on the United States of America – Report of the Office of the United Nations High Commissioner for Human Rights. U.N. Doc. A/HRC/WG.6/36/ USA/2 (2020). The United Nations.

Connors, Jane. The Human Rights Treaty Body System, in The Oxford Handbook of United Nations Treaties (Simon Chesterman et al., eds. 2019). Oxford University Press. Copyright © 2019.

Corporations and Human Rights: A Survey of the Scope and Patterns of Alleged Corporate-Related Human Rights Abuse Report of the Special Representative of the Secretary-General on the Issue of Human Rights and Transnational Corporations and Other Business Enterprises, UN Doc. A/HRC/8/5/Add.2 (2008). The United Nations.

Daugirdas, Kristina. "How and Why International Law Binds International Organizations," Harvard International Law Journal, Vol. 57, No. 2 (Spring 2016). Harvard Law School. Reprinted with permission from the author.

Declarations Under Article 41 of the Covenant General Comment No. 24, UN Doc. CCPR/C/21/Rev.1/Add.6 (1994). The United Nations.

Draper, G. I. A. D. Human Rights and the Law of War, Virginia Journal of International Law, Vol. 12 (1971-1972). The Virginia Journal of International Law Association. Copyright © 1972.

Fifth periodic report submitted by the United States of America under article 40 of the Covenant under the optional reporting procedure, due in 2020. U.N. Doc. CCPR/C/USA/5 (2020). The United Nations.

Fitzpatrick, Joan. Human Rights in Crisis: The International System for Protecting Rights During States of Emergency (1994). University of Pennsylvania Press. Copyright © 1994.

Ginsburg, Ruth Bader. A Decent Respect to the Opinions of [Human]Kind: The Value of a Comparative Perspective in Constitutional Adjudication. Address to the International Academy of Comparative Law, American University (July 30, 2010).

Guiding Principles on Business and Human Rights at 10: Taking Stock of the First Decade Report of the Working Group on the issue of human rights and transnational corporations and other business enterprises, U.N. Doc. A/HRC/47/39 (2021). The United Nations.

Guiding Principles on Business and Human Rights: Implementing the United Nations "Protect, Respect and Remedy Framework," UN Doc. A/HRC/17/31 (2011). The United Nations.

Hannum, Hurst. "The Rights of Persons Belonging to Minorities" in Human Rights: Concepts and Standards (Janusz Symonides ed. 2000). Routledge. Copyright © 2000.

Hathaway, Oona A., Sabria Mc Elroy & Sara Aronchick Solow. "International Law at Home: Enforcing Treaties in US Courts," Yale Journal of International Law, Vol. 37 (2012). Yale Law School. Reprinted with permission.

Heyns, Christof. "The African Regional Human Rights System: The African Charter," Dickinson Law Review, Vol. 108, Issue 3 (2004). Penn State Dickinson Law. Reprinted with permission from the publisher.

Howse, Robert and Makau Mutua. Protecting Human Rights in a Global Economy: Challenges for the World Trade Organization (2000). Institute for Agriculture & Trade Policy. Reprinted with permission.

Human Rights Committee. Concluding observations on the fourth periodic report of the United States of America. UN Doc. CCPR/C/USA/CO/4 (2014). The United Nations.

Human Rights Committee. Consideration of Reports Submitted by States Parties Under Article 40 of the Covenant, Comments of the Committee on the Report of the United States of America, UN Doc. CCPR/C/79/Add.50 (1995). The United Nations.

Human Rights Committee. Continuity of Obligations General Comment No. 26, UN Doc. A/53/40 (1997), Annex VII. The United Nations.

Human Rights Committee, General Comment No. 23 (50) (Art. 27) UN Doc. CCPR/C/21/Rev.1/Add.5 (1994). The United Nations.

Human Rights Committee, The Nature of the General Legal Obligation Imposed on States Parties to the Covenant on Civil and Political Rights. General Comment No. 31, UN Doc. CCPR/C/21/Rev.1/Add.13 (2004). The United Nations.

Human Rights Committee. States of Emergency (Article 4), General Comment No. 29. UN Doc. CCPR/C/21/Rev.1/Add.11 (2001). The United Nations.

Humphrey, John P. "The Universal Declaration of Human Rights: Its History, Impact and Juridical Character" in Human Rights: Thirty Years after the Universal Declaration (B.G. Ramcharan, editor, 1979). Brill. Copyright © 1979.

Huneeus, Alexandra. "Courts Resisting Courts: Lessons from the Inter-American Court's Struggle to Enforce Human Rights," Cornell International Law Journal, Vol. 44, No. 3 (Fall 2011). Cornell Law School. Reprinted with permission from the author.

Inter-American Court of Human Rights Advisory Opinion OC-28/21, June 7, 2021. Series A No 28. Licensed under CC BY-NC-ND 3.0, https://creativecomm ons.org/licenses/by-nc-nd/3.0/deed.en.

International Law Association. Committee on the Enforcement of Human Rights Law, Final Report on the Status of the Universal Declaration of Human Rights in National and International Law. ILA Report of the Sixty-Sixth Conference (Buenos Aires 1995). Reprinted with permission from the International Law Association.

International Law Commission. Guide to Practice on Reservations to Treaties, U.N. Doc. A/66/10, para. 75 (2011). The United Nations.

International Law Commission. Draft articles on the responsibility of international organizations, with commentaries. UN Doc. A/RES/66/100 (2011). The United Nations.

Fitzpatrick, Joan. "The Role of Domestic Courts in Enforcing International Human Rights Law" in Guide to International Human Rights Practice (Hurst Hannum ed., 3d ed. 1999). Transnational Publishers, Inc. Copyright © 1999.

Knox, John. Report of the Special Rapporteur on the issue of human rights obligations relating to the enjoyment of a safe, clean, healthy and sustainable environment. U.N. Doc A/73/188 (2018). The United Nations.

Koh, Harold Hongju. "Why Do Nations Obey International Law?" Yale Law Journal, Vol. 106, Iss. 8 (June 1997). The Yale Law Journal Company, Inc. Reprinted with permission from the author.

Koh, Harold Jongju. "Global Tobacco as a Health and Human Rights Imperative," Harvard International Law Journal, Vol. 57, No. 2 (Spring 2016). Harvard Law School. Reprinted with permission from the author.

Levesque, Christian A. "The International Covenant on Civil and Political Rights: A Primer for Raising a Defense Against the Juvenile Death Penalty in Federal Courts," American University Law Review, Vol. 50 (2001). American University Washington College of Law. Copyright © 2001.

Lieutenant Duffy's Statement in Crimes of War: A Legal, Political-Documentary, and Psychological Inquiry into the Responsibility of Leaders, Citizens, and

Soldiers for Criminal Acts in Wars (Richard A. Falk, Gabriel Kolko, and Robert Lifton, eds., 1971). Penguin Random House. Copyright © 1971.

Macklem, Patrick. The Sovereignty of Human Rights (2015). Oxford University Press. Copyright © 2015. Reprinted with permission from the author.

Medina, Cecilia. "The Inter-American Commission on Human Rights and the Inter-American Court of Human Rights: Reflections on a Joint Venture," Human Rights Quarterly, Vol. 12 (1990). The Johns Hopkins University Press. Copyright © 1990.

National report submitted in accordance with paragraph 5 of the annex to Human Rights Council resolution 16/21 - United States of America. U.N. Doc. A/HRC/WG.6/36/USA/1 (2020). The United Nations.

Office of the United Nations High Commissioner for Human Rights, Reporting to the United Nations Human Rights Treaty Bodies: Training Guide Part 1 – Manual. U.N. Doc. HR/P/PT/20 (Part I) (2017). The United Nations.

Orentlicher, Diane. "Settling Accounts: The Duty to Prosecute Human Rights Violations of a Prior Regime," Yale Law Journal, Vol. 100, No. 8 (June 1991). The Yale Law Journal Company, Inc. Reprinted with permission from the author.

Promotion and Protection of the Human Rights and Fundamental Freedoms of Africans and of People of African Descent against Excessive Use of Force and Human Rights Violations by Law Enforcement Officer, U.N. Doc. A/HRC/47/53 (June 1, 2021). The United Nations.

Protect, Respect, and Remedy: A Framework for Business and Human Rights, UN Doc. A/HRC/8/5 (2008). The United Nations.

Ramina, Larissa. "TWAIL – 'Third World Approaches to International Law' and Human Rights: Some Considerations," Revista de Investigações Constitucionais (2018). Licensed under CC-BY-NC, https://creativecommons.org/licenses/by-nc/2.0/.

Report of the Independent Expert on protection against violence and discrimination based on sexual orientation and gender identity. U.N. Doc. A/HRC/35/36 (2017). The United Nations.

Report of the Secretary-General: Special Measures for Protection from Sexual Exploitation and Sexual Abuse. UN Doc. A/70/729 (2016). The United Nations.

Report of the Working Group on the Universal Periodic Review – United States of America. U.N. Doc. A/HRC/46/15 (2020). The United Nations.

Robertson, A. H. Human Rights in the World: An Introduction to the Study of International Protection of Human Rights (3rd. ed., J. G. Merrills, editor). Manchester University Press. Copyright © 1989.

Schachter, Oscar. "The Charter and the Constitution: The Human Rights Provisions in American Law," Vanderbilt Law Review, Vol. 4, Issue 3 (1951). Vanderbilt Law School. Reprinted with permission from the publisher.

Schwelb, Egon. The Influence of the Universal Declaration of Human Rights on International and National Law. Proceedings of the American Society of International Law at Its Annual Meeting (1921-1969), vol. 53. American Society of International Law. Copyright © 1959.

Sen, Amartya. "Human Rights and Asian Values." The New Republic (July 14-21, 1997).

Shelton, Dinah. "Commentary and Conclusions" in Commitment and Compli-
    ance: The Role of Non-Binding Instruments in the International Legal System
    (2000). Oxford University Press. Copyright © 2000.

Simmons, Beth A. Mobilizing for Human Rights: International Law in Domestic
    Politics. Cambridge University Press. Copyright © 2009.

Steinhardt, Ralph G. "Losing the 'Right' Way Preserves the Narrow Scope of
    the Alien Tort Statute: NESTLE USA, Inc., v. John DOE; A Special Edition
    Response." On the Docket (July 31, 2021). Retrieved from https://www.gwlr
    .org/losing-the-right-way-preserves-the-narrow-scope-of-the-ats/. Reprinted
    with permission from the author.

Summary of stakeholders' submissions on the United States of America. U.N. Doc.
    A/HRC/WG.6/36/USA/3 (2020). The United Nations.

The ASEAN Declaration of Human Rights: A Legal Analysis, Rule of Law Initiative
    (ABA-ROLI). Copyright ©2014 by the American Bar Association. Reprinted
    with permission. All rights reserved. This information or any portion thereof
    may not be copied or disseminated in any form or by any means or stored in an
    electronic database or retrieval system without the express written consent of
    the American Bar Association.

The human right to a clean, healthy and sustainable environment. H.R.C. Res. 48/13,
    U.N. Doc. A/HRC/48/L.3/Rev.1 (2021). The United Nations.

The United Nations and Human Rights: Eighteenth Report of the Commission to
    Study the Organization of Peace 1-4 (1968). The United Nations.

Tzay, José Calí. Report of the Special Rapporteur on the rights of indigenous peo-
    ples, U.N. Doc. A/75/185 (2020). The United Nations.

# INTERNATIONAL HUMAN RIGHTS

# CHAPTER 1

# INTRODUCTION TO INTERNATIONAL HUMAN RIGHTS

## WHAT ARE HUMAN RIGHTS AND WHAT ARE THEIR SIGNIFICANCE TODAY?

# I.  INTRODUCTION: THE CONCEPT OF HUMAN RIGHTS AND ITS EVOLUTION

What do we mean by "human rights"? There is no simple answer, despite the widespread usage of the term or its equivalent in diverse languages. At its core, however, the concept of human rights embraces a certain universe of values having to do with human dignity. These values, and the claims to which they give rise, are understood to apply across national boundaries and cultural divides. Although deemed universal in some sense, human rights draw their content from diverse sources—for some, fundamental moral or ethical precepts discerned through rational thought; for others, religious ideals handed down over time; and, for still others, an understanding of social consensus at some level. Whatever the source of human rights, the widespread perception is that they necessarily belong to everyone *inherently*; temporal authority does not grant human rights, but exists to recognize and allow for their exercise.

The concept of human rights can be seen at work in the Declaration of Independence of the thirteen colonies that became the original United States, through which its drafters defied the British sovereignty asserted over them on the grounds of "truths" held "self-evident, that all men are created equal, that they are endowed by their Creator with certain inalienable Rights, that among these are Life, Liberty and the pursuit of Happiness."

The Western liberal tradition of the eighteenth century that inspired these words, and similar words that heralded the French Revolution, is often regarded as the intellectual wellspring of what we know today as human rights. Yet non-Western philosophical and intellectual traditions also lay claim to precepts of universal and inherent human rights, giving the concept of human rights a multicultural foundation for its common postulates of human dignity.

In his concurring opinion in the Namibia case before the International Court of Justice, Judge Ammoun linked the idea of human equality with "[t]wo streams of thought established on the two opposite shores of the Mediterranean, a Graeco-Roman stream represented by Epictetus, Lucan, Cicero and Marcus Aurelius; and an Asian and African stream, comprising the monks of Sinai and Saint John Climac, Alexandria with Plotinus and Philo the Jew, Carthage to which Saint Augustine gave new lustre." See *Legal Consequences for States of the Continued Presence of South Africa in Namibia (South West Africa) notwithstanding Security Council Resolution 276* (1970), Advisory Opinion, 1971 I.C.J. 16, 77.

Equality and other human rights precepts can also be found in expressions of thinking developed among peoples indigenous to the Americas and Asia. For the Navajo of North America, for example, "the idea of being superior to a fellow Navajo or nature is discouraged. There is an innate knowledge in each one of us that we are to treat with respect all persons and nature with whom we share this world." Judicial Branch of the Navajo Nation, *Annual Report: The Navajo Concept of Justice* 1 (1988). Based on this tradition, Navajo customary law continues to be invoked in Navajo courts to protect human rights such as freedom of expression and political participation. See, e.g., *Navajo Nation v. Crockett,* 24 Indian L. Rep. 6027 (Navajo 1996); *Bennett v. Navajo Board of Election Supervisors,* 17 Indian L. Rep. 6099 (1990). See generally Raymond Austin, *Navajo Courts and Navajo Common Law: A Tradition of Tribal Self-Governance* (2009).

Asian authors expressed the idea of human rights from at least the fifth century B.C.E. Chinese philosopher Hsün-tzu wrote that: "In order to relieve anxiety and eradicate strife, nothing is as effective as the institution of corporate life based on a clear recognition of individual rights." UNESCO, *Birthright of Man* 39 (1969). The Code of Hammurabi (1795-1750 B.C.E.), the oldest written legal code known today, represented a codification and development of the customary law of the region and was probably based upon earlier codes that are now lost. In the Preamble to the Code, Hammurabi expressed the fundamental purposes of government: "to bring about the rule of righteousness in the land, to destroy the wicked and the evil-doers, so that the strong should not harm the weak . . . and enlighten the land, to further the well-being of mankind." For related background, see Paul Gordon Lauren, "The Foundations of Justice and Human Rights in Early Legal Texts and Thought," in *Oxford Handbook of International Human Rights Law* 163 (D. Shelton ed., 2013).

Yet, however much broad convergence there may be around basic conceptions of human rights, abuses of human rights have abounded over time and space. In part, this is because of shifting ideas about what is right and wrong; in many cases, what is today considered an affront to human rights was once deemed acceptable behavior, at least by a sizable or powerful group. In part, human rights abuses occur simply because of the persistent and often widespread tendency of persons in positions of authority to overstep limits on the exercise of power. Throughout the world there have been powerful opponents of human rights who have sought to retain privilege, hierarchy, hereditary rule, and property. In eighteenth-century Europe, human rights proponents challenged and in turn were challenged by vested interests: Thomas Paine was hung in effigy in English cities; Voltaire's writings were banned. Reactionary authors referred to the "monstrous fiction" of human equality. Jeremy Bentham rejected the idea of natural or inherent rights, labeling it "nonsense on stilts." In his strongly held view, people should know "their proper place."

Still, individuals and groups have long joined to assert basic rights against perceived wrongs through actions that have eventually influenced official law, policy, and, at least to some extent, actual behavior. The contemporary international human rights movement is characterized by such actions that transcend national boundaries and that influence the formation of international as well as domestic law, policy, and behavior.

## A.   The Movement Against Slavery

An important antecedent to the contemporary human rights movement is the movement to abolish slavery and the slave trade. The challenge to and eventual official demise of slavery illustrates the process by which the concept of human rights is harnessed to generate changes in law and practice, including at the international level. Notwithstanding the American Declaration of Independence and its proclamation of equality for all (men), slavery was legal in much of the United States for nearly a century after the country's birth, just as it was in much of the world. Slavery had existed throughout history and across the globe, but it changed fundamentally in the sixteenth century with the onset of the trans-Atlantic slave trade from Africa. Between 1519 and 1866, an estimated nine and a half million Africans were forcibly transported to and enslaved in North America, while a further million died on the voyage. The trade reached its peak in the 1780s, when an average of 100,000 people were transported to the Americas annually to be sold as slaves. See James A. Rawley, *The Transatlantic Slave Trade: A History* (rev. ed. 2005). Countless other enslaved persons were carried to Europe, the Caribbean, and Central and South America. Slavery came with the emergence of ideologies of racism, apartheid, and segregation. From the sixteenth to the nineteenth centuries, the international slave trade flourished, and slavery was legal in most countries of the world.

Almost from the beginning of the transcontinental slave trade, a small but vocal minority in the slave-trading countries expressed its determined opposition to slavery, joining the mostly unheard voices of enslaved persons. These individuals began to organize the world's first human rights nongovernmental organizations. They published articles and pamphlets; they spoke out against slavery; and they organized active campaigns of protest. Enslaved persons themselves engaged in uprisings in Saint-Dominigue, Haiti, and elsewhere. Many of the most outspoken abolitionists were themselves former slave traders or slave owners. Unlike many others, they saw a gap between the proclamations of rights—especially in England, the United States, and France—and the practice of slavery. They thus drew intellectual and moral strength from the general proclamations of human rights. As economic factors evolved to allow for the rapid accumulation of wealth without dependence on slavery, the abolitionist movement gained strength.

By the late nineteenth century, the tide had turned, and both the trade in slaves and slavery itself was made illegal in most of the countries that had engaged in or benefited from the slave trade. In the United States, it took a civil war on top of the human rights demands and shifts in economic and political forces to abolish slavery, but in other countries it did not. Governments committed to each other to abolish and impose criminal penalties for the trade in humans through the 1890 General Act for the Repression of the African Slave Trade. The Charter of the League of Nations, the predecessor to the United Nations, and the Convention to Suppress the Slave Trade and Slavery of 1926, along with subsequent treaties and programs developed by the International Labor Organization, succeeded in consolidating in international law a strong norm upholding the fundamental human right to not be subjected to involuntary servitude. The work of the UN's Working Group on contemporary forms of slavery, its causes and consequences, among others, highlights that continuing action is needed to eradicate forms of involuntary servitude that persist today. See generally *Critical Readings on Global Slavery* (D. A. Pargas and F. Roçu, eds., 2017).

## B.  *International Human Rights Today*

Today, there is a substantial body of human rights norms over a range of topics, in various international instruments of law and policy, accompanied by procedures to promote their implementation. Human rights have become part of international law and transnational relations out of efforts to shape perceptions about the essence of human dignity and to bring behavior in line with those perceptions and the values they represent.

The United Nations has developed a wide array of globally applicable international treaties and declarations, which guide the work of the several UN institutions devoted to advancing human rights. There are also well-developed regional human rights protection systems in Europe, the Americas, and Africa. Additionally, regional human rights regimes are emerging in Asia and the Middle East. National constitutions and courts, among other domestic institutions, have also played roles in consolidating understanding of what human rights are today.

This contemporary international human rights system emerged in the aftermath of World War II. This conflict is well-known to have resulted in unbearable loss of life, including the execution of about six million Jews at the hands of Nazi Germany and its allies. See generally *Introduction to the Holocaust,* United States Memorial Holocaust Museum, https://encyclopedia.ushmm.org/content/en/article/introduction-to-the-holocaust (last visited April 25, 2022). The post-war period was a critical time for the development of the international human rights regime that exists today. The United Nations Charter, adopted in 1945, placed human rights at the forefront of the organization's founding purposes and principles, along with peace and economic and social progress. It was soon followed by the adoption of the Universal Declaration of Human Rights, which recognizes key rights later expanded upon in leading human rights treaties, including the rights to life, to equality, to be free from involuntary servitude and from torture, and to enjoy basic economic and social rights such as the rights to health and education.

The Universal Declaration and many of the human rights instruments that subsequently developed reflect the need to place limits on the actions of states that affect the persons inhabiting their territories, out of concern especially with totalitarian and repressive regimes. Given this concern, the post-World War II human rights system has prioritized the development of civil and political rights to ensure democratic governance, participation, representation, free expression, and the ability to protest and to oppose majorities. However, international human rights law has evolved to cover not only what is considered the public sphere, but also, increasingly, the private, including personal relations and business activity. The UN and regional regimes are also giving ever-more content to economic, social, and cultural rights.

The scope of the issues addressed by the international human rights system has expanded over time. There are issues — such as slavery, abuses committed during armed conflicts and by dictatorships, the suppression of free speech, and torture — that have been historically considered problems to be addressed by international human rights or humanitarian law. Other pressing issues today — such as the problems of police violence, violence against women, and the conditions of indigenous peoples — are the subjects of growing attention as international human rights matters, and new human rights norms are quickly developing to address concerns in areas such as the environment, climate change, and the digital space. The content and reach of human rights principles and norms are not static, but rather they evolve according to the issues of the time and perceived needs.

The next section of this Chapter introduces some of the key and emblematic human rights issues today. That is followed by a survey of theoretical and critical approaches to international human rights, including reactionary challenges and backlash. Finally, the Chapter provides an overview of the steps in the development of contemporary international human rights law and institutions.


## II.   SALIENT HUMAN RIGHTS ISSUES TODAY

The readings below highlight examples of salient issues that are at the forefront of discussions about human rights today and that are drawing substantial attention within the international human rights system. The materials reflect how the concept of human rights and derivative principles drive inquiry and prescriptions through avenues of discourse that extend into the international arena. The documents extracted include reports and statements from United Nations and regional agencies and experts, and one from a well-respected non-governmental organization, as these have leading roles in the documentation and awareness-raising of human rights concerns. The origins and work of all these and similar entities are discussed throughout this book.

As you read about each of the issues, consider the following questions (and do so without referencing any particular human rights treaty or other instrument):

- Based on your intuitive sense of human rights or general knowledge, which specific human rights are involved or violated?
- Who are the perpetrators of the human rights violations or threats of violations?
- What obligations might states or others have in relation to the violations or threats?
- Why is the issue a matter of concern internationally?
- What action at the domestic and international levels might be taken to address these human rights concerns?

## A. Racial Discrimination and Police Violence

The prohibition of discrimination is a foundational principle of international human rights law, as manifested by its inclusion in most human rights treaties. It is generally understood that states have the obligation both to avoid discrimination and to take positive measures to address discrimination and achieve substantive equality. These measures entail the adoption of legislation, policies, and programs to prevent discrimination and build societies free from associated prejudices and stereotypes. Human rights treaties, as will be discussed further in Chapter 2, prohibit discrimination based on sex, race, language, religion, political or other opinion, and national or social origin, among other factors. Additionally, human rights treaties and other instruments have been interpreted to prohibit discrimination based on sexual orientation, gender identity, and gender expression.

One of the most deeply-seated forms of discrimination is on the basis of race. Racial discrimination is intimately connected to the legacy of slavery and a history of inferior treatment of persons of African-descent and others belonging to ethnically or culturally distinctive minority or non-dominant groups. Racial discrimination persists and is sometimes lethal, as manifested by the killing of George Floyd, a Black man, by a police officer in the United States in 2020. George Floyd's killing, which led to massive protests, was not isolated and is part of a historical pattern of unjustified police killings of African-Americans and others marked by difference. Although George Floyd's killer was convicted of murder, more often than not such police killings historically have gone unpunished. The United States like other countries is still a nation profoundly affected by racial discrimination, despite its strong legal institutions and governance and formal commitment to equality. Widespread condemnation of the killing of George Floyd contributed to renewed resolve globally in the fight against racism and racial discrimination. It prompted a report by the United Nations High Commissioner for Human Rights calling on states to strengthen their efforts against racial discrimination, especially in the context of law enforcement. An extract of the report follows. The High Commissioner has the status of an under secretary-general of the United Nations and has a leading role in the UN's efforts to promote and protect human rights.

## Promotion and protection of the human rights and fundamental freedoms of Africans and of people of African descent against excessive use of force and other human rights violations by law enforcement officers

Report of the United Nations High Commissioner for Human Rights
U.N. Doc. A/HRC/47/53 (2021) (citations omitted)

SUMMARY

The murder of George Floyd on 25 May 2020 and the ensuing mass protests worldwide have marked a watershed in the fight against racism. In some countries, there is now broader acknowledgment of the systemic nature of the racism that affects the lives of Africans and people of African descent and of the need to address the past in order to secure future conditions of life that uphold the dignity and rights of all. It is our collective duty to address these issues—immediately and everywhere.

Prepared . . . in recognition of the unprecedented opportunity for change, the present comprehensive report . . . presents an agenda towards transformative change for racial justice and equality.

The objectives of this transformative agenda . . . are to reverse cultures of denial, dismantle systemic racism and accelerate the pace of action; end impunity for human rights violations by law enforcement officials and close trust deficits in this area; ensure that the voices of people of African descent and those who stand up against racism are heard and that their concerns are acted upon; and acknowledge and confront legacies, including through accountability and redress. . . .

### II. REVERSING CULTURES OF DENIAL, DISMANTLING SYSTEMIC RACISM AND ACCELERATING THE PACE OF ACTION

10 . . . [P]eople of African descent face interconnected, intersectional and compounded forms of racial discrimination, marginalization and exclusion that are shaped by historical legacies and mutually reinforced through cycles of structural inequalities that have lasted for generations, affecting the enjoyment of human rights in every part of life. Systemic racism persists, in large part, due to misconceptions that the abolition of slavery, the end of the transatlantic trade in enslaved Africans and colonialism, and measures taken by States to date, have removed the racially discriminatory structures built by those practices and created equal societies.

11. Stark socioeconomic and political marginalization shapes the lives of people of African descent in many States. In countries where there are sizable communities of people of African descent, the members of these communities are more likely to live in or to be vulnerable to poverty, suffer disproportionately high unemployment rates, earn lower wages and occupy less-skilled positions. They are more likely to lack access to adequate housing and to live in segregated, disadvantaged and hazardous neighborhoods. In several countries, they also suffer disproportionately from environmental pollution and lack of access to clean water. In some instances, measures relating to citizenship and immigration status have reportedly resulted in discriminatory outcomes for some people of African descent. Despite

some formal measures to protect land rights, people of African descent continue to experience displacement, dispossession, exclusion from and expropriation of their lands in some countries. . . .

13. With the racialization of poverty, disparate outcomes in terms of the enjoyment of economic and social rights are compounded by the insufficient meaningful participation and representation of people of African descent in decision-making processes and in public life. The level of representation in elected and other decision-making bodies in States where there are sizable communities of people of African descent is substantially lower than the percentage of the population they represent. In the United States, for instance, some people of African descent are disenfranchised through measures that affect them disproportionately, including measures that deny voting rights to individuals with felony convictions.

14. The systemic racism experienced by Africans and people of African descent is shaped by intersectionality or the combination of several identities, including sex, gender, sexual orientation, gender identity, nationality, migration status, disability, religion, socioeconomic and other status. Women of African descent stand at the crossroads of intersectionality and inequality and therefore face multiple forms of discrimination arising from their racial or ethnic origin combined with gender-based discrimination and harmful gender stereotyping.

15. The dehumanization of people of African descent—a practice rooted in false social constructions of race historically created to justify enslavement, pervasive racial stereotypes and widely accepted harmful practices and traditions—has sustained and cultivated a tolerance for racial discrimination, inequality and violence. Narratives that falsely associate Africans and people of African descent, including migrants, with criminal activities or that play on economic or even national security anxieties continue to be used to justify laws and practices governing criminal justice systems, migration policy and border governance. Racially motivated violence and hatred, including hate speech, are instruments of far right and populist strategies that draw on supremacist ideologies. . . .

29 . . . OHCHR [Office of the High Commissioner for Human Rights] has received information concerning over 190 incidents of deaths of Africans and people of African descent in contact with law enforcement officials, 98 percent of which were reported in Europe, Latin America and North America, mostly during the past 10 years. Although most of the victims were men—particularly young men from impoverished communities and men with psychosocial disabilities—approximately 16 per cent were women, 11 per cent were children and 4 per cent were lesbian, gay, bisexual, transgender or intersex persons.

30. The analysis of these incidents carried out by OHCHR suggests that three key contexts underlie over 85 per cent of police-related fatalities: first is the policing of minor offenses, traffic stops and stops-and-searches, as in the cases of George Floyd (United States), Adama Traoré (France) and Luana Barbosa dos Reis Santos (Brazil); second is the intervention of law enforcement officials as first responders in mental health crises, as in the case of Kevin Clarke (United Kingdom); and third is the conduct of special police operations, as in the cases of Breonna Taylor (United States), Janner García Palomino (Colombia) and João Pedro Mattos Pinto (Brazil). Many such interventions have been characterized as actions taken in the context of the "war on drugs" or as gang-related operations. . . .

31. In these three contexts, racial bias, stereotypes and profiling appear to play recurrent roles. It appears that erroneous and stereotypical portrayals or perceptions of what or who is dangerous continue to drive inferences made in the context of law enforcement. This situation is compounded and aggravated by intersectional factors. Racial stereotypes have reportedly led to use-of-force violations and to the failure to deliver appropriate care in cases where law enforcement officials have acted as first responders in situations involving people experiencing mental health crises. . . .

34. Research indicates patterns of weak cultures of institutional accountability for race-related misconduct. While some States have undertaken reviews and inquiries producing clear recommendations for change, lessons-learned have not been routinely embedded in policymaking. As a result, there is a high risk that problematic cycles and patterns repeat themselves. With rare exceptions, investigations and judicial decisions fail to consider the role that racial discrimination and institutional bias may have played in the deaths.

35. Consultations and submissions revealed that people of African descent feel continuously betrayed by the system and that there are striking similarities across countries in terms of the challenges they face in gaining access to justice. Many expressed a profound lack of trust in law enforcement and the criminal justice system, primarily due to impunity. It often falls on victims and families to fight for accountability, without adequate support, when they have already been overpoliced and traumatized.

### B.   *Violence Against Women: An Ongoing Crisis*

Violence against women is one of the most widespread and harmful human rights problems. Women constitute more than half of the world's population, and, according to the World Health Organization, one in three women have experienced either physical or sexual violence in their lifetimes. See *Global and Regional Estimates of Violence against Women*, World Health Organization (Oct. 20, 2013), http://www.who.int/reproductivehealth/publications/violence/9789241564625/en/.

Violence against women occurs irrespective of age, race or ethnicity, nationality, or economic class. It takes place within the family and in numerous public settings, such as prisons, places of employment, schools and universities, hospitals, and religious institutions. It may be perpetrated by partners and family members, strangers, government officials and security forces, doctors, teachers, and employees of public and private entities. These serious acts are also largely underreported, which hinders an accurate estimate of their true scope and reach. International human rights law was slow to recognize violence against women as a distinct human rights violation, but today the issue receives considerable attention both within the United Nations and regional human rights bodies. An important development in the area of violence against women has been the recent extension of international legal protection to transgender, lesbian, bisexual, and intersex women. There have been important developments in legal terminology—which now includes sexual orientation, gender identity, gender expression, and sex characteristics—and the consolidation of international norms in the areas of equality and privacy in relation to women.

Violence against women is pervasive during times of unrest, political instability, armed conflict, and government repression. One of the most widely documented situations of violence against women has been the dire reality of women belonging to the Rohingya Muslim minority in Myanmar, which is a Buddhist-majority country. A number of international organizations, including the United Nations, have documented continuous attacks against the Rohingya by the government and its forces. These attacks have included the raping of women and girls, the destruction of their villages and homes, and forced displacement. See United Nations High Commissioner for Human Rights (OHCHR), *Situation of human rights of Rohingya Muslim minority and other minorities in Myanmar—Report of the United Nations High Commissioner for Human Rights,* U.N. Doc. A/HRC/43/18 (2020), paras. 4-24; United Nations, *Detailed findings of the Independent International Fact-Finding Mission on Myanmar,* UN doc. A/HRC/42/CRP.5 (2019), paras. 528-534.

Included below is an extract of a report on this situation by Human Rights Watch, one of the leading non-governmental organizations in the world working in the field of international human rights law.

## All of My Body Was Pain: Sexual Violence against Rohingya Women and Girls in Burma

Human Rights Watch (November 16, 2017)
https://www.hrw.org/report/2017/11/16/all-my-body-was-pain/sexual-violence-against-rohingya-women-and-girls-burma#

. . . Since August 25, 2017, Burmese security forces have committed widespread rape against women and girls as part of a campaign of ethnic cleansing against Rohingya Muslims in Burma's Rakhine State.

Killings, rapes, arbitrary arrests, and mass arson of homes by Burmese security forces in hundreds of predominantly Rohingya villages have forced more than 600,000 Rohingya to flee to neighboring Bangladesh. Rohingya women, men, and children have arrived in Bangladesh in desperate condition—hungry, exhausted, and sometimes with rape, bullet, or burn injuries. The humanitarian crisis caused by Burma's atrocities against the Rohingya has been staggering in both scale and speed.

The Burmese military's brutal campaign follows attacks on 30 police posts and an army base by the Arakan Rohingya Salvation Army (ARSA) on the morning of August 25, 2017 in northern Rakhine State. The government reported that 11 security force personnel were killed. While the government had a duty to respond to the attacks, the Burmese military, supported by Border Police and armed ethnic Rakhine villagers, not only pursued those responsible, but immediately launched large-scale attacks against scores of Rohingya villages under the guise of counter-insurgency operations. Human Rights Watch has found that the violations committed by members of Burma's security forces against the Rohingya population in northern Rakhine State since August 25 amount to crimes against humanity under international law.

This report is based on 52 interviews with Rohingya women and girls, including 29 survivors of rape, who fled to Bangladesh since these operations began.

Rape survivors were from 19 different villages in Burma's Rakhine State, mostly in northern Buthiduang and Maungdaw Townships. They described similarly brutal circumstances of the rapes.  Human Rights Watch also spoke to 17 representatives of humanitarian organizations providing health services to women and girls in the refugee camps, including representatives of United Nations agencies and international and national nongovernmental organizations. We also interviewed two Bangladeshi government health officials.

Human Rights Watch found that Burmese security forces raped and sexually assaulted women and girls both during major attacks on villages but also in the weeks prior to these major attacks sometimes after repeated harassment. In every case described to us, the perpetrators were uniformed members of security forces, almost all military personnel. While it is difficult to estimate the numbers of rapes that occurred, humanitarian organizations working with refugees in the camps in Bangladesh have reported receiving dozens or sometimes hundreds of cases.

These likely only represent a proportion of the actual number of women and girls who were raped. Some witnesses reported seeing women raped and then killed. Others do not report rape because of the deep stigma that makes survivors reluctant to seek assistance. Fear of having to pay medical fees that they cannot afford, or the lack of confidence in ever obtaining redress, also are factors. Of the survivors that Human Rights Watch interviewed, almost two-thirds had not reported their rape to authorities or humanitarian organizations.

All but one of the rapes reported to Human Rights Watch were gang rapes, involving two or more perpetrators. In eight cases women and girls reported being raped by five or more soldiers. They described being raped in their homes and while fleeing burning villages. Human Rights Watch documented six cases of "mass rape" by the Burmese military. In these instances, survivors said that soldiers gathered them together in groups and then gang raped or raped them. Ethnic Rakhine villagers, acting alongside and in apparent coordination with government security forces, were also responsible for sexual harassment, often connected with looting. . . .

Attention to the specific abuses suffered by Rohingya women and girls, including sexual violence, should be integrated into every aspect of the international response to these human rights and humanitarian crisis. This includes efforts to fully investigate the scope of sexual violence and other crimes against the Rohingya, putting in place measures to protect displaced Rohingya in Bangladesh from gender-based violence in refugee camps, and promoting their full participation and leadership in consultations with the Rohingya community.

### C.  Challenges Faced by Indigenous Peoples

The human rights challenges common to indigenous peoples across the globe are a matter of special concern within the United Nations and regional human rights systems. Peoples indigenous to the Western Hemisphere and elsewhere have experienced histories of extreme oppression and systemic racism, beginning with the patterns of European colonization that started in the early sixteenth century that were in many instances genocidal. In addition to having suffered loss of life, indigenous peoples have experienced dispossession of lands and natural resources crucial to their survival, suppression of their cultural identities, and systematic undermining of their own systems of governance. In many instances, these patterns of oppression continue, including as a result of powerful forces that seek to exploit the natural resources on lands that still sustain them. Both state and private actors often implement development and economic activities in the territories of indigenous peoples without their effective participation, with results that can include poverty; food and water insecurity; barriers to access natural resources needed for survival; violence; and cultural upheaval.

Generally, indigenous peoples have remained remarkably resilient, determined to maintain their distinct identities and build healthy communities, but they continue to face obstacles to the realization of their aspirations and the full enjoyment of their human rights. Still lacking are the conditions necessary to ensure that indigenous peoples' rights are adequately respected and secured.

Given their situations, indigenous peoples faced unique challenges during the global COVID-19 pandemic. The following report by the UN Human Rights Council's Special Rapporteur on the rights of indigenous peoples examines these challenges based on information gathered in the early months of the pandemic. As discussed in Chapter 7, the Human Rights Council, which is composed of 47 UN member states, appoints Special Rapporteurs and other independent experts to assist with its work of investigating and addressing human rights issues around the world.

## Report of the Special Rapporteur on the Rights of Indigenous Peoples, José Francisco Calí Tzay

U.N. Doc. A/75/185 (2020) (footnotes omitted)

. . . 17. Indigenous collective memory is marked by pandemics, as diseases such as smallpox, measles and influenza were spread by colonizers, sometimes deliberately, ravaging and decimating their communities. In the COVID-19 pandemic, indigenous peoples have already reported alarming levels of transmission among their communities and sometimes higher rates of fatalities.

18. Respiratory infections, diabetes, cardiovascular illnesses and HIV/AIDS, as well as malnutrition, are already common in many indigenous populations. Often depending on fragile ecosystems for their subsistence, they also suffer particular health impacts from environmental degradation, including pollution of water resources on their traditional lands caused by extractive industries and pesticides from monoculture. Indigenous persons with chronic health conditions or disabilities requiring regular medical check-ups or treatment experience disproportionately the consequences of lockdown measures, overwhelmed national health systems and depletion of medical equipment.

19. Indigenous peoples in voluntary isolation have reduced immunity to imported diseases and are farther from medical services if they contract a disease. In the Amazon, these peoples are already on the brink of cultural extinction. They

report exponential rates of transmission of the virus introduced by logging and mining workers, religious missionaries and, in certain cases, health professionals who had not been tested for COVID or quarantined themselves before entering their territories. . . .

21. While community-living practices such as extended family co-residence, communal labour, food sharing and spiritual ceremonial practices are a fundamental aspect of many indigenous cultures, measures adopted by States to control the virus do not always acknowledge or respect their deep and particular importance for indigenous peoples.

22. Across the world, neo-colonialism and globalization contribute to dispossession of indigenous peoples' lands and keep their societies in a state of marginalization and extreme poverty. Indigenous communities are at increased risk because of the systemic inequities and discrimination they face, and COVID-19 has further exacerbated racism against indigenous men and women across all continents, including stigmatization when indigenous communities are accused of not respecting preventive measures or of having high infection rates. Indigenous peoples also suffer the consequences of food insecurity and lack access to clean water, soap and sanitation.

23. Indigenous peoples often face obstacles in accessing public health services and medication: many indigenous peoples live long distances from health structures, cannot afford the cost of consultations and treatment, face discriminatory attitudes and are denied the right to speak in their own language or to receive care that takes into account their cultural specificities. Public health care structures servicing indigenous territories may be insufficiently equipped. . . .

24. Reports from Africa, Latin America and Asia indicate that indigenous peoples outside urban areas may not have access to testing. Many cannot afford personal protective equipment, and distribution by public authorities may reach remote communities too late or not at all. In certain communities, indigenous peoples are reluctant to access public health care because of more general practices of avoiding outside contact and distrust that they will be treated with dignity. . . .

27. COVID-19 prevention guidelines and advisories are not always translated into indigenous languages, may not be culturally relevant in content or presentation or may be disseminated only via television, online or in other formats inaccessible to certain indigenous peoples. Information for indigenous persons with visual, hearing or intellectual impairment is also rarely available. Communication platforms, such as local radio, phone calls, texting and social networks, should be used, depending on the medium most accessible by the communities, to convey information in accessible and culturally appropriate formats. . . .

44. Unfortunately, indigenous peoples appear to have been largely left out of the COVID response. While the level of preparedness for the pandemic was low around the globe, indigenous peoples were even less likely to be included in any form of national pandemic contingency plan. Nationwide measures to stop the pandemic were applied to indigenous territories without their free, prior and informed consent and did not take into account the systemic barriers faced by recipients. Some Governments relied entirely on civil society or volunteers to ensure the care of indigenous peoples.

### D.  *Suppression of Speech, Social Protest, and the Defense of Human Rights*

Arbitrary limitations on speech, particularly speech in opposition to those in power or that advances controversial agendas, are commonplace in many parts of the world. Limitations on speech can be targeted at political opposition groups, human rights defenders and activists, journalists, or academics. Violence is often used as a means to silence and repress speech. The situation of human rights defenders is of particular concern, as across the globe there are frequent murders of, acts of harassment against, and forms of discrediting those who defend causes that upset powerful interests, including those who advocate for indigenous peoples opposing extractive industries within their lands, the respect and integrity of the environment, the advancement of sexual and reproductive rights, and the rights of LGBTI persons, among others.

This repression is particularly concerning in a global context in which protest is still a major strategy to raise awareness of human rights issues, call for better government responses, and demand accountability for social challenges. The world has continually seen the use of protest in the streets—with various forms of messaging including art—to effect change. The extract below refers to the massive protests in Chile in December 2019, which sounded a call against corruption, the cost of living, privatization efforts, and persistent forms of discrimination in the country. The following press release was issued by the Inter-American Commission on Human Rights, one of the two organs of the regional human rights protection system of the Organization of American States, which will be discussed in detail in Chapter 8.

## IACHR Condemns the Excessive Use of Force during Social Protests in Chile, Expresses Its Grave Concern at the High Number of Reported Human Rights Violations, and Rejects All Forms of Violence

Inter-Am. Comm'n H.R. Press Release No. 317/19 (December 6, 2019)

The Inter-American Commission on Human Rights (IACHR) spoke out against the excessive use of force during the recent social protests in Chile and the serious abuses of power waged during some demonstrations. It also condemned the high number of reports of human rights violations levied against state organizations since the demonstrations started.

As part of its mandate to permanently monitor the human rights situation in Chile, the IACHR has received various reports indicating that people who were arrested were subjected to acts of sexual violence, torture, and cruel, inhuman, and degrading treatment, among others. In response to these serious allegations, the IACHR decided to establish a Rapid and Integrated Response Coordination Unit (SACROI) to monitor and respond to the human rights situation in Chile.

The IACHR noted that the president of Chile made a public statement on November 17, 2019, acknowledging that human rights were violated during the social protests and that state security forces had made excessive use of force in some cases.

According to the information received by the IACHR, there have been 26 fatal victims since the start of the social protests on October 18, at least five of whom died as a consequence of direct action on the part of state security forces, and two of whom died while being held in state custody. According to information from the Ministry of Health, the country's emergency medical services treated 12,652 people who were injured in connection with the demonstrations, and the National Institute of Human Rights (INDH) confirmed that 2,808 people had been hospitalized after being injured during the demonstrations. . . . The IACHR urged the Chilean authorities to investigate these acts of violence with due diligence, to identify and sanction those responsible for such acts, and to inform the public of the outcomes.

To that effect, the IACHR expresses grave concern about the high number of serious human rights violations reported by various international organizations and state bodies. It also expresses concern over the nature of these violations, which point to the existence of repeated patterns of violence against demonstrators during the recent protests. The IACHR welcomes the president of Chile's public commitment to ensuring that these cases are duly investigated, prosecuted, and sanctioned and to guaranteeing that victims will be assisted during the recovery process.

In this regard, the IACHR received information on the excessive and disproportionate use of force against demonstrators at the hands of Chile's national police force (Carabineros de Chile). The IACHR noted that in their respective reports, both the INDH and the Office of Children's Ombuds reported a disproportionate use of force against people who were taking part in peaceful protests, which implied a serious breach of the Protocols for Maintaining Public Order, and of Carabineros Circular No. 1,832 on the use of force. Specifically, these organizations have reported that shots were fired from pellet guns, targeting demonstrators' bodies, necks, and faces; teargas canisters were thrown at demonstrators' bodies; there has been a lack of gradual escalation techniques in the use of force without prior warning; teargas was used around the elderly, children, and pregnant women; and there have been serious injuries from pepper gas, pellets, teargas canisters, and gas guns. The IACHR acknowledged that on November 10 and 17, the Ministry of the Interior sent written instructions to the national police force regarding compliance with protocols on the use of pellet guns. . . .

The IACHR expresses its extreme concern over the large number of people who have suffered eye injuries during the social protests due to the national police force's use of pellet guns or teargas canisters to scatter protesters. . . .

The IACHR also expresses its concern over the high numbers of people who have been arrested since October 18, 2019, in connection with the social protests. According to the information it has received, at least 20,645 people have been arrested since the protests began and at least 950 are being held in pretrial detention. . . .

The IACHR expresses its grave concern over information it received indicating that torture and cruel, inhuman, and degrading treatment took place during arrests. It also notes its alarm at the information published by national human rights institutions that described the national police force's treatment of detainees, which included simulated executions, severe physical and verbal abuse, beatings, overcrowding in unventilated places, and the harassment of children and adolescents.

The IACHR is also alarmed at the large number of allegations of sexual abuse during arrests. According to the information it received, detainees were allegedly raped, subjected to sexual abuse and other forms of sexual ill-treatment, threatened with rape, and forced to strip or squat. The SACROI received information on instances of sexual abuse and inappropriate physical contact with children and adolescents. . . .

The IACHR calls on the authorities to order state security forces to immediately cease their disproportionate use of force. In this regard, the IACHR reminded the state that the national police force's actions to maintain public order must comply strictly with international human rights standards that govern the use of force through the principles of exceptionality, proportionality, and absolute necessity. . . .

Finally, the IACHR urges Chilean society to engage in effective, inclusive dialogue to address the population's legitimate demands while fully respecting human rights and the democratic rule of law. On this point, the IACHR welcomed efforts to establish a new constitution for the country.

### E.  *Environmental Degradation and Climate Change*

The past decades have seen a significant surge of attention to environmental concerns such as pollution from the burning of fossil fuels, contamination of waters and soils from various kinds of industrial activity, deforestation, and biodiversity loss. As it progresses, climate change is rising to the top of the global environmental agenda.

The 1992 Conference on the Environment and Development in Rio de Janeiro produced, in addition to the comprehensive Rio Declaration on the Environment and Development, two groundbreaking treaties: the Convention on Biological Diversity and the UN Framework Convention on Climate Change. A later watershed moment was the adoption in 2015 of the Paris Agreement on Climate Change, by which states commit to addressing the harmful and human-driven effects of climate change by reducing greenhouse emissions fast enough to keep temperature rise this century to well below 2 degrees Celsius and by reinforcing adaptation and mitigation efforts. See Paris Agreement, U.N. Doc. FCCC/CP/2015/10/Add.1 (2016), Annex; *Historic Paris Agreement on Climate Change: 195 Nations Set Path to Keep Temperature Rise Well Below 2 Degrees Celsius*, United Nations Climate Change (Dec. 13, 2015), https://unfccc.int/news/finale-cop21. One noteworthy aspect of the Paris Agreement is that the leading superpowers, United States and China, became parties to it. As of April 25, 2022, the Paris Agreement had 193 state parties and 195 signatories. See *Status of Treaties: 7.d Paris Agreement*, United Nations Treaty Collection, https://treaties.un.org/Pages/ViewDetails.aspx?src=TREATY&mtdsg_no= XXVII-7-d&chapter=27&clang=_en (last updated April 25, 2022).

As concerns over environmental degradation and climate change have increased, so too have these issues been increasingly seen through a human rights lens. The right to a healthy environment is affirmed in several regional treaties, and it was recently recognized at the global level by means of two United Nations resolutions adopted in 2021 and 2022, as will be discussed in Chapter 2. See The human right to a safe, clean, healthy and sustainable environment, H.R.C. Res. 48/13, U.N. Doc. A/HRC/48/L.23/Rev. 1 (Oct. 8, 2021) (resolution by the UN Human Rights Council); The human right to a clean, healthy, and sustainable environment, G.A. Res. 76/300, A/76/L.75 (July 26, 2022) (resolution by the UN General Assembly).

With these developments there are ongoing debates on how to use international human rights law more generally to advance a clean and healthy environment in light of the impacts of environmental degradation and climate change on a range of human rights, such as the rights to life and health. There also has been noteworthy attention to groups whose human rights are particularly affected by environmental degradation and climate change, including indigenous peoples, women, children, older persons, and others. The extract below, of a resolution by the Parliamentary Assembly of the Council of Europe, illustrates a human rights approach to environmental concerns, with attention to inequalities in this context. The Council of Europe, which exists independently of the European Union, promotes democracy and human rights throughout the Council's 46 member states, as discussed in Chapter 9.

## Council of Europe Parliamentary Assembly

## Combating Inequalities in the Right to a Safe, Healthy and Clean Environment

Resolution 2400 (2021)

1. The United Nations Environment Programme states that "human rights cannot be enjoyed without a safe, clean and healthy environment; and sustainable environmental governance cannot exist without the establishment of and respect for human rights." The relationship between the exercise of human rights and the environment is increasingly recognised, and the right to a healthy environment is currently set out in over 100 constitutions worldwide. Despite this, the United Nations High Commissioner for Human Rights has estimated that at least three people a week are killed protecting our environmental rights, while many more are harassed, intimidated, criminalized and forced from their lands. . . .

4. The Assembly also recalls the Preamble of the Paris Agreement that states "Parties should, when taking action to address climate change, respect, promote and consider their respective obligations on human rights, the right to health, the rights of indigenous peoples, local communities, migrants, children, persons with disabilities and people in vulnerable situations and the right to development, as well as gender equality, empowerment of women and intergenerational equity".

6. Just as access to the substantive right to a safe, clean and healthy environment is unequally shared between regions, countries and individuals, so is access to the procedural rights deriving from them, which include the right to information, participation in policy and decision making and training. The Assembly urges all member States to work to ensure that environmental rights are not only a reality for all, but are developed in cooperation between all represented groups, in particular those most affected by climate change and adaptation policies.

7. According to the World Bank, between 2008 and 2013, global inequality fell for the first time since the industrial revolution, but the climate crisis is now reversing this positive trend. The effects of climate change impact poor countries disproportionately, via both a rise in economic damages due to extreme weather and a disproportionate cost of reducing emissions. The Covid crisis has also reopened the rifts between rich and poor countries.

8. Individuals affected by inequalities in access to environmental rights are caught up in a "vicious circle" of multiple discrimination. People already affected by racism are harder hit by climate change, for instance, and the same goes for the poorest groups, as adaptation to climate depends largely on household wealth. Disadvantaged groups are more exposed to the adverse effects of climate change, which in turn increases their vulnerability to damage caused by natural hazards and lowers their capacity to cope and recover.

9. Socially disadvantaged people and minorities also suffer from stigmatization that associates them with their living conditions, which are most often forced upon them. Roma are relegated to sites located on the margins of urban settlements, where they are obliged to share the space with polluting industries, landfills, waste dumps and other contaminated and contaminating installations. Their health and safety are threatened, and in addition they become associated with the negative images of their surroundings by the rest of the population. Member States must distance reception areas for Roma and Travelers from polluted areas, work with them to disassociate their way of life from stigmatizing and discriminating stereotypes and provide them with adequate facilities to allow them to live safe and healthy lives.

10. With regard to gendered differences, 70% of women living in the countries hardest hit by climate change work in agriculture. And 70% of the poorest people in the world are women. Climate change affects children, the oldest individuals, sick people and those in financial hardship. On average, more women than men are elderly and/or suffer from poverty. And it is predominantly women who look after children and the sick. Climate change therefore places a disproportionate burden on women worldwide. . . .

12. With respect to inequalities in access to the right to a safe, healthy and clean environment resulting from economic differences between and within countries, the Assembly calls for:

12.1. the implementation and strengthening of the mechanism for financial assistance from "rich" to "poor" countries provided for in the 1992 United Nations Convention on Biological Diversity, by including additional obligations on developed countries under the 1992 Framework Convention on Climate Change—in particular, the obligation to provide financial assistance to developing countries and to facilitate the technology transfer; . . .

12.3. the strengthening and implementation of the commitment by developed countries to help developing countries inherent in the 2015 Paris agreements, in particular by implementing Article 9 of the Paris Agreement, which provides for financial support in mitigation of and adaptation to climate change, multi-source mobilisation of climate finance, and regular quantitative and qualitative reporting on this action;

12.4. respect and reinforcement of the principle of common but differentiated responsibilities;

12.5. stronger regulations on housing development within countries, drawing lessons from the Covid-19 pandemic which showed that for the benefit of the whole population everyone must have adequate living space and healthy living conditions, and that access to green spaces is essential.

13. With respect to indigenous peoples, the Assembly:

13.1. insists on the necessity for all new legislation to tap into the knowledge and experience developed over centuries by communities whose traditions have preserved the strongest links with and respect for the living world and are less anthropocentric than others, in order for future policies to place higher priority on the environment and take into account this world view;

13.2. calls on countries where indigenous peoples are living to ensure they are consulted and take part in decisions related to their lands and ways of living, and in particular that measures taken in the name of protection of the environment (wind farms or green constructions, for instance) do not affect their lives and livelihoods; . . .

14. With respect to women's access to and contribution to the enjoyment of environmental rights, the Assembly calls for:

14.1. more gender-responsive climate finance to be allocated, in particular at grass-roots and rural levels, to enable women to work and increase their competences;

14.2. equal access to property and tenure rights for women in all member States, in order for them to be in a secure position from which they can build on their knowledge and experience, in particular through community co-operation;

14.3. empowerment of women and girls to lead a just transition to a green economy;

14.4. more quantitative and qualitative data collection on the link between gender and the environment, and a more enabling environment for women and girls through education and training.

15. Concerning young people, the Assembly stresses the absolute necessity to involve youth organizations and other young people in the design of any new legally binding framework for environmental rights, as a condition for success.


## F.  Human Rights Concerns in the Digital Space

An emerging area of human rights concern is the digital world. The fast development of information and communications technology (ICT's), social media outlets, and virtual platforms such as Zoom have revolutionized the way we communicate, interact, and express our ideas. A catalyst for this revolution was the COVID-19 pandemic the world experienced between 2020-2022, which resulted in the closing of schools, businesses, and in-person social activity, producing a significant increase in the use of digital technology and its spaces to continue daily life. Beyond facilitating life through the pandemic, this increase undoubtedly has amplified the voices of many individuals and groups and expanded the ways they are able to communicate. However, it has also added another space in which human rights violations occur, through forms of harassment, hate speech, and infringements of privacy.

Below is an extract of a joint press release by several Special Rapporteurs and other experts appointed by the United Nations Human Rights Council, issued in connection with the 2021 RightsCon summit on human rights in the digital age.

## Pandemic recovery: Digital rights key to inclusive and resilient world — RightsCon, June 7-11, 2021

UN OHCHR Press Release (June 4, 2021),
https://www.ohchr.org/EN/NewsEvents/Pages/DisplayNews.aspx?NewsID=27140&LangID=E

As the world rebuilds civic space during and after the COVID-19 pandemic and beyond, UN experts stress that human rights apply online, as offline, and digital rights must be a top priority.

"Despite the instrumental role of the internet and digital technologies, which have provided new avenues for the exercise of public freedoms and access to health and related information and care in particular during the COVID-19 pandemic, States continue to leverage these technologies to muzzle dissent, surveil, and quash online and offline collective action and the tech companies have done too little to avert such abuse of human rights," the experts said.

"We are deeply concerned that these patterns of abuse, which have further accelerated under the exigencies of the pandemic, will continue and exacerbate inequalities worldwide."

"We need to act together to embrace the fast-pace expansion of digital space and technological solutions that are safe, inclusive and rights-based," nine U.N. human rights experts said ahead of the annual RightsCon summit on human rights in the digital age from June 7-11.

COVID-19 recovery efforts to "build back better" must address serious threats contributing to the closing of civic space and suppression of free speech and media freedom, the experts said, along with ongoing global crises such as systemic violence, climate change, structural inequality, institutional racism, and gender-based violence.

They specifically pointed to internet shutdowns during peaceful protests, digital divides and accessibility barriers including to basic human rights and services, disinformation and misinformation; attacks independent and diverse media; algorithmic discrimination, online threats against human rights defenders, mass and targeted surveillance, cyberattacks and attempts to undermine encryption.

The experts said the pandemic had particularly heightened digital inequalities and discrimination against, among others: people of African descent, ethnic groups, minority groups and communities facing religious, and ethnic discrimination, persons with disabilities, indigenous peoples, internally displaced people, people affected by extreme poverty, women and girls, older persons, migrants and refugees, LGBTQ+, gender diverse persons, human rights and environmental defenders, journalists and activists, worldwide.

They also raised concern about ongoing repression of peaceful protests around the world and an unprecedented spike in reports of child sexual abuse material online.

The experts stressed that States—and the tech sector—must take additional systemic measures so that their efforts reach those who are most at risk of being disproportionately affected. Platforms must be inclusive through engaging people in the ground and improving their investments in least developed countries. "We must leave no one behind—online or offline," they said.

The experts reiterated the need for States to maintain their positive obligation to promote and protect human rights, including through rights-respecting regulations on tech companies. Initiatives to regulate online spaces need to be participatory and fully grounded in human rights standards. Businesses need to uphold their responsibility to respect human rights, including by reviewing their business models, and be held accountable for acts of digital repression, such as the non-transparent content takedowns and manipulation recently witnessed in various regions of the world. "The opacity that prevails in the ways content is moderated by Governments and companies reinforces global perceptions of discrimination, inefficiency and censorship. There is an urgent need for transparency", stressed the experts.

The experts further called on companies to stop supplying governments with technologies—such as spyware tools and applications claiming to recognize faces, genders, disabilities and emotions—which reinforce risks for defenders and civil society actors when exercising their legitimate right to voice critical concerns and defend human rights. Businesses need to prevent and address these risks and avoid contributing consciously or inadvertently to further shrinking civic space.

The experts also cautioned against the repurposing of security and counter-terrorism measures, specifically the use of new technologies, data collection, surveillance and biometric technologies to securitize health and regulate a health pandemic whose effects are most severely felt by minority and groups at heightened risk. They demanded that already controversial public-private security partnerships be subjected to additional scrutiny when leveraged into the public health arena.

The experts reiterated that "only with concerted multilateral efforts to restore solidarity and mutual trust, will we overcome the pandemic while becoming more resilient and united". They also warned particularly against using the pandemic as an excuse to rush forward "digital transformation", as exemplified in digital vaccine certificates, without prioritizing foundational digital rights safeguards.

## Comments and Questions

1. What similarities and differences do you see among the human rights issues discussed above—discrimination and racism; violence against women; oppression of indigenous peoples; barriers to speech and protest; environmental degradation and climate change; and human rights concerns in the digital setting? One important similarity is that they affect persons and groups in large numbers and with elevated frequency. Another is that these are issues closely related to the exercise of human rights that have been recognized in major global and regional human rights treaties. Regarding potential differences, some of the issues are related to the content of specific substantive rights, such as the prohibition of discrimination, and others are intimately connected with the enjoyment of procedural rights such as participation in public and private life and access to information. Why do you

think these six issues (among others) are at the forefront of international attention in the human rights sphere?

2. As we see from the discussion above, the concept of human rights applies in a number of different settings. At the same time, as pointed out at the beginning of this Chapter, human rights are considered inherently universal, applying equally to all segments of humanity. How is the inherent universality of human rights demonstrated or not in relation to the different issues discussed above? Do indigenous peoples or women have rights specific to them? If so, how is that consistent with the universality of human rights?

3. Are all social problems connected to human rights issues? What is the value of considering a social problem as human rights related? What criteria should be used to determine whether an issue should be covered by international human rights law? What does the movement against slavery, discussed in the introduction, have to say about such criteria? Is it better to have more or fewer issues addressed by international human rights law? For critical discussions of the current proliferation of human rights norms and mechanism in international law, see Hurst Hannum, *Rescuing Human Rights: A Radically Moderate Approach* (2019), and *Reinvigorating Human Rights for the Twenty-First Century*, 16 Hum. Rts L. R. 409, 413-419, 429-451 (2016).

## III. THEORETICAL AND CRITICAL APPROACHES TO HUMAN RIGHTS

### A. Natural Law

A range of human rights are now affirmed in international law, as we have seen. But these rights have been asserted well before they became prescribed by treaties, international custom, or generally accepted international legal principles. Characteristic of human rights discourse, assertions of human rights often do not depend at their inception on legal authority emanating from the acts of states. Instead, human rights demands can rely primarily on non-legalistic ideas of justice or morality and in doing so challenge legal authority. Did you find yourself resorting to basic notions of justice or morality in thinking about the human rights issues discussed in the materials above?

Appeals of this type to theories or notions of justice as "higher authority" are a core element of contemporary human rights discourse. Such appeals also are central to the natural law tradition, which has deep jurisprudential roots.

An example is in Lord Mansfield's judgment in the celebrated case of James Sommersett, a Black man, who in eighteenth-century England was held by a ship commander for transport to Jamaica at the behest of an American who claimed ownership of him as a slave. In the absence of specific legal authority to support the ship commander's holding of Sommersett, Lord Mansfield reasoned, "The state of slavery is of such a nature, that it is incapable of being introduced on any reasons, moral or political, but only by positive law. . . . Whatever inconveniences, therefore, may follow from the decision, I cannot say this case is allowed or approved by the law of England; and therefore the black must be discharged." *Sommersett's Case*, 12 George III A.D.1771-71, Lofft 1-18, 98 Eng. Rep. 499-510 (King's Bench, June 22, 1772).

Natural law theory and methodology was at the foundation of the works of Renaissance-era theorists associated with the beginnings of international law. Featured among these early works, articulating the building blocks of a system of law applying broadly to relations among peoples, was examination of the legality of the colonial onslaught brought upon the indigenous peoples of the Americas.

## S. James Anaya

## Indigenous Peoples in International Law

16-19 (2d ed. 2004) (endnotes omitted)

The advent of European exploration and conquest in the Western Hemisphere following the arrival of Christopher Columbus brought on questions of the first order regarding the relationship between Europeans and the indigenous peoples they encountered. Within a frame of thinking traditionally linked to the rise of modern international law, prominent European theorists questioned the legality and morality of claims to the "New World" and of the ensuing, often brutal, settlement patterns. . . .

. . . The early European jurisprudence concerned with indigenous peoples and associated with the early development of international law was the legacy of medieval European ecclesiastical humanism. This jurisprudence perceived a normative order independent of and higher than the positive law or decisions of temporal authority. Conceptions about the source of higher authority, characterized as natural or divine law, varied. For [Francisco de] Vitoria and other Spanish school theorists, God figured prominently as the source of legal authority, and law merged with theology. [Hugo] Grotius moved toward a secular characterization of the law of nature, defining it as a "dictate of right reason" in conformity with the social nature of human beings. This perceived higher authority, whatever its source, provided the jurisprudential grounds for theorists to conceive of and examine norms from a fundamentally humanist, moral perspective, and to withhold the imprimatur of law from acts of earthly sovereigns found to violate the moral code. Thus the early international law theorists were prepared to confront official practices and declare unlawful even the acts of monarchs when these acts were at odds with the perceived natural law. Further, the naturalist theorists viewed the law applying to sovereigns as part of an integrated normative order encompassing all levels of human interaction. . . .

Within this historical jurisprudential frame, the threshold question for determining the rights and status of the American Indians was whether they were rational human beings. In his published lectures, *On the Indians Lately Discovered* (1532), Vitoria answered this question in the affirmative. He surmised that

> the Indians are not of unsound mind, but have, according to their kind, the use of reason. This is clear, because there is a certain method in their affairs. . . .

While unambiguously rejecting title by discovery or papal grant, Vitoria found more palatable the argument that the Spaniards could legitimately assume authority over Indian lands for the Indians' own benefit. Although Vitoria found the Indians sufficiently rational to possess original rights and dominion over lands, he entertained the view that they

> are unfit to found or administer a lawful State up to the standard required by human and civil claims. Accordingly they have no proper laws nor magistrates, and are not even capable of controlling their family affairs; they are without any literature or arts, not only the liberal arts, but the mechanical arts also; . . .

Vitoria pondered this view with ambivalence. He said, "I dare not affirm it at all, nor do I entirely condemn it." Nonetheless, the argument articulated but not adopted by Vitoria to justify Spanish administration over Indian lands was a precursor to the trusteeship doctrine later adopted and acted upon by nineteenth-century states. Of more generally foreboding significance, implicit in Vitoria's pejorative characterization of American Indians, was the measurement of cultural expression and social organization by the European standard: Although they met some standard of rationality sufficient to possess rights, the Indians could be characterized as "unfit" because they failed to conform to the European forms of civilization with which Vitoria was familiar.

Against the backdrop of this Eurocentric bias, Vitoria ultimately constructed a theory of just war to justify Spanish claims to Indian lands in the absence of Indian consent. Within the early naturalist frame, Indians not only had rights but obligations as well. According to Vitoria, under the Roman *jus gentium*, which he viewed as either "natural law or . . . derived from natural law," Indians were bound to allow foreigners to travel to their lands, trade among them, and proselytize in favor of Christianity. In his lecture, *On the Indians, or On the Law of War Made by the Spaniards on the Barbarians*, Vitoria concluded that the Indians' persistent interference in Spanish efforts to carry out these activities could lead to "just" war and conquest. Vitoria counseled, however, against sham assertions of "imaginary causes of war."

Thus, Vitoria articulated a duality in the normative construct deemed applicable to European contact with non-European indigenous peoples. On the one hand, the American Indians were held to have rights by virtue of their essential humanity. On the other hand, the Indians could lose their rights through conquest following a "just" war, and the criteria for determining whether a war was "just" were grounded in a European value system. The essential elements of this normative duality were advanced by other important European theorists of the period associated with the beginnings of international law, including Francisco Suarez (1548-1617), Domingo de Soto (1494-1560), Balthasar Ayala (1548-1584), and Alberico Gentilis (1552-1608).

---

The foregoing extract identifies the methodology and major doctrinal features of an early inquiry into the rights and status of indigenous peoples, within a normative order that was deemed to apply universally to relations among peoples. At the same time, it illustrates how reliance on natural law precepts necessarily is wedded to a certain set of values that can be historically or culturally bound. The legacies of the colonial onslaught experienced by indigenous peoples is the subject of international human rights law today, as discussed in Chapter 3.

## B. Legal Positivism

The natural law tradition, as well as the analytical method by which human rights proponents of diverse backgrounds converge on common fundamental demands, contrasts with legal positivism. Positivism focuses attention on the state as the relevant source of authority and thus sees norms only as the positive enactments of states. Legal positivism came to dominate international legal theory in the late nineteenth and early twentieth centuries, as reflected in, e.g., John Westlake, *Chapters on the Principles of International Law* (1894); William E. Hall, *A Treatise on International Law* 47-49, 65 (Alexander P. Higgins ed., 8th ed. 1924); and Charles C. Hyde, *International Law Chiefly as Applied and Interpreted by the United States* (1922). For a discussion of legal positivism, international law, and international human rights norms, see Martin V. Totaro, *Legal Positivism, Constructivism, and International Human Rights Law: The Case of Participatory Development*, 28 VA. J. INT'L L. 719, 723-731 (2008)

Illustrating positivism in both international and domestic legal discourse is John Marshall's opinion for the U.S. Supreme Court in *The Antelope*, 23 U.S. (10 Wheat.) 66 (1825), a case that arose from the seizure, in international waters off the coast of Florida, of a slave-transporting ship, The Antelope, by a US revenue cutter for suspected violations of federal statutes prohibiting the international slave trade. Spain and Portugal claimed the Africans on board the ship as property of citizens of their countries and argued that, under international law, US law could not apply to infringe upon the trade in that property being transported on the high seas for delivery to Brazil, where the slave trade remained legal. The applicability of the federal statutes prohibiting the trade in slaves turned on an interpretation of the relevant international law, then also called *the law of nations*, on the slave trade and commercial transit on the sea. The Court ultimately agreed that the United States must recognize the claims of Spain and Portugal to the return of the enslaved Africans. Distinguishing between natural and positive law, Justice Marshall opted for the latter in justifying the Court's decision:

> That [the slave trade] is contrary to the law of nature will scarcely be denied. That every man has a natural right to the fruits of his own labour, is generally admitted; and that no other person can rightfully deprive him of those fruits, and appropriate them against his will, seems to be the necessary result of this admission. . . .
>
> Throughout Christendom . . . war is no longer considered as giving a right to enslave captives. But this triumph of humanity has not been universal. The parties to the modern law of nations do not propagate their principles by force; and Africa has not yet adopted them. Throughout the whole extent of that immense continent, so far as we know its history, it is still the law of nations that prisoners are slaves. Can those who have themselves renounced this law, be permitted to participate in its effects by purchasing the beings who are its victims?

Whatever might be the answer of a moralist to this question, a jurist must search for its legal solution, in those principles of action which are sanctioned by the usages, the national acts, and the general assent, of that portion of the world of which he considers himself as a part, and to whose law the appeal is made. If we resort to this standard as the test of international law, the question, as has already been observed, is decided in favour of the legality of the trade. Both Europe and America embarked in it; and for nearly two centuries, it was carried on without opposition, and without censure. A jurist could not say, that a practice thus supported was illegal, and that those engaged in it might be punished, either personally, or by deprivation of property.

It follows that a foreign vessel engaged in the African slave trade, captured on the high seas in time of peace, by and American Cruiser, and brought in for adjudication, would be restored.

Id. at 120-23.

Today slavery is made illegal by treaties and other sources that would qualify as binding positive law under Marshall's analysis. Moreover, an extensive body of human rights norms can now be found in numerous treaties adopted by states or can be deemed to have been consented to by states through custom, as this book demonstrates (see especially Chapters 2 and 3). Hence, it is now possible to embrace human rights from even a purely positivist perspective; for example, the rights of children as articulated in the Convention on the Rights of Child have now been accepted as legally binding by the 196 parties to that treaty.

Nonetheless, as we shall address throughout this book, the modern scope of human rights activism engages not just states but also international institutions, nongovernmental organizations, individual claimants, private actors, and others. Human rights practice involves much more than the straightforward application of existing legal texts or readily discernible custom. Human rights activists continue to propose new human rights norms, and the line between what the law *is* and what the law *ought* to be is often blurred. As a result, human rights discourse inevitably draws heavily on pre-positive notions of justice, very much in the natural law tradition.

## C.  Structural/Functional Approaches

Beyond examining the philosophical underpinnings of human rights, another focus of inquiry is on the function of human rights within the overall state-centric structure of the international legal system, which reflects the fundamental norm of state sovereignty. An example of this approach follows.

Patrick Macklem

## The Sovereignty of Human Rights

22-23, 25-26 (2015) (footnotes omitted)

. . . Human rights in international law are similar to other legal norms that comprise the field in the sense that they are part of customary international law or are enshrined in treaties. But unlike other international legal norms, which characteristically vest entitlements in States and regulate relations between and among sovereign States, international human rights vest rights in individuals and collectivities not necessarily coextensive with the populations of States. They thus perform a distinct function in international law. They speak to adverse consequences of how international law deploys the concept of sovereignty to organize global politics into a legal order—consequences that generate political projects aimed at their amelioration. Some of these projects successfully receive international legal validation in the form of human rights. Determining the purpose of an international human right thus involves identifying the ameliorative role that it performs in relation to the structure and operation of international law itself. . . .

As a result, the possibility that human rights might possess universal and non-universal properties does not threaten the legitimacy of legally comprehending them in these terms. Their role in our international legal order makes sense of the fact that some international human rights legally vest entitlements in, and impose obligations on, some individuals and communities and not others. Nor does the possibility that an international human right imposes positive obligations on others threaten its standing as a human right. If the point of international human rights law is to mitigate harms produced by the structure and operation of international law, then—depending on the nature of these harms and the ways in which international law participates in their production—international human rights may well give rise to positive legal obligations to provide assistance to others. And although their purposes rest on moral considerations that extend beyond the positive fact of their legal existence, the normativity on which they rely is one that is internal—not external—to international law. . . .

The central claim of this [author], then, is that the purpose of international human rights law is to identify and mitigate adverse effects of the structure and operation of the international legal order. International human rights speak to distributional consequences of the fact that international law deploys sovereignty, as a legal entitlement, to organize global economic and political realities into an international legal order. International human rights monitor the distribution and exercise of sovereign power to which international law extends legal validity. They impose positive and negative obligations on sovereign and other legal actors to exercise the authority they receive from international law in ways that respect the right of all individuals and not simply those who fall within their domestic jurisdiction. They focus on the extent to which international legal structuring of global politics by means of a system of sovereign States participates in the production of global economic inequality. They impose international legal duties on all of us to improve the social and economic conditions of impoverished people around the world—conditions for which the structure and operation of international law are partly responsible.

Understanding international human rights law this way does not eliminate deep political disagreement over what global justice might mean and how it might be promoted. Nor does it relegate human rights law to a merely functional role in international political discourse. It ascribes a richer mission to the field by placing the legitimacy of the international legal order under its watch. It comprehends human rights as legal sites of moral and political contestation over fundamental questions about the structure and operation of international law, but it casts these debates in distinctively legal terms. It focuses on how international law distinguishes between legal and illegal claims of power, including sovereign power, and how international human rights possess the potential to monitor the distribution and exercise of international legal authority. In doing so, this account shapes legal judgment on more precise legal questions that punctuate the field—such as what constitutes the scope and content of specific human rights, what interests various human rights protect, and what duties they generate—by directing these questions toward the effects of the structure and operation of international law itself.

———————————

Compare the above approach to the views of Steven Ratner, who sees respect for human rights as one of the foundational purposes of the international legal system. For Professor Ratner, international law embodies, or should embody, a standard of "global justice"—albeit a "thin" standard—and to do so the norms of international law should be "assessed in terms of two principles, or 'pillars'—their advancement of international and intrastate peace and their respect for basic human rights." Steven R. Ratner, *The Thin Justice of International Law: A Moral Reckoning of the Law of Nations* 2 (2015).

## D. Critical Legal Studies

Adding to the discussion of the nature of human rights and their place within the international system are critical perspectives such as those associated with the body of legal theory commonly known as "critical legal studies" (CLS). The CLS approach involves inquiry into political context, power structures, and paradigms of thinking related to the articulation of legal norms and to the processes within which they function. See generally David Trubek, *Where the Action Is: Critical Legal Studies and Empiricism*, 36 STAN. L. REV. 575 (1984); Phillip Trimble, *International Law, World Order, and Critical Legal Studies*, 42 STAN. L. REV. 811 (1990); Nigel Purvis, *Critical Legal Studies in Public International Law*, 32 HARV. INT'L L.J. 81 (1991).

While advancing widely disparate avenues of criticism, the CLS movement includes as one of its central contentions that law is indeterminate and ultimately subject to political choice, rather than politically neutral in its conception and application. CLS scholars tend to see international human rights law in particular as limited by or even favoring power structures grounded in the primacy of states within the construct of an international legal order that is perpetuated by the world's powerful actors and political elites, so that the ability of international human rights law to act as a force against oppression in many contexts is hamstrung or nonexistent. David Kennedy, one of the principal proponents of this criticism, has written:

> Although the human rights vocabulary expresses relentless suspicion of the state, by structuring emancipation as a relationship between an individual right holder and the state, human rights place the state at the center of the emancipatory promise. However much one may insist on

the priority or pre-existence of rights, in the end rights are enforced, granted, recognized, implemented, their violations remedied, by the state. By consolidating human experience into the exercise of legal entitlements, human rights strengthens the national governmental structure and equates the structure of the state with the structure of freedom. To be free is . . . to have an appropriately organized state. We might say that the right-holder imagines and experiences freedom only as a *citizen*. This encourages autochthonous political tendencies and alienates the "citizen" from both his or her own experience as a person and from the possibility of alternative communal forms.

David Kennedy, *The International Human Rights Movement: Part of the Problem?*, 15 HARV. HUM. RTS. J. 101, 113 (2002).

A variant of CLS resides in what is known as Third World Approaches to International Law, or TWAIL. The extract below explains strains of TWAIL's criticisms of international human rights law.

Larissa Ramina

## "Third World Approaches to International Law" and Human Rights: Some Considerations

5(1) Revista de Investigações Constitucionais 261, 263-65 (2018) (footnotes omitted)

. . . TWAIL scholars contend that a TWAIL perspective of international human rights law is crucial to identify many problems concerning the mainstream discourse. . . .

Bhupinder Singh Chimni reminds that the contradictions which mark contemporary international law is perhaps best manifested in the field of international human rights law which even as it legitimizes the internationalization of property rights and hegemonic interventions, codifies a range of civil, political, social, cultural and economic rights which can be invoked on behalf of the poor and the marginal groups.

Rémi Bachand, at his turn, points out that the normative and political goals of TWAILers have guided them to question important issues regarding international law, and beside the focus on the historical evolution of their field, they have concentrated also on the critique of human rights. According to him, there are three types of critiques which are addressed to human rights. The first one is centered on the relationship between universality and particularity, that is, TWAILers argue that the current "universal" and "official" human rights corpus is based essentially in European philosophy, although the concept of human rights is not unique to European societies. Further, they attack the universalizing imaginary based on the premise that they are neutral, objective and apolitical, and the example is the emphasis on civil and political rights.

The second critique addressed to human rights by TWAIL pointed out by Rémi Bachand is that they are a way to civilize peoples mired in a savage and barbaric culture (that is, the Third World), and a way to impose European standards often used as a toll for colonialist or imperialist practices and interventions. Makau

MUTUA's work focus on that issue, talking about what he calls the "SVS metaphore"—savages, victims, saviors. . . .

The third critique addressed to human rights by TWAIL pointed out by Rémi Bachand concerns the imposition of a form of political organization and a form of state as such: the liberal state adopting representative democracy, as it can easily be demonstrated by the focus on civil and political rights, which seek to strengthen, legitimize, and export political or liberal democracy. Makau Mutua states that the human rights "have become synonymous with the human rights movement," and he argues also that liberalism does not tackle the causes of real and economic inequality, which is the main challenge of Third World. Further, Rémi Bachand observes that TWAILers' analysis remains less radical than their political militancy, even if some scholars are openly Marxists. The author reminds also that the European historical origins of human rights (the protection of emerging bourgeoisie against authoritarian monarchical regimes) are enough to demonstrate that they are far from being adequate to protect Third World against violation of the same rights, that is, imperialist and neocolonialist practices. In other words, those human rights have not been made to fight against imperialism and neocolonialism. According to Rémi Bachand: "Nevertheless, the criticisms made by Twail, interpreted in the light of our own comments, reveal that a subalternist theory of international law can only take human rights as strategic tools, if not tactics from the struggle for emancipation, and that it would be a mistake to raise them to the level of the ultimate goal to be attained."

### E.  Feminist Perspectives

As discussed earlier, a major goal in the creation of the international human rights system was to restrain state abuses towards individuals. Civil and political rights were given foremost attention in the early instruments and treaties as part of this goal. Even though the Universal Declaration of Human Rights and several major treaties prohibit discrimination on the basis of sex, these instruments have been seen as failing to capture the broad nature of women's experiences with discrimination and gender-based violence, both in the home and public spaces. Many feminist scholars have criticized these voids in the inception and development of international human rights law, as illustrated in the following extract.

Hilary Charlesworth

### Feminist Methods in International Law

93 Am. J. Int'l L. 379, 382-83, 387-88 (1999) (footnotes omitted)

. . . Feminist methods emphasize conversations and dialogue rather than the production of a single, triumphant truth. They will not lead to neat "legal" answers because they are challenging the very categories of "law" and "nonlaw." Feminist methods seek to expose and question the limited bases of international law's claim to objectivity and impartiality and insist on the importance of gender relations as a category of analysis. The term "gender" here refers to the social construction of differences between women and men and ideas of "femininity" and "masculinity"—the excess cultural baggage associated with biological sex. . . .

One technique for identifying and decoding the silences in international law is paying attention to the way that various dichotomies are used in its structure. International legal discourse rests on a series of distinctions; for example, objective/subjective, legal/political, logic/emotion, order/anarchy, mind/body, culture/nature, action/passivity, public/private, protector/protected, independence/dependence. . . .

The operation of public/private distinctions in international law provides an example of the way that the discipline can factor out the realities of women's lives and build its objectivity on a limited base. One such distinction is the line drawn between the "public" world of politics, government and the state and the "private" world of home, hearth and family. Thus, the definition of torture in the Convention against Torture requires the involvement of a public (governmental) official. On this account, sexual violence against women constitutes an abuse of human rights only if it can be connected with the public realm; for example, if a woman is raped by a person holding a public position for some type of public end. The Declaration on the Elimination of Violence against Women, adopted by the General Assembly in 1993, makes violence against women an issue of international concern but refrains from categorizing violence against women as a human rights issue in its operative provisions. The failure to create a nexus between violence against women and human rights was due to a fear that this might dilute the traditional notion of human rights. It was said that the idea of human rights abuses required direct state involvement and that extending the concept to cover private behavior would reduce the status of the human rights canon as a whole.

This type of public/private distinction in international human rights law is not a neutral or objective qualification. Its consequences are gendered because in all societies men dominate the public sphere of politics and government and women are associated with the private sphere of home and family. Its effect is to blot out the experiences of many women and to silence their voices in international law. . . .

Another public/private distinction incorporated (albeit unevenly) in international criminal law—via human rights law—is that between the acts of state and nonstate actors. Such a dichotomy has gendered aspects when mapped onto the reality of violence against women. Significantly, the ICC statute defines torture more broadly than the Convention against Torture, omitting any reference to the involvement of public officials. Steven Ratner has suggested, however, that some sort of distinction based on "official" involvement is useful as a criterion to sort out those actions against human dignity that should engender state and individual international criminal responsibility and those (such as common assault) that should not. The problem, from a feminist perspective, is not the drawing of public/private, or regulated/nonregulated, distinctions as such, but rather the reinforcement of gender inequality through the use of such distinctions. We need, then, to pay attention to the actual operation of boundary drawing in international law and whether it ends up affecting women's and men's lives differently. For example, the consequence of defining certain rapes as public in international law is to make private rapes seem somehow less serious. The distinction is made, not by reference to women's experiences, but by the implications for the male-dominated public sphere.

———————

For additional reading on feminist perspectives, see Rosa Celorio, "Discrimination against Women: Doctrine, Practice, and the Path Forward," in *Women and International Human Rights in Modern Times: A Contemporary Casebook* 1-18 (2022); and *International Law: Modern Feminist Approaches* (Doris Buss and Ambreena Manji eds., 2005); Hillary Charlesworth, Christine Chinkin, and Shelly Wright, *Feminist Approaches to International Law*, 85 AM J. INT'L L. 613 (1991); *Human Rights of Women: National and International Perspectives* (Rebecca Cook ed., 1994); Suzan M. Pritchett, *Entrenched Hegemony, Efficient Procedure, or Selective Justice?: An Inquiry into Charges for Gender-Based Violence at the International Criminal Court*, 17 TRANSNAT'L L. & CONTEMP. PROBS. 265 (2008); Barbara Stark, *Nurturing Rights: An Essay on Women, Peace, and International Human Rights*, 13 MICH. J. INT'L L. 144 (1991). But see Catherine Harries, *Daughters of Our Peoples: International Feminism Meets Ugandan Law and Custom*, 25 COLUM. HUM. RTS. REV. 493 (1994) (criticizing the standard feminist perspective for its Western orientation at the expense of the problems of women in underdeveloped countries).

## F.  Cultural Relativism

The very idea of universal human rights has been criticized on the grounds that it is necessarily linked to a particular cultural perspective to the exclusion or at the expense of others. In essence, critics assert that the moral assessments implicit in identifying and asserting human rights, like the assessments for discerning natural law, are inevitably driven by cultural conditioning. The diversity of cultures in the world is said to give rise to diverse moral assessments, the existence of which undermines the concept of human rights as universal and inherent. It is thus no surprise that international human rights law has a very complex relationship with culture, including potential conflicts and the need for ways to reconcile rights in this area.

Many of the arguments asserting that specific regional or cultural values differ from established human rights norms have come from Asia, as discussed in Chapter 9. Nobel laureate Amartya Sen responds to cultural relativism concerns in the following extract.

Amartya Sen

## Human Rights and Asian Values
The New Republic, July 14-July 21, 1997

I want to examine the thesis that Asian values are less supportive of freedom and more concerned with order and discipline, and that the claims of human rights in the areas of political and civil liberties, therefore, are less relevant and less appropriate in Asia than in the West. The defense of authoritarianism in Asia on the grounds of the special nature of Asian values calls for historical scrutiny. . . .

II . . .

The size of Asia is itself a problem. Asia is where about 60 percent of the world's population lives. What can we take to be the values of so vast a region, with so much diversity? It is important to state at the outset that there are no quintessential values that separate the Asians as a group from people in the rest of the world and which fit all parts of this immensely large and heterogeneous population. The temptation to see Asia as a single unit reveals a distinctly Eurocentric perspective. Indeed, the term "the Orient," which was widely used for a long time to mean essentially what Asia means today, referred to the positional vision of Europe, as it contemplated the direction of the rising sun. . . .

Still, the recognition of heterogeneity in the traditions of Asia does not settle the issue of the presence or the absence of a commitment to individual freedom and political liberty in Asian culture. . . . The advocates of Asian particularism allow internal heterogeneity within Asia, but in the context of a shared mistrust of the claims of political liberalism. Authoritarian lines of reasoning often receive indirect backing from certain strains of thought in the West itself. There is clearly a tendency in America and Europe to assume, if only implicitly, the primacy of political freedom and democracy as a fundamental and ancient feature of Western culture, one not to be easily found in Asia. There is a contrast, it is alleged, between the authoritarianism implicit in, say, Confucianism and the respect for liberty and autonomy allegedly deeply rooted in Western liberal culture. Western promoters of personal and political freedom in the non-Western world often see such an analysis as a necessary preliminary to bringing Western values to Asia and Africa.

In all this, there is a substantial tendency to extrapolate backwards from the present. Values that the European enlightenment and other relatively recent developments have made widespread cannot really be seen as part of the Western heritage as it was experienced over millennia. In answer to the question, "at what date, in what circumstances, the notion of individual liberty . . . first became explicit in the West," Isaiah Berlin has noted: "I have found no convincing evidence of any clear formulation of it in the ancient world." This view has been disputed by Orlando Patterson, among others. He points to particular features in Western culture, particularly in Greece and Rome, and in the tradition of Christianity, which indicate the presence of selective championing of individual liberty.

The question that does not get adequately answered — it is scarcely even asked — is whether similar elements are absent in other cultures. Berlin's thesis concerns the notion of individual freedom as we now understand it, and the absence of "any clear formulation" of this can certainly co-exist with the advocacy of selected components of the comprehensive notion that makes up the contemporary idea of individual liberty. Such components are found in the Greco-Roman world and in the world of Jewish and Christian thought. But such an acknowledgment has to be followed up by examining whether these components are absent elsewhere — that is, in non-Western cultures. We have to search for the parts rather than the whole, in the West and in Asia and elsewhere. . . .

In the terms of such an analysis, the question has to be asked whether these constitutive components can be found in Asian writings in the way they can be found in Western thought. The presence of these components must not be confused with the absence of the opposite, that is, with the presence of ideas and doctrines that clearly do not emphasize freedom and tolerance. The championing of order and discipline can be found in Western classics as well. Indeed, it is by no means clear to me that Confucius is more authoritarian than, say, Plato or Augustine. The real issue is not whether these non-freedom perspectives are present in Asian traditions, but whether the freedom-oriented perspectives are absent from them.

This is where the diversity of Asian value systems becomes quite central. An obvious example is the role of Buddhism as a form of thought. In Buddhist tradition, great importance is attached to freedom, and the traditions of earlier Indian thinking to which Buddhist thoughts relate allow much room for volition and free choice. Nobility of conduct has to be achieved in freedom, and even the ideas of liberation (such as moksha) include this feature. The presence of these elements in Buddhist thought does not obliterate the importance of discipline emphasized by Confucianism, but it would be a mistake to take Confucianism to be the only tradition in Asia — or in China. Since so much of the contemporary authoritarian interpretation of Asian values concentrates on Confucianism, this diversity is particularly worth emphasizing.

---

Many works raise various approaches and responses to relativism. See, e.g., Abdullah Ahmed An-Na'im, *Human Rights in the Muslim World: Socio-Political Conditions and Scriptural Imperatives*, 3 HARV. HUM. RTS. J. 13 (1990); Mashood A. Baderin, *International Human Rights and Islamic Law* (2003); Edna Boyle-Lewicki, *Need World's Collide: The Hudad Crimes of Islamic Law and International Human Rights*, 13 N.Y. INT'L L. REV. 43 (2000); Eva Brems, *Enemies or Allies? Feminism and Cultural Relativism as Dissident Voices in Human Rights Discourse*, 19 HUM. RTS. Q. 136 (1997); Chris Brown, *Universal Human Rights: A Critique*, 1 INT'L J. HUM. RTS. 41 (1997); *Confucianism and Human Rights* (Wm. Theodore de Bary and Tu Weiming eds., 1998); *The East Asian Challenge for Human Rights* (Joanne R. Bauer and Daniel A. Bell eds., 1999); Ann Elizabeth Mayer, *Islam and Human Rights: Traditions and Politics* (3d ed. 1999); Chandra Muzaffar, "Human Rights and Hypocrisy in the International Order," in *Dominance of the West over the Rest* (Chandra Muzaffar ed., 1995); Ann-Belinda S. Preis, *Human Rights as Cultural Practice: An Anthropological Critique*, 18 HUM. RTS. Q. 286 (1996); Alison Dundes Renteln, *The Cultural Defense* (2004).

### G.   Nationalism, Populism, and Anti-Multilateralism

In the early twenty-first century the world has seen a resurgence of populism and nationalism, which has fed on grievances about the actual or perceived harms from globalization, migration patterns, and other factors. Populist and nationalist movements in many countries have embraced multiple critiques of the functioning of international institutions, including the United Nations and regional organizations with regard to their human rights protection systems. Populist elected leaders, politicians, activists, and others have attacked the perceived ineffectiveness of multilateral institutions in general and challenged their efforts to promote the implementation of international human rights norms. Many of the verbal attacks have included hateful speech and discriminatory language. In some cases, nationalist or populist tendencies have led to very public withdrawals of states from key multilateral institutions or to the undermining of the financial sustainability of many international and regional organizations.

The extract below, written by a well-informed person, provides insight on these populist anti-multilateralist forces, their impacts on the international human rights movement, and how to address them.


Philip Alston

## The Populist Challenge to Human Rights

9 Journal H. R. Practice 1, 1-7 (2018) (citations and footnotes omitted)


. . .The world as we in the human rights movement have known it in recent years is no longer. The populist agenda that has made such dramatic inroads recently is often avowedly nationalistic, xenophobic, misogynistic, and explicitly antagonistic to all or much of the human rights agenda. As a result, the challenges the human rights movement now faces are fundamentally different from much of what has gone before. This does not mean, as scholars have told us, that these are "the end times of human rights," that human rights are so compromised by their liberal elite association that they are of little use in the fight against populism, or that we have entered "the post-human rights era." Nor does it mean that we should all despair and move on, or that there is a "desperate need" to find tools other than human rights with which to combat the many challenges brought by the new populism combined with an old authoritarianism with which we are all too familiar.

But it does mean that human rights proponents need to rethink many of their assumptions, re-evaluate their strategies, and broaden their outreach, while not giving up on the basic principles. As each new wave of bad news sweeps in, most of us are now suffering from commentary and analysis fatigue. But there has not been enough reflection by human rights advocates on the innovative thinking and creative strategizing that are urgently needed. . . .

Before reflecting on how best the international human rights community can respond to challenges that will undoubtedly be more severe and sustained than anything we have witnessed since the depths of the cold war, it is useful to keep some general principles in mind.

First, we need to maintain perspective, despite the magnitude of the challenges. Defending human rights has never been a consensus project. It has almost always been the product of struggle. The modern human rights regime emerged out of the ashes of the deepest authoritarian dysfunction and the greatest conflagration the world had ever seen. It has dueled with and been shaped by the eras of reluctant decolonization, the cold war, neoliberalism, and now populism. Dejection and despair are pointless and self-defeating. It's assuredly not a lost cause, but we should not be fooled into thinking that it's ever going to be a winning cause; it's an ongoing struggle.

Second, this is the start of a long-term effort; it won't be over in four years. I don't need to read out the "honor" roll of recently triumphant populists, nor the list of those waiting in the wings, shortly to gain their moment of glory. But there are many, and no continent is immune — unless we count Antarctica, but even there I suspect that there are some very alienated and angry penguins! The main characteristic of the new populist-authoritarian era is disdain for social conventions, a currency on which respect for human rights norms has long been heavily dependent. The devaluation of that currency opens up immense horizons for the enemies of human rights.

Third, the human rights movement needs to develop a spirit of introspection and openness. Historically, it has not responded well to criticism. As long as the critics were mainly governments seeking to defend themselves or despairing deconstructionist scholars, it was not difficult to continue with business as usual. Going forward, it will be highly desirable for the movement to be open to reflecting on its past shortcomings and to involve a broader range of interlocutors in its reflections than has been the case in the past. . . .

In terms of specifics, there are a great many issues that will demand our attention in the years ahead. I want to focus on just five, all of which seem to me to be central to the challenges that we now confront.

The first is the populist threat to democracy. While this is a complex phenomenon, much of the problem is linked to post-9/11 era security concerns, some of which have blended seamlessly into an actual or constructed fear and hatred of foreigners or minorities. The resulting concerns have been exploited to justify huge trade-offs. This is not only a strategy pursued by governments of many different stripes, but one that has been sold with remarkable success to the broader public. People are now widely convinced that security can only be achieved through making enormous trade-offs, whether in terms of freedom of movement, privacy, non-discrimination norms, or even personal integrity guarantees. The new era of internal threats, which have dramatically increased in recent years, is bringing with it a move to normalize states of emergency. For example, remarkably little attention has been paid as the French government continues to extend and enthusiastically implement a rather draconian state of emergency. This is not for a moment to suggest that the seriousness of the threats that may have been identified, and the horrors that have taken place, should be downplayed, but the fact that the depth and scope of the emergency provisions have been so little debated is both stunning and instructive. . . .

The second major issue is the role of civil society. It is now fashionable among human rights proponents to decry the fact that the "space for civil society is shrinking." But this phrase is all too often a euphemism, when the reality is that the space has already closed in a great many countries. The opportunities for civil society to operate are being closed down, and very effectively so in many countries. . . . Many organizations thus have to operate without authorization, which brings the possibility of being arrested and imprisoned at any moment. . . .

The third issue is the linkage between inequality and exclusion. Populism is driven in part by fear and resentment. To the extent that economic policies are thus critical, it is noteworthy that mainstream human rights advocacy addresses economic and social rights issues in a tokenistic manner at best, and the issue of inequality almost not at all. Similarly, the focus of most human rights advocacy is on marginal and oppressed individuals and minority groups. From our traditional perspective, that is how it should be — they are the ones who most need the help. People like me do not need help — elderly white males are fine thank you, we are doing well. But the reality is that the majority in society feel that they have no stake in the human rights enterprise, and that human rights groups really are just working for "asylum seekers," "felons," "terrorists," and the like. This societal majority seems far less likely today than it might have been in the past to be supportive of the rights of the most disadvantaged merely out of some disappearing ethos of solidarity. I believe that a renewed focus on social rights and on diminishing inequality must be part of a new human rights agenda which promises to take into account the concerns, indeed the human rights, of those who feel badly done by as a result of what we loosely call globalization-driven economic change.

The fourth issue that I want to highlight is the undermining of the international rule of law. This is a potentially huge area and I will focus on just two aspects of it. The first is the systematic undermining of the rules governing the international use of force. . . . When I was involved in my capacity as UN Special Rapporteur on extrajudicial executions in the debate over targeted killings, I warned that the countries justifying these practices were setting precedents that would inevitably be invoked by much less well-meaning forces in the future, and by administrations that had even fewer qualms about legality. Those practices are now coming back to haunt us. . . .

The fifth and final issue concerns the fragility of international institutions. The International Criminal Court (ICC) is under sustained attack with various African states announcing their planned withdrawals. And the announcement by the Office of the Prosecutor that she is actively investigating the activities of the CIA and other forces in Afghanistan and related countries will also further endear the court to the Trump Administration. We are in for an extremely tough ride in terms of trying to withstand and protect what has been achieved by the ICC and its immense potential. . . .

### Comments and Questions

1. Contrast Lord Mansfield's reasoning in the *Sommersett's Case*, referenced *supra* page 23, with that of Chief Justice John Marshall's in *The Antelope*, *supra* page 26. Note that both recognized that slavery was immoral and against natural rights, but in *Sommersett's Case* morality prevailed and in *The Antelope* it did not. What can explain the difference in the weight given natural law precepts, relative to positive law, in these cases? In judicial decision-making and legal analysis today, how do concepts of morality or fundamental values work in association with statutes, treaties and other sources that can be described as positive law? This question will be taken up in relation to treaty interpretation in Chapter 2.

2. Recall from the material above, at page 24, that Francisco de Vitoria was able to perceive in the indigenous people of "newly discovered" lands certain inherent rights based on their prior occupancy of those lands; but the same body of natural law that recognized those rights was deemed to limit and condition them within a religious and cultural perspective that, according to Professor Anaya, ultimately favored the non-indigenous "discoverers." Assuming that Vitoria's ultimate

conclusions about the rights and status of indigenous peoples in the Americas were flawed under today's standards of justice, did Vitoria's reasoning on this subject nonetheless contribute to human rights? In what way, if any, was Vitoria's method of reasoning similar to that invoked by many who today challenge conditions of oppression? What does Vitoria's analysis tell us about the significance of cultural perspective for natural law reasoning? Does cultural perspective similarly influence human rights discourse today?

3. Contemporary human rights discourse largely eschews the rhetoric of "natural law" or "natural rights," but it nonetheless assumes that there are certain basic values that are common to all or most cultures of the world today, even though such values may have evolved differentially across cultures over time. Do you agree with this assumption of the existence of universal or broadly held values? Are values such as liberty and freedom truly universal, as Amartya Sen suggests? Assuming there are such universal values, does contemporary international human law adequately capture them, or does it yield to Western liberal perspectives so as to undermine its claim to universality and legitimacy, as suggested by TWAIL scholars, in respect to much of the developing world?

4. Can culture ever justify a practice even if it violates human rights norms? One practice that has been conducted historically against women and girls within a number of cultures is female genital mutilation. The United Nations Committee on the Elimination of All Forms of Discrimination against Women and the Committee on the Rights of the Child have defined this practice as "the practice of partially or wholly removing the external female genitalia or otherwise injuring the female genital organs for non-medical or non-health reasons." Committee on the Elimination of Discrimination against Women and Committee on the Rights of the Child, *Joint General recommendation no. 31 of the Committee on the Elimination of Discrimination against Women/General comment no. 18 of the Committee on the Rights of the Child on harmful practices*, UN Doc. CEDAW/C/GC/31-CRC/C/GC/18 (2014), para. 19. Both committees have identified female genital mutilation as a harmful practice contrary to universal human rights treaties and have expressed concern over its harmful health effects, including extreme pain and childbirth complications. See id. How can this assessment carry weight where the practice is entrenched?

5. Consider Macklem's argument that, given the state-centered character of the international legal order, the function of human rights norms in international law is to mitigate the adverse consequences of the way international law has otherwise validated the distribution of sovereignty among states. Does this argument ascribe to human rights too little of a role in the international legal order or instead one that is too ambitious? Is this argument a persuasive way around the criticism that the state-centered character of international human rights law is debilitating, a criticism made within CLS?

6. Do you agree with Charlesworth's criticism of the public/private distinction in international human rights law? Which factors would justify state interference with family matters or spousal relations? How can states prevent human rights violations that may occur within a home setting? Other than by maintaining this distinction, what other consequences might result from the historically male-dominated world in which international human rights law has developed?

7. What accounts for the resistance within nationalist and populist movements to the international human rights system? Is it the content of human rights norms,

the international institutional apparatus that works to implement the norms, some of both, or something else? What is the response to those who challenge the legitimacy of international institutions generally and international human rights institutions in particular? Note that many of the populist challenges to international institutions are based on economic or labor grievances. Can human rights norms themselves help resolve these grievances?

## IV.   A BRIEF HISTORY OF HUMAN RIGHTS IN INTERNATIONAL LAW AND INSTITUTIONS

The author of the following piece, who is a Holocaust survivor, had many roles in the international human rights system, including as a former judge on the International Court of Justice and the Inter-American Court of Human Rights. This essay was a contribution to the centenary celebration of the *American Journal of International Law*.

Thomas Buergenthal

### The Evolving International Human Rights System

100 Am. J. Int'l L. 783, 784-801, 803, 807 (2006) (footnotes omitted)

The regional human rights machinery in existence today, as well as the plethora of United Nations human rights bodies, traces its antecedents to League of Nations institutions that dealt with minorities' rights and mandated territories. After World War I, the Allied and Associated Powers concluded a series of treaties with Austria, Bulgaria, Czechoslovakia, Greece, Poland, Romania, Turkey, and Yugoslavia for the protection of the rights of the minorities living in those countries. The League agreed to become the guarantor of the obligations the states parties assumed in these treaties. . . .

The League of Nations mandates system applied only to the former colonies of the states that were defeated in World War I. Under Article 22 of the League's Covenant, these colonies were transformed into mandates to be administered by some of the victorious powers in that war. Article 22 further provided that the mandatory states were to administer the mandated territories in accordance with "the principle that the well-being and development of [indigenous] peoples form a sacred trust of civilisation." . . .

### II.  THE UNITED NATIONS CHARTER

International human rights law, as we know it today, begins with the Charter of the United Nations. According to its Article 1 (3), one of the purposes of the United Nations is the achievement of "international co-operation in . . . promoting and encouraging respect for human rights and for fundamental freedoms for all without distinction as to race, sex, language, or religion." That the UN Charter should have listed this subject among the Organization's purposes is not surprising, considering that it was drafted in the aftermath of World War II, the Holocaust, and the murder of millions of innocent human beings. But contrary to what might have been expected given this background, the Charter did not impose any concrete human rights obligations on the UN member states. Although a group of smaller countries and nongovernmental organizations (NGOs) attending the San Francisco Conference fought for the inclusion of an international bill of rights in the Charter, these efforts failed, principally because they were opposed by the major powers.

Instead of a bill of rights, the San Francisco Conference adopted some intentionally vague Charter provisions on human rights. . . .

Despite their vagueness, however, the human rights provisions of the Charter did prove to have important consequences. In time, the membership of the United Nations came to accept the proposition that the Charter had internationalized the concept of human rights. This did not mean that as soon as the Charter entered into force, all human rights issues were ipso facto no longer essentially within the domestic jurisdiction of states. It did mean, though, that states were deemed to have assumed some international obligations relating to human rights. Although the full scope of these rights remained to be defined, states could no longer validly claim that human rights as such were essentially domestic in character. Equally important, the obligation imposed by Article 56 on UN member states, which requires them to cooperate with the Organization in the promotion of human rights, provided the United Nations with the requisite legal authority to embark on what became a massive lawmaking effort to define and codify these rights. The centerpiece of this effort was the proclamation in 1948 of the Universal Declaration of Human Rights. The adoption of a large number of human rights conventions followed, including the two International Covenants on Human Rights in 1966. These two treaties, together with the human rights provisions of the Charter and the Universal Declaration, constitute the International Bill of Rights. Although the Universal Declaration was adopted as a nonbinding UN General Assembly resolution and was intended, as its preamble indicates, to provide "a common understanding" of the human rights and fundamental freedoms mentioned in the Charter, it has come to be accepted as a normative instrument in its own right. Together with the Charter, the Universal Declaration is now considered to spell out the general human rights obligations of all UN member states.

## III. UN Human Rights Law and Practice

UN human rights law has evolved over the past sixty years along two parallel paths, one based on the UN Charter, the other on the human rights treaties adopted by the Organization. The Charter-based system comprises the human rights principles and institutional mechanisms that different UN organs have developed in the exercise of their Charter powers. The treaty-based system consists of a large number of human rights treaties drafted under UN auspices that codify much of the international human rights law in existence today. Some of these treaties also establish institutional mechanisms to monitor compliance by the states parties with the obligations imposed by these instruments.

THE CHARTER-BASED SYSTEM

The UN Human Rights Council, the successor to the Human Rights Commission, lies at the center of the Charter-based system, followed by the Commission on the Status of Women and various subsidiary bodies of the Council. . . . Although the Human Rights Commission took the position into the mid-1960s that it lacked the power to act on violations of human rights brought to its attention, that attitude began to change as more and more newly independent states joined the United Nations and campaigned for UN antiapartheid measures. They argued that the United Nations had the requisite authority to take such action because a state that practiced apartheid could not be said to be "promoting" human rights without discrimination, as required by Articles 55 and 56 of the Charter. This argument gradually prevailed, prompting the General Assembly to call on South Africa to end apartheid and on Southern Rhodesia to do away with its racial discrimination policies. The Economic and Social Council followed up with a series of resolutions on the subject. In one of the earliest, ECOSOC authorized the Human Rights Commission "to make a thorough study of situations which reveal a consistent pattern of violations of human rights, as exemplified by the policy of apartheid as practised in the Republic of South Africa . . . , and racial discrimination as practiced notably in Southern Rhodesia." This narrow mandate was expanded a few years later when ECOSOC empowered the Commission and its subcommission to act on complaints from groups and individuals that revealed "a consistent pattern of gross and reliably attested violations of human rights." This resolution opened the way for the Commission and subcommission to deal with gross violations of human rights in general, that is, whether or not they involved apartheid or racial discrimination.

These and related ECOSOC resolutions enabled the Human Rights Commission gradually to develop a growing number of UN Charter-based mechanisms for dealing with large-scale human rights violations. Today the system consists of mushrooming rapporteur and special mission components, as well as the Office of the United Nations High Commissioner for Human Rights with its own bureaucracy. . . . These institutions derive their normative legitimacy from the Charter itself and from the Universal Declaration of Human Rights.

THE TREATY-BASED SYSTEM

The treaty-based human rights system of the United Nations began with the adoption by the General Assembly of the Convention on the Prevention and Punishment of the Crime of Genocide on December 9, 1948, one day before the proclamation of the Universal Declaration of Human Rights. Since then the United Nations has adopted a large number of human rights treaties. [These include] the International Convention on the Elimination of All Forms of Racial Discrimination; the International Covenant on Civil and Political Rights and the International Covenant on Economic, Social and Cultural Rights [and other treaties that are discussed in Chapter 2]. With the exception of the Genocide Convention and the Covenant on Economic, Social and Cultural Rights, each of the foregoing treaties provides for a so-called "treaty body," which consists of a committee of independent experts that monitors compliance by the states parties with the obligations they assumed by ratifying these conventions. Some years after the Covenant on

Economic, Social and Cultural Rights entered into force, ECOSOC created a similar body for that Covenant by resolution. . . .

### OVERALL ACHIEVEMENT OF THE UNITED NATIONS

The most important contribution of the United Nations to the protection of human rights consists of the many human rights instruments — resolutions, declarations, and conventions — it has adopted since it came into being. These instruments, together with the human rights provisions of the Charter, laid the normative foundation of the contemporary international human rights revolution. They inspired the lawmaking processes that created the European, inter-American, and African human rights systems. They have also influenced, in part at least, the contents of the legal norms under which international criminal tribunals operate today.

The . . . UN treaty bodies, which currently supervise the implementation of the major UN human rights conventions, have played an important role over the years in strengthening the international human rights system. Although their powers are limited, these bodies have been able gradually to examine ever more intrusively the human rights policies and practices of the states parties to these conventions. This process — the review of the periodic reports these states must submit to the treaty bodies — has required the states publicly to explain and defend their human rights policies every few years. The very knowledge that their human rights policies will be scrutinized in this fashion by one or the other treaty body puts pressure on states to reexamine these policies and may lead to an improvement in the human rights situation in some countries at a minimum. This entire process also makes those states that are not parties to these treaties aware of the progressive internationalization of almost all aspects of their national human rights policies. That, in turn, cannot but have beneficial consequences in at least some countries as far as their human rights situations are concerned. . . .

## IV. REGIONAL HUMAN RIGHTS SYSTEMS

The European Convention on Human Rights ushered in the first regional system for the protection of human rights. It was followed by the inter-American and African systems. All three of the existing systems seek in one form or another to supplement the human rights efforts of the United Nations by providing protective mechanisms suited to their regions. In addition to guaranteeing many of the human rights that various UN instruments proclaim, each regional system also codifies those rights to which the region attaches particular importance because of its political and legal traditions, its history and culture.

### THE EUROPEAN HUMAN RIGHTS SYSTEM

The European Convention for the Protection of Human Rights and Fundamental Freedoms established what has become the most effective international system for the protection of individual human rights to date. It has also served as a model for the two other regional human rights systems. The Convention traces its origin to the late 1940s, when the states constituting the Council of Europe, then a grouping of Western European states only, concluded that UN efforts to produce a treaty transforming the lofty principles proclaimed in the Universal Declaration of Human Rights into a binding international bill of rights would take many years to come to fruition. Rather than wait, they decided that the Council of Europe should proceed on its own. The justification for not waiting was expressed in the preamble to the European Convention, which stated that the members of the Council of Europe were "resolved, as the Governments of European countries which are likeminded and have a common heritage of political traditions, ideals, freedom and the rule of law, to take the first steps for the collective enforcement of certain of the rights stated in the Universal Declaration." . . .

. . .The original Convention machinery consisted of a European Commission and Court of Human Rights. The main function of the Commission was to pass on the admissibility of all applications, both interstate and individual. . . .

The institutional structure of the European system was substantially changed with the adoption of Protocol No. 11 to the Convention, which entered into force in 1998. It abolished the Commission and gave individuals direct access to the Court. The Convention thus became the first human rights treaty to give individuals standing to file cases directly with the appropriate tribunal. . . . Over time, the European Court of Human Rights for all practical purposes has become Europe's constitutional court in matters of civil and political rights. Its judgments are routinely followed by the national courts of the states parties to the Convention, their legislatures, and their national governments. The Convention itself has acquired the status of domestic law in most of the states parties and can be invoked as such in their courts. While at times some of the newer states parties find it difficult to live up to their obligations under the Convention, a substantial majority of states applies the Convention faithfully and routinely. . . .

THE INTER-AMERICAN HUMAN RIGHTS SYSTEM

When the Charter of the Organization of American States (OAS) was adopted in Bogota, Colombia, in 1948, it made only general references to human rights. But the same Bogota conference also proclaimed the American Declaration of the Rights and Duties of Man, though merely in the form of a nonbinding conference resolution. Before the American Convention on Human Rights entered into force in 1978, the human rights provisions of the OAS Charter, read together with the American Declaration, provided the sole, albeit rather weak, legal basis for the protection of human rights by the OAS.

Until 1960, the OAS made no serious effort to create a mechanism for the enforcement of these rights. That year the Inter-American Commission on Human Rights was established. Composed of seven independent experts elected by the General Assembly of the OAS, the Commission was charged with the promotion of the rights proclaimed in the American Declaration. . . .

The American Convention on Human Rights was concluded in San Jose, Costa Rica, in 1969 and came into force in 1978. Like the European Convention, the American Convention guarantees only civil and political rights. . . .

The institutional structure of the American Convention is modeled on that of the European Convention as originally drafted, that is, before its Protocol No. 11 entered into force. The American Convention provides for a seven-member Inter-American Commission on Human Rights and an Inter-American Court of Human Rights of seven judges. . . .

Today the Inter-American Court of Human Rights, which has both contentious and advisory jurisdiction, plays an ever more important role in the inter-American human rights system. Most of the states that have ratified the Convention to date have now also accepted the Court's contentious jurisdiction. . . .

### The African Human Rights System

The African human rights system evolved in two distinct stages in a manner somewhat similar to that of its inter-American counterpart. The first stage consisted of the adoption in 1981 by the Organization of African Unity, now the African Union, of the African Charter on Human and Peoples' Rights. It entered into force in 1986 and in the meantime has been ratified by all fifty-three member states of the African Union. The Charter created an African Commission on Human and Peoples' Rights, but not a court. The African Court of Human and Peoples' Rights was established later by means of a separate protocol that came into force in 2004. The Court was formally inaugurated only in 2006.

The catalog of rights that the African Charter guarantees differs from its European and inter-American counterparts in several important respects. The Charter proclaims not only rights but also duties, and it guarantees both individual and peoples' rights. In addition to civil and political rights, the African Charter sets out a series of economic and social rights. . . .

The Commission's mandate is "to promote human and peoples' rights and ensure their protection in Africa." It is composed of eleven elected members who serve in their individual capacities. The Commission has promotional and quasi-judicial powers. . . .

The [subsequently-established] African Court of Human and Peoples' Rights, whose function it is to "complement the protective mandate" of the African Commission, has contentious and advisory jurisdiction. Its contentious jurisdiction is broader than that of the European and inter-American Courts; it extends to disputes arising not only under the Charter and the Protocol establishing the Court, but also "under any other relevant Human Rights instrument ratified by the States concerned.". . .

### V.  Other Developments

. . .

### Nongovernmental Organizations

Another important and relatively recent development can be seen in the phenomenal growth of human rights NGOs. As UN and regional human rights institutions have multiplied, so have NGOs that monitor, promote, and criticize their activities. Some of them were created to advance the protection of human rights in general or in various organizations, such as the United Nations; others concern themselves only with the regional human rights bodies or institutions, for example, the Organization for Security and Co-operation in Europe. Some NGOs are international in character and have offices or links in different regions of the world; others work only at the national level. Depending upon their charters, these organizations perform a variety of functions. They represent petitioners before international judicial and quasijudicial human rights institutions; they lobby national and international political bodies on human rights issues; and they publicize human rights violations in their own countries or abroad. Some of them focus on one specific issue, such as health; others deal with a whole range of issues. A few NGOs prepare reports on human rights conditions in specific countries. They frequently submit these reports to UN human rights rapporteurs and to members of UN human rights treaty bodies to challenge the claims governments make in their official periodic human rights reports. . . .

As a group, the human rights NGOs have been playing an ever more important role in helping to transform the conglomerate of weak institutions that constitute the international human rights system into an institutional machinery that will make it increasingly more difficult for states to give mere lip service to their international human rights obligations. . . .

## VI. Conclusion

As this overview of the evolution of the contemporary international human rights system demonstrates, this branch of international law has experienced phenomenal growth over the past one hundred years. . . . Today international law accords individuals a plethora of internationally guaranteed human rights. But because so much international human rights law has come into force and so many intergovernmental institutions have been created to give effect to it, one might be led to believe that the system as a whole is functioning well and that it is effective in protecting rights of human beings the world over. That is certainly not true! Although the international human rights system as it exists today is undeniably functioning better than many would have believed possible twenty or thirty years ago, it has not prevented the massive violations that have been, and continue to be, committed in many parts of the world. Equally, though, the system in place today—and here I refer not only to the formal institutions and legal norms, but also to the work being done by NGOs and various human rights bureaucracies both national and intergovernmental—has saved lives, improved the human rights conditions in many countries, and is succeeding in forcing an increasing number of governments to take their human rights obligations more seriously than before. That is progress regardless of how one defines it.

One phenomenon above all others has been a major contributing factor to the growing political impact of human rights on the conduct of international relations and the behavior of governments: the ever more pervasive and readily observable conviction of human beings around the world that they are entitled to the enjoyment of human rights. . . . This phenomenon, I would argue, has taken on almost universal proportions and is attributable to several factors. First is the massive corpus of human rights legislation that the United Nations, its specialized agencies, and various regional organizations have promulgated and publicized over the years. Of equal impact is the growing importance the international community has come to attach to human rights as a priority item on the agendas of international diplomatic conferences and in bilateral and multilateral relations. This development grew out of the decades-long efforts by various NGOs and a handful of governments to call attention to human rights violations, to stigmatize the violators, and, in general, to make international human rights law more effective. Not to be overlooked, finally, is the global electronic communications explosion. It has played and continues to play an important role in focusing the world's attention almost instantaneously on violations of human rights no matter where they occur. While over the years some government leaders in various countries and different extremist political groups have sought in a variety of ways to undermine these developments, their efforts have on the whole been unsuccessful. They have been unable to halt what has become a worldwide movement that has captured the imagination of human beings yearning to be treated humanely and with dignity.

---

The above extract of Professor Buergenthal's essay provides a foundation for understanding the basic components of the international human rights system as it exists today, as well as for understanding the historical underpinnings of this system. The readings that follow in this book will build upon this outline and the other materials in this introductory chapter, with attention to that constantly evolving "imagination of human beings yearning to be treated humanely and with dignity" referred to by Professor Buergenthal.

## V. FINAL COMMENTS AND QUESTIONS

1. As international human rights institutions and instruments grow in scope and number, so too does the complexity of the international human rights system. And there are many persistent questions. How to adequately respond to social change and new problems? How to properly reflect the concerns of all segments of humanity in international human rights programming? Can or should treaties cover every issue that bears upon human rights? How can the international human rights system better work to achieve substantive equality and other fundamental rights in practice? These questions come into better focus and answers begin to emerge with the building of knowledge about the components of the international human rights system and their place in international law and institutions, the objective of this book.

2. Other questions — regarding our humanity — still provoke reflection, with future potential repercussions on the development of international human rights law. What makes us qualify for human rights in the first place? What is the essence of our humanity? What makes human rights *inherent*? Consider that elephants mourn their dead, bonobos transmit learning (i.e., cultural practices) to their young, chimpanzees use tools and can communicate in sign language, and dolphins as well as primates have exhibited altruistic behavior. See *Minding Animals: Awareness, Emotions, and Heart* (Marc Bekoff ed., 2002); Jeffrey Moussaieff Masson and Susan McCarthy, *When Elephants Weep: The Emotional Lives of Animals* (1994). We share 98 percent of our genome with higher primates. And what might the future hold for artificial intelligence (AI)?

3. Consider also the quickly developing technology that recently has led to the capacity to clone humans. There appears to be general agreement worldwide that, despite such capacity, human reproductive cloning should be discouraged, although governments are deeply divided on the validity of research cloning of

human embryos, which scientists claim could yield important medical advances. See generally National Research Council, *Scientific and Medical Aspects of Human Reproductive Cloning* (2002).

In 2005, the UN General Assembly adopted, by a vote of 84 to 34 with 37 abstentions, a Declaration on Human Cloning, GA Res. 59/280 (Mar. 8, 2005). The Declaration calls upon states to "prohibit all forms of human cloning inasmuch as they are incompatible with human dignity and the protection of human life." Id., para. (b). But the declaration is non-binding and does not reflect a consensus of states. Several states and the European Union do prohibit human cloning, but most do not. It could be only a matter of time before human reproductive cloning will occur, despite the myriad ethical concerns. See generally Adèle Langlois, *The Global Governance of Human Cloning: The Case of UNESCO*, Palgrave Communications 3, 17019 (March 17, 2017), https://www.nature.com/articles/palcomms201 719; Kerry Lynn Macintosh, *Illegal Beings: Human Clones and the Law* (2005); Stephen P. Marks, *Human Rights Assumptions of Restrictive and Permissive Approaches to Human Reproductive Cloning*, 6 J. HEALTH & HUM. RTS. 81 (2002).

Contrary to popular belief, human clones would not be exact replicas of existing or dead persons; the identity in DNA would yield similarities fewer than those that exist between identical twins. See Macintosh *supra* at 12-14. Nonetheless, if human clones are produced, they may be stigmatized by a continuing aversion to reproductive cloning. Do current efforts to ban human cloning contribute to stigmatizing potential human clones? Assuming that human clones may one day exist, how should the international human rights movement respond to any such stigmatization of clones or other difficulties they may encounter? Would extending human rights protections to clones in some way validate human cloning? Consider the clone army in the *Star Wars* movies, the compassionate clone hatched to continue the life of a dying man with the latter's young family in the 2021 *Swan Song* film, and the following lyrics from the Pat Benatar song, "My Clone Sleeps Alone," which reflect likely stereotypes:

You know and I know my clone sleeps alone
She's out on her own—forever
She's programmed to work hard, she's never profane
She won't go insane, not ever. . . .

Your clone loves my clone, but yours cannot see
That's no way to be, in heaven
No sorrow, no heartache, just clone harmony
So, obviously, it's heaven.

No naughty clone ladies allowed in the eighties
No bed names, no sex games, just clone names and clone games
And you know and I know my clone sleeps alone. . . .

But they won't remember or ever be tender
No loving, no caring, no program for pairing
No VD, no cancer, on TV's the answer
No father, no mother, she's just like the other. . . .
And you know and I know my clone sleeps alone. . . .

# CHAPTER 2

# GUARANTEEING HUMAN RIGHTS BY TREATY

## HOW MANY TREATIES AND HOW MANY RIGHTS?

## I.   *INTRODUCTION: TREATIES AND INTERNATIONAL HUMAN RIGHTS LAW*

As indicated in Chapter 1, efforts to protect human rights through international measures initially addressed only isolated issues of concern to more than one state, such as the slave trade and armed conflict. It took the cataclysm of World War II to demonstrate the critical need for more general international efforts to promote and protect human rights. An important means to do so was through treaties setting forth guaranteed rights and imposing obligations on states to secure them. Treaties, often referred to by various other terms such as conventions or covenants, are binding agreements that constitute one of the primary sources of international law. See Statute of the International Court of Justice, Article 38.* "So much is well known. What is less well understood is, why would individual governments—only a short time ago considered internally supreme—choose to further this project of international accountability? What disturbed the conspiracy of mutual state silence that prevailed until the second half of the twentieth century? And why would an individual government choose to commit itself internationally to limit its freedom of action domestically?" Beth A. Simmons, *Mobilizing for Human Rights: International Law in Domestic Politics* 4 (2009).

As these questions might suggest, the making of human rights treaties is not free from controversy. It requires convincing governments, whose powers are limited by the treaties, to negotiate, conclude, and bind their states to the obligations therein. In addition, it requires achieving consensus on the content of human rights, which is by no means easy in a heterogeneous world, especially when new human rights treaties are proposed to address specific areas of concern. The duties of states that correspond to the rights must be articulated and agreement must be reached on the terms of any monitoring institutions and mechanisms. In many instances, positive results are achieved only due to the efforts of nongovernmental organizations and the leadership of key states. Other factors also may encourage international law-making in the field of human rights, such as transition to democratic governance, which may encourage new governments to seek an "international safety net" in an attempt to prevent regression in human rights observance.

After human rights treaties are concluded and enter into force, other issues arise: How should the agreements be interpreted and gaps in their provisions be filled? To what extent can states opt out of provisions through reservations, limitations, or derogations? Do the bodies established to monitor the treaties have implied as well as express powers? More generally, are human rights treaties different from other international agreements, and are special rules required to govern them? To what extent should matters of social concern, such as the environment and climate change, be addressed by treaties specifically framed through the lens

---

* Article 38 of the ICJ Statute sets forth the sources of authority that the International Court of Justice is to apply in deciding cases on the basis of international law. This provision of the ICJ's governing document is understood to be the most authoritative statement of the sources of international law. According to Article 38, the Court shall apply:

   a. international conventions, whether general or particular, establishing rules expressly recognized by the contesting states;
   b. international custom, as evidence of a general practice accepted as law;
   c. the general principles of law recognized by civilized nations;
   d. subject to the provisions of Article 59, judicial decisions and the teachings of the most highly qualified publicists of the various nations, as subsidiary means for the determination of rules of law.

of human rights? And more fundamentally, what is the value of addressing human rights matters by treaty? This Chapter touches upon all of these questions, beginning with the last, and surveys the major globally-applicable treaties.

## II. THE PROTECTION OF HUMAN RIGHTS THROUGH TREATIES

### A.   Why Treaties?

Beth A. Simmons

## Mobilizing for Human Rights: International Law in Domestic Politics

4-5, 6, 7, 12-14, 21 (2009) (references omitted)

Whether treaty law has done much to improve rights practices around the world is an open question. Has the growing set of legal agreements that governments have negotiated and acceded to over the past half century improved the "rights chances" of those whom such rules were designed to protect? Attempts to answer this question have—in the absence of much systematic evidence—been based on naïve faith or cynical skepticism. Basic divisions exist over who has the burden of proof—those who believe that international law compliance is pervasive and therefore conclude that it falls to the skeptics to prove otherwise versus those who view international law as inherently weak and epiphenomenal and require firm causal evidence of its impact. Supporters of each approach can adduce a set of anecdotes to lend credence to their claims. Yet, broader patterns and causally persuasive evidence remain illusive.

. . . I argue that once made, formal commitments to treaties can have noticeably positive consequences. Depending on the domestic context into which they are inserted, treaties can affect domestic politics in ways that tend to exert important influences over how governments behave toward their own citizens. Treaties are the clearest statements available about the content of globally sanctioned decent rights practices. Certainly, it is possible for governments to differ over what a particular treaty requires—this is so with domestic laws as well—but it is less plausible to argue that the right to be free from torture, for example, is not something people have a right to demand and into which the international community has no right to inquire; less plausible to contend that children should be drafted to carry AK-47s; and less plausible to justify educating boys over girls on the basis of limited resources when governments have explicitly and voluntarily agreed to the contrary. Treaties serve notice that governments are *accountable*—domestically and externally—for refraining from the abuses proscribed by their own mutual agreements. Treaties signal a seriousness of intent that is difficult to replicate in other ways. They reflect politics but they also shape political behavior, setting the stage for new political alliances, empowering new political actors, and heightening public scrutiny.

*Accountability!*

When treaties alter politics in these ways, they have the potential to change government behaviors and public policies. It is precisely because of their potential power to constrain that treaty commitments are contentious in domestic and international politics. Were they but scraps of paper, one might expect every universal treaty to be ratified swiftly by every government on earth, which has simply not happened. Rather, human rights treaties are pushed by passionate advocates—domestically and transnationally—and are opposed just as strenuously by those who feel the most threatened by their acceptance. . . .

. . . Respect for international legal obligations is one of the few policy tolls that public and private members of the international community have to bring to bear on governments that abuse or neglect their people's rights. . . . [T]he evidence presented in this study suggests that under some conditions, international legal commitments have generally promoted the kinds of outcomes for which they were designed. This argues for a continued commitment to the international rule of law as a possible lever, in conjunction with monitoring, advocacy, and resource assistance, in persuading governments that they have little to gain by systematically violating their explicit rights promises. . . .

The reason is simple. The development of international legal rules has been the central *collective* project to address human rights for the past 60 years. Whenever the community of nations as a whole has attempted to address these issues, it has groped toward the development of a legal framework by which certain rights might become understood as "fundamental." . . . The international legal structure, and especially those parts to which governments have explicitly and voluntarily committed via treaty ratification, provides the central "hook" by which the oppressed and their allies can legitimately call for behavioral change.

This is not, of course, a view that is universally held. . . .

Even mainstream scholars increasingly warn of the dangers of too much legalization at the international level. A common theme is that international adjudication is a step too far for most governments and a problematic development for the human rights regime generally. . . . These accounts reflect a growing skepticism that the world's idealists have thrown *too much* law at the problems of human rights, to the neglect of underlying political conditions essential for rights to flourish. . . .

But why focus on law, some may ask, rather on the power of norms themselves to affect change in rights practices? . . . The key here is commitment: the making of an explicit, public, and lawlike promise by public authorities to act within particular boundaries in their relationships with individual persons. Governments can make such commitments without treaties, but . . . treaties are understood by domestic and international audiences as especially clear statements of intended behavior. . . . [L]egal commitments have a further unique advantage: In some polities they are in fact legally enforceable. . . .

Treaties reflect politics. Their negotiation and ratification reflect the power, organization, and aspirations of the governments that negotiate and sign them, the legislatures that ratify them, and the groups that lobby on their behalf. But treaties also *alter politics*, especially in fluid domestic political settings. Treaties set visible goals for public policy and practice that alter political coalitions and the strength, clarity, and legitimacy of their demands. Human rights treaties matter most where they have domestic political and legal traction. . . .

Why should a government commit itself to an international legal agreement to respect the rights of its own people? The primary reason is that the government anticipates its ability and willingness to comply. Governments participate in negotiations, sign drafts, and expend political capital on ratification in most cases because they support the treaty goals and generally want to implement them. They tend to drag their feet in negotiating treaties they find threatening, potentially costly, or socially alienating. Polities participate most readily and enthusiastically in treaty regimes that reflect values consonant with their own. In this sense, the treaty-making and ratifying processes "screen" the participants themselves, leaving a pool of adherents that *generally* are likely to support their goals. Were this not the case, treaty ratification would be empirically random and theoretically uninteresting — a meaningless gesture to which it would be impossible to attach political, social, or legal significance. If we expect treaties to have effects, we should expect them to be something other than random noise on the international political landscape.

Treaties are not perfect screens, however — far from it. . . . The single strongest motive for ratification in the absence of a strong value commitment is the preference that nearly all governments have to avoid the social and political pressures of remaining aloof from a multilateral agreement to which most of their peers have already committed themselves. As more countries — especially regional peers — ratify human rights accords, it becomes more difficult to justify nonadherence and to deflect criticism for remaining a non-party. . . .

Treaties are also imperfect screens because countries vary widely in their treaty-relevant national institutions. Legal traditions, ratification procedures, and the degree of decentralization impact the politics of the treaty-acceptance process. Because governments sometimes anticipate that ratification will impose political costs that they are not ready to bear, they sometimes self-screen. . . . The point is this: Two governments with similar values may appear on opposite sides of the ratification divide because of their domestic institutions rather than their preferences for the content of the treaty itself.

. . . Treaties are perhaps the best instrument available to sovereign states to sharpen the focus on particularly accepted and proscribed behaviors. Indeed, they are valued by sovereign states as well as nongovernmental actors for precisely this reason. Treaties constrain governments because they help define the size of the *expectations gap* when governments fail to life up to their provisions. This expectations gap has the power to alter political demands for compliance, primarily from domestic constituencies, but sometimes by the international community as well. . . .

The conclusions are . . . cautiously optimistic, because while this study has considered many alternative explanations, these apparently do not overwhelm the influence of a public promise to one's citizens as well as to the international community to abide by specific human rights standards. The rigor of these tests suggests to me a causal relationship, but it is crucial to reiterate that the statistical evidence is, strictly speaking, no more than correlative. At a minimum, with very high confidence we can conclude that the ratification of human rights treaties is associated with improvements in outcomes that many of us care deeply about.

## B.   Human Rights Provisions of the UN Charter

We now turn to the treaty that is foundational to the international human rights system, the United Nation Charter. The Charter establishes the institutional architecture of the United Nations and provides the normative grounding of the post-World War II world order. As was briefly introduced in Chapter 1, this normative grounding includes a range of prescriptions linked to human rights.

### 1.   The Content of the Charter

## The United Nations and Human Rights

*Eighteenth Report of the Commission to Study the Organization of Peace* 1-4 (1968)

### I. THE DEVELOPMENT OF THE CONCEPT OF INTERNATIONAL PROTECTION OF HUMAN RIGHTS

It was during one of the darkest hours of the war, when the Axis powers achieved almost complete control of the European continent that President Roosevelt provided in his "Four Freedoms"—freedom of speech, freedom of religion, freedom from want and freedom from fear—a rallying cry for all those suffering from the ravages of war and totalitarianism. After another disaster, the Pearl Harbor attack, the Allied Governments agreed in Washington on the "Declaration by United Nations" which named as the basic goal of victory the preservation of "human rights and justice in their own lands as well as in other lands." Encouraged by this statement, various official and unofficial groups, both in the United States and other countries, started immediately to work on an International Bill of Rights which would be proclaimed by the United Nations after their victory and which would become one of the cornerstones of the new world order to be built after the war. While the official enthusiasm for a codification of the basic principles for the protection of human rights later cooled down, active pressure of non-governmental organizations led to the inclusion in the Charter of the United Nations of several provisions on human rights.

### II. THE CHARTER OF THE UNITED NATIONS

In the preamble to the Charter, the peoples of the United Nations have reaffirmed their "faith in fundamental human rights, in the dignity and worth of the human person, in the equal rights of men and women and of nations large and small," and their determination "to promote social progress and better standards of life in larger freedom." Article 1 of the Charter lists among the main purposes of the United Nations the achievement of international cooperation "in promoting and encouraging respect for human rights and for fundamental freedoms for all without distinction as to race, sex, language, or religion." Similarly, in accordance with Article 55 of the Charter, the United Nations has the duty to promote "universal respect for, and observance of human rights and fundamental freedoms for all without distinction as to race, sex, language, or religion." In Article 56, all Members of the United Nations "pledge themselves to take joint and separate action in cooperation with the Organization for the achievement of the purposes set forth in Article 55."

The Charter of the United Nations contains also significant grants of power to various organs of the United Nations. Thus, under Article 13, the General Assembly has the duty to initiate studies and make recommendations for the purpose of "assisting in the realization of human rights and fundamental freedoms for all without distinction as to race, sex, language, or religion." Responsibility for the discharge of the functions set forth in Chapter IX of the Charter (which includes Articles 55 and 56 mentioned above) is vested by Article 60 in the General Assembly and, under the authority of the General Assembly, in the Economic and Social Council. In discharging this responsibility the Economic and Social Council may, according to Article 62, "make recommendations for the purpose of promoting respect for, and observance of, human rights and fundamental freedoms for all"; under Article 68, it has an obligation to set up a commission "for the promotion of human rights," which is the only functional commission expressly provided for by the Charter itself; and, under Article 64, it may make arrangements with the Members of the United Nations to obtain reports on steps taken by them to give effect to the recommendations of the General Assembly and of the Council. . . .

These provisions define clearly the obligations of all Members and the powers of the Organization in the field of human rights. While the provisions are general, nevertheless they have the force of positive international law and create basic duties which all Members must fulfill in good faith. They must cooperate with the United Nations in promoting both universal respect for and observance of human rights and fundamental freedoms for all without distinction as to race, sex, language, or religion. For this purpose, they have pledged themselves to take such joint and separate action as may be necessary. The General Assembly and, under the Assembly's authority, the Economic and Social Council are responsible, under Article 60 of the Charter, for the discharge of the functions of the United Nations in this area, and for this purpose may initiate such studies and make such recommendations as they may deem necessary. Any refusal to participate in the United Nations program to promote the observance of human rights constitutes a violation of the Charter. The General Assembly may recommend, under Article 14 of the Charter, "measures for the peaceful adjustment of any situation, regardless of origin, which it deems likely to impair the general welfare or friendly relations among nations, including situations resulting from a violation of the provisions of the present Charter setting forth the Purposes and Principles of the United Nations." As the obligation to promote and encourage respect for human rights is set forth in the statement of Purposes in Article 1 of the Charter, the broad powers of the General Assembly under Article 14 clearly apply in case of a violation of the duty to cooperate with the United Nations in this area.

As far as the United States is concerned, the Charter of the United Nations . . . has been ratified by the United States. . . . Being embodied in a treaty, the obligations under the Charter form part of the law of the United States. They impose directly an obligation upon the federal government to promote the observance of human rights by all means at its disposal.

## 2.   The Legal Obligations of UN Member States Under the Charter

On the international level, the human rights clauses of the UN Charter have been invoked frequently, despite debate over exactly what obligations are contained in their provisions. It is noteworthy that the obligations of UN member states pursuant to Articles 55 and 56 of the Charter are explicitly referred to in the preambles of nearly all UN human rights treaties. In interstate relations generally, these obligations are raised in the course of UN debates or other diplomatic exchanges and have been since the inception of the organization. The Charter references to self-determination and nondiscrimination were the focus of most of the early matters raised in the General Assembly. India, for example, criticized segregation in the United States, which responded by pointing to the caste system in India. During the first session of the UN General Assembly, Egypt, supported by Latin American states, introduced a resolution that passed unanimously to condemn racial and religious persecution. See Persecution and Discrimination, G.A. Res. 103 (I) (1946). India then sought a resolution to condemn South Africa for its policies of racial discrimination, accusing the government of gross and systematic human rights violations in breach of the principles and purposes of the Charter. The resolution passed with the required two-thirds majority, despite opposition from Australia, Great Britain, Canada, and the United States, each of which had its own racial policies that contravened the Charter guarantees. See Treatment of Indians in the Union of South Africa, G.A. Res. 44(I) (1946). The issue of South Africa's racial policies remained on the agenda of the UN in every session until the end of apartheid. The first session of the General Assembly also declared genocide a crime under international law. See generally Paul Gordon Lauren, *The Evolution of International Human Rights: Visions Seen* 217 (1998); Dinah Shelton, *International Human Rights Law: Principled, Double, or Absent Standards?*, 25 J.L. & INEQUALITY 467 (2007).

Concern over South Africa's racial policies extended to its imposition of those policies in neighboring South West Africa (Namibia), over which South Africa exercised authority for a period after World War I. At the close of World War I, the League of Nations, the predecessor to the UN, established a system of "Mandates," by which the territories that had been colonized by Germany and the Ottoman Empire, among others, were transferred to other countries to be administered for the benefit of the inhabitants of the territories. The League of Nations approved a Mandate for South Africa to administer South West Africa, which had been colonized by Germany. When the League of Nations ceased to exist and the UN came into being, the oversight of the system of Mandates was assumed by the UN.

In its Resolution 2145 (XXI) of October 27, 1966, the UN General Assembly expressed its conviction "that the administration of the Mandated territory by South Africa has been conducted in a manner contrary to the Mandate, the Charter of the United Nations and the Universal Declaration of Human Rights," and "that South Africa has failed to fulfill its obligations in respect of the administration of the Mandated Territory and to ensure the moral and material wellbeing and security of the indigenous inhabitants of South West Africa and has, in fact, disavowed the Mandate." Accordingly, the General Assembly decided that "the Mandate conferred upon . . . South Africa is therefore terminated" and "that South Africa has no other right to administer the Territory." Subsequently, the Security Council, which is the UN institution with primary responsibility for peace and security, called on South Africa to withdraw its administration from the territory. See S.C. Res. 264 (1969). When South Africa refused to do so, the Security Council declared South Africa's presence in the territory illegal, see S.C. Res. 276 (1970), and submitted the matter to the International Court of Justice, the principal judicial organ of the UN, for an advisory opinion. Reflect on the following two relevant paragraphs of the Court's opinion.

> 130. It is undisputed, and is amply supported by documents annexed to South Africa's written statement in these proceedings, that the official governmental policy pursued by South Africa in Namibia is to achieve a complete physical separation of races and ethnic groups in separate areas within the Territory. The application of this policy has required, as has been conceded by South Africa, restrictive measures of control officially adopted and enforced in the Territory by the coercive power of the former Mandatory. These measures establish limitations, exclusions or restrictions for the members of the indigenous population groups in respect of their participation in certain types of activities, fields of study or of training, labour or employment and also submit them to restrictions or exclusions of residence and movement in large parts of the "territory."
>
> 131. Under the Charter of the United Nations, the former Mandatory [South Africa] had pledged itself to observe and respect, in a territory having an international status, human rights and fundamental freedoms for all without distinction as to race. To establish instead, and to enforce, distinctions, exclusions, restrictions and limitations exclusively based on grounds of race, colour, descent or national or ethnic origin which constitute a denial of fundamental human rights is a flagrant violation of the purposes and principles of the Charter.

*Legal Consequences for States of the Continued Presence of South Africa in Namibia (South West Africa)*, Advisory Opinion, 1971 I.C.J. 16, 37.

Both the Security Council and the General Assembly subsequently adopted resolutions commending the Court's advisory opinion. The Security Council noted it "with appreciation" (S.C. Res. 301 (1971)), while the General Assembly took similar notice "with satisfaction" (G.A. Res. 2871 (1971)). Thus, South Africa was found to be in breach of its specific human rights obligations under the Charter in relation to its administration of Namibia.

The following extract elaborates upon the human rights obligations of states under the Charter more generally.

Oscar Schachter

## The Charter and the Constitution: The Human Rights Provisions in American Law

4 Vand. L. Rev. 643, 646-53 (1951) (footnotes omitted)

### DO THE HUMAN RIGHTS PROVISIONS INVOLVE LEGAL OBLIGATIONS ON THE PART OF MEMBER STATES?

. . .

The principal provisions of the Charter involved are Articles 55(c) and 56. . . . It has been maintained by some authorities that in spite of the "pledge" expressly taken in Article 56, these provisions do not impose upon Members of the United Nations the legal obligation to respect and observe human rights and fundamental freedoms. The provisions of the Charter are characterized as statements of "guiding principles" or "general purposes," or indeed, as "legally meaningless and redundant." In support of this conclusion, the essential argument is that the United Nations has no compulsory powers in regard to human rights; this is an argument based first on the fact that the organs concerned with human rights (i.e. the General Assembly and the Economic and Social Council) may make only recommendations which have no obligatory effect and secondly on Article 2(7), forbidding United Nations intervention in matters of domestic jurisdiction. Kelsen also supports this position with special reference to the language of Article 56. He points out that the pledge is "to take joint and separate action operation with the Organization;" he then states that the only effective way to cooperate with the Organization is by compliance with the recommendations of the appropriate organs; but the Charter does not make such recommendations obligation; hence (he infers) it is left solely to the Members to decide what kind of action they think appropriate to achieve the cooperation sought by the Organization. Consequently, Kelsen concludes, the pledge does not express a "true obligation." [See H. Kelsen, *The Law of the United Nations* (1950).]

This brings us to the crux of the problem: Is the pledge to take action in co-operation with the Organization negated by the fact that the Organization admittedly cannot make mandatory decisions in regard to human rights? Or, stated in another way, if it is admitted (as it must be) that an organ may not "order" a Member to take action regarding human rights, does that mean that the Member may act as it deems appropriate, entirely free from legal limitations under Article 56? Is it possible to have [a] legal obligation to act "in co-operation" which does not require full compliance with the recommendations of the Organization?

In considering these questions it is necessary to review briefly the language and history of the human rights provisions. It may be useful to begin with the word "pledge" as used in Article 56. A pledge in its ordinary English meaning is a solemn promise or an undertaking; as used in a legal instrument, the word itself connotes a legal obligation. In the French version "les Membres s'engagent . . . à agir;" this too is the language of legal obligation. The discussions at San Francisco show that this was not accidental; it was stated that "pledge" has been used as a term at least as "strong" as the word "undertake" and that the Technical Committee which drafted the provision attached particular importance to this point. It is therefore difficult to avoid at least a prima facie conclusion that the pledge in Article 56 was intended to constitute a legal commitment on the part of Members.

Now, it is also true that in the course of formulating Article 56 many of the delegations insisted that this provision would not mean that the Organization would have the right to interfere with the internal affairs of Members. It was the understanding that Article 2(7), the "domestic jurisdiction" clause, applied to Articles 55 and 56 and consequently that "intervention" (or enforcement) of human rights by the United Nations was prohibited. But whatever may be the precise meaning of this clause it in no way implies that the pledge in Article 56 is without legal force. It is after all a common-place in international law that States assume duties of a legal character which are not enforceable by international organs. The Charter itself has many other articles imposing obligations with no provision for enforcement or implementation. Of course, some jurists consider that these are not true legal obligations since they do not involve sanctions for contrary conduct; but this is a specific use of the term obligation which is not generally accepted in international law or in the interpretation of the Charter. Throughout the Charter it is evident that obligations are imposed upon Members, even though in most cases these obligations do not have sanctions. Indeed, it may even be persuasively argued that the concern of the draftsmen in connection with Article 56 with the prohibition against intervention was based on their understanding and intention that this Article should constitute a legal undertaking, for if it were only a statement of purpose, there would have been little reason to stress noninterference by the Organization.

It is also of considerable significance that in the actual application of the Charter, the Members of the United Nations have found no incompatibility between the principle of nonintervention in Article 2(7) and the position that Members have a definite legal responsibility with respect to human rights by virtue of Article 56. In more than one resolution adopted by the General Assembly, it is clearly stated that Members have made a legal commitment to respect and observe human rights; and in the course of UN discussions, numerous representatives including several of legal eminence, have consistently maintained the position that the Charter imposes obligations of a legal character on Member States in regard to the observance of human rights.

This brings us to a further point of controversy; even if it is conceded that there is a legal commitment in Article 56, is it not merely a general duty to cooperate which can be construed by each State as it sees fit, and does this not in effect nullify the notion of a legal obligation? Here again, the travaux préparatoires afford some illumination. It appears from the San Francisco records that, at one stage, the pledge in Article 56 was threefold: it called for joint action, for separate action, and for co-operation with the Organization. The U.S. delegation then expressed doubt concerning the pledge to take separate action; it preferred simply a pledge to co-operate. But the Australian delegation, the original sponsor of this provision, continued to urge inclusion of a pledge to take separate action as distinguished from co-operation; this position was supported by the Belgian and British delegations. The final text represented a compromise: the pledge to take separate action was qualified by the phrase "in co-operation with the organization." This compromise text does not seem to have received further clarification in the San Francisco discussions; and no opinions were expressed specifically on what was meant by "co-operation with the Organization." It appears that the U.S. delegation favoured this qualification in order to eliminate the possibility of an interpretation under which the obligation would extend to "internal economic matters . . . and therefore the Organization would be permitted to intervene in them."

The foregoing history seems to bring out several points of significance in connection with this problem. First, it reveals that the draftsmen in San Francisco rejected a text which provided merely for a pledge to co-operate with the Organization and that they attached importance to the words "separate action," although such action was to be "in co-operation with the Organization." Secondly, it indicates that this latter expression was mainly intended to avoid the implication that "separate action" would open the door to intervention by the United Nations in domestic affairs. Thirdly, there is no indication that the phrase "co-operation" was intended to confer unlimited discretion on the Member States — a result which would be almost the direct opposite of the normal meaning of co-operation and of the committee's intentions. Admittedly, the record also indicates that the obligation is far from precise and leaves considerable latitude to each Member State to carry it out in its own way. But does this mean that it cannot be considered a legal obligation? In view of both the history and the language of this Article, this would certainly be an extreme conclusion; it would, in effect, make a mockery of the efforts of the draftsmen at San Francisco to formulate a pledge which would have legal significance and effectiveness. There is certainly no overriding reason to arrive at this result.

It must be borne in mind, in this respect, that the degree of precision required in a treaty is not the same as that demanded of a criminal statute. Treaty obligations are often expressed in general terms and leave broad discretion to the States which are Parties. But the fact that a State is free to carry out those obligations by its own methods and its own way does not destroy the legal character of this obligation. In the case of Article 56 there is no compelling reason to define a priori and in detail all the implications of the obligation it is evident that there are large areas where the purposes under Article 55 are as yet so undefined that it is impossible to say what kind of action would be required if a State is to co-operate with the Organization.

However, it is equally evident that in other respects the broad language of Article 55 has specific meaning and effect; this is particularly true of clause (c) relating to human rights and fundamental freedoms. The clause itself contains the significant prohibition against discrimination because of race, sex, language or religion, a theme which is recurrent throughout tire Charter and which in itself furnishes considerable content to the notion of human rights. Moreover, it must not be forgotten that the concept of human rights is not an abstract notion introduced for the first time in the Charter; it has had (under various names) a long and rich history in constitutional law, in the practice of states and in the development of the law of nations. Nor is it irrelevant in this connection to consider the wide measure of agreement regarding most specific rights and freedoms which was revealed during the preparation of the Declaration on Human Rights and by the specific resolutions adopted by the General Assembly and other principal organs. Through the outer boundaries of "human rights" remain undefined (perhaps undefinable) it can hardly be denied that the concept has a special core of meaning which is widely recognized and accepted. Certainly an American lawyer familiar with the due process and equal protection clauses and the other broad phrases of the U.S. Constitution is not likely take the position that a concept such as human rights must be denied legal effect because of its breadth and generality.

There is therefore no sufficient reason to characterize Article 56 as a mere statement of purpose, devoid of legal effect. To do so as we have seen, would be contrary to both the language and the ascertainable intentions of the framers of the Charter. And even if it be granted that there is some obscurity in the text or the intent of the drafters, the choice between alternative interpretations should legitimately be resolved in favour of that construction which best effectuates the major purposes of the provision. In this case, obviously the major purpose is the promotion of human rights; if a "pledge" to take action to achieve that purpose is interpreted as having no obligatory effect, the whole point of the pledge is lost and it becomes entirely superfluous. A construction which renders an article virtually meaningless is certainly contrary to the principle of effectiveness in the interpretation of treaties. Undoubtedly, there are occasions when the rule of effectiveness may run counter to the manifest intention of the parties; in this case, however, effectiveness—at least to the extent of a legal commitment—is precisely what most of the drafters desired.

Thus, both major rules of interpretation—that based on intent and that on effectiveness—reinforce each other and, taken together, practically make inescapable the conclusion that the pledge in Article 56 constitutes a legal commitment on the part of Members to take action in co-operation with the Organization to achieve "respect for and observance of human rights and fundamental freedoms for all. . . ."

## *Note: Article 2(7) Of The UN Charter*

A question with diminishing significance has been how to read the human rights clauses in the UN Charter against Article 2(7) thereof, which provides: "Nothing contained in the present Charter shall authorize the United Nations to intervene in matters which are essentially within the domestic jurisdiction of any state or shall require the Members to submit such matters to settlement under the present Charter; but this principle shall not prejudice the application of enforcement measures [by the Security Council] under Chapter VII." Note that at the time the Charter was negotiated, each of the major powers had a troublesome human rights record of its own. The Soviet Union had its Gulag, the United States its de jure racial discrimination, and France and Great Britain their colonial empires. Given their own vulnerabilities as far as human rights were concerned, it was not in the political interests of these countries to draft a Charter that established an effective international system for the protection of human rights, which is what some smaller democratic nations advocated.

Article 2(7) was intended to ensure that none of the human rights clauses of the Charter should "be construed as giving authority to the Organization to intervene in the domestic affairs of member states." 10 *Documents of the United Nations Conference on International Organization, San Francisco* 83 (1945) (United States). But in those cases where the Security Council determines that a state's human rights violations constitute either a "breach of the peace" or a "threat to the peace" under Article 39 of the Charter, Article 2(7) itself clearly renders the "domestic jurisdiction" clause inoperable by specifically authorizing the adoption of economic sanctions or even the use of armed force against the offending state pursuant to Articles 41 and 42 of Chapter VII of the Charter.

A vast body of literature exists concerning the "domestic jurisdiction" clause of the Chapter VII and the kind of UN "intervention" it was intended to prohibit. See, e.g., Felix Ermacora, *Human Rights and Domestic Jurisdiction (Article 2, §7, of the Charter)*, 124 RECUEIL DES COURS, HAGUE ACADEMY OF INTERNATIONAL LAW 371 (1968-II). Suffice it to say that, over the years, human rights questions have come to be regarded by the United Nations as no longer "essentially within the domestic jurisdiction" of states. See Rosalyn Higgins, *The Development of International Law Through the Political Organs of the United Nations* 58 (1963); Louis B. Sohn and Thomas Buergenthal, *International Protection of Human Rights* 556 (1973); Louis B. Sohn, *Rights in Conflict: The United Nations and South Africa* 48, 63 (1994). See also Antonio Cassese, "The General Assembly: Historical Perspective, 1945-1989," in *The United Nations and Human Rights: A Critical Appraisal* 25 (Philip Alston ed., 1992). How important is subsequent practice in interpreting the constituting documents of international organizations? See Vienna Convention on the Law of Treaties, Art. 31, discussed at pages 75-76, *infra*.

### Note: US Recognition of the Legal Status of The Human Rights Clauses

The United States upon numerous occasions has adopted Professor Schachter's reasoning *sub silentio* and argued that the human rights clauses of the UN Charter give rise to international legal obligations on the part of member states. Thus, when in early 1969 the revolutionary government of Iraq summarily tried, convicted, and publicly hanged 14 of its nationals (nine of them Jews) — and displayed their bodies in a grisly carnival atmosphere — on the premise that they were Israeli spies, the US ambassador to the United Nations, Charles Yost, raised the matter with the Security Council in a letter, reprinted in 24 UN SCOR Supp. (Jan.-Mar. 1969) at 65, UN Doc. S/8987 (1969)), which said in part:

> The Government of the United States recognizes the legal right of any government to bring to trial and administer justice to any of its citizens. However, the manner in which these executions and the trials that preceded them were conducted scarcely conforms to normally accepted standards of respect for human rights and human dignity or to the obligations in this regard that the United Nations Charter imposes upon all Members. . . . The United States hopes that the worldwide revulsion aroused by the reports of these trials and executions will induce those responsible to carry out their solemn Charter obligations to promote "universal respect for and observance of human rights and fundamental freedoms for all without distinction as to race, sex, language or religion."

If you had been a Department of State lawyer assigned to the US Mission to the United Nations, to which articles would you have referred had Security Council

President Max Jakobson's office telephoned for further explanation of "the obligations in this regard that the United Nations Charter imposes upon all Members"?
In response to an inquiry two years later, the Office of the Legal Adviser of the
Department of State, in a letter dated March 18, 1971, explained that "it is the
view of the United States Government that the right to a fair trial before an impartial tribunal is a 'fundamental freedom' and that the specific facts in the situation
described in [the above letter] justified the statement by Ambassador Yost that the
obligations of the Charter had not been met." Is this explanation satisfactory? Does
it provide much guidance in identifying other international human rights obligations of states under the UN Charter?

The right to a fair trial is specifically guaranteed by Article 10 of the Universal
Declaration of Human Rights, which was proclaimed by the UN General Assembly
in 1945, and Article 14 of the International Covenant on Civil and Political Rights,
a widely ratified treaty including by the United States. See generally David Weissbrodt, *The Right to a Fair Trial Under the Universal Declaration of Human Rights and the
International Covenant on Civil and Political Rights: Articles 8, 10 and 11 of the Universal
Declaration of Human Rights* (2001). Why did Ambassador Yost not mention these
instruments explicitly? Would not his argument have been strengthened by their
reference? Can the fair trial provision of the Universal Declaration be read back
into the UN Charter, as Professor Schachter suggests, to bind states as treaty law?
Cf. Louis Henkin, *The Constitution at Sea*, 36 ME. L. REV. 201, 209 n.31 (1984) ("The
United States . . . is a party to the UN Charter which includes general human rights
obligations, and it may be bound by some of the provisions of the Universal Declaration of Human Rights, either as elaborations of the Charter obligation or under
customary international law."). Since the Yost letter, the United States repeatedly
has taken the position that the human rights clauses of the UN Charter have legal
effect and thus must be observed by all countries, including the United States.

### *Comments and Questions*

1. The Court in the *South West Africa* case specifically held that South Africa's
imposition of the policy of apartheid in Namibia constituted a "flagrant violation"
of the human rights clauses of the UN Charter. How important to this conclusion
is the fact that most Charter references to human rights are accompanied by the
phrase "without distinction as to race, sex, language or religion?" Would segregation of women from public life similarly constitute a "flagrant violation"? Are "non-
flagrant" human rights violations within the Court's rationale? If so, why? If not,
how can one justify the US assertion (see *supra* pages 63-64) that the UN Charter
imposed a legal obligation on Iraq to accord criminal defendants a fair trial?

2. Since the Charter nowhere defines the scope or content of the "human rights
and fundamental freedoms" that the United Nations shall promote and that member
states shall help achieve, just what are the obligations assumed by states under the
Charter? Does it matter when a state became a member of the United Nations?

3. To what extent is Article 2(7) still relevant today when human rights issues
are raised? Under what circumstances might an argument based on Article 2(7) be
persuasive in a state's effort to avoid scrutiny for a human rights problem?

4. What is the importance of inclusion in the UN Charter of its human rights
clauses? What difference does it make whether or not the Charter's human rights

clauses establish international legal obligations? Consider that, under the Charter, the UN can take enforcement action only when the UN Security Council deems that there is a threat to "international peace and security" and when none of the Council's five permanent members opposes the action. The UN General Assembly, Economic and Social Council, and Human Rights Council each has authority that in human rights matters is limited to making "recommendations" and promoting investigations and programs. The International Court of Justice can only pronounce binding judgements in cases in which a state makes a claim against another state and both have accepted the jurisdiction of the Court over the dispute. The powers and functions of the principal UN organs are established by Chapters III, IV, V, X, and XIV of the UN Charter. The Human Rights Council was established by a resolution of the General Assembly, as detailed in Chapter 7, and the Commission on Human Rights, predecessor to the Human Rights Council, was established by a resolution of the Economic and Social Council, as discussed subsequently.

### C.   UN Human Rights Law-Making

The previous section examined the meaning and effect of the human rights clauses of the UN Charter, a treaty binding the organization's member states. The present section analyzes what traditionally has been regarded as the UN's principal means of achieving universal respect for human rights—the sponsoring of multilateral treaties for the protection of specifically enumerated human rights.

When the San Francisco conference that adopted the UN Charter ended without concluding an international bill of rights to be ratified with the Charter, the issue did not disappear. A group of states remained insistent on the need to articulate a catalog of the human rights to which the Charter referred. The Preparatory Commission of the United Nations recommended that the Economic and Social Council (ECOSOC) immediately establish a Commission on Human Rights to formulate an "international bill of rights" and to prepare studies and recommendations that "would encourage the acceptance of higher standards in this field and help to check and eliminate discrimination and other abuses." United Nations, *Report of the Preparatory Commission of the United Nations* 36 (1946). The recommendation was approved by the General Assembly on February 12, 1946. G.A. Res. 7 (I) (1946). Four days later, ECOSOC created the Commission on Human Rights to be composed of a subgroup of UN member states. See E.S.C. Res. 5 (I) (1946). A subsequent ECOSOC resolution conferred on the Commission the mandate to submit to the Council "proposals, recommendations and reports" regarding:

(a)   an international bill of rights;
(b)   international declarations or conventions on civil liberties, the status of women, freedom of information and similar matters;
(c)   the protection of minorities;
(d)   the prevention of discrimination on grounds of race, sex, language or religion; and
(e)   any other matter concerning human rights not covered by other items.

E.S.C. Res. 9 (II) (1946).

Standard setting, in particular the formulation of an international bill of rights, was thus to be the focus of the Commission's early work. Indeed, some observers, like John Humphrey, criticized the Commission for its focus on standard setting rather than on preventing and responding to violations. See John Humphrey, "The United Nations Commission on Human Rights and Its Parent Body," in I *Amicorum Discipulorumque Liber* 111 (René Cassin ed., 1969).

The Human Rights Commission was an important locus of standard setting, but it was not the only body engaged in this process nor was it the origin of most human rights treaties. The Commission most often reviewed, debated, and adopted initiatives originating elsewhere, including projects coming from NGO's and, occasionally, from within the Secretariat. In addition, quite a few major human rights instruments were concluded without any input from the Commission. Topics falling within the mandate of a specialized agency, such as labor rights and education, understandably have been dealt with by the relevant agency, but it is also apparent that, in other instances, states or UN bodies chose to bypass the Commission and initiate the drafting and adoption of new instruments in other UN organs. The Genocide Convention of 1948, for example, was mostly negotiated in the Economic and Social Council. Similarly, the Commission had no input into the drafting of conventions on the rights of women, which were instead drafted within the Commission on the Status of Women. The 1990 International Convention on the Rights of Migrant Workers and Their Families was drafted by a sessional General Assembly working group of open-ended membership. In the end, the Assembly transmitted the draft Migrant Workers Convention to the Human Rights Commission for a "technical review." G.A. Res. 44/155 (1989), para. 2.

The process of elaborating treaties thus involves numerous actors, with individual states sometimes taking leadership on an issue. This multiplicity of actors has both a positive and a negative dimension. On the negative side, the desire for consensus sometimes leads to vague, weakened, and, some claim, inconsistent obligations. On the positive side, states tend to become invested in the final product, which may produce positive changes in national laws and practices even before the text is finalized. Thus, the politics of the negotiations are not always detrimental to human rights.

UN treaties have gone much farther than most of the earlier agreements, discussed in Chapter 1, in obligating states to make changes—sometimes drastic changes—in their own domestic legal regimes to bring them into conformity with the treaties. It is one thing for a state to agree to eradicate a practice that takes place on faraway continents or on the high seas; it is quite another to agree to take steps to protect individuals from oppression at home. In this respect, to the extent that states have ratified them, UN treaties represent a great advance in the cause of human rights.

Before examining specific human rights treaties of the UN, consider the diversity of human rights problems addressed by the major UN human rights treaties in force as of April 2022. (See the Documentary Supplement for the texts of these treaties.) The United Nations, in addition to promulgating general human rights treaties containing numerous articles covering a wide variety of individual rights (e.g., the International Covenant on Civil and Political Rights), has used treaties to combat specific human rights problems (e.g., torture, forced disappearances) and to protect specific parts of the population (e.g., women, children, migrant workers, persons with disabilities). Cross-cutting themes in these treaties are the guarantee of the right to life; the prohibition of discrimination and equal protection of the law; concerns over access to justice and due process; freedom of expression, religion, and personal liberty; and the protection of privacy and the family, among others.

It is important to note that the human rights treaty-adoption process has not been limited to the global level. Many leading human rights treaties have been developed by regional intergovernmental organizations in Africa, the Americas, and Europe, as referenced in Chapter 1, and as will be discussed in more detail in Chapters 8 and 9 of this book.

### 1.  Completing the International Bill of Rights

With the adoption of the Universal Declaration of Human Rights in 1948 (which is referenced in Chapter 1 and discussed further in Chapter 3), the Commission's attention turned to negotiating what became the International Covenant on Civil and Political Rights and the International Covenant on Economic, Social, and Cultural Rights. The precedent this action set—of first adopting a declaration, then concluding a treaty on the same topic—was one followed with some consistency during the Commission's tenure. On controversial subjects, a declaration often proved to be the only text on which states could agree. In a few instances, even a non-binding set of standards proved unacceptable.

The Covenants are predominantly a product of the Commission, but with input from its Sub-Commission, the General Assembly, the Secretariat, and several specialized agencies. The Commission originally forwarded to ECOSOC in 1947, at the same time as the Declaration, a text entitled "Convention on Human Rights" that was largely based on a proposal from the United Kingdom. The Commission changed the name to Covenant on Human Rights in December 1947 and approved 27 articles, most of them defining civil and political rights. The drafting committee revised the draft Covenant in the light of comments from governments and transmitted the new draft to the Commission, which simply forwarded it to ECOSOC without changes. ECOSOC in turn sent it to the General Assembly without comment. The General Assembly, on the same day it adopted the Universal Declaration, requested the Commission through ECOSOC to continue to make drafting the Covenant a priority.

Work continued throughout 1949. By this point, several states (Australia, the Soviet Union, and Yugoslavia among them) strongly advocated including economic, social, and cultural rights in the Covenant. The Commission rejected this, however, agreeing only to consider additional treaties or measures dealing with economic, social, cultural, and other categories of human rights at some time in the future. The Economic and Social Council, having received the text after the Commission completed the first reading, sent it to the General Assembly for "basic policy decisions." E.S.C. Res. 303 I (XI) (1950).

The General Assembly took an active role from this point. It directed the Commission to draft a single covenant containing economic, social, cultural, civil, and political rights, concluding that the draft that was forwarded did not contain "certain of the most elementary rights," and that economic, social, and cultural rights should be included "in a manner which relates them to the civic and political freedoms proclaimed by the draft Covenant." It said that the wording of some articles "should be improved to protect more effectively the rights to which they refer." Finally, it said that both the rights and any limitations on them should be defined with the greatest possible precision." G.A. Res. 421 (V) (1950). The Commission took up this mandate at its 1951 session and drafted articles on economic, social, and cultural rights, expanding the Covenant to some 73 articles.

When ECOSOC received the 1951 report of the Commission, it recommended, by a vote of 11 to 7, that the General Assembly reconsider its decision on including all rights in a single covenant because of fundamental differences of opinion among states, especially concerning implementation and monitoring mechanisms. See E. S.C. Res. 384 (XIII) (1951). The General Assembly was even more divided, agreeing on a vote of 29 to 25, with four abstentions, to separate civil and political rights from economic, social, and cultural rights, after Western representatives agreed that the two covenants could be approved and opened for signature at the same time. See G.A. Res. 543 (VI) (1952). Based on a proposal from Arab states, and after lengthy debate and controversy, the General Assembly also decided that the Commission should include an article on self-determination, which became Article 1 common to the Covenants. The Assembly later added provisions on the rights of children, as proposed by Poland, and the duty to ensure the equal rights of men and women. The Assembly also proposed, drafted, and adopted the first Optional Protocol to the Covenant on Civil and Political Rights, which provided an individual complaint procedure.

Other parts of the UN system, besides the General Assembly and its committees, contributed to the drafting. The Sub-Commission submitted what became Article 27 on minority rights. Officials from the Secretariat suggested implementation measures. ECOSOC played a limited role, mostly in debating the right of self-determination. Specialized agencies participated in negotiations for the Economic and Social Covenant, proposing specific provisions. The International Labor Organization addressed labor rights, UNESCO the right to education, and WHO the right to health. The Food and Agriculture Organization succeeded in obtaining a reference to the "fundamental right to freedom from hunger."

In addition to adding rights that were not mentioned in the Universal Declaration, the negotiating process led to omitting or modifying some Declaration guarantees. Debate over property rights concluded with a decision that disagreement was so great that no reference to the right to property should be included in either Covenant. The right to seek asylum and the prohibition on arbitrary exile were also omitted, despite being included in the Universal Declaration.

The Commission on Human Rights completed drafting the two Covenants during its next three sessions (1952-54) and presented them to ECOSOC and the General Assembly in 1954, where negotiations took another 12 years. For an extensive discussion of the history of the International Bill of Rights, see *United Nations and Human Rights: Eighteenth Report of the Commission to Study the Organization of Peace* 59-169 (1968); Johannes Morsink, *The Universal Declaration of Human Rights: Origins, Drafting, and Intent* (2000); Marc Bossuyt, *Guide to the "Travaux Preparatoires" of the*

*International Covenant on Civil and Political Rights* (1987); Manfred Nowak, *U.N. Covenant on Civil and Political Rights: CCPR Commentary* (2d rev. ed. 2005).

## 2. Issue-Specific Human Rights Treaties

Concurrent with its effort to promulgate general human rights norms and enforcement procedures through an International Bill of Rights, the UN began to use the treaty approach to combat human rights problems in specific subject areas, usually under pressure from nongovernmental human rights organizations. The first such treaty was the Convention on the Prevention and Punishment of the Crime of Genocide (the Genocide Convention). Drafted in 1948, the same year as the Universal Declaration, it came into force in 1951. The Genocide Convention was made more acceptable to states by delegating enforcement power to each state party individually; no international supervisory mechanism was created. The United States ratified the Genocide Convention 40 years after its conclusion. The Convention declares that genocide, whether committed in time of peace or time of war, is a crime under international law, a concept discussed in Chapter 5. See generally *Encyclopedia of Genocide and Crimes against Humanity* (Dinah Shelton ed., 2004); Rafael Lemkin, *Genocide as a Crime under International Law*, 41 AM. J. INT'L L. 145 (1947); William Schabas, *Genocide in International Law* (2000).

The International Convention on the Elimination of All Forms of Racial Discrimination (ICERD) marked a significant advance over the Genocide Convention, in that it contains monitoring provisions similar to those adopted a year later for the Covenant on Civil and Political Rights, creating procedures that would ultimately become standard practice. The ICERD has been described as "the most comprehensive and unambiguous codification in treaty form of the idea of the equality of races." Egon Schwelb, *The International Convention on the Elimination of Racial Discrimination*, 15 INT'L & COMP. L.Q. 996, 1057 (1966). The Convention was largely an international response to outbursts of neo-Nazi activities around the world in 1959-1960. The General Assembly first adopted a Declaration on the Elimination of All Forms of Racial Discrimination (G.A. Res. 1904 (XVIII) (1963)), and the Convention followed. The Convention came into force in 1969, and the United States ratified it in 1994.

Sex discrimination, like racial discrimination, is prohibited by the human rights provisions of the United Nations Charter and by Article 2 of the Universal Declaration. The prohibition is repeated in Article 2(1) of the Covenant on Civil and Political Rights and in Article 3, which obligates states parties "to ensure the equal rights of men and women to the enjoyment of all civil and political rights set forth in the present Covenant." The UN General Assembly adopted a rather minimalist treaty on the political rights of women in 1953 and a more comprehensive treaty in 1979, the Convention on the Elimination of All Forms of Discrimination against Women (CEDAW), which entered into force in 1981. CEDAW seeks to do away with discrimination against women, which it defines as "any distinction, exclusion, or restriction made on the basis of sex" that impairs the enjoyment by women of "human rights and fundamental freedoms in the political, economic, social, cultural, civil, or any other field" (Article 1). In addition to the obligation to condemn discrimination against women, states undertake, inter alia, "to embody the principle of equality of men and women in their national constitutions or other appropriate legislation" and to adopt laws or other measures "including sanctions where appropriate, prohibiting all discrimination against women" (Article 2). The Convention also requires that states take a series of measures in the political, social, economic, and cultural realms to advance the enjoyment of equal rights by women in all walks of life. In one of its more far-reaching provisions, Article 5(a) requires states to take "all appropriate measures . . . [t]o modify the social and cultural patterns of conduct of men and women, with a view to achieving the elimination of prejudices and customary and all other practices which are based on the idea of the inferiority or superiority of either of the sexes or on stereotyped roles for men and women."

Torture is condemned by Article 5 of the Universal Declaration and is also prohibited by Article 7 of the Civil and Political Covenant. The origins of the Convention against Torture and Other Cruel, Inhuman, and Degrading Treatment, an instrument largely drafted by a working group of the Commission, are quite diverse. In 1973, Amnesty International began a campaign against torture, supported by the International Commission of Jurists, the International Red Cross, the Swiss Committee against Torture, and the World Council of Churches Commission on International Affairs. Two years later, the Fifth United Nations Congress on the Prevention of Crime and the Treatment of Offenders recommended to the General Assembly a draft Declaration on the Protection of All Persons from Being Subjected to Torture and Other Cruel, Inhuman, or Degrading Treatment or Punishment. The General Assembly approved the text in 1975; the Commission on Human Rights was not part of the process. In 1977, the General Assembly took further action on the subject by accepting a Swedish proposal to confer on the Commission the mandate to draft a treaty against torture. Experts from Amnesty International and the International Committee of the Red Cross provided technical advice during the negotiations and made substantive proposals during the drafting. In 1980, Costa Rica introduced a draft optional protocol on implementation that had been recommended by the International Commission of Jurists and the Swiss Committee against Torture. Disagreement among the participating states on various matters lessened but could not be overcome during the negotiations. In 1984 a text with several provisions in brackets was sent to the General Assembly's Third (social, humanitarian, and culture) Committee, which succeeded in resolving issues about the implementation machinery and in finalizing the text by December 10, 1984. The Committee then approved the text and the General Assembly adopted the convention.

Children not only are covered by the all-inclusive language of the Universal Declaration and the Civil and Political Covenant (e.g., "everyone"), but also "are entitled to special care and assistance" under Article 25(2) of the former and are singled out for special protection by Articles 23(3) and 24 of the latter. In 1979, while work was proceeding on the Torture Convention, Poland introduced at the Commission a draft convention on the rights of the child. The same process was used to negotiate this convention as was used for the Torture Convention, with a pre-sessional open-ended working group seeking consensus on each provision. By 1986, the group had agreed on 19 articles but remained divided on others. The convention eventually was completed and adopted in 1989. While the length of the negotiations reflects the many difficult issues addressed, the process also helped create a consensus evidenced by the almost universal ratification of the agreement.

More recently, the 1990 International Convention on the Rights of Migrant Workers and Their Families was drafted by a sessional open-ended General Assembly working group meeting at the beginning of the Third Committee's session and between sessions. The process was criticized for having limited involvement of state delegates, lack of Secretariat technical support, and even greater lack of expertise in the drafting. The Sub-Commission of the Commission on Human Rights, an expert body, had studied the problems of trafficking and ill treatment of migrant workers, and the issue was discussed in the Commission itself, but the General Assembly was still chosen as the negotiating forum. In the end, the Assembly transmitted the draft Migrant Workers Convention to the Commission for only a "technical review."

The General Assembly, also, was the forum for negotiations for the Convention on Disability Rights, following an initiative of Mexico to create an ad hoc committee that in turn established a working group to draft the first text of the Convention. The General Assembly directed the process to involve persons with disabilities, representatives of disability organizations, and experts on the subject, and it urged governments to include persons with disabilities in their delegations. In response, over half of the working group's 40 members were persons with disabilities, and the group also had twelve NGO members. See *Report of the Second Session of the Ad Hoc Committee on a Comprehensive and Integral International Convention on the Protection and Promotion of the Rights and Dignity of Persons with Disabilities*, UN Doc. A/58/118 and Corr.1. See also Janet E. Lord, *NGO Participation in Human Rights Law and Process: Latest Developments in the Effort to Develop an International Treaty on the Rights of People with Disabilities*, 10 ILSA J. INT'L & COMP. L. 311 (2004).

In some instances, certain issues were set aside, seemingly because they were either too controversial or politically fraught. A draft convention on freedom of information was considered by the General Assembly, but it was never concluded despite being on the agenda from 1950 to 1980. Similarly, the Declaration on the Elimination of All Forms of Intolerance and of Discrimination Based on Religion or Belief, G.A. Res. 36/55 (1981), did not lead to adoption of a convention on the subject.

In short, there is no particular template for drafting human rights treaties within the United Nations, although the ultimate authority to approve a treaty and open it for signature and ratification rests with the General Assembly.

### 3.  Specialized Agencies

The United Nations' specialized agencies are legally independent organizations created by their own constitutions or charters, through which they establish their own organs and subsidiary bodies to fulfill their particular mandates. States must apply for membership and ratify the respective constituting treaties. Nonetheless, specialized agencies having responsibility for economic, social, cultural, educational, health, and related fields have been brought into relationship with the United Nations through special agreements, concluded in accordance with Article 63 of the UN Charter. An Inter-Agency Standing Committee helps to harmonize the activities of organizations that are part of the UN system.

Agencies such as the International Labor Organization, the United Nations Economic, Social and Cultural Organization, the Food and Agriculture Organization, and the World Health Organization are directly involved in a number of specific human rights activities. Others, such as the World Bank Group, the International Monetary Fund, and the World Trade Organization, indirectly may have significant impact on human rights (see Chapter 4). The interaction of specialized agencies with the UN in the promotion of human rights is described in detail in UN Centre for Human Rights, *United Nations Action in the Field of Human Rights* (1994); and Stephen P. Marks, "Human Rights, Activities of Universal Organizations," in 2 *Encyclopedia of Public International Law* 893 (1995).

### (a) The International Labor Organization

The International Labor Organization (ILO) was founded in 1919 and is the oldest organization concerned with human rights. Its tripartite system of governance, whereby each member state delegation is composed of government representatives, along with representatives from employers' and workers' associations, ensures that the views of non-state actors are heard. The ILO focuses on those human rights related to the right to work and to working conditions, including the right to form trade unions, the right to strike, the right to be free from slavery and forced labor, the right to equal employment and training opportunities, the right to safe and healthy working conditions, and the right to social security. The ILO also provides protections for groups in vulnerable situations and has adopted standards on child labor, employment of women, migrant workers, and indigenous and tribal peoples. It seeks to guarantee these rights through the adoption of conventions (now 190) and recommendations containing core minimum standards, and additional flexible provisions that enhance the likelihood of ratification by states. These latter provisions are of particular importance, because the ILO does not allow reservations to its conventions.

Some of the most important ILO conventions include those on Forced Labor (No. 29) of 1930; Freedom of Association and Protection of the Right to Organize (No. 98) of 1949; Equal Remuneration (No. 100) of 1957; Abolition of Forced Labor (No. 105) of 1957; Discrimination (Employment and Occupation) (No. 111) of 1958; Indigenous and Tribal Peoples (No. 169) of 1989; the Worst Forms of Child Labor (No. 182) of 1999; Maternity Protection (No. 183) of 2000; and Violence and Harassment (No. 190) of 2019. In 1998, the ILO responded to increasing concerns about the impact of globalization on worker rights by adopting a Declaration of Fundamental Rights and Principles at Work, together with a follow-up procedure. The Declaration insists that all ILO member states, by virtue of joining the organization, have an obligation to ensure the protection of four areas of human rights or core labor standards: freedom of association and the right to collectively bargain; freedom from child labor; freedom from forced or compulsory labor; and nondiscrimination in employment. All member states must report annually if they have not ratified the relevant ILO conventions on these subjects, indicating the obstacles to ratification.

The ILO has also developed a supervisory system that requires states to report not only on ratified but also on unratified conventions. Monitoring is carried out in the first place by a Committee of Experts, composed of 20 independent experts.

The Committee meets annually to examine reports and may follow up with "Direct Requests" to governments and to organizations of workers and employers in the state concerned. If the Committee discovers more serious or persistent problems, it may make "Observations" to the government, which are published in the Committee's annual report to the Conference. The second supervisory body is the Committee on the Application of Standards, a standing Conference Committee with representatives of government, employers, and workers. On the basis of the Committee of Experts' Report, the Conference Committee on the Applicaton of Standards selects specific important or persistent cases and asks the government to appear to discuss the situation. The Conference Committee then reports to the full Conference. In addition, the ILO has an individual complaint procedures. See Lee Swepston, "Human Rights Complaint Procedures of the International Labour Organization," in *Guide to International Human Rights Practice* (Hurst Hannum ed., 4th ed. 2004).

### (b) UN Educational, Scientific, and Cultural Organization

The UN Educational, Scientific, and Cultural Organization (UNESCO), founded in 1945 and headquartered in Paris, is the primary agency responsible for cultural rights, including the right to education and rights in cultural property. Among its primary conventions are the 1954 Convention for the Protection of Cultural Property in the Event of Armed Conflict, the 1962 Convention Against Discrimination in Education, and the 2005 Convention on the Protection and Promotion of the Diversity of Cultural Expressions. It also adopted in 1997 a Universal Declaration on the Human Genome and Human Rights, the first international instrument to address human rights and modern biotechnology and to reject the cloning of human beings. UNESCO has a nonjudicial communications procedure that was established in 1978, which allows a victim or anyone with reliable knowledge about a human rights violation concerned with education, science, or culture to submit a petition to UNESCO. See Stephen P. Marks, "The UN Educational, Scientific, and Cultural Organization," in *Guide to International Human Rights Practice* (Hurst Hannum ed., 4th ed. 2004).

### (c) The World Health Organization and Food and Agriculture Organization

The Constitution of the World Health Organization refers to the right to health, meaning the right to access to facilities, goods, services, and conditions necessary to enjoy the highest attainable standard of health. The Constitution defines health as a state of complete physical, mental, and social well-being and not merely as the absence of disease or infirmity. WHO has established a global program on HIV/AIDS that has been involved in standard setting. During the COVID-19 pandemic, the World Health Organization produced extensive technical guidance for health authorities and government officials on how to manage its effects and widespread nature. See, e.g., World Health Organization, *Prevention, Identification, and Management of Health Worker Infection in the Context of COVID-19* (October 30, 2020), https://www.who.int/publications/i/item/10665-336265.

Finally, the Food and Agriculture Organization, one of the UN's largest specialized agencies, aims to ensure food security and alleviate hunger. In 2004, the

FAO's Committee on World Food Security endorsed a set of voluntary guidelines to support the progressive realization of the right to adequate food in the context of national food security. The text was approved by the FAO Council in November 2004. (FAO Doc. CL 127/REP, appendix D). The Guidelines are intended to demonstrate how to integrate a human rights approach in the operational activities of states, UN bodies, and NGOs to ensure national food security. At the same time, the Guidelines indicate measures that states should adopt to implement the Covenant on Economic, Social, and Cultural Rights.

### Comments and Questions

1. Some scholars have attempted to articulate criteria for defining human rights. See, e.g., Bertrand G. Ramcharan, *The Concept of Human Rights in Contemporary International Law*, 1983 CAN. HUM. RTS. Y.B. 267, 280 ("Human rights are legal rights which possess one or more of certain qualitative characteristics, such as: appurtenance to the human person or group[;] universality[;] essentiality to human life, security, survival, dignity, liberty, equality[;] essentiality for international order[;] essentiality in the conscience of mankind[;] essentiality for the protection of vulnerable groups."); Francis G. Jacobs, *The Extension of the European Convention on Human Rights to Include Economic, Social, and Cultural Rights*, 3 HUM. RTS. REV. 166, 170, 172 (1978) (arguing that a human right must be: (1) fundamental; (2) universal in the sense both that it is universally or very widely recognized and that it is guaranteed to everyone; and (3) capable of sufficiently precise formulation to give rise to legal obligations on the part of the state rather than merely setting a standard). Are these criteria reflected in the various treaties referenced above?

2. The International Covenant on Civil and Political Rights (ICCPR) — which can be reviewed in the Documentary Supplement — is a cornerstone treaty in the international human rights law system. It codifies a wide array of human rights, inspired by the Universal Declaration of Human Rights. Among the most important rights that it protects are those related to life and freedom of expression, thought and religion, and the rights to be free from discrimination, torture, and slavery. The International Covenant on Economic, Social, and Cultural Rights (ICESCR) focuses instead on rights that entail systemic responses from states in their application, including rights to education, employment, health, social security, food, and others. What linkages can you see between civil and political rights, on the one hand, and economic, social and cultural rights, on the other? How are the rights in these treaties related to the topics of the other treaties referred to above?

3. The United States ratified, in 1992, the International Covenant on Civil and Political Rights, but it has not ratified the International Covenant on Economic, Social and Cultural Rights. Why do you think this is the case? How are these two treaties different from other treaties referred to *supra*, for example, the Convention on the Elimination of All Forms of Discrimination against Women?

4. An important aspect of United Nations human rights treaties such as the ICCPR and the ICESCR is the system of monitoring committees that have been created to supervise and oversee their compliance, which is discussed in Chapter 7. Briefly, the ICCPR is monitored by the Human Rights Committee and the ICESCR by the Committee on Economic, Social, and Cultural Rights. These monitoring

committees, typically referred to as "treaty-monitoring bodies" consider state party reports and issue observations on the reports and recommendations to improve treaty compliance. In their assessment of state reports, the committees can consider information presented by nongovernmental organizations. These committees also adopt "General Comments" or "General Recommendations" providing authoritative guidance for states on how to comply with specific treaty provisions. They can also adjudicate and issue views on complaints presented by individuals claiming human rights violations under the relevant treaty. The complaints can be presented against states that are parties to the first optional protocol to the ICCPR and that to the ICESCR.

## III.  THE INTERNATIONAL RULES GOVERNING TREATIES: ARE THEY DIFFERENT FROM HUMAN RIGHTS TREATIES?

Until the second half of the nineteenth century, most treaties were bilateral and contained equal and reciprocal benefits and burdens for each of the two parties. Multilateral treaty-making emerged as a source of legal obligation with the advent of international conferences like the Congress of Vienna (1815) but only became prevalent with the creation of permanent international organizations. Such treaties may adopt uniform technical standards or "rules of the road," such as the treaties and regulations adopted within the framework of the International Civil Aviation Organization or the World Trade Organization. Multilateral human rights treaties do not grant direct reciprocal benefits to the parties in the same way that trade or extradition treaties do, but instead impose obligations often referred to as "unilateral," because the primary beneficiaries of the obligations are within the ratifying or acceding state itself.

Given this characteristic of human rights treaties, in addition to their moral foundations, some scholars and human rights bodies have questioned whether they constitute a "special regime" in which the normal rules governing treaties are modified in key respects. This section examines key aspects of these rules, which constitute the law of treaties, and how they apply to human rights treaties, in light of the considerations just stated. The issues in this connection inevitably implicate the views of courts and supervisory bodies created by human rights treaties.

### A.  Interpretation

## Vienna Convention on the Law of Treaties

Adopted May 23, 1969, entered into force Jan. 27, 1980, 1155 U.N.T.S. 331

ARTICLE 31  INTERPRETATION OF TREATIES

1. A treaty shall be interpreted in good faith in accordance with the ordinary meaning to be given to the terms of the treaty in their context and in the light of its object and purpose.

2. The context for the purpose of the interpretation of a treaty shall comprise, in addition to the text, including its preamble and annexes:

(a) any agreement relating to the treaty which was made between all the parties in connection with the conclusion of the treaty;

(b) any instrument which was made by one or more parties in connection with the conclusion of the treaty and accepted by the other parties as an instrument related to the treaty.

3. There shall be taken into account, together with the context:

(a) any subsequent agreement between the parties regarding the interpretation of the treaty or the application of its provisions;

(b) any subsequent practice in the application of the treaty which establishes the agreement of the parties regarding its interpretation;

(c) any relevant rules of international law applicable in the relations between the parties.

4. A special meaning shall be given to a term if it is established that the parties so intended.

### ARTICLE 32  SUPPLEMENTARY MEANS OF INTERPRETATION

Recourse may be had to supplementary means of interpretation, including the preparatory work of the treaty and the circumstances of its conclusion, in order to confirm the meaning resulting from the application of article 31, or to determine the meaning when the interpretation according to article 31:

(a) leaves the meaning ambiguous or obscure; or

(b) leads to a result which is manifestly absurd or unreasonable.

---

In addition to these basic rules of interpretation, which are generally accepted as codifying customary international law, human rights treaties may contain their own provisions governing interpretation, such as the following.

## American Convention on Human Rights

Done November 22, 1969, O.A.S.T.S. No. 36

### ARTICLE 29.  RESTRICTIONS REGARDING INTERPRETATION

No provision of this Convention shall be interpreted as:

(a) permitting any State Party, group, or person to suppress the enjoyment or exercise of the rights and freedoms recognized in this Convention or to restrict them to a greater extent than is provided herein;

(b) restricting the enjoyment or exercise of any right or freedom recognized by virtue of the laws of any State party or by virtue of another convention to which one of the said states is a party;

(c) precluding other rights or guarantees that are inherent in the human personality or derived from representative democracy as a form of government; or

(d) excluding or limiting the effect that the American Declaration of the Rights and Duties of Man and other international acts of the same nature may have.

––––––––––––––

The following case suggests that a particularly expansive mode of interpretation may be appropriate in the context of human rights.

## Demir and Baykara v. Turkey

Eur. Ct. H.R. (GC), App. 34503/97, Judgment of Nov. 12

1. The case originated in an application against the Republic of Turkey lodged with the European Commission of Human Rights under former Article 25 of the Convention for the Protection of Human Rights and Fundamental Freedoms by two Turkish nationals, Mr. Kemal Demir and Mrs. Vicdan Baykara, the latter in her capacity as president of the trade union Tüm Bel Sen, on 8 October 1996. . . .

3. The applicants complained that, in breach of Article 11 of the Convention, by itself or in conjunction with Article 14, the domestic courts had denied them, first, the right to form trade unions and, second, the right to engage in collective bargaining and enter into collective agreements . . . ⎱ ⎰ *H arg*

### I. The Circumstances of the Case

15. The trade union Tüm Bel Sen was founded in 1990 by civil servants from various municipalities whose employment was governed by the Public Service Act (Law no. 657). Under Article 2 of its constitution, the union's objective is to promote democratic trade unionism and thereby assist its members in their aspirations and claims. Its head office is located in Istanbul.

16. On 27 February 1993 Tüm Bel Sen entered into a collective agreement with the Gaziantep Municipal Council for a period of two years effective from 1 January 1993. The agreement concerned all aspects of the working conditions of the Gaziantep Municipal Council's employees, such as salaries, allowances and welfare services.

17. As the Gaziantep Municipal Council had failed to fulfil certain of its obligations under the agreement, in particular financial obligations, the second applicant, as president of the union, brought civil proceedings against it in the Gaziantep District Court on 18 June 1993. [Domestic remedies provided no relief; members of the union were in fact ordered to reimburse income received pursuant to the collective bargaining agreement.]

. . .

The Law

## II. Alleged Violation of Article 11 of the Convention

59. The applicants complained that the domestic courts had denied them the right to form trade unions and to enter into collective agreements. In this connection they relied on Article 11 of the Convention, which reads as follows:

> 1. Everyone has the right to freedom of peaceful assembly and to freedom of association with others, including the right to form and to join trade unions for the protection of his interests.
>
> 2. No restrictions shall be placed on the exercise of these rights other than such as are prescribed by law and are necessary in a democratic society in the interests of national security or public safety, for the prevention of disorder or crime, for the protection of health or morals or for the protection of the rights and freedoms of others. This Article shall not prevent the imposition of lawful restrictions on the exercise of these rights by members of the armed forces, of the police or of the administration of the State.

### A. Interpretation of the Convention in The Light of Other International Instruments

60. The Court decided above to examine at the merits stage the Government's submission to the effect that, in adjudicating a case, it was impossible to rely against Turkey on international instruments other than the Convention, particularly instruments that Turkey had not ratified. As it relates more to the methodology to be adopted in an examination of the merits of the complaints submitted under Article 11 of the Convention, the Court considers it necessary to dispose of this submission before turning to any other question. . . .

3. The Practice of Interpreting Convention Provisions in the Light of other International Texts and Instruments

*(a) Basis*

65. In order to determine the meaning of the terms and phrases used in the Convention, the Court is guided mainly by the rules of interpretation provided for in Articles 31 to 33 of the Vienna Convention on the Law of Treaties. In accordance with the Vienna Convention the Court is required to ascertain the ordinary meaning to be given to the words in their context and in the light of the object and purpose of the provision from which they are drawn (see . . . Article 31 §1 of the Vienna Convention). Recourse may also be had to supplementary means of interpretation, either to confirm a meaning determined in accordance with the above steps, or to establish the meaning where it would otherwise be ambiguous, obscure, or manifestly absurd or unreasonable.

66. Since the Convention is first and foremost a system for the protection of human rights, the Court must interpret and apply it in a manner which renders its rights practical and effective, not theoretical and illusory. The Convention must

also be read as a whole, and interpreted in such a way as to promote internal consistency and harmony between its various provisions. . . .

67. In addition, the Court has never considered the provisions of the Convention as the sole framework of reference for the interpretation of the rights and freedoms enshrined therein. On the contrary, it must also take into account any relevant rules and principles of international law applicable in relations between the Contracting Parties.

68. The Court further observes that it has always referred to the "living" nature of the Convention, which must be interpreted in the light of present-day conditions, and that it has taken account of evolving norms of national and international law in its interpretation of Convention provisions.

*(b) Diversity of international texts and instruments used for the interpretation of the Convention*

(i) General international law

69. The precise obligations that the substantive provisions of the Convention impose on Contracting States may be interpreted, firstly, in the light of relevant international treaties that are applicable in the particular sphere (thus, for example, the Court has interpreted Article 8 of the Convention in the light of the United Nations Convention of 20 November 1989 on the Rights of the Child and the European Convention on the Adoption of Children of 24 April 1967).

70. In another case where reference was made to international treaties other than the Convention, the Court, in order to establish the State's positive obligation concerning "the prohibition on domestic slavery" took into account the provisions of universal international conventions (the ILO Forced Labour Convention, the Supplementary Convention on the Abolition of Slavery, the Slave Trade, and Institutions and Practices Similar to Slavery, and the International Convention on the Rights of the Child). After referring to the relevant provisions of these international instruments, the Court considered that limiting the question of compliance with Article 4 of the Convention only to direct action by the State authorities would be inconsistent with the international instruments specifically concerned with this issue and would amount to rendering it ineffective.

71. Moreover, as the Court indicated in the *Golder* case (cited above, §35), the relevant rules of international law applicable in the relations between the parties also include "general principles of law recognized by civilized nations" (see Article 38 §1 (c) of the Statute of the International Court of Justice). The Legal Committee of the Consultative Assembly of the Council of Europe foresaw in August 1950 that "the Commission and the Court [would] necessarily [have to] apply such principles" in the execution of their duties and thus considered it to be "unnecessary" to insert a specific clause to this effect in the Convention.

72. In the *Soering* judgment, the Court took into consideration the principles laid down by texts of universal scope in developing its case-law concerning Article 3 of the Convention in respect of extradition to third countries. Firstly, it considered, with reference to the 1966 International Covenant on Civil and Political Rights and the 1969 American Convention on Human Rights, that the prohibition of treatment contrary to Article 3 of the Convention had become an internationally accepted standard. Secondly, it considered that the fact that the United Nations Convention

Against Torture and Other Cruel, Inhuman or Degrading Treatment or Punishment
prohibited the extradition of a person to another State where he would be in danger
of being subjected to torture did not mean that an essentially similar obligation was
not already inherent in the general terms of Article 3 of the European Convention.

73. Furthermore, the Court found in its *Al-Adsani* judgment, with reference
to universal instruments (Article 5 of the Universal Declaration of Human Rights,
Article 7 of the International Covenant on Civil and Political Rights, Articles 2
and 4 of the United Nations Convention against Torture and Other Cruel, Inhuman and Degrading Treatment or Punishment) and their interpretation by international criminal courts and domestic courts, that the prohibition of torture had
attained the status of a peremptory norm of international law, or *jus cogens*, which it
incorporated into its case-law in this sphere.

### (ii) Council of Europe instruments

74. In a number of judgments the Court has used, for the purpose of interpreting the Convention, intrinsically non-binding instruments of Council of Europe
organs, in particular recommendations and resolutions of the Committee of Ministers and the Parliamentary Assembly.

75. These methods of interpretation have also led the Court to support its reasoning by reference to norms emanating from other Council of Europe organs, even
though those organs have no function of representing States Parties to the Convention, whether supervisory mechanisms or expert bodies. In order to interpret the exact
scope of the rights and freedoms guaranteed by the Convention, the Court has, for
example, made use of the work of the European Commission for Democracy through
Law or "Venice Commission" and of the reports of the European Committee for the
Prevention of Torture and Inhuman or Degrading Treatment or Punishment (CPT).

### (iii) Consideration by the Court

76. The Court recently confirmed, in the *Saadi v. the United Kingdom* judgment,
that when it considers the object and purpose of the Convention provisions, it also
takes into account the international law background to the legal question before it.
Being made up of a set of rules and principles that are accepted by the vast majority
of States, the common international or domestic law standards of European States
reflect a reality that the Court cannot disregard when it is called upon to clarify the
scope of a Convention provision that more conventional means of interpretation
have not enabled it to establish with a sufficient degree of certainty.

77. By way of example, in finding that the right to organise had a negative
aspect which excluded closed-shop agreements, the Court considered, largely on
the basis of the European Social Charter and the case-law of its supervisory organs,
together with other European or universal instruments, that there was a growing
measure of agreement on the subject at international level.

78. The Court observes in this connection that in searching for common
ground among the norms of international law it has never distinguished between
sources of law according to whether or not they have been signed or ratified by the
respondent State.

79. Thus, in the *Marckx v. Belgium* case, concerning the legal status of children born out of wedlock, the Court based its interpretation on two international

conventions of 1962 and 1975 that Belgium, like other States Parties to the Convention, had not yet ratified at the time. The Court considered that the small number of ratifications of these instruments could not be relied on in opposition to the continuing evolution of the domestic law of the great majority of the member States, together with the relevant international instruments, towards full juridical recognition of the maxim *"mater semper certa est"*.

80. Moreover, in the cases of *Christine Goodwin v. the United Kingdom, Vilho Eskelinen and Others v. Finland*, and *Sørensen and Rasmussen v. Denmark* the Court was guided by the European Union's Charter of Fundamental Rights, even though this instrument was not binding. Furthermore, in the cases of *McElhinney v. Ireland Al-Adsani v. the United Kingdom* and *Fogarty v. the United Kingdom*, the Court took note of the European Convention on State Immunity, which had only been ratified at the time by eight member States.

81. In addition, in its *Glass v. the United Kingdom* judgment, the Court took account, in interpreting Article 8 of the Convention, of the standards enshrined in the Oviedo Convention on Human Rights and Biomedicine of 4 April 1997, even though that instrument had not been ratified by all the States parties to the Convention.

82. In order to determine the criteria for State responsibility under Article 2 of the Convention in respect of dangerous activities, the Court, in the *Öneryıldız v. Turkey* judgment, referred among other texts to the Convention on Civil Liability for Damage resulting from Activities Dangerous to the Environment and the Convention on the Protection of the Environment through Criminal Law. The majority of member States, including Turkey, had neither signed nor ratified these two Conventions.

83. In the *Taşkın and Others v. Turkey* case, the Court built on its caselaw concerning Article 8 of the Convention in matters of environmental protection (an aspect regarded as forming part of the individual's private life) largely on the basis of principles enshrined in the Aarhus Convention on Access to Information, Public Participation in Decision-making and Access to Justice in Environmental Matters. Turkey had not signed the Aarhus Convention.

84. The Court notes that the Government further invoked the absence of political support on the part of member States, in the context of the work of the Steering Committee for Human Rights, for the creation of an additional protocol to extend the Convention system to certain economic and social rights. The Court observes, however, that this attitude of member States was accompanied, as acknowledged by the Government, by a wish to strengthen the mechanism of the Social Charter. The Court regards this as an argument in support of the existence of a consensus among Contracting States to promote economic and social rights. It is not precluded from taking this general wish of Contracting States into consideration when interpreting the provisions of the Convention.

4. Conclusion

. . .

86. In this context, it is not necessary for the respondent State to have ratified the entire collection of instruments that are applicable in respect of the precise subject matter of the case concerned. It will be sufficient for the Court that the

relevant international instruments denote a continuous evolution in the norms and principles applied in international law or in the domestic law of the majority of member States of the Council of Europe and show, in a precise area, that there is common ground in modern societies. . . .

[The Court concluded that "members of the administration of the State" cannot be excluded from the scope of Article 11. Thus, national authorities are entitled to impose "lawful restrictions" on those persons only in accordance with Article 11, paragraph 2. Since the government had failed to show how the nature of the duties performed by the applicants, as municipal civil servants, required them to be regarded as "members of the administration of the State" subject to such restrictions, the applicants could rely on Article 11 of the Convention; any interference with the exercise of the right concerned must satisfy the requirements of paragraph 2 of that Article].

. . .

147. The Court observes that in international law, the right to bargain collectively is protected by ILO Convention No. 98 concerning the Right to Organise and to Bargain Collectively. Adopted in 1949, this text, which is one of the fundamental instruments concerning international labour standards, was ratified by Turkey in 1952. It states in Article 6 that it does not deal with the position of "public servants engaged in the administration of the State". However, the ILO's Committee of Experts interpreted this provision as excluding only those officials whose activities were specific to the administration of the State. With that exception, all other persons employed by government, by public enterprises or by autonomous public institutions should benefit, according to the Committee, from the guarantees provided for in Convention No. 98 in the same manner as other employees, and consequently should be able to engage in collective bargaining in respect of their conditions of employment, including wages.

148. The Court further notes that ILO Convention No. 151 (which was adopted in 1978, entered into force in 1981 and has been ratified by Turkey) on labour relations in the public service ("Convention concerning Protection of the Right to Organise and Procedures for Determining Conditions of Employment in the Public Service") leaves States free to choose whether or not members of the armed forces or of the police should be accorded the right to take part in the determination of working conditions, but provides that this right applies everywhere else in the public service, if need be under specific conditions. In addition, the provisions of Convention No. 151, under its Article 1 §1, cannot be used to reduce the extent of the guarantees provided for in Convention No. 98.

149. As to European instruments, the Court finds that the European Social Charter, in its Article 6 §2 (which Turkey has not ratified), affords to all workers, and to all unions, the right to bargain collectively, thus imposing on the public authorities the corresponding obligation to promote actively a culture of dialogue and negotiation in the economy, so as to ensure broad coverage for collective agreements. The Court observes, however, that this obligation does not oblige authorities to enter into collective agreements. According to the meaning attributed by the European Committee of Social Rights (ECSR) to Article 6 §2 of the Charter, which in fact fully applies to public officials, States which impose restrictions on collective bargaining in the public sector have an obligation, in order to comply with this

provision, to arrange for the involvement of staff representatives in the drafting of the applicable employment regulations.

150. As to the European Union's Charter of Fundamental Rights, which is one of the most recent European instruments, it provides in Article 28 that workers and employers, or their respective organisations, have, in accordance with Community law and national laws and practices, the right to negotiate and conclude collective agreements at the appropriate levels.

*EU Charter on Fund. Rights*

151. As to the practice of European States, the Court reiterates that, in the vast majority of them, the right of civil servants to bargain collectively with the authorities has been recognised, subject to various exceptions so as to exclude certain areas regarded as sensitive or certain categories of civil servants who hold exclusive powers of the State. In particular, the right of public servants employed by local authorities and not holding State powers to engage in collective bargaining in order to determine their wages and working conditions has been recognised in the majority of Contracting States. The remaining exceptions can be justified only by particular circumstances.

*practices of EU states*

152. It is also appropriate to take into account the evolution in the Turkish situation since the application was lodged. Following its ratification of Convention No. 87 on freedom of association and the protection of the right to organise, Turkey amended, in 1995, Article 53 of its Constitution by inserting a paragraph providing for the right of unions formed by public officials to take or defend court proceedings and to engage in collective bargaining with authorities. Later on, Law no. 4688 of 25 June 2001 laid down the terms governing the exercise by civil servants of their right to bargain collectively.

*Turkish law*

153. In the light of these developments, the Court considers that its caselaw to the effect that the right to bargain collectively and to enter into collective agreements does not constitute an inherent element of Article 11 (*Swedish Engine Drivers' Union* and *Schmidt and Dahlström*) should be reconsidered, so as to take account of the perceptible evolution in such matters, in both international law and domestic legal systems. While it is in the interests of legal certainty, foreseeability and equality before the law that the Court should not depart, without good reason, from precedents established in previous cases, a failure by the Court to maintain a dynamic and evolutive approach would risk rendering it a bar to reform or improvement.

154. Consequently, the Court considers that, having regard to the developments in labour law, both international and national, and to the practice of Contracting States in such matters, the right to bargain collectively with the employer has, in principle, become one of the essential elements of the "right to form and to join trade unions for the protection of [one's] interests" set forth in Article 11 of the Convention, it being understood that States remain free to organise their system so as, if appropriate, to grant special status to representative trade unions. Like other workers, civil servants, except in very specific cases, should enjoy such rights, but without prejudice to the effects of any "lawful restrictions" that may have to be imposed on "members of the administration of the State" within the meaning of Article 11 §2 — a category to which the applicants in the present case do not, however, belong. . . .

[Applying this test, the Court found that the annulment of the collective agreement entered into by the applicants' union following collective bargaining with the authority was not "necessary in a democratic society" and that there had been therefore a violation of Article 11 of the Convention on this point also, in respect of both the applicants' trade union and the applicants themselves.]

### Comments and Questions

1. Does the European Court of Human Rights—discussed in more detail in Chapter 9—faithfully follow the rules of interpretation set forth in the Vienna Convention on the Law of Treaties, *supra* page 75-76?

2. By what reasoning in *Demir* did the Court determine that it is appropriate to apply treaties to which Turkey was not a party? Does the Court's approach reflect anything about the source of international obligation, traditionally viewed as being based on consent?

3. Does the Court indicate whether or not this decision is retroactive? Should it be?

4. Is there anything in the case that suggests the reasoning would be limited to Article 11 of the European Convention on Human Rights? Can it be used for all rights in the Convention?

5. The Court refers at several points in the judgment to the state's "margin of appreciation," which is a concept mostly unique to the European human rights system, as discussed in Chapter 9. This concept was first enunciated by the European Court in the case of *Handyside v. the United Kingdom*, 24-A Eur. Ct. H.R. (1976), 1 EHRR 737, paras. 48-49, a case involving allegations of obscenity. The Court held that "by reason of their direct and continuous contact with the vital forces of their countries," state authorities are better placed to determine the requirements of morality and the measures necessary to uphold it—subject to European supervision. Therefore, a certain degree of deference is afforded the state, a deference that varies with the right involved and the context of the case. The deference is considerable when the Court finds no consensus within the member states of the Council of Europe about the importance of the interest at stake or the best means of protecting it. See *Evans v. United Kingdom*, 46 EHRR 728 (2007); *VO v. France*, 2004-III, 40 EHRR 259 (abortion). Issues of social or economic policy and national emergencies are similarly reviewed under a deferential margin of appreciation, while there is a very slim margin of appreciation in matters relating to personal security (e.g., torture).

6. To the extent that the Court is relying on texts and jurisprudence from other systems, is this likely in the long run to lead to a coherent body of global human rights norms? Should it?

### B.   Reservations

Most United Nations human rights treaties do not include any provision on reservations, but the ability to make reservations to parts of a treaty may be an essential condition for a state to accept being bound to the treaty. The following provisions of the Vienna Convention on the Law of Treaties are generally considered to restate customary international law on the subject of reservations.

## Vienna Convention on the Law of Treaties

Adopted May 23, 1969, entered into force Jan. 27, 1980, 1155 U.N.T.S. 331

### Article 19   Formulation of Reservations

A State may, when signing, ratifying, accepting, approving or acceding to a treaty, formulate a reservation unless:

(a) the reservation is prohibited by the treaty;

(b) the treaty provides that only specified reservations, which do not include the reservation in question, may be made; or

(c) in cases not falling under sub-paragraphs (a) and (b), the reservation is incompatible with the object and purpose of the treaty.

### Article 20   Acceptance of and Objection to Reservations

1. A reservation expressly authorized by a treaty does not require any subsequent acceptance by the other contracting States unless the treaty so provides.

2. When it appears from the limited number of the negotiating States and the object and purpose of a treaty that the application of the treaty in its entirety between all the parties is an essential condition of the consent of each one to be bound by the treaty, a reservation requires acceptance by all the parties.

3. When a treaty is a constituent instrument of an international organization and unless it otherwise provides, a reservation requires the acceptance of the competent organ of that organization.

4. In cases not falling under the preceding paragraphs and unless the treaty otherwise provides:

(a) acceptance by another contracting State of a reservation constitutes the reserving State a party to the treaty in relation to that other State if or when the treaty is in force for those States;

(b) an objection by another contracting State to a reservation does not preclude the entry into force of the treaty as between the objecting and reserving States unless a contrary intention is definitely expressed by the objecting State;

(c) an act expressing a State's consent to be bound by the treaty and containing a reservation is effective as soon as at least one other contracting State has accepted the reservation.

5. For the purposes of paragraphs 2 and 4 and unless the treaty otherwise provides, a reservation is considered to have been accepted by a State if it shall have raised no objection to the reservation by the end of a period of twelve months after it was notified of the reservation or by the date on which it expressed its consent to be bound by the treaty, whichever is later.

### Article 21   Legal Effects of Reservations and of Objections to Reservations

1. A reservation established with regard to another party in accordance with articles 19, 20 and 23:

(a) modifies for the reserving State in its relations with that other party the provisions of the treaty to which the reservation relates to the extent of the reservation; and

(b) modifies those provisions to the same extent for that other party in its relations with the reserving State.

2. The reservation does not modify the provisions of the treaty for the other parties to the treaty *inter se*.

3. When a State objecting to a reservation has not opposed the entry into force of the treaty between itself and the reserving State, the provisions to which the reservation relates do not apply as between the two States to the extent of the reservation.

———————

Thus, reservations are permitted unless a treaty prohibits them. States have filed numerous reservations both to substantive and procedural provisions of human rights treaties, and roughly one-half the states parties to the Covenant on Civil and Political Rights (CCPR) have submitted one or more reservations. Very few objections to these reservations have been filed, although examples include the objections of France, Germany, and the Netherlands to a statement by India that the right of self-determination applies only to peoples under foreign domination, and the declarations by Belgium and the Netherlands that no reservation to a non-derogable right is permissible.

The ratification record and number of reservations vary among human rights treaties. The effectiveness of the Convention on the Elimination of All Forms of Discrimination against Women (CEDAW) has been weakened significantly by the many reservations made by states in ratifying this treaty. For an analysis of some of these reservations, see Katarina Tomaševski, "Women's Rights," in *Human Rights: Concepts and Standards* 231, 235-38 (Janusz Symonides ed., 2000); Linda M. Keller, *Impact of States Parties' Reservations to the Convention on the Elimination of All Forms of Discrimination against Women*, 2014 MICH. ST. L. REV. 309, 315-326 (2014). The reservations to CEDAW generally seek to preserve various national or religious institutions that might otherwise be in conflict with the Convention. Some of these reservations raise serious questions about their legality, given that Article 28(2) of CEDAW—in line with Article 19(c) of the Vienna Convention— declares that "a reservation incompatible with the object and purpose of the present Convention shall not be permitted." See generally Belinda Clerk, *The Vienna Convention Reservations Regime and the Convention on Discrimination Against Women*, 85 AM. J. Int'l L. 281 (1991).

### *Note: US Reservations, Understandings, and Declarations to the Covenant on Civil and Political Rights*

Despite the similarity of the Covenant on Civil and Political Rights to the US Constitution and laws, one of President Carter's legacies to the ratification process was the precedent he created of recommending a reservation or other qualifying proviso not only in cases where the Covenant actually might conflict with the Constitution's guarantees (e.g., Article 20's restrictions on incitement to war and "hate speech" that might run afoul of the First Amendment), but also in any case where the Covenant, by setting a more humane standard than the Constitution, would at the time of ratification require a modification of US law (e.g., Article 6's prohibition of capital punishment in the case of crimes committed by persons below 18 years of age).

President Carter finally recommended the adoption of four reservations, one understanding, one statement, and two declarations. President Bush, following President Carter's path, went several steps further; his promise of "few essential reservations and understandings" turned out to include a "package" of five reservations, five understandings, and four declarations. They are set out and then assessed in the following extracts.

## International Covenant on Civil and Political Rights: The Administration's Proposed Reservations, Understandings, and Declarations in International Covenant on Civil and Political Rights

Hearing Before the Senate Comm. on Foreign Relations, 102d Cong., 1st Sess. 8-9 (1991)

### A. RESERVATIONS

#### 1. FREE SPEECH

Article 20 does not authorize or require legislation or other action by the United States that would restrict the right of free speech and association protected by the Constitution and laws of the United States.

#### 2. CAPITAL PUNISHMENT

The United States reserves the right, subject to its Constitutional constraints, to impose capital punishment on any person (other than a pregnant woman) duly convicted under existing or future laws permitting the imposition of capital punishment, including such punishment for crimes committed by persons below, eighteen years of age.*

#### 3. CRUEL, INHUMAN OR DEGRADING TREATMENT OR PUNISHMENT

The United States considers itself bound by Article 7 to the extent that "cruel, inhuman or degrading treatment or punishment" means the cruel and unusual treatment or punishment prohibited by the Fifth, Eighth and/or Fourteenth Amendments to the Constitution of the United States.

*found incompatible w/ obj/purp pg 96*

---

* [In *Roper v. Simmons*, 543 U.S. 551 (2005), the Supreme Court held that imposition of capital punishment on minors violates the US Constitution. The majority opinion referred to international opinion, the practice of other states, and human rights treaties, including the Civil and Political Rights Covenant. Id. at 1198-99. See the discussion of *Roper* in Chapter 6, pages 370-377.—Eds.]

4. Criminal Penalties

Because U.s. Law Generally applies to an offender the penalty in force at the time the offense was committed, the United States does not adhere to the third clause of paragraph 1 of Article 15.

5. Juveniles

The policy and practice of the United States are generally in compliance with and supportive of the Covenant's provisions regarding treatment of juveniles in the criminal justice system. Nevertheless, the United States reserves the right, in exceptional circumstances, to treat juveniles as adults, notwithstanding paragraphs 2(b) and 3 of Article 10 and paragraph 9 of Article 14. The United States further reserves to these provisions with respect to individuals who volunteer for military service prior to age 18.

B. Understandings

1. Non-Discrimination and Equal Protection

The Constitution and laws of the United States guarantee all persons equal protection of the law and provide extensive protections against discrimination. The United States understands distinctions based upon race, colour, sex, language, religion, political or other opinion, national or social origin, property, birth or any other status—as those terms are used in Article 2, paragraph 1 and Article 26—to be permitted when such distinctions are, at minimum, rationally related to a legitimate governmental objective. The United States further understands the prohibition in paragraph of Article 4 upon discrimination, in time of public emergency, based "solely" on the status of race, colour, sex, language, religion or social origin not to bar distinctions that may have a disproportionate effect upon persons of a particular status.

2. Right to Compensation for Illegal Arrest and
   Miscarriage Of Justice

The United States understands the right to compensation referred to in Articles 9(5) and 14(6) to require the provision of effective and enforceable mechanisms by which a victim of an unlawful arrest or detention or a miscarriage of justice may seek and, where justified, obtain compensation from either the responsible individual or the appropriate governmental entity. Entitlement to compensation may be subject to the reasonable requirements of domestic law.

3. Separate Treatment of The Accused and Juveniles

The United States understands the reference to "exceptional circumstances" in paragraph 2(a) of Article 10 to permit the imprisonment of an accused person with convicted persons where appropriate in light of an individual's overall dangerousness, and to permit accused persons to waive their right to segregation from convicted persons. The United States further understands that paragraph 3 of Article 10 does not diminish the goals of punishment, deterrence, and incapacitation as additional legitimate purposes for a penitentiary system.

4. Right to Counsel, Compelled Witnesses, Double Jeopardy

The United States understands that subparagraphs 3(b) and (d) do not require the provision of a criminal defendant's counsel of choice when the defendant is provided with court-appointed counsel on grounds of indigence, when the defendant is financially able to retain alternative counsel, or when imprisonment is not imposed. The United States further understands that paragraph 3(e) does not prohibit a requirement that the defendant make a showing that any witness whose attendance he seeks to compel is necessary for his defense. The United States understands the prohibition upon double jeopardy in paragraph 7 to apply only when the judgment of acquittal has been rendered by a court of the same governmental unit, whether the Federal Government or a constituent unit, as is seeking a new trial for the same cause.

5. Federalism

The United States understands that this Convention shall be implemented by the federal Government to the extent that it exercises legislative and judicial jurisdiction over the matters covered therein, and otherwise by the state and local governments; to the extent that state and local governments exercise jurisdiction over such matters, the Federal Government shall take measures appropriate to the Federal system to the end that the competent authorities of the state or local governments may take appropriate measures for the fulfillment of the Convention.

C. Declarations

1. Non-Self-Executing

The United States declares that the provisions of Articles 1 through 27 of the Covenant are not self-executing.

2. Limitations on Rights

It is the view of the United States that States Party to the Covenant should wherever possible refrain from imposing any restrictions or limitations on the exercise of the rights recognized and protected by the Covenant, even when such restrictions and limitations are permissible under the terms of the Covenant. For the United States, Article 5, paragraph 2, which provides that fundamental human rights existing in any State Party may not be diminished on the pretext that the Covenant recognizes them to a lesser extent, has particular relevance to Article 19, paragraph 3, which would permit certain restrictions on the freedom of expression. The United States declares that it will continue to adhere to the requirements and constraints of its Constitution in respect of all such restrictions and limitations.

3. Competence of The Human Rights Committee

The United States declares that it accepts the competence of the Human Rights Committee to receive and consider communications under Article 41 in which a State Party claims that another State Party is not fulfilling its obligations under the Covenant.

4. Natural Wealth and Resources

The United States declares that the right referred to in Article 47 may be exercised only in accordance with international law.

---

The United States reservations to the Covenant on Civil and Political Rights drew significant criticism. See, e.g., Annika K. Carlsten, *Young Enough to Die? Executing Juvenile Offenders in Violation of International Law*, 29 Denv. J. Int'l L. & Pol'y 181, 187-89 (2001); William A. Schabas, *Invalid Reservations to the International Covenant on Civil and Political Rights: Is the United States Still a Party?*, 21 Brook. J. Int'l L. 277 (1995); Penny M. Venetis, *Making Human Rights Treaty Law Actionable in the United States: The Case for Universal Implementing Legislation*, 63 Ala. L. Rev. 97 (2011).

As pointed out earlier and discussed in Chapter 7, most of the bodies that oversee human rights treaties have the possibility of adopting "General Comments" or "General Recommendations." Such comments or recommendations are addressed to all of the parties to a treaty and are designed to provide guidance to them in discharging their reporting obligations and interpreting the substantive provisions of the treaty. General Comments and Recommendations are relied upon by the committees in evaluating compliance by states with their obligations, be it in examining state reports or in giving "views" or decisions on individual complaints. Concerned about the numerous reservations made by states to the Covenant on Civil and Political Rights, the Human Rights Committee adopted the following General Comment in 1994.


Human Rights Committee

General Comment No. 24: Issues relating to reservations made upon ratification or accession to the Covenant or the Optional Protocols thereto, or in relation to declarations Under Article 41 of the Covenant

UN Doc. CCPR/C/21/Rev.1/Add.6 (1994)

1. As of 1 November 1994, 46 of the 127 States parties to the International Covenant on Civil and Political Rights had, between them, entered 150 reservations of varying significance to their acceptance of the obligations of the Covenant. Some of these reservations exclude the duty to provide and guarantee particular rights in the Covenant. Others are couched in more general terms, often directed to ensuring the continued paramountcy of certain domestic legal provisions. Still others are directed at the competence of the Committee. The number of reservations, their content and their scope may undermine the effective implementation of the Covenant and tend to weaken respect for the obligations of States parties. It is important for States parties to know exactly what obligations they, and other States parties, have in fact undertaken. And the Committee, in the performance of its duties under either article 40 of the Covenant or under the Optional Protocols, must know whether a State is bound by a particular obligation or to what extent.

This will require a determination as to whether a unilateral statement is a reservation or an interpretative declaration and a determination of its acceptability and effects.

2. For these reasons the Committee has deemed it useful to address in a General Comment the issues of international law and human rights policy that arise. The General Comment identifies the principles of international law that apply to the making of reservations and by reference to which their acceptability is to be tested and their purport to be interpreted. It addresses the role of States parties in relation to the reservations of others. It further addresses the role of the Committee itself in relation to reservations. And it makes certain recommendations to present States parties for a reviewing of reservations and to those States that are not yet parties about legal and human rights policy considerations to be borne in mind should they consider ratifying or acceding with particular reservations.

3. It is not always easy to distinguish a reservation from a declaration as to a State's understanding of the interpretation of a provision, or from a statement of policy. Regard will be had to the intention of the State, rather than the form of the instrument. If a statement, irrespective of its name or title, purports to exclude or modify the legal effect of a treaty in its application to the State, it constitutes a reservation. Conversely, if a so-called reservation merely offers a State's understanding of a provision but does not exclude or modify that provision in its application to that State, it is, in reality, not a reservation.

4. The possibility of entering reservations may encourage States which consider that they have difficulties in guaranteeing all the rights in the Covenant none the less to accept the generality of obligations in that instrument. Reservations may serve a useful function to enable States to adapt specific elements in their laws to the inherent rights of each person as articulated in the Covenant. However, it is desirable in principle that States accept the full range of obligations, because the human rights norms are the legal expression of the essential rights that every person is entitled to as a human being. . . .

6. The absence of a prohibition on reservations does not mean that any reservation is permitted. The matter of reservations under the Covenant and the first Optional Protocol is governed by international law. Article 19 (3) of the Vienna Convention on the Law of Treaties provides relevant guidance. . . . Even though, unlike some other human rights treaties, the Covenant does not incorporate a specific reference to the object and purpose test, that test governs the matter of interpretation and acceptability of reservations.

7. In an instrument which articulates very many civil and political rights, each of the many articles, and indeed their interplay, secures the objectives of the Covenant. The object and purpose of the Covenant is to create legally binding standards for human rights by defining certain civil and political rights and placing them in a framework of obligations which are legally binding for those States which ratify; and to provide an efficacious supervisory machinery for the obligations undertaken.

8. . . . Although treaties that are mere exchanges of obligations between States allow them to reserve *inter se* application of rules of general international law, it is otherwise in human rights treaties, which are for the benefit of persons within their jurisdiction. Accordingly, provisions in the Covenant that represent customary international law (and *a fortiori* when they have the character of peremptory

norms) may not be the subject of reservations. Accordingly, a State may not reserve the right to engage in slavery, to torture, to subject persons to cruel, inhuman or degrading treatment or punishment, to arbitrarily deprive persons of their lives, to arbitrarily arrest and detain persons, to deny freedom of thought, conscience and religion, to presume a person guilty unless he proves his innocence, to execute pregnant women or children, to permit the advocacy of national, racial or religious hatred, to deny to persons of marriageable age the right to marry, or to deny to minorities the right to enjoy their own culture, profess their own religion, or use their own language. And while reservations to particular clauses of article 14 may be acceptable, a general reservation to the right to a fair trial would not be.

9. Applying more generally the object and purpose test to the Covenant, the Committee notes that, for example, reservation [sic] to article 1 denying peoples the right to determine their own political status and to pursue their economic, social and cultural development, would be incompatible with the object and purpose of the Covenant. Equally, a reservation to the obligation to respect and ensure the rights, and to do so on a non-discriminatory basis (article 2 (1)) would not be acceptable. Nor may a state reserve an entitlement not to take the necessary steps at the domestic level to give effect to the rights of the Covenant (article 2 (2)).

10. The Committee has further examined whether categories of reservations may offend the "object and purpose" test. In particular, it falls for consideration as to whether reservations to the non-derogable provisions of the Covenant are compatible with its object and purpose. While there is no hierarchy of importance of rights under the Covenant, the operation of certain rights may not be suspended, even in times of national emergency. This underlines the great importance of non-derogable rights. But not all rights of profound importance, such as articles 9 and 27 of the Covenant, have in fact been made non-derogable. One reason for certain rights being made non-derogable is because their suspension is irrelevant to the legitimate control of the state of national emergency (for example, no imprisonment for debt, in article 11). Another reason is that derogation may indeed be impossible (as, for example, freedom of conscience). At the same time, some provisions are non-derogable exactly because without them there would be no rule of law. A reservation to the provisions of article 4 itself, which precisely stipulates the balance to be struck between the interests of the State and the rights of the individual in times of emergency, would fall in this category. And some non-derogable rights, which in any event cannot be reserved because of their status as peremptory norms, are also of this character—the prohibition of torture and arbitrary deprivation of life are examples. While there is no automatic correlation between reservations to non-derogable provisions, and reservations which offend against the object and purpose of the Covenant, a State has a heavy onus to justify such a reservation.

11. The Covenant consists not just of the specified rights, but of important supportive guarantees. These guarantees provide the necessary framework for securing the rights in the Covenant and are thus essential to its object and purpose. Some operate at the national level and some at the international level. Reservations designed to remove these guarantees are thus not acceptable. Thus, a State could not make a reservation to article 2, paragraph 3, of the Covenant, indicating that it intends to provide no remedies for human rights violations. Guarantees such as these are an integral part of the structure of the Covenant and underpin its

efficacy. The Covenant also envisages, for the better attainment of its stated objectives, a monitoring role for the Committee. Reservations that purport to evade that essential element in the design of the Covenant, which is also directed to securing the enjoyment of the rights, are also incompatible with its object and purpose. A State may not reserve the right not to present a report and have it considered by the Committee. The Committee's role under the Covenant, whether under article 40 or under the Optional Protocols, necessarily entails interpreting the provisions of the Covenant and the development of a jurisprudence. Accordingly, a reservation that rejects the Committee's competence to interpret the requirements of any provisions of the Covenant would also be contrary to the object and purpose of that treaty.

12. The intention of the Covenant is that the rights contained therein should be ensured to all those under a State party's jurisdiction. To this end certain attendant requirements are likely to be necessary. Domestic laws may need to be altered properly to reflect the requirements of the Covenant; and mechanisms at the domestic level will be needed to allow the Covenant rights to be enforceable at the local level. Reservations often reveal a tendency of States not to want to change a particular law. And sometimes that tendency is elevated to a general policy. Of particular concern are widely formulated reservations which essentially render ineffective all Covenant rights which would require any change in national law to ensure compliance with Covenant obligations. No real international rights or obligations have thus been accepted. And when there is an absence of provisions to ensure that Covenant rights may be sued on in domestic courts, and, further, a failure to allow individual complaints to be brought to the Committee under the first Optional Protocol, all the essential elements of the Covenant guarantees have been removed. . . .

16. The Committee finds it important to address which body has the legal authority to make determinations as to whether specific reservations are compatible with the object and purpose of the Covenant. As for international treaties in general, the International Court of Justice has indicated in the *Reservations to the Genocide Convention Case* (1951) that a State which objected to a reservation on the grounds of incompatibility with the object and purpose of a treaty could, through objecting, regard the treaty as not in effect as between itself and the reserving State. Article 20, paragraph 4, of the Vienna Convention on the Law of Treaties 1969 contains provisions most relevant to the present case on acceptance of and objection to reservations. This provides for the possibility of a State to object to a reservation made by another State. Article 21 deals with the legal effects of objections by States to reservations made by other States. Essentially, a reservation precludes the operation, as between the reserving and other States, of the provision reserved; and an objection thereto leads to the reservation being in operation as between the reserving and objecting State only to the extent that it has not been objected to.

17. As indicated above, it is the Vienna Convention on the Law of Treaties that provides the definition of reservations and also the application of the object and purpose test in the absence of other specific provisions. But the Committee believes that its provisions on the role of State objections in relation to reservations are inappropriate to address the problem of reservations to human rights treaties. Such treaties, and the Covenant specifically, are not a web of inter-State

exchanges of mutual obligations. They concern the endowment of individuals with rights. The principle of inter-State reciprocity has no place, save perhaps in the limited context of reservations to declarations on the Committee's competence under article 41. And because the operation of the classic rules on reservations is so inadequate for the Covenant, States have often not seen any legal interest in or need to object to reservations. The absence of protest by States cannot imply that a reservation is either compatible or incompatible with the object and purpose of the Covenant. Objections have been occasional, made by some States but not others, and on grounds not always specified; when an objection is made, it often does not specify a legal consequence, or sometimes even indicates that the objecting party none the less does not regard the Covenant as not in effect as between the parties concerned. In short, the pattern is so unclear that it is not safe to assume that a non-objecting State thinks that a particular reservation is acceptable. In the view of the Committee, because of the special characteristics of the Covenant as a human rights treaty, it is open to question what effect objections have between States *inter se*. However, an objection to a reservation made by States may provide some guidance to the Committee in its interpretation as to its compatibility with the object and purpose of the Covenant.

18. It necessarily falls to the Committee to determine whether a specific reservation is compatible with the object and purpose of the Covenant. This is in part because, as indicated above, it is an inappropriate task for States parties in relation to human rights treaties, and in part because it is a task that the Committee cannot avoid in the performance of its functions. In order to know the scope of its duty to examine a State's compliance under article 40 or a communication under the first Optional Protocol, the Committee has necessarily to take a view on the compatibility of a reservation with the object and purpose of the Covenant and with general international law. Because of the special character of a human rights treaty, the compatibility of a reservation with the object and purpose of the Covenant must be established objectively, by reference to legal principles, and the Committee is particularly well placed to perform this task. The normal consequence of an unacceptable reservation is not that the Covenant will not be in effect at all for a reserving party. Rather, such a reservation will generally be severable, in the sense that the Covenant will be operative for the reserving party without benefit of the reservation.

19. Reservations must be specific and transparent, so that the Committee, those under the jurisdiction of the reserving State and other States parties may be clear as to what obligations of human rights compliance have or have not been undertaken. Reservations may thus not be general, but must refer to a particular provision of the Covenant and indicate in precise terms its scope in relation thereto. When considering the compatibility of possible reservations with the object and purpose of the Covenant, States should also take into consideration the overall effect of a group of reservations, as well as the effect of each reservation on the integrity of the Covenant, which remains an essential consideration. States should not enter so many reservations that they are in effect accepting a limited number of human rights obligations, and not the Covenant as such. So that reservations do not lead to a perpetual non-attainment of international human rights standards, reservations should not systematically reduce the obligations undertaken only to

those presently existing in less demanding standards of domestic law. Nor should interpretative declarations or reservations seek to remove an autonomous meaning to Covenant obligations, by pronouncing them to be identical, or to be accepted only in so far as they are identical, with existing provisions of domestic law. States should not seek through reservations or interpretative declarations to determine that the meaning of a provision of the Covenant is the same as that given by an organ of any other international treaty body.

20. States should institute procedures to ensure that each and every proposed reservation is compatible with the object and purpose of the Covenant. It is desirable for a State entering a reservation to indicate in precise terms the domestic legislation or practices which it believes to be incompatible with the Covenant obligation reserved; and to explain the time period it requires to render its own laws and practices compatible with the Covenant, or why it is unable to render its own laws and practices compatible with the Covenant. States should also ensure that the necessity for maintaining reservations is periodically reviewed, taking into account any observations and recommendations made by the Committee during examination of their reports. Reservations should be withdrawn at the earliest possible moment. Reports to the Committee should contain information on what action has been taken to review, reconsider or withdraw reservations.

---

The following extract provides an example of how the Human Rights Committee, given its General Comment 24, has assessed reservations made by states parties to the International Covenant on Civil and Political Rights. It is from comments issued by the Committee on the first periodic report presented by the United States pursuant to its reporting obligation under the Covenant.

Human Rights Committee

## Consideration of Reports Submitted by States Parties Under Article 40 of the Covenant, Comments of the Committee on the Report of the United States of America

UN Doc. CCPR/C/79/Add.50 (1995), paras. 267-304

267. The Committee expresses its appreciation at the high quality of the report submitted by the State party, which was detailed, informative and drafted in accordance with the guidelines. The Committee regrets, however, that, while containing comprehensive information on the laws and regulations giving effect to the rights provided in the Covenant at the federal level, the report contained few references to the implementation of Covenant rights at the state level.

### 4.  Principal Subjects of Concern

278. The Committee has taken note of the concerns addressed by the delegation in writing to its Chairman about the Committee's General Comment No. 24

(52) on issues relating to reservations made upon ratification or accession to the Covenant or the Optional Protocols thereto (CCPR/C/21/Rev.1/Add.6). Attention is drawn to the observations made by the Chairman of the Committee at the 1406th meeting, on 31 March 1995 (CCPR/C/SR.1406).

279. The Committee regrets the extent of the State party's reservations, declarations and understandings to the Covenant. It believes that, taken together, they intended to ensure that the United States has accepted only what is already the law of the United States. The Committee is also particularly concerned at reservations to article 6, paragraph 5, and article 7 of the Covenant, which it believes to be incompatible with the object and purpose of the Covenant. . . .

5. Suggestions and Recommendations

292. The Committee recommends that the State party review its reservations, declarations and understandings with a view to withdrawing them, in particular reservations to article 6, paragraph 5, and article 7 of the Covenant.

---

The reaction to the Human Rights Committee's General Comment 24 on reservations was divided. While many human rights activists welcomed it, generally states were far less positive. At the next election of members to the Committee, Mr. Mavrommatis, who had chaired the Committee since its beginning, was not reelected.

Another response to the controversy came through the UN's International Law Commission (ILC), a body of experts designated to "codify" and "progressively develop" international law. The ILC, which was responsible for the original draft of the Vienna Convention on the Law of Treaties, proposed to take up the issue of reservations to treaties with a clear focus on the practice of human rights bodies in general and the Committee in particular. The General Assembly approved the ILC's proposal, following which the ILC appointed its French member, Professor Alain Pellet, as rapporteur on the topic.

Professor Pellet submitted 16 reports between 1994 and 2005 (for the 2005 report, see UN Doc. A/CN.4/558 and Add.1 (2005)). Following consideration of his first report by the ILC, Professor Pellet summarized the conclusions he drew from the Commission's discussion, including what he perceived as a consensus that there should be no change in the relevant provisions of the Vienna Convention. In 1997, the ILC adopted preliminary conclusions on reservations to normative multilateral treaties, including human rights treaties. A multi-year process of deliberations on reservations to treaties led to a set of ILC guidelines, which represented somewhat of a compromise. For a recapitulation and analysis of the ICL's lengthy process, see Alain Pellet, *The ILC Guide to Practice on Reservations to Treaties: A General Presentation by the Special Rapporteur*, 24 Eur. J. Int'l. 1061 (2013).

By adopting a set of guidelines, the ILC altered its normal practice of adopting a final report in the form of a draft treaty on the topic under consideration. Adopted in 2011, the Commission's *Guide to Practice on Reservations to Treaties* and an extensive accompanying commentary were published together in the Commission's annual report to the General Assembly. Some of the ILC's guidelines that are particularly relevant to human rights treaties and treaty monitoring bodies are set forth below.

## International Law Commission

## Guide to Practice on Reservations to Treaties

UN Doc. A/66/10, para. 75 (2011) (citations omitted)

### 2.1.2. STATEMENT OF REASONS FOR RESERVATIONS

A reservation should, to the extent possible, indicate the reasons why it is being formulated. . . .

### 2.8.2. TACIT ACCEPTANCE OF RESERVATIONS

Unless the treaty otherwise provides, a reservation is considered to have been accepted by a State or an international organization if it shall have raised no objection to the reservation. . . .

### 3.1.5. INCOMPATIBILITY OF A RESERVATION WITH THE OBJECT AND PURPOSE OF THE TREATY

A reservation is incompatible with the object and purpose of the treaty if it affects an essential element of the treaty that is necessary to its general tenour, in such a way that the reservation impairs the raison d'être of the treaty.

### 3.1.5.1. DETERMINATION OF THE OBJECT AND PURPOSE OF THE TREATY

The object and purpose of the treaty is to be determined in good faith, taking account of the terms of the treaty in their context, in particular the title and the preamble of the treaty. Recourse may also be had to the preparatory work of the treaty and the circumstances of its conclusion and, where appropriate, the subsequent practice of the parties.

### 3.1.5.2. VAGUE OR GENERAL RESERVATIONS

A reservation shall be worded in such a way as to allow its meaning to be understood, in order to assess in particular its compatibility with the object and purpose of the treaty.

### 3.1.5.3. RESERVATIONS TO A PROVISION REFLECTING A CUSTOMARY RULE

The fact that a treaty provision reflects a rule of customary international law does not in itself constitute an obstacle to the formulation of a reservation to that provision.

### 3.1.5.4. RESERVATIONS TO PROVISIONS CONCERNING RIGHTS FROM WHICH NO DEROGATION IS PERMISSIBLE UNDER ANY CIRCUMSTANCES

A State or an international organization may not formulate a reservation to a treaty provision concerning rights from which no derogation is permissible under any circumstances, unless the reservation in question is compatible with the essential rights and obligations arising out of that treaty. In assessing that compatibility, account shall be taken of the importance which the parties have conferred upon the rights at issue by making them non-derogable. . . .

### 3.2. ASSESSMENT OF THE PERMISSIBILITY OF RESERVATIONS

The following may assess, within their respective competences, the permissibility of reservations to a treaty formulated by a State or an international organization:

- contracting States or contracting organizations;
- dispute settlement bodies;
- treaty monitoring bodies.

### 3.2.1. COMPETENCE OF THE TREATY MONITORING BODIES TO ASSESS THE PERMISSIBILITY OF RESERVATIONS

1. A treaty monitoring body may, for the purpose of discharging the functions entrusted to it, assess the permissibility of reservations formulated by a State or an international organization.
2. The assessment made by such a body in the exercise of this competence has no greater legal effect than that of the act which contains it.

### 3.2.2. SPECIFICATION OF THE COMPETENCE OF TREATY MONITORING BODIES TO ASSESS THE PERMISSIBILITY OF RESERVATIONS.

When providing bodies with the competence to monitor the application of treaties, States or international organizations should specify, where appropriate, the nature and the limits of the competence of such bodies to assess the permissibility of reservations.

### 3.2.3. CONSIDERATION OF THE ASSESSMENTS OF TREATY MONITORING BODIES

States and international organizations that have formulated reservations to a treaty establishing a treaty monitoring body shall give consideration to that body's assessment of the permissibility of the reservations.

### 3.2.4. BODIES COMPETENT TO ASSESS THE PERMISSIBILITY OF RESERVATIONS IN THE EVENT OF THE ESTABLISHMENT OF A TREATY MONITORING BODY

When a treaty establishes a treaty monitoring body, the competence of that body is without prejudice to the competence of the contracting States or contracting organizations to assess the permissibility of reservations to that treaty, or to that of dispute settlement bodies competent to interpret or apply the treaty. . . .

### 3.2.5. Competence of Dispute Settlement Bodies to Assess the Permissibility of Reservations

When a dispute settlement body is competent to adopt decisions binding upon the parties to a dispute, and the assessment of the permissibility of a reservation is necessary for the discharge of such competence by that body, such assessment is, as an element of the decision, legally binding upon the parties. . . .

### 4.5.3. Status of the Author of an Invalid Reservation In Relation to the Treaty

1. The status of the author of an invalid reservation in relation to a treaty depends on the intention expressed by the reserving State or international organization on whether it intends to be bound by the treaty without the benefit of the reservation or whether it considers that it is not bound by the treaty.

2. Unless the author of the invalid reservation has expressed a contrary intention or such an intention is otherwise established, it is considered a contracting State or a contracting organization without the benefit of the reservation.

3. Notwithstanding paragraphs 1 and 2, the author of the invalid reservation may express at any time its intention not to be bound by the treaty without the benefit of the reservation.

4. If a treaty monitoring body expresses the view that a reservation is invalid and the reserving State or international organization intends not to be bound by the treaty without the benefit of the reservation, it should express its intention to that effect within a period of twelve months from the date at which the treaty monitoring body made its assessment.

---

The ILC Guide to Practice on Reservations and Treaties includes an Annex of "Conclusions on the reservations dialogue." The Conclusions add that, where the validity of a reservation is questioned, "States and international organizations, as well as monitoring bodies, should cooperate as closely as possible in order to exchange views on reservations in respect of which concerns have been raised and coordinate the measures to be taken. . . . [Those concerned should] initiate and pursue such a reservations dialogue in a pragmatic and transparent manner." ILC Guide, *supra*, Annex, paras. 9-10.

## C.  Termination of Treaties

While some human rights treaties (e.g., the Convention on the Elimination of All Forms of Racial Discrimination and the Convention against Torture) contain provisions permitting parties to withdraw from them after a period of time following notification to the other parties, the two Covenants contain no denunciation clauses. Article 56 of the Vienna Convention on the Law of Treaties states the following:

> 1. A treaty which contains no provision regarding its termination and which does not provide for denunciation or withdrawal is not subject to denunciation or withdrawal unless:
> (a) it is established that the parties intended to admit the possibility of denunciation or withdrawal; or
> (b) a right of denunciation or withdrawal may be implied by the nature of the treaty.
> 2. A party shall give not less than twelve months' notice of its intention to denounce or withdraw from a treaty under paragraph 1.

In 1988, the government of the Netherlands considered withdrawing from the Covenant on Civil and Political Rights as a result of disagreement with the Human Rights Committee's case law on Article 26 (see *Broeks v. the Netherlands*, No. 172/1984, views of April 9, 1987, UN Doc. CCPR/C/29/D/172/1984; and *Zwaan-de Vries v. the Netherlands*, No. 182/1984, views of April 9, 1987, UN Doc. CCPR/C/28/D/182/1984,). After a legal opinion by P.J. Kooijmans (a judge on the International Court of Justice from 1997-2006) concluded that denunciation was impermissible, the government decided not to pursue the matter. In 1997, however, the Democratic People's Republic of Korea (North Korea) circulated a "notification of withdrawal" to other states parties. The Committee quickly adopted the following General Comment.

## Human Rights Committee

## General Comment No. 26: Continuity of Obligations

UN Doc. A/53/40 (1997), Annex VII

1. The International Covenant on Civil and Political Rights does not contain any provision regarding its termination and does not provide for denunciation or withdrawal. Consequently, the possibility of termination, denunciation or withdrawal must be considered in the light of applicable rules of customary international law which are reflected in the Vienna Convention on the Law of Treaties. On this basis, the Covenant is not subject to denunciation or withdrawal unless it is established that the parties intended to admit the possibility of denunciation or withdrawal or a right to do so is implied from the nature of the treaty.

2. That the parties to the Covenant did not admit the possibility of denunciation and that it was not a mere oversight on their part to omit reference to denunciation is demonstrated by the fact that article 41(2) of the Covenant does permit a State party to withdraw its acceptance of the competence of the Committee to examine inter-State communications by filing an appropriate notice to that effect while there is no such provision for denunciation of or withdrawal from the Covenant itself. Moreover, the Optional Protocol to the Covenant, negotiated and adopted contemporaneously with it, permits States parties to denounce it. Additionally, by way of comparison, the International Convention on the Elimination

of All Forms of Racial Discrimination, which was adopted one year prior to the Covenant, expressly permits denunciation. It can therefore be concluded that the drafters of the Covenant deliberately intended to exclude the possibility of denunciation. The same conclusion applies to the Second Optional Protocol in the drafting of which a denunciation clause was deliberately omitted.

3. Furthermore, it is clear that the Covenant is not the type of treaty which, by its nature, implies a right of denunciation. Together with the simultaneously prepared and adopted International Covenant on Economic, Social and Cultural Rights, the Covenant codifies in treaty form the universal human rights enshrined in the Universal Declaration of Human Rights, the three instruments together often being referred to as the "International Bill of Human Rights". As such, the Covenant does not have a temporary character typical of treaties where a right of denunciation is deemed to be admitted, notwithstanding the absence of a specific provision to that effect.

4. The rights enshrined in the Covenant belong to the people living in the territory of the State party. The Human Rights Committee has consistently taken the view, as evidenced by its long-standing practice, that once the people are accorded the protection of the rights under the Covenant, such protection devolves with territory and continues to belong to them, notwithstanding change in government of the State party, including dismemberment in more than one State or State succession or any subsequent action of the State party designed to divest them of the rights guaranteed by the Covenant.

5. The Committee is therefore firmly of the view that international law does not permit a State which has ratified or acceded or succeeded to the Covenant to denounce it or withdraw from it.

---

A concerning tendency is in the recent withdrawals from regional treaties of a number of countries in Europe, the Americas, and Africa. The most recent of the violence against women treaties is the Council of Europe's Convention on Preventing and Combating Violence against Women and Domestic Violence (hereinafter "Istanbul Convention"), adopted in 2011. The treaty has been ratified by 34 members of the Council of Europe. Turkey's withdrawal from it, effective June 30, 2021, was met with intense global criticism. See *Turkey's withdrawal from the Istanbul Convention rallies the fight for women's rights across the world*, Amnesty International (July 1st, 2021), https://www.amnesty.org/en/latest/news/2021/07/turkeys-withdrawal-from-the-istanbul-convention-rallies-the-fight-for-womens-rights-across-the-world-2/.

In the Americas, Trinidad and Tobago has withdrawn from the American Convention on Human Rights. See generally Natasha Parassram Concepcion, *The Legal Implications of Trinidad & Tobago's Withdrawal from the American Convention on Human Rights,* 16 AM. U. INT.L L. REV. 847-890 (2002), https://digitalcommons.wcl.american.edu/auilr/vol16/iss3/4/. Venezuela, on September 10, 2012, also made public a decision to denounce the American Convention. See *IACHR Deeply Concerned over Result of Venezuela's Denunciation of the American Convention*, Inter-Am. Comm'n H.R. Press Release No. 64/13 (September 10, 2013), https://www.oas.org/en/

iachr/media_center/preleases/2013/064.asp. In the same vein, in Africa key states including Benin, Côte d'Ivoire, Rwanda, and Tanzania have withdrawn their declarations recognizing the competency of the African Court of Human and Peoples' Rights. See Nicole de Silva and Micha Plagis, *A Court in Crisis: African States' Increasing Resistance to Africa's Human Rights Court*, OpinioJuris (May 19, 2020), https://opiniojuris.org/2020/05/19/a-court-in-crisis-african-states-increasing-resistance-to-africas-human-rights-court/.

## Comments and Questions

1. Is it clear that the Vienna Convention on the Law of Treaties applies to international human rights treaties?

2. Some of the US reservations to the Covenant on Civil and Political Rights were objected to by Belgium, Denmark, Finland, France, Germany, Italy, the Netherlands, Norway, Portugal, Spain, and Sweden. What is the legal effect of these objections?

3. Do you agree that the Human Rights Committee has the power to review and render inoperative the acceptability of reservations to the Covenant? Do all human rights bodies have such powers? How does the view of the International Law Commission compare to that of the Human Rights Committee on these questions?

4. Are reservations always an obstacle to domestic compliance with a human rights treaty? For more reading on reservations and human rights treaties, see Center for Global Legal Challenges, Yales Law School, *General Principles Regarding the Legal Validity of Reservations, Understandings, and Declarations* (2015), https://law.yale.edu/sites/default/files/yale_glc_legal_validity_of_ruds_2015.pdf; Ryan Goodman, *Human Rights Treaties, Invalid Reservations, and State Consent*, 96 Am. J. Int'l L. 531 (2002).

5. After the Human Rights Committee adopted General Comment No. 26, the North Korean government submitted a long overdue state report and sent a delegation to appear before the Committee. Does this suggest agreement with the Committee's opinion on denunciation? Can you think of potential situations in which a withdrawal from a human rights treaty may be justified? What is the value for a state in remaining a party to a human rights treaty despite concerns over the treaty's provisions?

6. What does the Committee mean in General Comment No. 26 when it says that the Covenant does not have a temporary character and that protection of the rights enshrined in the Covenant, once granted, devolves with the territory of the state? How does this affect the successor states of the former Soviet Union and Yugoslavia, both of which were parties to the Covenants? Note that Great Britain extended the Covenant to Hong Kong while it still administered the territory (as did Portugal to Macau). Does this mean that the government of China was bound to apply the Covenant in Hong Kong before China itself ratified the treaty?

7. Should human rights treaties be treated differently from other international legal instruments, given that they characteristically have direct or indirect beneficiaries other than states? Can human rights bodies persuasively argue that there is a special regime for human rights treaties with respect to reservations but

reject the notion of a special regime regarding denunciations? See generally Liesbeth Lijnzaad, *Reservations to UN Human Rights Treaties: Ratify and Ruin?* (1994).

## IV. EMERGING ISSUES IN INTERNATIONAL HUMAN RIGHTS LAW AND TREATIES: THE ENVIRONMENT AND CLIMATE CHANGE

As discussed in Chapter 1, among the subjects of significant international human rights concern at the moment are challenges related to the environment and the harmful effects of climate change. This set of topics is also an area in which international law is quickly developing. On July 26, 2022, the UN General Assembly recognized for the first time a "right to a clean, healthy, and sustainable environment." G.A. Res. 76/300, UN Doc A/76/L.75 (2022) (reprinted in substantial part, *infra* page 112). The General Assembly followed the lead of the Human Rights Council, which during the previous year had adopted its own resolution titled, The human right to a clean, healthy and sustainable environment, H.R.C. Res. 48/13, UN Doc. A/HRC/RES/48/13 (2021). The Council Resolution affirmed and sought to operationalize this right and invited similar action by the General Assembly.

However, a human right to good environmental quality has not yet been codified in any United Nations treaty. This is a void frequently noted by advocates and relevant United Nations experts, who have increasingly called on states to take steps to recognize the substantive and procedural components of such a right. See, e.g., *Report of the Special Rapporteur on the issue of human rights obligations relating to the enjoyment of a safe, clean, healthy, and sustainable environment*, John H. Knox, UN Doc. A/HRC/37/59 (2018), paras. 14-16. The adoption of the 2015 Paris Agreement on climate change and the inclusion of environmental issues in the UN's 2030 Agenda for Sustainable Development have also fueled demands for a treaty at the global level addressing human rights concerns relating to the environment. See Paris Agreement to the United Nations Framework Convention on Climate Change, December 12, 2015, T.I.A.S. No 16-1104; UN General Assembly, *Transforming our World: the 2030 Agenda for Sustainable Development Goals*, G.A Res. 70/1 (Oct. 21, 2015), Goals 13-15.

Most UN human rights treaties were drafted before environmental protection gained the international attention it has today. There are thus few references to environmental matters in most human rights instruments, although the formulation of the right to health sometimes includes environmental matters. The International Covenant on Economic, Social, and Cultural Rights, for example, guarantees the right to safe and healthy working conditions (Article 7(b)) and the right of children and young persons to be free from work harmful to their health (Article 10(3)). The provision on the right to health (Article 12) calls on states to take steps for "the improvement of all aspects of environmental and industrial hygiene" and "the prevention, treatment and control of epidemic, endemic, occupational, and other diseases." The Convention on the Rights of the Child refers to aspects of environmental protection in respect to children's right to health. Its Article 24 requires parties to take appropriate measures to combat disease and malnutrition "through the provision of adequate nutritious foods and clean drinking water, taking into consideration the dangers and risks of environmental pollution." The same article also requires that states parties provide information and education on hygiene and environmental sanitation to all segments of society.

ILO Convention No. 169 concerning Indigenous and Tribal Peoples in Independent Countries (1989) contains numerous references to the lands, resources, and environment of indigenous peoples (e.g., Articles 2, 6, 7, 15). Part II of the Convention addresses land issues, including the rights of indigenous peoples to the natural resources pertaining to their lands. Further, governments are to ensure adequate health services are available or provide resources to indigenous peoples "so that they may enjoy the highest attainable standard of physical and mental health." (Article 25(1)).

At present, formulations of a human right to an adequate level of environmental quality are found in some national constitutions and laws. It is also noteworthy that the right to a healthy environment has been recognized in several regional, as opposed to United Nations, treaties, as discussed in the next extract.

As you read the remainder of this chapter, question whether in fact a gap exists in current human rights law. If so, does it require a UN or other globally applicable treaty recognizing a right to a healthy environment and establishing corresponding obligations, or would such a treaty weaken existing guarantees by "devaluing the currency" of human rights treaties generally? How would a treaty recognizing such a right contribute to environmental protection or to the enjoyment of other human rights? Is a "human rights" treaty the best or even a useful way of addressing such a complex issue as climate change?

The following report by an independent expert appointed by the UN Human Rights Council (the system of Human Rights Council Special Rapporteurs and other experts is discussed in Chapter 7) addresses the interconnection between human rights and the environment and argues for recognition in a UN treaty or other instrument of a "right to a safe, clean, healthy, and sustainable environment."

## Report of the Special Rapporteur on the issue of human rights obligations relating to the enjoyment of a safe, clean, healthy and sustainable environment, John Knox

U.N. Doc A/73/188 (2018) (most footnotes omitted)

. . .

### II. "GREENING" HUMAN RIGHTS

12. From the beginning of the modern environmental movement in the late 1960s, it has been clear that a healthy environment is necessary for the full enjoyment of human rights, including the rights to life and health. Fifty years ago, the General Assembly, in its resolution 2398 (XXII), decided to convene the first international environmental conference on the environment, noting its concern about

the effects of "the continuing and accelerating impairment of the quality of the human environment . . . on the condition of man, his physical, mental and social well-being, his dignity and his enjoyment of basic human rights, in developing as well as developed countries". At the ensuing United Nations Conference on the Human Environment, held in Stockholm in 1972, Governments adopted a declaration in which it is stated, in the first paragraph of the proclamation, that "both aspects of man's environment, the natural and the man-made, are essential to his well-being and to the enjoyment of basic human rights — even the right to life itself".

13. In recent decades, human rights bodies have elaborated on the understanding that a healthy environment is of fundamental importance to the full enjoyment of a vast range of human rights. Treaty bodies, regional tribunals, special rapporteurs and other international human rights bodies have described how environmental degradation interferes with specific rights, including the rights to life, health, food, water, housing, culture, development, property and home and private life. In effect, they have "greened" existing human rights. They have also explained that the obligations of States to respect, protect and fulfil human rights apply in the environmental context no less than in any other.

14. In the framework principles presented earlier in 2018 to the Human Rights Council [see U.N. Doc. A/HRC/37/59 (2018)], the Special Rapporteur summarizes the obligations of States under human rights law relating to the enjoyment of a safe, clean, healthy and sustainable environment. The framework principles include specific procedural obligations, such as the duties of States to respect and protect the rights to freedom of expression, association and peaceful assembly in relation to environmental matters, provide for environmental education and public awareness, provide public access to environmental information, require the prior assessment of the possible environmental and human rights impacts of proposed projects and policies, provide for and facilitate public participation in decision-making related to the environment and provide for access to effective remedies for violations of human rights and domestic laws relating to the environment.

15. The framework principles also set out human rights obligations relating to substantive standards. Ideally, environmental standards would be set and implemented at levels that would prevent all environmental harm from human sources and ensure a safe, clean, healthy and sustainable environment. However, limited resources may prevent the immediate realization of the rights to health, food and water and other economic, social and cultural rights. The obligation of States to achieve progressively the full realization of these rights by all appropriate means requires States to take deliberate, concrete and targeted measures towards that goal, but States have some discretion in deciding which means are appropriate in view of available resources. Similarly, human rights bodies applying civil and political rights, such as the rights to life and private and family life, have held that States have some discretion in determining the appropriate levels of environmental protection, taking into account the need to balance the goal of preventing all environmental harm with other social goals.

16. This discretion is not unlimited. One constraint is that decisions as to the establishment and implementation of appropriate levels of environmental protection must always comply with obligations of non-discrimination. Another constraint

is the strong presumption against retrogressive measures in relation to the progressive realization of economic, social and cultural rights. . . .

17. Once adopted, the standards must be implemented and enforced to be effective. Governmental authorities must comply with the relevant environmental standards in their own operations. They must also monitor and effectively enforce compliance with the standards by preventing, investigating, punishing and redressing violations of the standards by private actors as well as governmental authorities. In particular, States must regulate business enterprises to protect against human rights abuses resulting from environmental harm and to provide for remedies for such abuses.

18. Moreover, in accordance with the Guiding Principles on Business and Human Rights [discussed Chapter 4, *infra*], the responsibility of business enterprises to respect human rights includes the responsibility to avoid causing or contributing to adverse human rights impacts through environmental harm, to address such impacts when they occur and to seek to prevent or mitigate adverse human rights impacts that are directly linked to their operations, products or services by their business relationships. Businesses should comply with all applicable environmental laws, issue clear policy commitments to meet their responsibility to respect human rights through environmental protection, implement human rights due diligence processes, including human rights impact assessments, to identify, prevent, mitigate and account for how they address their environmental impacts on human rights, and enable the remediation of any adverse environmental human rights impacts that they cause or to which they contribute.

19. Many environmental challenges, such as climate change, ozone depletion, the loss of biological diversity, long-range air pollution, marine pollution, plastic pollution and trade in hazardous substances, have global or transboundary dimensions. The obligation of States to cooperate to achieve universal respect for and observance of human rights requires States to work together to address transboundary and global environmental threats to human rights. . . .

20. The obligation of international cooperation does not require every State to take exactly the same actions. The responsibilities that are necessary and appropriate for each State will depend in part on its situation, and agreements between States may appropriately tailor their commitments to take account of their respective capabilities and challenges. Multilateral environmental agreements often include different requirements for States in different economic situations and provide for technical and financial assistance from wealthy States to other States. . . .

22. Finally, human rights law requires States to take special care to respect, protect and fulfill the rights of those who are most at risk from environmental harm. As the Human Rights Council has recognized, while the human rights implications of environmental damage are felt by individuals and communities around the world, the consequences are felt most acutely by those segments of the population that are already in vulnerable situations. Persons may be vulnerable because they are unusually susceptible to certain types of environmental harm or because they are denied their human rights, or both. Those who are at greater risk from environmental harm for either or both reasons often include women, children, persons living in poverty, members of indigenous peoples and traditional communities, older

persons, persons with disabilities, national, ethnic, religious or linguistic minorities and displaced persons. Many persons are vulnerable and subject to discrimination along more than one dimension, such as children living in poverty or indigenous women. . . .

25. The obligations of States to prohibit discrimination and to ensure equal and effective protection against discrimination apply to the equal enjoyment of human rights relating to a safe, clean, healthy and sustainable environment. States therefore have obligations, among others, to protect against environmental harm that results from or contributes to discrimination, to provide for equal access to environmental benefits and to ensure that their actions relating to the environment do not themselves discriminate. . . .

26. Finally, States have obligations to protect environmental human rights defenders, namely, individuals and groups striving to protect and promote human rights relating to the environment. Those who work to protect the environment on which the enjoyment of human rights depends are protecting and promoting human rights as well, whether or not they self-identify as human rights defenders. They are among the human rights defenders most at risk. On average, four environmental defenders are killed every week because of their work, and countless more receive threats, suffer violence, are unlawfully detained or are otherwise harassed. . . .

### III. National and Regional Recognition of the Human Right to a Safe, Clean, Healthy and Sustainable Environment

28. In addition to the greening of human rights, including the rights to life, health, food, water, housing, culture, development, property and home and private life, there has been a second critical development in the field of human rights and the environment since the General Assembly first took note of the nexus between those issues in 1968. This involves the emergence of a new human right: the right to a safe, clean, healthy and sustainable environment, or, more simply, the right to a healthy environment. The roots of this new human right can be traced back to the Declaration of the United Nations Conference on the Human Environment (Stockholm Declaration) of 1972, in which, in the very first principle, it is stated that "man has the fundamental right to freedom, equality and adequate conditions of life, in an environment of a quality that permits a life of dignity and well-being, and he bears a solemn responsibility to protect and improve the environment for present and future generations."

29. Since 1972, the right to a healthy environment has gained widespread public and legal recognition across the world. Governments have incorporated it into constitutions and environmental legislation. The right to a healthy environment has also been incorporated into regional human rights agreements and regional environmental treaties. Governments have made genuine efforts, with varying degrees of success, to respect, protect, fulfill and promote this right. Over the past forty years, national courts, regional tribunals, treaty bodies, special procedures and many international institutions have contributed to defining the content, scope and parameters of the right to a healthy environment, as well as its relationship with other human rights. . . .

33. At the regional level, human rights agreements drafted after the 1970s have also included the right to a healthy environment. The African Charter on Human and Peoples' Rights of 1981 provides that "all peoples shall have the right to a general satisfactory environment favorable to their development" (art. 24). In the 1988 Additional Protocol to the American Convention on Human Rights in the Area of Economic, Social and Cultural Rights (Protocol of San Salvador), it is stated that "everyone shall have the right to live in a healthy environment" (art. 11, para. 1). In 2003, the African Union adopted the Protocol to the African Charter on Human and Peoples' Rights on the Rights of Women in Africa, in which it is stated that women shall have "the right to live in a healthy and sustainable environment" (art. 18) and "the right to fully enjoy their right to sustainable development" (art. 19). The Arab Charter on Human Rights of 2004 includes the right to a healthy environment as part of the right to an adequate standard of living that ensures well-being and a decent life (art. 38). Similarly, the Human Rights Declaration adopted by the Association of Southeast Asian Nations in 2012 incorporates a "right to a safe, clean and sustainable environment" as an element of the right to an adequate standard of living (para. 28 (f)).

34. Also at the regional level, the Convention on Access to Information, Public Participation in Decision-Making and Access to Justice in Environmental Matters (Aarhus Convention) of 1998, drafted under the auspices of the Economic Commission for Europe, refers to "the right of every person of present and future generations to live in an environment adequate to his or her health and well-being" (art. 1). Finally, the Regional Agreement on Access to Information, Public Participation and Justice in Environmental Matters in Latin America and the Caribbean (Escazú Agreement), concluded and opened for signature in 2018, is a regional agreement similar to the Aarhus Convention but covering Latin America and the Caribbean. One of the objectives of the Escazú Agreement is "contributing to the protection of the right of every person of present and future generations to live in a healthy environment and to sustainable development" (art. 1). The agreement also requires that "each Party shall guarantee the right of every person to live in a healthy environment" (art. 4). The above-mentioned regional human rights agreements and environmental treaties, all explicitly recognizing the right to a healthy environment, have been ratified by more than 130 States to date.

35. At both the regional and national levels, human rights commissions and courts have played an active role in defining the scope of the right to a healthy environment and the corresponding obligations upon Governments. The African Commission on Human and Peoples' Rights produced a ground-breaking decision in 2001 in a case involving pollution caused by the oil industry that violated the Ogoni people's right to a healthy environment under the African Charter. [An edtied version of the Ogoni case has been included in Chapter 4, *infra* page 195.] The Commission determined that Governments have clear obligations "to take reasonable and other measures to prevent pollution and ecological degradation, to promote conservation, and to secure an ecologically sustainable development and use of natural resources." In 2017, the Inter-American Court of Human Rights ruled that the right to a healthy environment under the Protocol of San Salvador protects individuals and collectives, including future generations, and can be used to hold States responsible for cross-border violations that are within their

"effective control."[3] The Inter-American Court stated that: "Environmental damage can cause irreparable damage to human beings. As such, a healthy environment is a fundamental right for the existence of humanity." Although the Convention for the Protection of Human Rights and Fundamental Freedoms does not include any explicit references to the environment, the jurisprudence of the European Court of Human Rights has repeatedly referred to the right to a healthy environment. For example, in a case involving the dangers of using sodium cyanide for gold mining in Romania, the European Court concluded that the State's failure to take positive steps to prevent an environmental disaster violated the rights to life, private and family life and, more generally, to the enjoyment of a healthy and protected environment.[4] Similarly, the European Committee of Social Rights has interpreted the right to protection of health in article 11 of the European Social Charter to include an implicit right to a healthy environment.[5]

36. Taking into consideration the ratification of regional human rights agreements and environmental treaties, constitutions and national legislation, more than 150 States have already established legal recognition of the right to a healthy environment, with corresponding obligations. . . .

### IV.  United Nations Recognition of the Human Right to a Safe, Clean, Healthy and Sustainable Environment

37. The time has come for the United Nations to formally recognize the human right to a safe, clean, healthy and sustainable environment, or, more simply, the human right to a healthy environment. It is understandable that the central United Nations human rights instruments — the Universal Declaration of Human Rights, the International Covenant on Economic, Social and Cultural Rights and the International Covenant on Civil and Political Rights — do not include an explicit right to a healthy environment. They were drafted and adopted before the modern environmental movement raised awareness of the breadth and depth of the environmental challenges facing humanity. Today, however, it is beyond debate that human beings are wholly dependent on a healthy environment in order to lead dignified, healthy and fulfilling lives. The ecological systems, biological diversity and planetary conditions that are the vital foundations of human existence are under unprecedented stress. Were the Universal Declaration of Human Rights to be drafted today, it is hard to imagine that it would fail to include the right to a healthy environment, a right so essential to human well-being and so widely recognized in national constitutions, legislation and regional agreements.

38. States may be understandably reluctant to recognize a "new" human right if its content appears to be uncertain or its implications seem unclear. . . . As the extensive reports of the Special Rapporteur forcefully demonstrate, the human

---

3. Inter-American Court of Human Rights, Advisory Opinion, OC-23/17, 15 November 2017.

4. European Court of Human Rights, *Tatar v. Romania*, Application No. 67021/01, Judgment, 27 January 2009, paras. 107 and 112.

5. See European Committee of Social Rights, *Marangopoulos Foundation for Human Rights* v. *Greece*, Complaint No. 30/2005, Decision on the Merits, 6 December 2006, para. 195.

right to a healthy environment is not an empty vessel waiting to be filled; on the contrary, its content has already been exhaustively discussed, debated, defined and clarified over the past 45 years.

39. Recognition of the right to a healthy environment by the United Nations would not only be consistent with the state of the law in most of the world, but would also provide a series of important and tangible benefits. It would raise awareness of and reinforce the understanding that human rights norms require protection of the environment and that environmental protection depends on the exercise of human rights. It would highlight that environmental protection must be assigned the same level of importance as other interests that are fundamental to human dignity, equality and freedom. It would also help to ensure that human rights norms relating to the environment continue to develop in a coherent, consistent and integrated manner. Recognition of the right to a healthy environment by the United Nations would complement, reinforce and amplify the regional and national norms and jurisprudence developed over the past 45 years.

40. Examining experience at the national level demonstrates the many advantages of formal recognition of this right. Recognition of the right to a healthy environment in national constitutions has raised the profile and importance of environmental protection and provided a basis for the enactment of stronger environmental laws, standards, regulations and policies. At least 80 States enacted stronger environmental laws in direct response to the incorporation of the right to a healthy environment into their national constitutions. In States including Argentina, Brazil, Colombia, Costa Rica, France, Portugal, South Africa and Spain, the right to a healthy environment is one of the fundamental principles shaping, strengthening and unifying the entire body of environmental law. In India, Nepal and Uganda, the right to a healthy environment has been used to fill legislative or regulatory gaps related to air pollution, plastic pollution and forest conservation.

41. Recognition of the right to a healthy environment enables individuals, government agencies, communities, indigenous peoples, civil society organizations and the judiciary to contribute to improved implementation and enforcement of environmental laws and, concurrently, greater respect for human rights. When applied by the judiciary, constitutional environmental rights have helped to provide a safety net to protect against gaps in statutory laws, created opportunities for better access to justice and, most importantly, contributed to stopping or preventing human rights violations. Courts in many States are increasingly applying the right, as is illustrated by the interest in the regional judicial workshops held by UNEP and the Special Rapporteur. Thousands of cases decided by courts in more than 50 States have involved alleged violations of the right to a healthy environment over the past four decades. An impressive example comes from Costa Rica, where the constitutional recognition of the right to a healthy environment in 1994 contributed to a significant increase in the implementation and enforcement of environmental laws. In cases involving solid waste, sewage treatment, air pollution, groundwater and endangered species, the Constitutional Court has protected the right to a healthy environment and ruled that it includes a number of key principles, including the precautionary, polluter-pays and intergenerational equity principles.

42. Recognition of the right to a healthy environment has also contributed to substantial increases in the role of the public in environmental governance. People and organizations are empowered by the procedural elements of this right, including access to information, participation in decision-making and access to justice. In many nations that recognize the right to a healthy environment, legislative processes, administrative procedures and courthouse doors are now open to citizens seeking to protect both their individual right to a healthy environment and society's collective interest in a healthy environment. According to the Environmental Democracy Index, Colombia, Latvia, Lithuania and South Africa are among the global leaders in enhancing access to justice to protect human rights, including the right to a healthy environment. The Philippines has developed special rules of procedure for environmental litigation, which are specifically intended to facilitate protection of the right to a healthy environment.

43. Recognition of the right to a healthy environment has been a catalyst for national laws related to environmental education in States including Armenia, Brazil, the Philippines and the Republic of Korea. In addition, extensive efforts have been made by international agencies and the Special Rapporteur to educate judges, enforcement agencies, prosecutors and other groups involved in the implementation and enforcement of environmental laws about the right to a healthy environment. . . .

45. Of particular importance are the positive effects of the recognition of the right to a healthy environment on vulnerable populations, including women, children, persons living in poverty, members of indigenous peoples and traditional communities, older persons, persons with disabilities, minorities and displaced persons. Respecting and fulfilling the right to a healthy environment should ensure a minimum level of environmental quality for all members of society, consistent with international standards, with a particular emphasis on those populations that currently shoulder a disproportionate share of the burden of pollution and other environmental harms or that do not enjoy adequate access to essential environmental goods and services, such as safe water and adequate sanitation. . . .

46. On the basis of the extensive experience with the right to a healthy environment and its critical importance in protecting human rights threatened by the multiple current environmental challenges, the Special Rapporteur recommends that the General Assembly recognize the right in a global instrument. One possible vehicle for such recognition would be a new international treaty. . . .

47. A second option would involve the development of an additional protocol to an existing human rights treaty. For example, the right to a safe, clean, healthy and sustainable environment could be the focus of an optional protocol to the International Covenant on Economic, Social and Cultural Rights. . . .

48. A third and potentially more expeditious approach would be for the General Assembly to adopt a resolution focused on the right to a healthy environment. A model could be the resolution in which the Assembly recognized the rights to water and sanitation, which, like the right to a healthy environment, were not explicitly recognized in United Nations human rights treaties but are clearly necessary to the full enjoyment of human rights. . . .

49. Through any of the foregoing mechanisms, which are not mutually exclusive, recognition of the right to a safe, clean, healthy and sustainable environment

by the United Nations would serve as acknowledgement that the right to a healthy environment must be universally protected (rather than subject to the current patchwork of protection measures), serve as an impetus for more nations to incorporate this right into their constitutions and legislation and potentially provide a mechanism for increased accountability where national governments violate or fail to protect this vital human right.

---

After the above report was published, the UN Human Rights Council adopted its resolution, mentioned earlier, recognizing a human right to a clean, healthy and sustainable environment and affirming its relation to other rights. See H.R.C. Res. 48/13 (1921). This was followed by the General Assembly's adoption of its resolution on the matter, which is reproduced below.

These resolutions — like resolutions of the Human Rights Council and the General Assembly generally — are by definition not treaties and do not in their own right establish any legal obligations. But resolutions of this type at least have political force, reflect international consensus on the gravity of a human rights issue, and may precede treaties on the topics addressed. The nature and legal implications of resolutions by the UN General Assembly and other inter-governmental bodies are discussed in Chapter 3.

## The Human Right to a Clean, Healthy, and Sustainable Environment

United Nations General Assembly Resolution 76/300, U.N. Doc. A/76/L.75 (July 26, 2022) (footnotes omitted)

*The General Assembly,*

*Guided* by the purposes and principles of the Charter of the United Nations,

*Reaffirming* the Universal Declaration of Human Rights and the Vienna Declaration and Programme of Action, recalling the Declaration on the Right to Development, the Declaration of the United Nations Conference on the Human Environment (Stockholm Declaration), the Rio Declaration on Environment and Development, and relevant international human rights treaties, and noting other relevant regional human rights instruments,

*Reaffirming* also that all human rights are universal, indivisible, interdependent and interrelated,

*Reaffirming* further its resolution 70/1 of 25 September 2015, entitled "Transforming our world: the 2030 Agenda for Sustainable Development", in which it adopted a comprehensive, far-reaching and people-centred set of universal and transformative Sustainable Development Goals and targets, its commitment to working tirelessly for the full implementation of the Agenda by 2030 ensuring that no one is left behind, its recognition that eradicating poverty in all its forms and dimensions, including extreme poverty, is the greatest global challenge and an indispensable requirement for sustainable development, and its commitment to achieving sustainable development in its three dimensions — economic, social and environmental — in a balanced and integrated manner,

*Recalling* States' obligations and commitments under multilateral environmental instruments and agreements, including on climate change, and the outcome of the United Nations Conference on Sustainable Development, held in Rio de Janeiro, Brazil, in June 2012, and its outcome document entitled "The future we want", which reaffirmed the principles of the Rio Declaration on Environment and Development,

*Recalling* also Human Rights Council resolution 48/13 of 8 October 2021, entitled "The human right to a clean, healthy and sustainable environment",

*Recalling* further all Human Rights Council resolutions on human rights and the environment, including resolutions 44/7 of 16 July 2020, 45/17 of 6 October 2020, 45/30 of 7 October 202010 and 46/7 of 23 March 2021, and relevant resolutions of the General Assembly,

*Recognizing* that sustainable development, in its three dimensions (social, economic and environmental), and the protection of the environment, including ecosystems, contribute to and promote human well-being and the full enjoyment of all human rights, for present and future generations,

*Recognizing also* that, conversely, the impact of climate change, the unsustainable management and use of natural resources, the pollution of air, land and water, the unsound management of chemicals and waste, the resulting loss of biodiversity and the decline in services provided by ecosystems interfere with the enjoyment of a clean, healthy and sustainable environment and that environmental damage has negative implications, both direct and indirect, for the effective enjoyment of all human rights,

*Reaffirming* that international cooperation has an essential role in assisting developing countries, including highly indebted poor countries, least developed countries, landlocked developing countries, small island developing States, as well as the specific challenges faced by middle-income countries, in strengthening their human, institutional and technological capacity,

*Recognizing* that, while the human rights implications of environmental damage are felt by individuals and communities around the world, the consequences are felt most acutely by women and girls and those segments of the population that are already in vulnerable situations, including indigenous peoples, children, older persons and persons with disabilities,

*Recognizing* also the importance of gender equality, gender-responsive action to address climate change and environmental degradation, the empowerment, leadership, decision-making and full, equal and meaningful participation of women and girls, and the role that women play as managers, leaders and defenders of natural resources and agents of change in safeguarding the environment,

*Recognizing further* that environmental degradation, climate change, biodiversity loss, desertification and unsustainable development constitute some of the most pressing and serious threats to the ability of present and future generations to effectively enjoy all human rights,

*Recognizing* that the exercise of human rights, including the rights to seek, receive and impart information, to participate effectively in the conduct of government and public affairs and to an effective remedy, is vital to the protection of a clean, healthy and sustainable environment,

*Reaffirming* that States have the obligation to respect, protect and promote human rights, including in all actions undertaken to address environmental challenges, and to take measures to protect the human rights of all, as recognized in different international instruments, and that additional measures should be taken for those who are particularly vulnerable to environmental degradation, noting the framework principles on human rights and the environment,

*Recalling* the Guiding Principles on Business and Human Rights, which underscore the responsibility of all business enterprises to respect human rights,

*Affirming* the importance of a clean, healthy and sustainable environment for the enjoyment of all human rights,

*Taking note* of all the reports of the Special Rapporteur (formerly the Independent Expert) on the issue of human rights obligations relating to the enjoyment of a safe, clean, healthy and sustainable environment,

*Noting* "The highest aspiration: a call to action for human rights", which the Secretary-General presented to the Human Rights Council on 24 February 2020,

*Noting also* that a vast majority of States have recognized some form of the right to a clean, healthy and sustainable environment through international agreements, their national constitutions, legislation, laws or policies,

1. *Recognizes* the right to a clean, healthy and sustainable environment as a human right;
2. *Notes* that the right to a clean, healthy and sustainable environment is related to other rights and existing international law;
3. *Affirms* that the promotion of the human right to a clean, healthy and sustainable environment requires the full implementation of the multilateral environmental agreements under the principles of international environmental law;
4. *Calls upon* States, international organizations, business enterprises and other relevant stakeholders to adopt policies, to enhance international cooperation, strengthen capacity-building and continue to share good practices in order to scale up efforts to ensure a clean, healthy and sustainable environment for all.

---

The UN General Assembly adopted the above resolution with 161 votes in favor and none against. Eight states — Belarus, Cambodia, China, Ethiopia, Iran, Kyrgyzstan, the Russian Federation, and Syria — abstained.

Notably the United States voted in favor of the General Assembly resolution, after having previously expressed concerns about addressing environmental issues in the context of human rights. Those concerns were consistent with the US's longtime position skeptical of rights other than traditional civil and political rights such as those found in the US-ratified International Covenant on Civil and Political Rights. The US has also questioned whether human rights bodies such as the Human Rights Council have adequate expertise to address environmental issues. See, e.g., *U.S. Explanation of Position on Human Rights and the Environment*, U.S. Mission to International Organizations in Geneva (March 14, 2017), https://gen eva.usmission.gov/2017/03/24/u-s-explanation-of-position-on-human-rights-and -the-environment. Thus, according to media and other informed sources, US diplomats expressed their lack of support for the Human Rights Council resolution of October 2021 that preceded the Generally Assembly resolution and that similarly affirmed a right to clean, healthy, and sustainable environment. The United States was not a member of the Human Rights Council at the time of the vote in the Council, but it reportedly let its views known to Council members. What could have made the US change its position and vote in favor of the General Assembly resolution less than a year later?

That previous position of the United States coincided with a strain of questioning the soundness of articulating ever more "new" human rights.

A.H. Robertson and J.G. Merrills,

## Human Rights in the World: An Introduction to the Study of the International Protection of Human Rights

255-59 (3d ed. 1989)

In recent years a good deal of thought has been given to the question of extending the scope of human rights beyond those to be found in the Universal Declaration and the two international Covenants. An early indication of this tendency was the proclamation of a 'right to development'. The thinking here is that, quite apart from moral considerations, the economic development of the poorer countries of the world is essential to their social well-being and political stability and that without it they are in no position to guarantee the civil, political, economic, social and cultural rights prescribed in the major international texts. As a consequence, the 'right to development' is asserted as a human right.

In a similar way, the concern felt in many countries and international organizations about the need for the protection of the environment, particularly against the pollution generated by modern industrial societies, has led some to the conclusion that there is a human right to a clean and healthy environment.

Then there are those who go further and consider that there is a human right to peace and a human right to share in the 'common heritage of mankind', that is the natural resources of the deep-sea bed and other areas not subject to territorial sovereignty. . . .

A distinct but related question, which has been much discussed in the United Nations in recent years, is the establishment of a new international economic order. [The author devotes four paragraphs to describing the rise (but not the fall) of the new international economic order (NIEO).]

This brings us back to the so-called 'new rights': the right to development, the right to the environment, the right to share in the common heritage of mankind, the right to peace, and so on. Are these concepts human rights in any meaningful sense of that term? In trying to answer this question, there are several factors to be borne in mind.

In the first place, the word 'human' in the expression 'human rights' has a specific meaning. It indicates that the rights under consideration are rights pertaining to human beings by virtue of their humanity. As stated in both the UN Covenants, 'these rights derive from the inherent dignity of the human person.' In our view this means that the rights which can properly be called 'human rights' are rights of individual human beings stemming from their nature as human beings, and not rights of groups, associations, or other collectivities. This is borne out of the wording repeatedly used in the Universal Declaration and in the Covenant on Civil and Political Rights, 'Everyone has the right . . .'; while the Covenant on Economic, Social and Cultural Rights repeatedly stipulates that 'the States Parties . . . recognize the right of everyone to . . .' the different rights protected. It is quite clear from this language that what the Universal Declaration and the Covenants are concerned with is the rights of individual human beings. True, there is an exception in Article 1 of both Covenants, which states, 'All peoples have the right of self-determination.' But it is clear from the travaux that this was regarded as a special provision, and its exceptional character is underlined by the fact that [it] is placed in a distinct chapter of each Covenant, and separated from the articles relating to individual human rights.

This being so, is it accurate to designate as 'human-rights' so-called which pertain not to individuals but to groups or collectivities? Usage, of course, is a matter of convention and there is room for more than one view as to what is appropriate here. In our view, however, language and thinking will be clearer if we use the expression 'human rights' to designate individual rights and 'collective rights' to designate the rights of groups and collectivities, a distinction which also has the advantage of being consistent with much generally accepted practice.

The second consideration relates to the use of the word 'rights' in the expression 'new human rights.' Economic development, the protection of the environment, the common heritage of mankind and peace: are these concepts 'rights' in a meaningful sense? They can, and should, be objectives of social policy. They may be items in a political programme. However, they are certainly not legally enforceable claims. Most people no doubt prefer peace. But if one's country is at war, it is certain that there is no legally enforceable 'right to peace.' Naturally, it would be possible to define 'rights' in such a way as to include all desirable objectives of social policy, and in that event, the 'new human rights' would become 'rights' by virtue of the definition. But this would be to distort the ordinary meaning given to the term 'human rights' and, more seriously, would run together goals which enlightened humanity ought to pursue with claims which are already protected by international law. The trouble arises, then, because advocates of the 'new human rights' are confusing objectives of social policy with rights in the lawyers' sense. If one wishes to see some objective achieved—a clean and healthy environment, for example—it is tempting to say that this is a right to which we are all entitled. But it is not a good idea to take wishes for reality.

The last point to be borne in mind is that there is a crucial distinction between legal rights and moral rights. We may consider that we have a moral right to something—consideration from others, perhaps—when we have no legal right to it at all. Countless examples could be given. If advocates of the 'new human rights' assert that we have a moral right to peace, to the environment, and so on, then many will be inclined to agree. But there is all the difference in the world between these and other moral rights, on the one hand, and, on the other, rights, whether civil and political or economic and social, which have been incorporated in international treaties. While it is true that moral ideas provide both an incentive to create new law and a yardstick for its interpretation, until the process of law-making has taken place, 'new human rights' must remain in the realm of speculation.

––––––––––––––

As reflected in the above report by the Special Rapporteur on human rights and the environment, environmental issues can be addressed on the basis of already widely recognized human rights, apart from a newly articulated free-standing right to a clean, healthy, and sustainable environment. Human-caused pollution, contamination, deforestation, burning fossil fuels, biodiversity loss, and climate change are all major environmental issues that implicate the rights to life, health, development, and other recognized human rights. These issues have been addressed by different regional human rights institutions in the application of general regional human rights treaties.

The judgment in *Lopez Ostra v. Spain* by the European Court of Human Rights exemplifies this approach. In that case, the Court examined allegations of environmental pollution and waste. The industrial plant at issue produced gas fumes, odors, and other forms of contamination resulting in health problems for the residents of the town of Lorca, Spain. The Court found that environmental pollution can endanger health, threaten well-being, and negatively impact the enjoyment of home, private and family life, and hence the Court found a violation of Article 8 (right to private and family life) of the European Convention given Spain's failure to act diligently to protect against such harms. See Eur. Ct. H.R., App. 16798/90, Judgment of Dec. 9, 1994, pages 7-9; 44-48. There are currently calls for the Council of Europe to adopt a treaty on the right to a healthy environment. See *ENNHRI calls on the Council of Europe to adopt a binding instrument on the right to a healthy environment*, European Network of National Human Rights Institutions, (Nov. 19, 2021), *https://ennhri.org/news-and-blog/cddh-env-contribution-right-to-healthy-environment/* If the right to a clean, healthy, and sustainable environment is codified in a new treaty adopted by the Council of Europe, how might one argue future cases of environmental pollution and waste before the European Court of Human Rights? Do you think this treaty recognition would make a difference in future rulings from the European Court of Human Rights?

There has been a recent surge of efforts to secure justice for human rights violations linked to environmental harm before United Nations bodies. For example, the case of *Sacchi v. Argentina*, before the Committee on the Rights of the Child, was part of a group of five cases filed by 16 individuals under the age of 18 from Argentina, Brazil, France, Germany, and Turkey. The claimants alleged that these states failed to act diligently to reduce carbon emissions and to mitigate or provide adaptation measures for the negative effects of climate change. Even though the complaint was held inadmissible due to non-exhaustion of domestic remedies, the Committee presented ground-breaking analysis concerning the scope of state responsibility and the content of state obligations under the Convention on the Rights of the Child when transboundary harm related to climate change occurs. The Committee referred to the important precedent set by the Inter-American Court of Human Rights in its Advisory Opinion OC-23/17, in which the Court confirmed that states may be held responsible for significant damage caused to persons outside their borders from human-driven activities originating in their territories or under their effective control or authority. See Inter-Am. Court of H.R., *The Environment and Human Rights*, Advisory Opinion OC-23/17 of November 15, 2017, Ser. A No. 23, paras. 101-104.

The Committee in *Sacchi v. Argentina* also confirmed that there are ways to establish connections between harm to the life and health of children and state failures to act diligently to reduce carbon emissions. The Committee called this harm foreseeable and identified a heightened obligation for states to act immediately to prevent the damaging impacts of climate change on children throughout their lifetimes. See *Chiara Sacchi et al.*, Communication No. 104/2019, Decision Adopted by the Committee under the Optional Protocol to the Convention on the Rights of the Child, UN Doc. CRC/C/88/D/104/2019 (Nov. 11, 2021), paras. 1-2, 3.1-3.2, 10.2-10.18, 10.20. See also Maria Antonia Tigre and Victoria Lichet, *The CRC Decision in Sacchi v. Argentina*, ASIL Insights, Dec. 13, 2021, https://www.asil.org/insights/volume/25/issue/26.

A number of complaints have also been presented before regional human rights bodies alleging the violation of existing human rights treaties due to state failures to properly address climate change and its harmful effects. Cases have been presented by children raising allegations similar to the ones in *Sacchi v. Argentina*. For example, the European Court of Human Rights has admitted the case of *Duarte Agostinho and Others v. Portugal and Others*, in which it is alleged that global greenhouse gas emissions from 33 Member States of the Council of Europe are contributing to the harms produced by global warming and climate change. The petition was brought by six Portuguese children and young people, with support from Global Legal Action Network, claiming that their generation will be especially harmed by the effects of climate change. They refer in particular to the damaging effects of states permitting the release of carbon emissions and allowing the export of fossil fuels. See *Duarte Agostinho and Others v. Portugal and Others (relinquishment)*, Eur. Ct. H.R., App. 39371/20, Information Note on the Court's case-law No. 263 of June 2022 (relinquishment, or transference, of the case to the Grand Chamber), https://hudoc.echr.coe.int/eng#{%22itemid%22:[%22002-13724%22]}.

The Inter-American Commission on Human Rights has also received a petition related to climate change. Presented in 2021 by the Haitian Children from Cité de Soleil, the petition alleges that toxic trash disposal in the residential district of Cité de Soleil in Port-au-Prince is harming the children's health — harm that will be exacerbated by climate change, environmental displacement, and waterborne diseases. See *Petition to the Inter-American Commission on Human Rights Seeking to Redress Violations of the Rights of Children in Cité Soleil, Haiti*, Professors James R. May and Erin Daly (Representatives) (Feb. 4, 2021), http://climatecasechart.com/climate-change-litigation/wp-content/uploads/sites/16/non-us-case-documents/2021/20210204_13174_petition.pdf.

Given these and other developments, what does the General Assembly's recognition of a free-standing right to a clean, healthy, and sustainable environment add? And what might a treaty recognizing such a free-standing right accomplish?

## *Note: A Human Rights Treaty for Older Persons*

On June 15, 2015, the Organization of American States adopted the Inter-American Convention on Protecting the Human Rights of Older Persons (OAS T.S. A-70). This is one of the newest regional treaties, and there is no comparable United Nations treaty. The Preamble of the Convention expresses its rationale: "Recognizing the need to address matters of old age and aging from a human-rights perspective that recognizes the valuable current and potential contributions of older persons to the common good, to cultural identity, to the diversity of their communities, to human, social, and economic development, and to the eradication of poverty." The Convention substantially reflects the earlier United Nations Principles for Older Persons (1991), the Proclamation on Ageing (1992), the Political Declaration and Madrid International Plan of Action on Ageing (2002), and other prior declarations and action plans including at the regional level. The Convention has in part a programmatic focus; its preamble expresses the determination "to incorporate and prioritize the subject of ageing in public policy, and to raise and allocate the human, material, and financial resources needed to achieve appropriate implementation and evaluation of the special measures undertaken."

Article 3 defines "older person" as "a person aged 60 or older, except where domestic legislation determines an age that is lesser or greater, provided that it is not over 65 years. This concept includes, among others, elderly persons" [undefined]. The Convention reaffirms the rights found in general UN and regional human rights instruments, including the right to equality and nondiscrimination (art. 5); right to life (art. 6); right to freedom from torture and cruel, inhuman, and degrading treatment (art. 10); right to give free and informed consent on health matters (art. 11); right to personal liberty (art. 13); right to freedom of expression and opinion, and access to information (art. 14); right to nationality and freedom of movement (art. 15); right to privacy and intimacy (art. 16); right to social security (art. 17); right to work (art. 18); right to health (art. 19); right to education (art. 20); right to culture (art. 21); right to property (art. 23); right to a healthy environment (art. 25); political rights (art. 27) and freedom of association and assembly (art. 28); equality before the law (art. 30).

Other articles contain innovations, although some if not all of these provisions could be inferred from more general guarantees in the International Bill of Rights. Article 19(a), however, specifies that states undertake to ensure "preferential care" for the elderly; Article 21 similarly calls on states to promote "preferential access for older persons to cultural goods and services in accessible formats and conditions." Other guarantees are found in Article 8 (participation and community integration); Article 9 (right to safety and freedom from violence); Article 22 (right to recreation, leisure and sports); Article 24 (a lengthy article on the right to housing); and Article 26 (guaranteeing a right to accessibility and personal mobility).

Review the text of the Inter-American Convention on Protecting the Rights of Older Persons in the Documentary Supplement and reflect on the following questions:

1.  What arguments support the existence of this new treaty?
2.  Is this treaty necessary? Why?

3. Are all the guarantees included in this new OAS treaty correctly considered human rights?

4. When you review the provisions, do you see any similarities and differences with the United Nations human rights treaties discussed in this Chapter?

5. Should there be a United Nation treaty protecting the rights of older persons?

6. What other groups should have a specific treaty dedicated to their concerns?

7. Is the proliferation of human rights instruments (and a growing catalog of rights) positive or negative for human rights in general?

## V.   FINAL COMMENTS AND QUESTIONS

1. Consider the pros and cons of addressing issues at the intersection of human rights and the environment through treaties. Do you think a globally applicable, UN human rights treaty would be beneficial in this area? Can you see any disadvantages? Is General Assembly Resolution 76/300, reproduced above, actually useful in the effort to move states and other actors to address human rights concerns related to the environment?

2. Do you agree with the criteria advanced by Robertson and Merrills to identify new human rights? How might these criteria be applied in the identification of new human rights deserving attention, including a human right to a clean, healthy, and sustainable environment? Is there a difference between, on the one hand, recognizing a new human right as such and, on the other, developing a new treaty to address a new area of human rights concern? Can you envision a new treaty on human rights and the environment without recognition of a specific human right to a clean, healthy, and sustainable environment? Does the relatively new Inter-American Convention on the Protection of Older Persons, referred to above recognize any new human right? If not, what does it accomplish?

3. What criteria can you use to distinguish between the nature-made and human-driven effects of climate change? And what criteria should guide a determination of foreseeable harm that a state should have acted diligently to prevent? Would a treaty in the area of human rights and climate change be helpful in this determination? For in depth discussion of the obligations of states to exercise due diligence to protect human rights generally, see Chapter 4, *infra* pages 212-236.

4. Treaties are important for setting standards of state behavior and are influential in the international community's definition of priorities. However, and as indicated in this Chapter, some important questions remain. Should the United Nations conclude additional human rights treaties? If so, which other groups should be the subject of a specific treaty? What other rights or topics might be considered appropriate to address in a new global treaty in light of modern developments and concerns? A right to a clean, healthy, and sustainable environment? A right to peace? A right to protection against human trafficking? A right to genetic integrity? The rights of lesbian, gay, bisexual, transgender, and intersex persons? Business and human rights? Should there be harmonization between the global

and regional human rights treaties? Continue to reflect on these questions as you navigate the chapters and other topics in this textbook.

5. Another lingering issue is how preferences emerge as claims and become translated into rights. Who sets the agenda? In the fields of racial and sex-based discrimination, many of those most affected and marginalized have not participated in treaty-negotiation processes to address their concerns. What kind of spaces can be created for individuals and groups to effectively participate in treaty-negotiation processes? How can these spaces be diverse, inclusive, and meaningful?

6. Is every social problem a human rights concern? There are many social values that vary from state to state or even within states, such as the degree of equity to be pursued as part of economic policy, government spending priorities, the criminalization of private actions (such as drug use), the role of religion, relationships within the family, and others. Even if wide consensus could be achieved on some of these issues, do you consider that certain social or political goods may *not* be suitable for inclusion in a human rights treaty? If everything falls under the rubric of "human rights," does human rights lose all meaning?

# CHAPTER 3

# THE DEVELOPMENT OF HUMAN RIGHTS NORMS THROUGH NON-BINDING INSTRUMENTS

## HOW AND WHY DO NEW INTERNATIONAL HUMAN RIGHTS NORMS EMERGE OTHER THAN BY TREATY?

# I.   INTRODUCTION: THE ROLE OF "SOFT LAW" IN HUMAN RIGHTS LAW-MAKING

As discussed in Chapter 2, human rights law-making takes place primarily through the development of treaties to which states affirmatively commit themselves by means of formal procedures of signature and ratification or accession. But is international human rights law only made by treaties? Numerous other documents are in some way endorsed by states or international institutions but not adopted as treaties. United Nations declarations, for example, also express human rights standards with varying degrees of specificity and on an expanding range of topics. In and of themselves, these documents are not legally binding, but they nonetheless have some measure of authority and impact when they are invoked. Because of their character, UN declarations and other such non-treaty documents proclaiming human rights or related standards are sometimes referred to as "soft" law. But does the "soft" metaphor adequately capture the nature of these documents and their place in decision-making by states and others? The answer to this question lies in an examination of the way in which declarations and other non-treaty human rights documents are drafted and adopted and in the role they play in decision-making. Implicit in much of the discussion is the distinction between legal and political obligations, and we will see that the line between the two is often blurred — although one should be careful not to ignore that line entirely.

The materials in this Chapter explore the process of human rights norm-building and application through instruments other than treaties, beginning with an introductory discussion of various types of soft law instruments and related practice. The Chapter then examines the drafting and legal character of the Universal Declaration of Human Rights, the very first human rights declaration to emanate from the United Nations. Succeeding sections offer examples of how soft law norms develop in interaction with treaty norms, focusing on indigenous peoples, minorities, and the related issue of self-determination.

Dinah Shelton

## "Commentary and Conclusions"

in *Compliance and Commitment: The Role of Non-Binding Instruments in the International Legal System* 449-63 (Dinah Shelton ed., 2000) (footnotes omitted)

International human rights law since the Second World War has utilized a combination of binding and non-binding instruments to set forth human rights guarantees and the obligations of states in regard to them. The United Nations Charter contains references to human rights, including the obligation of member states to take joint and separate action in cooperation with the organization to achieve universal respect for, and observance of, human rights and fundamental freedoms. The first instrument adopted by the member states to define the rights referred to in the Charter was the 1948 Universal Declaration of Human Rights (UDHR), a non-binding resolution of the UN General Assembly.

From the beginning, however, the drafters of the UDHR intended that it be the first step, "a common standard of achievement" that would lead to a binding agreement on the subject. The 1966 Covenants on Civil and Political Rights and on Economic, Social and Cultural Rights fulfilled the drafters' expectations by incorporating the UDHR rights in binding international agreements. . . .

It is unusual to find human rights norms that exist only in soft law form, given the complex interweaving of treaty and non-binding instruments, global and regional texts. Human rights law also is complicated by the existence of judicial and quasi-judicial bodies that decide cases and build a jurisprudence that itself is a combination of hard and soft law. A decision of the European Court of Human Rights or the Inter-American Court of Human Rights, for example, is legally binding on the state party to the case, but is not binding on other parties to the treaty. [*binding, but not*] In the field of human rights, therefore, it may be useful to attempt to categorize non-binding norms, as follows:

*Primary soft law* can be considered as those normative texts not adopted in treaty form that are addressed to the international community as a whole or to the entire membership of the adopting institution or organization. Such an instrument may declare new norms, often as an intended precursor to adoption of a later treaty, or it may reaffirm or further elaborate norms previously set forth in binding or non-binding texts. The UN Standard Minimum Rules for the Treatment of Prisoners, adopted by the First United Nations Congress on the Prevention of Crime and Treatment of Offenders, 1955, and approved by the UN Economic and Social Council in 1957 is an example of a primary declarative text. . . .

In many instances, primary soft law elaborates previously-accepted general or vague norms found in binding agreements or non-binding instruments. The Universal Declaration of Human Rights defines the term human rights as it is used in the United Nations Charter. The UN Declaration on the Rights of the Child in turn calls the Universal Declaration of Human Rights the "basis" for its adoption. The UN Declaration on the Rights of Persons Belonging to National or Ethnic, Religious and Linguistic Minorities is comprehensive in its references . . . [to standards in existing existing treaties].

*Secondary soft law* includes the recommendations and general comments of international human rights supervisory organs, the jurisprudence of courts and commissions, decisions of special rapporteurs and other *ad hoc* bodies, and the resolutions of political organs of international organizations applying primary norms. Most of this secondary soft law is pronounced by institutions whose existence and jurisdiction is derived from a treaty and who apply norms contained in the same treaty. . . . [E]ven institutions are created by soft law. . . .

Secondary soft law has expanded in large part due to the proliferation of primary treaty standards and monitoring institutions created to supervise state compliance with the treaty obligations. In some cases, human rights treaty bodies have asserted their implied powers to encourage compliance and have developed a considerable body of secondary soft law. An important source of soft law norms is the set of General Comments issued by many of the UN treaty bodies, including the Human Rights Committee and the Committee on Economic, Social and Cultural Rights. General Comments interpret and add detail to the rights and obligations contained in the respective treaties. . . .

Finally, secondary soft law derives from the increasingly important work of specially appointed individuals or working groups. Both in the United Nations and regional organizations, thematic rapporteurs or ad hoc committees have become a common device for monitoring state compliance with particular human rights. Thematic mandates may be based on a particular treaty norm or a primary soft law text. The UN Special Rapporteur on Religious Intolerance, for example, has a mandate based on the 1981 General Assembly Declaration on the Elimination of All Forms of Intolerance and of Discrimination Based on Religion or Belief. Rapporteurs create both primary and secondary soft law. . . .

### Conclusions

Soft law is used regularly for international human rights norm-setting, either as an ultimate or an intermediate expression of international consensus. In developing human rights treaties, it is now common to pass through a soft law, declarative stage. Probably even more common is the "secondary" soft law that is not preliminary or declaratory in nature, but is intended to be the ultimate and authoritative determination of a legal question. In this regard, hard law and soft law interact to shape the content of international obligations. Soft law formulates and reformulates the hard law of human rights treaties in the application of this law to specific states and cases. Paradoxically, this secondary soft law may be harder than the primary soft law declaring new standards.

Soft law is clearly useful in enunciating broad principles in new areas of law-making, where details of obligation remain to be elaborated. In addition, soft law can be seen as a necessary mechanism related to the traditional consensual nature of international law formation, which only allows hard law to be made and imposed on those who agree. Even where there is overwhelming consensus on the need for action and on the negative impact that inaction will have on all states, norms cannot be imposed on objectors. Soft law can express standards and broad international consensus when unanimity is lacking in state practice and thus the will to establish hard law is absent. Ultimately, as compliance increases soft law may serve to pressure the few non-consenting states to comply with the majority views. . . .

Whether the norms are binding or non-binding, compliance seems most directly linked to the existence of effective monitoring and independent supervision. The role of non-governmental organizations has been crucial, but without a forum to which to take the results of their investigations and the evidence they gather, they are limited in their effectiveness. In short, it is the synergy between human rights bodies created by inter-governmental organizations and non-governmental organizations that leads to greater compliance by states. The existence of non-binding norms and the consensus that emerges as states begin to comply with them also appears to stimulate the development of legally-binding norms.

The studies indicate that states do comply with non-binding human rights norms some of the time. They also comply with binding human rights norms some of the time. No state is free of human rights problems and it is utopian to think that either international or national human rights norms, binding or non-binding, will ever be complied with by all states all of the time. The use of non-binding instruments in human rights law as a precursor to binding norms probably limits state compliance, because the use of the non-binding form is often a reflection of disagreement over the content of the norm or norms in question. It at least reflec"s "unfinished business" in defining the details of the rights guaranteed within the instrument. . . .

## II.  THE UNIVERSAL DECLARATION OF HUMAN RIGHTS

The Universal Declaration of Human Rights, introduced in the first chapter, was adopted in 1948 without a dissenting vote by the UN General Assembly, the organization's most broadly representative body. It preceded the many human rights treaties that have emanated from the United Nations and that are discussed in Chapter 2. Although the General Assembly has no formal legislative or law-making power, adoption of the Declaration was a process by which states developed and endorsed a common understanding of basic human rights standards that are to apply universally, building on the general human rights clauses of the UN Charter. The following materials discuss the adoption of the declaration and its evolving influence on law and policy, both domestically and internationally.


## A.  *The Making of the Universal Declaration*

John P. Humphrey[*]

## "The Universal Declaration of Human Rights: Its History, Impact, and Juridical Character"

in *Human Rights: Thirty Years after the Universal Declaration* 21-37
(B.G. Ramcharan ed., 1979) (footnotes omitted)


The catalyst to which we owe the Universal Declaration of Human Rights and indeed much of the new international law of human rights which has so radically changed the theory and practice of the law of nations was the gross violations of human rights that were committed in and by certain countries during and immediately before the Second World War. For it was these atrocities that fostered the climate of world opinion which made it possible . . . to make the promotion of respect for human rights and fundamental freedoms "for all without distinction as to race, sex, language or religion" one of the pillars on which the United Nations was erected and a stated purpose of the Organization. It was on these foundations that the new international law of human rights was built. . . .

The most important business of the Commission [on Human Rights—predecessor to the Human Rights Council] when it met under Mrs. Roosevelt's chairmanship in its first regular session on 27 January. 1947, was to make arrangements for the drafting of [an International Bill of Rights]. No decision had yet been taken as to its form. . . . Although the Australian and Indian delegations strongly advocated a convention, the great majority of the governments represented at this first session of the Commission favoured a declaration and it was in that form that the first draft, the so-called Secretariat Outline, was prepared. It was only at its second session that the Commission decided to draft a bill in three parts: a declaration, a multilateral convention (soon known as the Covenant and later as the Covenants after the General Assembly decided that there would be two conventions) and measures of implementation.

The Commission made no attempt at its first session to draft the declaration, but it did appoint a committee consisting of its chairman (Mrs. Roosevelt of the United States), its vice-chairman (P.C. Chang of China) and its rapporteur (Charles Malik of the Lebanon) to prepare a first draft. This Committee of three held only one meeting—a tea-party really in Mrs. Roosevelt's Washington Square apartment on the Sunday following the adjournment of the Commission—and soon found itself without a mandate. Nor did it draft any articles, partly because Chang and

---

* [Humphrey served as Director of the Division of Human Rights of the UN from 1946 to 1966 and was a leading participant in the drafting of the Universal Declaration.—Eds.]

Malik—two of the most brilliant men ever to sit on the Human Rights Commission and who would later be among the principal architects of the International Bill of Rights—were poles apart philosophically and could seldom agree on anything; but the committee did ask the Director of the Human Rights Division [the author] in the Secretariat to prepare a draft declaration. He eventually did so. . . . This draft, which was based on a number of drafts that had been prepared by a number of individuals and organizations, contained forty-eight short articles in which both civil and political and economic and social rights were catalogued and defined. With two exceptions all the texts on which the Director worked came from English-speaking sources and all of them from the democratic West;* but the documentation which the Secretariat later brought together in support of his draft included texts extracted from the constitutions of many countries.

[Humphrey describes the ensuing negotiations around the initial Secretariat draft that took place within and outside a drafting committee that had been reconfigured and expanded to meet the political concerns of certain states.]

With the help of the Commission on the Status of Women, the Commission's two sub-commissions on freedom of information and the prevention of discrimination, the 1948 Geneva Conference on Freedom of Information, the Specialized Agencies and non-governmental organizations, the Human Rights Commission and its Drafting Committee continued to work on the declaration until the late Spring of 1948. Its work on the two covenants, as they later became, would not be completed until 1954; but on 18 June, 1948, at the end of its third session the Commission adopted its draft of the Declaration with twelve of its members voting in favour. Byelorussia, the Soviet Union, the Ukraine and Yugoslavia—anticipating the stand they would later take in the General Assembly—all abstained from voting. The draft declaration was therefore ready for consideration by the Assembly at its third session.

Although the Economic and Social Council through which the Commission's text was transmitted to the General Assembly had so many human rights items on the agenda of its seventh session, including the draft convention on genocide and the Final Act of the Information Conference, that exceptionally it set up a special committee to deal with them, the Council made no changes in the text of the Declaration which when it reached the Assembly was sent to the Third Committee [of the General Assembly]. In the light of the many difficulties which then arose, it was fortunate that the chairman of this committee was Charles Malik who as rapporteur of the Commission was familiar with all the details of the legislative history of the draft. It was a tribute to the work of the Commission that many of the governments

---

* [It should be noted that the first draft of a bill of human rights, which was to be included in the UN Charter, came from Cuba, Chile, and Panama in 1945. This text was used by the Commission's drafting committee and by Humphrey, along with an influential text submitted by the Inter-American Juridical Committee. In 1968, French jurist Rene Cassin, who represented France on the Commission and was later a judge on the European Court of Human Rights, was awarded the Nobel Peace Prize for his work on the Declaration. Further information on the role of Cassin, Malik (Lebanon), Hernan Santa Cruz (Chile), and Alexie Pavlov (USSR) can be found in Johannes Morsink, *The Universal Declaration of Human Rights: Origins, Drafting and Intent* (1999).—Eds.]

represented in the Assembly would have accepted the text as it stood; but in the end the Third Committee devoted eighty-one long meetings to it and dealt with one hundred and sixty-eight resolutions containing amendments. In the circumstances it is remarkable that the text finally adopted was so much like the Commission's text. . . .

Attempts to postpone the adoption of the Declaration were . . . defeated. It was, however only in the night of 6 December that the Third Committee finished its task and forwarded its report to the plenary session of the Assembly, just in time for that body to adopt the Declaration in the night of 10 December, only two days before the end of the session. There were no dissenting votes but the six communist countries which were then members of the United Nations, Saudi Arabia and South Africa all abstained.

This is no place to review the legislative history of the Declaration or even to analyse its thirty articles. Some of the articles could have been better formulated and the document suffers from the inclusion in it of certain assertions which do not enunciate justiciable rights; but having regard to the very great number of people who in one way or another contributed to the text it is a remarkably well drafted document. There were some important omissions including the failure to include any article on the protection of minorities and to recognize any right of petition even at the national level—a right so fundamental that it is recognized even by some authoritarian countries—let alone by the United Nations.

Remembering that the final arbiters of the text were governments it is perhaps just as well that no serious attempt was made to catalogue or define those duties which are correlative to human rights; but the principle that everyone owes duties to the community is recognized in article 29. This important article also stipulates the conditions under which limitations may be legitimately placed on the exercise of human rights and freedoms, the only permitted limitations being such "as are determined by law solely for the purpose of securing due recognition and respect for the rights and freedoms of others and of meeting the just requirements of morality, public order and the general welfare in a democratic society." The reference here to public order can be compared with advantage to the use in the Covenant on Civil and Political Rights of the expression "public order (*ordre public*)" which insofar as that instrument is concerned in any even introduces the nebulous and dangerous concept of public order in civil law jurisdictions.

The Declaration gives pride of place to the traditional civil and political rights which are catalogued and defined in its first twenty-one articles. There then follows, after an "umbrella article," a list and definitions of economic, social and cultural rights which, in 1948, were still controversial in many countries; witness the principal reason that motivated the division of the Covenant into two parts. It was indeed the inclusion of these rights in the declaration which was one of the reasons for its great historical importance.

---

Professor Humphrey, whose insider's account of the adoption of the Universal Declaration makes fascinating reading, concludes in another of his many writings on the subject that "[i]ts impact on world public opinion has been as great as if not greater than that of any contemporary international instrument, including the Charter of the United Nations." John Humphrey, *Human Rights and the United Nations: A Great Adventure* 76 (1984).

The Declaration consists of 30 articles, which Professor Henkin asserts "are in their essence American constitutional rights projected around the world." Louis Henkin, "International Human Rights and Rights in the United States," in *1 Human Rights in International Law: Legal and Policy Issues* 25, 39 (T. Meron ed. 1984). This statement may not be entirely accurate, however, since the Declaration also includes economic and social rights not included in the U.S. Constitution. Compare Stephen P. Marks, *From the "Single Confused Page" to the "Decalogue for Six Billion Persons": The Roots of the Universal Declaration of Human Rights in the French Revolution,* 20 HUM. RTS. Q. 459 (1998). Before proceeding to the materials and cases that follow, take this opportunity to read the Declaration (in the Documentary Supplement) in its entirety.

Over one-half of the articles in the Universal Declaration (Articles 3-18) guarantee the civil rights of individuals. Another three articles (Articles 19-21) protect their political rights. Finally, six articles (Articles 22-27) grant individuals certain minimal economic, social, and cultural rights. Since the Declaration was considered by all its drafters to be a standard-setting exercise rather than an instrument with binding legal character, no measures of implementation are included.

## B.  *The Legal Status of the Declaration*

### 1.  **The Historical Perspective**

In giving our approval to the declaration today, it is of primary importance that we keep clearly in mind the basic character of the document. It is not a treaty; it is not an international agreement. It is not and does not purport to be a statement of law or of legal obligation. It is a declaration of basic principles of human rights and freedoms, to be stamped with the approval of the General Assembly by formal vote of its members, and to serve as a common standard of achievement for all peoples of all nations.

Statement of Mrs. Eleanor Roosevelt, Chairman of the Commission on Human Rights, immediately preceding the General Assembly's vote in 1948 on the Universal Declaration, quoted in M. Whiteman, *5 Digest of International Law* 243 (1965).

Egon Schwelb

## The Influence of the Universal Declaration of Human Rights on International and National Law

1959 Am. Socy. Intl. Law Proceedings 217

Mr. Alejandro Alvarez, the former judge of the International Court of Justice, said in his dissenting opinion on Competence of the Assembly for the Admission of a State to the United Nations that a treaty or a text that has once been established acquires a life of its own. Consequently, in interpreting it, we must have regard to the exigencies of contemporary life rather than to the intentions of those who framed it.

This dictum can hardly be said to be an accepted statement of present-day international law. One is, however, tempted to add that if there ever has been a development which would induce the student to accept it, it has been the fate of the Universal Declaration of Human Rights in the ten years which followed upon its proclamation by the General Assembly of the United Nations on December 10, 1948.

The *travaux préparatoires* [preparatory work—akin to legislative history] make it clear that the overwhelming majority of the speakers in the various organs of the United Nations did not intend the Declaration to become a statement of law or of legal obligations, but a statement of principles devoid of any obligatory character, and which would have moral force "only." One finds in the debates statements which suggest that the Declaration might be considered a complement to the Charter, as its authoritative or "authentic" interpretation, or a formulation of "the general principles of law recognized by civilized nations" within the meaning of Article 38, paragraph 1(c), of the Statute of the Court. Now the difficulty with these suggestions is that the General Assembly, which adopted the Declaration, does not have the constitutional authority to give an authentic interpretation of the Charter. And as to the question of the "general principles of law," the correct answer is, perhaps, this: that while the substance of most, though by no means all, of the provisions of the Declaration may well be said to be identical with general principles of law recognized by civilized nations, the proposition that the Declaration is a codification of these general principles is not warranted.

With a few exceptions, publicists also agree that the Declaration is a "nonbinding pronouncement." Nevertheless, a complete denial of the legal relevance of the Universal Declaration does not do justice to a document which was adopted—without a dissenting vote—by the governments forming the most representative body of the international community. The General Assembly adopted the Declaration not only as "a common standard of achievement," but also stressed that a "common understanding" of rights and freedoms, to which the pledge of Member States expressed in Article 56 of the Charter applies, was of the greatest importance. Nor can the developments be disregarded which have taken place since December 10, 1948. . . .

There are three main areas in which the influence of the Declaration can be traced.

The first such area comes . . . under the term "invocation" which . . . "consists of making a preliminary appeal to a prescription in the hope of influencing results," if it is admissible, that is, to apply the term "invocation" in connection with an instrument like the Declaration. There are innumerable instances of the use of the Declaration as a yardstick to measure the degree of respect for human rights: by governments by international conferences, by regional inter-governmental organizations, by specialized agencies and by the United Nations, or as a basis for action or exhortation. . . .

The second area of influence of the Declaration is international treaties and conventions. In this regard we must distinguish between various types of agreements. Some instruments have simply made the Universal Declaration part and parcel of their substantive and immediately applicable law. The earliest and best-known example is the Special Statute for Trieste of 1954. Another example of full incorporation may be found in the Franco-Tunisian Conventions of 1955, in which Tunisia undertook to grant all persons resident in its territory the rights and personal guarantees proclaimed in the Declaration. . . .

This brings me to the third area of the impact of the Declaration, i.e., its direct influence on national constitutions and on municipal legislation and, in some instances, on court decisions. It may be objected that the fact that a constitution or municipal enactment uses the phraseology of the Declaration is by no means proof that the rights thereby proclaimed or defined are in fact respected. This, of course, is true. . . . An audience of American Lawyers will perhaps respond with greater understanding than any other to the suggestion that general principles embodied, and general phraseology used, in a basic document sometimes have a decisive effect on subsequent legal history. The Constitutional law of the United States might be different if the Fifth and Fourteenth Amendments had not prohibited deprivation of life, liberty, or property "without due process of law," or if general expressions such as "the privileges and immunities of citizens" and "equal protection of the laws" had not been used. There are already cases on record where the general language of the Universal Declaration has tended to encourage similar developments.

It is not surprising that constitutions drafted in co-operation with the United Nations, such as those of Libya and Eritrea, show the marked influence of the Universal Declaration, although they fall short of its provisions in one important respect, viz., the right of women to vote. It can be seen from express references to the Declaration in many other constitutions and statutes from various regions of the world, and, in the absence of such references, from extraneous evidence, that the influence of the Declaration is also reflected in many instruments not written under United Nations sponsorship. . . .

The influence of the Universal Declaration is also reflected in the constitutional law of two great European states, the Federal Republic of Germany and France. . . .

Now a few examples of the Declaration having influenced or having at least been quoted in [United States] judicial decisions: . . .

American Federation of Labor v. American Sash and Door Company involved the constitutionality of an Arizona Constitutional Amendment which prohibited union security arrangements (the closed shop). Mr. Justice Frankfurter, in concurring with the decision of the Court which upheld the Arizona Constitutional Amendment, referred to Article 20(2) of the Universal Declaration providing that "No one may be compelled to belong to an association." Again, it is not for me to say whether this provision of the Declaration applies to trade unions, a matter which is controversial. What we are interested in this connection is the fact that the Declaration was invoked by one of the justices of the Supreme Court.

In a case which also dealt with trade union matters, the New York Supreme Court, in Wilson v. Hacker, considered whether it may condemn discrimination based upon sex "as a violation of fundamental principle and judge the legitimacy of union activities in the light of the principle." In this connection, the court stated: "Indicative of the spirit of our times are the provisions of the Universal

Declaration," and went on to quote the nondiscrimination provision of Article 2 and also Article 23, which provides that everyone has the right to work, to free choice of employment, to just and favorable conditions of work and to protection against unemployment.

The influence of the Declaration is not limited to cases in this country. [Schwelb identifies the use of the Declaration in a number of judicial decisions in other countries, including in the Netherlands, Belgium, Italy, and the Philippines.] . . .

There are also a few instances in which the Universal Declaration has been referred to by judges of the International Court of Justice, albeit in dissenting opinions:

Judge Azevedo stated in the *Asylum* Case that the new Declaration of Human Rights should not remain a dead letter. Judge Levi Carneiro, in the *Anglo-Iranian Oil Company* Case, invoked Article 17 of the Declaration, which deals with the right to own property and provides that no one shall be arbitrarily deprived of his property. Judge Ad Hoc Guggenheim stressed in the Nottebohm Case that to dissociate diplomatic protection from nationality will weaken even further the protection of the individual, which is so precarious under existing international law. He considered that this would be contrary to the basic principle embodied in Article 15(1) of the Declaration, according to which everyone has a right to a nationality.

The state of affairs which has been created by all these developments is certainly not neat or logical. We are faced with a haphazard growth, not with a methodical legislative process; International legislation on human rights has been attempted on a grand scale by the ambitious project of the draft International Covenants on Human Rights [which are discussed in Chapter 2].

———

After the delivery of the preceding paper in 1959, the evolution of understandings about the status of the Universal Declaration in international law continued apace. By 1968, the twentieth anniversary of its adoption, arguments were being made that the Declaration was not just in the nature of "soft law" but had become part of customary international law. The non-governmental Assembly for Human Rights meeting in Montreal that year adopted what has become known as the Montreal Statement, which included the assertion that the "Universal Declaration of Human Rights . . . has over the years become a part of customary international law." Montreal Statement, reproduced in 9 J. INT. COMM'N JURISTS 94, 95 (1968). Also in 1968, the year designated by the United Nations as Human Rights Year, came a similar statement by the UN-sponsored International Conference on Human Rights meeting in Teheran. The Proclamation of Teheran stated that "[t]he Universal Declaration of Human Rights . . . constitutes an obligation for members of the international community." UN Doc. A/CONF.32/41 at 3 (1968), para. 2. See Final Act of the International Conference on Human Rights, Teheran, 1968, https://legal.un.org/avl/pdf/ha/fatchr/Final_Act_of_TehranConf.pdf.

### Note: Customary International Law

Customary international law is among the principal sources of international law in addition to treaties. A norm of customary international law emerges — or *crystallizes*—when a preponderance of states (and other actors with international legal personality) from different regions of the world converge on a common understanding of the norm's content and expect future behavior to conform to the norm. Customary law is "generally observed to include two key elements: a 'material' element in certain past uniformities in behavior and a 'psychological' element, or *opinio juris*, in certain subjectivities of 'oughtness' attending such uniformities in behavior." Myres McDougal et al., *Human Rights and World Public Order: The Basic Policies of an International Law of Human Dignity* 269 (1980). See also James Crawford, *Brownlie's Principles of Public International Law* 21-28 (9th ed. 2019). Article 38 of the Statute of the International Court of Justice identifies in its listing of the sources of law to be applied by the Court "international custom, as evidence of a general practice accepted as law." Complete uniformity in a practice assenting to or acquiescing in a norm is not required, although it must be sufficiently widespread and coherent among states to give rise to expectations of compliance with the norm.

Traditionally, the relevant state practice for the development of customary international law was considered to be limited to or to primarily involve the actual physical behavior or episodic conduct of states, for example, a state's actual treatment of foreign diplomats in relation to diplomatic immunity. There has been significant debate about the constituitive elements of customary international law, especially in relation to state practice. See William A. Schabas, *The Customary International Law of Human Rights* 41-53 (1921) (surveying different approaches). The unmistakable trend, however, is to not just rely on actual state conduct but also on what states say, especially in writing. The now prevalent view is that forms of practice other than actual conduct also contribute to the formation of customary international law. *Brownlie's Principles of Public International Law*, for example, includes among the "very numerous" sources of custom the following:

> [D]iplomatic correspondence, policy statements, press releases, the opinions of government legal advisers, official manuals on legal questions (e.g. manuals of military law), executive decisions and practices, orders to military forces (e.g. rules of engagement), comments by governments on ILC drafts and accompanying commentary, legislation, international and national judicial decisions, recitals in treaties and other international instruments (epecially when in 'all states' form), an extensive pattern of treaties in the same terms, the practice of international organs, and resolutions relating to legal questions in UN organs, notably the General Assembly.

*Brownlie's, supra,* at 21-22 (citations omitted). This assessment of the sources of international custom is generally reinforced in connection with international human rights law by Schabas, *supra*. To identify customary human rights norms Schabas relies substantially on written sources associated with UN human rights processes, including human rights reports by states and standard setting instruments, in particular General Assembly declarations and treaties, that reflect patterns of widespread norm recognition. See also Oscar Schachter, *International Law in Theory and Practice* 84-105 (1991) (on the legal effect of resolutions and political texts).

The existence of customary law does not negate the basic principle of international law that a state may not be bound without its consent, however. Although silence in the face of a developing customary norm is presumed to evidence consent, a state will not be bound to such a norm if it clearly and persistently objects to it (unless the norm is one of *jus cogens*, a peremptory or non-derogable norm). See *Brownlie's, supra*, at 26. At least one prominent scholar asserts that because "[t]he international community is much less anarchic and individualistic, and far more integrated than in the past. . . . [c]ommunity pressure . . . is such that it proves difficult for a State to avoid being bound by a new general rule." Antonio Cassese, *International Law* 155 (2d ed. 2005). However, this observation does not easily fit within the traditional understanding of customary international law.

Another and somewhat related source of international law is identified in Article 38 of ICJ Statute as "general principles of law recognized by civilized nations." The distinction between customary international law and general principles of law is ambiguous in modern doctrine. The classic distinction is that, while customary international law evolves from the actual day-to-day practice of states, "general principles" embrace the principles of private and public law administered in domestic courts where such principles are applicable to international relations. See J.L. Brierly, *The Law of Nations* 57-63 (Humphrey Waldock ed., 6th ed. 1963). The rubric of general principles, however, is now often understood to include not just such shared principles of domestic law, but also principles reflected on a widespread basis in state practice in the international arena, discernible from numerous international treaties or other standard-setting documents, or which are necessary as logical propositions of legal reasoning. See generally *Brownlie's, supra*, at 31-34; Mark Janis, *An Introduction to International Law* 58-62 (5th ed. 2008).

Also noteworthy are the "subsidiary" sources that endeavor to reveal the content of rules deriving from the primary sources of international law, including custom. In the words of Article 38 of the ICJ Statute, these subsidiary sources include "judicial decisions and the teachings of the most highly qualified publicists of the various nations." For US attitudes toward the sources of international law, see *Restatement (Third) of the Foreign Relations Law of the United States* §102 (1988).

Assertions that the Universal Declaration on Human Rights constitutes or reflects customary international law attempt to fit the Declaration into one of the standard sources of international law and thereby establish its legally binding character. But merely stating that the Universal Declaration on Human Rights is legally binding as customary international law, of course, does not make it so. Although the views of "highly qualified publicists" are a subsidiary source for determining customary international law, what counts primarily is the actual practice of states, in one form or another, demonstrating uniformity of expectation among them consistent with the Declaration, or states' recognition that the Declaration's norms reflect general principles of law. At the very least, however, the Montreal Statement and the Proclamation of Teheran, referred to above, were important indications that a law-making consensus as to the Declaration's legal status was evolving.

## 2.  Subsequent Developments in the Legal Significance of the Declaration

After the 1968 International Conference on Human Rights and its ensuing Proclamation of Teheran, an expanding group of scholars argued that the

Universal Declaration had developed into customary international law. Among these scholars was Professor Louis B. Sohn, who posited that the Universal Declaration is not only "an authoritative interpretation of the Charter obligations but also a binding instrument in its own right." Louis B. Sohn, *The Human Rights Law of the Charter*, 12 TEX. INTL. L.J. 129, 133 (1977). But while the Declaration has been invoked repeatedly by states at the United Nations, before international tribunals and in the diplomatic context, this is usually done without explicitly ascribing to the Declaration the force of law.

Indeed, in the instances where states have expressed their views regarding the basis of the obligation to observe human rights under international law, they usually have either mentioned the provisions of one or more of the human rights treaties or have relied upon the incorporation of the Declaration's articles into the human rights clauses of the UN Charter. See, for example, L.H. Legault, *Canadian Practice in International Law During 1979 as Reflected Mainly in Public Correspondence and Statements of the Department of External Affairs*, 18 CAN. Y.B. INTL. L. 301, 326 (1980):

> It is the view of the Canadian Government that the observance of human rights is obligatory under international law. The Canadian Government views the Universal Declaration of Human Rights as a valid interpretation and elaboration of the references to human rights and fundamental freedoms in the Charter of the United Nations. Consequently, the obligation on states to observe the human rights and fundamental freedoms enunciated in the Universal Declaration derives from their adherence to the Charter of the United Nations.

This view contrasts with the latter half of Professor Sohn's statement that the Declaration is "a binding instrument in its own right."

Insofar as the Executive Branch of the US government is concerned, explicit recognition that at least *some* articles of the Universal Declaration reflect or embody obligations for states as a matter of international law came in the US Memorial to the International Court of Justice in the *Hostages* case, 1980 I.C.J. 3, where, after marshalling traditional international law precedents to demonstrate "that States have an international legal obligation to observe certain minimum standards in their treatment of aliens," the government added the following brief passage about the nature and scope of fundamental human rights:

> It has been argued that no such standard can or should exist, but such force as that position may have had has gradually diminished as recognition of the existence of certain fundamental human rights has spread throughout the international community. The existence of such fundamental rights for all human beings, nationals and aliens alike, and the existence of a corresponding duty on the part of every State to respect and observe them, are now reflected, inter alia, in the Charter of the United Nations, the Universal Declaration of Human Rights and corresponding portions of the International Covenant on Civil and Political Rights. . . .
>
> In view of the universal contemporary recognition that such fundamental human rights exist . . . Iran's obligation to provide "the most

constant protection and security" to United States nationals in Iran includes an obligation to observe those rights. . . .

Memorial of the United States (*U.S. v. Iran*), 1980 I.C.J. Pleadings (Case Concerning United States Diplomatic and Consular Staff in Tehran) 182 (Jan. 12, 1980). As evidence of the fundamental human rights to which all individuals are entitled and which all states must guarantee, the Memorial cited Articles 3, 5, 7, 9, 12, and 13 of the Declaration, which cover, respectively, the right to life, liberty, and security of person; the prohibition of torture and cruel, inhuman, or degrading treatment or punishment; the right to equality before the law and to non-discrimination in its application; the prohibition of arbitrary arrest or detention; the right to privacy; and the right to freedom of movement.

Compare this catalogue of "fundamental rights" with that found in the following extract from the American Law Institute's *Restatement (Third) of the Foreign Relations Law of the United States.*

## Restatement (Third) of the Foreign Relations Law of the United States

§702 (1987)

### §702. Customary International Law of Human Rights

A state violates international law if, as a matter of state policy, it practices, encourages, or condones

(a)  genocide,
(b)  slavery or slave trade,
(c)  the murder or causing the disappearance of individuals,
(d)  torture or other cruel, inhuman, or degrading treatment or punishment,
(e)  prolonged arbitrary detention,
(f)  systematic racial discrimination, or
(g)  a consistent pattern of gross violations of internationally recognized human rights.

———

Although Section 702 remained unchanged from the initial draft in 1982 through the final version in 1987, the Reporters who drafted this section did add a comment that "[t]he list is not necessarily complete, and is not closed: human rights not listed in this section may have achieved the status of customary international law, and some rights might achieve that status in the future." Id. §702 comment a, at 162. Possible candidates listed for prohibited acts under customary international law are systematic religious discrimination, arbitrary deprivations of property, and gender discrimination (id. at 165-166), all of which are guaranteed by the Universal Declaration.

The *Restatement of the Foreign Relations Law of the United States*, which is currently being revised, roughly synthesizes the "blackletter" law as practiced by the United States courts and executive agencies engaged in foreign relations. However, US

government attitudes, while important and, indeed, perhaps controlling domestically, are only the views of one state and, thus, not necessarily determinative internationally. See generally Bruno Simma and Philip Alston, *The Sources of Human Rights
Law: Custom, Jus Cogens, and General Principles*, 12 AUSTL. Y.B. INTL. L. 12 (1992).
The following extract, based upon a six-year study of the practice of numerous UN
member states, reveals widespread support for the proposition that a substantial
number of the rights contained in the Universal Declaration had achieved the status of customary international law by the mid-1990s or before.


## International Law Association, Committee on the Enforcement of Human Rights Law

## Final Report on the Status of the Universal Declaration of Human Rights in National and International Law

ILA, Report of the Sixty-Sixth Conference 525, 544-549 (Buenos Aires 1995)*
(footnotes omitted)


Those who urge acceptance of the Declaration *in toto* as customary law are
in a clear minority, and there is insufficient state practice to support such a wide-
ranging proposition at present. . . .

However, there would seem to be little argument that many provisions of the
Declaration today do reflect customary international law. . . .

It would be presumptuous for the present report to pretend to analyse com-
prehensively each of the rights set forth in the Universal Declaration. Nevertheless,
the evidence of state practice identified by the rapporteur suggests the following
tentative conclusions with respect to the various articles of the Declaration.

*Articles 1, 2, and 7* express the fundamental right of equal treatment and non-
discrimination *with respect to guaranteed human rights* "without distinction of any
kind." It would seem difficult to deny the widespread acceptance of such a right to
equal treatment under the law, subject to the caveats below.

Of course, even with respect to protected rights, state practice does not
support a conclusion that there is full compliance with the principle of equality.
Women are prevented from exercising their human rights on an equal footing with
men in many states; distinctions based on religious and political beliefs are found
in many constitutions; and the effective guarantee of respective rights and obligations to the wealthy and the poor is often quite different.

One specific kind of discrimination, that based on race, is held by all commentators to be prohibited under customary international law, at least when it is
pervasive.

---

* One of the authors, Professor Hannum, served as Rapporteur of the Committee. He
and the chairman of the Committee, Professor Richard Lillich, were primarily responsible
for the preparation of this report. The substance of the report is reprinted in Hurst Hannum, *The Status of the Universal Declaration of Human Rights in National and International Law*,
25 GA. J. INT'L & COMP. L. 287 (1995/96). —Eds.

*Article 3*, guaranteeing "the right to life, liberty and security of person," may be too general to be a useful international norm, although protection of the right to life has been cited frequently as falling within customary international law. The prohibition against murder and causing "disappearances" is included in the Restatement's list, and the prohibition against the arbitrary deprivation of life has been referred to by many other commentators.

The prohibition against slavery in *article 4* is also universally held to form part of customary law; it is further prohibited by a series of widely ratified conventions.

*Article 5*'s prohibition against "torture or . . . cruel, inhuman or degrading treatment or punishment" is perhaps the most widely commented upon right in the Declaration (with the possible exception of the prohibition against racial discrimination). Its place in customary international law is confirmed by the *Restatement,* and many other sources could be cited. The Vienna World Conference on Human Rights "reaffirm[ed] that under human rights law and international humanitarian law, freedom from torture is a right which must be protected under all circumstances."

One of the most comprehensive examinations of the evidence of the status of the prohibition against torture in customary international law is the U.S. case of *Filartiga v. Peña-Irala,* in which the Court of Appeals for the Second Circuit found that the right to be free from torture is one of the rights conferred by international law "upon all people vis-à-vis their own governments." It relied for its conclusion on provisions of the Universal Declaration and a number of other international instruments (most unratified by the United States), national statutes, U.S. government statements, and the opinions of legal experts.

*Article 6* states simply that "[e]veryone has the right to recognition everywhere as a person before the law." Although no direct support for this principle is found in scholarly literature, it would seem impossible to deny the status of custom to such a fundamental expression of the essential equality and value of natural persons. The relegation of certain categories of individuals to the status of "non-persons" without rights may unfortunately exist in practice, but no state publicly adheres to such a view.

*Article 8*'s guarantee of an effective remedy before domestic courts for violations of human rights would seem to be an essential prerequisite to ensure the enjoyment of other human rights, but it is not generally included in lists of customary human rights and has not been the subject of significant domestic jurisprudence.

The prohibition in *article 9* against arbitrary arrest, detention, or exile is included in the *Restatement* list only if it is "prolonged;" other commentators have not made such a fine distinction, although the definition of what is "arbitrary" obviously limits the norm's usefulness in all but the most blatant cases. The International Court of Justice has stated:

> Wrongfully to deprive human beings of their freedom and to subject them to the physical constraint in conditions of hardship is in itself manifestly incompatible with the principles of the Charter of the United Nations, as well as with the fundamental principles enunciated in the Universal Declaration of Human Rights.

The prohibition against arbitrary detention is closely linked to provisions relating to the right to a fair trial, found in *articles 10 and 11*. A comprehensive survey of provisions relating to criminal justice recently concluded that "at times there seems to be an uncanny resemblance between the terminology of more recent constitutions and that of the Universal Declaration and the ICCPR [International Covenant on Civil and Political Rights]," and many observers include the right to a fair trial (without more specific examination of the components of the right) among those now guaranteed under customary law.

*Article 12*, which deals, inter alia, with the right to privacy, was cited by the U.S. Government in the *Hostages* case as being encompassed in customary law and is included in other major human rights treaties. However, the content of the right varies considerably among states, and the contours of that realm of personal privacy which is beyond the reach of government is perhaps too vague to be deemed a useful part of customary law at present.

*Article 13*, which is concerned with freedom of movement and the right to leave and return, also was cited by the United States in the *Hostages* case. Meron believes that these rights should be added to those considered to be part of customary law, but there does not seem to be sufficient consensus on this point at present to draw firm conclusions.

Despite widespread acceptance of the 1951 Convention on the Status of Refugees and the 1967 Protocol thereto, the right to seek (not to receive) asylum set forth in *article 14* has not been identified by commentators or states as falling within customary international law. However, returning a person to a country where he would be tortured or persecuted might well violate a developing customary norm against the *refoulement* of refugees.

German courts have recognized that the right to a nationality set forth in *article 15* is "the expression of customary international law in the sense of article 25 of the Basic Law [German Constitution]." The Inter-American Court of Human Rights referred to article 15 of the Declaration as supporting its conclusion that "[t]he right of every human being to a nationality has been recognized as such by international law." However, no other source for including this specific right within customary law has been found.

A German court has likewise found that "there is a consensus under international law that freedom of marriage is one of the fundamental human rights," citing the European Convention of Human Rights and *article 16* of the Universal Declaration.

The right to property, included in *article 17*, of the Universal Declaration, was omitted from both of the two human rights Covenants. However, a recent UN study on the right to property concludes that the Declaration's standards "became rules of customary international law and which as such were regarded as mandatory in the doctrine and practice of international law." One must assume that the right to property would be included as one of these "mandatory" rules, so long as one excludes from the right broader issues such as the international norms governing expropriation and other controversial topics. The rapporteur did observe that the right to property is not universally recognized, thus casting some doubt on its status or scope as a customary norm. Nonetheless, it would seem difficult to maintain that a state's power to expropriate or seize individual property is wholly unlimited.

*Article 18* guarantees the right to freedom of thought, conscience, and religion; its provisions were expanded upon in the 1981 Declaration on the Elimination of All Forms of Intolerance and of Discrimination Based on Religion or Belief adopted by the UN General Assembly. The Declaration's Preamble considers that "religion or belief, for anyone who professes either, is one of the fundamental elements in his conception of life and that freedom of religion or belief should be firmly respected and guaranteed." Although the Special Rapporteur on Iran of the UN Commission on Human Rights has stated that freedom of thought, conscience, and religion has "the character of *jus cogens*," the degree of de facto and de jure suppression of the practice of certain religions makes acceptance of such an assertion problematic. In addition, some Islamic countries have denied that Muslims have a right to change their religion.

Similarly, the widespread restrictions on freedom of opinion and expression, set forth in *article 19* of the Declaration, make it difficult to conclude that this provision is now part of customary international law, unless one accepts that the restrictions to freedom of expression which states believe are permissible can be so broad as to swallow the right itself. Similar observations might be made with respect to *article 20's* guarantee of the right of peaceful assembly.

Despite the arguments of some that a "right to democracy" may be emerging as a norm of international customary law, it is apparent that many states have not accepted *article 21's* guarantee of the right to participate in the political life of one's country.

*Articles 22 through 27* deal primarily with economic, social, and cultural rights, including social security, the right to work, the right to rest and leisure, the right to an adequate standard of living, the right to education, and the right to participate in cultural life. Despite the fact that the United States, in particular, has often denied the status of "rights" to these norms, they may enjoy wider international support than some of the civil and political rights traditionally emphasized in U.S. jurisprudence. However, they are rarely referred [to] by either commentators or courts in discussions of the content of customary international human rights law.

The following rights would seem to enjoy sufficiently widespread support as to be at least potential candidates for rights recognized under customary international law: the right to free choice of employment; the right to form and join trade unions; and the right to free primary education, subject to a state's available resources. Many rights included within these articles are closely related to other rights, such as the right to life and the prohibition against arbitrary discrimination. The Appeals Board of the Council of Europe has found that "[t]he absence of discrimination based on sex, and equal pay for workers of either sex constitute, at the present time, one of the general principles of law."

*Article 28*, which calls for "a social and international order" in which the Declaration's rights can be realized is clearly hortatory and insufficiently precise to constitute an international legal norm.

Although it does not set forth a substantive right, *article 29's* reference to permissible restrictions on rights might be considered as a general principle of international law, if it is interpreted to mean that international human rights may not be restricted arbitrarily. On the other hand, human rights treaties do permit limitations or restrictions on rights to be imposed on grounds other than those specified in article 29, which suggests that the literal terms of the article cannot he taken to represent international custom.

Finally, the savings clause in *article 30* is found in essentially all subsequent human rights treaties and may be seen as an admonition that the Declaration's provisions must be implemented in good faith, so as not to undermine its very purpose. This may simply reflect the general principle of international law which does not allow a treaty party to act in a way which would defeat the object and purpose of the treaty while purporting to rely on its provisions.

Firm conclusions as to the status of any of the provisions of the Universal Declaration of Human Rights in customary international law cannot be drawn without a much more thorough and comprehensive survey of state practice than is possible in the present report. However, these cursory observations may suggest the rights with respect to which such a survey might be most productive.

---

The above study found that, at the time of its completion in the mid 1990s, more than 90 national constitutions had included statements of fundamental rights inspired by the Universal Declaration of Human Rights, and Annex 2 of the study lists more than 200 judicial opinions from 27 countries citing the Declaration. In his study published in 2021, William Schabas confirmed the customary international law status of many of the rights affirmed in the Declaration. See Schabas, *supra.*

Whatever its precise legal character, the Universal Declaration of Human Rigths has had an elevated status in the international human rights system for some time. At the 1993 World Conference on Human Rights, more than 100 countries reaffirmed "their commitment to the purposes and principles contained in the Charter of the United Nations and the Universal Declaration of Human Rights" and emphasized that the Universal Declaration of Human Rights "is the source of inspiration and has been the basis for the United Nations making advances in standard setting as contained in the existing international human rights instruments." Vienna Declaration and Programme of Action, World Conference on Human Rights, pmbl, para. 3, 8, UN Doc. A/CONF.157/24 (Part 1) at 20-46 (1993). The General Assembly emphasized the need to observe the Declaration when it created the post of UN High Commissioner for Human Rights, whose mandate is to function within the framework of the Charter and the Universal Declaration of Human Rights. See G.A. Res. 48/141 (Dec. 20, 1993), Pmbl.

## Note: Other United Nations and Regional Human Rights Declarations

Since the adoption of the Universal of Declaration of Human Rights, the UN General Assembly has passed resolutions adopting numerous additional declarations articulating human standards on particular subjects of concern. Like the Universal Declaration, which was followed by the two covenants that fill out the International Bill of Human Rights, many of these declarations have been followed by treaties on the same subjects. Various ad hoc conferences convened by the United Nations—such as the 1993 World Conference on Human Rights, the Fourth World Conference on Women in 1995, the 2001 World Conference Against Racism, and the 2014 World Conference on Indigenous Peoples — have also resulted in UN member states collectively adopting standard-setting and programmatic declarations related to matters of human rights. In addition, specialized agencies of the United Nations, especially the UN Educational, Scientific, and Cultural Organization (UNESCO) and the International Labour Organization (ILO), have adopted topical statements or declarations on human rights. Even when not followed by treaties, the numerous declarations by the United Nations and its specialized agencies have contributed to a growing corpus of common understandings about human rights and, at least arguably, to new norms of customary international law. Examples of UN declarations or other normative statements are those involving minorities, indigenous peoples, self-determination, and criminal justice, as well as other declarations and resolutions that are referenced later in this chapter, elsewhere in this volume, or included in the Documentary Supplement. For a comprehensive compilation of UN instruments, including non-binding declarations, see the website of the UN Office of the High Commissioner for Human Rights, www.ohchr.org.

Regional intergovernmental organizations also have adopted resolutions proclaiming, or promoting compliance with, human rights standards. States participating in the inaugural session of the 1975 Conference (now Organization) on Security and Cooperation in Europe (CSCE) in Helsinki in 1975, for example, adopted a Final Act setting forth a program of cooperation in multiple spheres and declaring adherence to principles of human rights and, in particular, the Universal Declaration on Human Rights. See Helsinki Final Act, adopted Aug. 1, 1975. reprinted in 14 Int'l Legal Mat. 1292. At a subsequent session, in Copenhagen in 1990, the CSCE adopted a final document that set forth a wide and detailed range of human rights principles to which the participating states expressed commitment. See Final Document of the Copenhagen Meeting of the Conference on the Human Dimension of the CSCE, adopted June 29, 1990, reprinted in 29 Int'l Legal Mat. 1305. While it was explicitly understood by the participating states that texts such as the 1975 Helsinki and 1990 Copenhagen documents were not legally binding, the political impact of their having been adopted by all states by consensus has been considerable.

The Organization of American States (OAS) has been the source of important human rights declarations, in addition to promulgating treaties for ratification by the states members of that organization. In a development parallel to the UN's adoption in 1948 of the Universal Declaration on Human Rights, the OAS unanimously passed a resolution earlier that year proclaiming the American Declaration on the Rights and Duties of Man, the first of several human rights declarations to be adopted by OAS member states through the organization's General Assembly. The American Declaration (in the Documentary Supplement) in many ways mirrors the catalogue of civil, political, social, economic, and cultural rights subsequently included in the Universal Declaration of Human Rights. In what many describe as an attempt by its drafters to incorporate values of individual responsibility — in addition to values of individual autonomy — deemed common to many Western Hemispheric, especially Latin American, countries, the American Declaration also includes a recitation of various "duties" owed by the individual.

These include duties of self-development and productive engagement, to children, and to certain minimum obligations of citizenship such as paying taxes and participating in elections.

During the deliberations leading to the adoption of the American Declaration, it was uniformly considered that the American Declaration would not impose binding legal obligations on states. See Lawrence LeBlanc, *The OAS and the Promotion and Protection of Human Rights* 13 (1977). However, since its adoption the Declaration has functioned as a benchmark for action by the OAS in the area of human rights, particularly in regard to the work of its specialized institutions that are charged with promoting human rights throughout the hemisphere, as discussed in Chapter 8. Furthermore, to the extent the American Declaration incorporates many of the same rights expressed in the Universal Declaration of Human Rights that may be considered customary international law, it too may be understood to incorporate or reflect customary international law. According to the Inter-American Court of Human Rights, "by means of an authoritative interpretation, the member states of the Organization have signaled their agreement that the Declaration contains and defines the fundamental human rights referred to in the [OAS] Charter. . . . For the member states of the Organization, the Declaration is the text that defines the human rights referred to in the Charter." *Interpretation of the American Declaration of the Rights and Duties of Man Within the Framework of Article 64 of the American Convention on Human Rights,* Inter-Am. Ct. H.R., Advisory Opinion OC-10/89 of July 14, 1989, Ser. A No. 10, paras. 43, 45. An edited version of this Advisory Opinion appears and is discussed in Chapter 8.

While the Universal Declaration of Human Rights and other instruments by their terms apply to all segments of humanity, international standard-setting activities often have been aimed at developing norms concerning particular groups. As will be discussed in some detail below, standards have been or are being developed to address indigenous peoples and minorities, because of the vulnerable situations of these groups. International standards have been developed to address other groups in vulnerable situations as well, through UN declarations and other "soft law" instruments. For example, the following declarations have been adopted by the UN General Assembly: Declaration on the Human Rights of Individuals Who Are Not Nationals of the Country in which They Live, G.A. Res. 40/144 (1985); Declaration on Social and Legal Principles Relating to the Protection and Welfare of Children, with Special Reference to Foster Placement and Adoption Nationally and Internationally, G.A. Res. 41/85 (1986); Principles for the Protection of the Rights of Persons with Mental Illness and for the Improvement of Mental Health Care, G.A. Res. 46/119 (1991), Annex; Declaration of Commitment on HIV/AIDS, G.A. Res. S-26/2 (2001), Annex. None of these declarations has been succeeded by a binding convention specifically on the same subject, although UN conventions have been adopted on the rights of the child (declaration 1959, convention 1989), racial discrimination (declaration 1963, convention 1965), discrimination against women (declaration 1967, convention 1979), the prohibition of torture (declaration 1975, convention 1984), and persons with disabilities (declaration 1975, convention 2006).

Criminal justice has been a particular concern of UN declarations and other non-treaty instruments. The many instruments in this field constitute a regime of "soft law" that includes standards on prisoners' rights; juvenile offenders; judicial, prosecutorial, and police conduct; and related fields. One of the most influential of these instruments has been the Standard Minimum Rules for the Treatment of Prisoners, which was adopted by the UN Economic and Social Council in 1957. See E.S.C. Res. 663C (1957).

Space constraints prohibit more than a simple listing of some of the most important of these instruments, but their titles indicate the range of issues they address. The texts of these documents may be found in United Nations Office on Drugs and Crime. *Compendium of United Nations Standards and Norms in Crime Prevention and Criminal Justice* (2016), https://www.unodc.org/documents/justice-and-prison-reform/English_book.pdf.

### Treatment of Prisoners

Principles of Medical Ethics, G.A. Res. 37/194 (1982)

Safeguards Guaranteeing Protection of the Rights of Those Facing the Death Penalty, E.S.C. Res. 1984/50 (1984), Annex

Declaration of Basic Principles of Justice for Victims of Crime and Abuse of Power, G.A. Res. 40/34 (1985)

Body of Principles for the Protection of All Persons Under Any Form of Detention or Imprisonment, G.A. Res. 43/173 (1988)

Standard Minimum Rules for Non-Custodial Measures (The Tokyo Rules), G.A. Res. 45/110 (1990)

Basic Principles for the Treatment of Prisoners, G.A. Res. 45/111 (1990)

Standard Minimum Rules for the Treatment of Prisoners, E.S.C. Res. 2015/20 (2015)

### Juvenile Offenders

Standard Minimum Rules for the Administration of Juvenile Justice (The Beijing Rules), G.A. Res. 40/33 (1985)

Guidelines for the Prevention of Juvenile Delinquency (The Riyadh Guidelines), G.A. Res. 45/112 (1990)

United Nations Rules for the Protection of Juveniles Deprived of Their Liberty, G.A. Res. 45/113 (1990)

United Nations Rules for the Treatment of Women Prisoners and Non-custodial Measures for Women Offenders (the Bangkok Rules), G.A. Res. 65/229, Annex (2010)

### Standards for the Administration of Justice

Code of Conduct for Law Enforcement Officials, G.A. Res. 34/169 (1979)

Basic Principles on the Independence of the Judiciary, Seventh UN Congress on the Prevention of Crime and the Treatment of Offenders, Report Prepared by the Secretariat, UN Doc. A/CONF. 121/22/Rev. 1, at 58 (1985)

Basic Principles on the Use of Force and Firearms by Law Enforcement Officials, Eighth UN Congress on the Prevention of Crime and Treatment of Offenders, Report Prepared by the Secretariat, UN Doc. A/CONF.144/28, at 110 (1990)

Basic Principles on the Role of Lawyers, Eighth UN Congress on the Prevention of Crime and the Treatment of Offenders, Report Prepared by the Secretariat, UN Doc. A/CONF.144/28, at 117 (1990)

Guidelines on the Role of Prosecutors, Eighth UN Congress on the Prevention of Crime and the Treatment of Offenders, Report Prepared by the Secretariat, UN Doc. A/CONF.144/28, at 188 (1990)

Basic Principles on the Use of Restorative Justice Programmes in Criminal Matters, and Action to Promote Effective Crime Prevention, E.S.C. Res. 2002/12, Annex (2002)

United Nations Principles and Guidelines on Access to Legal Aid in Criminal Justice Systems, G.A. Res. 67/187, Annex (2012)

Improving the Quality and Availability of Statistics on Crime and Criminal Justice for Policy Development, E.S.C. Res. 2015/24 (July 21, 2015)

Doha Declaration on Integrating Crime Prevention and Criminal Justice, G.A. Res. 70/174 (December 17, 2015)

### *Comments and Questions*

1. As the readings indicate, the Universal Declaration is seen as at least partly embodying or reflecting customary international law. The Declaration is alternatively held, as asserted by the Canadian Department of External Affairs, to constitute an authoritative interpretation of the UN Charter's human rights clauses. The Declaration may also be regarded as articulating what are now considered to be general principles of law. What are the differences among these formulations? Do those differences have any practical consequences? See the discussion in Chapter 6 regarding the treatment of treaty and customary international law in US courts.

2. A declaration may be an initial step toward the formation of customary international law, as is widely understood to have been the case with the Universal Declaration of Human Rights. Can the votes of states in favor of a declaration and the collective act of adopting it themselves be seen as forms of practice contributing to the formation of customary international law? See *TOPCO/CALASIATIC v. Libyan Arab Republic*, International Arbitration Tribunal Merits (1977) 17 Int'l Legal Mat. 1 (1978) (René Dupuy, arbitrator) (finding applicable customary law in part on the basis of patterns of voting on UN General Assembly resolutions).

3. The UN Human Rights Council, which consists of 47 UN member states, like its predecessor the Commission on Human Rights, and other UN institutions have utilized the norms of the Universal Declaration of Human Rights as a matter of routine in evaluating the many country situations that have come before them. Note that the Human Rights Council explicitly specified that the Declaration, along with the UN Charter and relevant treaties, would be a basis of its "universal periodic review" (UPR) of the human rights records of UN member states. H.R.C. Res. 5/1, para. 1 (2007) (see Chapter 7 for a discussion of the UPR and other UN human rights procedures.) UN human rights bodies typically apply the Declaration without questioning or establishing its legal character, just as the US Department of State does in its annual reports surveying human rights practices around the world. See *Country Reports on Human Rights Practices*, U.S. Department of State, https://www.state.gov/

reports-bureau-of-democracy-human-rights-and-labor/country-reports-on-human-rig hts-practices/ (last visited on April 29, 2022). Does the foregoing prove that the Universal Declaration is customary international law or some other species of law? Or does it indicate that discussions about the legal character of the Universal Declaration are no longer very relevant, at least in some settings and to the extent that the Declaration does in fact express standards that are rooted in a strong consensus?

4. While the technical legal status of the Universal Declaration may be less significant today, lawyers still need to bear in mind the distinction between political and legal obligations. That distinction may be unimportant in a political forum, such as the UN Human Rights Council, but it remains vital if one is addressing a domestic or international judicial body. See Chapter 7. Nonetheless, the role that "soft law" instruments may play even in judicial or quasi-judicial settings can be significant, as discussed in the next section.

5. The United Nations has produced many more non-binding human rights instruments than treaties. Why is this so? Consider the following possible factors:

(a) The general unwillingness of states to subscribe to additional international human rights instruments;
(b) The realization of some states that declarations or model laws and guidelines, being just that, carry with them no international legal obligation;
(c) The greater flexibility that comes with applying non-binding norms and the need to maintain such flexibility in light of the diversity in country situations;
(d) The recognition that, even when an international human rights instrument has been ratified, it has little "legal bite" absent good faith compliance, so that it may be better to agree to declarations of "soft law," which implicitly accept that voluntary compliance is the sine qua non of effective international human rights law.

Is it "safer" for states to adopt declarations, guidelines, and principles, on the ground that they are non-binding? Consider the relationship between declarations and customary or general principles of law, discussed *supra*.

## III. THE EMERGENCE OF NEW HUMAN RIGHTS NORMS: THE RIGHTS OF INDIGENOUS PEOPLES AND MAYA LAND CLAIMS IN SOUTHERN BELIZE

Illustrating the conceptualization of new international human rights norms in a specific area of concern, substantially through declarations and other soft law, are the developments leading to a relatively new body of norms on indigenous peoples. These developments also illustrate the intersection of soft law, binding treaties, and general human rights principles.

### A. The Rights of Indigenous Peoples

Prominent among the more recent declarations to emerge from the United Nations and regional human rights systems are the UN Declaration on the Rights of Indigenous Peoples, G.A. Res. 62/295, adopted by the UN General Assembly in 2007, and the American Declaration on the Rights of Indigenous Peoples, AG/RES.2888 (XLVI-0/16), adopted by the OAS General Assembly in 2016. These declarations are the culmination of decades of efforts to elevate internationally the concerns of indigenous peoples and achieve recognition of their rights as such, led by a worldwide movement of indigenous communities and supportive nongovernmental organizations. See generally Ronald Niezen, *The Origins of Indigenism: Human Rights and the Politics of Identity* 29-52 (2003) (describing the origins and development of this movement). One of the authors of this volume has observed:

> As generally understood today within the international human rights system, the rubric of indigenous peoples includes the diverse Indian and aboriginal societies of the Western Hemisphere, the Inuit and Aleut of the Arctic, the aboriginal peoples of Australia, the Maori of Aoteoroa (New Zealand), Native Hawaiians and other Pacific Islanders, the Sami of the European far North, and at least many of the tribal or culturally distinctive non-dominant peoples of Asia and Africa. They are *indigenous* because their ancestral roots are embedded in the lands on which they live, or would like to live, much more deeply than the roots of more powerful sectors of society living on the same lands or in close proximity. And they are *peoples* in that they comprise distinct communities with a continuity of existence and identity that links them to the communities, tribes, or nations of their ancestral past.

S. James Anaya, *International Human Rights and Indigenous Peoples* 1 (2009) (emphasis in original). The UN and OAS indigenous rights declarations are central components of the international human rights system's response to the demands of these peoples, which historically have fallen victim to patterns and legacies of European empire building and colonial settlement, or to similar invasions, and which now seek to maintain and transmit to future generations their distinctive cultural attributes and associational bonds.

As pointed out in Chapter 1, the history of indigenous peoples has been one of conflict, conquest, marginalization, and even genocide. In many countries indigenous peoples have been treated as impediments to territorial expansion; in others they have been accorded special status, often in order to deny them full participation in the surrounding society.

France, England, Canada, the United States, and other states entered into treaties with Indian governments. Nonetheless, the conquering Europeans ultimately refused to recognize that indigenous societies were among the "civilized nations" that participated in the formulation of and enjoyed the benefits of international law. See S. James Anaya, *Indigenous Peoples in International Law* 19-34 (2d ed. 2004); Robert Williams, Jr., *The American Indian in Western Legal Thought* (1990).

In the United States, Chief Justice Marshall's acceptance of the doctrine of discovery in *Johnson v. McIntosh*, 21 U.S. (8 Wheat.) 543 (1823), and his later characterization of Indian tribes as "domestic dependent nations" in *Cherokee Nation v. Georgia*, 30 U.S. (5 Pet.) 1 (1831), confirmed that Indian tribes and their governments were subject to the jurisdiction of the United States. Only a year later, however, Marshall refined his characterization and described Indian tribes as "distinct people, divided into separate nations, independent of each other, and of the rest of the world, having institutions of their own, and governing themselves by their own laws." *Worcester v. Georgia*, 21 U.S. (6 Pet.) 515, 542-543 (1832). See generally Russell Barsh and John Henderson, *The Road* 50-61 (1980) (discussing the international and domestic legal status of Indian tribes).

As one author has noted, "Indian law is a complex field, and generalizations are subject to exceptions and can be misleading." Dean Suagee, *Self-Determination for Indigenous Peoples at the Dawn of the Solar Age*, 25 MICH. J. L. REFORM 671, 698 (1992). This is not the place to summarize the convoluted history of relations between the US federal government and Indian tribes, which generally led to the assertion of ever greater authority by the former over the latter until a change of policy in the 1970s. Congress has asserted "plenary power" to legislate over Indian tribes, but, while affirming that power, the federal courts have held that tribes retain residual governmental powers as an aspect of their original or inherent sovereignty. "Within their reservations, tribes generally retain all powers other than those they gave up in treaties, had taken away by an express act of Congress, or had taken away by implicit divestiture as a result of their dependent status." Id. at 699.

At whatever stage of such developments one chooses, however, it is abundantly clear that claims to resources, territory, and governmental powers have remained central to the concerns of Indian Nations and indigenous peoples elsewhere. The inherent conflict of authority—often debated in terms of sovereignty—between national and indigenous governments led the former to claim that relations with indigenous tribes were purely a matter of domestic jurisdiction. As a result, despite the existence of treaties between some indigenous peoples and European settler states, indigenous rights came to be regarded as outside the domain of international concern until well into the last century.

The International Labor Organization (ILO) had been concerned with the status and condition of indigenous workers since the 1920s, but no multilateral treaty addressed the issue of indigenous rights per se until the adoption in 1957 of ILO Convention No. 107 Concerning the Protection and Integration of Indigenous and Other Tribal and Semi-Tribal Populations in Independent Countries. For background on the ILO's involvement in indigenous issues, see Luis Rodriguez-Piñero, *Indigenous Peoples, Post Colonialism, and International Law: The ILO Regime (1919-1989)* (2005).

As movement at the UN toward a new declaration on indigenous rights progressed, the assimilationist orientation of Convention No. 107 was challenged and ultimately rejected by the ILO. In 1989, the ILO replaced Convention No. 107 with Convention No. 169 Concerning Indigenous and Tribal Peoples in Independent Countries, which entered into force in 1991. The basic theme of Convention 169 is indicated by the Convention's preamble, which recognizes "the aspirations of [indigenous] peoples to exercise control over their own institutions, ways of life and economic development and to maintain and develop their identities, languages and religions, within the framework of the States in which they live." The Convention requires, inter alia, that indigenous peoples be consulted whenever laws or administrative regulations affecting them are considered, and that "special measures" be adopted to safeguard indigenous interests. Additionally, the Convention recognizes rights of ownership over traditional lands and the right to maintain indigenous customs and institutions. Note also should be taken of the shift in terminology from indigenous "populations" to "peoples," the latter being understood to reflect an affirmation of indigenous group identity and collective rights. However, responding to state fears of indigenous self-determination claims, Article 1(3) of the Convention superfluously provides that "use of the term 'peoples' in this Convention shall not be construed as having any implications as regards the rights which may attach to the term under international law." States are obliged to report on their implementation of the Convention, and may be subject to complaints for failure to comply with its terms, through the ILO's regular and comprehensive supervisory machinery. See Lee Swepston, "The ILO Indigenous and Tribal Peoples Convention (No. 169): Eight Years After Adoption," in *The Human Rights of Indigenous Peoples* 17, 28-30 (Cynthia Price Cohen ed., 1998); Luis Rodriguez-Piñero, *Contemporary Consequences: The ILO Convention of Indigenous and Tribal Peoples (No. 169),* 12 LAW AND ANTHROPOLOGY 55 (2005). As of April of 2022, almost all Latin American states (14 of them) had ratified the Convention, while ten other states (Central African Republic, Denmark, Dominica, Fiji, Germany, Luxembourg, Nepal, Netherlands, Norway, and Spain) had done so.

When ILO Convention No. 169 came into being in 1989, drafting of a declaration on indigenous rights was underway at the United Nations, in a much more ambitious attempt to define international standards in this area. Formal steps to draft a UN declaration on indigenous rights began with the creation in 1982 of an expert Working Group on Indigenous Populations of the UN Sub-Commission on the Prevention of Discrimination and the Protection of Minorities (parts of the now expired machinery of the Commission on Human Rights). In 1994, a draft declaration was forwarded to the Commission on Human Rights, which in turn established its own working group to study the draft declaration. State delegates took a much more active role in the discussions of this working group than in those of the Sub-Commission working group, and the deliberations over the declaration proceeded for another several years amid ongoing disagreement over many aspects of the proposed declaration. Many governments and indigenous representatives continued to disagree over language related to issues such as collective rights, self-determination, the extent of indigenous self-government, and indigenous control over land, resources, and development activities. See, e.g., *Report of the working group established in accordance with Commission on Human Rights resolution 1995/32 of 3 March 1995 on its tenth session,* UN Doc. E/CN.4/2005/04 (2005).

As the life of the Commission working group came to a close with the reorganization of the UN human rights political machinery (see Chapter 7), a new draft text of the declaration emerged. In one of its first substantive acts upon replacing the Commission, the UN Human Rights Council approved that text in June 2006 and submitted it to the General Assembly. See H.R.C. Res. 2006/2 (2006). It would take another year of discussions, however, before the General Assembly would finally adopt the Declaration, see G.A. Res. 61/295 (2007), by a vote of 143 in favor, four against, and 11 abstentions. Notably, the four states that voted against the Declaration — Australia, Canada, New Zealand, and the United States — all eventually reversed positions and issued statements endorsing the Declaration.

With its 24 paragraphs of preamble and 46 operative articles, the Declaration is anchored in the complementary norms of equality and self-determination.

"Indigenous peoples and individuals" are declared in Article 2 to be "equal to all other peoples and individuals." Accordingly, Article 3 of the Declaration claims for indigenous peoples the same right of self-determination that is affirmed as a right of "All peoples" in common article 1 of the widely ratified International Covenant on Civil and Political Rights, and the International Covenant Economic, Social and Cultural Rights. Article 3 proclaims:

> Indigenous Peoples have a right to self-determination. By virtue of that right they freely determine their political status and freely pursue their their economic, social and cultural Development.

(See discussion of self-determination, *infra.*) On this grounding, the Declaration affirms the collective rights of indigenous peoples in relation to autonomy and self-government, culture, traditional knowledge, development, education, social services, the environment, and rights over traditional lands and natural resources; and it mandates respect for indigenous-state historical treaties and modern compacts.

The Declaration can be seen as remedial in nature, premised on the recognition "that indigenous peoples have suffered from historic injustices" and that they have been prevented from enjoying human rights (preamble, para. 6). Thus, the Declaration calls for affirmative measures to implement the rights affirmed. It generally mandates that "States, in consultation and cooperation with indigenous peoples, shall take the appropriate measures, including legislative measures, to achieve the ends of this Declaration" (Art. 37), and it further includes particularized requirements of affirmative measures in connection with most of the provisions. For a compilation of works on the Declaration and its background written by individuals close to its development, see *Making the Declaration Work: The United Nations Declaration on the Rights of Indigenous Peoples* (Claire Charters and Rodolfo Stavenhagen eds., 2009). See also *Reflections on the UN Declaration on the Rights of Indigenous Peoples* (Stephen Allan and Alexandra Xantaki eds., 2011); Mauro Barelli, *Seeking Justice in International Law: The Significance and Implications of the UN Declaration on the Rights of Indigenous Peoples* (2016).

As developments around the adoption of the UN Declaration on the Rights of Indigenous Peoples illustrate, there has been progressive movement toward an ever greater and more defined international consensus on norms of indigenous rights. In the "Outcome document" of the "high-level plenary meeting of the [UN] General Assembly known as the World Conference on Indigenous Peoples," in 2014, UN member states reaffirmed their "solemn commitment to respect, promote and advance and in no way diminish the rights of indigenous peoples and to uphold the principles of the Declaration." G.A. Res. 69/2 (2014), para. 4.

In a major development, in 2016, the Organization of American States, after 17 years of deliberation, adopted by acclamation the American Declaration on the Rights of Indigenous Peoples, which restates in similar terms the rights articulated by the UN Declaration, in particular for indigenous and tribal peoples in the Western Hemisphere. The OAS indigenous declaration adds prescriptions on indigenous law, peoples in voluntary isolation or initial contact, women, labor conditions, security, and genocide, among others. Notably, while the UN Declaration specifically avoids defining its scope of coverage, the American Declaration specifies that

"Self-identification as indigenous will be a fundamental criteria for determining to whom this Declaration applies" (Article I.2.).

The consensus on indigenous rights is also evidenced in numerous developments parallel to the adoption of the indigenous-specific declarations and ILO Convention No. 169. For example, the Convention on the Rights of the Child affirms in Article 30 that indigenous children "shall not be denied the right, in community with other members of his or her group, to enjoy his or her own culture, to profess and practice his or her own religion, or to use his or her own language." Resolutions adopted at the 1992 United Nations Conference on Environment and Development include provisions on indigenous people and their communities. The Rio Declaration, and the more detailed environmental program and policy statement known as Agenda 21, reiterate precepts of indigenous peoples' rights and seek to incorporate them within the larger agenda of global environmentalism and sustainable development. Resolutions adopted at subsequent major UN conferences — the 1993 World Conference on Human Rights, the 1994 UN Conference on Population and Development, the 1995 World Summit on Social Development, the Fourth World Conference on Women in 1995, the 2001 World Conference Against Racism, and the 2012 Conference on Sustainable Development (Rio + 20) — similarly include provisions that affirm or are consistent with prevailing normative assumptions in this regard.

Also noteworthy are the World Bank's policy prescriptions to guide its activities in financing development projects affecting indigenous peoples, the most recent iteration of which is found in its Environmental and Social Framework, which became effective on October 1st, 2018 and is discussed in Chapter 4. The Framework can be found at: https://thedocs.worldbank.org/en/doc/8377215 22762050108-0290022018/original/ESFFramework.pdf. Although its terms fall short of those advocated by indigenous groups, Standard 7 of the Framework establishes safeguards for "Indigenous Peoples/Sub-Saharan Historically Underserved Traditional Local Communities," including guidance for identifying conditions requiring their "free, prior, and informed consent" in relation to bank-funded projects affecting them.

These and other developments signify that indigenous peoples are undoubtedly now a matter of international concern and that there exists a certain core of recognized indigenous rights. For an edited compilation of documents and commentary synthesizing the developments in standard-setting and institutional arrangements concerning indigenous peoples, see S. James Anaya, *International Human Rights and Indigenous Peoples* (2009). See also Mattias Åhrén, *Indigenous Peoples' Status in the International Legal System* (2016); Ben Saul, *Indigenous Peoples and Human Rights: International and Regional Jurisprudence* (2016). Cf. Indigenous Peoples Rights International, *Digest: Legislation and Jurisprudence: Global, Regional, and National Developments*, January 2019-March 2022 (a compilation of summaries or extracts of recent jurisprudence and legislation on indigenous peoples from various jurisdictions), https://iprights.org/resources/publications/digest-legislat ion-and-jurisprudence-global-regional-and-national-developments.

As can be seen, the rights of indigenous peoples are specifically articulated in a number of international written instruments, most of which are aptly described as soft law instruments, in particular the UN and OAS instruments. Additionally, however, it is evident that these rights have their grounding in and are in some way derivative of the broader universe of human rights principles, including rights to non-discrimination, cultural integrity, property, and self-determination. This characteristic of indigenous rights can be seen in the interpretive comments and views of United Nations treaty bodies referenced *infra* pages 179-180, in relation to human rights treaties of general applicability. It is especially evident in the jurisprudence of the inter-American human rights institutions, as illustrated in the Maya land claims case discussed below. These interpretive comments and jurisprudence fall within the category of *secondary* soft law described by Professor Shelton, *supra*, page 125.

## B.    The Adjudication of Maya Land Claims by the Inter-American Commission on Human Rights

Representative of the kinds of claims asserted by indigenous peoples worldwide is the concerted effort by Maya communities of southern Belize to obtain respect for their rights to their traditional lands in the face of government-permitted logging and oil development on those lands. After initial failed attempts within the domestic judicial system, they took their case to the Inter-American Commission on Human Rights (whose jurisdiction and functions are addressed in Chapter 8), before which they asserted collective land and natural resource rights in terms similar to those set forth in the UN and OAS indigenous declarations and in ILO Convention No. 169. At the time that the Maya communities presented their petition to the Inter-American Commission and the Commission issued its findings and report, Belize was not a party to ILO Convention No. 169, and both the UN and OAS instruments on indigenous rights remained in draft form. The petition ultimately rested on an expansive interpretation of the American Declaration on the Rights and Duties of Man, referred to *supra*, page 144, which is not a treaty and which nowhere specifically mentions indigenous peoples. Extracts of the Commission's report on the case are included below, after the following note on important antecedents in the inter-American human rights system's jurisprudence on indigenous peoples.

### Note: The Awas Tingni and Dann cases

As the Maya petition was being considered by the Inter-American Commission on Human Rights, other indigenous claims were being processed by the Commission and its related institution, the Inter-American Court of Human Rights. In 1998, the Commission issued a confidential report finding Nicaragua in violation of the human rights of the indigenous Mayagna Community of Awas Tingni, because it failed to recognize the traditional land tenure of the community and instead authorized a major logging concession without the community's consent, a scenario similar to that of the Maya communities of Belize. See *Mayagna (Sumo) Awas Tingni Community v. Nicaragua*, Inter-Am Ct. H.R. Judgment on merits and reparations of August 31, 2001, Ser. C No. 79, paras. 25-26 (summarizing the report). A major difference between the situations is that, unlike Belize, Nicaragua through its constitutional and domestic legislation did recognize in general terms the communal property of indigenous communities. When Nicaragua, a party to the American Convention on Human Rights, did not respond to the Commission's report to the latter's satisfaction, the Commission initiated the procedure available under the Convention and submitted the case to the Inter-American Court. (See Chapter 8 for a description of this procedure.) After a lengthy proceeding, the Court issued a judgment in favor of Awas Tingni largely in agreement with the Commission's position. The Court held that the general right to property articulated in article 21 of the American Convention on Human Rights extends to the protection of traditional indigenous land tenure, even when that land tenure is not authorized by a deed of title or otherwise specifically recognized by the state. In interpreting Article 21, the Court stated:

> 143. Article 21 of the American Convention recognizes the right to private property. In this regard, it establishes: a) that "[e]veryone has the right to the use and enjoyment of his property;" b) that such use and enjoyment can be subordinate, according to a legal mandate, to "social interest;" c) that a person may be deprived of his or her property for reasons of "public utility or social interest, and in the cases and according to the forms established by law;" and d) that when so deprived, a just compensation must be paid.

> 144. "Property" can be defined as those material things which can be possessed, as well as any right which may be part of a person's patrimony; that concept includes all movables and immovables, corporeal and incorporeal elements and any other intangible object capable of having value. . . .

> 146. The terms of an international human rights treaty have an autonomous meaning, for which reason they cannot be made equivalent to the meaning given to them in domestic law. Furthermore, such human rights treaties are live instruments whose interpretation must adapt to the evolution of the times and, specifically, to current living conditions.

> 147. Article 29(b) of the Convention, in turn, establishes that no provision may be interpreted as "restricting the enjoyment or exercise of any right or freedom recognized by virtue of the laws of any State Party or by virtue of another convention to which one of the said states is a party".

> 148. Through an evolutionary interpretation of international instruments for the protection of human rights, taking into account applicable norms of interpretation and pursuant to article 29(b) of the Convention — which precludes a restrictive interpretation of rights —, it is the opinion of this Court that article 21 of the Convention protects the right to property in a sense which includes, among others, the rights of members of the indigenous communities within the framework of communal property, which is also recognized by the Constitution of Nicaragua.

> 149. Given the characteristics of the instant case, some specifications are required on the concept of property in indigenous communities. Among indigenous peoples there is a communitarian tradition regarding a communal form of collective property of the land, in the sense that ownership of the land is not centered on an individual but rather on the group and its community. Indigenous groups, by the fact of their very

existence, have the right to live freely in their own territory; the close ties of indigenous people with the land must be recognized and understood as the fundamental basis of their cultures, their spiritual life, their integrity, and their economic survival. For indigenous communities, relations to the land are not merely a matter of possession and production but a material and spiritual element which they must fully enjoy, even to preserve their cultural legacy and transmit it to future generations.

Id., paras. 143-149 (notes omitted).

The Court in *Awas Tingni* determined that indigenous peoples not only have property rights to their traditional lands but that they are also entitled under the American Convention to affirmative state measures to secure those rights through land titling or other appropriate mechanism. The Court found that Nicaragua violated Article 21 by not taking such affirmative measures and by granting the logging concession. Id., paras. 153-155. It further found that, because the Nicaraguan administrative and judicial systems failed to respond adequately to repeated petitions from Awas Tingni for land titling and to halt the concession, Nicaragua violated Article 25 of the Convention, which affirms the right to judicial protection, in connection with Articles 1 and 2, which obligate state parties to adopt measures necessary to secure the enjoyment of fundamental rights. See generally S. James Anaya and Claudio Grossman, *The Case of Awas Tingni v. Nicaragua: A New Step in the International Law of Indigenous Peoples*, 19 ARIZ. J. INT'L & COMP. LAW 1 (2002).

The "evolutionary interpretation" of the right to property in relation to indigenous lands was expanded in a subsequent decision that addressed a dispute concerning the Western Shoshone people of the Great Basin region of the United States. In the case of *Mary and Carrie Dann v. United States*, the Inter-American Commission extended the interpretation of the right to property of the American Convention on Human Rights advanced in the *Awas Tingni* case to the similar property rights provision of the American Declaration on the Rights and Duties of Man, emphasizing the due process and equal protections prescriptions that attach to indigenous property interests in lands and natural resources. See *Mary and Carrie Dann v. United States*, Case 11.140, Inter-Am. Comm'n. H.R., Report No. 75/02, OAS Doc. OEA/Ser.L/V/II.117 Doc. 5 rev. 1, at 860 (2003). The case arose from the refusal of Western Shoshone sisters Mary and Carrie Dann to submit to the permit system imposed by the United States for grazing on large parts of Western Shoshone traditional lands. Faced with efforts by the United States government to forcibly stop them from grazing cattle without a permit and to impose substantial fines on them for doing so, the Danns argued that the permit system contravened Western Shoshone land rights. The United States conceded that the land in question was Western Shoshone ancestral land but contended that Western Shoshone rights in the land had been "extinguished" through a series of administrative and judicial determinations.

The Commission rejected the United States theory of extinguishment as out of step with modern human rights concepts, in light of a lack of procedural fairness in the domestic proceedings upon which that theory relied. See generally John O'Connell, *Constructive Conquest in the Courts: A Legal History of the Western Shoshone Lands Struggle - 1864 to 1991*, 42 NAT. RESOURCES J. 765 (2003). Instead, the Commission found that the United States had "failed to ensure the Danns' right to property under conditions of equality contrary to Articles II [right to equal protection, XVIII [right to fair trial] and XXIII [right to property] of the American Declaration in connection with their claims to property rights in the Western Shoshone ancestral lands." Report 75/02, *supra*, para. 172.

In applying and interpreting the American Declaration in the *Dann* case, the Commission was explicit in its reliance on developments and trends in the international legal system regarding the rights of indigenous peoples. Significantly the Commission referred to its own Proposed American Declaration on the Rights of Indigenous Peoples, a document that was a precursor to the indigenous rights declaration referenced earlier that was adopted much later by the OAS General Assembly. See *Annual Report of the Inter-American Commission on Human Rights 1996*, ch. IV, OEA/Ser.L/V/II.95, Doc. 7 rev. (1997) (providing the text and the background of the Inter-American Commission's proposed declaration). The Commission affirmed that the "basic principles reflected in many of the provisions" of its proposed declaration, "including aspects of [its] article XVIII, reflect general international legal principles developing out of and applicable inside and outside of the inter-American system and to this extent are properly considered in interpreting and applying the provisions of the American Declaration in the context of indigenous peoples." Report 75/02, *supra*, para. 129. Article XVIII of the proposed declaration provided for the protection of traditional forms of land tenure in terms similar to those found ILO Convention 169, which the Commission also highlighted in its analysis. Id., paras. 127-128.

With the *Awas Tingni* and *Dann* decisions in hand, the Inter-American Commission proceeded to issue its report in the Maya case.

## Maya Indigenous Communities v. Belize

Case 12.053, Inter-Am. Comm'n H.R, Report 40/04, OAS. Doc. OEA/Ser.L/V/II.122, Doc. 5 rev. 1 (2005)

### I. SUMMARY

1. This report concerns a petition presented to the Inter-American Commission of Human Rights (the "Commission") against the State of Belize (the "State" or "Belize") on August 7, 1998 by the Indian Law Resource Center and the Toledo Maya Cultural Council (the "Petitioners"). The petition claims that the State is responsible for violating rights under the American Declaration of the Rights and Duties of Man (the "American Declaration") that the Mopan and Ke'kchi Maya People of the Toledo District of Southern Belize (the "Maya people of the Toledo District" or the "Maya people") are alleged to have over certain lands and natural resources.

2. The Petitioners claim that the State has violated . . . the American Declaration in respect of lands traditionally used and occupied by the Maya people, by granting logging and oil concessions in and otherwise failing to adequately protect those lands, failing to recognize and secure the territorial rights of the Maya people in those lands, and failing to afford the Maya people judicial protection of their

rights and interests in the lands due to delays in court proceedings instituted by them. According to the Petitioners, the State's contraventions have impacted negatively on the natural environment upon which the Maya people depend for subsistence, have jeopardized the Maya people and their culture, and threaten to cause further damage in the future. . . .

45. The Petitioners contend that the State of Belize is responsible for violations of the following human rights of the Maya people under the American Declaration, in conjunction with assorted other international instruments . . . : Articles XXIII (right to property), III (right to religious freedom), VI (right to family and protection thereof), XIV (right to take part in the cultural life of the community), I (right to life), XI (right to preservation of health and well-being) and XX (right to participate in government) all in relation to the logging and oil concessions granted by the government on lands used and occupied by the Maya in the Toledo District; Articles II (right to equality under the law) and XXIII (right to property) and general principles of international law concerning the failure of Belize to recognize and secure Maya territorial rights more broadly; and Article XVIII (right to a fair trial) in respect of the ineffectiveness of efforts by the Maya people to obtain domestic redress for their situation. . . .

### IV. ANALYSIS

#### A. APPLICATION AND INTERPRETATION OF THE AMERICAN DECLARATION OF THE RIGHTS AND DUTIES OF MAN

85. . . . . [T]he American Declaration constitutes a source of international legal obligation for all member states of the Organization of American States, including Belize. [To support this proposition, the Commission cited Advisory Opinion OC-10/89 of the Inter-American Court of Human Rights, which is quoted in Chapter 8] Moreover, the Commission is empowered under Article 20 of its Statute and Articles 49 and 50 of its Rules of Procedure to receive and examine any petition that contains a denunciation of alleged violations of the human rights set forth in the American Declaration in relation to OAS member states that are not parties to the American Convention.

86. According to the jurisprudence of the inter-American human rights system, the provisions of its governing instruments, including the American Declaration, should be interpreted and applied in context of developments in the field of international human rights law since those instruments were first composed and with due regard to other relevant rules of international law applicable to member states against which complaints of human rights violations are properly lodged.

87. In particular, the organs of the inter-American system have previously held that developments in the corpus of international human rights law relevant to interpreting and applying the American Declaration may be drawn from the provisions of other prevailing international and regional human rights instruments. . . .

88. Accordingly, in determining the present case, the Commission will, to the extent appropriate, interpret and apply the pertinent provisions of the American Declaration in light of current developments in the field of international human

rights law, as evidenced by treaties, custom and other relevant sources of international law.

### B. The Maya Communities of the Toledo District of Belize and International Human Rights Pertaining to Indigenous Peoples

89. In determining the norms and principles of human rights law that are properly applicable in the present case, the Commission first observes that the Petitioners claims relate to human rights violations that are alleged to have been committed against the members of an indigenous people located in the Toledo District of Belize.

90. According to the information available, the Toledo District is one of two administrative districts in Southern Belize, which together are home to approximately 14,000 Mopan and Ke'kchi-speaking Maya people. The Toledo District encompasses an area of approximately 1,500 square miles, bordered roughly by the Monkey River and the Maya Mountains in the north, the Gulf of Honduras in the East, and Belize's border with Guatemala to the West and South. . . .

95. In this regard, a review of pertinent treaties, legislation and jurisprudence reveals the development over more than 80 years of particular human rights norms and principles applicable to the circumstances and treatment of indigenous peoples. Central to these norms and principles has been the recognition of the need for special measures by states to compensate for the exploitation and discrimination to which these societies have been subjected at the hands of the non-indigenous.

96. In the context of the inter-American human rights system, this Commission has long recognized and promoted respect for the rights of indigenous peoples of this Hemisphere. In the Commission's 1972 resolution on the problem of "Special Protection for Indigenous Populations - Action to combat racism and racial discrimination," for example, the Commission proclaimed that "for historical reasons and because of moral and humanitarian principles, special protection for indigenous populations constitutes a sacred commitment of the states." This notion of special protection has also been considered in a number of country and individual reports adopted by the Commission and has been recognized and applied in the context of numerous rights and freedoms under both the American Declaration and the American Convention on Human Rights, including the right to life, the right to humane treatment, the right to judicial protection and to a fair trial, and the right to property. . . .

97. The Commission's approach in acknowledging and giving effect to particular protections in the context of human rights of indigenous populations is consistent with developments in the field of international human rights law more broadly. Special measures for securing indigenous human rights have been recognized and applied by other international and domestic bodies, including the Inter-American Court of Human Rights, the International Labour Organisation, the United Nations through its Human Rights Committee and Committee to Eradicate [sic] All Forms of Racial Discrimination, and the domestic legal systems of states.

98. In deciding upon the complaints in the present petition, therefore, the Commission will afford due consideration to the particular norms and principles of international human rights law governing the individual and collective interests

of indigenous peoples, including consideration of any special measures that may be appropriate and necessary in giving proper effect to these rights and interests.

### C. RIGHT TO PROPERTY

99. In their complaint, the Petitioners contend that the State's practice in granting numerous logging concessions and at least one oil concession on lands used and occupied by the Maya people in the Toledo District has violated the Maya people's right to property under Article XXIII of the American Declaration. The Petitioners also contend that this practice of granting concessions is a component of a more general failure of the State of Belize to recognize and effectively secure the territorial rights of the Maya people, also contrary to their right to property.

100. Article XXIII, of the American Declaration provides:

> Every person has a right to own such private property as meets the essential needs of decent living and helps to maintain the dignity of the individual and of the home. . . .

### 1. The Right to Property and Indigenous Peoples under Contemporary International Human Rights Law

112. In evaluating the nature and content of the right to property under Article XXIII of the American Declaration in the context of the present case, several aspects of the evolution of international human rights protections pertaining to indigenous peoples are particularly pertinent.

113. Among the developments arising from the advancement of indigenous human rights has been recognition that rights and freedoms are frequently exercised and enjoyed by indigenous communities in a collective manner, in the sense that they can only be properly ensured through their guarantee to an indigenous community as a whole. The right to property has been recognized as one of the rights having such a collective aspect.

114. More particularly, the organs of the inter-American human rights system have acknowledged that indigenous peoples enjoy a particular relationship with the lands and resources traditionally occupied and used by them, by which those lands and resources are considered to be owned and enjoyed by the indigenous community as a whole and according to which the use and enjoyment of the land and its resources are integral components of the physical and cultural survival of the indigenous communities and the effective realization of their human rights more broadly. . . .

115. The Commission, through its reports on individual petitions and on the general situation of human rights in member states, as well as in its authorization of precautionary measures, has pronounced upon the necessity of states to take the measures aimed at restoring, protecting and preserving the rights of indigenous peoples to their ancestral territories. It has also held that respect for the collective rights of property and possession of indigenous people to the ancestral lands and territories constitutes an obligation of OAS member states, and that the failure to fulfill this obligation engages the international responsibility of the states. According to the Commission, the right to property under the American Declaration must be interpreted and applied in the context of indigenous communities with due

consideration of principles relating to the protection of traditional forms of ownership and cultural survival and rights to land, territories and resources. These have been held to include the right of indigenous peoples to legal recognition of their varied and specific forms and modalities of their control, ownership, use and enjoyment of territories and property, and the recognition of their property and ownership rights with respect to lands, territories and resources they have historically occupied.

116. The Inter-American Court [in the *Awas Tingni* case] has taken a similar approach to the right to property in the context of indigenous peoples, by recognizing the communal form of indigenous land tenure as well as the distinctive relationship that indigenous people maintain with their land. . . .

117. Accordingly, the organs of the inter-American human rights system have recognized that the property rights protected by the system are not limited to those property interests that are already recognized by states or that are defined by domestic law, but rather that the right to property has an autonomous meaning in international human rights law. In this sense, the jurisprudence of the system has acknowledged that the property rights of indigenous peoples are not defined exclusively by entitlements within a state's formal legal regime, but also include that indigenous communal property that arises from and is grounded in indigenous custom and tradition. . . .

118. This interpretive approach is supported by the terms of other international instruments and deliberations, which serve as further indicia of international attitudes on the role of traditional system of land tenure in modern systems of human rights protection. The International Labour Organisation Convention (N° 169) concerning Indigenous and Tribal Peoples, for example, affirms indigenous peoples' rights of ownership and possession of the lands they traditionally occupy, and requires governments to safeguard those rights and to provide adequate procedures to resolve land claims. Additionally, both the Proposed American Declaration on the Rights of Indigenous Peoples and the Draft United Nations Declaration on the Rights of Indigenous Peoples affirm the rights of indigenous people to own, develop, control and use the lands and resources they have traditionally owned or otherwise occupied and used.

119. In this connection, the Commission believes that respect for and protection of the private property of indigenous peoples on their territories is equivalent in importance to non-indigenous property, and, as discussed further below, is mandated by the fundamental principle of non-discrimination enshrined in Article II of the American Declaration. . . .

120. For the organs of the inter-American system, the protection of the right to property of the indigenous people to their ancestral territories is a matter of particular importance, because the effective protection of ancestral territories implies not only the protection of an economic unit but the protection of the human rights of a collective that bases its economic, social and cultural development upon their relationship with the land. It has been the Commission's longstanding view that the protection of the culture of indigenous peoples encompasses the preservation of "the aspects linked to productive organization, which includes, among other things, the issue of ancestral and communal lands. . . ."

2. The Situation of the Maya People of the Toledo District

121. In the context of the norms and principles outlined above, it is necessary to determine whether the Maya people of the Toledo District are the beneficiaries of a right to property under Article XXIII of the Declaration in respect of lands in the southern region of Belize and, if so, the nature of the State's obligations concerning respect for and protection of this right.

### a. The Right to Property and the Traditional Lands of the Maya People in the Toledo District

122. . . . . [T]he Commission is satisfied, based upon the information available, that the members of the Mopan and Ke'kchi Maya communities of the Toledo District of Southern Belize constitute an indigenous people whose ancestors inhabited the Toledo District prior to the arrival of the Europeans and the colonial institutions that gave way to the present State of Belize. . . .

127. Based upon the arguments and evidence before it, the Commission is satisfied that the Mopan and Ke'kchi Maya people have demonstrated a communal property right to the lands that they currently inhabit in the Toledo District. These rights have arisen from the longstanding use and occupancy of the territory by the Maya people, which the parties have agreed pre-dated European colonization, and have extended to the use of the land and its resources for purposes relating to the physical and cultural survival of the Maya communities. . . .

131. The Commission also considers that this communal property right of the Maya people is the subject of protection under Article XXIII of the American Declaration, interpreted in accordance with the principles outlined above relating to the situation of indigenous peoples, including the obligation to take special measures to ensure recognition of the particular and collective interest that indigenous people have in the occupation and use of their traditional lands and resources. In this connection, the Maya people's communal property right has an autonomous meaning and foundation under international law. While the Commission has considered the legislation and jurisprudence of certain domestic legal systems in identifying international legal developments relating to the status and treatment of indigenous people, the communal property right of the Maya people is not dependent upon particular interpretations of domestic judicial decisions concerning the possible existence of aboriginal rights under common law.

132. Accompanying the existence of the Maya people's communal right to property under Article XXIII of the Declaration is a correspondent obligation on the State to recognize and guarantee the enjoyment of this right. In this regard, the Commission shares the view of the Inter-American Court of Human Rights that this obligation necessarily requires the State to effectively delimit and demarcate the territory to which the Maya people's property right extends and to take the appropriate measures to protect the right of the Maya people in their territory, including official recognition of that right [citing the *Awas Tingni* case]. In the Commission's view, this necessarily includes engaging in effective and informed consultations with the Maya people concerning the boundaries of their territory, and that the traditional land use practices and customary land tenure system be taken into account in this process. . . .

135. The Commission therefore concludes that the Mopan and Ke'kchi Maya people have demonstrated a communal property right to the lands that they currently inhabit in the Toledo District, that this communal property right of the Maya people is the subject of protection under Article XXIII of the American Declaration, and that the State has failed to delimit, demarcate and title or otherwise establish the legal mechanisms necessary to clarify and protect the territory on which their right exists. Accordingly, the Commission finds that the State of Belize violated the right to property enshrined in Article XXIII of the American Declaration to the detriment of the Maya people.

### b. The Granting of Concessions in the Toledo District

136. The Petitioners have also argued that by granting concessions to companies to extract logging and oil resources from the traditional lands of the Maya people, without properly delimiting and demarcating those lands and without any effective consultation with or agreement by the affected communities, the State has similarly violated the right to property of the Maya people under Article XXIII of the American Declaration. . . .

140. In evaluating this aspect of the Petitioners' complaint, the Commission considers that the right to use and enjoy property may be impeded when the State itself, or third parties acting with the acquiescence or tolerance of the State, affect the existence, value, use or enjoyment of that property without due consideration of and informed consultations with those having rights in the property. . . .

142. The Commission . . . observes in this connection that one of the central elements to the protection of indigenous property rights is the requirement that states undertake effective and fully informed consultations with indigenous communities regarding acts or decisions that may affect their traditional territories. As the Commission has previously noted, Articles XVIII and XXIII of the American Declaration specially oblige a member state to ensure that any determination of the extent to which indigenous claimants maintain interests in the lands to which they have traditionally held title and have occupied and used is based upon a process of fully informed consent on the part of the indigenous community as a whole. This requires, at a minimum, that all of the members of the community are fully and accurately informed of the nature and consequences of the process and provided with an effective opportunity to participate individually or as collectives. In the Commission's view, these requirements are equally applicable to decisions by the State that will have an impact upon indigenous lands and their communities, such as the granting of concessions to exploit the natural resources of indigenous territories.

143. Based upon the record in the present case, the Commission finds that the State granted logging and oil concessions to third parties to utilize property and resources that could fall within the traditional lands of the Maya people of the Toledo District, and that the State failed to take appropriate or adequate measures to consult with the Maya people concerning these concessions. . . .

144. The Commission therefore concludes that logging and oil concessions were granted by the State to third parties to utilize property and resources that could fall within the traditional lands of the Maya people of the Toledo District and that the State failed to take appropriate or adequate measures to consult with the

Maya people concerning these concessions. Based upon these acts and omissions, the Commission finds that the State of Belize further violated the right to property enshrined in Article XXIII of the American Declaration to the detriment of the Maya people. . . .

[The Commission went on to find violations of Article II of the Declaration (equal protection under the law), on the ground that Belize failed to protect Maya customary land tenure under terms equal to the protections provided non-indigenous forms of property, and Article XVIII (right to judicial protection), because of the ineffectiveness of the judicial proceedings initiated by Maya parties to attempt to resolve the land and resource issues. The Commission recommended that Belize adopt legislative and administrative measures to identify and recognize Maya lands and related rights according to Maya customary tenure; that it abstain from any act that might result in its agents, or private parties acting with their permission or acquiescence, that would undermine the property interests of the Maya people; and that it repair the environmental damage caused by the logging concessions.]

---

Continued inaction by the Government of Belize following the Inter-American Commission's decision led two Maya villages to return to the domestic courts in an effort to secure their land rights, with the backing of the same group of Maya leaders that had taken the matter to the Commission. In a remarkable decision, the trial court judge of the Supreme Court of Belize found in favor of the villages, basing his affirmation of Maya land rights on the equality and property rights provisions of the Belize Constitution, interpreting those provisions in light of Inter-American Commission's decision and the then newly-adopted UN Declaration on the Rights of Indigenous Peoples. See *Cal et al. v. Attorney General (Claims Nos. 171 and 172 of 2007)*, Belize S. Ct. Judgment of 18 October 2007.

The government of Belize, however, soon adopted the position that the judgment only applied to the two claimant Maya villages and continued to administer lands claimed by other Maya villages as government lands. This prompted another lawsuit before the same judge, this one a class action on behalf of all the Maya villages. The judge again ruled in favor of the Maya, reiterating his earlier analysis of the relevant constitutional norms. See *Maya Leaders Alliance et al. v. Attorney General (Claim No. 366 of 2008)*, Belize S. Ct. Judgment of June 28, 2010. This judgment was largely upheld on appeal, see [2015] CCJ 15 (AJ) (Caribbean Court of Justice), and in a consent order the government agreed to "develop the legislative, administrative and/or other measures necessary to create an effective mechanism to identify and protect the property and other rights arising from Maya customary land tenure, in accordance with Maya customary laws and land tenure practices," Consent Order of April 22, 2015, CCJ Appeal No. BZCV2014/002. As of this writing, however, that commitment remains unfulfilled.

For an overview of jurisprudence of the Inter-American Commission on Human Rights and Inter-American Court of Human Rights regarding indigenous peoples' rights over lands and resources, see Inter-Am. Comm. H.R., *Indigenous and Tribal Peoples' Rights Overs Their Ancestral Lands and Natural Resources*, OAS Doc.

OEA Ser. L/V/II, Doc. 56/09 (2009). Since its judgment in *Awas Tingni*, the Inter-American Court itself has upheld and expanded upon the interpretation advanced in that case of the right to property, in a series of subsequent cases. See, e.g., *Yakye Axa Indigenous Community v. Paraguay*, Inter-Am. Ct. H.R. (Ser. C) No. 125 (17 June 2005); *Moiwana Community v. Suriname*, Inter-Am. Ct. H.R. (Ser. C) No. 145 (8 Feb. 2006); *Sawhoyamaxa Indigenous Community v. Paraguay*, Inter-Am. Ct. H.R. (Ser. C) No. 146 (Mar. 29, 2006); *Saramaka People v. Suriname*, Inter-Am. Ct. H.R. (Ser. C) No. 172 (28 Nov. 2007); *Pueblos Indígena Kichwa de Sarayaku v. Ecuador*, Inter-Am. Ct. H.R. (Ser. C.) No. 245 (June 27, 2012); *Garifuna Community of Punta Piedra v. Honduras*, Inter-Am. Ct. H.R. (Ser. C) No. 304 (Oct. 8, 2015); *Kaliña and Lokono Peoples v. Suriname*, Inter-Am. Ct. H.R. (Ser. C) No. 309 (Nov. 25, 2015); *Kuna Indigenous People of Madungandi and the Emberá Indigenous People of Bayamo and their Members v. Panama*, Inter-Am. Ct. H.R., (Ser. C), No. 284 (Oct. 14, 2014); *Indigenous Communities of the Lhaka Honhat Association (Our Land) v. Argentina*, Inter-Am. Ct. H.R. (Ser. C), No. 400 (Feb. 6, 2020).

The African human rights systems has also addressed indigenous issues, reinforcing prevailing normative assumptions globally about indigenous rights. Notably, in the case of *Endorois v. Kenya*, discussed in Chapter 9, the African Commission and Peoples Rights essentially transposed the jurisprudence of the inter-American system to interpret in a similar manner the related provisions on peoples' rights in the African Charter on Human and Peoples Rights. See African Commission on Human and Peoples' Rights, *Centre for Minority Rights Development (Kenya) and Minority Rights Group International on behalf of Endorois Welfare Council v Kenya*, Case No. 276/2003 (Report of May 2009). The decision was approved by the African Union at its January 2010 session. Following the lead of its Working Group of Experts on Indigenous Populations/Communities, the African Commission considers certain tribal and other groups that have marks of disadvantage and strong roots in defined territories to fall within the rubric of "indigenous." By contrast, the Association of Southeast Asian Nations (ASEAN) Intergovernmental Commission on Human Rights has thus far been unable to adopt a normative statement on indigenous peoples, despite the urging of groups self-identifying as indigenous within the region.

## Comments and Questions

1. In interpreting the right to property of the American Declaration on the Rights and Duties of Man, is the Inter-American Commission on Human Rights stating a rule of binding international law? If so, in what sense? Recall that the American Declaration is a resolution of the OAS General Assembly, not a treaty. But, like the Universal Declaration on Human Rights, the American Declaration could be deemed to reflect or incorporate customary international law. For their part, the Inter-American Commission and the Inter-American Court on Human Rights have consistently taken the view that the Declaration is an authoritative statement of the human rights that states commit to uphold under the general human rights clauses of the OAS Charter, which is a treaty. See Report 75/02 (*Dann v United States*), *supra*, paras. 162-164; *Interpretation of the American Declaration of the Rights and Duties of Man Within the Framework of Article 64 of the American Convention*

*on Human Rights,* Inter-Am. Ct. H.R. (Ser. A) No. 10, paras. 43, 45 (1989), discussed in Chapter 8.

2. The Commission in the *Maya Communities* and *Dann* cases interpreted the right to property to extend to indigenous peoples' customary or traditional land tenure systems. Indigenous land tenure systems typically derive from patterns of land use and occupancy prior to the existence of the state and have their origins apart from the state's formal property regime. Is it plausible that states, when they adopted the property rights provision of Article XXIII of the American Declaration in 1948, had in mind protection of traditional indigenous land tenure? If not, on what basis does the Commission read such protection into Article XXIII? Note that in both cases, the Commission refers to, among other sources, the Proposed American Declaration on the Rights of Indigenous Peoples. Is this use of a draft instrument appropriate, particularly when the Commission itself drafted the text on which it relies? In its response to the Commission's report in the *Dann* case, the United States disputed the Commission's references to the proposed declaration, arguing that—since the instrument was merely a draft of an eventually non-binding declaration—it did not represent general principles of international law and that the assertion that such principles exist could not be used to convert the American Declaration, which is not a treaty, into a source of legal obligation for the United States. See Report 75/02, *supra,* at 161-163. Did the US have a point?

3. In assessing whether or not there are indeed customary or general principles of international law upholding indigenous land rights, what is one to make of the fact that states continue to act contrary to those rights in many parts of the world? One answer is in the view, supported by the jurisprudence of the International Court of Justice, that state behavior that fails to conform to an existing or emerging customary norm does not undermine the norm unless that behavior is persistent and held out by the nonconforming state as acceptable. See Theodor Meron, *Human Rights and Humanitarian Norms in Customary International Law* 58-60 (1989).

4. A declaration of the UN or another international body might confirm or restate already established or developing customary norms or general principles, as was the case with the 1970 Declaration on Principles of International Law Concerning Friendly Relations and Co-Operation Among States in Accordance with the Charter of the United Nations. Was this the case for the case (at least in part) for the UN and OAS indigenous rights declarations? Or did these declarations help motivate new customary rules?

5. Note the relationship—illustrated in the *Maya Communities, Dann,* and *Awas Tingni* cases—between human rights of presumed universal applicability, such as the right to property, and particular rights or standards applying to indigenous peoples, such as collective rights over lands and resources. As stated earlier, standards of indigenous rights can also be seen as grounded in other universal human rights principles, such as non-discrimination and self-determination, as manifested by numerous decisions and comments by authoritive bodies of the United Nations as well as inter-American and African human rights systems. See S. James Anaya, *Human Rights and Indigenous Peoples* (2011). For example, years before the Declaration was adopted by the General Assembly, the UN Committee on the Elimination of Racial Discrimination (CERD), which oversees compliance

with the International Convention on the Elimination of All Forms of Racial Discrimination, issued a "General Recommendation" on indigenous peoples. Even though the Convention does not explicitly mention indigenous peoples, CERD affirms "that discrimination against indigenous peoples falls under the scope of the Convention and that all appropriate means must be taken to combat and eliminate such discrimination." CERD, *General Recommendation 23: Indigenous Peoples*, U.N. Doc. A/52/18, Annex V (1997), para. 1. Accordingly, CERD calls upon states, inter alia, to "[r]ecognize and respect indigenous distinct culture, history, language and way of life," id. para. 4(a), and especially to "recognize and protect the rights of indigenous peoples to own, develop, control and use their communal lands, territories and resources," id., para. 5. What do these materials suggest about how one can justify according special treatment to particular groups in a human rights instrument—as the Declaration on the Rights of Indigenous Peoples does—when human rights are by definition universal?

5. Note that the UN and OAS indigenous rights declarations ascribe rights to "peoples" as such, including collective rights over lands and natural resources; whereas human rights instruments ordinarily have ascribed rights to individuals, as do the American Declaration of the Rights and Duties of Man and the American Convention on Human Rights, which affirm the right of "Every person" or "Everyone" to property, among other individual rights. In what sense are the collective rights of indigenous peoples properly construed as human rights or derived from human rights? Are human rights by definition individual as opposed to group rights? Is there an inherent tension between individual and collective rights? What light is shed on these questions by the decisions of the Inter-American Commission on Human Rights and the Inter-American Court on Human Rights in the *Maya Communities* and *Awas Tingni* cases, which interpret the right to property?

### Note: The Duty to Consult and "Free, Prior, and Informed Consent"

In the *Maya Communities* case, the Inter-American Commission on Human Rights stated that "one of the central elements to the protection of indigenous property rights is the requirement that states undertake effective and fully informed consultations with indigenous communities regarding acts or decisions that may affect their traditional territories" and that "any determination of the extent to which indigenous claimants maintain interests in the lands to which they have traditionally held title and have occupied and used is based upon a process of fully informed consent on the part of the indigenous community as a whole." *Maya Communities*, *supra*, at para. 142.

Article 19 of the UN Declaration on the Rights of Indigenous Peoples, in language mirrored in Article XXIII(2) the OAS indigenous declaration, similarly provides:

> States shall consult and cooperate in good faith with the indigenous peoples concerned through their own representative institutions in order to obtain their free, prior and informed consent before adopting and implementing legislative or administrative measures that may affect them.

See also Article 32 of the UN declaration (articulating the same standard in regard to "approval of any project affecting their lands or territories and other resources") and Article XXIX(4) of the OAS declaration (similar provision); ILO Convention No. 169, Article 6 (requiring states to consult with indigenous peoples on matters affecting them, with "the objective of achieving agreement or consent").

A general duty of states to consult with indigenous peoples on matters affecting them can now be seen as well-rooted in international human rights law and as central to the architecture of the contemporary international indigenous rights regime. In *Sarayaku v. Ecuador*, the Inter-American Court of Human Rights surveyed state and international practice, recounted its own jurisprudence interpreting provisions of relevant treaties, and concluded that "the obligation to consult, in addition to being a treaty-based provision, is also a general principle of international law. . . . In other words, nowadays the obligation of States to carry out special and differentiated consultation processes when certain interests of indigenous peoples and communities are about to be affected is an obligation that has been clearly recognized." *Case of the Kichwa Indigenous People of Sarayaku v. Ecuador,* Inter-Am. Ct. H.R., Judgment on Merits and Reparations of June 27, 2012, Ser. C. No. 245, paras. 164-165. Much less certain, however, is the extent to which states are required by international law not just to consult with indigenous peoples but to obtain their "free, prior, and informed consent" (FPIC) for decisions or measures affecting them.

In the prior case of *Saramaka v. Suriname,* in which the Inter-American Court first articulated a consent standard in association with the duty to consult, the court observed the significant impacts that logging and mining could have on the Saramaka tribal people in the exercise of their human rights. The court stated, "regarding large-scale development or investment projects that would have a major impact within Saramaka territory, the State has a duty, not only to consult with the Saramakas, but also to obtain their free, prior, and informed consent, according to their customs and traditions." *Saramaka People v. Suriname,* Inter-Am. Ct. H.R., Judgment of November 28, 2007, Ser. C No. 172, para. 134. Animated by the *Saramaka* and subsequent decisions by the Inter-American Court, references to a standard of "free, prior and informed consent" by UN treaty bodies and in the UN and OAS declarations, many indigenous rights advocates now vigorously assert what amounts to a veto power on the part of indigenous peoples. For their part, however, states generally continue to reject such a veto power as unworkable, undemocratic, or incompatible with state sovereignty.

The precise reach and contours of an FPIC standard thus remain a matter of debate, especially in the context of extractive or other development projects within indigenous territories. One of the authors of this volume offered the following views of the FPIC standard in that context, in his former capacity as UN Special Rapporteur on the Rights of Indigenous Peoples. (The system of UN special rapporteurs and other special procedures mandate-holders is discussed in Chapter 7.)

> 27. The Declaration [on the Rights of Indigenous Peoples] and various other international sources of authority, along with practical considerations, lead to a general rule that extractive activities should not take

place within the territories of indigenous peoples without their free, prior and informed consent. . . .

28. The general rule identified here derives from the character of free, prior and informed consent as a safeguard for the internationally recognized rights of indigenous peoples that are typically affected by extractive activities that occur within their territories. As explained previously by the Special Rapporteur, together, principles of consultation and consent function as instrumental to rights of participation and self-determination, and as safeguards for all those rights of indigenous peoples that may be affected by external actors . . . These rights include, in addition to rights of participation and self-determination, rights to property, culture, religion and non-discrimination in relation to lands, territories and natural resources, including sacred places and objects; rights to health and physical well-being in relation to a clean and healthy environment; and the right of indigenous peoples to set and pursue their own priorities for development, including with regard to natural resources. It can readily be seen that, given the invasive nature of industrial-scale extraction of natural resources, the enjoyment of these rights is invariably affected in one way or another when extractive activities occur within indigenous territories—thus the general rule that indigenous consent is required for extractive activities within indigenous territories.

29. This general rule is reinforced by practical considerations. It is increasingly understood that when proposed extractive projects might affect indigenous peoples or their territories, it is simply good practice for the States or companies that promote the projects to acquire the consent or agreement of the indigenous peoples concerned. Such consent or agreement provides needed social license and lays the groundwork for the operators of extractive projects to have positive relations with those most immediately affected by the projects, lending needed stability to the projects. . . .

31. The general requirement of indigenous consent for extractive activities within indigenous territories may be subject to certain exceptions, but only within narrowly defined parameters. First, consent may not be required for extractive activities within indigenous territories in cases in which it can be conclusively established that the activities will not substantially affect indigenous peoples in the exercise of any of their substantive rights in relation to the lands and resources within their territories—perhaps mostly a theoretical possibility given the invasive nature of extractive activities, especially when indigenous peoples are living in close proximity to the area where the activities are being carried out. More plausibly, consent may not be required when it can be established that the extractive activity would only impose such limitations on indigenous peoples' substantive rights as are permissible within certain narrow bounds established by international human rights law.

32. Within established doctrine of international human rights law, and in accordance with explicit provisions of international human rights treaties, States may impose limitations on the exercise of certain human

rights, such as the rights to property and to freedom of religion and expression. In order to be valid, however, the limitations must comply with certain standards of necessity and proportionality with regard to a valid public purpose, defined within an overall framework of respect for human rights. . . .

33. It will be recalled that consent performs a safeguard role for indigenous peoples' fundamental rights. When indigenous peoples freely give consent to extractive projects under terms that are aimed to be protective of their rights, there can be a presumption that any limitation on the exercise of rights is permissible and that rights are not being infringed. On the other hand, when indigenous peoples withhold their consent to extractive projects within their territories, no such presumption applies, and in order for a project to be implemented the State has the burden of demonstrating either that no rights are being limited or that, if they are, the limitation is valid.

34. In order for a limitation to be valid, first, the right involved must be one subject to limitation by the State and, second, . . . the limitation must be necessary and proportional in relation to a valid State objective motivated by concern for the human rights of others. The Inter-American Court of Human Rights has pointed out that indigenous peoples' proprietary interests in lands and resources, while being protected the American Convention on Human Rights, are subject to limitations by the State, but only those limitations that meet criteria of necessity and proportionality in relation to a valid objective.

*Extractive industries and indigenous peoples—Report of the Special Rapporteur on the rights of indigenous Peoples, James Anaya,* U.N. Doc. A/HRC/24/41 (2013). Do you agree that, consistent with Article 19 of the Declaration on the Rights of Indigenous Peoples, states may impose limitations on indigenous peoples' rights in certain circumstances involving a legitimate public purpose and implement development projects without their consent? Note that the Declaration itself states, in Article 46, that the rights articulated therein are "subject only to such limitations as are determined by law and in accordance with international human rights obligations. Any such limitations shall be non-discriminatory and strictly necessary solely for the purpose of securing due recognition and respect for the rights and freedoms of others and for meeting the just and most compelling requirements of a democratic society." The American Declaration on the Rights of Indigenous Peoples includes a similar provision (Article XXXVI).

Does the exception to the general rule of indigenous consent stated above threaten to swallow the rule? Note that the Special Rapporteur report went on to say:

> Even if a valid public purpose can be established for the limitation of property or other rights related to indigenous territories, the limitation must be necessary and proportional to that purpose. This requirement will generally be difficult to meet for extractive industries that are carried out within the territories of indigenous peoples without their consent. In determining necessity and proportionality, due account must be taken

of the significance to the survival of indigenous peoples of the range of rights potentially affected by the project. Account should also be taken of the fact that in many if not the vast majority of cases, indigenous peoples continue to claim rights to subsurface resources within their territories on the basis of their own laws or customs, despite State law to the contrary. These factors weigh heavily against a finding of proportionality of State-imposed rights limitations, reinforcing the general rule of indigenous consent to extractive activities within indigenous territories.

*Extractive Industries and Indigenous Peoples, supra*, para 36. Is the foregoing consistent or not with the decision of the Inter-American Court of Human Rights in the *Saramaka* case, *supra*, in which the Court stated that consent was required for logging and mining projects having a "major impact" in the Saramaka territory? Does the Special Rapporteur's interpretation of the FPIC standard itself constitute soft law? If so, is it soft law on soft law, or soft law intertpreting a treaty obligation, or both? In this regard, see Professor Shelton's description of secondary soft law, *supra* page 125.

For further discussion of the FPIC standard, see Office of the High Commissioner for Human Rights, *Free, Prior and Informed Consent of Indigeneous Peoples* (2013), http://www.ohchr.org/Documents/Issues/IPeoples/FreePriorandInformed Consent.pdf; Mauro Barelli, *Free, Prior and Informed Consent in the Aftermath of the UN Declaration on the Rights of Indigenous Peoples: Developments and Challenges Ahead*, 16(1) INT'L J. H.R. 1 (2012); Cathal Doyle, *Indigenous Peoples, Title to Territory, Rights and Resources: The Transformative Role of Free, Prior and Informed Consent* (2014); *Study of the United Nations Expert Mechanism on the Rights of Indigenous Peoples—Free, Prior and Informed consent: a human rights-based approach*, U.N. Doc. U.NA/HRC/39/62 (2018), paras. 20-41.

## IV.  *NORM BUILDING IN RELATED AREAS*

### A.  *Minorities*

Prior and eventually parallel to developments specifically concerning the rights of indigenous peoples is the formulation of "minority rights" in various written instruments. Indigenous peoples typically are numerical minorities in the countries in which they live and are in non-dominant positions vis-à-vis the larger or majority populations. Yet they are distinct from other groups that share such characteristics and that are commonly identified as national, ethnic, religious, or linguistic minorities. As illustrated by the *Maya Communities* case, indigenous peoples assert claims based on histories of prior occupancy and colonial encounter, and their claims go beyond the traditional concerns of minorities for protection of culture, language, and religion. It is thus understandable that indigenous peoples themselves have consistently rejected classification as minorities, both conceptually and politically. But it would be a mistake to overlook the fact that indigenous peoples do have many of the same concerns as groups generally identified as minorities and that the human rights claimed by groups in both categories to a significant extent draw from common core principles, such as non-discrimination and respect for diversity. For a discussion of the theoretical approaches to the status of indigenous peoples, as distinct from minority groups, see Benedict Kingsbury, "Reconciling Five Competing Conceptual Structures of Indigenous Peoples' Claims in International and Comparative Law," in *Peoples' Rights* 69 (Philip Alston ed., 2001).

Hurst Hannum

## "The Rights of Persons Belonging to Minorities"

in *Human Rights: Concepts and Standards* 277-294 passim (Janusz Symonides ed., 2000) (emphasis in original; footnotes omitted)

Many vulnerable categories of people have been singled out for protection by the international community in the past 50 years, as more specific norms have been developed to complement the general norms found in the Universal Declaration of Human Rights. Among these categories are workers, refugees, women, prisoners, indigenous peoples, children, disabled persons and migrant workers; prohibitions against discrimination on the basis of race and religion have also been adopted. . . .

### HISTORICAL DEVELOPMENTS

The reluctance to consider minorities as worthy of particular attention is a phenomenon only of the second half of the twentieth century, which has recently begun to change. For example, most early empires considered at least religious minorities worthy of recognition. The "millet" system developed under the Ottoman empire allowed religious communities a degree of personal and cultural autonomy, although it has been observed that the millets were "the solution devised by a government that did not know what nationality meant and, therefore, was unfamiliar with the majority-minority concept." The development of autonomous, religious-based communities was also consistent with Koranic injunctions of tolerance for other religions, and large non-Muslim communities continued to flourish throughout the Ottoman Empire.

In Europe, international protection of minorities can be traced to the Treaty of Westphalia in 1648, under the terms of which the parties agreed to respect the rights of certain religious minorities within their jurisdiction. However, given the historical congruence of religious and secular authority prior to this period, such agreements could just as easily be seen as recognizing the power of certain political groups rather than guaranteeing religious rights *per se.*

In the nineteenth century, the development of nationalism in Europe was based on the theory that political power was best exercised by groups that shared ethnic or linguistic ties. "Nations" sought to establish a separate political identity, whether by incorporating peoples spread over many countries (Germany, Italy) or by demanding greater political power for groups which had formerly been considered as minorities within existing empires (Greece, Hungary, Serbia, Poland, the Baltic States, and others).

The overriding concern in the nineteenth century with nationalism and the protection of cultural, linguistic and ethnic minorities led to a conscious and comprehensive attempt to protect minorities in the early twentieth century, with adoption of the so-called "minority treaties" at the end of World War I and their monitoring by the League of Nations. . . .

Among the protections commonly included . . . were the right to equality of treatment and non-discrimination; the right to citizenship (although a minority group member could opt to retain another citizenship if desired); the right to use one's own language; the right of minorities to establish and control their own charitable, religious and social institutions; a State obligation to provide "equitable" financial support to minority schools (in which primary school instruction would be in the minority language) and other institutions; and recognition of the supremacy of laws protecting minority rights over other statutes.

A major advance of this period was the legitimization of international interest in protecting minority rights, evidenced by the supervisory role of the League of Nations in monitoring the treaties. . . .

The existence of German-speaking minorities outside Germany had provided one excuse for Hitler's aggression in the 1930s, and there was thus little concern for the rights of "national minorities" on the part of the victorious Allies after World War II. The Charter of the United Nations does not specifically mention minority rights. Instead, emphasis was placed on the importance of respect for (individual) human rights "for all without distinction as to race, sex, language, or religion" and the principle of (collective) "self-determination of peoples."

The drafters of the UN Charter seemed to assume 1) that European and other minorities would be satisfied if their individual rights, particularly those of equality and non-discrimination, were respected; and 2) that the principle of self-determination would be adequate to resolve the larger problem of colonial territories. Despite the disastrous consequences for the individual victims of, e.g., the Greek-Turkish population "exchange" of 1920-22, migration became the preferred solution for post-1945 European minorities; it was largely the people (especially Germans) who moved, not the boundaries. Unfortunately, there is thus ample historical precedent for the solution of "ethnic cleansing" that re-emerged in the former Yugoslavia in the 1990s.

There were occasional exceptions to this general refusal to consider minority problems *per se*, although such ad hoc initiatives lacked the regular international supervision offered by the League of Nations. The German-speaking minority in the Italian South Tyrol, for example, was the subject of a 1946 agreement between Italy and Austria. The Austrian State Treaty, which re-established Austria within its pre-1938 borders, contains specific provisions for the protection of the Slovene and Croat minorities. The UN proposal for a Free Territory of Trieste and the UN-approved establishment of an autonomous Eritrea federated with Ethiopia were also designed to address minority situations, although each envisioned a greater degree of political autonomy than would traditionally have been reserved to a minority group. . . .

The 1948 Universal Declaration of Human Rights makes no specific mention of minority rights, and a separate part of the same resolution (ominously titled "fate of minorities") noted accurately, if somewhat disingenuously, that "it was difficult to adopt a uniform solution for this complex and delicate question [of minorities], which had special aspects in each State in which it arose." The UN Commission on

Human Rights did establish a Sub-Commission on Prevention of Discrimination and Protection of Minorities, but early attempts by the Sub-Commission to address minority issues were essentially rebuffed by the Commission. . . .

Drafting of binding international agreements to implement the Universal Declaration began soon after the Declaration's adoption, and article 27 of the Covenant on Civil and Political Rights does specifically address the issue of minority rights. It provides, in full:

> In those States in which ethnic, religious or linguistic minorities exist, persons belonging to such minorities shall not be denied the right, in community with the other members of their group, to enjoy their own culture, to profess and practise their own religion, or to use their own language.

The Covenant addresses only minimal, traditional, minority rights, that is, cultural, religious and linguistic rights. The fact that rights are granted to "persons belonging to such minorities" rather than to minority groups themselves is an indication of the individualistic orientation of the Covenant on Civil and Political Rights, as well as its reluctance to recognize the rights of groups which had yet to be satisfactorily defined.

Often forgotten in discussions of minority rights is the International Convention on the Elimination of All Forms of Racial Discrimination, which entered into force in 1969 and has been ratified by 182 States as of May of 2022, treaty also discussed in Chapter 2. "Racial discrimination" under the convention is defined in article 1 as any distinction "based on race, colour, descent, *or* national or ethnic origin" which impairs the exercise of human rights (emphasis added). Article 2 of the convention requires, *inter alia*, that parties take, in appropriate circumstances, "special and concrete measures to ensure the adequate development and protection of certain racial groups or individuals belonging to them, for the purpose of guaranteeing them the full and equal enjoyment of human rights and fundamental freedoms." An analogous provision is found in the UNESCO Declaration on Race and Racial Prejudice. . . .

The Declaration on the Rights of Persons belonging to National or Ethnic, Religious or Linguistic Minorities was finally completed and adopted by the General Assembly in 1992. There is little doubt that progress on the Declaration was greatly aided by the end of East-West rivalry, although it is ironic that the Declaration was completed after the disintegration of its original sponsoring State, Yugoslavia. While it continues the individualistic orientation of article 27 of the Covenant on Civil and Political Rights by referring to "the rights of persons" belonging to minorities, the Declaration does expand on existing provisions and contains progressive language related to minority participation in the political and economic life of the State. In addition, the Preamble recognizes that protecting minority rights will "contribute to the political and social stability of States in which they live" and, in turn, "contribute to the strengthening of friendship and co-operation among peoples and States.". . .

It was not until 1995 that the Commission on Human Rights created a mechanism to monitor observance of the Declaration, when it authorized the Sub-Commission to establish a five-member working group to "review the promotion and practical realization" of the Declaration, "examine possible solutions to problems involving minorities [and recommend] further measures, as appropriate, for the promotion and protection of the rights of persons belonging to national or ethnic, religious and linguistic minorities."

Other UN initiatives which have contributed to developing standards for the protection of minorities include the adoption of the 1981 Declaration on the Elimination of All Forms of Intolerance and Discrimination Based on Religion or Belief; appointment of special rapporteurs by the Commission on Human Rights and its Sub-Commission in the 1980s to consider specific aspects of religious intolerance and discrimination; and a 1993 report by the Sub-Commission on "the possible ways and means of facilitating the peaceful and constructive solution of problems involving minorities."

Just as Europe was the center of concern with minority rights from the mid-nineteenth century until World War II, it has been Europe which has devoted the most attention to the issue of minority rights since the end of the Cold War in the late 1980s. Perhaps spurred by renewed concerns over "ethnic" conflicts in both Eastern and Western Europe, European governments have attempted to set new standards for minority rights and have at least begun to devise new means of monitoring those standards.

The first indication that agreement on an expanded definition of minority rights was possible came in 1990, when a Final Document was adopted by consensus at the Copenhagen meeting of the Conference on the Human Dimension of the Conference on Security and Cooperation in Europe (CSCE). This remarkable document (which also contains detailed provisions relating to democracy, the rule of law and other human rights) was drafted and agreed to in only six weeks, and it represented the first detailed articulation of minority rights by governments since the post-First World War minorities treaties. It addressed, in particular, minority rights in the areas of language use, education and political participation, each of which is discussed further in the next section.

Two years later, the CSCE (known since 1995 as the Organization on Security and Cooperation in Europe (OSCE)) created the position of High Commissioner on National Minorities, in order to provide "early warning and, as appropriate, early action at the earliest possible stage in regard to tensions involving national minority issues that have the potential to develop into a conflict within the CSCE area, affecting peace, stability, or relations between participating States." Although the High Commissioner's mandate is to prevent conflict rather than protect minority rights *per se*, his interventions thus far appear to have contributed to both goals.

In recent years, it has almost appeared as though the Council of Europe was competing with the CSCE to see which organization could most quickly define rights to protect minorities and establish procedures to implement those rights. In 1992, the Council of Europe adopted and opened for ratification a Charter on the Protection of Minority and Regional Languages. Modelled on the European Social Charter, its provisions offer a wide range of guarantees from among which States may choose the level of obligations they are willing to accept. The following year, the Parliamentary Assembly recommended that a protocol on minority rights be added to the European Convention on Human Rights. A more ambitious Framework Convention on minorities was adopted in 1994. . . . [Both of these treaties entered into force in 1998.]

THE CONTEMPORARY CONTENT OF MINORITY RIGHTS

Most recent instruments concerning minority rights have taken the form of "soft law," that is, declarations or resolutions which constitute solemn political commitments but which do not constitute binding legal obligations. However, as readily demonstrated by the political impact of the CSCE since 1975 and many other international human rights instruments, political commitments can sometimes be as influential as legally binding treaties. What is significant is that these documents, whether universal or regional, provide evidence that there is an emerging consensus over at least the minimum content of internationally recognized minority rights. This section outlines the substance of those rights.

Two preliminary questions must be addressed before the content of the current rights of minorities can be identified. The first issue is that of defining a "minority" or its members; the second is whether states' obligations with respect to minorities are limited to non-interference and non-discrimination, or whether states may be under a more demanding obligation to take affirmative measures to promote minority cultures. . . .

It should first be recognized that definitional questions are important only if they carry with them legal or political consequences. In the case of minorities, emerging international norms would obviously benefit groups which fall within their scope, while they would be unavailable to groups considered to be only political, regional or social groups. However, there are also some potentially negative consequences to being classified as a minority; for example, "minorities" do not enjoy any right to self-determination, while "peoples" do enjoy that right. . . .

[There is at least a] consensus that any definition of minority must include both objective factors (the existence of shared ethnicity, language, religion or similar cultural traits) and subjective factors (individuals must identify themselves as members of minority group). Whether or not a minority exists is a question of fact and does not depend on a formal determination by the State. . . .

The question of whether "minority rights" are essentially group rights or individual rights may be of theoretical interest, but the practical implications of the debate are more difficult to discern. For example, Article 27 of the Covenant and all other intergovernmental instruments relating to minorities apply formally only to "persons belonging to" minorities, but Article 1 of the Minorities Declaration does oblige States to protect "the existence and [. . .] identity of minorities within their respective territories," not just individual members of minorities.

The very concept of a "minority" implies a community or group, and the reference in international instruments to the rights of "persons" should be understood primarily as a jurisdictional rather than a substantive limitation. For example, if rights were accorded only to minority groups *qua* groups, difficult questions might arise as to who was entitled to represent the minority and what persons should be considered to be members of the minority. In general it is easier (and more supportive of the underlying rights) to adopt the individually oriented approach of the Covenant and other documents, under which any aggrieved member of a minority may complain about alleged violations of his or her rights.

The second preliminary issue that is relevant to all minority rights is the extent to which States are under a positive obligation to promote such rights, as

IV. Norm Building in Related Areas

opposed to a merely negative obligation not to interfere with or impede development of a minority's culture. Article 27 of the International Covenant on Civil and Political Rights is phrased in the negative, i.e., minorities "shall not be denied" rights by the State. However, after noting that the rights set forth in article 27 "depend in turn on the ability of the minority group to maintain its culture, language or religion," the Human Rights Committee has stated that "positive measures by States may [. . .] be necessary to protect the identity of a minority.". . .

As the number of instruments on minority rights proliferates, it becomes easier to conclude that some state action to promote the rights of persons belonging to minorities may be required. Nonetheless, the scope of such positive obligations on states to promote minority culture remains unclear, and it is perhaps best analyzed by referring to specific provisions concerning, for example, language, access to the media and education. . . .

Turning to the substantive content of specific rights, the most basic obligation on States is to *protect the existence and identity* of minorities and their members. In many instances, this may mean simply guaranteeing the most basic human rights - to life and physical integrity, freedom from arrest and torture, due process, property and freedom of expression. It also implies a prohibition against forced assimilation, a prohibition made explicit in several instruments. . . .

The principles of *equality before the law and non-discrimination* are equally fundamental in all statements of minority rights, and they have by now acquired the status of customary international law binding on all states. . . .

Linked to the principle of equality is the notion that members of minorities are to be equal to members of the majority in fact, as well as in law. This concept, borrowed from the decision of the Permanent Court of International Justice in the "Minority Schools in Albania" case, implies that minorities must enjoy not only formal legal equality, but that they have the right to effective equality of opportunity or result *vis-à-vis* the majority community. This may necessitate that special measures, sometimes known as "positive discrimination or "affirmative action", be taken to ensure that the minority has the same rights in practice as the majority. . . .

[The author goes on to discuss the rights to freedom of religion, to enjoy one's own culture, to maintain contact with other members of the group, to learn and use one's language, and to education.]

Perhaps the most controversial set of rights concerns the ability of minorities to *participate effectively in decisions* which affect them, a right which was not generally recognized in the treaties supervised by the League of Nations. The earliest formulation of this right was by the CSCE in 1990, when the participating CSCE States agreed to "respect the right of persons belonging to national minorities to effective participation in public affairs, including participation in the affairs relating to the protection and promotion of the identity of such minorities." The Declaration adopted by the UN General Assembly two years later expands the right of participation to include "cultural, religious, social, economic and public life," although the right to participate in decision-making is limited to "a manner not incompatible with national legislation." Although the text is formulated rather weakly, Article 4(5) of the Minorities Declaration also provides that "states should consider appropriate measures so that persons belonging to minorities may participate fully in the economic progress and development in their country."

The CSCE Copenhagen Document "notes," as one way of achieving the aim of effective participation, the establishment of "appropriate local or autonomous administrations corresponding to the specific historical and territorial circumstances of such minorities and in accordance with the policies of the State concerned." The protocol recommended by the Parliamentary Assembly of the Council of Europe is even more specific, providing that "in regions where they are in a majority the persons belonging to a national minority shall have the right to have at their disposal appropriate local or autonomous authorities or to have a special status". . . .

Such provisions obviously reach far beyond the scope of "ordinary" human rights, insofar as they mandate that States adopt forms of government which make "effective participation" of minorities possible. Even though no particular constitutional or legislative structure is required, this is a much more delicate task than simply prohibiting torture or providing social security. Of course, "participation" does not necessarily mean "control", and the precise balance between minority and majority rights will need to be determined on a case-by-case basis. At the same time, however, a purely formal democracy in which members of minorities are consistently denied any share in power might well violate the emerging international norms of minority rights.

### CONCLUDING OBSERVATIONS

Members of minorities have suffered discrimination, land seizures, forced assimilation, deportation and even death at the hand of intolerant majorities and territorially ambitious governments. Despite such pressures, however, minorities will always exist within State boundaries: it is impossible (and perhaps not even desirable) for every state to be ethnically, linguistically and religiously homogeneous. While one must be careful not to undermine the legitimate rights of the majority, upon which democracy is based, the challenge for the twenty-first century is to do a better job of protecting the more vulnerable, often minority, members of society than was evidenced in the twentieth century. . . .

Ultimately, the challenge of protecting the rights of persons belonging to minorities is to balance the legitimate concerns of majority and minority communities, so that broader political and economic decisions may be reached in an atmosphere of full equality and respect for human rights. The international community has made significant strides in articulating this balance in only a few years. As with other human rights, the task now is to ensure that the political and legal commitments accepted by States are monitored and implemented in good faith.

---

As noted in the above extract, Article 27 of the International Covenant and Civil and Political Rights explicitly affirms minority rights. The UN Human Rights Committee, the expert body that oversees state compliance with the Covenant (see Chapter 7) has provided the following interpretation of Article 27.

Human Rights Committee

## General Comment No. 23: Article 27 (Rights of Minorities)

UN Doc. CCPR/C/21/Rev.1/Add.5 (1994)

5.1. The terms used in article 27 indicate that the persons designed to be protected are those who belong to a group and who share in common a culture, a religion and/or a language. Those terms also indicate that the individuals designed to be protected need not be citizens of the State party. . . .

5.2. Article 27 confers rights on persons belonging to minorities which "exist" in a State party. Given the nature and scope of the rights envisaged under that article, it is not relevant to determine the degree of permanence that the term "exist" connotes. Those rights simply are that individuals belonging to those minorities should not be denied the right, in community with members of their group, to enjoy their own culture, to practice their religion and speak their language. Just as they need not be nationals or citizens, they need not be permanent residents. Thus, migrant workers or even visitors in a State party constituting such minorities are entitled not to be denied the exercise of those rights. As any other individual in the territory of the State party, they would, also for this purpose, have the general rights, for example, to freedom of association, of assembly, and of expression. The existence of an ethnic, religious or linguistic minority in a given State party does not depend upon a decision by that State party but requires [the existence of a minority] to be established by objective criteria. . . .

6.1. Although article 27 is expressed in negative terms, that article, nevertheless, does recognize the existence of a "right" and requires that it shall not be denied. Consequently, a State party is under an obligation to ensure that the existence and the exercise of this right are protected against their denial or violation. Positive measures of protection are, therefore, required not only against the acts of the State party itself, whether through its legislative, judicial or administrative authorities, but also against the acts of other persons within the State party.

6.2 Although the rights protected under article 27 are individual rights, they depend in turn on the ability of the minority group to maintain its culture, language or religion. Accordingly, positive measures by States may also be necessary to protect the identity of a minority and the rights of its members to enjoy and develop their culture and language and to practice their religion, in community with the other members of the group. . . . [A]s long as those measures are aimed at correcting conditions which prevent or impair the enjoyment of the rights guaranteed under article 27, they may constitute a legitimate differentiation under the Covenant, provided that they are based on reasonable and objective criteria. . . .

7. With regard to the exercise of the cultural rights protected under article 27, the Committee observes that culture manifests itself in many forms, including a particular way of life associated with the use of land resources, especially in the case of indigenous peoples. That right may include such traditional activities as fishing or hunting and the right to live in reserves protected by law. The enjoyment of those rights may require positive legal measures of protection and measures to ensure the effective participation of members of minority communities in decisions which affect them. . . .

9. The Committee concludes that article 27 relates to rights whose these rights is directed to ensure the survival and continued development of the cultural, religious and social identity of the minorities concerned, thus enriching the fabric of society as a whole. Accordingly, the Committee observes that these rights must be protected as such and should not be confused with other personal rights conferred on one and all under the Covenant. States parties, therefore, have an obligation to ensure that the exercise of these rights is fully protected and they should indicate in their reports the measures they have adopted to this end.

––––––––––

The Human Rights Committee has considered minority issues in its examination of states' periodic reports which are mandated by the Covenant on Civil and Political Rights, and it has examined a number of complaints concerning alleged violations of Article 27, brought under the First Optional Protocol to the Covenant. These complaints have come from a wide variety of sources, including members of indigenous groups. See generally Ben Saul, *Indigenous Peoples and Human Rights: International and Regional Jurisprudence* 59-73 (2016); Sia Spiliopoulou, "Protection of Minorities Under Article 27 of the International Covenant on Civil and Political Rights and the Reporting System," in *Writings in Human and Minority Rights* (Frank Horn and Tuula Tervashenka eds., 1994); *Leading Cases of the Human Rights Committee* 375-399 (Raija Hanski and Martin Scheinin eds., 2003).

Despite the Committee's generally expansive reading of Article 27, as demonstrated by its General Comment 23, complainants have not often been successful in pressing their claims under this article outside the context of indigenous peoples. Many cases have been declared inadmissible for failure to exhaust local remedies, which is a requirement under most international human rights complaint procedures. All of the cases against France have been declared inadmissible as to Article 27, because the Committee determined that it is bound by a French reservation to Article 27 stating that the article is "not applicable" (although technically the French statement was entitled a "declaration"). Successful cases in the indigenous context include: *Ominayak and the Lubicon Lake Band v. Canada*, Communication No. 167/1984, Human Rights Cmte., views of March 26 1990, UN Doc. CCPR/C/D/167/1984 (1990) (finding that Canada threatened the way of life and the culture of the Lubicon Lake Band in violation of Article 27 of the Covenant by engaging in oil and gas development on traditional Lubicon lands); *Poma Poma v. Peru*, Communication No. 11457/2006, Human Rights Cmte., views of March 16, 2009, UN Doc. CCPR/C/95/D/1457/2006 (2009) (finding Peru violated the right of Ms. Poma Poma under Article 27 to enjoy her own culture together with the other members of her group by diverting groundwater from her land, drying out the wetlands, and desecrating the community's livestock and livelihood). See also *Hopu & Bessert v. France*, Communication No. 549/1993, Human Rights Cmte., views of July 29 1997, UN Doc. CCPR/E/60/D/549/1993/Rev. 1 (1997) (finding that France violated rights to family and privacy under Articles 17 and 23 of the Covenant by permitting hotel construction on ancestral burial grounds of indigenous Polynesians in Tahiti).

## B.   Self-Determination

Inevitably looming in the background of most discussions about the rights of indigenous peoples and minorities is the right of self-determination. The UN Charter includes among the founding principles of the United Nations the "principle of self-determination and equal rights of peoples." UN Charter, Article 1. The International Covenant on Civil and Political Rights and the International Covenant on Economic, Social, and Cultural Rights include identical language, in each one's Article 1, affirming the right of "[a]ll peoples have the right of self-determination;" and the African Charter on Human and Peoples rights similarly embraces self-determination, designating it an "inalienable right" of all peoples, African Charter on Human and Peoples Rights, Article 20.1 *adopted* June 27, 1981, OAU Doc. CAB/LEG/67/3 rev. 5, 21 I.L.M. 58 (1982), *entered into force* Oct. 21, 1986.

Beyond its affirmation in widely ratified treaties, self-determination is generally understood to be a norm of customary international law, at least in the context of classic decolonization. However, this development occurred initially not through a treaty, but on the basis of General Assembly resolutions, which eventually came to be supported by the practice of states. The language affirming the right of self-determination in the Covenants, and now in the UN Declaration on the Rights of Indigenous Peoples, is found in the 1960 Declaration on the Granting of Independence to Colonial Countries and Peoples, G.A. Res. 1514 (1960), which was the most significant formal statement on the topic at the time it was adopted. The 1960 Declaration sets forth the fundamental principle of self-determination, along with an equally fundamental limitation on its application:

> 2. All peoples have the right to self-determination; by virtue of that right they freely determine their political status and freely pursue their economic, social and cultural development. . . .
>
> 6. Any attempt aimed at the partial or total disruption of the national unity and the territorial integrity of a country is incompatible with the purposes and principles of the Charter of the United Nations.

Since 1960, these principles have been reiterated on numerous occasions, most notably in the authoritative 1970 Declaration on Principles of International Law Concerning Friendly Relations and Co-Operation Among States in Accordance with the Charter of the United Nations, G.A. Res. 2625 (1970), and in the Vienna Declaration and Programme of Action, World Conference on Human Rights, Vienna, 14-25 June 1993, U.N. Doc A/CONF.157/23 (1993). Significantly, the UN Declaration on Rights of Indigenous Peoples, in its Article 46, similarly balances the right of self-determination with principles of state territorial integrity and political unity. Article 46 was added in order to achieve consensus on the Declaration in the General Assembly a year after its adoption by the Human Rights Council in 2006. The American Declaration on the Rights of Indigenous Peoples also includes a territorial integrity provision (Article IV).

The territorial integrity and political unity principles, with their grounding in the UN Charter (Article 2), were not barriers to decolonization and the emergence of new states. The General Assembly resolution on decolonization already cited admonished, "Immediate steps shall be taken, in Trust and Non-Self-Governing territories or all other territories that have not yet attained independence, to transfer all powers to the peoples of those territories, in accordance with their freely expressed will and desire." G. A. Res. 1514 (1960), para. 5.

A companion resolution issued the day after Resolution 1514 was adopted observed that "[t]he authors of the Charter of the United Nations had in mind that Chapter XI [on non-self-governing territories] should be applicable to territories which were then known to be of the colonial type." Principles Which Should Guide Members in Determining Whether or not an Obligation Exists to Transmit the Information Called for in Article 73(e) [regarding "non-self-governing territories"] of the Charter of the United Nations, G.A. Res. 1541 (1960), Principle I. It also provided that "a full measure of self-government" could be achieved by "(a) Emergence as a sovereign independent state; (b) Free association with an independent state; or (c) Integration with an independent state." Id., Principle VI.

Debate has persisted about the extent to or manner in which the right of self-determination applies beyond the classical decolonization context. Secessionist movements by ethnic and other groups have occurred often; these movements typically invoke the right of self-determination and have often led to violent conflict when such demands are refused. The post-1989 dissolutions of the Soviet Union, Yugoslavia, Czechoslovakia, and Ethiopia emboldened groups seeking either independence or some form of self-government and, at the same time, generated opposition to efforts to broaden any legal entitlement to self-determination. No treaty body or other international institution has yet upheld the right of "peoples" to independence, outside the context of decolonization.

The UN and OAS indigenous rights declarations, which affirm indigenous self-determination within a set of standards and rights that contemplate reforms within existing states, may be seen as breakthroughs in the conceptualization of self-determination in the modern world.

The Human Rights Committee, which monitors compliance with the Covenant on Civil and Political Rights, thus far has declined to consider alleged violations of the right to self-determination proclaimed in Article 1 of the Covenant in the context of individual complaints lodged under the Optional Protocol to the Covenant, on the grounds that the Optional Protocol only allows complaints based on individual rights, not on the rights of "peoples." However, the Committee has applied Article 1 in reviewing state periodic reports. The Committee's General Comment on Article 1 indicates that the right of self-determination is relevant to concerns outside the secessionist or decolonization contexts and requests states to include in their reports, in connection with Article 1, descriptions of "the constitutional and political processes which in practice allow the exercise of this right." *General Comment 12, Article 1 (Right to Self-Determination)*, UN Doc. A/39/40, Annex VI, para. 4 (1984). This examination has included not only states' internal political processes but also their handling of indigenous peoples' claims. For example, in reviewing Canada's fourth periodic report under the Covenant, the Committee urged that "the practice of extinguishing inherent aboriginal rights be abandoned as incompatible with article 1 of the Covenant." *Concluding Observations of the Human Rights Committee: Canada*, UN Doc. CCPR/C/79/Add.105 (1999), para. 7. In the same vein, the Committee expressed concerns about state laws and policies in Australia and Norway relating to indigenous lands, making references to obligations derived from Article 1. See *Concluding Observations of the Human Rights Committee: Norway*, UN Doc. CCPR/C/79/Add.112 (1999), paras. 16, 17; *Concluding Observations of the Human Rights Committee: Australia*, UN Doc. A/55/40 (2000), paras. 509-510. Additionally, the Committee has stated that it may consider Article 1 to interpret other articles of the Covenant. See, e.g., *Mahuika et. al. v. New Zealand*, Communication No. 547/1993, Hum. Rts. Cmte., views of Oct. 27, 2000, UN Doc. DDPR/C/70/D/537/1993 (2000), paras. 3, 9.2 (Article 1 could be relevant to complaint under Article 27 in relation to Maori claims over fisheries).

Another UN treaty monitoring body, the Committee on the Elimination of Racial Discrimination, adopted an approach consistent with that of the Human Rights Committee, as evidenced in the following General Recommendation.

## Committee on the Elimination of Racial Discrimination

## General Recommandation 21: The right to self-determination

UN Doc. A/51/18 (1996)

1. The Committee notes that ethnic or religious groups or minorities frequently refer to the right to self-determination as a basis for an alleged right to secession. In this connection the Committee wishes to express the following views.

2. The right to self-determination of peoples is a fundamental principle of international law. It is enshrined in article 1 of the Charter of the United Nations, in article 1 of the International Covenant on Economic, Social and Cultural Rights and article 1 of the International Covenant on Civil and Political Rights, as well as in other international human rights instruments. The International Covenant on Civil and Political Rights provides for the rights of peoples to self-determination besides the right of ethnic, religious or linguistic minorities to enjoy their own culture, to profess and practie their own religion or to use their own language.

3. The Committee emphasizes that in accordance with the Declaration on Principles of International Law concerning Friendly Relations and Cooperation among States in accordance with the Charter of the United Nations, approved by the United Nations General Assembly in its resolution 2625 (XXV) of 24 October 1970, it is the duty of States to promote the right to self-determination of peoples. But the implementation of the principle of self-determination requires every State to promote, through joint and separate action, universal respect for and observance of human rights and fundamental freedoms in accordance with the Charter of the United Nations. In this context the Committee draws the attention of Governments to the Declaration on the Rights of Persons Belonging to National or Ethnic, Religious and Linguistic Minorities . . .

4. In respect of the self-determination of peoples two aspects have to be distinguished. The right to self-determination of peoples has an internal aspect, that is to say, the rights of all peoples to pursue freely their economic, social and cultural development without outside interference. In that respect there exists a link with the right of every citizen to take part in the conduct of public affairs at any level, as referred to in article 5 (c) of the International Convention on the Elimination of All Forms of Racial Discrimination. In consequence, Governments are to represent

the whole population without distinction as to race, colour, descent or national or ethnic origin. The external aspect of self-determination implies that all peoples have the right to determine freely their political status and their place in the international community based upon the principle of equal rights and exemplified by the liberation of peoples from colonialism and by the prohibition to subject peoples to alien subjugation, domination and exploitation.

5. In order to respect fully the rights of all peoples within a State, Governments are again called upon to adhere to and implement fully the international human rights instruments and in particular the International Convention on the Elimination of All Forms of Racial Discrimination. Concern for the protection of individual rights without discrimination on racial, ethnic, tribal, religious or other grounds must guide the policies of Governments. In accordance with article 2 of the International Convention on the Elimination of All Forms of Racial Discrimination and other relevant international documents, Governments should be sensitive towards the rights of persons belonging to ethnic groups, particularly their right to lead lives of dignity, to preserve their culture, to share equitably in the fruits of national growth and to play their part in the Government of the country of which they are citizens. Also, Governments should consider, within their respective constitutional frameworks, vesting persons belonging to ethnic or linguistic groups comprised of their citizens, where appropriate, with the right to engage in activities which are particularly relevant to the preservation of the identity of such persons or groups.

6. The Committee emphasizes that, in accordance with the Declaration on Friendly Relations, none of the Committee's actions shall be construed as authorizing or encouraging any action which would dismember or impair, totally or in part, the territorial integrity or political unity of sovereign and independent States conducting themselves in compliance with the principle of equal rights and self-determination of peoples and possessing a Government representing the whole people belonging to the territory, without distinction as to race, creed or colour. In the view of the Committee, international law has not recognized a general right of peoples unilaterally to declare secession from a State. In this respect, the Committee follows the views expressed in An Agenda for Peace (paras. 17 and following), namely, that a fragmentation of States may be detrimental to the protection of human rights, as well as to the preservation of peace and security. This does not, however, exclude the possibility of arrangements reached by free agreement of all parties concerned.

---

The interpretation of the right of self-determination advanced by the Committee on the Elimination of Racial Discrimination views that right as part of the larger universe of human rights and not necessarily implying a right of secession or independent statehood. The implicit message is that self-determination claims, with their potentially profound impact on the very structure of the state, can be better considered from a human rights perspective, rather than being subject exclusively to the geopolitical calculations that typically have guided responses to such claims. For arguments in favor of such a human rights approach, see S. James Anaya, *A*

*Contemporary Definition of the International Norm of Self-Determination*, 3 TRANSNATL. L. & CONTEMP. PROBS. 131 (1993); Hurst Hannum, *Rethinking Self-Determination*, 34 VA. J. INT'L L. 1 (1993); Robert McCorquodale, *Self-Determination: A Human Rights Approach*, 43 INT'L & COMP. L. Q. 857 (1994).

Among many other works that address the issue of self-determination from a primarily legal perspective are Ulrike Barten, *Minorities, Minority Rights and Internal Self-Determination* (2015); Antonio Cassese, *Self-Determination of Peoples, A Legal Reappraisal* (1995); Ryan D. Griffiths, *Age of Secession: The International and Domestic Determinants of State Birth* (2016); Jane A. Hofbauer, *Sovereignty in the Exercise of the Right to Self-Determination* (2016); Hurst Hannum, *Autonomy, Sovereignty, and Self-Determination, The Accommodation of Conflicting Rights* (2d ed. 1996); Edward McWhinney, *Self-Determination of Peoples and Plural-Ethnic States in Contemporary International Law: Failed States, Nation-Building and the Alternative, Federal Option* (2007); Michla Pomerance, *Self-Determination in Law and Practice* (1982); Volker Prott, *The Politics of Self-Determination: Remaking Territories and National Identities in Europe, 1917-1923* (2016); *Self-Determination and Secession in International Law* (Christian Walter et al. eds., 2014); A. Rigo Sureda, *The Evolution of the Right of Self-Determination* (1973); Joshua Castellino, *Territorial Integrity and the "Right" to Self-Determination: An Examination of the Conceptual Tools*, 33 BROOKLYN J. INT'L L. 503 (2008); United Nations, *The Right to Self Determination: Historical and Current Developments on the Basis of the United Nations Instruments* [Aureliu Cristescu, Special Rapporteur], U.N. Sales No. E.80.XIV3 (1981); United Nations, *The Right to Self-Determination –Implementation of United Nations Resolutions* [Hector Gros Espiell, Special Rapporteur], U.N. Sales No. E.79.XIV.5 (1980); *Report of the United Nations Expert Mechanism on the Rights of Indigenous Peoples — Efforts to Implement the United Nations Declaration on the Rights of Indigenous Peoples: Indigenous Peoples and the Right to Self-determination*, UN Doc. A/HRC/48/75 (2021); Inter-Am. Comm'n H.R., *Right to Self-Determination of Indigenous and Tribal Peoples*, OAS Doc. OEA/Ser.L/V/II. Doc. 413 (2021).

## *Note: Self-Determination and Kosovo*

There are very few examples of successful unilateral secessionist movements in the post-1945 era (excluding decolonization, which in some instances might technically have involved secession of a territory that had been considered to be an integral part of the administering state). For example, the independence of Bangladesh was not widely recognized until Pakistan first recognized the new state; the "Turkish Republic of Northern Cyprus" has been recognized only by Turkey, and its proclaimed independence has been rejected by the United Nations and the Council of Europe; the breakaway regions of Abkhazia and South Ossetia in Georgia have been recognized as independent by eight states, only five of which are themselves universally recognized as sovereign states. As of 2022, no universally recognized state recognizes the regions of Transdniester or Nagorno-Karabakh; and the independence of the former constituent republics of Yugoslavia was deemed by the international community to have resulted from the "dissolution" of the Yugoslav state, not the secession of any of its parts. The dissolutions of the Soviet Union and Czechoslovakia were by mutual consent, not unilateral, as was the 2006 division of

Serbia and Montenegro and the secession of South Sudan from Sudan in 2011 (the latter resulting from a peace treaty that ended three decades of civil war).

The independence of Kosovo, proclaimed in February 2008, may or may not be an exception. Kosovo had been recognized by 109 states as of mid-2022, including most Western states and most of its neighbors. However, Serbia, the state from which Kosovo purported to secede, has adamantly refused to recognize the new state, and its position is supported by such major actors as Russia, China, India, and most of Asia and Latin America.

At Serbia's initiative, the UN General Assembly requested that the International Court of Justice give an advisory opinion on the following question: "Is the unilateral declaration of independence by the Provisional Institutions of Self-Government of Kosovo in accordance with international law?" G.A. Res. 63/3 (2008). In giving its opinion, the I.C.J. relied on the narrow phrasing of the question to avoid examining the broader issue of the extent of post-colonial self-determination or secession. Adopting the traditional view that what is not prohibited by international law must be permissible ("general international law contains no applicable prohibition of declarations of independence"), the Court's carefully circumscribed opinion concludes merely that Kosovo's declaration of independence "did not violate general international law." *Accordance with International Law of the Unilateral Declaration of Independence in respect of Kosovo*, I.C.J. Advisory Opinion of July 22, 2010, para. 84. Approximately midway through its opinion, the Court notes the "radically different views" expressed to it on the question of whether either "self-determination" or a purported right of "remedial secession" would grant part of an existing state a right to separate from that state. Id., para. 82. The Court rather lamely—although correctly—decided that "it is not necessary to resolve these questions in the present case. . . . [which] is beyond the scope of the question posed by the General Assembly." Id., para. 83. We are thus left with the status quo ante, as the silence of international law identified by the Court leads to the conclusion that there is at present neither a positive right nor a prohibition under international law for a territory to attempt to secede, although one might query whether recognition of a seceding region against the wishes of the state whose territory it is found might constitute illegal interference with the territorial integrity or political independence of the parent state.

## Note: Peoples, Minorities, and Self-Determination

Although two UN-appointed experts have proposed definitions that have been generally accepted, states have resisted reaching formal agreement on a definition of either minorities or indigenous peoples, and none of the indigenous or minorities declarations contains a definition, although, as noted earlier, the OAS indigenous declaration does emphasize self-identification as a crucial criteria. See generally United Nations, *Study on the Rights of Persons Belonging to Ethnic, Religious and Linguistic Minorities* 96 [Francesco Capotorti, Special Rapporteur], U.N. Sales No. E.91.XIV.2 (1977, reprinted 1991); United Nations, *Study of the Problem of Discrimination Against Indigenous Populations*, Conclusions and Recommendations 50, 51 [Jose Martínez Cobo, Special Rapporteur], U.N. Sales No. E.86.XIV.3 (1986). Can one develop meaningful norms in this area without defining such essential terms as minority, indigenous, and peoples? How expansive is the concept of "indigenous peoples," and what is its relationship to the concept of "minorities"? Recall the description of the groups generally considered to be indigenous provided at page 149, *supra*.

Several African states led the effort to delay final adoption of the UN Declaration on the Rights of Indigenous Peoples after it was approved by the Human Rights Council, expressing concerns about the way in which the Declaration might apply to them. Asian states expressed similar concerns. Does the following extract from a report of a working group of the African Commission on Human and Peoples' Rights help identify the distinctions between indigenous peoples and minorities?

> It is our position that it is important to accept [that] the use of the term indigenous peoples more adequately encapsulates the real situation of the groups and communities concerned. However, there obviously can be overlaps between the [terms "minorities" and "indigenous peoples"]. . . .
>
> The major and crucial difference between minority rights and indigenous rights is that minority rights are formulated as individual rights whereas indigenous rights are collective rights. The specific rights of persons belonging to national or ethnic, religious or linguistic minorities . . . may be exercised by persons belonging to minorities individually as well as in community with other members of their group.
>
> Indigenous rights are clearly collective rights, even though they also recognize the foundation of individual human rights. Some of the most central elements in the indigenous rights regime are the collective rights to land, territory and natural resources. The Minority Declaration contains no such rights whereas land and natural resource rights are core elements in ILO Convention 169 (arts 13-19) and in the [then] draft indigenous declaration (arts 25-30). . . .
>
> The types of human rights protection that groups such as the San, Pygmies, Ogiek, Maasai, Barabaig, Tuareg, Berber etc. are seeking are of course individual human rights protections just like all other individuals in the world. However, it goes beyond this. These groups seek recognition as peoples and protection of their cultures and particular ways of living. A major issue for these groups is the protection of collective rights and access to their traditional land and the natural resources upon which the upholding of their way of life depends. As the protection of their collective rights, including land rights, is at the core of the matter, many of these groups feel that the indigenous human rights regime is a more relevant platform than the minority rights arena.

*Report of the African Commission's Working Group of Experts on Indigenous Populations/ Communities*, at 95-97, adopted by the African Commission and Peoples' Rights at its 34th Ordinary Sess. (Nov. 6-23, 2003), http://www.pro169.org/res/materials/en/ identification/ACHPR%20Report%20on%20indigenous%20populations -communities.pdf.

In the above extract the African Commission's working group clearly articulates the collective dimension of some indigenous rights and the individual dimension of the rights of persons belonging to minorities. However, this does not appear to be of much use if one considers it important to determine to which category a particular collectivity may belong. Note that in the African context specific rights are granted to "peoples" in the African Charter. For an expansive interpretation of the term "peoples" and discussion of the right of self-determination, see *Kevin Mgwanga Gunme v Cameroon*, Communication No. 266/2003, Afr. Comm'n H.P.R., EX.CL/529 (XV), 45th Ordinary Session, Annex 4 (2009). Can a group constitute both a minority and an indigenous people at the same time? For example, the Human Rights Committee has frequently examined petitions under the provisions of Article 27 of the Covenant, which deals with persons belonging to minorities, that have been filed by groups that are clearly "indigenous." What, then, are the distinctions among the terms minority, indigenous, and peoples?

The distinction between minority and indigenous is not a merely theoretical issue, since the rights attributed to members of the two groups and to the two groups per se are quite different in many respects, and different mechanisms within the human rights system are formally constituted to focus specifically on one or the other. Chief among these rights, according to some, is the right of self-determination, which is set forth in both the UN and OAS declarations but which appears nowhere in any articulation of minority rights. Many other "indigenous" rights—e.g., to self-government, land, natural resources, and culture—also are much broader than the rights normally ascribed to minorities.

The Human Rights Committee's General Comment 23 on Article 27 includes the following distinction between the right of self-determination and the minority rights set forth in Article 27 of the Covenant on Civil and Political Rights:

> 3.1 The Covenant draws a distinction between the right to self-determination and the rights protected under article 27. The former is expressed to be a right belonging to peoples and is dealt with in a separate part (Part I) of the Covenant. Self-determination is not a right cognizable under the Optional Protocol. Article 27, on the other hand, relates to rights conferred on individuals as such and is included, like the articles relating to other personal rights conferred on individuals, in Part III of the Covenant and is cognizable under the Optional Protocol.
>
> 3.2 The enjoyment of the rights to which article 27 relates does not prejudice the sovereignty and territorial integrity of a State party. At the same time, one or [the] other aspect of the rights of individuals protected under that article - for example to enjoy a particular culture - may consist in a way of life which is closely associated with territory and use of its resources. This may particularly be true of members of indigenous communities constituting a minority.

Is this distinction consistent with the views taken by the Committee on the Elimination of Racial Discrimination in its General Recommendation on Self-Determination, *supra* page 183?

A prevalent argument for recognizing a right of self-determination for indigenous peoples is their historical attachment to territory. But do not many other groups also have a strong sense of territory or "homeland"? Consider the following from William Shakespeare's, *King Richard II*, Act 2, Scene 1:

> This royal throne of kings, this sceptred isle,
> This earth of majesty, this seat of Mars,
> This other Eden, demi-paradise,
> This fortress built by Nature for herself
> Against infection and the hand of war,
> This happy breed of men, this little world,
> This precious stone set in the silver sea,
> Which serves it in the office of a wall
> Or as a moat defensive to a house,
> Against the envy of less happier lands,—
> This blessed plot, this earth, this realm, this England.

In 1975, the U.S. Congress adopted the Indian Self-Determination and Education Assistance Act, 25 U.S.C. §§13a, 450-450n, 455-458e, 42 U.S. §2004b (1994), which permits tribes to enter into contracts with the federal government and assume responsibility for various federally administered programs. Is this an appropriate use of the term "self-determination," as that term may be understood in international law?

Is the fact of colonization relevant to whether or how a group should enjoy self-determination? If so, should it be only European colonization that is relevant, or are conquest and incorporation by a neighboring expansionist power — which describes the history of most of the world's current states — effectively the same phenomenon? One or more of these and related questions are taken up in the following works: Hurst Hannum, *The Specter of Secession: Responding to Ethnic Self-Determination Claims*, 77 FOREIGN AFFAIRS 13 (1998); Maivân Lâm, *At the Edge of the State: Indigenous Peoples and Self-Determination* (2000); Thomas Duncan Musgrave, *Self-Determination and National Minorities* (1997); Jennifer Jackson-Preece, *National Minorities and the European Nation-State System* (1998); *The Rights of Peoples* (James Crawford ed. 1988); Patrick Thornberry, *International Law and the Rights of Minorities* (1993).

## V.   FINAL COMMENTS AND QUESTIONS

1. How expansive is the Human Rights Committee's interpretation of Article 27 of the Covenant on Civil and Political Rights in its General Comment on that article, *supra* page 179? Does paragraph 6.1 of the General Comment mean that private employers cannot prohibit employees from speaking their own language on the job? What kinds of "positive measures" might be necessary to protect the identity of a minority? Do you think that states intended that Article 27 protect indigenous rights over lands and resources, as held by the Committee? Do you think that states intended to grant minority rights to migrant workers and tourists? Does it matter what states thought? Recall the materials on treaty interpretation in Chapter 2.

2. One common theme in discussions about indigenous peoples, minorities, and self-determination is the call for respect for cultural diversity. Note in this regard the UNESCO Universal Declaration on Cultural Diversity, adopted in 2001 by the General Conference of the UN Educational, Scientific and Cultural Organization (UNESCO), and the subsequent UNESCO Convention on the Protection

and Promotion of the Diversity of Cultural Expressions, Oct. 20, 2005, CLT-2005. For the purposes of advancing cultural diversity, does it matter that a group is denominated a "minority" or "indigenous"?

3. Is the term "peoples" used in the same sense in (1) the declarations referring to decolonization and ascribing to "peoples" a right of self-determination; (2) common Article 1 of the Covenants proclaiming a right to self-determination for "All peoples"; and (3) the provisions of the UN and OAS indigenous rights declarations that affirm that "All indigenous peoples" have a right to self-determination? Is the right of self-determination the same in all contexts?

4. We can see from the above materials that expert bodies, such as the Inter-American Commission on Human Rights and the UN treaty monitoring bodies, are assuming roles in shaping international human rights standards through their interpretive statements and decisions. What is the legal effect of these statements and decisions? These bodies are made up of individuals acting in their own capacities and not as representatives of states; they are created by states through multilateral treaties; and they are authorized only to make recommendations, not to adopt legally binding decisions or interpretations. Are the statements and decisions of such institutions secondary sources akin to the "judicial decisions and teachings of the most highly qualified publicists" mentioned in Article 38 of the Statute of the International Court of Justice? Are they a form of practice contributing to the formation of customary international law? Or are they merely statements about "best practices" (or wishful thinking), whose ultimate legal effect will depend on their acceptance by states? Is it a satisfactory response simply call all of these non-treaty documents "soft law?"

# CHAPTER 4

# ACCOUNTABILITY FOR HUMAN RIGHTS

## WHAT ARE THE OBLIGATIONS OR RESPONSIBILITIES OF STATES, AND OTHERS, IN RELATION TO HUMAN RIGHTS?

## I.  INTRODUCTION: DEFINING THE SCOPE OF HUMAN RIGHTS OBLIGATIONS

Agreeing on the content and sources of human rights guaranteed by international law is not sufficient to ensure that rights are exercised in practice. The duties that correspond to the rights must also be agreed to and established. From the beginning of the modern human rights era, human rights law had its focus directed towards restraining powerful state actors. This approach corresponded to the framework of international society, which, at least since the seventeenth century, has been largely organized to address the exercise of state authority. Thus, the United Nations Charter and human rights treaties obligate states parties to observe the rights and freedoms the treaties guarantee; and the treaties, along with international human rights law more generally, provide principles for establishing the duties of states witin this obligation.

Yet, apart from states, there are many transnational entities and organizations with their own governing structures and claims of loyalty on those who belong to them, from corporations and inter-governmental organizations, to religious bodies, non-governmental organizations, terrorist networks, and organized crime syndicates. As non-state sectors have grown in size and power, authoritative international bodies and experts have begun to address—albeit tentatively and in a piecemeal manner—the question of whether or to what extext human rights norms apply to the conduct of actors other than states.

Inter-governmental organizations such as the UN themselves are objects of this inquiry, as they grow in authority and power internationally. They are deemed to have "international personality," the quality of having rights and duties under international law, a quality that was once reserved only to states. See *Reparations for Injuries Suffered in the Service of the United Nations*, Advisory Opinion, 1949 I.C.J. 174 (April 11). But complex issues remain about the extent to which these duties are framed by international human rights law and the extent to which the powers of international organizations can or should be harnessed to address human rights.

Also complex is the very different question of the link between international human rights law and the activities of business enterprises. In general, international law has encouraged the formation and operation of multinational companies. Parties to the many bilateral investment treaties pledge to recognize each other's respective legal business forms and permit each others' companies to establish subsidiaries, financial investments, joint ventures, and franchises. Bilateral investment treaties provide basic rights to foreign businesses, including protection against expropriation and guarantees of most-favored nation status, and identify the accepted dispute resolution mechanisms. See Bettwy, David Shea, *The Human Rights and Wrongs of Foreign Direct Investment: Addressing the Need for an Analytical Framework*, 2012 Rich. J. Global L.& Bus. 239-272 (2012).

Additionally, the World Trade Organization (WTO) has adopted Trade-Related Investment Measures (TRIMs) that limit the ability of states to regulate foreign-owned or foreign-controlled firms or joint ventures. The overall picture is one of relative freedom of economic movement and activity. The power of large multinational businesses in this environment, bringing with it the potential for abuse of workers and others, has led many human rights activists and developing countries to mount efforts to establish international legal obligations for business entities, especially since the era of governmental deregulation and privatization that began in the 1980s. As discussed in this Chapter, to date at the international level only non-binding standards have been explicitly adopted. There are also numerous voluntary codes of conduct and some effective consumer action through boycotts, labelling campaigns, and procurement policies like anti-sweatshop initiatives. Increasing attention is also being given to whether and to what extent parent companies should be subject to the law and jurisdiction of their home countries in relation to their subsidiaries and operations abroad.

The actions of private individuals, undoubtedly, also have bearing on the enjoyment of human rights. International human rights law may hold states responsible for the conduct of individuals in some situations, as we will see below. But international human rights law for the most part does not directly obligate individuals or hold them responsible for violations. Nonetheless, several human rights texts contain one or more provisions that speak to the duties of persons in society. See, e.g., Universal Declaration of Human Rights Article 29(1) (providing that "Everyone has duties to the community in which alone the free and full development of his personality is possible."). The International Covenant on Civil and Political Rights in its Preamble refers to individual duties, while the American Convention considers that "Every person has responsibilities to his family, his community, and mankind." The African Charter on Human and Peoples' Rights mentions individual duties in the Preamble and lists them in Articles 27-29, while the Arab Charter on Human Rights uniquely implies human duties in the statement of its aims contained in Article 1.

A more recently adopted regional instrument, the Human Rights Declaration of the Association of Southeast Nations (ASEAN), provides that the enjoyment of human rights and fundamental freedoms "must be balanced" with the performance of corresponding duties. The notion of conditioning respect for human rights on fulfillment of duties was troubling to civil society organizations and led the UN High Commissioner for Human Rights to affirm that "the balancing of human rights with individual duties is not a part of international human rights law, misrepresents the positive dynamic between rights and duties and should not be included in a human rights instrument." *Statement by the High Commissioner for Human Rights at the Bali Democracy Forum*, UN Office of the Hight Commissioner for Human Rights (Nov. 7, 2012), https://www.ohchr.org/en/statements/2012/11/statement-high-commissioner-human-rights-bali-democracy-forum.

Beyond the mostly abstract articulation of general individual duties to family and society in a number of treaties and declarations, private individuals can be held responsible under international law for human right violations in limited contexts. Private actor liability exists for acts of genocide, slavery, war crimes, and certain other gross violations of human rights. Therefore, individuals may be responsible for certain attacks on physical security and integrity during peace and war. The international law obligations of individual persons to avoid gross human rights violations and war crimes are addressed in Chapter 5.

This Chapter examines the general duties of states under international human rights law and examines the extent to which business enterprises and intergovernmental organizations also are or should be accountable for upholding human rights. Additionally, the readings in this chapter consider the attribution of responsibility for violations of international human rights law and how such attribution has been addressed by global and regional human rights bodies.

## II. THE GENERAL OBLIGATIONS OF STATES: "NEGATIVE" AND "POSITIVE" OBLIGATIONS

Human rights treaties use a variety of verbs to describe the duties they impose on states. The International Covenant on Civil and Political Rights and the American Convention on Human Rights require state parties to "respect" and "ensure" the rights proclaimed in the respective treaties. In contrast, under the International

Covenant on Economic, Social, and Cultural Rights each state party "recognizes" the rights therein and "undertakes to take steps, individually and through international assistance and cooperation, especially economic and technical, to the maximum of its available resources, with a view to achieving progressively the full realization of the rights . . . by all appropriate means, including particularly the adoption of legislative measures." The European Convention on Human Rights obliges states parties to "secure" the rights in the Convention and its Protocols, while the African Charter calls on its parties to "recognize" and "give effect" to the rights it affirms. What do these various terms mean in practice? Do the obligations respecting civil and political rights differ significantly from those concerning economic, social, and cultural rights? Are all obligations in the areas of social and economic rights subjected to progressive realization and the availability of resources?

The following materials explore the views of global and regional human rights bodies on the scope of state obligations. As we will see, the above treaty terms signify a combination of "negative" and "positive" obligations, and they are supplemented by certain generally recognized principles. Immediately following is an extract of a landmark decision of the African Commission on Human and Peoples' Rights, under its communications procedure, on the general human rights obligations of states particularly in connection with the African Charter on Human and Peoples' Rights, a regional multilateral human rights treaty introduced in Chapter 1. Further background on the African human rights system is provided in Chapter 9.

## The Social and Economic Rights Action Center (SERAC) and the Center for Economic and Social Rights v. Nigeria

Communication No. 155/96, African Comm'n H.P.R., decision of Oct. 27, 2001 (most footnotes and references omitted)

SUMMARY OF FACTS

1. The communication alleges that the military government of Nigeria has been directly involved in oil production through the State oil company, the Nigerian National Petroleum Company (NNPC), the majority shareholder in a consortium with Shell Petroleum Development Corporation (SPDC), and that these operations have caused environmental degradation and health problems resulting from the contamination of the environment among the Ogoni People.

2. The communication alleges that the oil consortium has exploited oil reserves in Ogoniland with no regard for the health or environment of the local communities, disposing toxic wastes into the environment and local waterways in violation of applicable international environmental standards. The consortium also neglected and/or failed to maintain its facilities causing numerous avoidable spills in the proximity of villages. The resulting contamination of water, soil and air has had serious short and long-term health impacts, including skin infections, gastrointestinal and respiratory ailments, and increased risk of cancers, and neurological and reproductive problems.

3. The communication alleges that the Nigerian Government has condoned and facilitated these violations by placing the legal and military powers of the state

at the disposal of the oil companies. The communication contains a memo from the Rivers State Internal Security Task Force, calling for "ruthless military operations."

4. The communication alleges that the government has neither monitored operations of the oil companies nor required safety measures that are standard procedure within the industry. The government has withheld from Ogoni communities information on the dangers created by oil activities. Ogoni communities have not been involved in the decisions affecting the development of Ogoniland.

5. The government has not required oil companies or its own agencies to produce basic health and environmental impact studies regarding hazardous operations and materials relating to oil production, despite the obvious health and environmental crisis in Ogoniland. The government has even refused to permit scientists and environmental organisations from entering Ogoniland to undertake such studies. The government has also ignored the concerns of Ogoni communities regarding oil development, and has responded to protests with massive violence and executions of Ogoni leaders.

6. The communication alleges that the Nigerian government does not require oil companies to consult communities before beginning operations, even if the operations pose direct threats to community or individual lands.

7. The communication alleges that in the course of the last three years, Nigerian security forces have attacked, burned and destroyed several Ogoni villages and homes under the pretext of dislodging officials and supporters of the Movement of the Survival of Ogoni People (MOSOP). These attacks have come in response to MOSOP's non-violent campaign in opposition to the destruction of their environment by oil companies. Some of the attacks have involved uniformed combined forces of the police, the army, the air-force, and the navy, armed with armoured tanks and other sophisticated weapons. In other instances, the attacks have been conducted by unidentified gunmen, mostly at night. The military-type methods and the calibre of weapons used in such attacks strongly suggest the involvement of the Nigerian security forces. The complete failure of the Government of Nigeria to investigate these attacks, let alone punish the perpetrators, further implicates the Nigerian authorities.

8. The Nigerian Army has admitted its role in the ruthless operations which have left thousands of villagers homeless. The admission is recorded in several memos exchanged between officials of the SPDC and the Rivers State Internal Security Task Force, which has devoted itself to the suppression of the Ogoni campaign. One such memo calls for "ruthless military operations" and "wasting operations coupled with psychological tactics of displacement." At a public meeting recorded on video, Major Okuntimo, head of the Task Force, described the repeated invasion of Ogoni villages by his troops, how unarmed villagers running from the troops were shot from behind, and the homes of suspected MOSOP activists were ransacked and destroyed. He stated his commitment to rid the communities of members and supporters of MOSOP.

9. The communication alleges that the Nigerian government has destroyed and threatened Ogoni food sources through a variety of means. The government has participated in irresponsible oil development that has poisoned much of the soil and water upon which Ogoni farming and fishing depended. In their raids on villages, Nigerian security forces have destroyed crops and killed farm animals. The security forces have created a state of terror and insecurity that has made it

impossible for many Ogoni villagers to return to their fields and animals. The destruction of farmlands, rivers, crops and animals has created malnutrition and starvation among certain Ogoni communities.

10. The communication alleges violations of Articles 2, 4, 14, 16, 18(1), 21, and 24 of the African Charter.

PROCEDURE

11. The communication was received by the Commission on 14th March 1996. The documents were sent with a video. . . .

[Between 1996 and 2000, the Commission tried unsuccessfully to obtain a respon from the Nigerian government on the allegations in the communication.]

30. During . . . [the spring 2001] session, the Respondent State submitted a Note Verbale stating the actions taken by the Government of the Federal Republic of Nigeria in respect of all the communications filed against it, including the present one. In respect of the instant communication, the note verbale admitted the gravamen of the complaints [which were against the former Abacha regime, not the authorities that finally responded in 2000]. . . .

34. At its 30th session held in Banjul, the Gambia from 13th to 27th October 2001, the African Commission reached a decision on the merits of this communication.

LAW

. . .

MERITS

. . .

43. The present Communication alleges a concerted violation of a wide range of rights guaranteed under the African Charter for Human and People' Rights. Before we venture into the inquiry whether the Government of Nigeria has violated the said rights as alleged in the Complaint, it would be proper to establish what is generally expected of governments under the Charter and more specifically vis-à-vis the rights themselves.

44. Internationally accepted ideas of the various obligations engendered by human rights indicate that all rights—both civil and political rights and social and economic—generate at least four levels of duties for a State that undertakes to adhere to a rights regime, namely the duty to respect, protect, promote, and fulfil these rights. These obligations universally apply to all rights and entail a combination of negative and positive duties. As a human rights instrument, the African Charter is not alien to these concepts and the order in which they are dealt with here is chosen as a matter of convenience and in no way should it imply the priority accorded to them. Each layer of obligation is equally relevant to the rights in question.[2]

_4 levels of duties_

---

2.  See generally, Asbjørn Eide, "Economic, Social and Cultural Rights As Human Rights" in Asbjørn Eide, Catarina Krause and Allan Rosas (Eds.) *Economic, Social, and Cultural Right: A Textbook* (1995) pp. 21-40.

*Respect*

45. At a primary level, the obligation to respect entails that the State should refrain from interfering in the enjoyment of all fundamental rights; it should respect right-holders, their freedoms, autonomy, resources, and liberty of their action.[3] With respect to socio economic rights, this means that the State is obliged to respect the free use of resources owned or at the disposal of the individual alone or in any form of association with others, including the household or the family, for the purpose of rights-related needs. And with regard to a collective group, the resources belonging to it should be respected, as it has to use the same resources to satisfy its needs.

*Protect*

*Promote*

46. At a secondary level, the State is obliged to protect right-holders against other subjects by legislation and provision of effective remedies. This obligation requires the State to take measures to protect beneficiaries of the protected rights against political, economic and social interferences. Protection generally entails the creation and maintenance of an atmosphere or framework by an effective interplay of laws and regulations so that individuals will be able to freely realize their rights and freedoms. This is very much intertwined with the tertiary obligation of the State to promote the enjoyment of all human rights. The State should make sure that individuals are able to exercise their rights and freedoms, for example, by promoting tolerance, raising awareness, and even building infrastructures.

*Fulfill*

47. The last layer of obligation requires the State to fulfill the rights and freedoms it freely undertook under the various human rights regimes. It is more of a positive expectation on the part of the State to move its machinery towards the actual realization of the rights. This is also very much intertwined with the duty to promote mentioned in the preceding paragraph. It could consist in the direct provision of basic needs such as food or resources that can be used for food (direct food aid or social security). . . .

49. In accordance with Articles 60 and 61 of the African Charter, this communication is examined in the light of the provisions of the African Charter and the relevant international and regional human rights instruments and principles. The Commission thanks the two human rights NGOs who brought the matter under its purview: the Social and Economic Rights Action Center (Nigeria) and the Center for Economic and Social Rights (USA). Such is a demonstration of the usefulness to the Commission and individuals of actio popul(Aris, which is wisely allowed under the African Charter. It is a matter of regret that the only written response from the government of Nigeria is an admission of the gravamen of the complaints which is contained in a note verbale . . . In the circumstances, the Commission is compelled to proceed with the examination of the matter on the basis of the uncontested allegations of the Complainants, which are consequently accepted by the Commission.

50. The Complainants allege that the Nigerian government violated the right to health and the right to clean environment as recognized under Articles 16 and 24 of the African Charter by failing to fulfill the minimum duties required by these rights. This, the Complainants allege, the government has done by:

---

3. Krzysztof Drzewicki, "Internationalization of Human Rights and Their Juridization" in Raija Hanski and Markku Suksi (Eds.), Second Revised Edition, *An Introduction to the International Protection of Human Rights: A Textbook* (1999), p. 31.

— Directly participating in the contamination of air, water and soil and thereby harming the health of the Ogoni population,

— Failing to protect the Ogoni population from the harm caused by the NNPC Shell Consortium but instead using its security forces to facilitate the damage,

— Failing to provide or permit studies of potential or actual environmental and health risks caused by the oil operations

Article 16 of the African Charter reads:

(1) Every individual shall have the right to enjoy the best attainable state of physical and mental health.
(2) States Parties to the present Charter shall take the necessary measures to protect the health of their people and to ensure that they receive medical attention when they are sick.

Article 24 of the African Charter reads:

All peoples shall have the right to a general satisfactory environment favourable to their development.

51. These rights recognize the importance of a clean and safe environment that is closely linked to economic and social rights in so far as the environment affects the quality of life and safety of the individual. As has been rightly observed by Alexander Kiss, "an environment degraded by pollution and defaced by the destruction of all beauty and variety is as contrary to satisfactory living conditions and the development as the breakdown of the fundamental ecologic equilibria is harmful to physical and moral health."

52. The right to a general satisfactory environment, as guaranteed under Article 24 of the African Charter or the right to a healthy environment, as it is widely known, therefore imposes clear obligations upon a government. It requires the State to take reasonable and other measures to prevent pollution and ecological degradation, to promote conservation, and to secure an ecologically sustainable development and use of natural resources. Article 12 of the International Covenant on Economic, Social and Cultural Rights (ICESCR), to which Nigeria is a party, requires governments to take necessary steps for the improvement of all aspects of environmental and industrial hygiene. The right to enjoy the best attainable state of physical and mental health enunciated in Article 16(1) of the African Charter and the right to a general satisfactory environment favourable to development (Article 16(3)) already noted obligate governments to desist from directly threatening the health and environment of their citizens. The State is under an obligation to respect the just noted rights and this entails largely non-interventionist conduct from the State for example, not from carrying out, sponsoring or tolerating any practice, policy or legal measures violating the integrity of the individual.

53. Government compliance with the spirit of Articles 16 and 24 of the African Charter must also include ordering or at least permitting independent scientific monitoring of threatened environments, requiring and publicizing environmental and social impact studies prior to any major industrial development, undertaking appropriate monitoring and providing information to those communities exposed to hazardous materials and activities and providing meaningful opportunities for individuals to be heard and to participate in the development decisions affecting their communities.

54. We now examine the conduct of the government of Nigeria in relation to Articles 16 and 24 of the African Charter. Undoubtedly and admittedly, the government of Nigeria, through NNPC has the right to produce oil, the income from which will be used to fulfill the economic and social rights of Nigerians. But the care that should have been taken as outlined in the preceding paragraph and which would have protected the rights of the victims of the violations complained of was not taken. To exacerbate the situation, the security forces of the government engaged in conduct in violation of the rights of the Ogonis by attacking, burning and destroying several Ogoni villages and homes. . . .

55. . . . The destructive and selfish role-played by oil development in Ogoniland, closely tied with repressive tactics of the Nigerian Government, and the lack of material benefits accruing to the local population, may well be said to constitute a violation of Article 21.

Article 21 provides

> All peoples shall freely dispose of their wealth and natural resources. This right shall be exercised in the exclusive interest of the people. In no case shall a people be deprived of it. In case of spoliation the dispossessed people shall have the right to the lawful recovery of its property as well as to an adequate compensation. The free disposal of wealth and natural resources shall be exercised without prejudice to the obligation of promoting international economic co-operation based on mutual respect, equitable exchange and the principles of international law. . . .

57. Governments have a duty to protect their citizens, not only through appropriate legislation and effective enforcement but also by protecting them from damaging acts that may be perpetrated by private parties. This duty calls for positive action on part of governments in fulfilling their obligation under human rights instruments. The practice before other tribunals also enhances this requirement as is evidenced in the case Velásquez Rodríguez v. Honduras [see pages 212-217, *infra*]. In this landmark judgment, the Inter-American Court of Human Rights held that when a State allows private persons or groups to act freely and with impunity to the detriment of the rights recognized, it would be in clear violation of its obligations to protect the human rights of its citizens. Similarly, this obligation of the State is further emphasized in the practice of the European Court of Human Rights, in X and Y v. Netherlands [91 ECHR (1985) (Ser. A) at 32]. In that case, the Court pronounced that there was an obligation on authorities to take steps to make sure that the enjoyment of the rights is not interfered with by any other private person.

58. The Commission notes that in the present case, despite its obligation to protect persons against interferences in the enjoyment of their rights, the Government of Nigeria facilitated the destruction of the Ogoniland. Contrary to its Charter obligations and despite such internationally established principles, the Nigerian Government has given the green light to private actors, and the oil Companies in particular, to devastatingly affect the well-being of the Ogonis. By any measure of standards, its practice falls short of the minimum conduct expected of governments, and therefore, is in violation of Article 21 of the African Charter.

59. The Complainants also assert that the Military government of Nigeria massively and systematically violated the right to adequate housing of members of the

Ogoni community under Article 14 and implicitly recognized by Articles 16 and 18(1) of the African Charter. . . .

60. Although the right to housing or shelter is not explicitly provided for under the African Charter, the corollary of the combination of the provisions protecting the right to enjoy the best attainable state of mental and physical health, cited under Article 16 above, the right to property, and the protection accorded to the family forbids the wanton destruction of shelter because when housing is destroyed, property, health, and family life are adversely affected. It is thus noted that the combined effect of Articles 14, 16 and 18(1) reads into the Charter a right to shelter or housing which the Nigerian Government has apparently violated.

61. At a very minimum, the right to shelter obliges the Nigerian government not to destroy the housing of its citizens and not to obstruct efforts by individuals or communities to rebuild lost homes. The State's obligation to respect housing rights requires it, and thereby all of its organs and agents, to abstain from carrying out, sponsoring or tolerating any practice, policy or legal measure violating the integrity of the individual or infringing upon his or her freedom to use those material or other resources available to them in a way they find most appropriate to satisfy individual, family, household or community housing needs. Its obligations to protect obliges it to prevent the violation of any individual's right to housing by any other individual or non-state actors like landlords, property developers, and land owners, and where such infringements occur, it should act to preclude further deprivations as well as guaranteeing access to legal remedies. The right to shelter even goes further than a roof over ones head. It extends to embody the individual's right to be let alone and to live in peace– whether under a roof or not.

62. The protection of the rights guaranteed in Articles 14, 16 and 18 (1) leads to the same conclusion. As regards the earlier right, and in the case of the Ogoni People, the Government of Nigeria has failed to fulfill these two minimum obligations. The government has destroyed Ogoni houses and villages and then, through its security forces, obstructed, harassed, beaten and, in some cases, shot and killed innocent citizens who have attempted to return to rebuild their ruined homes. These actions constitute massive violations of the right to shelter, in violation of Articles 14, 16, and 18(1) of the African Charter.

63. The particular violation by the Nigerian Government of the right to adequate housing as implicitly protected in the Charter also encompasses the right to protection against forced evictions. The African Commission draws inspiration from the definition of the term "forced evictions" by the Committee on Economic Social and Cultural Rights which defines this term as "the permanent removal against their will of individuals, families and/or communities from the homes and/or which they occupy, without the provision of, and access to, appropriate forms of legal or other protection". Wherever and whenever they occur, forced evictions are extremely traumatic. They cause physical, psychological and emotional distress; they entail losses of means of economic sustenance and increase impoverishment. They can also cause physical injury and in some cases sporadic deaths. . . . Evictions break up families and increase existing levels of homelessness. In this regard, General Comment No. 4 (1991) of the Committee on Economic, Social and Cultural Rights on the right to adequate housing states that "all persons should possess a degree of security of tenure which guarantees legal protection against forced

eviction, harassment and other threats". The conduct of the Nigerian government clearly demonstrates a violation of this right enjoyed by the Ogonis as a collective right.

64. The Communication argues that the right to food is implicit in the African Charter, in such provisions as the right to life (Art. 4), the right to health (Art. 16) and the right to economic, social and cultural development (Art. 22). By its violation of these rights, the Nigerian Government trampled upon not only the explicitly protected rights but also upon the right to food implicitly guaranteed.

65. The right to food is inseparably linked to the dignity of human beings and is therefore essential for the enjoyment and fulfilment of such other rights as health, education, work and political participation. The African Charter and international law require and bind Nigeria to protect and improve existing food sources and to ensure access to adequate food for all citizens. Without touching on the duty to improve food production and to guarantee access, the minimum core of the right to food requires that the Nigerian Government should not destroy or contaminate food sources. It should not allow private parties to destroy or contaminate food sources, and prevent peoples' efforts to feed themselves.

66. The government's treatment of the Ogonis has violated all three minimum duties of the right to food. The government has destroyed food sources through its security forces and State Oil Company; has allowed private oil companies to destroy food sources; and, through terror, has created significant obstacles to Ogoni communities trying to feed themselves. The Nigerian government has again fallen short of what is expected of it as under the provisions of the African Charter and international human rights standards, and hence, is in violation of the right to food of the Ogonis.

67. The Complainants also allege that the Nigerian Government has violated Article 4 of the Charter which guarantees the inviolability of human beings and everyone's right to life and integrity of the person respected. Given the wide spread violations perpetrated by the Government of Nigeria and by private actors (be it following its clear blessing or not), the most fundamental of all human rights, the right to life has been violated. The Security forces were given the green light to decisively deal with the Ogonis, which was illustrated by the wide spread terrorisations and killings. The pollution and environmental degradation to a level humanly unacceptable has made it living in the Ogoni land a nightmare. The survival of the Ogonis depended on their land and farms that were destroyed by the direct involvement of the Government. These and similar brutalities not only persecuted individuals in Ogoniland but also the whole of the Ogoni Community as a whole. They affected the life of the Ogoni Society as a whole. The Commission conducted a mission to Nigeria from the 7th-14th March 1997 and witnessed first-hand the deplorable situation in Ogoni land including the environmental degradation.

68. The uniqueness of the African situation and the special qualities of the African Charter on Human and Peoples' Rights imposes upon the African Commission an important task. International law and human rights must be responsive to African circumstances. Clearly, collective rights, environmental rights, and economic and social rights are essential elements of human rights in Africa. The African Commission will apply any of the diverse rights contained in the African Charter. It welcomes this opportunity to make clear that there is no right in the

African Charter that cannot be made effective. As indicated in the preceding paragraphs, however, the Nigerian Government did not live up to the minimum expectations of the African Charter.

69. The Commission does not wish to fault governments that are labouring under difficult circumstances to improve the lives of their people. The situation of the people of Ogoniland, however, requires, in the view of the Commission, a reconsideration of the Government's attitude to the allegations contained in the instant communication. The intervention of multinational corporations may be a potentially positive force for development if the State and the people concerned are ever mindful of the common good and the sacred rights of individuals and communities. The Commission however takes note of the efforts of the present civilian administration to redress the atrocities that were committed by the previous military administration as illustrated in the Note Verbale referred to in paragraph 30 of this decision.

FOR THE ABOVE REASONS, THE COMMISSION,

FINDS the Federal Republic of Nigeria in violation of Articles 2, 4, 14, 16, 18(1), 21 and 24 of the African Charter on Human and Peoples' Rights;

APPEALS to the government of the Federal Republic of Nigeria to ensure protection of the environment, health and livelihood of the people of Ogoniland by:

> Stopping all attacks on Ogoni communities and leaders by the Rivers State Internal Securities Task Force and permitting citizens and independent investigators free access to the territory;
>
> Conducting an investigation into the human rights violations described above and prosecuting officials of the security forces, NNPC and relevant agencies involved in human rights violations;
>
> Ensuring adequate compensation to victims of the human rights violations, including relief and resettlement assistance to victims of government sponsored raids, and undertaking a comprehensive cleanup of lands and rivers damaged by oil operations;
>
> Ensuring that appropriate environmental and social impact assessments are prepared for any future oil development and that the safe operation of any further oil development is guaranteed through effective and independent oversight bodies for the petroleum industry; and
>
> Providing information on health and environmental risks and meaningful access to regulatory and decision-making bodies to communities likely to be affected by oil operations.

---

The pattern of violence against Ogoni people, addressed by the African Commission on Human and Peoples' Rights in its decision above, included the much-condemned detentions and hangings of well-known activist Ken Saro-Wiwa and other leaders of the peaceful Movement for the Survival of the Ogoni People by the Nigerian military dictatorship. Family members of these and other victims filed lawsuits in US federal district court under the federal Alien Tort Statute (ATS) against

Royal Dutch/Shell, it's CEO, and it's Nigerian subsidiary Shell Petroleum Development Company. The lawsuits alleged complicity in the human rights abuses against the Ogoni people. In 2006, after ten years of litigation and appeals, these lawsuits were settled on the eve of trial, with Shell agreeing to provide the victims a total of $15.5 million in compensation. A group of Nigerian political asylees residing in the United States filed another ATS lawsuit in US federal court against the same defendants, similarly alleging aiding and abetting in human rights violations in Ogoniland. In that case, *Kiobel v. Royal Dutch Petroluem*, 569 U.S 108 (2013), the US Supreme Court ultimately upheld dismissal of the complaint on the ground that the ATS does not allow for a cause of action for acts committed outside the United States. The Court did not reach the issue, raised in the litigation, of whether or not the ATS or international law provide a basis for claims against corporations for human rights violations. The Alien Tort Statute is discussed in Chapter 6, along with an edited version of the *Kiobel* opinion by the Supreme Court. The issue of corporate responsibility in relation to international human rights is addressed in section III of this Chapter. For now, the readings continue with examination of the scope of state obligations.

In light of the above decision by the African Commission concerning the Ogoni, consider the following statements of two UN treaty-monitory bodies on the general legal obligations of states under, respectively, the International Covenant on Civil and Political Rights, and the International Covenant on Economic, Social and Cultural Rights. The UN system of committees established to monitor and promote compliance with the UN human rights treaties to which they are attached is discussed in Chapter 7. Among their functions, the committees created by UN human rights treaties, typically called "treaty-monitoring bodies," issue "General Comments" or "General Recommendations" that interpret specific treaty provisions and provide guidance on their implementation.

## Human Rights Committee

## General Comment 31: The Nature of the General Legal Obligation Imposed on States Parties to the Covenant on Civil and Political Rights

UN Doc. CCPR/C/21/Rev.1/Add.13 (2004)

3. Article 2 defines the scope of the legal obligations undertaken by States Parties to the Covenant. A general obligation is imposed on States Parties to respect the Covenant rights and to ensure them to all individuals in their territory and subject to their jurisdiction (see paragraph 10 below). Pursuant to the principle articulated in article 26 of the Vienna Convention on the Law of Treaties, States Parties are required to give effect to the obligations under the Covenant in good faith.

4. The obligations of the Covenant in general and article 2 in particular are binding on every State Party as a whole. All branches of government (executive, legislative and judicial), and other public or governmental authorities, at whatever level — national, regional or local — are in a position to engage the responsibility of the State Party. The executive branch that usually represents the State Party internationally, including before the Committee, may not point to the fact that an

action incompatible with the provisions of the Covenant was carried out by another branch of government as a means of seeking to relieve the State Party from responsibility for the action and consequent incompatibility. This understanding flows directly from the principle contained in article 27 of the Vienna Convention on the Law of Treaties, according to which a State Party 'may not invoke the provisions of its internal law as justification for its failure to perform a treaty'. Although article 2, paragraph 2, allows States Parties to give effect to Covenant rights in accordance with domestic constitutional processes, the same principle operates so as to prevent States parties from invoking provisions of the constitutional law or other aspects of domestic law to justify a failure to perform or give effect to obligations under the treaty. In this respect, the Committee reminds States Parties with a federal structure of the terms of article 50, according to which the Covenant's provisions 'shall extend to all parts of federal states without any limitations or exceptions'. . . .

6. The legal obligation under article 2, paragraph 1, is both negative and positive in nature. States Parties must refrain from violation of the rights recognized by the Covenant, and any restrictions on any of those rights must be permissible under the relevant provisions of the Covenant. Where such restrictions are made, States must demonstrate their necessity and only take such measures as are proportionate to the pursuance of legitimate aims in order to ensure continuous and effective protection of Covenant rights. In no case may the restrictions be applied or invoked in a manner that would impair the essence of a Covenant right.

7. Article 2 requires that States Parties adopt legislative, judicial, administrative, educative and other appropriate measures in order to fulfill their legal obligations. The Committee believes that it is important to raise levels of awareness about the Covenant not only among public officials and State agents but also among the population at large.

8. The article 2, paragraph 1, obligations are binding on States [Parties] and do not, as such, have direct horizontal effect as a matter of international law. The Covenant cannot be viewed as a substitute for domestic criminal or civil law. However the positive obligations on States Parties to ensure Covenant rights will only be fully discharged if individuals are protected by the State, not just against violations of Covenant rights by its agents, but also against acts committed by private persons or entities that would impair the enjoyment of Covenant rights in so far as they are amenable to application between private persons or entities. There may be circumstances in which a failure to ensure Covenant rights as required by article 2 would give rise to violations by States Parties of those rights, as a result of States Parties' permitting or failing to take appropriate measures or to exercise due diligence to prevent, punish, investigate or redress the harm caused by such acts by private persons or entities. States are reminded of the interrelationship between the positive obligations imposed under article 2 and the need to provide effective remedies in the event of breach under article 2, paragraph 3. The Covenant itself envisages in some articles certain areas where there are positive obligations on States Parties to address the activities of private persons or entities. For example, the privacy-related guarantees of article 17 must be protected by law. It is also implicit in article 7 that States Parties have to take positive measures to ensure that private persons or entities do not inflict torture or cruel, inhuman or degrading treatment or punishment on others within their power. In fields affecting basic aspects of ordinary life such

as work or housing, individuals are to be protected from discrimination within the meaning of article 26.

9. The beneficiaries of the rights recognized by the Covenant are individuals. Although, with the exception of article 1, the Covenant does not mention the rights of legal persons or similar entities or collectivities, many of the rights recognized by the Covenant, such as the freedom to manifest one's religion or belief (article 18), the freedom of association (article 22) or the rights of members of minorities (article 27), may be enjoyed in community with others. The fact that the competence of the Committee to receive and consider communications is restricted to those submitted by or on behalf of individuals (article 1 of the Optional Protocol) does not prevent such individuals from claiming that actions or omissions that concern legal persons and similar entities amount to a violation of their own rights.

10. States Parties are required by article 2, paragraph 1, to respect and to ensure the Covenant rights to all persons who may be within their territory and to all persons subject to their jurisdiction. This means that a State party must respect and ensure the rights laid down in the Covenant to anyone within the power or effective control of that State Party, even if not situated within the territory of the State Party. As indicated in General Comment 15 adopted at the twenty-seventh session (1986), the enjoyment of Covenant rights is not limited to citizens of States Parties but must also be available to all individuals, regardless of nationality or statelessness, such as asylum seekers, refugees, migrant workers and other persons, who may find themselves in the territory or subject to the jurisdiction of the State Party. This principle also applies to those within the power or effective control of the forces of a State Party acting outside its territory, regardless of the circumstances in which such power or effective control was obtained, such as forces constituting a national contingent of a State Party assigned to an international peace-keeping or peace-enforcement operation. . . .

13. Article 2, paragraph 2, requires that States Parties take the necessary steps to give effect to the Covenant rights in the domestic order. It follows that, unless Covenant rights are already protected by their domestic laws or practices, States Parties are required on ratification to make such changes to domestic laws and practices as are necessary to ensure their conformity with the Covenant. Where there are inconsistencies between domestic law and the Covenant, article 2 requires that the domestic law or practice be changed to meet the standards imposed by the Covenant's substantive guarantees. Article 2 allows a State Party to pursue this in accordance with its own domestic constitutional structure and accordingly does not require that the Covenant be directly applicable in the courts, by incorporation of the Covenant into national law. The Committee takes the view, however, that Covenant guarantees may receive enhanced protection in those States where the Covenant is automatically or through specific incorporation part of the domestic legal order. The Committee invites those States Parties in which the Covenant does not form part of the domestic legal order to consider incorporation of the Covenant to render it part of domestic law to facilitate full realization of Covenant rights as required by article 2.

14. The requirement under article 2, paragraph 2, to take steps to give effect to the Covenant rights is unqualified and of immediate effect. A failure to comply

with this obligation cannot be justified by reference to political, social, cultural or economic considerations within the State.

15. Article 2, paragraph 3, requires that in addition to effective protection of Covenant rights States Parties must ensure that individuals also have accessible and effective remedies to vindicate those rights. Such remedies should be appropriately adapted so as to take account of the special vulnerability of certain categories of person, including in particular children. The Committee attaches importance to States Parties' establishing appropriate judicial and administrative mechanisms for addressing claims of rights violations under domestic law. The Committee notes that the enjoyment of the rights recognized under the Covenant can be effectively assured by the judiciary in many different ways, including direct applicability of the Covenant, application of comparable constitutional or other provisions of law, or the interpretive effect of the Covenant in the application of national law. Administrative mechanisms are particularly required to give effect to the general obligation to investigate allegations of violations promptly, thoroughly and effectively through independent and impartial bodies. National human rights institutions, endowed with appropriate powers, can contribute to this end. A failure by a State Party to investigate allegations of violations could in and of itself give rise to a separate breach of the Covenant. Cessation of an ongoing violation is an essential element of the right to an effective remedy.

16. Article 2, paragraph 3, requires that States Parties make reparation to individuals whose Covenant rights have been violated. Without reparation to individuals whose Covenant rights have been violated, the obligation to provide an effective remedy, which is central to the efficacy of article 2, paragraph 3, is not discharged. In addition to the explicit reparation required by articles 9, paragraph 5, and 14, paragraph 6, the Committee considers that the Covenant generally entails appropriate compensation. The Committee notes that, where appropriate, reparation can involve restitution, rehabilitation and measures of satisfaction, such as public apologies, public memorials, guarantees of non-repetition and changes in relevant laws and practices, as well as bringing to justice the perpetrators of human rights violations.

## Committee on Economic, Social, and Cultural Rights

## General Comment 3: The Nature of States Parties Obligations (Art. 2, para. 1)

UN Doc. E/1991/23 (1990) (footnotes omitted)

1. Article 2 is of particular importance to a full understanding of the Covenant and must be seen as having a dynamic relationship with all of the other provisions of the Covenant. It describes the nature of the general legal obligations undertaken by States parties to the Covenant. Those obligations include both what may be termed (following the work of the International Law Commission) obligations of conduct and obligations of result. While great emphasis has sometimes been placed on the difference between the formulations used in this provision and that contained in the equivalent article 2 of the International Covenant on Civil and

Political Rights, it is not always recognized that there are also significant similarities. In particular, while the Covenant provides for progressive realization and acknowledges the constraints due to the limits of available resources, it also imposes various obligations which are of immediate effect. Of these, two are of particular importance in understanding the precise nature of States parties obligations. One of these, which is dealt with in a separate general comment, and which is to be considered by the Committee at its sixth session, is the "undertaking to guarantee" that relevant rights "will be exercised without discrimination. . . ."

2. The other is the undertaking in article 2 (1) "to take steps", which in itself, is not qualified or limited by other considerations. The full meaning of the phrase can also be gauged by noting some of the different language versions. In English the undertaking is "to take steps", in French it is "to act" ("s'engage à agir") and in Spanish it is "to adopt measures" ("a adoptar medidas"). Thus while the full realization of the relevant rights may be achieved progressively, steps towards that goal must be taken within a reasonably short time after the Covenant's entry into force for the States concerned. Such steps should be deliberate, concrete and targeted as clearly as possible towards meeting the obligations recognized in the Covenant. . . .

5. Among the measures which might be considered appropriate, in addition to legislation, is the provision of judicial remedies with respect to rights which may, in accordance with the national legal system, be considered justiciable. The Committee notes, for example, that the enjoyment of the rights recognized, without discrimination, will often be appropriately promoted, in part, through the provision of judicial or other effective remedies. Indeed, those States parties which are also parties to the International Covenant on Civil and Political Rights are already obligated (by virtue of arts. 2 (paras. 1 and 3), 3 and 26) of that Covenant to ensure that any person whose rights or freedoms (including the right to equality and non-discrimination) recognized in that Covenant are violated, "shall have an effective remedy" (art. 2 (3) (a)). In addition, there are a number of other provisions in the International Covenant on Economic, Social and Cultural Rights, including articles 3, 7 (a) (i), 8, 10 (3), 13 (2) (a), (3) and (4) and 15 (3) which would seem to be capable of immediate application by judicial and other organs in many national legal systems. Any suggestion that the provisions indicated are inherently non-self-executing would seem to be difficult to sustain. . . .

9. The principal obligation of result reflected in article 2 (1) is to take steps "with a view to achieving progressively the full realization of the rights recognized" in the Covenant. The term "progressive realization" is often used to describe the intent of this phrase. The concept of progressive realization constitutes a recognition of the fact that full realization of all economic, social and cultural rights will generally not be able to be achieved in a short period of time. In this sense the obligation differs significantly from that contained in article 2 of the International Covenant on Civil and Political Rights which embodies an immediate obligation to respect and ensure all of the relevant rights. Nevertheless, the fact that realization over time, or in other words progressively, is foreseen under the Covenant should not be misinterpreted as depriving the obligation of all meaningful content. It is on the one hand a necessary flexibility device, reflecting the realities of the real world and the difficulties involved for any country in ensuring full realization of economic, social and cultural rights. On the other hand, the phrase must be read

in the light of the overall objective, indeed the raison d'être, of the Covenant which is to establish clear obligations for States parties in respect of the full realization of the rights in question. It thus imposes an obligation to move as expeditiously and effectively as possible towards that goal. Moreover, any deliberately retrogressive measures in that regard would require the most careful consideration and would need to be fully justified by reference to the totality of the rights provided for in the Covenant and in the context of the full use of the maximum available resources.

10. On the basis of the extensive experience gained by the Committee, as well as by the body that preceded it, over a period of more than a decade of examining States parties' reports the Committee is of the view that a minimum core obligation to ensure the satisfaction of, at the very least, minimum essential levels of each of the rights is incumbent upon every State party. Thus, for example, a State party in which any significant number of individuals is deprived of essential foodstuffs, of essential primary health care, of basic shelter and housing, or of the most basic forms of education is, prima facie, failing to discharge its obligations under the Covenant. If the Covenant were to be read in such a way as not to establish such a minimum core obligation, it would be largely deprived of its raison d'être. By the same token, it must be noted that any assessment as to whether a State has discharged its minimum core obligation must also take account of resource constraints applying within the country concerned. Article 2 (1) obligates each State party to take the necessary steps "to the maximum of its available resources". In order for a State party to be able to attribute its failure to meet at least its minimum core obligations to a lack of available resources it must demonstrate that every effort has been made to use all resources that are at its disposition in an effort to satisfy, as a matter of priority, those minimum obligations.

11. The Committee wishes to emphasize, however, that even where the available resources are demonstrably inadequate, the obligation remains for a State party to strive to ensure the widest possible enjoyment of the relevant rights under the prevailing circumstances. Moreover, the obligations to monitor the extent of the realization, or more especially of the non-realization, of economic, social and cultural rights, and to devise strategies and programmes for their promotion, are not in any way eliminated as a result of resource constraints. The Committee has already dealt with these issues in its General Comment 1 (1989). . . .

13. A final element of article 2 (1), to which attention must be drawn, is that the undertaking given by all States parties is "to take steps, individually and through international assistance and cooperation, especially economic and technical. . . ." The Committee notes that the phrase "to the maximum of its available resources" was intended by the drafters of the Covenant to refer to both the resources existing within a State and those available from the international community through international cooperation and assistance. Moreover, the essential role of such cooperation in facilitating the full realization of the relevant rights is further underlined by the specific provisions contained in articles 11, 15, 22 and 23. With respect to article 22 the Committee has already drawn attention, in General Comment 2 (1990), to some of the opportunities and responsibilities that exist in relation to international cooperation. Article 23 also specifically identifies "the furnishing of technical assistance" as well as other activities, as being among the means of "international action for the achievement of the rights recognized. . . ."

14. The Committee wishes to emphasize that in accordance with Articles 55 and 56 of the Charter of the United Nations, with well-established principles of international law, and with the provisions of the Covenant itself, international cooperation for development and thus for the realization of economic, social and cultural rights is an obligation of all States. It is particularly incumbent upon those States which are in a position to assist others in this regard. The Committee notes in particular the importance of the Declaration on the Right to Development adopted by the General Assembly in its resolution 41/128 of 4 December 1986 and the need for States parties to take full account of all of the principles recognized therein. It emphasizes that, in the absence of an active programme of international assistance and cooperation on the part of all those States that are in a position to undertake one, the full realization of economic, social and cultural rights will remain an unfulfilled aspiration in many countries.

## Comments and Questions

1. Recall that in *SERAC v. Nigeria*, the African Commission on Human and Peoples Rights described "four levels of duties for a State that undertakes to adhere to a rights regime, namely the duty to respect, protect, promote, and fulfill these rights." This four-part framework does not appear in the African Charter on Human and Peoples Rights or any other treaty. Rather, the Commission referred to "[i]nternationally-accepted ideas of the various obligations engendered by these human rights" and cited scholarly works. Is the Commission's four-part framework based on law? Is that framework fairly derived or commensurate with the obligations expressed in the African Charter to "recognize" and "give effect" to the rights enshrined in the Charter? How does the framework compare with the analysis in the comments, above, by the two human rights treaty bodies in connection with the general human rights duties of states under the two treaties. Note that the respect, protect, promote, and fulfill framework, or some variation of it, is espoused in numerous secondary sources, including those relied upon by the Commission. The website of the Office of the UN High Commissioner of Human Rights, in describing the rights affirmed in and obligations arising out of the UN human rights treaties, refers to the duties of states to "respect, protect, and fulfull" human rights. See *International Human Rights Law*, United Nations, Office of the High Commissioner for Human Rights, https://www.ohchr.org/en/instruments -and-mechanisms/international-human-rights-law (last visited April 29, 2022).

2. Note that among the rights alleged to have been violated in *SERAC* was the "right to a general satisfactory environment favorable to their development" affirmed in Article 24 of the African Charter. How does the state duty to respect, protect, promote and fullfill apply to this right, and how did Nigeria fail to uphold it? How does this right, with its attendant duties or obligations, compare to the right to a "clean, healthy, and sustainable environment" affirmed by the UN General Assembly in its resolution reproduced in part in Chapter 2, *supra* page 112.

3. In what way did Nigeria in the *SERAC* case fail to meet its obligations in relation to social and economic rights, such as the rights to health (Art. 16) and the rights to food and housing that were found to be derivative of other African

Charter rights. Is the state duty to respect, protect, promote, and fullfill different for the right to life? The Commission in *SERAC* referred to and quoted Article 21 of the African Charter, which affirms, "All peoples shall freely dispose of their wealth and natural resources. This right shall be exercise in the exclusive interest of the people. . . ." What are states' duties or obligations with regard to this right?

4.  What are the different elements of states' obligations "to respect" and "to ensure" rights affirmed in the International Covenant on Civil and Political Rights (ICCPR) under its Article 2 and according to General Comment 31 of the Human Rights Committee? Consider, for example, how those elements apply in the context of police violence in the United States, a problem discussed in Chapter 1, in relation to the rights to life (Art. 6); freedom form torture and inhumane treatment (Art. 7); freedom from arbitrary arrest or detention (Art. 9); humane treatment in detention (Art. 10); equality before the courts and fair trial with minimum guarantees (Art. 14); and non-discrmination generally (Art. 2.1).

5.  How are state oblitations under the ICCPR the same or different from state obligations under the International Covenant on Economic, Social, and Cultural Rights? What does it mean for a state to be obligated under Article 2 of the latter Covent to "to take steps, . . . to the maximun degree of its available resources" to achieve the full realiazation of the rights in that Covenant? For example, what is a state party with very limited resource concretely obligated to do about a general situation in which half the child population does not live within 100 miles of any healthcare facility and 20 percent of all children die before the age of 12? What does the Economic, Social, and Cultural Committee mean by "a core minimum obligation" in its General Comment No. 3? What of the obligation to refrain from infringing social and economic rights pressed by the Arican Commission in *SERAC*?

5.  The UN Human Rights Committee states in its General Comment No. 31 that the requirement to "take steps" to "give effect" to the Covenant on Civil and Political Rights "is unqualified and of immediate effect," while most of the rights in the Covenant on Economic, Social, and Cultural Rights are to be achieved progressively. How does a country lacking in resources give "immediate effect" to the right to a fair trial (Art 14, ICCPR), which requires the expenditure of substantial resources on an entire judicial and criminal justice system? Would a state be justified in funding criminal defense attorneys before it staffed secondary schools or public health clinics? Must a state address the problem of widespread violence against women before the right to housing and an adequate standard of living? The Vienna Declaration and Programme of Action that resulted from the 1993 World Conference on Human Rights proclaimed that human rights are "indivisible" and "interdependent." If all human rights are on the same footing, how should a state establish priorities according to these principles?

---

The negative obligation to "respect"—that is, refrain from acts that infringe human rights—and the positive obligation to "ensure" appears not only in the Covenant on Civil and Political Rights, Article 2, but also in Article 1 of the American Convention on Human Rights. The following judgment of the Inter-American Court of Human Rights is one of the most widely cited sources of authority on the scope of state duties to respect and ensure or protect human rights, and on the attribution of conduct to states in relation to these duties. As indicated in Chapter 1 and further discussed in Chapter 8, the Inter-American Court of Human Rights and the Amercian Convention on Human Rights are key components of the Inter-American system for the protection of human rights.

## Velásquez Rodríguez v. Honduras

Inter-Am. Ct. H.R., Judgment of July 29, 1988, Ser. C No. 4

1. The Inter-American Commission on Human Rights submitted the instant case to the Inter-American Court of Human Rights . . . on April 24, 1986. It originated in a petition (No. 7920) against the State of Honduras . . . , which the Secretariat of the Commission received on October 7, 1981. . . .

3. According to the petition filed with the Commission, and the supplementary information received subsequently, Manfredo Velásquez, a student at the National Autonomous University of Honduras, "was violently detained without a warrant for his arrest by members of the National Office of Investigations (DNI) and G-2 of the Armed Forces of Honduras.". . .

[After extensive proceedings and a hearing, the Court found the following facts proven]:

147. . . .

"a. During the period 1981 to 1984, 100 to 150 persons disappeared in the Republic of Honduras, and many were never heard from again. . . .

b. Those disappearances followed a similar pattern, beginning with the kidnapping of the victims by force, often in broad daylight and in public places, by armed men in civilian clothes and disguises, who acted with apparent impunity and who used vehicles without any official identification, with tinted windows and with false license plates or no plates. . . .

c. It was public and notorious knowledge in Honduras that the kidnappings were carried out by military personnel or the police, or persons acting under their orders. . . .

d. The disappearances were carried out in a systematic manner, regarding which the Court considers the following circumstances particularly relevant:

i. The victims were usually persons whom Honduran officials considered dangerous to State security . . . ;

iii. The kidnappers blindfolded the victims, took them to secret, unofficial detention centers and moved them from one center to another. They interrogated the victims and subjected them to cruel and humiliating treatment and torture. Some were ultimately murdered and their bodies were buried in clandestine cemeteries . . . ;

v. Military and police officials as well as those from the Executive and Judicial Branches either denied the disappearances or were incapable of preventing or investigating them, punishing those responsible, or helping those interested discover the whereabouts and fate of the victims or the location of their remains. The investigative committees created by the Government and the Armed Forces did not produce any results. The judicial proceedings brought were processed slowly with a clear lack of interest and some were ultimately dismissed . . . ;

e. On September 12, 1981, between 4:30 and 5:00 p.m., several heavily-armed men in civilian clothes driving a white Ford without license plates kidnapped Manfredo Velásquez from a parking lot in downtown Tegucigalpa. Today, nearly seven years later, he remains disappeared, which creates a reasonable presumption that he is dead. . . .

f. Persons connected with the Armed Forces or under its direction carried out that kidnapping. . . ."

159. The Commission has asked the Court to find that Honduras has violated the rights guaranteed to Manfredo Velásquez by Articles 4 [right to life], 5 [right to humane treatment] and 7 [freedom from slavery] of the Convention. The Government has denied the charges and seeks to be absolved.

160. This requires the Court to examine the conditions under which a particular act, which violates one of the rights recognized by the Convention, can be imputed to a State Party thereby establishing its international responsibility.

161. Article 1 (1) of the Convention provides:

ARTICLE 1. OBLIGATION TO RESPECT RIGHTS
1. The States Parties to this Convention undertake to respect the rights and freedoms recognized herein and to ensure to all persons subject to their jurisdiction the free and full exercise of those rights and freedoms, without any discrimination for reasons of race, color, sex, language, religion, political or other opinion, national or social origin, economic status, birth, or any other social condition.

162. This article specifies the obligation assumed by the States Parties in relation to each of the rights protected. Each claim alleging that one of those rights has been infringed necessarily implies that Article 1 (1) of the Convention has also been violated.

163. The Commission did not specifically allege the violation of Article 1 (1) of the Convention, but that does not preclude the Court from applying it. The precept contained therein constitutes the generic basis of the protection of the rights recognized by the Convention and would be applicable, in any case, by virtue of a general principle of law, iura novit curia, on which international jurisprudence has repeatedly relied and under which a court has the power and the duty to apply the juridical provisions relevant to a proceeding, even when the parties do not expressly invoke them ("Lotus", Judgment No. 9, 1927, P.C.I.J., Series A No. 10, p. 31 and Eur. Court H.R., Handyside Case, Judgment of 7 December 1976, Series A No. 24, para. 41).

164. Article 1 (1) is essential in determining whether a violation of the human rights recognized by the Convention can be imputed to a State Party. In effect, that article charges the States Parties with the fundamental duty to respect and guarantee the rights recognized in the Convention. Any impairment of those rights which can be attributed under the rules of international law to the action or omission of any public authority constitutes an act imputable to the State, which assumes responsibility in the terms provided by the Convention.

165. The first obligation assumed by the States Parties under Article 1 (1) is "to respect the rights and freedoms" recognized by the Convention. The exercise of public authority has certain limits which derive from the fact that human rights are inherent attributes of human dignity and are, therefore, superior to the power of the State. On another occasion, this court stated:

> The protection of human rights, particularly the civil and political rights set forth in the Convention, is in effect based on the affirmation of the existence of certain inviolable attributes of the individual that cannot be legitimately restricted through the exercise of governmental power. There are individual domains that are beyond the reach of the State or to which the State has but limited access. Thus, the protection of human rights must necessarily comprise the concept of the restriction of the exercise of state power (The Word "Laws" in Article 30 of the American Convention on Human Rights, Advisory Opinion OC-6/86 of May 9, 1986. Series A No. 6, para 21).

166. The second obligation of the States Parties is to "ensure" the free and full exercise of the rights recognized by the Convention to every person subject to its jurisdiction. This obligation implies the duty of States Parties to organize the governmental apparatus and, in general, all the structures through which public power is exercised, so that they are capable of juridically ensuring the free and full enjoyment of human rights. As a consequence of this obligation, the States must prevent, investigate and punish any violation of the rights recognized by the Convention and, moreover, if possible attempt to restore the right violated and provide compensation as warranted for damages resulting from the violation.

167. The obligation to ensure the free and full exercise of human rights is not fulfilled by the existence of a legal system designed to make it possible to comply with this obligation—it also requires the government to conduct itself so as to effectively ensure the free and full exercise of human rights.

168. The obligation of the States is, thus, much more direct than that contained in Article 2, which reads:

ARTICLE 2. DOMESTIC LEGAL EFFECTS
> Where the exercise of any of the rights or freedoms referred to in Article 1 is not already ensured by legislative or other provisions, the States Parties undertake to adopt, in accordance with their constitutional processes and the provisions of this Convention, such legislative or other measures as may be necessary to give effect to those rights or freedoms.

169. According to Article 1 (1), any exercise of public power that violates the rights recognized by the Convention is illegal. Whenever a State organ, official or public entity violates one of those rights, this constitutes a failure of the duty to respect the rights and freedoms set forth in the Convention.

170. This conclusion is independent of whether the organ or official has contravened provisions of internal law or overstepped the limits of his authority: under international law a State is responsible for the acts of its agents undertaken in their official capacity and for their omissions, even when those agents act outside the sphere of their authority or violate internal law.

171. This principle suits perfectly the nature of the Convention, which is violated whenever public power is used to infringe the rights recognized therein. If acts of public power that exceed the State's authority or are illegal under its own laws were not considered to compromise that State's obligations under the treaty, the system of protection provided for in the Convention would be illusory.

172. Thus, in principle, any violation of rights recognized by the Convention carried out by an act of public authority or by persons who use their position of authority is imputable to the State. However, this does not define all the circumstances in which a State is obligated to prevent, investigate and punish human rights violations, nor all the cases in which the State might be found responsible for an infringement of those rights. An illegal act which violates human rights and which is initially not directly imputable to a State (for example, because it is the act of a private person or because the person responsible has not been identified) can lead to international responsibility of the State, not because of the act itself, but because of the lack of due diligence to prevent the violation or to respond to it as required by the Convention.

173. Violations of the Convention cannot be founded upon rules that take psychological factors into account in establishing individual culpability. For the purposes of analysis, the intent or motivation of the agent who has violated the rights recognized by the Convention is irrelevant—the violation can be established even if the identity of the individual perpetrator is unknown. What is decisive is whether a violation of the rights recognized by the Convention has occurred with the support or the acquiescence of the government, or whether the State has allowed the act to take place without taking measures to prevent it or to punish those responsible. Thus, the Court's task is to determine whether the violation is the result of a State's failure to fulfill its duty to respect and guarantee those rights, as required by Article 1 (1) of the Convention.

174. The State has a legal duty to take reasonable steps to prevent human rights violations and to use the means at its disposal to carry out a serious investigation of violations committed within its jurisdiction, to identify those responsible, to impose the appropriate punishment and to ensure the victim adequate compensation.

175. This duty to prevent includes all those means of a legal, political, administrative and cultural nature that promote the protection of human rights and ensure that any violations are considered and treated as illegal acts, which, as such, may lead to the punishment of those responsible and the obligation to indemnify the victims for damages. It is not possible to make a detailed list of all such measures, since they vary with the law and the conditions of each State Party. Of course, while the State is obligated to prevent human rights abuses, the existence of a particular violation does not, in itself, prove the failure to take preventive measures. On the other hand, subjecting a person to official, repressive bodies that practice torture and assassination with impunity is itself a breach of the duty to prevent violations of the rights to life and physical integrity of the person, even if that particular person is not tortured or assassinated, or if those facts cannot be proven in a concrete case.

176. The State is obligated to investigate every situation involving a violation of the rights protected by the Convention. If the State apparatus acts in such a way that the violation goes unpunished and the victim's full enjoyment of such

rights is not restored as soon as possible, the State has failed to comply with its duty to ensure the free and full exercise of those rights to the persons within its jurisdiction. The same is true when the State allows private persons or groups to act freely and with impunity to the detriment of the rights recognized by the Convention.

177. In certain circumstances, it may be difficult to investigate acts that violate an individual's rights. The duty to investigate, like the duty to prevent, is not breached merely because the investigation does not produce a satisfactory result. Nevertheless, it must be undertaken in a serious manner and not as a mere formality preordained to be ineffective. An investigation must have an objective and be assumed by the State as its own legal duty, not as a step taken by private interests that depends upon the initiative of the victim or his family or upon their offer of proof, without an effective search for the truth by the government. This is true regardless of what agent is eventually found responsible for the violation. Where the acts of private parties that violate the Convention are not seriously investigated, those parties are aided in a sense by the government, thereby making the State responsible on the international plane.

178. In the instant case, the evidence shows a complete inability of the procedures of the State of Honduras, which were theoretically adequate, to carry out an investigation into the disappearance of Manfredo Velásquez, and of the fulfillment of its duties to pay compensation and punish those responsible, as set out in Article 1 (1) of the Convention.

179. As the Court has verified above, the failure of the judicial system to act upon the writs brought before various tribunals in the instant case has been proven. Not one writ of habeas corpus was processed. No judge has access to the places where Manfredo Velásquez might have been detained. The criminal complaint was dismissed.

180. Nor did the organs of the Executive Branch carry out a serious investigation to establish the fate of Manfredo Velásquez. There was no investigation of public allegations of a practice of disappearances nor a determination of whether Manfredo Velásquez had been a victim of that practice. The Commission's requests for information were ignored to the point that the Commission had to presume, under Article 42 of its Regulations, that the allegations were true. The offer of an investigation in accord with Resolution 30/83 of the Commission resulted in an investigation by the Armed Forces, the same body accused of direct responsibility for the disappearances. This raises grave questions regarding the seriousness of the investigation. The Government often resorted to asking relatives of the victims to present conclusive proof of their allegations even though those allegations, because they involved crimes against the person, should have been investigated on the Government's own initiative in fulfillment of the State's duty to ensure public order. This is especially true when the allegations refer to a practice carried out within the Armed Forces, which, because of its nature, is not subject to private investigations. No proceeding was initiated to establish responsibility for the disappearance of Manfredo Velásquez and apply punishment under internal law. All of the above leads to the conclusion that the Honduran authorities did not take effective action to ensure respect for human rights within the jurisdiction of that State as required by Article 1 (1) of the Convention.

181. The duty to investigate facts of this type continues as long as there is uncertainty about the fate of the person who has disappeared. Even in the hypothetical case that those individually responsible for crimes of this type cannot be legally punished under certain circumstances, the State is obligated to use the means at its disposal to inform the relatives of the fate of the victims and, if they have been killed, the location of their remains.

182. The Court is convinced, and has so found, that the disappearance of Manfredo Velásquez was carried out by agents who acted under cover of public authority. However, even had that fact not been proven, the failure of the State apparatus to act, which is clearly proven, is a failure on the part of Honduras to fulfill the duties it assumed under Article 1 (1) of the Convention, which obligated it to ensure Manfredo Velásquez the free and full exercise of his human rights.

183. The Court notes that the legal order of Honduras does not authorize such acts and that internal law defines them as crimes. The Court also recognizes that not all levels of the Government of Honduras were necessarily aware of those acts, nor is there any evidence that such acts were the result of official orders. Nevertheless, those circumstances are irrelevant for the purposes of establishing whether Honduras is responsible under international law for the violations of human rights perpetrated within the practice of disappearances.

184. According to the principle of the continuity of the State in international law, responsibility exists both independently of changes of government over a period of time and continuously from the time of the act that creates responsibility to the time when the act is declared illegal. The foregoing is also valid in the area of human rights although, from an ethical or political point of view, the attitude of the new government may be much more respectful of those rights than that of the government in power when the violations occurred.

185. The Court, therefore, concludes that the facts found in this proceeding show that the State of Honduras is responsible for the involuntary disappearance of Angel Manfredo Velásquez Rodríguez. Thus, Honduras has violated Articles 7, 5 and 4 of the Convention.

---

The following decision by the European Court of Human Rights addresses the relevant standard of care arising from the protective duty in connection with obligations established by the European Convention on Human Rights, and in the context of waste management. The European regional human rights system was also introduced in Chapter 1, and further background on it can be found in Chapter 9.

## Öneryildiz v. Turkey

Eur. Ct. H.R. (GC), App. No. 48938/99, Judgment of of Nov. 30, 2004
(references omitted)

. . .

9. The applicant was born in 1955 and is now living in the district of Şirvan . . . the area where he was born. At the material time he was living with twelve close

relatives in the slum quarter . . . of Kazim Karabekir in Ümraniye, a district of Istanbul, where he had moved after resigning from his post as a village guard in southeastern Turkey.

10. Since the early 1970s a household-refuse tip had been in operation in Hekimbaş, a slum area adjoining Kazim Karabekir. On 22 January 1960 Istanbul City Council . . . had been granted use of the land, which belonged to the Forestry Commission (and therefore to the Treasury), for a term of ninety-nine years.

Situated on a slope overlooking a valley, the site spread out over a surface area of approximately 350,000 sq. m and from 1972 onwards was used as a rubbish tip by the districts of Beykoz, Üsküdar, Kadiköy and Ümraniye under the authority and responsibility of the city council and, ultimately, the ministerial authorities. When the rubbish tip started being used, the area was uninhabited and the closest built-up area was approximately 3.5 km away. However, as the years passed, rudimentary dwellings were built without any authorisation in the area surrounding the rubbish tip, which eventually developed into the slums of Ümraniye. . . .

13. On 9 April 1991 Ümraniye District Council applied to the Third Division of the Üsküdar District Court for experts to be appointed to determine whether the rubbish tip complied with the relevant regulations, in particular the Regulations of 14 March 1991 on Solid-Waste Control. The district council also applied for an assessment of the damage it had sustained, as evidence in support of an action for damages it was preparing to bring against the city council and the councils of the three other districts that used the tip. . . .

According to the experts' report, drawn up on 7 May 1991, the rubbish tip in question did not conform to the technical requirements set forth, inter alia, in regulations 24-27, 30 and 38 of the Regulations of 14 March 1991 and, accordingly, presented a number of dangers liable to give rise to a major health risk for the inhabitants of the valley, particularly those living in the slum areas: no walls or fencing separated the tip from the dwellings fifty metres away from the mountain of refuse; the tip was not equipped with collection, composting, recycling or combustion systems; and no drainage or drainage-water purification systems had been installed. The experts concluded that the Ümraniye tip "exposed humans, animals and the environment to all kinds of risks." In that connection the report, drawing attention first to the fact that some twenty contagious diseases might spread, underlined the following:

> . . . In any waste-collection site gases such as methane, carbon dioxide and hydrogen sulphide form. These substances must be collected and . . . burnt under supervision. However, the tip in question is not equipped with such a system. If methane is mixed with air in a particular proportion, it can explode. This installation contains no means of preventing an explosion of the methane produced as a result of the decomposition [of the waste]. May God preserve us, as the damage could be very substantial given the neighbouring dwellings. . . .

On 27 May 1991 the report was brought to the attention of the four councils in question, and on 7 June 1991 the governor was informed of it and asked to brief the Ministry of Health and the Prime Minister's Environment Office ("the Environment Office").

14. Kadiköy and Üsküdar District Councils and the city council applied on 3, 5 and 9 June 1991 respectively to have the expert report set aside. In their notice of application the councils' lawyers simply stated that the report, which had been ordered and drawn up without their knowledge, contravened the Code of Civil Procedure. The three lawyers reserved the right to file supplementary pleadings in support of their objections once they had obtained all the necessary information and documents from their authorities. As none of the parties filed supplementary pleadings to that end, the proceedings were discontinued.

15. However, the Environment Office, which had been advised of the report on 18 June 1991, made a recommendation (no. 09513) urging the Istanbul Governor's Office, the city council and Ümraniye District Council to remedy the problems identified in the present case. . . .

16. On 27 August 1992 Şinasi Öktem, the mayor of Ümraniye, applied to the First Division of the Üsküdar District Court for the implementation of temporary measures to prevent the city council and the neighbouring district councils from using the waste-collection site. He requested, in particular, that no further waste be dumped, that the tip be closed and that redress be provided in respect of the damage sustained by his district.

On 3 November 1992 Istanbul City Council's representative opposed that request. Emphasising the city council's efforts to maintain the roads leading to the rubbish tip and to prevent the spread of diseases, the emission of odours and the destruction of stray dogs, the representative submitted, in particular, that a plan to redevelop the site of the tip had been put out to tender. As regards the request for the temporary closure of the tip, the representative asserted that Ümraniye District Council was acting in bad faith in that, since it had been set up in 1987, it had done nothing to decontaminate the site.

The City Council had indeed issued a call for tenders for the development of new sites conforming to modern standards. The first planning contract was awarded to the American firm CVH2M Hill International Ltd, and on 21 December 1992 and 17 February 1993 new sites were designed for the European and Anatolian sides of Istanbul respectively. The project was due for completion in the course of 1993.

17. While those proceedings were still pending, Ümraniye District Council informed the mayor of Istanbul that from 15 May 1993 the dumping of waste would no longer be authorised.

18. On 28 April 1993 at about 11 a.m. a methane explosion occurred at the site. Following a landslide caused by mounting pressure, the refuse erupted from the mountain of waste and engulfed some ten slum dwellings situated below it, including the one belonging to the applicant. Thirty-nine people died in the accident. . . .

## I. Alleged Violation of Article 2 of the Convention

69. Taking the parties' arguments as a whole, the Court reiterates, firstly, that its approach to the interpretation of Article 2 [right to life] is guided by the idea that the object and purpose of the Convention as an instrument for the protection of individual human beings requires its provisions to be interpreted and applied in such a way as to make its safeguards practical and effective.

70. In the instant case the complaint before the Court is that the national authorities did not do all that could have been expected of them to prevent the deaths of the applicant's close relatives in the accident of 28 April 1993 at the Ümraniye municipal rubbish tip, which was operated under the authorities' control.

71. In this connection, the Court reiterates that Article 2 does not solely concern deaths resulting from the use of force by agents of the State but also, in the first sentence of its first paragraph ["Everyon's right to life shall be protected by law"], lays down a positive obligation on States to take appropriate steps to safeguard the lives of those within their jurisdiction.

The Court considers that this obligation must be construed as applying in the context of any activity, whether public or not, in which the right to life may be at stake, and a fortiori in the case of industrial activities, which by their very nature are dangerous, such as the operation of waste-collection sites. . . .

74. To sum up, it considers that the applicant's complaint undoubtedly falls within the ambit of the first sentence of Article 2, which is therefore applicable in the instant case. . . .

B. COMPLIANCE

(a) General principles applicable in the present case

(i) *Principles relating to the prevention of infringements of the right to life as a result of dangerous activities: the substantive aspect of Article 2 of the Convention*

89. The positive obligation to take all appropriate steps to safeguard life for the purposes of Article 2 entails above all a primary duty on the State to put in place a legislative and administrative framework designed to provide effective deterrence against threats to the right to life.

90. This obligation indisputably applies in the particular context of dangerous activities, where, in addition, special emphasis must be placed on regulations geared to the special features of the activity in question, particularly with regard to the level of the potential risk to human lives. They must govern the licensing, setting up, operation, security and supervision of the activity and must make it compulsory for all those concerned to take practical measures to ensure the effective protection of citizens whose lives might be endangered by the inherent risks. . . .

(ii) *Principles relating to the judicial response required in the event of alleged infringements of the right to life: the procedural aspect of Article 2 of the Convention.*

91. The obligations deriving from Article 2 do not end there. Where lives have been lost in circumstances potentially engaging the responsibility of the State, that provision entails a duty for the State to ensure, by all means at its disposal, an adequate response—judicial or otherwise—so that the legislative and administrative framework set up to protect the right to life is properly implemented and any breaches of that right are repressed and punished.

92. In this connection, the Court has held that if the infringement of the right to life or to physical integrity is not caused intentionally, the positive obligation to set up an "effective judicial system" does not necessarily require criminal proceedings to be brought in every case and may be satisfied if civil, administrative or even disciplinary remedies were available to the victims.

93. However, in areas such as that in issue in the instant case, the applicable principles are rather to be found in those which the Court has already had occasion to develop in relation notably to the use of lethal force, principles which lend themselves to application in other categories of cases. In this connection, it should be pointed out that in cases of homicide the interpretation of Article 2 as entailing an obligation to conduct an official investigation is justified not only because any allegations of such an offence normally give rise to criminal liability, but also because often, in practice, the true circumstances of the death are, or may be, largely confined within the knowledge of State officials or authorities.

In the Court's view, such considerations are indisputably valid in the context of dangerous activities, when lives have been lost as a result of events occurring under the responsibility of the public authorities, which are often the only entities to have sufficient relevant knowledge to identify and establish the complex phenomena that might have caused such incidents.

Where it is established that the negligence attributable to State officials or bodies on that account goes beyond an error of judgment or carelessness, in that the authorities in question, fully realising the likely consequences and disregarding the powers vested in them, failed to take measures that were necessary and sufficient to avert the risks inherent in a dangerous activity, the fact that those responsible for endangering life have not been charged with a criminal offence or prosecuted may amount to a violation of Article 2, irrespective of any other types of remedy which individuals may exercise on their own initiative; this is amply evidenced by developments in the relevant European standards.

94. To sum up, the judicial system required by Article 2 must make provision for an independent and impartial official investigation procedure that satisfies certain minimum standards as to effectiveness and is capable of ensuring that criminal penalties are applied where lives are lost as a result of a dangerous activity if and to the extent that this is justified by the findings of the investigation. In such cases, the competent authorities must act with exemplary diligence and promptness and must of their own motion initiate investigations capable of, firstly, ascertaining the circumstances in which the incident took place and any shortcomings in the operation of the regulatory system and, secondly, identifying the State officials or authorities involved in whatever capacity in the chain of events in issue.

95. That said, the requirements of Article 2 go beyond the stage of the official investigation, where this has led to the institution of proceedings in the national courts; the proceedings as a whole, including the trial stage, must satisfy the requirements of the positive obligation to protect lives through the law.

96. It should in no way be inferred from the foregoing that Article 2 may entail the right for an applicant to have third parties prosecuted or sentenced for a criminal offence or an absolute obligation for all prosecutions to result in conviction, or indeed in a particular sentence.

On the other hand, the national courts should not under any circumstances be prepared to allow life-endangering offences to go unpunished. This is essential for maintaining public confidence and ensuring adherence to the rule of law and for preventing any appearance of tolerance of or collusion in unlawful acts. The Court's task therefore consists in reviewing whether and to what extent the courts, in reaching their conclusion, may be deemed to have submitted the case to the careful scrutiny required by Article 2 of the Convention, so that the deterrent effect of the judicial system in place and the significance of the role it is required to play in preventing violations of the right to life are not undermined.

(b) Assessment of the facts of the case in the light of these principles

*(i) Responsibility borne by the State for the deaths in the instant case, in the light of the substantive aspect of Article 2 of the Convention.*

97. In the instant case the Court notes at the outset that in both of the fields of activity central to the present case — the operation of household-refuse tips . . . and the rehabilitation and clearance of slum areas . . . there are safety regulations in force in Turkey.

It must therefore determine whether the legal measures applicable to the situation in issue in the instant case call for criticism and whether the national authorities actually complied with the relevant regulations.

98. To that end, the Court considers that it should begin by noting a decisive factor for the assessment of the circumstances of the case, namely that there was practical information available to the effect that the inhabitants of certain slum areas of Ümraniye were faced with a threat to their physical integrity on account of the technical shortcomings of the municipal rubbish tip. . . .

100. The Court considers that neither the reality nor the immediacy of the danger in question is in dispute, seeing that the risk of an explosion had clearly come into being long before it was highlighted in the report of 7 May 1991 and that, as the site continued to operate in the same conditions, that risk could only have increased during the period until it materialised on 28 April 1993.

101. The Grand Chamber accordingly agrees with the Chamber that it was impossible for the administrative and municipal departments responsible for supervising and managing the tip not to have known of the risks inherent in methanogenesis or of the necessary preventive measures, particularly as there were specific regulations on the matter. Furthermore, the Court likewise regards it as established that various authorities were also aware of those risks, at least by 27 May 1991, when they were notified of the report of 7 May 1991.

It follows that the Turkish authorities at several levels knew or ought to have known that there was a real and immediate risk to a number of persons living near the Ümraniye municipal rubbish tip. They consequently had a positive obligation under Article 2 of the Convention to take such preventive operational measures as were necessary and sufficient to protect those individuals, especially as they themselves had set up the site and authorised its operation, which gave rise to the risk in question. . . .

103. . . . The Government also . . . criticised the applicant for having knowingly chosen to break the law and live in the vicinity of the rubbish tip. . . .

However, those arguments do not stand up to scrutiny for the following reasons.

104. . . . The Court concludes . . . that in spite of the statutory prohibitions in the field of town planning, the State's consistent policy on slum areas encouraged the integration of such areas into the urban environment and hence acknowledged their existence and the way of life of the citizens who had gradually caused

them to build up since 1960, whether of their own free will or simply as a result of that policy. Seeing that this policy effectively established an amnesty for breaches of town-planning regulations, including the unlawful occupation of public property, it must have created uncertainty as to the extent of the discretion enjoyed by the administrative authorities responsible for applying the measures prescribed by law, which could not therefore have been regarded as foreseeable by the public.

105. . . . The authorities let the applicant and his close relatives live entirely undisturbed in their house, in the social and family environment they had created. Furthermore, regard being had to the concrete evidence adduced before the Court and not rebutted by the Government, there is no cause to call into question the applicant's assertion that the authorities also levied council tax on him and on the other inhabitants of the Ümraniye slums and provided them with public services, for which they were charged.

106. In those circumstances, it would be hard for the Government to maintain legitimately that any negligence or lack of foresight should be attributed to the victims of the accident of 28 April 1993. . . .

It remains for the Court to address the Government's other arguments relating, in general, to: the scale of the rehabilitation projects carried out by the city council at the time in order to alleviate the problems caused by the Ümraniye waste-collection site; the amount invested, which was said to have influenced the way in which the national authorities chose to deal with the situation at the site; and, lastly, the humanitarian considerations which at the time allegedly precluded any measure entailing the immediate and wholesale destruction of the slum areas.

107. The Court acknowledges that it is not its task to substitute for the views of the local authorities its own view of the best policy to adopt in dealing with the social, economic and urban problems in this part of Istanbul. It therefore accepts the Government's argument that in this respect, an impossible or disproportionate burden must not be imposed on the authorities without consideration being given, in particular, to the operational choices which they must make in terms of priorities and resources; this results from the wide margin of appreciation which States enjoy, as the Court has previously held, in difficult social and technical spheres such as the one in issue in the instant case.

However, even when seen from this perspective, the Court does not find the Government's arguments convincing. The preventive measures required by the positive obligation in question fall precisely within the powers conferred on the authorities and may reasonably be regarded as a suitable means of averting the risk brought to their attention. The Court considers that the timely installation of a gas-extraction system at the Ümraniye tip before the situation became fatal could have been an effective measure without diverting the State's resources to an excessive degree in breach of Article 65 of the Turkish Constitution or giving rise to policy problems to the extent alleged by the Government. Such a measure would not only have complied with Turkish regulations and general practice in the area, but would also have been a much better reflection of the humanitarian considerations which the Government relied on before the Court. . . .

109. In the light of the foregoing, the Court cannot see any reason to cast doubt on the domestic investigating authorities' findings of fact and considers that

the circumstances examined above show that in the instant case the State's responsibility was engaged under Article 2 in several respects.

Firstly, the regulatory framework proved defective in that the Ümraniye
municipal waste-collection site was opened and operated despite not conforming
to the relevant technical standards and there was no coherent supervisory system
to encourage those responsible to take steps to ensure adequate protection of
the public and coordination and cooperation between the various administrative
authorities so that the risks brought to their attention did not become so serious as
to endanger human lives. . . .

110. Such circumstances give rise to a violation of Article 2 of the Convention
in its substantive aspect; the Government's submission relating to the favourable
outcome of the administrative action brought in the instant case . . . is of no consequence here, for the reasons set . . . out . . . below.

*(ii) Responsibility borne by the State as regards the judicial response required on account of
the deaths, in the light of the procedural aspect of Article 2 of the Convention. . . .*

112. . . . It remains to be determined whether the measures taken in the framework of the Turkish criminal-law system following the accident at the Ümraniye
municipal rubbish tip were satisfactory in practice, regard being had to the requirements of the Convention in this respect. . . .

113. In this connection, the Court notes that immediately after the accident
had occurred on 28 April 1993 at about 11 a.m., the police arrived on the scene and
interviewed the victims' families. In addition, the Istanbul Governor's Office set up
a crisis unit, whose members went to the site on the same day. On the following day,
29 April 1993, the Ministry of the Interior ordered, of its own motion, the opening
of an administrative investigation to determine the extent to which the authorities
had been responsible for the accident. On 30 April 1993 the Üsküdar public prosecutor began a criminal investigation. Lastly, the official inquiries ended on 15 July
1993, when the two mayors, Mr Sözen and Mr Öktem, were committed for trial in
the criminal courts.

Accordingly, the investigating authorities may be regarded as having acted
with exemplary promptness and as having shown diligence in seeking to establish
the circumstances that led both to the accident of 28 April 1993 and to the ensuing
deaths. . . .

116. In the instant case, in a judgment of 4 April 1996 the Istanbul Criminal
Court sentenced the two mayors in question to fines of TRL 610,000 (an amount
equivalent at the time to approximately EUR 9.70), suspended, for negligent omissions in the performance of their duties within the meaning of Article 230 §1 of the
Criminal Code. Before the Court, the Government attempted to explain why that
provision alone had been applied in respect of the two mayors and why they had
been sentenced to the minimum penalty applicable. However, it is not for the Court
to address such issues of domestic law concerning individual criminal responsibility, that being a matter for assessment by the national courts, or to deliver guilty or
not-guilty verdicts in that regard.

Having regard to its task, the Court would simply observe that in the instant
case the sole purpose of the criminal proceedings in issue was to establish whether
the authorities could be held liable for "negligence in the performance of their
duties" under Article 230 of the Criminal Code, which provision does not in any

way relate to life-endangering acts or to the protection of the right to life within the meaning of Article 2.

Indeed, it appears from the judgment of 4 April 1996 that the trial court did not see any reason to depart from the reasoning set out in the committal order issued by the Administrative Council and left in abeyance any question of the authorities' possible responsibility for the death of the applicant's nine relatives. The judgment of 4 April 1996 does, admittedly, contain passages referring to the deaths that occurred on 28 April 1993 as a factual element. However, that cannot be taken to mean that there was an acknowledgment of any responsibility for failing to protect the right to life. . . .

117. Accordingly, it cannot be said that the manner in which the Turkish criminal-justice system operated in response to the tragedy secured the full accountability of State officials or authorities for their role in it and the effective implementation of provisions of domestic law guaranteeing respect for the right to life, in particular the deterrent function of the criminal law.

118. In short, it must be concluded in the instant case that there has been a violation of Article 2 of the Convention in its procedural aspect also, on account of the lack, in connection with a fatal accident provoked by the operation of a dangerous activity, of adequate protection "by law" safeguarding the right to life and deterring similar life-endangering conduct in future. . . .

[The Court also held by a vote of 15 to 2 that there had been a violation of the right to property, contained in Article 1 of Protocol 1, and the right to a remedy, found in Article 13.]

---

Along with addressing the affirmative duties of states to ensure human rights, the *SERAC, Velásquez Rodríguez,* and *Öneryildiz* judgments applied the rules of international law by which conduct can be attributable to a state for the purposes of determining whether the state is in breach of its obligations under international law.

Those rules also are reflected in the UN International Law Commission's articles on Responsibility of States for Internationally Wrongful Acts (2001), G.A. Res. 56/83 (2001), Annnex. Article 4 of this document states:

> 1. The conduct of any State organ shall be considered an act of that State under international law, whether the organ exercises legislative, executive, judicial or any function . . . ,
> 2. An organ includes a person or entity which has that status. . . .

The facts in *SERAC, Velazquez Rodriquez,* and *Öneryildiz* involved the conduct of state actors—that is, respectively, state security forces and an oil consortium in which the state was a majority partner, military and justice authorities, and municipal authorities. Hence, the conduct that was found to be in violation of human rights was held attributable to the state. However, the African Commission in *SERAC* (at para. 57) and the Inter-American Court in *Velazquez Rodriquez* (at para. 172) affirmed that a state could be held responsible for an act by a private party—an act *not* attributable to the state—if the state failed to uphold its duty of protection and due diligence. This principle is illustrated by the following case, which involves an extreme pattern of violence against women.

## González et. al. ("Cotton Field") v. Mexico

Inter.-Am. Court H.R., Judgment of Nov. 16, 2009, Series C No. 205
(footnotes omitted).

. . .

2. The application relates to the State's alleged international responsibility for "the disappearance and subsequent death" of the Ms. Claudia Ivette González, Esmeralda Herrera Monreal and Laura Berenice Ramos Monárrez (hereinafter "Ms. González, Herrera and Ramos"), whose bodies were found in a cotton field in Ciudad Juárez on November 6, 2001. The State is considered responsible for "the lack of measures for the protection of the victims, two of whom were minor children, the lack of prevention of these crimes, in spite of full awareness of the existence of a pattern of gender-related violence that had resulted in hundreds of women and girls murdered, the lack of response of the authorities to the disappearance [. . .]; the lack of due diligence in the investigation of the homicides [. . .], as well as the denial of justice and the lack of an adequate reparation.". . .

111. Despite acknowledging "the serious nature of these murders," the State denied that it had committed "any violation" of the rights to life, humane treatment and personal liberty. According to the State, neither the Commission nor the representatives "had proved that State agents were in any way responsible for the murders." In addition, it argued that, during the second stage of the investigations into the three cases starting in 2004, "the irregularities were fully rectified, the case files were reactivated and the investigations were started up again on a scientific basis, and even with international support." According to the State, "impunity does not exist. The investigations into the cases are still open and measures are still being taken to identify those responsible."

### 1. Context

#### 1.1. Ciudad Juárez

113. Ciudad Juárez is located in the north of the state of Chihuahua, on the border with El Paso, Texas. It has a population of more than 1.2 million inhabitants, and is an industrial city – where the "*maquila* industry" (manufacturing and/ or assembly plants, hereinafter referred to as "*maquila*," "*maquiladora*" or "*maquilas*") has flourished—and a place of transit for Mexican and foreign migrants. The State, as well as various national and international reports, mention a series of factors that converge in Ciudad Juárez, such as social inequalities and the proximity of the international border, that have contributed to the development of different types of organized crime, such as drug-trafficking, people trafficking, arms smuggling and money-laundering, which have increased the levels of insecurity and violence.

1.2. Phenomenon of The Murder of Women, and Numbers

114. The Commission and the representatives alleged that, since 1993, the number of disappearances and murders of women and girls in Ciudad Juárez has increased significantly. According to the Commission, "Ciudad Juárez has become a focus of attention of both the national and the international communities because of the particularly critical situation of violence against women which has prevailed since 1993, and the deficient State response to these crimes."

115. The State acknowledged "the problem it faces owing to the situation of violence against women in Ciudad Juárez, above all, the murders that have been recorded since the beginning of the 1990s in the last century."

116. Various national and international human rights monitoring mechanisms have been following the situation in Ciudad Juárez and have called the international community's attention to it. . . . .

117. The report of the IACHR Rapporteur underscores that, although Ciudad Juárez has been characterized by a significant increase in crimes against women and men, several aspects of the increase are "anomalous" with regard to women because: (i) murders of women increased significantly in 1993; (ii) the coefficients for murders of women doubled compared to those for men; and (iii) the homicide rate for women in Ciudad Juárez is disproportionately higher than that for other border cities with similar characteristics. For its part, the State provided evidence that, in 2006, Ciudad Juárez was ranked fourth among all Mexican cities for the murder of women.

118. From the information provided by the parties, the Court observes that no clear data exists on the exact number of women who have been murdered in Ciudad Juárez since 1993. Reports quote figures ranging from 260 to 370 women from 1993 to 2003. . . .

1.3 Victims

. . .

123. The plaintiffs' allegations were based on different reports prepared by national and international agencies establishing that the murder victims appeared to be, above all, young women, including girls, women workers — especially those working in the *maquilas* – who are underprivileged, students or migrants.

1.4. Method

. . .

125. Diverse reports establish the following common factors in several of the murders: the women were abducted and kept in captivity, their next of kin reported their disappearance and, after days or months, their bodies were found on empty lots with signs of violence, including rape and other types of sexual abuse, torture and mutilation.

1.5. Gender-based Violence

128. According to the representatives [of the victims?], the issue of gender is the common denominator of the violence in Ciudad Juárez, which "occurs as a

culmination of a situation characterized by the reiterated and systematic violation of human rights." They alleged that "cruel acts of violence are perpetrated against girls and women merely because of their gender and, only in some cases, are they murdered as a culmination of this public and private violence.". . .

1.7. INVESTIGATION INTO THE MURDERS OF WOMEN

146. According to the Commission and the representatives, another factor that characterizes these murders of women is the failure to clarify them and the irregularities in the respective investigations which, they consider, have given rise to a climate of impunity. In this regard, the Tribunal [Inter-American Court] takes note of the State's acknowledgement of "the commission of several irregularities in the investigation and processing of the murders of women perpetrated between 1993 and 2004 in Ciudad Juárez." The State also regretted "the mistakes committed up until 2004 by public servants who took part in some of these investigations.". . .

1.7.2. Discriminatory attitude of the authorities

151. The Commission and the representatives alleged that the attitude of the State authorities to the killings of women in Ciudad Juárez was extremely discriminatory and dilatory, a situation that the Commission described as an "alarming pattern of response and stereotyped conceptions of the missing women." In particular, the pattern "was reflected on the part of the [S]tate officials that the search and protection of women reported as having disappeared was not important" and meant that, initially, the authorities refused to investigate. . . .

4.2.1. Obligation of prevention in relation to the right to personal liberty, to personal integrity and to life of the victims

252. The Court has established that the obligation of prevention encompasses all those measures of a legal, political, administrative and cultural nature that ensure the safeguard of human rights, and that any possible violation of these rights is considered and treated as an unlawful act, which, as such, may result in the punishment of the person who commits it, as well as the obligation to compensate the victims for the harmful consequences. It is also clear that the obligation to prevent is one of means or conduct, and failure to comply with it is not proved merely because the right has been violated.

253. The Convention of Belém do Pará defines violence against women and its Article 7(b) obliges the States Parties to use due diligence to prevent, punish and eliminate this violence.

254. . . . [After referring to the Convention on the Elimination of Discrimination Against Women, the UN Declaration on the Elimination of Violence against Women, and the Platform for Action of the Beijing World Conference on Women, the Court cited a 2006 report of the U.N. Special Rapporteur on violence against women, who conclude that "there is a norm of customary international law that obliges States to prevent and respond with due diligence to acts of violence against women."]

. . .

256. In addition, the U.N. Special Rapporteur on violence against women has provided guidelines on the measures that States should take to comply with their international obligations of due diligence with regard to prevention, namely: ratification of the international human rights instruments; constitutional guarantees on equality for women; existence of national legislation and administrative sanctions providing adequate redress for women victims of violence; executive policies or plans of action that attempt to deal with the question of violence against women; sensitization of the criminal justice system and the police to gender issues; availability and accessibility of support services; existence of measures in the field of education and the media to raise awareness and modify practices that discriminate against women, and collection of data and statistics on violence against women. . . .

258. The foregoing reveals that States should adopt comprehensive measures to comply with due diligence in cases of violence against women. In particular, they should have an appropriate legal framework for protection that is enforced effectively, and prevention policies and practices that allow effective measures to be taken in response to the respective complaints. The prevention strategy should also be comprehensive; in other words, it should prevent the risk factors and, at the same time, strengthen the institutions that can provide an effective response in cases of violence against women. Furthermore, the State should adopt preventive measures in specific cases in which it is evident that certain women and girls may be victims of violence. This should take into account that, in cases of violence against women, the States also have the general obligation established in the American Convention, an obligation reinforced since the Convention of Belém do Pará came into force. The Court will now examine the measures adopted by the State prior to the facts of this case to comply with its obligation of prevention. . . .

279. Even though the State was fully aware of the danger faced by these women of being subjected to violence, it has not shown that, prior to November 2001, it had adopted effective measures of prevention that would have reduced the risk factors for the women. Although the obligation of prevention is one of means and not of results, the State has not demonstrated that the creation of the FEIHM [Spanish acronym for the Office of the Special Prosecutor for the Investigation of the Murders of Women in Ciudad Juárez, created in 1998] and some additions to its legislative framework, although necessary and revealing a commitment by the State, were sufficient and effective to prevent the serious manifestations of violence against women that occurred in Ciudad Juárez at the time of this case.

280. Nevertheless, according to the Court's jurisprudence, it is evident that a State cannot be held responsible for every human rights violation committed between private individuals within its jurisdiction. Indeed, a State's obligation of guarantee under the Convention does not imply its unlimited responsibility for any act or deed of private individuals, because its obligation to adopt measures of prevention and protection for private individuals in their relations with each other is conditional on its awareness of a situation of real and imminent danger for a specific individual or group of individuals and the reasonable possibility of preventing or avoiding that danger. . . .

281. In this case, there are two crucial moments in which the obligation of prevention must be examined. The first is prior to the disappearance of the victims and the second is before the discovery of their bodies.

282. Regarding the first moment – before the disappearance of the victims — the Tribunal finds that the failure to prevent the disappearance does not *per se* result in the State's international responsibility because, even though the State was aware of the situation of risk for women in Ciudad Juárez, it has not been established that it knew of a real and imminent danger for the victims in this case. Even though the context of this case and the State's international obligations impose on it a greater responsibility with regard to the protection of women in Ciudad Juárez, who are in a vulnerable situation, particularly young women from humble backgrounds, these factors do not impose unlimited responsibility for any unlawful act against such women. Moreover, the Court can only note that the absence of a general policy which could have been initiated at least in 1998 — when the CNDH warned of the pattern of violence against women in Ciudad Juárez — is a failure of the State to comply in general with its obligation of prevention.

283. With regard to the second moment — before the discovery of the bodies — given the context of the case, the State was aware that there was a real and imminent risk that the victims would be sexually abused, subjected to ill-treatment and killed. The Tribunal finds that, in this context, an obligation of strict due diligence arises in regard to reports of missing women, with respect to search operations during the first hours and days. Since this obligation of means is more rigorous, it requires that exhaustive search activities be conducted. Above all, it is essential that police authorities, prosecutors and judicial officials take prompt immediate action by ordering, without delay, the necessary measures to determine the whereabouts of the victims or the place where they may have been retained. Adequate procedures should exist for reporting disappearances, which should result in an immediate effective investigation. The authorities should presume that the disappeared person has been deprived of liberty and is still alive until there is no longer any uncertainty about her fate.

284. Mexico did not prove that it had adopted reasonable measures, according to the circumstances surrounding these cases, to find the victims alive. The State did not act promptly during the first hours and days following the reports of the disappearances, losing valuable time. In the period between the reports and the discovery of the victims' bodies, the State merely carried out formalities and took statements that, although important, lost their value when they failed to lead to specific search actions. In addition, the attitude of the officials towards the victims' next of kin, suggesting that the missing persons' reports should not be dealt with urgently and immediately, leads the Court to conclude reasonably that there were unjustified delays following the filing of these reports. The foregoing reveals that the State did not act with the required due diligence to prevent the death and abuse suffered by the victims adequately and did not act, as could reasonably be expected, in accordance with the circumstances of the case, to end their deprivation of liberty. This failure to comply with the obligation to guarantee is particularly serious owing to the context of which the State was aware — which placed women in a particularly vulnerable situation — and of the even greater obligations imposed

in cases of violence against women by Article 7(b) of the Convention of Belém do Pará.

285. In addition, the Tribunal finds that the State did not prove that it had adopted norms or implemented the necessary measures, pursuant to Article 2 of the American Convention and Article 7(c) of the Convention of Belém do Pará, that would have allowed the authorities to provide an immediate and effective response to the reports of disappearance and to adequately prevent the violence against women. Furthermore, it did not prove that it had adopted norms or taken measures to ensure that the officials in charge of receiving the missing reports had the capacity and the sensitivity to understand the seriousness of the phenomenon of violence against women and the willingness to act immediately.

286. Based on the foregoing, the Court finds that the State violated the rights to life, personal integrity and personal liberty recognized in Articles 4(1), 5(1), 5(2) and 7(1) of the American Convention, in relation to the general obligation to guarantee contained in Article 1(1) and the obligation to adopt domestic legal provisions contained in Article 2 thereof, as well as the obligations established in Article 7(b) and 7(c) of the Convention of Belém do Pará, to the detriment of Claudia Ivette González, Laura Berenice Ramos Monárrez and Esmeralda Herrera Monreal.

## *Note: State Responsibility for Violence Against Women*

The above case represents a harrowing example of a pattern of violence against women and illustrates how a state can be held responsible for such violence. As discussed in Chapter 1, violence against women is an ongoing, dire, and endemic human rights issue. It is frequently perpetrated by both state and private actors.

Even though the international bill of rights, and indeed the UN Charter, guarantees the enjoyment of human rights without discrimination on the basis of sex, advocates believed it necessary to adopt a specialized treaty on this topic. After earlier adoption of two limited conventions concerned with certain aspects of women's rights (the 1952 Convention on the Political Rights of Women, 193 U.N.T.S. 135, and the 1957 Convention on the Nationality of Married Women, 309 U.N.T.S. 65), in 1979 the comprehensive Convention on the Elimination of all Forms of Discrimination against Women (CEDAW) was adopted. CEDAW is the second most widely ratified of all human rights treaties (189 parties), and has been supplemented by 38 General Recommendations adopted by the committee entrusted with its monitoring. For more discussion on the history of CEDAW and the work of the CEDAW Committee, see Rosa Celorio, "Discrimination Against Women: Doctrine, Practice, and the Path Forward," in *Women and International Human Rights in Modern Times: A Contemporary Casebook* 1 (2022).

Highly significant as it is, CEDAW is noticeably silent on the issue of violence against women and the obligations of states to address it. In response to this gap and in light of growing recognition of the worldwide scope of the problem, in 1992 the Committee on the Elimination of Discrimination against Women adopted General Recommendation 19. This General Recommendation, an extract of which follows, addresses state obligations under CEDAW in this context.

Committee on the Elimination of Discrimination against Women

## General Recommendation No. 19: Violence against Women

UN Doc. A/47/38 (1992).

. . . .

6. The Convention in article 1 defines discrimination against women. The definition of discrimination includes gender-based violence, that is, violence that is directed against a woman because she is a woman or that affects women disproportionately. It includes acts that inflict physical, mental or sexual harm or suffering, threats of such acts, coercion and other deprivations of liberty. Gender-based violence may breach specific provisions of the Convention, regardless of whether those provisions expressly mention violence.

7. Gender-based violence, which impairs or nullifies the enjoyment by women of human rights and fundamental freedoms under general international law or under human rights conventions, is discrimination within the meaning of article 1 of the Convention. . . .

8. The Convention applies to violence perpetrated by public authorities. Such acts of violence may breach that State's obligations under general international human rights law and under other conventions, in addition to breaching this Convention.

9. It is emphasized, however, that discrimination under the Convention is not restricted to action by or on behalf of Governments (see articles 2(e), 2(f) and 5). For example, under article 2(e) the Convention calls on States parties to take all appropriate measures to eliminate discrimination against women by any person, organization or enterprise. Under general international law and specific human rights covenants, States may also be responsible for private acts if they fail to act with due diligence to prevent violations of rights or to investigate and punish acts of violence, and for providing compensation.

*Comments on Specific Articles of the Convention*

ARTICLES 2 AND 3

10. Articles 2 and 3 establish a comprehensive obligation to eliminate discrimination in all its forms in addition to the specific obligations under articles 5-16.

ARTICLES 2(f), 5 AND 10(c)

11. Traditional attitudes by which women are regarded as subordinate to men or as having stereotyped roles perpetuate widespread practices involving violence or coercion, such as family violence and abuse, forced marriage, dowry deaths, acid attacks and female circumcision. Such prejudices and practices may justify gender-based violence as a form of protection or control of women. The effect of such violence on the physical and mental integrity of women is to deprive them the equal enjoyment, exercise and knowledge of human rights and fundamental freedoms. While this comment addresses mainly actual or threatened violence the underlying consequences of these forms of gender-based violence help to maintain women in

subordinate roles and contribute to the low level of political participation and to their lower level of education, skills and work opportunities.

12. These attitudes also contribute to the propagation of pornography and the depiction and other commercial exploitation of women as sexual objects, rather than as individuals. This in turn contributes to gender-based violence. . . .

ARTICLE 11

17. Equality in employment can be seriously impaired when women are subjected to gender-specific violence, such as sexual harassment in the workplace.

18. Sexual harassment includes such unwelcome sexually determined behaviour as physical contact and advances, sexually coloured remarks, showing pornography and sexual demand, whether by words or actions. Such conduct can be humiliating and may constitute a health and safety problem; it is discriminatory when the woman has reasonable grounds to believe that her objection would disadvantage her in connection with her employment, including recruitment or promotion, or when it creates a hostile working environment.

ARTICLE 12

19. States parties are required by article 12 to take measures to ensure equal access to health care. Violence against women puts their health and lives at risk.

20. In some States there are traditional practices perpetuated by culture and tradition that are harmful to the health of women and children. These practices include dietary restrictions for pregnant women, preference for male children and female circumcision or genital mutilation.

ARTICLE 14

21. Rural women are at risk of gender-based violence because traditional attitudes regarding the subordinate role of women that persist in many rural communities. Girls from rural communities are at special risk of violence and sexual exploitation when they leave the rural community to seek employment in towns.

ARTICLE 16 (AND ARTICLE 5)

22. Compulsory sterilization or abortion adversely affects women's physical and mental health, and infringes the right of women to decide on the number and spacing of their children.

23. Family violence is one of the most insidious forms of violence against women. It is prevalent in all societies. Within family relationships women of all ages are subjected to violence of all kinds, including battering, rape, other forms of sexual assault, mental and other forms of violence, which are perpetuated by traditional attitudes. Lack of economic independence forces many women to stay in violent relationships. The abrogation of their family responsibilities by men can be a form of violence, and coercion. These forms of violence put women's health at risk and impair their ability to participate in family life and public life on a basis of equality.

SPECIFIC RECOMMENDATION

24. In light of these comments, the Committee on the Elimination of Discrimination against Women recommends that:

a) States parties should take appropriate and effective measures to overcome all forms of gender-based violence, whether by public or private act;

b) States parties should ensure that laws against family violence and abuse, rape, sexual assault and other gender-based violence give adequate protection to all women, and respect their integrity and dignity. Appropriate protective and support services should be provided for victims. Gender-sensitive training of judicial and law enforcement officers and other public officials is essential for the effective implementation of the Convention;

c) States parties should encourage the compilation of statistics and research on the extent, causes and effects of violence, and on the effectiveness of measures to prevent and deal with violence;

d) States parties in their reports should identify the nature and extent of attitudes, customs and practices that perpetuate violence against women and the kinds of violence that result. They should report on the measures that they have undertaken to overcome violence and the effect of those measures. . . .

---

The foregoing materials affirm that the states' duty to protect or ensure human rights entails a standard of due diligence toward both public and private conduct. The due diligence standard has been an important feature of international law, considered applicable to cases with human rights implications in general. See J. Hessbruegge, *The Historical Development of the Doctrines of Attribution and Due Diligence in International Law*, 36 N.Y.U. J. INT'L L. 265 (2004); Robert P. Barnidge, Jr., *The Due Diligence Principle under International Law*, 8 INT'L COMMUNITY L. REV. 81 (2006); Johanna Bourke-Martignoni, "The History and Development of the Due Diligence Standard in International Law and Its Role in the Protection of Women Against Violence," in *Due Diligence and Iits Application to Protect Women from Violence* (Carin Benniger-Budel ed., 2008); *The Due Diligence Standard as a Tool for the Elimination of Violence against Women—Report of the Special Rapporteur on Violence Against Women, Its Causes and Consequences, Yakin Ertürk*, UN Doc. E/CN.4/2006/61 (2006).

## Comments and Questions

1. The Inter-American Court of Human Rights first referred to the due diligence standard in its landmark judgment in the case of *Velasquez Rodriguez*, concerning the issue of forced disappearances in Honduras. In that case the conduct of state military and security agents was held attributable to the state. What is the difference between attribution of responsibility to the state and the state oligation

of due diligence? Can the state be attributed responsibility for the acts of private presons? Can the state violate its obligation of due diligence in regard to the conduct of private persons?

2.  Do you agree with the *Öneryildiz* judgment? Should (gross) negligence by state authorities result in a finding that human rights have been violated? In another case, *Makaratzis v. Greece*, App. No. 50385/99, Euro Ct. H.R. (GC), Judgment of Dec. 20, 2004, the European Court of Human Rights held that physical ill-treatment by state officials that does not result in death may, in exceptional circumstances, bring the facts of a case within the scope of Article 2's obligation to protect life. The facts of the case indicated that policemen had engaged in a high-speed car chase with the applicant and repeatedly fired their weapons at him. While they had not intended to kill him, the fact that he did not die was fortuitous, because the conduct had put his life at risk; Article 2 was thus applicable. The conduct of the authorities lacked appropriate structure in domestic law or practice setting out clear guidelines and criteria governing the use of force. Therefore, the authorities had not complied with their positive obligation to protect life under Article 2 and the applicant had been the victim of a violation. Does such a standard place too great a burden on the state? Contrast these cases with the U.S. Supreme Court decisions in *DeShaney v. County of Winnebago Dep't of Social Services*, 489 U.S. 189 (1989) and *Castle Rock v. Gonzales* 545 U.S. 748 (2005), each of which held that the US Constitution imposes no positive obligations on the government to protect life and personal security from violence by private actors.

3.  The readings above reflect that states are obligated to provide appropriorate judicial or administrative remedies when protected rights are violated. In light of *Öneryildiz* and the due diligence standard, how far do judicial or adminstrative remedies need to go — beyond what is provided in domestic law — for state responsibility to be avoided for a violation of an internationally-protected human right?

4.  The Inter-American Court of Human Rights shed important light on the content of the due diligence standard in the *Cotton Field* case. The Inter-American Court clarified that state duties to respect and guarantee rights under Article 1(1) of the American Convention on Human Right require state officials to investigate all human rights violations promptly and exhaustively in order to prevent impunity. The Court also established that the due diligence standard entails a broad duty to prevent human rights violations, including in certain cases those committed by private individuals. The Court underscored that this duty is comprehensive and encompasses the adoption of legal, public policy, and institutional measures. Which criteria should be used to determine that a state complied with its obligation in the sphere of prevention? How relevant should knowledge of a context of disappearances and murders be in this analysis? Does it make a difference that the act was perpetrated by a public official or a private actor? Reflect on this question in light of the difference the Court establishes between the duty of prevention before the disappearances were reported to the authorities and afterwards, as well as the fact that the Court did not have conclusive evidence confirming the involvement of public officials in the events at issue.

5.  How does the scope of state obligations in the context of violence against women articulated in *Cotton Field* compare with state obligations set forth in General Recommendation No. 19 of the Committee on the Elimination of Violence

against Women? The Court in *Cotton Field* focused its analysis on the investigation of cases of violence against women and the broad obligation of states to investigate these cases without delay and with a gender perspective. The CEDAW Committee in General Recommendation 19 calls on state parties to take appropriate and effective measures—in their legislation, public policies, and programs—to eradicate all forms of gender-based violence, such violence being a form of discrimination. How are the state obligations referred to by the Inter-American Court in *Cotton Field* and the CEDAW Committee in its General Recommendation 19 connected? Note that in *Cotton Field*, the Inter-American Court of Human Rights largely bases its analysis on a treaty of general applicability—the American Convention on Human Rights—while the CEDAW Committee is interpreting the scope of state obligations under a specialized treaty.

Is there a heightened, sui generis standard of duty diligence and duty of prevention in the context of violence against women? If so what justifies such a sui generis standard? Might a similar sui generis standard of hightened duty of due diligence and prevention be justified in other areas of concern?

6. What do the due diligence and negligence standards in the above cases suggest about the scope of state obligations in the context of environmental harm or climate change? Is there a duty to prevent foreseeable harm? How can foreseeable harm be verified? Recall that in the *SERAC* case, the African Commission found Nigeria responsible, among other things, for failing to prevent or adequately address the human rights impacts of the environmental degradation generated by Shell's oil operations. Might states be responsible under international human rights law for negligently allowing the causes of climate change, and consequent human rights impacts, to accumulate? Or might they be failing to exercise due diligence to adequately address the human rights impacts of climate change? Should states be responsible for the activity of private actors in this area? See the cases discussed in Chapter 2, at pages 117-118, at least partially answering these questions.Can you construct the basic elements of a complaint, based on international human rights law, that could be presented to an appropriate international body for a state's failure to prevent foreseeable harm concerning the environment and climate change? See generally Office of the High Commissioner for Human Rights, *Frequently Asked Questions on Human Rights and Climate Change* (2021), https://www.ohchr.org/sites/default/files/Documents/Publications/FSheet38_FAQ_HR_CC_EN.pdf.

## III.  *BUSINESS ENTERPRISES AND HUMAN RIGHTS*

The effort to limit or prohibit private-sector conduct detrimental to human rights is as old as the effort to protect human rights through international and national law. The movement to combat the transatlantic slave trade—a major multinational business from the sixteenth through the nineteenth centuries—was among the first global human rights actions. In recent years, several developments have placed international human rights norms on the agenda of corporations and other business organizations. Consumer awareness has increased, as consumers are

to adequate food, clothing and housing were as likely to appear in cases concerning the living conditions of workers residing at a manufacturing facility campus as they were to appear in relation to communities affected by extractive or infrastructure projects. Regarding the right to education, a heavy manufacturing firm was alleged to have contributed to infringement of the right because it sold equipment that was subsequently used to block access to local schools while a supplier firm was alleged to employ children full-time in its factory without regard to their schooling. Alleged impacts on the right to privacy occurred where company-affiliated security forces arbitrarily attacked private homes and also in cases where companies set up surveillance systems and methods to intercept e-mail communications.

27. In addition . . . , nearly a third of cases alleged environmental harms that had corresponding impacts on human rights. Environmental concerns were raised in relation to all sectors. In these cases, various forms of pollution, contamination, and degradation translated into alleged impacts on a number of rights, including on the right to health, the right to life, rights to adequate food and housing, minority rights to culture, and the right to benefit from scientific progress. A number of environmental issues also prompted allegations that a firm had either impeded access to clean water or polluted a clean water supply, an issue raised in 20 per cent of cases.

28. Corruption issues were regularly raised in relation to the realization of non-labor rights, with transparency emerging as the key issue of concern. Transparency was expected but allegedly not delivered in relation to a number of issues, ranging from project impact assessments to corporate political and trade association payments.

## B.  The UN Guiding Principles on Business and Human Rights

In 2011, the UN Human Rights Council endorsed the Guiding Principles on Business and Human Rights, which were developed by the Special Representative on business and human rights, John Ruggie. The Guiding Principles are discussed and reproduced in substantial part below. While the UN Guiding Principles are now foremost among efforts to articulate the human right obligations and responsibilities related to business activity, they were preceded by a number of important developments related to the topic.

### 1.  Background

An early step in the United Nations' effort to promote alignment of corporate behavior with human rights occurred in 1999, when the UN adopted an initative known as the Global Compact. This initiative encourages business enterprises to adhere to a set of principles intended to ensure more responsible forms of globalization. In announcing the Global Compact, UN Secretary-General Kofi Annan urged corporations to increase transparency and integrate social responsibility into their business operations. The first two principles of the Global Compact address human rights directly and provide that businesses should: (1) "support and respect the protection of internationally proclaimed human rights," and (2) make sure they are not complicit in human rights abuses. See UN Global Compact, https://www.unglobalcompact.org/. Other principles address labor standards, the environment, and combating corruption. At a conference to review the UN Global Compact, which took place in June 2016, more than 600 business leaders from 75 countries met with representatives from nongovernmental organizations, the United Nations, and governments to discuss how corporate activity can best achieve the 17 Sustainable Development Goals set forth in the UN's Agenda 2030. See *UN Global Compact Leaders Summit 2016*, United Nations Global Compact, https://www.unglobalcompact.org/take-action/events/leaders-summit (last visited Sept. 14, 2022).

Another UN attempt to articulate the proper relationship between business and human rights produced the Norms on the Responsibilities of Transnational Corporations and Other Business Enterprises with Regard to Human Rights, UN Doc. E/CN.4/Sub.2/2003/12/Rev.2 (2003), which were adopted by the Sub-Commission on the Promotion and Protection of Human Rights in 2003. The Sub-Commission was previously under the Commission on Human Rights, which was replaced in 2006 by the Human Rights Council; see Chapter 7. When commenting on the draft of the Norms, its primary author, then Sub-Commission member David Weissbrodt, stated that "the document was binding in the sense that it applied human rights law under ratified conventions to the activities of transnational corporations and other business enterprises. Moreover, the language of the document emphasized binding responsibilities through the use of the term 'shall' rather than 'should,' and the draft norms included measures for implementation." Sub-Commission on the Promotion and Protection of Human Rights, *Report of the sessional working group on the working methods and activities of transnational corporations on its fourth session*, UN Doc. E/CN.4/Sub.2/2002/13 (2002), para. 14. For a discussion of the UN Sub-Commission Norms, see David Weissbrodt and Muria Kruger, *Norms on the Responsibilities of Transnational Corporations and Other Business Enterprises with Regard to Human Rights*, 97 Am. J. Int'l L. 901 (2003).

Reaction to the Sub-Commission's work by the Commission on Human Rights was less than enthusiastic, however. The Commission explicitly noted that it had not requested that the norms be prepared and pointed out that, "as a draft proposal, [the Sub-Commission document] has no legal standing." The Commission directed that the Sub-Commission not perform any monitoring function with regard to the Norms. Comm'n H.R., Decision 2004/116 (2004), para. (c). The Commission nonetheless requested the High Commissioner for Human Rights, among other things, "to compile a report setting out the scope and legal status of existing initiatives and standards relating to the responsibility of transnational corporations and related business enterprises with regard to human rights." Id., para. (b).

The *Report of the United Nations High Commissioner for Human Rights on the responsibilities of transnational corporations and related business enterprises with regard to human rights*, UN Doc. E/CN.4/2005/91 (2005), helped lay the groundwork for further work on the topic. Notably, the report affirmed that "[e]nsuring that business respects human rights is first a matter of State action at the domestic level," in conformity with obligations under international law to protect human rights against the actions of third parties, including corporations. Id., para. 43. At the same time, the report addressed "the responsibilities of business with regard to human rights," identifying multiple issues that arise in identifying the nature and scope of those responsibilities. It referred to the "non-legal concept of 'sphere of influence'" as a means of discerning when business enterprises should support human rights or set limits to avoid complicity with human rights violations. The report observed how, as a practical matter business can promote human rights within their operations. Id., paras. 37-38, 44. Exploring means of addressing "accountability gaps," the report identified the possibility of companies being subject to the law and jurisdiction of their home countries in relation to their operations abroad. Id., para. 47.

Following the issuance of the High Commissioner's report, the UN Secretary-General, at the request of the UN Commission on Human Rights, appointed a "Special Representative on the issue of human rights and transnational corporations and other business enterprises." The mandate of the Sapecial Representative, as established by the Commission, was as follows:

> (*a*) To identify and clarify standards of corporate responsibility and accountability for transnational corporations and other business enterprises with regard to human rights;
>
> (*b*) To elaborate on the role of states in effectively regulating and adjudicating the role of transnational corporations and other business enterprises with regard to human rights, including through international cooperation;
>
> (*c*) To research and clarify the implications for transnational corporations and other business enterprises of concepts such as "complicity" and "sphere of influence;"
>
> (*d*) develop materials and methodologies for undertaking human rights impact assessments of the activities of transnational corporations and other business enterprises; and
>
> (*e*) To compile a compendium of best practices of States and transnational corporations and other business enterprises.

Comm'n H.R. Res. 2005/69 (2005), para. 1.

## 2.   The Protect, Respect, and Remedy Framework

The Special Representative, John Ruggie, a professor at Harvard's Kennedy School, submitted a series of reports, which included mapping patterns of corporate-related human rights abuse and defining principles he believed should guide the conduct of states and businesses. These principles were articulated in *Protect, Respect and Remedy: A Framework for Business and Human Rights*, UN Doc. A/HRC/8/5 (2008):

> The framework rests on differentiated but complementary responsibilities. It comprises three core principles: the State duty to protect against human rights abuses by third parties, including business; the corporate responsibility to respect human rights; and the need for more effective access to remedies. Each principle is an essential component of the framework: the State duty to protect because it lies at the very core of the international human rights regime; the corporate responsibility to respect because it is the basic expectation society has of business; and access to remedy, because even the most concerted efforts cannot prevent

all abuse, while access to judicial redress is often problematic, and non-judicial means are limited in number, scope and effectiveness. The three principles form a complementary whole in that each supports the others in achieving sustainable progress.

. . .

Take first the State duty to protect. It has both legal and policy dimensions. As documented in the Special Representative's 2007 report, international law provides that States have a duty to protect against human rights abuses by non-State actors, including by business, affecting persons within their territory or jurisdiction. To help States interpret how this duty applies under the core United Nations human rights conventions, the treaty monitoring bodies generally recommend that States take all necessary steps to protect against such abuse, including to prevent, investigate, and punish the abuse, and to provide access to redress. States have discretion to decide what measures to take, but the treaty bodies indicate that both regulation and adjudication of corporate activities vis-à-vis human rights are appropriate. They also suggest that the duty applies to the activities of all types of businesses—national and transnational, large and small—and that it applies to all rights private parties are capable of impairing. Regional human rights systems have reached similar conclusions.

. . .

The corporate responsibility to respect human rights is the second principle. It is recognized in such soft law instruments as the Tripartite Declaration of Principles Concerning Multinational Enterprises and Social Policy, and the OECD Guidelines for Multinational Enterprises. It is invoked by the largest global business organizations in their submission to the mandate, which states that companies "are expected to obey the law, even if it is not enforced, and to respect the principles of relevant international instruments where national law is absent". It is one of the commitments companies undertake in joining the Global Compact. And the Special Representative's surveys document the fact that companies worldwide increasingly claim they respect human rights.

To respect rights essentially means not to infringe on the rights of others—put simply, to do no harm. Because companies can affect virtually all internationally recognized rights, they should consider the responsibility to respect in relation to all such rights, although some may require greater attention in particular contexts. There are situations in which companies may have additional responsibilities—for example, where they perform certain public functions, or because they have undertaken additional commitments voluntarily. But the responsibility to respect is the baseline expectation for all companies in all situations.

. . .

Access to remedy is the third principle. Even where institutions operate optimally, disputes over the human rights impact of companies are likely to occur. Currently, access to formal judicial systems is often most difficult where the need is greatest. And non-judicial mechanisms are seriously underdeveloped—from the company level up through national and international levels.

Effective grievance mechanisms play an important role in the State duty to protect, in both its legal and policy dimensions, as well as in the corporate responsibility to respect. State regulation proscribing certain corporate conduct will have little impact without accompanying mechanisms to investigate, punish, and redress abuses. Equally, the corporate responsibility to respect requires a means for those who believe they have been harmed to bring this to the attention of the company and seek remediation, without prejudice to legal channels available. Providing access to remedy does not presume that all allegations represent real abuses or bona fide complaints.

Id. At 9, 18, 23, 24, 26, 82.

The Human Rights Council (shortly after having replaced the Commission on Human Rights) welcomed the report articulating the protect, respect and remedy framework, and renewed the mandate of the Special Representative. After extensive consultations with governments, business leaders, NGOs, and others, the Special Representative in 2011 issued his final report, introducing his Guiding Principles on Business and Human Rights, which were included in an annex to the report. The Special Representative prefaced the Guiding Principles by saying:

> What do these Guiding Principles do? And how should they be read? Council endorsement of the Guiding Principles, by itself, will not bring business and human rights challenges to an end. But it will mark the end of the beginning: by establishing a common global platform for action, on which cumulative progress can be built, step-by-step, without foreclosing any other promising longer-term developments.

*Report of the Special Representative of the Secretary-General on the issue of human rights and transnational corporations and other business enterprises, John Ruggie,* UN Doc. A/HRC/17/31 (2011), para. 13.

The Human Rights Council endorsed the Special Representative's Guiding Principles on Business and Human Rights in its Resolution 17/4 (2011), thereby effectively providing them a heightened political, if not legal, status. An edited version of the Guiding Principles follows.

## Guiding Principles on Business and Human Rights

UN Doc. HR/PUB/11/04 (2011) (emphasis in original)

. . . .

These Guiding Principles are grounded in recognition of:

a) States' existing obligations to respect, protect and fulfill human rights and fundamental freedoms;

b) The role of business enterprises as specialized organs of society performing specialized functions, required to comply with all applicable
   laws and to respect human rights;
c) The need for rights and obligations to be matched to appropriate and
   effective remedies when breached.

These Guiding Principles apply to all States and to all business enterprises,
both transnational and others, regardless of their size, sector, location, ownership
and structure.

These Guiding Principles should be understood as a coherent whole and
should be read, individually and collectively, in terms of their objective of enhancing standards and practices with regard to business and human rights so as to
achieve tangible results for affected individuals and communities, and thereby also
contributing to a socially sustainable globalization.

Nothing in these Guiding Principles should be read as creating new international law obligations, or as limiting or undermining any legal obligations a State
may have undertaken or be subject to under international law with regard to
human rights.

These Guiding Principles should be implemented in a non-discriminatory
manner, with particular attention to the rights and needs of, as well as the challenges faced by, individuals from groups or populations that may be at heightened
risk of becoming vulnerable or marginalized, and with due regard to the different
risks that may be faced by women and men.

## I. The State Duty to Protect Human Rights

### A. Foundational Principles

**1. States must protect against human rights abuse within their territory and/
or jurisdiction by third parties, including business enterprises. This requires taking
appropriate steps to prevent, investigate, punish and redress such abuse through
effective policies, legislation, regulations and adjudication.**

*Commentary*

States' international human rights law obligations require that they respect, protect
and fulfill the human rights of individuals within their territory and/or jurisdiction. This includes the duty to protect against human rights abuse by third parties,
including business enterprises.

The State duty to protect is a standard of conduct. Therefore, States are not
per se responsible for human rights abuse by private actors. However, States may
breach their international human rights law obligations where such abuse can
be attributed to them, or where they fail to take appropriate steps to prevent,
investigate, punish and redress private actors' abuse. While States generally have
discretion in deciding upon these steps, they should consider the full range of permissible preventative and remedial measures, including policies, legislation, regulations and adjudication. States also have the duty to protect and promote the rule
of law, including by taking measures to ensure equality before the law, fairness in

its application, and by providing for adequate accountability, legal certainty, and procedural and legal transparency.

**2. States should set out clearly the expectation that all business enterprises domiciled in their territory and/or jurisdiction respect human rights throughout their operations.**

*Commentary*

At present States are not generally required under international human rights law to regulate the extraterritorial activities of businesses domiciled in their territory and/or jurisdiction. Nor are they generally prohibited from doing so, provided there is a recognized jurisdictional basis. Within these parameters some human rights treaty bodies recommend that home States take steps to prevent abuse abroad by business enterprises within their jurisdiction.

There are strong policy reasons for home States to set out clearly the expectation that businesses respect human rights abroad, especially where the State itself is involved in or supports those businesses. The reasons include ensuring predictability for business enterprises by providing coherent and consistent messages, and preserving the State's own reputation. . . .

## II. The Corporate Responsibility to Respect Human Rights

### A. Foundational Principles

**11. Business enterprises should respect human rights. This means that they should avoid infringing on the human rights of others and should address adverse human rights impacts with which they are involved.**

*Commentary*

The responsibility to respect human rights is a global standard of expected conduct for all business enterprises wherever they operate. It exists independently of States' abilities and/or willingness to fulfil their own human rights obligations, and does not diminish those obligations. And it exists over and above compliance with national laws and regulations protecting human rights.

Addressing adverse human rights impacts requires taking adequate measures for their prevention, mitigation and, where appropriate, remediation. . . .

**12. The responsibility of business enterprises to respect human rights refers to internationally recognized human rights – understood, at a minimum, as those expressed in the International Bill of Human Rights and the principles concerning fundamental rights set out in the International Labour Organization's Declaration on Fundamental Principles and Rights at Work.**

*Commentary*

Because business enterprises can have an impact on virtually the entire spectrum of internationally recognized human rights, their responsibility to respect applies to all such rights. In practice, some human rights may be at greater risk than others in particular industries or contexts, and therefore will be the focus of heightened attention. However, situations may change, so all human rights should be the subject of periodic review . . .

**13. The responsibility to respect human rights requires that business enterprises:**

**(a) Avoid causing or contributing to adverse human rights impacts through their own activities, and address such impacts when they occur;**

**(b) Seek to prevent or mitigate adverse human rights impacts that are directly linked to their operations, products or services by their business relationships, even if they have not contributed to those impacts.**

*Commentary*

Business enterprises may be involved with adverse human rights impacts either through their own activities or as a result of their business relationships with other parties. . . . For the purpose of these Guiding Principles a business enterprise's "activities" are understood to include both actions and omissions; and its "business relationships" are understood to include relationships with business partners, entities in its value chain, and any other non-State or State entity directly linked to its business operations, products or services.

**14. The responsibility of business enterprises to respect human rights applies to all enterprises regardless of their size, sector, operational context, ownership and structure. Nevertheless, the scale and complexity of the means through which enterprises meet that responsibility may vary according to these factors and with the severity of the enterprise's adverse human rights impacts.**
  . . . .

**15. In order to meet their responsibility to respect human rights, business enterprises should have in place policies and processes appropriate to their size and circumstances, including:**

**(a) A policy commitment to meet their responsibility to respect human rights;**

**(b) A human rights due-diligence process to identify, prevent, mitigate and account for how they address their impacts on human rights;**

**(c) Processes to enable the remediation of any adverse human rights impacts they cause or to which they contribute.**
  . . . .

**17. In order to identify, prevent, mitigate and account for how they address their adverse human rights impacts, business enterprises should carry out human rights due diligence. The process should include assessing actual and potential human rights impacts, integrating and acting upon the findings, tracking responses, and communicating how impacts are addressed. Human rights due diligence:**

(a) **Should cover adverse human rights impacts that the business enterprise may cause or contribute to through its own activities, or which may be directly linked to its operations, products or services by its business relationships;**

(b) **Will vary in complexity with the size of the business enterprise, the risk of severe human rights impacts, and the nature and context of its operations;**

(c) **Should be ongoing, recognizing that the human rights risks may change over time as the business enterprise's operations and operating context evolve.**

*Commentary*

. . . Human rights risks are understood to be the business enterprise's potential adverse human rights impacts. Potential impacts should be addressed through prevention or mitigation, while actual impacts—those that have already occurred—should be a subject for remediation (Principle 22).

. . . Human rights due diligence should be initiated as early as possible in the development of a new activity or relationship, given that human rights risks can be increased or mitigated already at the stage of structuring contracts or other agreements, and may be inherited through mergers or acquisitions.

Where business enterprises have large numbers of entities in their value chains it may be unreasonably difficult to conduct due diligence for adverse human rights impacts across them all. If so, business enterprises should identify general areas where the risk of adverse human rights impacts is most significant, whether due to certain suppliers' or clients' operating context, the particular operations, products or services involved, or other relevant considerations, and prioritize these for human rights due diligence.

Questions of complicity may arise when a business enterprise contributes to, or is seen as contributing to, adverse human rights impacts caused by other parties. Complicity has both non-legal and legal meanings. As a non-legal matter, business enterprises may be perceived as being "complicit" in the acts of another party where, for example, they are seen to benefit from an abuse committed by that party.

As a legal matter, most national jurisdictions prohibit complicity in the commission of a crime, and a number allow for criminal liability of business enterprises in such cases. Typically, civil actions can also be based on an enterprise's alleged contr'bution to a harm, although these may not be framed in human rights terms. The weight of international criminal law jurisprudence indicates that the relevant standard for aiding and abetting is knowingly providing practical assistance or encouragement that has a substantial effect on the commission of a crime.

Conducting appropriate human rights due diligence should help business enterprises address the risk of legal claims against them by showing that they took every reasonable step to avoid involvement with an alleged human rights abuse. However, business enterprises conducting such due diligence should not assume that, by itself, this will automatically and fully absolve them from liability for causing or contributing to human rights abuses. . . .

. . . .

III. Access to Remedy

A. Foundational Principle

**25. As part of their duty to protect against business-related human rights abuse, States must take appropriate steps to ensure, through judicial, administrative, legislative or other appropriate means, that when such abuses occur within their territory and/or jurisdiction those affected have access to effective remedy.**

. . .

Non-State-based grievance mechanisms

**28. States should consider ways to facilitate access to effective non-State-based grievance mechanisms dealing with business-related human rights harms.**

*Commentary*

One category of non-State-based grievance mechanisms encompasses those administered by a business enterprise alone or with stakeholders, by an industry association or a multi-stakeholder group. They are non-judicial, but may use adjudicative, dialogue-based or other culturally appropriate and rights-compatible processes. These mechanisms may offer particular benefits such as speed of access and remediation, reduced costs and/or transnational reach.

Another category comprises regional and international human rights bodies. These have dealt most often with alleged violations by States of their obligations to respect human rights. However, some have also dealt with the failure of a State to meet its duty to protect against human rights abuse by business enterprises.

States can play a helpful role in raising awareness of, or otherwise facilitating access to, such options, alongside the mechanisms provided by States themselves.

**29. To make it possible for grievances to be addressed early and remediated directly, business enterprises should establish or participate in effective operational-level grievance mechanisms for individuals and communities who may be adversely impacted.**

*Commentary*

Operational-level grievance mechanisms are accessible directly to individuals and communities who may be adversely impacted by a business enterprise. They are typically administered by enterprises, alone or in collaboration with others, including relevant stakeholders. They may also be provided through recourse to a mutually acceptable external expert or body. They do not require that those bringing a complaint first access other means of recourse. They can engage the business enterprise directly in assessing the issues and seeking remediation of any harm.

Operational-level grievance mechanisms perform two key functions regarding the responsibility of business enterprises to respect human rights.

- First, they support the identification of adverse human rights impacts as a part of an enterprise's on-going human rights due diligence. They do so by providing a channel for those directly impacted by the enterprise's operations to raise concerns when they believe they are being or will be adversely impacted. By analyzing trends and patterns in complaints, business enterprises can also identify systemic problems and adapt their practices accordingly

- Second, these mechanisms make it possible for grievances, once identified, to be addressed and for adverse impacts to be remediated early and directly by the business enterprise, thereby preventing harms from compounding and grievances from escalating.

Such mechanisms need not require that a complaint or grievance amount to an alleged human rights abuse before it can be raised, but specifically aim to identify any legitimate concerns of those who may be adversely impacted. If those concerns are not identified and addressed, they may over time escalate into more major disputes and human rights abuses. . . .

———————

The business and NGO communities both initially had mixed reactions to the work of the Special Representative, although eventually the 2008 Framework and the 2011 Guiding Principles received general support from major business associations and social investors. A number of NGOs remained critical, primarily on the grounds that the Guiding Principles did not firmly establish obligations for companies or mechanisms for close scrutiny of their behavior. While recognizing the "protect, respect, and remedy" framework as an important step forward, several NGOs called on the Human Rights Council to expand beyond the articulated framework and to "include an explicit capacity to examine situations of corporate abuse." See *Joint NGO Statement to the Eighth Session of the Human Rights Council*, Human Rights Watch (May 19, 2008), https://www.hrw.org/legacy/english/docs/2008/05/20/global18884.htm.

This NGO proposal was not adopted by the Council, although the Council did create in 2011 a new Working Group on the issue of human rights and transnational corporations and other business enterprises, and hosts an annual two-day Forum on Business and Human Rights led by this Working Group. See H.R.C. Res. 17/4 (2011). The Working Group's mandate is to promote awareness of the Guiding Principles and business practices consistent with them. Through its communications procedure the Working Group receives information on alleged human rights violations related to business practices and, when it deems appropriate, intervenes directly with states, companies and others regarding the allegations. See *Methods of work*, U.N. Doc. A/HRC/WG.12/10/1 (2015), Annex.

Contrasting with the UN Guiding Principles on Business and Human Rights is the approach taken by the Inter-American Commission on Human Rights in its report, *Business and Human Rights: Inter-American Standards*, OAS Doc. OEA/Ser.L/V/II (Nov. 1, 2019) (co-authored with the Commission's Special Rapporteur on economic, social and cultural rights (REDESCA, by the initials in Spanish)). Consistent with the protect, respect, and remedy framework, the Guiding Principles appear to pay equal attention to the articulated *legal* obligation of states to protect human rights in this context and the asserted separate responsibility of businesses enterprises to respect human rights in their operations, a responsibility that is identified as "a global standard of expected conduct." The Inter-American Commission's lengthy report, instead, is almost entirely focused on state obligations.

In the introduction to the report, the Commission and REDESCA acknowledge the Guiding Principles, but stress that they are not the "last word" on the subject; rather they "provide a dynamic and conceptual foundation, which permeates the aspects of discourse in the field of business and human rights in coexistence with other, binding legal standards." Id., para. 11. Accordingly, the principal points of departure in the report are the international obligations that states are deemed to have on the basis of the Inter-American human rights instruments, and the topic is addressed with emphasis on the jurisprudence of the Inter-American institutions and with reference to the kinds of problems that have arisen in the region. While the lengthy report mentions the human rights responsibilities of business enterprises at several points, its main emphasis is on the multilayered obligations of states, including their duties to regulate, supervise, and monitor activities of business enterprises; to prevent businesses from engaging in activities that present risks to human rights; and to guarantee an adequate access to justice when human rights violations occur in these contexts.

The Inter-American Commission on Human Rights, therefore, has emphasized state obligations and gives considerably less attention to any independent human rights responsibilities (moral or other) of business enterprises. Which approach do you think is more effective?

In any event, the UN Guiding Principles have become an important benchmark within the UN human rights system and beyond for addressing matters of business and human rights. For example, the Guiding Principles were a key point of reference in the work of the UN Special Rapporteur on the rights of indigenous peoples to define the scope of human rights duties and responsibilities in the context of oil and gas development and mining activity affecting indigenous peoples. Below are extracts of a report (written by one of the authors of this volume when he was the Special Rapporteur) incorporating the Guiding Principles into his analysis of the human rights concerns presented by extractive industries in relation to indigenous peoples.

## Extractive industries and indigenous peoples

Report of the Special Rapporteur on the rights of indigenous peoples, James Anaya

UN Doc. A/HRC/21/47 (2012) (footnotes omitted)

. . .

34. The worldwide drive to extract and develop minerals and fossil fuels (oil, gas and coal), coupled with the fact that much of what remains of these natural resources is situated on the lands of indigenous peoples, results in increasing and ever more widespread effects on indigenous peoples' lives. As has been amply documented in previous reports by the Special Rapporteur (see, for example, A/HRC/18/35, paras. 30-55), indigenous peoples around the world have suffered negative, even devastating, consequences from extractive industries. . . .

DUTY OF STATES TO PROTECT AND THE RESPONSIBILITY OF
CORPORATIONS TO RESPECT THE HUMAN RIGHTS OF INDIGENOUS
PEOPLES IN RELATION TO EXTRACTIVE ACTIVITIES

. . . .

55. While the Special Rapporteur has observed a high level of acceptance of
the Guiding Principles [on Business and Human Rights] and their "protect, respect
and remedy" framework, he has also noted ambiguity among Government and corporate actors about the extent to or manner in which the Guiding Principles relate
to the standards of human rights that specifically concern indigenous peoples. This
ambiguity should be dispelled in favour of a clear understanding that the Guiding
Principles apply to advance the specific rights of indigenous peoples in the same
way as they advance human rights more generally, when those rights are affected
or potentially affected by business activities, including extractive industries. There
is no sound reason to exclude the human rights standards that apply specifically to
indigenous peoples from the application of the Guiding Principles, and to do so
would be contrary to the injunction, found among the Guiding Principles' introductory paragraphs, that they should be applied "in a non-discriminatory manner,"
with particular attention to the rights and needs of groups that are vulnerable or
marginalized.

56. The Special Rapporteur notes that the Expert Mechanism [on the Rights
of Indigenous Peoples, an expert body of the UN Human Rights Council], in
its recent follow-up report on indigenous peoples and the right to participate in
decision-making (A/HRC/EMRIP/2011/2), discussed the relationship between
the Guiding Principles and the rights of indigenous peoples. The Special Rapporteur joins the Expert Mechanism in affirming that all the Guiding Principles are
to be applied specifically to indigenous peoples with due regard to the relevant
international standards, and he urges all concerned to take account of the Expert
Mechanism's exposition of the particular implications of the Guiding Principles in
the context of extractive industries operating or seeking to operate within or near
indigenous territories (A/HRC/EMRIP/2011/2, paras. 26-28).

57. It bears reiterating here that the State's protective role in the context of
extractive industries entails ensuring a regulatory framework that fully recognizes
indigenous peoples' rights over lands and natural resources and other rights that
may be affected by extractive operations; that mandates respect for those rights both
in all relevant State administrative decision-making and in corporate behaviour;
and that provides effective sanctions and remedies when those rights are infringed
either by Governments or corporate actors. Such a regulatory framework requires
legislation or regulations that incorporate international standards of indigenous
rights and that make them operational through the various components of State
administration that govern land tenure, mining, oil, gas and other natural resource
extraction or development.

58. The Special Rapporteur regrets that he has found, across the globe, deficient regulatory frameworks such that in many respects indigenous peoples' rights
remain inadequately protected, and in all too many cases entirely unprotected, in
the face of extractive industries. Major legislative and administrative reforms are
needed in virtually all countries in which indigenous peoples live to adequately

define and protect their rights over lands and resources and other rights that may be affected by extractive industries. Yet at the same time and in the same countries in which this need persists, extractive industries are permitted to encroach upon indigenous habitats, a situation that the Special Rapporteur finds alarming and in need of urgent attention.

59. For their part, business enterprises have a responsibility to respect human rights, including the rights of indigenous peoples, and this responsibility is independent of the State duty to protect. . . .

61. This independence of responsibility notwithstanding, the Special Rapporteur has learned of numerous instances in which business enterprises engaged in extractive industries do not go further than compliance with domestic laws or regulations, regardless of the ineffectiveness of those laws and regulations for the protection of indigenous rights. Corporate attitudes that regard compliance with domestic laws or regulation as sufficient should give way to understanding that fulfillment of the responsibility to respect human rights often entails due diligence beyond compliance with domestic law. Due diligence requires, instead, ensuring that corporate behaviour does not infringe or contribute to the infringement of the rights of indigenous peoples that are internationally recognized, regardless of the reach of domestic laws.

---

The following document provides an assessment of the progress and challenges in the implementation of the UN Guiding Principles, ten years after they were published and endorsed by the Human Rights Council.

## Guiding Principles on Business and Human Rights at 10: taking stock of the first decade

Report of the Working Group on the issue of human rights and transnational corporations and other business enterprises

U.N. Doc. A/HRC/47/39 (2021) (foonotes omitted)

. . .

### II.  A COMMON GLOBAL PLATFORM FOR ACTION AND ACCOUNTABILITY

#### A.  AN AUTHORITATIVE STANDARD FOR RESPONSIBLE BUSINESS

11. There is no doubt that the Guiding Principles have succeeded in providing a globally agreed-upon authoritative standard for what States and businesses need to do to respectively protect and respect the full range of human rights across all business contexts – something which did not exist before 2011. . . .

15. Within the United Nations human rights system, treaty bodies and special procedure mandate holders have increasingly applied the Guiding Principles in their work, including through direct engagement with States and business, such

as via "communications" addressing allegations of business-related human rights abuse. A mapping carried out for the UNGPs 10+ project of such communications handled by the Working Group and other special procedure mandates from 2011 to 2020 found that the Guiding Principles were expressly referenced in responses by business enterprises and States.

16. The Guiding Principles have also been used as an authoritative normative framework to support the essential efforts of regional human rights mechanisms, in Africa and Latin America, as well as of trade unions, indigenous peoples, civil society organizations and national human rights institutions, to monitor States and businesses and hold them accountable.

17. Finally, and as importantly, the Guiding Principles have helped enable multi-stakeholder dialogue grounded in a "lingua franca" — a common language understood by both private and State actors. The growing number of stakeholders coming together since 2012 to discuss trends and challenges in implementing the Guiding Principles at global and regional forums confirms a movement coalescing around the Guiding Principles.

### B. Human Rights Due Diligence

18. Monitoring of and achieving accountability for business-related human rights abuses is still a work in progress. Yet, a decade of implementation of the Guiding Principles has been marked by its most notable normative innovation – the expectation that businesses exercise human rights due diligence — morphing towards a legally binding standard of conduct, while States and businesses have begun to implement the framework to prevent and address business-related harms to people.

19. Introduced by the Guiding Principles, human rights due diligence requires businesses to identify, prevent and mitigate their adverse impacts and to account for how they address them. This normative clarification is the cornerstone of the business responsibility to respect human rights, and is likely the most influential contribution of the Guiding Principles. . . .

20. The institutional uptake of human rights due diligence by various entities has contributed to fulfilling one of the central objectives of the Guiding Principles by fostering convergence among the many different institutions that shape business conduct. This growing web of uptake has helped to compensate for each entity's respective weaknesses and in mutually reinforcing one another's roles.25

21. Besides the widely known mirroring between the Guiding Principles and the OECD Guidelines for Multinational Enterprises, corporate human rights due diligence has also been incorporated into the ISO 26000 standard on social responsibility and the International Labour Organization's revised 2017 Tripartite Declaration of Principles concerning Multinational Enterprises and Social Policy. It is also the standard of reference for the United Nations Global Compact and its participants on the policies and processes they should implement in order to ensure that they follow the Global Compact principles. Organizations such as the Fédération Internationale de Football Association (FIFA) and the International Olympic Committee have also adopted the standard.

22. Importantly, human rights due diligence has started to permeate the world of financial institutions, albeit unevenly and relatively narrowly. The recognition

by such institutions of their responsibility under the Guiding Principles and their integration of human rights due diligence into business relationships is an essential step in fostering corporate respect for human rights, considering the leverage that they have in providing services and influencing public and private economic actors.

23. In the context of multilateral lenders, the European Investment Bank, the European Bank for Reconstruction and Development, the International Finance Corporation and most recently the Inter-American Development Bank refer to human rights due diligence in their operational policies, or in broader policy statements for other development finance institutions, such as the World Bank and the African Development Bank. These developments have provided a foundation for strengthening human rights safeguards, but overall integration of human rights due diligence into projects financed by development finance and international financial institutions remains low, including as a tool for managing risks to people in mega-infrastructure projects. There remains a need to demonstrate that human rights due diligence is carried out effectively by these institutions and that they require the same from businesses and States benefiting from their services. . . .

25. Similarly, other key international financial institutions must do better and show leadership. For example, the continued apparent inability of the International Monetary Fund to connect social protection and a sustainable economy led the Special Rapporteur on extreme poverty and human rights to conclude it had "relegated social impact to an afterthought".

26. The few developments in the development finance world, however partial, highlight by contrast the lack of engagement by the United Nations as an organization, beyond the efforts of particular entities such as the Office of the United Nations High Commissioner for Human Rights, the International Labour Organization, the United Nations Children's Fund (UNICEF) and the United Nations Development Programme (UNDP) to promote the Guiding Principles.

27. Despite repeated calls from the Secretary-General for the United Nations system to lead by example, and some initiatives across different fields and entities such as procurement, partnerships, broader risk analysis and programming, and on an issue-specific basis, the United Nations still falls short in integrating human rights due diligence into its own activities and business relationships.

28. The consequence is a lost opportunity for the United Nations system to walk its own talk, to spur uptake on a larger scale and to contribute to greater overall coherence in global governance frameworks. Almost a decade of inaction at the executive level of these institutions also reflects the limited number of requests from Member States to integrate and promote the Guiding Principles. To date, the United Nations system has not developed sufficient structures or tools to further reinforce implementation support, including systematic data gathering, wide-ranging capacity-building, or a global "help desk" for businesses, States, civil society and other stakeholders.

29. Several business and industry platforms have embedded human rights due diligence into their respective expectations toward member companies, such as the China Chamber of Commerce of Metals, Minerals and Chemicals Importers and Exporters and the International Council on Mining and Metals. In 2020, the World Business Council for Sustainable Development made having in place a policy to respect human rights and a human rights due diligence process one of its five

criteria for membership. The potential of global business organizations has yet to be tapped more fully. For example, the International Chamber of Commerce and the International Organisation of Employers have strongly supported the Guiding Principles but are yet to make human rights due diligence a requirement for members.

---

Elsewhere in the report the Working Group on business and human rights examined the performance of states in relation to their duty to protect human rights in the context of business, identifying significant advances such as the development of national action plans on business and human rights by several states. However, the Working Group found most states still lacking in living up to the standards articulated in the Guiding Principles, including in regard to States' own economic or business activity. For example, "the embedding of the Guiding Principles into international economic agreements, or where States act as an economic actor—in State-ownded enterprises, in public procurement, and through sovereign wealth fund and export credits, among other things—has not seen seen much progress." Id., para. 49. Similarly, the Working Group found advances but for the most part shortfalls in the business uptake of the Guiding Principles. There is a notable trend among major corporations toward the adoption of human rights policies consistent with the Guiding Principles. The Working Group observed, however, that many more companies still fail to incorporate into their operations rigorous attention to human rights or adopt explicit human rights policies. See id., para. 49-13.

Investment and business activities are of course related to (and some would say required for) economic development, especially in low income countries, and development itself constitutes an area of human rights concern. The UN Declaration on the Right to Development, G.A. Res. 41/128 (1986), proclaims in its article 1:

> The right to development is an inalienable human right by virtue of which every human person and all peoples are entitled to participate in, contribute to, and enjoy economic, social, cultural and political development, in which all human rights and fundamental freedoms can be fully realized.

In 2015, the UN General Assembly adopted the 2030 Agenda for Sustainable Development, which includes 17 goals to be achieved by the year 2030. This resolution identifies areas of critical importance for humanity and the planet, including ending poverty and creating "conditions for sustainable, inclusive and sustained growth, shared prosperity and decent work for all, taking account different levels of national development and capacities." UN General Assembly Res. 70/1 (2015), para. 3. As a preface to the goals, the resolution "envisages a world of universal respect for human rights, human dignity, and the rule of law." Id., para. 8. This language was a modest victory for those advocates who insist on economic development consistent with human rights. Nonetheless, the Working Group on business and human rights criticized the 2030 Agenda, as well as the Paris Agreement on climate change, for not explicitly referencing or adequately aligning with the UN Guiding Principles on Business and Human Rights. Taking Stock of the First Decade, *supra* page 252, para. 52.

## Comments and Questions

1. Both economic development and full respect for human rights are seen as important goals, but what is the relationship between the two? Does the concept of "sustainable development" provide a vehicle for harmonizing the two? Recall the above report by former UN Special Representative John Ruggie on the myriad human rights problems faced by workers and communities as a result of direct foreign investment and associated business activities. Reflect also on the observation by the UN Special Rapporteur on the rights to freedom of peaceful assembly and of association that "[g]lobal competition for investment is fierce, and businesses, by their nature, tend to favor environments with less regulation so that they can maximize profits. There is thus something of a 'race to the bottom' among States in terms of creating an enabling environment for business." UN Doc. A/HRC/29/25 (2015), para. 31. While the "race to the bottom" is universally condemned, are lower-wage countries nonetheless justified in taking advantage of their competitive edge in this respect in order to further their own development? If a business relocates to take advantage of lower wages, does this necessarily mean that human rights will inevitably be violated?

2. In one of his reports that preceded the articulation of the Guiding Principles, Special Representative Ruggie clarified that use of the word "responsibility" rather than "duty" or "obligation" when referring to corporations "is meant to indicate that respecting rights is not an obligation that current international human rights law generally imposes directly on companies. . . ." *Business and Human Rights: Further Steps Toward the Operationalization of the "Protect, Respect and Remedy" Framework*, UN Doc. A/HRC/14/27 (2010), para. 55. Ruggie's final report reiterates that "[t]he Guiding Principles' normative contribution lies not in the creation of new international law obligations but in elaborating the implications of existing standards and practices for States and businesses; integrating them within a single, logically coherent and comprehensive template; and identifying where the current regime falls short and how it should be improved." What is the difference between the "responsibility" of companies and the "duty" of states in this context? Are they coextensive? If the responsibility of companies to respect human rights is not a *legal* one, what is it? To what extent do the Guiding Principles reflect the *legal* obligations of states?

3. It has long been argued—and often authoritatively held—that international law directly obligates corporations to refrain from committing certain gross violations of human rights such as genocide, torture, extrajudicial killing, slavery and other acts defined as crimes against humanity, just as natural persons are so obligated. See, e.g., *Brief of Yale Law School Center for Global Legal Challenges as Amicus Curiae in Support of Petirioners, Ester Kiobel v. Royal Dutch Petroleum, Supreme Court of the United States Nos. 10-1491 and 11-88* (2011). However, as will be discussed in Chapter 5, the jurisdiction of the International Criminal Court to adjudicate such

violations is limited to natural persons, although that does not necessarily foreclose elsewhere the legal application to corporations of the international norms against gross human rights violations. Also note that states widely differ on whether and the extent to which they recognize, on the basis of international as opposed to domestic law, corporate liability for gross violations of human rights or corporate crimes. See generally Jennifer Zerk, *Corporate Liability for Gross Human Rights Abuses; Towards a Fairer and More Effective System of Domestic Law Remedies* (2012). (For a discussion of corporate liability for human rights violations under the US Alien Tort Statute, see Chapter 6.) What does the discussion above on the human rights duties of states, and the UN Guiding Principles themselves, say about the need for states to establish domestic legal arrangements to hold corporations and other business enterprises accountable for gross human rights violations and international crimes (and for other infractions of human rights)? In this regard, see Basic Principles and Guidelines on the Right to a Remedy and Reparations for Victims of Gross Violation of International Human Rights Law and Serious Violations of International Human Rights Law, G.A. Res. 60/147 (2005).

4. In 2014, a deeply divided UN Human Rights Council created an open-ended intergovernmental Working Group to explore the possibility of an international legally binding instrument on transnational corporations and human rights. While the resolution refers to "transnational corporations and other business entities," a footnote specifies that the initiative applies only to businesses of a transnational character, not to "local"—i.e., domestic—business. See Hum. Rts. Council Res. 26/9 (2014), adopted by a vote of 20 to 14, with 13 abstentions. The UN initiative begun in 2014 to explore the adoption of a treaty on transnational businesses and human rights echoes similar attempts to regulate transnational corporations in the 1990s. Given the divisions that have appeared within the Human Rights Council itself at the outset of this initiative, do you think that the political-economic climate has changed much in the past three decades? A number of academic and other papers have already emerged with suggestions regarding a potential treaty's content; see, e.g., Anita Ramasastry and Douglas Cassel, *White Paper: Options for a Treaty on Business and Human Rights*, 6 Notre Dame J. Int'l & Comp. L. 1 (2016); Olivier de Schutter, *Towards a New Treaty on Business and Human Rights*, Bus. & H. R. J. (2016), https://www.cambridge.org/core/journals/business-and-human -rights-journal/article/towards-a-new-treaty-on-business-and-human-rights/45E25 BD824C6EEB18CD8050752C119E7; David Bilchitz, *The Moral and Legal Necessity for a Business and Human Rights Treaty* (2015), https://business-humanrights.org/en/ treaty-on-business-human-rights-necessary-to-fill-gaps-in-intl-law-says-academic.

5. Recall that the commentary on principle 2 of the Guiding Principles, *supra* at page 245, takes the view that "States are not generally required under international law to regulate the extraterritorial activities of businesses domiciled in their territories. Nor are they generally prohibited from doing so." The commentary goes on, nonetheless, to affirm that there are good policy reasons for states "to set out clearly the expectation that businesses respect human rights abroad, especially where the State itself is involved in or supports those businesses." Do you agree? Should those expectations take the form of legal requirements that can be enforced through judicial action in the home states' courts? As noted by the commentary some UN treaty-monitory bodies have called on states to take steps to

prevent human rights abuses abroad by companies domiciled in their respective
jurisdictions. While some states, such as Spain, the United Kingdom and The Netherlands, have permitted tort claims to be filed against companies stemming from
activities by their subsidiaries abroad, the broad assertion of extra-territorial jurisdiction by states does not appear to enjoy wide support. Why is that? At least some
of the reasons are reflected in *Kiobel v. Royal Dutch Petroleum*,__US__, 133 S.Ct. 1659
(2013), a case in which the US Supreme Court ruled against use of the Alien Tort
Statute for claims arising from alleged human rights violations outside the United
States. See Chapter 6, *infra* page 422.

6. The report of the Working Goup on business and human rights assessing
the Guiding Principles ten years after their adoption identified other non-binding
documents as generally aligning with the Guiding Principles. These included the
*OECD* [Organization for Economic Co-operation and Development] *Guidelines for
Multinational Enterprises* (2011), http://mneguidelines.oecd.org, and the International Labour Organization's *Tripartite Declaration of Principles concerning Multinational Enterprises and Social Policy* (5th ed. 2017), https://www.ilo.org/wcmsp5/gro
ups/public/---ed_emp/---emp_ent/---multi/documents/publication/wcms_094
386.pdf. The Working Group report also observed that an increasing number of
companies have publicly committed to the Guiding Principles, and many of them
have done so along with developing their own human rights or corporate responsibility policies. For a collection of the human rights and corporate responsibility policies of major companies, see Business and Human Rights Resource Center,
https://www.business-humanrights.org/en/ (last updated Sept. 16, 2016). How
likely are these non-binding standards and internal voluntary corporate policies to
actually influence corporate behavior?

7. A number of scholarly critiques have been directed at the UN Guiding
Principles since they were published. Representative of these is the following:

> [The Guiding Principles] Framework underestimates the radical nature
> of what is required for states to take "appropriate steps" to regulate busi-
> ness respect for human rights including the role of the state in "reg-
> ulatory space" interacting with other actors especially where the state
> itself is directly involved in subsidizing or supporting business. . . .[The]
> Framework equally underestimates what is required for businesses
> to take "due diligence" to discharge their responsibility to respect . . .
> human rights, and provide victims with access to remedies. We argue
> that businesses will always seek to neutralize critiques of their adverse
> human rights impacts and to bring any new initiatives to regulate busi-
> ness and rights back within the rubric of the "business case" and "risk
> management" since this provides greater opportunity for management
> discretion and profit-orientation in the way they respond to human
> rights concerns.

Christine Parker & John Howe, "Ruggie's Diplomatic Project and Its Missing
Regulatory Infrastructure," in *The UN Guiding Principles on Business and Human
Rights: Foundations and Implementation* 273 (R. Mares ed., 2012). Do you agree with
this analysis?

For further reading on the Guiding Principles and on the relationship between the international human rights regime and business, see Surya Deva, *The UN Guiding Principles' Orbit and Other Regulatory Regimes in the Business and Human Rights Universe: Managing the Interface*, Cambridge University Press (Online) (June 22, 2021), https://www.cambridge.org/core/journals/business-and-human-rights-journal/article/abs/un-guiding-principles-orbit-and-other-regulatory-regimes-in-the-business-and-human-rights-universe-managing-the-interface/A28A098B954A4A4D2FF2AE311C2D6835; Larry Catá Backer, *Moving Forward the UN Guiding Principles for Business and Human Rights: Between Enterprise Social Norm, State Domestic Legal Orders, and the Treaty Law That Might Bind Them All*, 38 FORDHAM INT'L L.J. 457 (2015).

# IV.  INTERNATIONAL ORGANIZATIONS AND HUMAN RIGHTS

The United Nations and other international organizations are taking on a multitude of new roles, from observing elections to establishing criminal tribunals to acting as de facto governments in states emerging from violent conflict. With these roles, they are being pushed to accept accountability for their own conduct, as measured by international human rights and humanitarian law. The materials in this section focus on two issues in this regard. The first is whether international organizations themselves have binding obligations under international human rights law, including the duty to prevent and remedy human rights violations when they occur. A second issue is the extent to which international financial and trade institutions, such as the World Bank, the International Monetary Fund and the World Trade Organization, should incorporate a human rights approach into their operations.

## A.  *International Organizations and Obligations Under International Law*

The International Law Commission (ILC) has engaged in a long and ongoing effort to codify rules on the responsibility of states for acts considered internationally wrongful. In 2002, the ILC began to develop standards of responsibility specific to international organizations. This effort resulted in draft articles adopted in 2011, an extract of which follows.

International Law Commission

## Responsibility of international organizations (draft articles)

UN Doc. A/RES/66/100 (2011), Annex

. . . .

ARTICLE 3 RESPONSIBILITY OF AN INTERNATIONAL ORGANIZATION FOR
ITS INTERNATIONALLY WRONGFUL ACTS

Every internationally wrongful act of an international organization entails the
international responsibility of that organization.

ARTICLE 4 ELEMENTS OF AN INTERNATIONALLY WRONGFUL ACT OF AN
INTERNATIONAL ORGANIZATION

There is an internationally wrongful act of an international organization when
conduct consisting of an action or omission:

(a)  is attributable to that organization under international law; and
(b)  constitutes a breach of an international obligation of that organization.

. . .

ARTICLE 6 CONDUCT OF ORGANS OR AGENTS OF AN INTERNATIONAL
ORGANIZATION

1. The conduct of an organ or agent of an international organization in the
performance of functions of that organ or agent shall be considered an act of that
organization under international law, whatever position the organ or agent holds
in respect of the organization.
2. The rules of the organization shall apply in the determination of the functions of its organs and agents.

———————

As the foregoing extract makes clear, the ILC rules in no way decide which, if
any, norms of international human rights law directly bind international organizations. Do any? This question has been tackled by a number of scholars, as exemplified by the extract below.

Kristina Daugirdas

## How and Why International Law Binds International Organizations

57 Harv. Int. L. J. 325 (2016)

Which international law rules bind international organizations? Does the
Security Council have a legal obligation to prevent genocide? Does the International Monetary Fund have an obligation to ensure that its loan conditions do not
impede borrowing states' efforts to provide an education? Must the World Trade
Organization recognize the precautionary principle in international environmental law? The charters of the United Nations, the IMF, and the WTO do not clearly
impose these obligations. Nor are these IOs [international organizations] party to
treaties that impose such obligations. So if these obligations bind these IOs—and
many commentators think they do—it must be for another reason. . . .

. . . [T]he debate about IOs' legal obligations boils down to this question: when and why should obligations that were created by states and for states also bind IOs? To begin to answer this question, it is helpful to consider IOs' relationship to states in the international legal system. A defining feature of IOs is that they are simultaneously in a vertical and a horizontal relationship with states. IOs are subordinate to states because states are the entities that create, sustain, and—potentially—dismantle IOs (the vertical relationship). States are the principals, IOs are the agents. At the same time, IOs are separate legal persons under international law with a significant degree of autonomy (the horizontal relationship). Among other things, IOs can call states to account for violations of international obligations using the same methods that states, as sovereign equals, use to resolve disputes among themselves. In addition, comprehensive immunity shields IOs from the regulatory authority of individual states. Both features distinguish IOs from other nonstate actors, including corporations and nongovernmental organizations ("NGOs"). The vertical relationship suggests that IOs are appropriately characterized as vehicles through which states operate. The horizontal relationship, by contrast, suggests that IOs are states' peers on the international plane.

Of course, these two perspectives are not genuinely dichotomous. No IO is purely a vehicle, and no IO is wholly autonomous. The two conceptions are poles at the ends of a wide spectrum. Some IOs will be closer to the peer end, perhaps because of their resources or authorities. Others will be closer to the vehicle end, perhaps because of their decision-making structure or limited membership. Indeed, the same IO might look more like a peer or more like a vehicle depending on the angle from which it is scrutinized. Focus on the Secretary-General, and the United Nations looks more like a peer; focus on the Security Council or the General Assembly, and it looks more like a vehicle. These two conceptions correspond to two distinct apprehensions that motivate the arguments about IOs' obligations. If IOs are conceived as vehicles through which states operate, the fear is that states might exploit IOs to evade their international obligations. If IOs are conceived as peers, however, the underlying concern is quite different: states have created entities with significant authorities and power that states do not or cannot fully control. This latter concern might be labeled the Frankenstein problem.

Both conceptions of IOs lead to the same conclusion about their international obligations: general international law and treaties bind IOs to the same degree that they bind states. In other words, I argue that regardless of whether IOs are seen as peers or vehicles, the same international obligations bind them . . .

A number of IOs have in fact communicated their views on the scope of their international obligations to the International Law Commission ("ILC"). . . . They have emphatically rejected the possibility that treaties bind them without their consent. They have, at times, directly endorsed the conclusion that they are bound by jus cogens and customary international law. Finally, participating IOs have asserted that their charters constitute lex specialis—that is, that their charters reflect action by states to alter the application of customary international law or general principles by elaborating or carving out exceptions to it. The view that IO charters constitute lex specialis necessarily rests on the understanding that general international law binds IOs except to the extent that those IOs or their member states have contracted around it. In other words, there is some evidence that IOs themselves recognize that general international law binds them, but only as a default matter. At the end of the day, then, states enjoy wide latitude to create lex specialis and to adjust the legal obligations that bind the IOs they establish. States can exercise that discretion to create IOs that are free to ignore certain international rules vis-`a-vis their member states. States might choose to do so because they believe that such institutions will be more efficient or effective at achieving their policy goals. The result may be problematic along some dimensions: IOs that are licensed to ignore certain international norms might undermine those norms or work at cross-purposes to policy goals that states are advancing in other arenas. But such conflicts are an inevitable feature of an international legal system that is based largely on state consent. Although IOs are creatures of international law, it does not follow that they are obliged to follow or reinforce all international norms. . . .

. . . Most scholars writing about IO obligations have not addressed IOs' own views on the question of which rules of international law bind them. . . . Whether IOs' views are relevant may depend on the theoretical perspective one takes. If IOs are treated simply as vehicles through which states act, IOs' views may not matter much. But IOs' own views would seem to count if they are peers of states and full-status members of the international community. The very existence of such a community depends in part on its members sharing the conviction that they are part of a community that is governed by certain rules. In addition to their theoretical significance, IOs' own views about their legal obligations matter for practical reasons. Formal mechanisms for adjudicating and enforcing IOs' international obligations are few and far between. IOs are simply more likely to comply with obligations that they themselves accept as binding. . . .

### B.  UN Peacekeeping Operations

An area of United Nations activity that has highlighted issues about an organization's human rights obligations is peacekeeping. The United Nations has carried out more than 70 peacekeeping operations since its creation, to which approximately 128 member states have contributed. As of mid-2022, it was engaged in 12 peacekeeping operations around the world involving more than 100,000 military and civilian police personnel. For more background, see *Our History*, United Nations Peacekeeping, https://peacekeeping.un.org/en/our-history (last verified May 2, 2022).

While the operations are undertaken with the authorization of and under the direction of the United Nations, troop-contributing countries continue to be responsible for the conduct of their own forces. The United Nations itself enjoys immunity from civil and criminal liability in the countries in which it operates, equivalent to the immunities enjoyed by states and their diplomats. But as the report by the UN Secretary-General below illustrates, the UN assumes some level of responsibility, if not clearly legal, when UN peacekeepers violate human rights.

While many peacekeeping operations have contributed substantially to stability, they have also been the subject of allegations of human rights abuse, particularly sexual exploitation, and there have been issues of accountability for the conduct of peacekeepers. The following extract describes the extent of the problem and identifies some of the steps taken by the United Nations to address it.

## Special Measures for Protection from Sexual Exploitation and Sexual Abuse

Report of the Secretary General

UN Doc. A/70/729 (2016) (footnotes omitted)

### I. INTRODUCTION

1. The Secretary-General remains distressed by continuing instances of sexual exploitation and abuse but resolute in ensuring ever more effective means to prevent and address the profound betrayal through such acts by United Nations personnel against the people they are charged with protecting. During 2015, the Secretary-General took determined action to implement the strengthened programme of action described in his previous report on sexual exploitation and sexual abuse (A/69/779), which was welcomed by the General Assembly in its resolution 69/307. . . .

3. The present report provides data on allegations of sexual exploitation and abuse in the United Nations system received in 2015 and on the status of investigations into those allegations, as well as an update on the enhanced measures being taken to implement the Secretary-General's zero-tolerance policy and new initiatives, building on work done to date, to address gaps and emerging issues. In addition, information is included further to the report of the external independent panel to review the United Nations response to allegations of sexual exploitation and abuse and other serious crimes by members of foreign military forces not under United Nations command in the Central African Republic.

### II. REPORTS OF SEXUAL EXPLOITATION AND ABUSE IN 2015

1. The number of new allegations of sexual exploitation or sexual abuse received from the departments and offices of the Secretariat and agencies, funds and programmes of the United Nations system totalled 99 in 2015, compared with 80 allegations in 2014. This regrettable increase in the number of new allegations signifies that more needs to be done to reduce the number of allegations and, more importantly, the number of victims affected by sexual exploitation and abuse perpetrated by United Nations personnel.

5. In 2015, 30 allegations of sexual exploitation and abuse were made against United Nations staff members and related personnel other than those deployed in peacekeeping operations and special political missions. . . .

6. In 2015, 69 allegations of sexual exploitation and abuse were reported in nine current and one closed peacekeeping missions. Of those allegations, 15 involved staff members or United Nations Volunteers; 38 involved members of

military contingents or United Nations military observers; and 16 involved United Nations police officers, members of formed police units and government-provided personnel. Of the 17 completed investigations as at 31 January 2016, 7 allegations were substantiated and 10 were unsubstantiated. . . .

### III. Observations

21. The Secretary-General remains committed to ensuring that reported allegations are investigated fully and promptly. When allegations are substantiated through investigations, the Secretary-General will continue to take measures within his authority and to request that Member States ensure that those responsible are held accountable through disciplinary actions or criminal accountability measures when so warranted. The Secretary-General is determined to take measures to prevent misconduct and to assist complainants and victims of sexual exploitation and abuse.

22. A total of 69 allegations of sexual exploitation and abuse were reported in 2015, a marked increase from the number of allegations recorded in 2014 (52)4 and in 2013 (66). Only in 2011 (75) and earlier were higher numbers of allegations recorded per year. The increase in the number of allegations is deeply worrisome. A significant proportion can be attributed to MINUSCA [United Nations Multidimensional Integrated Stabilization Mission in the Central African Republic], although there were also increases for MONUSCO [United Nations Organization Stabilization Mission in the Democratic Republic of the Congo] and, to a lesser extent, for UNOCI [United Nations Operation in Côte d'Ivoire] and MINUSMA [United Nations Multidimensional Integrated Stabilization Mission in Mali].

23. A significant amount of attention was focused on allegations reported for MINUSCA. While there may be a number of reasons for this increase, two sets of factors have been determined to have had a particular impact.

24. The first set of factors is associated with the situation in the Central African Republic, with the high level of sexual violence associated with the conflict, extreme poverty, the displacement of vulnerable populations and women and girls being forced into prostitution. These factors can create a heightened vulnerability for sexual exploitation and abuse. It is deplorable that United Nations personnel would take advantage of this situation, and the United Nations is committed to taking measures to eradicate this behaviour. The situation in the Central African Republic requires a holistic response, from the United Nations system and Member States, which considers accountability for acts of misconduct, including sexual exploitation and abuse, as well as programmatic action to address underlying political, security and socioeconomic factors.

25. The second set of factors is the rehatting of troops (similar situations to those observed previously for MINUSMA and the United Nations Mission in the Central African Republic and Chad); the absence of predeployment training on standards of conduct; the excessive length of the deployment for certain contingents; the living conditions of contingents, including lack of welfare and communication facilities to stay in contact with home, and camps in proximity to and not properly separated from the local population; and a lack of discipline among some of the contingents. The factors associated with encampments of contingents, welfare and the length of deployments can be addressed through better planning in

the deployments and rotations of troops. The preparation of troops to be deployed or rehatted will require greater attention. The Departments of Peacekeeping Operations and Field Support have, where necessary, addressed problems of the lack of discipline by certain contingents, including through the repatriation and termination of the deployment of all military personnel from a Member State, as was recently decided for MINUSCA.

## IV.  STRENGTHENING MEASURES FOR PROTECTION FROM SEXUAL EXPLOITATION AND ABUSE

37. There can be no impunity for personnel who commit sexual exploitation and abuse, nor does immunity serve as a shield for those who serve with the United Nations.

38. Troop-contributing and police-contributing countries, with support from the Secretariat, have a particular responsibility to ensure that they are prepared to perform in difficult and complex United Nations peace operations, which includes a readiness to respect the United Nations standards of conduct. . . .

47. In 2015, the Secretary-General stated his intention to develop a community-based complaint reception mechanism to encourage complainants to come forward. It is critical to ensuring that complainants report through confidential pathways in local communities. The Secretariat has issued a framework to support missions in establishing complaint reception mechanisms, guided by consultations with interested stakeholders. Missions have identified common challenges, including a lack of knowledge of reporting mechanisms, difficulties reaching communities for outreach efforts and reluctance to report transactional sex. The Department of Field Support will continue to monitor progress.

48. All peacekeeping missions have established standing task forces on sexual exploitation and abuse, and have put in place sexual exploitation and abuse focal points to provide consistent guidance and monitoring in the application of the zero-tolerance policy.

49. In 2015, the Secretary-General, in collaboration with Member States, continued work to improve the speed and quality of investigations. Urgent action upon receipt of a report of sexual exploitation and abuse creates the best conditions for investigation and, as outlined in the previous report of the Secretary-General, immediate response teams were established in peacekeeping missions to gather and preserve evidence, pending the initiation of an investigation. The Secretariat has provided peacekeeping missions with interim operational guidance and is working with external partners, as well as OIOS [UN Office of Internal Oversight Services] and the Standing Police Capacity of the Department of Peacekeeping Operations, to implement a sustainable training and capacity-building programme for team members. It is anticipated that a training programme will be piloted in the first quarter of 2016 and expanded to other missions throughout the year. . . .

54. The Secretary-General indicated in his previous report that he would request that troop-contributing countries include National Investigation Officers within deployments as a means of expediting investigations. . . .

55. To further enhance the Organization's capacity to respond, Member States are requested to expand the scope of action open to the United Nations in cases of alleged sexual exploitation and abuse by contingent members. This exceptional

consent would allow OIOS and/or an immediate response team to interview witnesses, including contingent members, where no National Investigation Officer is available. Such evidence will be promptly shared with the National Investigation Officer upon arrival in mission.

56. It is proposed that troop-contributing countries enter into bilateral agreements with OIOS authorizing the Office to investigate alleged sexual exploitation and abuse by military contingent members, either alone or in cooperation with National Investigation Office.

---

Relevant to assessing responsibility for the human rights violations alluded to in the above report is Article 7 of the ILC draft articles on the Responsibility of International Organizations. Reflect on the extract of the Secretary-General's report in light of Article 7 and the ILC commentary to it, which follow.

> Article 7—Conduct of organs of a State or organs or agents of an international organization placed at the disposal of another international organization
>
> The conduct of an organ of a State or an organ or agent of an international organization that is placed at the disposal of another international organization shall be considered under international law an act of the latter organization if the organization exercises effective control over that conduct.
>
> *Commentary*
>
> (1) . . . Article 7 deals with the . . . situation in which the seconded organ or agent still acts to a certain extent as organ of the seconding State or as organ or agent of the seconding organization. This occurs for instance in the case of military contingents that a State places at the disposal of the United Nations for a peacekeeping operation, since the State retains disciplinary powers and criminal jurisdiction over the members of the national contingent. In this situation the problem arises whether a specific conduct of the seconded organ or agent is to be attributed to the receiving organization or to the seconding State or organization. . . .
>
> (3) The seconding State or organization may conclude an agreement with the receiving organization over placing an organ or agent at the latter organization's disposal. The agreement may state which State or organization would be responsible for conduct of that organ or agent. For example, according to the model contribution agreement relating to military contingents placed at the disposal of the United Nations by one of its Member States, the United Nations is regarded as liable towards third parties, but has a right of recovery from the contributing State under circumstances such as "loss, damage, death or injury [arising] from gross negligence or wilful misconduct of the personnel provided by the Government". The agreement appears to deal only with distribution of responsibility and not with attribution of conduct. At any event, this type of agreement is not conclusive because it governs only the relations between the contributing State or organization and the receiving organization and could thus not have the effect of depriving a third party of any right that that party may have towards the State or organization which is responsible under the general rules.

(4) The criterion for attribution of conduct either to the contributing State or organization or to the receiving organization is based according to article 7 on the factual control that is exercised over the specific conduct taken by the organ or agent placed at the receiving organization's disposal. As was noted in the comment by one State, account needs to be taken of the "full factual circumstances and particular context". . . .

(6) The United Nations assumes that in principle it has exclusive control of the deployment of national contingents in a peacekeeping force. This premise led the United Nations Legal Counsel to state:

> As a subsidiary organ of the United Nations, an act of a peacekeeping force is, in principle, imputable to the Organization, and if committed in violation of an international obligation entails the international responsibility of the Organization and its liability in compensation.

This statement sums up United Nations practice relating to the United Nations Operation in the Congo (ONUC), the United Nations Peacekeeping Force in Cyprus (UNFICYP) and later peacekeeping forces. In a recent comment, the United Nations Secretariat observed that "[f]or a number of reasons, notably political," the practice of the United Nations had been that of "maintaining the principle of United Nations responsibility vis-à-vis third parties" in connection with peacekeeping operations. . . .

(9) The United Nations Secretary-General held that the criterion of the "degree of effective control" was decisive with regard to joint operations:

> The international responsibility of the United Nations for combat-related activities of United Nations forces is premised on the assumption that the operation in question is under the exclusive command and control of the United Nations [. . .] In joint operations, international responsibility for the conduct of the troops lies where operational command and control is vested according to the arrangements establishing the modalities of cooperation between the State or States providing the troops and the United Nations. In the absence of formal arrangements between the United Nations and the State or States providing troops, responsibility would be determined in each and every case according to the degree of effective control exercised by either party in the conduct of the operation.

International Law Commission, Draft articles on responsibility of international Organizations, with commentaries 19-23 (2011), https://legal.un.org/ilc/texts/instruments/english/commentaries/9_11_2011.pdf.

### *Note: Haiti, Cholera Epidemic, and UN Accountability*

A well-publicized cholera epidemic broke out in Haiti in 2010. From the outset, there were indications that the spread of the disease was linked to the arrival of a new contingent of peacekeeping troops from Nepal there to join the UN Stabilization Mission (MINUSTAH). Since then, civil society organizations as well as several UN rapporteurs have criticized the United Nations for not assuming its responsibility for the spread of cholera in Haiti.

In the United States, this problem was at issue in the case of *Delama George*, in which U.S. and Haitian citizens filed a class action in federal court seeking to hold the UN and several of its officials responsible for the individual effects of the cholera epidemic in Haiti. In particular, they named in their complaints UN Secretary General Ban Ki-Moon, the United Nations, its former Under Secretary-General Edmond Mulet, and MINUSTAH.

The plaintiffs argued that the defendants knowingly ignored the high risk of transmitting cholera in Haiti by deploying 1,000 UN personnel from Nepal without screening them properly, despite knowing the disease was endemic in Nepal. In 2015, the U.S. District Court for the Southern District of New York dismissed the plaintiff's claims due to lack of subject matter jurisdiction upon finding that the defendants were immune from suit under the UN Charter, the Convention on Privileges and Immunities of the United Nations (hereinafter "CPIUN"), and the Vienna Convention on Diplomatic Relations. *Delama Georges, et al. v. United Nations, et al.*, 84 F. Supp. 3d 246, 2015 U.S. Dist. LEXIS 2657 (S.D.N.Y., 2015). The U.S. Court of Appeals for the Second Circuit affirmed the District Court holding. *Georges v. United Nations*, 2016 U.S. App. LEXIS 15210 (2d Cir. N.Y. Aug. 18, 2016).

In response to the Second Circuit decision, a spokesman for the UN Secretary-General issued the following statement:

> [T]he Secretary-General deeply regrets the terrible suffering the people of Haiti have endured as a result of the cholera epidemic. The United Nations has a moral responsibility to the victims of the cholera epidemic and for supporting Haiti in overcoming the epidemic and building sound water, sanitation, and health systems. Sustained efforts by national authorities and the international community have contributed to a 90 per cent reduction in the number of cases since the peak in 2011. However, eliminating cholera from Haiti will take the full commitment of the Haitian government and the international community, and crucially, the resources to fulfill our shared duty . . . The Secretary-General urges Member States to demonstrate their solidarity with the people of Haiti by increasing their contributions to eliminate cholera and provide assistance to those affected.

See *Noting Court Decision Upholding United Nations Immunity in Haiti Cholera Case, Secretary-General Urges Member States to Boost Support for Overcoming Epidemic*, United Nations Press Release (Aug. 19, 2016), http://www.un.org/press/en/2016/sgsm17991.doc.htm.

Although one might query the relationship of cholera in Haiti to his mandate, the UN Rapporteur on extreme poverty and human rights heavily criticized the UN response to the cholera outbreak in Haiti in a report published in 2016, which included the following statement:

> The UN's legal position to date has involved denial of legal responsibility for the outbreak, rejection of all claims for compensation, a refusal to establish the procedure required to resolve such private law matters, and entirely unjustified suggestions that the UN's absolute immunity from suit would be jeopardized by adopting a different approach. The existing approach is morally unconscionable, legally indefensible, and politically self-defeating. It is also entirely unnecessary.

*Report of the UN Special Rapporteur on extreme poverty and human rights,* UN Doc. A/71/40823 (2016). See also *Statement [to the Third Committee of the UN General Assembly] by Professor Philip Alston, Special Rapporteur on extreme poverty and human rights, UN responsibility for the introduction of cholera into Haiti,* UN Office of the High Commissioner for Human Rights (Oct. 25, 2016), http://www.ohchr.org/EN/NewsEvents/Pages/DisplayNews.aspx?NewsID=2 0794&LangID=E#sthash.Uc3vPH16.dpuf.

Following the UN Rapporteur's criticism, the United Nations leadership announced the creation of a Haiti Cholera Response Multi-Partner Trust Fund (MPTF) with the goals of (1) strengthening efforts to eradicate and treat the disease and (2) encouraging Member States to assist those Haitians most affected by the epidemic since 2010. The final aim is to raise approximately $400 million to fund these two goals. For more on the MPTF, see *United Nations Haiti Cholera Response Multi-Partner Trust Fund Launched to Help Country Overcome Epidemic, Build Sound Systems, Strengthen Resilience,* UN Press Release Dev/3248 (Oct. 14, 2016), http://www.un.org/press/en/2016/dev3248.doc.htm. The Pan-American Health Organization reported in January 2020 that Haiti had reached one year free from cholera, after the death of 9,792 people and the infection of 820,000. See *Haiti Reaches One Year Free of Cholera,* Pan-American Health Organization (January 23, 2020), https://www3.paho.org/hq/index.php?option=com_content&view=article&id=15684:haiti-reaches-one-year-free-of-cholera&Itemid=1926&lang=en.

## C. International Financial and Trade Institutions

### 1. The World Bank

International financial institutions established by multilateral arrangements among states, such as the World Bank, engage in financing or promoting development projects that can have significant impacts on human rights, for better or sometimes worse. The World Bank, along with the International Monetary Fund (IMF), was created in 1944 to assist in the reconstruction of Europe and Asia after the Second World War, although the Bank has since turned its attention to the economic problems of developing countries. The IMF works closely with the Bank on economic policy but is more concerned with financial markets and stability than with development and poverty. The Bank is founded on Articles of Agreement supplemented with bylaws approved by its member states. A Board of Governors meets once a year to set policy for the Bank, and ongoing operations are overseen by a 24-member Board of Executive Directors that meets weekly. Voting in the Bank is weighted and based upon financial shares that correspond in large part to the global economic rank of each member state. The seven largest industrial states (G-7) control about 45% of the votes, but decisions are generally taken by consensus.

Since the World Bank was created, a number of financial institutions have been established by multilateral agreements at the regional level. The conglomerate of institutions constituting the World Bank Group, however, stands out for its unmatched influence in the developing world and scope of operations geographically and programmatically.

The World Bank Group is composed of five associated institutions: the International Bank for Reconstruction and Development, the International Development Association, the International Finance Corporation, the Multilateral Investment Guarantee Agency, and the International Center for the Settlement of Investment Disputes. The Group uses financial instruments to promote sustainable development, including through loan arrangements, long-term low-interest concessional credits and grants made to the poorest countries, partial risk guarantees, and private-sector debt and equity. The World Bank's primary mission is to achieve poverty reduction "through an inclusive and sustainable globalization." *History*, The World Bank, http://www.worldbank.org/en/about/history (last visited Sept. 16, 2022).

The World Bank's Articles of Agreement do not mention human rights, and historically that has led Bank lawyers to assert that the Bank is not obligated to adhere to international human rights law. Another question, however, is the extent to which the World Bank's activities can be harnessed to advance human rights, including but not limited to the right to development, which is central to the Bank's work.

In recent decades, the World Bank has addressed social issues that bear upon human rights through its "Safeguard Policies" and through the work of an Inspection Panel established in 1993 that evaluates compliance with those policies. The Bank established its Inspection Panel because of growing concerns about the accountability of international development agencies if they support projects and programs that negatively affect the enjoyment of human rights. The Panel is an independent investigatory body that receives and investigates complaints from those in the territory of a borrower whose rights or interests have been adversely affected by the Bank's failure to comply with its policies and procedures in the design, appraisal, and implementation of a Bank-financed project. The Panel may investigate complaints upon authorization by the Bank's Board of Executive Directors and assess to what extent the Bank has complied with its own standards. At the first stage, the Panel registers the request and asks management to respond to the concerns expressed in it. The Panel then assesses whether the request meets the eligibility requirements—in particular, whether prima facie the Bank has engaged in a serious violation of its operational policies and procedures, resulting or likely to result in material and adverse harm to those making the request and to which management has failed to respond adequately. On the basis of this assessment, the Panel recommends to the Executive Directors whether or not to authorize an investigation. If authorized, the Panel investigates the merits and reaches findings. The process can result in a remedial action plan requiring management to take action.

In 2016, the World Bank revised its safeguard policies through adoption of a new Environmental and Social Framework (ESF) that expands protections for people and the environment in Bank-financed investment projects. The revisions resulted from a consultation process that involved close to 8,000 stakeholders from 83 countries, including governments, international organizations, development experts, indigenous peoples, and civil society groups. Among the Bank's goals in the framework are to protect persons and communities, including indigenous peoples, in the context of the investment projects it finances; to promote non-discrimination, social inclusion and public participation; and to mitigate project risks and impacts on disadvantaged and vulnerable groups. The new framework—which became effective on October 1, 2018—also expands the competencies of the grievance redress mechanisms instituted by the World Bank. See The World Bank, *Environment and Social Framework* (2017), https://thedocs.worldb ank.org/en/doc/837721522762050108-0290022018/original/ESFFramework.pdf.

Despite these developments in its policy and programmatic architecture, the World Bank has been extensively criticized over the years for not employing sufficient attention to human rights in its operations. Many NGOs have expressed dissatisfaction with the World Bank's revised safeguard policies, asserting that they lack an adequate human rights focus and weaken protection for indigenous peoples—a position that is generally disputed by Bank officials. See, e.g., *World Bank undermines decades of progress on building protections for the rights of indigenous peoples*, Forest Peoples Programme (July 28, 2016), https://www.forestpeoples.org/en/top ics/world-bank/news/2016/07/world-bank-undermines-decades-progress-build ing-protections-rights-in; *World Bank: Human Rights All But Absent in New Policy*, Human Rights Watch (July 21, 2016), https://www.hrw.org/news/2016/07/21/ world-bank-human-rights-all-absent-new-policy. Additionally, the new World Bank Directive on Vulnerable Groups has also been criticized for lacking a reference to discrimination on the basis of sexual orientation and gender identity, even though the World Bank has created a position of Senior Advisor on LGBTI issues. See generally *World Bank Announces New Advisor on Sexual Orientation and Gender Identity Issues*, The World Bank (October 27, 2016), https://www.worldbank.org/en/news/ press-release/2016/10/27/world-bank-announces-new-advisor-on-sexual-orientat ion-and-gender-identity-issues.

The following report summarizes many of the concerns about the Bank's policies and operations in relation to human rights.

## Report of the United Nations Special Rapporteur on extreme poverty and human rights, Philip Alston

UN Doc. A/70/274 (2015) (citations omitted)

### I. INTRODUCTION

. . .

2. In the context of a mandate dealing with extreme poverty and human rights, the World Bank is arguably the single most important international agency. Some might question this characterization on the grounds that the $40 billion or more that the Bank provided to borrowing countries in 2014 represents only a fraction of total private capital flows to developing countries from all multilateral and national development banks, bilateral donors and private investors. However, not only is the elimination of extreme poverty one of its two central goals, its research is more voluminous and influential than that of its peers. It remains the key standard-setter in many areas, its knowledge and expertise are often crucial and its seal of approval frequently encourages the participation of other donors or investors.

3. The Special Rapporteur begins his report by looking at how human rights are approached within the following contexts in the work of the Bank: legal policy,

public relations, policy analysis, operations and safeguards. He then seeks to explain the reasons for the historical aversion of the Bank to human rights, argues that it needs a new approach and explores what difference that might make. Finally, he reflects on what a World Bank policy on human rights might look like.

4. The thrust of the report is that the existing approach of the Bank is incoherent, counterproductive and unsustainable. It is based on outdated legal analysis and shaped by deep misperceptions of what a human rights policy would require. What is needed is a transparent dialogue designed to generate an informed and nuanced policy that will avoid undoubted perils, while enabling the Bank and its members to make constructive and productive use of the universally accepted human rights framework.

## II.    HUMAN RIGHTS POLICY OF THE WORLD BANK

5. The World Bank does not have a single comprehensive human rights policy. Rather, it has many different and competing approaches to the issue. For analytical purposes it can be seen to have adopted different human rights policies in each of the following contexts: legal policy, public relations, policy analysis, operations and safeguards. . . .

## III.    EXPLAINING THE AVERSION OF THE WORLD BANK TO HUMAN RIGHTS

34. Before considering why the Bank should change its approach, it is essential to seek to understand why there is currently such an aversion to human rights within the management of the Bank. Six factors would seem to be especially important.

### INSTITUTIONAL CULTURE

35. From its creation in 1944, the Bank has sought to present itself as a functional, technical agency and hence one that is above the political fray. That was deemed essential to avoid the appearance of choosing sides in the aftermath of the Second World War and subsequently in the fraught climate of the cold war. That technocratic image is mirrored in the internal culture of the Bank, which is dominated by economists. That in turn affects how institutional goals are shaped and justifications framed. To become relevant, human rights factors need to be presented in terms of economic impact, rather than as matters of values, law, or dignity. Just as human rights proponents are uncomfortable with the consequentialism of economics, economists often perceive rights as being rigid, anti-market and overly State-centric. The concern is that the engagement of the Bank with human rights would bring about a radical paradigm shift with unknown consequences.

36. Another institutional element is the pressure to approve loans, or as a famous Bank report put it, to "push money out the door." Despite official denials, those pressures continue. In such a setting, it is unsurprising that some see social safeguards and even more so human rights as factors likely to raise costs and delay lending. An internal Bank report observed that management is often uninterested in, or resistant to, work on safeguards and treats it as a box to be checked. However,

minimizing safeguard concerns enhances the likelihood of flawed project design, which neglects elements important for success, overlooks likely opposition and resistance, creates ill will and damages the credibility of the Bank. It also assumes, contrary to the findings of a report by the Independent Evaluation Group, that the costs of safeguards outweigh their benefits.

MISPLACED LEGALISM

37. The goals and policies of the Bank have changed radically since 1944. The Articles of Agreement contain no mention of either of its current proclaimed "twin goals" of ending extreme poverty and promoting shared prosperity. The General Counsels have played a key role in the necessarily dynamic interpretation of the Articles required to reflect and justify that evolution.

38. Interpretation of the Articles is decided by the Executive Directors by a simple majority vote, with the possibility of appeal to the Board of Governors. In practice, legal opinions by the General Counsel have provided the basis for most such interpretations. General Counsels also provide regular advice to the Executive Directors and the President and senior management, including on interpretation of the mandate. The most influential General Counsels have acknowledged the need to adopt a purposive or teleological approach.

39. The principal exception to that general rule has been the issue of human rights. As theories of development have changed and the Bank has confronted new challenges, legal counsels have had no difficulty in justifying the engagement of the Bank with issues such as corruption, the rule of law, environmental degradation and other novel issues. Alone among those new issues, human rights is classified as political rather than economic, despite the view of a former General Counsel that "human rights are an intrinsic part of the Bank's mission". Today, it is still the Legal Department that takes the lead in "policing" the human rights taboo within the Bank. That is said to apply even within the discussions in the Executive Board. . . .

CULTURAL RELATIVISM

41. Ironically, given the widespread perception that the Bank is dominated by Western interests and values, the argument is often heard that the Bank needs to avoid human rights discourse because it may be perceived as imposing Western values on non-Western countries. Thus, the authors of a report on gender and human rights-based approaches in development felt the need to address such concerns in a separate annex. While the debate over cultural relativism is a very vibrant one in both political and scholarly circles, the justifiable issue of concern is not the basic universality of the standards, which has long been reaffirmed, but the degree of cultural appropriateness shown in their application. For the Bank to invoke a relativist justification to refuse all engagement with the universal standards is contrary to international law. Particular interpretations of human rights will always be contested, but so too will definitions of poverty, the rule of law, corruption and a great many other notions which lie at the heart of its work. Avoidance is no substitute for sophisticated and nuanced engagement.

SHADOW OF SANCTIONS

42. The Bank has a long, and generally unhappy, history in which human rights concerns have been linked to demands for it to impose sanctions on client States. . . . In principle, the Bank has rejected most such calls on the grounds that they involve politics rather than economics. In practice, however, it has occasionally succumbed to political pressure and delayed or withheld funds, albeit insisting that its actions did not amount to sanctioning.

43. An especially problematic, if well-intentioned, case was the decision in February 2014 to delay a $90 million health project loan to Uganda after the country adopted a draconian anti-homosexuality act. The Bank suggested that it had acted only to ensure that the health project would not be adversely affected by the act. However, the President of the Bank explained that he had acted because he was not convinced that the loan would not lead to discrimination or even endangerment of the lesbian, gay, bisexual and transgender community.

44. . . . No convincing justification was put forward by the Bank as to why Uganda alone was singled out among the various countries that have laws that criminalize homosexuality. No explanation was given as to why discrimination against lesbian, gay, bisexual, transgender and intersex communities was the trigger for action, rather than often deeply entrenched official discrimination against various other groups. Nor was the action based on any policy document that had previously been elaborated. And finally, if the Bank itself had been directly implicated in the issue at hand, urgent remedial action would have been much more readily defensible, but it was not.

45. While it was clearly not intended as such, the most significant impact of the decision was probably to convince an even larger number of countries that the Bank should indeed be kept away from human rights issues for fear that it would start to apply sanctions more broadly and in an equally unpredictable and ad hoc manner. . . .

TURNING THE WORLD BANK INTO A HUMAN RIGHTS COP

47. On various occasions, senior Bank officials have warned of the dire consequences that would follow if the Bank were to become some sort of global policeman, responsible for enforcing respect for human rights by its client Governments. Because of the sanctions mentality described above, that fear is not altogether unfounded.

48. There is a vast difference, however, between having a carefully tailored human rights policy and becoming an enforcer of rights. Many other international organizations have adopted such policies; none of them have become enforcers. The established international human rights regime exists to engage with States that are accused of violations and to find ways to encourage, facilitate and promote compliance with international norms. There is no reason why that task would or should move to the Bank if it were to acknowledge that human rights are also relevant to its operations. . . . It is especially noteworthy in this respect that the Bank safeguards already require it to take account of the international environmental treaty obligations of a country when undertaking an environmental assessment and it has managed to do that without giving rise to undue controversy.

COMPETITION WITH OTHER LENDERS

49. It is often suggested that obliging the Bank to take human rights into account would place it at a disadvantage to other lenders, which might not do so. In 2006, the then President of the Bank, Paul Wolfowitz, criticized the Government and banks of China for not attaching human rights and environmental standards to their loans to Africa. In 2011, China overtook the Bank in the volume of its development lending. The creation of new multilateral investment banks and the growth of national development banks in countries like Brazil and India, means ever more competition in the market for lenders. While the World Bank has always downplayed such suggestions, most commentators suggest that those developments have placed it under competitive pressure.

50. In fact, if the major new banks do not adopt appropriate social protection policies, there would be good reason to assume that the Bank will be less able to compete in terms of the time taken for project planning, the conditions offered to borrowers and the speed of disbursement. Both the New Development Bank, which proclaims itself "as an alternative to the existing US-dominated World Bank and International Monetary Fund", and the Asian Infrastructure Investment Bank were set up in 2015. The Articles of Agreement of both banks reproduce the same political prohibition clause as is contained in the Articles of Agreement of the World Bank. The Asian Infrastructure Investment Bank is committed to addressing environmental and social impacts, but it remains to be seen what type of standards and safeguards will be adopted and how, if at all, human rights will be factored in. Those are issues that will warrant the most careful scrutiny going forward.

51. The immediate question for the World Bank is whether the best strategy is to compete with the new lenders in a race to the bottom or to adopt a principled stance. Despite obvious temptations, there are strong arguments for the latter approach. Strong safeguards, as noted above, ensure sound planning, reduce subsequent problems, facilitate public support, minimize reputational costs for the lender and facilitate better overall outcomes. Loans that are made in secrecy and without such precautions carry with them the seeds of eventual disaster for both the borrower and the lender. The real comparative advantage for the World Bank lies in underwriting high-quality projects and maintaining its role as an innovator, rather than in a race to lend more at whatever cost. Of course, none of that means that the Bank should not explore efficiency gains that might be achieved through means other than cutting standards and avoiding human rights considerations.

## IV. TIME FOR CHANGE: WHY THE WORLD BANK NEEDS A NEW APPROACH TO HUMAN RIGHTS

52. Based on the preceding review, the following propositions seem to encapsulate the actual practice of the World Bank: (a) pay lip service to human rights in official settings, as long as there are no consequences; (b) acknowledge the theoretical significance of human rights in studies and analyses of issues in relation to which they are incontestably relevant; (c) ensure that, as a general rule, the Bank does not engage with any aspect of human rights in its actual operations and lending; and (d) be prepared to make exceptions when political imperatives require it, even if that involves a high degree of inconsistency.

53. There are many reasons why a new approach is needed. The following six seem especially compelling.

54. First, an inconsistent, ad hoc and opaque policy of the type that exists today is in no one's interests. The world has changed dramatically since the 1980s and human rights are an unavoidable feature of national and international policies and debates. It is illusory to believe that the Bank can be fully effective without any meaningful engagement with that entire field of activity. By treating human rights as a taboo issue, the Bank has ensured that a whole range of issues that are universally acknowledged to be crucial to the development and poverty eradication agendas cannot be openly addressed or factored into its work. As noted below, the valiant effort to rely upon surrogate terms can never be an adequate substitute for engaging with the human rights framework and norms. The result is a staff and management with relatively little understanding of the complexity of the international human rights regime, which in turn results in unfounded fears, avoidance of debates that would otherwise be a matter of course, a poor sense of how to respond when human rights problems force themselves onto the agenda and the absence of a credible Bank voice when those issues are discussed in other settings.

55. Second, the policies of the Bank need to reflect the current status of international human rights law, rather than the situation in the 1960s or the 1980s, when its existing policies were frozen into place. . . .

56. Third, rather than being an outlier, the Bank needs to bring its approach into line with that of almost every other major international organization. . . .

59. Fourth, the Bank needs to bring its operational policies into line with mainstream development theory, especially its own. In 1999, Amartya Sen published a landmark study entitled *Development as Freedom*, based on lectures given at the Bank. [A brief extract of Sen's study may be found in Chapter 1, *supra* pages 33-35.] . . . The Bank itself has often paid lip service to the consensus that has emerged since the end of the cold war that recognizes that "democracy, development and respect for human rights and fundamental freedoms are interdependent and mutually reinforcing," as proclaimed in the Vienna Declaration and Programme of Action, adopted by consensus by 171 States in 1993.

60. Fifth, the Bank needs at least a convincing due diligence policy to enable it to adjust or reject projects that would otherwise lead to, or support, human rights violations. Its safeguard policies have long been referred to as "do-no-harm" policies, but their very limited coverage in terms of the full gamut of the human rights obligations of States has meant that many serious violations are alleged to have occurred in the context of projects funded by the Bank. . . .

61. Sixth, by refusing to take account of any information emanating from human rights sources, the Bank places itself in an artificial bubble, which excludes information that could greatly enrich its understanding of the situations and contexts in which it works. That includes especially the materials generated by human rights treaty bodies, special procedures mandate holders and the universal periodic review process of the Human Rights Council, as well as analyses generated by NGOs. It is striking that the Bank regularly consults religious leaders, such as the faith-based and religious leaders' round table it held in 2015, but has no comparable meetings with human rights experts.

For more reading on the World Bank in relation to human rights, see Dana Clark, *The World Bank and Human Rights: The Need for Greater Accountability*, 15 HARV. HUM. RTS J. 210 (2002); Mac Darrow, *Between Light and Shadow: The World Bank, the IMF, and International Human Rights Law* (2003); Siobhán McInerney-Lankford, *Human Rights and Development: A Comment on Challenges and Opportunities from a Legal Perspective*, 2009 J. HUM. RTS. PRACTICE; Megan Natheson, *The World Bank Group's Human Rights Obligations Under the United Nations Guiding Principles on Business and Human Rights*, 33 BERKELEY J. INT'L L. 489 (2015); Human Rights Watch, *Abuse-Free Development: How the World Bank should Safeguard against Human Rights Violations* (2013), https://www.hrw.org/sites/default/files/reports/worldbank0713_ForUpl oad.pdf; Amartya Sen, *Development as Freedom* (1998); Amartya Sen, *Human Rights and the Limits of Law*, 27 CARDOZO L. REV. 2913 (2006); *Human Rights and Development: Towards Mutual Reinforcement* (Philip Alston and Mary Robinson eds., 2005); World Bank, *World Bank, Development and Human Rights: The Role of the World Bank* (1998). The Bank's Operational Policies can be found at https://policies.worldb ank.org/en/policies/operational-manual.

## 2.  The World Trade Organization

The World Trade Organization (WTO), which is dedicated to facilitating trade liberalization, is another major conduit for activities that can have an impact on human rights. The increasing role of the WTO has raised concerns about the possible impact that liberalized economic policies might have on human rights. Issues of particular concern include protecting labor rights, upholding economic and social rights (such as the right to health, which may conflict with intellectual property protection for pharmaceutical companies), and permitting (or reject-ing) the use of economic sanctions or boycotts for human rights purposes that may be incompatibility with free trade. The following reading explores some of these issues.

Robert Howse and Makau Mutua

## Protecting Human Rights in a Global Economy: Challenges for the World Trade Organization

6 Hum. Rts. & Devt. Yearbk. 51 (2001) (endnotes omitted)

Over the past decade, trade agreements have come under increased scrutiny from the public. More and more people—peasants, trade unionists, human rights activists, small businesses, environmentalists, farmers, students and others—are expressing concern about how trade agreements are affecting their lives. For all the talk of the benefits of globalization and its presumed contribution to economic growth, the undeniable reality is that globally, and within most countries, the gap between the rich and the poor is widening, and hundreds of millions of people are denied the basic human rights provided for by the United Nations. The creation of the World Trade Organization (WTO), outside the auspices of the UN, has aggra-vated many of civil society's concerns.

There is no consensus on how trade liberalization affects human rights, nor even a well-developed methodology for determining the human rights impacts of trade agreements. Many people in the mainstream trade policy community see no linkage whatsoever with human rights and consider such concerns outside their realm. Likewise, many human rights groups lack familiarity with trade issues. They are puzzled by the language and suspicious of the entire process: from the negotiations of tariffs to the settlement of disputes. The two communities are so far apart that they do not even use the same vocabulary, let alone share a common philosophy.

Both trade and human rights have been codified in highly developed legal regimes, negotiated by governments since the end of World War II. These two legal regimes have developed however in splendid isolation from one another. Both trade law and human rights law narrow the range of policy options that are available to governments. And yet, it seems that the question of whether the two legal regimes are contradictory has rarely been asked. . . .

As the postwar GATT regime evolved into the World Trade Organization in late 1994, so its rules and those of its accompanying agreements evolved into a detailed legal code, which is interpreted and defined through a dispute settlement process. This process, however, has not been transparent and has not viewed dispute resolution through the lens of human rights impacts. Provisions of WTO Agreements on domestic food safety and other technical standards, as well as on intellectual property directly affect the ability of governments to fulfill their human rights obligations to their citizens. This is especially true in the case of social and economic rights, which should be understood in connection with, not in isolation from, civil and political rights.

. . . The preamble of the WTO Agreement, which establishes the framework for the entire WTO system, does not make free trade an end in itself. Rather, it establishes the objectives of the system as related to the fulfillment of basic human values, including the improvement of living standards for all people and sustainable development. As is widely recognized now, both in development literature as well as in numerous documents of international policy, these objectives cannot be reached without respect for human rights. . . .

Although the GATT text — now part of the broader WTO system of treaties — reflects the recognition of non-trade public values, which are meant to prevail in the event of conflict with its free trade rules, institutional isolation has contributed to a very limited interpretation of this principle. Specifically, GATT Article XX, which was designed to be a fundamental pillar of the international trade regime, has often been construed so restrictively as to almost read it out of text, or to marginalize it. Compounding the problems created by institutional isolation is the atmosphere of secrecy and the lack of transparency in the dispute settlement and appellate process within the WTO. The GATT has often been interpreted as creating a general right to free trade; however, as emphasized in a few recent decisions of the WTO Appellate Body, the GATT and the other WTO treaties contain fine balances of rights and obligations. And the provisions that limit or balance trade liberalization, protecting other human interests, are as fundamental a part of the international law of trade, as those that support the globalization of markets. They must not be read out or down.

Enlightened interpretation of the GATT and other WTO agreements, however, will not in and of itself address the needs of under-development, inequality
and the corresponding violations of fundamental human rights around the world.
Trade rules must be looked at in their relationship to other phenomena connected
to globalization, such as free capital movements and the practices of the international financial institutions. We must understand the effects of trade laws and
policies in the broadest sense, and evolve new laws and policies in a manner that
overcomes the isolation between human rights institutions and economic institutions, including those preoccupied with the trading system.

### Highlights

—The relationship of trade law and human rights law: In the event of a conflict between a universally recognized human right and a commitment ensuing
from international treaty law such as a trade agreement, the latter must be interpreted to be consistent with the former. When properly interpreted and applied,
the trade regime recognizes that human rights are fundamental and prior to free
trade itself.

—Labour: It is often claimed that the GATT prohibits members from regulating access of imports based on the manner in which those products have been
produced, even if such regulations are applied equally to domestic products. However, this view is inconsistent with a close analysis of the jurisprudence, despite its
presence in two notorious panel rulings, which were not adopted as legally binding
by the GATT membership. The correct reading of the GATT text would permit a
country to impose conditions on imports related to the labour practices involved in
their production.

—Government Procurement: The current negotiation of government procurement rules with respect to services provides the opportunity to develop the
position that human rights-based procurement conditions are consistent with WTO
law. As well, the existing Government Procurement Agreement, which concerns
trade in goods, should be interpreted so as to permit ethical purchasing policies by
governments. Not permitting members of the WTO to impose the kind of requirements on foreign suppliers that they routinely impose on domestic suppliers (such
as anti-discrimination requirements) would amount to an obligation to favour foreign suppliers, which the GPA could not possibly be read as to entrench. Further,
the public order exception in the GPA must be interpreted in light of the international law of human rights.

—Trade Policy Review: WTO member states are currently subject to a review
process which examines their policies and practices in relation to their promotion
of free trade. This is inconsistent with the actual full objective of the review process,
which is to review policies in their relation to the "functioning of the multilateral
trading system". The objective of the trading system is not free trade as such, but
rather "ensuring full employment", "optimal use of the world's resources" and "sustainable development". National trade policy and practice should be examined in
relation to the achievement of these goals.

—Dispute Settlement: Consideration of the human rights impact of dispute
settlement rulings would be facilitated by the acceptance of amicus briefs by panel
and appellate body members. In the Shrimp/Turtle case, a precedent has been

established for the submission of amicus briefs to both the panels and the Appellate Body. Secrecy of pleadings and oral argument in WTO dispute settlement, however, may limit the effectiveness of amicus participation, and these provisions of the Dispute Settlement Understanding should be revisited as soon as possible.

— Global Governance: Interpretation of WTO law has not incorporated the expertise of other institutions governing the various regimes of international law. Nor has there been serious dialogue or interaction between the WTO as an institution and other relevant international institutions. However, the agreement establishing the WTO requires that this be the case. The implementation of this obligation should be the subject of a formal review.

---

The following extract of an article written several years later gives a different perspective.

Harold Hongju Koh

## Global Tobacco as a Health and Human Rights Imperative

23 Harvard Int'l L. J. 433 (2016) (footnotes omitted)

It has long been settled that, in deciding trade disputes, WTO panels may consider human rights and public health concerns as legitimate background for interpretation. After all, trade liberalization is fundamentally ameans, not an end. The preamble to the Marrakesh Agreement, which established the framework for the WTO system, declares the system's objectives not as free trade per se, but rather, fulfillment of basic human values, including the improvement of living standards for all people and sustainable development. Such improvement cannot reasonably be achieved unless adequate respect is given to legitimate governmental concerns regarding public health and human rights. Far from being a novel view, trade commentators and officials have widely accepted this position dating back to before the WTO's founding.12 Perhaps then-WTO Director General Pascal Lamy put it most directly in 2010 when he suggested, "One could almost claim that trade is human rights in practice! . . . It is [at least in part the] responsibility [of the WTO and UN human rights bodies] to coordinate our actions in a meaningful and efficient manner to ensure that trade does not impair human rights, but rather strengthens them."

In the twenty-first century, one of those human rights should be a right to be free from preventable communicable and noncommunicable disease. Under international law, the International Covenant on Economic, Social and Cultural Rights ("ICESCR") obligates all States Parties to recognize the right to "enjoyment of the highest attainable standard of physical and mental health," as well as to take steps necessary to prevent, treat, and control disease.14 General Comment 14 from the ICESCR Treaty Committee ("CESCR") states: "Health is a fundamental human right indispensable for the exercise of other human rights. Every human being is entitled to the enjoyment of the highest attainable standard of health conducive to living a life in dignity," and such rights may be enforceable in law. In the tobacco setting, this concept should be understood to encompass the notion that human beings have an enforceable right to avoid preventable noncommunicable disease caused by tobacco addiction and promoted by underregulated private production, marketing, and consumption.

Whether that individual human right can be adequately protected by responsible governments turns critically upon whether dispute settlement bodies acknowledge that those nations themselves have a right under international law to protect public health through reasonable government regulation. Because tobacco use is the world's leading preventable cause of death, the ICESCR and customary international law do not just empower—they oblige—national governments to regulate to protect those rights effectively. . . .

That leads to my second proposition: under certain circumstances, human rights and public health concerns can be both a shield and a sword—a valid defense against a claimed WTO violation and a valid way to challenge national action that undermines these concerns. Human rights and public health considerations can act as a shield: they can justify a WTO member state's exercise of the police power to engage in what might otherwise be seen as a WTO violation. From the outset, the GATT's drafters included Article XX, which provided that "nothing in this Agreement shall be construed to prevent the adoption or enforcement by any contracting party of measures," inter alia, "necessary to protect public morals," "necessary to protect human, animal or plant life or health," or "relating to the conservation of exhaustible natural resources if such measures are made effective in conjunction with restrictions on domestic production or consumption."25 On their face, measures to protect "human . . . life or health" against disease, such as those taken under the Framework Convention on Tobacco Control, would seem to fall within this language. . . .

In recent years, the WTO Appellate Body offered a more expansive interpretive approach in the United States—Shrimp/Turtle case, when it construed the term "exhaustible natural resources" in an environmental trade dispute. Rather than woodenly seeking a less restrictive alternative, the Appellate Body interpreted Article XX to include living "endangered species" within "exhaustible natural resources," a phrase it construed in light of a modern understanding of international environmental law as it had evolved since the GATT was first negotiated. By so saying, the Appellate Body suggested that when examining WTO claims, other human-focused bodies of public international law can offer a justification that precludes a panel from finding that WTO law has been breached.

Jurisdictionally, WTO panels may only decide claims raised under agreements covered by the WTO. But Article 3.2 of the Dispute Settlement Understanding ("DSU") directs panels to interpret WTO-covered agreements "in accordance with customary rules of interpretation of public internationallaw." In turn, Article 31(3) of the Vienna Convention on the Law of Treaties (which states generally applicable rules of treaty interpretation) instructs that when interpreting any treaty, the interpreter must account not just for the treaty at hand but also for "[a]ny subsequent agreement between the parties regarding the interpretation of the treaty or the application of its provisions," as well as "[a]ny relevant rules of international law applicable in the relations between the parties."

All of this suggests that a WTO panel may interpret the relevant WTO rules in the context of relevant human rights or public health treaties. A party to the panel proceedings could thus raise a public health or human rights defense against a WTO claim in cases in which a public health or human rights treaty required or authorized the state action, in which case the WTO obligation should be read flexibly in the context of that other body of international law. In a case in which following an explicit WTO obligation would put the member state in violation of its legal obligations under health and human rights law (and if the complainant state were also bound by the same health or human rights norm), the WTO Dispute Settlement Body would need to decide which of the two norms prevailed under interpretive rules governing conflicts of international laws. To be sure, the defending nation would not automatically win by invoking the health and human rights "trump card." For example, the defending nation could not interpose the health and human rights concern as a pretext to engage in violation of well-accepted free trade rules forbidding arbitrary and discriminatory treatment. But if the health or human rights norm were found to be legitimate and a conflict unavoidable, the panel could accept the human focused legal justification and decline to find a WTO violation.

Perhaps the most controversial use of a health and human rights argument would arise if a state used that argument as a sword. A party could invoke human rights "offensively" to authorize executive action: for example, human rights clauses in economic agreements concluded with the European Union could authorize a party to take "appropriate measures" tosuspend the trade preferences afforded to a state party that failed to comply with human rights principles. A complainant could also invoke human rights offensively in WTO adjudication, asking a panel to invalidate another state's law whose legality was being defended on grounds of compliance with WTO law. Assuming that the panel had jurisdiction to decide the claims of any WTO violations, the panel should also be able to apply other bodies of international law, including human rights and public health law, in assessing the legality of the national regulations. While it seems unlikely that a WTO panel would entertain, for example, a direct claim of violation under the International Covenant on Civil and Political Rights, the terms of the TBT Agreement permit challenges to a state's deviation from an "international standard"—defined as "standards that are developed by international bodies." If the meaning and application of the human rights rule were clear—for example, a jus cogens rule—a WTO panel could apply it directly. But if the meaning of the human rights rule were ambiguous, advice from the authoritative interpretive body regarding the human rights treaty could be sought, not just to help the WTO panel to reach the most correct decision, but also to maintain uniformity in the interpretation of the human rights treaty.

## V.   FINAL COMMENTS AND QUESTIONS

1. What are the primary sources of human rights obligations for international organizations under international law? Should international organizations automatically be bound by all human rights norms that are international customary

law? Should international organizations follow the obligations contained in human rights treaties, even though most such treaties include no provision for their ratification by such organizations? Should the views of international organizations of their obligations be considered to promote compliance, as argued by Daugirdas? Keep in mind that the 2011 ILC draft articles indicate that "nothing in the draft articles should be read as implying the existence or otherwise of any particular primary rule binding on international organizations."

2. The UN Secretary General's report on sexual abuse by UN peacekeeping forces reflects how peacekeeping operations present unique human rights challenges. What human rights norms are implicit in the report? Does the report concede the applicability of these norms as a matter of international human rights law?

3. Note that Chapter VII of the UN Charter originally envisaged special agreements between the UN and member states to provide for military contingents to be readily available to the UN under the strategic direction of a Military Staff Committee. Instead, control over peacekeeping and enforcement forces remains subject to the specific agreements developed between and the UN and the states that contribute forces to particular UN missions. How does this affect the determination of UN responsibility for abuses committed by peacekeepers acting under the auspices of a UN misson, keeping in mind Article 7 of the ILC draft articles? Difficulties in drawing a line between operational and organizational control are underscored in Luigi Condorelli, *Le statut des forces de l'ONU et le droit international humanitaire,* 78 RIVISTA DI DIRITTO INTERNAZIONALE 881 (1995); Tom Dannenbaum, *Translating the Standard of Effective Control into a System of Effective Accountability: How Liability Should be Apportioned for Violations of Human Rights by Member State Troop Contingents Serving as United Nations Peacekeepers,* 51 HARV. INT'L L. J. 113 (2010).

4. In *Agim Behrami and Bekir Behrami v. France; Ruzhdi Saramati v. France, Gernamy and Norway,* Eur. Ct. H.R. (GC), Apps. 71412/01 and 78166/01, Admissibility decision of May 2, 2007, the European Court of Human Rights declined to admit complaints against France and Germany arising from alleged conduct of troops and personnel those countries contributed to UN missions in Kosovo. The Court reasoned that the responsible party in the case was instead the UN, in light of the relevant UN Security Council resolution delegating broad security authority to the UNKFOR peace enforcement mission and establishing UNMIK as a subsidiary organ of the UN to exercise administrative authority over Kosovo (and the Court had no jurisdiction over the UN). How does this decision influence your answer to the fomer question?

5. The UN Secretary-General's 2016 statement concerning the Haiti cholera epidemic, *supra* page 268, alludes to the UN's "moral responsibility" toward "the victims of the cholera epidemic and for supporting Haiti in overcoming the epidemic and building sound water, sanitation, and health systems." Does this statement implicitly reject the argument that the United Nations is *legally* responsible under international law?

6. Why is it important for the World Bank and other international financial institutions to incorporate a human rights approach to their daily work and operations? How should this be done — more lawyers and fewer economists? Should every UN specialized agency and other international organizations adopt a similar stance? The International Finance Corporation, a part of the World Bank, finances

private projects through commercial bank intermediaries. Should World Bank private sector lending be equally subject to human rights norms?

7. Are there inherent tensions between the goals of development pursued by the World Bank and respect for human rights? Can advancing human rights in itself have a positive economic impact? Can one advance respect for human rights by fostering economic development? Does this debate assume a false distinction between civil-political rights and economic-social-cultural rights, since development is implicitly necessary to achieve many of the latter?

8. As pointed out above, a number of human rights can be implicated in international trade relations, including those linked to labor issues, the environment, health, indigenous peoples, and women. Can you think of other civil, political, economic, social, or cultural rights that may be affected by trade? Do you agree with Harold Hongju Koh that trade can advance human rights protections?

9. A state's compliance with human rights obligations that requires restrictions on the operations of foreign investors can place it at risk of complaints for violating its trade obligations as a WTO member or under bilateral or multilateral investment treaties. This can occur for example in the area of extraction or exploitation of natural resources. How should this potential conflict be resolved? Consider the harmonizing approach proposed by Harold Hongju Koh, which essentially is to interpret obligations under the WTO agreements consistent with human rights. Does this approach have merit or is it realistic? Cf. *Agreement Reached on WTO Waiver for "Conflict Diamonds" Under the Kimberley Process Certification Scheme for Rough Diamonds*, World Trade Organization (Feb. 26, 2003), http://www.wto.org/english/news_e/news03_e/goods_council_26fev03_e.htm.

# CHAPTER 5

# HUMAN RIGHTS IN EXTREMIS

## HOW CAN HUMAN RIGHTS BE PROTECTED IN TIMES OF ARMED CONFLICT, TERRORISM, AND UNREST?

# I.  *INTRODUCTION: INTERNATIONAL LAW AND CONFLICT*

Traditional international law made sharp distinctions between peace and war, between civil war and international conflict, between civilians and soldiers. In a time that was based on the rights and duties of states as such, that approach may have made sense. For contemporary international human rights law, however, the fundamental task of which is the protection of the rights of human beings, these distinctions often seem woefully artificial. The first four chapters examined the substantial body of international human rights law—conventional, customary, and "soft" law—that has been developed for times of peace. This Chapter is concerned with the law that applies in times of conflict and unrest, whether internal or international, ranging from sporadic emergency situations to sustained war (generally referred to somewhat euphemistically as "armed conflict").

Humanity does not seem to have made much progress in ridding itself of war. Indeed, war, whether against terrorism, rogue states, or internal enemies, is becoming increasingly internationalized, and demands for accountability and punishment have become more frequent and more strident. While we wait for peace to break out, it may be useful to develop a more coherent, comprehensive, and effective body of international human rights and humanitarian law so that the traditional barriers between the law of war and the law of peace are broken down and innocent victims are not left without protection. This Chapter provides some of the raw materials for that effort.

## The Russian Invasion of Ukraine

Russia's invasion of Ukraine, which began on February 24, 2022, starkly reminds us that humanity has not overcome the plague of war, including war between sovereign states. The invasion is the largest military confrontation in Europe since World War II. It has been characterized by air strikes and bombings, and targeted attacks against residential areas, hospitals, schools, train stations, and nuclear power plants. As the war progressed, there were reports of increasing numbers of civilian casualties, with women, children, older persons, and persons with disabilities among those suffering injury or death. As of early May 2022, well over five million refugees from Ukraine had fled to neighboring countries. The Ukrainian people have mounted significant resistance to defend their country and have become a symbol of the struggle to preserve liberal democracy and self-determination. For further details on the conflict's outbreak, see *Ukraine*

*Conflict: What We Know about the Invasion,* BBC News (Feb. 24, 2022), https://www.bbc.com/news/world-europe-60504334; *Russian Military Commits Indiscriminate Attacks During the Invasion of Ukraine,* Amnesty International (Feb. 25, 2022), https://www.amnesty.org/en/latest/news/2022/02/russian-military-commits -indiscriminate-attacks-during-the-invasion-of-ukraine/; *Russia-Ukraine War, List of Key Events on Day 68,* Aljazeera, https://www.aljazeera.com/news/2022/5/2/russia -ukraine-war-list-of-key-events-on-day-68 (last updated May 2, 2022),

The invasion has been widely condemned by the international community and has sparked fears of another World War. It has been called by the United Nations General Assembly and a variety of entities and experts as a brazen violation of international law and an act of aggression contrary to Article 2(4) of the United Nations Charter. Additionally, Russia has been accused of war crimes and violations of the laws of war. Ukraine took its grievances against Russia to the International Court of Justice, which in vain ordered Russia on March 16, 2022 to cease its military operations in Ukraine. The International Criminal Court opened an investigation into war crimes, and the United Nations High Commissioner for Human Rights established an Independent International Commission of Inquiry to investigate human rights violations in relation to the conflict. The North Atlantic Treaty Organization (NATO) took steps to guard against any potential spread of the conflict. The European Union, the United States, and other countries mobilized to impose far-reaching economic sanctions on Russia. Russia has become an international pariah and is being excluded from global sporting events and other activities. As of May 2022, this war is ongoing.

Ukraine was once a part of the Soviet Union, until the latter was dissolved on December 26, 1991. Ukraine declared its independence from the Soviet Union on August 24, 1991, after a national referendum. An apparent motive for the war has been Russian President Vladimir Putin's concern over the possibility of Ukraine joining (NATO) and developing ever closer ties to Western countries. For a detailed account of the increasing tensions between the two countries, see Matthew Mpoke Bigg, *A Timeline of Tensions between Russia and Ukraine,* The New York Times, Feb. 18, 2022, https://www.nytimes.com/2022/02/18/world/europe/russia -ukraine-timeline.html.

This war has shaken the world in many ways, given its scale and brutality. Concerns are elevated because Russia is one of the world's leading military powers, with the world's largest nuclear arsenal at its disposal. For its part, Ukraine is a middle-income country that has opted to pursue democracy and strengthen ties to the West. Erupting in the Eastern flank of Europe and in the age of round-the-clock news, the war is highly visible to the world and serves as a reminder of the enormous human toll and suffering that war imparts. The war also poses a major test to the effectiveness of international law and institutions to address armed conflicts, and thus far on display is the weakness of the UN security system which is held hostage to Russia's veto-wielding power as a permanent member of the Security Council.

The following statement by Michelle Bachelet, made when she was the United Nations' chief human rights officer, captures the dimension of the human rights problems unfolding early in the conflict.

Michelle Bachelet, UN High Commissioner for Human Rights

## Statement on the situation of human rights in Ukraine stemming from Russian aggression

Human Rights Council, 49th Session, March 3, 2022, https://www.ohchr.org/en/statements/2022/03/ukraine-high-commissioner-cites-new-and-dangerous-threats-human-rights

One week ago, the Russian Federation's military attack on Ukraine opened a new and dangerous chapter in world history.

The Secretary-General has termed this "the most serious global peace and security crisis in recent years;" he added, "a country has been thrown into chaos; a region has been upended; and the reverberations are being felt around the world."

The attack that began on 24 February is generating massive impact on the human rights of millions of people across Ukraine. Elevated threat levels for nuclear weapons underline the gravity of the risks to all of humanity.

Military operations are escalating further as we speak, with military strikes on and near large cities, including Chernihiv, Kharkiv, Kherson, Lysychansk, Sievierodonetsk, Sumy, Mariupol and Zhytomyr, and the capital, Kyiv. The town of Volnovakha in Donetsk region has been almost completely destroyed by shelling, and its remaining residents have been hiding in basements.

By Tuesday night, my Office had recorded and confirmed 752 civilian casualties, including 227 killed — 15 of them children. At least 525 have been injured, including 28 children. I will disaggregate these figures in terms of the regions affected: 323 casualties (65 killed and 258 injured) were recorded in Donetsk and Luhansk regions. 429 casualties (162 killed and 267 injured) were recorded in other regions of Ukraine — the city of Kyiv, and Cherkasy, Chernihiv, Kharkiv, Kherson, Kyiv, Odesa, Sumy, Zaporizhzhia, and Zhytomyr regions.

I must emphasize that the real figures will be far higher, since numerous other casualties are pending confirmation, and information from some areas engaged in intense hostilities has been delayed. A member of the OSCE Monitoring Unit in Ukraine was killed last night in Kharkiv while getting supplies for her family. We grieve all the deaths that have occurred.

Most civilian casualties were caused by the use of heavy artillery, multi-launch rocket systems and air strikes in populated areas, with concerning reports of use of cluster munitions striking civilian targets. Massive damage to residential buildings has been inflicted. The use of weapons with wide area effects in populated urban areas risks being inherently indiscriminate, and I call for the immediate cessation of such force.

There has also been substantial damage to a significant number of civilian objects, including a hospital, schools and kindergartens. Essential infrastructure has been heavily damaged — cutting off critical supplies and services, including electricity, water and access to healthcare. On 26 February, Russian troops near Kherson reportedly fired on an ambulance that was transporting seriously wounded victims; the driver was killed and one paramedic was injured.

Over two million people have been forced to flee their homes. One million, according to UNHCR estimates, are internally displaced. A further 1,040,000 refugees have sought safety in neighbouring countries in the past seven days—often after travelling for days by bicycle or on foot, in freezing conditions. UNHCR has estimated that up to four million people could leave the country in the coming weeks if the conflict continues.

I commend the welcome that Ukrainians leaving the country have received. This welcome must be extended to all those fleeing conflict, regardless of their citizenship, ethnicity, migration or other status. There have been disturbing indications of discrimination against African and Asian nationals while fleeing, and the Office will be watching this situation attentively.

Tens of millions of people remain in the country, in potentially mortal danger. I am deeply concerned that the current escalation of military operations will further heighten the harm they face. Thousands of people, including older people, pregnant women, as well as children and people with disabilities, are being forced to gather in underground shelters and subway stations to escape explosions. Many people in situations of vulnerability are separated from families and effectively trapped. My staff in Ukraine have been contacted by several groups who fear persecution if Russian troops advance, including members of the Crimean Tatar community in mainland Ukraine, as well as prominent human rights defenders and journalists.

Excellencies,

We are here to demonstrate and uphold our commitment to multilateralism and human rights. I echo the powerful call by the General Assembly yesterday for an immediate resolution of the conflict through peaceful means.

States must abide by international law and the core principles that protect human life and human dignity.

It is imperative that full access for the delivery of humanitarian assistance to civilians across the entire country be enabled.

I also strongly urge the full protection of civilians, as well as captured soldiers, as required under international humanitarian law.

It is a reality that, in armed conflict, there are incidents that violate the binding norms of international armed conflict. It is in all States' interest to ensure that those standards are met, and that there is due accountability where they are not.

I note that, at the international level, the International Court of Justice has been formally seized of proceedings connected to the conflict, and will begin hearings Monday on a request for provisional measures. In addition, the Prosecutor of the International Criminal Court has announced his decision to immediately proceed with active investigations on the situation in Ukraine, following referrals by a broad number of States. And this Council has before it an important proposal, building on established practice, to widen accountability avenues through an independent international commission of inquiry.

The Office has for eight years extensively and consistently monitored the human rights situation in Ukraine with particular focus on the regions of the Donbas engaged in conflict, as well as the Autonomous Republic of Crimea and the city of Sevastopol, which have been occupied by the Russian Federation since 2014. The 40 reports the Office has published are publicly accessible, and document violations of international human rights and humanitarian law by multiple actors over that period.

Our human rights monitors will continue to operate across the country to the full extent of their capacity. I believe this crisis demonstrates the vital importance of our objective monitoring and reporting in Ukraine—and in many other countries—and I take this opportunity to publicly thank the staff of the Office, particularly our colleagues in the field, for their dedication.

Excellencies,

As the Secretary-General has said, the UN Charter has always "stood firm on the side of peace, security, development, justice, international law and human rights—and time after time, when the international community has rallied together in solidarity, those values have prevailed."

It is vital that they prevail today, in Ukraine—and elsewhere.

My thoughts are with all people who suffer unbearable fear, pain and deprivation because of the senseless destruction of warfare.

Thank you, Mr. President.

---

As this Chapter is written, there are lingering questions that will only be answered as the armed conflict between Russia and Ukraine unfolds. Will the pressure of the international community make a difference to avoid a prolonged war? What role will international law and the existing global and regional organizations play, if any, in curbing suffering? Will sanctions and other non-military measures work to end the armed conflict, or will they mostly just work to bring hardship on innocent people in Russia and elsewhere? Will the international legal order ever be the same? What will happen to the over 41 million Ukrainians, many of whom are now or will be refugees? Will the strong spirit of resistance of Ukrainians wane at some point?

With the crises in Ukraine as a backdrop, this Chapter provides an overview of international human rights law specifically applicable to states of emergency, the international law of armed conflict, and international criminal law. Other crises or conflict situations will also be introduced to highlight issues arising in connection with these interrelated areas of international law.

## II.   *HUMAN RIGHTS IN STATES OF EMERGENCY, ARMED CONFLICTS, AND CIVIL STRIFE*

The government of Ukraine declared a state of emergency, initially to last 30 days, on February 23, 2022 due to the impending Russia invasion. Among the measures imposed were restrictions in the freedom of movement, curfews, the verification of identification and security inspections, among others. Additionally, the airspace was closed to all commercial flights. See Pavel Polityuk and Maria Tsvetkova, *Ukraine to Impose State of Emergency but No Martial Law Yet*, Reuters (Feb. 23, 2022), https://www.reuters.com/world/europe/ukraine-impose-state-emergency-says-top-security-official-2022-02-23/.

Such states of emergency are common during times of war or threat of war. Even if they do not rise to such a level of armed confrontation, situations of civil strife can be serious enough to cause governments to assume emergency powers or restrict the enjoyment of certain rights. When they do, there is always the possibility that human rights may be abused.

Much of this Chapter concerns the law of war, or international humanitarian law, applicable during international and non-international conflicts. The applicability of this body of law, however, depends on the existence of an "armed conflict." The International Committee of the Red Cross has proposed that the following definitions (distinguishing between international and non-international conflicts) "reflect the strong prevailing legal opinion":

> 1. International armed conflicts exist whenever there is *resort to armed force between two or more States.*
>
> 2. Non-international armed conflicts are *protracted armed confrontations* occurring between governmental armed forces and the forces of one or more armed groups, or between such groups arising on the territory of a State [party to the Geneva Conventions]. The armed confrontation must reach a *minimum* level of intensity and the parties involved in the conflict must show a *minimum of organisation.*

International Committee of the Red Cross, *How Is the Term "Armed Conflict" Defined in International Humanitarian Law?* (2008), at 5 (emphasis original), https://www .icrc.org/eng/assets/files/other/opinion-paper-armed-conflict.pdf.

International human rights law applies concurrently with relevant humanitarian law in times of both international armed conflict, such as the one now occurring between Russia and Ukraine, and non-international armed conflict. However, of the two areas of law *only* international human rights law applies during civil strife and states of emergency that governments may declare during situations in which tensions and disturbances within the state fall short of actual armed conflict. Therefore, human rights law is important not only for the additional protection it may afford during armed conflicts, but also for its role during internal disturbances or other emergencies.

## A.   The Bounds of Permissible Derogation of Rights

The drafters of the International Covenant on Civil and Political Rights and the European Convention on Human Rights, treaties to which Ukraine and Russia were parties at the outset of the war, were aware that human rights could not apply normally in all conceivable situations. Therefore, provisions of both treaties, as well as those of the American Convention on Human Rights, concede the necessity of permitting states to derogate from their normal human rights obligations in times of genuine public emergency. However, these provisions also seek to ensure that the most basic human rights remain respected by listing certain core rights from which no derogation is permitted, even in time of emergency.

Before reading on, please take a moment to examine Article 4 of the International Covenant on Civil and Political Rights, Article 15 of the European Convention on Human Rights, and Article 27 of the American Convention on Human Rights (in the Documentary Supplement). The following reading compares these derogation provisions of the three treaties.


Joan Fitzpatrick

## Human Rights in Crisis: The International System for Protecting Rights During States of Emergency

37-38, 52-66 (1994) (notes omitted)

In a United Nations survey of governments, the rights most often mentioned as having been the subject of derogations during emergencies were liberty and security of the person, liberty of movement, protection of privacy, freedom of expression and opinion, and the right of peaceful assembly. Many monitors have noted that excessive invasions of these and other rights have occurred during many emergencies, often in association with deprivations of non-derogable rights, such as the right to life and the prohibition on torture. But, as the International Commission of Jurists observed:

> Some writers have emphasized the effects of states of emergency on individual rights, particularly the right to be free from arbitrary deprivation of freedom and the right to a fair trial. This tends to create a somewhat false image of states of emergency, for one of their most fundamental characteristics is precisely the breadth of their impact on a society. They typically affect trade union rights, freedom of opinion, freedom of expression, freedom of association, the right of access to information and ideas, the right to an education, the right to participate in public affairs . . . not only individual rights but also collective rights and rights of peoples, such as the right to development and the right to self-determination.

The scope of these effects naturally results in a potential concern with states of emergency by all the monitoring bodies with an interest in any of this wide range of rights. These potentially extensive effects have also influenced the debate over the drafting of non-treaty-based substantive standards for government behavior during states of emergency. . . .

. . . Article 15 of the European Convention was drafted primarily during early 1950 with the benefit of almost three years of discussion by drafters of the Covenant on Civil and Political Rights within the United Nations. The derogation article of the European Convention served as a focal point for the debate between two alternate approaches to treaty drafting, which might be called "general enumeration" and "precise definition." The proponents of general enumeration favored drafting a document with positive definitions of rights and no exceptions or restrictions other than a single general limitations clause, similar to Article 29 of the Universal Declaration. The proponents of precise definition, on the other hand, wanted not only specific limitations clauses in many provisions defining particular rights but also a derogation article for emergencies, arguing that these clauses would actually prevent abusive suspension or denial of rights. During the final stages of the drafting process, the attraction of entrenching a list of non-derogable rights swayed a majority to favor inclusion of the derogation article.

Whereas the drafting of the Covenant on Civil and Political Rights dragged on until 1966, debate on the advisability and specific terms of a derogation article occurred during the relatively compressed period between 1947 and 1952. Article 4 became the focus of the division of opinion between the general-enumeration and precise-definition camps, as had Article 15 in the case of the European Convention. Another key division, leading to an awkward compromise, developed on the question whether the clause on non-derogable rights should include only those rights most important and central to human dignity and most at risk during typical emergencies, or should be expanded to include all rights that no reasonable government would need to limit substantially in any conceivable emergency.

The drafters of the American Convention on Human Rights, who began work in earnest in the 1960s, had the benefit of earlier-drafted human rights treaties as a model and began with an apparent consensus on the precise-definition approach. Moreover, the OAS had the benefit of a specific study of the problem of the protection of human rights during states of emergency, conducted by the Inter-American Commission on Human Rights. This study was undertaken with three aims, which sound rather familiar to anyone who has worked in this field: (1) to examine the history of states of siege in the Americas to see how human rights had been violated; (2) to determine if it would be possible to articulate general principles that could be binding on all countries in the region and that might be incorporated into the internal laws of those countries; and (3) to determine if there might be international organs that could control the juridical and practical regimes of states of siege. The special interest developed with the OAS on protecting human rights during states of emergency may help explain the rather different form the derogation article takes in the American Convention, as compared to those in the European Convention and the Covenant.

A brief comparison of the three derogation articles in the human rights treaties to the relevant portions of the major humanitarian law instruments reveals some interesting similarities and differences, as well as "lacunae," that have attracted ongoing efforts to formulate additional, more complete standards. . . .

## 1. Severity

While the threshold for a legitimate derogation under the three human rights treaties is largely similar, there are interesting variations in terminology. The Covenant offers the simplest formulation: a public emergency threatening the life of the nation. The European Convention in addition makes explicit reference to "war," but the inclusion of war as a ground for derogation is implicit in the Covenant. The text of Article 27 of the American Convention differs strikingly: "war, public danger, or other emergency that threatens the independence or security of a State Party." On the surface, the American Convention might appear to set a lower threshold than the two earlier treaties, but the drafting history of the provision suggests the contrary.

While "the life of the nation" is clearly intended to have a restrictive meaning, its scope is not self-evident. An emergency that threatens the life of the nation must imperil some fundamental element of statehood or survival of the population—for example, the functioning of a major constitutional organ, such as the judiciary or legislature, or the flow of vital supplies. Threats to a discrete segment of the national territory are particularly problematic, although a risk of detachment or loss of control over an important region, which would have a significant impact on central institutions and the general population, would appear to be sufficient. Though not arising out of political causes, certain natural disasters might meet the criteria for derogation.

War presents its own special problems. As a textual matter, it has been suggested that a reference to "war" in a derogation clause encompasses only external war and not internal armed conflict, though the latter would fit under the general term "emergency." Satisfaction of technical criteria for the existence of a state of war is neither necessary nor sufficient for derogation from human rights treaties, though it bears obvious importance with respect to the applicability of international humanitarian law. Derogation would not be permissible in the case of a war that did not threaten the "life of the nation" or "the independence or security" of the derogating state. For example, involvement in foreign hostilities that did not threaten attack or have a significant impact on domestic institutions, or the mere existence of a state of war without active hostilities, would not meet the threshold of severity to justify substantial restrictions on the domestic enjoyment of fundamental rights.

Despite the benefit of the high threshold set in the earlier two human rights treaties and significant experience within the region of problems arising out of states of emergency, initial proposed drafts of the American Convention would have set a very low threshold of severity for derogation. The version prepared by the Inter-American Council of Jurists (IACJ) permitted derogation in undefined "exceptional situations"; the proposals of Chile and Uruguay also adopted this formula, while making if explicit that each state could define such "exceptional situations" for itself. The IACHR [Inter-American Commission on Human Rights], with the benefit of the Martins study, criticized this terminology and adopted a resolution in 1968 stating that suspension of guarantees should be permissible only "when adopted in case of war or other serious public emergency threatening the life of the nation or the security of the State." . . .

During the Conference, the term "public danger" was inserted. Norris and Reiton explain that while this phrase may seem "strikingly broad," it was intended to cover "public calamity" that was "not necessarily a threat to internal or external security." They question the need for this provision, suggesting that the limitations clauses in particular treaty articles would be adequate to permit governments to deal with such natural disasters.

## 2.   Notification and Proclamation

For the present, it is sufficient to note that all three treaties require formal notification, though the details vary in three respects: (1) while the Covenant and the American Convention require that the other states parties be notified through the intermediary of the secretaries-general of the United Nations and the Organization of American States, respectively, the European Convention simply requires notification to the Secretary-General of the Council of Europe, without mentioning the states parties; (2) the Covenant and the American Convention require that this notice be supplied "immediately," while the European Convention is silent as to timing; and (3) the Covenant requires information concerning the provisions from which the state has derogated, the European Convention demands an explanation of the "measures which it has taken," and the American Convention requires information concerning "the provisions the application of which it has suspended, the reasons that gave rise to the suspension, and the date set for the termination of such suspension."

The Covenant is unique among the three in also requiring proclamation of a public emergency. The aim of this provision was to ensure that derogating states also complied with domestic legal requirements for states of emergency.

### 3.   GOOD FAITH MOTIVATION

This requirement is merely implicit in the derogation articles themselves, though it is express in certain other clauses of the three treaties, which provide that no state party may perform any act aimed at the destruction or undue limitation of rights and freedoms protected by the treaties. Thus, a state of emergency declared in order to destroy a democratic system of government would arguably be invalid.

### 4.   OTHER INTERNATIONAL OBLIGATIONS

Each of the three human rights treaties specifically forbids derogations that are inconsistent with the state's other obligations under international law. Chief among these obligations in relevance would be non-derogable rights in customary and conventional international humanitarian law, as well as the more restrictive or demanding provisions of other human rights treaties and customary human rights law (e.g., any human rights that are jus cogens and thus not subject to suspension or denial under any circumstances). An intriguing question is whether these other international obligations are thereby substantively incorporated into the derogation articles and thus subject to the treaty-based monitoring mechanisms.

### 5.   PROPORTIONALITY

Along with the threshold of severity, the principle of proportionality is the most important and yet most elusive of the substantive limits imposed on the privilege of derogation. The three treaties impose a similar standard—measures in derogation of treaty rights are permitted only to the extent "strictly required by the exigencies of the situation," although the American Convention also makes explicit the preeminently important requirement that such measures may be imposed only "for the period of time strictly required." The principle of proportionality embodied in the derogation clauses has its roots in the principle of necessity, which also forms one of the key pillars of international humanitarian law. The existence of competent, active, and informed organs of supervision, both at the national as well as at the international level, is vital if the proportionality principle is to have meaning in practice. . . . [B]oth logistical (access to information and ability to act promptly) and attitudinal (deference to national authorities, e.g., by extension of a "margin of appreciation") factors affect the functioning of the various treaty implementation organs.

## 6. Non-Discrimination

The Covenant and the American Convention include clauses specifying that derogation measures may not be imposed in a manner that discriminates on the grounds of race, color, sex, language, religion, or social origin. Three interesting issues are raised by these clauses: (1) why no similar provision exists in the European Convention, and whether its absence denotes a real substantive difference among the treaties; (2) what the term "discrimination" is intended to mean; and (3) whether this meaning is affected by the further inclusion of the qualifying term "solely" in the Covenant.

Article 15 of the European Convention is silent on the issue of discrimination in the application of emergency measures. Of course the European Convention, like the other two treaties, elsewhere prohibits discrimination on the grounds listed. But these various non-discrimination provisions outside the derogation articles are generally subject to derogation. The issue of discriminatory treatment of minorities in the application of emergency measures was touched on during the drafting of the European Convention, but it never achieved prominence in the discussions, and no concrete proposals for a non-discrimination clause were made. Nevertheless, arbitrary discrimination against disfavored groups of various types would be difficult to justify as being "strictly required." Thus, there may be no substantive difference between the silence of the European Convention and the explicit non-discrimination clauses of the other two treaties, if only arbitrary distinctions are outlawed by the latter. . . .

The idea that only arbitrary discrimination is outlawed by Article 4(1) is underlined by the deliberate inclusion of the word "solely" in its text. Even without this term, however, the reference to discrimination in Article 4 conveys the implication that only arbitrary and unjustifiable distinctions in the application of emergency measures would be outlawed. Thus, where an identifiable racial or religious group poses a distinct security threat not posed by other members of the community, presumably, emergency measures could be deliberately targeted against the group, despite the non-discrimination clause.

The absence of the word "solely" from the non-discrimination clause in Article 27(1) of the American Convention on Human Rights apparently has no intended significance. The word was included in the draft prepared by the IACHR but "disappeared from the final text, and the records of the conference provide no clue as to the reason." Thus, the three treaties would seem to impose a virtually identical non-discrimination obligation, despite disparate phraseology.

## 7. Non-Derogable Rights

The three treaties diverge dramatically with respect to defining absolute rights never subject to suspension. The process of defining non-derogable rights has been a markedly progressive one, with each later-drafted instrument expanding the core of non-derogable rights. The European Convention begins with just four, sparsely defined: the right to life, excepting deaths resulting from lawful acts of war (Article 2); the ban on torture or inhuman or degrading treatment or punishment (Article 3); the prohibition on slavery or servitude (Article 4(1)); and the prohibition on retroactive criminal penalties (Article 7) . . . .

EU : 4

*Covenant*

*American*

The drafters of the Covenant touched on the basic issue whether defining non-derogable rights should proceed from the perspective of identifying those rights most vital to human integrity and most likely at risk during abusive emergencies, or whether those rights should include all provisions whose suspension could not conceivably be necessary during times of public emergency. Article 4(2) appears to be an uneasy compromise between these two camps, especially with respect to the anomalous inclusion of the ban on imprisonment for contractual debt and the provision on freedom of religion, which has the distinction of being non-derogable, yet subject to limitation at all times.

The American Convention is somewhat more consistent in its approach and includes many rights that are not as central as the right to life or the protection against torture, but whose suspension would not be justifiable in an imaginable emergency. The 1966 study by IACHR member Martins favored the approach of listing rights subject to derogation and suggested making suspendable only the provisions on arbitrary detention and prompt notice of charges, interference with private life and correspondence, and prior restraint on publication; the rights of assembly, association, and movement would not need to be included because they would be subject to limitation even under ordinary circumstances, The IACHR draft presented to the Conference of San Jose did not follow this recommendation, but offered instead a list of non-derogable rights only slightly more expansive than that of the Covenant.

During Conference debate, the suggestion was made that the IACHR draft was too vague, and a working group was appointed to redraft the clause. Their product was a major transformation of the IACHR draft, adding not just numerical references to particular treaty articles that would be non-derogable, but deleting three rights and including five new rights. The handiwork of the working group was later modified by the addition to Article 27(2) of the key phrase "the judicial guarantees essential for the protection of such rights," which includes at least some aspects of the protections against arbitrary detention and for due process of law that would have been non-suspendable under the original IACHR proposal.

The gradual expansion of the list of non-derogable rights in the three major human rights treaties and, particularly, the recognition of a core of fundamental process rights for detainees in the American Convention have stimulated non-treaty-based efforts to articulate standards for protection of human rights during states of emergency. Efforts to refine and perfect these standards continue to the present. An awareness that, in some respects, the principles of international humanitarian law are more advanced than those of the human rights treaties has been an especially important factor in stimulating some of these standard-drafting efforts.

———————

The Human Rights Committee has issued two General Comments concerning derogations of rights affirmed in the International Covenant on Civil and Political Rights. While the first (1981) Comment did little more than paraphrase the

Covenant, the second (which replaced the first) offers a great deal more detail to guide states in their interpretation of Article 4. It also clarifies that even some rights not listed as non-derogable under Article 4(2) may nonetheless be protected from suspension. Below are extracts from General Comment 29.

## Human Rights Committee

## General Comment No. 29: States of Emergency (Article 4)

UN Doc. CCPR/C/21/Rev.1/Add.11 (2001) (notes omitted)

1. Article 4 of the Covenant is of paramount importance for the system of protection for human rights under the Covenant. On the one hand, it allows for a State party unilaterally to derogate temporarily from a part of its obligations under the Covenant. On the other hand, article 4 subjects both this very measure of derogation, as well as its material consequences, to a specific regime of safeguards. The restoration of a state of normalcy where full respect for the Covenant can again be secured must be the predominant objective of a State party derogating from the Covenant. In this general comment, replacing its General Comment No 5, adopted at the thirteenth session (1981), the Committee seeks to assist States parties to meet the requirements of article 4.

2. Measures derogating from the provisions of the Covenant must be of an exceptional and temporary nature. Before a State moves to invoke article 4, two fundamental conditions must be met: the situation must amount to a public emergency which threatens the life of the nation, and the State party must have officially proclaimed a state of emergency. The latter requirement is essential for the maintenance of the principles of legality and rule of law at times when they are most needed. When proclaiming a state of emergency with consequences that could entail derogation from any provision of the Covenant, States must act within their constitutional and other provisions of law that govern such proclamation and the exercise of emergency powers; it is the task of the Committee to monitor the laws in question with respect to whether they enable and secure compliance with article 4. In order that the Committee can perform its task, States parties to the Covenant should include in their reports submitted under article 40 sufficient and precise information about their law and practice in the field of emergency powers.

3. . . . Not every disturbance or catastrophe qualifies as a public emergency which threatens the life of the nation, as required by article 4, paragraph 1. During armed conflict, whether international or non-international, rules of international humanitarian law become applicable and help, in addition to the provisions in article 4 and article 5, paragraph 1, of the Covenant, to prevent the abuse of a State's emergency powers. The Covenant requires that even during an armed conflict measures derogating from the Covenant are allowed only if and to the extent that the situation constitutes a threat to the life of the nation. If States parties consider invoking article 4 in other situations than an armed conflict, they should carefully consider the justification and why such a measure is necessary and legitimate in the circumstances. On a number of occasions the Committee has expressed its concern

*2 conditions must be met* [handwritten annotation]

over States parties that appear to have derogated from rights protected by the Covenant, or whose domestic law appears to allow such derogation in situations not covered by article 4.1. . . .

6. The fact that some of the provisions of the Covenant have been listed in article 4 (paragraph 2), as not being subject to derogation does not mean that other articles in the Covenant may be subjected to derogations at will, even where a threat to the life of the nation exists. . . .

11. . . . States parties may in no circumstances invoke article 4 of the Covenant as justification for acting in violation of humanitarian law or peremptory norms of international law, for instance by taking hostages, by imposing collective punishments, through arbitrary deprivations of liberty or by deviating from fundamental principles of fair trial, including the presumption of innocence. . . .

13. In those provisions of the Covenant that are not listed in article 4, paragraph 2, there are elements that in the Committee's opinion cannot be made subject to lawful derogation under article 4. Some illustrative examples are presented below.

(a)  All persons deprived of their liberty shall be treated with humanity and with respect for the inherent dignity of the human person. Although this right, prescribed in article 10 of the Covenant, is not separately mentioned in the list of non-derogable rights in article 4, paragraph 2, the Committee believes that here the Covenant expresses a norm of general international law not subject to derogation. This is supported by the reference to the inherent dignity of the human person in the preamble to the Covenant and by the close connection between articles 7 and 10.

(b)  The prohibitions against taking of hostages, abductions or unacknowledged detention are not subject to derogation. The absolute nature of these prohibitions, even in times of emergency, is justified by their status as norms of general international law.

(c)  The Committee is of the opinion that the international protection of the rights of persons belonging to minorities includes elements that must be respected in all circumstances. This is reflected in the prohibition against genocide in international law, in the inclusion of a non-discrimination clause in article 4 itself (paragraph 1), as well as in the non-derogable nature of article 18.

(d)  As confirmed by the Rome Statute of the International Criminal Court, deportation or forcible transfer of population without grounds permitted under international law, in the form of forced displacement by expulsion or other coercive means from the area in which the persons concerned are lawfully present, constitutes a crime against humanity. The legitimate right to derogate from article 12 of the Covenant during a state of emergency can never be accepted as justifying such measures.

(e)  No declaration of a state of emergency made pursuant to article 4, paragraph 1, may be invoked as justification for a State party to engage itself, contrary to article 20, in propaganda for war, or in advocacy of national, racial or religious hatred that would constitute incitement to discrimination, hostility or violence. . . .

16. Safeguards related to derogation, as embodied in article 4 of the Covenant, are based on the principles of legality and the rule of law inherent in the Covenant as a whole. As certain elements of the right to a fair trial are explicitly guaranteed under international humanitarian law during armed conflict, the Committee finds no justification for derogation from these guarantees during other emergency situations. The Committee is of the opinion that the principles of legality and the rule of law require that fundamental requirements of fair trial must be respected during a state of emergency. Only a court of law may try and convict a person for a criminal offence. The presumption of innocence must be respected. In order to protect non-derogable rights, the right to take proceedings before a court to enable the court to decide without delay on the lawfulness of detention, must not be diminished by a State party's decision to derogate from the Covenant.

## Note: Non-Derogable Rights in the Russia-Ukraine Conflict

In the context of the Russia-Ukraine conflict, some of the rights included in relevant treaties could be derogated under the criteria discussed above, but only if those criteria could be met and the proper declarations of derogations were made. Other rights, however, such as the right to life, are not at all subject to derogation and in all cases must be protected at least for noncombatants. Finding threats to the right to life and other rights of the civilian population in Ukraine, the European Court of Human Rights granted interim measures (preliminary relief) against Russia in the early days of the conflict. On March 1, 2022, the Court ordered Russia in particular:

> to refrain from military attacks against civilians and civilian objects, including residential premises, emergency vehicles and other specially protected civilian objects such as schools and hospitals, and to ensure immediately the safety of the medical establishments, personnel and emergency vehicles within the territory under attack or siege by Russian troops.

*The European Court Grants Urgent Interim Measures in Application Concerning Russian Military Operations on Ukrainian Territory*, Euro. Ct. H. R. Press Release (Mar. 1, 2022). The interim measures were based on a determination that Russia's military actions gave rise to risk of serious violations of rights affirmed in the European Convention on Human Rights — to which both Russia and Ukraine at the time were parties — including the Convention's Article 2 (right to life), Article 3 (prohibition of torture and inhuman or degrading treatment or punishment), and Article 8 (respect for private and family life).

On what basis, however, can Russia be held responsible for violations of the European Convention on Human Rights outside its territory? Note that under Article 1 of the European Convention on Human Rights, state parties are to "secure within their jurisdiction the rights and freedoms [of] this Convention." The issue of extraterritorial application of obligations under the European Convention is taken up in Chapter 9. Compare the European approach with that advanced by the UN Human Rights Committee in interpreting the scope of extraterritorial obligations under the International Covenant on Civil and Political Rights: "In the light of [a similar jurisdictional provision], a State party has an obligation to respect and ensure the rights under article 6 [life] of all persons who are within its territory and all persons subject to its jurisdiction, that is, all persons over whose enjoyment of the right to life it exercises power or effective control." Human Rights Committee, *General Comment No. 36* (2018) on Article 6 (right to life) of the International Covenant on Civil and Political Rights, para. 63.

Soon after the pronouncement of the European Court, on March 16, 2022 Russia withdrew from the European Convention on Human Rights and the Council of Europe. It did so under threat of expulsion from the Council. The next day, the Council's Committee of Ministers declared Russia excluded from the Council. See Committee of Ministers, Council of Europe, Resolution CM/Res. (2022) on the cessation of the membership of the Russian Federation to the Council of Europe (Mar. 16, 2022). Was Russia's withdrawal from the European Convention and exclusion from the Council of Europe, an organization that was established to promote democracy and human rights in the region, a positive development?

### B.    States of Emergency and Counterterrorism

On the morning of September 11, 2001, the United States and the world watched in horror as two commercial airplanes, hijacked by terrorists, flew into the twin towers of the World Trade Center in New York City, and a third slammed into the Pentagon. A fourth plane crashed into a field in Pennsylvania. In all, nearly 3,000 people died. A week later, President George W. Bush addressed the nation at a joint session of Congress.

George W. Bush

## Address to a Joint Session of Congress and to the American People

Sept. 20, 2001, https://georgewbush-whitehouse.archives.gov/news/releases/2001/09/20010920-8.html

Mr. Speaker, Mr. President Pro Tempore, members of Congress, and fellow Americans:

In the normal course of events, Presidents come to this chamber to report on the state of the Union. Tonight, no such report is needed.

. . . . Tonight we are a country awakened to danger and called to defend freedom. Our grief has turned to anger, and anger to resolution. Whether we bring our enemies to justice, or bring justice to our enemies, justice will be done.

. . . . On September the 11th, enemies of freedom committed an act of war against our country. Americans have known wars — but for the past 136 years, they have been wars on foreign soil, except for one Sunday in 1941. Americans have known the casualties of war — but not at the center of a great city on a peaceful morning. Americans have known surprise attacks — but never before on thousands of civilians. All of this was brought upon us in a single day — and night fell on a different world, a world where freedom itself is under attack.

Americans have many questions tonight. Americans are asking: Who attacked our country? The evidence we have gathered all points to a collection of loosely affiliated terrorist organizations known as al Qaeda.

. . . . This group and its leader — a person named Osama bin Laden — are linked to many other organizations in different countries, including the Egyptian Islamic Jihad and the Islamic Movement of Uzbekistan. There are thousands of these terrorists in more than 60 countries. They are recruited from their own nations and neighborhoods and brought to camps in places like Afghanistan, where they are trained in the tactics of terror. They are sent back to their homes or sent to hide in countries around the world to plot evil and destruction.

. . . . Our war on terror begins with al Qaeda, but it does not end there. It will not end until every terrorist group of global reach has been found, stopped and defeated.

Americans are asking: How will we fight and win this war? We will direct every resource at our command — every means of diplomacy, every tool of intelligence, every instrument of law enforcement, every financial influence, and every necessary weapon of war — to the disruption and to the defeat of the global terror network. . . .

This war will not be like the war against Iraq a decade ago, with a decisive liberation of territory and a swift conclusion. It will not look like the air war above Kosovo two years ago, where no ground troops were used and not a single American was lost in combat.

Our response involves far more than instant retaliation and isolated strikes. Americans should not expect one battle, but a lengthy campaign, unlike any other we have ever seen. It may include dramatic strikes, visible on TV, and covert operations, secret even in success. We will starve terrorists of funding, turn them one against another, drive them from place to place, until there is no refuge or no rest. And we will pursue nations that provide aid or safe haven to terrorism. Every nation, in every region, now has a decision to make. Either you are with us, or you are with the terrorists. From this day forward, any nation that continues to harbor or support terrorism will be regarded by the United States as a hostile regime.

. . . . Great harm has been done to us. We have suffered great loss. And in our grief and anger we have found our mission and our moment. Freedom and fear are at war. The advance of human freedom — the great achievement of our time, and the great hope of every time — now depends on us. Our nation — this generation — will lift a dark threat of violence from our people and our future. We will rally the world to this cause by our efforts, by our courage. We will not tire, we will not falter, and we will not fail.

---

The "war on terror" proclaimed by the United States and other countries following the attacks on September 11, 2001 blurs the lines separating peace, civil strife, and armed conflict. In any event, President Bush declared a state of emergency in the days after the terrorist attacks on the US. See President of the United States of America, *Declaration of National Emergency by Reason of Certain Terrorist Attacks*, The White House (Sept. 14, 2001), https://georgewbush-whitehouse.archi ves.gov/news/releases/2001/09/20010914-4.html. The declaration allowed for presidential emergency powers over the active and reserve military forces. It did not involve any formal derogation of rights, although in fact legislative and administrative provisions, including through the Patriot Act, were implemented to curtail certain investigative and judicial processes involving terrorism.

The United Kingdom also declared a state of emergency in the immediate aftermath of the September 11 attacks. But unlike the United States, it did so with a specific derogation of the right against arbitrary detention (referring specifically to Article 5(4) of the European Convention on Human Rights), and it enacted legislation to authorize the detention without trial of non-British nationals who were suspected of planning terrorist acts within the UK. The legislation was challenged and eventually rejected by the House of Lords on the ground that it impermissibly discriminated against non-nationals. The applicants appealed aspects of the case to the European Court of Human Rights, as did the British government.

## A. and Others v. United Kingdom

> Eur. Ct. H.R. (GC), App. 3455/05, Judgment of Feb. 19, 2009 (most internal references deleted)

1. The case originated in an application (no. 3455/05) against the United Kingdom of Great Britain and Northern Ireland lodged with the Court under Article 34 of the Convention for the Protection of Human Rights and Fundamental Freedoms ("the Convention") by eleven non-United Kingdom nationals ("the applicants"), on 21 January 2005. The President acceded to the applicants' request not to have their names disclosed (Rule 47 § 3 of the Rules of Court). . . .

3. The applicants alleged, in particular, that they had been unlawfully detained, in breach of Articles 3 [freedom from torture], 5§1 [liberty of security of person] and 14 [prohibition of discrimination] of the Convention and that they had not had adequate remedies at their disposal, in breach of Articles 5 § 4 and 13 of the Convention. . . .

10. The Government contended that the events of 11 September 2001 demonstrated that international terrorists, notably those associated with al-Qaeda, had the intention and capacity to mount attacks against civilian targets on an unprecedented scale. Further, given the loose-knit, global structure of al-Qaeda and its affiliates and their fanaticism, ruthlessness and determination, it would be difficult for the State to prevent future attacks. In the Government's assessment, the United Kingdom, because of its close links with the United States of America, was a particular target. They considered that there was an emergency of a most serious kind threatening the life of the nation. Moreover, they considered that the threat came principally, but not exclusively, from a number of foreign nationals present in the United Kingdom, who were providing a support network for Islamist terrorist operations linked to al-Qaeda. A number of these foreign nationals could not be deported because of the risk that they would suffer treatment contrary to Article 3 of the Convention in their countries of origin.

11. On 11 November 2001 the Secretary of State made a derogation order under section 14 of the Human Rights Act 1998 ("the 1998 Act" in which he set out the terms of a proposed notification to the Secretary General of the Council of

Europe of a derogation pursuant to Article 15 of the Convention. On 18 December 2001 the Government lodged the derogation with the Secretary General of the Council of Europe. The derogation notice provided as follows:

> Public Emergency in the United Kingdom
>
> The terrorist attacks in New York, Washington, D.C. and Pennsylvania on 11 September 2001 resulted in several thousand deaths, including many British victims and others from seventy different countries. In its Resolutions 1368 (2001) and 1373 (2001), the United Nations Security Council recognised the attacks as a threat to international peace and security.
>
> The threat from international terrorism is a continuing one. In its Resolution 1373 (2001), the Security Council, acting under Chapter VII of the United Nations Charter, required all States to take measures to prevent the commission of terrorist attacks, including by denying safe haven to those who finance, plan, support or commit terrorist attacks.
>
> There exists a terrorist threat to the United Kingdom from persons suspected of involvement in international terrorism. In particular, there are foreign nationals present in the United Kingdom who are suspected of being concerned in the commission, preparation or instigation of acts of international terrorism, of being members of organisations or groups which are so concerned or of having links with members of such organisations or groups, and who are a threat to the national security of the United Kingdom.
>
> As a result, a public emergency, within the meaning of Article 15 §1 of the Convention, exists in the United Kingdom. . . .

12.  On 12 November 2001 the Anti-terrorism, Crime and Security Bill, containing the clauses which were to eventually become Part 4 of the Anti-terrorism, Crime and Security Act 2001 ("the 2001 Act"), was introduced into the House of Commons. The Bill was passed by Parliament in two weeks . . .

13.  The 2001 Act came into force on 4 December 2001. During the lifetime of the legislation, sixteen individuals, including the present eleven applicants, were certified under section 21 and detained. . . .

[The court considered and rejected claims that the applicants had been subjected to torture or inhuman treatment, in violation of Article 3 of the European Convention. It then proceeded to examine their detention without trial pursuant to the emergency legislation.]

## II.  Whether There Was a "Public Emergency Threatening the Life of the Nation"

178.  . . . While the United Nations Human Rights Committee has observed that measures derogating from the provisions of the International Covenant on Civil and Political Rights must be of "an exceptional and temporary nature" (see paragraph 110 above), the Court's case-law has never, to date, explicitly incorporated the requirement that the emergency be temporary, although the question of the proportionality of the response may be linked to the duration of the emergency.

Indeed, the cases cited above, relating to the security situation in Northern Ireland, demonstrate that it is possible for a "public emergency" within the meaning of Article 15 to continue for many years. The Court does not consider that derogating measures put in place in the immediate aftermath of the al-Qaeda attacks in the United States of America, and reviewed on an annual basis by Parliament, can be said to be invalid on the ground that they were not "temporary".

179.  The applicants' argument that the life of the nation was not threatened is principally founded on the dissenting opinion of Lord Hoffman [in the prior proceedings on the matter before the House of Lords, the United Kingdom's highest court at the time], who interpreted the words as requiring a threat to the organised life of the community which went beyond a threat of serious physical damage and loss of life. It had, in his view, to threaten "our institutions of government or our existence as a civil community." However, the Court has in previous cases been prepared to take into account a much broader range of factors in determining the nature and degree of the actual or imminent threat to the "nation" and has in the past concluded that emergency situations have existed even though the institutions of the State did not appear to be imperilled to the extent envisaged by Lord Hoffman.

180.  As previously stated, the national authorities enjoy a wide margin of appreciation under Article 15 in assessing whether the life of their nation is threatened by a public emergency. While it is striking that the United Kingdom was the only Convention State to have lodged a derogation in response to the danger from al-Qaeda, although other States were also the subject of threats, the Court accepts that it was for each Government, as the guardian of their own people's safety, to make their own assessment on the basis of the facts known to them. Weight must, therefore, attach to the judgment of the United Kingdom's executive and Parliament on this question. In addition, significant weight must be accorded to the views of the national courts, which were better placed to assess the evidence relating to the existence of an emergency.

181.  On this first question, the Court accordingly shares the view of the majority of the House of Lords that there was a public emergency threatening the life of the nation.

## III. Whether the Measures Were Strictly Required by the Exigencies of the Situation

182.  Article 15 provides that the State may take measures derogating from its obligations under the Convention only "to the extent strictly required by the exigencies of the situation." As previously stated, the Court considers that it should in principle follow the judgment of the House of Lords on the question of the proportionality of the applicants' detention, unless it can be shown that the national court misinterpreted the Convention or the Court's case-law or reached a conclusion which was manifestly unreasonable. It will consider the Government's challenges to the House of Lords' judgment against this background.

183.  The Government contended, firstly, that the majority of the House of Lords should have afforded a much wider margin of appreciation to the executive and Parliament to decide whether the applicants' detention was necessary.

A similar argument was advanced before the House of Lords, where the Attorney-General submitted that the assessment of what was needed to protect the public was a matter of political rather than judicial judgment.

184.   When the Court comes to consider a derogation under Article 15, it allows the national authorities a wide margin of appreciation to decide on the nature and scope of the derogating measures necessary to avert the emergency. Nonetheless, it is ultimately for the Court to rule whether the measures were "strictly required". In particular, where a derogating measure encroaches upon a fundamental Convention right, such as the right to liberty, the Court must be satisfied that it was a genuine response to the emergency situation, that it was fully justified by the special circumstances of the emergency and that adequate safeguards were provided against abuse. The doctrine of the margin of appreciation has always been meant as a tool to define relations between the domestic authorities and the Court. It cannot have the same application to the relations between the organs of State at the domestic level. As the House of Lords held, the question of proportionality is ultimately a judicial decision, particularly in a case such as the present where the applicants were deprived of their fundamental right to liberty over a long period of time. In any event, having regard to the careful way in which the House of Lords approached the issues, it cannot be said that inadequate weight was given to the views of the executive or of Parliament.

185.   The Government also submitted that the House of Lords erred in examining the legislation in the abstract rather than considering the applicants' concrete cases. However, in the Court's view, the approach under Article 15 is necessarily focused on the general situation pertaining in the country concerned, in the sense that the court—whether national or international—is required to examine the measures that have been adopted in derogation of the Convention rights in question and to weigh them against the nature of the threat to the nation posed by the emergency. Where, as here, the measures are found to be disproportionate to that threat and to be discriminatory in their effect, there is no need to go further and examine their application in the concrete case of each applicant.

186.   The Government's third ground of challenge to the House of Lords' decision was directed principally at the approach taken towards the comparison between non-national and national suspected terrorists. The Court, however, considers that the House of Lords was correct in holding that the impugned powers were not to be seen as immigration measures, where a distinction between nationals and non-nationals would be legitimate, but instead as concerned with national security. Part 4 of the 2001 Act was designed to avert a real and imminent threat of terrorist attack which, on the evidence, was posed by both nationals and non-nationals. The choice by the Government and Parliament of an immigration measure to address what was essentially a security issue had the result of failing adequately to address the problem, while imposing a disproportionate and discriminatory burden of indefinite detention on one group of suspected terrorists. As the House of Lords found, there was no significant difference in the potential adverse impact of detention without charge on a national or on a non-national who in practice could not leave the country because of fear of torture abroad.

187.   Finally, the Government advanced two arguments which the applicants claimed had not been relied on before the national courts. Certainly, there does

not appear to be any reference to them in the national courts' judgments or in the open material which has been put before the Court. In these circumstances, even assuming that the principle of subsidiarity does not prevent the Court from examining new grounds, it would require persuasive evidence in support of them.

188. The first of the allegedly new arguments was that it was legitimate for the State, in confining the measures to non-nationals, to take into account the sensitivities of the British Muslim population in order to reduce the chances of recruitment among them by extremists. However, the Government have not placed before the Court any evidence to suggest that British Muslims were significantly more likely to react negatively to the detention without charge of national rather than foreign Muslims reasonably suspected of links to al-Qaeda. In this respect the Court notes that the system of control orders, put in place by the Prevention of Terrorism Act 2005, does not discriminate between national and non-national suspects.

189. The second allegedly new ground relied on by the Government was that the State could better respond to the terrorist threat if it were able to detain its most serious source, namely non-nationals. In this connection, again the Court has not been provided with any evidence which could persuade it to overturn the conclusion of the House of Lords that the difference in treatment was unjustified. Indeed, the Court notes that the national courts, including SIAC, which saw both the open and the closed material, were not convinced that the threat from non-nationals was more serious than that from nationals.

190. In conclusion, therefore, the Court, like the House of Lords, and contrary to the Government's contention, finds that the derogating measures were disproportionate in that they discriminated unjustifiably between nationals and non-nationals. It follows that there has been a violation of Article 5 §1 in respect of the first, third, fifth, sixth, seventh, eighth, ninth, tenth and eleventh applicants. [The Court found that the right to due process under Article 5(4) had been violated as to four of the 11 applicants and that the right to compensation for deprivation of liberty under Article 5(5) had been violated as to nine of them.]

### Note: States of Emergency and Derogations during the COVID-19 Pandemic

The COVID-19 pandemic gripped the world between 2020 through at least part of 2022. By May 2, 2022, there were 6,236,836 documented deaths and 513,895,939 cases of infection worldwide, https://coronavirus.jhu.edu/map.html. During the pandemic, many countries enforced a range of measures to curb contagion, including the imposition of mask mandates; orders of strict social distancing; the closing of all schools and businesses; decrees to shelter in place; lockdowns; and curfews.

To support these measures, officials declared states of emergency, exception, or disaster on the ground of health, by means of decrees or regulations. In the Americas for example, Argentina, Bolivia, Chile, Colombia, Ecuador, El Salvador, Guatemala, Honduras, Panama, and Peru officially communicated to the Organization of the American States that they had suspended guarantees as per Article 27 of the American Convention. See *IACHR Calls on the OAS States to Ensure That the Emergency Measures They Adopt to Address the COVID-19 Pandemic Are Compatible with Their International Obligations*, Inter-Am. Comm'n H.R. Press Release No. 076/20 (April 17, 2020), https://www.oas.org/en/iachr/media_center/PReleases/2020/076.asp. Additionally, a number of Council of Europe member states notified the Secretary General of their decision to invoke Article 15 of the European Convention in the context of the pandemic, including Latvia, Romania, Armenia, the Republic of Moldova, Estonia, Georgia, Albania, North Macedonia, Serbia, and San Marino. See European Court of Human Rights, *Factsheet: Derogation in Times of Emergency* (2020), https://www.echr.coe.int/documents/fs_derogation_eng.pdf.

In response to these declarations and measures, a number of regional human rights bodies issued guidelines urging that all state restrictions of any human rights be justified by the principles of legality, necessity and proportionality, and that they have temporal limitations. The Council of Europe developed an important toolkit for its member states underscoring that all rights derogations would be assessed by the European Court of Human Rights in cases brought before it; that they needed to be formally communicated to the Secretary General of the Council of Europe; and that certain Convention rights never allow for derogations. The non-derogable rights include the rights to life (Article 2), the prohibition of torture and inhuman or degrading treatment or punishment (Article 3), the prohibition of slavery and servitude (Article 4.1), and the rule of "no punishment without law" (Article 7). The Council of Europe also stressed the principle of non-discrimination as critical when assessing whether derogating measures are "strictly required" under Article 15 of the European Convention and how these restrictions may negatively impact disadvantaged groups. See Council of Europe, *Respecting Democracy, Rule of Law, and Human Rights in the Framework of the COVID-19 Sanitary Crisis: A Toolkit for Member States, Council of Europe* (April 7, 2020), at 2-4, 7-8, https://rm.coe.int/sg-inf-2020-11-respecting-democracy-rule-of-law-and-human-rights-in-th/16809e1f40.

The Inter-American Commission on Human Rights, for its part, issued a resolution referring to COVID-19 as an "unprecedented global health emergency," stating in part the following.

> f. Measures taken by states . . . follow the *pro persona* principle, and the principles of proportionality, and temporary basis, and should have as their legitimate purpose strict compliance with comprehensive public health and protection objectives, such as proper, timely care for the population, over and above any other consideration or interests of a public or private nature.
>
> g. Even in the most extreme and exceptional cases in which suspension of certain rights may become necessary, international law lays down a series of requirements such as legality, necessity, proportionality and timeliness, which are designed to prevent measures such a state of emergency from being used illegally or in an abusive or disproportionate way, causing human rights violations or harm to the democratic system of government.

*Pandemic and Human Rights in the Americas*, Int.-Am. Comm'n H.R., Res. No. 1/2020, April 10, 2020, para. C.3(f) & (g) (emphasis original), https://www.oas.org/en/iachr/decisions/pdf/Resolution-1-20-en.pdf.

Additionally, the Inter-American Commission in its resolution urged states to pursue measures to curb infection rates guided by a human rights approach, considering the problems of intersectional discrimination and violence; the need for a gender perspective taking into account increased risks for women and girls; the interdependence of civil, political, economic, social, and cultural rights; and accountability measures when human rights violations take place. See id., paras. 49-53.

Even though the African Charter on Human and Peoples Rights does not provide for rights derogations, the African Commission on Human and Peoples Rights did issue a statement on February 28, 2020 urging states to ensure that COVID-19 restrictions were lawful, necessary, and proportional. See Press Statement of the African Commission on Human and Peoples' Rights on the Coronavirus (COVID-19 crisis) (Feb. 28, 2020), https://www.achpr.org/pressrelease/detail?id=480. The African Commission also urged African states to ensure that their efforts to prevent and contain the disease "include vulnerable and marginalized groups, are gender-sensitive, child-friendly and disability-sensitive." Id., Point 6.

## Comments and Questions

1. Ukraine became a party to the International Covenant on Civil and Political Rights on November 12, 1973. Review again Article 4 of the Covenant and General Comment 29 of the Human Rights Committee. Identify specific rights articulated in the Covenant that could justifiably be derogated due to Russia's aggression. Given the gravity and scope of Russia's invasion, consider steps that the Ukrainian government could take to ensure that the derogations are proportional, exceptional, and temporary in accordance with General Comment 29 of the Human Rights Committee.

2. Note that a number of the rights affirmed in the International Covenant on Civil and Political Rights are explicitly subject to limitations. For example, Article 18(3) of the Covenant states, "Freedom to manifest one's religion or beliefs may be subject only to such limitations as are prescribed by law and are necessary to protect public safety, order, health, or morals or the fundamental rights and freedoms of others." Do such limitation provisions substantially undermine the rights affirmed? How are such provisions different from the treaty provisions, such as Article 4 of the Covenant, allowing for derogations?

3. The concept of "margin of appreciation"—discussed further in Chapter 9 as a leading doctrine applied by the European Court of Human Rights—has frequently been criticized for granting too much discretion to states, precisely in situations when human rights are likely to be at risk. In *A and Others v. United Kingdom*, the European Court stated that "national authorities are in principle in a better position than the international judge to decide both on the presence of . . . an emergency and on the nature and scope of derogations necessary to avert it." What then justified the Court's decision effectively invalidating one of the UK's emergency measures?

4. Reread President Bush's address in the aftermath of the September 11, 2001, attacks, *supra* page 302. Did the "war on terror" constitute an "emergency which threatens the life of the nation" under Article 4 of the Covenant on Civil and Political Rights, to which the United States is a party? If so, why did the United

States not file a notice of derogation under Article 4(3)? Given the threat that's involved, is the war on terror an emergency that could continue indefinitely? If so, is that a reason for not notifying derogations of rights under the Covenant? The United States is not a party to the European Convention on Human Rights, but what is the significance in this regard of the European Court's comment, *supra* page 304, that its case law "has never . . . explicitly incorporated the requirement that the emergency be temporary" in order for there to be a valid derogation?

5. Following terrorist attacks in Paris in 2015 and 2016, France declared a state of emergency, which was extended several times. See Robert Zaretsky, *France's Perpetual State of Emergency*, Foreign Policy (July 16, 2016), http://foreignpolicy.com/2016/07/16/frances-perpetual-state-of-emergency/; *France's ermanent state of emergency*, Amnesty International (Sept. 26, 2017), https://www.amnesty.org/en/latest/news/2017/09/a-permanent-state-of-emergency-in-france/. Between the November 2015 attacks and August 2016, France conducted approximately 3,600 warrantless house searches, which resulted in only six terrorist-related inquiries; and many French Muslims and rights groups reportedly "regard the state of emergency as a public relations exercise rather than a genuine security policy." Ramzi Kassem, *France's Real State of Emergency*, The New York Times, Aug. 4, 2016. See also Adam Nossiter, *What Price to Keep France Safe? Perhaps a Nation's Core Values, Many Fear*, The New York Times, Aug. 5, 2016. Given the irregularity and unpredictable nature of the terrorist acts, are the standards applicable to derogations of rights well-suited to this context?

6. The African Charter on Human and Peoples' Rights contains no reference to derogation, which has been interpreted as meaning that no derogation is possible. Why do you think that the African system takes this different approach?

7. Reflect on the objections in the United States to Covid restrictions that appeared to be politically aligned. In what way can political alignments influence determinations of the validity of rights derogations? Are there genuinely objective international standards for assessing derogations that belie politics? As indicated earlier, a major concern of the regional human rights bodies in the Americas and Europe with rights derogations during the COVID-19 pandemic was the potential negative impact of these restrictions on the enjoyment of the right to non-discrimination. Is the prohibition of discrimination itself a non-derogable norm? Can you think of ways in which the COVID-19-related restrictions had harmful effects on disadvantaged groups and groups at risk of human rights violations?

## III. INTERNATIONAL HUMANITARIAN LAW

As already noted, international humanitarian law is a set of rules applicable to situations of armed conflict and warfare. Its main goal is to limit the negative effects of armed conflicts. This body of international law protects persons who are participating in hostilities and those who are considered civilians and are not participating in the armed conflict. International humanitarian law is also referred to as the law of war or the law of armed conflict.

Since soon after Russia-Ukraine conflict began, key international actors have repeatedly called for observance of international humanitarian law, especially in relation to the protection of civilians. The International Committee of the Red Cross (ICRC) quickly identified the situation to be an international armed conflict in which the Geneva Conventions are fully applicable. Accordingly, the ICRC called for fulfillment of the legal obligations to prevent civilian casualties, loss of life, and suffering. See Peter Kenny, *Red Cross Calls for Protecting Civilians in Russia-Ukraine War*, Anadolu Agency (Mar. 4, 2022), https://www.aa.com.tr/en/russia-ukraine-crisis/red-cross-calls-for-protecting-civilians-in-russia-ukraine-war/2523821.

Additionally, the UN Secretary General urged a ceasefire to facilitate civilian departure from conflict areas in Ukraine. See *Gutierres Appeals for Urgent Humanitarian Ceasefire in Ukraine*, United Nations News (Apr. 18, 2022), https://news.un.org/en/story/2022/04/1116412#:~:text=UN%20Secretary%2DGeneral%20Ant%C3%B3nio%20Guterres,his%20spokesperson%20said%20on%20Monday. As of mid-April 2022, the UN High Commissioner for Human Rights had recorded at least 4,890 civilian deaths since the beginning of the invasion. See United Nation High Commissioner for Human Rights, *Ukraine: Civilian Casualty Update 18 April 2022*, https://www.ohchr.org/en/news/2022/04/ukraine-civilian-casualty-update-18-april-2022.

After some historical background, this section discusses the Geneva Conventions of 1949 and relates them to the context of modern warfare and counter-terrorism efforts. The Geneva regime constitutes much of international humanitarian law as it exists today.

## A.　*Historical Roots of the Concern for Human Rights in the Law of War*

Beginning at least as far back as the Middle Ages (and probably a good deal farther), people have thought about the association between justice and warfare from two basic perspectives: from the standpoint of the decision to resort to war (*jus ad bellum*) and from the standpoint of the actual conduct of the war once hostilities have begun (*jus in bello*). By the nineteenth century, international lawyers had more or less abandoned questions of jus ad bellum — the justifications for war — to philosophers and theologians. Lawyers by then had accepted the view that states had the sovereign right to settle their differences by resorting to arms if they so chose. Instead, they concentrated their energies on the questions of *jus in bello*, on right and wrong ways of making war.

For a long time, little attention was accorded to the development of detailed rules for the protection of civilians. The assumption behind this inattention was that the best way of protecting civilians was by ensuring that the horrors of battle affected only the military forces of the participating states. Civilians were sought (and thought) to be protected by the sharp distinction drawn between them and combatants. If civilians could be kept out of the fray altogether, the reasoning ran, then a detailed body of rules for their protection would be unnecessary. On that supposition, the nineteenth-century pioneers of the modern law of war devoted their attention to developing rules for the humane treatment of soldiers — for the wounded and sick, for prisoners of war, for the banning of particularly inhumane types of weapons, and so forth. Only during the course of the twentieth century did it become apparent that it would be necessary for the law of war to broaden its concerns in certain important ways.


G.I.A.D. Draper

## Human Rights and the Law of War

12 Va. J. Int' L. 326, 326-33 (1972)

By the mid-19th century, the humanitarian movement gathered force under the impact of a number of diverse, social, moral, political, scientific, military and economic factors. Religious considerations, so decisive in the early formation of the old Law of Arms, the precursor of our Law of War, were not controlling in the infusion of humanitarian considerations into the 19th century Law of War. It will be recalled that the Red Cross emblem has no Christian connotation, but is merely the heraldic arms of the Swiss Confederation, a white cross on a red background, reversed, as tribute to the origin of the Red Cross movement in that country inspired by Henry Dunant. [The red crescent and red crystal also have been recognized as official emblems, the latter by Protocol additional to the Geneva Conventions of 12 August 1949, and relating to the Adoption of an Additional Distinctive Emblem (Protocol III), 8 December 2005.]

The ideas lying behind the first Geneva Convention of 1864, the direct outcome of the appalling suffering on the battlefield of Solferino in 1854, dealing exclusively with the treatment of the sick and wounded as well as medical services and installations, and the powerful de Martens preamble to the Hague Convention No. IV of 1907 on the Law of War on Land, both give us the climate of humanitarian sentiment of the second half of the 19th century. De Martens, a Lutheran by religion, and a German-Balt by parentage, was converted to the Russian Orthodox faith. He became Professor of International Law at the Imperial University of St. Petersburg and held a senior position in the Imperial Foreign Ministry as well as his Chair at the University. He published his main work, in two volumes entitled International Law of Civilized Nations, in 1882. He was one of the moving forces at the First Hague Peace Conference of 1899, convened by his master, Czar Nicholas II. In particular he was the draftsman of the famous Preamble to the Hague Convention No. IV, of 1907, which, in part, reads thus:

> Being animated by the desire to serve, even in this extreme case (the resort to armed conflict), the interest of humanity and the ever progressive needs of civilization; . . . Until a more complete code of the laws of war can be drawn up, the High Contracting Parties deem it expedient to declare that, in cases not covered by the rules adopted by them, the inhabitants and the belligerents remain under the protection and governance of the principles of the law of nations, derived from the usages established among civilized peoples, from the laws of humanity and from the dictates of the public conscience.

Given the alleged widespread atrocities by Russia during its invasion of
Ukraine, it is ironic that the Russian Czar Nicholas II was one of the early proponents of international humanitarian law. Nonetheless, the above formulation
from the 1907 Hague Convention is repeated and inserted into each of the
four Geneva Conventions of 1949, which today form much of the architecture
of international humanitarian law. The Geneva Conventions of 1949 are discussed below.

## B.   The Traditional Law of War: International Armed Conflict

### 1.   Protecting Combatants: The First Three 1949 Geneva Conventions

Several treaties and customary rules apply to the conduct of war and prohibit
certain types of weapons or methods of warfare. See, e.g., Convention on the Prohibition of the Development, Production, Stockpiling and Use of Chemical Weapons
and on their Destruction (1993); Convention on Prohibitions or Restrictions on
the Use of Certain Conventional Weapons Which May Be Deemed to Be Excessively
Injurious or Have Indiscriminate Effects (1980, amended 2001). Our focus here,
by contrast, is on the significant part of the body of international humanitarian law
applying to those not or no longer participating in an armed conflict. This latter
part of international humanitarian law is codified in the four Geneva Conventions
of 1949, which have been widely ratified globally. The four Geneva Conventions
were adopted in 1949, three years after the completion of the Nuremberg Trials.
Three of these Conventions replaced earlier instruments: Convention (I) for the
Amelioration of the Condition of the Wounded and Sick in Armed Forces in the
Field; Convention (II) for the Amelioration of the Condition of Wounded, Sick
and Shipwrecked Members of Armed Forces at Sea; and Convention (III) Relative
to the Treatment of Prisoners of War.

The following extract of the Third Geneva Convention reflects the tenor of
all first three Conventions, which protect combatants no longer participating in
armed conflict. An important provision of the Third Convention is Article 4, which
defines who qualifies as a combatant that if captured by the enemy is to be treated
as a prisoner of war with the protections of the Convention. Article 4 is also relevant to defining, by negative implication, who is a civilian and entitled to protection as such, as we shall see further below.

## (Third) Geneva Convention Relative to the Treatment of Prisoners of War

75 U.N.T.S. 135 (Aug. 12, 1949)

ARTICLE 4

Prisoners of war, in the sense of the present Convention, are persons belonging to one of the following categories, who have fallen into the power of the enemy:

(1) Members of the armed forces of a Party to the conflict as well as members of militias or volunteer corps forming part of such armed forces.

(2) Members of other militias and members of other volunteer corps, including those of organized resistance movements, belonging to a Party to the conflict and operating in or outside their own territory, even if this territory is occupied, provided that such militias or volunteer corps, including such organized resistance movements, fulfil the following conditions:

(a) that of being commanded by a person responsible for his subordinates;

(b) that of having a fixed distinctive sign recognizable at a distance;

(c) that of carrying arms openly;

(d) that of conducting their operations in accordance with the laws and customs of war.

(3) Members of regular armed forces who profess allegiance to a government or an authority not recognized by the Detaining Power.

(4) Persons who accompany the armed forces without actually being members thereof, such as civilian members of military aircraft crews, war correspondents, supply contractors, members of labour units or of services responsible for the welfare of the armed forces, provided that they have received authorization from the armed forces which they accompany, who shall provide them for that purpose with an identity card similar to the annexed model.

(5) Members of crews, including masters, pilots and apprentices, of the merchant marine and the crews of civil aircraft of the Parties to the conflict, who do not benefit by more favourable treatment under any other provisions of international law.

(6) Inhabitants of a non-occupied territory, who on the approach of the enemy spontaneously take up arms to resist the invading forces, without having had time to form themselves into regular armed units, provided they carry arms openly and respect the laws and customs of war.

B. [Others who have participated in the war and are subject to internment in specified circumstances.]

C. This Article shall in no way affect the status of medical personnel and chaplains as provided for in Article 33 of the present Convention.

ARTICLE 5

The present Convention shall apply to the persons referred to in Article 4 from the time they fall into the power of the enemy and until their final release and repatriation.

Should any doubt arise as to whether persons, having committed a belligerent act and having fallen into the hands of the enemy, belong to any of the categories enumerated in Article 4, such persons shall enjoy the protection of the present Convention until such time as their status has been determined by a competent tribunal.

REQUIREMENT OF HUMANE TREATMENT

ARTICLE 13

Prisoners of war must at all times be humanely treated. Any unlawful act or omission by the Detaining Power causing death or seriously endangering the health of a prisoner of war in its custody is prohibited, and will be regarded as a serious breach of the present Convention. In particular, no prisoner of war may be subjected to physical mutilation or to medical or scientific experiments of any kind which are not justified by the medical, dental or hospital treatment of the prisoner concerned and carried out in his interest.

Likewise, prisoners of war must at all times be protected, particularly against acts of violence or intimidation and against insults and public curiosity.

Measures of reprisal against prisoners of war are prohibited.

ARTICLE 14

Prisoners of war are entitled in all circumstances to respect for their persons and their honour.

Women shall be treated with all the regard due to their sex and shall in all cases benefit by treatment as favorable as that granted to men.

Prisoners of war shall retain the full civil capacity which they enjoyed at the time of their capture. The Detaining Power may not restrict the exercise, either within or without its own territory, of the rights such capacity confers except in so far as the captivity requires.

## 2.   Protecting Civilians: The Fourth Geneva Convention

The Fourth Geneva Convention was the first attempt to codify what the Nuremberg Tribunal referred to as "crimes against humanity." It applies to civilian persons in occupied territories, for example German occupied France in in World War II. Thus, Geneva IV does not directly apply, for example, to the many civilians in unoccupied territory in Ukraine who have directly experienced the effects of the war. The following seven articles include some of the Convention's most important provisions.

## (Fourth) Geneva Convention on the Protection of Civilian Persons in Time of War

75 U.N.T.S. 287 (Aug. 12, 1949)

ARTICLE 4

Persons protected by the Convention are those who, at a given moment and in any manner whatsoever, find themselves, in case of a conflict or occupation, in the hands of a Party to the conflict or Occupying Power of which they are not nationals.

Nationals of a State which is not bound by the Convention are not protected by it. Nationals of a neutral State who find themselves in the territory of a belligerent

State, and nationals of a co-belligerent State, shall not be regarded as protected persons while the State of which they are nationals has normal diplomatic representation in the State in whose hands they are. . . .

Persons protected by . . . [any of the first three Geneva Conventions] shall not be considered as protected persons within the meaning of the present Convention.

ARTICLE 5

Where in the territory of a Party to the conflict, the latter is satisfied that an individual protected person is definitely suspected of or engaged in activities hostile to the security of the State, such individual person shall not be entitled to claim such rights and privileges under the present Convention as would, if exercised in the favor of such individual person, be prejudicial to the security of such State.

Where in occupied territory an individual protected person is detained as a spy or saboteur, or as a person under definite suspicion of activity hostile to the security of the Occupying Power, such person shall, in those cases where absolute military security so requires, be regarded as having forfeited rights of communication under the present Convention.

In each case, such persons shall nevertheless be treated with humanity and, in case of trial, shall not be deprived of the rights of fair and regular trial prescribed by the present Convention. They shall also be granted the full rights and privileges of a protected person under the present Convention at the earliest date consistent with the security of the State or Occupying Power, as the case may be.

ARTICLE 27

Protected persons are entitled, in all circumstances, to respect for their persons, their honour, their family rights, their religious convictions and practices, and their manners and customs. They shall at all times be humanely treated, and shall be protected especially against all acts of violence or threats thereof and against insults and public curiosity.

Women shall be especially protected against any attack on their honour, in particular against rape, enforced prostitution, or any form of indecent assault.

Without prejudice to the provisions relating to their state of health, age and sex, all protected persons shall be treated with the same consideration by the Party to the conflict in whose power they are, without any adverse distinction based, in particular, on race, religion or political opinion.

However, the Parties to the conflict may take such measures of control and security in regard to protected persons as may be necessary as a result of the war.

ARTICLE 31

No physical or moral coercion shall be exercised against protected persons, in particular to obtain information from them or from third parties.

ARTICLE 32

The High Contracting Parties specifically agree that each of them is prohibited from taking any measure of such a character as to cause the physical suffering or extermination of protected persons in their hands. This prohibition applies not only to murder, torture, corporal punishment, mutilation and medical or scientific experiments not necessitated by the medical treatment of a protected person, but also to any other measures of brutality whether applied by civilian or military agents.

ARTICLE 33

No protected person may be punished for an offence he or she has not personally committed. Collective penalties and likewise all measures of intimidation or of terrorism are prohibited.
    Pillage is prohibited.
    Reprisals against protected persons and their property are prohibited.

ARTICLE 34

The taking of hostages is prohibited.

———————

The rest of the Fourth Geneva Convention may be summarized briefly. It encourages agreements between parties to a conflict for the protection of wounded and sick civilians, with particular provision for expectant mothers (Article 14). It encourages opposing armed forces to reach local agreements for the evacuation of civilian populations from zones of combat (Article 17). It contains provisions for the protection of civilian hospitals from attack (Articles 18 to 20) and for the protection of civilian evacuees (Articles 21 and 22). Free passage is to be guaranteed for hospital and medical stores for civilians, together with articles for religious worship (Article 23). There is a specific provision for the care of orphans (Article 24). Communication between family members is to be guaranteed (Article 25), and armed forces are to take steps to assist with the reunion of dispersed families (Article 25). Articles 35 to 46 concern aliens found in the territory of parties to an armed conflict. The administration of occupied territories is covered by Articles 47 to 78. Finally, provisions relating to civilian internees are contained in Articles 79 to 135.
    The 196 states parties to the Convention (including the United States, which became a party in 1955) are under a general obligation, set forth in Article 1, "to ensure respect for the present Convention in all circumstances." More specifically, states parties are obligated, under Article 146, to enact legislation providing "effective penal sanctions" for persons committing certain specified "grave breaches" of the Convention. Article 147 identifies these grave breaches as:

> willful killing, torture or inhuman treatment, including biological experiments, willfully causing great suffering or serious bodily injury to body or health, unlawful deportation or transfer or unlawful confinement of a protected person, compelling a protected person to serve in the forces of a hostile Power, or willfully depriving a protected person of the rights of

fair and regular trial . . . taking of hostages and extensive destruction and appropriation of property, not justified by military necessity and carried out unlawfully and wantonly.

The United States has implemented this obligation through the Uniform Code of Military Justice.

### 3. Subsequent Developments: Protocol I

During the early 1970s, the International Committee of the Red Cross (ICRC) convened a diplomatic conference to reaffirm and develop the international humanitarian law applicable in armed conflicts. The result, in 1977, was the adoption of two protocols to the four Geneva Conventions. Protocol I is concerned with international armed conflicts, the traditional subject matter of the law of war, but it defines such conflicts to include those "in which peoples are fighting against colonial domination and alien occupation and against racial regimes in the exercise of their right of self-determination"—that is, wars of "national liberation." Protocol Additional to the Geneva Conventions of 12 August 1949, and Relating to the Protection of Victims of International Armed Conflicts (Protocol I), Art. 1(4), 1125 U.N.T.S. 3. Protocol II, which will be taken up in the next sub-section, is concerned with internal or non-international armed conflicts (i.e., conflicts that take place within the territory of a single country) and thus breaks even more new ground. See Protocol Additional to the Geneva Conventions of 12 August 1949, and Relating to the Protection of Victims of Non-International Armed Conflicts (Protocol II), 1125 U.N.T.S. 609.

Part IV of Protocol I (Articles 48 to 79) deals with the protection of civilians and contains much of interest. In contrast to the Fourth Geneva Convention, Protocol I's protections for civilians are not limited to those in "occupied territories." Article 48 sets forth a "basic rule" that the parties to the conflict "shall at all times distinguish between the civilian population and combatants and between civilian objects and military objectives and accordingly shall direct their operations only against military objectives." However another provision, objected to by the United States and others in connection with the wars of "national liberation" provision, states: "recognizing that there are situations in armed conflicts where, owing to the nature of the hostilities an armed combatant cannot so distinguish himself, he shall retain his status as a combatant, provided that, in such situations, he carries his arms openly" (Art. 43.3).

In any case, many of the substantive norms set forth in Protocol I, including those found in Articles 51 and 75, quoted immediately below, are now recognized to constitute norms of customary international law. For example, the "fundamental guarantees" in Article 75 were recognized as forming part of customary international law by a State Department Deputy Legal Adviser. See Michael J. Matheson, *The United States Position on the Relation of Customary International Law to the 1977 Protocols Additional to the 1949 Geneva Conventions*, 2 AM. U. J. Int'l L. & POL'Y 419 (1987). See also Jean-Marie Henckaerts and Louise Doswald-Beck, *Customary International Humanitarian Law, Volume I: Rules* 299-491 (2005).

## Protocol Additional to the Geneva Conventions of August 12, 1949, and Relating to the Protection of Victims of International Armed Conflicts (Protocol I)

1125 U.N.T.S. 3 (Dec. 12, 1977)

### ARTICLE 50 — DEFINITION OF CIVILIANS AND CIVILIAN POPULATION

1. A civilian is any person who does not belong to one of the categories of persons referred to in Article 4 (A) (1), (2), (3) and (6) of the Third Convention [included above] and in Article 43 [defining armed forces as subject to an organized chain of command] of this Protocol. In case of doubt whether a person is a civilian, that person shall be considered to be a civilian.

### ARTICLE 51 — PROTECTION OF THE CIVILIAN POPULATION

1. The civilian population and individual civilians shall enjoy general protection against dangers arising from military operations. To give effect to this protection, the following rules, which are additional to other applicable rules of international law, shall be observed in all circumstances.
2. The civilian population as such, as well as individual civilians, shall not be the object of attack. Acts or threats of violence the primary purpose of which is to spread terror among the civilian population are prohibited.
3. Civilians shall enjoy the protection afforded by this Section, unless and for such time as they take a direct part in hostilities.
4. Indiscriminate attacks are prohibited. Indiscriminate attacks are:

  (a)  those which are not directed at a specific military objective;

  (b)  those which employ a method or means of combat which cannot be directed at a specific military's objective; or

  (c)  those which employ a method or means of combat the effects of which cannot be limited as required by this Protocol; and consequently, in each such case, are of a nature to strike military objectives amid civilians or civilian objects without distinction.

5. Among others, the following types of attacks are to be considered as indiscriminate:

  (a)  an attack by bombardment by any methods or means which treats as a single military objective a number of clearly separated and distinct military objectives located in a city, town, village or other area containing a similar concentration of civilians or civilian objects; and

  (b)  an attack which may be expected to cause incidental loss of civilian life, injury to civilians, damage to civilian objects, or a combination thereof, which would be excessive in relation to the concrete and direct military advantage anticipated.

6. Attacks against the civilian population or civilians by way of reprisals are prohibited.
7. The presence or movements of the civilian population or individual civilians shall not be used to render certain points or areas immune from military

operations, in particular in attempts to shield military objectives from attacks or to shield, favour or impede military operations. The Parties to the conflict shall not direct the movement of the civilian population or individual civilians in order to attempt to shield military objectives from attacks or to shield military operations.

8. Any violation of these prohibitions shall not release the Parties to the conflict from their legal obligations with respect to the civilian population and civilians, including the obligations to take the precautionary measures provided for in Article 57.

ARTICLE 75 — FUNDAMENTAL GUARANTEES

1. In so far as they are affected by a situation referred to in Article I of this Protocol, persons who are in the power of a Party to the conflict and who do not benefit from more favourable treatment under the Conventions or under this Protocol shall be treated humanely in all circumstances and shall enjoy, as a minimum, the protection provided by this Article without any adverse distinction based upon race, colour, sex, language, religion or belief, political or other opinion, national or social origin, wealth, birth or other status, or on any other similar criteria. Each Party shall respect the person, honour, convictions and religious practice of all such persons.

2. The following acts are and shall remain prohibited at any time and in any place whatsoever, whether committed by civilian or by military agents:

(a) violence to the life, health, or physical or mental well-being of persons, in particular:
(i) murder;
(ii) torture of all kinds, whether physical or mental;
(iii) corporal punishment; and
(iv) mutilation;
(b) outrages upon personal dignity, in particular humiliating and degrading treatment, enforced prostitution and any form of indecent assault;
(c) the taking of hostages;
(d) collective punishments; and
(e) threats to commit any of the foregoing acts.

3. Any person arrested, detained or interned for actions related to the armed conflict shall be informed promptly, in a language he understands, of the reasons why these measures have been taken. Except in cases of arrest or detention for penal offences, such persons shall be released with the minimum delay possible and in any event as soon as the circumstances justifying the arrest, detention or internment have ceased to exist.

4. No sentence may be passed and no penalty may be executed on a person found guilty of a penal offence related to the armed conflict except pursuant to a conviction pronounced by an impartial and regularly constituted court respecting the generally recognized principles of regular judicial procedure.

Protocol I has been widely ratified (there were 174 state parties as of early 2022). However, as of this writing, no state has invoked the services of the International Fact-Finding Commission, provided for in Article 90 and established in 1991, although more than 75 states have accepted its competence to inquire into alleged grave breaches of the 1949 Conventions or Protocol I and to offer its good offices to promote respect for humanitarian norms.

President Carter signed Protocol I in 1977, but the official US position since then appears to be that set forth by President Reagan in 1987 when he referred to Protocol I as:

> fundamentally and irreconcilably flawed. . . . It would give special status to "wars of national liberation," an ill-defined concept expressed in vague, subjective, politicized terminology. Another provision would grant combatant status to irregular forces even if they do not satisfy the traditional requirements to distinguish themselves from the civilian population and otherwise comply with the laws of war. This would endanger civilians among whom terrorists and other irregulars attempt to conceal themselves.

Message from the President Transmitting Protocol II Additional to the 1949 Geneva Conventions, and Relating to the Protection of Victims of Non-international Armed Conflicts, S. Treaty Doc. No. 2, 100th Cong, 1st Sess. III-V (1987).

### Note: War Crimes

Grave breaches of the Geneva Conventions and other rules of war constitute war crimes. See *infra*, Section V of this Chapter. Allegations of war crimes began to increase after the first several days of Russia's invasion of Ukraine. These allegations were based on what appeared to be indiscriminate attacks on civilians, hospitals, kindergartens, ambulances, residential areas, airports, train stations, and nuclear and other power facilities. Also, mass graves and civilian bodies lying on streets were discovered in several Ukrainian towns. See Vasco Cotovio, Frederik Pleitgen, Byron Blunt and Daria Markina, *The Horrors of Putin's Invasion of Ukraine are Increasing Coming to Light*, CNN (Apr. 4, 2022), https://www.cnn.com/2022/04/03/europe/ukraine-bucha-horrors/index.html. There has been ever more documentation of the use of rape as a weapon of war and as a strategy to terrorize Ukrainian civilians. See Bethan McKernan, *Rape as a Weapon: Huge Scale of Sexual Violence Inflicted in Ukraine Emerges*, The Guardian (Apr. 4, 2022), https://www.theguardian.com/world/2022/apr/03/all-wars-are-like-this-used-as-a-weapon-of-war-in-ukraine. As will be discussed in the following section, the International Criminal Court has opened an inquiry into serious crimes that allegedly have been committed in the context of the Russia-Ukraine war. For detailed accounts of events that could constitute war crimes committed in the context of the war, see David L. Stern et al. *Civilian Toll Mounts in Ukraine as World Leaders Raise Question of War Crimes*, The Washington Post, Mar. 6, 2022, https://www.washingtonpost.com/world/2022/03/06/russia-ukraine-war-news-putin-live-updates/; *Ukraine, Countries Request ICC War Crimes Inquiry*, Human Rights Watch (Mar. 2, 2022), https://www.hrw.org/news/2022/03/02/ukraine-countries-request-icc-war-crimes-inquiry#.

Regrettably, war crimes have occurred since rules of war were hatched. Even by the standards then applicable, the United States committed war crimes against Native people during many of the military campaigns against them through much of the country's history. A case in point is the brutal massacre of hundreds of defenseless Cheyenne and Arapaho people, most of them women and children, by a nearly 700-man force of the US Cavalry in southeastern Colorado Territory in 1864.

Perhaps the most infamous US war crime committed since World War II was the massacre of at least 128 (and probably many more) Vietnamese civilians at the village of My Lai, Vietnam, in March 1968. The only person convicted for the killings was Lieutenant William Calley, who was court-martialed and initially sentenced to imprisonment for life; in fact, he served only three and a half years in prison. A Gallup Poll conducted at the time, reported that 79 percent of the American public disagreed with the verdict. An army helicopter pilot, Hugh C. Thompson, Jr., who tried to stop the killing and saved perhaps a dozen Vietnamese, was awarded the Soldier's Medal — 28 years after the fact, in 1996. In 2009, Calley made his first public apology for his role in the My Lai massacre, at a Kiwanis Club meeting in Columbus, Georgia. The Calley case is discussed extensively in the third edition of this book, Richard B. Lillich and Hurst Hannum, *International Human Rights: Problems of Law, Policy, and Practice* 839-43, 859-75 (3d ed. 1995).

Allegations of war crimes have been a fixture of armed conflicts taking place in the past 40 years. During the 1991 or First Gulf War, which followed Iraq's invasion of Kuwait, most public condemnation was directed against the political and military leaders of the operations rather than individual soldiers — perhaps because the ground phase of the war lasted only 100 hours. However, no prosecutions appear to have been pressed by any side to the conflict, and there was no effort to establish a war crimes tribunal, despite early expressions of interest. Most of the alleged crimes were committed by Iraqi forces and might include the uncontroverted fact of the invasion of Kuwait itself (perhaps more accurately termed a crime against peace) and the firing of Scud missiles at cities in Israel, a state not otherwise involved in the conflict. Other allegations concerned the taking of diplomatic hostages and the treatment of Kuwaitis during the Iraqi occupation, including killing, rape, looting, and destruction of property. See Paul W. Kahn, *Lessons for International Law from the Gulf War*, 45 STAN. L. REV. 425 (1993); James S. Robbins, *War Crimes: The Case of Iraq*, 18 FLETCHER F. WORLD AFF. 45 (No. 2, 1994).

The "coalition forces," led by the United States, were accused of targeting civilian installations (including Iraq's water supply, a "munitions" factory that purportedly produced milk powder, and an air raid shelter in which hundreds of civilians were killed) and of unnecessarily killing Iraqi soldiers at the end of the brief ground war. The United States also was accused of having encouraged Saddam Hussein's attack on Kuwait and thus sharing guilt for the invasion itself. See Ramsey Clark, *Complaint to the Commission of Inquiry for the International War Crimes Tribunal*, 48 GUILD PRAC. 33 (1991); John G. Heidenrich, *The Gulf War: How Many Iraqis Died?*, 90 FOREIGN POLICY 108 (1993); Al Kamen, *Iraqi Factory's Product: Germ Warfare or Milk?*, The Washington Post, Feb. 8, 1991, at A1; Charles M. Madigan, *In War, the Bottom Line Is Death*, Chicago Tribune, Feb. 15, 1991, at 1.

The Second Gulf War, initiated by the United States and another "coalition of the willing" in 2003 against the Saddam Hussein regime in Iraq, also gave rise to serious allegations of war crimes arising from unjustified killing of civilians, in addition to the ill treatment at Abu Ghraib discussed *infra* section IV.A. Prosecutions for war crimes and crimes against humanity did occur, but they were not related to actions that took place during the First or the Second Gulf War. Instead, Saddam Hussein and other members of his government were prosecuted before Iraq's own Special Tribunal for Crimes Against Humanity, including for the use of chemical weapons and killings of Kurdish civilians during a military action in Northern Iraq. Saddam Hussein was condemned to death in 2006 and executed by hanging on December 30, 2006. Several human rights groups called the prosecution and conviction a "show trial." What does this suggest about accountability for war crimes?

Recent international efforts concerning Iraq have focused on documenting and holding accountable the Islamic State in Iraq and the Levant (ISIL/Da'esh) — a terrorist group — for international crimes. These have included the documented systemic rape of women from the Yazidi ethnic and religious minority, including Nadia Murad, who won the Nobel Peace Prize in 2018. See *"We Now Stand at a Turning Point" with Unexpected Hope, Head of United Nations Team Investigating ISIL/ Da'esh Atrocity Crimes in Iraq Tells Security Council*, UN Security Council Press Release (Dec. 2, 2021), https://www.un.org/press/en/2021/sc14715.doc.htm;, *Nadia Murad: Facts, the Nobel Peace Prize 2018*, The Nobel Prize https://www.nobelprize .org/prizes/peace/2018/murad/facts/ (last visited April 28, 2022).

There were also serious allegations of war crimes during the US invasion of Afghanistan related to presumed US complicity in the deaths of a large number of Taliban prisoners after the battle for Kunduz in November 2002. See, e.g., Kate Connolly and Rory McCarthy, *New Film Accuses U.S. of War Crimes*, The Guardian (June 13, 2002), https://www.theguardian.com/world/2002/jun/13/afghanistan.warcrimes. Bombing raids and attacks on mistaken targets continued to kill Afghan civilians. After a 20-year war, the United States formally completed its withdrawal from Afghanistan on August 30, 2021, and the Taliban shortly took over the country. See Michael D. Shear and Jim Tankersley, *Biden Defends Afghan Pullout and Declares an End to Nation-Building*, The New York Times, Aug. 31 2021 (updated Oct. 7, 2021) https://www.nytimes .com/2021/08/31/us/politics/biden-defends-afghanistan-withdrawal.html.

The International Criminal Court's Chief Prosecutor, Karim Khan filed a submission to the ICC Pre-Trial Chamber on September 28, 2021 requesting authorization to resume the investigation of international crimes that are taking place in Afghanistan. The investigation will focus on a diversity of international crimes committed by the Taliban and the Islamic State, including attacks on civilians, extrajudicial executions, violence against women and girls, and crimes against children. For more reading, see *Statement of the Prosecutor of the International Criminal Court, Karim A. A. Khan QC, following the application for an expedited order under article 18(2) seeking authorization to resume investigations in the Situation in Afghanistan*, International Criminal Court (Sept. 27, 2021), https://www.icc-cpi.int/Pages/item.aspx?name= 2021-09-27-otp-statement-afghanistan.

Serious allegations of violations of international humanitarian law have been leveled against all parties to the ongoing civil war in Syria, as in that conflict there appear to be no efforts by anyone to distinguish civilians from fighters. Bombings by Syrian government forces often target civilians in rebel-held areas, while suicide attacks in Syria and Iraq deliberately target civilians in markets, schools, mosques, and similar places. As of May 2022, intermittent negotiations among some (not all) of the warring factions have had little effect. Human Rights Watch documented in its 2021 annual report that the parties to the Syrian conflict continue to commit violations of international humanitarian law with impunity. These violations include aerial and artillery bombing attacks on civilians by government and allied forces, plus the government restriction of access to humanitarian and medical aid to civilians in government-controlled areas. Thousands of people are still being detained, disappeared, tortured, and subjected to other forms of ill treatment. See Human Right Watch, *Syria, Annual Report 2021*, https://www.amnesty .org/en/location/middle-east-and-north-africa/syria/report-syria/. For a history of the civil war in Syria, see Council on Foreign Relations, *Syria's Civil War: The Descent into Horror* (Mar. 17, 2021), https://www.cfr.org/article/syrias-civil-war.

## C.  *Expanding Traditional Protections: Internal Armed Conflicts*

At the 1949 Diplomatic Conference that negotiated the Geneva Conventions on the rules applicable during war, the delegates of many states believed the Geneva Conventions should apply to both civil and international armed conflicts. This position was certainly influenced by Francis Lieber, the principal author of the Civil War-era Lieber Code, who believed that rules of warfare could be observed during internal conflicts without giving recognition to the rebel forces. The initial proposal by the International Committee of the Red Cross (ICRC) incorporated this view, and explicitly provided that the application of the Geneva Conventions to internal armed conflicts would not affect the status of the parties. The proposal, however, met stiff resistance from a considerable number of delegates. Many states feared unqualified application of the Conventions to all internal armed conflicts would give rebels de facto status as belligerents and possibly even de jure legal recognition. They believed observance of the Conventions would hamper the legitimate repression of rebellions and wanted to limit the laws of war to traditional armed conflicts between states. These states particularly did not want to give rebels prisoner of war status, with its attendant immunity for actions on the battlefield.

### 1.  Common Article 3

Common to the four Geneva Conventions is Article 3 ("Common Article 3"), which was the compromise between the competing views just described. Common Article 3 provides some minimum protections for victims of internal armed conflicts, while avoiding any recognition of rebel forces or any rebel entitlement to prisoner of war status. See Daniel Smith, *New Protections for Victims of International Armed Conflicts: The Proposed Ratification of Protocol II by the United States,* 120 Mil. L. Rev. 59, 63-65 (1988). The text of Common Article 3 follows.

In the case of armed conflict not of an international character occurring in the territory of one of the High Contracting Parties, each Party to the conflict shall be bound to apply, as a minimum, the following provisions:

(1) Persons taking no active part in the hostilities, including members of armed forces who have laid down their arms and those placed hors de combat by sickness, wounds, detention, or any other cause, shall in all circumstances be treated humanely, without any adverse distinction founded on race, colour, religion or faith, sex, birth or wealth, or any other similar criteria.

To this end, the following acts are and shall remain prohibited at any time and in any place whatsoever with respect to the above-mentioned persons:

(a) violence to life and person, in particular murder of all kinds, mutilation, cruel treatment and torture;

(b) taking of hostages;

(c) outrages upon personal dignity, in particular humiliating and degrading treatment;

(d) the passing of sentences and the carrying out of executions without previous judgment pronounced by a regularly constituted court, affording all the judicial guarantees which are recognized as indispensable by civilized peoples.

(2) The wounded and sick shall be collected and cared for.

An impartial humanitarian body, such as the International Committee of the Red Cross, may offer its services to the Parties to the conflict.

The Parties to the conflict should further endeavor to bring into force, by means of special agreements, all or part of the other provisions of the present Convention.

The application of the preceding provisions shall not affect the legal status of the Parties to the conflict.

Common Article 3 was a major step toward recognizing the need for basic humanitarian protections for noncombatants in internal armed conflicts. It represented the first internationally accepted law that regulated a state's treatment of its own nationals in internal armed conflicts. The Article also established that the laws governing internal armed conflict were of legitimate international concern.

Although Common Article 3 advanced the laws governing internal armed conflicts, it has not been very effective from a practical standpoint. Some governments have explicitly accepted the applicability of Common Article 3 and have attempted to comply with it, but these have been the exception rather than the general rule. Most governments have been reluctant to admit the existence of "armed conflicts" within their states, because they fear that rebels will gain international legal status as insurgents or belligerents if Common Article 3 is applied to internal strife. To compound this problem, the text of Common Article 3 and its drafting history do not clearly define the term "non-international armed conflict." This has made it easier for states to deny that the provision applies. Finally, Common Article 3 sets forth very general principles rather than the precise standards of conduct necessary to regulate the conduct of states effectively.

III. International Humanitarian Law

Notwithstanding these concerns, the following case represents an application of the principles set forth in Common Article 3.

## Case Concerning Military and Paramilitary Activities in and Against Nicaragua (*Nicaragua v. United States*)

1986 I.C.J. 14, 66-69, 113-14, 129-30 (Judgment of 27 June) (Merits)

[Among the many questions raised in this complicated case was whether the United States incurred legal responsibility for the CIA's preparation and dissemination to the anti-government contra guerrillas in 1983 of a publication, in Spanish, entitled *Operaciones Sicológicas en Guerra de Guerillas* (*Psychological Operations in Guerrilla Warfare*).]

122. The Court concludes that in 1983 an agency of the United States Government supplied to the FDN [the so-called contras who were fighting to overthrow the Sandinista government in Nicaragua] a manual on psychological guerrilla warfare which, while expressly discouraging indiscriminate violence against civilians, considered the possible necessity of shooting civilians who were attempting to leave a town; and advised the "neutralization" for propaganda purposes of local judges, officials or notables after the semblance of trial in the presence of the population. The text supplied to the contras also advised the use of professional criminals to perform unspecified "jobs," and the use of provocation at mass demonstrations to produce violence on the part of the authorities so as to make "martyrs." . . .

218. The court [finds it unnecessary to decide whether Common Article 3 applies under the facts of this case,] since in its view the conduct of the United States may be judged according to the fundamental general principles of humanitarian law; in its view, the Geneva Conventions are in some respects a development, and in other respects no more than the expression, of such principles. . . . Article 3 which is common to all four Geneva Conventions of 12 August 1949 defines certain rules to be applied in the armed conflicts of a non-international character. There is no doubt that, in the event of international armed conflicts, these rules also constitute a minimum yardstick, in addition to the more elaborate rules which are also to apply to international conflicts; and they are rules which, in the Court's opinion, reflect what the Court in 1949 called "elementary considerations of humanity" (Corfu Channel, *Merits*, I.C.J. Reports 1949, p. 22 . . .). The Court may therefore find them applicable to the present dispute, and is thus not required to decide what role the United States multilateral treaty reservation might otherwise play in regard to the treaties in question.

219. The conflict between the contras' forces and those of the Government of Nicaragua is an armed conflict which is "not of an international character." The acts of the contras towards the Nicaraguan Government are therefore governed by the law applicable to conflicts of that character; whereas the actions of the United States in and against Nicaragua fall under the legal rules relating to international conflicts. Because the minimum rules applicable to international and to non-international conflicts are identical, there is no need to address the question whether those actions must be looked at in the context of the rules which operate

for the one or for the other category of conflict. The relevant principles are to be looked for in the provisions of Article 3 of each of the four Conventions of 12 August 1949, the text of which, identical in each Convention, expressly refers to conflicts not having an international character.

220. The Court considers that there is an obligation on the United States Government, in the terms of Article 1 of the Geneva Conventions, to "respect" the Conventions and even "to ensure respect" for them "in all circumstances," since such an obligation does not derive only from the Conventions themselves, but from the general principles of humanitarian law to which the Conventions merely give specific expression. The United States is thus under an obligation not to encourage persons or groups engaged in the conflict in Nicaragua to act in violation of the provisions of Article 3 common to the four 1949 Geneva Conventions. . . .

[The Court held, 14 votes to 1 (Judge Oda dissenting), that the United States, by producing the manual and disseminating it to the contras, had "encouraged the commission by them of acts contrary to general principles of humanitarian law; but does not find a basis for concluding that any such acts which may have been committed are imputable to the United States of America. . . ." 1986 I.C.J. at 148.]

## 2.  Protocol II

Protocol II to the Geneva Conventions, which supplements Common Article 3, emerged from the same diplomatic conference of 1974-1977 as did Protocol I. Many states, particularly developing ones, opposed efforts to regulate internal armed conflicts by international norms. While this position did not prevail at the diplomatic conference, Protocol II emerged a much weaker instrument than the ICRC, and most human rights activists, had hoped to see drafted. See Protocol II Additional to the Geneva Conventions of 12 August 1949, and Relating to the Protection of Victims of Non-International Armed Conflicts.

Richard R. Baxter

Modernizing the Law of War

78 Mil. L. Rev. 165, 168-73 (1978)

When the [International Committee of the Red Cross] began its work on the development of the humanitarian law of war, there were high hopes for a separate new Protocol (or convention) on non-international armed conflicts. . . . This proved to be too much for the majority of the states participating in the Conference. Opposition to the Protocol first took the form of raising the threshold of violence to which the Protocol would apply. Common Article 3 of the Geneva Conventions simply applies to "armed conflict not of an international character," but the new Protocol II was made to apply to

all armed conflicts . . . which take place in the territory of a High Contracting Party between its armed forces and dissident armed forces or other organized armed groups which, under responsible command, exercise such control over a pact of its territory as to enable them to carry out

sustained and concerted military operations and to implement this Protocol. [Art. 1(1)]

What was obviously in the minds of the draftsmen was a conflict resembling the
Civil War in Spain rather than the civil wars in Nigeria or the Congo. Through this
definition two levels of internal armed conflicts were created, even as to parties to
both the Conventions of 1949 and Protocol II—the lower level, governed by Article 3, and the higher level, governed by Protocol II. Such nice legal distinctions do
not make the correct application of the law any easier.

The second limitation on the scope of the Protocol came in the fourth session of the Conference when, at the initiative of Pakistan, the drafting of provisions
was changed from the form "The parties to the conflict shall . . ." to statements
of the protections which are to be extended to the participants and participants
in the conflict. A number of provisions already adopted were simply dropped, and
the simplified Protocol II was adopted in its reduced scale. There was some danger
that the Protocol would not have survived at all if this radical surgery had not been
employed. . . .

Political forces dominated the consideration of "non-international armed
conflicts" and "wars of national liberation." Developing countries, led by those who
had experienced civil wars, succeeded in blunting the edge of the movement for a
much more ample protection of the victims of civil wars. It was that same bloc of
developing countries, supported by the U.S.S.R. and its allies, that succeeded in
giving special status to wars of national liberation

---

As Baxter notes, one major concession made to states reluctant to develop a
legal regime to govern internal wars and civil strife concerned the "threshold" of
the Protocol's application. In addition to the definition in Article 1(1), Article 1(2)
of Protocol II specifies that it does *not* apply "to situations of internal disturbances
and tensions, such as riots, isolated and sporadic acts of violence and other acts of
a similar nature, as not being armed conflicts." These conditions effectively bar the
Protocol's application to many internal conflicts.

Assuming that the Protocol's threshold conditions are met, its core protective
provisions apply. These are contained in Article 4, which provides, inter alia, as
follows:

Article 4
Fundamental Guarantees

1. All persons who do not take a direct part or who have ceased to
take part in hostilities, whether or not their liberty has been restricted, are
entitled to respect for their person, honour and convictions and religious
practices. They shall in all circumstances be treated humanely, without
any adverse distinction. It is prohibited to order that there shall be no
survivors.

2. Without prejudice to the generality of the foregoing, the following
acts against the persons referred to in paragraph 1 are and shall remain
prohibited at any time and in any place whatsoever:

(a) violence to the life, health and physical or mental well-being of persons, in particular murder as well as cruel treatment such as torture, mutilation or any form of corporal punishment;
(b) collective punishments;
I taking of hostages;
(d) acts of terrorisI(e) outrages upon personal dignity, in particular humiliating and degrading treatment, rape, enforced prostitution and any form of indecent assault;
(f) slavery and the slave trade in all their forms;
(g) pillage;
(h) threats to commit any of the foregoing acts.

\* \* \*

Numerous other articles also extend protection to the civilian population, although Protocol II's provisions are much less extensive and specific than those found in Protocol I. See generally Charles Lysaght, *The Scope of Protocol II and Its Relation to Common Article 3 of the Geneva Conventions of 1949 and Other Human Rights Instruments*, 33 Am. U. L. Rev. 4, 24 (1983).

## Comments and Questions

1. Which provisions of the Geneva Conventions and their Protocols have potentially been infringed in the context of the Russia-Ukraine conflict? As implied by much of the discussion above, many of the rules of international humanitarian law are detailed, complex, and subject to differing interpretations. One of the best sources for analysis of this area of law is the website maintained by the International Committee of the Red Cross, *Customary IHL*, https://www.icrc.org/customary-ihl/eng/docs/home (last visited May 5, 2022). The site contains both legal analysis and references to state practice, and it is updated frequently.

2. As pointed out earlier, apart from international humanitarian law, which according to the classic terminology is *jus in bello* (law during war), international rules govern the decision to go to war, the so-called *jus ad bello*. Today, foremost among the rules on going to war is Article 2(4) of the UN Charter, which requires all UN members states "to refrain in their international relations from the threat or use of force against the territorial integrity or political independence of any state." Generally, in order to not run afoul of Article 2(4), the use of force must be for self-defense, authorized by the UN Security Council or, at least arguably, for humanitarian purposes. See Michael Wood, *International Law and the use of Force: What Happens in Practice?*, 53 Indian J. Int'l L. 345, 352 (2013). The UN General Assembly promptly condemned the Russian invasion of Ukraine as a violation of Article 2(4). See G.A. Res (ES-11/1) of 2 March 2022, para. 2. If the use of force is unlawful, is all killing by the aggressor state then unlawful? Does Russia's presumed illegal invasion and prosecution of its war render most all intentional taking of life by Russian soldiers in Ukraine, including the killing of Ukrainian combatants defending Ukrainian territory and people, a human rights violation? Consider the following

from the UN Human Rights Committee's *General Comment No. 36* (2018) on the right to life.

> States parties should, in general, disclose the criteria for attacking with lethal force individuals or objects whose targeting is expected to result in deprivation of life, including the legal basis for specific attacks, the process of identification of military targets and combatants or persons taking a direct part in hostilities, the circumstances in which relevant means and methods of warfare have been used, and whether less harmful alternatives were considered.

Id., para. 64 (endnote omitted) What are the implications of the foregoing interpretation of state obligations in relation to the right to life, in the context of armed conflict?

3. A total of 169 states have ratified Protocol II to the 1949 Geneva Conventions dealing with non-international armed conflicts. Is there any evidence that combatants in Afghanistan, Angola, Colombia, Democratic Republic of the Congo (DRC), Iraq, Liberia, Rwanda, Somalia, Sri Lanka, Sudan, South Sudan, Syria, and Yemen — to mention only a few recent civil wars that may meet the threshold requirements of Protocol II — abided by its proscriptions? Out of this list, Afghanistan, Angola, Colombia, DRC, Liberia, Mali, Rwanda, Sudan, and Yemen have ratified Protocol II; have their ratifications made any difference?

4. One objection to Protocol II is that its application might give greater credibility to insurgent or guerrilla forces engaged in a civil war, despite Article 3(1)'s injunction that "[n]othing in this Protocol shall be invoked for the purpose of affecting the sovereignty of a State or the responsibility of the government, by all legitimate means, to maintain or re-establish law and order in the State or to defend the national unity and territorial integrity of the State." Is this a legitimate concern? Is a state prohibited from treating terrorists as common criminals if Protocol II is applicable? Are terrorists bound by the same restrictions as the government, such as the requirement to distinguish between combatants and civilians?

5. As pointed out earlier, apart from the Geneva Conventions, several treaties specifically prohibit certain methods of war or weapons. Among these, in addition to the examples already mentioned *supra* page 313, are the Convention on the Prohibition of Biological Weapons (1972); and Protocol II (of the Convention on Prohibitions or Restrictions on the Use of Certain Conventional Weapons) on the Prohibitions of Restrictions on the Use of Mines, Booby-Traps and other Devices (1996). The 2017 Treaty on the Prohibition of Nuclear Weapons entered into force in 2021, but it has not been ratified by the world's major powers or by even a majority of UN member states. Is the use of nuclear weapons otherwise prohibited by the Geneva Conventions?

## D. Modern Warfare: Distinguishing Combatants from Civilians

The modern law of war is premised on the possibility and the necessity of distinguishing between combatants and non-combatants, between military targets and civilian inhabitants. Certainly nothing is more important insofar as the protection of the human rights of civilians is concerned. At the same time, nothing is more difficult. Moreover, the problem has become increasingly serious in the decades since the adoption of the Fourth Geneva Convention in 1949. For example, the Vietnam War, post-Cold War "peacekeeping," US-led attacks on Kosovo, Afghanistan, and Iraq, the Russia-Ukraine war, internal conflicts in several African countries, Sri Lanka, and Colombia, armed conflict between various parties in Syria, Iraq, and Yemen, and the increased focus on international terrorism are illustrations of the fact that the traditional law of war—designed to regulate international armed conflicts between states—may be inadequate to handle the complex issues arising during situations of civil strife, insurgencies, and terrorism.

Sometimes the most important decisions of all—whether particular persons are to live or die—must be made on the spot by the lowest ranking and least trained personnel in the armed services. Is it fair to assume that when war crimes occur in such a context, they are attributable only to the individual soldiers involved? Do conditions of warfare in many modern contexts resemble the battles between identifiable armies that characterized the first two world wars? How are soldiers supposed to combat irregular fighters who do not wear uniforms, hide their weapons, and deliberately target and mingle among civilians?

The situation of Lieutenant James T. Duffy, the holder of two Bronze Stars, the Purple Heart and seven other honorable citations, is a case in point. Duffy was court-martialed in 1970 for ordering a prisoner to be shot in cold blood during the war in Vietnam. At his trial, Duffy made the following observations.

## Lieutenant Duffy's Statement

*Crimes of War: A Legal, Political-Documentary, and Psychological Inquiry into the Responsibility of Leaders, Citizens, and Soldiers for Criminal Acts in Wars* 248, 249-54 (Richard A. Falk, Gabriel Kolko, and Robert Lifton eds., 1971)

There was only one thing that really upset me (and many other people in the platoon too). That was taking prisoners that we knew were VC [Viet Cong] and having them released by Brigade as innocent civilians. It's not hard to spot a VC after you've spent some time in the field. The only people who live out there are farmers and the VC. The farmers are only women and children and old men. They were always very friendly toward us. We would stop in a house for lunch or dinner and share our food with them, talk, play with the children and really have a good time. I almost never saw any young men in the rice paddies. Whenever we found any young men we immediately questioned them. I can think of only two young men that I ever found in the field and they were just 15 years old and still going to school. The only other young men I ever found in the field were VC who were shooting at us.

Once we ambushed a sampan in the Plain of Reeds, which is a free-fire zone and anybody who moves is fair game. This sampan came down a canal at about 2100 hours. When we opened up, two men were killed and two women were injured. The women were yelling, "Don't shoot, don't shoot, we are VC!" Sergeant Lanasa swam out and rescued the two women and brought them back to shore. The next morning he carried one of them three-quarters of a mile through swamps to an area where we dusted them off for medical treatment and interrogation. We found out two days later that both women had been released by Brigade as innocent civilians. This really upset me and many others in the platoon. . . . It's hard enough to find the enemy, but to catch and just let them go is ridiculous.

After that incident I decided I was not going to take any more prisoners. If at all possible I was not going to let the situation arise where a prisoner might be taken. I told all my squad leaders and my company commander of this. I told all my men that if they were going to engage someone, not to stop shooting until everyone was dead. I told them if they were going to shoot at somebody, they had better kill him. Nobody ever said anything against this policy and I think most of the men agreed to it. My company commander felt the same way I did about it. . . .

Sometimes innocent civilians are killed out there, but it just can't be helped. We were always careful not to shoot towards any populated areas when we prepped a woodline, and even in a contact we would try not to shoot towards civilians if at all possible. But still you would hit a few, especially at night. Many of the farmers would be out after curfew wandering around, or going over to a friend's house.

Whenever we did take prisoners, they were always roughed up and then questioned. When we worked with ARVN's [the South Vietnamese army] or national police, we found that they were excellent interrogators. You could tell that they really hated the VC by the way they beat them when they caught one. They do not mess around at all. I once had a national policeman with me when we chased a VC through a house. The VC got away but the national policemen wanted to take one of the women in the house with us for questioning. That night he beat and kicked that woman for about two hours while he questioned her. When he was finished he came over and told me she was okay, not a VC, and to let her go in the morning. I went along with his decision. I always listened to my Tiger Scouts, ARVN's or national police and would do what they say. They always seem to know who is a VC and who isn't. . . .

I know in my case, platoon leaders never got any guidance on treatment of prisoners. Battalion HQS never said anything about them. There was no SOP [standard operating procedure], there was never a request that we take any prisoners. The only thing we ever heard was to get more body count, kill more VC! We heard that all the time; it was really stressed. My squad leader told me that in his old unit they couldn't come in from the field unless they turned in a body count. Many units "pad" their body count so they can say they killed more than anybody else. The only way anybody judged a unit's effectiveness was by the number of body counts they had. If you had a lot of body counts, everybody would think you were really good. If you didn't have a lot of body counts, they would think you were a poor unit. . . . Some people might have thought it was wrong to judge a unit just by the number of kills they get. I think it is the only way a unit should be judged. That is really the only mission we have in the field, to kill the enemy. As far as I'm concerned that's why we were sent over here and that's what our job is. The only way to see how well a unit is performing its job is to see how many body counts they have. My platoon killed, found or captured about 50 enemy from mid-July to mid-September and I only had one man killed and only two seriously wounded. I always thought that was a pretty good record.

[Duffy was convicted of involuntary manslaughter and sentenced to six months imprisonment. Was this an appropriate outcome? See *United States v. Duffy*, 47 C.M.R. 658 (1973).]

---

Is the more recent experience of soldiers in Afghanistan, Iraq, Syria, Ukraine, and elsewhere much different from that described by Lieutenant Duffy in Vietnam more than 50 years ago, at least in terms of distinguishing between combatants and civilians? Consider Russian forces facing civilians who have taken up arms against them or organized, at the urging of Ukrainian government officials, to hurl Molotov cocktails on approaching Russian troops.

## Russia-Ukraine Conflict: From Making Molotov Cocktails to Taking up Arms, How Ukraine's Every Man Is Standing Up to Russian Troops

Firstpost, Feb. 28, 2022, https://www.firstpost.com/world/russia-ukraine-conflict -from-making-molotov-cocktails-to-taking-up-arms-how-ukraines-every-man-is -standing-up-to-russian-troops-10414511.html

Ordinary citizens all over Ukraine are taking up arms in the fight against Russian forces as they close in on the capital city following four days of heavy attacks and hundreds of casualties.

The civilians are turning into everyday heroes by putting up a stubborn resistance to the Russian invasion so far—despite being heavily mismatched in terms of military might.

It is important to note here that Ukraine has 196,600 active military personnel, whereas the Vladimir Putin-led country has around 900,000 active military personnel and two million reservists.

Nevertheless, the Ukrainians are refusing to give in, and digging in—taking up arms, making Molotov cocktails in their gardens, pushing back tanks with their bare hands.

### *Molotov Cocktails*

After Ukraine president Volodymyr Zelenskyy appealed to the citizens to defend the country, the the Ministry of Defence took to social media urging the civilians to make Molotov cocktails to neutralise the occupier.

In a post from the verified Twitter page of the Ministry of Defence of Ukraine, it said: "In Obolon . . . We ask citizens to inform about the movement of equipment! "Make Molotov cocktails, neutralise the occupier! Peaceful residents—be careful! Do not leave the house!"

News agency *AFP* reported that in Ukraine's main city Lviv, employees at the Pravda brewery have responded to the Russian invasion by switching from producing beer to Molotov cocktails.

Yuriy Zastavny, the owner of the brewery, was quoted as saying, "We do this because someone has to. We have the skills, we went through a street revolution in 2014."

### Taking Up Arms

Besides building Molotov cocktails, Ukrainian political leaders and ordinary citizens alike are taking up arms to defend their homeland against Russia's invasion this week.

President Volodymyr Zelenskyy had said on Thursday that the government would hand out weapons to anyone willing to take up arms.

And by Friday, Ukrainian officials had already handed out 18,000 guns, according to the *BBC.*

Kira Rudik, a member of Ukraine's parliament, posted multiple pictures of herself with guns, saying that "[women] will protect our soil the same way as our [men]."

"I planned to plant tulips and daffodils on my backyard today," Rudik tweeted on Saturday. "Instead, I learn to fire arms and get ready for the next night of attacks on [Kyiv] . . . We are not going anywhere. This is our [city], our [land], our soil. We will fight for it."

Former heavyweight boxing champion Vitali Klitschko, the mayor of Kyiv, said that he would stay and fight. His brother and fellow heavyweight boxing champion, Wladimir Klitschko, enrolled in Ukraine's reserve army as the country braced for the Russian invasion.

Twitter was also abuzz with images of former Miss Grand Ukraine holding up a rifle. Anastasiia Lenna, who represented her country in the 2015 Miss Grand International beauty contest, has joined the army to fight against the Russian invasion.

Lenna shared pictures of her wielding a gun with the hashtags #standwithukraine, #handsoffukraine. She also said, "Everyone who crosses the Ukrainian border with the intent to invade will be killed! (sic)"

### Blowing Up a Bridge

According to reported information, one Ukrainian sailor, Vitaly Skakun, is said to have blown himself up with a bridge to prevent Russian forces from advancing further. As per a *Buzzfeed* report, the 25-year sailor volunteered to place mines on the bridge on 24 February but did not have time to leave. The statement said that he significantly helped to slow Russian forces and allowed the unit to move and reorganise its defenses.

Another example of courage in the face of adversity is that of a man standing in front of an approaching Russian tank. The 30-second clip, shared by Ukrainian news outlet *HB,* shows a man standing in front of what appear to be military vehicles. As the vehicles try to swerve around him, the man jockeys to the side, seemingly in an attempt to block their progress.

The video sparked comparisons to the photo of a man standing down a line of four Chinese tanks in Beijing's Tiananmen Square.

---

What parameters do the Geneva Conventions provide for the use of force by Russian forces under these circumstances? Does it matter that Russia is the aggressor in the conflict?

## IV.   WHAT RULES APPLY IN THE "WAR ON TERROR"?

Terrorism is still a threat to the United States and a widespread practice globally. It typically involves the use of violence in the pursuit of political, religious, social, or economic objectives. The issues of when the detention of suspected terrorists is justified, the rights of the detainees, what fair trial guarantees are essential to any criminal proceedings, and what counterterrorism tactics are appropriate continue to be debated to this day.

### A.   Military Commissions and Torture

Following the September 11, 2001 attacks, President Bush issued an executive order permitting the detention of suspected terrorists and providing for trial by military commissions for members of al Qaida accused of being involved in terrorist acts. See Detention, Treatment, and Trial of Certain Noncitizens in the War Against Terrorism, Military Order of Nov. 13, 2011, 66 Fed. Reg. 57,831 (Nov. 16, 2001). On advice from the Department of Justice, the Bush administration took the position that the Geneva Conventions, including Common Article 3, did not apply to its operations against al Qaeda, the organization suspected of carrying out the September 11 attacks. See Memorandum from Assistant Attorney General Jay S. Bybee (Jan. 22, 2002), reprinted in *The Torture Papers: The Road to Abu Ghraib* (Karen J. Greenberg and Joshua L. Dratel eds., 2005).

To hold captured suspected terrorists in the aftermath of September 11, the United States opened a detention center at the US Naval base in Guantanamo Bay, Cuba. The detention and possible trials of Guantánamo detainees has been the subject of almost constant court challenges since 2001. While the initial goal of the Bush administration seems to have been to place detainees beyond the jurisdiction of any court or tribunal, domestic or international, the courts have refused to grant the US president such unlimited powers. In 2004, the US Supreme Court held that detainees in Guantánamo did not fall outside the jurisdiction of US courts, although it did not identify precisely what remedies might be available to such persons to challenge their detention. See *Hamdi v. Rumsfeld*, 542 U.S. 507 (2004). In partial response to that decision, the United States created "combatant status review tribunals" to review detentions. Nonetheless, the government attempted to subject detainees to trial by military commission. While a district court initially rejected those tribunals as insufficient, *Hamdan v. Rumsfeld*, 344 F. Supp. 2d 152 (D.D.C. 2004) (Memorandum Opinion), a court of appeals upheld the legality of the trials in *Hamdan v. Rumsfeld*, 415 F.3d 33 (D.C. Cir. 2005). By a divided vote, the Supreme Court reversed in the following judgment.

### Hamdan v. Rumsfeld

48 U.S. 557 (2006) (most internal references, citations, and footnotes omitted)

[The Court first considered and rejected the government's argument that enactment of the 2005 Detainee Treatment Act, which, inter alia, purported to remove federal court jurisdiction over Guantánamo detainees, prevented the Court from hearing the present case.]

The common law governing military commissions may be gleaned from past practice and what sparse legal precedent exists. Commissions historically have been used in three situations. First, they have substituted for civilian courts at times and in places where martial law has been declared. Their use in these circumstances has raised constitutional questions, but is well recognized. Second, commissions have been established to try civilians "as part of a temporary military government over occupied enemy territory or territory regained from an enemy where civilian government cannot and does not function." Illustrative of this second kind of commission is the one that was established, with jurisdiction to apply the German Criminal Code, in occupied Germany following the end of World War II. . . .

The third type of commission, convened as an "incident to the conduct of war" when there is a need "to seize and subject to disciplinary measures those enemies who in their attempt to thwart or impede our military effort have violated the law of war," has been described as "utterly different" from the other two. Not only is its jurisdiction limited to offenses cognizable during time of war, but its role is primarily a factfinding one — to determine, typically on the battlefield itself, whether the defendant has violated the law of war. The last time the U.S. Armed Forces used the law-of-war military commission was during World War II. In *Quirin*, this Court sanctioned President Roosevelt's use of such a tribunal to try Nazi saboteurs captured on American soil during the War. And in *Yamashita*, we held that a military commission had jurisdiction to try a Japanese commander for failing to prevent troops under his command from committing atrocities in the Philippines.

. . . Since Guantanamo Bay is neither enemy-occupied territory nor under martial law, the law-of-war commission is the only model available.

Whether or not the Government has charged Hamdan with an offense against the law of war cognizable by military commission, the commission lacks power to proceed. The UCMJ conditions the President's use of military commissions on compliance not only with the American common law of war, but also with the rest of the UCMJ itself, insofar as applicable, and with the "rules and precepts of the law of nations" — including, *inter alia*, the four Geneva Conventions signed in 1949. The procedures that the Government has decreed will govern Hamdan's trial by commission violate these laws.

Nothing in the record before us demonstrates that it would be impracticable to apply court-martial rules in this case. There is no suggestion, for example, of any logistical difficulty in securing properly sworn and authenticated evidence or in applying the usual principles of relevance and admissibility. Assuming, *arguendo*, that the reasons articulated in the President's Article 36(a) determination ought to be considered in evaluating the impracticability of applying court-martial rules, the only reason offered in support of that determination is the danger posed by international terrorism. Without for one moment underestimating that danger, it is not evident to us why it should require, in the case of Hamdan's trial, any variance from the rules that govern courts-martial. . . .

Under the circumstances, then, the rules applicable in courts-martial must apply. Since it is undisputed that Commission Order No. 1 deviates in many significant respects from those rules, it necessarily violates Article 36(b). . . .

The procedures adopted to try Hamdan also violate the Geneva Conventions. The Court of Appeals dismissed Hamdan's Geneva Convention challenge on three independent grounds: (1) the Geneva Conventions are not judicially enforceable; (2) Hamdan in any event is not entitled to their protections; and (3) even if he is entitled to their protections, *Councilman* abstention is appropriate. . . .

The conflict with al Qaeda is not, according to the Government, a conflict to which the full protections afforded detainees under the 1949 Geneva Conventions apply because Article 2 of those Conventions (which appears in all four Conventions) renders the full protections applicable only to "all cases of declared war or of any other armed conflict which may arise between two or more of the High Contracting Parties." Since Hamdan was captured and detained incident to the conflict with al Qaeda and not the conflict with the Taliban, and since al Qaeda, unlike Afghanistan, is not a "High Contracting Party" — *i.e.*, a signatory of the Conventions, the protections of those Conventions are not, it is argued, applicable to Hamdan. . . .

We need not decide the merits of this argument because there is at least one provision of the Geneva Conventions that applies here even if the relevant conflict is not one between signatories. Article 3, often referred to as Common Article 3 because, like Article 2, it appears in all four Geneva Conventions, provides that in a "conflict not of an international character occurring in the territory of one of the High Contracting Parties, each Party to the conflict shall be bound to apply, as a minimum," certain provisions protecting "[p]ersons taking no active part in the hostilities, including members of armed forces who have laid down their arms and those placed *hors de combat* by . . . detention." One such provision prohibits "the passing of sentences and the carrying out of executions without previous judgment pronounced by a regularly constituted court affording all the judicial guarantees which are recognized as indispensable by civilized peoples." . . .

The Court of Appeals thought, and the Government asserts, that Common Article 3 does not apply to Hamdan because the conflict with al Qaeda, being " 'international in scope,' " does not qualify as a " 'conflict not of an international character.' " That reasoning is erroneous. The term "conflict not of an international character" is used here in contradistinction to a conflict between nations. So much is demonstrated by the "fundamental logic [of] the Convention's provisions on its application." Common Article 2 provides that "the present Convention shall apply to all cases of declared war or of any other armed conflict which may arise between two or more of the High Contracting Parties." High Contracting Parties (signatories) also must abide by all terms of the Conventions vis-à-vis one another even if one party to the conflict is a nonsignatory "Power," and must so abide vis-à-vis the nonsignatory if "the latter accepts and applies" those terms. Common Article 3, by contrast, affords some minimal protection, falling short of full protection under the Conventions, to individuals associated with neither a signatory nor even a nonsignatory "Power" who are involved in a conflict "in the territory of" a signatory. The latter kind of conflict is distinguishable from the conflict described in Common Article 2 chiefly because it does not involve a clash between nations (whether signatories or not). In context, then, the phrase "not of an international character" bears its literal meaning. . . .

Common Article 3, then, is applicable here and, as indicated above, requires that Hamdan be tried by a "regularly constituted court affording all the judicial guarantees which are recognized as indispensable by civilized peoples." While the term "regularly constituted court" is not specifically defined in either Common Article 3 or its accompanying commentary, other sources disclose its core meaning. The commentary accompanying a provision of the Fourth Geneva Convention, for example, defines " 'regularly constituted' " tribunals to include "ordinary military courts" and "definitely exclud[ed] all special tribunals." . . .

Common Article 3 obviously tolerates a great degree of flexibility in trying individuals captured during armed conflict; its requirements are general, crafted to accommodate a wide variety of legal systems. But *requirements* they are nonetheless. The commission that the President has convened to try Hamdan does not meet those requirements. . . .

[The dissent by Justice Scalia, joined by Justices Thomas and Alito, is omitted.]

---

Human rights organizations and experts are still actively denouncing human rights violations against the prisoners in Guantanamo Bay and calling for the closure of the detention center. See *Close "Disgraceful" Guantánamo Camp — UN Experts Urge Incoming US Administration*, United Nations (Jan. 11, 2021), https://news.un .org/en/story/2021/01/1081842; Inter-American Commission on Human Rights, *Towards the Closure of Guantanamo* (June 3, 2015), OAS Doc. OAS/Ser.L/V/II. Doc. 20/15, http://www.oas.org/en/iachr/reports/pdfs/Towards-Closure-Guantan amo.pdf. President Joe Biden has expressed his intentions to close the Guantanamo Bay detention facility, which as of this writing still houses approximately 39 detainees. See generally Ellie Kaufman, *Biden Administration Has Made Little Progress Towards Goal of Closing Notorious Guantanamo Bay* Prison, CNN (Sept. 19, 2021), https://www.cnn.com/2021/09/19/politics/guantanamo-state-of-play/index .html.

On the other hand, the problem of terrorism persists, with responses from the UN and regional bodies whose effectiveness is difficult to gauge. The United Nations has addressed terrorism in various ways for decades. During the UN's 2005 World Summit, the Security Council unanimously adopted a resolution condemning terrorism and calling on states to combat it. The resolution also "[s]tresses that States must ensure that any measures taken to implement . . . this resolution comply with all of their obligations under international law, in particular international human rights law, refuge law, and humanitarian law." S.C. Res. 1624 (Sept. 14, 2005). The General Assembly adopted a Global Counter-Terrorism Strategy in 2006, G.A. Res. 60/288, which devotes a section to "[m]easures to ensure respect for human rights for all and the rule of law as the fundamental basis of the fight against terrorism." The UN Security Council has created a number of committees and adopted a number of resolutions to combat terrorism generally and in specific countries. A summary of the United Nations activities to counter terrorism is available at http://www.un.org/terrorism/.

## *Note: Torture and Inhuman Treatment at Abu Ghraib*

The adverse treatment of detainees by the United States came to light noto-riously when, on April 28, 2004, the CBS television program *60 Minutes II* broad-casted a series of disturbing photographs taken at Abu Ghraib prison, which is 20 miles from Baghdad. The now infamous photographs depicted naked Iraqi detainees being forced to engage in degrading simulated sex acts while US military personnel looked on with leering smiles, offering the thumbs-up sign. Other pho-tographs captured a hooded detainee standing on flimsy boxes with electrical cords attached to his fingertips and genitalia; a naked detainee prone on the floor with a leash around his neck, held by a female US soldier at the other end; naked detain-ees cowering as they are threatened with barking military dogs; and the bodies of dead Iraqis packed in ice. The photos became instant international news, and the United States' moral credibility plummeted around the world. While condemning the abuses, the Bush administration was unapologetic about the use of "enhanced" interrogation for collecting intelligence.

In an op-ed published in the month following the emergence of the Abu Ghraib photographs, John Yoo, Deputy Assistant Attorney General, wrote, "[I]n-terrogations of detainees captured in the war on terrorism are not regulated under Geneva. This is not to condone torture, which is still prohibited by the Torture Convention and federal criminal law. Nonetheless, Congress's definition of torture in those laws — the infliction of severe mental or physical pain — leaves room for interrogation methods that go beyond polite conversation." John Yoo, *Terrorists Have No Geneva Rights*, Wall St. J. (May 26, 2004). Subsequent investigations of Abu Ghraib resulted in the court-martial and conviction of a number of military person-nel, although the investigations also concluded that no officer had ordered abuse and that there was no policy of torture. For more reading on the lasting impacts of the events in Abu Ghraib, see Maha Hilal, *Abu Ghraib, The Legacy of Torture in the War on Terror* (Oct. 1, 2017), https://www.aljazeera.com/opinions/2017/10/1/abu-ghr aib-the-legacy-of-torture-in-the-war-on-terror.

### Comments and Questions

1. Although the Court in *Hamdan* held that Common Article 3 to the Geneva Conventions applied to Guantanamo Bay detainees, the Bush administration con-tinued to maintain that the other provisions of the Geneva Conventions, including those applying specifically to prisoners of war, did not apply to Guantanamo detain-ees. Subsequent administrations have maintained the same position. Is this position correct? Note that the Geneva Convention Relative to the Treatment of Prisoners of War (Geneva III), reproduced in part *supra* pages 314-316, by its terms applies "to all cases of declared war or of any other armed conflict which may arise between two or more of the High Contracting Parties, even if the state of war is not recog-nized by one of them." (Art. III) However, study Article 4 of Geneva III at page 314, *supra*, which includes as prisoners of war those members of "organized resistance movements" that meet certain criteria (Art. 4.2). What protections would Guan-tanamo detainees have under Geneva III beyond what they have under Common

Article 3? For an argument that Guantanamo detainees are at least entitled to an impartial determination of whether or not they qualify as prisoners of war, see Erin Chlopak, *Dealing with Detainees at Guantanamo Bay: Humanitarian and Human Rights Obligations under the Geneva Conventions*, 9 HUM RTS. BRIEF 6 (2002), https://digital commons.wcl.american.edu/cgi/viewcontent.cgi?referer=&httpsredir=1&article=1456&context=hrbrief.

2.  Why did the Supreme Court in *Hamdan* refuse to articulate the minimum standards necessary in order for detention or trial by military commission to pass US constitutional muster? Is it appropriate that judges determine habeas petitions on a case-by-case basis, without guidance from the country's highest court? See, e.g., Human Rights First and the Constitution Project, *Habeas Works: Federal Courts' Proven Capacity to Handle Guantánamo Cases* (2010), https://archive.constitution project.org/wp-content/uploads/2012/10/414.pdf; Benjamin Wittes et al., *The Emerging Law of Detention: The Guantánamo Cases as Lawmaking* (2010), http://ssrn .com/abstract=1540601.

3.  In 2005, the Human Rights Council established, as part of its system of "special procedures" (discussed in Chapter 7) the independent expert position of Special Rapporteur on the promotion and protection of human rights and fundamental freedoms while countering terrorism (H.R.C. Res. 2005/80). The Special Rapporteur, who reports regularly to the Human Rights Council and General Assembly, has conducted investigations in Turkey, Israel and the Occupied Palestinian Territories, the United States, South Africa, Spain, Egypt, Tunisia, and Uzbekistan. In May 2010, the Rapporteur identified 35 "elements of good practice" that should guide intelligence services in their collection of information about terrorism. See Report of the Special Rapporteur on the promotion and protection of human rights and fundamental freedoms while countering terrorism, *Compilation of Good Practices on Legal and Institutional Frameworks and Measures That Ensure Respect for Human Rights by Intelligence Agencies While Countering Terrorism, Including on Their Oversight*, UN Doc. A/HRC/14/46 (2010). In what might way might such a compilation of "good practices" be useful to the United States or to advocates trying to influence US behavior?

4.  The prohibition of torture is one of the few absolute protections in international human rights and humanitarian law. Do you agree with John Yoo's statement that the prohibition of torture "leaves room for interrogation methods that go beyond polite conversation?" What are the implications of such a statement coming from a high-level government lawyer? Note that the Convention against Torture and Other Cruel, Inhuman or Degrading Treatment or Punishment defines torture as "any act by which severe pain or suffering, whether physical or mental, is intentionally inflicted on a person" by a state actor for a coercive purpose (Art. 1.1). What qualifies as torture under this definition continues to be debated. Is torture (or cruel, inhuman, or degrading treatment) ever justified, despite the Convention's admonition that "no exceptional circumstances whatsoever . . . may be invoked as a justification of torture" (Art. 2(2))? See generally Steven Greer, *Is the Prohibition against Torture, Cruel, Inhuman and Degrading Treatment Really "Absolute" in International Human Rights Law?*, 0 HUM. RTS. L. REV. 1 (2015), https://www.corte idh.or.cr/tablas/r33346%20(2).pdf.

## B.   Use of Force: Drones and Targeted Killings

One of the distinguishing features of international humanitarian law is that it permits the use of force, including deadly force, in self-defense or in the conduct of war (at least where the use of force can be legally justified to start with, see page 330, *supra*). Thus, it is ordinarily not considered murder to kill enemy soldiers, and some "collateral damage" to noncombatants may be justifiable if it is militarily necessary and proportionate. Of course, these rules only apply in an "armed conflict." While there is no question that international humanitarian law applies to military actions by the United States in Iraq, Afghanistan and other countries, the killing of alleged, suspected, or actual members of the Taliban or al Qaeda outside of actual combat raises more complex issues. These killings are epitomized by the use of unmanned aircraft, popularly known as drones, to attack targets in Pakistan, Yemen, as well as in Afghanistan and elsewhere. The locations are often remote, and it is difficult to obtain conclusive evidence about how intended targets are selected and who has been killed.

UN experts have examined the legality of drone strikes under both human rights law and humanitarian law. See, e.g., *Report of the Special Rapporteur on the promotion and protection of human rights and fundamental freedoms while countering terrorism, Ben Emerson*, UN Doc. A/68/389 (2013); *Report of the Special Rapporteur on extrajudicial, summary, or arbitrary executions, Christof Heyns*, UN Doc. A/68/382 (2013); and id., UN Doc. A/HRC/14/24/Add.6 (2010). Their observations and analysis have been generally consistent with one another, and they emphasize that both transparency and accountability are essential elements in ensuring that drone strikes are consistent with international law. Christof Heyns's analysis concludes that existing international law sets forth "an adequate framework for the use of armed drones" and that "[t]he central norms of international law need not, and should not, be abandoned to meet the new challenges posed by terrorism." UN Doc. A/68/382 (2013), paras. 104, 102. Ben Emmerson "identifies . . . a number of legal questions on which there is currently no clear international consensus . . . [and] considers that there is an urgent and imperative need to seek agreement between States on these issues." UN Doc. A/38/389 (2013), para. 79.

Below is an extract of a 2020 report by the United Nations Special Rapporteur on extrajudicial, summary, or arbitrary executions, Agnès Callamard (successor to Christof Heyns) discussing the increased use of drones and its international law implications. The report calls for accountability when targeted killings are perpetrated by armed drones. Agnès Callamard, currently serves as Secretary General of Amnesty International.

## Report of the Special Rapporteur on Extrajudicial, Summary or Arbitrary Executions (Agnès Callamard)

U.N. Doc. A/HRC/44/38 (2020)

1. Armed drones, whether deployed by State or non-State actors, can nowadays strike deep into national territory, targeting individuals and public infrastructure. While some "incidents" such as the drone strike in January 2020 against

Iran's General Soleimani or that against Saudi Arabia's oil facilities generate strong political reaction, the vast majority of targeted killings by drones are subjected to little public scrutiny at either national or international levels. And yet, drone technologies and drone attacks generate fundamental challenges to international legal standards, the prohibition against arbitrary killings and the lawful limitations on permissible use of force, and the very institutions established to safeguard peace and security.

2. This is not to suggest that armed drones are mainly, or solely, responsible for a weakening compliance with applicable international law. Deliberate attacks on civilians and civilian objects such as schools, hospitals and ambulances in Afghanistan, Occupied Palestinian Territory, Syria, Yemen and Libya, to name but a few, evidence the tragic disregard of the most essential humanitarian principles. Yet, while investigations, commissions of inquiries, UNGA and UNSC deliberations have led to some condemnation of these breeches of international humanitarian law and the resulting mass violations, by comparison, and despite their significant civilian casualties, the consequences of targeted killings by armed drones have been relatively neglected by states and institutions.

3. A reasonable argument can be made that to single out drones is misplaced, given that many targeted killings are carried out by conventional means — e.g. Special Operations Forces. Indeed, these also raise serious concerns. The present report thus contains findings applicable to all forms of targeted killings, no matter their method. Nonetheless, understanding the particularities of armed drone technologies is crucial if we are to keep pace with current and expected developments impacting on the protection of the right to life . . .

7. As of 2020, at least 102 countries had acquired an active military drone inventory, and around 40 possess, or are in the process of procuring, armed drones. 35 States are believed to possess the largest and deadliest class. Since 2015, Israel, Iraq, Iran, UK, US, Turkey, UAE, Saudi Arabia, Egypt, Nigeria, and Pakistan have allegedly operated drones, including for the purpose of use of force, such as targeted killings.

8. Since 2015, armed drones have been used against domestic targets on national territories, within or outside non-international armed conflicts. Turkey has reportedly used drones domestically against the Kurdistan Worker's Party (PKK), while Nigeria first confirmed attack was carried out against a Boko Haram logistics base in 2016. In 2015 Pakistan allegedly used its armed drones for the very first time in an operation to kill three "high profile terrorists." Iraq has similarly purchased drones to carry out strikes against ISIS in Anbar province in 2016.

9. At least 20 armed non-State actors have reportedly obtained armed and unarmed drone systems including the Libyan National Army, Harakat Tahrir al-Sham, Palestinian Islamic Jihad, Venezuelan military defectors, Partiya Karkerên Kurdistanê, Maute Group, Cártel de Jalisco Nueva Generación, the Houthis and ISIS. Armed groups have accessed commercially available "off-the-shelf" systems, drones sold by States and internally developed their own. Multi-drone deployment (in multiples of 10) have also been used by non-State actors. In 2017 in Mosul, Iraq, for example, within a 24-hour period "there were no less than 82 drones of all shapes and sizes" striking at Iraqi, Kurdish, US, and French forces. The Haftar Armed Forces carried out over 600 drone strikes against opposition targets resulting

allegedly in massive civilian casualties, including, in August 2019, against a migrant detention center . . .

13. The allure of drone technologies explains their proliferation:

(a)  Efficiency: Drones are relatively cheap to produce, easy to deploy and offer economy of effort, meaning the option of targeted killing is a less financially onerous choice compared to the alternatives, such as "locate, detain/arrest".

(b)  Adaptability: Drones are truly "all terrain," deployable in a variety of settings for a range of purposes by various actors, and they are amenable to ongoing technological innovations.

(c)  Deniability: Operable at long range and clandestinely, the drone is both easy to deny and its operation more difficult to attribute. Drones further are not "indigenous" to their operators, bearing often similar look and design, range and lethal capability. The very same make and model may be deployed by different State and non-State actors operating in the same geographical area.

(d)  Effectiveness: Drones offer unprecedentedly asymmetrical advantage in favour of their deployer; promising limited damage to other than the intended target, with low-to-no risk of direct damage for the initiator.

(e)  Acceptability: Drone technologies are perceived as largely "bloodless, painless, and odorless", the guarantors thus of (more) virtuous war by providing "the technical capability and ethical imperative to threaten and, if necessary, actualize violence from a distance with virtually no casualties".

(f)  Political gain: As a number of drones' strikes have demonstrated, a country's ability to take-out big-name targets, without any casualties on its side, is a political gain for the government at the time, even though it may not see 'military victory' in the longer term.

14. Yet, these characteristics, each on their own and all together, raise troubling moral and human rights question and, as importantly, present dangerous myths. . . .

30. As argued by a previous Special Rapporteur, to be lawful a drone strike must satisfy the legal requirements under *all* applicable international legal regimes: the law regulating inter-state use of force (*jus ad bellum*); international humanitarian law (IHL) and international human rights law (IHRL).

31. On its own *jus ad bellum* is not sufficient to guide the use of force extra territorially. While *jus ad bellum* is a question between States under the UN-Charter, other obligations are owed to individuals. Accordingly, even the legality of a strike under Art. 51 of the UN Charter does not preclude its wrongfulness under humanitarian or human rights law. As the International Law Commission (ILC) Draft Articles on State Responsibility states: "*As to obligations under international humanitarian law and in relation to non-derogable human rights provisions, self-defense does not preclude the wrongfulness of conduct.*"

32. While previous Special Rapporteurs applied this approach to situations of "peace" and to non-international armed conflicts (NIAC), current events oblige the present Special Rapporteur to consider these legal questions in reference to

international armed conflicts (IAC) and the operationalization of the complementarity between IHL and IHRL.

33. The right to protection from arbitrary deprivation of life is a rule of customary international law as well as a general principle of international law and a rule of *jus cogens*. It is recognized by the UDHR, the ICCPR, and regional Conventions.

34. The complementarity of IHL and IHRL has been highlighted by States, international bodies and courts. The well-established principle that IHRL continues to apply during war and public emergencies has been confirmed by international jurisprudence and the text of human rights treaties, including their derogations.

35. That said, the legal assessment of targeted killings may result in different outcomes depending on the regime considered. As a general principle, under IHRL the intentional, premeditated killing of an individual would be unlawful, unless it is a means of last resort and strictly necessary to protect against an imminent threat to life. To be lawful under IHL, on the other hand, the target of a deliberate killing must be a *legitimate target*, i.e. a combatant or a civilian directly participating in hostilities and be guided by the principles of distinction, proportionality, and precautionary measures.

36. State parties engaged in acts of aggression as defined in international law, resulting in deprivation of life, violate, ipso facto, Article 6 of the ICCPR (GC36, para 64) whether or not they also violate IHL. State parties that fail to take all reasonable measures to settle their international disputes by peaceful means may fall short of compliance with their positive obligation to ensure the right to life (GC 36, para 70); a link not established by or under IHL . . .

41. The first priority is to determine whether, on the basis of a strict and objective reading of the elements constitutive of armed conflicts, a situation amounts to an international or non-international armed conflict. Four scenarios as far as drones targeted killings may be identified:

(a) The first scenario is, simply put, that of a strike but not in an international or non-international armed conflict: in such case it must be assessed under IHRL. That assessment should take into account the larger context, whether derogations have been activated, as is highlighted by the jurisprudence, and the specifics of the situation.

(b) Under a second scenario, the drone strike occurs in an IAC or NIAC in the midst of, or alongside, active and open hostilities involving exchange of fire, conventional air strikes and other military deployments.

(c) Under a third scenario although a country or region may be affected by an IAC or NIAC, the particular drone strike is distant from any battlefields: it takes place in areas, or at a time, of no military activity, presence, control or engagement in the immediate surrounds. This is a pertinent scenario: many contemporary conflicts involve sporadic, unpredictable frontlines, leaving often large areas of the same country or region with little to no exposure to active or ongoing exchange of enemy fire.

(d) Under a related scenario, the drone strike itself is a first strike, potentially triggering an IAC with no other elements or acts constitutive of a conflict preceding or at the time of the strike, or perhaps even in its aftermath. . . .

42. In the first scenario, the applicable body of law is clear. By comparison, assessment of the lawfulness of targeted killings in the last three, but particularly last two, scenarios, may vary.

43. One approach is to apply the legal regime that is the most protective of the victim(s), or which privileges individual rights over State rights. In these instances, however, IHL would always be displaced in favor of IHRL.

44. Under another approach—the *systemic integration* approach, derived from Article 31(3)(c) of the Vienna Convention on Treaties, and applied in the ICJs Oil Platforms case—mthe different rules of international law would be used to assess the situation and/or support a purposive interpretation of Convention-based rights. This approach is in keeping with the derogation clauses of the ICCPR and regional instruments, applicable in the exceptional circumstances of emergency or war. It is backed up by contemporary jurisprudence. In the aforementioned scenarios, a *systemic integration* approach would not consider humanitarian law alone but would consider human rights treaties obligations, the territoriality and scope of contemporaneous military actions and State behaviour overall . . .

50. It is the Special Rapporteur's opinion that such contextual and situational analyses are inherent to all effective assessments of the use of force including in the scenarios presented above. For compliance with IHRL, this means assessing necessity, proportionality and precaution through a situational analysis that takes into account the location, circumstances, possibilities of armed resistance and the planning involved. It also means that the lethal use of force cannot be justified or allowed when it is not necessary, it is likely to cause disproportionate harm, or it reasonably could have been avoided by feasible precautionary measures. . . .

65. Notwithstanding the legal gymnastics of a number of States as they attempt to justify drones targeted killings, many such killings qualify either as *arbitrary* under Article 6 of the ICCPR or as violations of *jus ad bellum*. Some killings, along with their so-called "collateral" casualties, may also violate international humanitarian law. However, an absence of investigation into these incidents leaves them sealed off from truth and accountability.

66. At the international level, where are we to go to have these matters reviewed in a consequential way; in a manner that encourages States to take their consideration and resulting conclusions seriously? Unfortunately, to date international oversight mechanisms have not been able to address the gravity that the situation requires. In an extensive 2017 study, UNIDIR, for example, found there was a pressing need to address (the lack of) transparency, oversight and accountability of armed drones . . .

83. When asked "Why did you want to climb Mount Everest?" a renowned mountaineer retorted "Because it's there." As public opinion turned against the loss of soldiers' lives in military actions abroad, the use of armed drones has increased exponentially. Drones have also emerged as a prestigious, effective and efficient weapon in this "second drone age," with many States eager to join the "drone power club." But their mere existence does not justify their indiscriminate deployment, as conventions against weapons of mass destruction, chemical weapons and other indiscriminate weapons exemplify.

84. What is especially troubling is the absence of public discussion about the ethics, legality, and effectiveness of the "decapitation" strategy at the heart

of drones targeted killings, whether or not they have their effect as claimed, and about the measures of their success, in terms of a long-term vision for the sustainable protection of human lives and global peace. Instead, war has been normalized as the legitimate and necessary companion to "peace," not as its opposite we must do all that we can to resist.

85. To tackle effectively the many challenges posed by armed drones and targeted killings, States, international decision-making bodies, and other concerned actors, should:

(a) Develop and commit to robust standards for transparency, oversight and accountability in the use of armed drones;

(b) Undertake effective measures to control their proliferation through export and multilateral arms control regimes and/or under international treaties;

(c) Openly discuss the challenges that drones' targeted killings pose to international law;

(d) Call out any use of force not in compliance with the UN Charter and reject their purported legal underpinnings;

(e) Investigate all allegations of unlawful deaths in relation to the use of drones, including through international bodies where States fail to do so . . .

## Comments and Questions

1. Paragraphs 8 and 9 of the preceding UN expert report discuss the use of drones by both state and non-state actors. Should state and non-state actor use of drones be treated the same in international law? Would the standard of due diligence discussed in Chapter 4 be a helpful tool for determining the legality of the use of drones?

2. Can you conceive of scenarios in which drones can be used without breaching international law? See generally Christof Heyns et al., *The International Law Framework Regulating the Use of Armed Drones*, 65 INT'L & COMP. L.Q. 791, 794-805, 810-814 (2016).

3. What are the practical advantages and disadvantages to use of drones, and what are the gaps in international law in this regard? Which international law regime do you consider best suited to determining the validity of the use of drones, international humanitarian law or international human rights law?

## V. INTERNATIONAL CRIMES AND HUMAN RIGHTS

### A. Introduction

As pointed out earlier, Russia has been accused of committing war crimes during its invasion of Ukraine for gross breaches of international humanitarian law. Persons who perpetrate such war crimes and other international crimes

are individually criminally liable, just as are persons who commit crimes under
~~domestic law.~~ In this respect, international crimes are to be distinguished from
human rights violations, which normally implicate the responsibility of a government. Human rights violations are not automatically crimes; indeed, most
violations—e.g., suppression of freedom of speech, discrimination, interference
with property, violations of a fair criminal procedure, failure to ensure adequate
housing or health care, interference with freedom of religion, and others—are
not criminal acts under either domestic or international law. Similarly, many
international crimes—e.g., piracy, terrorism, hijacking, drug trafficking, money
laundering—are simply crimes committed by individuals and do not implicate
human rights norms. Nonetheless, quite a few acts (such as torture, some killings,
and certain other abuses if committed systematically or during time of war) may be
considered to be both violations of international human rights law (when committed under color of governmental authority) and international crimes.

At the end of World War II, an ad hoc international tribunal sitting at Nuremberg applied legal standards set out in a special charter during the trials of Nazi
war criminals for crimes against peace, war crimes, and crimes against humanity. In
many ways, Nuremberg was and remains the high-water mark insofar as the use of
the international criminal process is concerned, although the International Criminal Court (see discussion i*nfra*) is showing signs of becoming an even more important actor.

Immediately after Nuremberg, efforts were made to codify certain large-scale or
particularly grave human rights violations as international crimes, the commission of
which would render the offender subject to trial in various domestic or international
courts. This period saw the UN General Assembly's adoption of the Genocide Convention, followed by the International Law Commission's formulation of the Nuremberg Principles (5 U.N. GAOR Supp. (No. 12) at 11-14, UN Doc. A/1316 (1950))
and the Draft Code of Offenses against the Peace and Security of Mankind (9 U.N.
GAOR Supp. (No. 9) at 11-12, UN Doc. A/2693 (1954)). Even at this early stage, the
United Nations considered the possible establishment of an international criminal
court, see *Report of the Committee on International Criminal Jurisdiction*, 9 U.N. GAOR
Supp. (No. 12) at 23-26, UN Doc. A/2645 (1954). In 1957, however, the General
Assembly decided to defer consideration of such a court until it had completed the
Draft Code and agreed on a definition of aggression. See G.A. Res. 1187 (1957). This
decision effectively delayed any consideration of an international criminal court for
nearly two decades, because the General Assembly took until 1974 to agree on an
official definition of aggression. See G.A. Res. 3314 (1974).

## B.  Ad Hoc Tribunals

By 1992 the situation in the former Yugoslavia, especially in Bosnia and Herzegovina, had produced a strong demand within and outside the United Nations for
the creation of a Yugoslav war crimes tribunal to hold criminally responsible those
persons involved in "ethnic cleansing," war crimes, and crimes against humanity. In
response, the UN Security Council created the International Criminal Tribunal for
the Former Yugoslavia (ICTY). See S.C. Res. 827 (May 25, 1993).

The massacre of perhaps 800,000 people that took place in Rwanda in 1994 also spurred calls for international trials of the perpetrators. These calls were all the more irresistible, given the establishment of the ICTY only a year earlier to address massacres in Europe. Consequently, the Security Council established a second ad hoc tribunal, this one to prosecute persons responsible for genocide and other violations of international humanitarian law in Rwanda taking place between January and December of 1994. See S.C. Res. 955 (Nov. 8, 1994).

Criminal tribunals with at least some formal elements of international involvement have been created in East Timor, Bosnia and Herzegovina, Kosovo, Cambodia, Sierra Leone, and Lebanon. In 2015, the UN Human Rights Council adopted a resolution encouraging Sri Lanka to include foreign judges and other officials in bodies created to investigate violations of international humanitarian law and human rights committed during the civil war that ended in 2009, see H.R.C. Res. 30/1 (Oct. 1, 2015), but the government seemed unlikely to accept a significant foreign component.

### C.    *The International Criminal Court*

On July 17, 1998, 120 states signed the Statute of the International Criminal Court (ICC) at the conclusion of the UN Diplomatic Conference of Plenipotentiaries convened in Rome to create the Court. To the surprise of some, ratifications of the Rome Statute followed relatively quickly, and it entered into force on July 1, 2002. As of May 2022, there were 124 parties to the Statute and the 2022 budget for the International Criminal Court was 154,855,000 euros. See *About the Court, Facts and Figures,* International Criminal Court, https://www.icc-cpi.int/about/the-court (last visited June 5, 2022).

Under the Rome Statute, the ICC has jurisdiction to consider charges against individuals for war crimes (breaches of the Geneva Conventions and others sources of the rules of war), genocide, and crimes against humanity, the latter defined as a number of specified abuses when committed as part and with knowledge of an attack against a civilian population. See Rome Statue, *supra,* Arts. 5-8. A person accused of such a crime is subject to the court's jurisdiction if the person is a national of a party to the Rome Statute or committed the crime within the territory of a state party (or in either case of a state that has accepted the court's jurisdiction), or the UN Security Council authorizes the person's prosecution. See id., Arts. 12, 13. Additionally, as of July 2018, a situation in which a crime of aggression — that is, the use of force against the independence, integrity or sovereignty of another state — appears to have occurred may be referred to the court by the Security Council.

An important feature of the ICC's jurisdiction is that it is to function as complementary to the domestic jurisdiction of states, not to supplant it. Article 17 of the Rome Statutes envisages that states maintain primary jurisdiction to prosecute international crimes and that the ICC will step in only when that primary jurisdiction fails. See generally Mohamed M. El Zeidy, *The Principle of Complementarity: A New Machinery to Implement International Criminal Law,* 23 MICH. J. INT'L L. 869 (2001-2002).

International criminal law, and the ICC in particular, has become a significant issue in political and academic debates for over three decades, and separate courses on the topic are offered in many law schools. As of May 2022, the ICC has over 30 cases under its review and has issued 35 arrests. Even though the work of the ICC has been mostly focused on African countries, it has also opened investigations in Afghanistan, Georgia, Bangladesh, Myanmar, Palestine, Philippines, and Venezuela. As discussed earlier, in February 2022, the ICC prosecutor opened an investigation into potential war crimes in connection with Russia's invasion of Ukraine. See Statement of ICC Prosecutor, Karim A.A. Khan QC, on the Situation in Ukraine: "I have decided to proceed with opening an investigation." (Feb. 28, 2022), https://www.icc-cpi.int/Pages/item.aspx?name=20220228-prosecutor-statement-ukraine; Sudarsan Raghavan, *Amid the Death and Rubble, Ukrainian Teams Hunt for Evidence of Possible War Crimes*, The Washington Post (Mar. 6, 2022), https://www.washingtonpost.com/world/2022/03/06/ukraine-russia-war-crimes/.

As an example of its recent judgments, the International Criminal Court declared Dominic Ongwen guilty on February 4, 2021 for 61 war crimes and crimes against humanity committed in Uganda between July 1, 2002 and December 31, 2005. The Trial Chamber found that these crimes were committed in the context of the armed rebellion of the Lord's Resistance Army (LRA) against the government of Uganda. He was sentenced to 25 years in prison. The judgment illustrates the approach of the Court to sexual and gender-based crimes, and for the first time finds a conviction for the crime of forced pregnancy under the Rome Statute. The ICC received accounts of women who were forced to marry Ongwen in this context, and the following extract of the Court's judgment underscores the long term and pernicious consequences of these marriages.

## The Prosecutor v. Dominic Ongwen

Int'l Crim. Ct., Trial Chamber IX (Feb. 4, 2021), ICC-02/04-01/15

. . .

### F. FORCED PREGNANCY (ARTICLE 7(1)(G) AND ARTICLE 8(2)(E)(VI)) [UNDER ROME STATUTE]

. . .

2717. This is the first time forced pregnancy is to be considered by a trial chamber of this Court. The crime of forced pregnancy is grounded in the woman's right to personal and reproductive autonomy and the right to family.

2718. The Statute adopted a "narrow" definition of forced pregnancy, largely because the provision was "one of the most difficult and controversial to draft." Negotiations for the crime of forced pregnancy were largely driven with atrocities of the Bosnian conflict in mind, where Bosnian women were raped and then unlawfully detained with the intent to change the ethnic composition of their group by giving birth to half-Serb children.

2719. Some States argued that the crime was unnecessary because its elements were already covered by the crimes of rape and unlawful detention in the Statute and there was no need to create a new crime to punish those acts committed in Bosnia. Another group of States, including Bosnia and Herzegovina and the United States of America, argued that this approach denied the existence of a distinct and terrible crime. Some States focused on fair labelling and how each gender-based crime, including forced pregnancy, should be specifically punished in the Statute.

2720. The Holy See and certain States were also concerned that the crime might be construed as interfering with national laws on abortion and wanted a high threshold of intent by limiting it to "ethnic-cleansing." Other States wanted a less restrictive approach because they argued that this crime might occur in other situations.

2721. The resulting definition of forced pregnancy in the Statute is a delicate compromise that specified the mens rea requirement as "affecting the ethnic composition of any population or carrying out other grave violations of international law." A final sentence was added, saying that this crime "shall not in any way be interpreted as affecting national laws related to pregnancy." This final sentence does not add a new element to the offence—and is thus not reproduced in the Elements of Crimes—but allays the concern that criminalizing forced pregnancy may be seen as legalizing abortion.

2722. As with any crime, forced pregnancy must be interpreted in a manner which gives this crime independent meaning from the other sexual and gender-based violence crimes in the Statute. This is demanded by the rule against surplusage, a basic principle of statutory interpretation that presumes that the legislator does nothing in vain and that the court must endeavor to give significance to every word of a statutory instrument. This also implicates the principle of fair labelling, and how the proper characterization of the evil committed, that is to say, calling the crime by its true name, is part of the justice sought by the victims. It is not enough to punish it merely as a combination of other crimes (e.g., rape and unlawful detention), or subsumed under the generic "any other form of sexual violence." The crime of forced pregnancy depends on the unlawful confinement of a (forcibly made) pregnant woman, with the effect that the woman is deprived of reproductive autonomy . . .

## I. Material Elements (actus reus)

2723. The crime of forced pregnancy, whether as a crime against humanity or a war crime, is committed when the perpetrator "confined one or more women forcibly made pregnant." The forcible conception of the woman could occur prior to or during the unlawful confinement. The perpetrator need not have personally made the victim forcibly pregnant—confining a woman made forcibly pregnant by another is necessary and sufficient for the crime of forced pregnancy.

2724. The material element of this crime can be split into two components. The first of these is "unlawful confinement," which means that the woman must have been restricted in her physical movement contrary to standards of international law. The Elements of Crimes do not indicate a specific duration of confinement, nor do they specify that the deprivation of liberty be "severe" as is explicitly required for the crime against humanity of imprisonment.

2725. The second component of the material element is that the woman has been "forcibly made pregnant." This is understood as encompassing the same coercive circumstances described for other sexual violence crimes in the Statute. This means that the woman need not have been made pregnant through physical violence alone. "Forcibly" in this context means force, or threat of force or coercion, such as that caused by fear of violence, duress, detention, psychological oppression or abuse of power, against her or another person, or by taking advantage of a coercive environment, or that the woman made pregnant was a person incapable of giving genuine consent. The existence of such coercive circumstances undermines the woman's ability to give voluntary and genuine consent.

### II. MENTAL ELEMENTS (MENS REA)

2726. Not every confinement of a forcibly impregnated woman constitutes the crime of forced pregnancy. In addition to the mental elements specified in Article 30, the perpetrator must act with the specific intent of "affecting the ethnic composition of any population or carrying out other grave violations of international law."

2727. This requirement of special intent is phrased alternatively, meaning that the crime of forced pregnancy under the Statute is committed with the intent either to affect the ethnic composition of the population or to carry out other grave violations of international law, e.g., confining a woman with the intent to rape, sexually enslave, enslave and/or torture her.

2728. It is not required that the accused intended to keep the woman pregnant beyond these alternative intentions. In the negotiations for the Elements of Crimes, there was a proposal to include an element that "the accused intended to keep the woman or women pregnant in order to affect the ethnic composition of a population or to carry out another grave violation of international law". . . .

3056. Under Counts 58-59, Dominic Ongwen is charged with forced pregnancy as a crime against humanity, pursuant to Article 7(1)(g)* of the Statute, and forced pregnancy as a war crime, pursuant to Article 8(2)(e)(vi)** of the Statute, of (P-0101, two pregnancies), between 1 July 2002 and July 2004 and (P-0214), sometime in 2005.

3057. The Chamber found that Dominic Ongwen had sex by force with his so-called "wives," including with P-0101 and P-0214. This happened on a repeated

---

* [Article 7 provides: "1. For the purpose of this Statute, 'crime against humanity' means any of the following acts when committed as part of a widespread or systematic attack directed against any civilian population, with knowledge of the attack: . . . [inter alia] (g) Rape, sexual slavery, enforced prostitution, forced pregnancy, enforced sterilization, or other form of sexual violence with comparable gravity; . . . . 2(f) 'Forced pregnancy' means the unlawful confinement of a woman forcibly made pregnant, with the intent of affecting the ethnic composition of any population or carrying out other grave violations of international law. This definition shall not in any way be interpreted as affecting national laws relating to pregnancy . . ."—Eds.]

** [Article 8.2 provides: "For the purposes of this State, 'war crimes' means: . . . [inter alia] (e)(vi) Committing rape, sexual slavery, enforced prostitution, forced pregnancy, as defined in article 7, paragraph 2 (f), enforced sterilization, and any other form of sexual violence also constituting a serious violation of article 3 common to the four Geneva Conventions."—Eds.]

basis whenever Dominic Ongwen wanted. P-0101 became pregnant and gave birth to a girl fathered by Dominic Ongwen sometime between July 2002 and July 2004. In 2004, P-0101 became pregnant and gave birth to a boy fathered by Dominic Ongwen.7725 In 2005, P0214 became pregnant and, in December 2005, gave birth to a girl fathered by Dominic Ongwen.

3058. The Chamber also found that during the time relevant to the charges the seven women 'distributed' to Dominic Ongwen, including P-0101 and P-0214 during their pregnancies, were not allowed to leave. Dominic Ongwen placed them under heavy guard. They were told or came to understand that if they tried to escape, they would be killed.

3059. On this basis, the Chamber finds that Dominic Ongwen confined P-0101 and P-0214, who had been forcibly made pregnant. The objective element of forced pregnancy as a crime against humanity, pursuant to Article 7(1)(g) of the Statute, and forced pregnancy, pursuant to Article 7(1)(g) of the Statute, and forced pregnancy as a war crime, pursuant to Article 8(2)(e)(vi) of the Statute is met.

3060. As concerns the mental elements, due to the nature of the acts performed by Dominic Ongwen and due to the sustained character of the acts over a long period of time, the Chamber considers that Dominic Ongwen meant to engage in the relevant conduct.

3061. Moreover, the Chamber finds that Dominic Ongwen confined P-0101 and P-0214, who had been forcibly made pregnant, with the intent of sustaining the continued commission of other crimes found, in particular of forced marriage, torture, rape and sexual slavery. The special intent requirement of the crime of forced pregnancy is therefore equally met.

3062. On the basis of the above, the Chamber therefore finds that Dominic Ongwen committed, as an individual, within the meaning of Article 25(3)(a) of the Statute, the crimes of forced pregnancy as a crime against humanity, pursuant to Article 7(1)(g) of the Statute (Count 58), and forced pregnancy as a war crime, pursuant to Article 8(2)(e)(vi) of the Statute (Count 59), of (P-0101) between 1 July 2002 and July 2004 (two pregnancies) and (P-0214) sometime in 2005.

---

The Rome Statute was heralded as a key advance for women and international prosecutions by codifying significant forms of gender-based violence as war crimes and crimes against humanity, including rape, sexual slavery, enforced prostitution, forced pregnancies, enforced sterilizations, and other forms of sexual violence. The International Criminal Tribunals for Rwanda and Yugoslavia also adopted a number of judgments prosecuting a range of gender-based crimes and defining the crime of rape broadly. See, e.g., *The Prosecutor v. Jean-Paul Akayesu (Appeal Judgment)*, ICTR-96-4-A, International Criminal Tribunal for Rwanda (ICTR), 1 June 2001; *Prosecutor v. Anto Furundzija (Trial Judgement)*, IT-95-17/1-T, International Criminal Tribunal for the former Yugoslavia (ICTY), 10 December 1998. The trial judgment in the case of Dominic Ongwen found him guilty for a range of sexual and gender-based crimes committed against women who were abducted and forced to live as his wives, including forced marriage and pregnancy, torture, rape, sexual slavery, and torture. The non-profit organization Human Rights Watch considers the Ongwen judgment a critical step in considering gender systematically across the ICC's work, filling the blanks and adding content to the provisions already included in the Rome Statute. See Nisha Varia, *LRA's Ongwen: A Critical First ICC Conviction*, Human Rights Watch, https://www.hrw.org/news/2021/03/13/lras-ongwen-critical-first-icc-conviction# (last updated March 13, 2021).

Apart from the ICC and other international tribunals, there are different means of enforcing international criminal law through domestic judicial systems. The following three sub-sections offer an overview of the most often employed options.

## D.   Universal Jurisdiction

Universal jurisdiction reflects the principle that some crimes are so heinous and are of such concern to the international community that individual states are entitled to prosecute, through their own domestic judicial systems, alleged perpetrators no matter where the crime was committed and no matter the nationality or residence of either victim or perpetrator.

While universal jurisdiction has long been asserted regarding piracy, it is now generally accepted that universal jurisdiction may (but need not be) claimed by a state over grave breaches of international humanitarian law (war crimes), crimes against humanity, genocide, and torture. In a survey it published in 2012, Amnesty International found that 163 states had established at least one of these four types of crimes as crimes under national law, and that many allowed prosecution of such crimes wherever and by whoever committed. See Amnesty International, *Universal Jurisdiction—A Preliminary Survey of Legislation Around the World* (2012), https://www.amnesty.org/en/documents/ior53/019/2012/en/. New Zealand law, for example, identifies war crimes, crimes against humanity, and genocide as crimes that may be prosecuted in New Zealand regardless of "(i) the nationality or citizenship of the person accused; or (ii) whether or not any act forming part of the offence occurred in New Zealand; or (iii) whether or not the person accused was in New Zealand at the time that the act constituting the offence occurred or at the time a decision was made to charge the person with an offence." International Crimes and International Criminal Court Act 2000 (New Zealand), Art. 8(1)(c).

This expansion of domestic criminal jurisdiction may be viewed as either a welcome response to criminals who would otherwise enjoy impunity or an unwarranted and dangerous assertion of authority by countries with respect to allegations of crimes they have no direct link to. In practice, most domestic jurisdiction over international crimes is exercised by states that have some connection to the crime, either through the nationality of the victim, or the accused — e.g., the investigation by a Spanish judge of alleged crimes against humanity committed by military regimes in Chile and Argentina, among whose victims were Spanish citizens. Residence in a country may also suffice, as has been the case with a few persons in the UK and Belgium accused of genocide or crimes against humanity in Rwanda.

In regards to the Russia-Ukraine war, a number of countries such as Germany and Sweden have opened investigations into suspected war crimes committed in the context of this war. See Bojan Pancevski, *Germany Opens Investigation into Suspected Russian War Crimes in Ukraine*, Wall Street Journal (Mar. 8, 2022), https://www.wsj.com/livecoverage/russia-ukraine-latest-news-2022-03-08/card/germany-opens-investigation-into-suspected-russian-war-crimes-in-ukraine-bNCphaIWE30f2REH8 BCi; *Swedish Prosecutors Open Preliminary Investigation into War Crimes in Ukraine*, Reuters (Apr. 5, 2022), https://www.reuters.com/world/europe/swedish-prosecutors-open-preliminary-investigation-into-war-crimes-ukraine-2022-04-05/.

### E.  The "Piecemeal" Convention Approach Coupled with Domestic Enforcement

The exercise of universal or less far-reaching jurisdiction to prosecute international crimes is required by a number of treaties. The 1949 Geneva Conventions obligate states to punish "grave breaches" of humanitarian law no matter where such crimes are committed. Other examples include treaties on slavery, genocide, apartheid and torture, which similarly obligate states to punish those crimes, although not in each case with such expansive jurisdiction.

The historical development of the prohibition against slavery is discussed in Chapter 1. As noted therein, slavery has been an international crime at least since the late nineteenth century, and today it is prohibited by general human rights treaties as well as the 1926 Slavery Convention and the 1956 Supplementary Convention on the Abolition of Slavery; both of which require states to impose criminal penalties for acts of slavery and the slave trade.

The Convention on the Prevention and Punishment of the Crime of Genocide, 78 U.N.T.S. 77, was adopted on December 9, 1948 (the day before the Universal Declaration of Human Rights) and obligated states to prosecute and punish the crime. The prohibition against genocide is universally considered to be part of customary international law or *jus cogens*. See, e.g., *Reservations to the Convention on the Prevention and Punishment of the Crime of Genocide*, 1951 I.C.J. 15, Advisory Opinion of May 28, 1951, at 23. While many see the Genocide Convention as the first modern human rights treaty, it is actually, as its title suggests, a treaty that creates an international crime. Like the slavery conventions, it creates no specific oversight mechanism, although states may bring to the International Court of Justice any dispute "relating to the interpretation, application or fulfillment" of the Convention; perhaps unfortunately, many states have entered a reservation rejecting this possibility. Genocide now falls within the jurisdiction of the International Criminal Court.

Under Article 1 of the Genocide Convention, states "confirm that genocide, whether committed in time of peace or in time of war, is a crime under international law which they undertake to prevent and to punish." The substantive scope of the Convention is relatively narrow, as Article 2 prohibits only certain acts "committed with intent to destroy, in whole or in part, a national, ethnical, racial or religious group, as such." Political groups were specifically excluded during the drafting of the Convention, and there must be a specific, subjective intent to destroy a protected group, in whole or in part.

The International Convention on the Suppression and Punishment of the Crime of Apartheid of 1973 was one of the clearest modern declarations of an international crime. Article I declares that apartheid is "a crime against humanity" and that inhuman acts resulting from it are "crimes violating the principles of international law." Article V provides explicitly that domestic courts may prosecute offenders over which the courts acquire jurisdiction and adds (in terms nearly identical to those found in Article 6 of the Genocide Convention) that prosecution also may occur before "an international penal tribunal having jurisdiction with respect to those States Parties which shall have accepted its jurisdiction." Today, this latter option is more than theoretical, since apartheid is included among the crimes against humanity that fall within the jurisdiction of the International Criminal Court.

The current relevance of the Apartheid Convention would seem to be limited at best. "It thus seems best to regard the Apartheid Convention as a potential source of law for imputing criminal responsibility for certain patterns of racial discrimination, but one which states have not yet shown much inclination to apply." Antonio Cassese, *International Criminal Law* (2d ed. 2008), at 123. It is noteworthy that most South Africans and human rights NGOs seem satisfied with the "truth and reconciliation" approach adopted by South Africa upon the abolishment of apartheid in the 1990s.

The Convention against Torture and Other Cruel, Inhuman or Degrading Treatment or Punishment, which the United States ratified in 1994, is the paradigmatic blend of human rights and international criminal law. The Torture Convention is typical of treaties that create criminal liability outside the field of the laws of war. After defining the crime in Article 1, it sets forth the specific obligations of each state party not only to abolish torture within its own territory, but also to ensure that no torturer found within its territory escapes responsibility, no matter where the crime was committed. It has been ratified by approximately 160 states, and, again, under certain circumstances, torture also falls within the jurisdiction of the ICC. The Inter-American Convention to Prevent and Punish Torture, adopted Dec. 9, 1985, also criminalizes torture.

More generally, states often include, within their domestic criminal codes, crimes that amount to international crimes and provide for prosecution of such crimes within ordinary jurisdictional bounds, whether or not in association with specific treaties. Recall that the jurisdiction of the ICC is complementary and presupposes that states will ordinarily prosecute international criminal acts over which they have jurisdiction. A prominent, recent example of the use of domestic jurisdiction to prosecute a war crime is the prosecution by Ukrainian prosecutors and conviction by a Ukrainian court of a Russian soldier charged with murdering a Ukrainian civilian during the armed conflict. See Bryan Pietsch, Annabelle Timsit, Michael Birnbaum and Sammy Westfall, *Russian Soldier Gets Life Imprisonment in Ukraine's First War Crimes Trial*, The Washington Post (May 23. 2022), https://www.washingtonpost.com/world/2022/05/23/ukraine-russia-soldier-war-crimes-verdict/.

### F.  The Exercise of National Jurisdiction: Amnesties and Prosecutions

As just indicated, all of the crimes referred to in this Chapter are likely to be crimes under domestic law as well as international law. If the crimes are committed within the territory of or by a citizen of a state, domestic courts will ordinarily have jurisdiction to try and punish the perpetrator. It bears reiterating that the Rome Statute establishes the jurisdiction of International Criminal Court as one that is complementary to domestic jurisdiction, such that the ICC prosecutes cases only when states are unwilling or unable to do so.

Domestic prosecution of egregious or systemic criminal behavior committed under a dictatorship or other oppressive regime often faces considerable obstacles even when the regime is no longer in power and there is a transition toward democracy and the rule of law. Not only the lingering forces of impunity, but also pleas for amnesty in the name of reconciliation can impede prosecution. The following extract makes the case for recognizing a limited international *obligation* to prosecute, including in such scenarios.

Diane Orentlicher

## Settling Accounts: The Duty to Prosecute Human Rights Violations of a Prior Regime

100 Yale L.J. 2537, 2541-42, 2550, 2551-52, 2583, 2595-96, 2599-2600 (1991) (citations omitted)

### I. WHY PUNISH?

The debate over post-transition prosecutions has focused on their potential role in ending cycles of state violence and promoting consolidation of democratic transitions. These considerations have, in turn, informed a broader debate about the role that international law should play in shaping governments' policy toward violations of a prior regime.

#### A. THE CASE FOR PROSECUTIONS

The fulcrum of the case for criminal punishment is that it is the most effective insurance against future repression. By laying bare the truth about violations of the past and condemning them, prosecutions can deter potential lawbreakers and inoculate the public against future temptation to be complicit in state-sponsored violence. Trials may, as well, inspire societies that are reexamining their basic values to affirm the fundamental principles of respect for the rule of law and for the inherent dignity of individuals.

Above all, however, the case for prosecutions turns on the consequences of failing to punish atrocious crimes committed by a prior regime on a sweeping scale. If law is unavailable to punish widespread brutality of the recent past, what lesson can be offered for the future? A complete failure of enforcement vitiates the authority of law itself, sapping its power to deter proscribed conduct. This may be tolerable when the law or the crime is of marginal consequence, but there can be no scope for eviscerating wholesale laws that forbid violence and that have been violated on a massive scale. Societies recently scourged by lawlessness need look no farther than their own past to discover the costs of impunity. Their history provides sobering cause to believe, with William Pitt, that tyranny begins where law ends. . . .

By drawing a bright line between crimes that must be punished and those for which amnesties are permissible, international law helps answer an agonizing question confronting many transitional societies: How is it possible to seek accountability without setting off an endless chain of divisive recriminations? . . .

## II. The Duty to Punish Under Current International Law

Increasingly, . . . international law has required states to punish certain human rights crimes committed in their territorial jurisdiction. Several human rights treaties require States Parties to criminalize particular abuses, such as genocide and torture, investigate violations and seek to punish the wrongdoers. On their face the more comprehensive treaties, such as the International Covenant on Civil and Political Rights, are silent about a duty to punish violations of the rights they ensure. But authoritative interpretations of these treaties make clear that a State Party fails in its duty to ensure the cluster of rights protecting physical integrity if it does not investigate violations and seek to punish those who are responsible. Moreover a state's failure to punish repeated or notorious violations breaches the customary obligation to respect the same set of preeminent rights. . . .

A wide range of activities of the United Nations and other intergovernmental organizations reinforce the view that punishment plays a necessary part in states' duty under customary law to ensure the rights to life, freedom from torture, and freedom from involuntary disappearance. For example, reports prepared by Special Rapporteurs, Special Representatives, and Working Groups appointed by the Commission on Human Rights of the United Nations to report on human rights conditions in particular countries or on particular types of human rights violations have repeatedly condemned governments' failure to punish torture, disappearances, and extra-legal executions. . . . [T]hese reports have asserted that a state's failure to punish repeated violations of physical integrity encourages further violations. Although these reports are not authoritative interpretations of international law, resolutions of the U.N. General Assembly have endorsed many of the reports' conclusions regarding punishment of persons responsible for torture, disappearances, and extra-legal executions.

If international law generally requires states to punish serious violations of physical integrity, must a successor government attempt to prosecute every such violation committed with impunity during a recent dictatorship? Or does international law provide a basis for "mitigating" the duty in light of the peculiar constraints prevailing in transitional societies?

In addressing these questions, it is important to begin by making clear what is not at issue. First, the fact that a democratically elected government succeeds a repressive regime has no bearing on the state's international obligations. It is well-established that a change in government does not relieve a state of its duties under international law. Accordingly, if an outgoing government failed to discharge its duty to punish atrocious crimes, its successor is generally bound to fulfill the obligation.

Second, that prosecutions may be inexpedient politically is no excuse for a government's failure to discharge its legal obligations. International law does not, of course, require states to take action that poses a serious threat to vital national interests. But a state cannot evade its duty to punish atrocious crimes merely to appease disaffected military forces or to promote national reconciliation. However desirable the objectives, the government must find other means to achieve them. Ratification of an amnesty law through some form of democratic procedure would not alter this conclusion; nations cannot extinguish their international obligations by enacting inconsistent domestic law . . .

### 1. Application of Customary International Law

The duty to punish human rights crimes imposed by customary law can readily accommodate the constraints faced by transitional societies. . . . [C]ustomary law would be violated by complete impunity for repeated or notorious instances of torture, extra-legal executions, and disappearances, but would not require prosecution of every person who committed such an offense. Prosecution of those who were most responsible for designing and implementing a system of human rights atrocities or for especially notorious crimes that were emblematic of past violations would seemingly discharge governments' customary-law obligation not to condone or encourage such violations, provided the criteria used to select potential defendants did not appear to condone or tolerate past abuses.

### 2. Application of Comprehensive Human Rights Conventions

More complex issues are raised by the question whether a government of a state that has ratified the International Covenant, the European Convention, or the American Convention must attempt to prosecute all serious violations of the right to physical integrity committed, following the convention's entry into force for the state, by or with the acquiescence of a previous regime. Decisions interpreting these conventions include some indications that States Parties are in general expected to investigate every violation of the rights to life, freedom from torture, and freedom from involuntary disappearances, and to prosecute those who are responsible. A rigid application of the general rule that a state's international obligations persist despite a change in government might, then, require successor governments to prosecute virtually every violation of those three rights that has not yet been punished. Yet, for reasons suggested above, such a requirement could produce untenable results.

Pursuant to general canons of construction, the comprehensive treaties should be interpreted in a manner that avoids imposing impossible obligations or duties whose discharge would prove harmful. A functional analysis of the general rule requiring prosecution of torture, extra-legal killings, and disappearances provides a principled basis for such an interpretation.

---

After authoring the above article, Professor Orentlicher was appointed as an independent expert to address issues of impunity by the UN Commission on Human Rights. She developed a draft set of principles, which may be found in *Report of the Independent Expert to Update the Set of Principles to Combat Impunity*, UN Doc. E/CN.4/2005/102/Add.1 (2005).

Much of the early attention to combating impunity and ensuring accountability came from Latin America, as the military regimes of the 1960s to 1980s gave way to more democratic governments. However, this transition from authoritarianism to democracy presents very different issues than the situation that often exists following a protracted civil war in which government institutions (often weak to begin with) are almost useless and where the transition is from a highly fractured society to (re)creating nearly all aspects of a functional system. This latter, more global, phenomena no doubt influenced the guidelines developed by a group of experts who met under the auspices of Ulster University's Transitional Justice Institute in 2011 and 2012.

## The Belfast Guidelines on Amnesty and Accountability

Http://www.ulster.ac.uk/__data/assets/pdf_file/0005/57839/TheBelfastGuidelines FINAL_000.pdf (2013) (footnotes omitted)

. . .

### GUIDELINE 6. AMNESTIES AND INTERNATIONAL OBLIGATIONS TO PROSECUTE

(a) Accountability should be pursued for international crimes and gross violations of human rights* but international law allows states some flexibility and discretion with respect to considering amnesties.

(b) No international treaty explicitly prohibits amnesties. Article 6(5) of Additional Protocol II to the Geneva Conventions, which relates to non-international armed conflicts, encourages states to enact amnesties at the end of hostilities. As a result, the status of amnesties under international law is generally evaluated for incompatibility with treaties prohibiting specific crimes, with interpretations of customary international law, and with the obligation to provide a remedy under international human rights law.

(c) International crimes, such as genocide, grave breaches of the Geneva Conventions, torture and enforced disappearances, are today generally prohibited by treaty. These treaties require states parties to enact domestic legislation to provide effective penalties for these crimes. The Geneva Conventions of 1949 also require states parties to search for persons alleged to have perpetrated grave breaches with the goal of bringing them to trial. The conventions on torture and enforced disappearances require states parties to submit cases to their competent authorities for the purpose of prosecution, but these treaties also stipulate that the authorities shall decide whether to prosecute in a similar manner as they would for ordinary offenses of a serious

---

* The Guidelines use the term gross violations of human rights "to denote acts that constitute serious crimes under national or international law and, if committed by a government, would violate the state's human rights obligations. This includes the most serious actions that are prohibited in universal and regional human rights treaties, such as torture and other cruel, inhuman or degrading treatment; extra-judicial, summary or arbitrary executions; slavery; enforced disappearances. It also includes rape and other forms of sexual violence, which depending on circumstances, can be forms of war crimes or torture."

nature. In making these decisions, national criminal justice systems can apply established principles of law, for example, by exercising discretion in developing selective prosecution strategies. Selective prosecution strategies are also employed by international and hybrid courts. As a result, states will not necessarily be violating their obligations if, due to the exercise of prosecutorial discretion, they do not prosecute all perpetrators or instances of these crimes. Decisions to select or prioritize cases should be made on the basis of transparent and objective criteria. As indicated in Guideline 5, carefully designed amnesties can complement selective prosecution strategies.

(d) Crimes against humanity and war crimes committed in non-international armed conflicts have been defined in the Rome Statute of the International Criminal Court (ICC) and where it has jurisdiction, the ICC can prosecute these crimes. These developments together with the case law of international courts and the opinions of authoritative bodies have provided greater clarity on the nature of these offenses and contributed to a body of opinion to support the existence of a customary prohibition on amnesties for international crimes. However, other sources of opinio juris from domestic and hybrid courts together with state practice on amnesties does not reflect an established, explicit and categorical customary prohibition of amnesties for international crimes.

(e) Within international human rights law, there are differences in the approach of the regional human rights courts on whether there is an obligation to prosecute gross violations of human rights or whether it is sufficient that states investigate such violations and provide remedies for those affected. Amnesties enacted in different regions of the world may be subject to different standards.

[The explanatory guidelines that accompany the principles offer additional analysis.]

Guideline 6 addresses the most controversial issue with respect to the legality and legitimacy of amnesties. In considering the duty to prosecute, the drafters sought to identify the scope of existing legal standards and to highlight where the law remains unsettled. Due to the contested nature of the duty to prosecute, Guideline 6 sets out to highlight areas in which states retain flexibility in determining their approach to amnesties. The drafters, however, declined to be prescriptive as the legal obligations relating to a national amnesty may depend on numerous factors, such as, when the crimes were committed, the nature of those offences, if and when the state has become a party to relevant treaties, and whether state is subject to the jurisdiction of international courts. . . .

### AMNESTIES AND CRIMES PROHIBITED BY INTERNATIONAL TREATY

Paragraph (c) reviews the obligation to prosecute created by treaties on genocide, "grave breaches" of the Geneva Conventions, torture, and enforced disappearances. It draws in particular on the wording of the conventions against torture and enforced disappearances, which state that decisions to prosecute those crimes should be taken by national prosecuting authorities "in the same manner as in the case of any ordinary offence of a serious nature under the law of that State Party."

In line with the discussion of selective prosecutions in Guideline 3, this paragraph notes that national prosecuting authorities could rely on established discretionary rules, which may in some instances result in a decision not to prosecute. This paragraph concludes by suggesting that even where treaties create an obligation to prosecute, states will not necessarily be violating their obligations if, due to the exercise of prosecutorial discretion, they do not prosecute all perpetrators or instances of these crimes. Decisions to select or prioritise cases should be made based on transparent and objective criteria.

### Amnesties and Customary International Law . . .

In sum, state practice suggests that states remain willing to enact amnesty laws and endorse amnesties in other states, even for the most serious crimes, and have consistently rejected proposals to limit their discretion in this area. In addition, amnesties for serious crimes have been upheld by some national courts. On this basis, in keeping with the views expressed by some hybrid courts, paragraph (d) concludes that no settled prohibition on amnesties exists under customary international law.

### International Human Rights Law

The duty to prosecute and punish is not explicitly mentioned in universal or regional human rights treaties. Instead, with respect to gross human rights violations, human rights courts and quasi-judicial bodies that monitor compliance with these treaties have read the duty to prosecute into the explicit duty on states to provide a remedy for human rights violations. The UN Human Rights Committee has issued many significant opinions on the status of amnesties under the International Covenant on Civil and Political Rights[;] however, paragraph (e) focuses on the case law of human rights courts with binding jurisdiction, namely the Inter-American Court of Human Rights and the European Court of Human Rights.

These courts have taken different approaches on whether there is an obligation to prosecute gross violations of human rights. The Inter-American Court has developed a rejection of broad, unconditional amnesties for serious human rights violations. Its jurisprudence has confirmed that where gross human rights violations have occurred, states must investigate, try, and where appropriate punish those responsible, and provide reparations to victims. The court has not ruled on conditional amnesties or amnesties that are combined with prosecutions. When it considered the reduced sentence regime for crimes against humanity created by the Justice and Peace Law in Colombia, the court rejected requests from the victims' lawyers to find that that it violated the convention. Furthermore, . . . a concurring opinion in the *El Mozote v El Salvador* case acknowledged that post-conflict states might need to balance the duty to prosecute against victims' right to peace.

Unlike its Inter-American counterpart, the European Court of Human Rights has no direct experience of dealing with amnesties. Where it has confronted cases of serious human rights violations, the court has declined to proclaim an outright duty to prosecute. Instead, in the 1996 *Aksoy v Turkey* case, the European Court of Human Rights said that with respect to violations of the right to life "the notion of an 'effective remedy' entails a thorough and effective investigation capable of leading to the identification and punishment of those responsible." The phrase "capable of leading to" describes the quality of the investigation, rather than imposing an obligation on the state to prosecute and punish those responsible. In recent decisions, the Court has commented, obiter, that amnesties for war crimes and torture committed by state agents would not be permissible under international law. However, in *Tarbuk v Croatia* the Court held

> even in such fundamental areas of the protection of human rights as the right to life, the State is justified in enacting, in the context of its criminal policy, any amnesty laws it might consider necessary, with the proviso, however, that a balance is maintained between the legitimate interests of the State and the interests of individual members of the public.

To date, the court has not ruled directly on whether a specific national amnesty is compatible with the European Convention on Human Rights. However, it can be inferred that the court might be tolerant of amnesties for gross human rights violations, such as violations of the right to life, and of amnesties that are enacted to deliver legitimate state interests such as achieving peace and reconciliation, and which seek to fulfil the needs of victims by for example facilitating investigations.

In conclusion, Paragraph (e) emphasizes that regional differences exist in the duty to prosecute under international human rights law and that as a result, the legality and legitimacy of amnesties enacted in different parts of the world would be subject to different standards.

---

A final word goes to former UN Secretary-General Kofi Annan, who articulated the classic dilemma of peace versus justice (narrowly construed) in a statement to the Security Council:

> Ending the climate of impunity is vital to restoring public confidence and building international support to implement peace agreements. At the same time, we should remember that the process of achieving justice for victims may take many years, and it must not come at the expense of the more immediate need to establish the rule of law on the ground. . . .
>
> At times, the goals of justice and reconciliation compete with each other. Each society needs to form a view about how to strike the right balance between them. . . .
>
> We also know that there cannot be real peace without justice. Yet the relentless pursuit of justice may sometimes be an obstacle to peace. If we insist, at all times, and in all places, on punishing those who are guilty of extreme violations of human rights, it may be difficult, or even impossible, to stop the bloodshed and save innocent civilians. If we always and everywhere insist on uncompromising standards of justice, a delicate peace may not survive.
>
> But equally, if we ignore the demands of justice simply to secure agreement, the foundations of that agreement will be fragile, and we will set bad precedents.

There are no easy answers to such moral, legal and philosophical dilemmas.

UN Press Release, UN Doc. SG/SM/8892, SC/7881 (2003).


## V.  FINAL COMMENTS AND QUESTIONS

1. Do you think that the "criminalization" of human rights violations is a step forward in the protection and promotion of rights? Does it privilege a certain category of violations of physical security, as opposed to (equally?) important economic, social, cultural, and political rights? Obtaining sufficient resources to promote human rights is never easy; would the more than $100 million that is spent annually on the ICC be better spent in expanding the work of the Office of the UN High Commissioner for Human Rights, which advances human rights broadly throughout the world? Is it realistic to do both?

2. Approaching the issue from the opposite perspective, what is gained by treating crimes as human rights violations? Is trafficking in persons likely to be more effectively combated by INTERPOL and law enforcement agencies or by UN human rights bodies and NGOs? Again, is there room for both, or might crime prevention and/or human rights priorities be skewed? Why do human rights NGOs and the UN High Commissioner regularly denounce terrorist attacks but not drug trafficking, murder, or other criminal acts? Besides protecting the rights of suspects, is there any other reason to link preventing terrorism and human rights?

3. Do you agree with Professor Orentlicher that international law mandates at least some prosecutions? Are "criminal sanctions . . . the most effective means of securing rights deemed of paramount importance"? Is her contention that prosecutions are essential because of their deterrent value borne out in practice? Orentlicher concedes that "[i]nternational law does not, of course, require states to take action that poses a serious threat to vital national interests." Does this have the effect of undermining her entire argument? Cf. Ellen Lutz and Kathryn Sikkink, *The Justice Cascade: The Evolution and Impact of Foreign Human Rights Trials in Latin America*, 2 Chi. J. Int'l L. 1 (2001). In July 2016, the Supreme Court of El Salvador voided a two-decades-old amnesty for crimes committed during that country's civil war, citing, inter alia, international human rights law and the state's obligation to investigate, try, and punish grave violations of human rights. See Elisabeth Malkin and Gene Palumbo, *Salvadoran Court Overturns Wartime Amnesty, Paving Way for Prosecutions*, The New York Times, July 16, 2016. Why wouldn't that be an acceptable arrangement?

4. As discussed in several parts of this book, there are well-developed legal standards advancing the respect, protection, and fulfillment of the human rights of women and outlining a range of state obligations in this area. International criminal law has the different goal of convicting individual perpetrators of mass or gross atrocities. Can you think of ways in which international human rights law and international criminal law can complement each other to prevent and protect women against gender-based violence? Where do you think the work of the ICC should be heading in the area of sexual and gender-based crimes in the future? See generally

Valerie Oosterveld, *The ICC Policy Paper on Sexual and Gender-Based Crimes: A Crucial Step for International Criminal Law*, 24 WM. & MARY J. WOMEN & L. 443 (2018); ICC, *Policy Paper on Sexual and Gender-Based Crimes* (June 2014), https://www.icc-cpi.int/iccdocs/otp/otp-policy-paper-on-sexual-and-gender-based-crimes–june-2014.pdf.

5. As discussed at the beginning of this Chapter, the Russia-Ukraine war is ongoing as of this writing, with an increasing number of civilian casualties and reports of international crimes. Is it genuinely plausible that Vladimir Putin himself could be prosecuted and tried by the ICC for war crimes, crimes against humanity, or even genocide? Who else might be prosecuted for war crimes in the Russia-Ukraine conflict? Note that neither Russia nor Ukraine is a party to the Rome Statute. However, Ukraine has declared it has accepted the jurisdiction of the ICC for crimes committed within its territory, and it is on that basis that the ICC Prosecutor has initiated an investigation. The prosecution process at the ICC takes time and there have only been ten convictions in the ICC's existence. Could this case be different? Can the work of the ICC help bring an end to this war? Might there be a need for a specific war crimes tribunal just for the Russia-Ukraine war? See generally Zachary B. Wolf, *Everything You Need to Know about War Crimes and How Putin Could Be Prosecuted*, CNN, https://www.cnn.com/2022/03/03/politics/putin-war-crimes-russia-ukraine-us-what-matters/index.html.

# CHAPTER 6

# DOMESTIC
# ENFORCEMENT OF
# INTERNATIONAL
# HUMAN RIGHTS LAW

## WHAT IS THE ROLE OF
## DOMESTIC COURTS?

# I.   INTRODUCTION: INTERNATIONAL HUMAN RIGHTS AND DOMESTIC LAW

Previous chapters have identified a broad array of international human rights standards contained in binding multilateral treaties and, to some extent, in customary international law, as well as standards articulated in "soft law" instruments that have not yet ripened into legally binding norms. It is one thing, however, for there to exist a well-developed universe of international human rights norms; it is quite another for those norms to affect the lives of real people. In all too many parts of the world, an enormous gap persists between internationally recognized rights and their enjoyment in practice. Even in Western democracies, such as the United States, that claim strong human rights traditions, infractions of human rights frequently occur. One should recall that the international human rights movement exists precisely because of this gap between the ideal and the reality of life for many.

As we will see in the chapters that follow, mechanisms associated with the United Nations and regional international institutions have been developed to promote the observance of human rights and, in limited circumstances, to provide remedies for human rights violations. Still, states remain the fundamental units of sovereignty and power in the world today; the international system looks to them, not international institutions, as the primary agents responsible for securing the observance of human rights.

As discussed in Chapter 4, states have a positive duty to safeguard human rights and provide remedies when they are violated. This duty entails arranging the domestic legal apparatus, through legislation and otherwise, to incorporate and apply international human rights norms that are binding on the state. An example of such legislation is the US Torture Victim Protection Act of 1991, 108 Stat.73, the long title of which is: "An Act to carry out obligations of the United States under the United Nations Charter and other international agreements pertaining to the protection of human rights by establishing a civil action for recovery of damages from an individual who engages in torture or extrajudicial killing." Another example is Australia's Racial Discrimination Act 1975, whose explicit purpose is to give effect to the International Convention on the Elimination of All Forms of Racial Discrimination.

Even without specific reference to international sources, domestic legislation or government programs can reflect or in some measure give effect to obligations under international human rights law—e.g., the US civil rights laws or Canada's extensive legislation and programing on housing and health care. It is also possible for the executive branch of government, within the bounds of enabling constitutional and legislative authority, to enact regulations or programming that advances implementation of international human rights law. In many countries, a comprehensive approach is taken by the adoption of constitutional provisions that generally incorporate international human rights treaties into domestic law, as discussed *infra*, at pages 440-441.

When domestic constitutional provisions or legislation incorporate or reflect international human rights norms, domestic courts are then usually able, in accordance with their institutional competencies, to provide remedies for the infringement of human rights that states are bound to uphold. For example, under the Torture Victim Protection Act, the US judiciary can adjudicate and provide remedies for violations of the right not to be tortured.

But what happens when such constitutional provisions, domestic legislation, or executive action incorporating or implementing international human rights norms is absent or falls short? What role can or should domestic courts then have in the fulfilment of the duty of states to protect human rights when that duty is not otherwise fulfilled in the existing domestic legal order? The answers to these questions lie in significant part in the definition of the relationship generally of international law to domestic law, which varies among countries across the globe.

International legal scholars have tried to make sense of divergent approaches to the treatment of international law in domestic legal systems, by organizing them into two categories. Under *monist* systems, international law is deemed to be automatically part of domestic law, with a status at least equivalent, and sometimes superior, to law enacted domestically. Domestic courts thus can directly apply international law even when relevant domestic law is absent. Under *dualist* systems, by contrast, international law becomes part of domestic law only by a domestic legislative or other official act of incorporation. Accordingly, actions attributable to the state can be in violation of international law, while at the same time complying with domestic law and there being no domestic judicial recourse. Many states have features of both monism and dualism, such that this framing is not always helpful. See generally J.G. Starke, *Monism and Dualism in the Theory of International Law*, 17 Brit. Y.B. Int'l L. 66 (1936); European Commission for Democracy through Law, *Report on the Implementation of International Human Rights Treaties in Domestic Law and the Role of Courts,* adopted by the Venice Commission at its 100th plenary session (Rome, 10-11 October 2014).

The United States Constitution provides that treaties are part of the "supreme law of the land," US Const., Article VI, Clause 2, and as such treaties are equivalent in theory to federal legislation, see *The Chinese Exclusion Case,* 130 U.S. 581, 578-99 (1889). In practice, however, in the absence of incorporating legislation, the status and role of both treaty and customary international law in US domestic law remain somewhat ambiguous, although both still play a role in domestic judicial and other decision-making. This Chapter first examines the role of sources of international human rights law in judicial decision-making in the United States, along with the limitations on that role, against the backdrop of international law's prohibition of the death penalty for juvenile criminal defendants. Next are materials on judicial application of international human rights law in other countries.

# II.   US COURTS AND THE RIGHTS OF JUVENILE OFFENDERS

## A.   The Use of International Norms to Discern the Parameters of Domestic Legal Protections

Several states of the United States applied the death penalty to persons convicted of committing capital offenses while under the age of 18 until the Supreme Court rendered its landmark decision in *Roper v. Simmons.*

## Roper v. Simmons

543 U.S. 551 (2005) (most references and citations omitted)

[Christopher Simmons was 17 years old when he and two other minors broke into the home of Shirley Crook and forcibly took her to a bridge, where they bound her with duct tape and wire, and threw her into the river below, where she drowned. Simmons later confessed to the murder. He was tried as an adult and convicted of murder in a Missouri state court. Despite arguments of his lawyer that his age at the time of the murder should count as a mitigating factor, Simmons was sentenced to death under Missouri state law. After his conviction, the U.S. Supreme Court decided *Atkins v. Virginia,* 536 U.S. 304 (2002), in which it held that the Eighth and Fourteenth Amendments to the US Constitution prohibit the execution of a mentally disabled person. Simmons filed a petition for state post-conviction relief, arguing that the reasoning of *Atkins* established that the Constitution prohibits the execution of a juvenile who was under 18 when the crime was committed. The Missouri Supreme Court agreed, and subsequently the case was reviewed by the US Supreme Court].

Justice KENNEDY delivered the opinion of the Court [in which Justices Stevens, Souter, Ginsberg, and Breyer joined].

. . . The Eighth Amendment [to the U.S. Constitution] provides: "Excessive bail shall not be required, nor excessive fines imposed, nor cruel and unusual punishments inflicted." The provision is applicable to the States through the Fourteenth Amendment. As the Court explained in Atkins, the Eighth Amendment guarantees individuals the right not to be subjected to excessive sanctions. The right flows from the basic " 'precept of justice that punishment for crime should be graduated and proportioned to [the] offense.' " By protecting even those convicted of heinous crimes, the Eighth Amendment reaffirms the duty of the government to respect the dignity of all persons.

The prohibition against "cruel and unusual punishments," like other expansive language in the Constitution, must be interpreted according to its text, by considering history, tradition, and precedent, and with due regard for its purpose and function in the constitutional design. To implement this framework we have established the propriety and affirmed the necessity of referring to "the evolving standards of decency that mark the progress of a maturing society" to determine which punishments are so disproportionate as to be cruel and unusual. *Trop v. Dulles*, 356 U.S. 86 (1958) (plurality opinion).

In *Thompson v. Oklahoma*, 487 U.S. 815 (1988), a plurality of the Court determined that our standards of decency do not permit the execution of any offender under the age of 16 at the time of the crime. (opinion of Stevens, J., joined by Brennan, Marshall, and Blackmun, JJ.). The plurality opinion explained that no death penalty State that had given express consideration to a minimum age for the death penalty had set the age lower than 16. . . .

The next year, in *Stanford v. Kentucky*, 492 U.S. 361 (1989), the Court, over a dissenting opinion joined by four Justices, referred to contemporary standards of decency in this country and concluded the Eighth and Fourteenth Amendments did not proscribe the execution of juvenile offenders over 15 but under 18. The Court noted that 22 of the 37 death penalty States permitted the death penalty for 16-year-old offenders, and, among these 37 States, 25 permitted it for 17-year-old offenders. These numbers, in the Court's view, indicated there was no national consensus "sufficient to label a particular punishment cruel and unusual.". . .

The same day the Court decided *Stanford*, it held that the Eighth Amendment did not mandate a categorical exemption from the death penalty for the mentally retarded. *Penry v. Lynaugh*, 492 U.S. 302 (1989). . . .

Three Terms ago the subject was reconsidered in *Atkins*. We held that standards of decency have evolved since *Penry* and now demonstrate that the execution of the mentally retarded is cruel and unusual punishment. The Court noted objective indicia of society's standards, as expressed in legislative enactments and state practice with respect to executions of the mentally retarded. When *Atkins* was decided only a minority of States permitted the practice, and even in those States it was rare. On the basis of these indicia the Court determined that executing mentally retarded offenders "has become truly unusual, and it is fair to say that a national consensus has developed against it."

. . .

III.

A.

The evidence of national consensus against the death penalty for juveniles is similar, and in some respects parallel, to the evidence *Atkins* held sufficient to demonstrate a national consensus against the death penalty for the mentally retarded. When *Atkins* was decided, 30 States prohibited the death penalty for the mentally retarded. This number comprised 12 that had abandoned the death penalty altogether, and 18 that maintained it but excluded the mentally retarded from its reach. By a similar calculation in this case, 30 States prohibit the juvenile death penalty, comprising 12 that have rejected the death penalty altogether and 18 that maintain it but, by express provision or judicial interpretation, exclude juveniles from its reach. *Atkins* emphasized that even in the 20 States without formal prohibition, the practice of executing the mentally retarded was infrequent. . . . In the present case, too, even in the 20 States without a formal prohibition on executing juveniles, the practice is infrequent. . . . [The Court described a trend among states in the years since *Stanford v. Kentucky* to reject the juvenile death penalty.]

Petitioner cannot show national consensus in favor of capital punishment for juveniles but still resists the conclusion that any consensus exists against it. Petitioner supports this position with, in particular, the observation that when the Senate ratified the International Covenant on Civil and Political Rights (ICCPR), Dec. 19, 1966, 999 U. N. T. S. 171 (entered into force Mar. 23, 1976), it did so subject to the President's proposed reservation regarding Article 6(5) of that treaty, which prohibits capital punishment for juveniles. Brief for Petitioner 27. This reservation at best provides only faint support for petitioner's argument. First, the reservation was passed in 1992; since then, five States have abandoned capital punishment for juveniles. Second, Congress considered the issue when enacting the Federal Death Penalty Act in 1994, and determined that the death penalty should not extend to juveniles. See 18 U. S. C. ß3591. The reservation to Article 6(5) of the ICCPR provides minimal evidence that there is not now a national consensus against juvenile executions.

As in *Atkins*, the objective indicia of consensus in this case — the rejection of the juvenile death penalty in the majority of States; the infrequency of its use even where it remains on the books; and the consistency in the trend toward abolition of the practice — provide sufficient evidence that today our society views juveniles, in the words *Atkins* used respecting the mentally retarded, as "categorically less culpable than the average criminal."

B.

A majority of States have rejected the imposition of the death penalty on juvenile offenders under 18, and we now hold this is required by the Eighth Amendment.

Because the death penalty is the most severe punishment, the Eighth Amendment applies to it with special force. . . . [T]he death penalty is reserved for a narrow category of crimes and offenders.

Three general differences between juveniles under 18 and adults demonstrate that juvenile offenders cannot with reliability be classified among the worst offenders. First, as any parent knows and as the scientific and sociological studies respondent and his *amici* cite tend to confirm, "[a] lack of maturity and an underdeveloped sense of responsibility are found in youth more often than in adults and are more understandable among the young." . . . The second area of difference is that juveniles are more vulnerable or susceptible to negative influences and outside pressures, including peer pressure. . . . The third broad difference is that the character of a juvenile is not as well formed as that of an adult. The personality traits of juveniles are more transitory, less fixed. . . . These differences render suspect any conclusion that a juvenile falls among the worst offenders. The susceptibility of juveniles to immature and irresponsible behavior means their "irresponsible conduct is not as morally reprehensible as that of an adult." *Thompson, supra*, at 835 (plurality opinion). Their own vulnerability and comparative lack of control over their immediate surroundings mean juveniles have a greater claim than adults to be forgiven for failing to escape negative influences in their whole environment. . . . Once the diminished culpability of juveniles is recognized, it is evident that the penological justifications [of retribution and deterrence] for the death penalty apply to them with lesser force than to adults.

## IV.

Our determination that the death penalty is disproportionate punishment for offenders under 18 finds confirmation in the stark reality that the United States is the only country in the world that continues to give official sanction to the juvenile death penalty. This reality does not become controlling, for the task of interpreting the Eighth Amendment remains our responsibility. Yet at least from the time of the Court's decision in *Trop*, the Court has referred to the laws of other countries and to international authorities as instructive for its interpretation of the Eighth Amendment's prohibition of "cruel and unusual punishments." (plurality opinion) ("The civilized nations of the world are in virtual unanimity that statelessness is not to be imposed as punishment for crime"); see also *Atkins, supra*, (recognizing that "within the world community, the imposition of the death penalty for crimes committed by mentally retarded offenders is overwhelmingly disapproved"); *Thompson, supra* (plurality opinion) (noting the abolition of the juvenile death penalty "by other nations that share our Anglo-American heritage, and by the leading members of the Western European community," and observing that "[w]e have previously recognized the relevance of the views of the international community in determining whether a punishment is cruel and unusual"); *Enmund, supra* (observing that "the doctrine of felony murder has been abolished in England and India, severely restricted in Canada and a number of other Commonwealth countries, and is unknown in continental Europe"); *Coker, supra* (plurality opinion) ("It is . . . not irrelevant here that out of 60 major nations in the world surveyed in 1965, only 3 retained the death penalty for rape where death did not ensue").

As respondent and a number of *amici* emphasize, Article 37 of the United Nations Convention on the Rights of the Child, which every country in the world has ratified save for the United States and Somalia, contains an express prohibition on capital punishment for crimes committed by juveniles under 18. No ratifying country has entered a reservation to the provision prohibiting the execution of juvenile offenders. Parallel prohibitions are contained in other significant international covenants. See ICCPR, Art. 6(5), (prohibiting capital punishment for anyone under 18 at the time of offense) (signed and ratified by the United States subject to a reservation regarding Article 6(5), as noted, *supra* ...); American Convention on Human Rights; African Charter on the Rights and Welfare of the Child, Art. 5(3) (same).

Respondent and his *amici* have submitted, and petitioner does not contest, that only seven countries other than the United States have executed juvenile offenders since 1990: Iran, Pakistan, Saudi Arabia, Yemen, Nigeria, the Democratic Republic of Congo, and China. Since then each of these countries has either abolished capital punishment for juveniles or made public disavowal of the practice. Brief for Respondent 49-50. In sum, it is fair to say that the United States now stands alone in a world that has turned its face against the juvenile death penalty.

Though the international covenants prohibiting the juvenile death penalty are of more recent date, it is instructive to note that the United Kingdom abolished the juvenile death penalty before these covenants came into being. The United Kingdom's experience bears particular relevance here in light of the historic ties between our countries and in light of the Eighth Amendment's own origins. The Amendment was modeled on a parallel provision in the English Declaration of Rights of 1689, which provided: "[E]xcessive Bail ought not to be required nor excessive Fines imposed; nor cruel and unusually Punishments inflicted." As of now, the United Kingdom has abolished the death penalty in its entirety; but, decades before it took this step, it recognized the disproportionate nature of the juvenile death penalty; and it abolished that penalty as a separate matter. In 1930 an official committee recommended that the minimum age for execution be raised to 21. Parliament then enacted the Children and Young Person's Act of 1933, which prevented execution of those aged 18 at the date of the sentence. And in 1948, Parliament enacted the Criminal Justice Act, prohibiting the execution of any person under 18 at the time of the offense. In the 56 years that have passed since the United Kingdom abolished the juvenile death penalty, the weight of authority against it there, and in the international community, has become well established.

It is proper that we acknowledge the overwhelming weight of international opinion against the juvenile death penalty, resting in large part on the understanding that the instability and emotional imbalance of young people may often be a factor in the crime. The opinion of the world community, while not controlling our outcome, does provide respected and significant confirmation for our own conclusions.

------

*Roper v. Simmons,* which was decided by a five to four majority, overruled *Stanford v. Kentucky,* 492 U.S. 361 (1989), which had upheld the prerogative of states to apply the death penalty to a juvenile offender between the ages of 16 and 18 at the time of the crime. Justice Scalia, writing for the plurality in that previous case, had declined to give weight to international opinion in determining whether the death penalty for juvenile offenders was inconsistent with the Eighth Amendment's prohibition against cruel and unusual punishment: "We emphasize that it is *American* conceptions of decency that are dispositive, rejecting the contention . . . that the sentencing practices of other countries are relevant." 492 U.S. at 370 n.1 (emphasis in original). That rejection of world opinion became the dissenting position in *Roper v. Simmons*. See 543 U.S. at 622-628 (dissenting opinion of Justice Scalia, joined by Chief Justice Rehnquist and Justice Thomas).

In any event, the majority's decision in *Roper v. Simmons* invalidating the death penalty for juvenile offenders rested on a reinterpretation of the Eighth Amendment that was buttressed by an understanding of world opinion, as manifested by the practice of other countries and provisions in a number of multilateral treaties. Simmons's lawyers and several amicus parties had provided extensive arguments detailing these and many additional manifestations of international condemnation of the juvenile death penalty. Highlighted were the overwhelming practice of states prohibiting the death penalty for offenders under 18 years of age, the repeated and numerous resolutions and statements against the practice by the UN General Assembly and UN human rights organs, and the global and regional human rights treaties prohibiting the practice. Amici pointed to a widespread international practice that left the United States isolated as the "only nation in the world that has not committed itself by treaty to bar the death penalty" for juvenile offenders, a position ultimately accepted by the court. *Roper v. Simmons*, Brief of Amici Curiae Nobel Peace Prize Laureates in Support of Respondent, at 9 (No. 03-633) 2004 WL 1636446 (2004). See also *Roper v. Simmons*, Brief of Amici Curiae Former U.S. Diplomats in Support of Respondent (No. 03-633) 2004 WL 1636448 (2004). On the basis of these multiple sources, the argument was pressed upon the Supreme Court that the prohibition of the juvenile penalty is an international norm of jus cogens from which the United States cannot derogate as a matter of international law. See *Roper v. Simmons*, Brief of Amici Curiae the European Union and Members of the International Community in Support of Respondent, at 19-21 (No. 03-633), 2004 WL 1619203 (2004).

Although it did not explicitly acknowledge that it was legally binding on the United States, the Court did, in effect, identify an international standard against the juvenile death penalty and applied it through a reinterpretation of the Eighth Amendment. This *indirect* method of incorporating an international norm into domestic law contrasts with the *direct* application by courts of treaty or customary international rules, and it is the most common use of international norms by courts in the United States.

> Direct incorporation of international law involves use of an international agreement or customary international law directly as law forming the basis for a claim, right, duty, power, civil cause of action, criminal prosecution, or other type of sanction. In such cases, direct incorporation occurs whether or not there is a specific statutory basis for such uses of international law.
>
> Another primary form of incorporation is indirect incorporation involving the use of international law as an interpretive aid. This form of incorporation can involve use of international law indirectly to clarify or supplement the meaning of, for example, the U.S. Constitution, a federal statute, a state constitution or statute, common law, a private contract, or some

other legal provision. In this instance, international law is not used directly as the basis for a civil claim or criminal prosecution, but indirectly to inform the meaning of some other law or legal instrument. When international law is used to clarify duties or powers under the U.S. Constitution, it is the Constitution that provides the direct basis for the duty or power addressed and international law is used indirectly as an interpretive aid concerning the identification, limitation, or enhancement of a duty or competence. . . . Indirect incorporation happens to be the most frequent use of international law throughout United States history. Even treaties that had not been ratified yet by the U.S. have been used indirectly to clarify or provide content of federal law. Since most lawyers and judges in the U.S. have never taken a course in international law, it is not surprising that some of the judges may be more comfortable applying a domestic law as the direct basis for a civil claim, but utilizing international law as an aid to interpret such domestic law.

Jordan J. Paust, *International Law as Law of the United States* 12-13 (2d ed. 2003) (endnotes omitted).

The outcome in *Roper v. Simmons*—making the juvenile death penalty a thing of the past—was the culmination of years of work by death penalty opponents both in the United States and abroad. Some of the individuals and nongovernmental organizations that submitted amicus briefs in favor of Simmons had been involved for years in efforts to see an end to the juvenile death penalty. These efforts included embarking on numerous prior challenges in US federal and state courts on the basis of a combination of constitutional and international law arguments. See, e.g., *Beazley v. Johnson*, 242 F.3d 248 (5th Cir. 2001), cert. denied, 534 U.S. 945 (2001); *Ex Parte Marcus Pressly*, 770 So. 2d 143 (Ala. 2000), cert denied, 531 U.S. 931 (2000); *Servin v. Nevada*, 117 Nev. 775, 794, 32 P.3d 1277 (2001); *Domingues v. State of Nevada*, 114 Nev. 783, 961 P.2d 1279 (1998), cert. denied 528 U.S. 963 (1999). The arguments advanced in these cases are exemplified in the following articles: Carly Baetz-Stangel, *The Role of International Law in the Abolition of the Juvenile Death Penalty*, 16 FLA. J. INT'L L. 955 (2004); Carrie Martin, *Spare the Death Penalty, Spoil the Child: How the Execution of Juveniles Violates the Eighth Amendment's Ban on Cruel and Unusual Punishment in 2005*, 46 S. TEX. L. REV. 695 (2005).

Juvenile death penalty opponents extended their efforts into the international arena, addressing appeals to UN and regional institutions, which in turn responded with statements of condemnation and expressions of concern, in some cases directed specifically at the United States. At the international level, the former UN Commission on Human Rights and its Sub-Commission on the Promotion and Protection of Human Rights issued a series of resolutions condemning the execution of juvenile offenders. See *Roper v. Simmons*, Brief of the Human Rights Committee of the Bar of England and Wales, Human Rights Advocates, Human Rights Watch, and the World Organization for Human Rights USA as Amici Curiae in Support of Respondents (No. 03-633) (2004). In the fall of 1997, after years of expressing concern about the practice of executing juvenile offenders in the United States, the UN Special Rapporteur on extrajudicial, summary or arbitrary executions visited the United States on a special mission to investigate the matter along with the issue of police killings. His report emphasized "that international law clearly indicates a prohibition of imposing a death sentence on juvenile offenders" and called on the United States to follow that prohibition. See *Report of the Special Rapporteur on extrajudicial, summary or arbitrary executions: Mission to the United States of America*, UN Doc E/CN.4/1998/68/Add.3 (1998), para. 55.

Some of the US judicial decisions that had upheld application of the juvenile death penalty were contested in petitions to the Inter-American Commission on Human Rights, which joined in condemning the US practice as a violation of international law. See *Domingues v. United States*, Case 12.285, Inter-Am. Comm'n H.R., Report No. 62/02, OAS doc. OEA/ Ser.L/V/II.116, doc. 33 (2002); *Napoleon Beazley v. United States*, Case 12.412, Inter-Am. Comm'n H.R., Report No. 101/03, OAS doc. OEA/Ser./L/V/II.114 Doc. 70 rev. 1 (2003); *Gary Graham v. United States*, Case No. 11.193, Inter-Am. Comm'n H.R., Report No. 97/03, OAS doc. OEA/Ser./L/V/II.114 Doc. 70 rev. 1 (2003); *Douglas Christopher Thomas v. United States*, Case No. 12.240, Inter-Am. Comm'n H.R., Report No. 100/03, OAS doc. OEA/Ser./L/V/II.114 Doc. 70 rev. 1 (2003).

Whether or not a causal link can be established, these efforts against the juvenile death penalty and manifestations of international concern about it were followed by, or contemporaneous with, the developments identified by the Supreme Court in *Roper* as crucial to its reinterpretation of the Eighth Amendment: a reduction in the number of US states that allowed or practiced the juvenile death penalty and a corresponding shift in public consensus away from allowing the penalty. The Supreme Court's decision in *Roper* was itself part of a gradual evolution in the views among the Court's members toward greater restrictions on the use of the death penalty, as indicated by the prior cases cited by the Court, *Thompson v. Oklahoma* (first prohibiting the death penalty for juvenile offenders under the age of 16) and *Atkins v. Virginia* (prohibiting the death penalty for the mentally retarded).

Given its place within a multifaceted advocacy effort that combined domestic and international dimensions and influenced multiple actors, *Roper* can be seen as part of what Professor Harold Hongju Koh refers to as the "transnational legal process" by which nations "obey" international law.


Harold Hongju Koh

## Why Do Nations Obey International Law?

Review Essay, 106 Yale L.J. 2599, 2635, 2645-46, 2655-58 (1997)
(footnotes omitted)

... [Recent scholarship] suggest[s] that the key [today] to better compliance [with international law] is more internalized compliance, or what I have called obedience. But by what process does norm-internalization occur? How do we transform occasional or grudging compliance with global norms into habitual obedience?

As I have already suggested, such a process can be viewed as having three phases. One or more transnational actors provokes an interaction (or series of interactions) with another, which forces an interpretation or enunciation of the global norm applicable to the situation. By so doing, the moving party seeks not simply to coerce the other party, but to internalize the new interpretation of the international norm into the other party's internal normative system. The aim is to "bind" that other party to obey the interpretation as part of its internal value set. Such a transnational legal process is normative, dynamic, and constitutive. The transaction generates a legal rule which will guide future transnational interactions between the parties; future transactions will further internalize those norms; and eventually, repeated participation in the process will help to reconstitute the interests and even the identities of the participants in the process. . . . As I have described it, transnational legal process presents both a theoretical explanation of why nations obey and a plan of strategic action for prodding nations to obey. How, then, to study this process? . . . [L]et me identify some basic inquiries, using international human rights as an example. In the human rights area, treaty regimes are notoriously weak, and national governments, for reasons of economics or realpolitik, are often hesitant to declare openly that another government engages in abuses. In such an area, where enforcement mechanisms are weak, but core customary norms are clearly defined and often peremptory (jus cogens), the best compliance strategies may not be "horizontal" regime management strategies, but rather, vertical strategies of interaction, interpretation, and internalization.

If transnational actors obey international law as a result of repeated interaction with other actors in the transnational legal process, a first step is to empower more actors to participate. It is here that expanding the role of intergovernmental organizations, nongovernmental organizations, private business entities, and "transnational moral entrepreneurs" deserves careful study. How, for example, do international human rights "issue networks" and epistemic communities form among international and regional intergovernmental organizations, international and domestic NGOs on human rights, and private foundations? How do these networks intersect with the "International Human Rights Regime," namely, the global system of rules and implementation procedures centered in and around the United Nations; regional regimes in Europe, the Americas, Africa, Asia, and the Middle East; single-issue human rights regimes regarding workers' rights, racial discrimination, women's rights; and "global prohibition regimes" against slavery, torture, and the like? Within national governments and intergovernmental organizations, what role do lawyers and legal advisers play in ensuring that the government's policies conform to international legal standards and in prompting governmental agencies to take proactive stances toward human rights abuses?

Second, if the goal of interaction is to produce interpretation of human rights norms, what fora are available for norm-enunciation and elaboration, both within and without existing human rights regimes? If dedicated fora do not already exist, how can existing fora be adapted for this purpose or new fora, such as the International Criminal Tribunal for Rwanda and the former Yugoslavia, be created?

Third, what are the best strategies for internalization of international human rights norms? One might distinguish among social, political, and legal internalization. Social internalization occurs when a norm acquires so much public legitimacy that there is widespread general obedience to it. Political internalization occurs when political elites accept an international norm, and adopt it as a matter of government policy. Legal internalization occurs when an international norm is incorporated into the domestic legal system through executive action, judicial interpretation, legislative action, or some combination of the three. The ABM Treaty controversy thus exemplified the incorporation of a norm (narrow treaty interpretation) into U.S. law and policy through the executive action of the President, acting through his delegate, the U.S. Arms Control and Disarmament Administration.

Judicial internalization can occur when domestic litigation provokes judicial incorporation of human rights norms either implicitly, by construing existing statutes consistently with international human rights norms, or explicitly, through what I have elsewhere called "transnational public law litigation." Legislative internalization occurs when domestic lobbying embeds international law norms into binding domestic legislation or even constitutional law that officials of a noncomplying government must then obey as part of the domestic legal fabric.

The relationship among social, political, and legal internalization can be complex. In the Haitian refugee case, for example, U.S. human rights advocates failed to achieve judicial internalization of an international treaty norm, but in tandem with the growing social outrage about the treatment of Haitian refugees, eventually achieved political internalization: a reversal of the Clinton Administration's policy with respect to Haiti. Similarly, beginning with Filartiga v. Pena-Irala [extracted and discussed *infra*, page 409] U.S. human rights litigators began to promote domestic judicial incorporation of the norm against torture in a manner that eventually helped push President Bush to ratify the U.N. Convention against Torture and Congress to enact the Torture Victim Protection Act of 1991. In the United Kingdom, the issue of legislative internalization has similarly been brought to the fore by the first general election in five years, in which the opposition Labour party has promised, if elected, to incorporate the European Convention on Human Rights into U.K. law. This issue has been a major human rights issue in British politics since the Clement Attlee government first ratified the Convention in the early 1950s. Since then, the Convention has been internalized in part through judicial construction. Yet judicial refusal to recognize explicit incorporation has given new impetus to a political internalization movement that at this writing seems likely to bring about legal internalization of the European Convention into U.K. law by an act of Parliament.

---

The extent to which US Courts should reference or apply sources of international law in their decisions is widely debated among judges, lawyers, scholars, and politicians. That debate is often conflated with debates about the propriety of referencing the law of *foreign* jurisdictions — that is, the domestic law of other countries. Below are remarks offered by a then-sitting Justice of the United States Supreme Court.

Ruth Bader Ginsburg

## A Decent Respect to the Opinions of [Human]kind: The Value of a Comparative Perspective in Constitutional Adjudication

Remarks at the International Academy of Comparative Law, American University
July 30, 2010

. . .

From the birth of the United States as a nation, foreign and international law influenced legal reasoning and judicial decision-making. Founding fathers, most notably, Alexander Hamilton and John Adams, were familiar with leading international law treatises, the law merchant, and English constitutional law. And they used that learning as advocates in legal contests.

The U.S. Constitution, in Article I, authorized Congress to define and punish "Offences against the Law of Nations," and the very first Congress passed the Alien Tort Act [discussed later in this chapter], which empowers federal courts to entertain civil actions brought by an alien for a tort "committed in violation of the law of nations or a treaty of the United States." . . .

The law of nations, Chief Justice Marshall famously said in 1815, is part of the law of our land. Decisions of the courts of other countries, Marshall explained, show how the law of nations is understood elsewhere, and will be considered in determining the rule which is to prevail here. Those decisions, he clarified, while not binding authority for U. S. courts, merit respectful attention for their potential persuasive value.

Decades later, in 1900, the U.S. Supreme Court reaffirmed that

> [i]nternational law is part of our law and must be ascertained and administered by [our] courts of justice . . . . [W]here there is no treaty, no controlling executive or legislative act or judicial decision, resort must be had to the customs and usages of civilized nations, and, as evidence of these, to the works of jurists and commentators, who by years of labor, research and experience, have made themselves peculiarly well acquainted with the subject of which they treat.

. . .

Flash forward with me now to the hearings held earlier this month on the nomination of Elena Kagan for a seat on the U.S. Supreme Court. Queries about international and foreign law were several times posed by members of the Senate Committee on the Judiciary. One Senator expressed "dismay" that, during Kagan's tenure as Dean of the Harvard Law School, "first year students [were required] to take a course in international law." Another ventured that "[n]owhere did the founders say anything about using foreign law." "[P]lease explain," that Senator asked, "why it is OK sometimes to use foreign law to interpret our Constitution or statutes, our treaties." Yet another asked "whether [judges should] ever look to foreign laws for good ideas" or "get inspiration for their decisions from foreign law."

Nominee Kagan responded: "I'm in favor of good ideas . . . wherever you can get them." "Having an awareness of what other nations are doing might be useful," she explained, offering as an example a brief she filed as Solicitor General a few months ago in a case concerning the immunity of foreign officials. Of course, she observed, on a point of U.S. law, foreign decisions do not rank as precedent, but they could be informative in much the same way as one might gain knowledge or insight from reading a law review article. "I'm troubled," a Senator told her, that she "believes we can turn to foreign law to get good ideas."

Contrast with those exchanges, the view of the Constitution's framers, expressed in *The Federalist*, on the "high importance" to the new nation of our adherence to "the laws of nations" in our commerce with other countries. The authors of *The Federalist*, schooled in history, looked abroad for both positive and negative examples to guide their course.

On judicial review for constitutionality, my own view is simply this: If U.S. experience and decisions may be instructive to systems that have more recently instituted or invigorated judicial review for constitutionality, so too can we learn from others now engaged in measuring ordinary laws and executive actions against fundamental instruments of government and charters securing basic rights.

Exposing laws to judicial review for constitutionality was once uncommon outside the United States. But particularly in the years following World War II, many nations installed constitutional review by courts as one safeguard against oppressive government and stirred-up majorities. National, multinational, and international human rights charters and courts today play a prominent part in our world. The U.S. judicial system will be the poorer, I have urged, if we do not both share our experience with, and learn from, legal systems with values and a commitment to democracy similar to our own.

In the value I place on comparative dialogue — on sharing with and learning from others — as I earlier noted, I draw on counsel from the founders of the United States. The drafters and signers of the Declaration of Independence showed their concern about the opinions of other peoples; they placed before the world the reasons why the States, joining together to become the United States of America, were impelled to separate from Great Britain. The Declarants stated their reasons out of "a decent Respect to the Opinions of Mankind." They sought to expose those reasons to the scrutiny of "a candid world."

The U.S. Supreme Court, early on, expressed a complementary view: The judicial power of the United States, the Court said in 1816, includes cases "in the correct adjudication of which foreign nations are deeply interested . . . [and] in which the principles of the law and comity of nations often form an essential inquiry." Just as the founding generation showed concern for how adjudication in our courts would affect other countries' regard for the United States, so today, even more than when the United States was a new nation, judgments rendered in the USA are subject to the scrutiny of "a candid World.". . .

True, there are generations-old and still persistent discordant views on concern about, and recourse to, the "Opinions of Mankind." As my quotations from the remarks of Senators at the Elena Kagan hearings indicate, U.S. jurists and political actors today divide sharply on the propriety of looking beyond our nation's borders, particularly on matters touching fundamental human rights. Expressing spirited opposition, my dear colleague, Justice Antonin Scalia, for example, counsels: The Court "should cease putting forth foreigners' views as part of the reasoned basis of its decisions. To invoke alien law when it agrees with one's own thinking, and ignore it otherwise, is not reasoned decisionmaking, but sophistry."

Another trenchant critic, Seventh Circuit U.S. Court of Appeals Judge Richard Posner, commented not long ago: "To cite foreign law as authority is to flirt with the discredited . . . idea of a universal natural law; or to suppose fantastically that the world's judges constitute a single, elite community of wisdom and conscience." Judge Posner's view rests, in part, on the concern that U.S. judges do not comprehend the social, historical, political, and institutional background from which foreign opinions emerge. Nor do most of us even understand the language in which laws and judgments, outside the common law realm, are written.

Judge Posner is right, of course, to this extent: Foreign opinions, as Elena Kagan reiterated in her responses to Senators, are not authoritative; they set no binding precedent for the U.S. judge. But they can add to the store of knowledge relevant to the solution of trying questions. Yes, we should approach foreign legal materials with sensitivity to our differences and imperfect understanding, but imperfection, I believe, should not lead us to abandon the effort to learn what we can from the experience and wisdom foreign sources may convey.

Comparative sideglances can sometimes aid us in deciding not only what we should do, but what we should not do. A notable example: In the "Steel Seizure Case" decided by the U. S. Supreme Court in 1952, Justice Jackson, in his separate opinion, pointed to features of the Weimar Constitution in Germany that allowed Adolf Hitler to assume dictatorial powers. Even in wartime, Jackson concluded, the U.S. President could not seize private property (in that case, the steel mills). Such a measure, in good times and bad, the Court held, required congressional authorization.

At the time Justice Jackson cast a comparative side glance at Weimar Germany, the United States itself was a source of "negative authority" abroad. The Attorney General pressed that point in an amicus brief for the United States filed in *Brown* v. *Board of Education*, the public schools desegregation case decided in 1954. Urging the Court to put an end to the "separate but equal doctrine," the Attorney General wrote:

> The existence of discrimination against minority groups in the United States has an adverse effect upon our relations with other countries. Racial discrimination . . . raises doubts even among friendly nations as to the intensity of our devotion to the democratic faith.

Judges in the United States, after all, are free to consult all manner of commentary—Restatements, Treatises, what law professors or even law students write copiously in law reviews, and, in the internet age, any number of legal blogs. If we can consult those sources, why not the analysis of a question similar to the one we confront contained, for example, in an opinion of the Supreme Court of Canada, the Constitutional Court of South Africa, the German Constitutional Court, or the European Court of Human Rights? . . .

Recognizing that forecasts are risky, I nonetheless believe the U. S. Supreme Court will continue to accord "a decent Respect to the Opinions of [Human]kind" as a matter of comity and in a spirit of humility. Comity, because projects vital to our well-being—combating international terrorism is a prime example—require trust and cooperation of nations the world over. And humility because, in Justice O'Connor's words: "Other legal systems continue to innovate, to experiment, and to find . . . solutions to the new legal problems that arise each day, [solutions] from which we can learn and benefit."

---

Less controversial than the use of international sources to interpret the U.S. Constitution is the use of international sources to interpret federal statutes or judge-made rules. In a famous early case, *Murray v. The Schooner Charming Betsy*, 6 U.S.

(2 Cranch) 64, 118 (1804), the Supreme Court affirmed, in an opinion written by Chief Justice John Marshall, that "an act of Congress ought never to be construed to violate the law of nations if any other possible construction remains." See, e.g., applying this rule: *Trans World Airlines, Inc. v. Franklin Mint Corp,* 466 U.S. 243, 252 (1984); *McCulloch v. Sociedad de Marineros,* 372 U.S. 10, 21-22 (1963); *Lauritzen v. Larsen,* 345 U.S. 571, 578, (1953); *Pigeon River Improvement, Slide & Boom Co. v. Charles W. Cox, Ltd.,* 291 U.S. 138, 160 (1934); *Chew Heong v. United States,* 112 U.S. 536, 539 (1884). This rule of interpretation is justified, not just by respect for international law, but by the practical imperative of not advancing, if at all possible, an interpretation that places the United States in breach of its international obligations. Thus, for example, a federal district court went to significant lengths to interpret the Anti-terrorism Act to not require the closure of the Palestine Liberation Organization's observer mission to the UN in New York, which would have been in violation of the UN Headquarters Agreement, a treaty binding on the United States. See *United States v. Palestine Liberation Organization,* 695 F. Supp. 1456, (S.D.N.Y. 1988).

There is ample authority, therefore, for interpreting a federal statute or judge-made rule so that it does not run afoul of international human rights norms that are binding on the United States. To what extent does this same authority support interpreting a federal law in light of international human rights law in order to enhance the normative content of the federal law, rather than to just ensure that the federal law does not conflict with international law? Can you think of any federal statute or judicial doctrine that could be improved, from a human rights standpoint, by interpreting it in light of applicable international human rights law?

### *Comments and Questions*

1. During the US Senate hearings for his confirmation as Chief Justice of the Supreme Court, which took place after *Roper v. Simmons* was decided, John Roberts echoed the sentiments of Justice Scalia, expressed in his dissent in *Roper,* in which Scalia stressed the primacy of American values over any international opinion. Roberts argued further that recourse to foreign sources as precedent inappropriately enhances the discretion of judges. See *Transcript: Day Three of the Roberts Confirmation Hearings,* The Washington Post, Sept. 14, 2005. As pointed out by Justice Ginsberg, a number of scholars and politicians have advanced arguments similar to those of Scalia and Roberts against applying international or foreign sources. Is Justice Ginsberg's response to those arguments convincing?

2. Justice Ginsburg referred to the value of both international sources—such as treaties—and the domestic law of other countries. Is there a different argument for relying on international sources as interpretive tools than there is for relying on foreign domestic sources? Should a court in the US give the same weight to the International Covenant on Civil and Political Rights in interpreting the US constitutional right to privacy as it should to a privacy statute of France or Mexico?

3. The Supreme Court has made reference in other constitutional cases to human rights standards as understood internationally or applied in other democracies. In *Lawrence v. Texas,* 539 U.S. 558, 576-577 (2003), for example, the Court noted that the right to engage in intimate same-sex conduct had been accepted as

an integral part of human freedom in many other countries and referenced jurisprudence of the European Court of Human Rights, as support for finding the right
to be within the privacy interest protected by the due process clause of the Constitution. See also *Washington v. Glucksberg*, 521 U.S. 702, 710 & n.8 (1997) (noting
that "almost every western democracy" criminalized physician-assisted suicide and
discussing laws in a number of nations in Western Europe); *Grutter v. Bollinger*, 539
U.S. 306, 342 (2003) (Ginsburg, J., concurring) (citing UN conventions and identifying the "international understanding" concerning affirmative action plans).
Subsequent to *Roper*, in *Graham v. Florida*, 560 U.S. 48 (2010), the Court made
similar references to international and foreign sources in interpreting the Eight
Amendment, and found that sentencing a minor with life imprisonment without
parole, for a nonhomicide crime, violated the amendment's prohibition of cruel
and unusual punishment. In all these cases, members of the Supreme Court identified patterns of normative understanding being adopted and applied transnationally, although they declined to explicitly recognize a binding international norm or
apply it directly. Despite not recognizing *binding* international norms, is the United
States, by virtue of these decisions, nonetheless "obeying" international law? Cf.
Elizabeth Burleson, *Juvenile Execution, Terrorist Extradition, and Supreme Court Discretion to Consider International Death Penalty Jurisprudence*, 68 ALB. L. REV. 909, 947
(2005) (discussing the interaction between international and domestic US law in
the area of the death penalty); David Sloss and Michael Van Alstine, "International
Law in Domestic Courts," in *Reasearch Handbook on the Politics of International Law*
(2017) (analyzing the approaches in various countries interpreting and analyzing
international legal rules).

4. Justice Ginsburg forecasted that the U.S. Supreme Court will continue to
accord " 'a decent Respect to the Opinions of [Human]kind' as a matter of comity
and in a spirit of humility." Do you share this optimism? In *Miller v. Alabama*, 567
U.S. 460 (2012), in which the Supreme Court held unconstitutional a sentence
of life imprisonment without parole for any crime committed by a minor, neither the majority opinion by Justice Kagan nor the concurring opinion by Justice
Breyer joined by Justice Sotomayor made reference to any international or foreign
sources. Can you speculate about a reason for this? Note that Justice Breyer has otherwise been one of the strongest proponents of a judicial philosophy that embraces
consideration of international and foreign sources. See Stephen Breyer, *The Court
and the World: American Law and the New Global Realities* (2015).

5. The current composition of the Court appears to include a majority of Justices whose judicial philosophies do not align with the approach reflected in *Roper*
that is favorable to using international and foreign sources. Nonetheless, members
of that majority—including Justices Roberts, Thomas, Alito, Gorsuch, and Kavanaugh—joined in an opinion in *Dept. of Commerce v. New York*, 588 U.S. __,139
S. Ct. 2551 (2019), upholding the Commerce Department's inclusion of a question
on citizenship in the national census, and in the course of the opinion they highlighted the government's observation that "the United Nations recommends collecting census-based citizenship information, and other major democracies such as
Australia . . . inquire about citizenship in their censuses." 139 S. Ct. at 2563. During
oral argument in the case, Justices Gorsuch and Kavanagh pressed that point on
the attorney arguing for those challenging the citizenship question. See Transcript

of oral argument in *Dept. of Commerce v. New York*, April 23, 2019, pages 52-55, 80. See also Adam Liptak, *Conservatives, Often Wary of Foreign Law, Embrace It in Census Case*, The New York Times, Apr. 29, 2019. Have these Justices had a change of heart? Or are they invoking international sources only because it supports their inclinations on the merits of the case? Does it matter?

6. Whatever path the U.S. Supreme Court takes in the foreseeable future in relation to international sources, lower federal and state courts can be encouraged to use those sources when relevant to the interpretation of domestic rules in cases before them. It can be observed that many judges are simply reluctant to use international law because they are not familiar with it, or view it as exotic. In the United States, there is a unique legal culture—which contrasts markedly with the legal environments in the rest of the world—in which international law is viewed with ambivalence if not hostility, and judges are part of this legal culture. See John F. Coyle, *The Case for Writing International Law into the U.S. Code*, 56 B.C. L. REV. 433 (2015). Does this mean that judges in the United States can never be educated to understand the value of international sources, especially those sources with which the United States has aligned, or be influenced to resort to them when they are relevant to interpreting an applicable domestic rule? For one of the many cases that suggest that they can, see *Pueblo of Jemez v. United States*, 350 F. Supp. 3d 1052, 1094 & n.15 (D.N.M. 2018) (referring to the UN Declaration on the Rights of Indigenous Peoples in construing origins of indigenous land rights, though adhering to federal doctrine of extinguishment of indigenous land rights contrary to the declaration).

7. Many of the international sources referred by the Supreme Court in *Roper* to invalidate the death penalty for minor criminal offenders were soft law and not strictly speaking binding on the United States, although arguably those sources reflected a customary international law norm against the death penalty for minor offenders. The Court in *Roper* used these sources as reinforcing its assessment of the Constitution, but not as legally controlling. What if the Court had found or conceded to a rule of customary international law or a treaty-based rule prohibiting the death penalty for minor offenders? More generally, what could be the international legal consequence if courts in the US interpret domestic law in a way that is inconsistent with international human rights law? Are binding norms of international human rights law merely instructive or in the nature of "good ideas?" For further discussion, see Grainne de Burca, *International Law Before the Courts, the EU and the US Compared*, 55 VA. J. INT'L. 685 (2015); Tai-Heng Cheng, *The Universal Declaration of Human Rights at Sixty: Is It Still Right for the United States?*, 41 CORNELL INT'L L.J. 251 (2008).

## B. Can Treaty Provisions Be Directly Applied by Domestic Courts?

Apart from being used to interpret domestic law, can international treaties furnish rules of decision for the courts, independently of law enacted domestically? Among the several international instruments cited by the Supreme Court in *Roper v. Simmons* to support its decision that the death penalty as applied to juvenile offenders is unconstitutional was the International Covenant on Civil and Political Rights. Article 6(5) of the Covenant provides, "Sentence of death shall not be imposed for crimes committed by persons before eighteen years of age and shall not be carried out on pregnant women." The United States became a party to the Covenant on June 8, 1992, years before the Supreme Court's ruling in *Roper*. But while specifically citing Article 6(5) of the Covenant, which explicitly prohibits the juvenile death penalty at issue in *Roper*, the Court did not directly apply it as a rule of decision. Absent from the Court's opinion is any suggestion that Article 6(5) could itself be an independent or alternative legal basis for invalidating state laws allowing execution of juvenile offenders. Article 6(5) of the Covenant effectively is reduced to one of many contributors to a policy backdrop for the Court's interpretation of the Eighth Amendment. In earlier cases in federal and state courts, defendants had sought without success to avoid the death penalty on the basis of Article 6(5) of the Covenant.

As indicated earlier, Article VI, Section 2 of the US Constitution affirms that treaties ratified by the United States are part of the "supreme Law of the Land," thereby establishing treaties as part of federal law with supremacy over state law. The Supreme Court confirmed this supremacy in *Ware v. Hylton*, 3 U.S. (3 Dall.) 199 (1796), and further cemented this principle in *United States v. Pink*, 315 U.S. 203, 230 (1942), emphasizing that "state law must yield when it is inconsistent with, or impairs the policy or provisions of, a treaty." See generally Jordan J. Paust, *International Law as Law of the United States*, 70-71 (2d ed. 2003) (discussing early Supreme Court cases in which "treaty law was accepted as operating directly as supreme federal law in the face of inconsistent state law"); Carlos Manuel Vázquez, *Treaties as Law of the Land: The Supremacy Clause and the Judicial Enforcement of Treaties*, 122 Harv. L. Rev. 599-695 (2008) (contending that the US Constitution establishes a straightforward rule establishing that treaties are the "supreme Law of the Land," and therefore they are enforceable in courts in the same circumstances as constitutional and statutory provisions of similar content).

To be sure, US courts have regarded treaties as equal but not superior to federal statutes; thus, if a treaty conflicts with a federal law, the more recent prevails, whichever it is. See *The Chinese Exclusion Case*, 130 U.S. 581, 578-99 (1889). Also, like federal statutes, treaties are held subject to constitutional protections for individual rights and other constitutional limitations. See *Reid v. Covert*, 354 U.S. 1, 16-17 (1957). But there can be no argument that the prohibition of the juvenile death penalty contained in Article 6(5) of the Covenant is itself prohibited by the Constitution. And no federal legislation subsequent to the ratification of the Covenant supplants Article 6(5) by authorizing the imposition of the death penalty on juvenile capital offenders. As in the *Roper* case, authorization for imposing the death penalty on juvenile offenders has been under state, not federal, law. At the time *Roper* was decided, 20 states had laws providing such authorization.

So why have courts in the United States not applied Article 6(5) of the Covenant on Civil and Political Rights to invalidate state laws authorizing the application of the death penalty to juvenile offenders? Treaties like the Covenant are part of US law to which state law is subordinate, given the Supremacy Clause and established Supreme Court doctrine. The most obvious answer lies in the reservations the United States attached to the Covenant upon ratification, as well as the allegedly non-self-executing character of the Covenant. We now turn to these issues.

## 1. Judicial Deference of Reservations to Multilateral Treaties

The United States ratified the Covenant on Civil and Political Rights subject to various reservations, understandings, and declarations, as discussed in Chapter 2. Among these was the affirmation that "the United States reserves the right, subject to its Constitutional constraints, to impose capital punishment on any person (other than a pregnant woman) duly convicted under existing or future laws permitting the imposition of capital punishment, including persons below eighteen years of age." See U.S. Senate Resolution of Advice and Consent to the Ratification of the International Covenant on Civil and Political Rights, art. I(2), 138 Con'g. Rec. S4781 (1991).

The Supreme Court in *Roper v. Simmons* referred to this reservation without questioning its validity, but found that the reservation provided little evidence against a national consensus against the death penalty. The validity of the reservation has been questioned by the UN Human Rights Committee, as discussed in Chapter 2, as well as by a significant number of scholars and human rights advocates. See, e.g., Annika K. Carlsten, *Young Enough to Die? Executing Juvenile Offenders in Violation of International Law*, 29 DENV. J. INT'L L. & POL'Y 181, 187- 189 (2001); William A. Schabas, *Invalid Reservations to the International Covenant on Civil and Political Rights: Is the United States Still a Party?*, 21 BROOKLYN J. INT'L L. 277 (1995).

Arguments that the reservation is invalid are based on the Covenant itself and on the general international law applicable to treaty reservations (see Chapter 2), as exemplified succinctly by the following.

> Turning first to the language of the treaty, Article 4(2) of the ICCPR [the Covenant on Civil and Political Rights] states that "no derogation from Articles 6, 7, 8 (paragraphs one and two), 11, 15, 16, and 18 may be made under this provision." Although there is no formula to determine under what conditions a reservation may be valid, the Inter-American Court on Human Rights issued an opinion linking the non-derogable provisions of a treaty with the incompatibility principle of the Law of Nations. [See Restrictions to the Death Penalty (Arts. 4(2) and 4(4) American Convention on Human Rights, Advisory Opinion No. OC-3/83 of Sept. 8, 1983.] In this advisory opinion, the court defined the incompatibility doctrine when it stated that a reservation violating a non-derogable right is incompatible with the object and purpose of the treaty and is therefore not permitted. The Human Rights Committee, established under the ICCPR, affirmed that some components of the death penalty reservation may be "incompatible with the object and purpose of the Covenant" causing these reservations to be invalid. [Human Right's Committee's observations on the United States' first report under the Covenant, UN Doc. CCPR/C/79/Add.50 (1995).] The Inter-American Court of Human Rights also discussed the object and purpose of treaties, stating that modern human rights treaties, such as the ICCPR, stand for the protection of "basic rights of individual human beings . . . against the State of their nationality and all other contracting States." [See The Effect of Reservations on the Entry into Force of the American Convention (Arts. 74 and 75), Advisory Opinion No. OC-2/82 of Sept. 24, 1982.] In light of the

above opinions, the Senate's reservation is incompatible with the purpose of the treaty and signifies the United States' non-compliance with its international obligations under Article Six.

External to the language of the ICCPR and decisions interpreting specific reservations to Article Six, Article 19(c) of the Vienna Convention on the Law of Treaties establishes that a party may not formulate a reservation that is incompatible with the object and purpose of the treaty. Although the United States has not ratified the Vienna Convention, the State Department recognizes this treaty as a guide to international law and practice.

Christian A. Levesque, *The International Covenant on Civil and Political Rights: A Primer for Raising a Defense Against the Juvenile Death Penalty in Federal Courts*, 50 Am. U.L. Rev. 755, 784-785 (2001) (footnotes changed into bracketed text).

The foregoing argument, however, has not carried the day in the courts. Before the US Supreme Court in *Roper v. Simmons* determined that the US Constitution itself prohibits capital punishment of juvenile offenders, federal and state courts consistently applied the US reservation to Article 6(5) of the Covenant to avoid that Article's prohibition of the juvenile death penalty. Generally, the courts applied the reservation without assessing its validity, essentially deferring to the posture of the federal executive and Senate in ratifying the treaty.

It is telling that, in *Roper v. Simmons*, the lawyers for Simmons did not urge the Court to consider Article 6(5) a binding treaty provision, effectively conceding the validity of the US reservation. See Brief for Respondent (Jul. 19, 2004), *Roper v. Simmons*, 125 S. Ct. 1183 (2005) (No. 03-633), WL 1947812. Neither, for the most part, did the several amicus parties that weighed in favor of *Simmons* urge rejection of the reservation to Article 6(5); instead, they presented a picture of applicable international law and world opinion that did not depend on finding that Article 6(5) was binding on the United States. See, e.g., Brief of Amici Curiae Nobel Peace Laureates in Support of Respondent, *Roper v. Simmons*, *supra*. But see Brief of Amici Curiae the European Union and Members of the International Community in Support of Respondent, *Roper v. Simmons*, *supra*, at 14-17 (asserting that the reservation is invalid). As noted, the Court itself did not question the validity of the reservation, although it did count Article 6(5) among the indicators of world opinion (something that attracted caustic criticism by Justice Scalia in his dissent). A rationale, if not justification, for this deference to the reservation was provided in the following article, written before the Court's decision in *Roper*.

Curtis A. Bradley

## The Juvenile Death Penalty and International Law

52 Duke L.J. 485, 541-44, 557 (2002) (notes omitted)

. . . [I]n order for an ICCPR-based challenge against the U.S. juvenile death penalty to succeed under international law, a decisionmaker would have to reach two questionable conclusions: that the U.S. reservation violates the object and purpose of the ICCPR [International Covenant on Civil and Political Rights], and that the proper remedy under international law is to sever the reservation and enforce the treaty against the United States as if it had never entered the reservation. Even those conclusions, however, would probably be insufficient to provide a *U.S. court* with a basis for disregarding the reservation.

Article II of the Constitution specifies the procedural requirements for treaty-making: the president has the power to make treaties, "by and with the Advice and Consent of the Senate . . . provided two thirds of the Senators present concur." The reservations to the ICCPR, including the reservation to the juvenile death penalty provision, comply with these requirements. The president and at least two-thirds of the senators present accepted these reservations, and they were included with the U.S. instrument of treaty ratification that was deposited by the president with the United Nations. . . .

In fact, enforcement of the juvenile death penalty provision by a U.S. court would not only lack support in U.S. law, it arguably would violate the U.S. Constitution. Under Articles II and VI of the Constitution, the president and two- thirds of the Senate must agree on the terms of a treaty before it becomes part of the "supreme Law of the Land." If a U.S. court disregarded the U.S. reservation and enforced the juvenile death penalty provision, it would be treating as supreme law of the land a treaty provision that had never been approved by the president and Senate. Even if one were to conclude that the proper *international law remedy* was to sever the reservation and enforce the treaty as if the reservation had never been entered, the procedural requirements of the Constitution would remain unsatisfied. This is true even if a court somehow concluded that the U.S. treatymakers would have ratified the treaty without the reservation if they had known that the reservation was invalid under international law, since Article II refers to what the treatymakers *actually* agreed upon, not to what they *would have* agreed upon.

More generally, courts would likely be reluctant to disregard the U.S. reservation because doing so would involve a substantial judicial intervention into the treaty process. U.S. courts have never exercised judicial review to invalidate either the domestic or international effects of a treaty. In part, this is because the text of the Constitution is relatively silent about the scope and exclusivity of the treaty power. U.S. courts also have recognized that, although treaties are legal instruments, their creation and especially their enforcement are heavily informed by political factors. Recognizing the lack of textual guidance and the importance of political contingency in this context, U.S. courts have taken a largely passive role in the institutional developments concerning the making and enforcement of treaties. They usually defer to the accommodations of the political branches (such as the allowance of congressional-executive agreements) or abstain from adjudicating disputes between the political branches (such as over the termination of treaties). Similarly, they consider many matters pertaining to the negotiation, observance, and status of treaties to be "political questions" committed to the discretion of the political branches. They also give "great weight" to the Executive Branch's interpretation of a treaty. And, of course, judicial deference to political branch arrangements is especially strong in situations, as with the reservations to the ICCPR, in which the political branches are in agreement. For all of these reasons, it is highly unlikely that a U.S. court would apply the customary international law of treaty reservations to invalidate the United States' juvenile death penalty reservation to the ICCPR. . . . I do not intend to suggest in this Article that the juvenile death penalty reflects wise policy or that it should be retained. Nor am I arguing that international practice is irrelevant to this policy question, or even to the Eighth Amendment analysis of what is cruel and unusual. My argument, rather, is that these policy and legal questions must ultimately be decided by the United States, in accordance with its constitutional processes. Claims by advocacy groups and scholars that these decisions have already been made for the United States distort the actual requirements of international law and, in any event, are not likely to be persuasive to U.S. decision makers.

## *Comments and Questions*

1. Do you find convincing the argument that the US reservation regarding Article 6(5) of the Covenant on Civil and Political Rights is invalid? Isn't the purpose of a reservation precisely to avoid obligations that a ratifying state, for whatever reasons, does not wish to accept? See the discussion of reservations in Chapter 2.

2. Should domestic courts always defer to reservations attached to human rights treaties upon ratification, or is the validity of a reservation appropriately resolved by a domestic court? Consider also the constitutional and policy argument advanced by Professor Bradley. What would happen if a domestic court determined a reservation to a human rights treaty invalid? Consider the discussion of how reservations might be determined to be invalid and the effects of such determinations in Chapter 2.

### 2.   The Doctrine of (Non) Self-Executing Treaties

As noted earlier, Article VI, section 2, of the Constitution establishes treaties ratified by the United States to be part of the "supreme Law of the Land." However, under principles first enunciated by Chief Justice Marshall in *Foster v. Neilson*, 27 U.S. (2 Pet.) 253, 314 (1829), the status accorded by courts in the United States to treaty provisions that are admitted to be binding on the country turns on whether the provisions are considered self-executing. "It is only when a treaty is self-executing, when it prescribes rules by which private rights may be determined that it may be relied upon for the enforcement of such rights." *Dreyfus v. Von Finck*, 534 F.2d 24, 30 (2d Cir.), cert. denied, 429 U.S. 835 (1976). Thus, even if the reservation to Article 6(5) of the Covenant on Civil and Political Rights did not exist or was somehow considered inoperative, the self-execution hurdle would have to be overcome for that provision—and the other provisions of the Covenant—to be judicially enforceable within the United States.

Ordinarily, the question of whether a treaty provision is self-executing and hence judicially enforceable is a matter of judicial interpretation. Nonetheless, presidential and Senate-approved declarations of non-self-execution appear to have foreclosed judicial determination of the issue with regard to the Covenant on Civil and Political Rights and other US-ratified human rights treaties.

## *The US Declarations of Non-Self-Execution*

The president attached to his ratification of the Covenant on Civil and Political Rights a "declaration" that the Covenant's substantive provisions "are not self-executing," and that declaration was approved by the Senate. U.S. Senate Resolution of Advice and Consent to the Ratification of the International Covenant on Civil and Political Rights, art. III(1),138 Con'g. Rec. S4781 (1991). Similar declarations were attached to US ratification of the International Convention on the Elimination All Forms of Racial Discrimination and the Convention Against Torture and Other Cruel, Inhuman, or Degrading Treatment or Punishment. For a review of the content of these non-self-execution declarations and their impact, see David Sloss, *The Domestication of International Human Rights: Non-Self-Executing Declarations and Human Rights Treaties*, 24 YALE J. INT'L L. 129 (1999).

Scholars and advocates have argued that the non-self-execution declaration is invalid on the ground that the question of self-execution is a matter of judicial determination that should not be predetermined by the president or Senate. See, e.g., Louis Henkin, *Comment, U.S. Ratification of Human Rights Convention: The Ghost of Senator Bricker*, 89 AM. J. INT'L L. 341, 346-347 (1995) (arguing that the Senate and president's attempt to foreclose judicial enforcement of the Covenant "may be unconstitutional"). An alternative argument is that the declaration is contrary to the object and purpose of the Covenant, since rendering the Covenant non-self-executing undermines the judicial remedies contemplated by the Covenant. See, e.g., Jordan J. Paust, *Customary International Law and Human Rights Treaties Are Law of the United States*, 20 MICH. J. INT'L L. 301, 322- 324 (1999).

Despite such arguments, the US Supreme Court, in *Sosa v. Alvarez-Machain*, 542 U.S. 692 (2004), followed the dominant trend in the lower federal courts and summarily construed the Covenant on Civil and Political Rights to be non-self-executing in light of the declaration. The Court concluded that, because of the declaration, the Covenant does not "itself create obligations enforceable in the federal courts" and hence could not "establish the relevant and applicable rule of international law" for an action under the federal Alien Tort Statute. Id. at 735 (an extract of the opinion in *Sosa* is set forth *infra*, page 414).

Assuming that the non-self-execution declaration is valid, how far-reaching is it? Does it render the Covenant, and other human rights treaties ratified with similar declarations of non-self-execution, without *any* possibility of providing a rule of decision in the domestic courts? Relevant to this question is the following statement from the Clinton administration, made during deliberations on the ratification of the Convention on the Elimination of All Forms of Racial Discrimination.

> . . . By making clear that this convention is not self-executing, we ensure that it does not create a new or independently enforceable private cause of action in U.S. courts. We have proposed and the Senate has concurred in the same approach to previous human rights treaties, such as . . . the International Covenant on Civil and Political Rights (1992).
>
> As was the case with the earlier treaties, existing U.S. law provides extensive protection and remedies. . . . We see no need for the establishment of additional causes of action to enforce the requirements of the convention.

Statement of Conrad Harper, Legal Advisor of the U.S. State Department, to the Senate Committee on Foreign Relations (May 11, 1994).

This statement has been used to argue that the effect of the non-self-execution declaration is not to prevent the substantive provisions of the Covenant on Civil and Political Rights from operating as rules of decision in all judicial proceedings, but only to ensure that the treaty does not itself give rise to any affirmative cause of action in domestic courts. The extension of this argument is that, notwithstanding the declaration, Article 6(5) of the Covenant on Civil and Political Rights may be applied defensively to prevent application of the death penalty to a juvenile defender (assuming that the reservation specific to that article is invalid), since such a defensive use of the Covenant is not the assertion of a cause of action. See Connie de la Vega, *Amici Curiae Urge the U.S. Supreme Court to Consider International Human Rights Law in Death Penalty Case*, 42 SANTA CLARA L. REV. 1041, 1056 (2002) (advancing this argument). See generally Paust, *Customary International Law and Human Rights Treaties Are Law of the United States, supra*, at 326 (arguing that "even generally non-self-executing treaties are still law of the United States and can be used [inter alia] . . . defensively in civil or criminal contexts"); Carlos Manuel Vazquez, *The Four Doctrines of Self-Executing Treaties*, 89 AM J. INT'L L. 695 (1995) (distinguishing between treaties that create affirmative causes of action and those that do not but that should still otherwise be judicially enforceable).

However, the sweeping language of the Supreme Court in *Sosa v. Alvarez-Machain*—stating that the Covenant does "not itself create obligations enforceable in the federal courts"—discourages this argument. This language can be read to suggest that the Covenant on Civil and Political Rights cannot for *any* purpose provide a judicially applicable rule of decision, including but not limited to establishing an affirmative cause of action. The quoted language read in this way might be considered mere dictum, since the matter before the Court was whether international law established an affirmative cause of action that could be pursued under the Alien Tort Statute (see extract of decision *infra*). It is strong dictum, nonetheless, supported by a number of cases in which courts have consistently deferred to the non-self-execution declaration and declined to directly apply the Covenant, including instances when the Covenant was defensively invoked. See, e.g., *Igartúa v. U.S.*, 626 F.3d 592 (1st Cir. 2010), petition for cert. denied; *Guaylupo-Moya v. Gonzales*, 423 F.3d 121 (2d Cir. 2005); *Beazley v. Johnson*, 242 F.3d 248, 267 (5th Cir. 2001), petition for cert. denied; *United States v. Duarte-Acero* 296 F.3d. 1277, 1283 (11th Cir. 2002), petition for cert. denied; *Igartua de la Rosa v. United States*, 32 F.3d 8, 10 n.1 (1st Cir. 1994), petition for cert. denied; *Ralk v. Lincoln County*, 81 F. Supp. 2d 1372, 1381 (S.D. Ga. 2000); *In re Matter of the Extradition of Cheung*, 968 F. Supp. 791, 803 n. 17 (D. Conn. 1997); *Rivera v. Warden*, 2001 U.S. Dist. LEXIS 24344, 13, 14 (M.D. Pa. June 12, 2001).

## *Judicial Assessments of Whether Treaties Are Self-Executing*

Prior to the Supreme Court's finding, in *Sosa v. Alvarez-Machain, infra* page 414, that the non-self-execution declaration regarding the Covenant on Civil and Political Rights is dispositive, a federal district court, in *White v. Paulsen*, 997 F. Supp. 1380, 1387 (E.D. Wash. 1998), declined to give such dispositive weight to either that declaration or a similar declaration attached to the US ratification of the Convention sgainst Torture and Other Cruel, Inhuman or Degrading Treatment or Punishment. The court held that neither the Covenant nor the Convention against Torture could ground a claim of prisoner mistreatment in connection with 28 U.S.C. §1331, which provides a statutory basis for federal jurisdiction over claims "arising under the Constitution, laws, or treaties of the United States." Taking a rare judicial posture, the court in *White* stated that the non-self-execution declaration "may not carry controlling weight on this issue," 997 F. Supp. at 1387, while it nonetheless found the substantive provisions of the Covenant to be non-self-executing on the basis of its own interpretation of the treaty:

> There is no set test for determining whether a treaty is self-executing; different courts have come up with various descriptions of factors relevant to this inquiry. *See, e.g., Frolova v. Union of Soviet Socialist Republics,* 761 F.2d 370, 373 (7th Cir. 1975) (listing six relevant factors). The Ninth Circuit has expressly stated that its subordinate courts must look to relevant "contextual factors," including:
>
> > the purposes of the treaty and the objectives of its creators, the existence of domestic procedures and institutions appropriate for direct implementation, the availability and feasibility of alternative enforcement methods, and the immediate and long-range social consequences of self- or non-self-execution.

*People of Saipan v. United States Dep't of Interior,* 502 F.2d 90, 97 (9th Cir. 1974). Of these four non-exclusive factors, "it is the first factor that is critical to determine whether an executive agreement is self-executing, while the other factors are most relevant to determine the extent to which the agreement is self-executing." *Iran,* 771 F.2d at 1283; *see also Frolova,* 761 F.2d at 373 ("if the parties' intent is clear from the treaty's language courts will not inquire into the remaining factors").

Plaintiffs contend two treaties to which the United States is a party contain self- executing prohibitions on torture that incorporate non-consensual medical experimentation: the previously discussed International Covenant on Civil and Political Rights ("ICCPR"), and the Convention Against Torture and Other Cruel, Inhuman or Degrading Treatment or Punishment. . . . [B]oth of these treaties expressly require that party-states take steps under their municipal laws to enforce the rights described in those treaties, suggesting strongly that parties to these agreements did not intend for them to be self-executing. *See Foster v. Neilson,* 27 U.S. 253, 314, 7 L. Ed. 415 (1829) ("When the terms of [a treaty] import a contract, when either of the parties engages to perform a particular act, the treaty addresses itself to the political, not the judicial department; and the legislature must execute the contract before it can become a rule for the Court."), *overruled on other grounds, United States v. Percheman,* 32 U.S. (7 Pet.) 51, 8 L. Ed. 604 (1833).

For example, although Article 2 of the ICCPR expressly addresses the duty of party-states to enforce the rights described in the ICCPR, it does not purport to expressly or implicitly create a private right of action for violations of those rights. On its face, Article 2 creates no express right, discussing only what the party-states have agreed to do to give effect to the rights discussed in the ICCPR. Moreover, the language is couched in terms of further actions that States agree to undertake, thereby suggesting that the agreement is subject to further domestic action rather than self-executing. *Compare with Iran*, 771 F.2d at 1283 (finding statements that United States "agrees to" undertake further actions does not evince intent that agreement be self-executing). Additionally, Article 2 expressly recognizes that the treaty imposes no obligation to take further action if effective remedies exist, non-judicial or otherwise, and also provides that the remedy need not be judicial in nature. Indeed, to the extent that Article 2 addresses itself to a requirement for a judicial remedy, it states only that its parties must "develop the possibilities of a judicial remedy." From this language, it is apparent that the parties to the ICCPR did not intend for its provisions to be self-executing in the sense of automatically creating a private right of action cognizable by citizens of a State. *See also Tel-Oren*, 726 F.2d at 818-19 & n. 26 (Bork, J. concurring) (language of Art. 2 of ICCPR implies convention is not self-executing).

*White v. Paulsen*, 997 F. Supp. at 1385-1387. See also *Akhtar v. Reno*, 123 F. Supp. 2d 191, 196 (S.D. N.Y. 2000) (finding the Torture Convention not to be self-executing upon an affirmation that the issue is one for judicial determination, while construing the relevant non-self-execution declaration to be a manifestation of the United States' intent in ratifying the treaty).

In the leading case of *Sei Fujii v. State*, 38 Cal. 2d 713, 242, P.2d 617 (1952), the California Supreme Court considered a claim based on the UN Charter and the US Constitution to render invalid the California Alien Property Initiative Act of 1920 (better known as the Alien Land Law), a blatantly discriminatory statute that prohibited immigrants who were ineligible for citizenship (principally, in effect, Japanese and Chinese immigrants) from owning property. The court held that that the human rights clauses of the UN Charter could not be a basis of the claim, finding the clauses to be non-self-executing:

> In determining whether a treaty is self-executing courts look to the intent of the signatory parties as manifested by the language of the instrument, and, if the instrument is uncertain, recourse may be had to the circumstances surrounding its execution. . . . In order for a treaty provision to be operative without the aid of implementing legislation and to have the force and effect of a statute, it must appear that the framers of the treaty intended to prescribe a rule that, standing alone, would be enforceable in the courts. . . .

> It is clear that the provisions of the preamble and of Article 1 of the charter which are claimed to be in conflict with the alien land law are not self-executing. They state general purposes and objectives of the United Nations Organization and do not purport to impose legal obligations on the individual member nations or to create rights in private persons. It is equally clear that none of the other provisions relied on by plaintiff is self-executing. Article 55 declares that the United Nations "shall promote . . .

universal respect for, and observance of, human rights and fundamental freedoms for all without distinction as to race, sex, language, or religion," and in Article 56. The member nations "pledge themselves to take joint and separate action in cooperation with the Organization of the achievement of the purposes set forth in Article 55." Although the member nations have obligated themselves to cooperate with the international organization in promoting respect for, and observance of human rights, it is plain that it was contemplated that future legislative action by the several nations would be required to accomplish the declared objectives, and there is nothing to indicate that these provisions were intended to become rules of law for the courts of this county upon the ratification of the charter.

*Sei Fujii v. State*, 38 Cal. 2d at 721-722. Having thus disposed of the issues relating to the UN Charter, the court proceeded to hold the Alien Land Law invalid on the ground that it violated the equal protection clause of the Fourteenth Amendment to the U.S. Constitution.

More recently, the U.S. Supreme Court resolved a question of self-execution where the treaties involved were relevant to the enforceability of a judgment by the International Court of Justice (ICJ). The majority and dissenting opinions in this case, extracts of which follow, reflect an ongoing debate about the methodology and criteria for determining self-execution.

## Medellin v. Texas

552 U.S. 491 (2008) (most footnotes and some citations omitted)

In 1969, the United States, upon the advice and consent of the Senate, ratified the Vienna Convention on Consular Relations (Vienna Convention or Convention) and the Optional Protocol Concerning the Compulsory Settlement of Disputes to the Vienna Convention (Optional Protocol or Protocol). The preamble to the Convention provides that its purpose is to "contribute to the development of friendly relations among nations." Toward that end, Article 36 of the Convention was drafted to "facilitat[e] the exercise of consular functions." It provides that if a person detained by a foreign country "so requests, the competent authorities of the receiving State shall, without delay, inform the consular post of the sending State" of such detention, and "inform the [detainee] of his righ[t]" to request assistance from the consul of his own state.

The Optional Protocol provides a venue for the resolution of disputes arising out of the interpretation or application of the Vienna Convention. Under the Protocol, such disputes "shall lie within the compulsory jurisdiction of the International Court of Justice" and "may accordingly be brought before the [ICJ] . . . by any party to the dispute being a Party to the present Protocol."

The ICJ is "the principal judicial organ of the United Nations." United Nations Charter, Art. 92. It was established in 1945 pursuant to the United Nations Charter. The ICJ Statute—annexed to the U. N. Charter—provides the organizational framework and governing procedures for cases brought before the ICJ. Statute of the International Court of Justice (ICJ Statute).

Under Article 94(1) of the U. N. Charter, "[e]ach Member of the United Nations undertakes to comply with the decision of the [ICJ] in any case to which it is a party. . . .

Petitioner Jose Ernesto Medellin, a Mexican national, has lived in the United States since preschool. A member of the "Black and Whites" gang, Medellin was convicted of capital murder and sentenced to death in Texas for the gang rape and brutal murders of two Houston teenagers. . . . Medellin was arrested at approximately 4 a.m. on June 29, 1993. A few hours later, between 5:54 and 7:23 a.m., Medellin was given *Miranda* warnings; he then signed a written waiver and gave a detailed written confession. Local law enforcement officers did not, however, inform Medellin of his Vienna Convention right to notify the Mexican consulate of his detention. Medellin was convicted of capital murder and sentenced to death; his conviction and sentence were affirmed on appeal. . . . While Medellin's application for a certificate of appealability [from denial of a writ of habeas corpus] was pending in the Fifth Circuit, the ICJ issued its decision in [*Case Concerning Avena and Other Mexican Nationals (Mex. v. U.S.)*, 2004 I.C.J. No. 12 (Judgment of Mar. 31) (*Avena*)]. The ICJ held that the United States had violated Article 36(1)(b) of the Vienna Convention by failing to inform the 51 named Mexican nationals, including Medellin, of their Vienna Convention rights. In the ICJ's determination, the United States was obligated "to provide, by means of its own choosing, review and reconsideration of the convictions and sentences of the [affected] Mexican nationals." The ICJ indicated that such review was required without regard to state procedural default rules. . . . No one disputes that the *Avena* decision — a decision that flows from the treaties through which the United States submitted to ICJ jurisdiction with respect to Vienna Convention disputes — constitutes an *international* law obligation on the part of the United States. But not all international law obligations automatically constitute binding federal law enforceable in United States courts. The question we confront here is whether the *Avena* judgment has automatic *domestic* legal effect such that the judgment of its own force applies in state and federal courts.

This Court has long recognized the distinction between treaties that automatically have effect as domestic law, and those that — while they constitute international law commitments — do not by themselves function as binding federal law. . . . Medellin and his *amici* nonetheless contend that the Optional Protocol, United Nations Charter, and ICJ Statute supply the "relevant obligation" to give the *Avena* judgment binding effect in the domestic courts of the United States.[4] Because none of these treaty sources creates binding federal law in the absence of implementing legislation, and because it is uncontested that no such legislation exists, we conclude that the *Avena* judgment is not automatically binding domestic law. . . . As a signatory to the Optional Protocol, the United States agreed to submit disputes arising out of the Vienna Convention to the ICJ. The Protocol provides: "Disputes arising out of the interpretation or application of the [Vienna] Convention shall

---

4. The question is whether the *Avena* judgment has binding effect in domestic courts under the Optional Protocol, ICJ Statute, and U. N. Charter. Consequently, it is unnecessary to resolve whether the Vienna Convention is itself "self-executing" or whether it grants Medellin individually enforceable rights.

lie within the compulsory jurisdiction of the International Court of Justice." Of course, submitting to jurisdiction and agreeing to be bound are two different things. A party could, for example, agree to compulsory nonbinding arbitration. Such an agreement would require the party to appear before the arbitral tribunal without obligating the party to treat the tribunal's decision as binding. See, *e.g.*, North American Free Trade Agreement, U. S.-Can.-Mex., Art. 2018(1), Dec. 17, 1992, 32 I. L. M. 605, 697 (1993) ("On receipt of the final report of [the arbitral panel requested by a Party to the agreement], the disputing Parties shall agree on the resolution of the dispute, which normally shall conform with the determinations and recommendations of the panel").

The most natural reading of the Optional Protocol is as a bare grant of jurisdiction. It provides only that "[d]isputes arising out of the interpretation or application of the [Vienna] Convention shall lie within the compulsory jurisdiction of the International Court of Justice" and "may accordingly be brought before the [ICJ] . . . by any party to the dispute being a Party to the present Protocol." The Protocol says nothing about the effect of an ICJ decision and does not itself commit signatories to comply with an ICJ judgment. The Protocol is similarly silent as to any enforcement mechanism.

The obligation on the part of signatory nations to comply with ICJ judgments derives not from the Optional Protocol, but rather from Article 94 of the United Nations Charter—the provision that specifically addresses the effect of ICJ decisions. Article 94(1) provides that "[e]ach Member of the United Nations *undertakes to comply* with the decision of the [ICJ] in any case to which it is a party." 59 Stat. 1051 (emphasis added). The Executive Branch contends that the phrase "undertakes to comply" is not "an acknowledgement that an ICJ decision will have immediate legal effect in the courts of U. N. members," but rather "a *commitment* on the part of U. N. members to take *future* action through their political branches to comply with an ICJ decision." Brief for United States as *Amicus Curiae* in *Medellin I*, O. T. 2004, No. 04-5928, p 34.

We agree with this construction of Article 94. The Article is not a directive to domestic courts. It does not provide that the United States "shall" or "must" comply with an ICJ decision, nor indicate that the Senate that ratified the U. N. Charter intended to vest ICJ decisions with immediate legal effect in domestic courts. Instead, "[t]he words of Article 94 . . . call upon governments to take certain action. . . . In other words, the U. N. Charter reads like "a compact between independent nations" that "depends for the enforcement of its provisions on the interest and the honor of the governments which are parties to it." *Head Money Cases*, 112 U.S., at 598. . . . The remainder of Article 94 confirms that the U. N. Charter does not contemplate the automatic enforceability of ICJ decisions in domestic courts. Article 94(2) — the enforcement provision — provides the sole remedy for noncompliance: referral to the United Nations Security Council by an aggrieved state.

The U. N. Charter's provision of an express diplomatic—that is, nonjudicial— remedy is itself evidence that ICJ judgments were not meant to be enforceable in domestic courts. See *Sanchez-Llamas*, 548 U.S., at *347*. And even this "quintessentially *international* remed[y]" is not absolute. First, the Security Council must "dee[m] necessary" the issuance of a recommendation or measure to effectuate the judgment. Art. 94(2). Second, as the President and Senate were undoubtedly aware in subscribing to the U. N. Charter and Optional Protocol, the United States retained the unqualified right to exercise its veto of any Security Council resolution.

This was the understanding of the Executive Branch when the President agreed to the U.N. Charter and the declaration accepting general compulsory ICJ jurisdiction. See, *e.g.*, The Charter of the United Nations for the Maintenance of International Peace and Security: Hearings before the Senate Committee on Foreign Relations, 79th Cong., 1st Sess., 124-125 (1945) ("[I]f a state fails to perform its obligations under a judgment of the [ICJ], the other party may have recourse to the Security Council"); *id.*, at 286 (statement of Leo Pasvolsky, Special Assistant to the Secretary of State for International Organizations and Security Affairs) ("[W]hen the Court has rendered a judgment and one of the parties refuses to accept it, then the dispute becomes political rather than legal. It is as a political dispute that the matter is referred to the Security Council"); A Resolution Proposing Acceptance of Compulsory Jurisdiction of International Court of Justice: Hearings on S. Res. 196 before the Subcommittee of the Senate Committee on Foreign Relations, 79th Cong., 2d Sess., 142 (1946) (statement of Charles Fahy, State Dept. Legal Adviser) (while parties that accept ICJ jurisdiction have "a moral obligation" to comply with ICJ decisions, Article 94(2) provides the exclusive means of enforcement).

If ICJ judgments were instead regarded as automatically enforceable domestic law, they would be immediately and directly binding on state and federal courts pursuant to the *Supremacy Clause.* Mexico or the ICJ would have no need to proceed to the Security Council to enforce the judgment in this case. Noncompliance with an ICJ judgment through exercise of the Security Council veto—always regarded as an option by the Executive and ratifying Senate during and after consideration of the U.N. Charter, Optional Protocol, and ICJ Statute—would no longer be a viable alternative. There would be nothing to veto. In light of the U. N. Charter's remedial scheme, there is no reason to believe that the President and Senate signed up for such a result.

In sum, Medellin's view that ICJ decisions are automatically enforceable as domestic law is fatally undermined by the enforcement structure established by Article 94. His construction would eliminate the option of noncompliance contemplated by Article 94(2), undermining the ability of the political branches to determine whether and how to comply with an ICJ judgment. Those sensitive foreign policy decisions would instead be transferred to state and federal courts charged with applying an ICJ judgment directly as domestic law. And those courts would not be empowered to decide whether to comply with the judgment—again, always regarded as an option by the political branches—any more than courts may consider whether to comply with any other species of domestic law. This result would be particularly anomalous in light of the principle that "[t]he conduct of the foreign relations of our Government is committed by the Constitution to the Executive and Legislative—'the political'—Departments." *Oetjen v. Central Leather Co.*, 246 U.S. 297, 302, 38 S. Ct. 309, 62 L. Ed. 726 (1918).

The ICJ Statute, incorporated into the U. N. Charter, provides further evidence that the ICJ's judgment in *Avena* does not automatically constitute federal law judicially enforceable in United States courts. To begin with, the ICJ's "principal purpose" is said to be to "arbitrate particular disputes between national governments." *Sanchez-Llamas, supra*, at 355. Accordingly, the ICJ can hear disputes only between nations, not individuals. Art. 34(1) ("Only states [*i.e.*, countries] may be parties in cases before the [ICJ]"). More important, Article 59 of the statute provides that "[t]he decision of the [ICJ] has *no binding force* except between the parties and in respect of that particular case." *Id.* (emphasis added). The dissent does not explain how Medellin, an individual, can be a party to the ICJ proceeding. . . . It is, moreover, well settled that the United States' interpretation of a treaty "is entitled to great weight." The Executive Branch has unfailingly adhered to its view that the relevant treaties do not create domestically enforceable federal law. . . . Moreover, the consequences of Medellin's argument give pause. An ICJ judgment, the argument goes, is not only binding domestic law but is also unassailable. As a result, neither Texas nor this Court may look behind a judgment and quarrel with its reasoning or result. (We already know, from *Sanchez-Llamas*, that this Court disagrees with both the reasoning and result in *Avena*.) Medellin's interpretation would allow ICJ judgments to override otherwise binding state law; there is nothing in his logic that would exempt contrary federal law from the same fate. See, *e.g., Cook v. United States*, 288 U.S. 102, 119, 53 S. Ct. 305, 77 L. Ed. 641 (1933) (later-in-time self-executing treaty supersedes a federal statute if there is a conflict). And there is nothing to prevent the ICJ from ordering state courts to annul criminal convictions and sentences, for any reason deemed sufficient by the ICJ. Indeed, that is precisely the relief Mexico requested. . . . In sum, while the ICJ's judgment in *Avena* creates an international law obligation on the part of the United States, it does not of its own force constitute binding federal law that pre-empts state restrictions on the filing of successive habeas petitions. As we noted in *Sanchez-Llamas*, a contrary conclusion would be extraordinary, given that basic rights guaranteed by our own Constitution do not have the effect of displacing state procedural rules. Nothing in the text, background, negotiating and drafting history, or practice among signatory nations suggests that the President or Senate intended the improbable result of giving the judgments of an international tribunal a higher status than that enjoyed by "many of our most fundamental constitutional protections."

. . .

Justice BREYER, with whom Justice SOUTER and Justice GINSBURG join, dissenting.

The *Constitution's Supremacy Clause* provides that "all Treaties . . . which shall be made . . . under the Authority of the United States, shall be the supreme Law of the Land; and the Judges in every State shall be bound thereby." *Art. VI, cl. 2.* The Clause means that the "courts" must regard "a treaty . . . as equivalent to an act of the legislature, whenever it operates of itself without the aid of any legislative provision." *Foster v. Neilson*, 27 U.S. 253, 2 Pet. 253, 314, 7 L. Ed. 415 (1829) (majority opinion of Marshall, C. J.). . . .

The case law provides no simple magic answer to the question whether a particular treaty provision is self-executing. But the case law does make clear that, insofar as today's majority looks for language about "self-execution" in the treaty itself and insofar as it erects "clear statement" presumptions designed to help find an answer, it is misguided. . . . The many treaty provisions that this Court [previously] has found self-executing contain no textual language on the point. [The dissent provided appendices with references to multiple Supreme Court cases and treaties to support its characterizations of case law and treaties.] . . . These many Supreme Court cases finding treaty provisions to be self-executing cannot be reconciled with the majority's demand for textual clarity. . . . In a word, for present purposes, the absence or presence of language in a treaty about a provision's self-execution proves nothing at all. At best the Court is hunting the snark. At worst it erects legalistic hurdles that can threaten the application of provisions in many existing commercial and other treaties and make it more difficult to negotiate new ones. . . .

The case law also suggests practical, context-specific criteria that this Court has previously used to help determine whether, for *Supremacy Clause* purposes, a treaty provision is self-executing. The provision's text matters very much. But that is not because it contains language that explicitly refers to self-execution. For reasons I have already explained, *supra*, one should not expect *that* kind of textual statement. Drafting history is also relevant. But, again, that is not because it will explicitly address the relevant question. Instead text and history, along with subject matter and related characteristics will help our courts determine whether, as Chief Justice Marshall put it, the treaty provision "addresses itself to the political . . . department[s]" for further action or to "the judicial department" for direct enforcement. *Foster*, 27 U.S. 253, 2 Pet., at 314; see also *Ware*, 3 U.S. 199, *3 Dall.*, at 244 (opinion of Chase, J.) ("No one can doubt that a treaty may stipulate, that certain acts shall be done by the Legislature; that other acts shall be done by the Executive; and others by the Judiciary").

In making this determination, this Court has found the provision's subject matter of particular importance. Does the treaty provision declare peace? Does it promise not to engage in hostilities? If so, it addresses itself to the political branches. Alternatively, does it concern the adjudication of traditional private legal rights such as rights to own property, to conduct a business, or to obtain civil tort recovery? If so, it may well address itself to the Judiciary. Enforcing such rights and setting their boundaries is the bread-and-butter work of the courts. See, *e.g.*, *Clark v. Allen*, 331 U.S. 503 (1947) (treating provision with such subject matter as self-executing); *Asakura v. Seattle*, 265 U.S. 332 (1924) (same).

One might also ask whether the treaty provision confers specific, detailed individual legal rights. Does it set forth definite standards that judges can readily enforce? Other things being equal, where rights are specific and readily enforceable, the treaty provision more likely "addresses" the judiciary.

Alternatively, would direct enforcement require the courts to create a new cause of action? Would such enforcement engender constitutional controversy? Would it create constitutionally undesirable conflict with the other branches? In such circumstances, it is not likely that the provision contemplates direct judicial enforcement. *See, e.g., Asakura, supra*, at 341 (although "not limited by any express provision of the Constitution," the treaty-making power of the United States "does not extend 'so far as to authorize what the Constitution forbids'").

Such questions, drawn from case law stretching back 200 years, do not create a simple test, let alone a magic formula. But they do help to constitute a practical, context-specific judicial approach, seeking to separate run-of-the-mill judicial matters from other matters, sometimes more politically charged, sometimes more clearly the responsibility of other branches, sometimes lacking those attributes that would permit courts to act on their own without more ado. And such an approach is all that we need to find an answer to the legal question now before us.

Applying the approach just described, I would find the relevant treaty provisions self-executing as applied to the ICJ judgment before us (giving that judgment domestic legal effect) for the following reasons, taken together [the dissent provides an exhaustive analysis of the relevant treaty provisions employing the approach described.]

---

The US Supreme Court judgment in *Medellin v. Texas* illustrates the complexity of reconciling international law with the workings of the United States legal system. The Court recognizes the United States possesses treaty obligations under international law, but establishes a clear difference between assuming these obligations, and considering them automatically enforceable in domestic courts. The following article explores further these questions and the legacy of the *Medellin v. Texas* judgment.

Oona A. Hathaway, Sabrina McElroy & Sara Aronchick Solow

## International Law at Home: Enforcing Treaties in US Courts

37 Yale J. Int'L. 51, 70-71, 76, 90-91, 105 (2012) (footnotes omitted)

A deep puzzle lies at the heart of international law. It is "law" binding on the United States, and yet it is not always enforceable in the courts. One of the great challenges for scholars, judges, and practitioners alike has been to make some sense of this puzzle—some might call it a paradox—and to figure out when international law can be used in U.S. courts and when it cannot . . .

During the first 170 years of U.S. history, courts generally applied a strong presumption that private litigants could use treaties to press their claims in court. That all began to change just after World War II, as international treaties—and international human rights treaties in particular—proliferated. Still, the old presumption remained in place for certain categories of treaties. . . .

The Supreme Court . . . [during] the post World War II period . . . . continued to consider a number of treaties—particularly those affecting economic or commercial relations between individuals and those addressing transnational liability or litigation—self-executing and capable of direct enforcement in U.S. courts It reached such judgments in cases involving aircraft liability treaties, a multilateral convention concerning ship-owners' liability, a treaty governing international discovery rules, and several bilateral treaties setting forth protections for investors and inheritors. Yet the Court adopted a newly skeptical posture to other types of treaties. The Court was hesitant to declare that the treaty provided a private right of action in cases that turned on the new International Covenant on Civil and Political Rights (ICCPR), an extradition treaty with human rights implications, and treaties regulating the maritime industry on the high seas.

The Supreme Court did not offer the lower courts a consistent standard by which to judge which treaties should be treated as self-executing and giving rise to a private right of action and which should not. Left without clear guidance, the lower federal courts developed a bifurcated approach to treaty enforcement that reflected and amplified the Supreme Court's approach. Like the Supreme Court, lower courts continued to infer a private right of action for treaties that involved economic or commercial relations. But they began taking a more skeptical approach toward treaties regulating relationships between sovereign states (such as international dispute settlement and international use of force) and those regulating the relationship between the state and individual (most notably the emerging body of human rights treaties and international criminal law regimes). Furthermore, when federal courts of appeal concluded there was no private right of action, they did so on one of two grounds: (1) either the treaty was not self-executing, and thus not judicially enforceable; or (2) regardless of whether the treaty was self-executing, it was not intended to benefit private individuals in the first place, and therefore did not give rise to a private right of action. . . .

Although it had long been assumed that the treaties granting jurisdiction to the ICJ constituted binding federal law in the United States, the Supreme Court held in Medellin that they were non-self-executing. . . . In what has become influential dicta, the Court stated, "Even when treaties are self-executing in the sense that they create federal law, the background presumption is that international agreements, even those directly benefiting private persons, generally do not create private rights or provide for a private cause of action in domestic courts." This statement by the Medellin Court appears to suggest that the presumption against finding a private right of action had previously been universally applied, which, as we have seen, is not the case.

Despite its inaccuracy and status as dicta, the blanket statement by the Medellin Court has led to a significant shift in U.S. courts' approach to Article II treaties. No longer is the presumption against private rights of action applied exclusively to public law treaties. Instead, as we shall show, lower courts are treating it as universal. After *Medellin*, the courts have begun applying the opposite presumption of that used by the courts during most of the country's history. Instead of presuming that treaties that create private rights necessarily create private rights of action, courts now generally presume that they do not, regardless of the type of treaty. . . .

Many will read our findings on the trend in the case law after Medellin as sounding a death knell for the enforcement of Article II treaties in U.S. courts. After all, it is commonly assumed that if an international treaty cannot be used as a source of a private right of action, then it cannot be enforced in a U.S. court at all. That common assumption, however, misses a significant part of the picture of international law enforcement in U.S. courts. In fact, treaties are regularly enforced in U.S. courts even when there is no private right of action. Understanding this bigger picture is essential to understanding the true impact of the courts' shifting position on the enforcement of treaties through private rights of action.

International treaties are enforced by courts in three circumstances in which the treaty itself does not give rise to a private right of action. First, treaties may create a right that can then be enforced through legislation that makes the right actionable. We call this "indirect enforcement." Second, a treaty may be invoked defensively by a private party who has been prosecuted or sued under a statute that is inconsistent with a treaty provision. We call this "defensive enforcement." Third, courts may look to treaties when interpreting statutes and, more controversially, constitutional provisions. We call this "interpretive enforcement."

. . . The gap left by the decline in direct enforcement has been filled in part by indirect enforcement, defensive enforcement, and interpretive enforcement. Yet there is more that can be done to ensure that once the United States makes an international legal commitment, it is able to honor that obligation.

Here we offer three proposals to ensure that the United States's Article II treaty commitments may be more effectively enforced in U.S.courts. First, Congress could pass legislation that provides for the judicial enforcement of obligations established in Article II treaties. Alternatively, the President and Congress could make individual international treaty obligations through the ordinary legislative process rather than through Article II. Second, the executive branch could adopt a clear statement rule, which the Legal Advisor's Office of the State Department would apply to newly concluded treaties. Finally, the executive branch could enforce international treaty obligations by seeking injunctions against state and municipal agencies violating those obligations in cases where the United States risks being placed in violation of a national treaty obligation. . . .

Today, more than ever before, international law is a part of daily life. The United States is party to hundreds of Article II treaties, many of them covering topics of the gravest importance to the country, ranging from the economy, to criminal law enforcement, to national security. It is thus of no small importance that the Supreme Court has cast the legal status of significant numbers of these treaties into doubt with its decision in *Medellin v. Texas.*

## Comments and Questions

1. What are the criteria for determining whether treaties are self-executing in the majority and dissenting opinions in *Medellin,* and how do those criteria differ? What merit or drawbacks do you see in each approach? See generally *Medellin: Intent, Presumptions, and Non-Self-Executing Treaties,* 102 AM. J. INT'L L. 540 (2008). Compare also the criteria applied in *White v. Paulsen, supra* page 393 to find the Covenant on Civil and Political Rights non-self-executing, and in *Sei Fujii, supra* page 394, to find the human rights clauses of UN Charter non-self-executing. For pre-*Medellin* analyses of divergent approaches employed by courts to determine whether or not a treaty is self-executing, see David Sloss, *When Do Treaties Create Individually Enforceable Rights? The Supreme Court Ducks the Issue in Hamdan and Sanchez-Llamas,* 45 COLUM. J. TRANSNAT'L L. 20 (2007) (discussing "nationalist" and "trans-nationalist" models of treaty enforcement); Carlos Manuel Vazquez, *The Four Doctrines of Self-Executing Treaties, supra* page 392.

2. Reread Articles 2 and 6(5) of the Covenant on Civil and Political Rights. Do you agree, as concluded in *White v. Paulsen,* that Article 2, which commits states to take measures domestically to give effect to the rights in the Covenant, is a strong indication that the Covenant is non-self-executing? Or does Article 2 instead

suggest that states should ensure the availability of judicial remedies for Covenant rights, even in the absence of relevant implementing legislation? Consider these questions in light of *Medellin*.

3. In *Asakura v. Seattle*, 265 U.S. 332 (1924), a case cited by the dissent in *Medellin,* the Supreme Court interpreted the US-Japan treaty of 1911, which provided that citizens of each country enjoyed the right to carry on a trade or business within the other country. Holding that this provision of the treaty was self-executing and created enforceable rights in individuals, the Court opined that "[t]reaties are to be construed in a broad and liberal spirit, and when two constructions are possible, one restrictive of rights which may be claimed under it, and the other favorable to them the latter is preferred." Id. at 342. Are *Sei Fujii, Medellin*, and *White* consistent with this mandate of a liberal reading of treaties? What factors might explain or justify holding the treaties in those cases to a higher standard of scrutiny, with the result that they were each deemed to be non-self-executing? The fact that each of those treaties — the UN Charter, the Covenant on Civil and Political Rights, and the Optional Protocol Concerning the Compulsory Settlement of Disputes to the Vienna Convention — is a multilateral treaty, as opposed to a bilateral treaty governing aspects of the reciprocal relationship between two countries and their citizens? In the case of the human rights provisions of the UN Charter and the Covenant, the fact that those provisions apply in favor of US citizens whose rights are otherwise defined and protected by domestic law? In the case of the Optional Protocol, the fact that it empowers the jurisdiction of an international tribunal that might interpret the substantive rights differently than the domestic judiciary?

4. Note also *People of Saipan ex rel. Guerrero v. U.S. Dept. of Interior*, 502 F.2d 90 (9th Cir.), cert. denied, 420 U.S. 1003 (1974), a case in which citizens of Micronesia sued to enforce the Trusteeship Agreement that the United States had entered into with the United Nations governing its administration of the Trust Territory of the Pacific Islands. In finding that international agreement to be self-executing, the court of appeals acknowledged that "the substantive rights guaranteed through the Trusteeship Agreement are not precisely defined. However, we do not believe that the agreement is too vague for judicial enforcement. Its language is no more general than such terms as 'due process of law,' 'seaworthiness,' 'equal protection of the law,' 'good faith,' or 'restraint of trade,' which courts interpret every day . . ." 502 F.2d at 99. Is there a distinction between U.S. courts interpreting vague constitutional or statutory language and these same courts construing similarly vague treaty provisions? Should there be?

5. In the above extract of their article, Hathaway, McElroy, and Solow observe that the Supreme Court and lower courts have inferred a right of action from treaties that involve economic or commercial relations, but not from human rights treaties. Why do you think that United States courts have been more hesitant historically to consider human rights treaties to be self-executing or to create a private right of action? Reflect on the explanation the authors give elsewhere in the article:

> We argue [a shift] can be traced at least in part to changes in the nature of the treaties creating individual rights during [the post-World War II period] and the response to that shift among the political branches and the public. The global human rights revolution and the very public backlash against it provoked increased scrutiny of treaties that could provide

a mechanism by which individuals could challenge government policies. This, in turn, led to greater wariness among the courts to find that
such treaties created private rights of action in U.S. courts. . . . Courts
were less familiar with these newer treaties and were wary of inferring private rights of action to enforce them.

Hathaway et al., *supra* page 401, at 68.

6. Which way did foreign policy and separation of powers considerations
favoring executive discretion cut in *Medellin*? In that case, the petitioner sought
to apply the ICJ's *Avena* judgment, not just on the basis of the relevant treaties,
but also relying on a memorandum by the president determining that the United
States would "discharge its international obligations" under *Avena* "by having State
courts give effect to the decision." See Memorandum of President George W. Bush
for the Attorney General (Feb. 28, 2005), as quoted in 552 U.S. at 498. (In the
extract of the Supreme Court's opinion in *Medellin, supra*, the part of the opinion
addressing the President's memorandum is not included.) Intervening as amicus
curiae, the United States sided with the petitioner on this point and maintained
that "while the *Avena* judgment does not of its own force require domestic courts
to set aside ordinary rules of procedural default, that judgment became the law
of the land with precisely that effect pursuant to the President's Memorandum
and his power 'to establish binding rules of decision that preempt contrary state
law.'" See 552 U.S. at 523 (quoting Brief for United States as *Amicus Curiae* 5).
The United States argued that the President's authority to implement the *Avena*
judgment in this way derived from the treaties relevant to the ICJ judgment and,
apart from that, an "independent" international dispute resolution power. See
552 U.S. at 525. The Court rejected the United States' argument, holding that the
President could not unilaterally transform non-self-executing treaties and an ICJ
judgment depending on them into self-executing obligations, and that the President's international-dispute resolution powers were not so expansive. The Court
also rejected the petitioner's argument that the President's authority in this regard
rested in his constitutional power to "take care" that the laws are executed. Id. at
525-532. Note that, in this case, federalism concerns competed with any policy that
would have allowed for executive discretion. Throughout the opinion, the Court
made references to concerns about the imposition of an international judgment on
state courts without clear congressional authorization. To what extent are such federalism concerns relevant to judicial interpretations and applications of treaties?

7. European colonizing states and the United States after them concluded
hundreds of treaties with the Indian tribes within the country's borders. Most of
these treaties have not been abrogated by subsequent acts of Congress, and they
continue to define many of the rights retained by tribes in exchange, usually, for
vast areas of land and other concessions. Indian treaties stand essentially on the
same footing in US domestic law as treaties with foreign nations. See *Worcester
v. Georgia*, 31 U.S. (6 Pet.) 515 (1832). However, Indian treaties have consistently
been judicially applied (or ignored), without regard to the non-self-execution
doctrine. See, e.g., id (affirming the territorial rights of the Cherokee Nation
as defined by the Treaty of Hopewell against incursions by the state of Georgia); *Puyallup Tribe v. Dep't of Game*, 391 U.S. 392 (1968) (enforcing treaty right
of tribal members to fish "at all usual and accustomed grounds and stations" in

off-reservation areas). Are Indian treaties exempt from scrutiny as to whether or not they possess the criteria of self-execution? Or is the pattern of judicial application of Indian treaties due to their manifestly self-executing character? Note that in *Robinson v. Salazar*, 885 F. Supp. 2d 1002 (2012), aff'd 2015 U.S. App. LEXIS 10446 (9th Cir. Cal., June 22, 2015) the court—in a case involving a land claim by a tribe against the corporations owned by another tribe—determined that the 1849 treaty with the Utah was non-self-executing, understanding that it only alluded to a future commitment to set aside land for the signatory tribes, but not directly granting land title or possession. Should courts apply the same criteria of self-execution to treaties with Indian Nations or tribes that it applies in connection with other treaties? Might the context matter?

## C.   *The Judicial Application of Customary International Law and the Alien Tort Statute*

Advocates and scholars have argued for years that, beyond any treaty obligation arising from Article 6(5) of the International Covenant on Civil and Political Rights, the prohibition of the juvenile death penalty is a norm of customary international law. Support for this position was submitted to the Supreme Court in *Roper v. Simmons* in an amicus brief, which argued for recognition of a norm against the juvenile death penalty as part of general international law and jus cogens. See Brief for the Human Rights Committee of the Bar of England and Wales, Human Rights Watch, Human Rights Advocates, and the World Organization for Human Rights as Amici Curiae in Support of Respondents, *Roper v. Simmons* (July 15, 2004), http://congressionaldigest .com/issue/executing-minors/human-rights-committee-of-the-bar-of-england -and-wales-human-rights-advocates-et-al/.

The Court in *Roper* agreed with the assessment of a widespread international practice and opinion against the death penalty, although without explicitly declaring the existence of a binding norm of general or customary international law, much less one of jus cogens.

Before the Court in *Roper* overruled precedent to find that the Eighth Amendment itself prohibits the juvenile death penalty, state and lower federal courts had rejected finding an alternative basis for protecting juveniles from the death penalty in either Article 6(5) of the Covenant on Civil and Political Rights (in light of the United States reservation to that article) or customary international law. The courts rejected arguments based on customary international law, not because they denied that a relevant norm of customary international law existed, but rather because they determined that such a norm could not be controlling over prior Supreme Court precedent allowing the juvenile death penalty. See, e.g., *Beazley v. Johnson*, 242 F.3d 248, 268-269 (5th Cir. Tex. 2001), cert. denied, 534 U.S. 945 (2001). Nonetheless, by reversing the earlier precedent and bringing the United States in conformity with international practice and opinion, albeit ultimately on the basis of the Eighth Amendment, the Supreme Court's decision in *Roper* added to the global practice and reinforced the customary international norm against the juvenile death penalty, and it nullified any persistent objector status the U.S. may have enjoyed in regard to the norm.

The Supreme Court in *Roper* both reinforced the customary norm and effectively applied it indirectly through a reinterpretation of the Eighth Amendment's prohibition against cruel and unusual punishment. As discussed previously, such indirect application of an international norm — whether treaty-based or customary — is the most common use of international law by domestic courts. But, like treaty-based ones, norms of customary international law can theoretically be applied *directly* by domestic courts, although such direct application of customary international norms has historically been limited.

Referring to customary international law in particular, the Supreme Court confirmed in *The Paquete Habana* that "[i]nternational law is part of our law, and must be ascertained and administered by the courts of justice of appropriate jurisdiction, as often as questions of right depending upon it are duly presented for their determination." 175 U.S. 677, 700 (1900). Still, one must ask, under what circumstances are questions that depend upon customary international law "duly presented" to the courts. These qualifying words to this famous utterance of the Supreme Court signify the complexities that are encountered in efforts to enforce rights in U.S. courts entirely on the basis of customary international law.

Joan Fitzpatrick

## The Role of Domestic Courts in Enforcing International Human Rights Law

*Guide to International Human Rights Practice*, 247, 253-54 (Hurst Hannum ed., 3d ed. 1999)

The weight of judicial and scholarly opinion holds that customary international law forms an aspect of federal common law and is thus part of the "supreme Law of the Land" for Article VI purposes. In the earliest days of the Republic, courts in the United States enforced the criminal prohibitions of international law, and the 1789 Alien Tort Claims Act (ATCA) [also known as the Alien Tort Statute] opened the federal courts to civil suits by aliens premised upon the law of nations.

Despite the impressive revival of the ATCA in relation to human rights violations occurring in foreign states [discussed below], plaintiffs rarely invoke customary international human rights law in litigation arising out of events occurring in the United States. The reasons for this relative rarity can be best explicated by considering concrete examples.

Assume that your client had been subjected to a specific use of force by police (for example, direct application of pepper spray to the unprotected eye in order to disrupt a non-violent demonstration) or had been excluded from public elementary education on the basis of her undocumented immigrant status. What obstacles might you encounter in bringing suit, in either federal or state court, against the responsible officials?

Human rights litigation of this type resembles civil rights litigation under the Constitution, statutes, and the common law of tort. Thus sovereign immunity and official immunities will have to be considered in selecting the appropriate defendants and judicial forum. Moreover, there may be alternate grounds (constitutional protections, statutory rights, or state common law) that provide a simpler avenue for relief.

An attorney representing a client asserting a right under customary international law must grapple with both substantive and jurisdictional puzzles. First, the advocate must prove that the actions of the defendants violated a norm of customary law that is specific, universal, and obligatory. While the process by which a norm of customary law may be proved is laid out in long-standing U.S. Supreme Court decisions, this process is complex and may require the expert testimony of recognized international law scholars.

In the police abuse example above, a litigant would have to prove that such use of pepper spray violates a customary prohibition on torture; cruel, inhuman, or degrading treatment; or other norms concerning humane treatment of persons detained by police. In the case of children excluded from school, the litigant would need to convince the court that, under a customary norm banning discrimination, the exclusion of minor children from education is unjustified and disproportionate to any legitimate governmental objective. Alternatively, an advocate might argue that a customary right to elementary education exists for all children within the national territory.

Even if the existence of the asserted norm in incontestable, an advocate must anticipate the argument that the norm is unenforceable. While the Supreme Court in *The Paquete Habana* recognized customary international law as "part of our law" to be enforced on behalf of injured individuals, the Court also suggested that the enforceability of international rights might be abrogated by contrary controlling acts of the Executive, Congress, or even the judiciary. Thus, an advocate must consider whether federal officials have authorized the act in question and show why such a contrary federal policy should not prevail. In the context of numerous cases involving indefinite detention of Cuban asylum-seekers, for example, U.S. courts have systematically rejected efforts to assert the primacy of the customary international norm against arbitrary detention, relying in part on this dictum from *Paquete Habana*. Where the challenged policies or acts are attributable to state officials, the likelihood that inconsistent federal law or policies may insulate the practice from challenge is diminished.

Finally, an advocate must establish that subject matter jurisdiction exists over the claim. This should not present a problem in state court, regardless of the citizenship of the litigants, because customary international law is incontestably a part of common law.

A claim premised solely upon customary international human rights law in federal court, in the absence of diversity of citizenship, requires establishing the asserted norm is one of federal law. The weight of authority holds that [federal court] jurisdiction exists over ATCA claims, regardless of the citizenship of the defendant. Where both plaintiff and defendant in a case arising under customary international law are U.S. citizens, just as where both are aliens, federal question jurisdiction must be shown to exist.

As noted in the above extract, customary international law is not commonly asserted as an independent basis for a cause of action, because of the significant barriers involved. However, the Alien Tort Statute (ATS), 28 U.S.C. §1350 (also referred to as the Alien Tort Claims Act) has provided a narrow avenue for claims based on customary international law.

The following is an extract of the decision in the first modern case under the ATS.

## Filartiga v. Peña-Irala

630 F.2d 876 (2d Cir. 1980) (footnotes omitted)

[Dr. Joel Filartiga and his daughter Dolly, both citizens of Paraguay who were living in the United States and who had applied for political asylum, brought this action in the Eastern District of New York against Americo Noberto Peña-Irala (Peña), also a citizen of Paraguay, for wrongfully causing the death of Dr. Filartiga's 17-year-old son, Joelito. The Filartigas contended that Joelito had been kidnapped and tortured to death by Peña, who was then Inspector General of Police in Asuncion, Paraguay, in retaliation for Dr. Filartiga's political activities and beliefs.

The Filartigas brought their action under the Alien Tort Statute, a then little-known federal law dating back to the original Judiciary Act of 1789, which provides: "The district courts shall have original jurisdiction of any civil action by an alien for a tort only, committed in violation of the law of nations or a treaty of the United States." The United States not being at the time a party to a treaty proscribing torture, jurisdiction under the statute turned upon whether or not torture now violated "the law of nations," i.e., customary international law. The District Court, in an unreported decision, felt constrained by precedent to dismiss the complaint on the ground that " 'the law of nations,' as employed in Section 1350, [excludes] that law which governs a state's treatment of its own citizens." This appeal followed.]

IRVING R. KAUFMAN, Circuit Judge:
Upon ratification of the Constitution, the thirteen former colonies were fused into a single nation, one which, in its relations with foreign states, is bound both to observe and construe the accepted norms of international law, formerly known as the law of nations. Under the Articles of Confederation, the several states had interpreted and applied this body of doctrine as a part of their common law, but with the founding of the "more perfect Union" of 1789, the law of nations became preeminently a federal concern.

Implementing the constitutional mandate for national control over foreign relations, the First Congress established original district court jurisdiction over "all causes where an alien sues for a tort only (committed) in violation of the law of nations." Judiciary Act of 1789, ch. 20, s 9(b), 1 Stat. 73, 77 (1789), codified at 28 U.S.C. §1350. Construing this rarely-invoked provision, we hold that deliberate torture perpetrated under color of official authority violates universally accepted norms of the international law of human rights, regardless of the nationality of the parties. Thus, whenever an alleged torturer is found and served with process by an alien within our borders, §1350 provides federal jurisdiction. Accordingly, we reverse the judgment of the district court dismissing the complaint for want of federal jurisdiction. . . .

Appellants rest their principal argument in support of federal jurisdiction upon the Alien Tort Statute, 28 U.S.C. §1350, which provides: "The district courts shall have original jurisdiction of any civil action by an alien for a tort only, committed in violation of the law of nations or a treaty of the United States." Since appellants do not contend that their action arises directly under a treaty of the United States, a threshold question on the jurisdictional issue is whether the conduct alleged violates the law of nations. In light of the universal condemnation of torture in numerous international agreements, and the renunciation of torture as an instrument of official policy by virtually all of the nations of the world (in principle if not in practice), we find that an act of torture committed by a state official against one held in detention violates established norms of the international law of human rights, and hence the law of nations.

The Supreme Court has enumerated the appropriate sources of international law. The law of nations "may be ascertained by consulting the works of jurists, writing professedly on public law; or by the general usage and practice of nations; or by judicial decisions recognizing and enforcing that law." *United States v. Smith*, 18 U.S. (5 Wheat.) 153, 160-61, 5 L.Ed. 57 (1820); Lopes v. Reederei Richard Schroder, 225 F.Supp. 292, 295 (E.D.Pa.1963). In Smith, a statute proscribing "the crime of piracy (on the high seas) as defined by the law of nations," 3 Stat. 510(a) (1819), was held sufficiently determinate in meaning to afford the basis for a death sentence. The Smith Court discovered among the works of Lord Bacon, Grotius, Bochard and other commentators a genuine consensus that rendered the crime "sufficiently and constitutionally defined." Smith, supra, 18 U.S. (5 Wheat.) at 162, 5 L.Ed. 57.

The Paquete Habana, 175 U.S. 677, 20 S.Ct. 290, 44 L.Ed. 320 (1900), reaffirmed that

> where there is no treaty, and no controlling executive or legislative act or judicial decision, resort must be had to the customs and usages of civilized nations; and, as evidence of these, to the works of jurists and commentators, who by years of labor, research and experience, have made themselves peculiarly well acquainted with the subjects of which they treat. Such works are resorted to by judicial tribunals, not for the speculations of their authors concerning what the law ought to be, but for trustworthy evidence of what the law really is.

Id. at 700, 20 S.Ct. at 299. Modern international sources confirm the propriety of this approach.

*Habana* is particularly instructive for present purposes, for it held that the traditional prohibition against seizure of an enemy's coastal fishing vessels during wartime, a standard that began as one of comity only, had ripened over the preceding century into "a settled rule of international law" by "the general assent of civilized nations." Id. at 694, 20 S. Ct. at 297; accord, id. at 686, 20 S. Ct. at 297. Thus it is clear that courts must interpret international law not as it was in 1789, but as it has evolved and exists among the nations of the world today. See *Ware v. Hylton*, 3 U.S.

(3 Dall.) 198, 1 L.Ed. 568 (1796) (distinguishing between "ancient" and "modern" law of nations).

The requirement that a rule command the "general assent of civilized nations" to become binding upon them all is a stringent one. Were this not so, the courts of one nation might feel free to impose idiosyncratic legal rules upon others, in the name of applying international law. Thus, in Banco Nacional de Cuba v. Sabbatino, 376 U.S. 398, 84 S. Ct. 923, 11 L.Ed.2d 804 (1964), the Court declined to pass on the validity of the Cuban government's expropriation of a foreign-owned corporation's assets, noting the sharply conflicting views on the issue propounded by the capital-exporting, capital-importing, socialist and capitalist nations. Id. at 428-30, 84 S. Ct. at 940-41.

The case at bar presents us with a situation diametrically opposed to the conflicted state of law that confronted the *Sabbatino* Court. Indeed, to paraphrase that Court's statement, id. at 428, 84 S. Ct. at 940, there are few, if any, issues in international law today on which opinion seems to be so united as the limitations on a state's power to torture persons held in its custody.

The United Nations Charter (a treaty of the United States, see 59 Stat. 1033 (1945)) makes it clear that in this modern age a state's treatment of its own citizens is a matter of international concern. [The court quotes Articles 55 and 56.]

While this broad mandate has been held not to be wholly self-executing, *Hitai v. Immigration and Naturalization Service*, 343 F.2d 466, 468 (2d Cir. 1965), this observation alone does not end our inquiry. For although there is no universal agreement as to the precise extent of the "human rights and fundamental freedoms" guaranteed to all by the Charter, there is at present no dissent from the view that the guaranties include, at a bare minimum, the right to be free from torture. This prohibition has become part of customary international law, as evidenced and defined by the Universal Declaration of Human Rights, General Assembly Resolution 217 (III)(A) (Dec. 10, 1948) which states, in the plainest of terms, "no one shall be subjected to torture." The General Assembly has declared that the Charter precepts embodied in this Universal Declaration "constitute basic principles of international law." G.A.Res. 2625 (XXV) (Oct. 24, 1970).

Particularly relevant is the Declaration on the Protection of All Persons from Being Subjected to Torture, General Assembly Resolution 3452, 30 U.N. GAOR Supp. (No. 34) 91, U.N.Doc. A/1034 (1975), which is set out in full in the margin. [FN11] The Declaration expressly prohibits any state from permitting the dastardly and totally inhuman act of torture. Torture, in turn, is defined as "any act by which severe pain and suffering, whether physical or mental, is intentionally inflicted by or at the instigation of a public official on a person for such purposes as . . . intimidating him or other persons." The Declaration goes on to provide that "(w)here it is proved that an act of torture or other cruel, inhuman or degrading treatment or punishment has been committed by or at the instigation of a public official, the victim shall be afforded redress and compensation, in accordance with national law." This Declaration, like the Declaration of Human Rights before it, was adopted without dissent by the General Assembly. Nayar, "Human Rights: The United Nations and United States Foreign Policy," 19 Harv. Int'l L.J. 813, 816 n.18 (1978).

These U.N. declarations are significant because they specify with great precision the obligations of member nations under the Charter. Since their adoption, "(m)embers can no longer contend that they do not know what human rights they promised in the Charter to promote." Sohn, "A Short History of United Nations Documents on Human Rights," in The United Nations and Human Rights, 18th Report of the Commission (Commission to Study the Organization of Peace ed. 1968). Moreover, a U.N. Declaration is, according to one authoritative definition, "a formal and solemn instrument, suitable for rare occasions when principles of great and lasting importance are being enunciated." 34 U.N. ESCOR, Supp. (No. 8) 15, U.N. Doc. E/cn.4/1/610 (1962) (memorandum of Office of Legal Affairs, U.N. Secretariat). Accordingly, it has been observed that the Universal Declaration of Human Rights "no longer fits into the dichotomy of 'binding treaty' against 'non- binding pronouncement,' but is rather an authoritative statement of the international community." E. Schwelb, Human Rights and the International Community 70 (1964). Thus, a Declaration creates an expectation of adherence, and "insofar as the expectation is gradually justified by State practice, a declaration may by custom become recognized as laying down rules binding upon the States." 34 U.N. ESCOR, supra. Indeed, several commentators have concluded that the Universal Declaration has become, in toto, a part of binding, customary international law. Nayar, supra, at 816-17; Waldlock, "Human Rights in Contemporary International Law and the Significance of the European Convention," Int'l & Comp. L.Q., Supp. Publ. No. 11 at 15 (1965).

Turning to the act of torture, we have little difficulty discerning its universal renunciation in the modern usage and practice of nations. Smith, supra, 18 U.S. (5 Wheat.) at 160-61, 5 L.Ed. 57. The international consensus surrounding torture has found expression in numerous international treaties and accords. E. g., American Convention on Human Rights, Art. 5, OAS Treaty Series No. 36 at 1, OAS Off. Rec. OEA/Ser 4 v/II 23, doc. 21, rev. 2 (English ed., 1975) ("No one shall be subjected to torture or to cruel, inhuman or degrading punishment or treatment"); International Covenant on Civil and Political Rights, U.N. General Assembly Res. 2200 (XXI)A, U.N. Doc. A/6316 (Dec. 16, 1966) (identical language); European Convention for the Protection of Human Rights and Fundamental Freedoms, Art. 3, Council of Europe, European Treaty Series No. 5 (1968), 213 U.N.T.S. 211 (semble). The substance of these international agreements is reflected in modern municipal — i.e. national — law as well. Although torture was once a routine concomitant of criminal interrogations in many nations, during the modern and hopefully more enlightened era it has been universally renounced. According to one survey, torture is prohibited, expressly or implicitly, by the constitutions of over fifty-five nations, including both the United States and Paraguay. Our State Department reports a general recognition of this principle:

> There now exists an international consensus that recognizes basic human rights and obligations owed by all governments to their citizens. . . . There is no doubt that these rights are often violated; but virtually all governments acknowledge their validity.

Department of State, Country Reports on Human Rights for 1979, published as Joint Comm. Print, House Comm. on Foreign Affairs, and Senate Comm. on Foreign Relations, 96th Cong. 2d Sess. (Feb. 4, 1980), Introduction at 1. We have been directed to no assertion by any contemporary state of a right to torture its own or another nation's citizens. Indeed, United States diplomatic contacts confirm the universal abhorrence with which torture is viewed:

> In exchanges between United States embassies and all foreign states with which the United States maintains relations, it has been the Department of State's general experience that no government has asserted a right to torture its own nationals. Where reports of torture elicit some credence, a state usually responds by denial or, less frequently, by asserting that the conduct was unauthorized or constituted rough treatment short of torture.

Memorandum of the United States as Amicus Curiae at 16 n.34.

Having examined the sources from which customary international law is derived the usage of nations, judicial opinions and the works of jurists we conclude that official torture is now prohibited by the law of nations. The prohibition is clear and unambiguous, and admits of no distinction between treatment of aliens and citizens. Accordingly, we must conclude that the dictum in *Dreyfus v. von Finck*, supra, 534 F.2d at 31, to the effect that "violations of international law do not occur when the aggrieved parties are nationals of the acting state," is clearly out of tune with the current usage and practice of international law. The treaties and accords cited above, as well as the express foreign policy of our own government, all make it clear that international law confers fundamental rights upon all people vis-à-vis their own governments. While the ultimate scope of those rights will be a subject for continuing refinement and elaboration, we hold that the right to be free from torture is now among them. . . . In the twentieth century the international community has come to recognize the common danger posed by the flagrant disregard of basic human rights and particularly the right to be free of torture. Spurred first by the Great War, and then the Second, civilized nations have banded together to prescribe acceptable norms of international behavior. From the ashes of the Second World War arose the United Nations Organization, amid hopes that an era of peace and cooperation had at last begun. Though many of these aspirations have remained elusive goals, that circumstance cannot diminish the true progress that has been made. In the modern age, humanitarian and practical considerations have combined to lead the nations of the world to recognize that respect for fundamental human rights is in their individual and collective interest. Among the rights universally proclaimed by all nations, as we have noted, is the right to be free of physical torture. Indeed, for purposes of civil liability, the torturer has become like the pirate and slave trader before him hostis humani generis, an enemy of all mankind. Our holding today, giving effect to a jurisdictional provision enacted by our First Congress, is a small but important step in the fulfillment of the ageless dream to free all people from brutal violence.

----

*Filartiga* was the first case to use the over 200-year-old Alien Torts Statute to vindicate rights based on the post-UN Charter international law of human rights. It generated considerable international human rights law litigation and was highly praised by numerous legal commentators. See, e.g., Carolyn Patty

Blum and Ralph G. Steinhardt, *Federal Jurisdiction over International Human Rights Claims: The Alien Tort Claims Act After Filartiga v. Peña-Irala*, 22 HARV. INTL. L.J. 53 (1981); *Human Rights Symposium*, 4 Hous. J. Intl. L. 1 (1981); *Symposium, Federal Jurisdiction, Human Rights and the Law of Nations: Essays on Filartiga v. Peña-Irala*, 11 GA. J. INTL. & COMP. L. 305 (1981); and the articles cited in Bert B. Lockwood, *The United Nations Charter and United States Civil Rights Litigation: 1946-1955*, 69 IOWA L. REV. 901, 925 (1984). Cf. *Comment, Torture as a Tort in Violation of International Law: Filartiga v. Peña-Irala*, 33 STAN. L. REV. 353 (1981). For a compilation of cases that have arisen under the Alien Tort Statute, a majority of them since *Filartiga*, see Kurtis A. Kemper, *Construction and Application of Alien Tort Statute (28 U.S.C. §1350) — Tort in Violation of Law of Nations or Treaty of the United States*, 64 A.L.R. Fed. 417 (updated to 2018).

The decision in *Filartiga*, however, also drew criticism. A leading protagonist of an attack on an expansive reading of the Alien Tort Statute was former Judge Robert H. Bork. In a concurring opinion, he contended, inter alia, that international human rights law could be invoked under the Alien Tort Statute only in those rare instances where the treaty or customary international law norm in question itself grants individuals a private, affirmative "cause of action," in addition to establishing obligations for states. See *Hanoch Tel-Oren v. Libyan Arab Republic*, 726 F.2d 774, 798-823 (D.C. Cir. 1984) (concurring opinion), cert. denied, 470 U.S. 1003 (1985). Contrary to the position taken by the Departments of State and Justice in *Filartiga*, see Memorandum for the United States as Amicus Curiae, *Filartiga v. Peña-Irala*, reprinted in 12 HASTING INT'L & COMP. L. REV. (1988), the Department of Justice adopted Judge Bork's "cause of action" approach in its amicus brief in *Trajano v. Marcos*, 878 F.2d 1439 (9th Cir. 1989).

Subsequently, Congress enacted the Torture Victim Protection of 1991 (TVPA), 28 U.S.C. §1350 note, which provides a cause of action against individuals who, acting under the authority of a foreign government, have committed torture or extrajudicial killing. A few years later, in 1994, the United States ratified the Convention against Torture.

The government eventually took a highly restrictive view of the Alien Tort Statute, arguing not only that the statute is purely jurisdictional but also that it allows only private actions related to the law of nations that Congress itself authorizes or creates by legislation apart from the ATS, as it did with the TVPA. The government tried to advance this view in the following case before the US Supreme Court.

## Sosa v. Alvarez-Machain

542 U.S. 692 (2004) (most references and citations omitted)

Justice SOUTER delivered the opinion of the Court.

. . .

### I

We have considered the underlying facts before, *United States v. Alvarez-Machain*, 504 U.S. 655 (1992). In 1985, an agent of the Drug Enforcement Administration (DEA),

Enrique Camarena-Salazar, was captured on assignment in Mexico and taken to a house in Guadalajara, where he was tortured over the course of a 2-day interrogation, then murdered. Based in part on eyewitness testimony, DEA officials in the United States came to believe that respondent Humberto Alvarez-Machain (Alvarez), a Mexican physician, was present at the house and acted to prolong the agent's life in order to extend the interrogation and torture.

In 1990, a federal grand jury indicted Alvarez for the torture and murder of Camarena-Salazar, and the United States District Court for the Central District of California issued a warrant for his arrest. 331 F.3d 604, 609 (CA9 2003) (en banc). The DEA asked the Mexican Government for help in getting Alvarez into the United States, but when the requests and negotiations proved fruitless, the DEA approved a plan to hire Mexican nationals to seize Alvarez and bring him to the United States for trial. As so planned, a group of Mexicans, including petitioner Jose Francisco Sosa, abducted Alvarez from his house, held him overnight in a motel, and brought him by private plane to El Paso, Texas, where he was arrested by federal officers. *Ibid.*

Once in American custody, Alvarez moved to dismiss the indictment on the ground that his seizure was "outrageous governmental conduct," and violated the extradition treaty between the United States and Mexico. The District Court agreed, the Ninth Circuit affirmed, and we reversed, *id.*, at 670, holding that the fact of Alvarez's forcible seizure did not affect the jurisdiction of a federal court. The case was tried in 1992, and ended at the close of the Government's case, when the District Court granted Alvarez's motion for a judgment of acquittal.

In 1993, after returning to Mexico, Alvarez began the civil action before us here. He sued Sosa, Mexican citizen and DEA operative Antonio Garate-Bustamante, five unnamed Mexican civilians, the United States, and four DEA agents. So far as it matters here, Alvarez sought damages from the United States under the FTCA [Federal Tort Claims Act], alleging false arrest, and from Sosa under the ATS [Alien Tort Statute], for a violation of the law of nations. The former statute authorizes suit "for . . . personal injury . . . caused by the negligent or wrongful act or omission of any employee of the Government while acting within the scope of his office or employment." 28 U.S.C. §1346(b)(1). The latter provides in its entirety that "[t]he district courts shall have original jurisdiction of any civil action by an alien for a tort only, committed in violation of the law of nations or a treaty of the United States." §1350.

The District Court granted the Government's motion to dismiss the FTCA claim, but awarded summary judgment and $25,000 in damages to Alvarez on the ATS claim. A three-judge panel of the Ninth Circuit then affirmed the ATS judgment, but reversed the dismissal of the FTCA claim.

A divided en banc court came to the same conclusion. As for the ATS claim, the court called on its own precedent, "that [the ATS] not only provides federal courts with subject matter jurisdiction, but also creates a cause of action for an alleged violation of the law of nations." The Circuit then relied upon what it called the "clear and universally recognized norm prohibiting arbitrary arrest and detention," to support the conclusion that Alvarez's arrest amounted to a tort in violation of international law. On the FTCA claim, the Ninth Circuit held that, because "the DEA had no authority to effect Alvarez's arrest and detention in Mexico," the United States was liable to him under California law for the tort of false arrest.

We granted certiorari in these companion cases to clarify the scope of both the FTCA and the ATS. We now reverse in each. . . . [The Court's analysis finding that the FTCA did not permit Alvarez's California law tort claim against the United States is omitted.]

### III

Alvarez has . . . brought an action under the ATS against petitioner, Sosa, who argues (as does the United States supporting him) that there is no relief under the ATS because the statute does no more than vest federal courts with jurisdiction, neither creating nor authorizing the courts to recognize any particular right of action without further congressional action. Although we agree the statute is in terms only jurisdictional, we think that at the time of enactment the jurisdiction enabled federal courts to hear claims in a very limited category defined by the law of nations and recognized at common law. We do not believe, however, that the limited, implicit sanction to entertain the handful of international law *cum* common law claims understood in 1789 should be taken as authority to recognize the right of action asserted by Alvarez here.

### A

. . .

The parties and *amici* here advance radically different historical interpretations of [the ATS]. Alvarez says that the ATS was intended not simply as a jurisdictional grant, but as authority for the creation of a new cause of action for torts in violation of international law. We think that reading is implausible. As enacted in 1789, the ATS gave the district courts "cognizance" of certain causes of action, and the term bespoke a grant of jurisdiction, not power to mold substantive law. See, *e.g.*, The Federalist No. 81, pp 447, 451 (J. Cooke ed. 1961) (A. Hamilton) (using "jurisdiction" interchangeably with "cognizance"). The fact that the ATS was placed in §9 of the Judiciary Act, a statute otherwise exclusively concerned with federal-court jurisdiction, is itself support for its strictly jurisdictional nature. Nor would the distinction between jurisdiction and cause of action have been elided by the drafters of the Act or those who voted on it. As Fisher Ames put it, "there is a substantial difference between the jurisdiction of courts and rules of decision." 1 Annals of Cong. 807 (Gales ed. 1834). It is unsurprising, then, that an authority on the historical origins of the ATS has written that "section 1350 clearly does not create a statutory cause of action," and that the contrary suggestion is "simply frivolous." Casto, The Federal Courts' Protective Jurisdiction Over Torts Committed in Violation of the Law of Nations, 18 Conn. L. Rev. 467, 479, 480 (1986) (hereinafter Casto, Law of Nations); Cf. Dodge, The Constitutionality of the Alien Tort Statute: Some Observations on Text and Context, 42 Va. J. Int'l L. 687, 689 (2002). In sum, we think the statute was intended as jurisdictional in the sense of addressing the power of the courts to entertain cases concerned with a certain subject.

But holding the ATS jurisdictional raises a new question, this one about the interaction between the ATS at the time of its enactment and the ambient law of the era. Sosa would have it that the ATS was stillborn because there could be no claim for relief without a further statute expressly authorizing adoption of causes of action. *Amici* professors of federal jurisdiction and legal history take a different tack, that federal courts could entertain claims once the jurisdictional grant was on the books, because torts in violation of the law of nations would have been recognized within the common law of the time. We think history and practice give the edge to this latter position . . .

. . . [D]espite considerable scholarly attention, it is fair to say that a consensus understanding of what Congress intended [by passage or the ATS] has proven elusive.

Still, the history does tend to support two propositions. First, there is every reason to suppose that the First Congress did not pass the ATS as a jurisdictional convenience to be placed on the shelf for use by a future Congress or state legislature that might, some day, authorize the creation of causes of action or itself decide to make some element of the law of nations actionable for the benefit of foreigners. The anxieties of the preconstitutional period cannot be ignored easily enough to think that the statute was not meant to have a practical effect. Consider that the principal draftsman of the ATS was apparently Oliver Ellsworth, previously a member of the Continental Congress that had passed the 1781 resolution [imploring states to vindicate rights under the law of nations] and a member of the Connecticut Legislature that made good on that congressional request. See generally W. Brown, The Life of Oliver Ellsworth (1905). Consider, too, that the First Congress was attentive enough to the law of nations to recognize certain offenses expressly as criminal, including the three mentioned by Blackstone. See An Act for the Punishment of Certain Crimes Against the United States, §8, 1 Stat. 113-114 (murder or robbery, or other capital crimes, punishable as piracy if committed on the high seas), and §28, *id.*, at 118 (violation of safe conducts and assaults against ambassadors punished by imprisonment and fines described as "infract[ions of] the law of nations"). It would have been passing strange for Ellsworth and this very Congress to vest federal courts expressly with jurisdiction to entertain civil causes brought by aliens alleging violations of the law of nations, but to no effect whatever until the Congress should take further action. There is too much in the historical record to believe that Congress would have enacted the ATS only to leave it lying fallow indefinitely.

The second inference to be drawn from the history is that Congress intended the ATS to furnish jurisdiction for a relatively modest set of actions alleging violations of the law of nations. Uppermost in the legislative mind appears to have been offenses against ambassadors, see *id.*, at 118; violations of safe conduct were probably understood to be actionable, *ibid.*, and individual actions arising out of prize captures and piracy may well have also been contemplated. *Id.*, at 113-114. But the common law appears to have understood only those three of the hybrid variety as definite and actionable, or at any rate, to have assumed only a very limited set of claims. As Blackstone had put it, "offences against this law [of nations] are principally incident to whole states or nations," and not individuals seeking relief in court. 4 Commentaries 68.

The sparse contemporaneous cases and legal materials referring to the ATS tend to confirm both inferences, that some, but few, torts in violation of the law of nations were understood to be within the common law. . . . In sum, although the ATS is a jurisdictional statute creating no new causes of action, the reasonable inference from the historical materials is that the statute was intended to have practical effect the moment it became law. The jurisdictional grant is best read as having been enacted on the understanding that the common law would provide a cause of action for the modest number of international law violations with a potential for personal liability at the time.

## IV

We think it is correct, then, to assume that the First Congress understood that the district courts would recognize private causes of action for certain torts in violation of the law of nations, though we have found no basis to suspect Congress had any examples in mind beyond those torts corresponding to Blackstone's three primary offenses: violation of safe conducts, infringement of the rights of ambassadors, and piracy. We assume, too, that no development in the two centuries from the enactment of §1350 to the birth of the modern line of cases beginning with *Filartiga* v. *Pena-Irala*, 630 F.2d 876 (CA2 1980), has categorically precluded federal courts from recognizing a claim under the law of nations as an element of common law; Congress has not in any relevant way amended §1350 or limited civil common law power by another statute. Still, there are good reasons for a restrained conception of the discretion a federal court should exercise in considering a new cause of action of this kind. Accordingly, we think courts should require any claim based on the present-day law of nations to rest on a norm of international character accepted by the civilized world and defined with a specificity comparable to the features of the 18th-century paradigms we have recognized. This requirement is fatal to Alvarez's claim.

### A

A series of reasons argue for judicial caution when considering the kinds of individual claims that might implement the jurisdiction conferred by the early statute. First, the prevailing conception of the common law has changed since 1789 in a way that counsels restraint in judicially applying internationally generated norms. When §1350 was enacted, the accepted conception was of the common law as "a transcendental body of law outside of any particular State but obligatory within it unless and until changed by statute." *Black and White Taxicab & Transfer Co.* v. *Brown and Yellow Taxicab & Transfer Co.*, 276 U.S. 518, 533, 72 L. Ed. 681, 48 S. Ct. 404 (1928) (Holmes, J., dissenting). Now, however, in most cases where a court is asked to state or formulate a common law principle in a new context, there is a general understanding that the law is not so much found or discovered as it is either made or created. . . .

Second, along with, and in part driven by, that conceptual development in understanding common law has come an equally significant rethinking of the role of the federal courts in making it. *Erie R. Co.* v. *Tompkins*, 304 U.S. 64 (1938), was the watershed in which we denied the existence of any federal "general" common law, which largely withdrew to havens of specialty, some of them defined by express congressional authorization to devise a body of law directly, *e.g.*, *Textile Workers* v. *Lincoln Mills of Ala.*, 353 U.S. 448, 1 L. Ed. 2d 972, 77 S. Ct. 912 (1957) (interpretation of collective-bargaining agreements); Fed. Rule Evid. 501 (evidentiary privileges in federal-question cases). Elsewhere, this Court has thought it was in order to create federal common law rules in interstitial areas of particular federal interest. *E.g.*, *United States v. Kimbell Foods, Inc.*, 440 U.S. 715, 726-727 (1979). And although we have even assumed competence to make judicial rules of decision of particular importance to foreign relations, such as the act of state doctrine, see *Banco Nacional de Cuba v. Sabbatino*, 376 U.S. 398, 427 (1964), the general practice has been to look for legislative guidance before exercising innovative authority over substantive law. It would be remarkable to take a more aggressive role in exercising a jurisdiction that remained largely in shadow for much of the prior two centuries.

Third, this Court has recently and repeatedly said that a decision to create a private right of action is one better left to legislative judgment in the great majority of cases. The creation of a private right of action raises issues beyond the mere consideration whether underlying primary conduct should be allowed or not, entailing, for example, a decision to permit enforcement without the check imposed by prosecutorial discretion. Accordingly, even when Congress has made it clear by statute that a rule applies to purely domestic conduct, we are reluctant to infer intent to provide a private cause of action where the statute does not supply one expressly. While the absence of congressional action addressing private rights of action under an international norm is more equivocal than its failure to provide such a right when it creates a statute, the possible collateral consequences of making international rules privately actionable argue for judicial caution.

Fourth, the subject of those collateral consequences is itself a reason for a high bar to new private causes of action for violating international law, for the potential implications for the foreign relations of the United States of recognizing such causes should make courts particularly wary of impinging on the discretion of the Legislative and Executive Branches in managing foreign affairs. It is one thing for American courts to enforce constitutional limits on our own State and Federal Governments' power, but quite another to consider suits under rules that would go so far as to claim a limit on the power of foreign governments over their own citizens, and to hold that a foreign government or its agent has transgressed those limits. Cf. *Sabbatino, supra*, at 431-432. Yet modern international law is very much concerned with just such questions, and apt to stimulate calls for vindicating private interests in §1350 cases. Since many attempts by federal courts to craft remedies for the violation of new norms of international law would raise risks of adverse foreign policy consequences, they should be undertaken, if at all, with great caution. Cf. *Tel-Oren* v. *Libyan Arab Republic*, 726 F.2d 774, 813 (CADC 1984) (Bork, J., concurring) (expressing doubt that §1350 should be read to require "our courts [to] sit in judgment of the conduct of foreign officials in their own countries with respect to their own citizens").

The fifth reason is particularly important in light of the first four. We have no congressional mandate to seek out and define new and debatable violations of the law of nations, and modern indications of congressional understanding of the judicial role in the field have not affirmatively encouraged greater judicial creativity. It is true that a clear mandate appears in the Torture Victim Protection Act of 1991, 106 Stat 73, providing authority that "establish[es] an unambiguous and modern basis for" federal claims of torture and extrajudicial killing, H. R. Rep. No. 102-367, pt. 1, p 3 (1991). But that affirmative authority is confined to specific subject matter, and although the legislative history includes the remark that §1350 should "remain intact to permit suits based on other norms that already exist or may ripen in the future into rules of customary international law," *id.*, at 4, Congress as a body has done nothing to promote such suits . . .

### C

We must still, however, derive a standard or set of standards for assessing the particular claim Alvarez raises, and for this case it suffices to look to the historical antecedents. Whatever the ultimate criteria for accepting a cause of action subject to jurisdiction under §1350, we are persuaded that federal courts should not recognize private claims under federal common law for violations of any international law norm with less definite content and acceptance among civilized nations than the historical paradigms familiar when §1350 was enacted. See, *e.g., United States* v. *Smith*, 18 U.S. 153, 5 Wheat. 153, 163-180, 5 L. Ed. 57 (1820) (illustrating the specificity with which the law of nations defined piracy). This limit upon judicial recognition is generally consistent with the reasoning of many of the courts and judges who faced the issue before it reached this Court. See *Filartiga, supra,* at 890 ("[F]or purposes of civil liability, the torturer has become — like the pirate and slave trader before him — *hostis humani generis,* an enemy of all mankind"); *Tel-Oren, supra,* at 781 (Edwards, J., concurring) (suggesting that the "limits of section 1350's reach" be defined by "a handful of heinous actions — each of which violates definable, universal and obligatory norms"); see also *In re Estate of Marcos Human Rights Litigation,* 25 F.3d 1467, 1475 (CA9 1994) ("Actionable violations of international law must be of a norm that is specific, universal, and obligatory"). And the determination whether a norm is sufficiently definite to support a cause of action should (and, indeed, inevitably must) involve an element of judgment about the practical consequences of making that cause available to litigants in the federal courts.

Thus, Alvarez's detention claim must be gauged against the current state of international law, looking to those sources we have long, albeit cautiously, recognized. . . .

Here, it is useful to examine Alvarez's complaint in greater detail . . . It is this position that Alvarez takes now: that . . . his arrest was arbitrary and as such forbidden by international law not because it infringed the prerogatives of Mexico, but because no applicable law authorized it.

Alvarez cites little authority that a rule so broad has the status of a binding customary norm today. He certainly cites nothing to justify the federal courts in taking his broad rule as the predicate for a federal lawsuit, for its implications would be breathtaking. His rule would support a cause of action in federal court for any arrest, anywhere in the world, unauthorized by the law of the jurisdiction in which it took place, and would create a cause of action for any seizure of an alien in violation of the Fourth Amendment, supplanting the actions under Rev Stat §1979, 42 U.S.C. §1983 [42 USCS §1983] and *Bivens v. Six Unknown Fed. Narcotics Agents,* 403 U.S. 388 (1971), that now provide damages remedies for such violations. It would create an action in federal court for arrests by state officers who simply exceed their authority; and for the violation of any limit that the law of any country might place on the authority of its own officers to arrest. And all of this assumes that Alvarez could establish that Sosa was acting on behalf of a government when he made the arrest, for otherwise he would need a rule broader still.

Alvarez's failure to marshal support for his proposed rule is underscored by the Restatement (Third) of Foreign Relations Law of the United States (1987), which says in its discussion of customary international human rights law that a "state violates international law if, as a matter of state policy, it practices, encourages, or condones . . . prolonged arbitrary detention." Although the Restatement does not explain its requirements of a "state policy" and of "prolonged" detention, the implication is clear. Any credible invocation of a principle against arbitrary detention that the civilized world accepts as binding customary international law requires a factual basis beyond relatively brief detention in excess of positive authority. Even the Restatement's limits are only the beginning of the enquiry, because although it is easy to say that some policies of prolonged arbitrary detentions are so bad that those who enforce them become enemies of the human race, it may be harder to say which policies cross that line with the certainty afforded by Blackstone's three common law offenses. In any event, the label would never fit the reckless policeman who botches his warrant, even though that same officer might pay damages under municipal law.

Whatever may be said for the broad principle Alvarez advances, in the present, imperfect world, it expresses an aspiration that exceeds any binding customary rule having the specificity we require. Creating a private cause of action to further that aspiration would go beyond any residual common law discretion we think it appropriate to exercise. It is enough to hold that a single illegal detention of less than a day, followed by the transfer of custody to lawful authorities and a prompt arraignment, violates no norm of customary international law so well defined as to support the creation of a federal remedy.

---

The Court's decision in *Sosa* dismissing Alvarez's ATS claim was unanimous, but only six of the nine justices agreed that the ATS could allow for claims beyond those historical causes of action associated with the ATS, albeit claims within the same paradigm of the historical ones (violation of safe conducts, infringement of the rights of ambassadors, and piracy). Justice Scalia authored a concurring opinion, joined by Chief Justice Rehnquist and Justice Thomas, arguing that the ATS is limited to the historical claims, an argument that Justice Thomas again pressed, along with Justice Gorsuch and Alito, in separate concurrences in later cases, *Jesner v. Arab Bank*, 137 S. Ct. 1432 (2018), and *Nestle USA, Inc. v. Doe*, 141 S. Ct. 1931 (2021), which are discussed below.

Since the earlier Second Circuit decision in *Filartiga*, a number of the claims presented under the ATS have involved allegations against corporations for harms caused outside the United States. See, e.g., *Doe v Unocal Corp.*, 395 F.3d 932 (9th Cir. 2002) (allowing ATS claims to proceed to trial against Unocal for gross human rights abuses—including of the kind to which private liability attaches—in connection with construction of a gas pipeline in Myanmar). As pointed out in Chapter 4, non-state actors can be held liable under international law for a limited set of human rights violations, in particular gross violations such as genocide, slavery, and other acts designated as international crimes. But does international law hold all non-state actors, including corporations, liable for such acts just as it does natural persons? And if it does, can corporate liability be established under the ATS? Both questions have been strongly debated, and lower federal courts have split on the issue of corporate liability under the ATS.

The US Supreme Court faced the issue in *Kiobel v. Royal Dutch Petroleum Co.*, 569 U.S. 108 (2013), a case involving claims under the ATS against Dutch, British, and Nigerian corporations for allegedly aiding and abetting the Nigerian government in committing systemic abuses in the Niger Delta. (The claims in *Kiobel* arose out of the same set of tragic circumstances that, as discussed in Chapter 4, pages 195-204, were addressed by the African Commission on Human Rights.) The Second Circuit dismissed the complaint, concluding that international law does not recognize corporate liability. The Supreme Court unanimously affirmed the judgment of the Second Circuit, but on quite different grounds. A majority of the Court pointed to a presumption against extraterritorial reach of any US statute and held that the presumption applies to claims under the ATS, given the statutes' text, its history, and foreign policy considerations. As to the particular claims brought in the case, the Court concluded:

> On these facts, all the relevant conduct took place outside the United States. And even where the claims touch and concern the territory of the United States, they must do so with sufficient force to displace the presumption against extraterritorial application. See *Morrison*,561 U.S. ___, 130 S. Ct., at 2883-2888. Corporations are often present in many countries, and it would reach too far to say that mere corporate presence suffices. If Congress were to determine otherwise, a statute more specific than the ATS would be required.

Id. at 1669.

The Court did address corporate liability in its next ATS decision, *Jesner v. Arab Bank*, 137 S. Ct. 1432 (2018). In that case the Court upheld, in a six to three decision, dismissal of a claim made under the ATS against Arab Bank, PLC for alleged complicity (including through transactions using the bank's New York office) in terrorist acts committed abroad. Applying the *Sosa* framework, Justice Kennedy's plurality opinion centered on the limitations of judicial capacity to create "new" causes of action under the ATS and found that—whatever the relevant international law—those limitations precluded recognizing a cause of action against *foreign* corporations under the statute. In separate opinions, a majority of the Court concurred that the claim against Arab Bank could not proceed under the ATS, but diverged on the rationale and on maintaining *Sosa*. In any event, the Court in *Jesner* foreclosed liability for foreign corporations, but not for domestic ones.

The Court once again construed the ATS in *Nestle USA, Inc. v. Doe*, 141 S. Ct. 1931 (1921). In that case, the Court disallowed an ATS claim against US companies for allegedly aiding and abetting in human trafficking and child slavery by cocoa farms in the Ivory Coast. The fact that the US companies bought cocoa from the farms and provided them with technical assistance, through operational decisions made in the US, was not sufficient to establish the requisite connection between the alleged wrongful conduct and the United States. Again, the Court majority that agreed on the disposition of the case was split on the underlying rationale. The majority, concurring, and dissenting opinions in the case reflected an ongoing debate within the Court about the ATS and the kind of claims it permits. The following extract provides an assessment of *Nestle* against the backdrop of the Court's previous ATS jurisprudence.

Ralph G. Steinhardt

## Losing the "Right" Way Preserves the Narrow Scope of the Alien Tort Statute: Nestle USA, Inc. v John Doe

George Washington University Law Review: On the Docket (2021), https://www .gwlr.org/losing-the-right-way-preserves-the-narrow-scope-of-the-ats/ (endnotes omitted)

In *Nestle v. Doe*, the Supreme Court again addressed the reach of the Alien Tort Statute of 1789 ("ATS"), which establishes a branch of subject matter jurisdiction in federal courts over "any civil action by an alien for torts in violation of the law of nations or a treaty of the United States." In *Nestle* and its companion case, *Cargill v. Doe*, the Court ruled that the ATS did not grant jurisdiction over certain Malian citizens' allegations against American corporations for aiding and abetting child slavery on cocoa plantations in Côte D'Ivoire. The fatal jurisdictional flaw was certainly not that child labor and other contemporary forms of slavery are lawful under international law or that such conduct could not qualify as a "tort." Nor was it that U.S. corporations cannot in principle be sued under the ATS, an issue that has been before the federal courts for over a decade. Nor was it that aiding-and-abetting liability is in principle unavailable under the ATS, which had been a highly-contested issue before the Ninth Circuit Court of Appeals in *Nestle* itself. Nor did the majority decide that the Erie Doctrine categorically prohibits the federal courts from inferring a private right of action from international law—as multiple *amici* had argued in support of the corporate defendants and as first advocated by self-styled "revisionists" a generation ago.

The majority's disposition rested instead on the conclusion that the allegations in the operative complaint were sufficiently extraterritorial to lie outside the reach of the ATS. Pleading the defendants' general corporate activity in the territory of the United States, including purchasing cocoa from the plantations where forced labor was alleged, "does not draw a sufficient connection between the cause of action the respondents seek and domestic conduct. *To plead facts sufficient to support a domestic application of the ATS, plaintiffs must allege more domestic conduct than general corporate activity common to most corporations.*" Given the breadth of the arguments advanced in the briefs of the parties (and *amici*) and the ratio of dicta to holding in the various opinions, *Nestle* is best viewed as narrowly laying out the pleading requirements for ATS cases against U.S.-based multinational corporations—in effect, a specialized application of the *Twombly-Iqbal* doctrine but tailored to a particular jurisdictional statute as applied to a particular class of defendants.

On the other hand, *Nestle* continues the unbroken losing streak for ATS claimants at the Supreme Court: *Argentina* v. *Amerada Hess* (1989) [holding that the Foreign Sovereign Immunities Act precluded an ATS claim against Argentina], *Sosa v. Alvarez-Machain* (2004), *Kiobel v. Royal Dutch Petroleum* (2013), and *Jesner v. Arab Bank PLC* (2018). So high a fatality rate at so high a level might be interpreted as the death knell of litigation under the statute—a death watch that started in earnest thirty-seven years ago. Of course, dozens of ATS cases have proceeded in the lower courts in that time which have never been reviewed—let alone repudiated—by the Supreme Court, and, in these four losing decisions, the Court itself has generally ruled narrowly that particular claims should be rejected, but leaving multiple questions unanswered. The consequence, in an example of what Justice Scalia memorably called the Court's "Never Say Never jurisprudence," is that *Nestle* invites more litigation than it resolves.

### *Sosa* Survives

The narrowness of the actual holding in *Nestle* obscures the breadth of its implications, especially a majority's reaffirmation of the principle from *Sosa v. Alvarez-Machain* that the actionable norms under the ATS were not frozen as of 1789: the recognition of a claim under the "present-day law of nations" as an element of common law extends to "norm[s] of international character accepted by the civilized world and defined with a specificity comparable to the features of the 18th-century paradigms we have recognized." What the actionable norms across the centuries have in common is a "specific, universal, and obligatory" character, combined with the "potential for personal liability"—a demanding limitation on the inference of causes of action that predates *Sosa* by two decades. Only three justices in *Nestle*—Thomas, Kavanaugh, and Alito—rejected that part of *Sosa* holding that the ATS authorizes federal courts to develop common law rules of liability where the underlying abuse violates such a norm. It takes a particularly selective form of originalism—not to mention an aggressive anti-literalism in the interpretation of statutes—to insist that the framers of the ATS would use the capacious language of "*any* civil action for a tort only in violation of" international law to confine ATS litigation (and the national interests it serves) to "violations of safe conducts, infringement of the rights of ambassadors, and piracy"—the three paradigmatic violations of international law articulated by Blackstone.

### The Potential Liability of U.S. Corporations Survives

Since the *Unocal* litigation, the federal courts have repeatedly faced the question whether multinational corporations may in principle bear international obligations to respect human rights norms and, if so, whether those obligations are enforceable through the ATS. Of course, no nation on the planet exempts juridical persons from legal liability for their torts, and it seems incongruous to create such an exemption for that subclass of torts that violate international law, which tend to be especially egregious. *Kiobel*'s specification that "mere corporate presence" is not enough to satisfy the pleading requirements of the ATS, reaffirmed in the majority opinion in *Nestle*, would be inexplicable if corporations were in principle immune from ATS liability. In *Jesner v. Arab Bank PLC*, the Supreme Court nevertheless ruled (5–4) that the ATS categorically forecloses claims against *foreign* corporations, and the corporate defendants in *Nestle* argued that U.S. corporations were entitled to the same treatment. As in *Kiobel* and *Jesner*, however, the *Nestle* Court avoided the question, despite having granted *certiorari* on the issue. In their separate concurrence in *Nestle*, Justices Gorsuch and Alito—joining the Court's "liberal" wing on the issue—concluded that "[t]he notion that corporations are immune from suit under the ATS cannot be reconciled with the statutory text and original understanding."

In the years since *Unocal* was filed, a robust, still-developing suite of international and domestic standards has emerged governing the human rights responsibilities and best practices of the corporation in the twenty-first century. From that perspective, the prospect of ATS liability from *Unocal* onward provided a kind of normative scaffolding for the creation of a regime. As in any construction project, the scaffolding serves an important function but is not an end in itself.

### The Ersatz Presumption Against Extraterritoriality Applies

As noted, the essence of the holding in *Nestle* is that the allegations of the defendants' conduct in the United States were considered insufficiently connected to the plaintiffs' injuries in Côte D'Ivoire. According to the majority, "nearly all the conduct [the plaintiffs] allege aided and abetted forced labor—providing training, equipment, and cash to overseas farmers—occurred in Ivory Coast." This is not a disposition that protects any other U.S.-based multinational corporation with more specific "connections" to the wrongs alleged, even if the injury that results is in foreign territory, but it is an apparent application of the rule from *Kiobel* that the "presumption against extraterritoriality applies to claims under the ATS." Of all the ways that the *Nestle* plaintiffs might have lost at the Supreme Court, this is the most case-specific and therefore the least destructive to future actions against U.S. companies that aid and abet human rights violations at home or abroad.

## Note: The State Action Requirement and Foreign Sovereign Immunity

The Court in *Sosa* noted that limitations exist for ATS claims in addition to the constraints on finding international norms that meet the required criteria of specificity. Among these limitations is that ATS plaintiffs must usually establish state action in the alleged violation, while simultaneously avoiding the barriers presented by the rules of foreign sovereign immunity. As discussed earlier in the book, international human rights law is mostly directed at establishing obligations for states, and it holds purely private conduct liable for only a limited number of wrongs such as genocide, crimes against humanity, and war crimes. Thus, unless the alleged wrongful conduct falls under one of the limited categories, an ATS plaintiff is required to established that the defendant acted with the kind of linkage to state action—such as in *Filartiga* in which the defendant committed torture while acting as a Paraguayan police official—that typically is required in constitutional or federal statutory civil rights claims. See, e.g., *Wiwa v. Royal Dutch Petroleum Co.*, 2002 U.S. Dis. LEXIS 3293, 43 (S.D. N.Y.) (plaintiffs' allegations of torture were sufficient to state a claim that private "defendants were 'willful participants in joint action with the state or its agents,' and can hence be treated as state actors for the purpose of the" ATS). See generally Natalie L. Bridgeman, *Human Rights Litigation Under the ATCA as a Proxy for Environmental Claims*, 6 YALE H.R. & DEV. L.J. 1, 8-17 (2003) (summarizing cases under the ATS applying the state action doctrine).

On the other hand, if a claim is in effect against a foreign state itself, and not just someone acting under color of state authority, then sovereign immunity rules come into play. While *Filartiga* and *Sosa* involved suits against individuals, nothing in the Alien Tort Statute itself prohibits suits against foreign states that seek to hold the state liable. The Supreme Court has held, however, that the Foreign Sovereign Immunities Act (FSIA) is the sole basis for obtaining jurisdiction over foreign states in US courts; the ATS does not provide an alternative avenue for jurisdiction, nor does it provide an exception to the immunity from suit provided foreign states by the FSIA. See *Argentine Republic v. Amerada Hess Shipping Corp.*, 488 U.S. 428, 434-440 (1989) (dismissing an ATS claim because of the FSIA). The FSIA provides for certain exceptions to sovereign immunity, including an exception for commercial activities or related acts occurring in the United States and an exception for non-commercial torts where the alleged damaged occurred in the United States. See 28 U.S.C. §1605(a). In *Amerada Hess*, which involved an incident on international waters during the Argentine-British war in the South Atlantic, the Court found the tort exception inapplicable because of the alleged wrongful act did not occur "within the United States" according to the FSIA's strict definition of that term. 488 U.S. at 439. Compare *Letelier v. Republic of Chile*, 488 F. Supp. 665 (D.D.C. 1980) (federal district court had jurisdiction under the FSIA to hear tort claim against Chile for its alleged role in lethal bombing in District of Columbia).

While the FSIA clearly governs suits against states themselves, another question is the extent to which government officials are entitled to some form of immunity. The FSIA defines "foreign states" to include states' political subdivisions and their "agencies and instrumentalities," the latter defined in turn to include "any entity . . . (1) which is a separate legal person, corporate or otherwise, and (2) which is an organ of a foreign state or political subdivision thereof." 28 U.S.C. §1603. In *Samantar v. Yousuf*, 560 U.S. 305 (2010), the Court held that by these terms the FISA does not govern the immunity of individual foreign officials. The Court pointed out, however, that the FSIA will apply in a suit plead against a foreign official where the state is a required party or the real party in interest. See id. at 324-325. The Court also indicated that, instead of the FSIA, the common law governs the immunity of foreign officials. See id. at 319-322.

Since *Samantar*, lower federal courts have varied in their approaches to common law immunity for foreign officials (other than heads of state), an immunity that is also based on international law. Professor Bradley has identified a conceptual division in the courts, between what he calls an "effect-of-judgment" approach and what he calls a "nature-of-act" approach. "Under an effect-of-judgment approach, foreign officials would have no immunity from damage claims when the plaintiff is seeking to recover the damages from the official personally rather than from the foreign state itself. By contrast, under a nature-of-act approach, foreign officials would generally have immunity if the suit is challenging conduct carried out on behalf of the foreign state, regardless of who is formally being asked to pay the judgment." Curtis A. Bradley, *Conflicting Approaches to Federal Common Law of Foreign Official Immunity*, 115 AM. J. IN'L L. 1, 2 (1921).

Where sitting heads of state are concerned, federal common law doctrine, in keeping with customary international law, ordinarily provides them with absolute immunity from lawsuits brought against them in the United States. See *Lafontant v. Aristide*, 844 F. Supp. 128 (E.D.N.Y. 1994). In order to assert head of state immunity, however, a government official must be recognized as a head of state by the United States and the foreign state concerned. See *United States v. Noriega*, 746 F. Supp. 1506 (S.D. Fla. 1990).

## Comments and Questions

1. The Court in *Sosa* affirmed that customary international law is part of the limited universe of federal common law that can appropriately be discerned and applied by the courts and from which a cause of action under the jurisdictional grant of the ATS can arise. Yet, in the end, the Court set a high bar for allowing an ATS claim based on an alleged violation of international law: Such a claim must be found "to rest on a norm of international character accepted by the civilized world and defined with a specificity comparable to the features of the 18th-century paradigms we have recognized." Additionally, and as highlighted by the Court subsequently, it must be determined that recognizing a cause or action under the ATS is a proper exercise of judicial discretion in light of several factors. As pointed out by Professor Steinhardt, the Court in *Kiobel* did not change the *Sosa* standard, and a plurality of the Court again reaffirmed it later in *Jesner v. Arab Bank*, 138 S. Ct. 1386 (1918). What, in particular, are the eighteenth-century paradigms? Why in *Sosa* did the right against arbitrary detention asserted by Alvarez not meet the threshold articulated by the Court? How can you distinguish that right and the prohibition against torture which was found to be actionable under the ATS in *Filartiga*? Did the Court in *Sosa* implicitly agree that *Filartiga* met the threshold? Note that the Court cited *Filartiga* in stating that its articulated limit for ATS claims "is generally consistent with the reasoning of many of the courts and judges who faced the issue before it reached this Court."

2. *Sosa* sounded a strong cautionary note against the recognition of new actionable customary international law norms and offered several reasons for judicial restraint in this regard. What specifically are those reasons? Do you agree with them? What are their implications generally for the application of international law by domestic courts?

3. Is it correct to say that *Sosa* and subsequent cases confirm that, for an international norm to be actionable under the ATS, it must meet a level of specificity in its definition and depth of worldwide acceptance *beyond that* which is ordinarily required for finding the existence of a customary international law norm? Consider that subsequent to the Supreme Court's decision in *Sosa*, the Eleventh Circuit Court of Appeals in *Aldaña v. Del Monte Fresh Produce, Inc.*, 416 F.3d 1242 (11th Cir. 2005), *reh'ing, en banc, denied*, 452 F.3d 1284 (2006), cert. denied, 549 U.S. 1032 (2006), ordered the dismissal of claims for "cruel, inhuman, degrading treatment or punishment" and arbitrary detention in connection with the alleged abduction and mistreatment of union leaders in Guatemala, while allowing a claim of torture arising from the same events to proceed. And Compare *Vietnam Ass'n for Victims of*

*Agent Orange v. Dow Chemical Co.*, 517 F.3d 104 (2d Cir. 2008) (finding no universally accepted norm with the specificity required by *Sosa* prohibiting the use of the herbicide known as "Agent Orange" during the Vietnam War); *Abagninin v. AMVAC Chem. Corp.*, 545 F.3d 733 (9th Cir. 2008) (affirming dismissal of claim of genocide and crimes against humanity under ATS where failure to allege that defendants acted with specific intent when exposing West African workers to pesticide, which caused male sterility); with *Abdullahi v. Pfizer, Inc.*, 562 F.3d 163, 187 (2d Cir. 2009), cert. denied, 2010 U.S. LEXIS 5541 (upholding an ATS cause of action "for a violation of the norm of customary international law prohibiting medical experimentation on human subjects without their consent," in a case in which Nigerian children were unknowingly subjected to testing of a new antibiotic by the defendant drug company); *Mastafa v. Chevron Corp.*, 770 F.3d 170 (2nd Cir. 2014) (finding valid complaints by Iraqi nationals under the ATS for war crimes, genocide, and other crimes against humanity perpetrated during the reign of Saddam Hussein regime, although dismissing the claims for insufficient facts to demonstrate liability by aiding and abetting).

4. How much of a barrier is the state action requirement to ATS claims? Are many of the ATS claims that can meet the *Sosa* criteria likely to entail human rights violations for which individuals can be liable without state action as a matter of international law? How was the state action requirement met in *Filartiga* and *Sosa*? If the FSIA precludes foreign states, and their agencies and instrumentalities, from being sued under the ATS, and common law immunity applies to individual foreign officials, then when can a state actor be sued under the ATS and for what kinds of claims? Consider the "effect-of-judgment" and "nature-of-act" approaches to determining official immunity, discussed *supra* page 426.

5. As discussed above, the Supreme Court has further limited the scope of potential ATS claims in cases subsequent to *Sosa*. Given the Supreme Court's jurisprudence, what are the parameters of permissible ATS claims now? Would the claim in *Filartiga* survive today? What kind of ATS claims can be brought against corporations?

## III. JUDICIAL ENFORCEMENT OF ECONOMIC, SOCIAL, AND CULTURAL RIGHTS IN SOUTH AFRICA: A COMPARATIVE PERSPECTIVE

Much as the US Constitution has its Bill of Rights, the constitutions of other countries typically contain provisions affirming individual or, in some cases, collective rights that are judicially enforceable. For the most part, these constitutional provisions in some measure reflect internationally-recognized human rights and to that extent advance the implementation of international human rights obligations. Many of the constitutions developed since the latter part of the twentieth century contain extensive catalogues of rights in terms similar to those of modern human rights instruments.

A case in point is the Constitution of South Africa, which includes a detailed Bill of Rights affirming a range of civil and political rights as well as economic, social, and cultural rights. See Constitution of the Republic of South Africa, 1996, as amended, Chapter 2, Bill of Rights, https://www.gov.za/documents/constitution/chapter-2-bill-rights. Implementation of South Africa's international human rights obligations is thus substantially advanced by the terms of the Constitution itself, especially insofar as the rights affirmed in the Constitution are enforceable by the country's courts. Under Section 231(4) of the Constitution, treaties ratified by Parliament are domestic law if they are enacted into domestic legislation or are self-executing (somewhat as in the United States). See generally Justice A. Mavedzenge, *Comparing the Role of International Law in South Africa and Kenya*, 1 CORNELL INT'L L.J. ONLINE 99 (2013). But in practice, because of South Africa's extensive constitutional Bill of Rights, the judicial enforcement of human rights is carried by enforcement of the constitutional rights, against the backdrop of applicable international law.

Section 39 of South African's Constitution provides: "In interpreting the Bill of Rights, a court, tribunal or forum . . . (b) must consider international law; and (c) may consider foreign law." Further, as to legislation, Section 233 states: "When interpreting any legislation, every court must prefer any reasonable interpretation that is consistent with international law over any alternative interpretations that is consistent with international law."

The following case illustrates the operation of aspects of these features of South Africa's constitutional arrangement, in relation to judicial enforcement of the right to health, a right affirmed both in international human rights law and in the Constitution of South African.

## Minister of Health and Others v. Treatment Action Campaign and Others

2002(5) SA (CC) (Constitutional Court of South Africa, Case CCT 8/02, Judgment of July 5, 2002) (most footnotes omitted)

### INTRODUCTION

[1] The HIV/AIDS pandemic in South Africa has been described as "an incomprehensible calamity" and "the most important challenge facing South Africa since the birth of our new democracy" and government's fight against "this scourge" as "a top priority." It "has claimed millions of lives, inflicting pain and grief, causing fear and uncertainty, and threatening the economy." These are not the words of alarmists but are taken from a Department of Health publication in 2000 and a ministerial foreword to an earlier departmental publication.

[2] This appeal is directed at reversing orders made in a high court against government because of perceived shortcomings in its response to an aspect of the HIV/ AIDS challenge. The court found that government had not reasonably addressed the need to reduce the risk of HIV-positive mothers transmitting the disease to their babies at birth. More specifically the finding was that government had acted unreasonably in (a) refusing to make an antiretroviral drug called

nevirapine[3] available in the public health sector where the attending doctor considered it medically indicated and (b) not setting out a timeframe for a national programme to prevent mother-to-child transmission of HIV.

[3] The case started as an application in the High Court in Pretoria on 21 August 2001. The applicants were a number of associations and members of civil society concerned with the treatment of people with HIV/AIDS and with the prevention of new infections. In this judgment they are referred to collectively as "the applicants." The principal actor among them was the Treatment Action Campaign (TAC). The respondents were the national Minister of Health and the respective members of the executive councils (MECs) responsible for health in all provinces save the Western Cape. They are referred to collectively as "the government" or "government."

[4] Government, as part of a formidable array of responses to the pandemic, devised a programme to deal with mother-to-child transmission of HIV at birth and identified nevirapine as its drug of choice for this purpose.[5] The programme imposes restrictions on the availability of nevirapine in the public health sector. This is where the first of two main issues in the case arose. The applicants contended that these restrictions are unreasonable when measured against the Constitution, which commands the state and all its organs to give effect to the rights guaranteed by the Bill of Rights. This duty is put thus by sections 7(2) and 8(1) of the Constitution respectively:

> "7(2) The state must respect, protect, promote and fulfil the rights in the Bill of Rights.
>
> . . .
>
> 8(1) The Bill of Rights applies to all law, and binds the legislature, the executive, the judiciary and all organs of state."

At issue here is the right given to everyone to have access to public health care services and the right of children to be afforded special protection. These rights are expressed in the following terms in the Bill of Rights:

> "27(1) Everyone has the right to have access to—
> (a) health care services, including reproductive health care;
> (2) The state must take reasonable legislative and other measures, within its available resources, to achieve the progressive realisation of each of these rights.
>
> . . .
>
> 28(1) Every child has the right—
>
> . . .
>
> (c) to basic nutrition, shelter, basic health care services and social services."

---

3. Nevirapine is a fast-acting and potent antiretroviral drug long since used worldwide in the treatment of HIV/AIDS and registered in South Africa since 1998. In January 2001 it was approved by the World Health Organization for use against intrapartum mother-to-child transmission of HIV, i.e., transmission of the virus from mother to child at birth. It was also approved for such use in South Africa. The nature and precise date of such approval were contested and this led to some vigorously debated subsidiary issues, dealt with more fully below. . . .

5. The drug is currently available free to government and its administration is simple: a single tablet taken by the mother at the onset of labour and a few drops fed to the baby within 72 hours after birth.

[5] The second main issue also arises out of the provisions of sections 27 and 28 of the Constitution. It is whether government is constitutionally obliged and had to be ordered forthwith to plan and implement an effective, comprehensive and progressive programme for the prevention of mother-to-child transmission of HIV throughout the country. The applicants also relied on other provisions of the Constitution which, in view of our conclusions, need not be considered.

[6] The affidavits lodged by the applicants addressed these two central issues from a variety of specialised perspectives, ranging from paediatrics, pharmacology and epidemiology to public health administration, economics and statistics. The applicants' papers also include the testimony of doctors, nurses and counsellors confronted daily with the human tragedies of HIV-infected mothers and their babies. In addition there are poignant accounts of HIV-positive pregnant women's pleas for access to nevirapine for themselves and their babies at public health institutions where its supply is prohibited. . . .

FACTUAL BACKGROUND

[10] The two principal issues had been in contention between the applicants and government for some considerable time prior to the launching of the application in the High Court. Thus, when the TAC in September 1999 pressed for acceleration of the government programme for the prevention of intrapartum mother-to-child transmission of HIV, it was told by the Minister that this could not be done because there were concerns about, among other things, the safety and efficacy of nevirapine. Nearly a year later (in August 2000), following the 13th International AIDS Conference in Durban and a follow-up meeting attended by the Minister and the MECs, the Minister announced that nevirapine would still not be made generally available. Instead each province was going to select two sites for further research and the use of the drug would be confined to such sites. . . .

[15] It can be accepted that an important reason for this decision was that government wanted to develop and monitor its human and material resources nationwide for the delivery of a comprehensive package of testing and counselling, dispensing of nevirapine and follow-up services to pregnant women attending at public health institutions. Where bottle-feeding was to be substituted for breastfeeding, appropriate methods and procedures had to be evolved for effective implementation, bearing in mind cultural problems, the absence of clean water in certain parts of the country and the increased risks to infants growing up with inadequate nutrition and sanitation. At the same time, data relating to administrative hitches and their solutions, staffing, costs and the like could be gathered and correlated. All of this obviously makes good sense from the public health point of view. These research and training sites could provide vital information on which in time the very best possible prevention programme for mother-to-child transmission could be developed.

[16] This point is also made in the *Protocol for providing a comprehensive package of care for the prevention of mother to child transmission of HIV in South Africa (draft version 4)* issued by government in April 2001. . . .

[17] The crux of the problem, however, lies elsewhere: what is to happen to those mothers and their babies who cannot afford access to private health care and do not have access to the research and training sites? It is not clear on the papers

how long it is planned to take before nevirapine will be made available outside these sites. Some of the provinces had not yet established any test sites by the time the application was launched in late August 2001. The first sites were established only in May 2001 following a meeting the previous month at which government had endorsed the establishment of the sites for a period of two years. These sites were to be selected according to stated criteria, one in an urban and one in a rural community in each province. Whether the programme was to be maintained strictly until the last of the provincial test sites had been functioning for two years or could possibly be extended beyond that period does not appear from the papers. What is plain, though, is that for a protracted period nevirapine would not be supplied at any public health institution other than one designated as part of a research site. . . .

[22] In their argument counsel for the government raised issues pertaining to the separation of powers. This may be relevant in two respects — (i) in the deference that courts should show to decisions taken by the executive concerning the formulation of its policies; and (ii) in the order to be made where a court finds that the executive has failed to comply with its constitutional obligations. These considerations are relevant to the manner in which a court should exercise the powers vested in it under the Constitution. It was not contended, nor could it have been, that they are relevant to the question of justiciability.

### ENFORCEMENT OF SOCIO-ECONOMIC RIGHTS

[23] This Court has had to consider claims for enforcement of socio-economic rights on two occasions.[6] On both occasions it was recognised that the state is under a constitutional duty to comply with the positive obligations imposed on it by sections 26 [right to housing] and 27 of the Constitution. It was stressed, however, that the obligations are subject to the qualifications expressed in sections 26(2) and 27(2). On the first occasion, in *Soobramoney*, the claim was dismissed because the applicant failed to establish that the state was in breach of its obligations under section 26 in so far as the provision of renal dialysis to chronically ill patients was concerned. In *Grootboom* the claim was upheld because the state's housing policy in the area of the Cape Metropolitan Council failed to make reasonable provision within available resources for people in that area who had no access to land and no roof over their heads and were living in intolerable conditions. . . .

[25] The question in the present case, therefore, is not whether socio-economic rights are justiciable. Clearly they are.[10] The question is whether the applicants have shown that the measures adopted by the government to provide access to health care services for HIV-positive mothers and their newborn babies fall short of its obligations under the Constitution.

---

6. Soobramoney v. Minister of Health, KwaZulu-Natal 1998 (1) SA 765 (CC); 1997 (12) BCLR 1696 (CC); Government of the Republic of South Africa and Others v. Grootboom and Others 2001 (1) SA 46 (CC); 2000 (11) BCLR 1169 (CC). . . .

10. Ex Parte Chairperson of the Constitutional Assembly: In re Certification of the Constitution of the Republic of South Africa, 1996 (4) SA 744 (CC); 1996 (10) BCLR 1253 (CC) para 78.

MINIMUM CORE

[26] . . . [I]t is necessary to consider a line of argument presented on behalf of the first and second amici. It was contended that section 27(1) of the Constitution establishes an individual right vested in everyone. This right, so the contention went, has a minimum core to which every person in need is entitled. The concept of "minimum core" was developed by the United Nations Committee on Economic, Social and Cultural Rights which is charged with monitoring the obligations undertaken by state parties to the International Covenant on Economic, Social and Cultural Rights. According to the Committee

> "a State party in which any significant number of individuals is deprived of essential foodstuffs, of essential primary health care, of basic shelter and housing, or of the most basic forms of education is, *prima facie*, failing to discharge its obligations under the Covenant. If the Covenant were to be read in such a way as not to establish such a minimum core obligation, it would be largely deprived of its *raison d'être*. By the same token, it must be noted that any assessment as to whether a State has discharged its minimum core obligations must also take account of resource constraints applying within the country concerned. Article 2(1) obligates each State party to take the necessary steps 'to the maximum of its available resources'. In order for a State party to be able to attribute its failure to meet at least its minimum core obligations to a lack of available resources it must demonstrate that every effort has been made to use all resources that are at its disposition in an effort to satisfy, as a matter of priority, those minimum obligations."[11]

. . .

[30] Section 26(1) refers to the "right" to have access to housing. Section 26(2), dealing with the state's obligation in that regard, requires it to "take reasonable legislative and other measures, within its available resources, to achieve the progressive realization of this right." The reference to "this right" is clearly a reference to the section 26(1) right. Similar language is used in section 27 which deals with health care services, including reproductive health care, sufficient food and water, and social security, including, if persons are unable to support themselves and their dependants, appropriate social assistance. Subsection (1) refers to the right everyone has to have "access" to these services; and subsection (2) obliges the state to take "reasonable legislative and other measures, within its available resources, to achieve the progressive realisation of each of these rights." The rights requiring progressive realisation are those referred to in sections 27(1)(a), (b) and (c).

[31] In *Soobramoney* it was said:

> "What is apparent from these provisions is that the obligations imposed on the State by ss 26 and 27 in regard to access to housing, health care, food, water and social security are dependent upon the resources available for

---

11. CESCR General Comment 3, "The nature of States parties obligations (Art. 2, par.1)" 4/12/90 para 10.

such purposes, *and that the corresponding rights themselves are limited by reason of the lack of resources.*"

The obligations referred to in this passage are clearly the obligations referred to in sections 26(2) and 27(2), and the "corresponding rights" are the rights referred to in sections 26(1) and 27(1).

[32] This passage is cited in *Grootboom*. It is made clear in that judgment that sections 26(1) and 26(2) "are related and must be read together." Yacoob J said: "The section has been carefully crafted. It contains three subsections. . . .

[33] In *Grootboom* reliance was also placed on the provisions of the Covenant. Yacoob J held that in terms of our Constitution the question is "whether the measures taken by the State to realise the right afforded by s 26 are reasonable."

[34] Although Yacoob J indicated that evidence in a particular case may show that there is a minimum core of a particular service that should be taken into account in determining whether measures adopted by the state are reasonable, the socio-economic rights of the Constitution should not be construed as entitling everyone to demand that the minimum core be provided to them. Minimum core was thus treated as possibly being relevant to reasonableness under section 26(2), and not as a self-standing right conferred on everyone under section 26(1).

[35] A purposive reading of sections 26 and 27 does not lead to any other conclusion. It is impossible to give everyone access even to a "core" service immediately. All that is possible, and all that can be expected of the state, is that it act reasonably to provide access to the socio-economic rights identified in sections 26 and 27 on a progressive basis. In *Grootboom* the relevant context in which socioeconomic rights need to be interpreted was said to be that

> "[m]illions of people are living in deplorable conditions and in great poverty. There is a high level of unemployment, inadequate social security, and many do not have access to clean water or to adequate health services. These conditions already existed when the Constitution was adopted. . . ."

[36] The state is obliged to take reasonable measures progressively to eliminate or reduce the large areas of severe deprivation that afflict our society. The courts will guarantee that the democratic processes are protected so as to ensure accountability, responsiveness and openness, as the Constitution requires in section 1. As the Bill of Rights indicates, their function in respect of socio-economic rights is directed towards ensuring that legislative and other measures taken by the state are reasonable. As this Court said in *Grootboom*, "[i]t is necessary to recognise that a wide range of possible measures could be adopted by the State to meet its obligations.". . .

[39] We therefore conclude that section 27(1) of the Constitution does not give rise to a self-standing and independent positive right enforceable irrespective of the considerations mentioned in section 27(2). Sections 27(1) and 27(2) must be read together as defining the scope of the positive rights that everyone has and the corresponding obligations on the state to "respect, protect, promote and fulfil" such rights. The rights conferred by sections 26(1) and 27(1) are to have "access" to the services that the state is obliged to provide in terms of sections 26(2) and 27(2). . . .

## Considerations Relevant to Reasonableness

[67] The policy of confining nevirapine to research and training sites fails to address the needs of mothers and their newborn children who do not have access to these sites. It fails to distinguish between the evaluation of programmes for reducing mother-to-child transmission and the need to provide access to health care services required by those who do not have access to the sites.

[69] The applicants do not suggest that nevirapine should be administered indiscriminately to mothers and babies throughout the public sector. They accept that the drug should be administered only to mothers who are shown to be HIV-positive and that it should not be administered unless it is medically indicated and, where necessary, counselling is available to the mother to enable her to take an informed decision as to whether or not to accept the treatment recommended. Those conditions form part of the order made by the High Court.

[70] In dealing with these questions it must be kept in mind that this case concerns particularly those who cannot afford to pay for medical services. To the extent that government limits the supply of nevirapine to its research sites, it is the poor outside the catchment areas of these sites who will suffer. There is a difference in the positions of those who can afford to pay for services and those who cannot. State policy must take account of these differences.

[71] The cost of nevirapine for preventing mother-to-child transmission is not an issue in the present proceedings. It is admittedly within the resources of the state. The relief claimed by the applicants on this aspect of the policy, and the order made by the High Court in that regard, contemplate that nevirapine will only be administered for the prevention of mother-to-child transmission at those hospitals and clinics where testing and counselling facilities are already in place. Therefore this aspect of the claim and the orders made will not attract any significant additional costs.

[72] In evaluating government's policy, regard must be had to the fact that this case is concerned with newborn babies whose lives might be saved by the administration of nevirapine to mother and child at the time of birth. The safety and efficacy of nevirapine for this purpose have been established and the drug is being provided by government itself to mothers and babies at the pilot sites in every province.

[73] The administration of nevirapine is a simple procedure. Where counselling and testing facilities exist, the administration of nevirapine is well within the available resources of the state and, in such circumstances, the provision of a single dose of nevirapine to mother and child where medically indicated is a simple, cheap and potentially lifesaving medical intervention. . . .

## Findings re Government's Programme

[93] In the present case this Court has the duty to determine whether the measures taken in respect of the prevention of mother-to-child transmission of HIV are reasonable. We know that throughout the country health services are overextended. HIV/AIDS is but one of many illnesses that require attention. It is, however, the greatest threat to public health in our country. . . .

[95] The rigidity of government's approach when these proceedings commenced affected its policy as a whole. If, as we have held, it was not reasonable to restrict the use of nevirapine to the research and training sites, the policy as a whole will have to be reviewed. Hospitals and clinics that have testing and counselling facilities should be able to prescribe nevirapine where that is medically indicated. The training of counselors ought now to include training for counselling on the use of nevirapine. As previously indicated, this is not a complex task and it should not be difficult to equip existing counsellors with the necessary additional knowledge. In addition, government will need to take reasonable measures to extend the testing and counselling facilities to hospitals and clinics throughout the public health sector beyond the test sites to facilitate and expedite the use of nevirapine for the purpose of reducing the risk of mother-to-child transmission of HIV . . .

## THE POWERS OF THE COURTS

[96] Counsel for the government contended that even if this Court should find that government policies fall short of what the Constitution requires, the only competent order that a court can make is to issue a declaration of rights to that effect. That leaves government free to pay heed to the declaration made and to adapt its policies in so far as this may be necessary to bring them into conformity with the court's judgment. This, so the argument went, is what the doctrine of separation of powers demands.

[97] In developing this argument counsel contended that under the separation of powers the making of policy is the prerogative of the executive and not the courts, and that courts cannot make orders that have the effect of requiring the executive to pursue a particular policy.

[98] This Court has made it clear on more than one occasion that although there are no bright lines that separate the roles of the legislature, the executive and the courts from one another, there are certain matters that are pre-eminently within the domain of one or other of the arms of government and not the others. All arms of government should be sensitive to and respect this separation. This does not mean, however, that courts cannot or should not make orders that have an impact on policy.

[99] The primary duty of courts is to the Constitution and the law, "which they must apply impartially and without fear, favour or prejudice." The Constitution requires the state to "respect, protect, promote, and fulfil the rights in the Bill of Rights." Where state policy is challenged as inconsistent with the Constitution, courts have to consider whether in formulating and implementing such policy the state has given effect to its constitutional obligations. If it should hold in any given case that the state has failed to do so, it is obliged by the Constitution to say so. In so far as that constitutes an intrusion into the domain of the executive, that is an intrusion mandated by the Constitution itself. . . .

[106] We thus reject the argument that the only power that this Court has in the present case is to issue a declaratory order. Where a breach of any right has taken place, including a socio-economic right, a court is under a duty to ensure that effective relief is granted. The nature of the right infringed and the nature of the infringement will provide guidance as to the appropriate relief in a particular

case. Where necessary this may include both the issuing of a mandamus and the exercise of supervisory jurisdiction.

[107] An examination of the jurisprudence of foreign jurisdictions on the question of remedies shows that courts in other countries also accept that it may be appropriate, depending on the circumstances of the particular case, to issue injunctive relief against the state. In the United States, for example, frequent use has been made of the structural injunction — a form of supervisory jurisdiction exercised by the courts over a government agency or institution. Most famously, the structural injunction was used in the case of *Brown v Board of Education* where the US Supreme Court held that lower courts would need to retain jurisdiction of *Brown* and similar cases. These lower courts would have the power to determine how much time was necessary for the school boards to achieve full compliance with the Court's decision and would also be able to consider the adequacy of any plan proposed by the school boards "to effectuate a transition to a racially nondiscriminatory school system."

[108] Even a cursory perusal of the relevant Indian case law demonstrates a willingness on the part of the Indian courts to grant far-reaching remedial orders. Most striking in this regard is the decision in *M.C. Mehta v. State of Tamil Nadu and Others*[6] where the Supreme Court granted a wide-ranging order concerning child labour that included highly detailed mandatory and structural injunctions.

[109] Although decisions of the German Federal Constitutional Court are mostly in the form of declaratory orders, the Court also has the power to prescribe for a temporary period which steps have to be taken in order to create a situation in conformity with the Basic Law. The most far-reaching execution order was probably that made by the Court in the *Second Abortion Case*, declaring several provisions of the Criminal Code unconstitutional and void and replacing them by a detailed interim law to remain in place until new legislation came into force. In Canada, it appears that both the supreme and the lower courts have the power to issue mandatory orders against organs of state. Canadian courts have, however, tended to be relatively cautious in this regard. For example, in *Eldridge v. British Columbia (Attorney General)*, the Supreme Court of Canada considered a declaration of unconstitutionality preferable to "some kind of injunctive relief" on the basis that "there are myriad options available to the government that may rectify the unconstitutionality of the current system." The Canadian courts have also tended to be wary of using the structural injunction.

[111] In the United Kingdom, although injunctive relief may be granted against officers of the Crown, the House of Lords has held that this should only be done in the "most limited circumstances. In the majority of situations so far as final relief is concerned, a declaration will continue to be the appropriate remedy on an application for judicial review involving officers of the Crown. As has been the position in the past, the Crown can be relied upon to co-operate fully with such declarations."

[112] [A] brief survey [of foreign jurisprudence] makes clear . . . that in none of the jurisdictions surveyed is there any suggestion that the granting of injunctive relief breaches the separation of powers. The various courts adopt different attitudes to when such remedies should be granted, but all accept that within the separation of powers they have the power to make use of such remedies — particularly when the state's obligations are not performed diligently and without delay. . . .

[114] A factor that needs to be kept in mind is that policy is and should be flexible. It may be changed at any time and the executive is always free to change policies where it considers it appropriate to do so. The only constraint is that policies must be consistent with the Constitution and the law. Court orders concerning policy choices made by the executive should therefore not be formulated in ways that preclude the executive from making such legitimate choices.

CIRCUMSTANCES RELEVANT TO THE ORDER TO BE MADE

. . . .

[122] In the present case we have identified aspects of government policy that are inconsistent with the Constitution. The decision not to make nevirapine available at hospitals and clinics other than the research and training sites is central to the entire policy. Once that restriction is removed, government will be able to devise and implement a more comprehensive policy that will give access to health care services to HIV-positive mothers and their newborn children, and will include the administration of nevirapine where that is appropriate. The policy as reformulated must meet the constitutional requirement of providing reasonable measures within available resources for the progressive realisation of the rights of such women and newborn children. This may also require, where that is necessary, that counsellors at places other than at the research and training sites be trained in counselling for the use of nevirapine. We will formulate a declaration to address these issues.

RELIEF . . .

[125] It is essential that there be a concerted national effort to combat the HIV/ AIDS pandemic. The government has committed itself to such an effort. We have held that its policy fails to meet constitutional standards because it excludes those who could reasonably be included where such treatment is medically indicated to combat mother-to-child transmission of HIV. That does not mean that everyone can immediately claim access to such treatment, although the ideal, as Dr Ntsaluba says [on behalf of the government], is to achieve that goal. Every effort must, however, be made to do so as soon as reasonably possible. The increases in the budget [about which we have been informed] will facilitate this.

[126] We consider it important that all sectors of the community, in particular civil society, should co-operate in the steps taken to achieve this goal. In our view that will be facilitated by spelling out the steps necessary to comply with the Constitution.

[127] We will do this on the basis of the policy that government has adopted as the best means of combating mother-to-child transmission of HIV, which is to make use of nevirapine for this purpose. Government must retain the right to adapt the policy, consistent with its constitutional obligations, should it consider it appropriate to do so. The order that we make has regard to this. . . .

[131] We do not underestimate the nature and extent of the problem facing government in its fight to combat HIV/AIDS and, in particular, to reduce the transmission of HIV from mother to child. We also understand the need to exercise caution when dealing with a potent and a relatively unknown drug. But the nature

of the problem is such that it demands urgent attention. Nevirapine is a potentially lifesaving drug. Its safety and efficacy have been established. There is a need to assess operational challenges for the best possible use of nevirapine on a comprehensive scale to reduce the risk of mother-to-child transmission of HIV. There is an additional need to monitor issues relevant to the safety and efficacy of and resistance to the use of nevirapine for this purpose. There is, however, also a pressing need to ensure that where possible loss of life is prevented in the meantime. . . .

ORDERS

[135] We accordingly make the following orders:

1. The orders made by the High Court are set aside and the following orders are substituted.
2. It is declared that:
    (a) Sections 27(1) and (2) of the Constitution require the government to devise and implement within its available resources a comprehensive and co-ordinated programme to realize progressively the rights of pregnant women and their newborn children to have access to health services to combat mother-to-child transmission of HIV.
    (b) The programme to be realised progressively within available resources must include reasonable measures for counselling and testing pregnant women for HIV, counselling HIV-positive pregnant women on the options open to them to reduce the risk of mother-to-child transmission of HIV, and making appropriate treatment available to them for such purposes.
    (c) The policy for reducing the risk of mother-to-child transmission of HIV as formulated and implemented by government fell short of compliance with the requirements in subparagraphs (a) and (b) in that:
        (i) Doctors at public hospitals and clinics other than the research and training sites were not enabled to prescribe nevirapine to reduce the risk of mother-to-child transmission of HIV even where it was medically indicated and adequate facilities existed for the testing and counselling of the pregnant women concerned.
        (ii) The policy failed to make provision for counsellors at hospitals and clinics other than at research and training sites to be trained in counselling for the use of nevirapine as a means of reducing the risk of mother- to-child transmission of HIV.
3. Government is ordered without delay to:
    (a) Remove the restrictions that prevent nevirapine from being made available for the purpose of reducing the risk of mother-to-child transmission of HIV at public hospitals and clinics that are not research and training sites.
    (b) Permit and facilitate the use of nevirapine for the purpose of reducing the risk of mother-to-child transmission of HIV and to make it available for this purpose at hospitals and clinics when in the judgment of the attending medical practitioner acting in consultation with the medical superintendent of the facility concerned this is medically indicated, which

shall if necessary include that the mother concerned has been appropriately tested and counselled.

(c)  Make provision if necessary for counsellors based at public hospitals and clinics other than the research and training sites to be trained for the counselling necessary for the use of nevirapine to reduce the risk of mother- to-child transmission of HIV.

(d)  Take reasonable measures to extend the testing and counseling facilities at hospitals and clinics throughout the public health sector to facilitate and expedite the use of nevirapine for the purpose of reducing the risk of mother-to-child transmission of HIV.

4. The orders made in paragraph 3 do not preclude government from adapting its policy in a manner consistent with the Constitution if equally appropriate or better methods become available to it for the prevention of mother-to-child transmission of HIV.

5. The government must pay the applicants' costs, including the costs of two counsel.

6. The application by government to adduce further evidence is refused.

## Note: The Application of International Human Rights Law in Other Foreign Jurisdictions

The above judgment in *Minister of Health and Others v. Treatment Action Campaign and Others* references international and foreign sources, reflecting the directive of Section 39(1)(b) of the South African Constitution to "consider international . . . and . . . foreign law" in cases applying provisions of the Constitution's Bill of Rights. Some constitutions other than South Africa's—for example, those of Spain, Romania, and Colombia—similarly include provisions requiring that constitutional rights be interpreted in a manner consistent with the treaties those countries have ratified. See Constitution of Colombia, Art. 93 (1992, as amended through March 2005); Constitution of Spain, Art. 10(2) (1978, as amended through Aug. 1992); Constitution of Romania, Art. 20(1) (1991).

Even in the absence of such constitutional mandates, the courts of many other countries—like the United State—can find it desirable to interpret domestic constitutional, statutory, or common law in light of applicable international human rights standards. In British commonwealth jurisdictions, in which international law generally has no domestic legal effect unless it is incorporated by legislation, international treaties and other instruments frequently inform the judicial application of domestic law in the area of human rights. In courts of the United Kingdom, the European Convention on Human Rights is a significant factor in the development of common law rights. See, e.g., *Derbyshire County Council v. Times Newspapers Ltd.*, 1992 Q.B. 770, 810-817 (European Convention and Civil and Political Covenant relevant in determining scope of common law free speech). See generally Andrew Clapham, "The European Convention on Human Rights in the British Courts: Problems Associated with the Incorporation of International Human Rights," in *Promoting Human Rights through Bills of Rights* 95 (Philip Alston, ed., 1999); Jeremy McBride and L.N. Brown, *The United Kingdom, the European Community and the European Convention on Human Rights*, 1981 Y.B. EUR. L. 167, 177. The Human Rights Act of 1998 incorporated the European Convention into British law, and it now may be invoked directly in domestic courts.

In Canada, courts look to international human rights law for interpretive guidance in construing the Canadian Charter of Rights and Freedoms, in applying statutes, and in identifying the contours of the common law. See, e.g, *Suresh v. Canada (Minister of Citizenship & Immigration)*, [2002] 1 S.C.R. 3, 31-32, 38; *Puspanathan v. Canada*, [1998] 1 S.C.R. 982 (using international human rights bodies' interpretations of the Convention relating to the Status of Refugees to interpret the Immigration Act implementing that Convention); *Mugesara v. Canada*, [2005] S.C.J. No. 39 (looking to international law of genocide to guide interpretation of the Criminal Code); *Baker v. Canada*, [1999] 2 S.C.R. 817 (using the Convention on the Rights of the Child to develop common law on administrative statutory discretion). The Supreme Court of Canada was asked the specific question of whether international or domestic law governs in the event of a conflict in relation to the right of peoples to self-determination, but the court failed to address the issue because no such conflict was determined to exist in that case. See *Quebec Secession Reference* [1998] 2 S.C.R. 217.

Australia's courts similarly look to international human rights law for interpretive guidance. A prominent instance of this interpretive use of international human rights occurred in *Mabo v. Queensland (No. 2)*, (1992) 175 C.L.R.1, in which the Australian High Court (the country's highest appellate court) overturned more than a century of common law doctrine based on the concept of terra nullius, a concept that regarded the land inhabited by Australian aboriginals prior to European settlement as legally vacant and that continued to serve to deny aboriginals rights to traditional lands. Justice Brennan of the High Court wrote that "unjust and discriminatory doctrine of that kind can no longer be accepted." Id. at 42. Instead, he reasoned, the common law in its present formulation should be interpreted in conformity with contemporary values embraced by Australian society and also in light of contemporary international law, which clearly prohibits racial discrimination: "If it were permissible in past centuries to keep the common law in step with international law, it is imperative in today's world that the common law should neither be nor be seen to be frozen in an age of racial discrimination." Id. at 41.

The constitutions of a number of countries explicitly incorporate the human rights affirmed in specified international sources. See Chapter 3 for a discussion of constitutions incorporating references to the Universal Declaration of Human Rights. The Constitution of Nicaragua, for example, affirms and guarantees enjoyment of the rights affirmed in the international bill of human rights, the American Declaration of the Rights and Duties of Man, and the American Convention on Human Rights (notwithstanding that country's dysfunctional judicial system amid broader tumultuous circumstances currently). See Constitution of Nicaragua, Art. 46 (1987, as amended through 2005). See also, e.g., Constitution of Colombia, Art. 93 (incorporating human rights treaties to which Colombia is a party and according them primacy in domestic law); Constitution of Romania, 20 (incorporating the Universal Declaration and ratified human rights treaties, and giving precedence to the treaties over internally-created law). Through such constitutional provisions, international human rights norms become more than mere interpretive backdrops; they are given constitutional status and may be directly applicable by courts of appropriate jurisdiction, usually without any assessment of self-execution. See, e.g., Colombian Const. Ct. Judgment No.C-139/96 (1996) (applying provisions of ILO Convention No. 169 on Indigenous and Tribal Peoples to declare invalid parts of the Ley de Resguardos, a domestic statute governing indigenous reserves).

International human rights norms can be incorporated into domestic law by general constitutional references to international law, such as that which appears in Article 25 of the German Constitution (Basic Law) (1949, with Amendments through 2014): "The general rules of international law shall be an integral part of federal law." Beyond such general incorporation of international law, Article 25 establishes that the rules of international law "shall take precedence over the laws and directly create rights and duties for the inhabitants of the federal territory." Hence, in accordance with Article 25, rules of customary international law and general international law may be directly applied by courts in appropriate cases. As for treaties, similarly to the constitutions of other countries, the German Constitution in its Article 59(2) requires parliamentary approval for certain categories of treaties, namely those that affect the country's political relationships and those that relate to the subjects of federal legislation, and by virtue of the parliamentary action such treaties are legislatively incorporated into domestic law and applicable by courts. See Holger Hestermeyer, *The Reception of International Law in the German Legal Order: An Introduction*, ResearchGate (2015), https://www.researchgate.net/publicat ion/306400927. Having been so incorporated into domestic law, the European Convention on Human Rights, given its subject corresponding with fundamental rights in the German Constitution, has been given quasi-constitutional status.

Similarly, in Mexico, Colombia and other Latin American countries, the American Convention of Human Rights—along with its interpretation by the Inter-American Court of Human Rights—has been judicially deemed to be within the countries' "constitutional block" (*"bloque constitucional"*). See Graciela Rodríguez Manzo et al., *Bloque de Constitucionalidad en México* 33-57 (2013). For discussion of the impact of inter-American human rights instruments and institutions on domestic legal developments in Latin American countries, see Sergio Garcia Ramirez, *The Relationship between Inter-American Jurisdiction and States (National Systems): Some Pertinent Questions*, 5 Notre Dame J. Int'l & Comp. Law:115 (2015).

## IV.   FINAL COMMENTS AND QUESTIONS

1. To what extent do the texts of sections 27 and 28 of South Africa's Constitution accomplish incorporating into that Constitution the human rights standard articulated in Article 12 (right to health) of the International Covenant on Economic, Social, and Cultural Rights? Compare sections 27 and 28, quoted in the judgement above, at paragraph 4, with Article 12 of the International Covenant on Economic, Social and Cultural Rights:

> 1. The States Parties to the present Covenant recognize the right of everyone to the enjoyment of the highest attainable standard of physical and mental health.

2. The steps to be taken by the States Parties to the present Covenant to achieve the full realization of this right shall include those necessary for:

(a) The provision for the reduction of the stillbirth-rate and of infant mortality and for the healthy development of the child;

(b) The improvement of all aspects of environmental and industrial hygiene;

(c) The prevention, treatment and control of epidemic, endemic, occupational and other diseases;

(d) The creation of conditions which would assure to all medical service and medical attention in the event of sickness.

Note also that the Covenant generally obligates states to take steps toward "achieving progressively the full realization of the rights recognized" therein "to the maximum of its available resources (Article 2)." Does the text of South Africa Constitution reflect or conform to this same obligation? Note also Section 7 of the Constitution, quoted in paragraph 4 of the judgment alongside sections 27 and 28.

2. Did the South African Constitutional Court interpret the South African constitutional protections for the right to health fully consistently with Article 12 of the International Covenant on Economic, Social, and Cultural Rights? In particular, did its interpretation of obligations flowing from Section 27 of the South African Constitution conform to the obligation under Article 12 of the Covenant to achieve progressively realization of the right to health? Did the Court follow the view of the Committee on Economic, Social and Cultural Rights, expressed in its General Comment 3, that the right to health carries with it a "minimum core" obligation for states? At the time of the judgment, South Africa had signed but not ratified the ESC Covenant; ratification came in 2015. Is that fact reflected in the Court's analysis? Note that in *Government of the Republic of South Africa and Others v. Grootboom and Others* 2001 (1) SA 46 (CC), a case heavily relied on in *Treatment Action Campaign*, the South African Court recalled its earlier jurisprudence affirming that, under the relevant section of the South Africa's Constitution:

> ... public international law would include non-binding as well as binding law. They may both be used under the section as tools of interpretation. International agreements and customary international law accordingly provide a framework within which [the Bill of Rights] can be evaluated and understood, and for that purpose, decisions of tribunals dealing with comparable instruments, such as the United Nations Committee on Human Rights, the Inter-American Commission on Human Rights, the Inter-American Court of Human Rights, the European Commission on Human Rights, and the European Court of Human Rights, and, in appropriate cases, reports of specialized agencies such as the International Labour Organisation, may provide guidance as to the correct interpretation of particular provisions of [the Bill of Rights].

*Grootboom*, SA 46 at para. 26 (quoting *S. v. Makwanyane and Another* 1995 (3) SA 391 (CC) at para. 35). Did the Court adequately consider international sources?

3. Do you agree that the right to health, as articulated South Africa's Constitution, is sufficiently concrete to be enforced through an adjudicative procedure? Is the right to health as articulated in the Covenant on Economic, Social, and

Cultural Rights any more concrete or justiciable? How much merit was there in the government's position in the *Treatment Action Campaign* case that the Court should refrain from imposing a specific remedy on the government, given the nature of the issue at hand? Compare *Mazibuko v. City of Johannesburg*, Const. Ct. S.A., Case CCT 8/02, Judgment of Sept. 2, 2009, 2010 (2) BCLR 239 (CC), in which the Constitutional Court drew on its previous jurisprudence to analyze the right of access to water as a component of the right to health of Section 27(1) of the Constitution. In that case, the Court stressed the importance of the constitutional right to water, but concluded that it was not appropriate for a court to quantify what constituted access to sufficient water when it applied the constitutional requirement that the government take reasonable steps toward the realization of the right. For further discussion on the justiciability of the right to health in South Africa and its impact on its health care system post-apartheid, see Katharine G. Young and Julieta Lemaitre, *The Comparative Fortunes of the Right to Health: Two Tales of Justiciability in Colombia and South Africa*, 26 HARVARD HUMAN RIGHTS L. J. 179 (2013).

4. To address the appropriateness of imposing a judicial remedy to enforce the right to health in Section 27, the Constitutional Court referred to several judicial decisions from foreign jurisdictions, including the US Supreme Court's decision in *Brown v. Board of Education*. Is that an apt use of *Brown*? The use of *Brown* aside, what would someone with the judicial posture of Justice Ginsburg say about this part of the Constitutional Court's judgment?

5. Might a right to health be read into the due process clauses of the Fifth and Fourteenth Amendments to the US Constitution, in light of the relevant provisions of the Universal Declaration on Human Rights and the International Covenant on Economic, Social, and Cultural Rights? The due process clauses of the Constitution, which provide that no one shall "be deprived of life, liberty, or property without due process of law," have been construed to protect "fundamental rights," including the right to privacy and, for example, derivative rights of reproductive choice that are not explicitly articulated in the Constitution. Would reading a right to health into the Constitution be more likely if the United States were to ratify the Covenant on Economic, Social, and Cultural Rights? Or is ratification of the Covenant impeded because of the absence of such a right in US constitutional and other domestic law?

6. Assume hypothetically that, by some change in political and philosophical alignments, the US has ratified the International Covenant on Economic, Social and Cultural Rights, and has done so without a declaration of non-self-execution. Based on the discussion advanced in this chapter previously, do you think that the Covenant could be enforced by US Courts?

7. Chapter 7 discusses the relatively new Optional Protocol to the Economic, Social, and Cultural Rights, which provides a procedure for the Committee on Economic, Social, and Cultural Rights to consider complaints of violations of the Covenant. Are arguments for consideration by an international body of alleged violations of economic, social, and cultural rights stronger or weaker than arguments for the determination of such claims by domestic courts? For an interesting discussion on the litigation of the right to health before treaty-based organs and international bodies, see Yamin, Alicia Ely and Duger, Angela, *Adjudicating Health-Related*

*Rights: Proposed Considerations for the United Nations Committee on Economic, Social and Cultural Rights, and Other Supra-National Tribunals*, 17 Chi. J. Int'l L. 80 (2016).

8. The Bill of Rights of the US Constitution and numerous federal and state laws protect many of the rights found in international human rights law. As demonstrated by its reservations to the treaties it has ratified and its failure to ratify other treaties, the United States has endeavored to limit its international legal obligations to the rights already or about to be included in domestic law. Is this because human rights protections in US law are generally adequate, or because of the notion that rights should be determined primarily, if not exclusively, through domestic decision-making? If it is the latter, is that a credible argument?

9. Why do other countries seem more willing to include international human rights standards in their domestic decision-making processes? To what extend do Supreme Court decisions, such as *Roper v. Simmons* and *Graham v. Florida*, represent a trend toward attention by US courts to international human rights standards, or is any such trend blunted by current atttitudes on the Supreme Court and overshadowed by the many barriers remaining to direct judicial enforcement of international norms? In this regard, what might be the future significance and legacy of US Supreme Court decisions in cases such as *Medellin v. Texas* and *Kiobel et al. v. Royal Dutch Petroleum Co. et al.*? Is there likely to still be room for the use international human rights law by US Courts and, if so, in what way?

# CHAPTER 7

# UN HUMAN RIGHTS MECHANISMS

## HOW ARE HUMAN RIGHTS IMPLEMENTED AT THE GLOBAL LEVEL?

## I.  INTRODUCTION

Rights without remedies, Justice Holmes is purported to have remarked, are no rights at all. What remedies exist in the international arena to enforce human rights? Previous chapters have discussed the development of international human rights norms and the corresponding obligations that fall on states to effectively implement them. While arising from dynamics that involve multiple actors extending their influence to the international arena, international human rights law is made operational primarily through procedures that engage the legislative, executive, and judicial institutions of states at the domestic level. However, it goes without saying that state institutions all too often fail at this task, which is the very reason that international law came to embrace human rights in the first place. Thus, the international system over time has not only generated norms but also has developed mechanisms to oversee their implementation. At the global level, these mechanisms and procedures lie primarily within the United Nations, and they are the subject of this Chapter.

The relationship between domestic and international procedural levels is regulated by the principle of non-interference in matters essentially within the domestic jurisdiction of states, a corollary to the doctrine of state sovereignty reflected in Article 2(7) of the UN Charter. This principle favors decision-making at the most local level possible, including decision-making on human rights, and it reflects the realities of a world system that is still largely state-centered.

The principle of non-interference in domestic affairs is not absolute, however, and it is less a barrier to international concern with human rights than in earlier periods in the development of international law. Today, the principle no longer shields states from international attention and criticism regarding human rights matters, and the intrusiveness of such procedures into the domestic realm is not always entirely a function of state consent to the procedures. Even without their consent, offending states may find themselves subject to a level of international scrutiny, depending upon the gravity of noncompliance with applicable norms or the degree to which violations of human rights are unchecked by domestic institutions and decision-makers.

International procedures to advance compliance with human rights take many forms, including diplomatic debates in political fora, formal state-to-state complaints under relevant treaties, and discussions by expert bodies of reports submitted by states. Intergovernmental bodies may focus attention on human rights violations through investigations of particular countries or issues. All of these techniques, it will be noted, are triggered for the most part by the decisions of states individually or collectively. Increasingly, however, the initiatives of individual persons and other non-state actors have a role in the international enforcement of human rights.

This Chapter focuses on human rights implementation procedures that are part of the UN system, including those derived from the general authority provided by the UN Charter to advance human rights, as well as the optional petition and mandatory reporting procedures connected to particular human rights treaties. Procedures created under regional human rights arrangements in Europe, the Americas, and Africa are discussed in Chapters 8 and 9. We will first turn our attention to treaties, continuing the discussion begun in Chapter 2.

## II.   *MONITORING COMPLIANCE WITH UN HUMAN RIGHTS TREATIES*

In addition to the Charter-based procedures discussed later in this Chapter, each of the nine major UN human rights treaties adopted since the mid-1960s—generally referred to as the "core" UN human rights treaties—has created or generated the creation of separate monitoring bodies and established compliance review procedures. See, e.g., International Covenant on Civil and Political Rights (ICCPR), Article 28 et seq. (establishing the Human Rights Committee and related procedures). States have been notably reluctant, however, to adopt measures that truly amount to enforcement, such as allowing binding judgments to be issued or sanctions imposed for noncompliance. Rather, the primary means of pressuring states to change their policies stems from the moral, political, and quasi-legal impact of the monitoring bodies and other mechanisms.

Self-reporting by states parties is an obligation under all the core UN human rights treaties, except for the International Convention for the Protection of all Persons from Enforced Disappearance. All of the treaties establish optional procedures that permit the filing of individual complaints by victims of alleged violations, and most of the treaties also have optional procedures for interstate complaints. The optional complaint procedures are authorized either in the text of the treaty itself or in a separate protocol. In addition to evaluating the reports and complaints, several of the treaty bodies may conduct inquiries or visits to investigate alleged widespread violations of their treaty's terms, even without a petition being filed, but this ability also depends in most cases on separate acceptance by states. Additionally, a number of the treaty bodies employ "urgent action" or "early warning" procedures pursuant to specific authorization or their general monitoring authority. A somewhat indirect monitoring practice of the treaty bodies is the adoption of "general comments" or "general recommendations." The adoption of such a comment or recommendation on the meaning of rights and the scope of obligations contained within a specific treaty has become an important means for interpreting treaty provisions, as illustrated in several parts of this book. For a detailed description of the procedures attached to the core UN human rights treaties, see International Service for Human Rights, *A Simple Guide to the UN Treaty Bodies* (2015), https://ishr.ch/defenders-toolbox/resources/updated-simple-guide-to-the-un-treaty-bodies-guide-simple-sur-les-organes-de-traites-des-nations-unies/. See also Jane Connors, "The Human Rights Treaty Body System," in *The Oxford Handbook of United Nations Treaties* 377 (Simon Chesterman et al. eds., 2019); *The UN Human Rights Treaty System in the 21st Century* (Anne Bayefsky ed., 2021).

The following subsections focus on the reporting, complaint, and urgent action procedures, and on efforts to strengthen the treaty body system.

### A.   *Review of State Reports*

The following extract explains the common elements of the mandatory reporting procedures under the core UN human rights treaties except for the treaty on enforced disappearances (which has a distinct monitoring mechanism specific to the subject of that treaty). The extract is from a manual developed by the Office of the United Nations High Commissioner for Human Rights, as part of the call by the General Assembly for enhanced capacity building within the ongoing effort to strengthen the UN treaty monitoring mechanisms.

Office of the United Nations High Commissioner for Human Rights

Reporting to the United Nations Human Rights Treaty Bodies:
Training Guide Part 1 — Manual

UN Doc. HR/P/PT/20 (Part I) (2017) (footnotes omitted) (emphasis in original)

. . . [W]hen a State becomes a party to a treaty, it assumes a legal obligation to implement the rights set out therein. In order to consider the progress that State parties make in meeting their human rights obligations, each of the nine core international human rights treaties establishes a human rights **Treaty Body**—an international committee of independent experts. In addition, the Optional Protocol to the Convention against Torture establishes the Subcommittee on Prevention of Torture, with a specific mandate on torture prevention. Thus the United Nations human rights Treaty Body System consists of **ten Treaty Bodies**, often referred to as Committees, as follows:

Table 2    Treaty Bodies and Human Rights Treaties

| Treaty Body | Founding treaty |
| --- | --- |
| **Human Rights Committee (HRCttee)** | International Covenant on Civil and Political Rights (ICCPR, 1966) |
| **Committee on Economic, Social and Cultural Rights (CESCR)** | International Covenant on Economic, Social and Cultural Rights (ICESCR, 1966)* |
| **Committee on the Elimination of Racial Discrimination (CERD)** | International Convention on the Elimination of All Forms of Racial Discrimination (ICERD, 1965) |
| **Committee on the Elimination of Discrimination against Women (CEDAW)** | Convention on the Elimination of All Forms of Discrimination against Women (CEDAW, 1979) |
| **Committee against Torture (CAT)** | Convention against Torture and Other Cruel, Inhuman or Degrading Treatment or Punishment (CAT, 1984) |
| **Committee on the Rights of the Child (CRC)** | Convention on the Rights of the Child (CRC, 1989) |
| **Committee on Migrant Workers (CMW)** | International Convention on the Protection of the Rights of All Migrant Workers and Members of Their Families (ICRMW, 1990) |
| **Committee on the Rights of Persons with Disabilities (CRPD)** | International Convention on the Rights of Persons with Disabilities (CRPD, 2006) |
| **Committee on Enforced Disappearances (CED)** | International Convention for the Protection of All Persons from Enforced Disappearance (ICPPED, 2006) |
| **The Subcommittee on Prevention of Torture (SPT)** | Optional Protocol of the Convention against Torture (OPCAT, 2002) |

*The Committee was established by ECOSOC Resolution 1985/17 of 28 May 1985 to carry out the functions set out in particular in articles 21 and 22 of the ICESCR. The Resolution is available at the following: http://www.un .org/en/ecosoc/docs/docs.shtml.*

### 1.3.1. Members

The criteria for being elected a committee member are in general terms established in each treaty. Members should be nationals of a State party to the human rights treaty in question. Typical criteria include high moral standing and the recognized competence in the field of human rights or the subject-matter of the respective treaty. Due consideration should be given to equitable geographical representation, to appropriate representation of different legal systems, and to balanced gender representation.

The treaties also stipulate that members should serve in their individual capacities. They should be independent and impartial. They should act in accordance with their conscience, with the terms of the treaty, and in the interests of the Treaty Body; and they should not act on behalf of other stakeholders. The Treaty Bodies also endorsed the self-regulatory Guidelines on the independence and impartiality of members of the human rights Treaty Bodies ("Addis Ababa Guidelines"), stipulating further safeguards for the independence and impartiality of Treaty Body members.

The members are elected at the meeting of the State parties to the respective treaty. They are elected for a four-year term. To ensure continuity in membership, elections are staggered—the State parties hold elections for one-half of the membership every two years.

Treaty Body members do not receive a salary for their work. The United Nations pays the travel costs of members and a daily subsistence allowance to cover their costs (accommodation, board, local transport) during the session. . . .

### 4. The Reporting Procedure

. . .

The reporting procedure is also known as the **reporting cycle**. It begins with preparation of the State party's report, followed by its consideration by a Treaty Body; and ends with the State party's follow-up and implementation of the recommendations issued by a Treaty Body. Each time a cycle ends and a new one starts, the concerned State is required to report back regularly on measures taken to implement the recommendations and on new measures aimed at realizing the rights set forth in the treaty. So the review of a State party forms a continuum and each cycle builds on the preceding one.

There are two reporting procedures available to State parties for submitting their reports, namely the **Standard** Treaty Reporting Procedure and the **Simplified** Reporting Procedure **(SRP)**. Unlike the Standard Reporting Procedure, the SRP is optional. States can seek to avail themselves of the procedure, and may or may not be granted the opportunity by the Treaty Body, or indeed accept a Treaty Body's offer to them. The other main difference relates to the manner of reporting, which under the SRP entails responding to specific questions sent in advance to the State party by a Treaty Body. . . .

Under the **Simplified Reporting Procedure (SRP)**, the State party does not prepare and submit a report as the first step. Instead, the State responds to a List of Issues Prior to Reporting (LoIPR) that contains specific questions on treaty implementation. The responses of the State party to the List of Issues Prior to Reporting constitute the report of the State party. Under this procedure a Treaty Body will not

**Figure 1.   Standard Reporting Procedure**

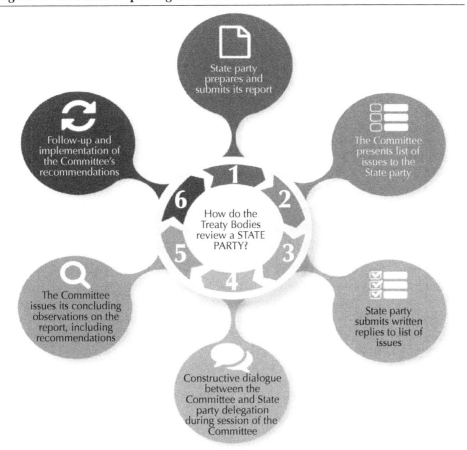

send a List of Issues to a State party after the submission of its report. Therefore a State party will not be required to submit further written information prior to the constructive dialogue. . . .

### 4.1.  The Report of the State party

. . . [T]he report of the State party constitutes the main element within the continuous review of a State party's progress in implementing the rights enshrined in the specific treaty. Before discussing in detail each of the stages of the reporting cycle, the following basic elements around the preparation of a State party report need clarification, namely the reporting periodicity, and the content and format of a report.

#### 4.1.1.  Reporting Periodicity

Most of the international human rights treaties establish a framework for regular reporting by State parties, known as "reporting periodicity", which covers

**initial** and **periodic** reports. The timetable for the submission of these reports is either explicitly set out in the provisions of the treaty or as indicated in the ICESCR and ICCPR at the discretion of the Treaty Body.

> While **initial** reports are required to be submitted **within one or two years** of the entry into force of the relevant treaty for the specific State party, the timeframe for submitting **periodic reports varies from two to six years depending on the treaty.**

In the case of the ICCPED, the Committee may request State parties to provide additional information on its implementation, even though the Convention does not provide for a regular reporting framework in its provisions (article 29 (4)). The practice of the Committee has been to request the submission of such complementary information no later than three or six years after the consideration of a State party report, depending on the situation of the State party with respect to the issues covered by the Convention. . . .

4.1.2.  Content of reports

In 2006 the Treaty Bodies adopted harmonized reporting guidelines on the content of State parties' reports, the aim being to strengthen State parties' capacity to fulfil their reporting obligations in a timely and efficient manner, including avoidance of unnecessary duplication of information. This harmonized approach also facilitates consistency by all committees in considering reports; helps each committee consider the human rights situation in every State party on an equal basis; and reduces the need for a committee to request supplementary information before considering a report. This approach was later supported and further encouraged by General Assembly Resolution 68/268 on strengthening and enhancing the effective functioning of the human rights Treaty Body system, adopted in April 2014 (A/RES/68/268).

In line with the foregoing, the report of a State party to any Treaty Body, irrespective of the reporting procedure under which such a report is submitted (Standard or Simplified) comprises two distinct but complementary documents, namely:

The **Common Core Document** (CCD) + the **Treaty-Specific Report** (initial or periodic)

The CCD and treaty-specific reports should elaborate on the *de jure* and *de facto* situation regarding implementation of the provisions of the treaties to which States are party. Reports should not be confined to lists of descriptions of legal instruments adopted in the country concerned in recent years, but should indicate how those legal instruments are reflected in the actual political, economic, social and cultural realities and general conditions of the country. They should provide evidence-based analysis supported by relevant statistical indicators and data, disaggregated by sex, age and population groups that may be more vulnerable, marginalized or at risk of discrimination. While statistics tables can usefully be **annexed** to the report, related analysis should be integrated into the main text. Such information should allow comparison over time and should indicate data sources. States should endeavour to analyse this information insofar as it is relevant to implementation of treaty obligations.

The ***Common Core Document (CCD)*** provides information of a general factual nature relating to the implementation of all treaties to which the reporting State is a party and which may be of relevance to all or several Treaty Bodies.30 It constitutes the common initial part of all State reports to the Treaty Bodies. Its aim is to avoid unnecessary duplication of information among the various reporting obligations of State parties. It should contain general information on the reporting State, for example on land, population and political structure; on the general framework for the protection and promotion of human rights; and on non-discrimination and equality issues, including effective remedies. The information submitted should take into consideration the list of indicators on the political system as well as on crime and administration of justice as provided in Annex 3 of the afore-mentioned Harmonized Guidelines on reporting under the international human rights treaties. The suggested structure for a Common Core Document is outlined below. . . .

State parties should submit the CCD only once, and they should update it regularly, usually every five years, or whenever major changes in the country take place. A Treaty Body may also request that the CCD be updated if it considers that the information it contains is out of date. Updates may be submitted in the form of an addendum to the existing CCD if only a few changes need to be incorporated, or a newly revised version if many changes have been made.31 State parties can submit the CCD at the same time as or independently of a treaty-specific report. It always remains a separate document but is transmitted to all relevant Treaty Bodies for upcoming reviews. . . .

**Initial treaty-specific reports** should focus on providing information relating to implementation of each of the rights (i.e., all substantive provisions) covered by the treaty concerned, including information on the State's constitutional and legal framework that is not provided in the common core document, as well as the legal and practical measures adopted to implement the treaty. It should contain an explanation, for example, of how a particular right is protected by national legislation, of which policies are in place to implement it, and of the types of mechanisms in place to monitor implementation of the right.

**Periodic treaty-specific reports** should in particular include recent developments affecting full realization of the rights recognized in the treaty, as well as information on measures taken and progress achieved to follow-up and implement the recommendations issued by the specific Treaty Body during the last consideration of the State party.

Periodic treaty-specific reports submitted under the Simplified Reporting Procedure should correspond to the List of Issues Prior to Reporting sent beforehand to State parties (see Section 4.3 on the SRP). . . .

4.2.2. Consideration of the report

As mentioned earlier, the State party report may be submitted under the Standard Reporting Procedure or the Simplified Reporting Procedure and, depending on the procedure selected, the reporting cycle may comprise six or seven stages. . . .

*i. Adoption of the List of Issues*

**(a) Preliminary review of the report—Standard Reporting Procedure.**   Once a report is submitted, the Treaty Body holds a preliminary review of the report with a view to determining any additional information it may need to request from the

State party. This internal discussion is often held during a so-called pre-session or country task force meeting. Such a meeting usually takes place several months ahead of the review, one or two sessions ahead of the session at which the Treaty Body formally considers the State party's report. Treaty Bodies appoint one or two country rapporteurs or a country task force, which are responsible for drafting the List of Issues on any given State party's report.

The Treaty Body considers information included in the State party report, along with reports from other sources, and adopts **a List of Issues** or **a List of Themes** (CERD). The purpose of this list is to indicate to the State party any additional required information that may have been omitted from the report, that may be out-dated, or that members consider necessary for an assessment of the state of implementation of the treaty in the country concerned. The List of Issues provides the State party with advance notice of issues of concern to the Treaty Body, so that the delegation can be duly prepared. Most Treaty Bodies structure their constructive dialogue around the List of Issues or themes.

It has become common practice for the UN system, national human rights institutions (NHRIs) and civil society organizations (CSOs) to submit written information to the committee or brief a country rapporteur, country task force or the entire committee on the issues of particular concern to them, once a List of Issues is discussed and adopted. . . .

**(b) List of Issues prior to Reporting—Simplified Reporting Procedure.**   In the case of the Simplified Reporting Procedure, the first step is a preparation of a List of Issues Prior to Reporting (LoIPR) by the Treaty Body. The preparation of a LoIPR is based on the previous concluding observations and on information provided to the Treaty Body by other sources such as the UN system, NHRIs and CSOs. These documents are included in the "**country file**" posted on the OHCHR website. . . .

*ii. Written replies to the List of Issues*

Under the **Standard Reporting Procedure,** the State party has the opportunity of supplementing and clarifying the information contained in the report in their replies to the List of Issues. In preparing its replies to LoIs, the State party should provide the Treaty Body with specific and fully updated information and data relating to the issues in question, including with statistics if available. . . .

In the case of **the Simplified Reporting Procedure**, the State party's written replies to the List of Issues Prior to Reporting constitute the State party report. . . .

*iii. Constructive dialogue*

The actual review of a State party's report by a Treaty Body is conducted through a six-hour **constructive dialogue** between members of the concerned Treaty Body and a State party delegation. In addition to the written reports received, the dialogue helps Treaty Bodies understand and review the human rights situation in the State party as it pertains to the treaty concerned. It serves as a basis for the concluding observations of the Treaty Bodies. The constructive dialogue provides an opportunity for State parties to receive expert advice on compliance with their international human rights commitments.

**(a) The State party's delegation.**   State parties are encouraged to have their delegations led by a senior State official with responsibility for implementation of the respective treaty, and also to include in their delegations, as far as possible, representatives with relevant technical expertise from key executive and other authorities responsible for implementation of the treaty concerned, with due regard to expertise. The delegation should have a gender balance in its composition. The State party may also wish to consider including in its delegation representatives of other relevant institutions or entities. . . .

(c) **Format of the constructive dialogue.** The constructive dialogue with State parties is conducted in public, usually in two sessions of up to three hours and will usually take place over two consecutive working days. An additional session of up to a further three hours may be held exceptionally when the Committee considers it appropriate and feasible. Observers, such as representatives of the United Nations System, national human rights institutions and of civil society organizations, may attend the constructive dialogue. . . .

*iv. Concluding observations*

Based on its dialogue with the State party and on information it has received from the State party and other sources — which assists it in conducting a well-informed country review — the Treaty Body adopts **concluding observations** which relate both to **positive aspects** of a State party's implementation of a treaty and also to **areas of concern** on which the Treaty Body makes **recommendations** on further action to be taken by the State party. . . .

4.2.3. Follow-up and implementation of concluding observations

. . .

*i. Treaty Bodies follow-up procedure*

Seven Treaty Bodies (HRCttee, CESCR, CERD, CAT, CEDAW, CED and CRPD) have adopted a **follow-up procedure** under which they identify between one and three recommendations from the concluding observations which require immediate attention and implementation; and, in consequence, request State parties to submit, within one or two years, **an interim follow-up report** on the measures taken to implement those priority recommendations. The procedure is a desk review which provides the opportunity for continuation of the State party's engagement with the Treaty Body. . . .

6. ENGAGEMENT OF NHRIs AND CSOs IN THE REPORTING PROCESS

. . .

NHRIs and CSOs (international, regional, national and local) working on the promotion and protection of human rights can engage at all stages of the work of the Treaty Bodies, namely on the reporting process, the communications procedure, the inquiry procedure, the country visits, any early warning and urgent action procedures where they exist, at Days of General or Thematic Discussions, and development of general comments. This involvement has been recognized by the Treaty Bodies as an essential element in the promotion and implementation of the international human rights treaties and their optional protocols at national level. While some treaties expressly provide for a role of CSOs or NHRIs in the work of the Treaty Body, most Treaty Bodies have formalized their cooperation with NHRIs and CSOs and have adopted procedures of interaction with them in various documents, such as in their working methods, official papers, statements and information notes. Most Treaty Bodies reach out to relevant NHRIs and encourage them to be involved in the upcoming review of their country of interest. This chapter will focus on the involvement of these stakeholders in the reporting process.

NHRIs and CSOs, usually national and local, can engage in the Treaty Bodies' reporting process by actively participating in the **national reporting preparations**. They can provide useful inputs into the State party reports by sharing their views and assessment of the State party's implementation of a particular international human rights treaty and of the relevant previous recommendations. . . .

NHRIs and CSOs can also engage directly in the reporting process by submitting their own reports, known as **alternative reports**, and by presenting oral information to the Treaty Bodies at different stages of the reporting cycle (see figure, below). NHRIS and CSOs wishing to brief a Treaty Body but do not have the means to travel to Geneva may avail themselves of the possibility of doing so by video-conference (VTC). They should contact the relevant Secretariat to make such a request. The country-specific information they provide, along with information provided by other sources such as the UN system, is deemed necessary by the Treaty Bodies as it assists them in ensuring a well-informed review of a State party. This means that NHRIs' and CSOs' participation in and inputs into the State party report should not exclude them from the opportunity of contributing independently to the reporting process. State parties must respect the independent role of these stakeholders in engaging directly with the Treaty Bodies. Furthermore, State parties are urged by Treaty Bodies to ensure that individuals and groups which provide information to and cooperate with a specific Treaty Body are not subjected to reprisals.

———————————

As noted in the above extract, the treaty bodies adopt concluding observations at the end of considering states' periodic reports. In the optional simplified reporting procedure, a treaty body's concluding observations become the starting point in preparing the list of issues to be addressed in the subsequent state report. The extract below of the concluding observations of the Human Rights Committee on the the United States fourth reporting cycle under the ICCPR is followed by an extract of the US's fifth periodic report. The US has accepted the simplified procedure in relation to that treaty.

Human Rights Committee

## Concluding observations on the fourth periodic report of the United States of America

UN Doc. CCPR/C/USA/CO/4 (2014) (emphasis in original)

. . .

B. Positive Aspects

3. The Committee notes with appreciation the many efforts undertaken by the State party and the progress made in protecting civil and political rights. The

Committee welcomes in particular the following legislative and institutional steps taken by the State party:

(a) Full implementation of article 6, paragraph 5, of the Covenant in the aftermath of the Supreme Court's judgment in Roper v. Simmons, 543 U.S. 551 (2005), despite the State party's reservation to the contrary;

(b) Recognition by the Supreme Court in Boumediene v. Bush, 553 U.S. 723 (2008) of the extraterritorial application of constitutional habeas corpus rights to aliens detained at Guantánamo Bay;

(c) Presidential Executive Orders 1349—Ensuring Lawful Interrogations, 13492—Review and Disposition of Individuals Detained at the Guantánamo Bay Naval Base and Closure of Detention Facilities and 13493—Review of Detention Policy Options, issued on 22 January 2009;

(d) Support for the United Nations Declaration on the Rights of Indigenous Peoples, announced by President Obama on 16 December 2010;

(e) Presidential Executive Order 13567 establishing a periodic review of detainees at the Guantánamo Bay detention facility who have not been charged, convicted or designated for transfer, issued on 7 March 2011.

## C. PRINCIPAL MATTERS OF CONCERN AND RECOMMENDATIONS

### APPLICABILITY OF THE COVENANT AT NATIONAL LEVEL

4. The Committee regrets that the State party continues to maintain the position that the Covenant does not apply with respect to individuals under its jurisdiction, but outside its territory, despite the interpretation to the contrary of article 2, paragraph 1, supported by the Committee's established jurisprudence, the jurisprudence of the International Court of Justice and State practice. The Committee further notes that the State party has only limited avenues to ensure that state and local governments respect and implement the Covenant, and that its provisions have been declared to be non-self-executing at the time of ratification. Taken together, these elements considerably limit the legal reach and practical relevance of the Covenant (art. 2).

**The State party should:**

**(a) Interpret the Covenant in good faith, in accordance with the ordinary meaning to be given to its terms in their context, including subsequent practice, and in the light of the object and purpose of the Covenant, and review its legal position so as to acknowledge the extraterritorial application of the Covenant under certain circumstances, as outlined, inter alia, in the Committee's general comment No. 31 (2004) on the nature of the general legal obligation imposed on States parties to the Covenant;**

**(b) Engage with stakeholders at all levels to identify ways to give greater effect to the Covenant at federal, state and local levels, taking into account that the obligations under the Covenant are binding on the State party as a whole, and that all branches of government and other public or governmental authorities at every level are in a position to engage the responsibility of the State party (general comment. No. 31, para. 4). . . .**

ACCOUNTABILITY FOR PAST HUMAN RIGHTS VIOLATIONS

5. The Committee is concerned at the limited number of investigations, prosecutions and convictions of members of the Armed Forces and other agents of
the United States Government, including private contractors, for unlawful killings
during its international operations, and the use of torture or other cruel, inhuman or degrading treatment or punishment of detainees in United States custody,
including outside its territory, as part of the so-called "enhanced interrogation
techniques". While welcoming Presidential Executive Order 13491 of 22 January
2009 terminating the programme of secret detention and interrogation operated
by the Central Intelligence Agency (CIA), the Committee notes with concern that
all reported investigations into enforced disappearances, torture and other cruel,
inhuman or degrading treatment committed in the context of the CIA secret ren-
dition, interrogation and detention programmes were closed in 2012, resulting in
only a meagre number of criminal charges being brought against low-level oper-
atives. The Committee is concerned that many details of the CIA programmes
remain secret, thereby creating barriers to accountability and redress for victims
(arts. 2, 6, 7, 9, 10 and 14). . . .

RACIAL DISPARITIES IN THE CRIMINAL JUSTICE SYSTEM

6. While appreciating the steps taken by the State party to address racial disparities in the criminal justice system, including the enactment in August 2010 of
the Fair Sentencing Act and plans to work on reforming mandatory minimum sentencing statutes, the Committee continues to be concerned about racial disparities
at different stages in the criminal justice system, as well as sentencing disparities
and the overrepresentation of individuals belonging to racial and ethnic minorities
in prisons and jails (arts. 2, 9, 14 and 26). . . .

TARGETED KILLINGS USING UNMANNED AERIAL VEHICLES (DRONES)

9. The Committee is concerned about the State party's practice of targeted
killings in extraterritorial counter-terrorism operations using unmanned aerial
vehicles (UAV), also known as "drones," the lack of transparency regarding the criteria for drone strikes, including the legal justification for specific attacks, and the
lack of accountability for the loss of life resulting from such attacks. The Committee notes the State party's position that drone strikes are conducted in the course
of its armed conflict with Al-Qaida, the Taliban and associated forces in accordance with its inherent right of national self-defence, and that they are governed
by international humanitarian law as well as by the Presidential Policy Guidance
that sets out standards for the use of lethal force outside areas of active hostilities.
Nevertheless, the Committee remains concerned about the State party's very broad
approach to the definition and geographical scope of "armed conflict", including
the end of hostilities, the unclear interpretation of what constitutes an "imminent
threat", who is a combatant or a civilian taking direct part in hostilities, the unclear
position on the nexus that should exist between any particular use of lethal force
and any specific theatre of hostilities, as well as the precautionary measures taken
to avoid civilian casualties in practice (arts. 2, 6 and 14). . . .

EXCESSIVE USE OF FORCE BY LAW ENFORCEMENT OFFICIALS

11. The Committee is concerned about the still high number of fatal shootings by certain police forces, including, for instance, in Chicago, and reports of excessive use of force by certain law enforcement officers, including the deadly use of tasers, which has a disparate impact on African Americans, and use of lethal force by Customs and Border Protection (CBP) officers at the United States-Mexico border (arts. 2, 6, 7 and 26).

**The State Party should:**

**(a)  Step up its efforts to prevent the excessive use of force by law enforcement officers by ensuring compliance with the 1990 Basic Principles on the Use of Force and Firearms by Law Enforcement Officials;**

**(b)  Ensure that the new CBP directive on the use of deadly force is applied and enforced in practice; and**

**(c)  Improve reporting of violations involving the excessive use of force and ensure that reported cases of excessive use of force are effectively investigated; that alleged perpetrators are prosecuted and, if convicted, punished with appropriate sanctions; that investigations are re-opened when new evidence becomes available; and that victims or their families are provided with adequate compensation. . . .**

DETAINEES AT GUANTÁNAMO BAY

21. While noting the President's commitment to closing the Guantánamo Bay facility and the appointment of Special Envoys at the United States Departments of State and of Defense to continue to pursue the transfer of designated detainees, the Committee regrets that no timeline for closure of the facility has been provided. The Committee is also concerned that detainees held in Guantánamo Bay and in military facilities in Afghanistan are not dealt with through the ordinary criminal justice system after a protracted period of over a decade, in some cases (arts. 7, 9, 10 and 14).

**The State party should expedite the transfer of detainees designated for transfer, including to Yemen, as well as the process of periodic review for Guantánamo detainees and ensure either their trial or their immediate release and the closure of the Guantánamo Bay facility. It should end the system of administrative detention without charge or trial and ensure that any criminal cases against detainees held in Guantánamo and in military facilities in Afghanistan are dealt with through the criminal justice system rather than military commissions, and that those detainees are afforded the fair trial guarantees enshrined in article 14 of the Covenant. . . .**

NATIONAL SECURITY AGENCY SURVEILLANCE

22. The Committee is concerned about the surveillance of communications in the interest of protecting national security, conducted by the National Security Agency (NSA) both within and outside the United States, through the bulk phone metadata surveillance programme (Section 215 of the USA PATRIOT Act) and, in particular, surveillance under Section 702 of the Foreign Intelligence Surveillance

Act (FISA) Amendment Act, conducted through PRISM (collection of communications content from United States-based Internet companies) and UPSTREAM (collection of communications metadata and content by tapping fiber-optic cables carrying Internet traffic) and the adverse impact on individuals' right to privacy. The Committee is concerned that, until recently, judicial interpretations of FISA and rulings of the Foreign Intelligence Surveillance Court (FISC) had largely been kept secret, thus not allowing affected persons to know the law with sufficient precision. The Committee is concerned that the current oversight system of the activities of the NSA fails to effectively protect the rights of the persons affected. While welcoming the recent Presidential Policy Directive/PPD-28, which now extends some safeguards to non-United States citizens "to the maximum extent feasible consistent with the national security," the Committee remains concerned that such persons enjoy only limited protection against excessive surveillance. Finally, the Committee is concerned that the persons affected have no access to effective remedies in case of abuse (arts. 2, 5 (1) and 17). . . .

[Additional matters addressed by the Committee were racial profiling, the death penalty, gun violence, legislation prohibiting torture, non-refoulement, human trafficking and forced labor, detention of immigrants, domestic violence, corporal punishment, non-consensual psychiatric treatment, criminalization of homelessness, conditions of detention and solitary confinement, juvenile justice, voting rights, and the rights of indigenous peoples.]

---

For the United States' subsequent reporting cycle, the Human Rights Committee compiled its list of issues, based largely on its concluding observations in the fourth cycle, and submitted the list to the United States. See Hum Rts. Cmte., *List of issues prior to submission of the fifth periodic report of the United States of America*, UN Doc. CCPR/C/USA/QPR/5 (2019). Under the simplified reporting procedure, the United States' response to the list of issues constituted its fifth periodic report. The extract below of the United States' 30-page fifth periodic report plus annexes gives but a sample of the issues raised by the Committee and the United States responses.

## Fifth periodic report submitted by the United States of America under article 40 of the Covenant under the optional reporting procedure, due in 2020

UN Doc. CCPR/C/USA/5 (2020) (footnotes omitted)

1. The United States of America ("United States") is pleased to present to the United Nations Human Rights Committee ("Committee") its Fifth Periodic Report concerning the implementation of its obligations under the International Covenant on Civil and Political Rights ("Covenant," "Convention" or "ICCPR") in accordance with Article 40 of the Convention. The substance and organization of this report is based on the April 2, 2019, List of Issues received from the Committee.

2. This report was prepared by the United States Department of State (DOS), with assistance from the Department of Justice (DOJ), the Department of Defense

(DoD), the Department of Homeland Security (DHS), the Department of Health and Human Services (HHS), the Department of Education (ED), the U.S. Agency for International Development (USAID) and other relevant components of the U.S. government. Representatives of U.S. government departments and agencies involved in implementation of the Convention also met with representatives of non-government organizations as part of outreach efforts in connection with drafting the report. Except where otherwise noted, the report covers the time period from 2015 to 2020. . . .

4. The United States observes that some of the questions posed by the Committee appear to request information regarding the U.S. legal framework with respect to the private actions of non-state actors. For example, Questions 14 and 18 concerning victims of gun violence, including in the context of domestic violence, and human trafficking appear to primarily relate to the conduct of persons or groups acting in a private rather than an official capacity. Similarly, questions on actions the U.S. Government has taken to combat interference with privacy by entities including Facebook (Paragraph 22) appear largely to concern the conduct of non-state actors. The United States reiterates its longstanding view that Article 2 of the Covenant contains no language stating that its obligations extend to private, non-governmental acts, and no such obligations can be inferred from Article 2. Moreover, neither the text nor the negotiating history of the Covenant support any obligation on the part of States Parties to take "reasonable positive measures" and to exercise "due diligence" to respond to foreseeable threats by private persons and entities. . . .

## USE OF LETHAL FORCE IN MILITARY CONTEXTS
### (ARTS. 2, 6, 7, 9, 10 AND 14)

### REPLY TO PARAGRAPH 6 OF THE LIST OF ISSUES — USE OF FORCE AND SAFEGUARDS AGAINST CIVILIAN HARM

16. The United States respectfully recalls that Article 2(1) of the ICCPR does not create obligations for a State Party with respect to individuals outside its territory and that international humanitarian law is the *lex specialis* with respect to armed conflict and, as such, is the controlling body of law in armed conflict with regard to the conduct of hostilities and the protection of war victims. However, in the spirit of cooperation, the United States has provided factual information related to this matter in Annex B.

## NON-DISCRIMINATION AND EQUAL RIGHTS OF MEN AND WOMEN
### (ARTS. 2, 3 AND 26)

### REPLY TO PARAGRAPH 7 OF THE LIST OF ISSUES — JUSTICE SYSTEM

17. The United States takes seriously addressing racial discrimination, including in our criminal justice system, and seeks to ensure that the justice system operates fairly and effectively for all. In 2010, the Fair Sentencing Act (Pub. L. No. 111–220) reduced the sentencing disparity between offenses involving powder cocaine and crack cocaine. It did not, however, apply retroactively, and thus did not ameliorate certain racial and ethnic disparities that had arisen among those

sentenced before 2010 for cocaine offenses carrying a mandatory minimum sentence. In December 2018, Congress passed, and the President signed into law, the First Step Act (Pub. L. 115–391), which authorized retroactive application of the Fair Sentencing Act of 2010. It also shortened mandatory minimum sentences for some non-violent drug offenses and firearm offenses and expanded the "drug safety valve" provision, thereby increasing opportunities for judges to deviate from mandatory minimums when sentencing for non-violent drug offenses. President Trump noted in his 2019 State of the Union Address: "*This legislation reformed sentencing laws that have wrongly and disproportionately harmed the African-American community. The First Step Act gives non-violent offenders the chance to reenter society as productive, law-abiding citizens. Now states across the country are following our lead.*"

18. The First Step Act also addresses issues affecting incarcerated offenders by requiring federal prisons to offer programs shown to reduce recidivism, prohibiting the shackling of pregnant women except in specifically delineated situations, expanding the availability of feminine healthcare products, increasing the effective cap on credit prisoners may receive for good behavior from 47 to 54 days per year, allowing inmates to earn time credits by participating in more vocational and rehabilitative programs, and calling for the placement of low-risk prisoners in home confinement to the extent permitted and the placement of prisoners in facilities closer to their families. . . .

### MATERNAL MORTALITY, TERMINATION OF PREGNANCY, AND REPRODUCTIVE RIGHTS (ARTS. 2, 3, 6, 7 AND 26)

### REPLY TO PARAGRAPH 12 OF THE LIST OF ISSUES—MATERNAL HEALTH ISSUES

32. The United States expresses its view that Paragraph 12, relating to "*mortality, termination of pregnancy and reproductive rights,*" contains a number of questions concerning issues outside the scope of the Covenant. The United States defends human dignity and life and supports access to high-quality health care for all women and girls across their lifespans. However, the United States rejects any interpretation of international human rights to require any State Party to provide access to abortion. In particular, the United States strongly opposes any interpretation of the Article 6 inherent right to life that purports to require State Parties to provide access to abortion. There is no international right to abortion, nor is there any duty on the part of States to finance or facilitate abortion.

33. Moreover, the United States reiterates its considered view that the Committee's views regarding the meaning of the ICCPR in its Draft General Comment No. 36 is unsupported "*with any treaty analysis grounded in VCLT Articles 31 and 32.*" In particular, the United States reiterates that "*State Parties to the ICCPR have not given authority to the Human Rights Committee or to any other entity to fashion or otherwise determine their treaty obligations,*" and the Committee has improperly attempted "*to fill what it may consider to be gaps in the reach and coverage of*" the ICCPR by interpreting Article 6 "*in ways that were proposed and debated by various negotiating delegations, but were excluded from the final text when agreement could not be reached,*" and by improperly "*importing requirements from other human rights treaties.*" In short, it remains the United States' view that "any issues concerning access to abortion . . . are outside the scope of Article 6" of the ICCPR. . . .

REPLY TO PARAGRAPH 14 OF THE LIST OF ISSUES — GUN VIOLENCE AND USE OF FORCE

46. With regard to the concluding observations concerning gun violence, according to the Centers for Disease Control and Prevention, there were 36,252 firearm-related deaths in the United States in 2015, 38,658 in 2016, 39,773 in 2017, and 39,740 in 2018. The United States provides the following information regarding its efforts to address gun violence. The U.S. government is concerned about, and responds aggressively to, gun violence. At the same time, the United States must pursue solutions to gun violence that do not infringe upon the Second Amendment guarantee that citizens may keep and bear arms, and we interpret nothing in the ICCPR to infringe upon that right. In December 2018, DOJ amended a regulation clarifying that bump stocks, which effectively turn semiautomatic firearms into automatic weapons, fall within the definition of "machine gun" under federal law, restricting possession of such devices, https://www.justice.gov/opa/pr/department-justice-announces-bump-stock-type-devices-final-rule. . . .

49. With regard to excessive use of force by law enforcement officials against civilians, particularly racial minorities, on June 16, 2020, President Trump signed an executive order on "Safe Policing for Safe Communities" to develop and incentivize critical policing reforms. . . .

50. With respect to the killing of George Floyd in Minnesota, the United States notes that this matter is being pursued by both the state and the federal government. The government in the state of Minnesota has filed second-degree murder and second-degree manslaughter charges against one officer, and aiding and abetting charges against three other officers. As it typically does in cases such as this, DOJ is conducting an independent investigation into whether the death of Mr. Floyd involved violations of federal civil rights laws.

51. Officers are held accountable for use of excessive force through a number of mechanisms. The first is administrative action by the applicable law enforcement agency. For example, officers may be fired, placed on leave, or otherwise punished for use of excessive force, whether or not criminal charges are filed. Officers may also face criminal charges under state law such as assault with bodily injury, abuse of official capacity, or official misconduct. Applicable laws vary from state to state. . . .

REPLY TO PARAGRAPH 17 OF THE LIST OF ISSUES — GUANTANAMO BAY

64. Recalling its views regarding Article 2(1) of the ICCPR and international humanitarian law, the United States nonetheless provides the following information in the spirit of cooperation. E.O. 13823 of January 30, 2018, Protecting America through Lawful Detention of Terrorists, revoked section 3 of E.O. 13492, which ordered the closure of the detention facilities at U.S. Naval Station Guantanamo Bay. The United States has no plans to close the detention facilities at Guantanamo Bay. Detention operations at Guantanamo are conducted consistent with all applicable U.S. and international law.

65. There are currently 40 individuals detained in U.S. detention facilities at Guantanamo Bay. Of these detainees, seven are being prosecuted in the military commissions established at Guantanamo Bay; one is awaiting sentencing by a military commission; one is serving a life sentence following conviction by a military commission; 25 are designated for continued law-of-war detention and

subject to periodic review under the procedures established in E.O. 13567 of March 7, 2011, and reaffirmed in E.O. 13823 of January 30, 2018; and six are deemed eligible for transfer. No new detainees have been transferred to Guantanamo during the reporting period.

## Comments and Questions

1. How useful is the reporting procedure? Are the concluding observations about the United States reasonable? How seriously is the United States taking the issues raised in the concluding observations and related list of issues submitted by the committee for the fifth reporting cycle? What benefit, if any, is the reporting procedure to the United States government or those who experience human rights problems in the United States? Might the usefulness or impact of the reporting procedure vary from country to country? For example, how might the significance of the reporting procedure for a developing country be different than it is for the United States?

2. In its introduction to its fifth periodic report, the United States complained that the "Committee's very lengthy LOI [list of issues], with 29 detailed questions and several sub-questions, belies its stated commitment to simplified reporting." Is the United States right? Or is the Committee correct to provide detail and context to the issues it raises? What does the "simplified" in "simplified reporting procedure" refer to?

3. In paragraph 4 of its fifth periodic report, the United States objected to questions regarding the US legal framework with regard to the actions of private or non-state actors. Do you agree that Article 2 of the Covenant on Civil and Political Rights, which establishes the obligation of states to "respect and ensure" the rights affirmed therein, "contains no language stating that its obligations extend to private, non-governmental acts, and no such obligations can be inferred from Article 2"? Recall the discussion of state obligations under the Covenant and international human rights law more generally in Chapter 4. Are there any consequences for the United States in persisting in disagreeing with the Committee, and the weight of international authority, on this issue? Note that the United States nonetheless went on to address, in an annex to its report, the privacy concerns raised by the Committee related the behavior of non-state actors. In what ways, if any, do these parts of the US report influence the rules of international human rights law on state responsibility with regard to private conduct?

4. Maternal health and abortion were not addressed in the Committee's concluding observations on the United States' fourth periodic report, yet the Committee included those matters in its list of issues in the fifth reporting cycle, illustrating how a treaty body might introduce new issues into the reporting procedure. The United States, however, emphasized in paragraph 33 of its report that it "rejects any interpretation of international human rights to require any State Party to provide access to abortion." In this connection, the US referred to and expressed disagreement with the Committee's General Comment No. 36 on the right to life. General Comment No. 36 states in relevant part:

> Although States parties may adopt measures designed to regulate voluntary terminations of pregnancy, such measures must not result in violation of the right to life of a pregnant woman or girl, or her other rights

under the Covenant. Thus, restrictions on the ability of women or girls to seek abortion must not, inter alia, jeopardize their lives, subject them to physical or mental pain or suffering which violates article 7, discriminate against them or arbitrarily interfere with their privacy. States parties must provide safe, legal and effective access to abortion where the life and health of the pregnant woman or girl is at risk, or where carrying a pregnancy to term would cause the pregnant woman or girl substantial pain or suffering, most notably where the pregnancy is the result of rape or incest or is not viable. In addition, States parties may not regulate pregnancy or abortion in all other cases in a manner that runs contrary to their duty to ensure that women and girls do not have to undertake unsafe abortions, and they should revise their abortion laws accordingly.

Human Rights Committee, *General comment No. 36 on article 6 of the International Covenant on Civil and Political Rights, on the right to life,* UN Doc. CCPR/C/GC/36 (2018), para. 8 (footnote omitted). In its report, the U.S asserted that the Committee's view is unsupported by any treaty analysis grounded in the Vienna Convention on the Law of Treaties and that the Committee has "improperly attempted to 'fill what it may consider to be gaps in the reach of coverage of' the ICCPR." Do you agree? Recall the discussion on treaty interpretation in Chapter 2.

   5. For additional analyses of state reporting, see *International Human Rights Monitoring Mechanisms* (Gudmundur Alfredsson et al. eds., 2d ed. 2009); Walter Kalin, "Examination of State Reports," in *UN Human Rights Treaty Bodies: Law and Legitimacy* (Helen Keller and Geir Ulfstein eds., 2012); Manfred Nowak, *U.N. Covenant on Civil and Political Rights: CCPR Commentary* 712-53 (2d ed. 2005); Michael O'Flaherty, *The Concluding Observations of United Nations Human Rights Treaty Bodies,* 6 Hum. Rts. L. Rev. 27 (2006); Cosette D. Creamer and Beth A. Simmons, *The Proof is in the Process: Self-Reporting Under International Human Rights Treaties,* 114 Am. J. Int'l L. 1 (2020).

## B.   Individual Complaints

   The right of individual petition has long been considered the key to effective implementation of international human rights law. Occasionally the procedure is made mandatory, as under the American and European human rights conventions, but more frequently it is optional. All nine of the core UN human rights treaties have optional procedures that permit individuals, or in some cases groups, to file complaints of alleged violations. Each such petition procedure is authorized in the text of the treaty itself or in a separate protocol. The United States has ratified the International Covenant on Civil and Political Rights; the International Convention on the Elimination of Racial Discrimination; the Convention against Torture; the Optional Protocol to the Convention on the Rights of the Child on the involvement of children in armed conflict; and the Optional Protocol to Rights of the Child on the sale of children, child prostitution, and child pornography. However, the US has not agreed to any of the petition procedures associated with the UN treaty bodies. Nonetheless, many states have, and the vast majority of the parties to the ICCPR have agreed to the often-used petition procedure associated with that treaty, which is set forth in a separate text called the Optional Protocol to the International Covenant on Civil and Political Rights.

The rules of admissibility of petitions established by the Optional Protocol to the ICCPR are in significant ways typical of the rules of admissibility associated with the various other individual petition procedures. The Optional Protocol provides:

### Article 1

A State Party to the Covenant that becomes a Party to the present Protocol recognizes the competence of the Committee to receive and consider communications from individuals subject to its jurisdiction who claim to be victims of a violation by that State Party of any of the rights set forth in the Covenant. No communication shall be received by the Committee if it concerns a State Party to the Covenant which is not a Party to the present Protocol.

### Article 2

Subject to the provisions of article 1, individuals who claim that any of their rights enumerated in the Covenant have been violated and who have exhausted all available domestic remedies may submit a written communication to the Committee for consideration.

### Article 3

The Committee shall consider inadmissible any communciation under the present Protocol which is anonymous, or which it considers to be an abuse of the right of submission of such communications or to be incompatible with the provisions of the Covenant.

### Article 4

1. Subject to the provisions of article 3, the Committee shall bring any communications submitted to it under the present Protocol to the attention of the State Party to the present Protocol alleged to be violating any provision of the Covenant.
2. Within six months, the receiving State shall submit to the Committee written explanations or statements clarifying the matter and the remedy, if any, that may have been taken by that State.

### Article 5

1. The Committee shall consider communications received under the present Protocol in the light of all written information made available to it by the individual and by the State Party concerned.
2. The Committee shall not consider any communication from an individual unless it has ascertained that:
   a. The same matter is not being examined under another procedure of international investigation or settlement;
   b. The individual has exhausted all available domestic remedies. This shall not be the rule where the application of the remedies is unreasonably prolonged.

3. The Committee shall hold closed meetings when examining communications under the present Protocol.

4. The Committee shall forward its views to the State Party concerned and to the individual.

The following case is indicative of how the Human Rights Committee interprets the rules of admissibility, as well as its own powers and functions, with regard to petitions under the Optional Protocol.

## Alekseev v. Russian Federation

Human Rights Committee, Communication No. 1873/2009, Views adopted October 25, 2013, UN Doc. CCPR/C/109/D/1873/2009 (2013)

1. The author of the communication is Nikolai Alekseev, a Russian national born in 1977. He claims to be a victim of violation by the Russian Federation of his rights under article 21 of the International Covenant on Civil and Political Rights. The author is not represented by counsel.

### The Facts as Submitted by the Author

2.1 The author is a homosexual and a human rights activist. From 2006 to 2008, the author, together with other activists, tried to organize a number of peaceful assemblies (gay pride marches) in Moscow, which were all banned by the municipal authorities.

2.2 On 11 July 2008, the author, together with two other activists, submitted a request to the Prefect of the Central Administrative District of Moscow to hold a stationary meeting—a picket—in front of the Iranian Embassy in Moscow. The purpose of the gathering was to express concern over the execution of homosexuals and minors in the Islamic Republic of Iran and to call for a ban on such executions. The author informed the authorities of the purpose, date, time and place of the event, which was scheduled to take place from 1 p.m. to 2 p.m. on 19 July 2008 in front of the Iranian Embassy, and which would involve no more than 30 participants.

2.3 On the same date, the Deputy Prefect of the Central Administrative District of Moscow refused to authorize the event, considering that the aim of the picket would trigger "a negative reaction in society" and could lead to "group violations of public order which can be dangerous to its participants."

2.4 On 16 July 2008, the author filed a complaint against this refusal with the Tagansky District Court of Moscow. He argued that Russian law does not permit a blanket ban on conducting a peaceful assembly, as long as the purpose of the assembly is in conformity with constitutional values. He added that if the Prefecture had any serious grounds to believe that the proposed picket would trigger mass riots, they should have arranged sufficient police protection for participants of the assembly in order to secure the exercise of their constitutional right to peaceful assembly.

2.5 On 18 September 2008, the Tagansky District Court rejected the complaint and endorsed the municipal authority's argument that it was impossible to ensure security of the participants of the event and avoid riots, as the proposed event would provoke strong public reaction. In the court's opinion, the decision of 11 July 2008 was in conformity with both national law and the provisions of the European Convention on Human Right and Fundamental Freedoms. On 5 October 2008, the author appealed the judgement before the Moscow City Court on cassation proceedings, but his appeal was rejected on 18 December 2008.

THE COMPLAINT

3. The author claims that the State party violated his right to peaceful assembly as protected by article 21 of the Covenant, as it imposed a blanket prohibition on the meeting that he had intended to organize. The authorities' refusal was not imposed "in conformity with the law" nor was it "necessary in a democratic society", In particular, national law clearly requires that the authorities take the necessary measures to ensure the security of the participants in an assembly and to secure its peaceful conduct. Moreover, the restriction imposed was not "necessary in a democratic society" and did not pursue any of the legitimate aims mentioned in article 21 of the Covenant. The authorities' refusal to propose an alternative location for the mass event in question and their assertion that they could not provide sufficient police force to protect the participants, demonstrate that the authorities' real aim was to prevent the gay and lesbian minority in Russia from becoming visible to the public and from attracting public attention to their concerns. Finally, the fact that a minority group's ideas might "offend, shock or disturb" the majority and might provoke violent opposition cannot justify a blanket ban on the expression of views of such groups by means of peaceful assembly. On the contrary, the State party must protect peaceful assemblies of minority groups against violent acts.

STATE PARTY'S OBSERVATIONS ON ADMISSIBILITY AND MERITS

4.1 On 29 June 2009, the State party submitted its observations on admissibility and merits. It recalls the facts of the case, and the proceedings engaged by the author. It further notes that the author's claims under article 21 of the Covenant are unfounded as the author was refused permission to hold the picket in order to ensure public order. In this connection, the State party notes that article 21 of the Covenant recognizes the right to peaceful assembly, but also provides for restriction to that right in conformity with the law in the interests of national security or public safety, public order, the protection of public health or morals or the protection of rights and freedoms of others. Articles 31 and 55 of the Constitution of the Russian Federation guarantee the right to peaceful assembly with similar restrictions to those set out in article 21 of the Covenant, and which are developed in the Federal Law on Rallies, Meetings, Demonstrations, Marches and Picketing (Federal Law on Mass Events). According to article 8, paragraph 1, of the Federal Law on Mass Events, public mass events may be held at any place suitable for the purposes of the event provided that such event does not endanger the security of persons participating in the event in question. The State party further notes that on 18 September 2008, the Tagansky District Court of Moscow concluded that in light of the negative public reaction towards such pickets, the authorities would not have been able to fully ensure the security of persons participating in such a mass event. The State party maintains that the authorities' refusal of 11 July 2008 was in line with the international norms and domestic legislation.

4.2 The State party adds that the author has not exhausted all domestic remedies as required by article 5, paragraph 2 (b), of the Optional Protocol to the Covenant, as according to articles 367, 376, 377 and chapter 41 of the Civil Procedure Code, the author could have sought a supervisory review of the decisions of the national courts from the Presidium of the Moscow City Court and thereafter, the Supreme Court.

### AUTHOR'S COMMENTS ON THE STATE PARTY'S OBSERVATIONS

5.1 On 9 November 2009, the author notes that the State party has erroneously referred to article 8 of the Federal Law on Mass Events. According to him, this provision guarantees the right to hold a public event at any place suitable for its purposes. However, the restrictions on holding public events are linked to the security considerations at a particular place due to its characteristics, such as risk of collapse of a building, for example. Nothing in the wording of this article suggests that its aim is to provide for general restrictions on the right of peaceful assembly due to security considerations, as invoked by the State party. Furthermore, the article referred to should, in any event, be interpreted in the context of "ensuring realization of the constitutionally mandated right of the citizens of the Russian Federation to peaceful assembly [. . .], to hold rallies, meetings, demonstrations, marches and picketing" as stated in the preamble of the Federal Law on Mass Events. . . .

5.3 As to the State party's comment regarding the exhaustion of domestic remedies, the author points out that the supervisory review proceedings do not constitute an effective remedy, as they do not ensure re-examination of the merits of the case under appeal by a panel of judges (the Presidium of the Moscow City Court or the Supreme Court). According to article 381 of the Civil Procedure Code, such an appeal is considered by a judge of the supervisory review court, who can reject it even without examining the case file materials. It is only if the judge finds the presented arguments convincing that he or she may request the case file and, at his or her discretion, remit the case to the panel of judges of the supervisory review court for consideration. In this regard, the author refers to a similar case in 2007, where the complainant had appealed the refusal to hold a rally for the purpose of calling for tolerance towards sexual minorities under a supervisory review, but a judge of the Supreme Court had concluded that the refusal was lawful as it was not possible to ensure the participants' safety, and decided not to grant a supervisory review of the case. As his case concerned similar circumstances, the author submits that appealing through the supervisory review process would have been futile and ineffective. . . .

### STATE PARTY'S FURTHER OBSERVATIONS

6.1 On 29 September 2010, the State party reiterates the facts of the case and the actions which the author undertook at the domestic level. It further reiterates that the author's claim under article 21 of the Covenant is unfounded and that similar restrictions on the enjoyment of the right to peaceful assembly, as set out in that article, are also provided for in article 55 of the Constitution and in article 8 of the Federal Law on Mass Events. It recalls that article 8 of the Federal Law on Mass Events stipulates that a public event may be held at any place suitable for the purpose of the event provided that the holding of the event does not endanger the security of the participants. In this connection, the State party maintains that the decision of the Deputy Prefect of the Central Administrative District of Moscow was based on the consideration of the above-mentioned security aspect.

6.2 It also reiterates that the author has failed to exhaust available domestic remedies within the supervisory review proceedings, therefore the present communication is inadmissible under article 5, paragraph 2 (b), of the Optional Protocol to the Covenant.

6.3 The State party adds that the author has abused the right to submit a communication, as the same matter is being examined by another procedure of international investigation or settlement. In particular, it draws attention to the fact that on 29 January 2007, 14 February 2008 and 10 March 2009, the author submitted applications to the European Court of Human Rights regarding the authorities' refusal to allow him to hold a mass event (gay pride march) and picket concerning the rights of sexual minorities. In this connection, it submits that the complaints before the European Court and the present communication are similar in nature as they have been submitted by the same person concerning the rights of the same group of persons (belonging to sexual minorities) and the actions of the same municipal authority.

### AUTHOR'S FURTHER COMMENTS

7.1 On 1 November 2010, the author informed the Committee that on 21 October 2010 the European Court of Human Rights had adopted a judgement in his case, concerning the authorities' refusal to allow him hold events similar to the ones mentioned in the present communication in 2006, 2007 and 2008. In that particular case, the European Court found a violation of the author's rights under article 11 of the European Convention on Human Rights (right to peaceful assembly).

7.2 On 30 November 2010, the author reiterated that the supervisory review proceedings could not be considered as an effective remedy for the purposes of admissibility. As to the State party's argument that the present communication should be viewed as an abuse of the right to complain because a similar matter was being examined by another international procedure, the author submits that the present complaint is based on and concerns different facts. The applications before the European Court of Human Rights concerned prohibitions to hold pride marches or pickets proposed by the author as alternatives to a pride march, while the present complaint concerns the prohibition to hold a picket protesting the execution of homosexuals and minors in the Islamic Republic of Iran. Therefore, the author considers that the present communication should be declared admissible under article 5 of the Optional Protocol to the Covenant.

### ISSUES AND PROCEEDINGS BEFORE THE COMMITTEE

#### CONSIDERATION OF ADMISSIBILITY

8.1 Before considering any claim contained in a communication, the Human Rights Committee must, in accordance with rule 93 of its rules of procedure, decide whether or not the case is admissible under the Optional Protocol to the Covenant.

8.2 As required under article 5, paragraph 2 (a), of the Optional Protocol, the Committee shall ascertain whether the same matter is being examined under another procedure of international investigation or settlement. In this regard, the Committee notes the State party's argument that on 29 January 2007, 14 February 2008 and 10 March 2009, the author submitted applications to the European Court of Human Rights regarding the State authorities' refusal to allow the author to hold mass events and a picket concerning the rights of sexual minorities and that they were registered by the European Court. The State party submits that the complaints before the European Court and the present communication are of a similar nature as they have been submitted by the same person, concern the rights of the same group of persons (belonging to sexual minorities) and concern the actions of the same authorities. The Committee further notes the author's explanation that the applications before the European Court of Human Rights concerned different factual circumstances, namely the prohibition to hold pride marches or pickets proposed by the author as an alternative to a pride march, in the years 2006 to 2008, while the present complaint concerns the prohibition to hold a picket protesting the execution of homosexuals and minors in the Islamic Republic of Iran.

8.3 The Committee recalls that the concept of "the same matter" within the meaning of article 5, paragraph (a), of the Optional Protocol is understood as including the same authors, the same facts and the same substantive rights. The Committee notes that it is clear from the available information on the case file that the author's applications to the European Court of Human Rights concern the same person and relate to the same substantive rights as those invoked in the present communication. However, the Committee observes that the respective applications before the European Court do not relate to the same facts, that is, the particular event referred to in the present communication. Consequently, the Committee considers that it is not precluded by article 5, paragraph 2 (a), of the Optional Protocol from examining the present communication for purposes of admissibility.

8.4 With regard to the requirement laid down in article 5, paragraph 2 (b), of the Optional Protocol, the Committee takes note of the State party's argument that the author failed to exhaust available domestic remedies within the supervisory review proceedings, therefore the communication is inadmissible. In this respect, the Committee notes that the author appealed to the Moscow City Court, which upheld the lower court's decision. The Committee refers to its case law, according to which supervisory review proceedings against court decisions which have entered into force constitute an extraordinary remedy, dependent on the discretionary power of a judge or prosecutor, and which do not need to be exhausted for purposes of admissibility. In the absence of any other pertinent information on file, the Committee considers that it is not precluded by article 5, paragraph 2 (b), of the Optional Protocol, from examining the present communication.

8.5 The Committee considers that the author has sufficiently substantiated, for purposes of admissibility, his claim under article 21 of the Covenant. It declares the communication admissible and proceeds to its examination on the merits.

CONSIDERATION OF THE MERITS

9.1 The Human Rights Committee has considered the present communication in the light of all the information received, in accordance with article 5, paragraph 1, of the Optional Protocol.

9.2. The first issue before the Committee is whether the State party's author- ities' restriction of the author's right to peaceful assembly was permissible under any of the criteria contained in article 21 of the Covenant.

9.3 The Committee recalls that the right of peaceful assembly, as guaranteed under article 21 of the Covenant, is essential for the public expression of a person's views and opinions, and indispensable in a democratic society. It also recalls that States parties must put in place effective measures to protect against attacks aimed at silencing those exercising their right to freedom of expression by means of an assembly. A restriction of the right of peaceful assembly is permissible only if it is (a) in conformity with the law, and (b) necessary in a democratic society in the interests of national security or public safety, public order, the protection of public health or morals or the protection of the rights and freedoms of others.

9.4 In the present case, the Committee observes that both the State party and the author agree that the denial of permission to hold a picket from 1 p.m. to 2 p.m. on 19 July 2008 in front of the Iranian Embassy in Moscow was an interfer- ence with the author's right of assembly, but the parties disagree as to whether it was a permissible restriction.

9.5 The Committee also notes that the State party defends the denial of per- mission to hold the picket concerned as necessary in the interest of public safety. Although the author contends that the safety rationale was a pretext for denying the permit, the Committee finds it unnecessary to evaluate this factual allegation, because the author's claim under article 21 can be decided on the assumption that the challenged restriction was motivated by concern for public safety.

9.6 The Committee notes that permission for the author's proposed picket was denied on the sole ground that the subject it addressed, namely, advocacy of respect for the human rights of persons belonging to sexual minorities, would pro- voke a negative reaction that could lead to violations of public order. The denial had nothing to do with the chosen location, date, time, duration or manner of the proposed public assembly. Thus the decision of the Deputy Prefect of the Central Administrative District of Moscow of 11 July 2008 amounted to a rejection of the author's right to organize a public assembly addressing the chosen subject, which is one of the most serious interferences with the freedom of peaceful assembly. The Committee notes that freedom of assembly protects demonstrations promot- ing ideas that may be regarded as annoying or offensive by others and that, in such cases, States parties have a duty to protect the participants in such a demonstra- tion in the exercise of their rights against violence by others. It also notes that an unspecified and general risk of a violent counterdemonstration or the mere possi- bility that the authorities would be unable to prevent or neutralize such violence is not sufficient to ban a demonstration. The State party has not provided the Com- mittee with any information in the present case to support the claim that a "neg- ative reaction" to the author's proposed picket by members of the public would involve violence or that the police would be unable to prevent such violence if they properly performed their duty. In such circumstances, the obligation of the State party was to protect the author in the exercise of his rights under the Covenant and not to contribute to suppressing those rights. The Committee therefore concludes that the restriction on the author's rights was not necessary in a democratic society in the interest of public safety, and violated article 21 of the Covenant.

9.7 In light of this conclusion, the Committee decides not to examine the author's additional claim that the denial of permission was not in conformity with the law on the grounds that the national law referred only to safety concerns such as the risk of collapse of a building, and that it obliged the authorities to designate an alternative location for the assembly when they rejected the original application.

10. The Human Rights Committee, acting under article 5, paragraph 4, of the Optional Protocol to the International Covenant on Civil and Political Rights, is of the view that the facts before it disclose a violation of the author's right under article 21 of the Covenant.

11. In accordance with article 2, paragraph 3 (a), of the Covenant, the State party is under an obligation to provide the author with an effective remedy, including adequate compensation and reimbursement of any legal costs paid by him. The State party is also under an obligation to take steps to prevent similar violations in the future.

12. Bearing in mind that, by becoming a party to the Optional Protocol, the State party has recognized the competence of the Committee to determine whether there has been a violation of the Covenant or not and that, pursuant to article 2 of the Covenant, the State party has undertaken to ensure to all individuals within its territory or subject to its jurisdiction the rights recognized in the Covenant and to provide an effective and enforceable remedy when a violation has been established, the Committee wishes to receive from the State party, within 180 days, information about the measures taken to give effect to the Committee's Views. The State party is also requested to publish the present Views and to have them widely disseminated in the official language of the State party.

## Comments and Questions

1. The above case raises issues of admissibility and merits. How does the case meet the requirements of admissibility stated in the Optional Protocol to the ICCPR? Why wasn't the case deemed inadmissible because of the collateral proceedings in the European Court of Human Rights or the complainant's failure to seek recourse through the domestic supervisory review proceedings?

2. What is the legal status of the decisions — or "views" in the wording of the Optional Protocol — of the Human Rights Committee adopted under the petition procedure? The provisions of the Optional Protocol most relevant to this question are Articles 1 and 5(4), reproduced *supra* pages 468-469. How does the Committee appear to understand the authoritativeness of its views in the above case? Can a state that agrees to the Optional Protocol in good faith ignore the views of a Committee in a case concerning it?

3. What happens after the Committee communicates its views to the state concerned? Overall, as the Human Rights Committee's Special Rapporteur for follow-up on views has noted, attempts to categorize replies by states are inherently imprecise and subjective. Many states indicate their willingness to implement the Committee's recommendations or to offer the complainant an appropriate remedy. Other replies either do not address the Committee's views at all or relate only to certain aspects of them, such as the issue of compensation. The remaining replies challenge the Committee's views on factual or legal grounds, promise

an investigation of the matter considered by the Committee, or indicate that the state will not, for one reason or another, give effect to the Committee's recommendations. For example, the response of the government to the Committee's views in *Alexander Smantser v. Belarus* (Communication no. 1178/2003, views of Oct. 23, 2008), was: "The State party contests the views and submits inter alia that the Courts acted with respect to the Belarus Constitution, and Criminal Procedural Code, as well as the Covenant. It denies that the author's rights under the Covenant were violated." What can the Committee do? In its follow-up report, given the state's refusal to implement the Committee's decision or to provide "any satisfactory response to any of the 16 findings of violations against it," the Committee decided to request a meeting between representatives of the state and the Rapporteur on follow-up. See UN Doc. CCPR/C/98/3 (2010), at 2-3. What then?

4. Under Rule 94 of the Human Rights Committee's Rules of Procedure, after the registration of a complaint, or communication, and before a determination on the merits, the Committee can request that the state party concerned adopt "interim measures" to avoid actions that could have irreparable consequences for the rights invoked by the complaining party. In practice, the interim measures are often ineffective. For example, in *Strakhov v. Uzbekistan* and *Fayzulaev v. Uzbekistan*, Communications Nos. 1017/2001 and 1066/2002, Human Rights Committee, views of July 20, 2007, UN Doc. A/64/40 (Vol. II) (2007), at 1-10, the Committee, acting through its Special Rapporteur on new communications and interim measures, requested the State party not to carry out the alleged victims' executions while their cases were under examination. The State party did not respond to the Committee's request and executed the alleged victims before the Committee concluded consideration and examination of the case. Given that the interim measures are not provided for in the Optional Protocol but rather in the Rules of Procedure adopted by the Committee itself, why should states pay attention to a request from the Committee for interim measures? And why do they sometimes? For example, Finland adhered to the Committee's request for interim measures in *Kalevi Paadar v. Finland*, Communication No. 2102/2011, Human Rights Committee, views on March 28 2014, UN Doc. CCPR/C/110/D/2102/2011 (2014) (interim measures to refrain from slaughtering reindeer pending review of case concerning Sami reindeer herding rights).

5. It still takes on average three years for complaints under the ICCPR Optional Protocol to be reviewed. Does this diminish the effectiveness of the procedure? Is such a delay less than, more than, or comparable to the time that it takes the highest domestic court of appeal in your country to hear cases at the national level?

6. As noted earlier, all of the core UN human rights treaties now have optional provisions granting a right of individual petition. Most follow a fairly common pattern. See generally Siân Lewis-Anthony and Martin Scheinin, "Treaty-Based Procedures for Making Human Rights Complaints Within the UN System," in *Guide to International Human Rights Practice* (Hurst Hannum ed., 4th ed. 2004); Andrew Byrnes, "An Effective Complaints Procedure in the Context of International Human Rights Law," in *The UN Human Rights Treaty System in the 21st Century*

139 (Anne Bayefsky ed., 2021); P.R. Ghandhi, *The Human Rights Committee and the Right of Individual Communication: Law and Practice* (2018); Michael O'Flaherty, *Human Rights and the UN: Practice Before the Treaty Bodies* (2002); Nowak, *supra* page 467, at 819-909. The website of the UN High Commissioner for Human Rights also includes specific instructions for filing complaints with the UN treaty bodies. See OHCHR, *Human Rights Treaty Bodies — Individual Communications*, http://www.ohchr.org/EN/HRBodies/TBPetitions/Pages/IndividualCommunications.aspx#proceduregenerale.

## C.  Early Warning and Urgent Action Procedures

Somewhat akin to the complaint procedures under the treaties or related protocols are the early warning or urgent actions procedures attached to some of the treaty bodies. Article 30 of the Convention for the Protection of All Persons from Enforced Disappearances authorizes the Committee on Enforced Disappearances (CED) to receive and act on requests for urgent action to seek and find disappeared persons. Upon receipt of relevant information from a concerned individual, the Committee may "request the State Party concerned to provide it with information of the persons sought, within a time limit set by the Committee." Albeit without specific treaty authorization, the Committee on the Rights of Persons with Disabilities (CRPD) and the Committee on the Elimination of Racial Discrimination (CERD) have developed, as part of their working methods, urgent action procedures by which they receive and act on information of threatened or unfolding rights violations. Related to the urgent action procedures of these two committees are the early warning (CERD) and early awareness (CRPD) procedures that seek to prevent human rights problems from escalating.

CERD's early warning and urgent action procedures, in particular, are well developed and draw on practice spanning nearly three decades. A "working paper" published by the Committee in 1993 first detailed its ideas for "early warning measures" and "urgent procedures" and set in motion the Committee's practice around them. See CERD, *Prevention of racial discrimination, including early warning and urgent procedures: working paper adopted by the Committee on the Elimination of Racial Discrimination*, UN Doc. A/48/18, Annex III (1993). The rationale provided for these procedures in the 1993 paper is linked to Secretary-General Boutros Boutros-Ghali's "Agenda for Peace," which identified the need for preventative action, and to a meeting of the chairs of the treaty bodies concluding that "'it is . . . appropriate for each treaty body to undertake an urgent examination of all possible measures that it might take, within its competence, both to prevent human rights violations from occurring and to monitor more closely emergency situations of all kinds arising within the jurisdiction of States parties.'" Id., para. 6 (quoting UN Doc. A/47/728, para. 44).

In 2007, the Committee adopted formal Guidelines for a consolidated early warning and urgent action procedure. An extract of the Guidelines follows.

Committee on the Elimination of Racial Discrimination

## Guidelines for the Early Warning and Urgent Action Procedure

UN Doc. A/62/18, Annex III (2007), para. 2.

. . .

### C. Indicators for the Early Warning and Urgent Action Procedure

12. The Committee shall act under its early warning and urgent action procedure when it deems it necessary to address serious violations of the Convention in an urgent manner. The Committee shall be guided by the indicators set out below which replace the criteria in the 1993 working paper. As these indicators may be present in situations not requiring immediate attention to prevent and limit serious violations of the Convention, the Committee shall assess their significance in light of the gravity and scale of the situation, including the escalation of violence or irreparable harm that may be caused to victims of discrimination on the grounds of race, colour, descent or national or ethnic origin:

(a) Presence of a significant and persistent pattern of racial discrimination, as evidenced in social and economic indicators;

(b) Presence of a pattern of escalating racial hatred and violence, or racist propaganda or appeals to racial intolerance by persons, groups or organizations, notably by elected or other State officials;

(c) Adoption of new discriminatory legislation;

(d) Segregation policies or de facto exclusion of members of a group from political, economic, social and cultural life;

(e) Lack of an adequate legislative framework defining and criminalizing all forms of racial discrimination or lack of effective mechanisms, including lack of recourse procedures;

### D. Possible Measures to be Taken Under the Early Warning and Urgent Action Procedure

13. The Committee shall decide to consider a specific situation under its early warning and urgent action procedure on the basis of the information made available to it by, inter alia, United Nations agencies and human rights bodies, special procedures of the Human Rights Council, regional human rights mechanisms, and national human rights institutions and nongovernmental organizations, that reflects serious violations of the Convention according to the above indicators.

14. The measures to be taken by the Committee under the early warning and urgent action procedure may include:

(a) To request the State party concerned for the urgent submission of information on the situation considered under the early warning and urgent action procedure;

(b) To request the Secretariat to collect information from field presences of the Office of the High Commissioner of Human Rights and specialized agencies of the United Nations, national human rights institutions, and non-governmental organizations on the situation under consideration;

(c) Adoption of a decision including the expression of specific concerns, along with recommendations for action, addressed to:

(i) The State party concerned;

(ii) The Special Rapporteur on contemporary forms of racism, racial discrimination and xenophobia and related intolerance, the Special Rapporteur on the situation of human rights and fundamental freedoms of indigenous people, or the independent expert on minority issues;

(iii) Other relevant human rights bodies or special procedures of the Human Rights Council;

(iv) Regional intergovernmental organizations and human rights mechanisms;

(v) The Human Rights Council;

(vi) The Special Adviser of the Secretary-General on the prevention of genocide;

(vii) The Secretary-General through the High Commissioner for Human Rights, together with a recommendation that the matter be brought to the attention of the Security Council.

(d) To offer to send to the State party concerned one or more of the members of the Committee in order to facilitate the implementation of international standards or the technical assistance to establish a human rights institutional infrastructure;

(e) Recommendation to the State party concerned to avail itself of the advisory services and technical assistance of the Office of the High Commissioner for Human Rights

(f) Policies or practice of impunity regarding: (a) Violence targeting members of a group identified on the basis of race, colour, descent or national or ethnic origin by State officials or private actors; (b) Grave statements by political leaders/prominent people that condone or justify violence against a group identified on the ground of race, colour, descent, national or ethnic origin; (c) Development and organization of militia groups and/or extreme political groups based on a racist platform;

(g) Significant flows of refugees or displaced persons, especially when those concerned belong to specific ethnic groups;

(h) Encroachment on the traditional lands of indigenous peoples or forced removal of these peoples from their lands, in particular for the purpose of exploitation of natural resources;

(i) Polluting or hazardous activities that reflect a pattern of racial discrimination with substantial harm to specific groups.

---

Through its early warning and urgent action procedure, CERD has engaged states and others in numerous situations, raising issues addressed by the Guidelines and its indicators. By its terms, CERD's early warning and early action procedure is applicable to all states parties to the Convention on the Elimination of all forms of Racial Discrimination, and it stands apart from the optional complaint procedure under Article 14 of the Convention. Thus, the procedure is presumptively applicable to the United States, which as noted earlier is a party to this and other UN human rights treaties but has not subscribed to any of the formal complaint procedures attached to the treaties.

On several occasions, the United States has been engaged by CERD under its early warning and urgent action procedure, including through statements, letters, or decisions about, for example, the murder of George Floyd in Minnesota; the effects of a tar sands pipeline on Anishinaabe people; the events in Charlottesville in 2017 and the brutality wrought by white supremacists there; and the impacts of a ski resort expansion on an indigenous sacred place. In its first engagement with the United States under the early warning and urgent action procedure, CERD issued the following decision.

## Committee on the Elimination of Racial Discrimination

## Decision 1 (68) — United States of America, Early Warning and Urgent Action Procedure

UN Doc. CERD/C/USA/DEC/1 (2006)

. . .

4. The Committee has received credible information alleging that the Western Shoshone indigenous peoples are being denied their traditional rights to land, and that measures taken and even accelerated lately by the State party in relation to the status, use and occupation of these lands may cumulatively lead to irreparable harm to these communities. In light of such information, and in the absence of any response from the State party, the Committee decided at its 68th session to adopt the present decision under its early warning and urgent action procedure. This procedure is clearly distinct from the communication procedure under article 14 of the Convention. Furthermore, the nature and urgency of the issue examined in this decision go well beyond the limits of the communication procedure.

### B. CONCERNS

5. The Committee expresses concern about the lack of action taken by the State party to follow up on its previous concluding observations, in relation to the situation of the Western Shoshone peoples (A/56/18, para. 400, adopted on 13 August 2001). Although these are indeed long-standing issues, as stressed by the State party in its letter, they warrant immediate and effective action from the State party. The Committee therefore considers that this issue should be dealt with as a matter of priority.

6. The Committee is concerned by the State party's position that Western Shoshone peoples' legal rights to ancestral lands have been extinguished through gradual encroachment, notwithstanding the fact that the Western Shoshone peoples have reportedly continued to use and occupy the lands and their natural

resources in accordance with their traditional land tenure patterns. The Committee further notes with concern that the State party's position is made on the basis of processes before the Indian Claims Commission, "which did not comply with contemporary international human rights norms, principles and standards that govern determination of indigenous property interests," as stressed by the Inter-American Commission on Human Rights in the case *Mary and Carrie Dann versus United States* (Case 11.140, 27 December 2002).

7. The Committee is of the view that past and new actions taken by the State party on Western Shoshone ancestral lands lead to a situation where, today, the obligations of the State party under the Convention are not respected, in particular the obligation to guarantee the right of everyone to equality before the law in the enjoyment of civil, political, economic, social and cultural rights, without discrimination based on race, colour, or national or ethnic origin. The Committee recalls its General recommendation 23 (1997) on the rights of indigenous peoples, in particular their right to own, develop, control and use their communal lands, territories and resources, and expresses particular concern about:

(a) Reported legislative efforts to privatize Western Shoshone ancestral lands for transfer to multinational extractive industries and energy developers.

(b) Information according to which destructive activities are conducted and/or planned on areas of spiritual and cultural significance to the Western Shoshone peoples, who are denied access to, and use of, such areas. It notes in particular the reinvigorated federal efforts to open a nuclear waste repository at the Yucca Mountain; the alleged use of explosives and open pit gold mining activities on Mont Tenabo and Horse Canyon; and the alleged issuance of geothermal energy leases at, or near, hot springs, and the processing of further applications to that end.

(c) The reported resumption of underground nuclear testing on Western Shoshone ancestral lands;

(d) The conduct and / or planning of all such activities without consultation with and despite protests of the Western Shoshone peoples;

(e) The reported intimidation and harassment of Western Shoshone people by the State party's authorities, through the imposition of grazing fees, trespass and collection notices, impounding of horse and livestock, restrictions on hunting, fishing and gathering, as well as arrests, which gravely disturb the enjoyment of their ancestral lands.

(f) The difficulties encountered by Western Shoshone peoples in appropriately challenging all such actions before national courts and in obtaining adjudication on the merits of their claims, due in particular to domestic technicalities.

C. RECOMMENDATIONS

8. The Committee recommends to the State party that it respect and protect the human rights of the Western Shoshone peoples, without discrimination based on race, colour, or national or ethnic origin, in accordance with the Convention. The State party is urged to pay particular attention to the right to health and cultural rights of the Western Shoshone people, which may be infringed upon by

activities threatening their environment and/or disregarding the spiritual and cultural significance they give to their ancestral lands.

9. The Committee urges the State party to take immediate action to initiate a dialogue with the representatives of the Western Shoshone peoples in order to find a solution acceptable to them, and which complies with their rights under, in particular, articles 5 and 6 of the Convention. In this regard also, the Committee draws the attention of the State party to its General recommendation 23 (1997) on the rights of indigenous peoples, in particular their right to own, develop, control and use their communal lands, territories and resources.

10. The Committee urges the State party to adopt the following measures until a final decision or settlement is reached on the status, use and occupation of Western Shoshone ancestral lands in accordance with due process of law and the State party's obligations under the Convention:

> (a) Freeze any plan to privatize Western Shoshone ancestral lands for transfer to multinational extractive industries and energy developers;
> (b) Desist from all activities planned and/or conducted on the ancestral lands of Western Shoshone or in relation to their natural resources, which are being carried out without consultation with and despite protests of the Western Shoshone peoples;
> (c) Stop imposing grazing fees, trespass and collection notices, horse and livestock impoundments, restrictions on hunting, fishing and gathering, as well as arrests, and rescind all notices already made to that end, inflicted on Western Shoshone people while using their ancestral lands.

11. In accordance with article 9 (1) of the Convention, the Committee requests that the State party provide it with information on action taken to implement the present decision by 15 July 2006.

## Comments and Questions

1. The United States did not respond to CERD about the above decision within the specified time frame. Instead, the U.S. responded in its next periodic report to the Committee. See UN Doc. CERD/C/USA/6 (2007) paras. 342-346 and Annex II. The United States maintained:

> its position that the issues raised by certain Western Shoshone descendents are not appropriate for consideration under early-warning measures and urgent procedures, which are not contemplated or described within the text of the Convention. In this context, it should be borne in mind that the United States has not made a declaration under article 14 of the Convention to accept individual complaints. As it indicated in response to the Committee's inquiry, the United States instead addresses these matters in this periodic report.

Id. para. 342. Does the United States have a point? What is the authority for CERD's early warning and urgent action procedure, and what is the argument that the US (and other countries that are parties to the Convention but have not made a declaration under Article 14) should be subject to it? Is it fair to say, as has often been asserted, that CERD's authority for its early warning and urgent action procedure lies in its authority to monitor state reporting? Since the US did respond, albeit not within the specified time frame and in a periodic report, was its objection to CERD's early warning and urgent action procedure more one of formality than of substance?

2. CERD's interventions under its early warning and urgent action procedure do not often by themselves result in any dramatic change in the circumstances addressed. In its lengthy response on the Western Shoshone situation, the United States did not concede anything but instead reiterated its faith in the very procedures resulting in the legal "extinguishment" of Western Shoshone land rights that CERD found concerning and that the Inter-American Commission on Human Rights, in a separate proceeding, found to violate the United States' human rights obligations. See Chapter 3, *supra*, page 156 (discussing the Commission's decision on the same matter). What, then, is the usefulness of the early warning and urgent action procedure?

3. Recall that CERD's overarching objective is to advance compliance with the Convention against racial discrimination. How are indigenous land rights protected by this treaty, which nowhere mentions indigenous peoples or their land rights?

## D. Interstate Complaints

Traditional international law has always envisaged the possibility for one state to initiate proceedings against another state, assuming that both states accept the jurisdiction of an appropriate judicial or arbitral tribunal. Similarly, human rights treaties often provide for the possibility of interstate complaints whenever one state alleges that another is acting in breach of the relevant treaty. Among the major UN treaties, the Convention against torture (Article 21), the migrant workers Convention (Article 76), the Convention against racial discrimination (Articles 11-13), the ICCPR (Articles 41-43), the ESCR Covenant (Optional Protocol), the Convention on the Rights of the Child (Third Optional Protocol), and the enforced disappearances Convention (Article 32) provide for the possibility of interstate complaints. However, only the Convention against racial discrimination makes this procedure mandatory. Under all of the other treaties, states may separately accept the interstate complaints procedure when or after ratifying the treaty.

Until 2018, no interstate complaints had been filed under any of these procedures. During that year, three such complaints, or communications, were submitted under Article 11 of the Convention on the Elimination of All Forms of Racial Discrimination. Two of these were by Qatar against Saudi Arabia and the United Arab Emirates, and a third was presented by Palestine against Israel. See *Inter-state communications: Committee on the Elimination of Racial Discrimination*, Office of the High Commissioner for Human Rights https://www.ohchr.org/en/treaty-bodies/cerd/inter-state-communications (last visited May 24, 2022).

The State of Palestine submitted a communication against Israel claiming Israel violated the Convention through policies and actions of Israel toward Palestinian citizens. See Committee on the Elimination of Racial Discrimination,

*Inter-state communication submitted by the State of Palestine against Israel*, UN Doc. CERD/C/100/3 (2019). Palestine has non-member observer state status at the UN and in 2014 it deposited an instrument of accession to the Convention. That same year Israel issued a statement objecting to Palestinian accession to the Convention, arguing that Palestine did not satisfy the criteria for statehood under international law and lacked the legal capacity to join the Convention. See Israel Communication, International Convention on the Elimination of All Forms of Racial Discrimination, C.N.293.2014.TREATIES-IV.2 (May 2014), https://treaties.un.org/doc/Publication/CN/2014/CN.293.2014-Eng.pdf. Based on this objection, Israel challenged the Palestinian inter-state communication as inadmissible, alleging that Palestine was not a state and not a party to the Convention and that no treaty relations existed between Palestine and Israel. See CERD, *Inter-state communication submitted by the State of Palestine against Israel, supra.* In response to a request for an opinion from the Committee, the UN Office of Legal Affairs (OLA) concluded that the Committee lacked authority to deal with the complaint because Israel's 2014 unilateral statement constituted a reservation as to Palestine that precluded the Committee from examining the inter-state communication submitted by Palestine. See Treaty Bodies Secretariate, *Transmission of the content of the OLA Memorandum at the request of the Committee on the Elimination of Racial Discrimination* (Aug. 23, 2019), https://tbinternet.ohchr.org/Treaties/CERD/Shared%20Documents/1_Global/INT_CERD_ISC_9360_E.pdf. Despite this response, the Committee found that it did have jurisdiction to adjudicate the Palestinian complaint against Israel, affirming that "a State party, cannot bar another State party, through a unilateral action, from triggering an enforcement mechanism created by the Convention, to the extent that such mechanism is essential to guarantee the equal enjoyment of the rights of individuals or groups set forth in the Convention." CERD, *Inter-state communication submitted by the State of Palestine against Israel, supra,* para. 3.37. In a subsequent decision, the Committee found the Palestinian complaint to be admissible, rejecting Israel's assertions of failure to exhaust domestic remedies. See Committee on the Elimination of Racial Discrimination, *Decision on the admissibility of the inter-State communication submitted by the State of Palestine Against Israel,* UN Doc. CERD/C/103/R.6 (2021). Pursuant to Article 12(1) of the Convention, the Committee requested its chair to appoint an ad hoc Conciliation Commission to "make its good offices available to the States concerned with a view to an amicable solution of the matter on the basis of States parties' compliance with the Convention." Id. at para 66.

In its communications against Saudi Arabia and the United Arab Emirates, Qatar alleged that both states violated the Convention in the context of sanctions taken by the respondent states in 2017 that discriminated against Qatari citizens. After confirming jurisdiction and admissibility for both communications, the Committee chair appointed an ad hoc Conciliation Commission to support the states in working toward settlement of the disputes. Following the Al Ula Agreement of January 5, 2021 between Qatar and its neighbors, whose section 2 sets out the terms of the settlement of disputes between the parties, including the respondents, Qatar requested the suspension of the proceedings. After both the United Arab Emirates and the Kingdom of Saudi Arabia consented to suspension, the ad hoc Conciliation Commissions suspended the proceedings. See *Decision of the ad hoc Conciliation Commission on the request for suspension submitted by Qatar concerning the interstate communication Qatar v. the United Arab Emirates* (March 15, 2021); *Decision of the ad hoc Conciliation Commission on the request for suspension submitted by Qatar concerning the interstate communication Qatar v. the Kingdom of Suadi Arabia* (March 15, 2021).

It is noteworthy that, around the same time it filed its complaint to CERD, in 2018, Qatar initiated proceedings against the United Arab Emirates in the International Court of Justice concerning the same dispute, alleging violations of the Convention against racial discrimination. See Application of International Convention on the Elimination of All Forms of Racial Discrimination (*Qatar v. United Arag Emirates*), 2021 I.C.J. 71 (Judgment of Feb. 4, 2021). Interestingly, the Court found that it did not have jurisdiction to hear the case in relation to the Convention, on the ground that the alleged violations did not fall within the scope of the Convention's prohibition of racial discrimination. Although acknowledging CERD's view to the contrary and purporting to give that view significant weight, the Court disagreed with the Committee and found that the Convention, which by its terms covers discrimination based on "national origin" (Art. 1), does not cover discrimination based on current citizenship. Id. at para. 74-105. Do you agree with this conclusion?

At the same time, more matters related to human rights are being submitted with increasing frequency to the International Court of Justice, and interstate cases have now been brought in all three regional systems. See, e.g., Case Concerning Application of the Convention on the Prevention and Punishment of the Crime of Genocide (*Bosnia and Herzegovina v. Serbia and Montenegro*), 1996 I.C.J. 595 (Judgment of Feb. 26, 2007); Application of the International Convention on the Elimination of All Forms of Racial Discrimination (*Georgia v. Russian Federation*), 2011 I.C.J. 70 (Judgment of April 1, 2011); *Democratic Republic of Congo v. Burundi, Rwanda, and Uganda*, Communication 227/99, Afr. Comm'n H.P.R., Report on the Merits, May 2003; *Nicaragua v. Costa Rica*, Interstate Case 01/06, Inter-Am. Comm'n H.R., Report No. 11/07, Admissibility decision of Mar. 8, 2007; *Ecuador v. Colombia*, Interstate Case 12.779, Inter-Am. Comm'n H.R., Report No. 96/13, Decision to archive of Nov. 4, 2013; *Georgia v. Russia*, Eur. Ct. H.R., App. No. 13255/07, Admissibility decision of July 3, 2009 (alleged harassment of Georgian migrants in Russia); *Slovenia v. Croatia*, Eur. Ct. H.R., App. No. 54155/16, Decision of Nov. 18, 2020 (alleged unpaid and overdue debts owed to Ljubljana Bank by various Croatian companies).

Why might states seek recourse against another state before a UN treaty body rather than the International Court of Justice? Can you think of any reasons other than the absence of jurisdiction by the ICJ in a given case?

## E.   *Strengthening the Treaty System*

Human rights treaties and their monitoring mechanisms have been developed largely in response to political pressure from NGOs and interested states. This piecemeal approach has meant that there has been little long-term thinking about the UN system or how to ensure that new instruments and treaty bodies complement existing procedures. For this and many other reasons, the system has suffered from substantial structural problems. The criticism of Manfred Nowak a decade ago remains in significant part true today:

[T]he proliferation of UN human rights treaties with different but overlapping reporting obligations and with separate treaty monitoring bodies working on an unpaid, voluntary and part-time basis, together with a trend towards universal ratification of these treaties, has led to an unmanageable and deeply frustrating situation for all involved. Governments complain about the high number of reports they are obliged to draft periodically, and which often are examined many years after their submission, and the expert bodies complain about the lack of discipline among governments and the limited time they are given to examine the numerous reports. . . . [O]nly a major structural reform can help to solve the ongoing crisis.

Nowak, *supra* page 467, at 718-19.

There have been many calls and several initiatives for reform from many quarters, both within and outside the United Nations. A summary of the UN initiatives compiled by the Office of the UN High Commissioner for Human Rights (OHCHR) may be found at http://www.ohchr.org/EN/HRBodies/HRTD/Pages/TBStrengthening.aspx. The following extract, from a book chapter written by a former OHCHR official, explains the modest progress of the UN reform initiatives.

Jane Connors

## "The Human Rights Treaty Body System"

in *The Oxford Handbook of United Nations Treaties* 377, 392-94 (Simon Chesterman et al., eds. 2019) (footnotes omitted)

The treaty bodies have continuously sought to improve their effectiveness. However, they face challenges, many related to the fact that their number has expanded significantly, but ad hoc, and they have developed their working methods to achieve the greatest impact on the promotion and protection of human rights to a large extent independently. While welcome, the broad acceptance of the human rights treaties by states has multiplied their tasks. Although they have sought to streamline and align their working methods and practices, there are differences in approach, despite their similar competence, including in the preparation of lists of issues, the procedure for the examination of reports, processes for formulating general recommendations, and the involvement of stakeholders in their work.

Since 1984, the chairs of each treaty body have met formally to discuss issues of common concern, in particular working methods and common approaches to thematic issues, such as reprisals against those who seek to interact with them, to enhance the effectiveness of the treaty body system as a whole. These meetings, which are now held annually and whose reports are transmitted to the General Assembly, are usually held in Geneva, but have been held in Brussels, Addis Ababa, New York, and Costa Rica in order to bring the treaty bodies closer to the site of implementation and strengthen links among international and regional mechanisms and institutions and stakeholders. On occasion, informal meetings are convened to deepen their work. Harmonization of the human rights treaty body system has been an issue since the chairs' first meeting. It has been the subject of many

UN reports, as well as academic commentary, and gained greater prominence as the system has become more overstretched.

In 2002, the UN Secretary-General identified modernization of the UN treaty system as a crucial element in the UN goal to promote and protect human rights. He called on the treaty bodies to craft a more coordinated approach to their activities by standardizing their reporting requirements and allowing states parties to produce a single report summarizing their compliance with the full range of treaties to which they are a party. The idea of a single report was not supported by the treaty bodies and many other stakeholders, but the treaty bodies were amenable to standardizing their reporting requirements. In 2005, Louise Arbour, then the High Commissioner for Human Rights, made a bold proposal for treaty body reform when she called for discussions on proposals for a unified treaty system and the replacement of the existing treaty bodies by a single, unified, standing treaty body. The OHCHR prepared a concept paper, which was discussed widely. A majority of stakeholders — many states parties, most treaty body experts, and numerous NGOs — were wary of the proposal. Many considered that the establishment of such a body would jeopardize, and perhaps undermine, the specificity of approach of the respective treaty bodies and the human rights treaties themselves. Some were concerned that this might be the first step toward the establishment of an international human rights court. Others considered that the creation of a single body merging all treaty body activities was politically unrealistic, but some form of unification, such as a single body for examination of complaints, might be feasible.

Succeeding high commissioners have not pursued High Commissioner Arbour's proposal. In 2009, the then High Commissioner Navi Pillay launched a process of reflection on ways to strengthen the treaty body system based on the premise that the legal parameters of the treaties should not be altered. Around 20 consultations involving states, treaty body experts, UN entities, NHRIs, academics, and civil society were organized by OHCHR. There was broad support for this multi-stakeholder process, but in 2011 some states expressed the view that states must play the primary role in any discussions relating to the treaty body system. As a result, in early 2012, the UNGA adopted a resolution requesting its President to launch an intergovernmental process on strengthening and enhancing the effective functioning of the human rights treaty body system. This process was initiated in July 2012, one month after the High Commissioner published a report setting out her vision for the future of the system.

The intergovernmental process concluded in April 2014 with the adoption of UNGA resolution 68/268 on strengthening and enhancing the effective functioning of the human rights treaty body system. The lengthy resolution reaffirms the independence of the treaty bodies and their members, but encourages them to align their methodology and harmonize their working methods. In so doing, however, they must pay attention to the views of states, and no new obligations for states should be created. The treaty bodies are encouraged to enhance the role of their chairs in relation to procedural matters, and there should be strengthened interaction between states parties and the chairs during their annual meetings so that these meetings constitute a forum where all issues, including those related to the independence and impartiality of treaty bodies, can be raised constructively. Efficiency strategies are promoted. These include: combining overdue reports to eliminate the backlog of outstanding reporting obligations; establishing word limits for documents produced by states parties, other stakeholders, and the treaty bodies themselves; and limiting treaty body working languages and translation of summary records. In order to enhance accessibility and visibility of the treaty bodies, they are encouraged to webcast their public meetings, and the Secretary-General is requested to make the system accessible to persons with disabilities to ensure their full and effective participation. To enable wider participation in the reporting process, the OHCHR is requested to facilitate participation of members of its delegations via videoconferencing, and states are encouraged to provide voluntary funds to facilitate the engagement of states parties, particularly those without representation in Geneva, with the treaty body system. Recommendations are made to sustain and strengthen the independence and impartiality of treaty body members, and all acts of intimidation and reprisals against individuals and groups contributing to the work of human rights treaty bodies are condemned. At the heart of the resolution, however, is the allocation of increased meeting time to the human rights treaty bodies, determined on the basis of a formula based on their workload in 2014, to be reviewed biennially. This is mirrored by a capacity-building program, including the deployment of dedicated officers in the OHCHR's regional offices, to support states parties in implementing their treaty obligations.

Full implementation of GA Resolution 68/268 began on January 1, 2015. The Secretary-General reports on progress made to the UNGA on a biennial basis: the first report was considered by the Assembly in 2016, and the second will be submitted to its 73rd session in 2018. The UNGA will review the state of the human rights treaty body system in 2020, including the measures taken in line with resolution 68/268 to ensure their sustainability, and, if appropriate, decide on further action to strengthen and enhance the effective functioning of the system. Discussions have begun on possible further action, including in the framework of an academic platform project on the 2020 review established by the Geneva Academy, which issued a report entitled "Optimizing the UN Treaty Body System" in May 2018.

———————

The reporting procedures described in the extract of the OHCHR Manual, *supra* pages 451-458, reflect both enhanced capacity building efforts and the effort at harmonization and simplification in reporting discussed above. The biennial reports on the status of the human rights treaty body system mandated by the General Assembly can be found on the relevant page of the website of the OHCHR, *supra* page 486. See also *Report on the process of the consideration of the state of the United Nations human rights treaty body system,* UN Doc. A/75/601 (2020) (report by ambassadors of Morocco and Switzerland resulting from consultations on the treaty system, with recommendations). For a critique of the treaty body reform process, see Jeremy Sarkin, *The 2020 United Nations Human Rights Treaty Body Review Process: Prioritising Resources, Independence and the Domestic State Reporting Process over Rationalising and Streamlining Treaty Bodies,* 25 INT'L. J. HUM. RTS. 8 (1921). Is there perhaps too much process going on in the reform process? At this stage, does the problem have less to do with the treaty body procedures themselves than, as Professor Sarkin suggests, the level of state commitment to the treaties, to funding the treaty body procedures, and to domestic efforts to implement treaty body recommendations?

## III.  UN CHARTER–BASED PROCEDURES

Apart from the treaty regimes discussed above, several institutions and mechanisms have been established under the authority of the UN Charter, which, as will be recalled, makes the promotion of human rights one of the founding purposes of the organization. Early in the history of the UN, the Commission on Human Rights was created as a subsidiary intergovernmental body of the Economic and Social Council to function as the UN's principal human rights forum. In the early 2000s, the UN embarked on an initiative to improve the Commission's credibility and performance, which eventually grew into an overhaul of the UN human rights machinery. Despite its undeniable accomplishments in advancing human rights at the global level, from its beginning the Commission had wrestled with geopolitics and the obstructionist tendencies of states that resisted elevating human rights above political ends. Concerns over the Commission's legitimacy loomed as states with abysmal human rights records found their way into the Commission's membership; states blocked human rights initiatives based primarily on political and ideological considerations; and the efficiency and transparency of some of the Commission's working methods were questioned. These and other issues were highlighted in a 2004 report by a panel of dignitaries appointed by Secretary-General Kofi Annan and a report the following year by the Secretary-General himself. See *Report of the Secretary-General's High-Level Panel on Threats, Challenges, and Changes—A More Secure World: Our Shared Responsibility*, UN Doc. A/59/565 (2004); *Report of the Secretary-General: In Larger Freedoms—Towards Development, Security, and Human Rights of All*, UN Doc. A/59/2005 (2005).

Major reform ensued with the decision by the UN General Assembly in 2006 to replace the Commission with a Human Rights Council, which would meet throughout the year and report directly to the Assembly. See G.A. Res. 60/251 (2006). The 47 member states of the Human Rights Council are elected by the General Assembly by secret ballot, with each candidate state standing for election on its own, rather than by regional blocs as had been the case for election to the Commission. Id., para. 7. To further improve the quality of membership, in electing members of the Council UN member states are supposed to "take into account the contribution of candidates to the promotion and protection of human rights and their voluntary pledges and commitments made thereto." Id., para. 8.

After a year of at times difficult debate, the new Council adopted an "institution-building plan" that defined its working methods and was approved by the General Assembly. See H.R.C. Res. 5/1, Annex (2007). For background and commentary on the reform, see *New Institutions for Human Rights Protection* (Kevin Boyle ed., 2008); *Symposium, Reviewing the UN Human Rights Council: Looking Back and Moving Forward*, 17 NEW ENG. J. INT'L & COMP. L. 193 (2011); Paul Gordon Lauren, *"To Preserve and Build on Its Achievements and to Redress Its Shortcomings": The Journey from the Commission on Human Rights to the Human Rights Council*, 29 HUM. RTS. Q. 307 (2007); Philip Alston, *Reconceiving the U.N. Human Rights Regime: Challenges Confronting the New Human Rights Council*, 7 MELB. J. INT'L L. 185 (2006); and Morton H. Halperin and Diane F. Orentlicher, *The New UN Human Rights Council*, 13 HUM. RTS. BR. 1 (2006).

With the reform, the Commission's Sub-Commission on the Promotion and Protection of Human Rights and its various working groups ceased to exist, but a somewhat similar Advisory Committee of independent experts was created to function under the authority of the Council. Additionally, the Council established an Expert Mechanism on the Rights of Indigenous Peoples to engage in research-based studies on issues of concern to indigenous peoples. The Council inherited a number of the mechanisms created by the Commission, including the confidential complaint procedure and the system of "special procedures," both of which are discussed below. We begin the discussion of the Human Rights Council by considering an additional mechanism, which was established along with the Council's creation—the "universal periodic review," under which each UN member state is subject to regular periodic examination of its human rights performance by the Council.

## A.   The Universal Periodic Review

When the Human Rights Council was created, the General Assembly mandated the Council to "[u]ndertake a universal periodic review, based on objective and reliable information, of the fulfillment of each State of its human rights obligations and commitments in a manner which ensure universality of coverage and equal treatment with respect to all States." G.A. Res. 60/251 (2006), para. 5(e). This universal periodic review (UPR) was conceived as a key component of a new approach that would strive to be more evenhanded and transparent, and less susceptible to power politics, than had been the Commission in its public examination of states. See Felice D. Gaer, *A Voice Not an Echo: Universal Periodic Review and the UN Treaty Body System*, 7 Hum. Rts. L. Rev. 109 (2007).

The UPR functions through a working group of the whole of the Council, which meets at regular intervals throughout the year to review one-fourth of the total number of member states each year. All UN member states may participate in the working group, in what is essentially a process of peer review. A state is reviewed on the basis of the UN Charter, the Universal Declaration of Human Rights, the treaties to which it is a party, its voluntary human rights commitments, and applicable international humanitarian law. Each state under review submits a "national report," which is discussed by the UPR working group in one of its sessions. The working group also considers information from relevant sources within the UN system and from other stakeholders, including NGOs and national human rights institutions. Information from these other sources is collected and summarized in reports complied by the Office of the High Commissioner for Human Rights. The UPR working group engages in an "interactive dialogue" with representatives of the state under review and then proceeds to develop an "outcome report" that includes recommendations made by the participating states.

The state under review offers its written responses (acceptance, partial acceptance, or rejection) to each of the recommendations (or at least to each of the recommendations to which it wished to respond), and those responses are appended to the outcome report. The final element in the UPR process is consideration of the working group's report at a plenary session of the Council, at which time both states and NGOs are given a relatively brief opportunity to comment on the review and the issues raised. The Council's formal approval of the review is descriptive rather than analytical, since it merely adopts the "outcome" of the review as set forth in the working group report and the state's voluntary commitments and replies presented before the adoption of the outcome by the plenary.

The materials that follow are drawn from the third review of the United States, which was undertaken in 2020-2021. The review touched upon a wide range of human rights issues, including ratification of human rights treaties not yet ratified by the U.S., discrimination and racial profiling, criminal justice, violence against women, human trafficking, indigenous issues, and issues arising in the context of national security. The extracts below, however, highlight issues related to economic and social rights that were also raised in this third review of the United States.

The extracts below are from, in the following order, the US national report submitted at the beginning of the third round of the UPR, the compilation of information from UN treaty bodies and special procedures, the summary of NGO submissions, and the US written responses to the recommendations made by individual states during the review. The references to recommendations in the following extract of the US's national report are to recommendations from the previous UPR cycle.

## National report submitted in accordance with paragraph 5 of the annex to Human Rights Council resolution 16/21 — United States of America

UN Doc. A/HRC/WG.6/36/USA/1 (2020)

. . .

HOMELESSNESS

Recommendation 310

58. The American economic system of free people and free markets has lifted millions of people out of poverty and been a model for other nations. Those who struggle with poverty and other mental, behavioral, and health problems that lead to homelessness have access to a wide variety of social programs sponsored by families, communities, businesses, nonprofit organizations, including faith-based organizations, and federal, state and local government. HUD, HHS, Department of Education (ED), the Department of Veterans Affairs (VA) and other members of the U.S. Interagency Council on Homelessness (USICH) have worked closely with state and local governments to alleviate the personal and social problems that lead to homelessness. In April of 2020, USICH and partner agencies launched a process to develop an updated comprehensive federal strategic plan to prevent and end homelessness using extensive stakeholder and direct provider input.

59. Through its 2019 Continuum of Care Program Competitions, HUD increased local flexibilities and enhanced provider ability to better help our vulnerable homeless populations. In order to increase self-sufficiency among homeless populations, HUD provided new flexibilities for grantees to implement service

participation requirements such as employment training, mental health care, substance abuse treatment after a person has been stably housed.

60. HUD estimates homelessness across the United States has declined by 11% since 2010. Homelessness among veterans is half of what was reported in 2010.

61. The Federal Interagency Council on Crime Prevention and Reentry, led by DOJ, has supported efforts to reduce recidivism and prepare individuals for successful reentry into society. USICH also released guidance to reentry service providers, corrections agencies, and state and local governments on removing barriers to housing and services for individuals with criminal records who are experiencing homelessness.

HEALTH CARE AND EDUCATION

Recommendations 124, 265, 309, 311–317, 319, 327

62. There is considerable debate in the United States about the best ways to make quality, affordable health care available to all. HHS' Title V Maternal and Child Health Services Block Grant Program seeks to improve maternal health outcomes, including rates of severe morbidity and maternal mortality. National and state level performance measure data is publicly accessible on the Title V Information System website. In 2019, HHS awarded $351 million to support families through the Maternal, Infant, and Early Childhood Home Visiting Program, which serves families living in almost one-third of U.S. counties. States and territories can tailor the program to serve the specific needs of their communities, targeting services to communities with concentrations of risk, such as premature birth, low-birth-weight infants, and infant mortality. A multi-pronged evaluation of the program found home visiting services result in positive effects for families. Additionally, results suggest that home visiting may improve maternal health. HHS also supports Tribal Maternal, Infant, and Early Childhood Home Visiting Program development grants. Evaluations are in progress and a release date will be forthcoming.

63. The Preventing Maternal Deaths Act of 2018[71] authorizes, amends, and expands the Safe Motherhood Initiative within the HHS Centers for Disease Control and Prevention, including authorizing support for state and tribal Maternal Mortality Review Committees, and directs HHS to make grants available to states to better track and examine the problem of maternal deaths; to establish maternal mortality review committees; and to ensure that state health departments have plans to educate healthcare providers about the findings of the review committees. CDC is now funding 25 states to conduct Maternal Mortality Review in the United States.

64. The United States remains committed to equal opportunity in education and, working with states and communities, helping students succeed in school and careers. In 2015, Congress enacted theEvery Student Succeeds Act (ESSA), which revised and reauthorized the Elementary and Secondary Education Act. Its support for states and communities includes investing in evidence-based and innovative local programs; providing intervention and support for schools and students that need the most help; and preserving protections for economically disadvantaged students, children with disabilities, English learners, and other vulnerable students. Consistent with the commitment to equal access, it is unlawful to deny elementary and secondary-level school children in the United States an education on the basis of actual or perceived immigration status.

65. Corporal punishment is governed by state law. In 2019, as a broader tool to help parents and educators create and maintain safe and positive learning environments in school, ED produced a guide on school climate resources for parents and educators. ED also has two centers that offer free assistance and resources related to school climate for states, school districts, schools, institutions of higher learning, and communities: (1) the National Center of Safe and Supportive Learning Environments, and (2) the Technical Assistance Center on Positive Behavioral Interventions and Supports.

WOMEN AND HEALTH

Recommendations 100, 164

66. As the world's largest bilateral donor to global health programs, the U.S. Government is committed to supporting health programs around the world, including life- saving services and helping women and children thrive, particularly in countries where the need is greatest. The United States remains resolute in its commitment to preventing conflict-related sexual violence and providing resources and support for survivors to address the trauma and stigma they experience as a step toward healing those afflicted, as well as mending their communities. As the United States has noted on many occasions, there is no international human right to abortion, whether under that name or under other terms like "sexual and reproductive health." Rather, as President Trump has stated, "our Nation proudly and strongly reaffirms our commitment to protect the precious gift of life at every stage, from conception until natural death." The United States believes in the sovereign right of nations to make their own laws to protect the unborn, and rejects any interpretation of international human rights to require any State to provide access to abortion. As President Trump has stated, "Every person — the born and the unborn, the poor, the downcast, the disabled, the infirm, and the elderly—has inherent value."

GENDER EQUALITY IN THE WORKPLACE

Recommendations 112, 114, 115, 116, 117

67. The United States promotes a non-discriminatory, inclusive, and integrated approach to work that ensures that all women and men are treated with human dignity. It is the policy of the United States to support and promote efforts that reinforce respect for the inherent dignity of both women and men, advance women's equality and promote and protect these rights.

68. Wage discrimination based on sex is illegal under the Equal Pay Act of 1963, 29 U.S.C. § 206(d) and Title VII of the Civil Rights Act of 1964, as amended. The National Security Strategy of the United States clearly identifies women's equality and empowerment worldwide as integral to our national security and a priority for the United States. We believe that investing in women's economic empowerment has a cascading effect for women, men, families, and communities, and is a key component to our national security approach.

69. U.S. law allows, but does not require, private employers to offer paid maternity leave. The Family and Medical Leave Act entitles eligible employees to 12 workweeks of unpaid, job-protected leave in a year for the birth and care of newborn or adopted/foster children. On December 20, 2019, President Trump signed

into law the Federal Employee Paid Leave Act, which provides up to 12 weeks of paid parental leave for over two million Federal civilian employees. The new law will apply to leave taken for births or adoption/foster placements that occur on or after October 1, 2020.

## Compilation on the United States of America — Report of the Office of the United Nations High Commissioner for Human Rights

UN Doc. A/HRC/WG.6/36/USA/2 (2020)

. . .

### C.  Economic, Social and Cultural Rights

44. The Special Rapporteur on extreme poverty noted that the United States had refused to accord domestic recognition to economic and social rights, except for some social rights, and especially the right to education.

#### 1.  Right to Work and to Just and Favourable Conditions of Work

45. The Special Rapporteur on extreme poverty stated that almost a quarter of full-time workers, and three quarters of part-time workers, received no paid sick leave.

46. The Special Rapporteur on trafficking recommended that the Government harmonize and strengthen laws that protected workers to enjoy fair terms of employment, including by increasing the minimum wage, strengthening paid and sick leave, ensuring access to affordable medical care and facilitating the formation of unions in all sectors.

47. The Special Rapporteur on freedom of peaceful assembly and of association recommended that the competent authorities strengthen sanctions against employers who engaged in unfair labour practices, adding fines, punitive damages and compensation provisions to deter future violations of workers' rights.

#### 2.  Right to an Adequate Standard of Living

48. The Special Rapporteur on extreme poverty noted high poverty and inequality levels. There was a dramatic contrast between the immense wealth of the few and the squalor and deprivation in which vast numbers of Americans existed. The face of poverty was not only black or Hispanic, but also white, Asian and many other backgrounds. The Working Group on the issue of discrimination against women in law and in practice noted that the percentage of women in poverty had increased at a higher rate than for men. That had predominantly affected women of colour, single-parent families and older women. The Special Rapporteur on extreme poverty stated that high child and youth poverty rates perpetuated the intergenerational transmission of poverty. The persistence of extreme poverty was a political choice and with political will it could be eliminated.

49. The same Special Rapporteur stated that punishing and imprisoning the poor was the distinctively American response to poverty. Workers who could not pay their debts, those who could not afford private probation services, minorities

targeted for traffic infractions, the mentally ill and fathers who could not pay child support were locked up. He noted that in many cities, homeless persons were effectively criminalized for the situation in which they found themselves. The Working Group of Experts on Persons of African Descent was concerned about the criminalization of poverty, which disproportionately affected African Americans.

50. The same Working Group observed that African Americans in many cities were facing a housing crisis, in which people were not able to pay their rents or mortgages. It was concerned about the persistence of a de facto residential segregation in many of the metropolitan areas.

51. The Special Rapporteur on adequate housing as a component of the right to an adequate standard of living, and on the right to non-discrimination in this context stated that the number of persons living in homelessness was an indication that the right to adequate housing was not being effectively implemented.

52. Two special procedure mandate holders encouraged the authorities to recognize the impact of the expanded role and unprecedented dominance of unregulated financial markets and corporations in the housing sector (financialization of housing) on the enjoyment of the right to adequate housing, particularly for minority and vulnerable groups, and to take steps towards returning housing to its core function as a social good.

53. Three special rapporteurs noted that the Flint case (contamination of the water supply of Flint, Michigan and the devastating consequences for its residents) illustrated the suffering and difficulties that flowed from failing to recognize that water is a human right and from failing to ensure that essential services were provided in a non-discriminatory manner.

54. Several special procedure mandate holders stated that a higher proportion of poor minorities lived near facilities that used, stored, processed or emitted chemicals. People of colour comprised nearly half of the populations living near potential sources of toxic emissions. Likewise, the Special Rapporteur on extreme poverty noted that poor rural communities were often located close to polluting industries.

3. RIGHT TO HEALTH

55. The Working Group on the issue of discrimination against women in law and in practice deplored the substantial disparities that persisted in the prevalence of certain diseases, such as obesity, cancer and HIV/AIDs, according to ethnicity, sex and level of education.

56. The Special Rapporteur on extreme poverty stated that the opioid crisis had devastated many communities, and that the addiction to pain-control opioids often led to heroin, methamphetamine and other substance abuse. Instead of responding with increased funding and improved access to vital care and support, the federal Government and many state governments had mounted concerted campaigns to reduce and restrict access to health care by the poorer members of the population.

57. The Working Group of Experts on People of African Descent stated that a number of factors contributed to the disparities faced by African Americans in realizing the right to the enjoyment of the highest attainable standard of health, including a lack of access to health insurance coverage and to preventive services

and care. While the implementation of the Patient Protection and Affordable Care Act had led to 20 million people getting health insurance coverage, states with some of the widest health disparities had rejected expansion of Medicaid, one of the main tools to cover the uninsured. The Working Group on the issue of discrimination against women in law and in practice regretted the absence of universal health insurance coverage.

58. The Working Group on the issue of discrimination against women in law and in practice regretted that women had seen their right to sexual and reproductive health eroded. Although women had a right under federal law to terminate a pregnancy in various circumstances, ever-increasing barriers were being created to prevent their access to abortion procedures. Women's access to reproductive health services had been truncated in some states by the imposition of constraints. The Human Rights Committee noted Presidential Executive Order 13798, which allowed employers and insurers to make "conscience-based objections" to the preventive care mandate of the Patient Protection and Affordable Care Act and thereby restricted women's access to reproductive care.

59. The Working Group on the issue of discrimination against women in law and in practice recommended ensuring that women could exercise their constitutional right to choose to terminate a pregnancy in the first trimester and that the provisions of the Patient Protection and Affordable Care Act regarding insured access to contraceptives were universally enforced. It also recommended disallowing conscientious objection by health-care personnel, providers and insurers to performing procedures to which women were legally entitled and for which there was no easily accessible, affordable and immediate alternative health provider.

60. Noting with concern the high rate of teenage pregnancy, the same Working Group recommended making contraception available and accessible at no cost, particularly for teenagers, with a view to combating teenage pregnancy.

61. Noting also an increase in the maternal mortality rate, the Working Group recommended addressing the root causes of increased maternal mortality, particularly among African-American women.

### 4. Right to Education

62. The Working Group of Experts on People of African Descent was concerned at the use of police in schools and at school discipline being criminalized, subjecting African American children in particular to severe punishments. It noted that those practices were a violation of children's rights and should be eliminated.

63. The same Working Group recommended that the school curriculum in each state reflect appropriately the history of the transatlantic trade in Africans, enslavement and segregation.

64. The Working Group on the issue of discrimination against women in law and in practice recommended ensuring mandatory human rights education in schools and adequate, scientifically based sex education in school curricula.

---

The extract of the summary of stakeholder views that follows is heavy on acronyms. "JS" refers to "joint submission" and the number along with the acronym refers to the number assigned to the joint submission. Because of the limited opportunities NGO's have to participate in the UPR procedure, they have increasingly been heeding advice to make joint submissions. The NGOs participating in the joint submissions can be found in the notes to the report, not included below.

## Summary of stakeholders' submissions on the United States of America

UN Doc. A/HRC/WG.6/36/USA/3 (2020) (endnotes omitted)

. . .

### 3.  Economic, Social and Cultural Rights

#### Right to Work and to Just and Favourable Conditions of Work

53. JS51 stated that though both federal and state law guaranteed protections to workers, penalties for non-compliant employers were minimal; and that the agencies charged with enforcing those laws lacked resources and were complaint-driven. JS51 also indicated that problems faced by workers to secure their wages and other workplace rights were exacerbated in industries with high subcontracting rates; and that migrant workers, especially those with irregular status, were particularly vulnerable to labour exploitation.

54. JS49 highlighted that domestic workers and farmworkers had been exempted from the protections afforded to most workers by the Federal Fair Labor Standards Act (FLSA) and the National Labor Relations Act. JS23 stated that due to exemptions to the FLSA, child protection was minimal for agriculture, and indicated that a high number of predominately Hispanic children harvested produce, working very long hours, and that the high-school dropout rate for these children was high.

55. JS51 recommended that the USA remove exemptions from the FLSA so that all workers receive minimum wage and overtime protections, regardless of industry or type of worker, especially in high risk industries such as construction, domestic service, and agriculture.

56. JS54 stated that penal labour carried out by government or private operations, exacerbated poverty as prisoners were paid far less than the federal minimum wage. Two submissions indicated that individuals in the Voluntary Work Programs in immigration detention centres were paid about $1 per day.

#### Right to an Adequate Standard of Living

57. JS47 stated that racial minority populations often experienced higher hunger rates linked to the poverty rates experienced by such groups, noting the higher poverty rates for African Americans and Hispanics. HRC [Human Rights Campaign] indicated that LGBTQ families and older adults were at an increased risk of poverty. JS53 highlighted that the Native American population suffered from high poverty and unemployment rates.

58. JS58 indicated that the law provided no entitlement to housing assistance for low income people; and that recognition of a right to even basic shelter was extremely limited to a few communities. Two submissions reported that

encampments had increased significantly since 2007. Several submissions referred to the criminalisation of homeless persons for engaging in life sustaining activities.

59. JS24 stated that institutional problems the Fair Housing Act was designed to solve, such as inequality in mortgage lending and landlords who avoided renting to minorities, endured. JS53 stressed that homelessness and the inability to access affordable housing was a reality for indigenous peoples, and that the 2018 cut of the US Department of Housing and Urban Development budget had severely impacted indigenous communities.

60. It was recommended that the USA affirm housing as a human right and commit to its implementation in a non-discriminatory way; and increase enforcement of existing fair housing and lending laws.

61. JS4 stated that many rural communities lacked access to basic sanitation162 and that there was a lack of political will to fully investigate the problem and its impacts and to provide adequate infrastructure funding.

RIGHT TO HEALTH

62. HRW stated that despite accepting UPR recommendations related to health-care, federal and state authorities continued to take actions to restrict access to health-care, targeting changes to the Medicaid program, private insurance subsidies, and other key elements of the 2010 Affordable Care Act (ACA).

63. JS1 stated that the wealth inequality increased inequality in health care because of the private insurance financing, with numerous coverage gaps. Higher levels of income inequality coincided with increased mortality for lower income individuals, and inequality in life expectancy was growing.

64. JS1 noted reports that from 2013-2016, medical problems and expenditures contributed to personal bankruptcies. JS37 stated that health issues increased the risk of homelessness and that individuals experiencing homelessness lacked access to quality health care.

65. JS1 stated that suicide was the 10th cause of mortality in 2017, rising every year from 2008 indicating that Native Americans and Alaska Natives had the highest rates and veterans took their lives at the rate of some 20 deaths per day.

66. JS42 stated that about one in every 5 deaths in the USA was due to tobacco.

67. HRW reported on the deaths of tens of thousands of Americans of drug overdose in 2017 and stated that the USA's response to the crisis was increasingly punitive. In many states, criminal laws blocked expansion of proven public health interventions, such as syringe exchange programs and supervised consumption sites. Reduced access to Medicaid, threatened to put drug treatment out of reach for millions of Americans.

68. Several submissions noted the high and increasing rates of maternal mortality; particularly among black women; but also among indigenous women, low income women and women in poor rural areas. PPFA [Planned Parenthood Federation of America] indicated that, according to reports, maternal mortality was the sixth most common cause of death among women aged 25-34. JS14 stated that the lack of systematically collected maternal mortality and morbidity data precluded comparisons across states and regions and undermined accountability for preventable maternal deaths.

69. AI was gravely concerned about the curtailment of sexual and reproductive rights, specifically, increasing efforts to criminalize pregnancy and abortion, and limiting access to reproductive health services.

70. Highlighting the Mexico City policy, several submissions were concerned about restrictions to foreign assistance related to abortion, while two submissions welcomed such restrictions.

71. HRW [Human Rights Watch] highlighted the adoption of a rule in 2019 to ban organizations providing abortion services from receiving federal family planning money, known as Title X, and to eliminate a requirement that doctors give neutral and factual information to pregnant women.

72. SRI stated that religious freedom had become an "opt out" strategy used to deny services related to health care, abortion and contraception, and that many such efforts promoted discrimination against often already-marginalized groups. JS14 stated that an array of federal and state laws permitted individual and institutional health care providers to opt out of providing critical health services, including abortion (46 states) and contraception (12 states). Two submissions welcomed action taken by the USA to support persons voicing religious or moral objections to abortion.

73. JS14 stated that a number of state legislatures were enacting increasingly extreme abortion bans, noting that these state laws were the subject of ongoing litigation. Several stakeholders indicated that some of these bans made no exceptions for rape or for ectopic pregnancies; and that many women seeking an abortion must now travel as abortion services were not available.

74. UFI was concerned about third party reproduction including surrogacy.

75. interACT [Advocates for Intersex Youth, Sudbary] reported that children with intersex traits had been, and continued to be, subjected to unnecessary medical interventions without their consent.

---

With the three documents immediately above, and written questions submitted in advance by states, the UPR working group proceeded with its interactive dialogue on the US, a process that is allotted three and a half hours and is broadcast live on the Internet. The working group's report is a summary record of the discussions and the recommendations submitted during the oral dialogue between US government representatives and other states.

## Report of the Working Group on the Universal Periodic Review — United States of America

UN Doc. A/HRC/46/15 (2020)

### INTRODUCTION

1. The Working Group on the Universal Periodic Review, established in accordance with Human Rights Council resolution 5/1, held its thirty-sixth session from 2 to 13 November 2020. The review of the United States of America was held at the

12th meeting, on 9 November 2020. The delegation of the United States of America was headed by the Permanent Representative of the United States to the Office of the United Nations and other international organizations in Geneva, Andrew Bremberg, the Assistant Secretary, Bureau of Democracy, Human Rights and Labor, United States Department of State, Robert Destro, and the Acting Legal Adviser, United States Department of State, Marik String. At its 17th meeting, held on 13 November 2020, the Working Group adopted the report on the United States. . . .

## I.  Summary of the Proceedings Under of the Review Process

. . .

### B.  Interactive Dialogue and Responses by the State Under Review

9. During the interactive dialogue, 116 delegations made statements. Recommendations made during the dialogue are to be found in section II of the present report. . . .

11. The Acting Legal Adviser, United States Department of State, noted that the United States was a party to many human rights treaties and took those obligations very seriously. The reasons for not ratifying all treaties varied from treaty to treaty. In accordance with the Constitution, only the Senate had the authority to provide advice on and to consent to treaty ratification through an affirmative vote by two thirds of its members. In many cases, such as in respect of the Convention on the Rights of Persons with Disabilities, United States domestic protections were even stronger than those of international treaties. The United States was committed to the effective implementation of its human rights obligations and welcomed continued input on how to improve it. . . .

14. A representative of the United States Department of Housing and Urban Development noted in June 2019 President Trump had established the White House Council on Eliminating Regulatory Barriers to Affordable Housing to remove obstacles to the construction of affordable homes, to boost economic growth and to provide economic mobility for more United States citizens. In October 2020, the Interagency Council on Homelessness released an updated strategic plan that focused on the root causes of homelessness and prioritized trauma-informed care to prevent and end homelessness. In its new strategic plan, the Council also promoted alternatives to criminalizing people experiencing homelessness through better partnerships between law enforcement and homeless service organizations and through increased capacity of social work and mental health programmes. The Council sought to reduce recidivism among individuals experiencing homelessness. In 2020, Congress had appropriated over $6.6 billion for homeless assistance programmes.

15. A representative of the United States Department of Health and Human Services said that the Government was committed to improving its understanding of the impact of COVID-19 on minority populations, who were often at higher risk of contracting the virus. The Government was also committed to preventing suicides and combating opioid misuse and abuse. The Department of Health and Human Services provided $286 million annually in grants to public and private organizations that offered a broad range of family planning methods and services,

primarily to those from low-income families. In addition, legislation passed in 2018 had expanded the Department's Safe Motherhood Initiative, including by authorizing support for state and tribal maternal mortality review committees. The Protecting Life in Global Health Policy, in effect since May 2019, focused United States discourse in multilateral settings on achieving better health for women, preserving human life at all stages, strengthening the family as the foundation of any healthy society and protecting every nation's sovereignty in global politics.

16. A representative of the United States Department of Labor emphasized United States leadership in promoting equal opportunities for women. United States law prohibited discrimination on the basis of sex, including factors such as pregnancy, childbirth and related medical conditions. The United States was fully committed to ensuring equal employment opportunities in all sectors of the workforce. By adhering to the Pledge to America's Workers, job creators around the country had committed themselves to providing more than 16 million new training, upskilling or reskilling opportunities for students and workers. Since January 2017, more than 800,000 people had entered apprenticeship programmes registered with the Department of Labor or its state-level counterparts. . . .

24. In addressing comments made on sexual and reproductive health, the Assistant Secretary [Bureau of Democracy, Human Rights and Labor, United States Department of State] noted that abortion remained legal in the United States but that the United States rejected the proposition that abortion was a matter of international human rights. The lives of all, born and unborn, should be protected. . . .

## II. Conclusions and/or recommendations

26. The following recommendations will be examined by the United States, which will provide responses in due time, but no later than the forty-sixth session of the Human Rights Council:

. . .

26.151 Intensify efforts to develop and strengthen the necessary legislative frameworks that address cross-sectoral environmental challenges, including climate change adaptation and mitigation frameworks (Fiji);

26.152 Pursue the fight against the global problem of climate change and its negative impacts, in particular by strengthening cooperation with the international community in this area (Haiti); . . .

26.286 Further enhance activities that will lead to reducing homelessness among vulnerable groups across the country (Ethiopia);

26.287 Develop strategies for addressing the housing and sanitary problems of marginalized communities such as indigenous and migrant communities (Azerbaijan);

26.288 Protect expanded and equitable access to health care (Poland); . . .

26.290 Take further measures to make health-care services accessible to vulnerable people not supported by the current health system (Angola);

26.291 Take measures for providing health-care services to all without prejudice to race, economic situation and citizenship status of persons under its jurisdiction (Azerbaijan);

26.292 Step up its efforts, both at home and abroad, to improve the health, dignity and well-being of women, children and their families (Ethiopia);

26.293 Ensure access to health care, drugs and treatment to all segments of society (Iraq);

26.294 Continue its ongoing efforts to build a more inclusive society and reduce inequalities, including by updating its strategic plans to address the disproportionate impact of the COVID-19 pandemic on vulnerable populations (Singapore);26.301 Ensure that laws permitting the refusal of care based on religious and moral beliefs do not restrict women's sexual and reproductive health and rights and that measures are put in place to monitor and prevent violations of these rights (Australia);

26.295 Ensure equal, full and rapid access for all segments of United States society to free health care in the face of the COVID-19 pandemic (Turkey);

26.296 Establish a public system that guarantees the right to health of its people, which has been decimated by the pandemic (Bolivarian Republic of Venezuela);

26.297 Urge politicians to respect people's right to life and right to health, and stop politicizing and stigmatizing the COVID-19 pandemic (China);

26.298 Guarantee the right to health, even in the context of COVID-19 (Cuba);

26.299 Lift funding restrictions on United States foreign assistance to promote women's full access to sexual and reproductive health and rights (Norway);

26.300 Clarify its approach to ensuring access to comprehensive sexual and reproductive health services (United Kingdom of Great Britain and Northern Ireland);

26.301 Ensure that laws permitting the refusal of care based on religious and moral beliefs do not restrict women's sexual and reproductive health and rights and that measures are put in place to monitor and prevent violations of these rights (Australia);

26.302 Reverse policies inhibiting comprehensive and universal access to voluntary sexual and reproductive health services, especially in emergency situations, and end related restrictions on foreign assistance (Austria);

26.303 Take action to support equitable access to sexual and reproductive health and rights services, and review policies that effectively limit foreign assistance for sexual and reproductive health and rights services abroad (Canada);

26.304 Rescind the Title X restrictions to ensure access to comprehensive family planning services for all (Denmark);

26.305 Make essential health services accessible to all women and girls, paying special attention to those who face multiple and intersecting forms of discrimination (Finland);

26.306 Ensure access by women and girls to sexual and reproductive rights and health (France);

26.307 Protect the sexual and reproductive health and rights of women and girls by ensuring their access to sexual and reproductive health information, commodities and services (Iceland);

26.308 Guarantee essential health services for all, including sexual and reproductive health services (Luxembourg);

26.309 Ensure universal access to sexual and reproductive health information, education and services for all (Malaysia);

26.310 Ensure access by all women to sexual and reproductive health information and services (Mexico);

26.311 Repeal the Helms Amendment and the Protecting Life in Global Health Assistance Policy and, in the interim, allow United States foreign assistance to be used, at a minimum, for safe abortion in cases of rape, incest and life endangerment (Netherlands);

26.312 Ensure that its international aid allows access to sexual and reproductive health services (New Zealand);

26.313 Take further robust and comprehensive measures to promote wider and equitable access to quality education at all levels (Botswana);

26.314 Strengthen legislation in order to eliminate all forms of gender discrimination in employment (Republic of Moldova);

26.315 Explore the option of introducing a by-law on mandatory paid minimum maternity leave (Romania);

26.316 Strengthen further equality in the workplace by moving towards universal paid maternity leave and advancing universal maternal health care (Sri Lanka);

26.317 Continue reinforcing legislation to eliminate all forms of gender discrimination in employment and ensure equal pay for work of equal value in the workplace (India);

26.318 Encourage further private employers to strengthen equality and to offer paid maternity leave (Israel); . . .

26.320 Strengthen further the existing non-discriminatory, inclusive and integrated approach to work to ensure women's equality and the promotion and protection of these rights (Montenegro);

26.321 Eliminate the wage gap and gender-based violence and guarantee access to justice and reparation for victims (Bolivarian Republic of Venezuela); . . .

26.325 Create a federal mechanism to provide the necessary support to boys and young men in order to avoid any delay in their psychosocial development (Haiti);

26.326 Develop norms that ensure free, prior and informed consultations with indigenous communities in relation to projects with a potential impact on their territories and traditional ways of life, in accordance with Sustainable Development Goals 10 and 16 (Paraguay);

---

In the penultimate stage of the process, before the review was discussed in a subsequent session of the plenary Council, the United States provided written responses to the above recommendations. Again, while the discussion on the UPR covered a wide range of human rights issues, the above extracts and the one that follows highlight the discussion on economic and social rights. Note that the numbered recommendations in the U.S. responses below refer to the numbered subparagraphs that include the recommendations by individual states in the immediately preceding report.

## Report of the Working Group on the Universal Periodic Review — United States of America, Addendum: Views on conclusions and/or recommendations, voluntary commitments and replies presented by the State under review

UN Doc. A/HRC/46/15/Add.1 (2021)

1. The United States (U.S.) has carefully reviewed the 347 recommendations received. This response reflects our continuing efforts, in consultation with civil society, to promote, protect, and respect human rights for all.

2. Some recommendations ask us to achieve an ideal, e.g., end discrimination or police brutality, and others request action not entirely within the power of our Federal Executive Branch, e.g., adopt legislation, ratify treaties, or act at the state level. We support or support in part these recommendations when we share their ideals, are making serious efforts to achieve their goals, and intend to continue doing so. Nonetheless, we recognize, realistically, that the United States may never completely accomplish what is described in the recommendations' literal terms. . . .

5. These responses should not be construed to suggest that the U.S. necessarily regards each of the matters addressed as subject to U.S. international human rights obligations. . . .

ECONOMIC, SOCIAL, AND CULTURAL RIGHTS AND MEASURES; INDIGENOUS ISSUES; AND THE ENVIRONMENT

. . .

12. We support:

- 152, 286-288, 290-294, 301, 318. [on climate change, homelessness, housing, healthcare, paid maternity leave]
- 151. Addressing climate change is a core priority for the U.S. We intend to take action consistent with U.S. law to develop and implement an ambitious plan to combat the climate crisis.
- 255, 284. The U.S. supports investing in direct solutions to alleviate the personal and social problems surrounding issues of poverty.
- 149, 299-300, 302-312. It is the policy of the U.S. to support women's and girls' sexual and reproductive health and rights in the U.S., as well as globally. On January 28, 2021, the President issued a "Memorandum on Protecting Women's Health at Home and Abroad," which revoked the January 23, 2017 Presidential Memorandum on the "Mexico City Policy," thereby rescinding the prior policy. As relevant to 304, this Memorandum also directed a review of the Title X family planning program and any other regulations governing the Title X program that impose undue restrictions on the use of federal funds for women's access to complete medical information. With respect to 149, the U.S. did not participate in the Nairobi Summit, but supports furthering efforts to prevent and address female genital mutilation and child, early, and forced marriages.
- 315-316. We support exploring possible legislation expanding the availability of paid parental leave for parents who seek it.

13. We support, in part:

- 283. We support the part of this recommendation asking us to work towards the ideal of equality, subject to the explanation in para. 2. Addressing inequities in our economy is a top priority for President Biden.

13.

- 285, 289, 296, 298. The U.S. is not a party to the ICESCR, and we understand that the rights therein are to be realized progressively. With respect to 285, we support the policy goals of reducing poverty and inequality. With respect to 289, 296, 298, we support the policy goal of improving access to quality, affordable healthcare.
- 295, 313. We support these recommendations in part, subject to para. 2, because we share the ideals of, respectively, improving access to healthcare and promoting access to quality education.
- 325. We support this recommendation to the extent it asks us to continue to support the development of boys and young men; the U.S. has no plan to create a new federal mechanism at this time.
- 326. We support in part this recommendation, which asks us to continue to consult with indigenous communities, insofar as consistent with our 2010 statement of support for the [UN Declaration on the Rights of Indigenous Peoples].

## Comments and Questions

1.  Does the UPR process appear to have influenced the behavior of the United States with respect to the issues addressed in the extracts, or is any change in the United States's positions simply the result of the intervening presidential election or other domestic factors? If the latter, what is the utility of the UPR process as to the United States, and what might this tell us about the utility of the process generally? The United States received 347 recommendations from states that participated in the process, many of them duplicative of one another. Like most states, the United States accepted the great majority of the recommendations and rejected relatively few. Will that acceptance bear on the US positions in the future, regardless of who is president?

2.  Note that the UPR process does not end in a collective evaluation or set of recommendations by the Human Rights Council as a whole. Rather, the outcome is limited to a record of the process itself, which consists primarily of the comments and views of the reviewing states and of the state under review. How might such an "outcome" actually improve human rights performance by states in the aggregate in the short or long term?

3.  How important is the role of NGOs in the UPR, given that their multiple individual submissions are reduced to a single ten-page compilation? NGOs have long played an active role in the UN human rights machinery, facilitated by the granting of official consultative status by the Economic and Social Council pursuant to Resolution 1996/31 (1996), which allowed NGOs with such status to participate in the deliberations of the Commission on Human Rights. The General Assembly extended the arrangements for consultative status to facilitate NGO participation

in the work of the Human Rights Council. Note, however, that no official consultative status is required to submit information in the UPR process. Neither is such status necessary in order to submit a petition or information under the Council's confidential complaint procedure or the special procedures, discussed below.

4. In its previous two UPR cycles the United States similarly reported on its performance in relation to economic and social rights. Is the United States conceding that it is obligated to such rights? Or is it simply reporting on policy? In the context of the UPR—which is about monitoring human rights commitments—can the distinction be maintained between obligation and policy? The United States is not a party to the International Covenant on Economic, Social, and Cultural Rights. The UPR, however, is framed not just by the treaties to which the state under review is a party but also by its stated human rights commitments otherwise and by the Universal Declaration on Human Rights, which affirms, among others, the rights to work, social security, an adequate standard of living, health, education, and culture. Might the United States be contributing to or acceding to a customary international law stature for these rights? Is any such inference blunted by paragraph 5 of the US report on its responses to recommendations, above? Paragraph 5 states: "These responses should not be construed to suggest that the U.S. necessarily regards each of the matters addressed as subject to U.S. international human rights obligations."

### B.   Country-Specific Debates and Resolutions

In the first decades of the Commission on Human Rights, diplomatic protocol and widespread resistance to discussing human rights in any but the most general terms made it difficult to raise the human rights situations within specific countries, let alone adopt resolutions condemning human rights violations or even expressing concern. While individual countries were occasionally criticized, it was not until 1967 that the Economic and Social Council welcomed the decision of the Commission on Human Rights to place on its annual agenda an item titled "Question of the violation of human rights and fundamental freedoms, including policies of racial discrimination and segregation and of apartheid, *in all countries*, with particular reference to colonial and other dependent countries and territories," E.S.C. Res. 1235 (XLII) (1967) (emphasis added). The same resolution empowered the Commission and its expert advisory body, the Sub-Commission on Prevention of Discrimination and Protection of Minorities (later renamed the Sub-Commission on the Promotion and Protection of Human Rights), "to examine information relevant to gross violations of human rights and fundamental freedoms;" where appropriate, to "make a thorough study of situations which reveal a consistent pattern of violations of human rights;" and to report and make recommendations to the Economic and Social Council. Id.

Direct criticism of countries became the norm under this agenda item, and the goal of many NGOs (and governments) became the adoption of a resolution critical of (or at least expressing concern about) a specific state or situation. Although such resolutions only rarely were couched in strong language, states fought vigorously to avoid being the subject of a critical Commission resolution. These often-heated debates led to allegations of selectivity and politicization and, eventually, contributed to the reform process that resulted in replacement of the Commission by the Human Rights Council.

Specific states and situations continue to be singled out during the Council's debates under various agenda items, and "human rights situations that require the Council's attention" continue to figure on the Council's agenda. However, the principles that guide the Council's program of work include universality, impartiality, non-selectiveness, constructive dialogue, and cooperation (H.R.C. Res. 5/1, Sec. V), and there is a clear preference among a majority of Council members to avoid the highly politicized debate over country-specific resolutions that characterized the Commission. States are asked "to secure the broadest possible support" for country-specific resolutions, preferably at least 15 members. Id., para. 112(d). The one exception to this reluctance to single out specific countries for formal attention is repeated attention to the situation of the Palestinian territories under Israeli control, which is deemed appropriate by a consistent Council majority but, for others, is indicative of vestiges of the selectiveness of the past. See, e.g., Israeli settlements in the Occupied Palestinian Territories, including East Jerusalem, H.RC. Res. 49/29 (2022).

Special sessions of the Council to address country situations or particular issues may be called at the request of two-thirds of its membership, a possibility not available to the former Commission on Human Rights. These sessions normally last only two days, and the agenda (and often a concluding resolution) are determined before the meeting. However, they do provide a politically significant opportunity to bring specific situations to the attention of the press and the public. By the end of 2021, 31 special sessions had been convened and covered a wide range of countries and situations. Six of the first 12 sessions concerned Israel, Lebanon, and/or the Israeli-occupied Palestinian territories, and five sessions since 2011 have considered the conflict in Syria. In addition, special sessions have examined the human rights situations in South Sudan, Burundi, Central African Republic, Libya, Ivory Coast, Sri Lanka, Democratic Republic of the Congo, Myanmar, Darfur, and Afghanistan. Two sessions have dealt with abuses committed by non-state actors, Boko Haram and the Islamic State/ISIL/ISIS, and sessions in 2008 and 2009 considered, respectively, the impact on the right to food of the worsening world food crisis and the impact on human rights of the global economic and financial crisis that began in 2008.

Since 2011, the Human Rights Council has created commissions of inquiry or fact-finding missions with respect to, among others, Syria, the 2014 conflict in Gaza, Sri Lanka, Eritrea, Libya, Democratic Republic of Korea, Burundi, South Sudan, Venezuela, Mali, the 2018 protests in the Occupied Territory, and the Russian invasion of Ukraine. These missions frequently focus on violations of international humanitarian law and individual accountability for international crimes (see generally the discussion in Chapter 5 at pages 311-354), although they address violations of human rights law as well. See generally Office of the High Commissioner for Human Rights, *Commissions of Inquiry and Fact-Finding Missions on International Human Rights and Humanitarian Law: Guidance and Practice* (2015), https://reliefweb.int/report/world/commissions-inquiry-and-fact-finding-missions -international-human-rights-and.

## C.   *The Confidential Complaint Procedure*

Today it may not seem remarkable that individuals and groups have a number of avenues within the United Nations system to lodge complaints of human rights abuse and have those complaints acted upon in one way or another. But it was not always so. Despite the fact that the United Nations received thousands of complaints from individuals alleging human rights violations throughout the world for over a decade after 1945, no UN organ would consider such petitions (except in the context of trust and non-self-governing territories). During its early years, the UN Commission on Human Rights, the predecessor to the Human Rights Council, focused on developing human rights standards, beginning with its drafting of the Universal Declaration on Human Rights. It was only in 1959 that the Commission was authorized to review summaries of communications received by the UN Secretary-General about human rights violations, and even then with the caveat that the Commission had no power to take any action in regard to any complaint concerning human rights. See E.S.C. Res. 728F (XXVIII) (1959).

A breakthrough came in 1970, when the Economic and Social Council adopted Resolution 1503 (XLVIII) (1970), which authorized the Commission and Sub-Commission to examine, in closed sessions, communications from individuals and other sources concerning "situations which appear to reveal a consistent pattern of gross and reliably attested violations of human rights." Together these resolutions broke the logjam at the United Nations that had until that time prevented it from discussing specific human rights violations except for those occurring in colonial territories, southern Africa, and (after 1967) the Israeli-occupied territories in the Middle East. The UN was now in the business (or so it might seem) of at least discussing violations of human rights worldwide. Moreover, the UN was now able to act — even if only in confidential sessions — on human rights complaints brought by individuals. Despite its confidential nature, the procedure under Resolution 1503 was an innovation that challenged the historical reluctance to subject states to international scrutiny for alleged human rights violations in specific cases, especially on the basis of petitions by individuals and other non-state sources.

When the Human Rights Council replaced the Commission in 2006, the "1503 procedure" was retained with some modifications, and today it is known simply as the "complaint procedure." The initial institution-building resolution of the Human Rights Council, HRC Res. 5/1 (2007), established the following criteria of admissibility for a complaint under this complaint procedure.

> 87. A communication related to a violation of human rights and fundamental freedoms, for the purpose of this procedure, shall be admissible, provided that:
>
> (*a*) It is not manifestly politically motivated and its object is consistent with the Charter of the United Nations, the Universal Declaration of Human Rights and other applicable instruments in the field of human rights law;
>
> (*b*) It gives a factual description of the alleged violations, including the rights which are alleged to be violated;
>
> (*c*) Its language is not abusive. However, such a communication may be considered if it meets the other criteria for admissibility after deletion of the abusive language;

(*d*) It is submitted by a person or a group of persons claiming to be the victims of violations of human rights and fundamental freedoms, or by any person or group of persons, including non-governmental organizations, acting in good faith . . .;

(*e*) It is not exclusively based on reports disseminated by mass media;

(*f*) It does not refer to a case that appears to reveal a consistent pattern of gross and reliably attested violations of human rights already being dealt with by a special procedure, a treaty body or other United Nations or similar regional complaints procedure in the field of human rights;

(*g*) Domestic remedies have been exhausted, unless it appears that such remedies would be ineffective or unreasonably prolonged.

––––––––––––

The track record of the Council's complaint procedure has been mixed, at best, and many activists place little faith in the procedure's ability to encourage change. In significant part because of its confidential nature, an assessment of its effectiveness is elusive. As of May 2022, the Human Rights Council's web page identified the following as having been considered by the full Council under its complaint procedure since 2006: situations in Kyrgyzstan, Iran, Uzbekistan, Turkmenistan, Maldives, Democratic Republic of the Congo, Guinea, Tajikistan, Iraq, Eritrea, and Cameroon. In 2006 and 2012, respectively, the Council decided to consider the situations in Kyrgyzstan and Eritrea in public rather than under the confidential procedure; Eritrea was subsequently the subject of a Human Rights Council commission of inquiry. In all of the other situations mentioned above, the Council's examination was discontinued (sometimes after having been kept under review for two or three years), sometimes with a recommendation that OHCHR provide capacity-building or technical assistance to the country concerned, but usually without any public comment.

Illustrating use of one of the options mentioned in para. 109 of HRC Res. 5/1, *supra*, the Commission on Human Rights — the Human Rights Council's predecessor — in 2002 appointed an independent expert to investigate and report back on the situation in Liberia. In a rare lifting of the shroud of confidentiality under which the 1503 procedure operated, the Commission decided to make public the report of the independent expert "so as to encourage assistance to the Government and the people of Liberia in restoring full respect for human rights and fundamental freedoms." Note by the Secretariate, UN Doc. E/CN.4/2004/8 (2003). The independent expert was appointed under the Commission's system of special procedures discussed below. See *Report of the Independent Expert of the Commission on Human Rights on the Situation of Human Rights in Liberia Submitted Under the 1503 Procedure*, UN Doc. E/CN.4/2004/8 (2003).

## Comments and Questions

1. One of the requirements of the confidential complaint procedure is that the petitioner must show a "consistent pattern of gross and reliably attested violations of human rights." What is a non-gross violation? Is there a consistent pattern

if the kind of violations varies over time? Can the procedure deal effectively with even gross violations that are not of a continuing nature, such as the poison gas attacks on Kurds in Iraq in the late 1980s or the massacre of demonstrators in Beijing's Tiananmen Square in 1989? Would the denial of indigenous land rights, such as that discussed in Chapter 3, qualify as a gross violation?

2.  The Commission eventually decided to make public the names of states being examined under the 1503 procedure. Under the Council's current practice, states are publicly identified in cases that reach the full Council, but public discussion of a country subsequent to consideration under the complaint procedure, such as that which occurred in connection with Liberia and Eritrea, has been rare. Given its confidential nature, in which contexts might the procedure be most useful in addressing violations of human rights? How does confidentiality assist or hinder in the promotion of solutions to violations? Under what circumstances is the Human Rights Council justified in deciding to make public its deliberations on a situation being examined under the procedure?

3.  Mere public disclosure of the states being considered under the confidential complaint procedure can itself serve to marshal world public opinion against them, which, in the case of Greece in the aftermath of the 1967 coup d'état, helped produce an amnesty for political prisoners literally on the eve of the Commission's working group meetings at which the communication against Greece was considered. A later communication concerning Brunei, initially ignored by the government, led directly to the release of a number of individuals who had been kept in detention beyond their sentences. Quiet diplomacy may, in some instances, be more effective than public condemnation in encouraging states to reform. For example, a communication filed against Japan in the 1980s alleged widespread official discrimination against members of the Korean minority in Japan and supplied valuable international support for domestic Japanese efforts to remedy the situation. It was deliberately filed under a confidential procedure, in the belief that the Japanese government would respond more positively to quiet pressure rather than public confrontation. Despite the confidentiality of the procedure, states continue to vigorously oppose any attempt to discuss them in the context of allegations of "a consistent pattern of gross violations."

## D.   The "Special Procedures"

Use of individual experts (denominated as "special rapporteurs" or "independent experts") to prepare reports on particular countries or human rights issues is another example of necessity (or at least desirability) being the mother of invention. While the former Commission on Human Rights became more willing and able to address specific human rights problems beginning in the late 1970s, there was still resistance to focusing publicly on particular countries (with the exception of apartheid-era South Africa and the Israeli-occupied territories). When the practice of enforced disappearances arose in the late 1970s in Argentina (see the discussion in Chapter 8), it was politically impossible to convince the Commission to investigate Argentina per se. A number of NGOs (prominent among them Amnesty International) and sympathetic governments thus decided to highlight the phenomenon of disappearances itself, as a new and pernicious form of human rights violation. The result was the creation by the Commission in 1980 of a five-person Working Group on Enforced or Involuntary Disappearances. See Comm'n Hum. Rts. Res. 20 (XXXVI) (1980).

This "thematic" body was the first in what has become an array of individual experts (and a few working groups) that came to be known collectively in UN parlance as "special procedures." The Commission eventually created a total of 28 thematic special procedures covering a wide range of topics. The early focus was on personal security (e.g., torture, arbitrary detention), but that was soon expanded to other civil or political rights (e.g., free expression, freedom of religion, the independence of judges and lawyers) and, by the late 1990s, to economic, social, and cultural rights (e.g., the rights to education, food, and housing).

When the Human Rights Council replaced the Commission in 2006, it was instructed to "review and, where necessary, improve and rationalize" all of the special procedures (G.A. Res. 60/251, para. 6); in fact, all of the thematic procedures were continued and many new ones were created, while country-specific mandates on Liberia, Cuba, and Belarus were discontinued without formal debate. As of May 2022, there were 13 country-specific mandates: on Myanmar (mandate created in 1992), the Palestinian Occupied Territories (1993), Somalia (1993), Cambodia (1993), Democratic People's Republic of Korea (2004), Iran (2011), Syria (2011), Belarus (2012), Eritrea (2012), Central African Republic (2013), Mali (2013), Afghanistan (2021), and Burundi (2021).

In addition, there were 45 thematic experts or working groups (none has ever been discontinued), whose respective mandates deal with enforced disappearances (1980), extrajudicial executions (1982), torture (1985), freedom of religion (1986), the sale of children and child prostitution and pornography (1990), arbitrary detention (1991), racism and xenophobia (1993), freedom of expression (1993), violence against women (1994), independence of lawyers and judges (1994), toxic and dangerous products and wastes (1995), children and armed conflict (1997), poverty (1998), education (1998), migrants (1999), housing (2000) human rights defenders (2000), economic reform policies and foreign debt (2000), indigenous peoples (2001), food (2002), persons of African descent (2002), physical and mental health (2002), people of African descent (2002), internally displaced persons (2004), human trafficking (2004), mercenaries (2005), minorities (2005), international solidarity (2005), protection of human rights while countering terrorism (2005), contemporary forms of slavery (2007), water and sanitation (2008), cultural rights (2009), discrimination against women and girls (2010); freedom of assembly and association (2020), human rights and business (2011); human rights and the environment (2011), truth, justice, and reparation (2011), equitable international order (2011), older person (2013), persons with disabilities (2014), unilateral coercive measures (2014), the rights of persons with albinism (2015), the right to privacy (2015), the right to development (2016), and sexual orientation and gender identity (2016), persons with leprosy and their families (2017), and climate change (2021). A current list of special procedures may be found on the OHCHR website, http://www.ohchr.org/EN/HRBodies/SP/Pages/Welcomepage.aspx.

The mandates of the special procedures vary (beyond the differences in the assigned countries or themes), in accordance with the specific resolutions of the Council reauthorizing or establishing them. Nonetheless, certain common features in the mandates and the corresponding work methods exist. Greater consistency in the special procedures has been encouraged by a Code of Conduct adopted by the Human Rights Council by its Resolution 5/2 (2006), which establishes rules that govern the work methods and behavior of all of them. There is also a uniform method and set of criteria for selection of mandate holders, which was created as part of the Council's institution-building package and which was further refined by the *Outcome of the review of the work and functioning of the United Nations Human Rights Council*, H.R.C. Res. 16/21, Annex, para 22. The Office of the High Commissioner for Human Rights (OHCHR), which provides support to the various UN human rights mechanisms, tends not to differentiate among the special procedures and promotes fairly uniform practices, and the special procedures mandate holders themselves have gravitated toward common work methods.

The following extract provides further details about the special procedures and reflects the commonalities of their mandates and work methods. In addition, the OHCHR has prepared a number of "fact sheets" on many of the procedures, which deal primarily with the substantive content of the rights concerned (see http://www.ohchr.org/EN/HRBodies/SP/Pages/Publications.aspx), and an OHCHR webpage provides instructions as to how a communication may be submitted to the procedures (see https://spsubmission.ohchr.org/).

## Manual of Operations of the Special Procedures of the Human Rights Council

(2008) (footnotes omitted), http://www.ohchr.org/EN/HRBodies/SP/Pages/Introduction.aspx

### I. Role and Functions of Special Procedures

#### A. Definition and Scope of Special Procedures

1. The term Special Procedures has been developed . . . to describe a diverse range of procedures established to promote and to protect human rights and to prevent violations in relation to specific themes or issues, or to examine the situation in specific countries. While the specific mandates and methods of work of the various Special Procedures differ, there are many commonalities in the ways in which they work . . . .

#### B. Main Characteristics of Special Procedures

4. Thematic Special Procedures are mandated by the HRC [Human Rights Council] to investigate the situation of human rights in all parts of the world, irrespective of whether a particular government is a party to any of the relevant human rights treaties. This requires them to take the measures necessary to monitor and respond quickly to allegations of human rights violations against individuals or groups, either globally or in a specific country or territory, and to report on their activities. In the case of country mandates, mandate-holders are called upon to take full account of all human rights (civil, cultural, economic, political and social) unless directed otherwise. In carrying out their activities, mandate holders are accountable to the Council.

The principal functions of Special Procedures include to:

— *analyze* the relevant thematic issue or country situation, including undertaking on-site missions;

— *advise* on the measures which should be taken by the Government(s) concerned and other relevant actors;

— *alert* United Nations organs and agencies, in particular, the HRC, and the international community in general to the need to address specific situations and issues. In this regard they have a role in providing "early warning" and encouraging preventive measures;

— *advocate* on behalf of the victims of violations through measures such as requesting urgent action by relevant States and calling upon Governments to respond to specific allegations of human rights violations and provide redress;

— *activate* and mobilize the international and national communities, and the HRC to address particular human rights issues and to encourage cooperation among Governments, civil society and inter-governmental organizations.

— *Follow-up to recommendations*

. . .

C. ESTABLISHMENT OF MANDATES

1. Terminology and Duration of Mandates

6. The term "Special Procedures" includes individuals variously designated as "Special Rapporteur", or "Independent Expert", Working Groups usually composed of five independent experts, "Special Representative of the Secretary-General" and "Representative of the Secretary-General".

7. Mandate-holder's tenure in a given function, whether a thematic or country mandate, will be no longer than six years (two terms of three years for thematic mandate-holders) . . . .

2. Appointment of Mandate-Holders

8. . . . On the basis of the recommendations of the Consultative Group and following broad consultations, in particular through the regional coordinators, the President of the Council will identify an appropriate candidate for each vacancy. The President will present to member States and observers a list of candidates to be proposed at least two weeks prior to the beginning of the session in which the Council will consider the appointments. The appointment of the special procedures mandate-holders will be completed upon the subsequent approval of the Council.

9. The individual mandate-holders are selected on the basis of their expertise, experience, independence, impartiality, integrity and objectivity. The requisite independence and impartiality are not compatible with the appointment of individuals currently holding decision-making positions within the executive or legislative branches of their Governments or in any other organization or entity which may give rise to a conflict of interest with the responsibilities inherent to the mandate . . . .

II. Methods of Work

. . .

B. Communications

1. Definition and Purpose

28. Most Special Procedures provide for the relevant mandate-holders to receive information from different sources and to act on credible information by sending a communication to the relevant Government(s). Such communications are sent through diplomatic channels, unless agreed otherwise between individual Governments and the Office of the High Commissioner for Human Rights, in relation to any actual or anticipated human rights violations which fall within the scope of their mandate.

29. Communications may deal with cases concerning individuals, groups or communities, with general trends and patterns of human rights violations in a particular country or more generally, or with the content of existing or draft legislation considered to be a matter of concern. Communications related to adopted or draft legislation may be formulated in various ways, as required by the specificities of each mandate.

30. Communications do not imply any kind of value judgment on the part of the Special Procedure concerned and are thus not per se accusatory. They are not intended as a substitute for judicial or other proceedings at the national level. Their main purpose is to obtain clarification in response to allegations of violations and to promote measures designed to protect human rights . . . .

36. In light of information received in response from the Government concerned, or of further information from sources, the mandate-holder will determine how best to proceed. This might include the initiation of further inquiries, the elaboration of recommendations or observations to be published in the relevant report, or other appropriate steps designed to achieve the objectives of the mandate.

37. The text of all communications sent and responses received thereon is confidential until such time as they are published in relevant reports of mandate-holders or mandate-holders determine that the specific circumstances require action to be taken before that time . . . .

2. Criteria for Taking Action

38. Information submitted to the Special Procedures alleging violations should be in written, printed or electronic form and include full details of the sender's identity and address, and full details of the relevant incident or situation. Information may be sent by a person or a group of persons claiming to have suffered a human rights violation. NGOs and other groups or individuals claiming to have direct or reliable knowledge of human rights violations, substantiated by clear information, may also submit information so long as they are acting in good faith in accordance with the principles of human rights and the provisions of the UN Charter, free from politically motivated stands. Anonymous communications are not considered. Communications may not be exclusively based on reports disseminated by mass media . . . .

40. A decision to take action on a case or situation rests in the discretion of the mandate-holder. That discretion should be exercised in light of the mandate entrusted to him or her as well as the criteria laid out in the Code of Conduct. The criteria will generally relate to: the reliability of the source and the credibility of information received; the details provided; and the scope of the mandate . . . .

42. Unlike the requirements of communication procedures established under human rights treaties, communications may be sent by the mandate holder even if local remedies in the country concerned have not been exhausted. The Special Procedures are not quasi-judicial mechanisms. Rather, they are premised upon the need for rapid action, designed to protect victims and potential victims, and do not preclude in any way the taking of appropriate judicial measures at the national level . . . .

### 5. Public and Press Statements

49. In appropriate situations, including those of grave concern or in which a Government has repeatedly failed to provide a substantive response to communications, a Special Procedure mandate-holder may issue a press statement, other public statement or hold a press conference, either individually or jointly with other mandate-holders . . . .

### C. COUNTRY VISITS

### 1. Definition and Purpose

52. Country visits are an essential means to obtain direct and first-hand information on human rights violations. They allow for direct observation of the human rights situation and facilitate an intensive dialogue with all relevant state authorities, including those in the executive, legislative and judicial branches. They also allow for contact with and information gathering from victims, relatives of victims, witnesses, national human rights institutions, international and local NGOs and other members of civil society, the academic community, and officials of international agencies present in the country concerned.

53. Country visits generally last between one and two weeks but can be shorter or longer if the circumstances so require. The visit occurs at the invitation of a State. Its purpose is to assess the actual human rights situation in the country concerned, including an examination of the relevant institutional, legal, judicial, and administrative aspects and to make recommendations thereon in relation to issues that arise under the relevant mandate.

54. Country visits by mandate-holders provide an opportunity to enhance awareness at the country, regional and international levels of the specific problems under consideration. This is done, *inter alia*, through meetings, briefings, press coverage of the visit and dissemination of the report.

### 2. Invitations and Requests for Visits

55. A Government may take the initiative to invite a mandate-holder to visit the country. Alternatively a mandate-holder may solicit an invitation by communicating with the Government concerned, by discussions with diplomats of the country concerned . . .

D. OTHER ACTIVITIES

1. Thematic Studies

75. In addition to any other reports, mandate-holders may opt to devote a separate report to a particular topic of relevance to the mandate. Such studies may be initiated by the mandate-holder or undertaken pursuant to a specific request by relevant bodies. The practical arrangements in relation to the drafting and publication of these reports will be determined in consultation with OHCHR.

76. Such studies should be thoroughly researched and where appropriate take account of replies to questionnaires or other requests for information transmitted to governments, United Nations agencies, NGOs, treaty bodies, regional organizations, other experts, or partners . . . .

F. REPORTING ON ACTIVITIES AND INTERACTION WITH GOVERNMENTS

84. Mandate-holders report on their activities on a regular basis to the relevant United Nations bodies, and particularly the HRC and the GA. With regard to the recommendations contained in their reports, mandate holders should ensure that their recommendations do not exceed their mandate or the mandate of the HRC. Recommendations may also serve to bring to the attention of the Council any suggestions of the mandate holder which will enhance his or her capacity to fulfill the mandate. . . .

86. An inter-active dialogue constitutes an important element in the presentation of reports by mandate-holders. Mandate holders present their reports to the HRC, and in some cases to the GA, and States are given the opportunity to respond to the contents of the reports and to pose questions to the mandate holders. Such dialogues are considered to be an integral part of cooperation between mandate holders and States.

87. Mandate-holders also maintain contact with relevant Governments through meetings and consultations in Geneva, New York, or elsewhere. Such meetings might focus on requests for visits, follow-up to visits, individual cases, or any other question related to the mandate. Such contacts are designed to facilitate smooth and fruitful cooperation between Governments and mandate-holders.

––––––––––––––

Within the broad outlines of the work methods described above, the independent experts and working groups employ different techniques. For example, the first of the special procedures mandates to be created, the Working Group on Enforced and Involuntary Disappearances, has developed well-defined procedures and criteria for screening, evaluating, and taking action on cases. See OHCHR, *Enforced or Involuntary Disappearances*, Fact Sheet No. 6/Rev.3 (2010). The same is true of the Working Group on Arbitrary Detention, which issues formal "opinions" on cases. See id., *The Working Group on Arbitrary Detention*, Fact Sheet No. 26 (n.d.). Both publications can be accessed via http://www.ohchr.org/EN/HRBodies/SP/Pages/Publications.aspx.

The treatment of complaints by other special procedures is typically less well defined and structured than those of the arbitrary detention and enforced disappearances working groups. The usual methodology under the "communications" procedure consists of: (1) making a discretionary decision to act (or not) on information received alleging a human rights violation or problem; (2) forwarding the information to the government concerned with a request for a response or a call for urgent action; and then (3) publishing the allegations, along with any response from the government in a consolidated annual communications report of all mandate holders. Increasingly, communications on cases are handled jointly by two or more mandate holders.

The following exchange concerning a situation in Tanzania illustrates the communications procedure. In accordance with protocol, the joint communication of February 9, 2022 was transmitted to the Ambassador who heads the Mission of United Republic of Tanzania to the UN Offices in Geneva.

## Joint Communication to Tanzania of Feb. 9, 2022 — Mandates of the Special Rapporteur on adequate housing as a component of the right to an adequate standard of living, and on the right to non-discrimination in this context; the Special Rapporteur in the field of cultural rights; the Special Rapporteur on the issue of human rights obligations relating to the enjoyment of a safe, clean, healthy and sustainable environment; the Special Rapporteur on the right to food; the Special Rapporteur on the rights of indigenous peoples; the Special Rapporteur on the human rights of internally displaced persons; the Special Rapporteur on extreme poverty and human rights and the Special Rapporteur on the human rights to safe drinking water and sanitation

*Communications report of special procedures*, UN Doc. A/HRC/C/50/3 (2022) (footnotes omitted) [original document available through link at https://spcomm reports.ohchr.org (last visited June 12, 2022)]

Excellency,

We have the honour to address you in our capacities as Special Rapporteur on adequate housing as a component of the right to an adequate standard of living, and on the right to non-discrimination in this context; Special Rapporteur in the field of cultural rights; Special Rapporteur on the issue of human rights obligations relating to the enjoyment of a safe, clean, healthy and sustainable environment; Special Rapporteur on the right to food; Special Rapporteur on the rights of indigenous peoples; Special Rapporteur on the human rights of internally displaced persons; Special Rapporteur on extreme poverty and human rights and Special Rapporteur on the human rights to safe drinking water and sanitation, pursuant to Human Rights Council resolutions 43/14, 46/9, 46/7, 32/8, 42/20, 41/15, 44/13 and 42/5.

In this connection, we would like to bring to the attention of your Excellency's Government information we have received concerning *plans for resettlement, forced evictions, home demolitions and additional restrictions which by 2027 are due to affect some 82,000 people, the vast majority being indigenous Maasai pastoralists whose traditional lands lie in the Ngorongoro Conservation Area. Such plans have allegedly not been consulted with the Maasai peoples in order to obtain their free, prior and informed consent. If pursued these plans could jeopardize their physical and cultural survival in the name of "nature conservation", ignoring the close relationship that the Maasai have traditionally had with their lands, territories, and resources and their stewardship role in protecting biodiversity. The plans also fail to address the root causes of the current threats to the healthy environment of these territories, notably touristic activity. . . .*

According to the information received:

Background

The Ngorongoro Conservation Area (NCA) is an area of 8,100 km2 [810,000 ha], bordering the Serengeti National Park, in Northern Tanzania and is home to indigenous Maasai pastoralists. The Maasai make up over 95% of the NCA's population, the rest being a small number of Datoga pastoralists and Hadzabe hunter-gatherers near Lake Eyasi as well as a small number of NCA employees and those employed in the tourism industry.

According to reports, when the proposal for the creation of the NCA was put forward in the 1950s, the Maasai were assured that they could continue inhabiting the NCA and were promised the development of better water resources as well as participation in the governance of the conservation area, among others, in exchange for leaving completely the region — Moru area — that is now part of the Serengeti National Park.

Over the years, the Maasai have been largely excluded from management positions in the Ngorongoro Conservation Area Authority (NCAA) and have been subjected to a series of subsequent evictions. These evictions have involved the burning of their *bomas* (a compound comprising the huts that house the Maasai and providing an enclosure for their cattle), the destruction of their livelihoods, food and water sources, the seizure of cattle and the forced displacement of tens of thousands from their lands, in the name of "preserving the ecosystems for tourism".

In 2010, the NCA was added to the UNESCO World Heritage Site List for its cultural values, after having already been listed in 1979 for its natural characteristics. Reportedly, for both designations, the indigenous communities in the NCA were not consulted and the decision resulted in a number of livelihood restrictions, including restrictions on crop cultivation and livestock raising.

In the recognition of the Outstanding Universal Value of the Ngorongoro Conservation Area and its inscription on the World Heritage List, it is stated that the primary management objectives are to (a) conserve the natural resources of the property, (b) protect the interests of the Maasai pastoralists, and (c) promote tourism. . . .

The Multiple Land Use Model review exercise, the resettlement plan and the threat to the Maasai's survival

In 2019, the UNESCO World Heritage Centre (WHC), the International Union for the Conservation of Nature (IUCN), and the International Council on Monuments and Sites (ICOMOS), in their capacity as official advisory bodies of the World Heritage Committee under the World Heritage Convention, visited the NCA and issued a joint mission report. In the report, they indicated that stringent measures were needed to control population growth in the NCA and its impact on the area. They requested the Government of Tanzania to complete a "multiple land-use model" (MLUM) review exercise and to share its results with the World Heritage Centre and its Advisory Bodies.

Following the recommendations included in the joint mission report, the Government developed a new MLUM and a related resettlement plan which would expand the size of the NCA from 8,100 km2 to 12,083 km2 by including areas from Loliondo Game Controlled Area (GCA)—already contested in the East African Court of Justice, and Lake Natron GCA. The new plan for the NCA envisages the division of the NCA into four management zones, namely a conservation core zone, a conservation sub- zone, a transition zone, and a settlement and development zone. According to reports, the proposed plan would restrict human settlement and development to an area equaling approximately 18 percent of the total area of the thus expanded NCA. The use of the core conservation area would be restricted to research and tourism development. Likewise, the conservation sub-zone will be mainly dedicated to research and tourism, while all settlement, grazing or cultivation activities will be prohibited. In the transition zone settlements and crop production are similarly prohibited, but seasonal grazing for livestock would be allowed. Allegedly, the new plan from the NCA would relegate the Maasai to areas without adequate water sources. Moreover, due to the planned expansion, the land available to the Maasai for pastoralism, settlements and farming will be further reduced, with devastating effects on their food security.

In order to implement the new NCA model, the Government developed the mentioned Resettlement Plan which sets out to relocate about 82,000 people by 2027. The Government considers that 40 percent of those living within the NCA are "immigrants," defined as "families, which were not present and those which were not resettled in NCA from Moru area in Serengeti National Park when the Conservation Area was established in 1959 and their descendants." According to the plan, 40,000 "immigrants" would be identified and moved back to their "place of origin" by the end of 2021. Reportedly, the full resettlement plan has not yet been made public and indigenous peoples have expressed their concern that, given the absence of documentation among pastoralist communities, it would be difficult for many people to prove their descent from the original inhabitants of the NCA—or the adjacent Moru area, with the risk that they will be forcibly relocated. The plan also envisages that 40,000 "destitute and very poor pastoralists" will be "interested to resettle out of NCA voluntarily to specified areas." . . .

According to the information received, the argument used to justify the MLUM and the resettlement plan, that is to say the impact of the growing population on the area, is unfounded and ignores the symbiotic relationship that the Maasai have developed over centuries with their territories. Their traditional knowledge has been recognized as having allowed biodiversity and a large mammal population to thrive. It is reported that the NCA hosts the highest density of mammalian predators in Africa including the lion population and endangered wildlife species such as the black rhino, wild dog, cheetah, and elephant. Nevertheless, according to reports, the approach followed by the Government as well as by the organizations which took part in the 2019 joint mission is to antagonize nature conservation and indigenous peoples' livelihoods, ignoring the root causes of the risks faced by the NCA, notably tourism. . . .

Current situation

On 16 April 2021, the Ngorongoro Conservation Area Authority (NCAA) issued eviction notices to 45 people and ordered more than 100 buildings to be destroyed on the ground that they lacked proper permits. The buildings included homes, public schools, religious centers, medical dispensaries and administrative offices. Reportedly, such buildings are not all built by community's members at their own initiative; the Government itself owns the public schools, dispensaries and police stations that have been listed for demolition. The occupants and owners of the buildings were given 30 days to comply with the orders. The NCAA also identified more than 150 'immigrants' within the NCA with a view to their future removal.

On 19 April 2021, representatives of NCA residents issued a statement asking the Government to halt the evictions and demolitions planned; investigate the human rights violations suffered by the Maasai; and create an independent and participatory commission to address the challenges of the NCA, among other requests.

On 20 April 2021, the NCAA suspended the relocation and demolition orders until further notice. Reportedly, the threat of relocation looms over the concerned communities, threatening the survival of the Maasai pastoralists who have stewarded the land and environment for generations and now risk losing access to them.

On 17 October 2021, the President of Tanzania delivered a public speech in which she indicated that people must be relocated from the NCA, which followed previous speeches with a similar message . . .

Without prejudging the accuracy of the information received, we wish to express our serious concern about plans for resettlement, forced evictions, home demolitions and additional restrictions to the livelihood of the residents of the Ngorongoro Conservation Area (NCA), which are expected to displace thousands of indigenous Maasai pastoralists from their traditional lands. We are also concerned that these plans have been developed without consulting the affected indigenous peoples, in violation of international human rights standards, including those related to the right to an adequate standard of living, including adequate food, housing, safe water and sanitation, and the right to take part in the definition, elaboration and implementation of policies and decisions that have an impact on the exercise of one's cultural rights.

We are deeply alarmed at the fact that, although the NCA is home to the indigenous Maasai and their active participation in all decision-making processes concerning the site is requested by the World Heritage Committee, they have reportedly not been involved in the elaboration of strategies for the sustainable management of the area including at the conservation level. We are also concerned that their free, prior and informed consent was not sought in connection with the plans mentioned above, which may have devastating consequences for their survival. . . . Our preoccupations extend to the lack of recognition of the Maasai's contributions to conservation and restoration of biodiversity on the territory, having substantial positive impacts on the right to a clean, healthy and sustainable environment. We also regret that your Excellency's Government fails to consider an approach to conservation that includes indigenous conservation skills and knowledge and to work collaboratively with indigenous peoples who have lived and protected the area for generations.

In connection with the above alleged facts and concerns, please refer to the *Annex on Reference to international human rights law*\* attached to this letter which cites international human rights instruments and standards relevant to these allegations.

As it is our responsibility, under the mandates provided to us by the Human Rights Council, to seek to clarify all cases brought to our attention, we would be grateful for your observations on the following matters:

1. Please provide any additional information and/or comment(s) you may have on the above-mentioned allegations.

2. Please provide information on the measures taken or envisaged by the Government to collaboratively work with the Maasai with a view to conserving the ecosystems within their traditional lands as well as indigenous livelihoods, skills and knowledge of conservation, which are all recognized as important features of natural and cultural World Heritage listing. Please indicate if, and to which extent, their involvement in conservation management and tourism activities in the NCA has been considered and undertaken, and how they share in the benefits of these developments.

3. Please provide information about how the MLUM balances the adverse impacts of tourism activities on the livelihoods of the traditional residents in the NCA. . . .

4. Please also provide details regarding the extent to which information about the proposed MLUM was provided to potentially affected indigenous communities, the opportunities provided for public participation in decision-making about it, and ways in which public feedback was reflected in decision-making.

5. Please provide information on the measures taken to confer legal security of tenure in the NCA, including information on the measures taken to demarcate

---

\* [The eight-page annex includes an extensive analysis of international human rights instruments and decisions of human rights bodies regarding rights to food, housing, culture, land, adequate standard of living, and indigenous peoples "special relationship" with their territories and ways of life. Among the human instruments featured are two human rights covenants, the Convention against racial discrimination, the Universal Declaration of Human Rights, the UN Declaration on the Rights of Indigenous Peoples, ILO (Employment and Occupation) Convention No. 111, and the African Union Convention for the Protection and Assistance of Internally Displaced Persons. —Eds.]

and allocate collective land rights to the Maasai, in consultation with them and in accordance with their customs, traditions, land tenure systems and evolving needs.

6. Please, provide information on the measures undertaken, legislative or otherwise, to protect the Maasai from forced evictions and arbitrary displacement, taking into consideration the fact that many persons and families may lack official documentation about the duration of their presence on the territory, and to ensure that any decision affecting their homes and lands, territories and resources is taken with their free, prior and informed consent and after agreement on just and fair compensation and, where possible, with the option of return. . . .

This communication and any response received from your Excellency's Government will be made public via the communications reporting website after 60 days. They will also subsequently be made available in the usual report to be presented to the Human Rights Council.

While awaiting a reply, we urge that all necessary interim measures be taken to halt the alleged violations and prevent their re-occurrence and in the event that the investigations support or suggest the allegations to be correct, to ensure the accountability of any person(s) responsible for the alleged violations.

We may publicly express our concerns in the near future as, in our view, the information upon which the press release will be based is sufficiently reliable to indicate a matter warranting immediate attention. We also believe that the wider public should be alerted to the potential implications of the above-mentioned allegations. If we do so, the press release will indicate that we have been in contact with your Excellency's Government's to clarify the issue/s in question.

———————

Via a note verbal dated April 8, 2022, the Permanent Mission of the United Republic of Tanzania to the United Nations Office in Geneva transmitted its response to the above joint communication. That response follows.

## Reply of Tanzania dated April 8, 2022 to Joint Communication of Feb. 9. 2022 — Joint Communication from the Special Rapporteur in the Field of Cultural Rights; The Special Rapporteur on the Issue of Human Rights Obligations Relating to the Enjoyment of a Safe, Clean, Healthy and Sustainable Environment; The Special Rapporteur On the Right to Food; The Special Rapporteur on the Rights of Indigenous Peoples; The Special Rapporteur on The Human Rights of Internally Displaced Persons; The Special Rapporteur on Extreme Poverty and Human Rights and The Special Rapporteur on the Human Rights to Safe Drinking Water and Sanitation

*Communications report of special procedures,* UN Doc. A/HRC/C/50/3 (2022) [original document available through link at https://spcommreports.ohchr.org (last visited June 12, 2022)]

The United Republic of Tanzania is in receipt of a Joint Communication sent by [the above special rapporteurs] dated 9 February 2022. The communication concerns allegations of human rights violations in the Ngorongoro Conservation Area

We would like to state at the outset that the United Republic of Tanzania is governed by rule of law, good governance and respect for human and peoples' rights. Therefore, there are no plans of forced evictions and demolition of homes of the inhabitants of the Ngorongoro Conservation Area as is being alleged.

### 1.0. BACKGROUND

The Ngorongoro was part of Serengeti National Park until 1959 when the two were separated into two different Protected Areas with different conservation status. The Ngorongoro Conservation Area (NCA) was established in 1959 as a multiple-land use area, where wildlife could co-exist with the semi-nomadic Maasai, who move from one place to another in search of water and pasture. The Maasai are a pastoral tribe that has managed to preserve its culture over hundreds of years, living in harmony with the wild animals. The NCA was therefore established as an experiment to maintain a balance between pastoralism, conservation, and tourism.

In order to ensure meaningful participation of the local communities in Ngorongoro, the government in 2000 established the Ngorongoro Pastoral Council (NPC) through the Government Notice No 234 published on 23/06/2000.

The NPC was established to ensure long-term success of the conservation area through the active involvement and participation of local communities in all aspects of the Ngorongoro Conservation Area management. The NPC has the following functions;

(i)  To oversee the actual needs of the pastoral communities living in NCA.

(ii)  It is an advisory body to the NCA's board of Directors on resident development and conservation matter of NCA.

(iii)  To ensure that other organs such as village governments and ward development committee are given opportunities to participate fully in providing their ideas on how to combat challenges facing the communities in NCA.

(iv)  To cooperate with other stakeholders mainly NCAA, donors, governmental and non-governmental organisations, the Ngorongoro District Council and other district authorities (neighbor district) in fulfilling its core activities.

(v)  To implement NPC activities and policies as approved by NCAA board of directors.

(vi)  To identify obstacles of resident's development and provide strategies for solving such problems by cooperating with other stakeholders.

Therefore, the concerns and views of the local communities and inhabitants of the NCA constitute Governments plans with regard to the development, traditional way of life, conservation and sustainability of the NCA.

### 2.0. CHANGING DYNAMICS

There have been concerns over increasing population, settlement, livestock and human activities that threaten the sustainability of the area listed by UNESCO as one of its World Heritage Site.

Initially, residents of the NCA who were estimated at 8,000 with 20 to 30 cows could live together with wildlife without any challenges. However, the population has rapidly increased to about 110,000 and the livestock has increased to 813,000. There is therefore need for sustainable conservation in the NCA.

### 3.0. RELOCATION PROPOSALS

The Government has indeed allocated land in Handeni district in Tanga Region where the Pastoralists will be relocated and provided with social services such as schools, hospitals and electricity.

The Government intends to construct 101 three-bedroom houses, with 336 plots for social services such as schools, health centers and water systems. Any relocation will be smooth and in compliance with the law of the land. People will be granted title deeds, houses as well as the land for grazing.

This re-allocation proposal has been tabled to residents of the NCA and is among the matters being discussed between the Government and the residents of the NCA.

### 4.0. THE PRINCIPLE OF PARTICIATION

As the United Republic of Tanzania is governed by good governance discussions on how to address situation in the NCA have involved the inhabitants of the NCA. They are being held in compliance with the principles of transparency and accountability.

The intention is for a win-win situation in order to ensure pastoral rights and ways of life are respected and environmental degradation to the Ngorongoro through conservation efforts are mitigated. This is the balance that the Government is striving to maintain through open and public discussion as is happening in the country.

The matter has been assigned the highest importance and is being steered by the Prime Minister of the United Republic of Tanzania and the Parliament has issued instructions for the Government to collect opinions and proposals from stakeholders in order to amicably reach a solution to the ongoing overpopulation and conservation challenges in the Ngorongoro Conservation Area.

The Government has also been allaying fears of forceful re-locations as peace and stability have to be maintained. Meetings and discussions are ongoing with community leaders and inhabitants of the NCA with local and high level Government delegations including the Prime Minister of the United Republic of Tanzania. These are being held in a transparent manner including all members of the local communities.

We believe that as the inhabitants of the NCA themselves are actively participating in the ongoing dialogue and are part of the process of coming up with solutions, there will be positive outcomes.

### 6.0. CONCLUSION

The United Republic of Tanzania is a country where human dignity and other human rights are respected and cherished.

We therefore refute allegations of arbitrary arrests and detention of journalists. Indeed, the NCA is being covered widely by local and international media as there is media pluralism in Tanzania. This is in compliance with the right to free-dom of expression and the right to information. In this regard, various views on how to address the NCA are being deliberated publicly by the people and experts in all media forums. However, it is important not to take the various opinions as the Government's position.

Kindly note that the deliberations over the NCA are still at preliminary stage with ongoing consultations with the inhabitants of the NCA in order to develop feasible and viable solutions. We reiterate that the inhabitants of the Ngorongoro Conservation Area are still being consulted as proposals are being developed with them and final and conclusive decisions are yet to be made as discussions are ongo-ing. Therefore, there have been no forceful evictions or any action taken. The mat-ter is still being discussed with the inhabitants of the NCA in consideration of the principle of participation.

Peaceful and constructive engagement with the inhabitants of the NCA is key in resolving the matter and this is the approach of the Government.

The Government will continue to ensure that the welfare of the inhabitants of the NCA is given top priority in Government activities and plans.

The United Republic of Tanzania remains allied to the spirit and mandate of the Human Rights Council and its Special Procedures Mechanisms.

---

Apart from addressing human rights problems on a case-by-case basis through written communications, special procedures function in a variety of ways to address issues within their respective mandates. Principal among their activi-ties are country visits and thematic studies. A country visit by a special procedures mandate holder typically involves engaging with high-level government officials, NGOs, and others to address human rights issues on a systemic level and to identify concerns as well as areas of improvement. The report that results from a visit usu-ally includes recommendations that address a wide range of issues that fall within the scope of the relevant mandate. See, e.g., *Visit to the United States of America — Report of the Special Rapporteur on minority issues, Fernande de Verennes*, UN Doc. A/HRC/49/48/Add.1 (2022); *Visit to Maldives — Report of the Special Rapporteur on torture and other cruel, inhuman or degrading treatment or punishment, Nils Melzer*, UN Doc. A/HRC/46/Add.1 (2020). Mandate holders often follow up on their rec-ommendations by written communications and sometimes do so through subse-quent visits.

Special procedures mandate holders also conduct thematic studies that, instead of focusing on country situations or specific cases, examine human issues of broad concern within the subjects of their respective mandates. These studies are often conducted in association with seminars or stakeholder consultations, and the resulting analyses and conclusions are typically included in the annual reports to the Human Rights Council and General Assembly. It is common for these the-matic studies to contribute to clarifying or building on international human rights standards relevant to specific issues. Some of the most innovative work of the UN human rights system is done through the thematic studies of special procedures mandate holders, and in some of the critical areas of human rights work, as illus-trated by the following extract.

## Report of the Independent Expert on protection against violence and discrimination based on sexual orientation and gender identity (Vitit Muntarbhorn)

UN Doc. A/HRC/35/36 (2017) (footnotes omitted)

. . .

17. The entry point for the mandate holder is action against violence and discrimination. This is based on existing international human rights law and its interrelationship with sexual orientation and gender identity; there is no advocacy of new rights for particular groups.

18. Also important is the context-specific nature of each country and situation. The situation is not necessarily the same for lesbian, gay, bisexual and transgender (and intersex) persons across the board, even though human rights are inherent to all persons without distinction: the situation is not homogeneous but heterogeneous. For instance, in one country, same-sex relationships are criminalized, with the threat of the death penalty. This is primarily targeted at homosexuals. However, in that same country, those who self-identify as transgender are assisted and recognized by the State (to undergo reassignment surgery). The lack of awareness or understanding or knowledge, and the biases and stereotypes, vary between countries and within each country—depending on diverse factors such as geography (urban vs. rural), demography (e.g. different educational and economic levels), and cultural affinity.

19. The reflections that follow are an initial response regarding the key elements under the mandate.

### A.  IMPLEMENTATION OF INTERNATIONAL INSTRUMENTS, WITH IDENTIFICATION OF GOOD PRACTICES AND GAPS

20. An array of international human rights instruments help to entrench calls for non-violence and the principle of non-discrimination in international law, with due respect for sexual orientation and gender identity. The genesis of human rights protection after the Second World War was the Universal Declaration of Human Rights, of 1948. There are now nine core international human rights treaties, complemented by various protocols. All of them interrelate with the issue of sexual orientation and gender identity, to a lesser or greater extent. For instance, the right to be free from discrimination is propounded in article 2 of the Universal Declaration of Human Rights and in all human rights treaties. Article 2 of the International Covenant on Civil and Political Rights stipulates:

> Each State Party to the present Covenant undertakes to respect and to ensure to all individuals within its territory and subject to its jurisdiction the rights recognized in the present Covenant, without distinction of any kind, such as race, colour, sex, language, religion, political or other opinion, national or social origin, property, birth or other status.

21. Other provisions (e.g. article 7 of the Universal Declaration of Human Rights and article 26 of the International Covenant on Civil and Political Rights) reaffirm the right to equality before the law and equal protection of the law without discrimination. The stricture against discrimination was deliberated upon by

the Human Rights Committee in regard to a seminal case, *Toonen v. Australia*, that concerned the presence of a local law that prohibited same-sex relations. The Committee found that the local law in question violated article 17 of the Covenant in regard to the right to privacy, and that the reference to "sex" in article 2 (1) (as well as in art. 26) covered sexual orientation. . . .

24. As evidenced by the wide range of international human rights treaties that are in force, international human rights bodies and procedures — ranging from the human rights treaty bodies, with their general comments and recommendations, to the universal periodic review, to the special procedures' coverage of sexual orientation and gender identity-related violations, to resolutions and studies — the international human rights system has been strengthening the promotion and protection of human rights without distinction. The protection of persons based on their sexual orientation and gender identity, and the mandate of the Independent Expert, are based on international law, complemented and supplemented by State practice.

25. Action against violence and discrimination has been espoused more recently in the 17 globally agreed Sustainable Development Goals, to which all countries are committed, with a framework of 2015-2030 for operationalization. Goal 16, which covers inclusive societies and access to justice, aims to bring about substantial reductions of violence and to promote anti-discrimination measures, on the basis of leaving no one behind. An all-inclusive approach invites effective coverage of all persons whatever their sexual orientation or gender identity.

26. The initiatives of regional organizations have led to constructive developments. The European human rights system has evolved greatly and proactively on the issue of sexual orientation and gender identity. . . . There have been a variety of cases before the European Court of Human Rights, covering a wide expanse of Europe and interlinking geographically with the furthest reaches of Asia, with much innovative thinking. In parallel to this, the European Union, with its Charter of Fundamental Rights, has strengthened measures against violence and discrimination on the basis of sexual orientation and gender identity, including via the collection and collation of data through the European Union Agency for Fundamental Rights to inform policymaking and action.

27. The inter-American system has offered many contributions to action against violence and discrimination. In addition to its important range of human rights-related declarations and conventions and its regional human rights court and commission, it has appointed a regional rapporteur specifically to cover the issue of lesbian, gay, bisexual, transgender and intersex persons. The General Assembly of the Organization of American States recently approved two treaties which refer to sexual orientation and gender identity directly as grounds on which discrimination must be prohibited: namely the Inter-American Convention Against All Forms of Discrimination and Intolerance and the Inter-American Convention on Protecting the Human Rights of Older Persons.

28. Complementing the measures outlined above, resolution 275 of the African Commission on Human and Peoples' Rights, on protection against violence and other human rights violations against persons on the basis of their real or imputed sexual orientation or gender identity, of 2014, resonates with the following message for the African region and beyond:

Strongly urges States to end all acts of violence and abuse, whether committed by State or non-State actors, including by enacting and effectively applying appropriate laws prohibiting and punishing all forms of violence including those targeting persons on the basis of their imputed or real sexual orientation or gender identities, ensuring proper investigation and diligent prosecution of perpetrators, and establishing judicial procedures responsive to the needs of victims.

. . .

30. Other regional human rights instruments offer opportunities for advocacy against violence and discrimination. For instance, it is stated in the Arab Charter on Human Rights, of 2004, in its article 3, that:

Each State party to the present Charter undertakes to ensure to all individuals subject to its jurisdiction the right to enjoy the rights and freedoms set forth herein, without distinction on grounds of race, colour, sex, language, religious belief, opinion, thought, national or social origin, wealth, birth or physical or mental disability.

31. The ASEAN Human Rights Declaration, of 2012, stipulates that:

Every person is entitled to the rights and freedoms set forth herein, without distinction of any kind, such as race, gender, age, language, religion, political or other opinion, national or social origin, economic status, birth, disability or other status.

32. A sample of recent constructive practices can be cited. A number of countries on every continent have seen reforms of antiquated and obstructive laws and policies, even though the progress is not always universal. Many South Asian countries and countries in other regions uphold the rights of transgender people, even where they have difficulty in accepting the rights of gays, lesbians and bisexuals. Same-sex couples are now allowed to marry officially in a number of countries, such as Canada, the United States of America, and a range of countries in Europe and Latin America. In 2016, a top court in Belize declared an old law, which had prohibited same-sex relations, to be unconstitutional. Seychelles reformed its law similarly on this front. In 2017, New Zealand agreed to expunge the criminal record of persons criminalized by the colonial law which had forbidden same-sex relations (the law itself having been abrogated a while ago). Germany also moved to annul Nazi-era homosexuality convictions (about 42,000 such convictions had been made under the Third Reich, under an old provision of the Penal Code (art. 175)) and to offer compensation.

33. Yet, there are evidently several gaps, interlinked with the root causes and environment behind the violence and discrimination, which will be elaborated upon in the sections below. Even in countries that are party to the human rights treaties and even where there are responsive laws, policies and programmes, there are sometimes major incidents of violence and discrimination, such as killings of transgender persons, attacks on sexual orientation and gender identity-related human rights defenders, and sexual orientation and gender identity-related hate speech on social networks, which invites sustained vigilance both at the national and the international levels.

## B. Awareness of the Violence and Discrimination Issue, and Linkage with Root Causes

34. The cross-cutting scenario of violence and discrimination is described by the World Health Organization (WHO) as follows:

> Many people in the world are stigmatized and discriminated against because of their actual or perceived sexual orientation or gender identity. Among other disparities, lesbian, gay and transgender people are significantly more likely than the general population to be targeted for violence and harassment, to contract HIV, and to be at risk for mental health concerns such as depression and suicide.

> In settings where same-sex consensual sexual behaviour is against the law, people may be deterred from seeking health services out of fear of being arrested and prosecuted.

35. How aware is the general population of the issue of sexual orientation and gender identity and the interface with violence and discrimination? The reality is often embedded in lack of awareness, misunderstanding, misconceptions and/or ambivalence. Violence and discrimination on the basis of sexual orientation and gender identity often starts being experienced in childhood, at home and in school, for example through bullying. The lack of awareness/knowledge might be compounded by stereotyping, homophobia and transphobia, virulent from the bottom to the top of the social, cultural and political ladder, tailed by the immediacy of social networks. Even among those who are educated, there is at times a cloistered mindset that wrongly looks upon lesbian, gay, bisexual and transgender people as being deviants and being mentally ill. Hate crimes, such as killings, rapes, incitement to violence, and cruel treatment on account of one's sexual orientation or gender identity, might be paralleled by prejudice, intolerance and bigotry from the personal level to the systemic level.

36. What are some of the root causes? While more empirical research is needed on the issue, behind the violence and discrimination there is an environment of negative elements: multiple factors, with longitudinal and intergenerational implications. . . .

37. In reality, there are many social, economic, cultural, legal and political factors behind the environment that breeds violence and discrimination. Various underpinnings deserve particular attention to help prevent and overcome the negative elements of that environment. These will be referred to initially below, and in more detail in future reports from the Independent Expert. In particular, the following underpinnings are essential as part of a strategy of preventing and protecting against violence and discrimination on the basis of sexual orientation and gender identity:

- Decriminalization of consensual same-sex relations;
- Effective anti-discrimination measures;
- Legal recognition of gender identity;
- Destigmatization linked with depathologization;
- Sociocultural inclusion; and
- Promotion of education and empathy.

Beyond communications, country visits, and thematic reports, there is a great deal of variation in the approaches of the various special procedures mandate holders due to their independence, relatively broad mandates, and the quite different topics that they address. It also should be remembered that a Special Rapporteur may hold the position for no more than two three-year terms, and there is no guarantee that rapporteurs on the same issue will necessarily adopt exactly the same approach.

The work of the special procedures is necessarily limited by resources. The system of special procedures, numbering 58 at the beginning of 2022, is increasingly seen as a strain on UN secretariat resources, both financial and staff. One staff person may service up to two mandate holders, and most mandate holders include two or more country visits in their annual activities, in addition to writing thematic reports and responding to communications. Nonetheless, the volume of work by the special procedures is impressive. In 2019, before the pandemic, the special procedures carried out 84 country visits to 57 countries and issued 419 public statements, including 60 statements issued jointly. They submitted a total of 168 reports to the Human Rights Council and 35 to the General Assembly. They sent 669 communications to 151 states and 54 non-state actors, which concerned at least 1,249 individuals and numerous groups of individuals—all this in addition to numerous thematic and annual reports. See OHCHR, Facts and Figures with regard to special Procedures 2019, UN Doc. A/HRC/43/64/Add.1 (2020).

## Comments and Questions

1. The rate of responses by governments to communications from the special procedures on specific cases of alleged human rights abuse has slowly increased. The OHCHR reported a rate of 48.46% for communications sent in 2020. See *Facts and Figures with regard to the special procedures in 2020*, UN Doc. A/HRC/46/61/Add.1 (2021), p. 3. However, as illustrated by the response of the government of Tanzania, *supra* page 522, many government responses simply reject any suggestion that their actions have been inconsistent with human rights norms. What, then, can be surmised to be the impact of the above joint communication to Tanzania? Is Tanzania likely to pay attention to the specific request for corrective and precautionary steps, even though it does not concede all the facts as transmitted in the communication? Why should it? In its response, did Tanzania contest, at least implicitly, any of the human rights norms implicitly invoked by in the joint communication (and made explicit in its annex)? The same group of mandate holders sent communications on the same situation to the World Heritage Committee of UNESCO, the International Union for the Conservation of Nature, and the International Council on Monuments and Sites. What is the nature of the international obligations, if any, that these organizations have with regard to the situation addressed?

2. Given the response rate and the usually defensive nature of government responses, how useful are the communications from the special procedures on specific cases? Under what circumstances might they be most useful? Note the absence

of a requirement of exhaustion of domestic remedies for mandate holders to intervene and the relative flexibility with which they carry out their tasks. Note also that
special procedures mandate holders often issue press statements in urgent situations or if a satisfactory response to a communication is not received, as the mandate holders in the joint communication above indicated they might.

3.  Most of the Human Rights Council resolutions establishing or reauthorizing thematic mandates do not specify the human rights instruments, be they declarations or treaties, that are to be utilized in framing the work of the mandate,
apparently leaving that to the judgment of the mandate holder. An exception is the
mandate for the Working Group on Arbitrary Detention, which stipulates that the
group is to apply "international standards set forth in the Universal Declaration of
Human Rights or in the relevant international legal instruments accepted by the
States concerned," H.R.C. Res. 6/4 (2007), a revised mandate that responded to
objections by some states that the working group exceeded its authority by relying
on instruments that a state had not accepted. Compare the 2007 resolution reauthorizing the indigenous mandate, which added to the operative aspects of that
mandate the directive "[t]o promote the United Nations Declaration on the Rights
of Indigenous Peoples and international instruments relevant to the advancement
of the rights of indigenous peoples, where appropriate." H.R.C. Res. 6/12 (2007),
para. (g). Before the communication concerning the Masai in the Ngorongoro
Conservation Area in Tanzania, the government of Tanzania had consistently maintained that the concept of indigenous peoples does not apply in that country. Why
would it maintain such a position with regard to the Masai? Was it proper for the
mandate holders to invoke the UN Declaration on the Rights of Indigenous Peoples in their communication in this case?

4.  The Human Rights Council established the mandate of the Independent
Expert on the protection against violence an discrimination based on sexual orientation and gender identity by a divided voted of 23 to 18, with 6 abstentions.
See H.R.C. Res. 32/2 (2016). All of the African, Middle Eastern and Asian states,
except for the Republic of Korea, that are members of the Council voted against
or abstained on the resolution establishing the mandate. The Russian Federation
joined the opposing states. How effectively can the Independent Expert on sexual orientation and gender identity be with this divided support for the mandate?
According to the Independent Expert in the above report, is the standard of non-
discrimination based on sexual orientation or gender identity a universal one, or
is it limited to certain regions? How can the work of the Independent Expert help
make this standard one that is universal or at least more broadly accepted?

5.  To which roles are the special procedures better suited: engaging in general
assessments of human rights conditions on a countrywide basis, as they frequently
do in conjunction with country visits; engaging in thematic studies or other promotional activities; or addressing specific situations on a case-by-case basis, as exemplified by the communication concerning Tanzania? Review the list of mandates *supra*
page 522 and consider how the answer to this question may vary depending on
the subject of the mandate. Consider also the fact that the special procedures are
provided limited resources and administrative support by OHCHR, as noted above.

6.  The Human Rights Council's Code of Conduct for the special procedures
has been criticized by a number of NGOs and mandate holders, who believe that

it is an effort to unduly restrict the special procedures and undermine their independence. For the most part, the Code of Conduct codifies the ethical standards of behavior appropriate to the presumably independent and impartial character of mandate holders as well as the practices of engagement with states and the public that had developed previously. The Code of Conduct stipulates, inter alia, that mandate holders are to:

> "[f]ocus exclusively on the implementation of their mandate;"
>
> take into account, "in a comprehensive and timely manner . . . information provided by the State concerned;"
>
> "seek to establish the facts, based on objective, reliable information emanating from relevant credible sources, that they have duly cross-checked to the best extent possible;"
>
> give the concerned state "the opportunity of commenting on mandate-holders' assessment and of responding to the allegations made against this State, and annex the State's written summary responses to their reports;"
>
> "[e]nsure that the concerned government authorities are the first recipients of their conclusions and recommendations concerning this State and are given adequate time to respond, and that likewise the Council is the first recipient of conclusions and recommendations addressed to this body;"
>
> "show restraint, moderation and discretion;" and
>
> "[k]eep in mind the mandate of the Council which is responsible for promoting universal respect for the protection of all human rights and fundamental freedoms for all, through dialogue and cooperation."

H.R.C. Res. 5/2 (2007). How might such provisions limit the effectiveness of the special procedures, if at all, or be used by governments to deflect legitimate criticism from the special procedures?

7. For additional perspectives on the special procedures, see Navanethem Pillay, *The Special Procedures of the Human Rights Council: A Brief Look from the Inside and Perspectives from Outside* (2015); *The United Nations Special Procedures System* (Aoife Nolan, Rosa Freedman, and Thérèse Murphy eds., 2017); Elvira Domínguez-Redondo, *In Defense of Politicization of Human Rights: The UN Special Procedures* (2020); *Symposium, The Role of the Special Rapporteurs of the United Nations Human Rights Council in the Development and Promotion of International Human Rights Norms*, 15(2) INT'L J. HUM. RTS. (2011); Ted Piccone, *Catalysts for Rights: The Unique Contribution of the UN's Independent Experts on Human Rights* (2010), https://www.brookings.edu/research/catalysts-for-rights-the-unique-contribution-of-the-uns-independent-experts-on-human-rights/.

### Note: Other Charter-Based Mechanisms

The Human Rights Council has created a number of subsidiary mechanisms to consider specific human rights issues. These include the Social Forum, Forum on Minority Issues, Forum on Business and Human Rights, and Forum on Human

Rights, Democracy and the Rule of Law. A description of their activities may be found via the Council's webpage on subsidiary bodies, http://www.ohchr.org/EN/HRBodies/HRC/Pages/OtherSubBodies.aspx. These mechanisms are essentially venues for discussion among states, NGOs, and individual experts on the topics indicated, although some (such as the Forum on Minority Issues) also may issue recommendations, conclusions, or "advice" at the end of their meetings.

Soon after it's creation the Council created an Expert Mechanism on the Rights of Indigenous Peoples, a standing body of fixed membership akin to the Council's Advisory Committee. In 2016, the Council increased the mechanism's membership to seven and amended its mandate to include, inter alia, providing assistance and advice upon a state's request in the implementation of the UN Declaration on the Rights of Indigenous Peoples. See H.R.C. Res. 33/25 (2016). Additionally, in 2019, the Human Rights Council decided to establish a five-member "expert mechanism to provide the Council with thematic expertise on the right to development." H.R.C. Res. 42/23 (2019). Known commonly as the Expert Mechanism on the Right to Development, this body meets annually and conducts thematic studies, engages in consultations and outreach, and identifies and shares best practices to implement the right to development. And in 2021 the Council authorized the establishment of the International Independent Expert Mechanism to Advance Racial Justice and Equality in Law Enforcement "in order to further transformative change for racial justice and equality in the context of law enforcement globally, especially where relating to the legacies of colonialism and the Transatlantic slave trade in enslaved Africans, [and] to investigate Governments' responses to peaceful anti-racism protests and all violations of international human rights law and to contribute to accountability and redress for victims." H.R.C. Res. 47/21 (2021).

Apart from the Human Rights Council, there are many other UN Charter-based bodies that are concerned with human rights, although there is no formal or direct route of access for individuals or NGOs to submit information to most of these other bodies. Many of these bodies lack the power to act directly in response to information on violations. Of course, the UN General Assembly has plenary authority to address human rights, as manifested by its long-standing activity in human rights matters associated with decolonization, the Israel-occupied territories, and South Africa before the end of apartheid. The Security Council also may be concerned with human rights within the framework of its work on peace and security, as illustrated by its attention to human rights concerns in Somalia, Haiti, Darfur, and the Central African Republic. The Economic and Social Council addresses human rights within its general mandate and as the parent body of the Commission on Crime Prevention and Criminal Justice, the Commission on the Status of Women, and the Permanent Forum on Indigenous Issues.

In the past decade, the intergovernmental Commission on the Status of Women, which was established by the UN Economic and Social Council (ECOSOC) in 1946, has taken "a leading role in monitoring and reviewing progress and problems in the implementation of the Beijing Declaration and Platform for Action, and in mainstreaming a gender perspective in UN activities." See http://www.unwomen.org/en/csw. It meets annually for two weeks, is based in New York, and is supported by the part of the UN secretariat called UN Women. The Commission has a confidential petition procedure, which functions pursuant to a series of Economic and Social Council resolutions. See http://www.unwomen.org/en/csw/communications-procedure. A Working Group on Communications meets privately during the Commission's annual session to consider complaints of violations of women's human rights and the corresponding replies of governments. It prepares a report that summarizes the communications according to specific categories of concern, but individual complainants are not provided copies of the report or government responses. The full Commission considers the Working Group report in a closed meeting and then reports to ECOSOC with any recommendations that it may deem appropriate. The description of the communications procedure specifically notes that "the Commission on the Status of Women does not take decisions on the merit of communications that are submitted to it and, therefore, the communications procedure does not provide an avenue for the redress of individual grievances." Id. The Commission also addresses women's rights in non-case-specific studies and discussions of a range of issues, such as violence against women and the need for equal pay for equal work; this work is summarized in the Commission's annual report to ECOSOC.

The Permanent Forum on Indigenous Issues is also a subsidiary body of ECOSOC. It was created in 2000, with a mandate to advise and make recommendations to ECOSOC specifically on indigenous peoples' concerns and to promote awareness and coordination of the activities concerning these issues within the UN system. See E.S.C. Res. 2000/22 (2000). Unlike other major UN bodies that are exclusively intergovernmental, the Permanent Forum is composed of independent experts, eight of whom are nominated by states and the other eight of whom are named by the president of the Economic and Social Council in consultation with indigenous peoples. The Permanent Forum opens its meetings to representatives of indigenous peoples and support groups from throughout the world, in addition to a wide range of government and international agency representatives, providing them the opportunity to raise their concerns and make recommendations in the Forum's public sessions. The Forum thus far has not developed a methodology to take action on specific allegations of violations of indigenous rights that have been brought to its attention. However, at times it has issued public expressions of concern about urgent situations and has conducted a few field visits (at the invitation of the states concerned), possibly indicating that it may adopt a more active monitoring role in the future.

In addition to the above bodies, the UN Secretary-General carries out a number of human rights activities both directly and through the Office of the High Commissioner on Human Rights. The High Commissioner has the rank of Under-Secretary-General and has principal responsibility for United Nations human rights activities under the direction and authority of the Secretary-General. G.A. Res 48/141 (1993). The High Commissioner often actively raises concern and advances inquiries on major human rights issues, an example being the work of the High Commissioner at the intersection of human rights and climate change. See, e.g., Office of the United Nations High Commissioner for Human Rights, *Analytical study on gender-responsive climate action for the full and effective enjoyment of the rights of women*, UN Doc. A/HRC/C/41/26 (2019). Similarly, the High Commissioner and other senior members of the secretariat often make public statements in the immediate context of urgent or crisis situations giving rise to human rights concerns.

The Office of the High Commissioner, based in Geneva, houses the permanent UN staff that provides services to the Human Rights Council, its special procedures and commissions of inquiry, and other UN bodies and programs concerned with human rights, including the treaty-monitoring bodies. In recent years, the Office has expanded its activities to gather and disseminate information on human rights and to provide technical and advisory services to states. Additionally, the Office has expanded the number and resources of its field offices, which often work in conjunction with other UN agencies, commissions of inquiry, or peacekeeping missions working in the field. The work of the field offices began as primarily promotional, although the "field presences" increasingly have taken on the role of on-site monitoring. Descriptions of the many field presences may be found on the OHCHR website, http://www.ohchr.org/EN/Countries/Pages/WorkInField.aspx.

## IV.  FINAL COMMENTS AND QUESTIONS

1. All of the mechanisms discussed in Section III of this chapter are based on the inherent authority of the United Nations to consider human rights issues; none of them imposes a formal legal obligation on states to respond or participate. Nonetheless, states have generally paid attention to the confidential complaint procedure and special procedures of the Human Rights Council, to a greater or lesser degree, and they have invariably submitted to examination and peer review under the Council's UPR. The sessions of the Council are regularly attended by hundreds, if not thousands of people, including state representatives (of both members and nonmembers of the Council), representatives of UN agencies, and NGOs. While one may certainly question the sincerity of many statements made during the sessions, it would be difficult to argue that many states believe that the best path is simply to ignore the UN's human rights activities altogether.

It is rarely possible to determine the impact of any UN procedure, or, indeed, of the United Nations human rights regime taken as a whole. What is certain, however, is that the vast majority of UN member states pay serious attention to issues that concern them directly, and it is not unusual for a country to expend significant diplomatic capital to fend off or support a particular initiative. An unusually public example of the significance of UN debates is offered by the paid announcement on page 536, which was placed in the Washington Post (Mar. 5, 1989), at A26, and other major US and European newspapers by the government of (then) Zaire. The announcement obviously ignores the required confidentiality of the 1503 procedure, but it also suggests that governments find even secret UN procedures to be of some relevance. It is also a reminder that most countries do care about their reputations, even if they are questioned "only" by a Human Rights Council resolution, a public statement by the High Commissioner for Human Rights, or critical comments by a treaty body or special procedure.

## UNITED NATIONS REPORT:
## HUMAN RIGHTS SITUATION IMPROVES MARKEDLY IN ZAIRE

The Embassy of the Republic of Zaire in Washington, D.C. is pleased to bring to your attention the conclusions of the United Nations Commission on Human Rights, based on our country's accomplishments in promoting and protecting human rights.

Zaire, true to President Mobutu's guidelines and goals, continues to demonstrate the commitment of its government to the principles of Human Rights and Democracy.

We would like to take this opportunity to salute the cordial and long standing relations between the United States of America and the Republic of Zaire.

H.E. Mushobekwa Kalimba wa Katana
Ambassador E. and P.

| OFFICE DES NATIONS UNIES A GENEVE | UNITED NATIONS OFFICE OF GENEVA |

**DECISION CONCERNING ZAIRE ADOPTED WITHOUT A VOTE
AT THE 38TH MEETING (CLOSED) OF THE COMMISSION
HELD ON 24 FEBRUARY 1989**

*The Commission on Human Rights,*

*Having examined the material concerning the human rights situation in Zaire brought before it under Economic and Social Council resolution 1503 (XLVIII), including the report of the Secretary-General on his direct contacts with the government of Zaire (E/CN.4/1989/R.4),*

*Noting with appreciation the willingness of the Government of Zaire, with the active participation of Maitre Nimy Mayidika Ngimbi, Commissaire d'Etat aux droits et libertes du citoyen, to co-operate with the Commission by furnishing replies and observations relating to the material which the Commission has before it,*

1. <u>Decides</u> to discontinue consideration of the matter;
2. <u>Encourages</u> the Government of Zaire in its efforts to promote and protect human rights;
3. <u>Requests</u> the Government of Zaire to inform the Commission at its forty-sixth session, of the results of the action already taken to this and at a special closed meeting;
4. <u>Requests</u> the Secretary-General to provide Zaire with all the assistance it desires under the advisory services program in order to help that country in its efforts to strengthen the machinery established for the purpose of protecting and promoting human rights;
5. <u>Requests</u> the Secretary-General to communicate this decision to the Government of Zaire.

2. How might an individual or NGO develop a strategy to use the various procedures of the Human Rights Council to press a concern about a human rights matter? Consider, for example, how you might attempt to help women migrant workers who have been victims of sexual assault and murder, or who fear being such victims, in a particular location where violence is widespread. Would it be possible or advisable for an NGO to submit a communication both under the confidential complaint procedure and under one or more of the special procedures to address such a situation? Could or should the matter also be submitted under the UPR at the appropriate time? What are the relative strengths and weaknesses of the various procedures, and how might they complement each other? Bear in mind that many procedures include provisions that specify whether a case submitted to one international procedure can be "appealed" to another or whether the same or a similar situation can be submitted to more than one procedure simultaneously.

3. A major problem of the UN system is that it is starved for resources. Indeed, the Office of the High Commissioner functions today only because of outside contributions; less than half of its funding comes from the regular UN budget. Might this compromise the priorities set by the High Commissioner? Is the High Commissioner likely to be less willing to criticize a state that has recently provided substantial money, equipment, or personnel to the Office?

4. On February 24, 2020, UN Secretary General António Guterres launched a "Call to Action for Human Rights," a seven-point blueprint for focused human rights action within the UN system and beyond. In a speech to the Human Rights Council launching the initiative, at the Council's its 43d session in Geneva, the Secretary-General affirmed, "Human rights are our ultimate tool to help societies grow in freedom." *With human rights under attack, UN chief unveils blueprint for positive change,* UN News (Feb. 24, 2020), https://news.un.org/en/story/2020/02/1057961. The Call to Action includes guiding principles under the following seven domains: (1) rights at the core of sustainable development; (2) rights in times of crisis; (3) gender equality and equal rights for women; (4) public participation and civic space; (5) rights of future generations, especially climate justice; (6) rights at the heart of collective action; and (7) new frontiers of human rights. See UN Secretary-General, *The Highest Aspiration–A Call to Action for Human Rights* (2020). While the initiative is not a new procedure or mechanism, it does suggest that human rights are unlikely to disappear from the UN's agenda any time soon.

# CHAPTER 8

# HUMAN RIGHTS IN THE AMERICAS

## THE PROCEDURES OF THE INTER-AMERICAN COMMISSION AND INTER-AMERICAN COURT OF HUMAN RIGHTS

# I.  INTRODUCTION: THE INTER-AMERICAN HUMAN RIGHTS SYSTEM

This Chapter examines the mechanisms of the Inter-American human rights system to protect and promote human rights in the Americas. In particular, it discusses the work of the two main organs entrusted by member states of the Organization of American States with the monitoring of human rights issues in the Americas — the Inter-American Commission on Human Rights and the Inter-American Court of Human Rights.

The readings in this Chapter shed light on the history and evolution of the Inter-American human rights system and on the broad range of procedures its organs have at their disposal to advance the protection of human rights. For the Inter-American Commission, these include an individual case petition system, precautionary measures, on-site visits, country reports and hearings, among others. The Inter-American Court of Human Rights for its part has issued more than 300 judgments and advisory opinions, including detailed orders of reparations and provisional measures. This Chapter discusses examples of how these procedures are applied to monitor and address human rights issues of great concern in the Americas, including forced disappearances, restrictions to freedom of expression and the right to protest, the killing of human rights defenders, violence against women, and obstacles to indigenous peoples' self-determination, among others.

This Chapter also explores important challenges that still shape the work of the Inter-American Commission and the Court. These include the lack of universal ratification among the OAS members states of the leading treaty of the Inter-American human rights system—the American Convention on Human Rights—and the continuing impunity for serious human rights violations committed during the wave of repressive regimes affecting Latin American countries in the 1970s and 1980s. It also addresses challenges to the full compliance with the case decisions of both the Inter-American Commission and Court. Lastly, the Chapter ends with a discussion on how Inter-American system procedures are addressing issues at the intersection of human rights and democratic governance in the Americas.

## II. EVOLUTION OF THE HUMAN RIGHTS SYSTEM IN THE AMERICAS

The Inter-American system as it exists today began with the transformation of the Pan American Union, which dates back to the nineteenth century, into the Organization of American States (OAS). Article 3 of the OAS Charter proclaims the "fundamental rights of the individual" as one of the Organization's basic principles. Concern with human rights not only inspired the Organization of American States to refer to human rights in its Charter, but also led it to adopt the American Declaration of the Rights and Duties of Man, in May 1948, half a year before the United Nations completed the Universal Declaration of Human Rights.

The Inter-American system has expanded its protections over time through the adoption of additional human rights instruments, including in the form of treaties. The Inter-American treaties are the following:

- American Convention on Human Rights (1969);
- Inter-American Convention for the Prevention and Punishment of Torture (1985);
- Additional Protocol to the American Convention on Human Rights in the Area of Economic, Social, and Cultural Rights (1988);
- Second Additional Protocol to the American Convention on Human Rights to Abolish the Death Penalty (1990);
- Inter-American Convention on the Prevention, Punishment, and Eradication of Violence Against Women (1994);
- Inter-American Convention on Forced Disappearance of Persons (1994);
- Inter-American Convention on the Elimination of all Forms of Discrimination Against Persons with Disabilities (1999);
- Inter-American Convention against All Forms of Discrimination and Intolerance (2013);

- Inter-American Convention against Racism, Racial Discrimination and Related Forms of Intolerance (2013);
- Inter-American Convention on Protecting the Human Rights of Older Persons (2015).

In addition, the Inter-American Commission on Human Rights and the OAS General Assembly have adopted important normative declarations, including the Declaration of Principles on Freedom of Expression (2000), the Principles and Best Practices on the Protection of Persons Deprived of Liberty in the Americas (2008), and the American Declaration on the Rights of Indigenous Peoples (2016), which is discussed in Chapter 3.

The Inter-American Commission on Human Rights, which was established by the OAS Charter, is composed of seven independent experts elected by the OAS member states. The other major institution of the Inter-American human rights system—the Inter-American Court of Huma Rights—was created by the American Convention on Human Rights and is composed of seven judges elected by the state parties to the American Convention.

The reading below offers background on the procedures and organs of the inter-American human right system.

Cecilia Medina

## The Inter-American Commission on Human Rights and the Inter-American Court of Human Rights: Reflections on a Joint Venture

12 Hum. Rts. Q. 439-47 (1990)

The Inter-American Commission on Human Rights was . . . originally conceived as a study group concerned with abstract investigations in the field of human rights. However, the creators of the Commission did not foresee the appeal this organ would have for the individual victims of human rights violations. As soon as it was known that the Commission had been created, individuals began to send complaints about human rights problems in their countries. Prompted by these complaints, the Commission started its activities with the conviction that in order to promote human rights it had to protect them.

A significant part of the Commission's work was addressing the problem of countries with gross, systematic violations of human rights, characterized by an absence or a lack of effective national mechanisms for the protection of human rights and a lack of cooperation on the part of the governments concerned. The main objective of the Commission was not to investigate isolated violations but to document the existence of these gross, systematic violations and to exercise pressure to improve the general condition of human rights in the country concerned. For this purpose, and by means of its regulatory powers, the Commission created a procedure to "take cognizance" of individual complaints and use them as a source of information about gross, systematic violations of human rights in the territories of the OAS member states.

The Commission's competence to handle individual communications was formalized in 1965, after the OAS reviewed and was satisfied with the Commission's work. The OAS passed Resolution XXII, which allowed the Commission to "examine" isolated human rights violations, with a particular focus on certain rights. This procedure, however, provided many obstacles for the Commission. Complaints could be handled only if domestic remedies had been exhausted, a requirement that prevented swift reactions to violations. Also, the procedure made the Commission more dependent on the governments for information. This resulted in the governments' either not answering the Commission's requests for information or answering with a blanket denial that did not contribute to a satisfactory solution of the problem.

Furthermore, once the Commission had given its opinion on the case, there was nothing else to be done; the Commission would declare that a government had violated the American Declaration of the Rights and Duties of Man and recommend the government take certain measures, knowing that this was unlikely to resolve the situation. The fact that some of the Commission's opinions could reach the political bodies of the OAS did not solve the problem, because the Commission's opinions on individual cases were never discussed at that level. Consequently, in order not to lose the flexibility it had, the Commission interpreted Resolution XXII as granting the Commission power to "examine" communications concerning individual violations of certain rights specified in the resolution without diminishing its power to "take cognizance" of communications concerning the rest of the human rights protected by the American Declaration. The Commission preserved this broader power for the purposes of identifying gross, systematic human rights violations.

The procedure to "take cognizance" of communications evolved and became the general case procedure and was later used in examining the general human rights situation in a country. This procedure, maturing with the Commission's practice, had several positive characteristics in view of the Commission's purposes. First, it could be started without checking whether the communications met any admissibility requirements or even in the absence of any communication. All that was necessary was for news to reach the Commission that serious violations were taking place in the territory of an OAS member state. Second, the Commission assumed a very active role by requesting and gathering information by telegram and telephone from witnesses, newspapers, and experts, and also requesting consent to visit the country at the Commission's convenience. Third, the Commission could publicize its findings in order to put pressure upon the governments. Finally, the report resulting from the investigation could be sent to the political bodies of the OAS, thereby allowing for a political discussion of the problem which, at least theoretically, could be followed by political measures against the governments involved. . . .

The [Inter-American Court of Human Rights] has contentious and advisory jurisdiction. In exercising its contentious jurisdiction, the Court settles controversies about the interpretation and application of the provisions of the American Convention through a special procedure designed to handle individual or state complaints against states parties to the Convention. Under its advisory jurisdiction, the Court may interpret not only the Convention but also any other treaty concerning the protection of human rights in the American states. The Court may also give its opinion regarding the compatibility of the domestic laws of any OAS member state with the requirements of the Convention or any human rights treaties to which the Convention refers. In addition, the Court is not prevented from giving its opinion regarding any question relating to the content or scope of the rights defined in the Convention or any question that might have to be considered by the Court in the exercise of its contentious jurisdiction or by the Commission's supervision of human rights. The advisory jurisdiction of the Court may be set in motion by any OAS member state, whether or not it is a party to the Convention, or by any OAS organ listed in Chapter X of the OAS Charter, which includes the Commission.

The Court may consider a case that is brought either by the Commission or by a state party to the Convention. For the Commission to refer a case to the Court, the case must have been admitted for investigation and the Commission's draft report sent to the state party. In addition, the state must recognize the Court's general contentious jurisdiction or a limited jurisdiction specified by a time period or case. For a state party to be able to place a case before the Court, the only requirement is that both states must have recognized the Court's contentious jurisdiction.

During the proceedings, the Court has powers to investigate the facts as it deems necessary. The Court ordinarily concludes its consideration of a case by issuing a judgment. If the Court finds that there has been a violation of a right or freedom protected by the Convention, it shall rule "that the injured party, be ensured the enjoyment of his right or freedom that was violated." If appropriate, it may also rule that "the consequences of the measure or situation that constituted the breach of such a right or freedom be remedied and that fair compensation be paid to the injured party." States are under the international obligation to comply with the judgment of the Court in any case to which they are parties. The part of the judgment that stipulates compensatory damages has executory force in the state concerned.

If a state does not comply with the decision of the Court, the Court may inform and make recommendations to the OAS General Assembly. There is no reference in the Convention to any action that the General Assembly might take; the assembly, being a political body, may take any political action it deems necessary to persuade the state to comply with its international obligations.

––––––––––––––––

The Inter-American human rights system is one of varying obligations, because not all OAS member states have ratified the American Convention and accepted the jurisdiction of the Inter-American Court to hear matters. This is one of the most important challenges affecting the Inter-American system today, as it is widely considered to limit the effectiveness of the system as a whole. Among the countries that have not ratified the American Convention, many are English-Speaking, including the United States, Canada, and several Caribbean countries. This fact reflects an important cultural, linguistic, and historic divide in the Inter-American system. See Paolo Carozza, *The Anglo-Latin Divide and the Future of the Inter-American System of Human Rights*, 5 NOTRE DAME J. OF INT'L & COMP. L. 153 (2015).

The Inter-American Commission on Human Rights has referred to "four levels of participation" in the Inter-American system in these terms:

> First, a universal, minimum level of protection exists with respect to
>     all 35 OAS member states, whose inhabitants enjoy [Inter-American

Commission on Human Rights]-supervised protection of the rights recognized in the American Declaration and the OAS Charter.

Second, a group of 23 member states has ratified the American Convention and continue being State parties to said instrument.

Third, a group of 20 member states has accepted the jurisdiction of the Inter-American Court and their acceptance is still in force.

Fourth, a group of 7 member states has ratified all the inter-American human rights treaties.

Inter-Am. Comm'n H.R., *Considerations Related to the Universal Ratification of the American Convention and other Inter-American Human Rights Treaties*, OEA/Ser.L/V/II.152 Doc. 21 (2014), para. 17 (discussing also the repercussions in human rights protection and monitoring of not ratifying Inter-American treaties).

All OAS member states are obligated by the OAS Charter and indirectly by the American Declaration as the following advisory opinion sets forth. States that have ratified the American Convention on Human Rights additionally are bound by its provisions. The Inter-American Commission on Human Rights can monitor the human rights observance of all countries throughout the Americas, including those that have not ratified the American Convention.

The following advisory opinion by the Inter-American Court of Human Rights discusses the legal status of the American Declaration and the Court's role in its interpretation.

## Interpretation of the American Declaration of the Rights and Duties of Man Within the Framework of Article 64 of the American Convention on Human Rights

Inter-Am. Ct. H.R., Advisory Opinion OC-10/89, July 14, 1989,
Ser. A No. 10 (1989) (some references omitted)

1. By note of February 17, 1988, the Government of the Republic of Colombia . . . submitted to the Inter-American Court of Human Rights a request for an advisory opinion on the interpretation of Article 64 of the American Convention on Human Rights . . . in relation to the American Declaration of the Rights and Duties of Man. . . .

2. The Government requests a reply to the following question:

Does Article 64 authorize the Inter-American Court of Human Rights to render advisory opinions at the request of a member state or one of the organs of the OAS, regarding the interpretation of the American Declaration of the Rights and Duties of Man, adopted by the Ninth International Conference of American States in Bogota in 1948?

The Government adds:

The Government of Colombia understands, of course, that the Declaration is not a treaty. But this conclusion does not automatically answer the question. It is perfectly reasonable to assume that the interpretation of the human rights provisions contained in the Charter of the OAS, as revised by the Protocol of Buenos Aires, involves, in principle, an analysis of the rights and duties of man proclaimed by the Declaration, and thus requires the determination of the normative status of the Declaration within the legal framework of the inter-American system for the protection of human rights.

. . .

12. The Government of the United States of America believes:

The American Declaration of the Rights and Duties of Man represents a noble statement of the human rights aspirations of the American States. Unlike the American Convention, however, it was not drafted as a legal instrument and lacks the precision necessary to resolve complex legal questions. Its normative value lies as a declaration of basic moral principles and broad political commitments and as a basis to review the general human rights performance of member states, not as a binding set of obligations.

The United States recognizes the good intentions of those who would transform the American Declaration from a statement of principles into a binding legal instrument. But good intentions do not make law. It would seriously undermine the process of international lawmaking — by which sovereign states voluntarily undertake specified legal obligations — to impose legal obligations on states through a process of "reinterpretation" or "inference" from a non-binding statement of principles.

29. The Court will now address the merits of the question before it.

30. Article 64(1) of the Convention authorizes the Court to render advisory opinions "regarding the interpretation of this Convention or of other treaties concerning the protection of human rights in the American states." That is, the object of the advisory opinions of the Court is treaties. . . .

31. According to the Vienna Convention on the Law of Treaties of 1969

"treaty" means an international agreement concluded between States in written form and governed by international law, whether embodied in a single instrument or in two or more related instruments and whatever its particular designation (Art. 2(1)(a)).

32. The Vienna Convention of 1986 on the Law of Treaties among States and International Organizations or among International Organizations provides as follows in Article 2(1)(a):

"treaty" means an international agreement governed by international law and concluded in written form:

(i)   between one or more States and one or more international organizations; or

(ii)  between international organizations, whether that agreement is embodied in a single instrument or in two or more related instruments and whatever its particular designation.

33. In attempting to define the word "treaty" as the term is employed in Article 64(1), it is sufficient for now to say that a "treaty" is, at the very least, an

international instrument of the type that is governed by the two Vienna Conventions. Whether the term includes other international instruments of a conventional nature whose existence is also recognized by those Conventions (Art. 3, Vienna Convention of 1969; Art. 3, Vienna Convention of 1986), need not be decided at this time. What is clear, however, is that the Declaration is not a treaty as defined by the Vienna Conventions because it was not approved as such, and that, consequently, it is also not a treaty within the meaning of Article 64(1).

34. Here it must be recalled that the American Declaration was adopted by the Ninth International Conference of American States (Bogotá, 1948) through a resolution adopted by the Conference itself. It was neither conceived nor drafted as a treaty. . . .

35. The mere fact that the Declaration is not a treaty does not necessarily compel the conclusion that the Court lacks the power to render an advisory opinion containing an interpretation of the American Declaration.

36. In fact, the American Convention refers to the Declaration in paragraph three of its Preamble which reads as follows:

> Considering that these principles have been set forth in the Charter of the Organization of the American States, in the American Declaration of the Rights and Duties of Man, and in the Universal Declaration of Human Rights, and that they have been reaffirmed and refined in other international instruments, worldwide as well as regional in scope.

And in Article 29(d) which indicates:

Restrictions Regarding Interpretation

No provision of this convention shall be interpreted as:

> d. excluding or limiting the effect that the American Declaration of the Rights and Duties of Man and other international acts of the same nature may have.

From the foregoing, it follows that, in interpreting the Convention in the exercise of its advisory jurisdiction, the Court may have to interpret the Declaration.

37. The American Declaration has its basis in the idea that "the international protection of the rights of man should be the principal guide of an evolving American law." This American law has evolved from 1948 to the present; international protective measures, subsidiary and complementary to national ones, have been shaped by new instruments. As the International Court of Justice said: "an international instrument must be interpreted and applied within the overall framework of the juridical system in force at the time of the interpretation" (*Legal Consequences for States of the Continued Presence of South Africa in Namibia (South West Africa) notwithstanding Security Council Resolution 276* (1970), Advisory Opinion, I.C.J. Reports 1971, p. 16 ad 31). That is why the Court finds it necessary to point out that to determine the legal status of the American Declaration it is appropriate to look to the inter-American system of today in the light of the evolution it has undergone since the adoption of the Declaration, rather than to examine the normative value and significance which that instrument was believed to have had in 1948.

38. The evolution of the here relevant "inter-American law" mirrors on the regional level the developments in contemporary international law and especially

in human rights law, which distinguished that law from classical international law to a significant extent. That is the case, for example, with the duty to respect certain essential human rights, which is today considered to be an erga omnes obligation (*Barcelona Traction, Light and Power Company, Limited,* Second Phase, Judgment, I.C.J. Reports 1970, p. 3. For an analysis following the same line of thought see also *Legal Consequences for States of the Continued Presence of South Africa in Namibia (South West Africa) notwithstanding Security Council Resolution 276* (1970) *supra* page 37, p. 16 ad 57; cfr. *United States Diplomatic and Consular Staff in Tehran,* I.C.J. Reports 1980, p. 3 ad 42).

39. The Charter of the Organization refers to the fundamental rights of man in its Preamble ((paragraph three) and in Arts. 3(j), 16, 43, 47, 51, 112 and 150; Preamble (paragraph four), Arts. 3(k), 16, 44, 48, 52, 111 and 150 of the Charter revised by the Protocol of Cartagena de Indias), but it does not list or define them. The member states of the Organization have, through its diverse organs, given specificity to the human rights mentioned in the Charter and to which the Declaration refers.

40. This is the case of Article 112 of the Charter (Art. 111 of the Charter as amended by the Protocol of Cartagena de Indias) which reads as follows:

> There shall be an Inter-American Commission on Human Rights, whose principal function shall be to promote the observance and protection of human rights and to serve as a consultative organ of the Organization in these matters. An inter-American convention on human rights shall determine the structure, competence, and procedure of this Commission, as well as those of other organs responsible for these matters.

Article 150 of the Charter provides as follows:

> Until the inter-American convention on human rights, referred to in Chapter XVIII (Chapter XVI of the Charter as amended by the Protocol of Cartagena de Indias), enters into force, the present Inter-American Commission on Human Rights shall keep vigilance over the observance of human rights.

41. These norms authorize the Inter-American Commission to protect human rights. These rights are none other than those enunciated and defined in the American Declaration. That conclusion results from Article 1 of the Commission's Statute, which was approved by Resolution No. 447, adopted by the General Assembly of the OAS at its Ninth Regular Period of Sessions, held in La Paz, Bolivia, in October, 1979. That Article reads as follows:

1. The Inter-American Commission on Human Rights is an organ of the Organization of the American States, created to promote the observance and defense of human rights and to serve as consultative organ of the Organization in this matter.
2. For the purposes of the present Statute, human rights are understood to be:
   a. The rights set forth in the American Convention on Human Rights, in relation to the States Parties thereto;
   b. The rights set forth in the American Declaration of the Rights and Duties of Man, in relation to the other member states.

Articles 18, 19 and 20 of the Statute enumerate these functions.

42. The General Assembly of the Organization has also repeatedly recognized that the American Declaration is a source of international obligations for the member states of the OAS. For example, in Resolution 314 (VII-O/77) of June 22, 1977, it charged the Inter-American Commission with the preparation of a study to "set forth their obligation to carry out the commitments assumed in the American Declaration of the Rights and Duties of Man." In Resolution 371 (VIII-O/78) of July 1, 1978, the General Assembly reaffirmed "its commitment to promote the observance of the American Declaration of the Rights and Duties of Man," and in Resolution 370 (VIII-O/78) of July 1, 1978, it referred to the "international commitments" of a member state of the Organization to respect the rights of man "recognized in the American Declaration of the Rights and Duties of Man." The Preamble of the American Convention to Prevent and Punish Torture, adopted and signed at the Fifteenth Regular Session of the General Assembly in Cartagena de Indias (December, 1985), reads as follows:

> Reaffirming that all acts of torture or any other cruel, inhuman, or degrading treatment or punishment constitute an offense against human dignity and a denial of the principles set forth in the Charter of the Organization of American States and in the Charter of the United Nations and are violations of the fundamental human rights and freedoms proclaimed in the American Declaration of the Rights and Duties of Man and the Universal Declaration of Human Rights.

43. Hence it may be said that by means of an authoritative interpretation, the member states of the Organization have signaled their agreement that the Declaration contains and defines the fundamental human rights referred to in the Charter. Thus, the Charter of the Organization cannot be interpreted and applied as far as human rights are concerned without relating its norms, consistent with the practice of the organs of the OAS, to the corresponding provisions of the Declaration.

44. In view of the fact that the Charter of the Organization and the American Convention are treaties with respect to which the Court has advisory jurisdiction by virtue of Article 64(1), it follows that the Court is authorized, within the framework and limits of its competence, to interpret the American Declaration and to render an advisory opinion relating to it whenever it is necessary to do so in interpreting those instruments.

45. For the member states of the Organization, the Declaration is the text that defines the human rights referred to in the Charter. Moreover, Articles 1(2)(b) and 20 of the Commission's Statute define the competence of that body with respect to the human rights enunciated in the Declaration, with the result that to this extent the American Declaration is for these States a source of international obligations related to the Charter of the Organization.

46. For the States Parties to the Convention, the specific source of their obligations with respect to the protection of human rights is, in principle, the Convention itself. It must be remembered, however, that, given the provisions of Article 29(d), these States cannot escape the obligations they have as members of the OAS under the Declaration, notwithstanding the fact that the Convention is the governing instrument for the States Parties thereto.

47. That the Declaration is not a treaty does not, then, lead to the conclusion that it does not have legal effect, nor that the Court lacks the power to interpret it within the framework of the principles set out above.

## Note: Advisory Opinions of the Court

The Inter-American Court of Human Rights spent most of its first decade of existence issuing advisory opinions, which are authorized by Article 64 of the American Convention. One reason for this history is the broad range of entities authorized to request advisory opinions, which includes all OAS member states, the Inter-American Commission, and other OAS organs. States accepted the Court's contentious jurisdiction only gradually, and advisory opinions were thus the only "business" the Court could conduct.

Contrast the European System, where Protocol No. 2 to the European Convention on Human Rights originally gave the European Court of Human Rights the authority to issue "advisory opinions on legal questions concerning the interpretation of the Convention" upon the request of the Committee of Ministers of the Council of Europe, but under very strict jurisdictional limitations. Protocol No. 16, adopted in 2013 and discussed in Chapter 9, extended the jurisdiction of the European Court of Human Rights to give national courts the opportunity to request advisory opinions concerning legal questions related to the European Convention and its protocols.

As the above Advisory Opinion OC-10 indicates, the Inter-American Court's advisory jurisdiction extends to interpreting "other treaties concerning the protection of human rights in the American states." Despite the potential for conflicting interpretations were the Court to consider non-American instruments, the Court has adopted a broad view of Article 64 that encompasses "any international treaty applicable in the American States," whether or not OAS members are parties to it, even if the primary object of the treaty is not the protection of human rights. See *The Right to Information on Consular Assistance*, Inter-Am. Ct. H.R., Advisory Opinion OC-16 of Oct. 1, 1999. At the same time this request for an advisory opinion was being heard, at the request of Mexico, the International Court of Justice was hearing the case of *Avena and Other Mexican Nationals (Mexico v. United States)*, which implicated the same treaty on consular assistance. Should the Inter-American Court have declined to give the opinion while the ICJ case was pending? Note that the ICJ declined to rule on the precise question asked of the Inter-American Court, perhaps to avoid an unfortunate conflict of rulings.

Two advisory opinions, in particular, have made a significant contribution to protecting rights during states of emergency by expanding the scope of non-derogable due process rights, such as habeas corpus and amparo. See *Habeas Corpus in Emergency Situations*, Inter-Am. Ct. H.R., Advisory Opinion OC-8/87 of Jan. 30, 1987, Ser. A No. 8; and *Judicial Guarantees in States of Emergency*, Inter-Am. Ct. H.R., Advisory Opinion OC-9/87 of Oct. 6, 1987, Ser. A No. 9.

A state may also request an advisory opinion to test the compatibility of its own law with the American Convention, while avoiding the legally binding result that would follow from a judgment by the Court. See, e.g., *Compulsory Membership in an Association Prescribed by Law for the Practice of Journalism*, Inter-Am. Ct. H.R., Advisory Opinion OC-5/85 of Nov. 13, 1985, Ser. A No. 5.

The Court adopted an advisory opinion confirming that legal entities like corporations are not entitled to human rights protections under the Inter-American human rights system. See *Entitlement of Legal Entities to Hold Rights under the Inter-American Human Rights System*, Inter-Am. Ct. H.R., Advisory Opinion OC-22/16 of February 26, 2016, Ser. A No. 22. The Court, however, reiterated that the human rights guarantees advanced by the Inter-American system and its treaties extend to indigenous and tribal communities as such. Id., paras 71-84. Additionally, the Court has adopted advisory opinions on matters related to the environment and human rights, marriage equality, the rights of LGBTI persons, collective bargaining with a gender perspective, and the human right to asylum. See Advisory Opinions OC-27/21, OC-25/18, OC-24,17, and OC-23/17, https://www.corteidh.or.cr/opiniones_consultivas .cfm?lang=en. The Inter-American Court on Human Rights also issued advisory opinions on presidential reelection without term limits and on the human rights consequences of denunciations to the American Convention on Human Rights and the OAS Charter. See Advisory Opinion 28/21, discussed later in this Chapter, and Advisory Opinion 26/20, https://www.corteidh.or.cr/opiniones_consultivas.cfm?lang=en.

On the Inter-American Court's advisory jurisdiction, see generally Eleanor Benz, *The Inter-American Court's Advisory Function Continues to Boom — A few comments on the requests currently pending*, EJIL:Talk (Nov. 25, 2019), https://www.ejiltalk.org/ the-inter-american-courts-advisory-function-continues-to-boom-a-few-comments-on -the-requests-currently-pending/; Jo M. Pasqualucci, *The Practice and Procedure of the Inter-American Court of Human Rights* (2013); Thomas Buergenthal, *The OAS and the Protection of Rights*, 3 EMORY J. INTL. DISPUTE RES. 1, 19-23 (1988); Thomas Buergenthal, *The Advisory Practice of the Inter-American Court of Human Rights*, 79 AM. J. INT'L L. 1 (1985).

## Comments and Questions

1. As noted, several state members of the OAS are not parties to the American Convention on Human Rights or other OAS treaties. Nonetheless, the American Declaration on the Rights and Duties of Man applies to all OAS member states. What is the juridical status of the American Declaration? Is it legally binding? If it is binding, why is it binding? Is it customary international law within the region? Does it take on binding qualities because of its link to treaties, including the OAS Charter? Review the discussion of customary law in Chapter 3.

2. The Commission has issued many historical decisions holding countries responsible for failing to fulfill their human rights obligations under the American Declaration, including in the *Maya Communities case* discussed in Chapter 3, pages 154-165. See also, e.g., *Djamel Ameziane v. United States*, Inter-Am. Comm'n H.R., Report No. 29/20 (Merits), OEA/Ser.L/V/II Doc. 39 (2020); *Kevin Cooper v. United States*, Case 12.831, Inter-Am. Comm., H.R. Report No. 78/15 (Merits) (2015); *Wayne Smith, Hugo Armendariz, et al. v. United States*, Case 12.562, Report No. 81/10 (2010). See also Inter-Am. Comm'n H.R., *Missing and Murdered Indigenous Women in British Columbia, Canada*, OEA/Ser.L/V/II.Doc.30/14 (2014). Are states subject to these decisions correct to question being held legally responsible under the American Declaration?

3. In general, how is the Inter-American Commission on Human Rights different from the Inter-American Court of Human Rights in relation to each one's authority to advance human rights among OAS member states? How potent is the

Inter-American Court's Advisory Opinion jurisdiction? Is there a valid concern that the Court might be going too far in its use of this jurisdiction?

4. For further introductory reading on the Inter-American system, see *Observations on the Process of Reflection on the Workings of the Inter-American Commission with a View to Strengthening the Inter-American Human Rights System*, Organization of American States Permanent Council (updated March 15, 2012), http://www.oas.org/council/reflexion.asp; Katya Salazar, "Between Reality and Appearances," in *The Reform of the Inter-American Commission on Human Rights*, Aportes DPLF Magazine, Number 9, Year 7 (April 2014), http://www.dplf.org/sites/default/files/apo rtes_19_english.pdf; Dinah Shelton, *The Rules and the Reality of Petition Procedures in the Inter-American Human Rights System*, Notre Dame Journal of International & Comparative Law: Vol. 5: Iss. 1, Article 2 (2015), https://www.corteidh.or.cr/tab las/r35064.pdf. See also Monica Pinto, *The Role of the Inter-American Commission and the Court of Human Rights in the Protection of Human Rights: Achievements and Contemporary Challenges*, Human Rights Brief 20, No. 2 (2013): 34-38, https://digital commons.wcl.american.edu/cgi/viewcontent.cgi?referer=&httpsredir=1&article= 1840&context=hrbrief.

## III. THE INTER-AMERICAN SYSTEM IN PRACTICE

In this section, we trace the various activities of the Inter-American Commission on Human Rights, including its monitoring of country situations and processing of individual case petitions, friendly settlement agreements, and precautionary measures. The section also discusses the work of the Inter-American Court of Human Rights in issuing judgments, reparations orders, and provisional measures in individual cases.

### A.  Country Reports and other Monitoring Mechanisms

As noted above, the Inter-American Commission on Human Rights has a number of mechanisms at its disposal to monitor the human rights situation of OAS Member States and to perform its protection and promotion functions. In addition to its ability to process individual case petitions, the Commission may "prepare such studies or reports as it considers advisable for the performance of its duties" American Convention, Article 41(c); Statute of the Commission, Article 18(c). This authority has been utilized to prepare a relatively large number of reports on "the situation of human rights" in particular countries. The reports may be undertaken in response to a series of individual complaints or NGO reports or at the Commission's own initiative, or even at a government's own request (e.g., report on Chile published in 2022 and reports on El Salvador, Nicaragua, and Brazil published on 2021).

Unless the human rights situation in a country improves dramatically, the Commission normally follows up an initial report with subsequent reports. These later reports may focus on particular aspects of human rights, or they may simply update previously reported information. For example, the Commission issued six reports on Colombia between 1981 and 2016, ten on Guatemala between 1981 and 2017, eight on Cuba between 1962 and 2020, five on Chile during and between 1974 and 2022, and nine reports on Haiti since 1969. Reports focused on countries may also be included in Chapter IV the Commission's annual report to the OAS General Assembly, under the heading "status of human rights in several countries." Inclusion in Chapter IV has signaled historically the Commission's particular concern about human rights in the designated countries. In the 2019 and 2020 annual reports, for example, Cuba, Nicaragua, and Venezuela were discussed. With more frequency, states are inviting the Commission to undertake on-site visits followed by country reports to avoid being included in Chapter IV of the annual report.

The country reports normally include a detailed analysis of the political and legal framework in the country, information on specific human rights violations, good practices, and the Commission's conclusions and recommendations. They are frequently based on on-site investigations by members of the Commission and its staff, although such visits require the consent of the country concerned. The reports are published and presented to the OAS General Assembly.

Below is an extract of an early country report by the Inter-American Commission on Human Rights, which was focused on Argentina and discusses the emergence of the practice of disappearances in that country after the military takeover in 1976.

Inter-American Commission on Human Rights

## Report on the Situation of Human Rights in Argentina

OEA/Ser.L/V/II.49, doc. 19, corr. 1 (1980), pp. 14-15, 18-19, 21, 53-56

A long phase of political and social instability began in Argentina in 1930. It gave rise to institutional crises, the establishment of irregular or de facto governments, an internal state of war, state of siege and martial law, attempts at totalitarian or joint rule, changes in the organization of state powers, enactment of repressive legislation and especially in the last ten years, an abrupt increase in terrorist violence by the extreme left and the extreme right, as a means of armed conflict. All of this has been detrimental to the rule of law.

In the last fifty years only two governments have completed their constitutional mandate: that of General Agustin P. Justo, 1932-1938, and that of General Juan Domingo Peron, 1946-1952. Military takeovers have prevented the completion of the other legal mandates during that same period and since 1952 [until 1980], no government has completed its constitutional term of office. . . .

With the military takeover of 1976, the constitutional system was altered by the new Government, by provisions which affect the full observance and exercise of human rights, despite the fact that in the Act issued on March 24 of that year, in which the purpose and basic objectives for the National Reorganization Process were set forth, a prime objective was "the validity of Christian moral values, national tradition and the dignity of the Argentine" and "a full enforcement of the juridical and social system."

When the change of government occurred in March 1976, the country was in a state of siege, pursuant to Article 23 of the Constitution, which made possible implementation of severe national security measures in order to eradicate subversion. . . .

By virtue of the Institutional Act of June 18, 1976, the Military Junta assumed, "the power and responsibility to consider the actions of those individuals who have injured the national interest," but on grounds as generic as "failure to observe basic moral principles in the exercise of public, political or union offices or activities that involve the public interest." Based on that Act, a number of special laws have been enacted, which, because of the discretionary nature of the powers granted, have led to the use of arbitrary measures, which have been the cause of intimidation and uncertainty. . . .

During [1976-1979], the IACHR . . . received a large number of claims affecting a considerable number of persons in Argentina. These claims allege that said persons have been apprehended either in their homes, their jobs, or on the public thoroughfares, by armed men, who are occasionally in uniform, in operations and under conditions that indicate, due to the characteristics in which they are carried out, that they are conducted by agents of the State. After these actions have occurred, the persons apprehended disappear, and nothing is ever known of their whereabouts. . . .

The Commission has in its files, lists with names, dates, and other data, as well as several studies that have been carried out regarding this problem. Without giving, for the time being, exact figures on the number of these disappeared persons, the information obtained makes it clear that there exists a situation of extreme irregularity requiring special discussion and analysis. . . .

In . . . denunciations or claims received by the IACHR it has been reported that the armed groups that carry out the operations in the homes apprehend the victim and occasionally his spouse and children, carry out a search of the home, looting the belongings of the residents, and as a general rule, take away all members of the family after placing hoods over their heads and eyes.

The persons affected by these operations, included in the lists at the IACHR, are mostly men and women between 20 and 30 years of age, although older persons and minors have also been known to disappear. Some of the children, kidnapped with their parents, have been released and delivered to relatives or have been abandoned in the streets. Other children, however, continue to be listed among the disappeared.

According to the Commission's information the phenomenon of the disappeared affects professionals, students, union workers, employees in various areas of business, journalists, religious leaders, military recruits and business men; in other words, most elements of Argentine society.

———————————

The Inter-American Commission on Human Rights now often conducts "working visits" to investigate human rights situations. These working visits are less formal and typically have a lower public profile than the Commission's official visits, but are nonetheless useful tools and can result in published reports. The following extract of the Commission's 2018 report of its working visit to Nicaragua in 2018 gives insights on the Commission's general and modern approach to reporting on country situations, the range of issues considered, and how it conducts on-site investigations.


Inter-American Commission on Human Rights

## Gross Human Rights Violations in the Context of Social Protests in Nicaragua

OEA/Ser.L/V/II., Doc. 86 (2018)


1. The instant report is about the human rights situation in Nicaragua as observed by the Inter-American Commission on Human Rights (IACHR) during its working visit to the country from May 17 to 21, 2018, in relation to the violent events that have been taking place since the State repressed the protests on April 18, 2018, and subsequent events over the following weeks. According to figures gathered by the IACHR, the State's repressive action has led to at least 212 deaths, 1,337 persons wounded as of June 19, and 507 persons deprived of liberty as of June 6, and hundreds of persons at risk of becoming victims of attacks, harassment, threats and other forms of intimidation.

2. The findings of the working visit suggest that the violence perpetrated by the State has been aimed at deterring participation in the demonstrations and putting down this expression of political dissent and that it follows a common pattern, marked by: (a) the excessive and arbitrary use of police force, (b) the use of parapolice forces or shock groups with the acquiescence and tolerance of State authorities, (c) obstacles in accessing emergency medical care for the wounded, as a form of retaliation for their participation in the demonstrations, (d) a pattern of arbitrary arrests of young people and adolescents who were participating in protests, (e) the dissemination of propaganda and stigmatization campaigns, measures of direct and indirect censorship, (f) intimidation and threats against leaders of social movements, and (g) lack of diligence in opening investigations into the killings and bodily injuries taking place in this context.

3. The demonstrators, including university students who took refuge on university campuses, the persons guarding the roadblocks known as *tranques* in different parts of the country, human rights defenders, journalists, victims and members of religious orders, comprise the groups most affected by the different forms of repression to which the Nicaraguan State has resorted.

4. The Nicaraguan authorities have cited maintaining public order and social peace as justification for their actions. Nonetheless, the IACHR notes that, in view of the scope of the State's violence and the type of strategies implemented by the State, it is obvious that there is coordinated action to control public spaces and repress social protest and not just a few illegal acts perpetrated by a few members of the security forces. In fact, the information received describes a pattern of state agents, mainly members of the National Police of Nicaragua and its anti-riot brigades, parapolice forces, as well as strike groups or mobs, acting in concert with the Police, setting into motion a repressive response aimed at deterring society from participating in the demonstrations.

5. The IACHR notes that this pattern has been implemented with the excessive and arbitrary use of force, including the use of lethal force, deliberately and systematically, by the above-mentioned actors. The IACHR notices that the State responded to the demonstrations in different stages and with different levels of intensity and that different tactics and methods of repression have been deployed against the demonstrators, as well as against the civilian population on the streets. Based on the information gathered by the IACHR, on April 18, 2018, the first day of the protests, the State response was first characterized by the excessive use of force, mostly, through the use of firearms and excessive use of less lethal weapons, such as tear gas, rubber bullets and buckshot, by the National Police and anti-riot squad, in order to break up protests and demonstrations in different cities of the country. Because the protests continued, from April 19 to 22 the State adopted a more aggressive repressive strategy against the demonstrators and even against individuals who were not taking part in the protests.

6. According to the testimonies received during the visit, snipers were deployed as another means of repression and evidence suggests a link of the snipers to State agents. The information received by the IACHR from staff members of public hospitals suggests that in the period referenced above numerous victims were treated for bullet wounds in the head, eyes, neck and the thorax, as well as in the back. The mechanics and trajectory of the shots would indicate arbitrary use of lethal force, or extrajudicial executions. According to the autopsy reports examined by the IACHR, projectile entry orifices, in many instances, were located in highly lethal areas of the body, which points to lethal intent of the shots.

7. Furthermore, the IACHR received extensive information and complaints of irregularities and denial of medical care and the blocking of humanitarian efforts to assist injured and wounded persons in the context of the violent events and repression occurring in the country on April 18, 2018. The restrictions reported on health care during the protests included not only obstacles within hospitals, but there were also reports about orders to restrict the departure and circulation of ambulances and humanitarian aid workers, such as firemen, Red Cross staff, as well as medical staff, paramedics, medical students and volunteers.

8. Additionally, a number of cases were identified where people did not go to State health care facilities out of mistrust or fear of being subjected to retaliation, and consequently they remained without any medical assistance or resorted to private hospitals, improvised health facilities or volunteer doctors, firemen and medical students, among others. According to testimonies received and public information, even schools, private homes and parishes were outfitted to tend to the wounded.

9. The IACHR views with concern that the mental health and emotional well-being of the population is being seriously jeopardized by the context of violence, harassment, threats and repression, in particular, those who report being victims of human rights violations, their family members, as well as students and residents who demonstrate against the government.

10. Additionally, the IACHR documented the existence of a pattern of arbitrary detentions occurring over the first days of the protests, mostly of individuals who were peacefully demonstrating, or were traveling on public roads in the area of the incidents. According to statistics, thus far, as of the date of the instant report, at

least 507 individuals were arrested, 421 of which are young people and adolescents. These detentions were carried out through the arbitrary and disproportional use of force, and were not based on the grounds provided for under the law, nor did they fulfill formal statutory requirements, but instead amounted to a punishment.

11. The IACHR also received many testimonies suggesting that most of the individuals detained in the context of the protests, that began on April 18, were subjected to different forms of cruel, inhuman and degrading treatment, with some of the treatment described beyond the threshold of torture, at the time of their apprehension and while they were deprived of liberty. In particular, according to information that was made available to the Commission, during their deprivation of liberty at the respective detention facilities mainly, "El Chipote" and "La Modelo," as well as when they were transferred to those facilities, the detainees were subjected to beatings and threats. According to the testimonies, the security agents threatened the detainees with death, as well as with assaulting them, their family members, and friends. The IACHR received complaints of the detainees being held incommunicado, inasmuch as they were not allowed to have any contact with their family members or legal representation.

12. Moreover, several testimonies taken by the IACHR cite attacks, acts of intimidation, threats, including death threats, and smear campaigns against young demonstrators, student leaders, human rights defenders, family members of the victims and members of religious orders in the country. In this regard, the Commission notes that several human rights defenders have been identified and assaulted in the context of the protests, in addition to accused and singled out for supporting the demonstrations. This has all led the Commission to reach the conclusion that in Nicaragua human rights defenders, the victims' family members and witnesses to human rights violations are at serious risk. Accordingly, the IACHR has requested the Nicaraguan State to immediately adopt precautionary measures to protect the lives and integrity of several individuals.

13. The Commission also received testimonies about state workers from different institutions, who reported being coerced into participating in pro-government acts, either under threat of being terminated or who actually have been terminated, under "orders from higher up" because they supported the protests. Some workers noted that the government has ordered the social media accounts of workers to be monitored in order to report who is sending messages or information perceived as running counter to the interests of the government.

14. The IACHR noticed that the State's response also included the dissemination of propaganda and stigmatization campaigns. Since the start of the protests, information has been disseminated which fails to recognize the grievances of the protests, any information about police repression is left out and the protesters, especially young people who block roads, are accused of being "delinquents" or "vandals" who are committing "acts of terrorism and of organized crime" and causing "chaos, pain and death" in the country and of violating the right to work of Nicaraguan families.

15. Additionally, during the visit and subsequent to it, the IACHR has noted that the State has adopted measures of direct and indirect censorship restricting the widest range of public information about what is happening in the country. Some media outlets or their journalists are being prevented from doing their job,

especially the independent media. During the demonstrations some media outlets were taken off the air, one journalist was murdered and others were wounded.

16. There were also reported cases of homes being attacked and burned by State actors and armed third parties, which has forced people to be displaced from their homes in search of safety and refuge.

17. The Commission has also observed several serious violations of access to justice and the right to the truth of victims and their family members, which is reflected mostly in the lack of diligence of the State to investigate the deaths and injuries occurring in the context of the protests, as well as serious irregularities in the recording of fundamental information for the elucidation of the facts, such as failure to conduct autopsies or conducting them based on documents (without any inspection of the bodies), untimely investigations and expert analysis, and shifting the burden of proof onto the victims or their family members. The IACHR ascertained with great concern the fact that the family members of the victims who died were instructed to sign waivers of transfer of the bodies to the Medical Examiner and to waive their right to file complaints as a requirement for receiving death certificates.

18. In particular, the IACHR underscores a climate of widespread distrust it has observed among victims, family members and representatives in filing complaints with the institutions in charge of investigating the crimes committed in the context of the protests. Victims and family members repeatedly cited a lack of trust in the National Police and the Office of the Public Prosecutor because these institutions would not offer any assurance of independence or impartiality. Additionally, the Commission notes that the victims' family members were afraid of filing complaints with the National Police because they felt intimidated by potential retaliation from this institution.

19. The IACHR identifies that there is growing violence in the country. The tension and reaction to the atmosphere of injustice and the failure of State actors to provide protection is leading to actions that fall outside the scope of peaceful protest. Social sectors sympathetic to the government and State agents in turn have been the targets of retaliation and harassment. According to figures provided by the State, from April 18 to June 6, 2018, at least 5 policemen have lost their lives and 65 have been injured in the context of the protests. The Commission also disapproves of these actions, which jeopardize the lives and safety of persons, and must be investigated and punished.

20. The IACHR condemns the escalation of State-perpetrated violence observed over the past weeks and reissues its call for the immediate cessation of repression. Likewise, it urges the Nicaraguan State to reach a constitutional, democratic and peaceful solution to this human rights crisis. The acts of violence must be investigated immediately, autonomously, independently and impartially, and with strict adherence to international norms and standards on seriousness, thoroughness and due diligence, in order to ensure the right to the truth and justice. In this context, the IACHR reiterates to the State the recommendations issued in its Preliminary Observations on the working visit and issues further recommendations.

21. In addition to providing a detailed analysis about the human rights situation in Nicaragua in the context of the protests that began in April, this report serves as a basis for the work of the GIEI in order to make a technical decision

about the lines of investigation as well as issuing recommendations of actions at the different levels of legal responsibility. Likewise, the instant report serves as guidance for the creation of the Special Follow-Up Mechanism of Nicaragua (MESENI), the purpose of which is to follow up on compliance with the recommendations issued in the reports produced in this context and the precautionary measures granted in the context of this document, as well as to continue to monitor the human rights situation of the country.

---

On June 24, 2018, with the acquiescence of Nicaragua, the Inter-American Commission created a Special Follow-Up Mechanisms for Nicaragua (MESENI) to follow-up on the recommendations made by the Inter-American Commission in the above report. The Commission has continued reporting on the deterioration of the human rights situation in Nicaragua in its annual reports, and it published in 2021 a report expressing alarm over the increasing power concentration in the Executive Branch and its negative impact in the rule of law and human rights situation in the country. See Inter-Am. Comm'n H.R., *Nicaragua: Concentration of Power and the Undermining of the Rule of Law*, OEA/Ser.L/V/II. Doc. 288 (2021), https://www.oas.org/en/iachr/reports/pdfs/2021_Nicaragua-EN.pdf.

The Inter-American Commission demonstrated its capacity for innovation in its human rights monitoring work through the creation of the ad hoc Interdisciplinary Group of Independent Experts (IGIE), in response to the alleged forced disappearance of 43 men in Guerrero, Mexico on September 26, 2014. The alleged victims were students of the Ayotzinapa Rural Teachers' College in Iguala who were traveling to Mexico City to commemorate the anniversary of the 1968 Tlatelolco Massacre. During the journey, they were presumably intercepted by the police, handed over to organized crime, and most likely brutally killed.

On November 18, 2014, the Inter-American Commission, with the agreement of Mexico, created the IGIE to provide technical assistance in the search for the missing students and in the investigation and sanctioning of those responsible. Under significant pressure to allow the independent investigation, the government of Mexico advanced considerable funding to the Inter-American Commission to finance IGIE's activities.

Since its creation, the IGIE has attracted significant media attention at the national, regional, and global levels. The IGIE, composed of well-known forensic and human rights experts in the region of the Americas, produced the report below with its main findings and recommendations.

## Interdisciplinary Group of Independent Experts

## Ayotzinapa Report: Research and Initial Conclusions of the Disappearances and Homicides of the Normalistas from Ayotzinapa (2015)

. . .

The Interdisciplinary Group of Independent Experts (IGIE) was appointed by the Inter-American Commission of Human Rights, with the agreement of the State of Mexico and that of the representatives of the victims of the case, to follow up on the investigation of the crimes and those responsible thereof, on the search for the disappeared, and on the care dispensed for the victims and their relatives. The IGIE has been working very intensely over these last six months as defined by its official mandate. At the end of this period, and while the possibilities or conditions for a follow-up of the case are defined, the Group wishes to publish its report. The idea is to account for all the work carried out, and describe all our findings, progress and proposals to the authorities of Mexico, to the victims' families and to the victims themselves, as well as to the human rights community, to the media and the people who have been following the case.

This report is a contribution to the fight against impunity. The IGIE has read and analyzed in depth the investigations carried out by the State Procurator General (PGJ) and the Procurator General of the Republic (PGR), and has used, as a fundamental part of its study, documents, declarations and evidence that were already included in their records. The Group has also carried out its own research on key aspects and has had independent expert reports drawn up by internationally-acclaimed independent experts in several of the necessary fields. . . .

The IGIE is sorry it cannot offer the relatives, the State and Mexican society as a whole, or the whole world, a final diagnosis on what happened with the 43 disappeared normalistas. There are many difficulties that are pointed out in this report. This report, however, does include facts that the Group considers proven, and a few others that it considers proven that they did not take place or on which there is such controversy that their validity is questionable. For the IGIE, the relationship with the relatives and other victims has been a key factor in this process.

The report attempts to gather their experiences, because in them there is much to be learned from the impact of forced disappearances and on the influence of the treatment received from the State authorities and social organizations. To have been able to approach this experience and to try to understand their situation has been a key element to be able to develop constructive policies both in terms of research and in terms of the search for victims and caring for them. . . .

The reasons and characteristics of this attack against the *normalistas* from Ayotzinapa, were extremely puzzling and bewildering for the students themselves, for Mexico and for the rest of the world: how can such serious crimes take place? And in fact, what exactly happened? The dimensions of the attack, however, have not been taken into account in a manner that would allow for an in-depth analysis of the facts. . . . . .

During these events there were over 180 people who were direct victims of various human rights violations, the great majority of them being young men, as well as many minors:

1. Six people were extra-judicially executed in four different crime scenes (including a *normalista* with clear signs of having been tortured, and another two who were shot to death at point-blank range, that is to say, from less than 15 cm away; and the three dead in the attack against the *Los Avispones* soccer team, among which there is one minor): at the crossroads between *Juan N. Alvarez and Periférico* Norte streets (in this case in two different episodes), on the *Andariego* road, on the way to the *Iguala* industrial area; on the highway leaving *Iguala*, in front the Palace of Justice; and on the *Santa Teresa* crossroads 15 km away from the town of Chilpancingo.

2.  Over 40 people were wounded, some of them seriously, and these were surgically operated on, one of which is still in comma and/or a state of stupor. These abuses took place during the referred facts in the initial crime scene in the *Juan N. Alvarez* and *Periférico Norte* crossroads, in the second attack three hours later in the same place, and at the Santa Teresa crossroads where another two consecutive attacks took place;

3.  Around another 80 people, including students from *Ayotzinapa* and teachers and other people who demonstrated their support endured different forms of persecution and attacks against their lives in at least three crime scenes, including the drivers of the buses involved: the *Juan N. Alvarez* and *Periférico Norte* street crossing; the area before the Palace of Justice and the *Pajaritos* colony; and the zone of 24th February Colony in *Iguala*.

4.  Another 30 people survived killing attempts in the case of the bus with the *Los Avispones* soccer team in the crime scene at the *Santa Teresa* crossroads.

5.  43 *normalistas* from *Ayotzinapa* were arrested from two different crime scenes and buses, one in the town centre and the other in the outskirts of the town of *Iguala*. They were later subjected to enforced disappearances.

6.  Among the victims it is also necessary to take into account the relatives of these direct victims -at least 700 people and that considering direct relatives only- and especially the relatives of the 43 disappeared *normalistas*.

Although the level of aggression and violence cannot be transformed into numeric data, these numbers show both the extension of the violence, and the different times and crime scenes in which they occurred, and the scope of the consequences that persist at present. . . .

The referred data shows the level of the aggression endured, the indiscriminate character thereof (shootouts against civilians, who were disarmed and fleeing), as well as the progressive increase of the level of aggression from the beginning of the commandeering of buses (chases and shots fired to the sky) to road blocks, shooting to kill, beatings, preparation of ambush actions, or long-standing persecution that were experienced at different periods.

The attack with shots fired in the very town centre, against buses with young people who had taken them from the bus station, before a numerous group of people who were in the street or at a concert in the town square, with a strong contingent and the deployment of police agents throughout the town appears to be completely out of proportion and devoid of sense, in comparison to the level of risk implied in the commandeering of buses or a possible confrontation with stones. The *normalistas* were unarmed, nor were they boycotting any political event whatsoever, nor had they attacked the population as has been indicated in different versions.

The Interdisciplinary Group of Independent Experts (IGIE) has been able to carry out its evaluation work, but has had to face an enormous level of fear, -still very much present nowadays- to be able to carry out its research activities in *Iguala*. Numerous witnesses did not want to speak; others did so in an atmosphere of considerable fear and requesting confidentiality, while others provided information only after numerous previous contacts carried out through confidence networks. Fear is not solely a response to the level of aggression endured, but also to the degree of control that is perceptible in the area by the perpetrators or their accomplices, and to the lack of protection felt by the witnesses against possible actions that could be carried out against them. Protection of witnesses is a key element in this process and its importance has been pointed out to the state authorities. . . .

In both scenes with *Estrella de Oro* buses 1568 and 1531, in which there were forced disappearances of *normalistas*, the aggressors were police agents from the *Iguala* and *Cocula* municipal police forces and perhaps others. In the crime scene at the Palace of Justice, according to witnesses, the perpetrators said that policemen or groups from *Huitzuco* were going to arrive in order to take part of the *normalistas* away.

Before that, the federal police, the state police, and the army had personnel posted in the *Iguala* turnpike at that time, which was where the normalistas had arranged to try to commandeer buses and where a state patrol car would have observed their arrival before leaving. According to the *normalistas'* testimony, the federal police was present close to the other place where they had foreseen to commandeer buses, the crossroads at *Huitzuco*. That is to say, before the facts, the *normalistas* had been followed by the federal police, the state police and the army, all of which knew these were students from *Ayotzinapa* engaged in fund raising activities and in the commandeering of buses. On the other hand, different witnesses also indicate the presence of the federal police in the crime scene at the Palace of Justice at two different points in time as well as that of ministerial police officers, according to the testimony of *normalistas*, other witnesses and municipal police officers; ministerial police were also seen in the crime scene at *Juan N. Alvarez*, according to some ministerial police agents; and army intelligence agents were also seen in the crime scene at *Galeana* street (exit to *Juan N. Alvarez*) and in that at the Palace of Justice, according to reports and statements by army members; and, according to the testimony of these survivors, ministerial police were also seen in the chase after normalistas in the *Pajaritos* Colony.

In addition to the municipal police forces of *Iguala* and *Cocula* that were the direct aggressors, in the two crime scenes at *Juan N. Alvarez* and at the Palace of Justice where *normalistas* were arrested and where there were forced disappearances, members of the army, the federal police and the ministerial police were also present at different times. After the arrests of the *normalistas*, an army patrol vehicle visited the Barandilla police station where a group of arrested normalistas would apparently have been taken, and later that same patrol vehicle went to the Hospital Cristina Clinic where a group of surviving normalistas and one of the severely wounded were sheltering. Also it protected the scene of the crime where two normalistas had been killed in the *Juan N Alvarez* and *Periférico Norte* street crossing after the second attack. Later, another army patrol vehicle arrived between 6 and 7am and protected the place where Julio Caesar Mondragón's tortured dead body had appeared, before the civilian authorities arrived. . . .

The IGIE in its research has considered several different hypotheses reference to the reasons that motivated the aggression. From an attack due to the fact that *Ayotzinapa* is considered a social base of political or insurgent movements, to the official thesis that was maintained for a certain amount of time on this being a confusion on the identity of the normalistas by the perpetrators. Another possibility considered was that this effectively was a punishment against the *normalistas* due to the existing precedents of confrontations and signaling against the Mayor, Mr. Abarca. Nevertheless, in opinion of the IGIE, those hypotheses explain neither the modus operandi nor the level of coordination and violence. It is probable that the contemptuous stereotypes on the *ayotzinapos* which different sectors brought to the attention of the IGIE on many occasions—even during their research activities—may be among the factors that could explain the aggression. Nevertheless, in opinion of the IGIE, this may have been a facilitating factor for the aggression, since scorn for others promotes violence, but never a detonating factor thereof nor an explanation for the level of violence used . . .

The scenes of violence that night of show a panorama of defenselessness of the victims before the aggressors. This not only due to the fact that it was the municipal police, but because no other police force of the State took action in protecting the *normalistas* in spite of having knowledge of the facts or being present in some of the crime scenes when the crimes took place and in spite of the fact that they had been witnessing the level of aggression and human rights violations. The mechanisms of protection or investigation of the government of the State of Guerrero did not work either. . . .

Nevertheless, it does not look as if a decision of this kind can be taken immediately and without preparing the necessary infrastructure to hide the fate of such a numerous group of people. The official version emphasizes a level of organization and a type of decision by a group of criminals which does not correspond as a whole with other criminal cases in the area, be it with murders or disappearances and concealment in graves. In this case it is a very numerous group of people, who are arrested by two municipal police forces in two different places and their fate is concealed with an enormous deployment of infrastructure and capacity of coordination that is necessary to carry out such an action. On the other hand, the contradictions in the different versions of the facts, by those accused of being members of *Guerreros Unidos*, and having carried out the murders and disappearances, show to the inconsistencies in this version of what happened and the disconnection of that version with respect to the levels of decision involved in the first part of the facts.

In addition the episodes of burning of corpses previously carried out bodies by *Guerreros Unidos* (in graves, and with firewood) left numerous pieces of proof and produce partial burning of bodies compatible with that kind of modus operandi, which allows for the identification of complete corpses which are sometimes even recognizable as complete bodies and not in that allegedly used in the case of the 43, in which they have been turned into "ashes." The only moment documented in the records in which a group of perpetrators gathers in the hours immediately after the facts is the proven meeting in the house belonging to Gilberto Lopez Astudillo, also known as El Gil, in *Loma de Coyotes* or *Pueblo Viejo*, according to the versions. This fact could probably show a moment in which the perpetrators analyzed the consequences of the facts and discussed possible steps to take. Be it then or at another time, be it by that group of perpetrators or in coordination with other intellectual or material authors, the decision on the disappearance had its continuity with the action carried out right from the beginning.

The decision to execute such an atrocious, sophisticated and unprecedented modus operandi, and therefore without counting on the necessary directives, practice, methods, materials etc. to carry it out and to turn the *normalistas* "into ashes," that is to say, to make them disappear to the point of turning their bodies into remains that cannot even be identified with DNA tests, similar to the calcinations that are obtained in a crematorium oven is unprecedented in terms of the place it was carried out in, nor in the modus operandi of the perpetrators of *Guerreros Unidos*, nor a motivation that corresponds to the considerable needs in terms of work, organization and adequate means to erase any kind of traces to such an extreme degree of sophistication.

The circumstances in which human remains were found mixed with ashes, earth and carbonized remains of combustible materials, and the later identification of the remains of a bone corresponding to one of the disappeared *normalistas*, shows both a pattern of concealment that comprises the crime of enforced disappearance, and the fact that at least one of the corpses of the *normalistas* was indeed incinerated. However, the conditions of this action and the versions on the facts continue being contradictory, although this report demonstrates that it is impossible for the waste dump at *Cocula* to be the scene of the crime, at least in the circumstances and times indicated in the investigation records. . . .

For the IGIE all these circumstances and findings show both the insufficiencies in the investigation and the tasks that are still pending in order to provide the relatives of the victims and Mexico as a whole with the justice they are entitled to expect in this case, including an effective investigation of the different responsibilities and the elucidation of the fate of the 43 missing *normalistas* which, as we have indicated is still uncertain. These circumstances and findings also indicate what is still to be done, and the way in which the search of the disappeared and the investigation of the facts and responsibilities and also the care for the victims and relatives should be oriented in the IGIE's opinion. All such matters are part of our mandate. In the opinion of this IGIE the advances made in these months in the investigation constitute a positive step. Nevertheless the IGIE considers that there should be general reconsideration of the investigation based on the results of this research.

––––––––––––––

On April 7, 2016, at the end of its 157th Period of Sessions, the Commission announced the termination of the technical agreement that created the IGIE and its intention to create a follow-up mechanism to monitor the situation. See Inter-Am. Comm'n H.R., *IACHR Wraps Up Its 157ʰ Period of Sessions*, Press Release No. 049/16 (Apr. 15, 2016), http://www.oas.org/en/iachr/media_center/PReleases/2016/049.asp. The Commission indicated in its announcement that the decision to terminate the IGIE was made at the request of the state of Mexico, noting the fact that the duration of the technical assistance agreement creating the expert group depended on its consent. It was not long, however, before Mexico did an about face, under continued international and domestic pressure to bring a resolution to the situation, and agreed to reinstate the IGIE. See *IACHR and Mexican State Sign Agreement to Reinstate the Interdisciplinary Group of Independent Experts (GIEI) for the Ayotzinapa Case*, Press Release (May 7, 2020), https://www.oas.org/en/iachr/media_center/PReleases/2020/104.asp. On March 28, 2022, the IGIE presented a report that discussed new findings concerning the disappearances and ongoing failures in the criminal investigations. See IGIE, *Informe Ayotzinapa III* (2022), https://centroprodh.org.mx/wp-content/uploads/2022/03/RESUMEN-GIEI-AYOTZINAPA-III.pdf. For discussion of this newer report, see Maureen Meyer and Stephanie Brewer, *Lies, Cover-Up, and Military Involvement: Third Expert Report Reveals Fresh Facts About*

*Ayotzinapa Disappearances*, Washington Office on Latin America (WOLA) (Apr. 4, 2022), https://www.wola.org/analysis/lies-cover-up-military-involvement-fresh -facts-ayotzinapa/.

In the same earlier 2016 press release, the Commission announced that family members of Berta Zúñiga Cáceres and other non-state actors had requested the formation of a similar independent group of experts to assist in the investigation of her killing in Honduras. Berta Cáceres was a renowned human rights activist in Honduras and a member of the Civic Council for Popular and Indigenous Organizations in Honduras (COPINH), advocating for causes related to the environment, extractive industries, and indigenous peoples. Her alleged murder brought international attention to the risks human rights defenders still face not only in Honduras but in the Americas in general. Her family indicated in hearings before the Commission, and during a visit of the Commission to Honduras, that they do not trust the local judicial authorities to conduct an exhaustive and credible investigation into her death. See Inter-Am. Comm'n H.R., Press Release No. 024/16, *IACHR Condemns the Killing of Berta Cáceres in Honduras* (Mar. 4, 2016), http://www.oas.org/en/iachr/media_center/ press_releases.asp; Inter-Am. Comm'n H.R., Hearing, *Human Rights Situation in Bajo Aguán, Honduras*, 157th Period of Sessions (April 5, 2016), http://www.oas.org/es/ cidh/audiencias/advanced.aspx?lang=en (audio).

## Comments and Questions

1. Under its governing statute, the Inter-American Commission on Human Rights could not have undertaken an on-site visit to Nicaragua without the consent of the government. Why would Nicaragua consent to such an investigation? Did the government think it would convince the Commission of the necessity of the repressive measures it had undertaken? Does it make a difference that the Commission was already monitoring the situation concerning the protests very closely and had issued a number of press releases? Can you see any benefit to a government that is collaborative during an on-site visit? Does state cooperation with the Commission in itself generate greater cooperation — the more a state cooperates with the Commission, the harder it is it to decline to cooperate?

2. What did Mexico stand to gain by agreeing to the inquiry of the IGIE with regard to the Ayotzinapa situation? And why would Mexico and the Inter-American Commission agree to an investigation by a group of highly qualified independent experts rather than by the Commission itself?

3. In the absence of an on-site visit with the consent of the government concerned, what is the value of a country report and its publication as an official OAS document?

### B.  Individual Case Petitions

### 1.  Admissibility and Merits

Even though the Inter-American Court of Human Rights has jurisdiction to adjudicate human rights claims, petitions by individuals or groups alleging human rights violations in specific cases are addressed first, and sometimes only, by the Inter-American Commission Human Rights. The following reading provides a summary of the rules and contemporary practice of the Commission for the processing of such petitions and for its public hearings and on-site visits related to these claims.

Dinah Shelton

## "The Inter-American Human Rights System"

in *Guide to International Human Rights Practice* 130-38 (Hurst Hannum ed., 4th ed. 2004) (notes omitted)

. . . Provided that the formal and substantive requirements are met, a petition may be filed with the Commission against any OAS member state. For states that are not party to the Convention, the recognized rights are those contained in the American Declaration. For parties to the American Convention, the rights contained in the Convention are protected in relation to all events which occur after the date of ratification, including continuing violations that may have begun prior to that date. Petitions also may be filed against a state party that violates its obligations under the Disappearances Convention or Article 7 of the Convention on Violence against Women.

The procedures governing complaints are set forth in the Commission's Statute and Regulations. The procedures are identical for all petitions, including criteria for admissibility, procedural stages, fact-finding, and decision-making, but only petitions arising under the American Convention or Disappearances Convention may be submitted to the Court (and then only if the state in question has accepted the Court's jurisdiction. [Editors' note: The Inter-American Court clarified in its 2009 *Cotton Field* Judgment, discussed in Chapter 4, pages 226-231, that petitions based on Article 7 of the Convention on Violence against Women are within the Court's jurisdiction].

The Commission is obliged to attempt a friendly settlement and may undertake a mission on-site if it deems it necessary and appropriate. The petition process may result in a Commission decision on the merits, together with specific recommendations to the state concerned. The Commission may call for the state to pay "appropriate" compensation when it finds a violation has occurred, but it does not itself set the amount of compensation it views as appropriate.

### Who May File

Any person, group of persons, or nongovernmental organization legally recognized in one or more of the member states of the OAS may submit a petition to the Inter-American Commission on Human Rights. The petition need not be filed directly by a victim but may be submitted by third parties, with or without the victim's knowledge or authorization. The petition may involve an individual or may indicate numerous victims of a specific incident or practice (a collective petition) . . .

## Exhaustion of Domestic Remedies

The Commission will not admit a petition unless all available and effective domestic remedies have been exhausted in accordance with general principles of international law. This means that domestic avenues of appeal must be pursued, unless it can be shown that no remedy exists or the purported remedies would be inadequate (i.e. incapable of producing the result sought) or ineffective (available in theory but not in practice). The petition therefore must include information on whether remedies under domestic law have been exhausted or whether it has been impossible or futile to proceed. . . .

The Commission has made clear that it is not a "court of fourth instance." The mere fact that the petitioner lost a case in the national courts is not grounds for bringing a petition to the Inter-American system. The Commission will not substitute its judgment for that of the trier of fact nor will it substitute its interpretation of a domestic statute or Constitutional norm for that of a domestic court. However, the Commission will accept a case if the proceedings in domestic court violated human rights guarantees of due process or fair hearing or were ineffective to remedy the violation, for example, if the domestic court lacked the power to strike down legislation incompatible with the Convention.

## Timeliness

Exhaustion of remedies is linked to the time limit within which a petition must be filed. Where domestic remedies have been pursued and exhausted, the petition must be filed within six months of the date on which the party whose rights have been violated was notified of the final ruling. This limit may be extended if the state has interfered with the petitioner's ability to file the complaint within the time period. If the requirement of exhaustion of remedies is excused because no remedies are available or effective, the petition must be filed within a reasonable period of time. If a third party is filing a petition for a victim unable to do so, the reasonableness criterion rather than the strict six-month rule may apply. The petition must include information on compliance with the relevant time period.

## Duplication of Procedures

The Commission cannot consider a petition if the subject matter is pending settlement in another international governmental organization or "essentially duplicates a petition pending or already examined and settled by the Commission or by another international governmental organization of which the state concerned is a member." However, the Commission will consider the matter if the other procedure examines only the general situation on human rights in the state in question, such as the UN's "1503 procedure," and there has been no decision on the specific facts in the petition submitted to the Commission, or if the other procedure will not effectively redress the violation. Although the situation is unlikely to arise in practice, the Commission also will consider the petition if the petitioner is the victim or a family member and the petitioner in the other proceeding is a third party acting without specific authorization from the victim. . . .

PROCEDURE

Petitions are considered in several distinct stages. Initially, petitions are received and processed by the Commission's Secretariat to see if they meet the requirements for consideration in accordance with Articles 26-28 of the Commission's rules . . .

Once the petition is complete and the Commission's *prima facie* competence is verified, the petition is registered and given a number, and the relevant parts of the petition are transmitted to the state in question. In transmitting the petition, the Secretariat deletes all details which would tend to identify the petitioner unless the petitioner has given authorization to have his or her identity revealed. The state is normally given two months from the date the petition is transmitted to respond to it. [Note from the authors: According to Article 30 of the current Rules of Procedure of the Commission, states are given three initial months to respond.] The state may request one additional month to reply, but it is not automatically entitled to an extension of time and its request must be evaluated by the Secretariat.

The Commission may invite further submissions from either party or may hold hearings prior to making a determination on admissibility. The Commission's regulations provide that, once observations have been received or the relevant time period has passed, the Commission must verify the admissibility of the petition; a working group on admissibility meets prior to each session to study the admissibility of petitions and make recommendations to the Commission. Only after the petition is deemed admissible is the petition registered as and considered "a case." In exceptional circumstances, where issues of admissibility are tied to the merits, the Commission may join consideration of the two issues and open the case by means of a written communication to both parties. . . .

HEARINGS AND ON-SITE VISITS

The Commission is authorized to hold a hearing to verify the facts, which is generally done in a chamber of three Commissioners, on its own initiative or at the request of one or more of the parties. . . .

In addition to holding hearings on cases, Commission practice now commonly includes informal visits to a country by the Commissioner who is the Rapporteur for the country along with a staff attorney. The visits typically concern more than one case and are directed at fact-finding, obtaining evidence or engaging the parties in friendly settlements. Where appropriate, the full Commission may undertake an on-site investigation in the country involved, at the request of the petitioner, state, or on its own motion. While on-site investigations are conducted much more frequently in the Inter-American system than in others, they are rarely undertaken solely to investigate a single or individual case. Instead, they are utilized to investigate allegations of widespread human rights violations within the target country, as part of which individual cases may be examined. No more than one or two such visits can be undertaken in a year.

FINAL DECISIONS AND REPORTS

The Commission examines all the evidence in the case and prepares a report stating the facts, arguments, and its conclusions regarding the case, including any proposals and recommendations it wishes to make. If the Commission finds there has been no violation, it states this in the report which it transmits to the parties and includes in its Annual Report. When the Commission finds one or more violations, it prepares a preliminary report with any proposals and recommendations it decides to make and transmits the preliminary report to the state in question. This is known as the Article 50 report, after the provision in the Convention that mandates it. The state is given two months to comply with the recommendations and is not authorized to publish the report until the Commission adopts its final decision. The petitioner is notified when the report is transmitted to the state and is given a summary of the findings. The short time limit for compliance and transmittal of information to the petitioner facilitates preparation for taking the case to the Court, if this can be done, within the three-month time limit imposed by the Convention.

If the state is party to the American Convention and has accepted the jurisdiction of the Court, the petitioner has one month to indicate a view on whether or not the Commission should submit the case to the Court and, if so, the reasons for this, the availability of evidence, claims concerning reparations, and personal information about the victim and the victim's family members.

---

In conection with the above, recall the Inter-American Commission's decision in the *Maya Communities* case in Chapter 3, page 157, which illustrates the Inter-American Commission's practice in issuing reports ruling on the merits of petitions and finding human rights violations under Inter-American instruments such as the American Declaration on the Rights and Duties of Man or the American Convention on Human Rights.

### *Note: Amnesties and Continuing Violations*

One of the most significant issues that has been brought to light in the context of transitions to democracy in the Americas has been the adoption of various amnesty laws, for example those adopted by Argentina during the 1980s. The Argentine amnesty laws were rejected by the Inter-American Commission in 1992 and ultimately by Argentina itself. See *Herrera v. Argentina*, Cases 10.147, 10.181, 10.240, 10.262, 10.309, and 10.311 (Argentina), Inter-Am. Comm'n H.R, Report No. 28/92, OEA/Ser.L/V/II.83, Doc. 14, corr. 1 (1993). The Commission held, inter alia, that the granting of amnesty and the refusal to account for disappearances and murders that occurred between 1976 and 1983 constituted continuing failures by the government to live up to its obligations under Article 1(1) of the American Convention on Human Rights, which Argentina ratified in 1984, a year after the last murder.

With respect to the temporal aspects of the Commission's decision in the Argentina amnesty situation, consider *Blake v. Guatemala*, extracts from which are set out below. Guatemala filed three preliminary objections to the Court's jurisdiction over a case of disappearance in that country. The first and most significant argued that the Inter-American Court was incompetent to examine the case inasmuch as Guatemala recognized the compulsory jurisdiction of the Court exclusively for cases that occurred after the date on which the declaration was deposited with the Secretariat of the Organization of American States. Blake disappeared on March 28, 1985 and was killed on March 29, 1985, according to the death certificate. Guatemala accepted the jurisdiction of the Court two years later, on March 9, 1987, with the explicit statement that such acceptance applied exclusively to events that "*occurred after the date on which the instrument of acceptance was deposited with the Secretariat of the Organization of American States.*" *Blake v. Guatemala,* Inter-Am. Ct. H.R. Judgment of July 2, 1996, Ser. C No. 27, para. 29 (emphasis in original).

The government maintained that the violations ended in March 1985, while the Inter-American Commission contended that the effects were continuous, since the deprivation of Mr. Blake's liberty and his death were discovered many years later and its consequences were still being felt, inasmuch as "they derive from Mr. Blake's kidnapping and subsequent forced disappearance by agents of the Guatemalan State and comprise, in addition to that crime, a series of violations including the cover-up of the disappearance by high-level Government officials and the Guatemalan Armed Forces, as well as the delay and consequent denial of justice by the Guatemalan State." The Court agreed that the acts of deprivation of Mr. Blake's liberty and his murder were indeed completed in March 1985 and that those events could not be considered per se to be continuous. The Court therefore lacked competence to rule on the government's liability for those acts. However, the Court distinguished those facts from the remaining allegations.

## Case of Blake v. Guatemala

Inter-Am. Ct. H.R., Jugement of July 2, 1996 (Preliminary Objections),
Ser. C No. 27 (notes omitted)

34. . . . [S]ince the question is one of forced disappearance, the consequences of those acts extended to June 14, 1992. As the Commission states in its application, government authorities or agents committed subsequent acts, and this, in the Commission's view, implies complicity in, and concealment of, Mr. Blake's arrest and murder. Although the victim's death was known to the authorities or agents, his relatives were not informed despite their unstinting efforts to discover his whereabouts, and because attempts had been made to dispose of the remains. The Commission also claims that there were further violations of the American Convention connected with these events.

35. In the first cases of disappearance of persons submitted to it this Court maintained that:

> [t]he forced disappearance of human beings is a multiple and continuous violation of many rights under the Convention that the States Parties are obligated to respect and guarantee . . . The practice of disappearance, in addition to directly violating many provisions of the Convention, such as those noted above, constitutes a radical breach of the treaty in that it shows a crass abandonment of the values which emanate from the concept of human dignity and of the most basic principles of the inter-American system and the Convention. The existence of this practice, moreover, evinces a disregard of the duty to organize the State is such a manner a

to guarantee the rights recognized in the Convention (*Velásquez Rodríguez Case*, Judgment of July 29, 1988. Series C No. 4, paras. 155 and 158, and *Godínez Cruz Case*, Judgment of January 20, 1989. Series C No. 5, paras. 163 and 166).

36. There is no treaty in force containing a legal definition of forced disappearance of persons which is applicable to the States Parties to the Convention. However, note should be taken of the texts of two instruments, the United Nations Declaration on the Protection of All Persons from Enforced Disappearance, of December 18, 1992, and the Inter-American Convention on Forced Disappearance of Persons, of June 9, 1994. Although the latter has not yet entered into force for Guatemala, these instruments embody several principles of international law on the subject and they may be invoked pursuant to Article 29(d) of the American Convention. In the terms of that article, no provision of this Convention shall be interpreted as *"excluding or limiting the effects that the American Declaration of the Rights and Duties of Man and other international acts of the same nature may have."*

37. Article 17(1) of the United Nations Declaration states that:

Acts constituting enforced disappearance shall be considered a continuing offense as long as its perpetrators continue to conceal the fate and the whereabouts of persons who have disappeared and as long as these facts remain unclarified.

Article III of the aforementioned Inter-American Convention provides that:

The States Parties undertake to adopt, in accordance with their constitutional procedures, the legislative measures that may be needed to define the forced disappearance of persons as an offense and to impose an appropriate punishment commensurate with its extreme gravity. This offense shall be deemed continuous or permanent as long as the fate or whereabouts of the victim has not been determined.

38. In addition, in Guatemala's domestic legislation, Article 201 TER of the Penal Code—amending decree No. 33-96 of the Congress of the Republic approved on May 22, 1996—stipulates in the pertinent part that the crime of forced disappearance *"shall be deemed to be continuing until such time as the victim is freed."*

39. The foregoing means that, in accordance with the aforementioned principles of international law which are also embodied in Guatemalan legislation, forced disappearance implies the violation of various human rights recognized in international human rights treaties, including the American Convention, and that the effects of such infringements—even though some may have been completed, as in the instant case—may be prolonged continuously or permanently until such time as the victim's fate or whereabouts are established.

40. In the light of the above, as Mr. Blake's fate or whereabouts were not known to his family until June 14, 1992, that is, after the date on which Guatemala accepted the contentious jurisdiction of this Court, the preliminary objection raised by the Government must be deemed to be without merit insofar as it relates to effects and actions subsequent to its acceptance. The Court is therefore competent to examine the possible violations which the Commission imputes to the Government in connection with those effects and actions.

## 2.   Precautionary and Provisional Measures

Article 25 of the Commission's Rules of Procedure provides that in serious and urgent cases, and wherever necessary according to the information available, the Commission may request that the state concerned adopt precautionary measures to prevent irreparable harm to persons. The Commission can decide on its own initiative to request a state to adopt measures, or at the request of the party affected. The Commission mostly reviews whether three requirements are present: urgency, gravity, and the potential or likelihood of irreparable harm. In many instances, the Commission requests information from the government before the measures are granted. There is no need for a petition to be before the system, and the mechanism applies to all 35 Member States of the OAS. The grant or denial of such measures does not constitute any prejudgment on the merits of the case.

In addition to the power to grant its own measures, the Commission may apply to the Court for provisional measures. Article 63(2) of the American Convention on Human Rights provides that "[i]n cases of extreme gravity and urgency, and when necessary to avoid irreparable damage to persons, the Court shall adopt such provisional measures as it deems pertinent in matters it has under consideration." With respect to a case not yet submitted to the Court, it may act at the request of the Commission. According to the 2020 annual report of the Inter-American Court, it was then monitoring compliance with a total of 24 provisional measures.

The following extract is indicative of the measures that may be sought by the Inter-American Commission on Human Rights and granted by the Inter-American Court of Human Rights.

## *Matter of B.* (El Salvador)

Inter-Am. Ct. H.R., Order of May 29, 2013 (Provisional Measures)

1. The brief of the Inter-American Commission on Human Rights (hereinafter "the Inter-American Commission" or "the Commission") received on May 27, 2013, and its annexes, in which it submitted to the Inter-American Court of Human Rights (hereinafter "the Inter-American Court" or "the Court") a request for provisional measures, pursuant to Articles 63(2) of the American Convention on Human Rights (hereinafter "the American Convention" or "the Convention") and 27 of the Rules of Procedure of the Court (hereinafter "the Rules of Procedure"), for the Court to require the Republic of El Salvador (hereinafter "El Salvador" or "the State") "to adopt immediately the necessary measures to protect the life, personal integrity, and health of B., in view of the urgent and imminent risk of irreparable damage as a result of the failure to implement the treatment indicated by the Medical Committee of the 'Dr. Raúl Arguello Escalón´ National Maternity Hospital" (hereinafter "the Medical Committee"). In addition, the Commission asked that the Inter-American Court "in its order on provisional measures, [ . . .] establish that the implementation of this treatment cannot be delayed by administrative or judicial measures or decisions," and that it "establish in its order that immediate and effective compliance with the provisional measures that it orders cannot, in any way, result in the exercise of the State's punitive powers . . ."

CONSIDERING THAT:

1. El Salvador has been a State Party to the American Convention since June 23, 1978, and accepted the contentious jurisdiction of the Court on June 6, 1995.

2. Article 63(2) of the American Convention stipulates that: "[i]n cases of extreme gravity and urgency, and when necessary to avoid irreparable damage to persons, the Court shall adopt such provisional measures as it deems pertinent in matters it has under consideration. With respect to a case not yet submitted to the Court, it may act at the request of the Commission . . ." . . .

4. This request for provisional measures does not arise from a case that the Court is hearing, nor has an initial petition been lodged before the Inter-American Commission for the facts that substantiate the request for provisional measures. However, this Court has established in previous cases that, "owing to the protective nature of provisional measures, exceptionally, these may be ordered, even when there is no contentious case before the inter-American system, in situations that, *prima facie*, may result in a grave and imminent impairment of human rights. In this regard, the Court has indicated that, in this type of situation, in addition to the requirements established in Article 63 of the Convention, it is necessary to take into account the situation described, the effectiveness of the State's actions in relation to this situation, and the degree of lack of protection in which the persons for whom the measures are requested would find themselves if these were not adopted. Thus, the Court reiterates that, in these cases, the Commission must present "sufficient grounds that include the criteria indicated. The Court also reiterates that the State has not revealed clearly and sufficiently the effectiveness of certain measures that it may have taken in the domestic jurisdiction."

5. This Court has established that, under international human rights law, provisional measures are not merely preventive, in that they preserve a juridical situation, but rather they are essentially protective, since they protect human rights inasmuch as they seek to avoid irreparable damage to persons. The preventive nature of provisional measures relates to the framework for international litigations; thus, the object and purpose of such measures is to preserve the rights that are possibly at risk until the dispute has been decided. Their object and purpose are to ensure the integrity and effectiveness of the decision on the merits and, in this way, to avoid harm to the rights in litigation, a situation that could nullify or render useless the practical effects of the final decision. Accordingly, provisional measures allow the State in question to comply with the final decision and, as appropriate, proceed to implement the reparations ordered. Regarding their protective nature, this Court has indicated that, provided that the basic requirements are met, provisional measures become a real jurisdictional guarantee of a preventive nature because they protect human rights inasmuch as they seek to avoid irreparable harm to persons.

6. The three conditions required by Article 63(2) of the Convention for the Court to be able to order provisional measures must co-exist in any situation in which they are requested. Based on its competence in the context of provisional measures the Court must consider only and strictly those arguments that are directly related to the extreme gravity, urgency and need to avoid irreparable damage to persons. Any other fact or argument may only be analyzed and decided during consideration of the merits of a contentious case . . .

7. Regarding the requirement of "gravity," in order to adopt provisional measures, the Convention requires that this be "extreme"; in other words, that it is at its highest or most intense level. The "urgent" nature means that the risk or threat involved must be imminent. Lastly, as regards the damage, there must be a reasonable probability that it will occur, and it should not relate to legal interests or rights that can be repaired.

8. This Court observes that, from the information provided by the Commission and uncontested by the State concerning the facts and the background of this matter, it has been proven that:

    a)  B. suffers from systemic lupus erythematosus (hereinafter "SLE"), aggravated by lupus nephritis;

    b)  Currently, B is 26 weeks pregnant and it has been determined that the fetus is anencephalic (without a brain), an anomaly incompatible with life outside the uterus;

    c)  The Medical Committee of the "Dr. Raúl Arguello Escolán" National Maternity Hospital "Dr. Raúl Arguello Escolán" (hereinafter "the Medical Committee") considered on April 12, 2013, that the pregnancy should be ended, taking into account that:

        1.  The prognosis for the survival of the fetus is nil in the short and medium term based on the prenatal diagnosis and, in the presence of anencephaly, there is a high possibility of severe fetal malformation.

        2.  The maternal disease previously described, mixed connective tissue disease overlapping with systemic lupus erythematosus and lupus nephritis, would certainly be aggravated as the pregnancy progresses and thus termination at an early stage of the pregnancy is necessary.

        3.  The actual moment of the pregnancy (less than 20 weeks) entails less risk for maternal complications than if the pregnancy progresses; thus, if it is prolonged there is a high risk of the occurrence of:

         _ Major obstetric hemorrhage
         _ Deterioration of the lupus
         _ Worsening of her kidney failure
         _ Severe preeclampsia, and complex forms of this condition such as hypertensive crisis, cerebral hemorrhage, arterial and venous thrombosis, and pulmonary thromboembolism
         _ Post-partum infections
         _ Maternal death

[ . . .]

11.  Bearing in mind the background information indicated above, the Court will now analyze the requirements established in Article 63 of the Convention; namely, extreme gravity and urgency, and the possibility of irreparable damage. However, before this, the Court recalls that the adoption of urgent or provisional measures does not presuppose or involve an eventual decision on the merits of the matter if the case should be submitted to the consideration of the Court, or prejudge the State's responsibility for the facts denounced.

12.  Regarding the first requirement, the Court underscores that all the medical reports cited have emphasized the severity of the health situation of

B. Indeed, the disease from which B. suffers, added to the other medical conditions that she has and the fact that she is pregnant, can result in a series of medical complications and even death. Indeed, the Court observes that, on April 22, 2013, the Latin American Center for Perinatology, Women and Reproductive Health" of the Pan-American Health Organization indicated that B. had [systemic lupus erythematosus] with exacerbated symptoms as of the first trimester of the pregnancy, and with two added complications of lupus nephrosis and hypertension, which have been treated to date with numerous medicines that could jeopardize her health [and, t]herefore, she has a high risk of dying," and also that "the patient suffers from lupus nephritis; namely, one of the highest causes of mortality in pregnant women with SLE." For its part, on May 7, 2013, the Institute of Forensic Medicine indicated that it was necessary to maintain "a strict medical supervision of the condition of the mother and fetus, and not to suspend the medical treatment for the chronic ailments from which she suffers, and [ . . .] required that she remain interned in a level three hospital." In addition, another example of the complex nature of her health situation is that the specialists agree that she must be kept under permanent medical supervision. Consequently, the Court considers that the gravity of the situation is high, so that the extreme gravity of this matter is proved *prima facie*.

13. Regarding the element of urgency, the Court observes that information was presented indicating that, actually, B. is stable and appears to be responding to the medical treatment that she is receiving (*supra* considering paragraph 8). Despite this, the Court underlines that, on May 2, 2013, the treating physician of B. indicated that "even though the patient's disease is stable, [ . . .] owing to the physiological changes inherent in pregnancy, added to the natural history of the underlying disease, a crisis could occur at any time, and it cannot be predicted when a medical emergency may occur." Similarly, the Constitutional Chamber's ruling of May 28, 2011, stressed that "the fact that B. is in a stable condition at this time, does not mean that the risk implicit in her medical history—which has been classified as severe and exceptional—has disappeared, owing to the unpredictable behavior of the underlying disease from which she suffers (SLE), and the biological changes that her body may undergo during the final stages of pregnancy during which the probability of the medical complications that she suffered during her first pregnancy is increased, or others may occur." It is precisely the fact that it is impossible to foresee whether the condition of B. will continue to be stable or whether, at any moment, a crisis could occur that creates a medical emergency that proves that it is urgent and necessary to take measures that prevent an impairment of her rights to life and to personal integrity. Moreover, the passage of time could have an impact on the right to the life and integrity of B., bearing in mind that the Constitutional Chamber itself noted that "the medical records" indicate that "as her pregnancy progresses, the patient may suffer from a worsening of the SLE and the above-mentioned obstetric complications, and these symptoms are aggravated by the fetal anencephaly, which would cause other problems," and that the Pan-American Health Organization indicated that "the physiological changes inherent in pregnancy may accelerate and exacerbate the disease of [B.] and even cause a series of obstetric complications, which had already occurred in her first pregnancy, including preeclampsia."

14. Regarding the alleged irreparable damage that could be produced if the necessary measures are not taken, the Court underscores that B.'s treating

physicians have concluded that her disease, added to the fact that she is pregnant with a fetus with "anencephaly, a major anomaly, incompatible with life outside the uterus," could entail risks to her health such as major obstetric hemorrhage, deterioration of the lupus, worsening of her kidney failure, severe preeclampsia and complex forms of this, such as hypertensive crisis, cerebral hemorrhage, arterial and venous thrombosis and pulmonary thromboembolism, post-partum infections or maternal death. In addition to the physical harm that B. could suffer, the Court emphasizes that her mental health would also be placed at risk. Indeed, the Court stresses that the documentation attached to this request contains some expressions of the intentions of B. in relation to her situation. In particular, B. has stated to the media that: "I want to live . . . yes, I want to live for my other child. I think that as this child is unfortunately ailing, and is going to die, then they should remove it . . . because my life is in danger." Also, on May 7, 2013, the Institute of Forensic Medicine indicated in its report that, "with regard to the emotional state of the individual examined, as she herself has said, she is under pressure, because she has been told that she is in danger of dying if they do not decide 'to remove the child.'" In addition, it indicated that "[t]he emotional situation of the individual examined is also affected by her belief that she could be faced with a prison sentence." It added that "[a]nother situation that causes her tension is her necessary separation from the family because, at the present time, she is hospitalized." The Institute of Forensic Medicine concluded that "[t]hese situations have led to the appearance of psychosomatic symptoms consistent with a state of emotional tension." Accordingly, the Court considers that the risk of irreparable damage to the life and physical and mental integrity of B. has been proved in this matter.

15. As previously mentioned, in matters in which the adoption of measures seeks to relate exclusively to their protective nature, it is necessary to analyze, in addition to the three requirements established in Article 63 of the Convention, the effectiveness of the State's actions to deal with the situation described and the degree of lack of protection in which the individuals for whom the measures are requested would find themselves if the measures are not adopted. In this regard, the Court considers that, in the context of the extreme situation to which this matter refers, the inter-American protection must reinforce and complement, to the greatest extent possible, the internal decisions adopted, so that B. does not find herself unprotected in regard to the possible harm that could be caused to her life and personal. In particular, the Court stresses that, in its ruling the Constitutional Chamber stated that "after the twentieth week, an eventual interruption of the pregnancy would not lead to or, in particular, have the purpose of the destruction of the fetus and, also, that the latter would be provided with the necessary measures to ensure, insofar as possible, its life outside the uterus." In addition, in the context of the decision taken by the Constitutional Chamber, "the defendant health authorities are obliged to continue monitoring the petitioner's health and to provide her with the treatment that, at any moment, is appropriate for her medical condition, as well as to implement the procedures that, according to medical science, are considered essential to deal with any future complications that may occur." Therefore, the State is obliged to guarantee that the team of treating physicians has the necessary protection to exercise fully their functions based on the decisions that, according to medical science, the said medical team may decide to adopt.

16. In addition, the Court takes note of the contents of the recent reports concerning this matter, in relation to the procedure that could be implemented, taking into account that B. is now in the twenty-sixth week of her pregnancy. Thus, on May 7, 2013, in its conclusions, the Institute of Forensic Medicine stated that, "from an obstetric perspective, [B.] is in the second trimester of her second pregnancy, so that, from a medical standpoint, one can no longer speak of abortion," and that "if complications occurred or a reactivation of the above-mentioned chronic diseases, [it would be possible] to proceed to terminate it by the corresponding means." Similarly, on May 17, 2013, the treating physician of the National Maternity Hospital indicated that "it should be clarified that, from a medical point of view, now at this stage of the pregnancy, [should it be required,] it would be necessary to effect an immature birth by caesarean section," and added that "a vaginal birth cannot be induced because the patient has had a previous caesarean section with a short period between pregnancies, and there is a risk of rupture of the uterus with the respective severe complications."

17. Based on all the above, the Inter-American Court considers that all the requirements have been met to adopt provisional measures in favor of B. in this matter. Therefore, the Court decides that the State must adopt and guarantee, urgently, all the necessary and effective measures so that the medical personnel who are treating B. can take, without interference, the medical measures they consider opportune and desirable to ensure due protection of the rights established in Articles 4 and 5 of the American Convention and, in this way, avoid any damage that could be irreparable to the rights to the life, personal integrity and health of B. In this regard, the State must take the necessary steps to ensure that B. is attended by the doctors of her choice.

———————

Precautionary measures can protect either one person or a group of persons, often covering entire populations or communities. A good example is the increasing use of the precautionary measures mechanism to protect the rights of indigenous peoples and communities in the Americas. The Commission granted measures on March 16, 2011 on behalf of all members of the Awá Indigenous Peoples in the Departments of Nariño and Putumayo in Colombia due to attacks, murders, and threats in the context of the Colombian armed conflict. See Inter-Am. Comm'n H.R. Res. 61/11, Precautionary Measures 61/11, *Members of the Awa Indigenous People of the Departments of Nariño and Putumayo, Colombia.*

Other examples include: On December 11, 2015, the Commission granted measures to protect all children and adolescents from the communities of Uribía, Manaure, Riohacha, and Maicao of the Wayúu people in the department of the Guajira. The request for precautionary measures alleged that the beneficiaries were at risk because of formidable barriers to access drinking water and malnutrition. According to the information presented to the Commission, 4,770 children had died as a result of this situation in the prior eight years. See Inter-Am. Comm'n H.R. Res. No 60/15, Precautionary Measures 51/15, *Children and adolescents of the communities of Uribia, Manaure, Riohacha, and Maicao of the Wayúu People, in the Department of the Guajira, Colombia* (2015). On April 16, 2021, the Inter-American Commission on Human Rights adopted precautionary measures to protect seven Wichí indigenous women in Formosa, Argentina who were pregnant and feared being submitted to forced C-sections, separation from their babies by state authorities, and deprivation of liberty. See Inter-Am. Comm'n H.R. Res. 32/21, Precautionary Measures 216/21, *Seven Pregnant Women of the Wichi Ethnic Group, Argentina* (2021). The Commission's precautionary measures are compiled at: http://www.oas.org/en/iachr/decisions/precautionary.asp.

### 3.  Friendly Settlement

The American Convention and the Commission's Rules of Procedure require the Commission to place itself at the disposal of the parties with a view to reaching a settlement of the dispute grounded in respect for human rights. The friendly settlement procedure requires the consent of both parties, and either of them may terminate it at any stage. The Commission, which acts as the moderator of meetings to facilitate agreement, is increasingly encouraging friendly settlement negotiations.

If a friendly settlement is reached, the Commission prepares a report that it transmits to the parties and refers to the Secretary-General of the OAS for publication. The increasing importance of the friendly settlement process is reflected in the creation at the Executive Secretariat of the Inter-American Commission of a section solely devoted to the handling of all stages of friendly settlements and the supervision of compliance. For more reading, see Inter-Am. Comm'n H.R., *Impact of the Friendly Settlement Procedure*, OEA/Ser.L/V/II. Doc. 45/13 (2013).

Below is an extract of a friendly settlement report published by the Commission concerning a case in Argentina.

## Inocencia Luca de Pergoraro et. al. v. Argentina

Case 242-03, Inter-Am. Comm'n H.R., Report No. 160/10 (2010)

2. The petitioners maintain that on June 18, 1977, Susana Pegoraro, who was five months pregnant at the time and the daughter of Inocencia Pegoraro, was arrested and taken to the Clandestine Detention Center that operated during the military dictatorship at the Naval Mechanics School (ESMA). According to the testimony of Inocencia Luca Pegoraro, Susana Pegoraro gave birth to a daughter inside the detention's facilities. The petitioners state that, in 1999, Inocencia Luca Pegoraro and Angélica Chimeno de Bauer became complainants and initiated a court proceeding, denouncing the abduction of their granddaughter, who they identified as Evelin Vásquez Ferra. Initially, the Federal National Court for Criminal and Correctional Matters No. 1 ordered expert testing to establish the identity of Evelin Vásquez Ferra. However, when this testing was challenged, the procedure was finally determined by the Supreme Court as not being mandatory because it felt that the testing was complementary for the purposes of the process given that the adoptive parents, Policarpo Luis Vásquez and Ana María Ferra, had confessed that Evelin Vásquez Ferra was not their biological child. The court also felt that mandatory testing violated the latter's right to privacy. The petitioners alleged that the ruling of the Supreme Court of Justice of the Nation closed the door to possible investigation into the disappearance of Susana Pegoraro and Raúl Santiago Bauer as well as the identification of Evelin Vásquez Ferra.

Friendly Settlement Agreement

. . .

Recognition of Facts. Adoption of Measures

The Government of the Argentine Republic recognizes the facts presented in Petition 242/03 of the registry of the Inter-American Commission on Human Rights. In this regard, and without prejudice to the legal debate that emerges regarding the collision of legally protected assets presented by the case and the decision adopted by the Supreme Court of Justice of the Nation, the State agrees with the petitioner on the need to adopt suitable measures that could effectively contribute to obtaining justice in those cases in which it is necessary to identify persons using scientific methods that require that samples be obtained.

2.1. On the right to identity

a. The National Executive Branch of the Argentine Republic agrees to send the Honorable Congress of the Nation a bill on establishing a procedure for obtaining DNA samples that protects the rights of those involved and effectively investigates and adjudicates the abduction of children during the military dictatorship.

b. The National Executive Branch of the Argentine Republic agrees to send to the Honorable Congress of the Nation a bill to amend the legislation governing the operation of the National Genetic Data Bank in order to adapt it to scientific advances in this area.

2.2. On the right of access to justice

a. The National Executive Branch of the Argentine Republic agrees to send to the Honorable Congress of the Nation a bill to more effectively guarantee the judicial participation of victims –understanding as such persons allegedly kidnapped and their legitimate family members – and intermediate associations set up to defend their rights in proceedings investigating the kidnapping of children.

b. The National Executive Branch of the Argentine Republic agrees to adopt, within a reasonable period of time, the measures necessary to optimize and expand on the implementation of Resolution No. 1229/09 of the Ministry of Justice, Security, and Human Rights.

c. The National Executive Branch of the Argentine Republic agrees to work on adopting measures to optimize the use of the power conferred upon it by Art. 27 of Law No. 24.946 (Organic Law of the Attorney General's Office) in order to propose that the Attorney General: 1) issue general instructions to prosecutors urging them to be present at residential searches conducted in cases in which the kidnapping of children is being investigated; and 2) design and execute a Special Investigation Plan on the kidnapping of children during the military dictatorship in order to optimize the resolution of cases, providing special prosecutors for the purpose in jurisdictions where the number of cases being processed justifies this.

2.3. On the training of judicial actors

a. The National Executive Branch of the Argentine Republic agrees to work on adopting measures associated with the use of the power conferred on it by Art.

27 of Law No. 24.946 (Organic Law of the Attorney General's Office) in order to propose that the Attorney General provide training for prosecutors and other employees of the Attorney General's Office in the appropriate handling of the victims of these serious crimes.

b. The National Executive Branch of the Argentine Republic agrees to urge the Council of the Judiciary of the Nation to plan training courses for judges, functionaries, and employees of the Judicial Branch in the appropriate handling of the victims of these serious crimes (see. Art. 7(11) of Law No. 24.937, o.t. Art. 3 of Law No. 26.080).

2.4. Regarding the task force

a. The National Executive Branch of the Argentine Republic agrees to establish specific mechanisms to facilitate the correction of national, provincial, and municipal public and private documentation and records of anyone whose identity was changed during the military dictatorship, in order to promote the restoration of identity.

b. The parties agree to hold periodic working meetings, in the Foreign Ministry, for purposes of evaluating progress made with the measures agreed to herein.

c. The Government of the Argentine Republic agrees to facilitate the activities of the task force, and provide it with technical support and the use of facilities as needed to develop its tasks, agreeing to report periodically to the Inter-American Commission on Human Rights.

2.5. On publicity

The Government of the Argentine Republic agrees to publicize this agreement in the Official Bulletin of the Argentine Republic and in the newspapers "Clarín," "La Nación," and "Página 12," once it is approved by the Inter-American Commission on Human Rights in accordance with the provisions of Article 49 of the American Convention on Human Rights.

III. PETITION

The Government of the Argentine Republic and the Petitioners celebrate the signing of this agreement, indicate their full agreement with its content and scope, and share their appreciation for the good will evidenced in the negotiating process. In this respect, it is noted that this agreement should be formalized through the approval by Decree of the National Executive Branch, at which time the Inter-American Commission on Human Rights will be asked to ratify the friendly settlement agreement reached by adopting the report indicated in Article 49 of the American Convention on Human Rights.

Buenos Aires, September 11, 2009

## Comments and Questions

1. How are the admissibility requirements for a petition to the Inter-American Commission on Human Rights similar to or different from those for communications under the Optional Protocol to the International Covenant on Civil and Political Rights discussed in Chapter 7?

2. As the number of petitions submitted to the Commission has grown each year, so has the number of requests for precautionary measures. During the past several years, the Commission has ordered more precautionary than any other international human rights body. Solely in 2020, the Commission granted 49 precautionary measures, lifted 40 precautionary measures in force, and 9 measures were extended. Throughout 2020, the Commission received 1,170 new requests for precautionary measures and 98.8% of these underwent review in accordance with Article 25 of the Commission's rules of procedure. See Inter-Am. Comm'n H.R., Annual Report 2020, OEA/Ser.L/V/II, Doc., Doc. 28, (2021), paras. 307 and 318. Which factors should the Commission consider in determining whether a particular situation meets the requirements of urgency, gravity, and irreparable harm in order to justify precautionary measures? At what point in a case can the Commission issue or request that the Court issue provisional measures?

3. How flexible is the concept of a "continuing violation" of human rights? Is there any violation committed in the past that does not continue to affect the victim or their relatives, or is there something unique about the phenomenon of disappearances addressed in the *Case of Blake v. Guatemala*?

4. What are the advantages of the friendly settlement procedure? The vast majority of cases adjudicated by the Inter-American Commission do not end in friendly settlement. Why is that? Under what circumstances might a state be most likely to agree to friendly settlement? What does the *Pergoraro* case suggest in this regard?

5. In 2020 alone, some 1,990 petitions claiming human rights violations were received by the Inter-American Commission on Human Rights. See Inter-American Comm'n H.R., Annual Report 2020, OEA/Ser.L/V/II, Doc. 28, March 30, 2021, Chapter II: The System of Petitions and Cases, Friendly Settlements, and Precautionary Measures, para. 14. The processing of individual cases by the Inter-American Commission has led it to set groundbreaking standards on amnesty, forced disappearances, the death penalty, violence against women, indigenous peoples, and freedom of expression, among other areas. Many of these standards have been expanded or consolidated through judgments issued by the Inter-American Court in the more than 300 cases presented to the Court by the Inter-American Commission. Yet, the Inter-American Commission has only seven part-time members and its legal staff consists of approximately 40 attorneys, of whom close to a quarter are fellows. Only half of these attorneys are funded by the regular financing of OAS member states. The rest are funded by voluntary contributions from donors. Of the nearly 2000 petitions submitted in any given year, the Commission takes formal decisions (to declare a petition admissible or inadmissible, approve a friendly settlement, adopt a report on the merits, or close a case for other reasons) on an average of only 10 percent of those cases annually. While most observers would agree that the Commission's procedures have improved significantly in recent years, can this situation continue? What reforms might you suggest, considering the financial challenges facing the Commission?

6. The Commission's mandate extends to promoting compliance with and knowledge of the legal standards issued by the Inter-American system—work that includes on-site visits, the production of country and thematic reports, as well as training for government officials, human rights advocates, and academic institutions. States have increasingly pushed the Commission to have more of a promotion

role, rather than a protection one through adjudication of complaints, due to their discomfort with individual case processing and the country-specific "naming" and "shaming" that can result from the adjudication of specific cases. Newly or emerging democracies in Latin American have also increasingly demanded from the Commission documentation of their good practices as a more effective way to promote compliance with human rights obligations. Furthermore, the Commission in the last decade suffered a financial crisis affecting its daily operations and human resources capacity. See *Severe Financial Crisis of the IACHR Leads to Suspension of Hearings and Imminent Layoff of Nearly Half its Staff*, Inter-Am. Comm'n H.R., Press Release No. 069/16, (May 23, 2016), http://www.oas.org/en/iachr/media_center/PReleases/2016/069.asp. Considering all of these historical, structural and financial factors, what kind of work should the Commission prioritize—its protection or promotion work? What would be the most effective combination or balance?

## C.  Inter-American Court of Human Rights Proceedings and Reparations

For the Inter-American Court of Human Rights to have jurisdiction over an individual case, the state concerned must be a party to the American Convention and have accepted the optional jurisdiction of the Court; and proceedings before the Commission must be completed. States are offered a timeframe by the Commission to comply with the recommendations contained in the Commission's merits report. An individual petitioner cannot invoke the Court's jurisdiction.

Under current rules, there is a presumption that all cases should go to the Court if the Commission has found one or more violations and the responsible state has not complied with the Commission's recommendations within the time period specified. A reasoned decision by an absolute majority of the Commission is required to withhold such a case from the Court. Other factors that the Commission may consider include the nature and seriousness of the violation, the need to develop or clarify case law, the future effect of the decision on member states, the quality of the evidence, and the position taken by the petitioner.

When a case is submitted to the Court by the Commission, three parties have representation before the Court. One is the Commission, which decides to submit the case to the Court after weighing the factors just mentioned. It is typically represented before the Court by delegates, who are usually one Commissioner and attorneys from the Commission's Executive Secretariat. The alleged victim(s) and their representative(s) also constitute a litigating party before the Court, and the state can be represented by its own agents.

Cases before the Inter-American Court follow both a written and an oral process. In the written process, the Court notifies both the alleged victim(s)' representative(s) and the state involved of the presentation of the case; and it offers the victim(s)' representative(s) the opportunity to file a written submission with supporting evidence. It also allows the state involved to present in writing its position on the case, including by the filing of preliminary objections to the processing of the case.

For individual cases, the Court also generally conducts oral proceedings in which all three parties may present their arguments and evidence. Witnesses may be called, who may include the victim or victims, witnesses to the issues litigated, family members, and expert witnesses on the legal or other issues involved in the case. These witnesses may be summoned to the public hearing by the Court or may be asked to render their evidence through affidavits. After the conclusion of the public hearing, the parties are offered the opportunity to file their final written arguments to the Court. According to Article 44 (3) of the Rules of Procedure of the Court, amicus briefs by outside persons or institutions can also be presented at any stage of the proceedings up to 15 days following the public hearing.

After the public hearing and the presentation of final written arguments, the Court issues its judgment on the merits of the case. The judgments usually include a description of the proceedings and the facts of the case; a summary of the submissions and legal arguments of the parties; the Court's conclusions on whether and which provisions of the relevant Inter-American treaties have been violated; and its decision concerning reparations and costs. The Court monitors compliance with its judgments through periodic reports from the three parties to the case and hearings.

Unlike the Commission, which can only make recommendations, the Court may order that a violation be remedied and may award compensation to the injured party. Compensation includes indemnification for actual damage and emotional or moral injury, but does not include punitive damages as such. Specific orders for nonmonetary relief may also be awarded, such as the release of wrongfully held detainees. The state concerned is legally obliged to comply with a judgment of the Court and related orders, and a remedial order may be enforced in domestic courts through the appropriate proceedings.

Recall the Court's judgment in the *Cotton Field* case, discussed in Chapter 4, at pages 226-231, in which the Court found Mexico responsible for the disappearances of women in and around Juarez, Mexico. The part of the judgement ordering reparations in that case is reproduced below in substantial part.

## González, et al. ("Cotton Field") v. Mexico

Inter-Am. Court H.R., Judgment of Nov. 16, 2009, Ser. C No. 205

. . .

### IX. REPARATIONS

450. The Court recalls that the concept of "integral reparation" (*restitutio in integrum*) entails the re-establishment of the previous situation and the elimination of the effects produced by the violation, as well as the payment of compensation for the damage caused. However, bearing in mind the context of structural discrimination in which the facts of this case occurred, which was acknowledged by the State. . . . the reparations must be designed to change this situation, so that their effect is not only of restitution, but also of rectification. In this regard, re-establishment of the same structural context of violence and discrimination is not acceptable. Similarly, the Tribunal recalls that the nature and amount of the reparations ordered depend on the characteristics of the violation and on the

pecuniary and non-pecuniary damage caused. Reparations should not make the victims or their next of kin either richer or poorer and they should be directly proportionate to the violations that have been declared. One or more measures can repair a specific damage, without this being considered double reparation.

451. In accordance with the foregoing, the Court will assess the measures of reparation requested by the Commission and the representatives to ensure that they: (i) refer directly to the violations declared by the Tribunal; (ii) repair the pecuniary and non-pecuniary damage proportionately; (iii) do not make the beneficiaries richer or poorer; (iv) restore the victims to their situation prior to the violation insofar as possible, to the extent that this does not interfere with the obligation not to discriminate; (v) are designed to identify and eliminate the factors that cause discrimination; (vi) are adopted from a gender perspective, bearing in mind the different impact that violence has on men and on women, and (vii) take into account all the juridical acts and actions in the case file which, according to the State, tend to repair the damage caused. . . .

THE COURT . . .
    . . .ORDERS,
    unanimously that,
    11. This judgement constitutes *per se* a form of reparation.
    12. The State shall, in accordance with . . . this Judgment, conduct the criminal proceeding that is underway effectively and, if applicable, any that are opened in the future to identify, prosecute and, if appropriate, punish the perpetrators and masterminds of the disappearances, ill-treatments and deprivations of life of Mss. González, Herrera and Ramos, in accordance with the following directives:

    (i) All legal or factual obstacles to the due investigation of the facts and the execution of the respective judicial proceedings shall be removed, and all available means used, to ensure that the investigations and judicial proceedings are prompt so as to avoid a repetition of the same or similar facts as those of the present case;

    (ii) The investigation shall include a gender perspective; undertake specific lines of inquiry concerning sexual violence, which must involve lines of inquiry into the respective patterns in the zone; be conducted in accordance with protocols and manuals that comply with the guidelines set out in this Judgment; provide the victims' next of kin with information on progress in the investigation regularly and give them full access to the case files, and be conducted by officials who are highly trained in similar cases and in dealing with victims of discrimination and gender-based violence;

    (iii) The different entities that take part in the investigation procedures and in the judicial proceedings shall have the necessary human and material resources to perform their tasks adequately, independently and impartially, and those who take part in the investigation shall be given due guarantees for their safety, and

    (iv) The results of the proceedings shall be published so that the Mexican society learns of the facts that are the object of the present case.

    13. The State shall, within a reasonable time, investigate, through the competent public institutions, the officials accused of irregularities and, after an

appropriate proceeding, apply the corresponding administrative, disciplinary or criminal sanctions to those found responsible . . .

14. The State shall, within a reasonable time, conduct the corresponding investigation and, if appropriate, punish those responsible for the harassment of Adrián Herrera Monreal, Benita Monárrez Salgado, Claudia Ivonne Ramos Monárrez, Daniel Ramos Monárrez, Ramón Antonio Aragón Monárrez, Claudia Dayana Bermúdez Ramos, Itzel Arely Bermúdez Ramos, Paola Alexandra Bermúdez Ramos and Atziri Geraldine Bermúdez Ramos, in accordance with paragraphs . . . this Judgment.

16. The State shall, within six months of notification of this Judgment, publish once in the Official Gazette of the Federation, in a daily newspaper with widespread national circulation and in a daily newspaper with widespread circulation in the state of Chihuahua, paragraphs 113 to 136, 146 to 168, 171 to 181, 185 to 195, 198 to 209 and 212 to 221 of the present Judgment [seting forth key facts and findings of the Court in the case], and the operative paragraphs, without the corresponding footnotes. Additionally, the State shall, within the same time frame, publish this Judgment in its entirety on an official web page of the State. . . .

17. The State shall, within one year of notification of this Judgment, organize a public act to acknowledge its international responsibility in relation to the facts of this case so as to honor the memory of Laura Berenice Ramos Monárrez, Esmeralda Herrera Monreal and Claudia Ivette González . . .

18. The State shall, within one year of notification of this Judgment, erect a monument in memory of the women victims of gender-based murders in Ciudad Juárez . . . The monument shall be unveiled at the ceremony during which the State publicly acknowledges its international responsibility, in compliance with the decision of the Court specified in the preceding operative paragraph.

19. The State shall, within a reasonable time, continue standardizing all its protocols, manuals, prosecutorial investigation criteria, expert services, and services to provide justice that are used to investigate all the crimes relating to the disappearance, sexual abuse and murders of women in accordance with the Istanbul Protocol, the United Nations Manual on the Effective Prevention and Investigation of Extralegal, Arbitrary and Summary Executions, and the international standards to search for disappeared persons, based on a gender perspective, in accordance with . . . this Judgment. In this regard, an annual report shall be presented for three years.

20. The State shall, within a reasonable time, and in accordance with . . . this Judgment, adapt the Alba Protocol [a special surveillance remigem]or else implement a similar new mechanism, pursuant to the following directives, and shall present an annual report for three years:

> (i)  Implement searches *ex officio* and without any delay, in cases of disappearance, as a measure designed to protect the life, personal liberty and personal integrity of the disappeared person;
>
> (ii)  Establish coordination among the different security agencies in order to find the person;
>
> (iii)  Eliminate any factual or legal obstacles that reduce the effectiveness of the search or that prevent it from starting, such as requiring preliminary inquiries or procedures;

(iv) Allocate the human, financial, logistic, scientific or any other type of resource required for the success of the search;

(v) Verify the missing report against the database of disappeared persons referred to in paragraphs 509 to 512 s*upra*, and

(vi) Give priority to searching areas where reason dictates that it is most probable to find the disappeared person, without disregarding arbitrarily other possibilities or areas. All of the above must be even more urgent and rigorous when it is a girl who has disappeared.

21. The State shall create, within six months of notification of this Judgment, a web page that it must update continually with the necessary personal information on all the women and girls who have disappeared in Chihuahua since 1993 and who remain missing. This web page must allow any individual to communicate with the authorities by any means, including anonymously, to provide relevant information on the whereabouts of the disappeared women or girls or, if applicable, of their remains, in accordance with . . . the present Judgment.

22. The State shall, within one year of notification of this Judgment . . . create or update a database with:

(i) The personal information available on disappeared women and girls at the national level:

(ii) The necessary personal information, principally DNA and tissue samples, of the next of kin of the disappeared who consent to this – or that is ordered by a judge – so that the State can store this personal information solely in order to locate a disappeared person, and

(iii) The genetic information and tissue samples from the body of any unidentified woman or girl deprived of life in the state of Chihuahua.

23. The State shall continue implementing permanent education and training programs and courses for public officials on human rights and gender, and on a gender perspective to ensure due diligence in conducting preliminary inquiries and judicial proceedings concerning gender-based discrimination, abuse and murder of women, and to overcome stereotyping about the role of women in society, in the terms of paragraphs 531 to 542 of this Judgment. Every year, for three years, the State shall report on the implementation of the courses and training sessions.

24. The State shall, within a reasonable time, conduct an educational program for the general population of the state of Chihuahua so as to overcome said situation. In this regard, the State shall present an annual report for three years, indicating the measures it has taken to this end, in the terms of paragraph 543 of this Judgment.

25. The State shall provide appropriate and effective medical, psychological or psychiatric treatment, immediately and free of charge, through its specialized health institutions to Irma Monreal Jaime, Benigno Herrera Monreal, Adrián Herrera Monreal, Juan Antonio Herrera Monreal, Cecilia Herrera Monreal, Zulema Montijo Monreal, Erick Montijo Monreal, Juana Ballín Castro, Irma Josefina González Rodríguez, Mayela Banda González, Gema Iris González, Karla Arizbeth Hernández Banda, Jacqueline Hernández, Carlos Hernández Llamas, Benita Monárrez Salgado, Claudia Ivonne Ramos Monárrez, Daniel Ramos Monárrez, Ramón Antonio Aragón Monárrez, Claudia Dayana Bermúdez Ramos, Itzel Arely

Bermúdez Ramos, Paola Alexandra Bermúdez Ramos and Atziri Geraldine Bermúdez Ramos, if they so wish, in the terms of paragraphs 544 to 549 of this Judgment.

26. The State shall, within one year of notification of the present Judgment,
pay the amounts established in paragraphs 565, 566, 577, 586 and 596 hereof
[amounts for funeral and other expenses, lost earnings, and moral damages] as
compensation for pecuniary and non-pecuniary damage and reimbursement of
costs and expenses, as appropriate, under the conditions and in the terms of . . .
this Judgment.

27. The Court will monitor full compliance with this Judgment in exercise of
its powers and in compliance with its obligations under the American Convention,
and will consider the case closed when the State has complied in full with all the
provisions herein. Within one year of notification of the Judgment, the State shall
provide the Court with a report on the measures adopted to comply with it.

The Court frequently refers to the *Aloeboetoe v. Suriname* case on the issue of
reparations. In that case, Suriname accepted responsibility for the kidnapping and
deaths of six young men and a 15-year-old boy of the Saramaka tribe. The victims
were forced to dig their own graves before six of them were killed. The seventh
was shot and seriously wounded while trying to escape. He later died of his wounds
after testifying about the massacre. On behalf of the victims' families, the Commission sought indemnification for material and moral damages, based on *restitutio
in integrum*, other nonmonetary reparations, and reimbursement of expenses and
costs incurred by the victims' next of kin. The Commission used questionnaire affidavits, administered with the permission of the Saramaca, to determine appropriate
remedies. These were reviewed by an actuary from the accounting firm of Coopers
and Lybrand to apply the "present value added" method to determine projected
earnings of the victims. The Commission identified 37 beneficiaries and submitted
a total demand for pecuniary damages comprising a lump sum of US$2,557,242
($557,000 for material damages to the children and an annual payment of $42,000,
adjusted for actual damages to the adult dependents).

In *Aloeboetoe*, the Court faced the difficult problem of identifying those among
the family members of the deceased who were entitled to compensation. The case
was brought by members of the Saramakas, or Maroons, descendants of African
slaves who maintain a traditional culture, including a matriarchal social structure
and polygamy. The Court, applying what it called a generally recognized choice of
law principle, determined that local law should apply to determine next of kin and
beneficiaries of the victims. Suriname law holds that a victim's next of kin includes
the legally recognized spouse, the children, and perhaps dependent parents of the
victims. The law does not recognize polygamy. In contrast, Saramaka tribal customary law accepts multiple marriages and the duty of adult children to care for their
parents. The Court found that Suriname's family law was not effective in the region
and was therefore not the local law for purposes of the case. As a result, the multiple wives and children of the victims were recognized by the Court. See Inter-Am.
Ct. H.R., *Case of Aloeboetoe et al. v. Suriname*, Judgment of September 10, 1993, Series
C No. 15.

The Inter-American Court has also decided a significant number of cases
concerning large-scale massacres, which have posed unique complexities when
it comes to determining the content of reparations. For example, in the case of
the *Rio Negro Massacres vs. Guatemala*, the Court dealt with a series of massacres

perpetrated by the Guatemalan army and members of the Civil Self-Defense Patrols in 1980 and 1982 and the failure to investigate and sanction these events. The Commission presented the case before the Court alleging that these massacres fit within a more general context of massacres in Guatemala which were planned by State agents as part of a 'scorched earth' policy executed against the Mayan people, considering them enemies. Due to the grave and massive scope of the massacres at issue, the Court was very expansive in the reparations granted. The Court acknowledged that it had not been possible to identify all victims of the massacres in this case. Therefore, it asked the state of Guatemala to establish an appropriate mechanism so that other members of the community of Río Negro could be eventually considered victims of any human rights violations declared in this judgment, and receive both individual and collective reparations. The Court also ordered the state to remove all obstacles in the investigation of these massacres, considering that 30 years had passed since their occurrence. The Court moreover reiterated that the exhumation and identification of the deceased victims is part of the obligation to investigate. On this aspect, the Court in particular indicated that:

> The discovery and identification of the victims reveals an historical truth that contributes to closing the mourning process of the Maya Achí community of Río Negro; contributes to the reconstruction of their cultural integrity; enhances the dignity of those who disappeared or who were presumably executed and that of their family members, who have struggled for decades to find their loved ones, and establishes a precedent to ensure that grave, massive and systematic violations such as those that occurred in this case never happen again.

*Case of the Río Negro Massacres v. Guatemala*, Inter-Am. Ct. H.R., Judgment of September 4, 2012, Ser. C No. 250, paragraph 265.

The Court in particular asked the state to prepare a meticulous plan to search for the members of the Río Negro community, who were forcibly disappeared, as well as to find, exhume, and identify the persons who were presumably executed. In particular, the Court ordered the state to create a genetic information bank to safeguard the information on the osseous remains that are found and exhumed, and of the next of kin of the persons who were presumably executed or disappeared during the acts perpetrated in the context of the massacres.

The Court also ordered a vast array of restitution, rehabilitation, and satisfaction measures, including: (a) the reproduction of the official summary of the Inter-American Court Judgment in Spanish and in the Maya Achí language; (b) a public act of acknowledgment of responsibility to be held in Pacux, in Spanish and in the Maya Achí language; (c) the creation of a museum to commemorate the victims; (d) measures oriented to improving the living conditions and health situation of the members of the community of Río Negro who live in the Pacux Settlement; and (e) the provision of free medical care and psychological services to the victims and their family members, among other measures. The Court went as far as ordering the creation of a program to rescue, promote, disseminate, and preserve the ancestral customs, principles and philosophies of the Maya Achí people and, in particular of the community of Río Negro. The Court also ordered compensation, including $30,000 for each victim of forced disappearance and $15,000 for each surviving victim of the massacres, among other measures.

---

For more reading on reparations, remedies and the Inter-American system, see Inter-Am. Comm'n H.R., *Truth, Justice, and Reparation in Transitional Contexts*, OEA/Ser.L/V/II. Doc. 121 (2021), Chapter 5: Reparation Standards Relevant to Transitional Contexts, http://www.oas.org/en/iachr/reports/pdfs/Compen diumTransitionalJustice.pdf; Dinah Shelton, *Remedies in International Human Rights Law* (3d ed. 2015); Thomas M. Antkowiak, *A Dark Side of Virtue: The Inter-American Court and Reparations for Indigenous Peoples*, 25 Duke J. Comp. & Int'l L. 1 (2014).

## *Comments and Questions*

1. What aspects, if any, of the reparations order in the *Cotton Field* case surprise you? Construction of a monument to commemorate victims may be appropriate, but do you agree that it is appropriate for a court to order that as a form of reparation? On what basis are nonmonetary awards made? What purpose do they serve? In *Cotton Field*, the Court ordered, in addition to pecuniary damages, a total of close to $300,000 for "moral" damages" for the three named victims and immediate relatives. The Court has distinguished moral form punitive damages and declined to grant the latter. What justifies such moral damages and how are they different from punitive damages?

2. The Inter-American Court of Human Rights in *Cotton Field* also introduced the element of *rectification* to a comprehensive reparations scheme. Reparations historically have focused instead on restitution and measures to support survivors in restoring their position and life plans to before the human rights violations at issue occurred. The Court in *Cotton Field* refers in addition to the need to change a cultural context of discrimination that fuels violence against women and girls in order to prevent such violence in the future. Can you think of reparations that can address a culture of discrimination against women beyond those already discussed by the Court in the *Cotton Field* judgment? See generally Rosa Celorio, "Gender-Based Violence as a Form of Discrimination," in *Women and International Human Rights in Modern Times: A Contemporary Casebook* 63-67 (2022).

3. How are damages for loss of life measured? Does the value of human life vary, depending on the country in which the victim or family lives? Consider these questions in light of the statement made by the Inter-American Court in its judgment in the case of *Almonacid-Arellano et al v. Chile* that reparations should not make victims or their family members wealthier or poorer. That case dealt with the lack of investigation and sanction of those responsible for the extrajudicial execution of Luis Alfredo Almonacid Arellano as well as the failure to provide adequate reparations. See *Case of Almonacid Arellano et al. v. Chile*, Inter-Am. Ct. H.R., Judgment of September 26, 2006, Ser. C No. 154.

## D.   *Compliance with the Decisions of the Inter-American System of Human Rights*

A key challenge for the Inter-American Commission and the Court is how to improve their supervision of state compliance with the decisions and judgments that they adopt. The Court has its own process of supervising compliance with judgments, including the imposition of deadlines for the parties to present relevant information on compliance as well as follow-up hearings. The Commission for its part has different mechanisms to supervise compliance with its recommendations, among these: (i) the ability to request information on compliance related to individual cases for inclusion in its annual reports; (ii) the holding of public hearings and working meetings on cases; and (iii) the organization of on-site visits including working meetings related to cases.

The Commission has a section in its annual report devoted to documenting state efforts, or the lack thereof, to comply with the recommendations it has made in its reports on the merits of cases. For example, the Commission confirmed in its 2020 annual report that it continues to use the following categories to measure the state level of compliance with its merits reports:

- *Total compliance:* those cases in which the State has fully complied with all of the recommendations/or FSA [Friendly Settlement Agreement] clauses published by the IACHR. The Commission considers as total compliance, any recommendation or FSA clause in which the State has begun and satisfactorily completed the measures for compliance.
- *Partial compliance:* those cases in which the State has partially complied with the recommendations/or FSA clauses published by the IACHR, either by having complied with only one or some of the recommendations or FSA clauses, or through incomplete compliance with all of the recommendations or FSA clauses; those cases in which the State has fully complied with all of the recommendations or FSA clauses published by the IACHR except for one of them, with which it has been unable to comply.
- *Compliance pending:* those cases in which the IACHR considers that there has been no compliance with the recommendations/or FSA clauses published by it, because no steps were taken to that end; or the steps taken have still not produced concrete results; because the State has expressly indicated that it will not comply with the recommendations or FSA clauses published by the IACHR; or the State has not reported to the IACHR and the Commission has no information from other sources to suggest otherwise.

Inter-Am. Comm'n H.R., Annual Report 2020, OEA/Ser.L/V/II, Doc., (2021), para. 141.

Experience has shown that more measures are needed to ensure full compliance with the recommendations and orders adopted by the Inter-American Commission and the Court. This need is particularly apparent for countries that have not ratified the American Convention or the other Inter-American treaties. According to the Commission's 2020 Annual Report, only nine cases show total compliance from a group of 105 cases under monitoring. All of these, with the exception of one, are related to countries that have ratified the American Convention. See

Inter-Am. Comm'n H.R., *Annual Report 2020*, OEA/Ser.L/V/II, Doc. 28 (2021), Chapter II: The System of Petitions and Cases, Friendly Settlements, and Precautionary Measures, para. 143 (and table). See also Inter-Am. Comm'n H.R., *Considerations Related to the Universal Ratification of the American Convention and other Inter-American Human Rights Treaties*, OAS/Ser.L/V/II.152 Doc. 21 (2014).

The first reading below discusses some of the challenges that impede full implementation of the judgments of the Inter-American Court and the crucial role of the justice system at the national level. The second article discusses the problem of effectiveness of regional human rights protection systems, underscoring the case of the Inter-American system of human rights and its treatment of ongoing forms of discrimination.

Alexandra Huneeus

## Courts Resisting Courts: Lessons from the Inter-American Court's Struggle to Enforce Human Rights

44 Cornell Int'l L.J. 493 (Fall 2011)

Leading scholars argue that autonomous national courts heighten compliance with international human rights regimes. But the Inter-American Court's ongoing experiments with innovative equitable remedies provide a new window into the challenges faced by international courts in enforcing human rights. An empirical examination of the Court's docket reveals two dynamics. First, in a majority of its contentious rulings, the Inter-American Court demands that some sort of prosecutorial or judicial action be taken, such as an investigation, a hearing, or a trial. Second, the judges and prosecutors of Latin America rarely comply. Latin American constitutions grant prosecutors autonomy from the executive, much like that of judges, to ensure accountability. But judges and prosecutors are far less likely to undertake the actions demanded by Inter-American Court rulings than are executives. While states implement the majority of orders that primarily require executive action, they implement only one in ten orders that invoke action by justice systems.

This Article will argue that the compliance gap between executives and justice system actors suggests that the Inter-American Court—and international human rights courts more generally—could increase compliance by more directly engaging national judges and prosecutors, deliberately cultivating national justice systems as partners in compliance. The reason for non-implementation of court orders is not only, as others have argued, that criminal prosecution of state-sponsored crime is "costly" or "difficult" to undertake, or that the government as a whole lacks political will. Nor is it a lack of judicial independence. Drawing on original data, this article shows that the problem is also—and often primarily—that implementation of orders involves disparate state actors whose interests, ideologies, and institutional settings differ from those of the executive, and who may be only dimly aware of the Inter-American Court. Prosecutorial and judicial politics must be viewed as separate, vital factors in explaining the performance of supra-national rights regimes and in devising strategies to enhance their effectiveness.

Of course, it is formally incorrect to say that judges and prosecutors disobey the Inter-American Court. International courts formally address themselves to the state, not to distinct actors within the state. And it is the state as a whole that does or does not comply with Court orders. But this formal legal description falls particularly flat in face of the Inter-American System's unique features. The Inter-American Court is "the only international human rights body with binding powers that has consistently ordered equitable remedies in conjunction with compensation." Whereas the ECHR typically allows governments to choose how they will remedy their state's violation, the Inter-American Court, which came of age in a region of dictatorships, prefers to be less deferential. It often requests that the state take specific remedial actions, and it often orders action that the executive cannot take single-handedly. In recent cases, it has ordered that judges in Mexico receive instruction in gender rights, that Chile amend its laws on freedom of expression and freedom of information, and that Guatemala's judges refrain from applying the death penalty. Notably, since it is not a criminal court but routinely hears cases of mass state-sponsored crimes, the Inter-American Court has ordered states to conduct criminal prosecution in a majority of its rulings. Full compliance thus typically turns on the will of justice system actors. To explain compliance patterns, we need to pry open the black box of domestic justice systems and examine the motives and institutional settings of judges and prosecutors. . . .

This observation has practical consequences. The Inter-American Court must make itself matter to local state actors beyond the foreign ministry to achieve greater implementation of its rulings. As Laurence Helfer writes, "compliance with international law increases when international institutions—including tribunals—can penetrate the surface of the state to interact with government decision-makers." One tool that the Inter-American Court has at hand is its self-styled remedial regime that, coupled with the Court's supervision of compliance with its rulings, establishes a link between the Court and particular state actors. This link provides a unique and, so far, under-utilized opportunity to deepen relationships with actors beyond the executive, and to shape those actors into compliance partners. Specifically, the Court could use its remedial regime to heighten actors' sense of accountability, and to demonstrate the benefits of partaking in transnational judicial dialogue by deferring to, citing to, and otherwise promoting national jurisprudence that embeds the Court and its rulings in national settings.

. . . The Inter-American Court is relatively young, in court years, and faces significant obstacles. Important challenges include its low budget and the threat of open confrontations from state parties. In the past, both Peru and Trinidad and Tobago have directly repudiated the Court's jurisdiction. Today, the greatest open challenge comes from Venezuela, whose Supreme Court has called on the government to withdraw from the American Convention, and whose president often speaks out against the Inter-American System. A final but critical challenge is the low rate of compliance with its rulings, the focus of this paper.

. . . The Court's compliance reports provide a rich record. These reports allow one to examine not only whether there has been full compliance in a particular case, but also whether individual orders issued in a particular ruling have been implemented. The Court's rulings typically order monetary compensation, amendment or repeal of offending laws, and a series of other injunctive remedies as varied as adding names to a memorial or resentencing in a particular case. If the act in violation of the American Convention is also a crime under national law, rulings demand that the state investigate, prosecute, and punish for criminal responsibility. Several recent studies analyze the orders by the kind of demands they make. They reveal that all states are most likely to comply with orders for monetary compensation, and least likely to comply with orders that implicate judicial investigation. Orders to provide monetary compensation are implemented over half of the time. Orders requesting legal reforms are implemented roughly 5-11% of the time. When asked to find criminal responsibility, states simply do not comply: The Court has never declared that a state has fully complied with an order to investigate, try, and punish those responsible for the crimes underlying a case.

While previous studies have analyzed the orders by what they request, it is also possible to disaggregate the Court's remedial orders by whom they address. Thus recast, the Court's compliance data reveals a strikingly pronounced trend: The more separate state branches or institutions an injunctive order involves, the less likely its implementation becomes. . . . If an injunctive order invokes only executive action, compliance is roughly 44%. But if an order requires action from the executive and one other institutional actor, compliance plummets. For orders that invoke action by the executive and the judiciary, compliance is 36%. A new generation of Latin American constitutions typically put prosecution in the hands of a public ministry that is formally independent from the executive and judiciary. For orders that invoke action by the executive and the public ministry, compliance is 21.1%. For orders that invoke action by the legislature and the executive, compliance is 22%. Orders requiring action by three autonomous state institutions — the executive, the public ministry, and the judiciary — receive 2% compliance. With each new state actor that is called upon to exercise discretion, the prospect of compliance fades. . . .

Once three actors are involved — the executive, the public prosecutor, and the judiciary — compliance drops even further to 2%. The orders that demand three actors mostly are comprised of orders to prosecute and punish for the underlying crimes. No state has ever fully complied with such an order. Here the thesis of the inherent difficulty of the task — as opposed to the particular disposition of specific actors — may have more force. Often, such prosecutions would implicate actors that those in power prefer to protect, including those serving political office, members of the military, and others connected to powerful social networks that assure impunity. But the explanation of difficulty is again incomplete. Even if we grant that "a climate of impunity characterizes the Americas," there is variation among states. Argentina and Chile have prosecuted more human rights violators of a former authoritarian regime than any other country in the hemisphere. Yet when it comes to specific Inter-American Court orders to prosecute, Argentina, Chile, and El Salvador have the same record: no compliance. The point is that to understand why prosecution in a particular case is difficult, one must study the politics of the local justice system.

. . . Of the distinct state institutions considered here — the executive, the judiciary, the legislature, and the public ministry — executives have many reasons to comply with Court orders. The executive is the branch charged with conducting foreign relations, and thus is the Inter-American Court's state interlocutor throughout litigation. More than any other branch, the executive is aware of the Court's ruling and its demands, and the executive is the one that has to answer and appear before the Court when it requests an update on compliance. . . .

The position of judiciaries is different. First, conducting the state's foreign affairs is not part of their job description. Second, they do not appear before the Inter-American Court, and the Court does not directly engage judges by faxing its orders to them or ordering them to appear in Costa Rica, its headquarters. Indeed (and third), in many states it is unclear exactly what position the rulings of the Court hold in national law, so the mandate to comply is formally weak. Fourth, judges may feel more threatened by the Court than do other state actors. Executives, too, resist and resent the intrusion from abroad when a ruling comes down, but for judges, each Court ruling is a direct incursion into their legal terrain. The Inter-American Court only reviews cases after victims have exhausted local judicial resources. For the IAS to take a case is thus already a judgment that the local judges got it wrong. Particularly in cases where the Inter-American Court demands a criminal case be reopened, local procedural rules notwithstanding, national courts may resent the intrusion on their turf. High courts may object to having their status as final instance usurped. Finally, in the many cases that demand states investigate and try the crimes of former authoritarian regimes, it is likely that this demand is made of the same judges that worked under the former authoritarian regime, and were in some ways complicit by failing to try the cases at the time. Whereas congress and the executive will have been renewed, the judges often remain, and the judiciary may be the branch most reluctant to turn against the former regime.

It is true that judiciaries in Latin America have undergone important changes in recent years, following constitutional change and heavy investment in judicial reforms. Today's judiciaries enjoy greater autonomy, and are generally more involved in judicial review of rights. This would seem to portend a judiciary more aware of and open to human rights adjudication. However, following Court orders is distinguishable from using the Court's rulings as a source in performing judicial review. In citing to the Inter-American Court for purposes of judicial review, national judges use the Court's rulings to fortify their own positions against other state actors. It bolsters their power. But in following Court orders, judges look to be yielding their position as ultimate arbiter, ceding power. Further, autonomy cuts two ways: While a more autonomous judiciary is more apt to hold the other branches accountable to the demands of the American Convention, it may also be better equipped to challenge the Inter-American Court and resist implementing orders despite executive pressure.

The underlying point is that executives and judges are in different institutional positions vis-a-vis compliance with the Inter-American Court, and that many institutional factors point to judicial resistance. . . .

. . . Finger pointing by a human rights institution in Costa Rica will not end impunity in Latin America. The impunity of powerful actors is rooted in entrenched social networks and social norms. But by systematically engaging national justice systems, the Court could enhance its influence, and it could gain compliance in the subset of cases in which the obstacles to prosecution are less deeply entrenched. To create such compliance partnerships, the Court has to be able to make itself attractive to local actors, fostering a pro-IAS posture beyond the executive. Such a policy would help judges and prosecutors learn about the Inter-American System and its jurisprudence, feel more directly responsible for compliance, and begin to identify as a part of the transnational judicial dialogue on human rights.

Skeptics will argue that there are some high courts in Latin America with whom a human rights court should not partner. Corruption, collusion with de facto powers, and other problems plague the region's judiciaries. It will not always make more sense to work with courts as partners rather than as subjects who must be disciplined. Indeed, the question of whet a horizontal or vertical relationship will be most effective will vary from judicial system to judicial system. The main point here, however, is only that potential partnerships with local justice systems should be a primary consideration for the Court as it issues orders and supervises compliance . . .

Rosa Celorio

## Discrimination and the Regional Human Rights Protection Systems: The Enigma of Effectiveness

40 U. PA. J. Int'l L. 784-90, 798-809 (2019) (footnotes omitted)

### I. Introduction

This article discusses the regional human rights protection systems in the Americas and Europe and ponders the following provocative question: Can they ever be fully effective in the prevention and response to the problem of discrimination and its different manifestations?

Despite their different conformations, both the Inter-American and European systems have taken advantage of their various mandates to issue many case decisions and pronouncements rejecting practices which are considered discriminatory, and issuing orders to states as to how to address these in the present and the future. Many of the human rights violations tackled by these systems relate to discrimination within the family, being perpetrated by partners against partners, by parents against children, and by the government authorities against families. Others have taken place in the health, education, employment, and various public settings. Women and children, racial and ethnic minorities, and persons discriminated against on the basis of their actual or perceived sexual orientation and gender identity have been very prominent in this work, frequently the target of discrimination, exclusion, and bias, both individually and structurally.

Nonetheless, the issues of discrimination, exclusion, and marginalization are still widespread in Europe and the Americas, posing formidable barriers for many persons to exercise their basic civil, political, economic, social, and cultural rights.

Both systems continue to receive in the present case petitions and information from different sectors claiming forms of discrimination, and a great deal of their work is dedicated to issuing rulings concerning these issues. Discrimination is also an evolving social issue, exemplified by the problems the Americas and Europe face today, including hate speech, xenophobia, and persistent systemic and institutional discrimination. Leaders of key countries have been elected after waging campaigns filled with messages contrary to the principles of discrimination, equality, inclusion, and human rights. The perpetrators are varied, going beyond the State, including businesses and individuals. The most extreme manifestation of discrimination, violence, has a more expansive definition and exemplification every day, extending beyond the rubrics of the physical, psychological, and sexual; occurring in the internet, cyber space, employment, and medical institutions, among others; and permeating many social spheres. There are mass movements all over the Americas and Europe demanding attention, prevention, and adequate response to violence and abuse, such as "me too," "Time's Up," and "Ni una Menos," which advocate for women to speak out and be heard regarding their experiences with sexual assault and harassment.

This complex context and developments raise the question of whether there are ways to make these regional protection systems more effective, or even preserve the level of impact they have today, in addressing the nuance of discrimination. In the author's view, the way the regional protection systems respond to these highly prevalent issues through their case law and other mechanisms is a window to their present and future relevance . . .

### 1.2. THE CHALLENGE OF EFFECTIVENESS IN INTERNATIONAL HUMAN RIGHTS

The author considers that it is important to examine the body of work and the legal standards set by a regional human rights system as a measure of present and future effectiveness. As indicated in her previous scholarship, a major part of the work of regional human rights protection systems is devoted to producing legal standards with important implications for states. A human rights standard constitutes a legal obligation for the state involved and sheds light on the content of this obligation. In this sense, the case decisions adopted by the European Court, and the Inter-American Commission and the Court, constitute legal and authoritative pronouncements related to the scope of individual articles of the European and Inter-American regional treaties and instruments. A standard issued by these regional protection systems can also offer an important guideline for the state implicated on how to adequately and effectively implement, at the national level, the individual rights contained in the governing instruments of these systems. These standards can be issued in the context of individual case decisions, but also in non-case work. The ability to produce legal standards and pronouncements which are well-researched, relevant, timely, and informed, which lead States to adopt measures at the ground level to comply with their internationally-assumed obligations, is an important variable in measuring the effectiveness of a regional protection system. This is key to achieve full protection from human rights violations and their short- and long-term prevention.

There is already some scholarship devoted to examining whether the regional systems in Europe and the Americas are effective as a whole in the area of human rights protection, in particular for individual case decisions. Scholars have also developed important doctrine concerning the treatment of discrimination and the legal developments in the two systems. The most important variable historically used to assess whether the European and Inter-American systems are effective in a given area has been whether states fully comply with their case decisions. The analysis usually centers on whether a state adjusted its conduct as a result of the case decision at issue. The conduct change can be in the form of completing an investigation or reforming the legislation, public policies, institutions, and programs in a given country as a result of the case at issue.

For the author, though, effectiveness is a broad and integral concept, extending beyond the objective notion of compliance with case decisions. A regional human rights system can have a significant subjective influence on state conduct and discourse without having those same states fully comply with its case decisions.

State conduct is also not the only measure of effectiveness of a regional human rights protection system. In the author's view, there are many variables that affect whether a given system is having impact on a human rights issue. Take for example an issue very linked to discrimination-the widespread problem of violence against women. Even though compliance with the judgments of the European and Inter-American Court is still lacking and the problem is widespread, it is undisputable today that the work of these systems on this issue has contributed to the following positives: the development of jurisprudence and legal standards with content conducive to enforcement; the collaboration between systems and cross-referencing of their work; the existence of progress and advances in the legislation, policies, and programs at the national level in Europe and the Americas; an increased participation of victims, states, civil society organizations, international entities, and academic institutions in the work of these systems in a specific area; and a plethora of initiatives to increase the capacity of states and their own entities in the enforcement of the judgments and orders of the regional human rights protection systems. The OAS and the Council of Europe have also adopted treaties solely devoted to violence against women, which is not a minor achievement, in an area with a great deal of deep-seated structural and cultural challenges . . .

The author considers these objective and subjective variables in concluding that the legal tendencies described in the following section entail potential opportunities for the European and Inter-American systems to set legal standards that increase their effectiveness in the area of discrimination [ . . .]

### 3. Opportunities and Challenges: The Road Ahead in the Regional Prevention and Response to Discrimination

It is important to note that the effectiveness of a regional human rights system to address complex discrimination issues is driven not only by its legal standards, but also by the context in which the legal standards are enforced, and on the strength of its institutions. In this sense, it is important for both the Inter-American and European systems to find creative ways to face contemporary political and institutional challenges. One important institutional obstacle is the enforcement problem of case rulings. In Europe, experts in the system have identified a number of states that have lingering enforcement issues, and compose also the largest caseload of the European system. In the Americas, the enforcement of judgments is very mixed, being particularly weak in the areas concerning the administration of justice and impunity issues. Important strategies have been employed by the different systems to improve compliance with judgments, including the adoption of Protocol 16 by the European Court of Human Rights and the Conventionality Control Doctrine of the Inter-American Court of Human Rights.

The Inter-American Commission on Human Rights has identified the supervision of compliance of rulings and judgments as one of the priority areas in its new strategic plan between 2017 and 2021, and the Inter-American Court has created a section solely devoted to this issue. It is important to follow closely strategies employed by these systems to improve compliance with judgments. In the Americas system, a related obstacle is the significant delays that affect the processing of case petitions. These institutional challenges negatively affect their overall work in the area of discrimination and any future strategies should consider the intricacies and complexities of addressing discrimination issues at the national level. These systems are also facing enormous political pressures today from different states, which affect their daily operations and effectiveness. Problems of this kind are inherent in these systems as they are inter-governmental in nature. Their proximity to states is both a challenge and an opportunity of influence. In the case of the Americas, two states have already withdrawn from the American Convention, and there is a group of states that is constantly criticizing the measures and pronouncements issued by the Inter-American Commission. Venezuela has already expressed its intention to withdraw from the OAS Charter. This is compounded by one of the most public financial crisis the Inter-American Commission has faced in its history, and difficulties in balancing its protection and promotion work. In Europe, the tensions with Russia and the exit process of the United Kingdom from the European Union bring fears of what kind of impact this all will have in the work of the European Court and its operations . . .

### 4. Concluding Thoughts

The continued existence of human rights protection systems in Europe and the Americas is fundamental for international dialogue and cooperation, as well as for the possibilities they offer to review issues at a supranational level, and as a second avenue for victims of human rights violations. In the author's view, finding ways to make them more effective is vital for their survival. The continued financial and political support of human rights systems is also key for them to succeed; support that depends greatly on their short-, medium-, and long-term effectiveness. In the author's view, the systems should prioritize not only finding creative ways to become more effective, but strategies to preserve their present impact or acquis, given the present challenges. Discrimination today in Europe and the Americas is an ongoing problem, with many layers and dimensions to address. Discrimination is direct and indirect, systemic and structural. It affects persons of every sex, gender, age, racial and ethnic background, and social class. It can be in the form of disparate or disadvantageous treatment without justification. It is illustrated in hate speech; cyber violence; sexual harassment; the "Me too" and "Time's Up" movements; and domestic and sexual violence. It happens in homes, schools, employment places, prisons, religious settings, and health institutions. The way regional protection systems address discrimination and its many forms in the present and the future is a key determinant of their continued relevance.

Despite the complexity of the current context and the intricate dynamics of discrimination and social exclusion, the author remains hopeful that the regional human rights protection systems do have windows of opportunity and are producing an important body of work which could have a measure of impact at the national level. A well-articulated strategy, including the participation of persons and groups who are the main bearers of social discrimination and continued exclusion, continues to be key to improve the effectiveness of the work and state compliance.

In the current global scheme, the author considers vital that the regional protection systems continue employing all means at their disposal to promote and serve as symbols of substantive equality, inclusion, leadership, and the full exercise of human rights for all. This is a key ingredient to resolve the enigma of effectiveness.

## Comments and Questions

1. One of the instances in which the Inter-American Commission noted "full compliance" with its recommendations was in the case of *Michael Dominguez*, which concerned the juvenile death penalty in the United States. The Commission declared full compliance after the United States Supreme Court issued its judgment in *Roper v. Simmons*, 543 U.S. 551 (2005), which is extracted in Chapter 6, at page 370. The Supreme Court did not mention the Commission's prior decision and recommendations in its judgment. Does there need to be or should there be a causal link between change in a State's law or policy and a Commission decision for the Commission to find compliance? From a human rights perspective, does it matter?

2. In its 2015 annual report, the Inter-American Court of Human Rights informed of the creation of a new unit in its Secretariat devoted exclusively to monitoring compliance with judgments, of its initiatives to enhance its relationships with national courts, and of the use of technology to increase knowledge of the content of its rulings among persons in the Americas hemisphere. See Inter-Am. Ct. Hum. Rts., *2015 Annual Report*, http://www.corteidh.or.cr/sitios/informes/docs/ENG/eng_2015.pdf. Can you think of any benefits a domestic justice system can derive from full compliance with relevant judgments of the Inter-American Court and general knowledge of those judgements?

3. As discussed in the article by Rosa Celorio, many factors impact the effectiveness of existing human rights instruments adopted by the Organization of American States to curb the problem of discrimination. A number of treaties and other instruments issued by the OAS prohibit discrimination explicitly, including the American Declaration, the American Convention, the Convention of Belém do Pará, and the discrimination conventions adopted in 2013, among others. Ongoing challenges include the lack of political will by states to comply with individual case decisions interpreting the content of these treaties; increased political pressure from states against the Inter-American human rights system and its decisions; and the scarcity of human and financial resources. Discrimination also frequently occurs at the rural and local levels—areas in which it is very difficult for international human rights law to make a real difference and have a positive impact. Many of the existing global and regional treaties establishing anti-discrimination obligations are still pending compliance, including those issued by the OAS. How do you measure compliance with a human rights treaty? Does partial compliance count? Should states be rewarded for complying with human rights treaties? See generally Ann Van Aaken and Betül Simsek, *Rewarding in International Law*, AM. J. OF INT'L LAW 115(2), 195-241, 195-199, 203-218 (2021).

## IV.   INTER-AMERICAN PROCEDURES TO STRENGTHEN DEMOCRATIC GOVERNANCE

This section discusses examples of how different Inter-American procedures have been applied to address challenges to the strength and effectiveness of democratic institutions in the Americas.

As background, it is noted that the links between human rights and democratic governance are reflected in provisions of the OAS Charter and actions taken by various OAS organs. The OAS General Assembly strengthened its norms on this matter in 2001 when it adopted the Inter-American Democratic Charter (a separate instrument from the OAS Charter). The Democratic Charter reaffirms "that the promotion and protection of human rights is a basic prerequisite for the existence of a democratic society, and recognize[s] the importance of the continuous development and strengthening of the Inter-American human rights system for the consolidation of democracy." Article 3 provides:

> Essential elements of representative democracy include, *inter alia*, respect for human rights and fundamental freedoms, access to and the exercise of power in accordance with the rule of law, the holding of periodic, free, and fair elections based on secret balloting and universal suffrage as an expression of the sovereignty of the people, the pluralistic system of political parties and organizations, and the separation of powers and independence of the branches of government.

Part II of the Charter further links democracy and human rights:

> Article 7
>
> Democracy is indispensable for the effective exercise of fundamental freedoms and human rights in their universality, indivisibility and interdependence, embodied in the respective constitutions of states and in inter-American and international human rights instruments.

> Article 8
>
> Any person or group of persons who consider that their human rights have been violated may present claims or petitions to the inter-American system for the promotion and protection of human rights in accordance with its established procedures.
>
> Member states reaffirm their intention to strengthen the inter-American system for the protection of human rights for the consolidation of democracy in the Hemisphere.

> Article 9
>
> The elimination of all forms of discrimination, especially gender, ethnic and race discrimination, as well as diverse forms of intolerance, the promotion and protection of human rights of indigenous peoples and migrants, and respect for ethnic, cultural and religious diversity in the Americas contribute to strengthening democracy and citizen participation.

Article 10

The promotion and strengthening of democracy requires the full and effective exercise of workers' rights and the application of core labor standards, as recognized in the International Labour Organization (ILO) Declaration on Fundamental Principles and Rights at Work, and its Follow-up, adopted in 1998, as well as other related fundamental ILO conventions. Democracy is strengthened by improving standards in the workplace and enhancing the quality of life for workers in the Hemisphere.

Part IV concerns the actions to be taken by the OAS in response to "an unconstitutional interruption of the democratic order or an unconstitutional alteration of the constitutional regime that seriously impairs the democratic order in a member state." Article 19 calls coups d'états and similar takeovers "an insurmountable obstacle" to a government's participation in the Organization. According to Article 20 of the Charter, any member state or the Secretary General may request the immediate convocation of the Organization's Permanent Council to undertake a collective assessment of the situation and to take such decisions as it deems appropriate. Pursuant to Article 23 of the Democratic Charter and Article 9 of the OAS Charter, the General Assembly may, by a two-thirds vote, suspend the participation of the state in question.

The Charter procedure has been invoked several times, including in 2002 against Venezuela; in 2003, 2005, and 2008 against Bolivia; in 2004 and 2005 against Nicaragua; against Peru in 2004; against Ecuador in 2005 and 2010; in 2009, after a coup d'état in Honduras; in 2016, in response to the acute humanitarian crisis facing Venezuela; and in 2021, to address human rights violations in Nicaragua and the government's decision to begin a two-year withdrawal process from the OAS. The following press release describes the decision to suspend Honduras's OAS membership.

## OAS Suspends Membership of Honduras

OAS Press Release E/219, July 5, 2009

The Special General Assembly of the Organization of American States (OAS) decided today to suspend immediately the right to participate in the institution of Honduras following the coup d'état that expelled President José Manuel Zelaya from power.

In a resolution adopted by acclamation by all Member States at the headquarters of the organization in Washington, DC, the Special General Assembly instructed the OAS Secretary General, José Miguel Insulza, "to reinforce all diplomatic initiatives and to promote other initiatives for the restoration of democracy and the rule of law in the Republic of Honduras and the reinstatement of President José Manuel Zelaya Rosales."

"No such initiative will imply recognition of the regime that emerged from this interruption of the constitutional order," specifies the resolution, that invoked for the first time Article 21 of the Inter-American Democratic Charter.

The document also encourages "the Member States and international organizations to review their relations with the Republic of Honduras during the period of the diplomatic initiatives." It also reaffirms that Honduras "must continue to fulfill its obligations as a member of the Organization, in particular with regard to human rights", and urges "the Inter-American Commission on Human Rights to continue to take all necessary measures to protect and defend human rights and fundamental freedoms in Honduras.". . . .

In his speech to the plenary session, [exiled] President Zelaya highlighted that "this is a very peculiar moment in the history of the Americas." After explaining the circumstances surrounding of the coup d'Etat, President Zelaya stressed that "the Honduran people have lived already six days of repression. The people are suffering." The Honduran leader praised the attitude of the OAS and its Member States: "You, by raising your voice, are giving hope to the Americas, and you are giving hope to the people of Honduras.". . . .

The General Assembly reached an agreement after listening to the report of Secretary General Insulza regarding the initiatives undertaken in the 72 previous hours trying to restore democracy, the Rule of Law and President Zelaya in power, as mandated by the resolution adopted by the same Special General Assembly on Wednesday. . . .

The Secretary General specified that it "should be clear that this is not an action against Honduras or against its people, but rather a means of pressure against the de facto government."

---

The Inter-American Commission on Human Rights actively documented the numerous human rights violations that occurred in the context of the coup d'état in Honduras and granted precautionary measures to safeguard the lives of hundreds of persons. The Commission reported killings, the arbitrary declaration of a state of emergency, the disproportionate use of force against public demonstrations, and the arbitrary detention of thousands of persons, among other human rights violations. The Inter-American Commission also conducted several working visits to monitor the human rights situation in the country during these events. See Inter.-Am. Comm'n H.R., *Honduras: Human Rights and the Coup d'État*, OEA/Ser.L/V/II. Doc. 55, (2009); Inter-Am. Comm'n H.R., *Preliminary Observations of the Inter-American Commission on Human Rights on Its Visit to Honduras*, May 15 to 18, 2010, OAS Doc. OEA/Ser.L/V/II, Doc. 68 (2010).

Honduras eventually returned to civilian rule. In December 2014, the Inter-American Commission undertook a highly public visit to the country, in which it expressed concerns over the process of reestablishing a democratic institutional framework in Honduras following the 2009 coup. The Commission documented alarming structural problems leading to violence, impunity, corruption and organized crime in the country, and expressed its concern over the intervention of the armed forces in many different state spheres and functions. The Commission also highlighted its concern over the persistent murder of many human rights defenders in the country and over how most of these murders remained unpunished. See Inter-Am. Comm'n H.R., *Situation of Human Rights in Honduras*, OEA/Ser.L/V/II. Doc. 42/15 (2015); *IACHR Wraps Up Onsite Visit to Honduras*, Inter-Am.

Comm'n H.R., Press Release 146/14 (Dec. 5, 2014), http://www.oas.org/en/iachr/media_center/PReleases/2014/146.asp; *Preliminary Observations concerning the Human Rights Situation in Honduras*, Inter-Am. Comm'n H.R., Press Release No. 146A/14 (Dec. 5, 2014); *IACHR Condemns Killing of Members of the Tolupán Indigenous Peoples in Honduras*, Inter-Am. Comm'n H.R., Press Release No. 028/16 (2016), http://www.oas.org/en/iachr/media_center/PReleases/2016/028.asp.

The Inter-American Commission on Human Rights has continued its close monitoring of the situation in Honduras. For example, it issued a press release on November 16, 2021, expressing concern over the potentially negative impact of criminal code reforms and money laundering laws on the exercise of the right to protest in Honduras. See *IACHR Concerned About the Implementation of Legislative Reforms with a Regressive Impact on the Exercise of the Right to Protest in Honduras*, Inter-Am. Comm'n H.R. Press Release, No. 304/21 (Nov. 16, 2021), https://www.oas.org/en/IACHR/jsForm/?File=/en/iachr/media_center/PReleases/2021/304.asp.

## *Note: Cuba and Human Rights Concerns*

The Inter-American Commission has also closely monitored the situation of Cuba, despite that country's complex relationship with the OAS and the lack of authorization to perform on-site visits. For example, Cuba has been traditionally included in of the Annual Report of the Inter-American Commission, where the Commission has documented many human rights violations, such as restrictions on rights to freedom of expression, persecution of human rights defenders, arbitrary imprisonment of political dissidents, and discrimination and violence against women, LGBTI persons, and afro-descendent individuals. See, e.g., Inter-Am. Comm'n H.R., *Annual Report 2020*, Chapter IV: Special Report: Cuba, http://www.oas.org/en/IACHR/reports/IA.asp?Year=2020.

Cuba was excluded from participation in the Inter-American system in 1962 by a resolution of the Eighth Meeting of Consultation of Ministers of Foreign Affairs of OAS member states. This exclusion was largely related to the assumption of power of Fidel Castro in 1959 and Cuba's new association with the Soviet Union (events that deeply reshaped the historical relationship between the Uited States and Cuba). In 2009, the OAS General Assembly revoked the 1962 decision and stated that "the participation of the Republic of Cuba in the OAS will be the result of a process of dialogue initiated at the request of the Government of Cuba, and in accordance with the practices, purposes, and principles of the OAS." OAS G.A. Res. 2438 (June 3, 2009).

As full participation of Cuba in the OAS remained pending, the Inter-American Commission published another detailed report on Cuba on February 3, 2020, covering the period between 2017 and 2019 and underscoring ongoing violations of the rights to freedom of expression and increased risks to the life and personal integrity of dissidents and human rights defenders. See Inter-Am. Comm'n H.R., *The Human Rights Situation in Cuba*, OEA/Ser.L/V/II (2020), https://www.oas.org/en/iachr/reports/pdfs/Cuba2020-en.pdf. On July 15, 2021, the Inter-American Commission on Human Rights and its Special Rapporteur on freedom of expression published a press release expressing concern over the violent repression of peaceful protests in Cuba, including the arbitrary use of force. This wave of protests, which made international news headlines, involved thousands of people demanding wider civil liberties and a change in the country's political structure. The protests were also triggered by mass shortages in food, medicine, and basic goods and services needed for survival. See *Inter-American Commission on Human Rights and Its Special Rapporteur on Freedom of Expression Condemn State Repression and the Use of Force during Peaceful Social Protests in Cuba, and Call for Dialogue on Citizen Demands,* Inter-Am. Comm'n H.R., Press Release No. 177/21 (July 15, 2021), http://www.oas.org/en/IACHR/jsForm/?File=/en/iachr/media_center/PReleases/2021/177.asp.

What factors will determine whether the protests in Cuba will lead to greater respect for human rights and democratization in the country?

### Comments and Questions

1.   The OAS General Assembly resolution suspending Honduras, discussed above, reaffirms in the same paragraph "the importance of strict respect for human rights" and "the principle of nonintervention in the internal affairs of other states." Is this a contradiction?

2.   What is the link between democracy and human rights? Is democracy a human right? Or are human rights a part of democracy? Or both? How does the OAS define democracy? On the link between democracy and human rights generally, see UN General Assembly Res. 60/164 (2006); UN Human Rights Council Res. 28/14 (2015); *Human Rights, Democracy and the Rule of Law,* UN Human Rights Council Res. 28/14, UN Doc. A/HRC/28/L.24 (2015); UN High Commissioner for Human Rights, *Outcome of the panel discussion on common challenges facing States in their efforts to secure democracy and the rule of law from a human rights perspective,* UN Doc. A/HRC/24/54 (2013); UN High Commissioner for Human Rights, *Study on common challenges facing States in their efforts to secure democracy and the rule of law from a human rights perspective,* UN Doc. A/HRC/22/29 (2012); UN Human Rights Committee, *General Comment 25: The right to participate in public affairs, voting rights and right of equal access to public service (Art. 25),* UN Doc. CCPR/C/21/ Rev.1/ Add.7 (1996); Thomas M. Franck, *The Emerging Right to Democratic Governance,* 86 Am. J. Int'l L. 46 (1992); Christoph Hanisch, *A Human Right to Democracy: For and Against,* 35 St. Louis U. Pub. L. Rev. 233 (2016); Matthew Lister, *There Is No Human Right to Democracy, but May We Promote It Anyway?,* 48 Stan. J Int'l 257 (2012); Sara McLaughlin and Paul F. Diehl, *Caution in What You Wish For: The Consequences of a Right to Democracy,* 48 Stan. J Int'l L. 289 (2012).

───────────

The Inter-American Court of Human Rights has used its advisory opinion authority to set important legal standards on democratic governance issues. Below is an extract of its 2021 advisory opinion on presidential reelection without term limits. This advisory opinion was requested by Colombia, which sought clarity on the international law and human rights implications of a particular set of challenges to democratic governance in the Americas context.

## Indefinite Presidential Re-election in Presidential Systems in the context of the Inter-American System of Human Rights

Inter-Am. Ct. H.R., Advisory Opinion OC-28/21, June 7, 2021. Ser. A No 28

. . .

66. The Court recalls that the object and purpose of the Convention is "the protection of the fundamental rights of the human being." It was therefore designed to protect the human rights of individuals regardless of their nationality, vis-à-vis their own State or any other. The State's commitment to full respect for and guarantee of human rights, as mandated by Article 1 of the American Convention, constitutes an essential precondition for consolidating a democracy and gives the State legitimacy before the international community.

67. According to the Inter-American Democratic Charter, "Essential elements of representative democracy include, *inter alia*, respect for human rights and fundamental freedoms, access to and the exercise of power in accordance with the rule of law, the holding of periodic, free, and fair elections based on secret balloting and universal suffrage as an expression of the sovereignty of the people, the pluralistic system of political parties and organizations, and the separation of powers and independence of the branches of government."

68. Also, its Article 4 establishes that "Transparency in government activities, probity, responsible public administration on the part of governments, respect for social rights, and freedom of expression and of the press are essential components of the exercise of democracy. The constitutional subordination of all state institutions to the legally constituted civilian authority and respect for the rule of law on the part of all institutions and sectors of society are equally essential to democracy."

69. These articles then define the basic characteristics of a representative democracy, without which a political system would cease to be one. To that extent, it is the Court's view that they constitute the guiding criteria for answering the questions posed in the request for an advisory opinion. Next, we will proceed to develop some of these characteristics, which are related to this advisory opinion.

70. In previous paragraphs of this opinion, the Court described respect for human rights and fundamental freedoms as one of the fundamental elements of a representative democracy. In this sense, the only way human rights can truly and effectively establish norms is through the recognition that they cannot be subject to majority rule, as it is precisely these rights that have been defined as limitations on the principle of majority rule. This Court has highlighted that the protection of human rights constitutes an insurmountable limit on majority rule — that is, on what is "susceptible to being decided" by the majority by democratic means. Indeed, the validity of a human right recognized by the Convention cannot be conditioned on the judgment of the majority and its compatibility with the objectives of public opinion, since that would remove all effectiveness from the Convention and international human rights treaties.

71. Second, Article 3 of the Inter-American Democratic Charter establishes access to power and its exercise — subject to the rule of law — as a constitutive element of representative democracy. In a representative democracy, the exercise of power must be subject to rules set in advance and of which citizens are informed

beforehand in order to avoid arbitrariness. This is precisely the meaning of the concept of the rule of law. To that extent, to protect minorities, the democratic process requires certain rules that limit the power of the majority as expressed at the polls. Therefore, those who are temporarily exercising political power cannot be allowed to make changes without limit to the rules on access to the exercise of power. Identifying popular sovereignty with the majority opinion as expressed at the polls is not enough to classify a system as democratic. True democratic systems respect minorities and the institutionalization of the exercise of political power, which is subject to legal limits and a set of controls.

72. The Democratic Charter, Article 23 of the American Convention, and Article XX of the American Declaration all establish an obligation to hold regular elections. In this regard, the Court has indicated that holding elections to choose the representatives of the people is a cornerstone of representative democracy. This obligation to hold regular elections indirectly implies that the terms of office of the Presidency of the Republic must have a fixed period. Presidents cannot be elected for indefinite terms. This Court highlights that the majority of the States Parties to the Convention include time limitations on the President's term.

73. This prohibition on indefinite terms in office aims to prevent people who hold popularly- elected office from keeping themselves in power. In this regard, the Court emphasizes that representative democracy is characterized by the fact that the people exercise power through their representatives as established by the Constitution, who are chosen through universal elections. When a person can hold a public office perpetually, there is a risk that the people will cease to be duly represented by their elected leaders, and that the system of government will come to resemble an autocracy more than a democracy. This can happen even with regular elections and limits on term lengths.

74. In this regard, the States in the region declared in the 1959 Declaration of Santiago that "Perpetuation in power, or the exercise of power without a fixed term and with the manifest intent of perpetuation, is incompatible with the effective exercise of democracy." Regarding this Declaration, the Inter-American Juridical Committee has indicated that it "enunciated some of the essential attributes of Democracy that are fully in effect and should be taken into account along with essential elements and fundamental components spelled out in the Inter- American Democratic Charter."

75. Consequently, this Court finds that it is possible to conclude from the obligation to hold periodic elections, together with the provisions of the Declaration of Santiago, that the principles of representative democracy on which the inter-American system is based include the obligation to prevent a person from remaining perpetually in power.

76. Additionally, the Court notes that the regularity of the elections also has the aim of ensuring that different political parties or ideological currents can access power. On this point, the Inter-American Democratic Charter establishes that another of the elements of representative democracy is the "the plural regimen of parties and political organizations." In this sense, this Court emphasizes that political groups and parties play an essential role in democratic development.

77. Political pluralism is fostered by the American Convention where it establishes the right of all citizens to be elected and to have access—under general conditions of equality—to public service in their country, freedom of thought

and expression, the right to assembly, the right of association, and the obligation to guarantee rights without discrimination. The Court has established that these rights make democracy possible. In this sense, the Inter-American Democratic Charter establishes that "Representative democracy is strengthened and deepened by permanent, ethical, and responsible participation of the citizenry within a legal framework conforming to the respective constitutional order . . ."

78. A democratic system means that the person with the most votes takes popularly-elected office. However, the right of minorities to propose alternative ideas and projects—as well as opportunities for them to be elected—must always be guaranteed. In this regard, political pluralism entails an obligation to guarantee rotation of power—that is, that a governance platform can be replaced by a different one once it has obtained the necessary electoral majority. There must be a real and effective possibility that different political movements and their candidates can win popular support and replace the ruling party.

79. On the other hand, Articles 3 and 4 of the Inter-American Democratic Charter emphasize that in democracies, power must be accessed and exercised subject to and under the rule of law. Democratic life is only possible if all parties respect the limits imposed by law that enable the very existence of democracy, such as limits on the length of presidential terms. In this sense, full respect for the rule of law means that changing the rules on access to power in a way that benefits the person in power and puts political minorities at a disadvantage is not something that can be done by majorities or their representatives. In this way, authoritarian governments are prevented from staying in power indefinitely by changing the rules of the democratic game and thereby eroding the protection of human rights.

80. Lastly, article 3 of the Inter-American Democratic Charter places the separation and independence of powers among the constitutive elements of a democracy. The separation of State powers into different branches and organs is linked closely with the aim of preserving related freedoms, with the understanding that concentration of power leads to tyranny and oppression. At the same time, the separation of State powers allows for the efficient fulfillment of the various aims entrusted to the State.

81. Therefore, the separation and independence of powers limits the scope of power exercised by each State body, thus preventing them from unduly interfering in the activities of the other bodies and guaranteeing the effective enjoyment of greater freedom.

82. However, the separation and independence of powers assumes the existence of a system of controls and oversight to constantly regulate the balance of powers. This so-called "checks and balances" model does not assume that harmony between the bodies playing the classic roles of branches of government will be a spontaneous consequence of adequate and functional delimitation of their powers and the absence of interference in their exercise thereof. On the contrary, the balance of powers is continuously struck and reestablished through the political oversight performed by some bodies of the tasks corresponding to others and the collaborative relationships between the different branches government in the exercise of their powers.

83. All the foregoing criteria are closely related. Indeed, the separation of powers, political pluralism, and holding of regular elections also function as guarantees of effective respect of fundamental rights and freedoms.

84. Therefore, this Court finds that the principles of representative democracy include, in addition to regular elections and political pluralism, the obligation to prevent a person from remaining in power and to guarantee the rotation of power and the separation of powers.

85. The measures that the State can take to prevent a person from holding onto power and to guarantee the separation of powers and the rotation of power are varied and will depend on the political system of the particular country.

86. The inter-American system, the American Declaration, and the Convention do not impose a particular political system on States, nor a specific modality of limitations on exercising political rights. States can establish their political systems and regulate political rights according to their historical, political, social and cultural needs, which may vary from one country to another and even within one country, at different historical moments. However, the regulations that States implement must be compatible with the American Convention and, therefore, with the principles of representative democracy that underpin the inter-American system, including those derived from the Inter-American Democratic Charter.

87. This Court notes that most of the States Parties to the American Convention have adopted a presidential political system. In this type of system, the duration of the President's mandate is not conditional on support from another branch of government but based rather on the length of time established by law for the term.

88. Although the powers of the presidents vary in each State, certain commonalities have been observed in constitutional executive systems. In general, the president is the head of the executive branch and acts as the head of State and head of government. The president is therefore in charge of appointing and removing the ministers and those leading the main government agencies. In fourteen OAS member States, the President is also the commander-in-chief of the armed forces.

89. Additionally, the Court observes that the checks and balances system that most OAS member States have implemented grants the President certain powers that influence how other branches of government function. In particular, Presidents often have the power to participate in the lawmaking process and can call special sessions of the legislative branch. In regard to how they relate to the judiciary, in six OAS Member States, the president appoints the judges of the Supreme Court, for subsequent approval by the legislative branch. In three States Parties to the American Convention, the President can also appoint certain judges.

90. In view of the broad powers that presidents have in presidential systems and the importance of ensuring that a person does not hold onto power, the legal systems of most OAS member States place limits on presidential reelection in presidential systems. Thus, presidential reelection is prohibited in Colombia, Guatemala, Mexico, and Paraguay; it is limited to a single additional term in Ecuador, the United States, and the Dominican Republic; reelection is limited to one consecutive term in Argentina, and allowed only non-consecutively in Brazil, Chile, Costa Rica, El Salvador, Panama, Peru, and Uruguay . . .

99. Therefore, although constitutional regulation of presidential reelection in OAS member States is mixed, currently only four of them allow "presidential reelection without term limits." Consequently, there is not enough of a State practice at a regional level with regard to the alleged human right to presidential reelection without term limits. In this sense, there is also no evidence that such a practice is

considered a right. On the contrary, the States of the region have assumed the obligation to guarantee that their system of government is a representative democracy, and one of the principles of this system of government is to guarantee rotation of power and prevent a person from holding onto it. Therefore, the Court rules out the customary recognition of presidential reelection without term limits as an autonomous right. Likewise, in the absence of a basis in international and domestic law, its recognition as a general principle of law must also be ruled out.

[The Court also concludes that prohibiting presidential reelection without term limits is compatible with the American Declaration, the American Convention, and the Inter-American Democratic Charter.]

---

The Commission and Court have issued a number of decisions concerning the scope of Article 23 (right to participate in government) of the American Convention and Article XX (right to vote and participate) of the American Declaration, underscoring the importance of the right to participate in government and public affairs. See, e.g. *Case of Petro Urrego v. Colombia*, Inter-Am. Ct. H.R., Judgment of July 8, 2020, Ser. C No. 406; *Case of Escaleras Mejía et al. v. Honduras*, Inter-Am. Ct. H.R., Judgment of September 26, 2018, Ser. C No. 361; *Case of Lopez Mendoza v. Venezuela*, Inter-Am. Ct. H.R., Judgment of Sept. 1, 2011, Ser. C No. 233; *Case of Castañeda Guzman*, Inter-Am. Ct. H.R., Judgment of Aug. 6, 2008, Ser. C No. 184; *Andres Aylwin Azocar et al. v. Chile*, Case 11.863, Inter-Am. Comm'n H.R., Report No. 137/99 (1999); *Susana Higuchi Miyagawa v. Peru*, Case 11.428, Inter-Am. Comm'n H.R., Report No. 119/99 (1999).

As illustrated by the case below, the Inter-American system has advanced the premise that effective representation and inclusion are crucial for strong democracies, and that the right to political participation should be respected and ensured free from all forms of discrimination. This guarantee may require the establishment of special electoral or representative arrangements.

## Case of Yatama v. Nicaragua

Inter-Am. Ct. H.R., Judgment of June 23, 2005, Ser. C No. 127.

2. The Commission presented the application for the Court to decide whether the State had violated Articles 8 (Right to a Fair Trial), 23 (Right to Participate in Government) and 25 (Judicial Protection) of the American Convention, all of them in relation to Articles 1(1) (Obligation to Respect Rights) and 2 (Domestic Legal Effects) thereof, to the detriment of the candidates for mayors, deputy mayors and councilors presented by the indigenous regional political party, Yapti Tasba Masraka Nanih Asla Takanka (hereinafter "YATAMA"). The Commission alleged that these candidates were excluded from participating in the municipal elections held on November 5, 2000, in the North Atlantic and the South Atlantic Autonomous Regions (hereinafter "RAAN" and "RAAS"), as a result of a decision issued on August 15, 2000, by the Supreme Electoral Council. The application stated that the alleged victims filed several recourses against this decision and, finally, on October

25, 2000, the Supreme Court of Justice of Nicaragua declared that the application for amparo that they had filed was inadmissible. The Commission indicated that the State had not provided a recourse that would have protected the right of these candidates to participate and to be elected in the municipal elections of November 5, 2000, and it had not adopted the legislative or other measures necessary to make these rights effective; above all, it had not provided for "norms in the electoral law that would facilitate the political participation of the indigenous organizations in the electoral processes of the Atlantic Coast Autonomous Region of Nicaragua, in accordance with the customary law, values, practices and customs of the indigenous people who reside there." . . .

## X. Violation of Articles 23 and 24 of the American Convention in relation to Articles 1(1) and 2 thereof (Right to Participate in Government and Right to Equal Protection)

. . .

184. The principle of the equal and effective protection of the law and of non-discrimination constitutes an outstanding element of the human rights protection system embodied in many international instruments and developed by international legal doctrine and case law. At the current stage of the evolution of international law, the fundamental principle of equality and non-discrimination has entered the realm of *jus cogens*. The juridical framework of national and international public order rests on it and it permeates the whole juridical system.

185. This principle is fundamental for the safeguard of human rights in both international and national law; it is a principle of peremptory law. Consequently, States are obliged not to introduce discriminatory regulations into their laws, to eliminate regulations of a discriminatory nature, to combat practices of this nature, and to establish norms and other measures that recognize and ensure the effective equality before the law of each individual. A distinction that lacks objective and reasonable justification is discriminatory.

186. Article 24 of the American Convention prohibits any type of discrimination, not only with regard to the rights embodied therein, but also with regard to all the laws that the State adopts and to their application. In other words, this Article does not merely reiterate the provisions of Article 1(1) of the Convention concerning the obligation of States to respect and ensure, without discrimination, the rights recognized therein, but, in addition, establishes a right that also entails obligations for the State to respect and ensure the principle of equality and non-discrimination in the safeguard of other rights and in all domestic laws that it adopts. . . .

190. In light of the proven facts in this case, the Court must determine whether Nicaragua restricted unduly the political rights embodied in Article 23 of the Convention and whether there has been a violation of the equal protection embodied in Article 24 thereof.

191. The Court has established that "[i]n a democratic society, the rights and freedoms inherent in the human person, the guarantee applicable to them and the rule of law form a triad," in which each component defines itself, complements and

depends on the others for its meaning. When deliberating on the importance of political rights, the Court observes that the Convention itself, in its Article 27, prohibits their suspension as well as that of the judicial guarantees essential for their protection.

192. This Court has stated that "[r]epresentative democracy is the determining factor throughout the system of which the Convention is a part," and "a 'principle' reaffirmed by the American States in the OAS Charter, the basic instrument of the inter-American system." The political rights protected in the American Convention, as well as in many international instruments, promote the strengthening of democracy and political pluralism. . . .

194. Article 23 of the Convention establishes the rights to take part in the conduct of public affairs, to vote and to be elected, and to have access to public service, which must be guaranteed by the State under conditions of equality.

195. It is essential that the State should generate the optimum conditions and mechanisms to ensure that these political rights can be exercised effectively, respecting the principles of equality and non-discrimination. The facts of the instant case refer principally to political participation through freely-elected representatives, the exercise of which is also protected in Article 50 of the Nicaraguan Constitution.

196. Political participation may include broad-ranging and varied activities that can be executed individually or in an organized manner, in order to intervene in the designation of those who will govern a State or who will be responsible for managing public affairs, as well as influencing the elaboration of State policy through direct participation mechanisms.

197. The exercise of the rights to be elected and to vote, which are closely related to each other, is the expression of the individual and social dimension of political participation.

198. Citizens have the right to take part in the management of public affairs through freely elected representatives. The right to vote is an essential element for the existence of democracy and one of the ways in which citizens exercise the right to political participation. This right implies that the citizens may freely elect those who will represent them, in conditions of equality.

199. Participation through the exercise of the right to be elected assumes that citizens can stand as candidates in conditions of equality and can occupy elected public office, if they obtain the necessary number of votes.

200. The right to have access to public office, under general conditions of equality, protects access to a direct form of participation in the design, implementation, development and execution of the State's political policies through public office. It is understood that these general conditions of equality refer to access to public office by popular election and by appointment or designation.

### 3. Obligation to Guarantee the Enjoyment of Political Rights

201. The Court understands that, in accordance with Articles 23, 24, 1(1) and 2 of the Convention, the State has the obligation to guarantee the enjoyment of political rights, which implies that the regulation of the exercise of such rights and its application shall be in keeping with the principle of equality and non-discrimination, and it should adopt the necessary measures to ensure their full

exercise. This obligation to guarantee is not fulfilled merely by issuing laws and regulations that formally recognize these rights, but requires the State to adopt the necessary measures to guarantee their full exercise considering the weakness or helplessness of the members of certain social groups or sectors.

202. When examining the enjoyment of these rights by the alleged victims in this case, it must be recalled that they are members of indigenous and ethnic communities of the Atlantic Coast of Nicaragua, who differ from most of the population, *inter alia*, owing to their languages, customs and forms of organization, and they face serious difficulties that place them in a situation of vulnerability and marginalization. . . .

206. Instituting and applying requirements for exercising political rights is not, *per se*, an undue restriction of political rights. These rights are not absolute and may be subject to limitations. Their regulation should respect the principles of legality, necessity and proportionality in a democratic society. Observance of the principle of legality requires the State to define precisely, by law, the requirements for voters to be able to take part in the elections, and to stipulate clearly the electoral procedures prior to the elections. According to Article 23(2) of the Convention, the law may regulate the exercise of the rights and opportunities referred to in the first paragraph of this Article, only for the reasons established in this second paragraph. The restriction should be established by law, non-discriminatory, based on reasonable criteria, respond to a useful and opportune purpose that makes it necessary to satisfy an urgent public interest, and be proportionate to this purpose. When there are several options to achieve this end, the one that is less restrictive of the protected right and more proportionate to the purpose sought should be chosen. . . .

213. With regard to the requirements in order to be elected established in the 2000 Electoral Act, the Court takes note that the Supreme Court of Justice of Nicaragua, in judgment No. 103 delivered on November 8, 2002, declared that paragraphs 1 and 2 of Article 65(9) of this law were unconstitutional, as well as Article 77(7) thereof, regarding the requirement for the presentation of the signatures of 3% of voters in order to present candidates, because it found that the provisions in the said paragraphs of Article 65 constituted "a barrier to the exercise of political rights" and that the provisions of Article 77(7) constitute[d] an undue and abhorrent interference in the political activity of the voters."

214. Furthermore, Electoral Act No. 331 of 2000, only permits participation in electoral processes through political parties, a form of organization that is not characteristic of the indigenous communities of the Atlantic Coast. It has been proved that YATAMA was able to obtain legal status to take part in the municipal elections of November 2000 as a political party, fulfilling the corresponding requirements. Nevertheless, the witnesses, Brooklyn Rivera Bryan and Jorge Teytom Fedrick, and the expert witness, María Dolores Álvarez Arzate, emphasized that the requirement to become a political party disregarded the customs, organization and culture of the candidates proposed by YATAMA, who are members of the indigenous and ethnic communities of the Atlantic Coast. . . .

218. . . . The State has not justified that this restriction obeyed a useful and opportune purpose, which made it necessary so as to satisfy an urgent public interest. To the contrary, this restriction implied an impediment to the full exercise of

the right to be elected of the members of the indigenous and ethnic communities that form part of YATAMA.

219. Based on the foregoing, the Court considers that the restriction examined in the preceding paragraphs constitutes an undue limitation of the exercise of a political right, entailing an unnecessary restriction of the right to be elected, taking into account the circumstances of the instant case, which are not necessarily comparable to the circumstances of all political groups that may be present in other national societies or sectors of a national society.

220. Having established the foregoing, the Court finds it necessary to indicate that any requirement for political participation designed for political parties, which cannot be fulfilled by groups with a different form of organization, is also contrary to Articles 23 and 24 of the American Convention, to the extent that it limits the full range of political rights more than strictly necessary, and becomes an impediment for citizens to participate effectively in the conduct of public affairs. The requirements for exercising the right to be elected must observe the parameters established in paragraphs 204, 206 and 207 of this judgment.

## V.  *FINAL COMMENTS AND QUESTIONS*

1. To what extent are states free to order their own governance institutions and practices, including in relation to presidential terms and electoral processes? What limits does the concept of democracy itself impose, and to what extent can the OAS legitimately work to enforce those limits? To what extent does the norm of non-discrimination require accommodation to diversity in governance institutions and electoral processes? Note that in Colombia two seats in the national senate are reserved for representatives of indigenous peoples. Does the rationale of the *Yatama* judgment support such a reservation? Might such a reservation not just be permissible but also required by Inter-American human rights instruments as interpreted by the Commission and the Court? Or would that go too far?

2. A critical challenge currently faced by both the Inter-American Commission and Court is how to effectively address human rights issues in transitioning democracies. The early work of the Inter-American system was deeply affected by the need to address systemic human rights abuses stemming from repressive regimes and dictatorships, including problems such as forced disappearances, amnesty laws and impunity, forms of torture, massacres, and others. Many of the Latin American countries affected by these regimes are striving to transition into working democracies. While not perfect, several of these democracies have strong executive, legislative and judicial branches, and well-functioning government institutions. Regional human rights treaties and their principles are reflected in constitutions, legislation, national policies, and programs. As will be explained in the next Chapter, the practice of the European system of human rights differs from the Inter-American system in that it considers national practices when defining the content of state obligations under the relevant human rights treaty—largely through the application of its margin of appreciation doctrine. Should the Inter-American Commission and Court do more to consider and reflect national and regional tendencies in their case rulings?

3. Note that under the Inter-American and African systems, as opposed to the European system, persons filing petitions need not be victims of the alleged human rights violations. "Victims" for the purposes of the European system can include corporate entities; in contrast, in the Inter-American system victims are only individuals or groups of individuals, not legal entities. This limitation is proving controversial in respect to freedom of expression, where the targets of suppression are often newspapers, radio stations, or television networks that are incorporated. Which system, or blend of systems, seems preferable? Why?

4. The Inter-American Commission's country reports have been rightly praised for their quality and usefulness. However, the Commission has not attempted to establish a periodic reporting process for states similar to that mandated by the UN human rights treaties or the African system. Article 43 of the American Convention permits the Commission to request information from states parties "as to the manner in which their domestic law, insures the effective application of any provision [of this Convention]." Could an innovative Commission seize upon this language to develop an effective state self-reporting process? Would such a process be valuable, or would it constitute an unwelcome diversion of Commission time and resources away from its own country reports and individual complaints? Could having such a self-reporting procedure in place dissuade states from ratifying the American Convention and other Inter-American instruments due to the already heavy reporting burden they have at the UN?

5. Compare the substantive rights protected under the American Convention with those protected under the European Convention, which will be discussed in Chapter 9. Would it still be correct to conclude that "some of the provisions of the American Convention are so advanced that it may be doubted whether there is a country in the Americas that is in full compliance with all of them," as a former president of the Inter-American Court remarked in 1984? Thomas Buergenthal, "The Inter-American System for the Protection of Human Rights," in 2 *Human Rights in International Law: Legal and Policy Issues* 439, 442 (Theodor Meron ed., 1984).

6. A body of specialized scholarship has developed which describes and analyzes particular aspects of the work of the Inter-American System of human rights. See, e.g., Thomas Antkowiak, *Remedial Approaches to Human Rights Violations: The Inter-American Court of Human Rights and Beyond*, 46 COLUM. J. TRANSNAT'L L. 351 (2008) and *A "Dignified Life" and the Resurgence of Social Rights*, 18 NW. J. HUM. RTS. 1 (2020); Rosa Celorio, *The Rights of Women in the Inter-American System of Human Rights: Current Opportunities and Challenges in Standard-Setting*, 65 U. MIAMI L. REV. 819 (2011), *The Case of Karen Atala and Daughters: Towards a Better Understanding of Discrimination, Equality, and the Rights of Women*, 15 CUNY L. REV. 335 (2012), and *Discrimination and the Regional Human Rights Protection Systems: The Enigma of Effectiveness*, 40 U. PA. J. INT'L L. 781 (2019); Jorge Contesse, *Subsidiarity in Global Governance: Contestation and Difference in the Inter-American Human Rights System*, 79 LAW & CONTEMP. PROB. 123 (2016); Tara Melish, *Rethinking "Less as More" Thesis: Supranational Litigation of Economic, Social and Cultural Rights in the Americas*, 39 NYU J. INT'L L. & POL. 1 (2006); Jo M. Pasqualucci, *International Indigenous Land Rights: A Critique of the Jurisprudence of the Inter-American Court of Human Rights in Light of the United Nations Declaration on the Rights of Indigenous Peoples*, 27 WIS.

INT'L L.J. 51 (2009); Diego Rodríguez-Pinzón, *The Future of the Inter-American System of Human Rights: Precautionary Measures of the Inter-American Commission on Human Rights: Legal Status and Importance*, 20 HUM. RTS. BR. 13 (2013); Dinah Shelton, *The Inter-American Human Rights Law of Indigenous Peoples*, 35 U. HAW. L. REV. 937 (2013); Brian D. Tittemore, *The Mandatory Death Penalty in the Commonwealth Caribbean and the Inter-American Human Rights System: An Evolution in the Development and Implementation of International Human Rights Protections*, 13 WM. & MARY BILL OF RTS. J. 445 (2004); James L. Cavallaro et al., *Doctrine, Practice, and Advocacy in the Inter-American Human Rights System* (2019).

CHAPTER 9

# THE EUROPEAN AND OTHER REGIONAL HUMAN RIGHTS SYSTEMS

## ESTABLISHED AND STILL EVOLVING INSTITUTIONS AND PROCEDURES

# I. INTRODUCTION: HUMAN RIGHTS MECHANISMS IN EUROPE, AFRICA, ASIA, AND THE ARAB WORLD

Apart from the Inter-American human rights system, regional human rights systems of varying strength and complexity exist in Europe, Africa, the Arab world, and Southeast Asia. As with the Inter-American system, these other systems in many ways reflect the legal and political histories and cultures in their respective regions.

This Chapter first examines the major components and procedures of the European human rights system, which is grounded in the Council of Europe. With its European Court of Human Rights, the European system is the world's most developed and functional regional human rights system, and it has been an important point of reference for the development of regional human rights systems in the Americas and elsewhere.

The emergence and evolution of the European human rights system has been shaped by two world wars, the desire for peace, the notion that regional cooperation is vital to prevent the recurrence of conflict, and an openness to the reform of institutions to make them ever more effective. Even though the European human rights protection machinery is strong, across Europe there are many human rights issues, including threats to the strength and transparency of democratic institutions, and to the rights to live free from discrimination and violence. Many of these issues have arisen against the backdrop of times of crisis and unrest, including Russia's invasion of Ukraine (discussed in Chapter 5), waves of migration and refugees, the COVID-19 pandemic, nationalist tendencies, and climate change, among other contexts. These concerns are testing the long history of multilateralism in Europe and the effectiveness of its treaties and institutions. While this Chapter focuses on the institutional architecture and procedures of the European human rights system, it touches on debates within Europe about how to respond to growing cultural and religious diversity and the resulting tensions.

This Chapter also discusses the components and procedures of the African human rights system, which is part of the African Union. The struggle for self-determination, freedom from racial discrimination, cultural integrity, peace, and stable institutions has deeply influenced the activities of the African Union and its human rights system. Lastly, the Chapter offers some insight into developments in Asia and the Arab world that are relevant to human rights protection.

## II.  THE EUROPEAN HUMAN RIGHTS SYSTEM

### A.  The Institutional and Normative Framework

In 1949, ten northern and western European countries created the Council of Europe, the first post-war European regional organization (which stands apart from the European Union and its predecessor organizations). The Statute of the Council provides that each member state must "[a]ccept the principles of the rule of law and of the enjoyment by all persons within its jurisdiction of human rights and fundamental freedoms." These states, self-described as "like-minded and hav[ing] a common heritage of political traditions, ideals, freedom and the rule of law," agreed to take the "first steps for the collective enforcement of certain of the rights stated in the Universal Declaration [of Human Rights]" and adopted the 1950 Convention for the Protection of Human Rights and Fundamental Freedoms (hereinafter European Convention of Human Rights or the European Convention).

The drafters of the European Convention chose to include a short list of civil and political rights, based on the language of the Universal Declaration of Human Rights, and prepared a single opening statement of the core obligation of state parties: "The High Contracting Parties shall secure to everyone within their jurisdiction the rights and freedoms defined in Section I of this Convention." The drafters gave greater attention to developing machinery to monitor implementation and compliance by the Contracting Parties and established two institutions "to ensure the observance of the engagements undertaken by the High Contracting Parties"—the European Commission of Human Rights and the European Court of Human Rights. This first attempt at creating compliance procedures was cautious, however, and both the Court's jurisdiction and the individual petition procedure for human rights violations were optional for each state party. The "normal" procedure thus envisaged was one of interstate complaints brought to the Commission and through it to the Committee of Ministers (composed of the foreign ministers of European Council member states), which would make the final decision on the merits and determine the consequences. The Commission met in closed sessions, engaged in fact-finding, and attempted to arrive at a friendly settlements of the matters before it. Only the Commission or the state concerned could refer a matter to the Court if the state in question had accepted the Court's jurisdiction. Enforcement of judgments of the Court and decisions of the Committee of Ministers lay with the Committee itself, which could suspend a state from its rights of representation or ask it to withdraw from the Council for serious violations of its obligations.

State acceptance of the right of individual petition and of the European Court's jurisdiction was gradual, but it expanded over time and led to an increase in the number of individual petitions, which roughly doubled every five years. A large surge of complaints began in the early 1990s after the political changes in Central and Eastern Europe brought new member states into the Council of Europe, which eventually led to its current membership of 46 states. By the end of the decade, delays caused by the procedures themselves and the rising caseload led the Council of Europe to adopt Protocol No. 11 to the Convention, which replaced the former Commission and Court with a new full-time Court that has compulsory jurisdiction to receive individual and interstate complaints of human rights violations.

The Court today is composed "of a number of members equal to that of the High Contracting Parties" to the European Convention. The judges are elected for a single nine-year term by the Parliamentary Assembly of the Council of Europe from a list of three nominees submitted by each member state. The judges serve in their individual capacities and must be persons of "high moral character," who "possess the qualifications required for appointment to high judicial office or be persons of recognized competence." The judges do not have to be nationals of the member states of the Council of Europe, although almost all of them have been. They serve full time during their term and may not undertake any activity incompatible with their judicial functions. They must retire at age 70. The permanent Court has its seat in Strasbourg, also the seat of the Council of Europe, and judges are expected to live in the area. The Court has a Registry with a full-time a staff. The Registrar is the chief clerk of the Court. See European Convention on Human Rights, Articles 19-24.

The Committee of Ministers, the governing body of the Council of Europe, continues to monitor compliance and exercise supervision over enforcement of the Court's judgments. It also approves protocols to the Convention and other European human rights treaties that are then submitted to states for ratification. Pursuant to a 1994 declaration on compliance with commitments, the Committee has expanded its thematic monitoring. The first theme it adopted for monitoring was freedom of expression and information; other themes include the functioning of democratic institutions, including political parties and free elections, the functioning of judicial systems, local democracy, capital punishment, police and security forces, the effectiveness of judicial remedies, nondiscrimination, freedom of conscience and religion, and gender equality.

Other organs and institutions also play important roles in facilitating the implementation of the European Convention. The Parliamentary Assembly has key functions in reviewing nominations to the Court and in vetting applicant states seeking to join the Council of Europe. The latter process involves an on-site visit and report on the state resulting in a set of commitments by the government of the applicant state. Compliance with these commitments is overseen by the Committee of Ministers, the Parliamentary Assembly, and the Secretariat. In addition, the Parliamentary Assembly's Committee on Human Rights adopts resolutions and declarations on key human rights issues, often leading to the conclusion of new treaties.

The 1993 Declaration adopted by the Council of Europe Heads of State and Government, meeting at the Vienna Summit, included a commitment to combat racism, xenophobia, anti-Semitism, and intolerance. The follow-up involved creation of a new mechanism, the European Commission against Racism and Intolerance (ECRI), established to review member states' legislation, policies, and other measures to combat racism and intolerance and to propose further action at local, national, and European levels. ECRI engages in studies of the situation in each of the member states, which are followed by specific proposals designed to resolve problems or remedy deficiencies. Draft texts are communicated to national liaison officers to allow national authorities to respond with observations. After a confidential dialogue, ECRI adopts a final report and submits it to the state concerned through the Committee of Ministers. State reports are made public two months after transmission to the government, unless the government expressly objects.

In 1999, the Council of Europe created the post of Commissioner for Human Rights, who is elected by the Parliamentary Assembly from a list of candidates drawn up by the Committee of Ministers and serves a nonrenewable six-year term. The independent and impartial Commissioner serves as "a non-judicial institution to promote education in, awareness of, and respect for human rights, as embodied in the human rights instruments of the Council of Europe." The functions are thus primarily promotional and preventive; the Commissioner has no power to accept complaints of rights violations.

The 17 protocols* to the European Convention have extended, for states ratifying the protocols, the initially short list of guaranteed rights, as well as modified its institutions and procedures. The first Protocol added a right to property, a right to education, and an undertaking by the state parties to hold free and secret elections at reasonable intervals. Protocol No. 4 enlarged the list further by prohibiting deprivation of liberty for failure to comply with contractual obligations, by guaranteeing the right to liberty of movement, and by barring forced exile of nationals and the collective expulsion of aliens. Protocol No. 6 provided for abolition of the death penalty except during wartime, and several years later Protocol 13 required doing away with the death penalty in all circumstances. Protocol No. 7 required states to accord aliens various due process safeguards before they may be expelled from a country where they reside. Protocol No. 7 also provided for rights of appeal in criminal proceedings, compensation in cases of miscarriage of justice, protection against double jeopardy, and equality of rights and responsibilities between spouses. Protocol No. 12 augmented the nondiscrimination guarantee in Article 14 of the European Convention by providing that "the enjoyment of any right set forth by law shall be secured without discrimination on any ground" and adding that "no one shall be discriminated against by any public authority."

Additionally, Protocol 14, which entered into force in 2010, amended the Convention to introduce new criteria for the admissibility of applications and the treatment of repetitive cases. Protocol 15, which entered into force on 2021, introduced references to the principle of subsidiarity and the doctrine of margin appreciation, which had previously been articulated by the European Court, as discussed *infra*, pages 628-640, and reduced the time limit for submitting a case to the Court. As referenced in Chapter 8, Protocol 16, which entered into force in 2018, extended the jurisdiction of the European Court of Human Rights to give national courts the opportunity to request advisory opinions concerning legal questions related to the European Convention and its protocols.

## B.  Taking a Complaint to the European Court

Today the states of the Council of Europe are locked into a system of collective responsibility for the protection of human rights, a system in which the jurisdiction of the Court provides the centerpiece. Pursuant to Article 34 of the Convention, the Court may receive applications from "any person, non-governmental

---

* The Protocols are numbered 1 through 16, but the adoption of Protocol 14bis means there are actually 17 in total. —Eds.

organization or group of individuals claiming to be the victim of a violation . . . of the rights set forth in the Convention or the protocols thereto." However, concern with the continually rising caseload has led to the inclusion in Protocol No. 14 of more restrictive admissibility criteria and a streamlined procedure for determining admissibility.

According to statistics published by the European Court of Human Rights, by the end of 2021 the Court had delivered 24,511 judgments since its establishment in 1959. Around 40% of those judgments concerned three member states of the Council of Europe, Turkey (3,820), the Russian Federation (3,116), and Italy (2,466). In 84% of these judgments, the Court found at least one violation of the Convention by the respondent state. Close to 40% of the violations found by the Court have been related to the right to fair trial under Article 6 of the European Convention on Human Rights, most raising issues of fairness (16.55%) or length of the proceedings (18.28%). The second most found violation has been related to the right to liberty and security under Article 5. In recent years, Convention violations have been found with increasing frequency in relation to the prohibition of torture and inhuman or degrading treatment (Article 3), and the right to liberty and security (Article 5). See European Court of Human Rights, *Overview 1959-2021* at 3, 6-7 (2022).

Other significant developments in recent years in the European system include a resurgence in interstate cases, many of which involve internal or international armed conflicts. There have been 20 interstate cases heard by the European Court and many of these have been brought against Russia by either Georgia or Ukraine. In July of 2021 Russia lodged an interstate application in 2021 against Ukraine alleging a practice of killings, abductions, forced displacement, interference with the right to vote, and other human rights abuses. In the context of the application, Russia submitted an urgent request for interim measures to order the Ukrainian government to stop restrictions on the rights of Russian-speaking persons to use their mother tongue in schools, the media, and the Internet, and to suspend the Ukrainian blockade of the North Crimean Canal. The Court rejected this request, considering that "it did not involve a serious risk of irreparable harm of a core right under the European Convention on Human Rights." See *Inter-State Application Brought by Russia against Ukraine*, Registrar of the Eur. Ct. H.R., Press Release (July 23, 2021). As discussed in Chapter 5, Ukraine made an application against Russia soon after it was invaded by Russia in early 2022. In relation to that application the European Court granted interim measures on March 1, 2022 calling on Russia to refrain from military attacks against civilians and civilian objects, including residential areas. See Eur. Ct. of H.R., Press Release, *The European Court grants urgent interim measures in application concerning Russian military operations on Ukrainian territory*, Registrar of Eur. Ct. of H.R., Press Release (Mar. 1, 2022).

### 1.   Jurisdiction and Admissibility

Like all human rights institutions, the jurisdiction of the European Court of Human Rights is limited by the provisions of its enabling treaty, which regulate subject matter jurisdiction, standing, and the temporal and territorial limits of the system. Unlike the other regional systems, the European Convention requires that an applicant be a "victim" of the alleged violation. The admissibility criteria are set forth in Articles 34 and 35 of the Convention, as amended by the relevant Protocols referred to above.

Article 34—Individual applications

The Court may receive applications from any person, non-governmental organization or group of individuals claiming to be the victim of a violation by one of the High Contracting Parties of the rights set forth in the Convention or the protocols thereto. The High Contracting Parties undertake not to hinder in any way the effective exercise of this right.

Article 35—Admissibility criteria

1. The Court may only deal with the matter after all domestic remedies have been exhausted, according to the generally recognized rules of international law, and within a period of four months from the date on which the final decision was taken.

2. The Court shall not deal with any application submitted under Article 34 that

a) is anonymous; or

b) is substantially the same as a matter that has already been examined by the Court or has already been submitted to another procedure of international investigation or settlement and contains no relevant new information.

3. The Court shall declare inadmissible any individual application submitted under Article 34 if it considers that:

a) the application is incompatible with the provisions of the Convention or the Protocols thereto, manifestly ill-founded, or an abuse of the right of individual application; or

b) the applicant has not suffered a significant disadvantage, unless respect for human rights as defined in the Convention and the Protocols thereto requires an examination of the application on the merits and provided that no case may be rejected on this ground which has not been duly considered by a domestic tribunal.

4. The Court shall reject any application which it considers inadmissible under this Article. It may do so at any stage of the proceedings.

Each aspect of the European Court's jurisdiction—temporal, personal, subject matter, and territorial—has been challenged in various cases submitted to it. Governments frequently raise preliminary issues of admissibility as well as jurisdictional challenges. In fact, a substantial majority of all applications never reach a merits determination and are dismissed on the ground of failure to exhaust domestic remedies.

In practice, the European Court's Registry plays a central role in case processing. It undertakes an initial evaluation of applications and decides whether the application should be assigned to a single judge, a Committee (three judges), or a Chamber (seven judges). Non-judicial rapporteurs from the Registry assist the single judges, see Rules of the European Court of Human Rights, Rule 18A, transmitting the lists of cases deemed clearly inadmissible to them for approval. The lists transmitted electronically to the single judges contain only one or two sentence summaries of each matter recommended for dismissal due to inadmissibility; the judges do not see the actual applications. See Iain Cameron, *The Court and the Member States: Procedural Aspects*, in *Constituting Europe: The European Court of Human Rights in a National, European and Global Context* 25, 31 (Andreas Follesdal et al. eds., 2013). Does this practice reduce the role of the judges to "rubber-stamping" admissibility decisions of the Registry, at least in certain cases? If an application is summarily rejected, the author is sent a form letter simply stating that "taking account of all the elements in its possession, and to the extent that it is able to evaluate the allegations formulated," the Court sees no reason to proceed. See *Gagliano Giorgi v. Italy*, App. 2353/07, Eur. Ct. H.R. Preliminary Judgment of March 6 2012, para. 40.

The following case raises the issue of territorial jurisdiction, against the backdrop of the kind of cross-cultural tension increasingly found in Europe. Consider in reading the following case whether the Court is overly or appropriately restrictive in rejecting the application.

## Ben El Mahi and Others v. Denmark

2006-XV Eur. Ct. H.R., App. No. 5853/06 (admissibility)

The first applicant, Mr. Mohammed Ben El Mahi, is a Moroccan national who was born in 1953 and lives in Morocco. He represents the second applicant, the Moroccan National Consumer Protection League, and the third applicant, the Moroccan Child Protection and Family Support Association. . . .

THE CIRCUMSTANCES OF THE CASE

The facts of the case, as submitted by the applicants, may be summarised as follows.

On 17 September 2005 a privately owned Danish newspaper, *Politiken*, ran an article under the headline "Profound fear of criticism of Islam" (*Dyb angst for kritik af islam*). It reported on the difficulties encountered by the writer of a children's book entitled *The Koran and the Life of the Prophet Muhammad* (*Koranen og profeten Muhammeds liv*) in finding an illustrator for the book.

On 30 September 2005 another privately owned Danish newspaper, *Morgenavisen Jyllands-Posten*, published twelve cartoons, most of which were caricatures of the Prophet Muhammad. The most controversial of the cartoons showed the Prophet Muhammad with a bomb in his turban. In the middle of the page carrying the cartoons was an explanatory text by the newspaper's cultural affairs editor which stated, *inter alia*, as follows:

> 1. Some Muslims reject modern secular society. They demand special status, insisting on special consideration of their own religious feelings. This is incompatible with contemporary democracy and freedom of expression, where one has to be prepared to put up with scorn, mockery and ridicule. While this is not always agreeable or pleasant to watch, and does not mean that religious feelings can be made fun of at any price, that is a minor consideration in the present context . . . we are on a slippery slope,

with no one able to predict where self-censorship will lead. That is why *Morgenavisen Jyllands-Posten* has invited members of the Danish Newspaper Illustrators' Union to draw Muhammad as they see him.

. . .

On 29 October 2005 several Muslim organisations in Denmark reported *Morgenavisen Jyllands-Posten* to the Danish police, maintaining that it had violated the provisions of the Criminal Code concerning blasphemy and insult on the basis of race or religious orientation.

By decision of 6 January 2006 the Regional Public Prosecutor for Viborg (*Statsadvokaten i Viborg*) decided not to initiate criminal proceedings against the newspaper. The Muslim organisations appealed against that decision to the Director of Public Prosecutions (*Rigsadvokaten*), who upheld the decision on 15 March 2006 . . .

Various Muslim organisations initiated civil proceedings for defamation against *Morgenavisen Jyllands-Posten* before the Århus City Court (*Retten i Århus*) which, in a judgment of 26 October 2006, found against them. . . .

THE LAW

The applicants complained that the publication of the cartoons at issue had breached their rights under Article 9 taken in conjunction with Article 14 of the Convention. They also relied on Article 17, taken together with Article 10 of the Convention.

Given that the first applicant lives in Morocco and the two applicant associations are based there, the question arises whether the applicants come within Denmark's "jurisdiction" within the meaning of Article 1 of the Convention. . . .

The established case-law in this area indicates that the concept of "jurisdiction" for the purposes of Article 1 of the Convention must be considered to reflect the term's meaning in public international law. Thus, from the standpoint of public international law, the words "within their jurisdiction" in Article 1 of the Convention must be understood to mean that a State's jurisdictional competence is primarily territorial and also that jurisdiction is presumed to be exercised normally throughout the State's territory. Only in exceptional circumstances may the acts of Contracting States performed outside their territory or which produce effects there ("extra-territorial acts") amount to an exercise by them of their jurisdiction within the meaning of Article 1 of the Convention. The Court has found clear confirmation of this essentially territorial notion of jurisdiction in the *travaux préparatoires*, given that the Expert Intergovernmental Committee replaced the words "all persons residing within their territories" with a reference to persons "within their jurisdiction" with a view to expanding the Convention's application to others who may not reside, in a legal sense, but who are, nevertheless, on the territory of the Contracting States. Hence, this preparatory material constitutes clear confirmatory evidence of the ordinary meaning of Article 1 of the Convention as already identified by the Court (see, among other authorities, *Banković and Others v. Belgium and 16 Other Contracting States*, Apps. 52207/99, §§59-65, ECHR 2001-XII, Admissibility dec. of Dec. 12, 2001 (GC), and *Issa and Others v. Turkey*, App. 31821/96, §§65-71, Admissibility dec. of Nov. 16, 2004).

. . .

. . . Here the applicants are, respectively, a Moroccan national resident in Morocco and two Moroccan associations which are based in Morocco and operate in that country. The Court considers that there is no jurisdictional link between any of the applicants and the relevant member State, namely Denmark, or that they can come within the jurisdiction of Denmark on account of any extra-territorial act. Accordingly, the Court has no competence to examine the applicants' substantive complaints under the Articles of the Convention relied upon.

The application must therefore be declared incompatible with the provisions of the Convention and, as such, inadmissible pursuant to Article 35 §§3 and 4 of the Convention.

For these reasons, the Court unanimously *Declares* the application inadmissible.

## Comments and Questions

1. The case of *Ben Al Mahi* illustrates how the European Court of Human Rights has interpreted the content and scope of states parties' territorial "jurisdiction" under Article 1 of the European Convention on Human Rights for admissibility purposes. The case poses the question of whether applicants from a foreign state — in this case Morocco — can be considered within the jurisdiction of Denmark and its human rights obligations under the European Convention on Human Rights. The Court found that there was no jurisdictional link between Denmark and the Moroccan applicants. Do you agree with the European Court's decision? Is there no link in fact?

2. Under what conditions should a state be held accountable for human rights violations caused by its agents when their actions have harmful effects beyond the State's territory? Given the 2022 Russian invasion of Ukraine, ongoing military activities around the world and the global reach of environmental harm and climate change among other issues, international tribunals are likely to face a growing number of cases raising questions about the extraterritorial scope of state obligations under specific instruments. Recall, as discussed in Chapter 5, pages 301-302, that the European Court of Human Rights granted interim measures in connection with alleged human rights violations in Ukraine resulting from Russia's belligerent actions. In *Catan and Others v. Moldova and Russia*, the European Court summarized its jurisprudence on territorial jurisdiction, corroborating that extraterritorial jurisdiction can take place in "exceptional circumstances," for example, when a state exercises effective control of an area outside of its territory. See *Catan and Others v. Moldova and Russia*, Eur. Ct. H.R. (GC), Apps. Nos. 43370/04, 8252/05, and 18454/06, Judgment of Oct. 19, 2012, paras. 103-106. The *Catan and Others* case addressed a complaint by both children and parents from the Moldovan community in Transdniestria regarding the harmful effects of a language policy imposed by a separatist regime prohibiting the use of the Latin alphabet in schools. Even though the events took place in Moldovan territory, the applicants argued that Russia also had jurisdiction over these human rights violations because it exercised decisive influence over the separatist Moldovan Republic of Transdniestria

(MRT) at the time. The Court considered that the case fell under Russia's jurisdiction since MRT had survived between 2002-2004 solely due to Russian military, economic, and political support. See *Catan and Others, supra,* paras. 108-123. See also *Öcalan v. Turkey,* Eur. Ct. H.R. (GC), App. No. 46221/99, Judgment of May 12, 2005, paras. 91-92 (capture in Kenya of a Kurdish guerilla leader by Turkish forces brought him within Turkish jurisdiction, although no violation found with regard to his treatment). And see generally Eur. Ct. H.R., *Factsheet: Extra-territorial jurisdiction of States Parties to the European Convention on Human Rights* (July 2018), https://www.echr.coe.int/documents/fs_extra-territorial_jurisdiction_eng.pdf.

4. Even if one takes an expansive view of extraterritorial obligations, should European governments be responsible for regulating publications, whether print, broadcast or Internet, that will almost certainly be transmitted outside the European region? If Muslims in Europe had an admissible case against Denmark, should the Court give any weight to the Danish prosecutor's finding that "[t]he religious writing of Islam cannot be said to contain a general and absolute prohibition on drawing the Prophet Mohammad"?

## 2. Applying the Substantive Rights in the European Convention: The Right to Freedom of Religion

Once a case has been admitted, the European Court must interpret and apply the rights within the Convention or its Protocols. While the Court has delivered opinions on a wide range of matters, a recurring set of issues are those related to the scope or content of freedom of religion and belief under Article 9 of the Convention. The Court has had a cluster of important cases concerning this right, including cases examining the interplay of Article 9 with Article 10, which guarantees freedom of speech, information, and expression.

The 46 states within the Council of Europe are diverse in culture, religion, legal systems, languages, and governments. And, like other parts of the world, Europe is no stranger to religious conflict. From the later Middle Ages to the early nineteenth century, church-sponsored inquisitions sought to fight heresy against the Catholic Church. Jews and Muslims were expelled from Spain in the late fifteenth century. The Protestant Reformation that challenged Catholic domination beginning in the early 1500s roiled Europe for over a century and fueled contests for power that erupted into the highly disruptive Thirty Years War. Anti-Semitism was rampant in France, Germany, and the Austro-Hungarian Empire, even prior to the rise of the Nazi regime in the 1930s.

More recently, in the post-colonial era, immigration has brought into Europe large numbers of Muslims, Hindus, Buddhists and Sikhs as well as adherents of newer religions. Governments and the public in many European states have responded with laws, policies, and practices that often appear intended to protect the majority (often officially state-supported) religions against minority religious beliefs and practices. Terrorism, often justified by religious extremism, has exacerbated hostility between groups; ethnic conflicts in the former Yugoslavia, although not necessarily religious in origin, led to the dissolution of the country. The widely reported publication of cartoons depicting the Prophet Mohammed, discussed in the *El Mahi* case *supra,* led to violence in several locales and later to a terrorist attack in Paris against the satirical publication *Charlie Hebdo*. Since 2011, new waves of primarily Muslim immigrants from Syria, Iraq, Libya, and elsewhere have further challenged European notions of tolerance and multiculturalism, and religious expression is frequently the phenomenon most reflective of larger socio-economic-cultural divides. The following examples introduce some of the issues arising in connection with religion in Europe.

*Ireland's blasphemy law.* Blasphemy was a common law offense under Irish law when the 1937 Constitution explicitly made it an offense punishable by law. Constitution of Ireland (July 1, 1937), Art. 40. The Defamation Act 2009, which entered into force on January 1, 2010, defines the crime of blasphemy as follows:

> 36. — (1) A person who publishes or utters blasphemous matter shall be guilty of an offence and shall be liable upon conviction on indictment to a fine not exceeding €25,000.
>
> (2) For the purposes of this section, a person publishes or utters blasphemous matter if—
>
>     *(a)* he or she publishes or utters matter that is grossly abusive or insulting in relation to matters held sacred by any religion, thereby causing outrage among a substantial number of the adherents of that religion, and
>
>     *(b)* he or she intends, by the publication or utterance of the matter concerned, to cause such outrage.
>
> (3) It shall be a defence to proceedings for an offence under this section for the defendant to prove that a reasonable person would find genuine literary, artistic, political, scientific, or academic value in the matter to which the offence relates.
>
> (4) In this section "religion" does not include an organisation or cult—
>
>     (*a*) the principal object of which is the making of profit, or
>
>     (*b*) that employs oppressive psychological manipulation—
>
>         (i)  of its followers, or
>
>         (ii) for the purpose of gaining new followers.

To test the law, the NGO Atheist Ireland immediately published 25 quotations on its website from various figures, including writers Mark Twain and Salman Rushdie, and films such as *Monty Python's Life of Brian*. The Blasphemy law was finally repealed after a constitutional referendum on October 26, 2018.

*The Swiss minaret law.* In late 2009, Switzerland adopted, by a 57.5 percent majority, a constitutional amendment by national referendum to ban the construction of new minarets in the country. At the time, only four mosques with minarets existed in Switzerland. Several months later, a UN Human Rights Council resolution strongly condemned the ban "and other recent discriminatory measures." It called the ban a "manifestation of Islamophobia that clearly contravenes international human rights obligations concerning freedom of religion, belief, conscience and expression." Seventeen, mostly Western, nations including the United States, opposed the resolution. Twenty states voted in favor of it and eight states abstained. Early cases submitted to the European Court of Human Rights were rejected on the ground that the applicants were not truly "victims" of a violation, which is a requirement under the European Convention on Human Rights. See *Ouardiri v. Switzerland,* Eur. Ct. H.R., App. No. 65840/09, Admissibility Decision of June 28, 2011.

*France bans concealing garments.* On July 13, 2010, the lower house of the French Parliament by a vote of 335 to 1 approved the *Loi interdisant la dissimulation du visage dans l'espace public* (Act prohibiting concealment of the face in public areas). The Senate gave its approval on September 14, 2010, and the law entered into force April 11, 2011, resulting in the first European ban on the wearing of face-covering clothing, including niqābs, burqas, and other veils covering the face. The law imposed a fine of €150 on those who contravened the rule and allowed for violators to be obliged to attend compulsory lessons in citizenship. It also provided for a fine of €30,000 and one year in prison for anyone who, by violence, threats, or abuse of power, forced another to wear face coverings; these penalties may be doubled if the victim is under the age of 18. The wearing of a head cover, or hijab, had already been banned in French (and Turkish) schools and public universities, although it was permitted in all other public places.

Against a backdrop of religious and other diversity, including diversity in approaches to balancing competing rights and interests, a constant source of debate and controversy in the region is the question of how far the European Court should insist on a uniform interpretation and application of the rights guaranteed by the Convention and its Protocols. The Court's doctrine of "margin of appreciation," as we have seen, permits some degree of local divergence, at least at the outer boundaries of some of the rights. For analyses of the Court's margin of appreciation doctrine, see generally Jeffrey A. Brauch, *The Margin of Appreciation and the Jurisprudence of the European Court of Human Rights: Threat to the Rule of Law,* 11 COLUM. J. EUR. L. 113 (2004); *Deference in International Courts and Tribunals: Standard of Review and Margin of Appreciation* (Lukasz Gruszczynski and Wouter Werner eds. 2014); D.J. Harris et al., *Harris, O'Boyle, and Warbrick: Law of the European Convention on Human Rights* (3d ed., 2014); Andrew Legg, *The Margin of Appreciation in International Human Rights Law: Deference and Proportionality* (2012); George Letsas, *Two Concepts of the Margin of Appreciation,* 26 OXFORD J. LEGAL STUDIES 705 (2006).

Very few human rights are absolute, and freedom of religion — particularly freedom to manifest one's religion — is no exception. But what are the permissible limitations, and how are they established? For the European Court, as the following case illustrates, the questions are bound by a social and inter-cultural context; and the Court's role is substantially determined by its margin of appreciation for national decision-making.

## S.A.S. v. France

Eur. Ct. H.R. (GC), App. No. 43835/11, Judgment of July 1, 2014

10. The applicant is a French national who was born in 1990 and lives in France. . . .

11. In the applicant's submission, she is a devout Muslim and she wears the burqa and niqab in accordance with her religious faith, culture and personal convictions. According to her explanation, the burqa is a full-body covering including a mesh over the face, and the niqab is a full-face veil leaving an opening only for

the eyes. The applicant emphasised that neither her husband nor any other member of her family put pressure on her to dress in this manner.

12. The applicant added that she wore the niqab in public and in private, but not systematically: she might not wear it, for example, when she visited the doctor, when meeting friends in a public place, or when she wanted to socialise in public. She was thus content not to wear the niqab in public places at all times but wished to be able to wear it when she chose to do so, depending in particular on her spiritual feelings. There were certain times (for example, during religious events such as Ramadan) when she believed that she ought to wear it in public in order to express her religious, personal and cultural faith. Her aim was not to annoy others but to feel at inner peace with herself.

13. The applicant did not claim that she should be able to keep the niqab on when undergoing a security check, at the bank or in airports, and she agreed to show her face when requested to do so for necessary identity checks.

14. Since 11 April 2011, the date of entry into force of Law no. 2010-1192 of 11 October 2010 throughout France, it has been prohibited for anyone to conceal their face in public places. . . .

MERITS

. . .

3. THE COURT'S ASSESSMENT

(a)  Alleged violation of Articles 8 and 9 of the Convention

106.  The ban on wearing clothing designed to conceal the face, in public places, raises questions in terms of the right to respect for private life (Article 8 of the Convention) of women who wish to wear the full-face veil for reasons related to their beliefs, and in terms of their freedom to manifest those beliefs (Article 9 of the Convention).

107.  The Court is thus of the view that personal choices as to an individual's desired appearance, whether in public or in private places, relate to the expression of his or her personality and thus fall within the notion of private life. It has found to this effect previously as regards a haircut (see *Popa v. Romania* (dec), no. 4233/09, §§32-33, 18 June 2013; see also the decision of the European Commission on Human Rights in *Sutter v. Switzerland*, no. 8209/78, 1 March 1979). It considers, like the Commission (see, in particular, the decisions in *McFeeley and Others v. the United Kingdom*, no. 8317/78, 15 May 1980, §83, Decisions and Reports (DR) 20, and *Kara v. the United Kingdom*, no. 36528/97, 22 October 1998), that this is also true for a choice of clothing. A measure emanating from a public authority which restricts a choice of this kind will therefore, in principle, constitute an interference with the exercise of the right to respect for private life within the meaning of Article 8 of the Convention (see the *Kara* decision, cited above). Consequently, the ban on wearing clothing designed to conceal the face in public places, pursuant to the Law of 11 October 2010, falls under Article 8 of the Convention.

108.  That being said, in so far as that ban is criticised by individuals who, like the applicant, complain that they are consequently prevented from wearing in public places clothing that the practice of their religion requires them to wear,

it mainly raises an issue with regard to the freedom to manifest one's religion or beliefs (see, in particular, *Ahmet Arslan and Others v. Turkey*, no. 41135/98, §35, 23 February 2010). The fact that this is a minority practice and appears to be contested is of no relevance in this connection.

109. The Court will thus examine this part of the application under both Article 8 and Article 9, but with emphasis on the second of those provisions.

(i) Whether There Has been a "Limitation" or an "Interference"

110. As the Court has already pointed out, the Law of 11 October 2010 confronts the applicant with a dilemma comparable to that which it identified in the *Dudgeon* and *Norris* judgments: either she complies with the ban and thus refrains from dressing in accordance with her approach to religion; or she refuses to comply and faces criminal sanctions. She thus finds herself, in the light of both Article 9 and Article 8 of the Convention, in a similar situation to that of the applicants in *Dudgeon* and *Norris*, where the Court found a "continuing interference" with the exercise of the rights guaranteed by the second of those provisions (judgments both cited above; see also, in particular, *Michaud*, cited above, §92). There has therefore been, in the present case, an "interference" with or a "limitation" of the exercise of the rights protected by Articles 8 and 9 of the Convention.

111. Such a limitation or interference will not be compatible with the second paragraphs of those Articles unless it is "prescribed by law", pursues one or more of the legitimate aims set out in those paragraphs and is "necessary in a democratic society", to achieve the aim or aims concerned.

(ii) Whether the Measure is "Prescribed by Law"

112. The Court finds that the limitation in question is prescribed by sections 1, 2 and 3 of the Law of 11 October 2010. It further notes that the applicant has not disputed that these provisions satisfy the criteria laid down in the Court's case-law concerning Article 8 §2 and Article 9 §2 of the Convention.

(iii) Whether There is a Legitimate Aim

113. The Court reiterates that the enumeration of the exceptions to the individual's freedom to manifest his or her religion or beliefs, as listed in Article 9 §2, is exhaustive and that their definition is restrictive (see, among other authorities, *Svyato-Mykhaylivska Parafiya v. Ukraine*, no. 77703/01, §132, 14 June 2007, and *Nolan and K. v. Russia*, no. 2512/04, §73, 12 February 2009). For it to be compatible with the Convention, a limitation of this freedom must, in particular, pursue an aim that can be linked to one of those listed in this provision. The same approach applies in respect of Article 8 of the Convention.

114. The Court's practice is to be quite succinct when it verifies the existence of a legitimate aim within the meaning of the second paragraphs of Articles 8 to 11 of the Convention (see, for example, the above-cited judgments of *Leyla Şahin*, §99, and *Ahmet Arslan and Others*, §43). However, in the present case, the substance of the objectives invoked in this connection by the Government, and strongly disputed by the applicant, call for an in-depth examination. The applicant took the view that the interference with the exercise of her freedom to manifest her religion and of her right to respect for her private life, as a result of the ban introduced by

the Law of 11 October 2010, did not correspond to any of the aims listed in the second paragraphs of Articles 8 and 9. The Government argued, for their part, that the Law pursued two legitimate aims: public safety and "respect for the minimum set of values of an open and democratic society". The Court observes that the second paragraphs of Articles 8 and 9 do not refer expressly to the second of those aims or to the three values mentioned by the Government in that connection.

115.  As regards the first of the aims invoked by the Government, the Court first observes that "public safety" is one of the aims enumerated in the second paragraph of Article 9 of the Convention (*sécurité publique* in the French text) and also in the second paragraph of Article 8 (*sûreté publique* in the French text). It further notes the Government's observation in this connection that the impugned ban on wearing, in public places, clothing designed to conceal the face satisfied the need to identify individuals in order to prevent danger for the safety of persons and property and to combat identity fraud. Having regard to the case file, it may admittedly be wondered whether the Law's drafters attached much weight to such concerns. It must nevertheless be observed that the explanatory memorandum which accompanied the Bill indicated — albeit secondarily — that the practice of concealing the face "could also represent a danger for public safety in certain situations", and that the Constitutional Council noted that the legislature had been of the view that this practice might be dangerous for public safety (see paragraph 30 above). Similarly, in its study report of 25 March 2010, the *Conseil d'État* indicated that public safety might constitute a basis for prohibiting concealment of the face, but pointed out that this could be the case only in specific circumstances (see paragraphs 22-23 above). Consequently, the Court accepts that, in adopting the impugned ban, the legislature sought to address questions of "public safety" within the meaning of the second paragraphs of Articles 8 and 9 of the Convention.

116.  As regards the second of the aims invoked — to ensure "respect for the minimum set of values of an open and democratic society" — the Government referred to three values: respect for equality between men and women, respect for human dignity and respect for the minimum requirements of life in society. They submitted that this aim could be linked to the "protection of the rights and freedoms of others", within the meaning of the second paragraphs of Articles 8 and 9 of the Convention.

117.  As the Court has previously noted, these three values do not expressly correspond to any of the legitimate aims enumerated in the second paragraphs of Articles 8 and 9 of the Convention. Among those aims, the only ones that may be relevant in the present case, in relation to the values in question, are "public order" and the "protection of the rights and freedoms of others". The former is not, however, mentioned in Article 8 §2. Moreover, the Government did not refer to it either in their written observations or in their answer to the question put to them in that connection during the public hearing, preferring to refer solely to the "protection of the rights and freedoms of others". The Court will thus focus its examination on the latter "legitimate aim", as it did previously in the cases of *Leyla Şahin* and *Ahmet Arslan and Others*.

118.  Firstly, the Court is not convinced by the Government's submission in so far as it concerns respect for equality between men and women.

119. It does not doubt that gender equality might rightly justify an interference with the exercise of certain rights and freedoms enshrined in the Convention (see, *mutatis mutandis, Staatkundig Gereformeerde Partij v. the Netherlands* (dec.), 10 July 2012). It reiterates in this connection that advancement of gender equality is today a major goal in the member States of the Council of Europe (ibid.; see also, among other authorities, *Schuler-Zgraggen v. Switzerland*, 24 June 1993, §67, Series A no. 263, and *Konstantin Markin v. Russia* [GC], no. 30078/06, §127, ECHR 2012). Thus a State Party which, in the name of gender equality, prohibits anyone from forcing women to conceal their face pursues an aim which corresponds to the "protection of the rights and freedoms of others" within the meaning of the second paragraphs of Articles 8 and 9 of the Convention (see *Leyla Şahin*, cited above, §111). The Court takes the view, however, that a State Party cannot invoke gender equality in order to ban a practice that is defended by women—such as the applicant—in the context of the exercise of the rights enshrined in those provisions, unless it were to be understood that individuals could be protected on that basis from the exercise of their own fundamental rights and freedoms. It further observes that the *Conseil d'État* reached a similar conclusion in its study report of 25 March 2010.

Moreover, in so far as the Government thus sought to show that the wearing of the full-face veil by certain women shocked the majority of the French population because it infringed the principle of gender equality as generally accepted in France, the Court would refer to its reasoning as to the other two values that they have invoked.

120. Secondly, the Court takes the view that, however essential it may be, respect for human dignity cannot legitimately justify a blanket ban on the wearing of the full-face veil in public places. The Court is aware that the clothing in question is perceived as strange by many of those who observe it. It would point out, however, that it is the expression of a cultural identity which contributes to the pluralism that is inherent in democracy. It notes in this connection the variability of the notions of virtuousness and decency that are applied to the uncovering of the human body. Moreover, it does not have any evidence capable of leading it to consider that women who wear the full-face veil seek to express a form of contempt against those they encounter or otherwise to offend against the dignity of others.

121. Thirdly, the Court finds, by contrast, that under certain conditions the "respect for the minimum requirements of life in society" referred to by the Government—or of "living together", as stated in the explanatory memorandum accompanying the Bill—can be linked to the legitimate aim of the "protection of the rights and freedoms of others."

122. The Court takes into account the respondent State's point that the face plays an important role in social interaction. It can understand the view that individuals who are present in places open to all may not wish to see practices or attitudes developing there which would fundamentally call into question the possibility of open interpersonal relationships, which, by virtue of an established consensus, forms an indispensable element of community life within the society in question. The Court is therefore able to accept that the barrier raised against others by a veil concealing the face is perceived by the respondent State as breaching the right of others to live in a space of socialisation which makes living together easier. That being said, in view of the flexibility of the notion of "living together"

and the resulting risk of abuse, the Court must engage in a careful examination of the necessity of the impugned limitation.

(iv)  Whether the Measure is Necessary in a Democratic Society

. . .

128.  Pluralism, tolerance and broadmindedness are hallmarks of a "democratic society." Although individual interests must on occasion be subordinated to those of a group, democracy does not simply mean that the views of a majority must always prevail: a balance must be achieved which ensures the fair treatment of people from minorities and avoids any abuse of a dominant position (see, *mutatis mutandis, Young, James and Webster v. the United Kingdom*, 13 August 1981, §63, Series A no. 44, and *Chassagnou and Others v. France* [GC], nos. 25088/94, 28331/95 and 28443/95, §112, ECHR 1999III). Pluralism and democracy must also be based on dialogue and a spirit of compromise necessarily entailing various concessions on the part of individuals or groups of individuals which are justified in order to maintain and promote the ideals and values of a democratic society (see, *mutatis mutandis, the United Communist Party of Turkey and Others*, cited above, §45, and *Refah Partisi (the Welfare Party) and Others*, cited above §99). Where these "rights and freedoms of others" are themselves among those guaranteed by the Convention or the Protocols thereto, it must be accepted that the need to protect them may lead States to restrict other rights or freedoms likewise set forth in the Convention. It is precisely this constant search for a balance between the fundamental rights of each individual which constitutes the foundation of a "democratic society" (see *Chassagnou and Others*, cited above, §113; see also *Leyla Şahin*, cited above, §108).

129.  It is also important to emphasise the fundamentally subsidiary role of the Convention mechanism. The national authorities have direct democratic legitimation and are, as the Court has held on many occasions, in principle better placed than an international court to evaluate local needs and conditions. In matters of general policy, on which opinions within a democratic society may reasonably differ widely, the role of the domestic policy-maker should be given special weight (see, for example, *Maurice v. France* [GC], no. 11810/03, §117, ECHR 2005IX). This is the case, in particular, where questions concerning the relationship between State and religions are at stake (see, *mutatis mutandis, Cha'are Shalom Ve Tsedek*, cited above, §84, and *Wingrove v. the United Kingdom*, 25 November 1996, §58, *Reports* 1996-V; see also *Leyla Şahin*, cited above, §109). As regards Article 9 of the Convention, the State should thus, in principle, be afforded a wide margin of appreciation in deciding whether and to what extent a limitation of the right to manifest one's religion or beliefs is "necessary". That being said, in delimiting the extent of the margin of appreciation in a given case, the Court must also have regard to what is at stake therein (see, among other authorities, *Manoussakis and Others*, cited above, §44, and *Leyla Şahin*, cited above, §110). It may also, if appropriate, have regard to any consensus and common values emerging from the practices of the States parties to the Convention (see, for example, *Bayatyan v. Armenia* [GC], no. 23459/03, §122, ECHR 2011).

130.  In the *Leyla Şahin* judgment, the Court pointed out that this would notably be the case when it came to regulating the wearing of religious symbols in educational institutions, especially in view of the diversity of the approaches taken by

national authorities on the issue. Referring to the *Otto-Preminger-Institut v. Austria*
judgment (20 September 1994, §50, Series A no. 295-A) and the *Dahlab v. Switzerland* decision (no. 42393/98, ECHR 2001-V), it added that it was thus not possible
to discern throughout Europe a uniform conception of the significance of religion
in society and that the meaning or impact of the public expression of a religious
belief would differ according to time and context. It observed that the rules in this
sphere would consequently vary from one country to another according to national
traditions and the requirements imposed by the need to protect the rights and
freedoms of others and to maintain public order. It concluded from this that the
choice of the extent and form of such rules must inevitably be left up to a point to
the State concerned, as it would depend on the specific domestic context (see *Leyla
Şahin*, cited above, §109).

131.  This margin of appreciation, however, goes hand in hand with a European supervision embracing both the law and the decisions applying it. The Court's
task is to determine whether the measures taken at national level were justified in
principle and proportionate (see, among other authorities, *Manoussakis and Others*,
cited above, §44, and *Leyla Şahin*, cited above, §110). . . .

(b)  Application of those Principles in Previous Cases

132.  The Court has had occasion to examine a number of situations in the
light of those principles.

133.  It has thus ruled on bans on the wearing of religious symbols in State
schools, imposed on teaching staff (see, *inter alia*, *Dahlab*, decision cited above,
and *Kurtulmuş v. Turkey* (dec.), no. 65500/01, ECHR 2006-II) and on pupils and
students (see, *inter alia*, *Leyla Şahin*, cited above; *Köse and Others v. Turkey* (dec.),
no. 26625/02, ECHR 2006-II; *Kervanci v. France*, no. 31645/04, 4 December 2008;
*Aktas v. France* (dec.), no. 43563/08, 30 June 2009; and *Ranjit Singh v. France* (dec.)
no. 27561/08, 30 June 2009), on an obligation to remove clothing with a religious
connotation in the context of a security check (*Phull v. France* (dec.), no. 35753/
03, ECHR 2005-I, and *El Morsli v. France* (dec.), no. 15585/06, 4 March 2008), and
on an obligation to appear bareheaded on identity photos for use on official documents (*Mann Singh v. France* (dec.), no. 24479/07, 11 June 2007). It did not find a
violation of Article 9 in any of these cases.

134. The Court has also examined two applications in which individuals complained in particular about restrictions imposed by their employers on the possibility for them to wear a cross visibly around their necks, arguing that domestic law
had not sufficiently protected their right to manifest their religion. One was an
employee of an airline company, the other was a nurse (see *Eweida and Others*, cited
above). The first of those cases, in which the Court found a violation of Article 9, is
the most pertinent for the present case. The Court took the view, *inter alia*, that the
domestic courts had given too much weight to the wishes of the employer—which
it nevertheless found legitimate—to project a certain corporate image, in relation
to the applicant's fundamental right to manifest her religious beliefs. On the latter
point, it observed that a healthy democratic society needed to tolerate and sustain
pluralism and diversity and that it was important for an individual who had made
religion a central tenet of her life to be able to communicate her beliefs to others.
It then noted that the cross had been discreet and could not have detracted from

the applicant's professional appearance. There was no evidence that the wearing of other, previously authorised, religious symbols had had any negative impact on the image of the airline company in question. While pointing out that the national authorities, in particular the courts, operated within a margin of appreciation when they were called upon to assess the proportionality of measures taken by a private company in respect of its employees, it thus found that there had been a violation of Article 9.

135.  The Court also examined, in the case of *Ahmet Arslan and Others* (cited above), the question of a ban on the wearing, outside religious ceremonies, of certain religious clothing in public places open to everyone, such as public streets or squares. The clothing in question, characteristic of the *Aczimendi tarikatı* group, consisted of a turban, a sirwal and a tunic, all in black, together with a baton. The Court accepted, having regard to the circumstances of the case and the decisions of the domestic courts, and particularly in view of the importance of the principle of secularism for the democratic system in Turkey, that, since the aim of the ban had been to uphold secular and democratic values, the interference pursued a number of the legitimate aims listed in Article 9 §2: the maintaining of public safety, the protection of public order and the protection of the rights and freedoms of others. It found, however, that the necessity of the measure in the light of those aims had not been established.

The Court thus noted that the ban affected not civil servants, who were bound by a certain discretion in the exercise of their duties, but ordinary citizens, with the result that its case-law on civil servants—and teachers in particular—did not apply. It then found that the ban was aimed at clothing worn in any public place, not only in specific public buildings, with the result that its case-law emphasising the particular weight to be given to the role of the domestic policy-maker, with regard to the wearing of religious symbols in State schools, did not apply either. The Court, moreover, observed that there was no evidence in the file to show that the manner in which the applicants had manifested their beliefs by wearing specific clothing—they had gathered in front of a mosque for the sole purpose of participating in a religious ceremony—constituted or risked constituting a threat to public order or a form of pressure on others. Lastly, in response to the Turkish Government's allegation of possible proselytising on the part of the applicants, the Court found that there was no evidence to show that they had sought to exert inappropriate pressure on passers-by in public streets and squares in order to promote their religious beliefs. The Court thus concluded that there had been a violation of Article 9 of the Convention.

136.  Among all these cases concerning Article 9, *Ahmet Arslan and Others* is that which the present case most closely resembles. However, while both cases concern a ban on wearing clothing with a religious connotation in public places, the present case differs significantly from *Ahmet Arslan and Others* in the fact that the full-face Islamic veil has the particularity of entirely concealing the face, with the possible exception of the eyes.

(c)  Application of those principles to the present case

137.  The Court would first emphasise that the argument put forward by the applicant and some of the third-party interveners, to the effect that the ban introduced by sections 1 to 3 of the Law of 11 October 2010 was based on the erroneous

supposition that the women concerned wore the full-face veil under duress, is not pertinent. It can be seen clearly from the explanatory memorandum accompanying the Bill that it was not the principal aim of the ban to protect women against a practice which was imposed on them or would be detrimental to them.

138.  That being clarified, the Court must verify whether the impugned interference is "necessary in a democratic society" for public safety (within the meaning of Articles 8 and 9 of the Convention) or for the "protection of the rights and freedoms of others".

139.  As regards the question of necessity in relation to public safety, within the meaning of Articles 8 and 9, the Court understands that a State may find it essential to be able to identify individuals in order to prevent danger for the safety of persons and property and to combat identity fraud. It has thus found no violation of Article 9 of the Convention in cases concerning the obligation to remove clothing with a religious connotation in the context of security checks and the obligation to appear bareheaded on identity photos for use on official documents. However, in view of its impact on the rights of women who wish to wear the full-face veil for religious reasons, a blanket ban on the wearing in public places of clothing designed to conceal the face can be regarded as proportionate only in a context where there is a general threat to public safety. The Government have not shown that the ban introduced by the Law of 11 October 2010 falls into such a context. As to the women concerned, they are thus obliged to give up completely an element of their identity that they consider important, together with their chosen manner of manifesting their religion or beliefs, whereas the objective alluded to by the Government could be attained by a mere obligation to show their face and to identify themselves where a risk for the safety of persons and property has been established, or where particular circumstances entail a suspicion of identity fraud. It cannot therefore be found that the blanket ban imposed by the Law of 11 October 2010 is necessary, in a democratic society, for public safety, within the meaning of Articles 8 and 9 of the Convention.

140.  The Court will now examine the questions raised by the other aim that it has found legitimate: to ensure the observance of the minimum requirements of life in society as part of the "protection of the rights and freedoms of others. . . ."

141.  The Court observes that this is an aim to which the authorities have given much weight. This can be seen, in particular, from the explanatory memorandum accompanying the Bill, which indicates that "[t]he voluntary and systematic concealment of the face is problematic because it is quite simply incompatible with the fundamental requirements of 'living together' in French society" and that "[t]he systematic concealment of the face in public places, contrary to the ideal of fraternity, . . . falls short of the minimum requirement of civility that is necessary for social interaction." It indeed falls within the powers of the State to secure the conditions whereby individuals can live together in their diversity. Moreover, the Court is able to accept that a State may find it essential to give particular weight in this connection to the interaction between individuals and may consider this to be adversely affected by the fact that some conceal their faces in public places.

142.  Consequently, the Court finds that the impugned ban can be regarded as justified in its principle solely in so far as it seeks to guarantee the conditions of "living together."

143.  It remains to be ascertained whether the ban is proportionate to that aim.

144. Some of the arguments put forward by the applicant and the intervening non-governmental organisations warrant particular attention.

145. Firstly, it is true that only a small number of women are concerned. It can be seen, among other things, from the report "on the wearing of the full-face veil on national territory" prepared by a commission of the National Assembly and deposited on 26 January 2010, that about 1,900 women wore the Islamic full-face veil in France at the end of 2009, of whom about 270 were living in French overseas administrative areas. This is a small proportion in relation to the French population of about sixty-five million and to the number of Muslims living in France. It may thus seem excessive to respond to such a situation by imposing a blanket ban.

146. In addition, there is no doubt that the ban has a significant negative impact on the situation of women who, like the applicant, have chosen to wear the full-face veil for reasons related to their beliefs. As stated previously, they are thus confronted with a complex dilemma, and the ban may have the effect of isolating them and restricting their autonomy, as well as impairing the exercise of their freedom to manifest their beliefs and their right to respect for their private life. It is also understandable that the women concerned may perceive the ban as a threat to their identity.

147. It should furthermore be observed that a large number of actors, both international and national, in the field of fundamental rights protection have found a blanket ban to be disproportionate. This is the case, for example, of the French National Advisory Commission on Human Rights, non-governmental organisations such as the third-party interveners, the Parliamentary Assembly of the Council of Europe and the Commissioner for Human Rights of the Council of Europe.

148. The Court is also aware that the Law of 11 October 2010, together with certain debates surrounding its drafting, may have upset part of the Muslim community, including some members who are not in favour of the full-face veil being worn.

149. In this connection, the Court is very concerned by the indications of some of the third-party interveners to the effect that certain Islamophobic remarks marked the debate which preceded the adoption of the Law of 11 October 2010 (see the observations of the Human Rights Centre of Ghent University and of the non-governmental organisations Liberty and Open Society Justice Initiative). It is admittedly not for the Court to rule on whether legislation is desirable in such matters. It would, however, emphasise that a State which enters into a legislative process of this kind takes the risk of contributing to the consolidation of the stereotypes which affect certain categories of the population and of encouraging the expression of intolerance, when it has a duty, on the contrary, to promote tolerance (see . . . the "Viewpoint" of the Commissioner for Human Rights of the Council of Europe, paragraph 37 above). The Court reiterates that remarks which constitute a general, vehement attack on a religious or ethnic group are incompatible with the values of tolerance, social peace and non-discrimination which underlie the Convention and do not fall within the right to freedom of expression that it protects (see, among other authorities, *Norwood v. the United Kingdom* (dec.), no. 23131/03, ECHR 2004XI, and *Ivanov v. Russia* (dec.), no. 35222/04, 20 February 2007).

150. The other arguments put forward in support of the application must, however, be qualified.

151. Thus, while it is true that the scope of the ban is broad, because all places accessible to the public are concerned (except for places of worship), the Law of 11 October 2010 does not affect the freedom to wear in public any garment or item of clothing—with or without a religious connotation—which does not have the effect of concealing the face. The Court is aware of the fact that the impugned ban mainly affects Muslim women who wish to wear the full-face veil. It nevertheless finds it to be of some significance that the ban is not expressly based on the religious connotation of the clothing in question but solely on the fact that it conceals the face. This distinguishes the present case from that of *Ahmet Arslan and Others* (cited above).

152. As to the fact that criminal sanctions are attached to the ban, this no doubt increases the impact of the measure on those concerned. It is certainly understandable that the idea of being prosecuted for concealing one's face in a public place is traumatising for women who have chosen to wear the full-face veil for reasons related to their beliefs. It should nevertheless be taken into account that the sanctions provided for by the Law's drafters are among the lightest that could be envisaged, because they consist of a fine at the rate applying to second-class petty offences (currently 150 euros maximum), with the possibility for the court to impose, in addition to or instead of the fine, an obligation to follow a citizenship course.

153. Furthermore, admittedly, as the applicant pointed out, by prohibiting everyone from wearing clothing designed to conceal the face in public places, the respondent State has to a certain extent restricted the reach of pluralism, since the ban prevents certain women from expressing their personality and their beliefs by wearing the full-face veil in public. However, for their part, the Government indicated that it was a question of responding to a practice that the State deemed incompatible, in French society, with the ground rules of social communication and more broadly the requirements of "living together". From that perspective, the respondent State is seeking to protect a principle of interaction between individuals, which in its view is essential for the expression not only of pluralism, but also of tolerance and broadmindedness without which there is no democratic society. It can thus be said that the question whether or not it should be permitted to wear the full-face veil in public places constitutes a choice of society.

154. In such circumstances, the Court has a duty to exercise a degree of restraint in its review of Convention compliance, since such review will lead it to assess a balance that has been struck by means of a democratic process within the society in question. The Court has, moreover, already had occasion to observe that in matters of general policy, on which opinions within a democratic society may reasonably differ widely, the role of the domestic policy-maker should be given special weight.

155. In other words, France had a wide margin of appreciation in the present case.

156. This is particularly true as there is little common ground amongst the member States of the Council of Europe (see, *mutatis mutandis, X, Y and Z v. the United Kingdom*, 22 April 1997, §44, *Reports* 1997II) as to the question of the wearing of the full-face veil in public. The Court thus observes that, contrary to the submission of one of the third-party interveners, there is no European consensus against

a ban. Admittedly, from a strictly normative standpoint, France is very much in a minority position in Europe: except for Belgium, no other member State of the Council of Europe has, to date, opted for such a measure. It must be observed, however, that the question of the wearing of the full-face veil in public is or has been a subject of debate in a number of European States. In some it has been decided not to opt for a blanket ban. In others, such a ban is still being considered (see paragraph 40 above). It should be added that, in all likelihood, the question of the wearing of the full-face veil in public is simply not an issue at all in a certain number of member States, where this practice is uncommon. It can thus be said that in Europe there is no consensus as to whether or not there should be a blanket ban on the wearing of the full-face veil in public places.

157.  Consequently, having regard in particular to the breadth of the margin of appreciation afforded to the respondent State in the present case, the Court finds that the ban imposed by the Law of 11 October 2010 can be regarded as proportionate to the aim pursued, namely the preservation of the conditions of "living together" as an element of the "protection of the rights and freedoms of others".

158.  The impugned limitation can thus be regarded as "necessary in a democratic society". This conclusion holds true with respect both to Article 8 of the Convention and to Article 9.

159.  Accordingly, there has been no violation either of Article 8 or of Article 9 of the Convention.

### *Comments and Questions*

1.  Should it make a difference to the outcome in *S.A.S.* or a similar case whether the wearing of a head or face covering (or any other garment or religious symbol) is required by the religion or merely authorized? Should the courts inquire as to whether there is such a requirement? What if religious authorities disagree on that? Should it make a difference if the item worn could be used as a weapon (a Sikh kirpan or ritual knife, for instance) or comes from an endangered species (such as an eagle feather when the eagles was thus classified)?

2.  The European Court's decision in *S.A.S.* relies heavily on its margin of appreciation doctrine, with substantial deference to France's internal decision-making and democratic processes. Does the Court strike the right balance between respect for democratic process and protection of a fundamental right? Does the answer to that question depend at least in part on the extent to which France's democratic processes leading to the ban on face coverings are adequate in relation to the Muslim minority in the country?

3.  Article 18 of the International Covenant on Civil and Political Rights (ICCPR) has language similar to that of Article 9 of the European Convention allowing for limitations on the right to religion. However, in *Matter of Sonia Yaker*, the UN Human Rights Committee examined the same ban as in the *S.A.S.* case and reached the opposite conclusion. The Human Rights Committee considered the ban a form of intersectional and indirect discrimination against Muslim women who choose to wear a veil, and an arbitrary distinction between them and those who wear other face coverings. See *Matter of Sonia Yaker*, Communication No. 2747/2016, Hum. Rts. Cmte., Views of Dec. 7, 2018, UN Doc. CCPR/C/123/D/2747/2016,

paras. 8.3 and 8.15. Which approach is correct—that of the European Court of Human Rights in *S.A.S.* or that of the Human Rights Committee in *Matter of Sonia Yaker*?

4. The Human Rights Committee issued General Comment 22 on Article 18 of the ICCPR in 1993, in which it said that Article 18 "protects theistic, non-theistic and atheistic beliefs, as well as the right not to profess any religion or belief. The terms belief and religion are to be broadly construed." Human Rights Committee, *General Comment 22: Article 18 (Freedom of Thought, Conscience or Religion)*, UN Doc. CCPR/C/21/Rev.1/Add.4 (1993), para. 2. Is there any ritual practice or belief system that is not included in the right to freedom of religion? Should there be? Note that Wiccans successfully fought to have their symbol included on the gravestones of adherents in Arlington National Cemetery. For cases declaring Wiccan beliefs to be a religion, see, e.g., *Dettmer v. Landon*, 799 F.2d 929 (4th Cir. 1986), and *Roberts v. Ravenwood Church of Wicca*, 249 Ga. 348 (1982).

5. The European system has developed a rich jurisprudence during its more than 50 years of existence, and the *S.A.S.* case merely gives the reader a flavor of the European Court's approach to one set of issues in which individual rights must be balanced against the legitimate interests of the larger community. The following offers a very brief summary of some of the other issues with which the system has dealt over the years.

> Most violations have concerned the right to a fair trial. Cases under Article 6 have brought to light many delays in the hearing of cases in breach of the right to "trial within a reasonable time." Other common infringements have concerned the right of access to a court and the requirements of an independent and impartial tribunal and of equality of arms. The next most problematic guarantee for states has been that of freedom of the person. Many breaches of Article 5 have been found concerning various aspects of defendants' rights, such as the right to pre-trial release, the length of detention on remand, and the need for a remedy to challenge detention. Other cases have involved the preventive detention of terrorists and the detention of the mentally disordered, vagrants, children and deportees. In recent years, the right to property in Article 1, First Protocol has generated a large jurisprudence and many breaches. Claims relying upon the right to respect for family life, privacy, etc. in Article 8 have been almost equally successful. In this context, the Court has made great use of its "dynamic" approach to the interpretation of the Convention in the light of changed social values and the idea that there may be positive obligations upon states, requiring them, for example, to legislate so as to respect the rights of homosexuals, children born out of wedlock, and transsexuals. Cases under Article 10 have confirmed the fundamental importance attached to freedom of expression, particularly freedom of the press. Violations of Article 3 have been found, in such diverse areas as the ill-treatment of persons in detention, judicial corporal punishment, and extradition to face the death row phenomenon. At the other extreme, the guarantees of freedom from slavery and forced labour (Article 4), the right to free elections (Article 3, First Protocol)

and all of the rights in the Fourth and Seventh Protocols have so far led to few adverse rulings.

D.J. Harris, M. O'Boyle, and C. Warbrick, *Law of the European Convention on Human Rights* 32-33 (2d ed., 2009).

### *Note: The European Union and Human Rights*

Separate from the Council of Europe, six of the Council's original members moved to reduce economic barriers between them through establishing the European Communities. The Communities gradually enlarged their membership and increased the power of their institutions, eventually forming the combined European Community (EC) and eventually becoming the European Union (EU). The absence of human rights protections in this organization, which was founded largely for purposes of trade, economic development and political cooperation, posed increasing problems as the role and powers of the European Union expanded and its legislative and administrative activities had an increasing impact on the rights of individuals and companies.

To fill the human rights gap and ensure the continued supremacy of EC law, the EC/EU's European Court of Justice (ECJ) declared in a series of decisions that respect for fundamental rights forms an integral part of the general principles of law that the Court is required to apply in interpreting EC law. In *Stauder v. City of Ulm*, Case 29/69, [1969] E.C.R. 419, the ECJ declared that a doctrine of fundamental human rights was enshrined as a general principle of Community law and was protected by the Court. In *Internationale Handelsgesellschaft v. EVGF*, Case 11/70 [1970] E.C.R. 1125, the ECJ announced a principle of autonomous human rights law, i.e., that the validity of EC law would be judged by the EC's own criteria for fundamental human rights. In the *Nold* case, Case 4/73 [1974] E.C.R. 491, 507, the Court of Justice held that "fundamental rights form an integral part of the general principles of law, the observance of which [the Court] ensures," relying on the constitutional traditions common to the member states and international treaties for the protection of human rights, especially the European Convention on Human Rights.

The Court's approach to the European Convention on Human Rights was confirmed by the 1977 Joint Declaration on Fundamental Rights and by the 1987 Single European Act, both of which mention the European Convention as one of the sources of the fundamental rights recognized by the European Community. Formal EU treaty status was given to the European Convention in Article F(2) of the Common Provisions of the Treaty on European Political Union, signed at the Maastricht Summit of December 1991. Nearly two decades later, the EU member states proclaimed the Charter of Fundamental Rights of the European Union, in 2000, and later incorporated the Charter into the Treaty of Lisbon. The Treaty of Lisbon (which amended the Maastricht Treaty on the European Union and the original Treaty of Rome on the European Community, without replacing either) entered into force in 2009 and is binding on all EU members.

The EU Commission and Council must respect fundamental rights as guaranteed by the European Convention on Human Rights and the constitutional traditions common to the member states. In cases raising human rights issues, the European Court of Justice utilizes the Charter of Fundamental Rights and, in applying it, is mandated to interpret the Charter with regard to case law developed by the European Court of Human Rights, although the broader wording of some provisions of the Charter may give rise to jurisprudence in the ECJ that diverges from that of the European Court of Human Rights. See generally Elizabeth F. Defeis, *Human Rights and the European Union: Who Decides? Possible Conflicts Between the European Court of Justice and the European Court of Human Rights*, 19 Dick. J. Int'l L. 301 (2001); Sionaidh Douglas-Scott, *The European Union and Human Rights after the Treaty of Lisbon*, 11 Hum. Rts. L. R. 645 (2011). For earlier EU developments, see Jean-Marie Henckaerts, *The Protection of Human Rights in the European Union: Overview and Bibliography*, 22 Int'l J. Legal Info. 228 (1994).

One proposed remedy for the potential conflicts of norms and jurisprudence is for the European Union to accede to the European Convention on Human Rights, which is mandated by the Treaty of Lisbon and, since 2010, has been authorized by the European Convention Protocol 14. The Parliamentary Assembly of the Council of Europe has supported accession to the Convention, but the European Court of Justice found legal barriers to accession in its Opinion 2/13 of Dec. 18, 2014, https://eur-lex.europa.eu/legal-content/EN/TXT/?uri=CELEX%3A62013CV0002. There are an ongoing discussions about the potential accession of the European Union to the European Convention on Human Rights. See *EU Accession to the European Convention on Human Rights*, Council of Europe, https://www.coe.int/en/web/human-rights-intergovernmental-cooperation/accession-of-the-european-union-to-the-european-convention-on-human-rights (last visited June 12, 2022).

The European Court of Justice may hear claims directly brought against member states or an institution, body, office, or agency of the European Union that assert that the respondent has not fulfilled its obligations under EU law. Under the provisions of the Treaty on the Functioning of the European Union (TFEU), these actions may be brought against a state either by the Commission or by another member state after it has brought the matter before the Commission. Actions against an EU institution may be brought by private parties who seek the annulment of a measure allegedly contrary to EU law or, in cases of infringement of EU law, where an institution, body, office, or agency has failed to act. Actions also may be brought by the member states, the EU institutions themselves, or any natural or legal person if the actions relate to a measure (in particular a regulation, directive, or decision) adopted by an EU institution, body, office, or agency and addressed to them. The European Court of Justice may declare an act void or that there has been a failure to act, in which case the institution at fault is required to take the necessary measures to comply with the Court's judgment.

Another common proceeding concerns questions of EU law raised before a national court or tribunal. National courts are normally responsible for applying EU law when a case so requires. However, when an issue relating to the interpretation of EU law is raised before a national court or tribunal, the court or tribunal may seek a preliminary ruling from the European Court of Justice. If it is a court of last instance, it is compulsory to refer the matter to the European Court.

The national court submits the question(s) about the interpretation or validity of a provision of EU law in accordance with the national procedural rules.


## III.   THE AFRICAN HUMAN RIGHTS SYSTEM

Regional systems, much like the UN system, are a product of the global concern with human rights that emerged at the end of the Second World War. Historical and political factors also encouraged each region to focus on human rights issues. In Europe, the horrors of World War II were only too clear and immediate, and the European system for protecting human rights was born in the early years after the war ended. In the Americas, as discussed in Chapter 8, the 1948 American Declaration on the Rights and Duties of Man actually predated by several months the UN's proclamation of the Universal Declaration of Human Rights. The Inter-American Commission on Human Rights, created in 1959, began actively to address human rights violations in the mid-1960s.

In Africa, the struggles for self-determination, decolonization, and national unity — as well as opposition to systematic racial discrimination in southern Africa — were the first concerns. Creation of formal African institutions to consider human rights did not occur until relatively late, after the continent's former colonies became independent. The African system has been in operation since 1986, and one should recall the somewhat faltering steps of even the European system in its early days. Review the African Charter on Human and Peoples' Rights in the Documentary Supplement before considering the following analysis.


Christof Heyns

### The African Regional Human Rights System: The African Charter

108 Penn St. L. Rev. 679, passim (2004) (footnotes omitted)


. . . [T]he struggle for human rights on the African continent is far from over or complete. The continent is plagued by widespread violations of human rights, often on a massive scale. The process to establish effective institutional structures that will help to consolidate and to protect the hard-earned gains of the freedom struggles of the past has become a struggle in its own right. No doubt, the most important task in this regard is to establish legal and political systems on the national level that protect human rights. But regional attempts to change the human rights practices of the continent, and to create safety nets for those cases not effectively dealt with on the national level, are assuming increased importance. . . .

The central document of the African regional system, the African Charter on Human and Peoples' Rights ("African Charter"), was opened for signature in 1981 and entered into force in 1986. It has been ratified by all fifty-three member states of the OAU/AU. . . .

In addition to the African Charter, the African regional human rights system is comprised of the OAU Convention Governing the Specific Aspects of Refugee Problems in Africa ("African Refugee Convention") of 1969, which entered into force in 1974 (44 ratifications); and the African Charter on the Rights and Welfare of the Child ("African Children's Charter") of 1990, which came into force in 1999 (32 ratifications).* A special monitoring body for the African Children's Charter has been created. The African Committee on the Rights and Welfare of the Child had its first meeting in 2002 in Addis Ababa, Ethiopia.

The relatively unknown Cultural Charter for Africa of 1976 came into force in 1990 (33 state parties). There are also two African treaties dealing with the environment, although not from a human rights perspective. . . .

. . . Several reasons have been advanced for why only a Commission, and not a Court, was provided for in the African Charter in 1981 as the body responsible for monitoring compliance of state parties with the Charter. On the one hand there is the more idealistic explanation that the traditional way of solving disputes in Africa is through mediation and conciliation, not through the adversarial, "win or lose" mechanism of a court. On the other hand there is the view that the member states of the OAU were protective of their newly found sovereignty, and did not wish to limit it by means of a supra-national court. . . .

The civil and political rights recognised in the African Charter are in many ways similar to those recognised in other international instruments, and these rights have in practical terms received most of the attention of the African Commission. . . .

The way in which the African Charter deals with restrictions on all rights, including civil and political rights, presents a significant obstacle. The African Charter does not contain a general limitation clause (although, as is noted below, article 27(2) is starting to play this role). This means that there are no general guidelines on how Charter rights should be limited — no clear "limits on the limitations," so to speak. A well-defined system of limitations is important. A society in which rights cannot be limited will be ungovernable, but it is essential that appropriate human rights norms be set for the limitations.

A number of the articles of the Charter setting out specific civil and political rights do contain limiting provisions applicable to those particular rights. Some of these internal limitations clearly spell out the procedural and substantive norms with which limitations should comply, while others only describe the substantive requirements that limitations must meet.

A last category of these limitation clauses merely poses the apparently procedural requirement that limitations should be done "within the law." An example of this category of internal limitations is article 9(2), which provides as follows: "Every individual shall have the right to express and disseminate his opinions within the law." This kind of limitation is generally known as "claw-back clauses." Claw-back clauses seem to recognise the right in question only to the extent that such a right is not infringed upon by national law.

If that is the correct interpretation, the claw-back clauses would obviously undermine the whole idea of international supervision of domestic law and practices and render the Charter meaningless in respect to the rights involved. Domestic

---

* [Additionally, a Protocol to the African Charter on Human and Peoples' Rights on the Rights of Women in Africa was adopted July 11, 2003. It entered into force on November 25, 2005, and as of June 1st, 2022, has been ratified by 42 states. — Eds.]

law will, in those cases, have to be measured according to domestic standards — a senseless exercise. What is given with the one hand is seemingly taken away with the other.

It should be noted . . . that the Charter has a very expansive approach in respect to interpretation. In terms of articles 60 and 61, the Commission has to draw inspiration from international human rights law in interpreting the provisions of the Charter. The Commission has used these provisions very liberally in a number of instances to bring the Charter in line with international practices, and the claw-back clauses are no exception.

In the context of the claw-back clauses, the African Commission has held that provisions in articles that allow rights to be limited "in accordance with law," should be understood to require such limitations to be done in terms of domestic legal provisions, which comply with international human rights standards.

Through this innovative interpretation, the Commission has gone a long way towards curing one of the most troublesome inherent deficiencies in the Charter. However, it remains unfortunate that the Charter, to those who have not had the benefit of exposure to the approach of the Commission, will continue to appear to condone infringements of human rights norms as long as it is done through domestic law. . . .

The socio-economic rights in the Charter have received scant attention from the Commission, but in a prominent case the Commission dealt with the issue and in effect held that the internationally recognised socio-economic rights that are not explicitly recognised in the Charter should be regarded as implicitly included. . . . [see *Social and Economic Rights Action Center and the Center for Economic and Social Rights v. Nigeria,* in Chapter 4, pages 195-204.]

There are other, more exotic features of the Charter that have attracted their fair share of academic and political commentary but have figured less in the pronouncements of the Commission.

The Charter, for example, recognises "peoples' rights." All "peoples," according to the Charter, have a right to be equal; to existence and self-determination; and to freely dispose of their wealth and natural resources. Clearly a major part of the motivation for the recognition of "peoples' rights" lies in the fact that entire "peoples" have been colonised and otherwise exploited in the history of Africa and have had to engage in protracted struggles to realise their human rights.

This concept has been referred to in some of the cases before the Commission, including the following two cases.

In a case concerning Katangese secessionists in the former Zaire, a complaint was brought on the basis that the Katangese people had a right, as a people, to self-determination in the form of independence. The Commission ruled against them on the basis that there was no evidence that a Charter provision had been violated because widespread human rights violations or a lack of political participation by the Katangese people had not been proven. This seems to suggest that if these conditions were met, secession by such a "people" could be a permissible option.

In a case concerning the 1994 coup d'etat against the democratically elected government of The Gambia, the Commission held that this violated the right to self-determination of the people of The Gambia as a whole.

The Charter recognises duties in addition to rights. For example, individuals have duties towards their families and society, and state parties have the duty to promote the Charter.

Perhaps the most significant provision under the heading "Duties" is article 27(2), which reads as follows: "The rights and freedoms of each individual shall be exercised with due regard to the rights of others, collective security, morality and common interest." This provision has now in effect been given the status of a general limitation clause by the African Commission. According to the Commission: "The only legitimate reasons for limitations to the rights and freedoms of the African Charter are found in article 27(2). . . ."

The Commission's use of article 27(2) as a general limitation clause seems to confirm the view that the concept of "duties" should not be understood as a sinister way of saying rights should first be earned, or that meeting certain duties is a precondition for enjoying human rights. Rather, it implies that the exercise of human rights, which are "natural" or valid in themselves, may be limited by the duties of individuals. Rights precede duties, and the recognition of duties is merely another way of signifying the kind of limitations that may be placed on rights. . . .

## 1. THE COMPLAINTS PROCEDURE

Both states and individuals may bring complaints to the African Commission alleging violations of the African Charter by state parties.

The procedure by which one state brings a complaint about an alleged human rights violation by another state has only been used once in a case. . . . [Communication 227/99—D. R. *Congo v. Burundi, Rwanda, and Uganda*, decided May 2003].

The so-called individual communication or complaints procedure is not clearly provided for in the African Charter. One reading of the Charter is that communications could be considered only where "serious or massive violations" are at stake, which then triggers the rather futile article 58 procedure described below. However, the African Commission has accepted from the start that it has the power to deal with complaints about any human rights violations under the Charter, provided the admissibility criteria are met.

The Charter is silent on the question of who can bring such complaints, but the Commission's practice is that complaints from individuals as well as non-governmental organizations are accepted. The individual complaints procedure is used much more frequently than the inter-state mechanism, although not as frequently as one might have expected on a continent with the kind of human rights problems like Africa's. The potential of this mechanism has not nearly been exhausted. . . .[Note from the Authors: In its Activity Report between December 4, 2020 to December 5, 2021, the African Commission had 216 Communications pending resolution. See African Commission on Human and Peoples' Rights, *50th and 51*st *Combined Activity Reports*, file:///C:/Users/Rosa/Downloads/50-51%20 Combined%20Activity%20Report_ENGl%20(1).pdf.]

Two of the more controversial articles of the Charter apply to the way in which the Commission is supposed to deal with individual communications. Article 58 provides that "special cases which reveal the existence of serious or massive violations of human and peoples' rights" must be referred by the Commission to the

Assembly, which "may then request the Commission to undertake an in-depth study of these cases." When the Commission has followed this route, the Assembly has failed to respond, but the Commission has nevertheless made findings that such massive violations have occurred. Today, the Commission does not seem to refer cases anymore to the Assembly in terms of article 58. . . .

### 2. CONSIDERATION OF STATE REPORTS . . .

Reporting under the Charter, as in other systems, is aimed at facilitating both introspection and inspection. "Introspection" refers to the process when the state, in writing its report, measures itself against the norms of the Charter. "Inspection" refers to the process when the Commission measures the performance of the state in question against the Charter. The objective is to facilitate a "constructive dialogue" between the Commission and the states.

Reporting has been very tardy, with [six] state parties not submitting any reports [and sixteen states having more than three reports overdue, as of the beginning of 2016. Fourteen states are up to date] . . .

### 3. SPECIAL RAPPORTEURS

The Commission has appointed a number of special rapporteurs, with varying degrees of success. . . . [By the beginning of 2016, special rapporteurs had been appointed concerned with persons living with HIV/AIDS; prisons and other places of detention; refugees, internally displaced persons, and migrants; the rights of women; human rights defenders; and freedom of expression and access to information. In addition, the Commission has working groups on indigenous peoples and communities; economic, social, and cultural rights; the death penalty; older persons and persons with disabilities; and on extractive industries and the environment.]

NGOs have a special relationship with the Commission. Large numbers have registered for affiliate status. NGOs are often instrumental in bringing cases to the Commission; they sometimes submit shadow reports, propose agenda items at the outset of Commission sessions, and provide logistical and other support to the Commission, for example by placing interns at the Commission and providing support to the special rapporteurs and missions of the Commission. NGOs often organise special NGO workshops just prior to Commission sessions and participate actively in the public sessions of the Commission. NGOs also collaborate with the Commission in developing normative resolutions and new protocols to the African Charter. [More than 400 NGOs had been formally granted observer status by the Commission as of May 2010. However, the Commission refused to grant such status to a South African NGO, the Coalition for African Lesbians, on the grounds that "the activities of the said Organisation do not promote and protect any of the rights enshrined in the African Charter." Report of the African Commission on Human and Peoples' Rights to the Executive Council of the African Union, EX.CL/600 (XVII) (July 2010), para. 33.]

The Charter does not contain a provision in terms of which the Commission has the power to take provisional or interim measures requesting state parties to abstain from causing irreparable harm. However, the Rules of Procedure of the

Commission grant the Commission the power to do so. The Commission has used these provisional or interim measures in a number of cases. . . .

### V. CONCLUSION

Much remains to be done to make the African human rights system effective. I would venture to say there are a number of determinants for the effectiveness of any regional human rights systems, which include the following.

An adequate level of compliance with human rights norms on the domestic level must occur in a significant number of the state parties. Working national human rights systems are the building blocks of an effective regional system. If the level of respect for human rights norms on the domestic level is low, and domestic courts are not effective in implementing these norms, there can be little hope for supra-national enforcement.

The necessary political will must be present in the regional organisation of which the system forms part, to ensure that the system really works and is not an empty facade. The regional organisation is the primary body through which peer pressure must be channelled. The all-important selection process of Commissioners and Judges must be taken seriously by the regional body. The budgets allocated to human rights organisations also often have an important influence on how effective they are. The system must be properly serviced and able administrators appointed.

Publicity for the work of the monitoring body or bodies of the system is essential. The decisions and resolutions of these bodies must be available, and disseminated on the national and regional level, to have an impact. Publicity is needed so that those who want to comply voluntarily know what is expected of them, but it is also necessary to ensure that shame or peer pressure can be mobilised against recalcitrant states. Peer pressure can change behaviour by inducing shame, or if that does not work, by mobilising stronger forms of sanctions against states. All of this is possible only when there is sufficient publicity. The responsibility to see to it that there is publicity lies on the regional system, the states, and civil society alike.

Trade and other links must exist between the state parties before a regional human rights system can be enforced effectively. Without trade, diplomatic communication, travel, and other links between state parties, the conditions to impose sanctions to affect the behaviour of states do not exist.

The independence, creativity, and wisdom of those who run the system are absolutely crucial. This includes the Commissioners (and judges) and the staff of the Commission (and Court), as well as the officials of the regional organisation.

Resources are important, but the proper management of whatever resources are available is more important. . . .

The continuous creation of new mechanisms for the protection of human rights in Africa is not necessarily helping the situation. Instead of focusing on getting the mechanism created by the African Charter, the African Commission, to function properly, new mechanisms are created, such as the African Human Rights Court. . . . In themselves all of these mechanisms could be a viable starting point, but the current proliferation of mechanisms means that there is a lack of focus of resources and effort, with the result that none of them might be in a position to make any difference.

The question should be asked which mechanism is mostly likely to make a significant impact on human rights in Africa, and that particular mechanism should be supported and developed until it is functioning properly before other mechanisms are created.

If all the effort that goes into developing new mechanisms goes into the Charter and the Commission, and thereafter the African Human Rights Court, we would be able to point to a specific mechanism that makes a real difference towards consolidating the gains of the struggles of the people of Africa.

———————

In addition to the activities mentioned in the previous extract, the African Commission has a procedure for urgent action, by which it sends Letters of Urgent Appeal in cases where individuals are threatened with immediate and irreparable harm, as well as a public process of sending Letters of Appreciation to states in response to their specific actions promoting or protecting human rights. Each commissioner also undertakes human rights promotion and advocacy missions between Commission sessions.

The case below exemplifies the work of the African Commission in the area of individual complaints. This case in particular illustrates the Commission's approach to groups with distinct cultural or ethnic identities, and to economic, social, and cultural rights.

## Centre for Minority Rights Development (Kenya) and Minority Rights Group (on behalf of Endorois Welfare Council) v. Kenya

Case 276/03, African Comm'n H.P.R, 46th Ordinary Session of the African Commission on Human and Peoples' Rights, 11–25 Nov, 11-15, 2009 (footnotes omitted)

. . .

3. The Complainants state that the Endorois are a community of approximately 60,000 people who, for centuries, have lived in the Lake Bogoria area. They claim that prior to the dispossession of Endorois land through the creation of the Lake Hannington Game Reserve in 1973, and a subsequent re-gazetting of the Lake Bogoria Game Reserve in 1978 by the Government of Kenya, the Endorois had established, and, for centuries, practised a sustainable way of life which was inextricably linked to their ancestral land. The Complainants allege that since 1978 the Endorois have been denied access to their land. . . .

6. The Complainants state that the area surrounding Lake Bogoria is fertile land, providing green pasture and medicinal salt licks, which help raise healthy cattle. The Complainants state that Lake Bogoria is central to the Endorois religious and traditional practices. They state that the community's historical prayer sites, places for circumcision rituals, and other cultural ceremonies are around Lake Bogoria. These sites were used on a weekly or monthly basis for smaller local ceremonies, and on an annual basis for cultural festivities involving Endorois from the whole region. The Complainants claim that the Endorois believe that the spirits of all Endorois, no matter where they are buried, live on in the lake, with

annual festivals taking place at the Lake. The Complainants further claim that the Endorois believe that the Monchongoi forest is considered the birthplace of the Endorois and the settlement of the first Endorois community. . . .

13. The Complainants allege that since the Kenyan High Court case in 2000 [which unsuccessfully sought recovery of their lands], the Endorois community has become aware that parts of their ancestral land have been demarcated and sold by the Respondent State to third parties.

14. The Complainants further allege that concessions for ruby mining on Endorois traditional land were granted in 2002 to a private company. This included the construction of a road in order to facilitate access for heavy mining machinery. The Complainants claim that these activities incur a high risk of polluting the waterways used by the Endorois community, both for their own personal consumption and for use by their livestock. Both mining operations and the demarcation and sale of land have continued despite the request by the African Commission to the President of Kenya to suspend these activities pending the outcome of the present communication.

16. The Complainants claim that land for the Endorois is held in very high esteem, since tribal land, in addition to securing subsistence and livelihood, is seen as sacred, being inextricably linked to the cultural integrity of the community and its traditional way of life. Land, they claim, belongs to the community and not the individual and is essential to the preservation and survival as a traditional people. The Complainants claim that the Endorois health, livelihood, religion and culture are all intimately connected with their traditional land, as grazing lands, sacred religious sites and plants used for traditional medicine are all situated around the shores of Lake Bogoria.

17. The Complainants claim that at present the Endorois live in a number of locations on the periphery of the reserve – that the Endorois are not only being forced from fertile lands to semi-arid areas, but have also been divided as a community and displaced from their traditional and ancestral lands. The Complainants claim that for the Endorois, access to the Lake Bogoria region, is a right for the community and the Government of Kenya continues to deny the community effective participation in decisions affecting their own land, in violation of their right to development. . . .

ARTICLES ALLEGED TO HAVE BEEN VIOLATED

22. The Complainants seek a declaration that the Republic of Kenya is in violation of Articles 8, 14, 17, 21 and 22 of the African Charter. The Complainants are also seeking:

- Restitution of their land, with legal title and clear demarcation.
- Compensation to the community for all the loss they have suffered through the loss of their property, development and natural resources, but also freedom to practice their religion and culture.

LAW

[After the government of Kenya failed to respond to the complaint during the admissibility phase, the Commission considered admissibility "based on the information at its disposal," and declared the case admissible.]

MERITS

. . .

147. . . . [T]he African Commission notes that the concepts of "peoples" and "indigenous peoples /communities" are contested terms. As far as "indigenous peoples" are concerned, there is no universal and unambiguous definition of the concept, since no single accepted definition captures the diversity of indigenous cultures, histories and current circumstances. The relationships between indigenous peoples and dominant or mainstream groups in society vary from country to country. The same is true of the concept of "peoples." The African Commission is thus aware of the political connotation that these concepts carry. Those controversies led the drafters of the African Charter to deliberately refrain from proposing any definitions for the notion of "people(s)." In its Report of the Working Group of Experts on Indigenous Populations/Communities, the African Commission describes its dilemma of defining the concept of "peoples" in the following terms:

> Despite its mandate to interpret all provisions of the African Charter as per Article 45.3, the African Commission initially shied away from interpreting the concept of 'peoples'. The African Charter itself does not define the concept. Initially the African Commission did not feel at ease in developing rights where there was little concrete international jurisprudence. The ICCPR and the ICESR do not define 'peoples.' It is evident that the drafters of the African Charter intended to distinguish between the traditional individual rights where the sections preceding Article 17 make reference to "every individual." Article 18 serves as a break by referring to the family. Articles 19 to 24 make specific reference to "all peoples."

148. The African Commission, nevertheless, notes that while the terms 'peoples' and 'indigenous community' arouse emotive debates, some marginalised and vulnerable groups in Africa are suffering from particular problems. It is aware that many of these groups have not been accommodated by dominating development paradigms and in many cases they are being victimised by mainstream development policies and thinking and their basic human rights violated. The African Commission is also aware that indigenous peoples have, due to past and ongoing processes, become marginalized in their own country and they need recognition and protection of their basic human rights and fundamental freedoms.

. . .

150. The African Commission also notes that the African Charter, in Articles 20 through 4, provides for peoples to retain rights as peoples, that is, as collectives. The African Commission through its Working Group of Experts on Indigenous Populations/Communities has set out four criteria for identifying indigenous peoples. These are: the occupation and use of a specific territory; the voluntary perpetuation of cultural distinctiveness; self-identification as a distinct collectivity, as well as recognition by other groups; an experience of subjugation, marginalisation, dispossession, exclusion or discrimination. The Working Group also demarcated some of the shared characteristics of African indigenous groups: . . . first and foremost (but not exclusively) different groups of hunter-gatherers or former hunter gatherers and certain groups of pastoralists. . . A key characteristic for most of them

is that the survival of their particular way of life depends on access and rights to their traditional land and the natural resources thereon.

151. The African Commission is thus aware that there is an emerging consensus on some objective features that a collective of individuals should manifest to be considered as "peoples", viz: a common historical tradition, racial or ethnic identity, cultural homogeneity, linguistic unity, religious and ideological affinities, territorial connection, and a common economic life or other bonds, identities and affinities they collectively enjoy—especially rights enumerated under Articles 19 to 24 of the African Charter—or suffer collectively from the deprivation of such rights. What is clear is that all attempts to define the concept of indigenous peoples recognise the linkages between peoples, their land, and culture and that such a group expresses its desire to be identified as a people or have the consciousness that they are a people.

152. As far as the present matter is concerned, the African Commission is also enjoined under Article 61 of the African Charter to be inspired by other subsidiary sources of international law or general principles in determining rights under the African Charter. It takes note of the working definition proposed by the UN Working Group on Indigenous Populations:

> . . . that indigenous peoples are . . . those which, having a historical continuity with pre-invasion and precolonial societies that developed on their territories, consider themselves distinct from other sectors of the societies now prevailing in those territories, or parts of them. They form at present non-dominant sectors of society and are determined to preserve, develop and transmit to future generations their ancestral territories, and their ethnic identity, as the basis of their continued existence as peoples, in accordance with their own cultural patterns, social institutions and legal systems.

153. But this working definition should be read in conjunction with the 2003 Report of the African Commission's Working Group of Experts on Indigenous Populations/Communities, which is the basis of its 'definition' of indigenous populations. Similarly it notes that the International Labour Organisation has proffered a definition of indigenous peoples in Convention No. 169 concerning Indigenous and Tribal Peoples in Independent Countries:

> Peoples in independent countries who are regarded as indigenous on account of their descent from the populations which inhabited the country, or a geographical region to which the country belongs, at the time of conquest or colonization or the establishment of present state boundaries and who, irrespective of their legal status, retain some or all of their own social, economic, cultural and political institutions.

154. The African Commission is also aware that though some indigenous populations might be first inhabitants, validation of rights is not automatically afforded to such pre-invasion and pre-colonial claims. In terms of ILO Convention 169, even though many African countries have not signed and ratified the said Convention, and like the UN Working Groups' conceptualization of the term, the African Commission notes that there is a common thread that runs through

all the various criteria that attempts to describe indigenous peoples—that indigenous peoples have an unambiguous relationship to a distinct territory and that all attempts to define the concept recognise the linkages between people, their land, and culture. In that regard, the African Commission notes the observation of the UN Special Rapporteur, where he states that in Kenya indigenous populations/communities include pastoralist communities such as the Endorois Borana, Gabra, Maasai, Pokot, Samburu, Turkana, and Somali, and hunter-gatherer communities whose livelihoods remain connected to the forest, such as the Awer (Boni), Ogiek, Sengwer, or Yaaku. The UN Special Rapporteur further observed that the Endorois community have lived for centuries in their traditional territory around Lake Bogoria, which was declared a wildlife sanctuary in 1973.

155. In the present communication the African Commission wishes to emphasise that the Charter recognises the rights of peoples. The Complainants argue that the Endorois are a people, a status that entitles them to benefit from provisions of the African Charter that protect collective rights. The Respondent State disagrees. The African Commission notes that the Constitution of Kenya, though incorporating the principle of non-discrimination and guaranteeing civil and political rights, does not recognise economic, social and cultural rights as such, as well as group rights. It further notes that the rights of indigenous pastoralist and hunter-gatherer communities are not recognised as such in Kenya's constitutional and legal framework, and no policies or governmental institutions deal directly with indigenous issues. . . .

156. After studying all the submissions of the Complainants and the Respondent State, the African Commission is of the view that Endorois culture, religion, and traditional way of life are intimately intertwined with their ancestral lands—Lake Bogoria and the surrounding area. It agrees that Lake Bogoria and the Monchongoi Forest are central to the Endorois' way of life and without access to their ancestral land, the Endorois are unable to fully exercise their cultural and religious rights, and feel disconnected from their land and ancestors.

157. In addition to a sacred relationship to their land, self-identification is another important criterion for determining indigenous peoples. The UN Special Rapporteur on the Rights and Fundamental Freedoms of Indigenous People also supports self-identification as a key criterion for determining who is indeed indigenous. The African Commission is aware that today many indigenous peoples are still excluded from society and often even deprived of their rights as equal citizens of a state. Nevertheless, many of these communities are determined to preserve, develop and transmit to future generations their ancestral territories and their ethnic identity. It accepts the arguments that the continued existence of indigenous communities as "peoples" is closely connected to the possibility of them influencing their own fate and to living in accordance with their own cultural patterns, social institutions and religious systems. The African Commission further notes that the Report of the African Commission's Working Group of Experts on Indigenous Populations/Communities (WGIP) emphasises that peoples' self-identification is an important ingredient to the concept of peoples' rights as laid out in the Charter. It agrees that the alleged violations of the African Charter by the Respondent State are those that go to the heart of indigenous rights—the right to preserve one's identity through identification with ancestral lands, cultural patterns, social

institutions and religious systems. The African Commission, therefore, accepts that self-identification for Endorois as indigenous individuals and acceptance as such by the group is an essential component of their sense of identity.

158. Furthermore, in drawing inspiration from international law on human and peoples' rights, the African Commission notes that the IACtHR has dealt with cases of self-identification where Afrodescendent communities were living in a collective manner, and had, for over 2-3 centuries, developed an ancestral link to their land. Moreover, the way of life of these communities depended heavily on the traditional use of their land, as did their cultural and spiritual survival due to the existence of ancestral graves on these lands.

159. The African Commission notes that while it has already accepted the existence of indigenous peoples in Africa through its WGIP reports, and through the adoption of its Advisory Opinion on the UN Declaration on the Rights of Indigenous Peoples, it notes the fact that the Inter-American Court has not hesitated in granting the collective rights protection to groups beyond the "narrow/aboriginal/preColombian" understanding of indigenous peoples traditionally adopted in the Americas. In that regard, the African Commission notes two relevant decisions from the IACtHR: *Moiwana v Suriname* and *Saramaka v Suriname*. The Saramaka case is of particular relevance to the Endorois case, given the views expressed by the Respondent State during the oral hearings on the Merits.

. . .

161. In the instant case, the African Commission, from all the evidence submitted to it, is satisfied that the Endorois can be defined as a distinct tribal group whose members enjoy and exercise certain rights, such as the right to property, in a distinctly collective manner from the Tugen sub-tribe or indeed the larger Kalenjin tribe.

. . .

### ALLEGED VIOLATION OF ARTICLE 8

[The African Commission first expressed its view that the Endorois' spiritual beliefs and ceremonial practices constitute a religion under the African Charter, then held that the respondent state by its actions and inactions violated the Endorois' right to religious freedom. It agreed that "in some situations it may be necessary to place some form of limited restrictions on a right protected by the African Charter. But such a restriction must be established by law and must not be applied in a manner that would completely vitiate the right." Denying the Endorois access to Lake Borgoria constituted a restriction on their freedom to practice their religion "not necessitated by any significant public security interest or other justification."]

### ALLEGED VIOLATION OF ARTICLE 14

174. The Complainants argue that the Endorois community have a right to property with regard to their ancestral land, the possessions attached to it, and their cattle. The Respondent State denies the allegation. . . .

178. In its oral and written testimonies, the Respondent State argues that the gazettement of a game reserve under the wildlife laws of Kenya is with the objective

of ensuring that wildlife is managed and conserved to yield to the nation in general and to individual areas in particular optimum returns in terms of cultural, aesthetic and scientific gains as well as economic gains as are incidental to proper wildlife management and conservation. The Respondent State also argues that national reserves unlike national parks, where the act expressly excludes human interference save for instances where one has got authorisation, are subject to agreements as to restrictions or conditions relating to the provisions of the area covered by the reserve. It also states that communities living around the national reserves have in some instances been allowed to drive their cattle to the reserve for the purposes of grazing, so long as they do not cause harm to the environment and the natural habitats of the wild animals. It states that with the establishment of a national reserve particularly from Trust Land, it is apparent that the community's right of access is not extinguished, but rather its propriety right as recognised under the law (that is, the right to deal with property as it pleases) is the one which is minimised and hence the requirement to compensate the affected people. . . .

181. The Respondent State argues further that the above Rules ensure that the livelihoods of the community are not compromised by the gazettement, in the sense that the people could obtain food and building materials, as well as run some economic activities such as beekeeping and grazing livestock in the Forest. They also say they were at liberty to practice their religion and culture. Further, it states that the due process of law regarding compensation was followed at the time of the said gazettement. . . .

185. Two issues that should be disposed of before going into the more substantive questions of whether the Respondent State has violated Article 14 are a determination of what is a 'property right' (within the context of indigenous populations) that accords with African and international law, and whether special measures are needed to protect such rights, if they exist and whether Endorois' land has been encroached upon by the Respondent State. The Complainants argue that "property rights" have an autonomous meaning under international human rights law, which supersedes national legal definitions. They state that both the European Court of Human Rights (ECHR) and IACtHR have examined the specific facts of individual situations to determine what should be classified as 'property rights', particularly for displaced persons, instead of limiting themselves to formal requirements in national law.

186. To determine that question, the African Commission will look, first, at its own jurisprudence and then at international case law. [The Commission cites to its decisions in *Malawi African Association and Others v. Mauritania* and the Ogoni case, *supra.*] The African Commission also notes that the ECHR have recognised that 'property rights' could also include the economic resources and rights over the common land of the applicants.

187. . . . The African Commission is of the view that the first step in the protection of traditional African communities is the acknowledgement that the rights, interests and benefits of such communities in their traditional lands constitute " 'property" ' under the Charter and that special measures may have to be taken to secure such " 'property rights" '.

188. The case of *Dogan and others v Turkey* is instructive in the instant communication. Although the applicants were unable to demonstrate registered title

of lands from which they had been forcibly evicted by the Turkish authorities, the European Court of Human Rights observed that:

> [T]he notion "'possessions"' in Article 1 has an autonomous meaning which is certainly not limited to ownership of physical goods: certain other rights and interests constituting assets can also be regarded as "'property rights"', and thus as 'possessions' for the purposes of this provision. . . .

190. The African Commission also notes the observation of the IActHR in the seminal case of The *Mayagna (Sumo) Awas Tingni v Nicaragua*, that the Inter-American Convention protected property rights in a sense which include the rights of members of the indigenous communities within the framework of communal property and argued that possession of the land should suffice for indigenous communities lacking real title to obtain official recognition of that property.

191. In the opinion of the African Commission, the Respondent State has an obligation under Article 14 of the African Charter not only to respect the 'right to property', but also to protect that right. In 'the Mauritania Cases', the African Commission concluded that the confiscation and pillaging of the property of black Mauritanians and the expropriation or destruction of their land and houses before forcing them to go abroad constituted a violation of the right to property as guaranteed in Article 14. . . .

199. The African Commission is of the view that even though the Constitution of Kenya provides that Trust Land may be alienated and that the Trust Land Act provides comprehensive procedure for the assessment of compensation, the Endorois property rights have been encroached upon, in particular by the expropriation and the effective denial of ownership of their land. It agrees with the Complainants that the Endorois were never given the full title to the land they had in practice before the British colonial administration. Their land was instead made subject to a trust, which gave them beneficial title, but denied them actual title. The African Commission further agrees that though for a decade they were able to exercise their traditional rights without restriction, the trust land system has proved inadequate to protect their rights.

200. The African Commission also notes the views expressed by the Committee on Economic, Social and Cultural Rights which has provided a legal test for forced removal from lands which is traditionally claimed by a group of people as their property. In its 'General Comment No. 4' it states that "instances of forced eviction are prima facie incompatible with the requirements of the Covenant and can only be justified in the most exceptional circumstances, and in accordance with the relevant principles of international law." This view has also been reaffirmed by the United Nations Commission on Human Rights which states that forced evictions are a gross violations of human rights, and in particular the right to adequate housing. The African Commission also notes General Comment No. 7 requiring States Parties, prior to carrying out any evictions, to explore all feasible alternatives in consultation with affected persons, with a view to avoiding, or at least minimizing, the need to use force. . . .

202. The African Commission also refers to *Akdivar and Others v. Turkey*. The European Court held that forced evictions constitute a violation of Article 1 of Protocol 1 to the European Convention. *Akdivar and Others* involved the destruction

of housing in the context of the ongoing conflict between the Government of Turkey and Kurdish separatist forces. The petitioners were forcibly evicted from their
properties, which were subsequently set on fire and destroyed. It was unclear which
party to the conflict was responsible. Nonetheless, the European Court held that
the Government of Turkey violated both Article 8 of the European Convention
and Article 1 of Protocol 1 to the European Convention because it has a duty to
both respect and protect the rights enshrined in the European Convention and its
Protocols. . . .

204. The African Commission notes that the UN Declaration on the Rights of
Indigenous Peoples, officially sanctioned by the African Commission through its
2007 Advisory Opinion, deals extensively with land rights. The jurisprudence under
international law bestows the right of ownership rather than mere access. The African Commission notes that if international law were to grant access only, indigenous peoples would remain vulnerable to further violations/dispossession by the
State or third parties. Ownership ensures that indigenous peoples can engage with
the state and third parties as active stakeholders rather than as passive beneficiaries.

205. The Inter-American Court jurisprudence also makes it clear that mere
access or de facto ownership of land is not compatible with principles of international law. Only de jure ownership can guarantee indigenous peoples' effective
protection. . . .

238. Taking all the submissions of both parties, the African Commission agrees
with the Complainants that the Property of the Endorois people has been severely
encroached upon and continues to be so encroached upon. The encroachment is
not proportionate to any public need and is not in accordance with national and
international law. Accordingly, the African Commission finds for the Complainants
that the Endorois as a distinct people have suffered a violation of Article 14 of the
Charter.

ALLEGED VIOLATION OF ARTICLE 17(2) AND 17(3)

239. The Complainants allege that the Endorois' cultural rights have been violated on two counts: first, the community has faced systematic restrictions on access
to cultural sites and, second, that the cultural rights of the community have been
violated by the serious damage caused by the Kenyan authorities to their pastoralist
way of life. . . .

241. The African Commission is of the view that protecting human rights goes
beyond the duty not to destroy or deliberately weaken minority groups, but requires
respect for, and protection of, their religious and cultural heritage essential to their
group identity, including buildings and sites such as libraries, churches, mosques,
temples and synagogues. Both the Complainants and the Respondent State seem
to agree on that. It notes that Article 17 of the Charter is of a dual dimension in
both its individual and collective nature, protecting, on the one hand, individuals' participation in the cultural life of their community and, on the other hand,
obliging the state to promote and protect traditional values recognised by a community. It thus understands culture to mean that complex whole which includes a
spiritual and physical association with one's ancestral land, knowledge, belief, art,
law, morals, customs, and any other capabilities and habits acquired by humankind
as a member of society—the sum total of the material and spiritual activities and

products of a given social group that distinguish it from other similar groups. It has also understood cultural identity to encompass a group's religion, language, and other defining characteristics. . . .

246. The African Commission is of the view that in its interpretation of the African Charter, it has recognised the duty of the state to tolerate diversity and to introduce measures that protect identity groups different from those of the majority/dominant group. It has thus interpreted 17(2) as requiring governments to take measures "aimed at the conservation, development and diffusion of culture," such as promoting "cultural identity as a factor of mutual appreciation among individuals, groups, nations and regions; . . . promoting awareness and enjoyment of cultural heritage of national ethnic groups and minorities and of indigenous sectors of the population. . . ."

251. By forcing the community to live on semi-arid lands without access to medicinal salt licks and other vital resources for the health of their livestock, the Respondent State have created a major threat to the Endorois pastoralist way of life. It is of the view that the very essence of the Endorois' right to culture has been denied, rendering the right, to all intents and purposes, illusory. Accordingly, the Respondent State is found to have violated

Article 17(2) and 17(3) of the Charter.

ALLEGED VIOLATION OF ARTICLE 21

. . .

256. The African Commission . . . refers to cases in the Inter-American Human Rights system to understand this area of the law. The American Convention does not have an equivalent of the African Charter's Article 21 on the Right to Natural Resources. It therefore reads the right to natural resources into the right to property (Article 21 of the American Convention), and in turn applies similar limitation rights on the issue of natural resources as it does on limitations of the right to property. The "test" in both cases makes for a much higher threshold when potential spoliation or development of the land is affecting indigenous land. . . .

263. The African Commission notes the opinion of the IACtHR [Inter-American Court of Human Rights] in the *Saramaka* case as regards the issue of permissible limitations. . . .

267. In the instant case of the Endorois, the Respondent State has a duty to evaluate whether a restriction of these [third party] private property rights is necessary to preserve the survival of the Endorois community. The African Commission is aware that the Endorois do not have an attachment to ruby. Nevertheless, it is instructive to note that the African Commission decided in The Ogoni case that the right to natural resources contained within their traditional lands vested in the indigenous people. This decision made clear that a people inhabiting a specific region within a state can claim the protection of Article 21. Article 14 of the African Charter indicates that the two-pronged test of 'in the interest of public need or in the general interest of the community' and 'in accordance with appropriate laws' should be satisfied.

268. As far as the African Commission is aware, that has not been done by the Respondent State. The African Commission is of the view the Endorois have the right to freely dispose of their wealth and natural resources in consultation

with the Respondent State. 21(2) also concerns the obligations of a State Party to the African Charter in cases of a violation by spoliation, through provision for restitution and compensation. The Endorois have never received adequate compensation or restitution of their land. Accordingly, the Respondent State is found to have violated Article 21 of the Charter.

ALLEGED VIOLATION OF ARTICLE 22

269. The Complainants allege that the Endorois' right to development have been violated as a result of the Respondent State's creation of a game reserve and the Respondent State's failure to adequately involve the Endorois in the development process. . . .

275. Responding to the allegation that the game reserve made it particularly difficult for the Endorois to access basic herbal medicine necessary for maintaining a healthy life, the Respondent State argues that the prime purpose of gazetting the national reserve is conservation. Also responding to the claim that the Respondent State has granted several mining and logging concessions to third parties, and from which the Endorois have not benefited, the Respondent State asserts that the community has been well informed of those prospecting for minerals in the area. It further states that the community's mining committee had entered into an agreement with the Kenyan company prospecting for minerals, implying that the Endorois are fully involved in all community decisions.

277. The African Commission is of the view that the right to development is a two-pronged test, that it is both constitutive and instrumental, or useful as both a means and an end. A violation of either the procedural or substantive element constitutes a violation of the right to development. Fulfilling only one of the two prongs will not satisfy the right to development. The African Commission notes the Complainants' arguments that recognising the right to development requires fulfilling five main criteria: it must be equitable, non-discriminatory, participatory, accountable, and transparent, with equity and choice as important, over-arching themes in the right to development.

278. In that regard it takes note of the report of the UN Independent Expert who said that development is not simply the state providing, for example, housing for particular individuals or peoples; development is instead about providing people with the ability to choose where to live. He states ". . . the state or any other authority cannot decide arbitrarily where an individual should live just because the supplies of such housing are made available". Freedom of choice must be present as a part of the right to development. . . .

281. The African Commission notes that its own standards state that a government must consult with respect to indigenous peoples especially when dealing with sensitive issues as land. The African Commission agrees with the Complainants that the consultations that the Respondent State did undertake with the community were inadequate and cannot be considered effective participation. The conditions of the consultation failed to fulfil the African Commission's standard of consultations in a form appropriate to the circumstances. It is convinced that community members were informed of the impending project as a fait accompli, and not given an opportunity to shape the policies or their role in the game reserve.

282. Furthermore, the community representatives were in an unequal bargaining position, an accusation not denied or argued by the Respondent State, being both illiterate and having a far different understanding of property use and ownership than that of the Kenyan Authorities. The African Commission agrees that it was incumbent upon the Respondent State to conduct the consultation process in such a manner that allowed the representatives to be fully informed of the agreement, and participate in developing parts crucial to the life of the community. It also agrees with the Complainants that the inadequacy of the consultation undertaken by the Respondent State is underscored by Endorois' actions after the creation of the game reserve. The Endorois believed, and continued to believe even after their eviction, that the game reserve and their pastoralist way of life would not be mutually exclusive and that they would have a right of re-entry on to their land. In failing to understand their permanent eviction, many families did not leave the location until 1986.

. . .

284. The case of the *Yakye Axa* is instructive. The Inter-American Court found that the members of the Yakye Axa community live in extremely destitute conditions as a consequence of lack of land and access to natural resources, caused by the facts that were the subject matter of proceedings in front of the Court as well as the precariousness of the temporary settlement where they have had to remain, waiting for a solution to their land claim. . . .

286. The precariousness of the Endorois' post-dispossession settlement has had similar effects. No collective land of equal value was ever accorded (thus failing the test of 'in accordance with the law', as the law requires adequate compensation). The Endorois were relegated to semi-arid land, which proved unsustainable for pastoralism, especially in view of the strict prohibition on access to the Lake area's medicinal salt licks or traditional water sources. Few Endorois got individual titles in the Mochongoi Forest, though the majority live on the arid land on the outskirts of the Reserve. . . .

288. In the instant communication in front of the African Commission, video evidence from the Complainants shows that access to clean drinking water was severely undermined as a result of loss of their ancestral land (Lake Bogoria) which has ample fresh water sources. Similarly, their traditional means of subsistence — through grazing their animals – has been curtailed due to lack of access to the green pastures of their traditional land. Elders commonly cite having lost more than half of their cattle since the displacement. The African Commission is of the view that the Respondent State has done very little to provide necessary assistance in these respects.

289. Closely allied with the right to development is the issue of participation. The IACtHR has stated that in ensuring the effective participation of the Saramaka people in development or investment plans within their territory, the State has a duty to actively consult with the said community according to their customs and traditions. This duty requires the State to both accept and disseminate information, and entails constant communication between the parties. These consultations must be in good faith, through culturally appropriate procedures and with the objective of reaching an agreement. . . .

291. . . . [T]he African Commission is of the view that any development or investment projects that would have a major impact within the Endorois territory, the State has a duty not only to consult with the community, but also to obtain their free, prior, and informed consent, according to their customs and traditions. . . .

293. In this sense, it is important to note that the U.N. Special Rapporteur on the Situation of Human Rights and Fundamental Freedoms of Indigenous People observed that: "[w]herever [large-scale projects] occur in areas occupied by indigenous peoples it is likely that their communities will undergo profound social and economic changes that are frequently not well understood, much less foreseen, by the authorities in charge of promoting them. [. . .] The principal human rights effects of these projects for indigenous peoples relate to loss of traditional territories and land, eviction, migration and eventual resettlement, depletion of resources necessary for physical and cultural survival, destruction and pollution of the traditional environment, social and community disorganization, long-term negative health and nutritional impacts as well as, in some cases, harassment and violence." Consequently, the U.N. Special Rapporteur determined that "[f]ree, prior and informed consent is essential for the [protection of] human rights of indigenous peoples in relation to major development projects. . ."

296. In this sense, the Committee on the Elimination of Racial Discrimination has recommended not only that the prior informed consent of communities must be sought when major exploitation activities are planned in indigenous territories but also "that the equitable sharing of benefits to be derived from such exploitation be ensured." In the instant case, the Respondent State should ensure mutually acceptable benefit sharing. In this context, pursuant to the spirit of the African Charter benefit sharing may be understood as a form of reasonable equitable compensation resulting from the exploitation of traditionally owned lands and of those natural resources necessary for the survival of the Endorois community. . . .

298. The African Commission is of the view that the Respondent State bears the burden for creating conditions favourable to a people's development. It is certainly not the responsibility of the Endorois themselves to find alternate places to graze their cattle or partake in religious ceremonies. The Respondent State, instead, is obligated to ensure that the Endorois are not left out of the development process or benefits. The African Commission agrees that the failure to provide adequate compensation and benefits, or provide suitable land for grazing indicates that the Respondent State did not adequately provide for the Endorois in the development process. It finds against the Respondent State that the Endorois community has suffered a violation of Article 22 of the Charter.

RECOMMENDATIONS OF THE AFRICAN COMMISSION

In view of the above, the African Commission finds that the Respondent State is in violation of Articles 1, 8, 14, 17, 21 and 22 of the African Charter. The African Commission recommends that the Respondent State:

(a) Recognise rights of ownership to the Endorois and Restitute Endorois ancestral land.

(b) Ensure that the Endorois community has unrestricted access to Lake Bogoria and surrounding sites for religious and cultural rites and for grazing their cattle.

(c) Pay adequate compensation to the community for all the loss suffered.

(d) Pay royalties to the Endorois from existing economic activities and ensure that they benefit from employment possibilities within the reserve.

(e) Grant registration to the Endorois Welfare Committee.

(f) Engage in dialogue with the Complainants for the effective implementation of these recommendations.

(g) Report on the implementation of these recommendations within three months from the date of notification.

---

An interesting feature of the African Commission on Human and Peoples' Rights is its ability to issue General Comments on specific provisions of the African human rights treaties. This is a mechanism similar to those for the issuance of intepretive statements by the UN human rights treaty-based organs—discussed in Chapter 7—and one that no other regional protection system has. In the following General Comment, the African Commission interprets the content of the right to life under the African Charter on Human and Peoples' Rights.

African Commission on Human and Peoples' Rights

## General Comment No. 3 on the African Charter on Human and Peoples Rights: The Right to Life (Article 4)

Adopted 57th Ordinary Session of the ACHPR, Nov. 4-18, 2015

(1) The African Commission on Human and Peoples' Rights (the Commission) has described the right to life as the fulcrum of all other rights. It is non-derogable, and applies to all persons at all times. In General Comment No. 3, the Commission clarifies the nature of the right to life as recognised in Article 4 of the African Charter on Human and Peoples' Rights (the Charter) and the extent of the obligation it imposes upon States Parties. It is designed to guide the interpretation and application of the right to life under the Charter and to ensure its coherent application to a range of situations, including its implementation at the domestic level. The General Comment does not put in place new standards or highlight best practices but rather sets out the Commission's perspective on dimensions of this universally recognised right.

(2) The Charter imposes on States a responsibility to prevent arbitrary deprivations of life caused by its own agents, and to protect individuals and groups from such deprivations at the hands of others. It also imposes a responsibility to investigate any killings that take place, and to hold the perpetrators accountable. This intersects with the general duty, recognised in the Charter, of all individuals to exercise their rights and freedoms with due regard to the rights of others. Organised crime and terrorism can pose significant threats to the enjoyment of the right to life and require a robust State response, but one that at all times takes into account the requirements of international human rights law.

(3) The General Comment proceeds from an understanding that the Charter envisages the protection not only of life in a narrow sense, but of dignified life.

This requires a broad interpretation of States' responsibilities to protect life. Such actions extend to preventive steps to preserve and protect the natural environment and humanitarian responses to natural disasters, famines, outbreaks of infectious diseases, or other emergencies. The State also has a responsibility to address more chronic yet pervasive threats to life, for example with respect to preventable maternal mortality, by establishing functioning health systems. Such an approach reflects the Charter's ambition to ensure a better life for all the people and peoples of Africa through its recognition of a wide range of rights, including the right to dignity, economic, social and cultural rights, and peoples' rights such as the right to existence and the right to peace. It is also rooted in widely shared communal values of the continent, according to which the value of one person's life is tied to the value of the lives of others.

(4) Article 4 of the Charter enshrines the right to life as follows: 'Human beings are inviolable. Every human being shall be entitled to respect for his life and the integrity of his person. No one may be arbitrarily deprived of this right.' Other African legal instruments protecting the right to life include: Article 4 of the Protocol to the African Charter on Human and Peoples' Rights on the Rights of Women in Africa; and Articles 5 and 30 of the African Charter on the Rights and Welfare of the Child.

(5) The right to life is universally recognised as a foundational human right. It is guaranteed by Article 4 of the African Charter and all of the other main global and regional human rights instruments. The right not to be arbitrarily deprived of one's life is recognised as part of customary international law and the general principles of law, and is also recognised as a jus cogens norm, universally binding at all times. The right to life is contained in the constitutions and other legal provisions of the vast majority of African and other States. All national legal systems criminalise murder, and arbitrary killings committed or tolerated by the State are a matter of the utmost gravity.

(6) The right to life should not be interpreted narrowly. In order to secure a dignified life for all, the right to life requires the realisation of all human rights recognised in the Charter, including civil, political, economic, social and cultural rights and peoples' rights, particularly the right to peace.

(7) States have a responsibility under the Charter to develop and implement a legal and practical framework to respect, protect, promote and fulfil the right to life. States must take steps both to prevent arbitrary deprivations of life and to conduct prompt, impartial, thorough and transparent investigations into any such deprivations that may have occurred, holding those responsible to account and providing for an effective remedy and reparation for the victim or victims, including, where appropriate, their immediate family and dependents. States are responsible for violations of this right by all their organs (executive, legislative and judicial), and other public or governmental authorities, at all levels (national, regional or local). Derogation from the right to life is not permissible in a time of emergency, including a situation of armed conflict, or in response to threats such as terrorism.

(8) Where a State or its agent has attempted unlawfully to kill a person, but that person survives, where it has unlawfully threatened the life of a person, or where it has forcibly caused a person to disappear and that person's fate remains unknown, in addition to the violation of other rights, a violation of the right to life has occurred.

(9) A State can be held responsible for killings by non-State actors if it approves, supports or acquiesces in those acts or if it fails to exercise due diligence to prevent such killings or to ensure proper investigation and accountability.

(10) Building blocks of a proper State system for the protection of the right to life will include the enactment of appropriate domestic laws that protect the right to life and define any limitations on the right in accordance with international standards, a law enforcement system with the necessary equipment and training, and a competent, independent and impartial judiciary and legal profession based on the rule of law. States should continuously update their laws and practices to comply with international standards. States should take steps to raise awareness of the human rights implications of the applicable legal framework through professional training and other measures.

(11) As part of their broader duty to secure the conditions for dignified life, States have a particular responsibility to protect the human rights, including the right to life, of individuals or groups who are frequently targeted or particularly at risk, including on the grounds listed in Article 2 of the Charter and those highlighted in resolutions of the Commission. . . .

(38) The State also has an obligation to protect individuals from violations or threats at the hands of other private individuals or entities, including corporations. The State should ensure that all individuals are able to exercise their rights and freedoms, for example, by promoting tolerance, non-discrimination, and mutual respect. Moreover, the State has a responsibility for those deaths where authorities knew or ought to have known of an immediate threat and failed to take measures that might have been expected to avoid those deaths. States shall take appropriate measures to investigate cases of enforced disappearances committed by persons or groups acting without the authorisation, support or acquiescence of the State, and to bring those responsible to justice.

(39) The State is responsible for killings by private individuals which are not adequately prevented, investigated or prosecuted by the authorities. These responsibilities are heightened when an observable pattern has been overlooked or ignored, such as is often the case with respect to mob-justice, gender-based violence, femicide, or harmful practices. States must take all appropriate measures effectively to respond to, prevent and eliminate such patterns or practices.

(40) The right to life cannot be enjoyed fully by individuals whose lives are threatened. In the case of death threats this implies that the State must investigate and take all reasonable steps to protect the threatened individuals. Similarly, States should not violate the principle of non-refoulement, through extradition or other mechanisms, by transferring or returning individuals to circumstances where their lives might be endangered.

## *Note: African Regional and Sub-Regional Courts*

In 1998, the Organization of African Unity (now the African Union) adopted a Protocol to the African Charter on the Establishment of an African Court on Human and Peoples' Rights. The Court is composed of eleven judges, nationals of Member States of the African Union. The judges of the Court are elected, after nomination by their respective States, in their individual capacities from among

African jurists of proven integrity and of recognized practical, judicial, or academic competence and experience in the field of human rights. The judges are elected for a six-year or four-year term renewable once. Unusually among international courts, the African Court is distinguished by the number of its judges who have served as judges in one or more of the domestic courts of their state.

According to the Court's Protocol, which entered into force in January 2004, the Commission, a complainant state, or a respondent state may submit cases to the Court concerning the interpretation and the application of the African Charter, the Protocol, or "any other applicable African Human Rights instrument." (Arts. 3, 5(1).) Optionally, states may declare that they accept the competence of the Court to receive cases and complaints from individuals and nongovernmental organizations with observer status (Arts. 5.1, 34(6)); only eight states had accepted and retained this optional competence as of June of 2022. See *Declarations*, African Court of Human and Peoples' Rights, https://www.african-court.org/wpafc/declarations/ (last verified June 5, 2022). As discussed in Chapter 2, a number of African states have withdrawn their declarations recognizing the competency of the African Court, including Tanzania, the state in which the Court is based and against which the most complaints have been presented. See Amnesty International, *The State of African Regional Human Rights Bodies and Mechanisms* 41-42 (2019-2020), https://www.amnesty.org/en/documents/afr01/3089/2020/en/.

The Court also has advisory jurisdiction over "any legal matter related to the Charter or any other relevant human rights instruments." (Art. 4(1).) Any member state of the African Union, any of the organs of the African Union, and any inter-govenmental organization recognized by the African Union may submit a request for an advisory opinion to the Court.

Arusha, Tanzania, was selected as the seat of the African Court, enabling it to utilize some of the facilities and staff of the International Tribunal for Rwanda, once that court concluded its mandate. The first 11 judges of the African Court on Human and Peoples' Rights were elected in 2006 and held their first session in July of that year. The Court issued its first judgment in 2009, declaring inadmissible a challenge to Senegal's decision to investigate and prosecute Chad's former head of state, Hissène Habré, because Senegal had not ratified the Protocol or accepted the Court's jurisdiction over individual or NGO complaints. *Jamil Ddamulira Mujuzi, Michelot Yogogombaye v. The Republic of Senegal: The African Court's First Decision*, 10 HUM. RTS. L. REV. 372 (2010). Since then, the large majority of applications have similarly been dismissed for lack of jurisdiction, but several important judgments on the merits and reparations have been issued since 2011, including *Konaté v. Burkina Faso*, App. No. 004.2013, Judgment of December 5, 2015 (on freedom of expression); *ARPDF and IHRDA v. Republic of Mali*, App. No. 046/2016, Judgment of May 11, 2018 (on women's rights); *Ally Rajabu v. Tanzania*, App. No. 007, 2015 (on the prohibition of the death penalty); and *African Commission on Human and Peoples' Rights v. Kenya*, App. No. 006/2012, Judgment of May 26, 2017 (communal rights over lands and natural resources).

On July 1, 2008, the AU adopted a Protocol intended to merge the African Court on Human and Peoples' Rights with the AU's Court of Justice; as of June of 2022, only eight states had ratified the Protocol, and it is not anticipated that the Protocol will enter into force in the near future. See *Protocol on the Statute of the African Court of Justice and Human Rights: List of Countries Which Have Signed, Ratified/Acceded to the Protocol on the Statute of the African Court of Justice and Human Rights,* African Union, https://au.int/sites/default/files/treaties/36396-sl-PROTO COL%20ON%20THE%20STATUTE%20OF%20THE%20AFRICAN%20CO URT%20OF%20JUSTICE%20AND%20HUMAN%20RIGHTS.pdf (last visited June 30, 2022).

Two sub-regional courts also were established to hear cases alleging violations of the African Charter and other human rights instruments. One is affiliated with the Economic Community of West African States (ECOWAS), which was created in1975 by the Treaty of Lagos to promote economic, social, and cultural cooperation and integration, and ultimately an economic and monetary union of member states. The founding of ECOWAS also aimed to raise the living standards of its peoples, maintain and enhance economic stability, foster good relations among member states, and contribute to the progress and development of the African continent. The Treaty of Lagos and subsequent treaties established the ECOWAS Parliament and other governance institutions, and provided for an ECOWAS Community Court of Justice. The fifteen members of ECOWAS are: Benin, Burkina Faso, Cabo Verde, Cote d'Ivoire, The Gambia, Ghana, Guinea, Guinea-Bissau, Liberia, Mali, Niger, Nigeria, Senegal, Sierra Leone, and Togo.

The seven-member ECOWAS Community Court of Justice was established by a Protocol signed July 6, 1991 and entered into force on November 5, 1996. Article 9(1) of the Protocol provides that the Court's competence includes "ensur[ing] the observance of law and of the principles of equity in the interpretation of the [organic] Treaty." The Court interpreted this provision as providing it jurisdiction over human rights cases, and that interpretation was codified in 2005 by a Supplementary Protocol, A/SP.1/01/05.

According to Article 10(d)(ii) of the 1991 Protocol, as amended, access to the Court is open to the following: (. . .)

> 1. individuals on application for relief for violation of their human rights; the submission of application for which shall:
>> i) not be anonymous; nor
>> ii) be made whilst the same matter has been instituted before another International Court for adjudication

There is no need to exhaust domestic remedies in order to apply to the ECOWAS Court. One of the Court's most significant early cases was *Hadijatou Mani Koraou v. The Republic of Niger*, Application No. ECW/CCJ/APP/08/08, ECOWAS Community Court of Justice, Judgment of October 27, 2008 (unofficial translation). In *Hadijatou Mani Koraou*, the Court issued a judgment finding Niger responsible for passively allowing practices of enslavement.

In addition to the ECOWAS tribunal, the South African Development Community (SADC) created a court that could hear cases alleging violations of human rights, although as a consequence of controversy over the exercise of this jurisdiction, as described below, in 2012 SADC removed the tribunal's jurisdiction to hear individual complaints. SADC is an intergovernmental organization of fifteen member states. Headquartered in Gaborone, Botswana, its goal is to further socioeconomic cooperation and integration, as well as political and security cooperation,

among its members. The SADC Tribunal was created by Article 9 of the 1992 SADC
Treaty to ensure adherence to, and the proper interpretation of, the provisions of
the treaty and the subsidiary instruments made thereunder, and to adjudicate such
disputes as may be referred to it. The scope of its jurisdiction, under Article 15(1)
of the Protocol on the Tribunal and its Rules of Procedure, originally included
adjudication of "disputes between States, and between natural and legal persons
and States," provided all available remedies were exhausted or the applicant was
unable to proceed under the domestic jurisdiction.

The first members of the Tribunal took office in 2005. Its first human rights
case, Case 2/2007, *Campbell and Others v. Republic of Zimbabwe,* challenged the
expropriation and other seizures of white-owned farms in Zimbabwe. The Tribunal held that the land expropriations and invasions, as well as the denial of access
to justice, violated the applicants' rights. According to the Tribunal, Article 21(b)
of its Protocol directed it to develop its own jurisprudence, "having regard to applicable treaties, [and] general principles and rules of public international law." The
Tribunal considered that no additional instrument on human rights was necessary
for it to give effect to the principles set out in the SADC Treaty, in light of the
express directive of Article 4(c) of the Treaty that "SADC and Member States are
required to act in accordance with the following principles . . . (c) human rights,
democracy and the rule of law." In accordance with this directive, the Tribunal
looked broadly at regional and global human rights law in deciding the merits in
favor of the applicants. The government objected to the judgment and lobbied
heavily to restrict the powers of the Tribunal. As a result, the Tribunal's jurisdiction to hear individual cases was removed in 2012. Later the Tribunal's activities
were suspended altogether.

### Comments and Questions

1. Recall Heyns' observation, *supra* page 649, that "[t]he continuous creation
of new mechanisms for the protection of human rights in Africa is not necessarily
helping the situation." Do you agree? Note that the Inter-American system is also
facing a proliferation of sub-regional bodies, in some instances created expressly to
provide an alternative to Inter-American supervision. Some of these sub-regional
bodies include MERCOSUR (Mercado Común del Sur), the members being
Argentina, Brazil, Paraguay, and Uruguay. Venezuela was suspended in 2016 and
Bolivia is in the process of joining; CELAC (Community of Latin American and
Caribbean States), comprising all OAS member states (except the US and Canada);
and the Caribbean Court of Justice, with original jurisdiction over fifteen members
of the Caribbean Community (CARICOM) and appellate jurisdiction over Barba-
dos, Belize, Dominica, and Guyana. Opposition to regional jurisprudence limiting application of the death penalty in part spurred the creation of the Caribbean
Court of Justice (CCJ).

2. One of the distinguishing characteristics of the African Charter is its protection of not only individual rights but also the rights of "peoples," as discussed
*supra* in the *Endorois* case. "Peoples" in the African Charter have the right to equality
(Article 19), to self-determination (Article 20), to freely dispose of their wealth and
natural resources (Article 21), to development (Article 22), to peace and security

(Article 23), and to a generally satisfactory environment (Article 24). The African Commission in its *Endorois* decision identifies criteria to consider a specific group a people for purposes of legal protection under the African Charter, including a shared historical tradition; racial or ethnic identity; a common culture, language, religious, and set of ideologies; links to lands and territories; and "bonds, identities, and affinities" that they enjoy. See *Endorois* case, *supra* page 650, para. 151. Can you think of advantages and disadvantages of this protection for the collective rights of peoples, which is in addition to the protection for individual human rights? Is it easy to draw the line between groups that qualify as "peoples" and those that do not? How does such line drawing matter? Recall the discussion of indigenous peoples, minorities, and self-determination in Chapter 3. Are the collective rights of peoples properly considered to be human rights? And can the collective rights of peoples always be reconciled with individual rights?

3. Note that in the *Endorois* case the African Commission, in interpreting the African Charter, relied significantly on the jurisprudence of the Inter-American Court of Human Rights interpreting the American Convention on Human Rights in relation to claims by indigenous peoples. How is this use of the Inter-American Court's jurisprudence justified? Are the rights the same, regardless of the fact that the American Convention on Human Rights does not explicitly recognize "peoples" rights? Are the issues or groups the same or similar? Are the Endorois an "indigenous people" or simply a "people"? And how does that matter or not matter?

4. The analysis of the African Commission of the content of peoples' rights is often linked to the right to development and the state obligation to create conditions favorable to the full enjoyment of these rights. As indicated by the African Commission in the *Endorois* case, states are mandated to ensure that indigenous peoples and other groups are not excluded from critical development processes or benefits. See *Endorois* case, *supra* page 650, para. 298. What steps can states take to comply with the right to development? Can you think of indicators of compliance with this right? Consider ways in which the procedures of the African system can be used to give content to and enforce the right to development.

5. In its General Comment No. 3, the African Commission interprets the right to life under the African Charter similarly to how the United Nations Human Rights Committee and the Inter-American Court of Human Rights have interpreted the right to life in connection with the treaties to which those other bodies are respectively attached. The African Commission interprets the right to life in a broad sense, as extending not only to the prevention of arbitrary loss of life but also to the pursuit of a dignified life. Likewise, the Inter-American Court of Human Rights in well-known indigenous peoples cases has established the principle that states have a duty to ensure that all individuals and groups live with dignity, adequate health conditions and housing, and sufficient food and water. See, e.g., *Yakye Axa Indigenous Community v. Paraguay, Merits Reparations, and Costs*, Inter-Am. Ct. H.R., Judgment of June 17, 2005, Ser. C No. 125, paras. 162-176. The UN Human Rights Committee has reaffirmed this position, calling on states to develop strategic and contingency plans to make the right to a dignified life a reality. See Human Right Committee, *General comment No. 36, Article 6: right to life*, UN Doc. CCPR/C/GC/36 (2019), para. 7. For more reading on the right to a "dignified life," see Thomas M. Antkowiak, *A "Dignified Life" and the Resurgency of Social Rights*, 18 NW. J. HUM. RTS. I, 16-39 (2020).

## IV.   EMERGING SYSTEMS IN ASIA AND THE ARAB WORLD

This section discusses the emerging approaches in Asia and the Arab World to human rights promotion and protection. Even though the most established regional human rights systems are found in the Americas, Europe and Africa, steps in Asia and the Middle East provide hope that there could be effective instruments and institutions in these regions in the future to address human rights concerns.

### A.   ASEAN

In the Asia-Pacific region, the Association of South-East Asian Nations (ASEAN), originally formed in 1967 by Indonesia, Malaysia, the Philippines, Singapore, and Thailand, and later joined by Vietnam, Laos, Myanmar, and Cambodia, has been a forum for cooperation. ASEAN Member States formalized their association in the ASEAN Charter, signed Nov. 20, 2007, https://asean.org/wp-content/uploads/images/archive/publications/ASEAN-Charter.pdf. The Charter declares that the organization's purposes include strengthening democracy, promoting the rule of law, and protecting human rights and fundamental freedoms. The Charter further includes as key principles to govern the conduct of ASEAN and its member states the "respect for fundamental freedoms, the promotion and protection of human rights, and the promotion of social justice" and "adherence to the rule of law, good governance, the principles of democracy and constitutional government." ASEAN's policy-making body, the ASEAN Summit, takes decisions on key issues pertaining to the realization of the objectives of ASEAN and addresses any emergency affecting the organization. The ASEAN Coordinating Council, composed of the ASEAN Foreign Ministers, prepares the meetings of the Summit, coordinates with the various councils to enhance policy coherence and cooperation, and undertakes tasks enumerated in the ASEAN Charter.

Article 14 of the ASEAN Charter calls for establishing an ASEAN human rights body, which was implemented through the creation in 2009 of the ASEAN Intergovernmental Commission on Human Rights (AICHR). Unlike other regional human rights bodies, the AICHR members are not independent; instead, each person named to the Commission is a representative of and serves at the pleasure of their government. See ASEAN Intergovernmental Commission on Human Rights (Terms or Reference) (TOR), Art. 5, subparagraphs 5 and 6, https://aichr.org/wp-content/uploads/2020/02/TOR-of-AICHR.pdf.

In contrast to the regional human rights commissions in the Americas and Africa, the ASEAN Commission is largely devoted to promotional work and it lacks an individual complaint system. When appointing their members to the Commission, ASEAN member states are obliged to pay "due consideration to gender equality, integrity and competence in the field of human rights." TOR, Art. 5.3. In practice, however, most Commissioners thus far have been current or former government officials. They must act by consensus and have limited powers conferred by the Terms of Reference, which lists the purposes of AICHR as follows: "To promote and protect human rights and fundamental freedoms of the peoples of ASEAN" and to uphold standards contained in "international human rights instruments to which ASEAN Member States are parties." The human rights promotion work is to be done "within the regional context, bearing in mind national and regional particularities and mutual respect for different historical, cultural and religious backgrounds, and taking into account the balance between rights and responsibilities." The mandate and functions include enhancing public awareness of human rights, promoting capacity building, encouraging member states "to consider acceding to and ratifying international human rights instruments," and promoting implementation of "ASEAN instruments related to human rights." Although human rights protection is mentioned, that function has not been spelled out through the grant of a specific mandate. In late March 2010, during the AICHR's first formal session in Jakarta, efforts to have the Commission receive a formal complaint were rejected, the Commission being unwilling to imply a power not formally granted in its Terms of Reference.

ASEAN also created a Commission on the Promotion and Protection of the Rights of Women and Children (ACWC), and a Committee on the Implementation of the Declaration on the Protection and Promotion of the Rights of Migrant Workers (ACMW). See *ASEAN Declaration on the Protection and Promotion of the Rights of Migrant Workers* (Jan. 13, 2007), https://www.ilo.org/dyn/migpractice/migmain.showPractice?p_lang=en&p_practice_id=41. Like the AICHR, these bodies are composed of governmental representatives.

In 2012, the Heads of State adopted the ASEAN Human Rights Declaration, recognizing certain human rights and related principles, and further clarified the mandate of the AICHR. See *ASEAN Human Rights Declaration* (Nov. 19, 2012), https://asean.org/asean-human-rights-declaration/. The ASEAN Declaration is seen by some as a precursor to a formal treaty for the region, as has happened with human rights declarations in the UN and in other regional systems.

The following reading discusses the development, content, and significance of the ASEAN Human Rights Declaration.

American Bar Association

## The ASEAN Declaration of Human Rights: A Legal Analysis

Rule of Law Initiative (ABA-ROLI), 2014, pp. 1-9 (footnotes omitted)

In November 2012, the ten Member States of the Association of Southeast Asian Nations (ASEAN) adopted the ASEAN Human Rights Declaration (AHRD or Declaration). The AHRD marked a significant step in the establishment of a formal ASEAN human rights system, which may, like its counterparts in Africa, the Americas, and Europe, help to form a solid foundation for the development of those legal instruments and independent mechanisms required to strengthen human rights protection in the region.

The AHRD text was the result of intense and protracted negotiations between the Member States, and reactions to it varied. Some commentators welcomed the Declaration, given the challenge of finding consensus on such a document among the different ASEAN states. Others, particularly human rights organizations, expressed disappointment about the omission of key rights and the inclusion of wording that appears to limit the enjoyment of rights in a manner inconsistent with international law. The AHRD reflects tensions between ASEAN governments' interests in preserving principles of sovereignty and non-interference and in promoting the development of a credible regional human rights system. From the point of view of international law, the AHRD contains both progressive and problematic elements.

As a non-binding declaration, the AHRD does not legally undermine ASEAN Member States' human rights obligations under United Nations (UN), International Labour Organisation (ILO) and other international treaties. Nevertheless, the AHRD represents the most recent articulation of human rights standards to which all ten ASEAN Member States have explicitly consented, and for that reason ought to carry substantial political weight and normative value. However, ASEAN governments have done little to engage with the AHRD at the national level, politically or legally. This perhaps is due to the vocal rejection of the AHRD by civil society organizations (CSOs) in the region, or reflects limited interest in applying it on the part of some ASEAN Member States. Although this does mean that Member States have not used the AHRD to actively undermine existing human rights protections, it also calls into question ASEAN's wider commitment to developing a credible regional human rights system, and the AHRD's utility as a foundation for such a system.

Thus, the AHRD's significance as a human rights text comes primarily from the fact that it represents the ASEAN Inter-governmental Commission on Human Rights' (AICHR) first attempt at human rights standard-setting. It does not create enforceable rights or protections for people within ASEAN, and does not create a body to interpret and apply the Declaration progressively, as was the case with the Inter-American Commission on Human Rights and its Declaration.

A regional human rights treaty, which members of the AICHR have already raised as a not-so-distant possibility, is another matter. A treaty, if not carefully drafted, could potentially undermine regional human rights standards by establishing lower expectations of compliance. Regional human rights treaties usually establish an independent body of experts to oversee treaty implementation and enforcement, and such lowered expectations could have an adverse impact on the development of human rights norms in the region. Thus, while a regional treaty between ASEAN Member States would still not serve to restrict the states' obligations under international agreements to which they are parties, as a treaty interpreted and applied amongst the Member States, it could serve to weaken human rights protection in the region. . . .

KEY FINDINGS

The AHRD includes both progressive and problematic elements. As mentioned above, it does not legally act to undermine ASEAN Member States' international treaty obligations. Article 40 of the AHRD and the Phnom Penh Statement adopted by ASEAN Heads of State alongside the Declaration furthermore require that the AHRD be interpreted in a manner consistent with the existing human rights obligations of ASEAN Member States. These elements provide grounds for reading down some of the Declaration's problematic provisions, and interpreting terms in favor of the right.

The AHRD includes a number of positive aspects:

- Highlights the importance of the rights of vulnerable and marginalised groups;
- Reinstates the UDHR right to property and protection against arbitrary deprivation of property which was omitted in the International Convention on Civil and Political Rights (ICCPR) and International Convention on Economic, Social and Civil Rights (ICESCR);
- Contains an expanded version of the right to an adequate standard of living which explicitly recognizes clean drinking water and sanitation, and a safe, clean and sustainable environment, as well as adequate and affordable housing and food, as elements of this right;
- Recognizes a need to prevent discrimination against persons with HIV/AIDS and other communicable diseases;
- Includes the right to development, while recognizing that the right to development must be exercised in a manner consistent with other human rights;
- Moves beyond the lowest common denominator as a standard for ASEAN human rights instruments, which in this case would be the UDHR, the Convention on Rights of the Child (CRC) and the Convention on the Elimination of Discrimination Against Women (CEDAW). The AHRD is largely based upon the UDHR, but elements of the ICESCR (special protection of motherhood, progressive realization of social, economic and cultural rights) and ICCPR (prohibition against double-jeopardy) are integrated into the AHRD text despite only six ASEAN Member States being party to the treaties.
- The problematic elements of the AHRD include provisions that could be invoked to undermine human rights in the region, those which represent a mischaracterisation of international human rights law, and those which present an inconsistency with the international obligations of ASEAN Member States. The negative impact of such elements on human rights protection in the region could be mitigated, however, by the establishment of an independent human rights body tasked to apply and enforce the AHRD in a manner consistent with international law.

However, there are several key points of concern:

- The AHRD's general limitation clause in article 8 of its opening principles undermines its acknowledgement of the non-derogable or absolute nature of several human rights under customary law and the ICCPR. Article 8 follows the UDHR but jurisprudence regarding rights limitations has developed since 1948 when the UDHR was adopted. International human rights instruments now tend to take a right by right approach, making the scope of permissible limitations narrower and more precise. In this context, the fact that the AHRD theoretically permits all enshrined rights to be limited "by law solely for the purpose of securing due recognition for the human rights and fundamental freedoms of others, and to meet the just requirements of national security, public order, public health, public safety, public morality, as well as the general welfare of the peoples in a democratic society" threatens to create inconsistency with ASEAN Member States' existing obligations. For example, freedom from slavery and torture are considered rights under customary law, and no state may permit torture or slavery to exist. However, the limitation clause could be used by Member States to justify their derogation from the established principle. Although there are few circumstances in which torture could imaginably assist to "secure" the human rights of others, it is arguably safer and legally correct to specify the absolute nature of the prohibition against torture and other non-derogable rights more generally.

- The AHRD calls for States to balance personal duties of an individual against their rights, and to take into account "national and regional contexts" in the realization of those rights. Articles 6 and 7 have their roots in previous Asian human rights declarations, and might constitute an attempt by ASEAN to infuse the AHRD with a regional flavour. Nevertheless, such language carries the risk of tying the realization of rights to unspecified "duties" or to social norms and mores which run counter to the requirements of international human rights treaties such as CEDAW and the CRC, both of which have been ratified by all ASEAN Member States. Whether these provisions will be interpreted and applied in a manner which violates international human rights norms remains to be seen, but the language raises some concerns.

- Absent from the AHRD are the right to self-determination, the right to freedom from forced labour, a clear prohibition against enforced disappearance, the freedom to manifest and change one's religion, and the right to freedom of association, all of which various ASEAN Member States have recognized in international declarations or treaties.

- The AHRD provides that rights be regulated by law or national law. Domestic legislation is certainly an effective way of achieving human rights protections, as long as such legislation actually comports with international human rights standards. The AHRD contains no clear statement requiring this compliance or consistency, meaning that it in theory permits ASEAN Member States to, for example, "guarantee" the right to a nationality simply through compliance with domestic immigration and citizenship laws, regardless of their content, effect, and compliance with relevant international instruments.

- Additionally, the AHRD could have better incorporated the more detailed obligations of Member States under ILO and UN human rights treaties to which they are all signatories or parties, but perhaps this detail is best addressed in a future convention.

- The inclusion of the right to peace in the AHRD, while novel, may not necessarily be a positive development, particularly insofar as it may shield from accountability alleged perpetrators of human rights abuse. Much depends upon how this right develops in international law, and how it is applied within the ASEAN region.

CONCLUSION

The AHRD provides an important foundation for the development of future binding human rights instruments in the ASEAN region, both in terms of lessons that can be learned from its drafting process as well as its substantive content.

From a process-based perspective, the drafting process for any further human rights instruments should be supported with substantial legal expertise from a team of individuals with in-depth knowledge of international human rights law, at all stages of the process. Although the AICHR's team of experts was present during the AHRD's initial drafting stages, they were not involved in the reformulation of the draft. Second, the process must include CSOs at all stages; such organizations bring substantial rights expertise to the table, as well as invaluable insight into the potential practical impacts of draft provisions.

From a content-based perspective, although the development of international legal texts is inevitably political and subject to negotiation, ASEAN should agree to a minimum set of human rights standards which future texts must at least meet and could conceivably surpass. This standard should be comprised of the complete international bill of human rights including the UDHR, ICCPR and the ICESCR. Additionally, explanatory notes could be provided alongside the text to allow for discussion of the meaning and interpretation of different terms, and to provide sufficient insight for human rights implementers who might look to the document for guidance.

Finally, ASEAN is fortunate in that it has decades of experience from other regional human rights systems to draw on which could serve as a model for its own. The basic components of the African, Inter-American and European regional human rights systems are:

> i) a binding human rights convention;
>
> ii) additional protocols to supplement the more general convention;
>
> iii) an independent body, established by treaty, to interpret and apply the convention; and
>
> iv) a range of treaty enforcement measures, including a complaint mechanism for individuals and/or states parties.

An ASEAN human rights convention must not only include a comprehensive bill of rights, but also the machinery required to establish an effective treaty enforcement mechanism. While text is an undeniably important first step, ultimately, the actual value of a human rights instrument—whether it be the AHRD or a later binding instrument—will be assessed by the role it plays in motivating concrete actions to improve human rights for the people of ASEAN.

---

For more reading on the ASEAN Declaration, see Catherine Shanahan Renshaw, *The ASEAN Human Rights Declaration 2012*, 13(3) HUM. RTS. L. REV. 557 (2013); Mathew Davies, *The ASEAN Synthesis: Human Rights, Non-Intervention, and the ASEAN Human Rights Declaration*, 14 GEO. J. INT'L AFF. 51 (2013).

## B.   The League of Arab States

The Middle East has been an area of conflict throughout human history, and illiberal tendencies have persisted in Arab states in the region through today. It is perhaps surprising, therefore, to see efforts to create a regional human rights system among the Arab states of this region. The League of Arab States was created around the same time the United Nations was established, and the topic of human rights has emerged increasingly on the agenda of the organization, particularly since the so-called Arab Spring began in 2011. This development, which has been uneven given the turmoil and lack of democracy in many states in the region, nonetheless led to the adoption of human rights treaties and to the creation of an Arab Court of Human Rights. Other mechanisms are also noteworthy, including the Arab Commission on Human Rights and an Arab Human Rights Committee. The evolution of attention to human rights in the Middle East is outlined in the following extract.

Mohammed Amin Al-Midani

## Human Rights Bodies in the League of Arab States

3 JINAN HUM. RTS. J. 109-34 (2012)

. . .

The promotion and protection of human rights was not originally among the issues that were stated in the Charter of the League of Arab States. The League's interest started seriously only in the 1960s, more specifically in 1968 when the Council of the League issued its decision on the establishment of the Arab Permanent Commission on Human Rights. The Council subsequently established a Human Rights Experts Committee in 2006, four decades after its inception, with the aim that these experts would help the Arab Permanent Commission on Human Rights in its work and activities. However, the big leap in the protection of human rights in the member states of the League took place when the members of the Arab Human Rights Committee were elected as a result of the adoption of the Arab Charter on Human Rights (May 23, 2004). The Charter entered into force on March 16, 2008. . . .

### II.   THE ARAB PERMANENT COMMISSION ON HUMAN RIGHTS

The Arab Permanent Commission on Human Rights was established as a result of an initiative by the United Nations. The UN Commission on Human Rights in its 24th meeting (March 23, 1967), dedicated to "dealing with the problem of establishing regional commissions on human rights," requested in resolution No. 6 (XXIII), that the UN General Secretary inquire from the regional organizations which had not established permanent commissions on human rights about the possibility of establishing such commissions. . . .

The Arab Permanent Commission on Human Rights was indeed established and held its first meeting from March 3-6, 1969. At this point, the Commission did not have its own statute. The statute governing the functional commissions of the League of Arab States instead was applied until the Council of the League issued ministerial resolution No. 6826 on September 1, 2010, approving a statute for the Arab Permanent Commission on Human Rights. . . .

### A. THE COMPOSITION OF THE ARAB PERMANENT COMMISSION ON HUMAN RIGHTS

This Commission is composed of representatives of the member states of the League of Arab States. . . .

The Council of the League, pursuant to Article 5 of the Statute of the Functional Commissions of the League and in accordance with the newer statute of the Commission, nominates the Chairperson for the Commission from among the candidates nominated by the member states of the League. . . .

The Secretary General of the League, pursuant to Article 6 of its statute, shall appoint a secretary in the League Secretariat to work on human rights. The "Department of Human Rights," established by the Secretary General of the League of Arab States on April 16, 1992, also helps the Arab Commission carrying out its tasks.

We note in this connection that the Department of Human Rights has carried out several activities in the area of promoting human rights in the Arab countries as it participated in a special Arab seminar on the updating of the first version of the Arab Charter for Human Rights 1994 in Sana'a on the December 21-22, 2002. The proceedings of this seminar were published under the title: "Towards Updating the Arab Charter on Human Rights." It also participated in the First Arab Conference on Human Rights, held in Doha on December 14-15, 2008. This Department called for a meeting in Cairo on July 4-5, 2009, regarding the Arab Charter on Human Rights. . . .

### 2. Powers of the Arab Permanent Commission on Human Rights

The Arab Permanent Commission on Human Rights, in its second meeting held on March 26, 1969, adopted its own action programme. The new statute of 2007 came to enhance this program and add to it other tasks. We can divide the powers of the Arab Permanent Commission on Human Rights into two parts; one at the Arab level, and the other, at the international level.

### 3. The Commission Powers at the Arab Level

The Arab Permanent Commission on Human Rights is concerned at the level of the member States of the League with all the issues relating to human rights. This Commission has had several activities, such as its contribution to the preparation for the first Arab Regional Conference on Human Rights in the Arab World, held in Beirut December 2-10, 1968, on the occasion of the International Year for Human Rights. This Conference asked the Arab Permanent Commission on Human Rights to prepare an Arab Charter on Human Rights.

At the request of the Arab States, the Permanent Commission on Human Rights also helped form national non-governmental commissions and organizations concerned with human rights. Some of these commissions and organizations then demanded that they be allowed to attend the meetings of the Arab Committee as observers. This prompted the Council of the League to issue resolution No. 4910 of March 10, 1989, which called for the League of Arab States General Secretariat "to accelerate the process of setting standards and conditions that shall regulate the invitation of human rights non-governmental organizations to participate in the works of the Commission as observers." The Council of the League also approved the recommendation of the Arab Permanent Commission on Human Rights on cooperation with Arab regional and international human rights Organizations in its resolution No. 5198 of April 29, 1992.

The Arab Permanent Commission on Human Rights, depending on what comes from the member states of the League, studies all the complaints and any information it receives from its communications with Arab non-governmental organizations and associations. This Commission usually tries to resolve all the issues presented to it by making recommendations to these countries. The Arab Commission celebrates the Arab Day for Human Rights on March 16 each year.

The Council of the League asked the Arab permanent Commission on Human Rights, based on its resolutions No. 4409 of April 25, 1984 and No. 4567 of March 27, 1986, to study a draft Arab convention to regulate the rights of Arab refugees in Arab countries. The Arab Permanent Commission studied the draft Convention and submitted it at the end of its seventh session, held in Tunis October 3-8, 1988, to the Legal Commission. The Council of the League subsequently approved the Arab Convention on Regulating the Status of Refugees in the Arab Countries on March 27, 1994. There are efforts now to update this Convention. The Arab Permanent Commission is also concerned with the issue of migrants' protection from racial discrimination. It also contributed to the preparation of the Arab Convention to Fight Terrorism in the Arab world.

The most important work done by the Arab Permanent Commission on human Rights in the area of protecting these rights in the member states of the League, and to keeping up with the achievements of other regional organizations, was its participation in the preparation of the first version of the Arab Charter on Human Rights 1994 and its contribution to updating it. . . . The 1994 Charter received a lot of criticism and objections from the legal and human rights specialists and the non-governmental organizations in the Arab world and Europe. Several meetings were held in various capitals and cities demanding that it be updated.

These efforts succeeded in drawing the attention of the Arab Permanent Commission on Human Rights to the need to update the Arab Charter. The League of Arab States Secretariat and the Secretary General himself took a special interest in this subject. The Arab Permanent Commission held meetings in June and October 2003 with the aim of providing some suggestions on updating the Arab Charter. But the important step in this regard came from the UN, thanks to a memorandum of understanding which was signed by the League of Arab States and the Office of High Commissioner for Human Rights in Geneva, and which stated that a committee comprising a group of Arab experts in the relevant committees emanating from International Conventions on Human Rights would be formed with the aim of updating the Arab Charter and introducing some amendments to it. This Committee met in Cairo between December 21-26, 2003, and prepared a revised draft of the Arab Charter taking into account the observations and contributions it received from the Arab NGOs and International Organizations. The Arab Permanent Commission on Human Rights members examined the draft again in their meeting held November 4-11, 2004. The new version of the Arab Charter on Human Rights was adopted by the Committee and presented to the Secretariat of the League, following which the Arab Summit, held in Tunis on May 23, 2004, adopted the revised Arab Charter on Human Rights.

4. The Commission Powers at the International Level

The Arab Permanent Commission on Human Rights Standing Committee on Human Rights participates at the international level in international conferences and meetings organized in various parts of the World. . . . The main concern for the Arab Permanent Commission remains the Israeli violations of human rights in the occupied Arab territories and the need to alert international public opinion and the various media to the dangers these violations create to international peace and security. . . .

D.  Critique

The fact that the members of the Arab Permanent Commission on Human Rights represent, as we have mentioned above, their governments, is, in our view, a serious drawback in the statute of this Arab Permanent Commission and a factor affecting, without any doubt, its effective functioning and the credibility of its decisions, recommendations, and draft conventions. Moreover, the Arab Permanent Commission on Human Rights did not have its own statute for several decades. The statute of the functional commissions of the League of Arab States was applied to it until a special statute for the Arab Permanent Commission was adopted on July 1, 2010. Secondly, the Arab Permanent Commission on Human Rights is limited to the role of "promoting" human rights, while it should adopt the role of protecting Arab human rights so that it proves its effectiveness, following the model of the regional American and African commissions. If the Israeli violations of human rights in the occupied Arab territories are on the agenda of all the sessions of the Arab Permanent Commission on Human Rights, do we not have the right to wonder if the protection of the rights of the citizens in the member states of the League of Arab States enjoys sufficient attention from this Arab Permanent Commission? And whether there is communication between the national commissions dealing with human rights and non-governmental organizations in these countries and this Arab Permanent Commission? Does the Arab Permanent Commission make recommendations to the member states regarding the protection of human rights or even the promotion of these rights? . . .

## IV.  The Arab Human Rights Committee Established by the Arab Charter on Human Rights 2004

The 2004 Arab Charter on Human Rights devoted Articles 45 to 48 to the mechanism of respecting its provisions by the States Parties through the establishment of the Arab Human Rights Committee.

### A. Composition of the Arab Human Rights Committee

Article 45(1) of the Arab Charter on Human Rights provided for the establishment of a committee under the name "The Arab Human Rights Committee" to consist of seven members. Paragraph 2 of the same Article sets forth the qualifications of the candidates to fill the position; they should be "highly experienced persons" in the field of work of the Committee. It is important here to note that these experts act in their "personal capacity" and that they should do their work "with full impartiality and integrity."

The Committee members are elected to a four year term by secret ballot from among the citizens of the States Parties (Articles 45(1), (2)). The Committee may not have more than one national of the same State (Article 45(3)). The same person, however, may be re-elected, but only once. The "principle of rotation" should be taken into account.

The first members of the Arab Human Rights Committee were from Algeria, Bahrain, Libya, Palestine, Saudi Arabia, Syria and the United Arab Emirates.

. . . .

Finally, Article 45(7) delegates to the Arab Human Rights Committee the task of "setting the regulations for its work and regular meetings," which means that it must adopt its own rules of procedure governing its functioning, just like the other regional commissions.

### B. Meetings of the Arab Human Rights Committee

The Arab Human Rights Committee holds its meetings at the League of Arab States headquarters in Cairo upon the invitation of the Secretary General of the League. These meetings also may be held in any State Party to the Arab Charter upon the invitation of the Secretary General of the League (Article 45(7)).

We wonder why the Secretary General has the power of calling the regular meetings of this Committee, whether at the League's headquarters or in any state party, instead of the Chairperson of the Committee calling for these meetings? . . . At least Article 45 of the Arab Charter does not grant the Secretary General of the League the right to attend the meetings of the Commission or to participate in the deliberations or vote on its resolutions. An additional responsibility is conferred by Article 46(5), which states that the Secretary General is to provide the necessary "financial resources, staff, and facilities" from within the budget of the League of Arab States for the effective "performance of the functions" of the Arab Human Rights Committee.

### C. Activities of the Arab Human Rights Commission

The monitoring of the Arab Charter on Human Rights 2004, indicated in the various paragraphs of Article 48, lies in the commitment of the party states to submit "reports" to the Secretary General of the League of Arab States, who, in his turn, refers them to the Arab Human Rights Committee. The nature of these reports varies, as the States Parties first submit preliminary reports, followed by regular reports and additional information. The Committee studies the reports and makes its remarks.

### 1. The Preliminary Reports

Each party State to the Arab Charter submits a preliminary report one year after the date the Charter enters into force for the State (Article 48(1)). The reports should explain the measures taken by that State "to give effect to the rights and freedoms recognized" in the Arab Charter.

### 2. Regular Reports

The States Parties are required to submit regular reports every three years to the Arab Human Rights Committee. (Article 48(2)), including on the measures they have taken. Although Article 48 does not expressly so provide, this is understood from the context of this Article. It was desirable for the Article to oblige the States Parties to indicate the progress or developments that have been made in the application of the Charter and to respect its provisions during the period between the preliminary report and the regular report. The Arab Human Rights Committee may request from a State Party "additional information relating to the implementation of the Charter" (Article 48(2)).

### 3. Studying the Reports and Providing Feedback and Recommendations

The Arab Human Rights Committee, in implementation of Article 48(3), shall study the preliminary and regular reports submitted by the States Parties "in the presence and with the collaboration of the representative of the State Parties whose report is being considered." We believe that the presence of the representatives during the Committee's discussion of the state report is necessary and helps in understanding the dimensions and content of the report and facilitates the work of the Committee. As noted above, the Committee also has the right to demand additional information about the fulfilment by the State Party of its obligations set forth in this Charter.

The Arab Human Rights Committee is also entitled to discuss "the report," so that the members can express their observations and make necessary recommendations "in accordance with the aims of the Charter." We believe that the word "report" in the singular means "reports" in the plural, as the Committee discusses both the preliminary and regular reports.

The Arab Human Rights Committee refers its annual report to the "the Council of the League through the Secretary General," in accordance with Article 48(5). The annual report includes the Committee's observations and recommendations on the reports. In addition, Article 48(6) states that the reports of the Arab Human Rights Committee, as well as its concluding remarks and recommendations, shall be considered "public documents which the Committee shall disseminate widely." Making the reports of this Committee 'public' is seen as a kind of "punishment" of the States Parties which do not respect the Charter's provisions. This publicity of the reports can also affect the public opinion in the Arab world and beyond.

Article 48(6), from our point of view, poses several questions: first, to what extent are the reports of the Committee and its observations are [sic] binding? Are these reports binding for the States Parties to the Arab Charter, or are they just "recommendations" to these countries? What is the role of the Council of the League of Arab States in monitoring the implementation of the observations and recommendations of the Committee? Is the purpose of disseminating these reports and making them public to expose the public in general to their content, or is the publicity to be confined to the States Parties to the Charter or member states of the League of Arab States?

There are, therefore, many questions regarding Article 48. Perhaps, the Arab Human Rights Committee's commencement of its activities and its adoption of its own statute will provide answers to these questions and clarify further its role in ensuring the proper application of the provisions of the Arab Charter on Human Rights. The Arab Charter on Human Rights, however, does not explain whether the Arab Human Rights Committee has the right to interpret the articles of the Arab Charter or to carry out tasks or activities other than those provided for in Article 48. The Arab Human Rights Committee cannot do that unless its statute, which it should adopt after the election of its members, includes, as it should, that it has the right to interpret the articles of the Arab Charter on Human Rights or to carry out additional tasks or activities.

Submission and examination of individual complaints is totally absent in the Arab Charter, which dates back around a quarter of a century. Most of the Arab countries that participated in the preparation of the UN's Optional Protocol to the CCPR had voted for its adoption, but by the beginning of February 2009, only four Arab countries had ratified this Protocol, namely Algeria, Djibouti, Libya and Somalia. We believe that it was incumbent upon the Arab countries to ask the experts who prepared the new version of the 2004 Arab Charter on Human Rights to add Articles that allow for individual, as well as government, complaints!

Although the adoption of a new version of the Arab Charter on Human Rights in 2004 has been a significant step in the process of promoting and protecting human rights in the Arab world and its entry into force on March 16, 2008 manifested a desire on the part of the states that have ratified it to respect human rights and fundamental freedoms, the institutions and procedures of the Arab Charter still fall short of the expectations of experts, activists, and defenders of human rights at the Arab and international levels.

We have dubbed the mechanism of the 1994 Arab Charter on Human Rights "primitive" and we believe that the mechanism of the 2004 Arab Charter on Human Rights has not been improved or developed it in a remarkable and clear way, compared to the mechanism of the Arab Charter of 1994. There is a wide gap between other regional mechanisms and their effectiveness and the mechanism of the Arab Charter and its effectiveness.

---

Neither the 1994 nor the 2004 Arab Charter included provisions foreseeing a human rights court, as was also the case with the 1981 African Charter. Despite being an update of the earlier 1994 Charter, the Arab Charter on Human Rights of 2004 has been heavily criticized for not conforming to human rights standards and principles well-recognized at the United Nations level and in other regional human rights promotion and protection systems. See generally Mervat Rishmawi, *The Revised Charter on Human Rights: A Step Forward?*, 5 Hum. Rts. L. Rev. 361 (2005) https://academic.oup.com/hrlr/article-abstract/5/2/361/789502?redirectedFrom=PDF. Read the 2004 Charter, which is in the Documentary Supplement. Do you agree with such criticisms?

Beginning in 2010, proponents of a court—influenced by studies of the European system—lobbied state parties to the Arab Charter to create a judicial body. Expert meetings were held to discuss the proposal and in late 2014 the Statute of the Arab Court of Human Rights (in the Documentary Supplement) was adopted, establishing the headquarters of the court in Manama, Bahrain. The following reading includes a critique of the Court's Statute by the International Commission of Jurists, an influential NGO.

International Commission of Jurists

## Arab League's Human Rights Court Will Not Bring Justice to Victims of Violations

(Sept. 4, 2014), http://www.icj.org/arab-leagues-human-rights-court-will-not-bring
-justice-to-victims-of-violations/

The ICJ [International Commission of Jurists] today dismissed the adoption by the League of Arab States (LAS) of the Statute of the Arab Court of Human Rights as an empty gesture that will do nothing for the victims of human rights violations in the Middle East and North African (MENA) region.

The Ministerial Council of the League adopted the Statute on 7 September 2014. The ICJ has called on the LAS member States to repudiate the flawed text and not to ratify it.

The Statute essentially restricts access to the Arab Court to States, rather than to the actual victims of the violations, relying on States to bring actions against other States, the ICJ says.

Such State-to State complaints are not likely to happen, as shown from the experience of other international human rights bodies.

Political considerations provide a disincentive for States to act on behalf of victims from other States.

Under the Statute, it may also be possible for some non-governmental organizations to bring a claim, but only where States have agreed to this in advance and the organization is State-approved.

A provision that allowed for the Arab Human Rights Committee to refer cases to the Arab Court was deleted from the draft that was submitted for approval by the Ministerial Council.

"The ICJ does not consider this Statute to have established a genuine human rights court. It is a gross departure from the human rights courts established in other regions of the world: Africa, the Americas, and Europe. Indeed, the Statute defeats the very purpose of establishing a human rights court: to provide those whose rights have been violated in the LAS member States with direct access to an effective judicial remedy," said Said Benarbia, Director of the ICJ MENA programme.

The ICJ expressed the view that several other provisions of the Statute, including those relating to the independence of the Court and its judges, the jurisdiction of the Court, and the admissibility of cases, fell far short of international standards and practice.

From the outset of the process of elaborating the Statute, the ICJ had repeatedly urged the LAS Secretariat and member States to ensure that the drafting process would be inclusive and transparent and that the adopted text would accord with international human rights law and standards.

In actuality, the process of elaborating the Statute was opaque, the ICJ says.

The identity of the members of the expert committee that drafted the Statute and its methods of work were never publicized.

The various drafts were never officially publicized nor subject to any meaningful consultation with civil society organizations and other key stakeholders.

———————

The Statute of the Arab Court of Human Rights has not yet received the required number of ratifications for the court to become operative. See generally Ahmed Almutawa, *The Failure of the Arab Court of Human Rights and the Conflicting Logics of Legitimacy, Sovereignty, Orientalism and Cultural Relativism*, 68 NETH. INT'L L. REV. 479 (2021).

For more reading on the development of human rights treaties, mechanisms, and institutions in the Middle East, see Armis Sadri, *The Arab human rights system: achievements and challenges*, 23 THE INT'L J. OF HUM. RTS., 1166 (2019), https://www.tandfonline.com/doi/citedby/10.1080/13642987.2019.1597713?scroll=top&needAccess=true.

## V.   FINAL COMMENTS AND QUESTIONS

1. Given the history of the European, Inter-American, and African systems, would it have been appropriate for the ASEAN Commission to infer that it has the power to receive and consider complaints of human rights violations without specific textual authority to do so? How about authority for precautionary or urgent measures? How might the structure and functioning of the ASEAN Commission influence its decision on this and other issues?

2. Reread the conclusions of the ABA's legal analysis of the ASEAN Declaration, *supra* page 675. Are civil society organizations normally involved at every stage of international negotiations, or is this a new "best practice" applicable primarily to human rights instruments?

3. Is it feasible that all or most of the provisions of the International Bill of Human Rights might be incorporated into future ASEAN instruments, given that not all ASEAN members are parties to the two UN human rights Covenants? Are there rights that you think are uniquely appropriate to southeast Asia and that should be included in any new treaty or other instrument, in addition to those already included in the two Covenants?

4. Consider the critiques of the Statute of the Arab Court by the International Commission of Jurists. Do you agree with all of them? Do you see other problems not mentioned by this influential NGO? Are there any positive innovations in the Statute? How much does this Statute appear to be based on those of other international courts? How does it differ? Should each new regional judicial body be consistent with those of other regions in terms of composition, jurisdiction, and functions? In other words, how much regional diversity is acceptable or desirable?

5. Developments in Asia and the Arab world are rudimentary, at best, but it is worth recalling the long gestation process of the Inter-American and European regimes considered in Chapter 8 and this one. It took over 60 years for Europe to move to a full-time court and to make acceptance of individual complaints mandatory rather than optional. As discussed in Chapter 8, of the 35 OAS member states, only 23 have ratified the American Convention on Human Rights (Venezuela and Trinidad and Tobago ratified the Convention but subsequently denounced it) and only 20 have accepted the optional jurisdiction of the Inter-American Court. There have been no new ratifications of the American Convention since that of Dominica in 1993.

6. Reflect on present human rights concerns that affect Asia and the Middle East. What would be the benefit of having stronger regional human rights protection systems in these regions? If these regions eventually have stronger individual complaint mechanisms, what kind of cases could be presented for their examination? Which rights would you invoke? See analysis on Asian and Middle Eastern countries in Human Rights Watch, *World Report* (2022), https://www.hrw .org/world-report/2022; and *Amnesty International Report 2021/2022: The state of the world's human rights*, https://www.amnesty.org/en/documents/pol10/4870/ 2022/en/#:~:text=The%20Amnesty%20International%20Report%202021,in%20 the%20corridors%20of%20power.

7. Having examined the law, institutions, and procedures of existing regional systems, how would you evaluate the differences between the UN and regional human rights mechanisms? What, specifically, is the value added by the latter? Do the newly emerging systems discussed in this chapter represent a strengthening or weakening of human rights law, or some combination of the two? If there is value in regional human rights promotion and protection, what strategies might be utilized to encourage the formation of additional regional systems for those parts of Asia and the Pacific currently lacking one? Do regional mechanisms for the protection of human rights always need to mirror those established at the global level?